West's
American
Government

Second Edition

West's American Government

Second Edition

ROGER LeROY MILLER

Institute for University Studies
Arlington, Texas

WEST EDUCATIONAL PUBLISHING

an International Thomson Publishing company I⊤P®

Cincinnati ✦ Albany, NY ✦ Belmont, CA ✦ Bonn ✦ Boston ✦ Detroit
✦ Johannesburg ✦ London ✦ Los Angeles ✦ Madrid ✦ Melbourne ✦ Mexico
City ✦ New York ✦ Paris ✦ Pacific Grove ✦ San Francisco ✦ St.
Paul/Minneapolis ✦ Singapore ✦ Tokyo ✦ Toronto ✦ Washington

PRODUCTION CREDITS

Project Manager   Phyllis Jelinek
Photo Research   Jan Seidel
Production Editor   Bette Darwin
Permissions   Elaine Arthur
Illustrator   Lee Anne Dollison
Copyediting   Beverly Peavler
Design   Lee Anne Dollison, John Orr
Dummy Artist   José Delgado
Maps   Lee Anne Dollison
Index   Bob Marsh
Cover Design   Lee Anne Dollison
Proofreader   Suzie De Fazio
Prepress Services   Clarinda Company

PHOTO ACKNOWLEDGMENTS

Cover
Flag: Image ©1998 PhotoDisc, Inc.
Capital Building: Digital Stock.

Contents vi Kevin Fleming/@Corbis; **viii** (top) SuperStock, Inc.; **viii** (bottom) National Archives; **ix** (top) Skjold Photographs; **ix** (bottom) Digital Stock; **x** (top) Jeff Greenberg/Archive Photos; **x** (bottom) Reuters/Archive Photos; **xi** (top) ©Rob Crandall/Stock•Boston; **xi** (bottom) UPI/Corbis-Bettmann; **xii** (top) Kelley-Mooney Photography/Corbis; **xii** (bottom) Image ©1998 PhotoDisc, Inc.; **xiii** (top) AP/Wide World Photos; **xiii** (bottom) ©Spencer Grant/Stock•Boston; **xiv** Corbis-Bettmann.

Unit Openers
2-3 ©1997 Richard T. Nowitz; **116-117** Kevin Fleming/@Corbis; **232-233** Peter Finger/Corbis; **368-369** Digital Stock; **448-449** Lambert/Archive Photos; **530-531** Joseph Sohm/©Tony Stone Images; **560-561** Digital Stock; **644-645** Joseph Sohm, ChromoSohm Inc./Corbis.

Chapter 1 4-5 Joseph Sohm, ChromoSohm Inc./Corbis; **7** Stock•Boston; **9** Bob Rowan, Progressive Image/Corbis; **10** AP/Wide World Photos; **12** The Purcell Team/Corbis; **15** Anonymous, Fall of the Bastille, Musee National des Chateau de Versailles, Giraudon/Art Resource, NY; **16** Cartoonist: Don Addis, Creators Syndicate; **18** (left) Digital Stock; **18** (right) ©Craig Blouin/Tony Stone Images; **20** Corbis-Bettmann; **21** Vince Streano/Corbis; **25** SuperStock, Inc.; **26** Image ©1998 PhotoDisc, Inc.

Chapter 2 30-31 Ted Spiegel/Corbis; **32** Corbis-Bettman; **33** North Wind Picture Archives; **34** North Wind Picture Archives; **36** (top) North Wind Picture Archives; **36** (bottom) Corbis-Bettmann; **39** (top) Colonial Williamsburg Foundation; **39** (bottom) Lee Snider/Corbis; **40** Library of Congress; **41** Smithsonian Institution; **42** Yale University Art Gallery; **43** Bequest of Winslow Warren, Courtesy Museum of Fine Arts, Boston; **46** Culver Pictures Inc.; **49** Corbis-Bettmann; **50** Corbis-Bettmann; **51** The Library of Congress/Photo Researchers; **52** Courtesy of the Mount Vernon Ladies' Association and the Founders Society; **55** Corbis-Bettmann; **57** North Wind Picture Archives.

Chapter 3 62-63 ©Ariel Skelley/The Stock Market; **64** James T. Potter, AIA; **66** National Archives; **67** National Archives; **69** Kelley-Mooney Photography/Corbis; **72** North Wind Picture Archives; **73** Corbis-Bettmann; **74** Archive Photos/American Stock; **80** U.S. Department of Defense/Corbis; **82** John F. Kennedy Library.

Chapter 4 86-87 Digital Stock; **90** Corbis-Bettman; **93** Draper Hill/©The Detroit News; **96** (top) AP/Wide World Photos; **96** (bottom) Karl Hubenthal Cartoon/L.A. Herald-Examiner; **98** ©Joseph Sohm/Stock•Boston; **99** Corbis-Bettmann; **101** UPI/Corbis-Bettmann; **102** FPG International; **103** (top) UPI/Corbis-Bettmann; **103** (bottom) Engraving by Alonzo Chappell, Collection of the Supreme Court of the United States; **106** Corbis-Bettmann; **108** (top) Courtesy of the U.S. Dept. of Justice/FBI; **108** (bottom) ©Bob Daemmrich/Stock•Boston.

Chapter 5 118-119 Digital Stock; **120** The National Archives/Corbis; **121** Corbis-Bettmann; **125** (top) Reuters/Nancy Andrews/Archive Photos; **125** (bottom) AP/Wide World Photos; **127** (left and right) ©Photos by Andy Starnes and Tom Ondrey/Pittsburgh Post Gazette, 1997. All rights reserved. Reprinted with permission; **128** ©Rob Crandall/Stock•Boston; **129** Skjold Photographs; **132** Portrait by Charles Sidney Hopkinson, Collection of the Supreme Court of the United States; **133** AP/Wide World Photos;

(Continued after Index)

Roger LeRoy Miller
Institute for University Studies
Arlington, Texas

REVIEWERS

Sue Alread
Conway Senior High School
Conway, Arkansas

Arthur Atkinson
Miller High School
Grand Terrace, California

Dorothy Barrett
West High School
North Mankato, Minnesota

Bob Bass
Roseburg High School
Roseburg, Oregon

Randy Boal
La Canada High School
La Canada, California

James Bradford
Social Studies Consultant
Midland, Texas

Orville G. Brown
San Diego Sr. High School
San Diego, California

Linda Cabell
John Tyler High School
Tyler, Texas

Jodee Cahalan
West Valley High School
Spokane, Washington

Bob Cantrell
McClelland Sr. High School
Little Rock, Arkansas

Anne Cole
Charlotte-Mecklenburg
 Schools
Charlotte, North Carolina

Frederick D. Cole
Dept. Chair, Social Studies
New Bedford School District
New Bedford, Massachusetts

Vince DeFalco
Villa Park High School
Villa Park, California

Don DiPalo
Saline High School
Saline, Michigan

Lewis Dunn
Edison High School
Fresno, California

Ruth Dunning
Germantown High School
Germantown, Tennessee

Jim Esau
Puyallup High School
Puyallup, Washington

Rebecca Ennis
Sharpstown Sr. High School
Houston, Texas

Professor Frank Feigert
University of North Texas
Denton, Texas

Professor Elizabeth Flores
Del Mar College
Corpus Christi, Texas

Kay Ford
Lee's Summit High School
Lee's Summit, Missouri

Robert Franzetti
David Crockett High School
Austin, Texas

David Goodwin
Virgil Grissom High School
Huntsville, Alabama

Robert Green
Plano Senior High School
Plano, Texas

Robert Hanson
Belleville High School
Belleville, Illinois

Joel Harding
Mead High School
Spokane, Washington

Martin Hajovsky
Robert E. Lee High School
Baytown, Texas

Professor Robert M.
 Herman
Moorpark College
Moorpark, California

Farley Hill
Havenview Jr. High School
Collierville, Tennessee

Nadolyn Hoskins
Northwestern High School
Detroit, Michigan

Tony Huddle
Los Altos High School
Chino Hills, California

LaFuan Humphreys
Eldorado High School
Albuquerque, New Mexico

Dodie Kasper
Plano Senior High School
Plano, Texas

Jerry Kennedy
Interboro High School
Prospect Park, Pennsylvania

Daniel Larsen
Stevenson High School
Lincolnshire, Illinois

Marilyn Lubarsky
Upland High School
Upland, California

Barbara MacDonald
Glen Oaks High School
Baton Rouge, Louisiana

Raymond Mattes
Lake Taylor High School
Norfolk, Virginia

Grace McGarvie
Wayzata High School
Plymouth, Minnesota

Janice McNeil
Cypress Falls High School
Cypress, Texas

Helen McPhaul
Scotland High School
Laurinburg, North Carolina

Patsy Meeks
Boiling Springs High School
Spartanburg, South Carolina

Robert Meggenberg
Addison Trail High School
Addison, Illinois

Willis Moran
North High School
Denver, Colorado

Karin Moore
Washington High School
Pensacola, Florida

Mary Murphy
Meadow Creek High School
Norcross, Georgia

Mark Neiweem
William Fremd High School
Palatine, Illinois

Kay Norman
Denton High School
Denton, Texas

John O'Brien
Centennial Sr. High School
Circle Pines, Minnesota

Linda Perl
Saguaro High School
Tempe, Arizona

Catherine Piszko
New Dorp High School
Staten Island, New York

Harvey Plaut
Bowie High School
El Paso, Texas

Jack Robin
Coral Gables Sr. High School
Miami, Florida

Stephen Shinnick
Norwood High School
Norwood, Massachusetts

Kay Stern
Kelso High School
Kelso, Washington

Carmela Tyre
Gaither High School
Tampa, Florida

Pat Wickman
Waco High School
Waco, Texas

David Williams
Skyview High School
Billings, Montana

George Worthington
Enumclaw High School
Enumclaw, Washington

Pamela Young
Eldorado High School
Las Vegas, Nevada

Contents in Brief

Contents

★ ★

UNIT TWO

The Rights and Responsibilities of All Citizens 116

UNIT SIX

The Federal Judicial Branch   530

UNIT SEVEN

American Policy in a Changing World   560

★ ★

UNIT EIGHT

State and Local Governments 644

Features

Features

BUILDING SOCIAL STUDIES SKILLS

CASE STUDY ★
Government in Action

Features

 THE GLOBAL VIEW

 PARTICIPATING IN YOUR GOVERNMENT

Features

THROUGH THE *Years*

Charts, Tables, Graphs and Maps

Charts, Tables, Graphs and Maps

Charts, Tables, Graphs and Maps

Introduction

Americans can be proud of their country, for they are living under a system of government that is quite special. Our Constitution is now over two hundred years old—it is the oldest written constitution in the world. Since this nation's beginning, we have had over forty presidential administrations, all of which have come into power without violence. Indeed, the American system of government is the envy of much of the world—and dozens of nations have copied the U.S. Constitution.

The book you hold in your hands, *West's American Government, Second Edition* is a significant tool for learning about the American political system and why it is important. In the following pages, you will examine the *process* of government and politics. Political events that happen today may be forgotten tomorrow, but the political process in this country changes very slowly. You will learn how this process works and how decisions reached through the political process affect the daily lives of all Americans. An understanding of the American process of governing will also help you understand the problems and political turmoils in other countries that you will undoubtedly learn about in newspapers, TV broadcasts, or on the Internet.

Learning about American government is the first step toward your full participation in that government as a citizen. Throughout this text, you will find information about how you can get involved in the political process and how, through this participation, you can help shape government decisions. We have a living democracy because people like you are willing to participate in it.

Controversies have always been part of the American political landscape. They started well before the Constitution was ratified, and they will continue to exist in the future. Learning about controversies and how they are resolved helps you better understand the American political system. That is why you will find at the end of every chapter a special feature called *America at Odds*. In each of these features, you will discover the positions taken by various groups of Americans on a current controversial issue, such as gun control, affirmative action, free speech on the Internet, school choice, or lawsuits against the president. At the end of each feature, you will be asked to come up with some ideas of your own. Take those assignments seriously, for developing your own views on particular issues helps you become an active participant in the American political process.

West's American Government

Second Edition

UNIT ONE

The Foundations of American Democracy

The American Revolution resulted in the birth of the first modern democracy. As the call for freedom went out through the colonies, many anti-British rallies were held here, in Boston's Faneuil Hall.

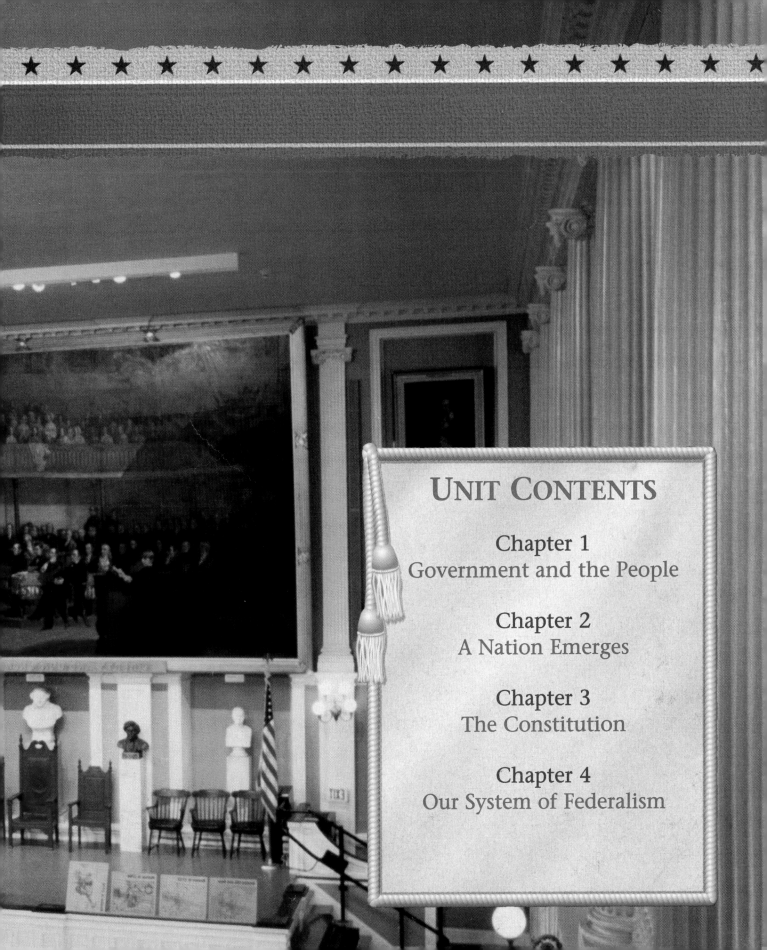

CHAPTER 1

Government and the People

INTRODUCTION

Imagine for a moment what life might be like if there were no government. There would be no public police force to protect you and your fellow citizens. You might have to hire a personal bodyguard just to walk out on the street. All of us might end up carrying weapons to protect ourselves.

If you made a business agreement with someone, you would have no judges and courts to turn to if that person cheated you. In short, life without government would be dangerous and difficult.

As James Madison stated over two hundred years ago, people are not angels. Human beings need an organized form of government and a set of rules by which to live. Thus, as the earliest societies developed, so did the need for government.

◄ This New York City ticker-tape parade celebrates the men and women who fought in the Desert Storm battles in 1991.

The Meaning of Politics and Government

Preview Questions:

🌐 What is politics?
🌐 What is government?
🌐 Why is participation in politics and government important?

Key Terms:

social conflict, politics, government, political participation

When we think of government, we often think of politics. Exactly what do those terms mean, and why is it important for you to learn about them?

What Is Politics?

Politics means many things to many people. To some, politics is an expensive game played at election time in Washington, D.C., in state capitols, and in city halls. To others, politics involves all the maneuvers carried out by the president and Congress as they struggle over national issues.

Most formal definitions of politics begin with the notion of **social conflict**—the idea that people in a society disagree over beliefs, values, and what the society's priorities should be. This conflict is seen as inevitable in any social system. Conflicts will naturally arise over how the society should use its scarce resources, such as land and water. People will also have conflicting ideas about who should receive various benefits, such as health care and higher education.

A civilized society must have a system that allows for the resolution of conflict among its members. That is where politics comes in. **Politics** can be defined as a way to resolve social conflict. In the words of political scientist Harold Lasswell, politics determines "who gets what, when, and how" in our society.

What Is Government?

Just as there are different ideas about the meaning of politics, there are different ideas about the mean-

ing of **government.** When you think of government, you might picture politicians campaigning loudly for reelection and debating issues in Washington, D.C. A citizen who has broken the law might view government as an interference, while another citizen might view government as a "rescuer" that provides public services such as transportation, health care, and protection from crime. To a social scientist, government is a permanent structure composed of decision makers who make society's rules about "who gets what" and who have the power and authority to enforce those rules.

Politics and government, then, are closely related. Politics is a process for resolving conflict. Government is a structure in which people make and enforce decisions about how conflicts will be resolved. Perhaps the best way to understand both politics and government is by understanding how they affect you.

Why Study Politics and Government?

One student of politics said that to most Americans, politics is "a sideshow on the circus of life." Generally, people's interest in government and politics ranks well below their interest in family, work, romance, and many other activities. Most of us, however, will at some time in our lives enter the political world. People usually enter that world through some form of political participation. **Political participation** occurs whenever a person says or does something that affects politics or government. Voting is the most common form of political participation. But there are many other ways that people participate in the political process. Discussing political issues with others, writing letters to the editor, and attending school board meetings are just a few of these ways.

More and more people with common interests are joining together to participate in politics because they see how government affects their own interests. African Americans, whites, Hispanic Americans, women, and older persons all promote policies con-

◄ *This Veterans Health Administration Medical Center is located in Big Spring, Texas. Why would the federal government provide health-care services for veterans?*

cerning equality in America. Consumers, farmers, small-business owners, and corporation managers all want government to make economic and political decisions that favor their interests. These groups have become involved in politics because they realize how profoundly politics touches their everyday lives.

Yet many people say they do not want to be involved in government and politics. These people do not realize that they are already involved. Apathy, or indifference, is as much a political statement as active participation. Both positions influence who gets what in society. Good school systems, safe communities, and adequate health standards are the results of political decisions. These decisions are influenced by who participates, who is prevented from participating, and who chooses not to participate in government and politics.

Every day, our lives are affected by someone's political choices. The quality of the food you had for breakfast was regulated by a government agency. The quality of the school you attend and the public transportation (or lack of it) in your community are the results of how your city or state government decided to allocate its resources.

Thus, the question is not *whether* to become involved in politics and government but *how* to become involved. Politics and government do affect us, and they will continue to do so throughout our lives. The choice is how we want to affect politics.

SECTION 1 REVIEW

1. What is social conflict, and how is it related to politics?
2. What is the relationship between government and politics?

Citizens of the United States are citizens of a democracy. As you have learned, democracy is government by the people, and citizen involvement is at the heart of democracy. If only a few people decided to become involved in government, public decisions would be left to those few. Such a government would no longer be an effective democracy. Being a citizen in a democratic society requires learning certain skills. These skills include the following:

1. **Acquiring and using information.** Citizens must know how to find answers to important questions. They can do this by reading books, magazines, and government publications and by using radio, television, and other electronic media. They must know how to ask questions, write letters, and make telephone calls to obtain the information they need. Throughout this book, you will learn how to gather and use various types of information.
2. **Making decisions.** Citizens need to recognize that there may be more than one solu-

PARTICIPATING IN YOUR GOVERNMENT

The Duties of Citizenship

tion to a given problem. They must be able to evaluate alternatives and be familiar with the decision-making process.
3. **Making sound judgments.** In order to make sound judgments, citizens must distinguish between fact and opinion, recognize their own biases and values, see both sides of an issue, and identify irrelevant and ambiguous information.
4. **Communicating.** Citizens must be able to express their views and communicate their ideas effectively, both in writing and in speaking.

5. **Cooperating.** Citizens must be able to work together to achieve common goals.
6. **Voting.** Exercising the right to vote is the basis of democracy.

These and many other citizenship skills are reviewed throughout this book.

TAKING ACTION

1. Choose a current issue facing your community, such as how to solve the problem of homelessness or how to reduce illegal drug use. Read as much as you can about the issue for two weeks. Put together a file of the newspaper and magazine (or Internet) articles that you have read about the subject.
2. Over the same period, watch TV or listen to the radio for news on the same topic. Take notes on what you learn.
3. Decide what you think can be done to solve the problem you have chosen. Make a list of your conclusions.

3. **For Critical Analysis:** Your school district is a local government, and the decision makers in that government are the members of the school board. Think about how your school board allocates its available resources (particularly money). Does it allocate too much (or too little) for such items as teachers' salaries, the salaries of administrative staff, learning resources such as books and computers, and new or improved school buildings? If you were a member of the board, what would your priorities be with regard to these needs?

The Purposes of Government

Preview Question:

🌐 What purposes does government serve?

Key Terms:

power, authority, public policies

The first step in understanding how government works is to understand what it actually does for people and society. Government serves five major purposes:

- It resolves conflicts.
- It provides public services.
- It provides for national security and common defense.
- It sets goals for public policies.
- It preserves culture.

Resolving Conflicts

People have lived together in groups throughout history. Still, we have not learned how to do so with-out social conflict, and we probably never will. This is because society's resources are limited, but people's wants are unlimited. Inevitably, disputes will arise over how our limited resources should be used. Consider the environment. There continues to be conflict over how best to protect it. Some citizens seem to want to protect the environment no matter what the cost to society. Others want to take into account the economic consequences of environmental protection. Who has the legitimate power and authority to resolve such conflicts? This is where government steps in.

Governments decide how conflicts will be resolved so that order can be maintained. Governments have **power**—the ability to cause others to change their behavior. Having power means being able to get someone to do something he or she would not do otherwise.

Just the Facts

Environmental pollution problems are not new to the modern era. According to a visitor to Chicago in the late 1800s, he "did not see in Chicago anything but darkness, smoke, [or] clouds of dirt."

◀ *These Los Angeles schoolchildren may not know it, but they are benefiting from a public service—an education for all citizens—provided by their local government. Who pays for public education?*

▶ *Workers from Granite Construction Company pour the first concrete sections for a new bridge on Mount Lemmon Highway near Tucson, Arizona. Why would the government pay a private company to improve highway conditions?*

The government, for example, has the power to make all children from the ages of six through sixteen go to school. The government has the power to force you to obey traffic laws. It has the power to punish you if you attack another person.

Governments also have **authority**—the right to cause citizens to behave in particular ways. Governments have authority only if their power is legitimate. *Legitimate power* means power that is recognized and accepted by society as legally and morally correct.

Power and authority are central to a government's ability to resolve conflicts. Without power and authority, a government could not make and enforce laws. It could not develop court systems to make final decisions about how laws should be applied to specific circumstances.

Providing Public Services

Another purpose of government is to provide public services. Governments undertake projects that individuals usually would not or could not do on their own, such as building and maintaining roads, providing welfare programs, operating public schools, and preserving national parks. Governments also provide such services as law enforcement, fire protection, and public health and safety programs. Abraham Lincoln once said:

> *The legitimate object of government is to do for a community of people whatever they need to have done but cannot do at all, or cannot so well do for themselves in their separate and individual capacities. But in all that people can individually do for themselves, government ought not to interfere.*

Providing for National Security and Common Defense

Governments also provide for a nation's security and defense against attacks from other nations. Historically, defense matters have been given high priority by governments. In the twentieth century, national defense has become an especially expensive and complex activity for almost every government in the world.

The government of the United States provides for defense and security with its Army, Navy, Air Force, Marines, and Coast Guard. The State Department, Defense Department, Central Intelligence Agency (CIA), and other agencies also contribute to this defense network.

Setting Goals for Public Policies

Governments set goals meant to improve the lives of their citizens. These goals may affect the people on a local, state, or national scale. To support or achieve the goals, governments design plans of action known as **public policies.**

Governments set goals and make policies in many areas. The goals and policies may be short term, such as improving a city's education system by adding new classes, or long term, such as discovering new energy sources by supporting research facilities. Political and social goals for the United States might include decisions to launch an orbiting space station by the year 2010, to eliminate discrimination against Americans with disabilities, or to clean up the environment in the first decade of the new century.

Preserving Culture

A nation's culture includes the customs, language, beliefs, and values of its people. Governments have worked to preserve their nations' cultures in ways that citizens cannot. For example, the observance of Independence Day in the United States helps carry on a tradition that celebrates our history. In France, Bastille Day is celebrated every July 14. You will learn more about the French Revolution in the *Case Study: Government in Action* feature on page 14.

In the People's Republic of China, National Day is celebrated October 10. Perhaps the ultimate way that governments preserve their national culture is by defending the nation against attacks by other nations. For example, consider what happened in Tibet. When that country was unable to defend itself against China, the conquering Chinese set out on a program to destroy Tibet's culture.

SECTION 2 REVIEW

1. List the five purposes government serves.
2. Explain the difference between power and authority.
3. What are public services? What are public policies?
4. **For Critical Analysis:** In the United States, there are many different ethnic groups that have different cultures, customs, languages, and values. Should the U.S. government help these groups preserve their cultures? Or should the government preserve one national culture that all can share?

SECTION 3

Nations and the Origins of Government

Preview Questions:

- What is a nation?
- What characteristics do all nations share?
- What are the theories regarding the origins of government?

Key Terms:

nation, unitary government, federal government, confederal government, sovereignty, evolutionary theory, force theory, institutions, social contract theory, revolution, natural rights

Where are governments actually found? You probably have a student government in your school that helps make decisions and rules for your student body. Your city has a government that makes decisions for its residents.

The largest group of people served by a government is the body of people living in a nation. A **nation** is a

▼ *One purpose of government is preserving a nation's culture in ways that citizens alone cannot. For example, this national celebration of Independence Day in Mexico helps carry on a tradition that celebrates that country's history.*

group of people occupying a specific area and organized under a government that makes and enforces laws *without the approval of a higher authority*. The nation is the basic political unit in the world today.

Characteristics of Nations

There are over two hundred nations in the world, spread over the seven continents on Earth. Just as the continents differ, so do the nations. No two nations are the same. Each has its own unique geographical, economic, and cultural features. In spite of their differences, though, nations share four fundamental characteristics: population, territory, government, and sovereignty.

Population Obviously, each nation contains people. National populations vary from several thousand people in Luxembourg to over a billion in the People's Republic of China. The population of the United States is over 270 million.

Territory A nation must have land on which its people can live, and its boundaries must be recognized by other nations. The total land area of the United States is 3,615,122 square miles (9,363,123 square kilometers). The People's Republic of China covers 3,691,901 square miles (9,562,024 square kilometers). Both the United States and China have expanded their territory since they were first established. Other nations, such as Mexico, have lost territory since their beginning.

The location of political boundaries between nations is often a source of conflict and has led to many wars throughout history. Wars have also resulted when nations have attempted to take over the territory of other nations. Sometimes stronger nations

FIGURE 1–1 Three Theories on the Origin of Government Three widely discussed theories of how government developed are described below. Which theory best describes the origins of American government?

Evolutionary Theory	Force Theory	Social Contract Theory
Government developed as families joined to form clans, which grew into tribes regulated by older members.	Government originated when strong groups conquered territories and then brought the inhabitants under their control.	Government arose out of a voluntary agreement (contract) among free individuals.

come to the aid of weaker ones that are invaded. That is what happened when the United States sent troops to the Middle East in reaction to the Iraqi invasion of Kuwait in 1990.

Government Every nation has some form of political organization through which public policies are made and enforced. Most nations have several levels of government, which operate according to an overall plan. Most governments today have either a unitary or a federal system of government. A **unitary government** is one in which all authority is vested in the central government. A **federal government,** such as that in the United States, divides its powers and authority between national and state governments. A third type of government is a **confederal government** made up of a group of independent states. You will learn more about these systems in Chapter 4.

Sovereignty An essential characteristic of any nation is **sovereignty**—the right, power, and authority to govern itself. A nation has complete authority to determine its form of government, its economic and legal systems, and its foreign policy. The United States claimed sovereignty in 1776 when it broke its ties with Great Britain and asserted its independence as a nation.

Who holds the sovereign power within a nation is extremely important. Some nations are ruled by one person or a small group of people. In a democratic government, the people hold the power and are sovereign.

How Did Government Begin?

What factors first brought about the existence of governments? This question has been examined and

debated for many centuries by political thinkers and historians. Over the years, many theories have been proposed, but none provides conclusive answers. Nonetheless, several of these theories have been widely discussed.

Evolution The **evolutionary theory** holds that government developed gradually, step by step. The first stage of human political development was the primitive family. Over a period of many years, families joined together into clans and worked cooperatively for protection. Clans gradually combined into larger units called tribes. Usually, one of the older individuals (or a group of them) led the tribe and was expected to make decisions and resolve conflicts between members. As the years went by, the number of families and clans in the tribe grew, and the "government" became larger and more formalized.

Force According to the **force theory,** governments first originated when strong persons or groups conquered territories and then forced everyone living in those territories to submit to their will. Then, institutions—such as police, courts, and tax collectors—were created to make people work and to collect all or part of what they produced for the conquerors. **Institutions** are long-standing structures or associations that perform functions for a society. The first leader of the modern German nation, Otto von Bismarck, said in 1862 that "the great questions of our day cannot be solved by speeches and majority votes . . . but by blood and iron." Obviously, Bismarck was a strong supporter of the force theory of government.

Social Contract The **social contract theory** was developed in the seventeenth and eighteenth centuries by such philosophers as John Locke (1632–1704) and

The French Revolution

Not all countries have a government as stable as ours in the United States. And some governments that are stable today were not always that way. Instead, they were created out of revolutions.

In a **revolution,** a government is overthrown by force and a new government is established. Revolutions often occur when many people in a society believe that the government is not meeting their needs.

One of the most important revolutions in the Western world was the French Revolution, which began in 1789. France at that time had long been governed by monarchs—kings or queens who made decisions as they pleased. In other words, they were not accountable to the people for their actions. They could not be "voted out of office."

Under this "old order," the nobility and the clergy (officials of the Church) were privileged classes. They received most of the society's resources, while the working classes paid most of the taxes, which were extremely high. The working classes grew increasingly unhappy as the government failed to solve these problems of inequality. Finally, they rebelled. On July 14, 1789, armed rebels in Paris stormed the Bastille, a state prison that had at one time held many famous political offenders.

By 1791, the old order had been overthrown and a new constitution written. The constitution established a government in which the power of citizens was greatly expanded. In the view of some scholars, the concept of popular sovereignty that emerged during the French Revolution became the basis for other new governmental systems that sprang up throughout Europe.

The United States, too, has a government that grew out of a revolution. The American Revolution ended in 1783. Since then, U.S. citizens have disagreed sharply over many issues. We have even suffered through a civil war. But we have never had to face another revolution. We are fortunate that our government was designed to be flexible and responsive to the demands of its citizens.

THINK ABOUT IT
....

1. Sometimes journalists and social commentators talk about a revolution in *ideas*. How is the term *revolution* in this phrase related to the term *revolution* as applied to political change?
2. Could a revolution take place in the United States today? Why or why not?

Thomas Hobbes (1588–1679) in England and Jean-Jacques Rousseau (1712–1778) in France. According to this theory, individuals voluntarily agree with one another to create a government and to give that government enough power to secure the protection and welfare of all individuals. This unwritten agreement is called a social contract.

John Locke, one writer who particularly influenced the American colonists, argued that people are born with **natural rights** to life, liberty, and property that no government can take away. He theorized that the purpose of government was to protect natural rights. Any government that abused its power by interfering with those rights should not be obeyed. Human beings, though, would voluntarily give up some of their freedoms to gain the benefits of orderly government.

Locke's theories greatly influenced many leaders of the American Revolution. Benjamin Franklin, James

▲ *Possibly inspired by the American Revolution against English rule, oppressed French citizens rose up against their own King Louis XVI in 1789. The French Revolution marked the beginning of the trend toward democracy in Europe.*

Madison, and Thomas Jefferson were all familiar with Locke's writings. Locke's thoughts and even some of his exact words were used in the Declaration of Independence and in the Constitution. Locke's thoughts also influenced many people in France. Like the leaders of the American Revolution, these people found that they had to fight to win popular sovereignty. (See the feature *Case Study: Government in Action—The French Revolution* on page 14.)

SECTION 3 REVIEW

1. What are the characteristics of a nation?
2. What theories have been proposed to explain the origins of government?
3. **For Critical Analysis:** Which theory of how government began is most applicable to the formation of the U.S. government?

How Do Governments Differ from One Another?

Preview Questions:

🌐 What are the main differences among the various types of government?

🌐 What is the difference between a direct democracy and an indirect democracy?

Key Terms:

autocracy, monarchy, divine right theory, dictatorship, authoritarian, totalitarian, democracy, direct democracy, representative democracy, republic

Through the centuries, governments have been organized in many different ways. A government's structure is influenced by a number of factors. These factors include history, customs, values, geography, climate, resources, and human experiences and needs. No two nations have exactly the same form of government. Political analysts, however, have developed several ways of classifying governments. One of the most meaningful ways to classify governments is according to *who* governs. Who has the power to make the rules and laws that all must obey?

BENT OFFERINGS By Don Addis

ABSOLUTE MONARCHY MEANS NEVER HAVING TO SAY YOU'RE SORRY

© 1991 Creators Syndicate, Inc.

▲ *This political cartoon highlights the power of an absolute monarch. Can an absolute monarch be voted out of office, as an American president can?*

Rule by One: Autocracy

In an **autocracy**, the power and authority of the government are in the hands of a single person, sometimes referred to as an autocrat. In ancient times, autocracy was one of the most common forms of government, and it still exists in some parts of the world. Autocrats usually obtained their power either by inheriting it or by using force.

Monarchy One of the forms of autocracy is a **monarchy**—government controlled by a king, queen, emperor, empress, tsar, or tsarina. The monarch, who usually acquires his or her power through inheritance, is the highest authority in the government.

Historically, most monarchies have been absolute monarchies, in which rulers held complete and unlimited power as a matter of divine right. Before the eighteenth century, the theory of divine right was widely accepted in Europe. It was also accepted in ancient Egypt, China, Greece, and Rome. The **divine right theory** held that God gave those of royal birth the unlimited right to govern other men and women—the "divine right" to rule. According to this theory, only God could judge those of royal birth. Thus, all citizens were bound to obey their monarchs, no matter how unfair or unjust they seemed to be. Challenging a monarch's power was regarded not only as treason against the government but also as a sin against God.

Just the Facts

One of the decisions facing the Russian government today is where to bury the recently discovered skeletal remains of Tsar Nicholas II, who was assassinated in 1917.

Most modern monarchies are constitutional monarchies, in which kings or queens share governmental power with elected lawmakers. Their power is limited, or checked, by other government leaders and by constitutions. In most constitutional monarchies, the people themselves elect these other leaders to office.

Dictatorship Autocracy can also take the form of a **dictatorship,** in which a single leader (or group of leaders) rules, although *not* through inheritance. Dictatorships are **authoritarian,** meaning the dictator has absolute power and is not subject to constitutional limitations. He or she is also not responsible to citizens or to their elected representatives. Changes in leadership can only come about by voluntary resignation, death, or forcible overthrow.

Dictatorships can also be **totalitarian,** which means the leader (or group of leaders) seeks to control almost all aspects of social and economic life. The needs of the nation come before the needs of individuals, and all citizens must work for the common goals established by the government. Examples of this form of government include Adolf Hitler's government in Nazi Germany from 1933 to 1945, Benito Mussolini's rule in Italy from 1922 to 1943, and Josef Stalin's rule in the Soviet Union from 1929 to 1953. More contemporary examples include Saddam Hussein in Iraq and Fidel Castro in Cuba.

Rule by Many: Democracy

The most familiar form of government to most Americans is **democracy,** in which the supreme political authority ultimately rests with the people. The word *democracy* comes from the Greek *demos,* meaning "the people," and *kratia,* meaning "rule." The main idea of democracy is that government exists only by the consent of the people and reflects the will of the majority.

The Athenian Model of Direct Democracy Democracy as a form of government began long ago. **Direct democracy** exists when the people participate directly in government decision making through mass meetings. In its purest form, direct democracy was practiced in Athens and other ancient Greek city-states about 2,500 years ago. Every Athenian *citizen* participated in the governing assembly and voted on all major issues. (Most residents of the Athenian city-state were not

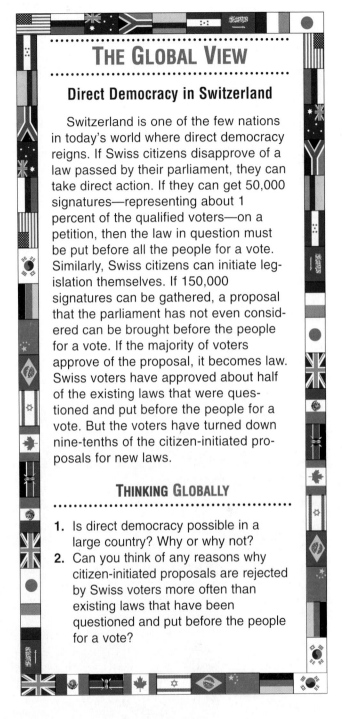

THE GLOBAL VIEW

Direct Democracy in Switzerland

Switzerland is one of the few nations in today's world where direct democracy reigns. If Swiss citizens disapprove of a law passed by their parliament, they can take direct action. If they can get 50,000 signatures—representing about 1 percent of the qualified voters—on a petition, then the law in question must be put before all the people for a vote. Similarly, Swiss citizens can initiate legislation themselves. If 150,000 signatures can be gathered, a proposal that the parliament has not even considered can be brought before the people for a vote. If the majority of voters approve of the proposal, it becomes law. Swiss voters have approved about half of the existing laws that were questioned and put before the people for a vote. But the voters have turned down nine-tenths of the citizen-initiated proposals for new laws.

THINKING GLOBALLY

1. Is direct democracy possible in a large country? Why or why not?
2. Can you think of any reasons why citizen-initiated proposals are rejected by Swiss voters more often than existing laws that have been questioned and put before the people for a vote?

citizens, however. Noncitizens—including women and slaves—did not participate in government.)

Clearly, direct democracy is possible only in small communities in which citizens can meet in a chosen place and decide key issues and policies. Some New

England town meetings still use a modified form of direct democracy.

Just the Facts

Before the Roman Empire was founded in 31 B.C., Rome had a republican form of government for more than five centuries.

Representative Democracy

The founders of the United States were aware of the Athenian model and agreed with the idea of government based on the consent of the governed. Many feared that a pure, direct democracy would deteriorate into mob rule, however. They believed that large groups of people meeting together would ignore the rights and opinions of people in the minority. Decisions, they feared, would be made without careful thought. The founders believed that a representative democracy would enable public decisions to be made more calmly and fairly.

In a **representative democracy** (also called indirect democracy), the will of the majority is expressed through a smaller group of individuals elected by the people to act as their representatives. These representatives are responsible to the people for their conduct, and they can be voted out of office. Our founders preferred to use the term **republic,** which is essentially the same as a representative democracy. As our population has grown, our democracy has become less and less like the Athenian model, as you will learn when you read the *America at Odds* feature on page 24.

In the modern world, there are two forms of representative democracy: presidential and parliamentary. A presidential democracy is one in which the lawmaking and law-implementing branches of government are separate. For example, in the United States, Congress has the power to make laws, and the president has the power to carry them out. In a parliamentary democracy, the lawmaking and law-implementing branches

◄ Direct democracy had its beginnings in Athens, Greece, where citizens and the ruling council met in the Parthenon. This tradition of direct democracy continues to this day, in the form of New England town meetings. Although there are significant differences in the buildings and in the form of the meetings, the tradition of direct democracy has been a lasting gift of the Greeks.

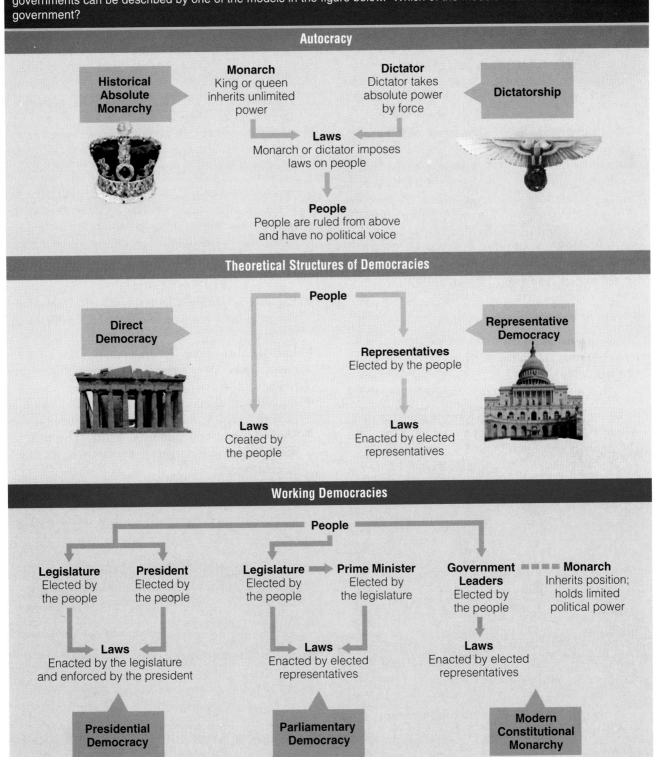

FIGURE 1–2 Forms of Government Although no two nations have exactly the same form of government, most governments can be described by one of the models in the figure below. Which of the models best describes the U.S. government?

Autocracy

Historical Absolute Monarchy

Monarch
King or queen inherits unlimited power

Dictator
Dictator takes absolute power by force

Dictatorship

Laws
Monarch or dictator imposes laws on people

People
People are ruled from above and have no political voice

Theoretical Structures of Democracies

People

Direct Democracy

Representatives
Elected by the people

Representative Democracy

Laws
Created by the people

Laws
Enacted by elected representatives

Working Democracies

People

Legislature
Elected by the people

President
Elected by the people

Legislature
Elected by the people

Prime Minister
Elected by the legislature

Government Leaders
Elected by the people

Monarch
Inherits position; holds limited political power

Laws
Enacted by the legislature and enforced by the president

Laws
Enacted by elected representatives

Laws
Enacted by elected representatives

Presidential Democracy

Parliamentary Democracy

Modern Constitutional Monarchy

ARCHITECTS
of Government

Thomas Jefferson
(1743–1826)

Born in Shadwell, Virginia, Thomas Jefferson attended the College of William and Mary. He drafted the Declaration of Independence while serving as a member of the Second Continental Congress. Jefferson was elected to the Virginia House of Delegates in 1776 and later served as governor of Virginia. He became ambassador to France in 1785 and secretary of state in 1789. After a term as vice president to John Adams, he served as president from 1801 to 1809.

HIS WORDS

"I have sworn upon the altar of God, eternal hostility against every form of tyranny over the mind of man."

(Letter, September 23, 1800)

"The republican is the only form of government which is not eternally at open or secret war with the rights of mankind."

(Letter, March 11, 1790)

"The boisterous sea of liberty is never without a wave."

(Letter, October 29, 1820)

DEVELOPING
CRITICAL THINKING SKILLS

1. What did Jefferson mean when he referred to "tyranny over the mind of man"?
2. Why do a republican form of government and the rights of humankind go well together?
3. The third quotation above states that the boisterous, or stormy, sea of liberty is never without a wave. Restate this quotation in another way.

---

of government overlap. In England, for example, the prime minister and the Cabinet are members of the legislature, or *Parliament*, and enact the laws as well as carry them out.

Principles of Democracy

This country, with all its institutions, belongs to the people who inhabit it. Whenever they shall grow weary of the existing government, they can exercise their constitutional right of amending it, or their revolutionary right to dismember or overthrow it.

With these words, Abraham Lincoln described the most basic concept of American government—that the people, not the government, are ultimately in control.

Democracy is based, in theory at least, on five principles listed below. All of them will be discussed throughout this text.

- **Equality in voting.** Citizens need equal opportunities to express their preferences about policies and leaders.
- **Individual freedom.** All individuals must have the greatest amount of freedom possible without interfering with the rights of others.
- **Equality of all persons.** The law must entitle all persons to equal treatment within the society.
- **Majority rule and minority rights.** The majority should rule, but the rights of minority groups should be guaranteed.
- **Voluntary consent to be governed.** The people who make up a democracy must agree voluntarily to be governed by the rules laid down by their representatives.

SECTION 4 REVIEW

1. What is the difference between a monarchy and a dictatorship?
2. What is direct democracy, and why did our founders oppose it?
3. What is the difference between a direct democracy and a representative, or indirect, democracy?
4. What are the principles of democracy?
5. **For Critical Analysis:** How do you think your life would be different if you were living in a country ruled by a dictatorship?

The World Is Getting Smaller

Preview Questions:

- What does interdependence mean?
- Why is interdependence among nations growing?

Key Term:

interdependence

You have read about how each nation is sovereign. This does not mean, though, that each nation is a world unto itself. Each nation is one among many, all sharing the same planet and the same environment. Many people say that "the world is getting smaller." In a sense, this is true. Improvements in transportation and communications systems have linked nations and their peoples in ways that were only dreamed of years ago. Today, people around the world are more aware of—and affected by—the goals and actions of others.

Nations, then, are becoming more and more interdependent. **Interdependence** means mutual reliance. Today, nations are relying on each other more for several reasons. Two important reasons have to do with environmental pollution and communications technology.

Our Shared Environment

Nations of the world are interdependent because they share the same air and water. Pollution in one nation can affect the people and the environment of other nations. As a result, the world's nations must depend on each other to protect an environment that knows no national boundaries.

An accident at a nuclear power plant in one country can affect the lives of millions of people thousands of miles away. The clear-cutting of the Brazilian rain forest may affect all of us if the world's oxygen level is severely reduced. In the United States, many electric utility plants generate air pollution that spreads hundreds of miles and creates the problem of acid rain in other regions of the country, as well as in Canada.

The possible depletion of the earth's ozone layer is a global problem. One of the causes is thought to be the

◀ *These workers are cleaning up an oil spill from a Texaco refinery in Anacortes Bay in Anacortes, Washington. As interdependence among nations increases, leaders and citizens alike are beginning to recognize the importance of working globally to manage environmental issues.*

▶ *A few years ago, just a handful of people had access to the Internet or could identify a Web site page as shown here. Now communication is instantaneous as people worldwide go online to find out what's happening in everything from fashion to politics. Why would a dictator be troubled by citizens' easy access to the Internet?*

QUICK SEARCH
TEXT OF BILLS
105th CONGRESS:

Search by Bill Number:

Ex: s. 435, H.R. 642
OR
Search by Word/Phrase:

Ex: line item veto, tax reform

Search   Clear

Frequently Asked Questions (FAQs)

105th Congress:
House Directories
Senate Directories

Congressional Internet Services:
House - Senate
Library of Congress
GPO - GAO - CBO
AOC - OTA - More

Library of Congress Web Links:
Legislative
Executive
Judicial
State/Local

THOMAS — Legislative Information on the Internet

■ CONGRESS NOW

House and Senate: Floor Activities
House: Latest Floor Actions - Floor Activities This Week **NEW**
National Bipartisan Commission on the Future of Medicare **NEW**

■ BILLS

Bill Summary & Status: 105th (1997-98)
Previous Congresses (1973 - 1996)

Bill Text:
105th (1997-98) - 104th (1995-96) - 103rd (1993-94) - 102nd (1991-93) **NEW** 101st (1989-90) **NEW**

House Roll Call Votes [Help]: 105th - 2nd (1998) - 105th - 1st (1997)
Previous Congresses (1990 - 1996)

Senate Roll Call Votes [Help]: 105th - 2nd (1998) - 105th - 1st (1997)

Public Laws By Law Number: 105th (1997-98)
Previous Congresses (1973 - 1996)

Major Legislation: [Definition]
105th: By topic - By popular/short title - By bill number/type - Enacted into law
104th: By topic - By popular/short title - By bill number/type - Enacted into law

■ CONGRESSIONAL RECORD

Congressional Record Text: Most Recent Issue **NEW**
105th (1997-98) - 104th (1995-96) - 103rd (1993-94) - 102nd (1991-92) **NEW** .
101st (1989-90) **NEW**

Congressional Record Index :
105th - 2nd (1998) - 105th - 1st (1997) - 104th - 2nd (1996) - 104th - 1st (1995) - 103rd - 2nd (1994)

Résumés of Congressional Activity :
105th - 1st (1997) - Previous Congresses (1969 - 1996)

Annals of Congress (Precursor of the Congressional Record) [About] **NEW**
1st Congress (1789-1791) - 2nd Congress (1791-1793)

■ COMMITTEE INFORMATION

Committee Reports: Congress: 105th (1997-98) - 104th (1995-96)

Committee Home Pages: House - Senate

House Committees: Today's Schedules - Schedules and Oversight Plans - Selected Hearing Transcripts

■ THE LEGISLATIVE PROCESS

How Our Laws Are Made (by Charles W. Johnson, House Parliamentarian)

Enactment of a Law (By Robert B. Dove, Senate Parliamentarian)

■ HISTORICAL DOCUMENTS

Historical documents including the Declaration of Independence, the Federalist Papers, early Congressional documents (Constitutional Convention and Continental Congress broadsides), and the Constitution. U.S. Congressional Documents and Debates: 1774 - 1873. **NEW**

---

release of chemicals called chlorofluorocarbons (CFCs) into the atmosphere. Some countries have banned the use of CFCs—for example, in the making of refrigerator coolant. But what happens if one country continues to produce products that cause more and more CFCs to be released into the air? Clearly, such an action creates a problem that other nations cannot ignore.

Nor can we ignore the problem of dangerous pesticides, such as DDT. A country may ban pesticide use within its own borders but still allow manufacturers to sell it to countries where it is not banned. What will the environmental effects of this practice be?

Communications Technology

Interdependence has also increased because of improvements in communications technology. Perhaps the most important development in recent years is the expanded use of the Internet, a huge, worldwide system of computer networks.

The Internet Explosion Through the Internet, anyone with a computer and a communications link can contact anyone else in the world who has these facilities. This phenomenon is called electronic mail, or e-mail. Estimates of the number of e-mail messages just within

Any textbook holds a vast amount of information that you can make your own. To help you, this textbook is divided into parts, each with its own function. Some parts help you understand information; other parts help you study and use that information. Using a textbook and its parts wisely is an important first move toward mastering its contents.

To get the most from this textbook, use the following guidelines.

1. **Study the table of contents to locate information.** Here, you can find where each chapter, section, and feature can be found.
2. **Examine the chapter-opening and unit-opening pages.** Read the titles and objectives. Ask yourself questions about the photos, such as how each relates to the chapter title. Read the introduction and familiarize yourself with the theme.
3. **Skim the chapter.** Preview the chapter, noting each section title and the subheadings. These will give you clues about how the chapter will progress. Read the section preview questions that start each section.
4. **Read the chapter carefully.** Use the headings and subheadings to get clues about the main and supporting ideas. Reread any paragraph that is unclear until you understand what it says. Pay attention to the boldfaced

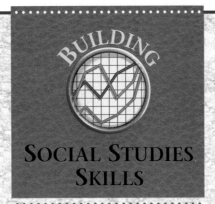

BUILDING
SOCIAL STUDIES SKILLS

Using This Textbook

words—they are highlighted because they are important. Use the review questions at the ends of the sections to check your understanding.
5. **Read the special features.** Each chapter has special features that will add to your knowledge of government. You will recognize them easily because they appear in boxes. You may prefer to read them as you go along or when you preview or review the section. When you read them is not as important as being sure you do read them.
6. **Summarize and review the chapter.** Each chapter ends with a summary that will help you recap the main ideas. Each chapter also has a set of review questions, critical thinking questions, activities and projects, a communication skills exercise, and a social studies skills exercise. All these review features

are designed to help you master the material.
7. **Use the glossary.** The glossary includes definitions for the important new words found in this book.
8. **Use the Resource Center.** The Resource Center found in the back of this book contains much useful material, including original source documents.

Remember, no textbook can teach you this course. A textbook cannot be a substitute for your instructor's skills and experience. This book, like all textbooks, is a tool. When used properly, it can enhance your knowledge and broaden your understanding.

PRACTICING YOUR SKILLS

1. Turn to the glossary and answer these questions: (a) On what page (or pages) in the glossary is the term *veto* found? (b) What is the last entry under L?
2. Turn to the table of contents and answer the following questions: (a) Who are the Americans profiled under *Architects of Government?* (b) How many units and chapters does the book have? (c) Name three *Case Study: Government in Action* features found in the book.
3. What is special about the Constitution as it is presented in the Resource Center?

Our Representative Democracy

Everybody accepts the notion that direct democracy as practiced in ancient Greece would not work in a nation of over 270 million people. Even if a small percentage of the total adult population wanted to participate in direct democracy, the result would be a mass meeting that could not be held in even the largest structure in the world. Representative democracy is therefore the most practical democratic system we can use in this country. Nonetheless, Americans are at odds over whether the current representative form of government is best. The key issue is how many people each representative to the U.S. Senate and Congress serves.

Our Representatives Represent Too Many People, Say Some

Some Americans have begun to question whether representative democracy can still work in the United States because of the continued rate of population growth. Consider that when our first president, George Washington, took office in 1789, the population numbered about four million. During the first election, twenty-two senators and fifty-nine representatives were elected. Therefore, each of the two senators from each state represented an average of 180,000 citizens.

The average member of the House of Representatives represented about 68,000 citizens.

Consider now the current situation. The population of the United States has grown to over 270 million. There is still one president. The number of senators has increased to 100, and the number of representatives to 435. That means that each senator represents an average of 2.7 million Americans. The average member of the House represents about 610,000 Americans. Is it possible for any one representative to truly reflect the "will of the people" when each congressional official in our government represents so many Americans?

Our Representative Democracy Will Continue to Work, Say Others

Other Americans point out that this nation is expected to reach its maximum, stable population sometime between the years 2020 and 2040. Although the population will probably increase to about 330 to 350 million, it will not be significantly larger than it is now. In other words, if representative democracy is working today, even with all of its faults, it will certainly work with 60 to 80 million more people. For example, assume that in the year 2030 the U.S. population is 340 million. Each senator will represent an average of

the United States run into trillions a year. Those who observe and analyze Internet growth believe that by the year 2005, virtually everyone in the United States will have an e-mail address.

Another important part of the Internet is electronic commerce—the ability to view products and order them electronically. While still in its infancy, electronic commerce promises to break down borders throughout the world. Because of the ease with which

commerce can occur, the interdependence of nations will become increasingly obvious during the twenty-first century.

The Information Age We are truly living in the age of information. It has become a simple matter to send still and moving images almost anywhere in the world at high speed. Facsimile (fax) machines now transmit clear photos around the globe at a moment's notice.

◀ *The strength of America has always been its people. The idea of giving everyday people the power to govern themselves was startling for subjects used to being ruled by a monarch. While a monarch requires obedience, a democracy demands an informed and concerned citizenry. What steps can high-school students take to help them meet the challenge of governing themselves?*

6.8 million people. For representatives, the average will be about 780,000 people. The effect and influence of any individual citizen on his or her elected officials should not markedly change.

The challenge to all U.S. citizens is to improve the representative nature of our democracy in spite of an increasing population. This can be done by increased voter participation, a greater understanding among all Americans (particularly young people) of the political process, and more limits on the degree to which our representatives are allowed to act in their own best interests rather than in those of the people they represent.

YOU DECIDE

1. Do you think that representative democracy worked better at the beginning of U.S. history, when each senator and representative represented fewer Americans? Explain.
2. Some argue that the number of representatives in the House should be increased. What problems might arise if that occurred?

Videos taken of a political demonstration in one country can be seen in another through satellite technology in a matter of seconds. Increasingly, countries that try to hide government brutality find themselves the object of international pressure. Why? Because someone was able to gather evidence of government brutality and rapidly transmit it to people in other countries.

Few significant events go unknown and unseen in the political world today, no matter where they take place. Indeed, some political analysts believe that the worldwide spread of relatively inexpensive telecommunications systems and products has been a major reason why some nondemocratic countries have had to change their governmental policies and systems. Their citizens know that better forms of government exist elsewhere in the world because they hear about them on the radio, see them on TV or in movie theaters, or learn about them on the Internet.

▶ Students throughout the nation often take computer classes, and many school districts now require that students successfully complete at least one computer class before graduation. These students, with the assistance of their teacher, are learning to access and conduct research via the Internet. Today, most schools and many public libraries provide computers with Internet access for student and public use.

You Have Easy Access to Information, Too Even if your school does not have computers connected to the Internet, you probably know someone who does. There are numerous government-related sites that you can access via the Internet. As you study the topics in this text, your teacher can guide you to those sites so that you can obtain further information.

Ethics and Interdependence

As mentioned, each nation has its own unique cultural system—customs, language, political and social values, and so on. In our increasingly interdependent world, what happens when the cultural system of one nation clashes with that of another? For example, the governments of several Middle Eastern countries call upon their religious tradition to keep certain groups, such as women, out of politics. The People's Republic of China has been accused by Americans and others of depriving its citizens of basic human rights and liberties.

The ethical question here is, who is right and who is wrong in these situations? If a nation is sovereign, shouldn't it be able to decide for itself what it should or should not do? Does any nation have the right to tell another nation how it should handle its affairs? As the

world grows smaller, such questions have come to the forefront. For example, one of the issues facing U.S. policymakers today has to do with China's internal policies and practices: Should the U.S. government continue to let China enjoy favorable trading arrangements with the United States in view of that country's lack of support for human rights within its borders?

SECTION 5 REVIEW

1. What does interdependence mean?
2. Why are nations becoming increasingly interdependent?
3. What are some ethical problems that result from this growing interdependence?
4. **For Critical Analysis:** Do you think that the increasing interdependence of the world's nations will have a positive or a negative effect on the United States? Explain your answer.

★ ★ ★ ★ **Chapter Summary** ★ ★ ★ ★

Section 1: The Meaning of Politics and Government

⭐ Politics is the set of procedures that we use to resolve questions about who receives which benefits in our society.

⭐ Government is a permanent structure composed of decision makers who make society's rules about "who gets what" and who have the power and authority to enforce those rules.

⭐ Political participation—for example, through voting—is important because politics and government affect our lives every day.

Section 2: The Purposes of Government

⭐ Government resolves conflicts, provides public services, and provides for national security and the common defense.

⭐ Government also sets goals for public policies and preserves culture.

Section 3: Nations and the Origins of Government

⭐ The nation is the basic political unit in the world today. Nations share four characteristics: population, territory, government, and sovereignty.

⭐ The evolutionary theory holds that government developed gradually as families gathered into clans and clans joined together into tribes.

⭐ The force theory holds that governments first originated when one person or group conquered a given territory and forced everyone in that territory into submission.

⭐ The social contract theory holds that government arose out of a voluntary agreement (contract) among free individuals.

Section 4: How Do Governments Differ from One Another?

⭐ In an autocracy, power is concentrated in the hands of an individual—either a monarch or a dictator.

⭐ In a democracy the supreme political authority rests with the people.

⭐ In a direct democracy, citizens participate directly in government decision making through mass meetings. In a representative democracy, decision making is carried out by representatives elected by the people.

⭐ The five basic principles of democracy are equality in voting, individual freedom, equality of all persons, majority rule and minority rights, and voluntary consent to be governed.

Section 5: The World Is Getting Smaller

⭐ Nations are becoming more interdependent—that is, more reliant on one another.

⭐ Nations are interdependent because they share the same environment and because the growth of technologies, including the Internet, has made communications faster and easier.

CHAPTER 1 Review

★ REVIEW QUESTIONS ★

1. Why do people living in groups need some form of government?
2. What are several forms of political participation?
3. What are the purposes of government?
4. List and explain the characteristics of a nation.
5. List and explain the three major theories of the origins of government.
6. Into what types can governments be classified?
7. How does a monarchy differ from a dictatorship?
8. What is the primary characteristic of any dictatorship?
9. Which form of government best describes the government of the United States?
10. Who holds the supreme political authority in a democracy?
11. Explain the difference between a direct democracy and a representative, or indirect, democracy. Which type best describes the system used in the United States?
12. What are the basic principles of democracy, and why are they important?
13. Explain why there is a growing interdependence among nations.
14. Has population growth weakened the representative nature of our democracy?

★ CRITICAL THINKING ★

1. Give three examples of why we must have rules in order to be free.
2. Historians have speculated that at one time humans lived without a form of organized government. Why do you think early peoples decided to devise laws and governments? What is your own theory of the origin of government?
3. Compare the three types of government outlined in this chapter and indicate who has ultimate authority in each one.

4. Consider the decision-making process in your city. Can you identify certain individuals or groups that seem to control the decision making? How are such groups controlled by the voters?
5. Nations are becoming more interdependent for many reasons. The reasons discussed in this chapter are world environmental problems and better and less expensive communications technology. Can you think of at least one other reason why nations are becoming more interdependent? Develop your answer.

★ IMPROVING YOUR SKILLS ★

Communication Skills

Listening Have you ever heard someone talking to you but been unable to remember anything that he or she said five minutes later? The person was probably insulted because you weren't really listening. Many individuals don't really listen to half of what they hear in life. We may hear the words but may not turn them into understandable and useful information. We consciously or unconsciously sort through what we've heard and focus on only *part* of the information.

You can become an effective listener at school, at work, and with family and friends by understanding the listening process:

- You hear what's being said.
- You make a decision as to its importance.
- You react to it.
- You file the information or discard it.

To become a more effective listener, you must gain more control over this process. Follow these guidelines:

1. ***Tell yourself that you want to retain what you are hearing.*** Concentrate on the speaker and tune out interference such as music, telephones, other con-

versations, and anything else about which you might be thinking. You must discipline yourself to become an active, involved listener, because it is easy to be distracted.

2. *Try to organize what you hear by listening to clues from the speaker.* For example, "The main point here is that . . . ." "The three reasons this happened are . . . ."

3. *If you know that a lecture or discussion is going to be based on something you have already heard or learned, review that information ahead of time.* It is much easier to retain new information if you can relate it to knowledge that you already have.

4. *Try to relate what you hear to your own knowledge and experience.* Coming up with concrete examples of what is being explained may help you understand. For example, if you are learning about the concepts of democracy, think of specific situations in which they apply to you.

5. *Ask questions if you don't understand or if you need more information.* If you need a point repeated or clarified, don't hesitate to ask the speaker.

Writing On a sheet of paper, complete the following statements.
1. The qualities that are most important for a high-ranking government policymaker to have are . . .
2. The best things about the United States are . . .
3. The president should work toward . . .

Form a team with three or four of your classmates. Take turns reading your responses to each other. Then take turns trying to repeat exactly how the others on your team have completed the statements.

Social Studies Skills

Learning about Forms of Government Use Figure 1–2 on page 19 to answer the following questions. This figure shows the forms of government. It simplifies the many complex forms that governments have taken since the beginning of organized society.

1. How does the upper panel, on autocracy, relate an absolute monarchy to a dictatorship?
2. In the middle panel, what is the distinction between laws developed under direct democracy and laws developed under representative democracy?
3. In the bottom panel, what is the distinction between a presidential democracy and a parliamentary democracy?
4. In the bottom panel, what distinguishes a modern constitutional monarchy from a parliamentary democracy?
5. In the bottom panel, why do you think the arrow pointing toward "monarch" is a broken line?

★ ACTIVITIES AND PROJECTS ★

1. Form small groups of five or six. Assume that each group has founded a new town that is growing quickly but as yet has no form of government. Each group should devise a plan of government for its town. Decide what the town goals will be, how a leader will be chosen, what rules will be made, and how the rules will be enforced.
2. Prepare a series of posters, each illustrating a form of government described in this chapter. Use pictures and words.

What If . . .

The United States Were Ruled by a King or Queen?

Many countries have been ruled by kings or queens. Imagine political and social life in the United States today. What if we were ruled by a king or queen? How would our lives be different?

CHAPTER 2

A Nation Emerges

CHAPTER OBJECTIVES

To learn about and understand . . .

⭐ The European origins of the American governmental system

⭐ The development of the American governmental system during the colonial era

⭐ The colonies' push for independence

⭐ The governmental arrangements set up by the Articles of Confederation

⭐ The Constitutional Convention and its compromises

⭐ The ratification of the Constitution

"The American Constitution [is] one of the few modern political documents drawn up by men who were forced by the sternest circumstances to think out what they really had to face, instead of chopping logic in a university classroom."

George Bernard Shaw
(1856–1950)
Anglo-Irish Playwright and Critic

INTRODUCTION

Imagine for a moment that you are sailing on a ship with hundreds of other people. The ship sinks off the coast of an uninhabited island. You and the others make it to shore, but you do not have access to any modern communications systems. You realize that all of you will be living on the island with no way for anyone to rescue you. Now you are faced with setting up a system of government for your new society.

That kind of situation is exactly what the playwright George Bernard Shaw was referring to in the above quotation. The framers of our Constitution were forced, by very strained conditions, to develop a document that would work. In this chapter, you will learn about some of those conditions.

◀ Actors recreate the drafting of the Declaration of Independence in the Assembly Room of Independence Hall, located in Philadelphia, Pennsylvania.

The European Origins of Our Governmental System

Preview Questions:

- What is limited government? Where did the concept of limited government come from?
- What is the system of representative government? Where did this system come from?
- What were some early influences on American political philosophy?

Key Terms:

Magna Carta, peers, limited government, representative government, representatives, Parliament, political philosophy

Although the American colonies were settled by people from many nations, most of the early American

▲ When England's King John signed the Magna Carta in 1215, it established the principal of limited government, ending the king's absolute power. In Chappels's painting, what does King John's attitude appear to be toward this historic event? Why is this event important for Americans?

settlers came from England. The English colonists brought with them the two principles *limited government* and *representative government*. These principles became important factors in forming the American political system. Also important were the works of English philosophers, as well as philosophers from other parts of Europe. Much of the political thought that has formed the way our nation governs itself originated in the theories of these philosophers.

Limited Government

For a long period in English history, the king or queen had almost unlimited powers. This situation changed in 1215, when King John was forced by his nobles to sign the **Magna Carta,** or great charter. (A copy of this document is included in the Resource Center at the back of this book.) This monumental document provided for trial by a jury of one's **peers,** or equals. It prohibited the taking of a person's life, liberty, and property except by the lawful judgment of that person's peers. The Magna Carta also forced the king to obtain the nobles' approval of any taxes he imposed on his royal subjects. Government became a contract between the king and the nobility.

The Magna Carta's importance to England cannot be overemphasized. It clearly established the principle of **limited government**—government on which strict limits are placed, usually by a constitution. Hence, the Magna Carta ended the monarch's absolute power. It is true that the rights provided under the Magna Carta originally applied only to the nobility. Eventually, however, these rights would be extended to all individuals in England and in the United States.

The principle of limited government was expanded in 1628, when King Charles I was forced to sign the Petition of Rights. Among other things, this petition prohibited the king from imprisoning political critics without a jury trial. Perhaps more importantly,' the petition declared that even the king or queen had to obey the law of the land.

In 1689, the English government passed the English Bill of Rights, which further extended the concept of limited government. Several important ideas were included in this document:

- The king or queen could not interfere with parliamentary elections.
- The king or queen had to have Parliament's approval to collect taxes or to maintain an army.
- The king or queen ruled with the consent of the people's representatives in Parliament.
- The people could not be subjected to cruel or unusual punishment or to excessive fines.

The British colonists in North America were also British citizens, and so they were familiar with the English Bill of Rights of 1689. Because of this, almost all the major concepts in the English Bill of Rights became part of the American system of government.

Representative Government

A **representative government** is one in which the people choose a limited number of individuals to make governmental decisions for all citizens. Those chosen by the citizens are called **representatives.** Usually, each representative is elected to office for a specific period of time.

In England, this group of representatives is called **Parliament.** Parliament consists of an upper chamber, called the House of Lords, and a lower chamber, called the House of Commons. In the eighteenth century, the House of Commons was mostly made up of merchants and property owners, and its members were elected by other merchants and property owners. Thus, in England, the concept of government by and for the people had become reality. The English system became a model by which the American colonies would govern themselves.

Early Philosophical Influences

Europeans were looking at the world in new ways in the 1600s and 1700s. One area of change was **political philosophy,** which involves ideas about how people should be governed. Political philosophers questioned such traditional doctrines as the divine right theory of government. The new ideas they proposed greatly influenced American colonists. In fact, as you will see, the ideas of these philosophers are clearly embodied in

▲ English philosopher John Locke argued that no one could be subjected to the political power of another without his own consent. Why was this such a radical concept in 1689?

the U.S. Constitution and other documents that outline the American philosophy of government. Influential European political philosophers included John Locke, Thomas Hobbes, Jean-Jacques Rousseau, and Charles de Secondat, the Baron of Montesquieu.

Locke, Hobbes, Rousseau, and the Social Contract It may seem obvious to you that any government should have the consent of the governed—that is, their permission and agreement. This notion, however, was still very new and revolutionary in the 1600s. An important English political philosopher, John Locke (1632–1704), wrote about this issue in *Two Treatises of Government* in 1689. He argued that "no one could be subjected to the political power of another, without his own consent." Government, therefore, was only legitimate as long as the people continued to consent to it.

Locke further argued that all persons were born free, equal, and independent. All persons had natural rights to life, liberty, and property—rights that everyone possessed even before governments existed. He held that the primary purpose of government was to protect those natural rights, and he believed that government

▲ In 1762, French philosopher Jean-Jacques Rousseau observed thousands of European peasants suffering under oppressive governments and stated, "Man is born free, yet everywhere he is found in chains." What did Rousseau believe was the main duty of government?

was really a social contract between the people and their government.

Locke theorized that before governments existed, people lived in "a state of nature" in which they had unlimited freedom and the right to do as they wished. In this respect, he agreed with an earlier English philosopher, Thomas Hobbes (1588–1679). Hobbes also discussed the "state of nature" in which people lived before governments were established. In contrast to Locke, however, Hobbes argued that this situation led to chaos and violence because the weak could not protect themselves against the strong. There were no natural rights. Rather, rights could be won only through force. Life in this "free" state of nature, therefore, was "nasty, brutish, and short."

Hobbes published his landmark political study *Leviathan* in 1651. In it, he said that human beings had voluntarily agreed to create a powerful government in order to gain security and safety. In exchange, they gave up the freedom to do as they chose in the state of nature. They therefore owed their complete loyalty to the government that protected them. Hobbes believed that a government in which a ruler had absolute authority would end the conflicts waged in the natural state. Only then would people enjoy rights, such as the right to life, liberty, or property. Few political thinkers agreed that the individual owed total loyalty to the government. Although Hobbes's writings supported the concept of monarchy, they also contributed to the growing idea that government was based on a negotiated agreement between the rulers and the ruled, rather than on raw force and power.

Like Hobbes and Locke, Jean-Jacques Rousseau (1712–1778), a French political philosopher, believed that people had once lived in a state of nature and freedom. Since then, though, many people had come under the control of unjust rulers who ruled at the expense of their citizens' personal freedom. In *The Social Contract*, published in 1762, Rousseau wrote, "Man is born free, yet everywhere he is found in chains." Rousseau was referring to the large number of people on the European continent living under oppressive governments. He argued that people alone had the right to determine how they should be governed. He proposed that because all human beings in a state of nature were born free, the main duty of government should be to maintain as much freedom as possible in a civilized society. This could be accomplished by allowing each person to have a say in decision making. At the same time, each person would have to agree to submit to the "will" of the majority.

Montesquieu and the Separation of Powers A French political philosopher, Charles de Secondat, the Baron of Montesquieu (1689–1755), was the first political writer to discuss dividing government into three separate branches with different duties and the ability to act as a check on each other's power. In his book *The Spirit of the Laws*, published in 1748, Montesquieu pointed out that no one person in the English government was allowed to make the laws, enforce the laws, and interpret the laws. This partial separation of governmental responsibilities helped to prevent the abuse of power and to protect the liberties of English people. The framers of our Constitution not only agreed with Montesquieu, but also went even further. They wanted to ensure that the American form of government had an even more distinct separation of powers. In this way, they hoped that liberty would be safer in the United States than in England.

SECTION 1 REVIEW

1. What is limited government? How did the American way of government evolve out of this concept?
2. What is representative government?

3. How did the theories of European political philosophers influence American political thinking?
4. **For Critical Analysis:** What are some common restrictions on government in the United States that follow the principle of limited government?

The Beginnings of Self-Government

Preview Questions:

- ⭐ What was the first British settlement in North America? What changes did this settlement go through?
- ⭐ What kind of government did the Pilgrims establish for themselves?
- ⭐ What was the nation's first written constitution? What kind of government did it establish?

Key Terms:

charter, representative assembly, Mayflower Compact, prototype, Fundamental Orders of Connecticut, legislatures

The American system of government has roots in English history and European political philosophy. It also has roots in the experiences of the colonists, as they struggled against nature, England, and each other to set up a system that would reflect their beliefs and meet their needs. Thus, to fully understand the American system, we must look back to the nation's beginnings.

The First British Settlements

In the 1580s, Sir Walter Raleigh, the adventurer and writer, convinced England's queen, Elizabeth I, to allow him to establish the first British outpost in North America. He did this by sending a ship of settlers in 1585 to Roanoke Island off the coast of North Car-

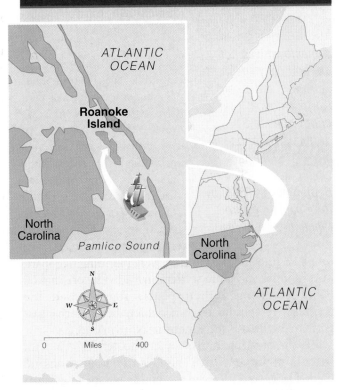

FIGURE 2–1 Roanoke Island The first British outpost in North America was established by Sir Walter Raleigh on Roanoke Island in 1585. What was the first permanent British settlement in North America?

olina. The map in Figure 2–1 shows the location of Roanoke Island. Raleigh's attempt to create a settlement was unsuccessful. The first permanent British settlement would not be established until the 1600s.

▶ *This nineteenth-century engraving depicts the arrival of the first English colonists at Jamestown. What happened to these colonists?*

Just the Facts

Jamestown was not the first permanent European settlement in North America. That honor goes to St. Augustine, Florida—a city that still exists— which was founded on September 8, 1565, by the Spaniard Pedro Menéndez de Avilés.

Jamestown In 1607, another group from London, the Virginia Company, established a trading post in Virginia. This group named its settlement Jamestown. In the first year of its existence, over 60 percent of the colony's 105 inhabitants died. In 1609, England sent over 800 new settlers. By the spring of the following year, only 60 were left. The survivors, admitting defeat, decided to return to England. Just as they were planning to depart, new supplies and more settlers arrived. The original 60 colonists changed their plans. Together, all the colonists rebuilt Jamestown, which became the first permanent British settlement in North America.

Of the six thousand people who left England for Virginia between 1607 and 1623, four thousand died. Those who survived established a type of government that would serve as a model for later colonial adventures.

The king of England had given the Virginia Company a **charter,** a written grant of authority, to make laws "for the good and welfare" of the Jamestown settlement. Jamestown's colonists used this charter to institute a **representative assembly,** a lawmaking body composed of individuals who represented the population. Representative assemblies became a typical form of government in the colonies.

▲ *Despite the fact that the* Mayflower *arrived well after Jamestown was established, the colonists who landed in New England strongly influenced the way government would be established in the New World. Why was the Pilgrims' influence so great?*

The Pilgrims and the Mayflower Compact The Plymouth Company established the first New England colony in 1620. A group of English Protestants, the Pilgrims, sailed to North America on the *Mayflower*. They landed at what is now Provincetown Harbor, at the tip of Cape Cod in Massachusetts. (They later moved the ship to Plymouth, Massachusetts, which became their new home.)

Before the Pilgrims went ashore, the adult males drew up the **Mayflower Compact,** an agreement in which they set up a government and promised to obey its laws. (A copy of the Mayflower Compact is included in the Resource Center.) It was signed by forty-one of the forty-four men aboard on November 21, 1620. No women were allowed to sign it, nor did they have any direct part in developing it, because women at that time did not have any political status. The Pilgrims established a written document for self-government because their leaders believed that they needed a set of rules to govern themselves and prevent civil disorder. They also wanted to create a government based on the consent of the governed.

The Mayflower Compact was in fact a *social contract* of the type that Locke had described. It was an agreement among individuals to establish a government and to live by its rules. This particular social contract had great historical significance because it served as a **prototype**—a model—for similar compacts in American history.

More Colonies Are Formed

Another settlement in New England was set up by the Massachusetts Bay Colony in 1620. By 1639, a number of Pilgrims who were being persecuted for their religious beliefs decided to leave the Massachusetts Bay Colony. They colonized the area that is now Connecticut. In the process, they developed America's first written constitution—the **Fundamental Orders of Connecticut.** This document called for a representative assembly. Elected representatives from each town would serve in the assembly and make laws. The document also called for the popular election of a governor and judges.

By 1732, all thirteen colonies had been established. The colonies are shown on the map in Figure 2–2. Each colony had its own political documents and constitution. For example, the Massachusetts Body of Liberties

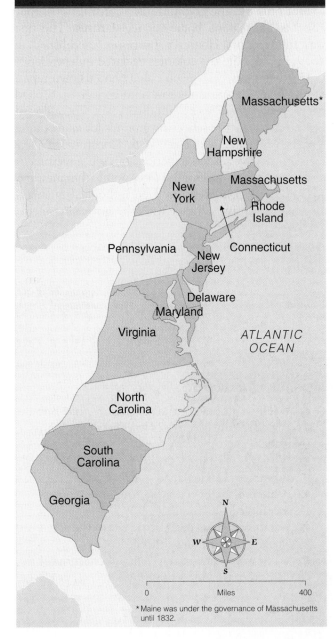

FIGURE 2–2 The Thirteen Colonies Georgia, the last of the thirteen colonies, was established in 1732. By this time, each of the thirteen colonies had developed its own political system complete with political documents and a constitution. Which colony had the first written constitution, and what was it called?

Massachusetts*

New Hampshire

New York

Massachusetts

Rhode Island

Pennsylvania

Connecticut

New Jersey

Delaware

Maryland

Virginia

ATLANTIC OCEAN

North Carolina

South Carolina

Georgia

N
W E
S

0   Miles   400

* Maine was under the governance of Massachusetts until 1832.

was adopted in 1641. It supported protection of individual rights and became part of colonial law. In 1683, the Pennsylvania Frame of Government was passed. This document, along with the Pennsylvania Charter of

Privileges of 1701, established some of the principles that were later expressed in the U.S. Constitution and the Bill of Rights.

Early Legislatures

Not only did the colonies have constitutions, they also had lawmaking bodies or **legislatures.** The first was the Virginia House of Burgesses, established in 1619. By the time the colonies declared independence from England in 1776, each colony had its own representative legislature, and most of these legislatures had been operating for over a hundred years. The colonial legislatures were the schooling grounds for many of the leaders who later wrote the U.S. Constitution. The legislatures gave leaders experience in self-government and provided a model for our later political framework.

Colonial legislatures and their individual members also had extensive contact with the governing methods of the native peoples. Indeed, some of the distinctive political beliefs of American life emerged out of a rich Native American democratic tradition.

SECTION 2 REVIEW

1. What major political concepts were brought to America by early English settlers?
2. What was the Mayflower Compact, and why was it written?
3. What kind of governing body did the Fundamental Orders of Connecticut establish? What was the role of the people under this constitution?
4. **For Critical Analysis:** Describe the historical significance of the Fundamental Orders of Connecticut. How do we see its principles in operation today?

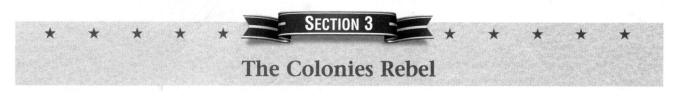

★ ★ ★ ★ ★ SECTION 3 ★ ★ ★ ★ ★

The Colonies Rebel

Preview Questions:

- What were some of the restrictions that Britain placed on the colonies? How did the colonists react?
- Why was the First Continental Congress called? What was decided at that meeting?
- What did the Second Continental Congress accomplish?
- What arguments and events led to the Declaration of Independence?
- What were some of the political concerns of the citizens of the first states?

Key Terms:

Navigation Acts, Sugar Act, Stamp Act, delegates, grievances, boycott, First Continental Congress, Second Continental Congress, legitimacy

Even though the thirteen colonies had been formed differently and were governed differently, all were under the rulership of the British monarchy. Britain wanted the colonies to act in England's best interest, but the British government did little to manage its outposts in the colonies. After all, they were located more than three thousand miles (almost five thousand kilometers) away, and it took almost two months to sail across the Atlantic. Therefore, the colonies gradually became self-governing, even though they were still officially ruled by the British king in London.

The British first placed general restrictions on the colonists in 1651 when the **Navigation Acts** were passed by the English Parliament. These acts required that only English ships (including ships of its colonies) be used for trade within the British empire. For the most part, however, the colonies were left alone to govern themselves until the mid-1700s. When the British began to tighten their restrictions on the colonies at that time, the colonists responded with increasing anger.

▶ *Even the teapots reflected the objections of the colonists to the severe taxes imposed by the British Parliament.*

Taxation without Representation

In 1760, George III was crowned king of England. After that, more restrictions were applied to colonial trade. The Proclamation of 1763 declared that no colonial settlement could be established west of the Appalachian Mountains. In 1764, the British Parliament passed the **Sugar Act.** This act imposed a tax on all sugar imported into the American colonies. The tax revenues helped pay for wars that the British had waged. These taxes were also used to support British troops in North America.

Further legislation soon followed. In 1765, the British Parliament passed the **Stamp Act,** placing the first direct tax on the colonies. The Stamp Act required the use of tax stamps on all legal documents, newspapers, pamphlets, and playing cards and certain business agreements. The colonists denounced the new taxes. Not only were the taxes a severe economic burden; they were also unjust, in the eyes of the colonists. The colonies had no elected official to represent their interests in Parliament. Colonists complained that this "taxation without representation" was unfair.

In October 1765, nine of the thirteen colonies sent **delegates** (representatives) to the Stamp Act Congress, held in New York City. The delegates prepared a declaration of rights and **grievances** (complaints) against the new British actions, which was sent to King George III. This action marked the first time that a majority of the colonies joined together to oppose a British law. As a result of the colonists' grievances, the British Parliament repealed the Stamp Act.

The British Crown passed new laws, however, designed to bind the colonies more tightly to the central government in London. Laws that imposed taxes on glass, paint, lead, and many other items were passed in 1767. The colonists protested the taxes by a **boycott,** a refusal to purchase all English goods. In 1773, anger over taxation reached a powerful climax at the famous Boston Tea Party. Colonists dressed as Mohawk Indians dumped almost 350 chests of British tea into the Boston Harbor as a gesture of tax protest.

The British Parliament was quick to respond to the Tea Party. It passed the Coercive Acts (sometimes called the Intolerable Acts) in 1774. The acts closed the harbor and placed the government of Boston under direct British control.

The First Continental Congress

In response to the Intolerable Acts, Rhode Island, Pennsylvania, and New York proposed that a colonial congress be held. The Massachusetts House of Representatives requested that all colonies select delegates to

▲ *The site of so much of our nation's early history, this Philadelphia building, Carpenters' Hall, was where the First Continental Congress met on September 5, 1774.*

send to Philadelphia for such a congress.

The **First Continental Congress** was held at Carpenters' Hall in Philadelphia on September 5, 1774. Of the thirteen colonies, only Georgia did not send delegates. The First Continental Congress decided that the colonies should send a petition to King George III to explain their grievances. Other resolutions were passed to continue the boycott of British goods and to require that each colony start an army. Almost immediately after receiving the petition, the British government condemned the congress's actions as open acts of rebellion.

The congressional delegates declared that each county and city in the colonies should form a committee to spy on people's actions and to report to the press the names of those who violated the trade boycott against Britain. The list of names would then be printed in the local papers. Over the next several months, all colonial legislators supported this and other actions taken by the First Continental Congress.

COMMON SENSE;

ADDRESSED TO THE

INHABITANTS

OF

AMERICA,

On the following interesting

SUBJECTS.

I. Of the Origin and Design of Government in general, with concise Remarks on the English Constitution.

II. Of Monarchy and Hereditary Succession.

III. Thoughts on the present State of American Affairs.

IV. Of the present Ability of America, with some miscellaneous Reflections.

Man knows no Master save creating Heaven,
Or those whom choice and common good ordain.
THOMSON.

PHILADELPHIA;
Printed, and Sold, by R. BELL, in Third-Street.
MDCCLXXVI.

Less than a month later, delegates from twelve colonies (Georgia's delegates did not arrive until the fall) gathered in Pennsylvania for the **Second Continental Congress.** The congress immediately assumed the powers of a central government. One of its main actions was to establish an army. Colonial citizen-soldiers had gathered around Boston, and the congress declared them an army. It named George Washington—a delegate to the Second Continental Congress who had some military experience—as the army's commander in chief.

The Second Continental Congress

Britain reacted to the resolution passed by the First Continental Congress with even more strict and repressive measures. On April 19, 1775, British soldiers, called Redcoats, fought with colonial citizen-soldiers, called Minutemen, in the towns of Lexington and Concord in Massachusetts. These were the first battles of the American Revolution. The Battle of Concord was later described by the poet Ralph Waldo Emerson as the "shot heard round the world."

Independence

Public debate raged bitterly about the problems with Great Britain, but the stage was set for independence. One of the most rousing arguments in favor of independence was presented by a former English corset maker, Thomas Paine, who wrote a brilliant pamphlet called *Common Sense*. In that pamphlet, he mocked King George III and attacked every argument that favored loyalty to the king. He wanted the developing colonies to become a model nation for democracy, in a world in which other nations were oppressed by strong central governments.

None of Paine's arguments was new. In fact, most of them were commonly heard in tavern debates throughout the land. The reason that *Common Sense* was so effective was Paine's ability to put these arguments together in such a convincing way:

> *A government of our own is our natural right: and when a man seriously reflects on the precariousness [uncertainty] of human affairs, he will become convinced, that it is infinitely wiser and safer, to form a constitution of our own in a cool and deliberate manner, while we have it in our power, than to trust such an interesting event to time and chance.*

The Resolution of Independence Many colonists began to call for independence. Samuel Adams, a patriot from Massachusetts, asked, "Is not America already independent? Why not then declare it?" In June 1776, after more than a year of fighting, Richard Henry Lee of Virginia introduced the Resolution of Independence to the Second Continental Congress. On July 2 of that year, the congress adopted the resolution:

> RESOLVED, That these United Colonies are, and of right ought to be free and independent States, that they are absolved from allegiance to the British Crown, and that all political connection between them and the state of Great Britain is, and ought to be, totally dissolved.

The Resolution of Independence was not a legally binding document. It was, however, one of the first necessary steps to establish the **legitimacy**—legal authority—of a new nation in the eyes of foreign governments. The new nation required supplies for its armies and foreign military aid. Unless officials of foreign nations believed that this new land was truly independent from Britain, they would not support its leaders.

The Declaration of Independence Soon after Richard Henry Lee proposed the Resolution of Independence, Thomas Jefferson, a tall, redheaded Virginia planter, began writing a draft of the Declaration of Independence. Jefferson worked alone on the document for the last two weeks in June.

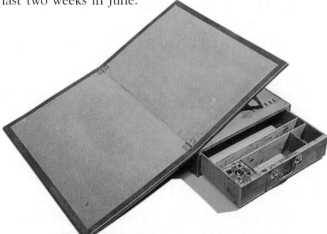

▲ It is believed that Jefferson wrote the first draft of the Declaration of Independence on this portable writing desk. Jefferson claimed that all persons had "unalienable rights." What are these rights?

On June 28, he asked John Adams and Benjamin Franklin to look over his work. They made few changes.

Immediately after adopting the Resolution of Independence, the congress was ready to pass Jefferson's declaration. Some changes were made so that all of the delegates would accept it. For example, his condemnation of slavery was eliminated to satisfy delegates from Georgia and North Carolina, where slaves were held on many farms and plantations. On July 4, 1776, one of the world's most famous documents, the Declaration of Independence, was adopted.

Further changes were made in the following two weeks. On July 19, the modified draft became the "unanimous declaration of the thirteen United States of America." On August 2, the members of the Continental Congress signed it.

Natural Rights and the Consent of the Governed The second paragraph of the Declaration of Independence begins with these words:

> We hold these Truths to be self-evident, that all Men are created equal, that they are endowed by their Creator with certain unalienable Rights, that among these are Life, Liberty, and the pursuit of Happiness—That to secure these Rights, Governments are instituted among Men, deriving their just Powers from the Consent of the Governed, that whenever any Form of Government becomes destructive of these Ends, it is the Right of the People to alter or to abolish it, and to institute new Government.

The unalienable—or natural—rights referred to in the Declaration of Independence are the same rights that Locke discussed in his political philosophy. Natural rights are *inherent* rights. That means they cannot be taken away from a person, and they are beyond the power of governments to grant or deny.

According to the Declaration of Independence, government exists to protect individuals' natural rights. In a democratic society, government derives its power from the consent of the governed. In other words, the people give government the power to rule. Because government is based on the will of the people, it can also be abolished by the people.

▲ This 1786 painting by John Trumbull depicts the signing of the Declaration of Independence. Though to us the scene looks formal and "historical," it actually shows a group of men taking a huge risk. What crime could these signers be accused of committing?

From Colonies to States

In May 1776, the Second Continental Congress directed the colonies to form "such governments as shall . . . be conducive to the happiness and safety of their constituents [voters]." During the next several years, all thirteen states formally adopted written constitutions to replace their colonial constitutions. Eleven of these constitutions were completely new. The other two, those of Rhode Island and Connecticut, were old royal charters with minor changes. Seven of the new constitutions contained bills of rights that defined the personal liberties of all state citizens. All the constitutions called for limited government.

Many citizens feared the establishment of a strong central government because of their experiences under British rule. They opposed any form of government that even seemed like monarchy. Thus, they did not favor government by a strong executive authority—a person with wide-reaching administrative powers. They preferred to place government in the hands of an elected legislative body. Where citizens were most strongly opposed to monarchy, the legislatures became all-powerful. The legislatures of Pennsylvania and Georgia were unchecked by executive authority. Indeed, the executive branch was weak in most states. This situation would continue until the U.S. Constitution was ratified.

Government in Action

Women and the American Revolution

We often read about the men who founded America, but few books written about the colonial era mention our country's "founding women." Although no women were present at the Constitutional Convention, women nonetheless contributed significantly to the political changes of the times.

In the years before the American Revolution, many women encouraged opposition to the British. Small groups of women who called themselves Daughters of Liberty helped spread the boycott of British goods. To pressure merchants into not importing British products, over three hundred "mistresses of families" in Boston refused to consume tea. Women of all social classes organized spinning bees to make fabric and sew clothing, so that it would not have to be imported.

Some women wrote political pamphlets that helped turn public opinion in favor of independence. Mercy Otis Warren (1728–1814) of Massachusetts was one of the first people to urge the Massachusetts delegates to the Second Continental Congress to vote for independence from England. Warren expressed her political ideas in written correspondence with John Adams and Thomas Jefferson. She also wrote a three-volume history of the American Revolution called *The History of the Rise, Progress, and Termination of the American Revolution*, which was published in 1805. She helped encourage revolutionary sentiments by making fun of the British colonial government in her plays *The Adulateur* (1773), *The Defeat* (1773), and *The Group* (1775).

During the revolution, many women served as nurses, seamstresses, and cooks. A few even disguised themselves as men and fought in battle. One such female soldier is buried in West Point Cemetery.

▲ This portrait of Mrs. James Warren (Mercy Otis) was painted by John Singleton Copley about 1763. What role did Warren play in the Patriot cause? (Bequest of Winslow Warren, Courtesy of Museum of Fine Arts, Boston.)

THINK ABOUT IT

1. Women contributed in many ways to the success of the American Revolution. They were not, however, given the right to vote when the new nation was established. Why?
2. How do you think the roles of women in World War I or World War II might have differed from their roles in the American Revolution?

3. Describe some of the resolutions passed by the First Continental Congress.
4. Describe the major events and common attitudes that led to the signing of the Declaration of Independence.
5. **For Critical Analysis:** Do you think experiences under English rule made it difficult for Americans to form a strong national government? Explain your answer.

1. What kind of relationships had developed between the British monarchy and the colonies by the mid-1700s? Why?
2. How did the thirteen colonies respond to the Stamp Act of 1765?

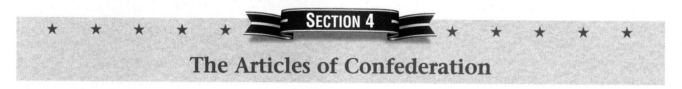

★ ★ ★ ★ ★ **SECTION 4** ★ ★ ★ ★ ★

The Articles of Confederation

Preview Questions:

- What were the basic provisions of the Articles of Confederation?
- What were the weaknesses of the Articles of Confederation?
- Why were the 1780s a critical period in American history?
- What major events and popular sentiments led to the Constitutional Convention of 1787?

Key Terms:

confederation, Northwest Ordinance, nationalists

The colonists' fear of a strong central government influenced the thinking of the delegates to the Second Continental Congress. A committee named by the congress to draft a plan for a national government drew up a plan for a **confederation**—a voluntary association of *independent* states. In a confederation, the member states agree to let the central government undertake a limited number of activities, such as forming an army. But the member states do not allow many restrictions on their own actions. They typically can govern most state affairs as they see fit.

On November 15, 1777, the Second Continental Congress agreed on a draft of the plan, which was finally signed by all thirteen states on March 1, 1781. The Articles of Confederation, the result of this plan, served as this nation's first national constitution. In spite of serious weaknesses, the Articles represented an important step in the creation of our governmental

system. (A copy of the Articles of Confederation is included in the Resource Center.)

The Government of the Confederation

Under the Articles of Confederation, the Congress of the Confederation was the central governing body for all the states. This body was an assembly of ambassadors, as they were called, from the various states. Each state could send from two to seven ambassadors to the congress; but each state, no matter what its size, had only one vote.

Sovereignty was an important issue in the Articles of Confederation:

Each State retains its sovereignty, freedom and independence, and every power, jurisdiction, and right, which is not by this Confederation expressly delegated to the United States in Congress assembled.

The structure of the government under the Articles of Confederation is shown in Figure 2–3 on page 46.

The Powers of Congress under the Articles

Congress had several powers under the Articles of Confederation, including the powers to do the following:

- Enter into treaties and alliances.
- Establish and control armed forces.

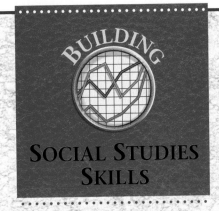
Every year, the government prints hundreds of publications. Many of them can help you understand American government and politics. Listed below are several government publications that may prove useful in your studies.

The *Statistical Abstract of the United States*, published by the Bureau of the Census, gives statistics on the social, political, and economic status of the United States. Its hundreds of charts, graphs, and tables cover topics such as population, law enforcement, immigration, and much more.

The *Book of the States* is published by the Council of State Governments. It contains information on state governments, economies, taxes, constitutions, and many other subjects.

A daily *Congressional Record* is published each day that Congress is in session. It contains everything that is said and done on the floors of both houses.

Using Government Publications

Issues are bound and indexed annually.

The *Congressional Directory* is a publication of the Congressional Joint Committee on Printing. It contains biographies of the members of Congress, lists of committees and committee assignments, statistics for recent congressional elections, and maps of congressional districts.

The *United States Government Manual* is a guide to the federal government. It contains information about the legislative, executive, and judicial branches of government and federal agencies and commissions. Addresses and telephone numbers of government offices are also included.

PRACTICING YOUR SKILLS

Go to your local library (or access the Internet) and use the sources listed above to find the following items and information:

1. A map of your congressional district.
2. A biography of one of the senators in your state.
3. The name of the state agency that can give you information about your state's welfare laws.

- Declare war and make peace.
- Regulate coinage (but not paper money).
- Borrow money from the people.
- Create a postal system.
- Regulate Indian affairs.
- Set standards of weights and measures.
- Create courts for problems related to ships at sea.
- Settle disputes between the states under certain circumstances.
- Guarantee that citizens visiting other states would have the same rights and privileges as the state's residents.

Under the Articles, the Congress of the Confederation accomplished a number of things. Certain states' claims to western land were settled with the **Northwest Ordinance.** This law established a basic pattern for how states should govern new territories north of the Ohio River. Additionally, and perhaps most importantly, the United States under the Articles of Confederation won the Revolutionary War. Congress was then able to negotiate a peace treaty with Great Britain, the Treaty of Paris, which was signed in 1783. Under the treaty, Britain recognized American independence. Britain also granted the United States all of the territory from the Atlantic Ocean to the Mississippi River and from the Great Lakes and Canada to what is now northern Florida.

The Articles of Confederation were, in a sense, an unplanned experiment that tested some of the principles of government set forth earlier in the Declaration of Independence. Some argue that without the experience of government under the Articles of Confederation, it would have been difficult, if not impossible, to arrive at the compromises that were put into the Constitution several years later.

Weaknesses of the Government of the Confederation

In spite of its accomplishments, the government created by the Articles was weak. Because of its lack of power, the central government had a difficult time coping with the problems

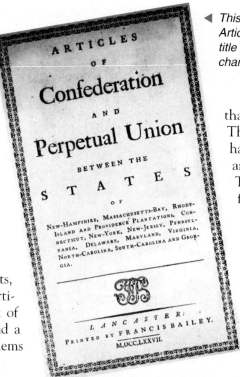

ARTICLES OF Confederation AND Perpetual Union BETWEEN THE STATES OF New-Hampshire, Massachusetts-Bay, Rhode-Island and Providence Plantations, Connecticut, New-York, New-Jersey, Pennsylvania, Delaware, Maryland, Virginia, North-Carolina, South-Carolina and Georgia.

LANCASTER: PRINTED BY FRANCIS BAILEY. M,DCC,LXXVII.

◀ *This is the cover of the official copy of the Articles of Confederation. What does the full title suggest? How have state names changed?*

that the growing nation was facing. The Articles of Confederation also had other major weaknesses, which are listed in Figure 2–4 on page 47. These weaknesses stemmed from the fact that the government under the Articles was made up of independent states that had no intention of giving up their sovereignty.

As you can see from Figure 2–4, much of the functioning of the government under the Articles depended on the goodwill of the states. Article 3, for example, simply established a "league of

---

FIGURE 2–3 American Government under the Articles of Confederation As you can see in the figure below, the individual states were supreme in power under the Articles of Confederation. Under the Articles of Confederation, how was a president chosen? Was the president very powerful?

States
★ Retained their independent political authority.
★ Held every power not expressly delegated to Congress.

Each state sent 2 to 7 representatives to the Congress of the Confederation.

President
★ Appointed by Congress to preside over meetings.
★ Had no real executive authority.

Other Committees and Civil Officers
★ Appointed by Congress to manage general affairs under the direction of Congress.

Congress
★ One-house assembly of state representatives, in which each state possessed one vote.
★ Needed the approval of at least nine states to exercise most powers.
★ Needed the consent of all states to amend the Articles.

Committee of States
★ Included one delegate from each state, appointed by Congress.
★ Authorized to act according to the wishes of Congress while Congress was in recess.

FIGURE 2–4 Weaknesses in the Articles of Confederation The lack of a strong government and the fierce independence of the states in the early years following the Revolutionary War led to several problems. Each of these problems was associated with a weakness in the Articles of Confederation. Which weakness led to financial problems for the central government?

Weakness	Result
Congress could not force the states to provide military troops.	Congress could not draft soldiers to form a standing army.
Congress could not regulate commerce between the states or with other nations.	Each state was free to set up its own system of taxes on goods imported from other states. Economic quarrels among the states broke out. Trading with other nations was difficult.
Congress could enter into treaties but could not enforce its agreements or control foreign relations.	The states were not forced to respect treaties. Many states entered into treaties independently of Congress.
Congress could not issue paper money.	Each state issued its own paper money; currencies among the states differed tremendously in value.
Congress could not directly tax the people.	Congress had to rely on the states to collect and forward taxes, which the states were reluctant to do. The central government was always short of money.
Congress had no power to enforce its laws.	The central government depended on the states to enforce its laws, which they rarely did.
Nine states had to approve any law before it was enacted.	Laws were difficult to enact.
Any amendment to the Articles required the consent of all thirteen states.	It was almost impossible to change the powers of the central government.
There was no national judicial system.	Most disputes among the states could not be settled by the national government.
There was no executive branch.	Coordinating the work of the central government was almost impossible.

friendship" among the states, with no central government intended.

A Time of Crisis—The 1780s The actual fighting during the Revolutionary War ended with the surrender of General Charles Cornwallis in Yorktown on October 18, 1781. Although peace with the British, formally achieved in 1783, may have been won, peace within the new nation was hard to find. The states bickered among themselves and refused to support the new central government in almost every way. The states also increasingly taxed each other's goods and at times even prevented trade altogether. As George Washington stated, "We are one nation today and thirteen tomorrow. Who will treat us on such terms?"

By 1784, the new nation was suffering from a serious economic depression. Banks were calling in old loans and refusing to give new ones. People who could not pay their debts were often thrown into prison. The tempers of angry farmers reached a boiling point in a well-known event that occurred in August 1786–Shays's Rebellion.

Think of a serious problem facing your community—for example, crime. Although everyone might agree that crime is a problem, chances are that not everyone agrees on how to solve it.

One vital citizenship skill is the ability to make thoughtful decisions about such matters. In making decisions, remember that there is almost always more than one solution to any problem. To make the best decision, you need to identify all possible alternatives and choose the one that will be the most effective for yourself and others. Doing this means knowing what goals or values are involved in each alternative and what the consequences of each choice may be.

The process outlined below can help you make wise decisions:

1. **Define what you need or want.** Try to pinpoint what you are trying to accomplish or what you need or want from your decision.
2. **Identify your choices.** There are at least two possible

PARTICIPATING IN YOUR GOVERNMENT

Making Decisions

choices, and usually more, for every decision. Sometimes you need to gather information and do research in order to identify your choices. Try to come up with as many possibilities as you can without eliminating any.
3. **Sort through your choices.** After you've listed all possible choices, take a good look at each one. Consider its advantages and disadvantages. Be sure that each option you are considering is legal and ethical.

4. **Compare your choices.** Use the information you have found to evaluate each possible choice. Compare them and see which one makes the most sense.
5. **Make the decision.**
6. **Make a plan to carry out your decision.**

TAKING ACTION

1. Think of a decision you made recently. Name two possible choices you had, and identify the advantages and disadvantages of each.
2. Think of a problem facing your community. Recommend a possible solution to the problem by using the decision-making process outlined above. Then send your recommendation to the council, commission, or official in charge of making such decisions.
3. Do you think the founders of this nation used any part of this decision-making process while they were drafting the Declaration of Independence or the Articles of Confederation? Explain your answer.

Shays's Rebellion

tionary War, Daniel Shays, along with approximately two thousand armed farmers, seized county courthouses and disrupted debtors' trials. Shays's men then launched an attack on the national government arsenal in Springfield, Massachusetts, where weapons were stored. The rebellion continued to spread and grow in intensity. It lasted into the winter, when it was finally stopped by the Massachusetts militia.

The revolt had an important effect. It frightened American political and business leaders and caused national government had to be created. That central government had to be strong enough to maintain order and to cope with the serious economic problems facing the nation.

The Annapolis Convention The Virginia legislature called for a meeting, or convention, of all of the states at Annapolis, Maryland, on September 11, 1786. Unhappy members of the Congress of the Confederation agreed. Five of the thirteen states sent delegates,

▲ *This engraving shows Shays's followers arguing with officials at a courthouse door. How did this rebellion spark a call for a stronger national government?*

called **nationalists.** They persuaded the other delegates to issue a report calling on the states to hold a convention in Philadelphia in May of the following year for the following purpose:

> to take into consideration the situation of the United States, to devise such further provisions as shall appear to them necessary to render the constitution of the Federal Government adequate to the exigencies of the Union.

The Congress of the Confederation at first was reluctant to give its approval to the Philadelphia convention. By mid-February 1787, however, seven of the states had named delegates to the Philadelphia meeting. Finally, on February 21, the Congress called on the states to send delegates to Philadelphia "for the sole and expressed purpose of revising the Articles of Confederation." That Philadelphia meeting became the Constitutional Convention.

SECTION 4 REVIEW

1. Describe the government set up by the Articles.
2. What were the powers of Congress under the Articles of Confederation?
3. What were the major weaknesses of the Articles, and what were the results of those weaknesses?
4. What did George Washington mean when he stated, "We are one nation today and thirteen tomorrow. Who will treat us on such terms?"
5. **For Critical Analysis:** Why do you think Shays's Rebellion frightened American business and political leaders?

two of whom were Alexander Hamilton of New York and James Madison of Virginia. Both of these men favored a strong central government. Thus, they were

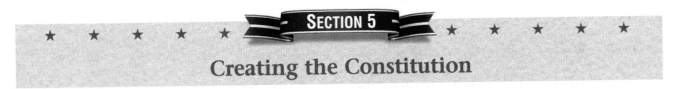

SECTION 5

Creating the Constitution

Preview Questions:

- On what basic concepts did the delegates to the Constitutional Convention agree?
- What compromises were necessary, and why?
- What were the final compromises reached?

Key Terms:

agenda, Virginia Plan, bicameral legislature, New Jersey Plan, Great Compromise, Three-Fifths Compromise, exports, interstate commerce

▲ *As the Declaration of Independence is read aloud for the first time to the waiting crowd, what emotions do you imagine the listeners might be experiencing?*

The Philadelphia convention was supposed to start on May 14, 1787, but few of the delegates had actually arrived in Philadelphia by that date. The convention formally opened in the East Room of the Pennsylvania State House (later named Independence Hall) on May 25. Fifty-five of the seventy-four delegates had arrived. Only Rhode Island, where feelings were strong against creating a more powerful central government, did not send any delegates.

Who Were the Delegates?

The fifty-five delegates were relatively young. James Madison was thirty-six, Alexander Hamilton was thirty-two, and Jonathan Dayton of New Jersey was twenty-six. Thirty-three of the delegates were members of the legal profession. Half of them were college graduates in a country in which less than 1 percent of the population finished college. Seven were former chief executives of their states; eight were important businessmen; six were large-plantation owners; and three were physicians.

Several men stood out as leaders. George Washington, who had served as commander in chief during the Revolutionary War, was already a national hero. Among all the prominent men assembled at the Philadelphia convention, Washington was immediately recognized as a leader. Benjamin Franklin was a world-famous scientist and diplomat. At eighty-one years old, he played an active role in the debates (even though he had to be carried in on a portable chair held by four prisoners from the local jail). Virginia had sent James Madison, a brilliant supporter of a strong central government. Madison's carefully taken notes are our primary source of information about what happened at the Constitutional Convention. He is often called the "Father of the Constitution" because he authored the basic plan of government that was ultimately adopted. Thomas Jefferson, unfortunately, could not be at the convention because he was serving as ambassador to France. John Adams could not attend either, as he was serving as ambassador to Great Britain.

Working Conditions

The delegates worked for 116 days and actually met on 89. In their meeting room, the windows were usually shut. None of the delegates wanted anyone to hear what they were doing. They did not want rumors spread about the form of government on which they would ultimately decide. Besides, if they opened the windows, hordes of flies would descend upon them. The air became humid and hot by noon of each day. At the end of each session, they retired to a nearby tavern, the Indian Queen.

George Washington was chosen to preside over the meetings. Each state had one vote on all questions, and a simple majority rule was used. Delegates from at least seven states had to be present in order for business to be transacted.

All of the delegates agreed on a number of basic concepts. They wanted the powers of the national government to be divided among three branches: legislative, executive, and judicial. They wanted the central government to limit the power of the states to print their own money. And they all wanted, in varying degrees, a more powerful central government. Delegates therefore did not debate these fundamental issues. Rather, they argued over how to put these principles into practice.

Revolutionary Plans and Compromises

James Madison had spent months reviewing European political theory before he went to the Philadelphia convention. His Virginia delegation arrived before anyone else, and he put the delegates to work immediately.

On the first day of the convention, governor Edmund Randolph of Virginia was able to present fifteen resolutions, which became known as the Virginia Plan. This was a masterful political stroke on the part of the Virginia delegation. It immediately set the **agenda**—the plan of things to be done—for the remainder of the convention.

The Virginia Plan The fifteen resolutions under the **Virginia Plan** proposed an entirely new national government. The plan, which favored large states such as Virginia, called for the following:

- A **bicameral legislature**—that is, a two-house legislature. Members of the lower house were to be chosen by the people. The upper house was to have fewer members, who were to be chosen by the elected members of the lower house. The number of representatives from each state would be based on the state's population, so the larger states would have more representatives. The national legislature could void any state laws.
- A national executive branch, which would be elected by the legislature.
- A national court system, created by the legislature.

The smaller states immediately complained. After all, under the Articles all states were equal, and the convention had no power to change this arrangement. After two weeks of debate, the smaller states offered their own plan.

The New Jersey Plan William Paterson of New Jersey presented an alternative plan favorable to the smaller states. The **New Jersey Plan,** as it was called, was based more closely on the Articles of Confederation. He suggested the following:

- That Congress be able to regulate trade and impose taxes.

◀ Patrick Henry was adamantly opposed to the new Constitution. How does the artist convey Henry's powerful oratorical style?

# of Government

George Washington
(1732–1799)

George Washington was born in Virginia in 1732. From 1754 to 1758, he served as a lieutenant colonel in the British army during the French and Indian War, a war fought between Britain and France over control of North America. He became a member of the Virginia colonial legislature, the House of Burgesses, in 1759 and was later a delegate to the First and Second Continental Congresses. In 1775, he was named general and commander in chief of the Continental Army. He presided over the Constitutional Convention in Philadelphia in 1787. In 1789, he was unanimously elected the new nation's first president, and he served as president for eight years.

HIS WORDS

"When we assumed the Soldier, we did not lay aside the Citizen."

(Address to the New York Legislature, June 26, 1775)

"'Tis our true policy to steer clear of permanent alliances, with any portion of the foreign world."

(Farewell address, September 17, 1796)

DEVELOPING
CRITICAL THINKING SKILLS
● ●

1. How does the first quotation relate to the importance of soldiers in our society?
2. Is Washington's advice about permanent alliances still relevant?

- That each state have only one vote.
- That acts of Congress be the supreme law of the land.
- That an executive office of more than one person be elected by Congress.
- That the executive office appoint a national supreme court.

The Great Compromise The Virginia Plan and the New Jersey Plan differed in several ways, but the major disagreement involved how states would be represented in the national legislature. Whereas the Virginia Plan would base representation on state population, the New Jersey Plan would provide equal representation for all the states.

As the summer grew hotter, so did the tempers of the delegates. Most were unwilling to consider the New Jersey Plan. When the Virginia Plan was brought up again, delegates from the smaller states threatened to leave, and the convention was in danger of dissolving. The convention was deadlocked.

On July 16, Roger Sherman of Connecticut proposed a plan to resolve the large-state/small-state controversy. His plan became known as the Connecticut Compromise, or the **Great Compromise.** Sherman's plan, which dealt only with the disagreement about how states would be represented in the national legislature, proposed a two-house legislature with the following parts:

- A lower house, the House of Representatives, in which the number of representatives from each state would be based on the number of people in the state.
- An upper house, the Senate, which would have two members from each state elected by the state legislatures.

The Great Compromise broke the deadlock. Like any good compromise, it gave something to both sides. Representation in the House would be based on population, as the larger states wanted. But all states would be equally represented in the Senate, which would benefit the smaller states.

The Slavery Question A second important compromise settled a disagreement over how to count slaves for the purposes of determining how many representatives each state would have in the House. Although slavery was legal in every state except Massachusetts, most slaves and slave owners lived in the South. The southern states wanted slaves to be counted equally in determining representation in Congress. Because they did not have many slaves, the northern states took the opposite position. They did not want slaves counted for representation purposes. The **Three-Fifths Compromise** broke this deadlock. Three-fifths of the slaves were to be counted for purposes of representation. (The three-fifths compromise was overturned in 1868 by the Fourteenth Amendment to the Constitution.)

The Three-Fifths Compromise did not satisfy everyone present. Many delegates wanted slavery banned completely in the United States. The delegates compromised on this question by agreeing that Congress could limit the number of slaves imported into the country after 1808, but the issue of slavery itself was never addressed. The South won twenty years of unrestricted slave trade and a requirement that slaves who escaped be returned to their owners.

Other Issues The delegates debated many other issues at the Constitutional Convention. These issues included the court system, the duration of the president's term of office, and the way the president should be elected. Commerce was also an issue. An important example involves export taxes.

The South's economic health depended in large part on its exports of agricultural products. (**Exports** are sales of goods to other countries.) The South feared that Congress might pass taxes on these exports. Another compromise was reached. The South agreed to let Congress have the power to regulate **interstate commerce**—commerce among the states—as well as commerce with other nations. In exchange, the South was guaranteed that no export taxes would ever be imposed on their products. Today, the United States is one of the few countries in the world that does not tax exports.

The Final Document

The Great Compromise had been reached by mid-July. Still to be determined was the makeup of the executive branch and the judiciary. A five-man committee, the Committee of Detail, undertook the remainder of this work. On August 6, the committee presented a rough draft of the Constitution to the convention. On September 8, a committee was named to "revise the stile [style] of, and arrange the Articles which had been agreed to" by the convention. This committee was headed by Gouverneur Morris of Pennsylvania. On September 17, 1787, the final draft of the Constitution was approved by thirty-nine of the remaining forty-two delegates.

Ethics and Political Compromises

The founders are sometimes taken to task for not having banned slavery outright. After all, the Declaration of Independence stated that "all Men are created equal." Additionally, many of the delegates to the Constitutional Convention thought that slavery was morally wrong. Why, then, did the founders ignore the slavery issue and leave it for future generations to resolve?

The fact is, those delegates who strongly believed that slavery should be banned had to face reality. The southern states would never accept the Constitution if it interfered with the practice of slavery. So, in order to create a new and stronger government, the founders compromised on the slavery question.

SECTION 5 REVIEW

1. Describe the Virginia Plan and the New Jersey Plan. What was the major difference between the two?
2. What were some of the major compromises reached by the convention delegates?
3. **For Critical Analysis:** Think of some compromises that could serve as alternatives to the Great Compromise. Explain your ideas.

Ratifying the Constitution

Preview Questions:

- What were the Federalists' advantages over the Anti-Federalists?
- Why did the Anti-Federalists object to ratifying the Constitution?

Key Terms:

ratified, Federalists, Anti-Federalists, factions, status quo

The delegates' approval of the Constitution did not mean that the Constitution was put into effect automatically. It had to be **ratified**—approved—by a majority of the states. The delegates to the convention agreed that each state should hold its own convention at which elected representatives would discuss and vote on the Constitution. The delegates also agreed that as soon as nine states approved the Constitution, it would take effect. Congress would then begin to organize the new government.

Look at Figure 2–5. You can see that the process of getting all the states to ratify the Constitution took nearly two and a half years.

FIGURE 2–5 Ratification of the Constitution The table below lists the date on which each of the new states ratified the Constitution. When did the Constitution formally go into effect?

State	Date	Vote For	Vote Against
Delaware	December 7, 1787	30	0
Pennsylvania	December 12, 1787	43	23
New Jersey	December 18, 1787	38	0
Georgia	January 2, 1788	26	0
Connecticut	January 9, 1788	128	40
Massachusetts	February 6, 1788	187	168
Maryland	April 28, 1788	63	11
South Carolina	May 23, 1788	149	73
New Hampshire	June 21, 1788	57	46
Virginia	June 25, 1788	89	79
New York	July 26, 1788	30	27
North Carolina	November 21, 1789*	194	77
Rhode Island	May 29, 1790	34	32

*Ratification was originally defeated on August 4, 1788, by a vote of 184 to 84; the numbers here represent the second vote.

The Battle Lines Are Drawn— Federalists versus Anti-Federalists

Ratifying the Constitution involved a tough battle, fought chiefly by two opposing groups. Those who favored a strong central government and the new Constitution were called **Federalists.** Those who opposed ratification were called **Anti-Federalists.** A national debate of unprecedented size arose between these two groups over the ratification issue.

The Federalists The Federalists had several advantages. In the first place, they adopted a positive name, leaving their opposition with a negative label. The Federalists had also attended the Constitutional Convention and knew about all of the discussions that had taken place. The Anti-Federalists had no actual knowledge of those discussions, which had been closed to the public. Thus, they were at a disadvantage. The Federalists also had time, money, and prestige on their side. Their impressive list of political thinkers and writers included Alexander Hamilton, John Jay, and James Madison. Federalists could communicate with each other more easily, because they were mostly bankers, lawyers, and merchants who lived in urban areas, where communication was better. The Federalists organized a quick and effective campaign to make sure that Federalists were elected as delegates to each state's ratifying convention. During that campaign, the Federalists published a series of papers collectively known as the *Federalist Papers*.

The *Federalist Papers* Alexander Hamilton, a leading Federalist, started answering critics of the Constitution in New York by writing newspaper columns. He used the signature "Caesar." When the Caesar letters appeared to have little effect, Hamilton switched his signature to "Publius." He also had John Jay and James Madison help him write more columns. In a period of less than a year, the three men wrote a series of eighty-five essays in defense of the Constitution. These essays were printed in New York newspapers, as well as in other papers throughout the states. Hamilton was responsible for about two-thirds of the essays, but Madison and Jay made important contributions. Madison's *Federalist Paper* No. 10 is considered a classic in political theory. It deals with the nature of interest groups, or **factions,** as he called them. (You can read *Federalist Paper* No. 10 in the Resource Center at the end of this book.)

Not everyone agrees about how important the *Federalist Papers* were in securing ratification. Even so, all admit to their lasting value as an authoritative explanation of the Constitution.

The Anti-Federalists Respond The major advantage of the Anti-Federalists was that they stood for the **status quo**—the way things were at the time. Usually, those who favor change face a more difficult task than those who favor staying with what is already known and understood. The Anti-Federalists published replies to the Federalists, using the names "Montezuma" and "Philadelphiensis." They also wrote brilliantly, attacking nearly every part of the new document. Many contended that the Constitution was written by aristocrats and would lead the nation to aristocratic tyranny. The Anti-Federalists argued that the Constitution would create an overly powerful central government that would limit personal freedom. The Anti-Federalists' strongest argument, however, was that the Constitution lacked a bill of rights. They warned that without a bill of rights, a strong national government might take away the political rights won during the American Revolution. They demanded that the new Constitution clearly guarantee personal freedoms.

Among the Anti-Federalists were such patriots as Patrick Henry and Samuel Adams. They argued in favor of what, in fact, was the leading view of the time. In this view, personal liberty was only safe in small societies governed either by direct democracy or by a large legislature with small districts. In contrast, many

▲ *John Jay, co-author of the* Federalist Papers, *served as the first chief justice of the Supreme Court. This position allowed him to actually apply the Constitution to specific situations facing the new nation.*

of the *Federalist Papers* argued a position that was unpopular at the time. As Patrick Henry said of the proposed Constitution, "I look upon that paper as the most fatal plan that could possibly be conceived to enslave a free people."

The Constitution Is Ratified

To gain support, the Federalists finally promised to add a bill of rights to the Constitution as the first order of business under the new government. This promise turned the tide in favor of the Constitution. The contest for ratification was close in several states, but the Federalists finally won in all of them.

Immigration

Except for a small number of Native Americans, all Americans are either immigrants or descendants of immigrants. Indeed, some of those who signed the Declaration of Independence were immigrants. Today, more immigrants are entering the United States than at any time since the early part of the twentieth century. In spite of the fact that we are indeed a nation of immigrants, Americans are at odds over the question of immigration. Some wish to reduce the numbers entering the United States, and some wish to make immigration policies more open.

Some Argue That Immigration Today Creates Too Many Problems

Americans in favor of reducing immigration rates argue that, even though immigration may have been beneficial in the past, it no longer is. They claim that immigrants increase the demand for government-provided social services, such as public education and welfare.

In addition, some people believe that increased immigration causes the wages of some American-born citizens to fall. In their view, increased immigration means more competition for jobs. This, in turn, allows employers to offer lower wages and still get enough workers.

Those who want to reduce immigration in the United States believe that immigrants cause more crime than American-born citizens. They believe that the crime rate would fall if fewer foreigners were allowed into this country.

Finally, some people are simply afraid of anything foreign. They do not want to be around an increasing number of individuals with different languages, cultures, and even cooking habits.

Others Believe That Continued Immigration Is Good for This Country

Those in favor of increased immigration argue that immigrants, over their lifetimes, pay more in taxes than they use in publicly provided services.

In addition, supporters of increased immigration argue that immigrants contribute to our economic prosperity. Those in favor of increased immigration point out that foreign-born Americans have been crucial in developing this nation's industries. For example, Andrew S. Grove came to the United States in 1957 with twenty dollars in his pocket. He ended up cofounding Intel Corporation, a multimillion-dollar company that sells 80 percent of the world's microprocessors. Other immigrants have either started or later presided over such high-technology companies as AST, Borland, Compaq, and Sun Microsystems. In fact, a foreign-born American—John Atanasoff, born in Bulgaria—did some of the earliest work on the principles used in modern digital computers. Other industries developed by the foreign-born include the American chemical industry, which was developed by a French immigrant, E. I. du Pont. Anheuser-Busch, Bausch & Lomb, Chrysler, and Hershey Foods were all the brainchildren of German-born Americans. In the last several decades, immigrants have started tens of thousands of small businesses.

YOU DECIDE

1. To what extent do you think a person's beliefs about immigration depend on whether his or her parents are immigrants?
2. Can you think of other arguments for or against increased immigration?

Ratification of the Constitution was unanimously approved in Delaware, New Jersey, and Georgia. Pennsylvania voted in favor of ratification by a margin of two to one and Connecticut by three to one. Even though the Anti-Federalists were perhaps the majority in Massachusetts, a brilliant political campaign by the Federalists led to ratification on February 6, 1788. On June 21, 1788, by a margin of fifty-seven to forty-six, New Hampshire became the ninth state to ratify. Thus, the Constitution was formally put into effect. Virginia ratified on June 25, 1788, and New York on July 26, 1788. North Carolina ratified on November 21 of the following year, and Rhode Island waited until May 29, 1790, after the new government had taken office.

◀ Americans have always loved a parade, and this celebration of ratification of the Constitution was a day for fun and excitement. Why do you think Hamilton's name is on the float?

such imitation most recently in the 1990s, as nations that were formerly part of the Soviet Union set up new governments. New democracies in Eastern Europe have almost exclusively imitated the U.S. Constitution. Figure 2–6 on page 58 shows a time line of the events that set the stage for the success of the American system.

The New Government Begins

On September 13, 1788, the Congress of the Confederation chose New York City as the temporary capital. On March 4, 1789, the new Congress convened in Federal Hall on Wall Street in New York City. On April 6, George Washington was elected the first president of the United States by a unanimous vote. His vice president, John Adams, was also elected. The first oath of office by a president of this country was taken on April 30 in New York City.

It is impossible to know for sure how far ahead the framers of the Constitution were looking when they met in Philadelphia. We can imagine, though, that they never dreamed that over two hundred years later, the U.S. Constitution would be the oldest living document of its type in the world. Nor is it likely that the first elected officials under the Constitution understood the truly global significance of what happened when they took office.

Through the years, the political system of democracy and the freedoms enjoyed by Americans have become the standard by which other countries measure themselves. At last count, the U.S. Constitution has been imitated by over 170 countries. We have seen

SECTION 6 REVIEW

1. What were the Anti-Federalists' objections to the Constitution? How did the Federalists respond to these objections?
2. Why did it take two and a half years for the states to ratify the Constitution?
3. **For Critical Analysis:** If a group today wanted to give the United States a new constitution, what problems would it encounter?

★ ★ ★ ★ Chapter Summary ★ ★ ★ ★

Section 1: The European Origins of Our Governmental System

🌐 The English colonists brought with them to North America the idea of limited government. Limited government in England began in 1215 with the Magna Carta, which ended the king's absolute power.
🌐 The English colonists also brought the idea of representative government to North America.
🌐 European political philosophers who influenced the American governmental system included John

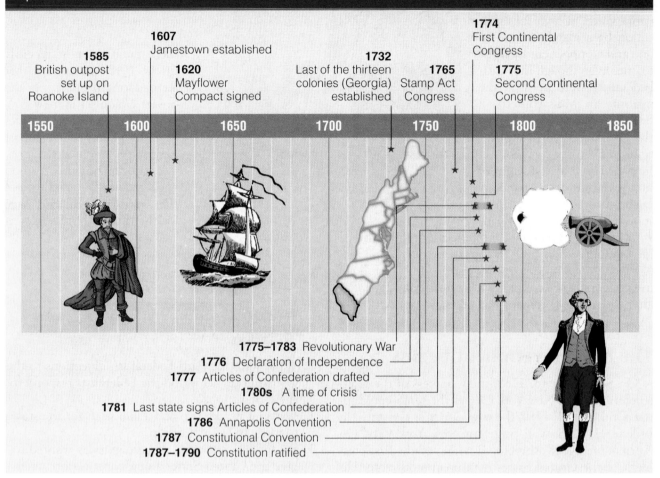

FIGURE 2–6 The Route to Lasting Self-Rule This time line lists important events that took place from 1585 through the ratification of the Constitution in 1790. Which of these dates do you think Americans would consider the most important?

1585 British outpost set up on Roanoke Island

1607 Jamestown established

1620 Mayflower Compact signed

1732 Last of the thirteen colonies (Georgia) established

1765 Stamp Act Congress

1774 First Continental Congress

1775 Second Continental Congress

1550   1600   1650   1700   1750   1800   1850

1775–1783 Revolutionary War
1776 Declaration of Independence
1777 Articles of Confederation drafted
1780s A time of crisis
1781 Last state signs Articles of Confederation
1786 Annapolis Convention
1787 Constitutional Convention
1787–1790 Constitution ratified

Locke, Thomas Hobbes, Jean-Jacques Rousseau, and Charles de Secondat, the Baron of Montesquieu. They wrote about such ideas as government by consent of the governed, natural rights, the social contract, and separation of powers in government.

Section 2: The Beginnings of Self-Government

🟢 Jamestown, established in 1607, was the first permanent British settlement in North America. Settlers in Jamestown instituted a representative assembly.

🟢 The Plymouth Company established the first New England colony in 1620. Their government was based on the Mayflower Compact.

🟢 Colonists in what is now Connecticut developed America's first written constitution, the Fundamental Orders of Connecticut.

🟢 By 1732, all thirteen colonies had been established, each with its own constitution and legislature.

Section 3: The Colonies Rebel

🟢 Beginning in the 1760s, Britain's rule of the colonies became more repressive. The British government imposed a series of new taxes, which colonists protested as "taxation without representation."

🟢 The colonies joined together in 1774 to hold the First Continental Congress to protest Britain's practices. The British government condemned the congress's actions as open acts of rebellion.

- On April 19, 1775, British soldiers and colonial citizen-soldiers fought in Lexington and Concord, Massachusetts, signaling the start of the Revolutionary War. The Second Continental Congress was called soon afterward and assumed the powers of a central government.
- The Declaration of Independence was written by Thomas Jefferson and adopted by the Second Continental Congress in 1776.

Section 4: The Articles of Confederation

- The Articles of Confederation, drawn up by the Second Continental Congress in 1777, served as the nation's first constitution.
- Because in general the colonists feared a strong central government, states retained their sovereignty under the Articles. Thus, the national government was weak.
- After achieving independence and peace with Britain, the new nation went through a time of crisis in the 1780s as states argued among themselves and economic conditions worsened.
- An armed rebellion of farmers led by Daniel Shays in 1786 led to a call to revise the Articles of Confederation and give the national government more power.

Section 5: Creating the Constitution

- Delegates met in Philadelphia from May to September, 1787, to revise the Articles; this meeting was the Constitutional Convention.
- The Virginia Plan, favored by larger states, called for an entirely new government. The New Jersey Plan, favored by smaller states, was based more closely on the Articles of Confederation. A major difference between the two plans involved how states would be represented in the national legislature.
- The Great Compromise resolved the difference by basing representation in the House of Representatives on population, but giving all states equal representation in the Senate.
- After reaching a series of compromises, a majority of the delegates approved the Constitution and submitted it to the states for ratification.

Section 6: Ratifying the Constitution

- In the process of ratification, conflict developed between the Federalists and the Anti-Federalists.
- The Federalists favored a strong central government and wanted the Constitution to be adopted. Their position is explained in the *Federalist Papers*, written by Alexander Hamilton, James Madison, and John Jay.
- The Anti-Federalists feared strong central government. They opposed the Constitution, in part because it had no bill of rights to guarantee personal freedom. The Federalists' promise to add a bill of rights turned the tide in favor of ratification.
- All the states ratified the Constitution, which formally took effect in 1788. A new Congress met in New York City, the temporary capital, in 1789, and George Washington was elected president.

CHAPTER 2 Review

★ REVIEW QUESTIONS ★

1. What two aspects of English government most strongly influenced the American style of government?
2. How did the British Parliament affect the way American government was organized?
3. What were the first British settlements in North America?
4. What contribution did the Pilgrims make to the development of American government?
5. Explain the major reasons for the colonists' revolt against Great Britain.
6. Describe the events that led up to the American Revolution.
7. Why were the First and Second Continental Congresses called?
8. Why is the Declaration of Independence important?
9. What is significant about the second paragraph of the Declaration of Independence?
10. How did the Articles of Confederation fail to create a strong central government?
11. What led George Washington to say, "We are one nation today and thirteen tomorrow. Who will treat us on such terms?"
12. Explain what the Great Compromise was and why it was necessary.
13. What major arguments did the Federalists offer in favor of the Constitution? Why did the Anti-Federalists oppose the Constitution?
14. What promise turned the tide in favor of ratifying the Constitution?

★ CRITICAL THINKING ★

1. If you had been a participant in the Constitutional Convention, would you have ended up a Federalist or an Anti-Federalist afterward? Explain why.
2. The Constitution has been described as a "bundle of compromises." When do you think political compromise is justifiable? When is it not justifiable? Support your answers with recent examples of political compromises.
3. Do you think it was right for the delegates to the Constitutional Convention to have met in secret? Would it be right for this to happen today?

★ IMPROVING YOUR SKILLS ★

Communication Skills

Note Taking The skills of listening and note taking are closely related. You must listen well in order to take good notes, and you must take notes—either mentally or on paper—in order to gain the most from listening. If you haven't done so already, read the section in Chapter 1 on listening.

There are many methods of note taking. Regardless of the method that you choose, the following guidelines will help you get the most from your note taking.

The Mechanics
1. *Use a loose-leaf binder with notepaper.* This way you can reorganize your notes or insert other materials. If you buy a spiral notebook instead, make sure it has pockets for handouts. Use a pen for readability.
2. *Always indicate the date, class, and name of your topic at the top of your notes.*
3. *Divide each page so that you have an empty column two to three inches wide on the right or left.* Use this space to make sketches to illustrate important points or to write helpful comments. Comments might include "T" for possible test question, "see textbook," or "use for term paper."

Prepare Your Mind
1. *Read any assigned work before going to class.* The lecture will make more sense, and you will be able to relate the ideas to what you have read.

2. *Review notes from the previous class a few minutes before class starts.*
3. *Reflect for a few minutes on any personal experiences or previous learning that relates to the subject.* New learning "sticks" most readily when it fits into a meaningful context.

Be a Keen Listener
1. *Get interested.* Being interested in the subject matter helps sharpen your attention and concentration, and it heightens your learning and remembering. It also helps you shut out distractions.
2. *Sort out the important points and significant details.* Listen for key phrases such as "on the one hand," "in summary," and "the important point is . . . ."
3. *Be mentally alert.* Listen to changes in a speaker's volume or tone. Pay attention to his or her voice and actions.

Record
1. *Take notes in your own words unless the subject is very technical.* Write in block, paragraph, or outline form, whichever you can manage most accurately and quickly.
2. *Skip a line whenever the lecturer moves to another topic.*
3. *Keep your notes brief, using words or phrases rather than sentences.* Use abbreviations and symbols whenever possible.

Review
1. *Review your notes as soon as possible after the class.* Fill in missing words and flesh out the concepts based on what you remember. Underline the most important ideas. Make corrections, summaries, and additions in the margin.

Writing
1. Watch an evening news program, taking notes as you watch. Then check to see if you followed the note-taking guidelines listed above.

2. Take notes during a lecture. Afterward, compare your notes with those of a classmate. Exchange suggestions and tips for improving each other's notes.

Social Studies Skills

Map Reading Use Figure 2–2 on page 37 to answer the following questions.

1. What is the approximate distance between the northernmost colony and the southernmost colony?
2. Which is the largest colony?
3. Which are the two smallest colonies?
4. Which colony doesn't have any coastline?

★ ACTIVITIES AND PROJECTS ★

1. Prepare a wall chart that lists the major weaknesses of the Articles of Confederation and shows how those weaknesses were remedied by the Constitution.
2. Stage a class Federalist/Anti-Federalist debate on this statement: *A strong federal government leads to violations of personal freedom.* In the course of the debate, discuss how the issue of balance between a strong central government and people's rights continues to be a major factor in American politics.

What If . . .

The Anti-Federalists Had Prevented the Constitution from Being Ratified?

You learned in this chapter that the Federalists wanted the Constitution ratified, while the Anti-Federalists were in favor of the status quo. The Federalists obviously won the ratification debate. How might government in the United States be different today if the Constitution had not been ratified? What form of government do you believe would have developed?

CHAPTER 3

The Constitution

CHAPTER OBJECTIVES

To learn about and understand . . .

⭐ The structure of the Constitution

⭐ The major principles of government on which the Constitution is based

⭐ The Bill of Rights and how it was created

⭐ The formal process of amending the Constitution

⭐ The informal process of amending the Constitution

"Our new Constitution is now established, and has an appearance that promises permanency; but in this world nothing can be said to be certain, except death and taxes."

Benjamin Franklin
(1706–1790)
U.S. Statesman and Writer

INTRODUCTION

As a student, you may disagree with Ben Franklin's statement above, for you are probably certain that at the end of every semester, you will have to take final exams. You are probably certain, too, that your teachers will judge you on the basis of the results of those exams.

You cannot, of course, be certain about the permanency of the Constitution, any more than Franklin could. But if Franklin was concerned about how well the Constitution would stand the test of time, he should not have been. The Constitution still serves today as the plan for government in the United States and as the supreme law of the land. The Constitution affects you, your family, and your friends as much as it affected those who wrote it over two hundred years ago.

◀ Throughout the United States, the Fourth of July is a time for celebration.

The Structure of Our Constitution

Preview Questions:

- 🌐 What are the three major parts of the Constitution?
- 🌐 What is the purpose of the Preamble?
- 🌐 What are the purposes of the seven articles in the Constitution?

Key Terms:

preamble, supremacy clause, amendments

In its original form, the U.S. Constitution contained only about five thousand words. Today, even after the addition of twenty-seven amendments, it contains only about seven thousand words. Compared with virtually all state constitutions and with the constitutions of other nations, the U.S. Constitution is brief and to the point. The founders of this nation did not attempt to spell out in detail exactly how the government should operate. Rather, they gave us a general framework for governing the nation. The Constitution has endured for more than two hundred years, and it has been copied in one form or another by numerous nations. In the words of Henry Clay (1777–1852), a nineteenth-century U.S. senator:

> The Constitution . . . was made not merely for the generation that then existed, but for posterity—unlimited, undefined, endless, perpetual posterity.

Clay recognized, along with others, that the framers of the Constitution knew that this nation would constantly change. So they made the document general enough for each of the many generations that would follow to interpret it according to the needs and values of the times. This is why our Constitution is often called a living, breathing document, created by people with a vision.

The Constitution consists of three major parts: a preamble, seven articles, and twenty-seven amend-

▲ *This painting by Albert Herter captures a historic moment during the Constitutional Convention. Why was this convention held?*

FIGURE 3–1 Structure of the U.S. Constitution The figure below outlines the structure of the U.S. Constitution. Where in the Constitution would you look to find the guarantee of freedom of speech?

The Constitution		Amendments to the Constitution	
Preamble		**Bill of Rights**	
		First Amendment	Religion, Speech, Assembly, and Petition (1791)
Article I	**Legislative Branch**	Second Amendment	Militia and the Right to Bear Arms (1791)
Section 1	Legislative Powers	Third Amendment	Quartering of Soldiers (1791)
Section 2	House of Representatives	Fourth Amendment	Searches and Seizures (1791)
Section 3	Senate	Fifth Amendment	Grand Juries, Self-Incrimination,
Section 4	Congressional Elections: Time, Place, and Manner		Double Jeopardy, Due Process, and Eminent Domain (1791)
Section 5	Powers and Duties of the Houses	Sixth Amendment	Criminal Court Procedures (1791)
Section 6	Rights of Members	Seventh Amendment	Trial by Jury in Civil Cases (1791)
Section 7	Legislative Powers: Bills and Resolutions	Eighth Amendment	Bail, Cruel and Unusual Punishment (1791)
Section 8	Powers of Congress	Ninth Amendment	Rights Retained by the People (1791)
Section 9	Powers Denied to Congress	Tenth Amendment	Reserved Powers of the States (1791)
Section 10	Powers Denied to the States		
		Pre-Civil War Amendments	
Article II	**Executive Branch**	Eleventh Amendment	Suits against States (1795)
Section 1	Nature and Scope of Presidential Power	Twelfth Amendment	Election of the President (1804)
Section 2	Powers of the President	**Civil War/Reconstruction Amendments**	
Section 3	Duties of the President	Thirteenth Amendment	Prohibition of Slavery (1865)
Section 4	Impeachment	Fourteenth Amendment	Citizenship, Due Process, and Equal Protection of the Laws (1868)
Article III	**Judicial Branch**	Fifteenth Amendment	Right to Vote (1870)
Section 1	Judicial Powers, Courts, and Judges	**Twentieth-Century Amendments**	
Section 2	Jurisdiction	Sixteenth Amendment	Income Taxes (1913)
Section 3	Treason	Seventeenth Amendment	Popular Election of Senators (1913)
		Eighteenth Amendment	Prohibition (1919)
Article IV	**Relations among the States**	Nineteenth Amendment	Women's Right to Vote (1920)
Section 1	Full Faith and Credit	Twentieth Amendment	Lame Duck Amendment (1933)
Section 2	Treatment of Citizens	Twenty-first Amendment	Repeal of Prohibition (1933)
Section 3	Admission of States	Twenty-second Amendment	Limitation of Presidential Terms (1951)
Section 4	Republican Form of Government	Twenty-third Amendment	Presidential Electors for the District of Columbia (1961)
		Twenty-fourth Amendment	Anti-Poll Tax Amendment (1964)
Article V	**Method of Amendment**	Twenty-fifth Amendment	Presidential Disability and Vice Presidential Vacancies (1967)
Article VI	**National Supremacy**	Twenty-sixth Amendment	Eighteen-Year-Old Vote (1971)
Article VII	**Ratification**	Twenty-seventh Amendment	Congressional Pay (1992)

ments. You can see an overview of the structure of the Constitution in Figure 3–1.

The Preamble

A **preamble** is an introductory statement. Such a statement at the beginning of a document generally explains the reasons and intentions behind what follows it. Hence, the Preamble of the U.S. Constitution sets forth the general purposes of American government.

We the People of the United States, in Order to form a more perfect Union, establish Justice, insure domestic Tranquility, provide for the common defence, promote the general Welfare, and secure the Blessings of Liberty to ourselves and our Posterity, do ordain and establish this Constitution for the United States of America.

The Preamble lists the major goals for which American government should strive. Rather than being law itself, as is the rest of the Constitution, it explains what the founders hoped the new government would accomplish. It shows that they wanted our government to provide law, order, and stability for this new country. They also wanted the government to serve the citizens while at the same time ensuring the liberty of each individual.

The Articles

There are seven articles in the Constitution, identified by the Roman numerals I through VII. The first three articles establish the structure and explain the functions of the three branches of government: the legislative, the executive, and the judicial.

Article I outlines the legislative powers given to Congress and describes how laws should be made. Article II, in a similar manner, tells how the executive branch—the presidency—is empowered to carry out the laws passed by Congress. It also tells how the president is elected.

Article III establishes the judicial branch of the federal government. Article III states that there shall be one Supreme Court and gives Congress the power to create lower courts. It also defines what kinds of cases the courts can hear.

The relations among states are outlined in Article IV, which describes how state governments and the federal government are linked together. The amendment process, or how to change the Constitution, is described in Article V. Article VI makes the Constitution, laws passed by Congress, and treaties of the United States

▲ The Great Charters of America's past—the Declaration of Independence, the Constitution, and the Bill of Rights— are permanently exhibited in the Shrine in the Rotunda at the National Archives.

the "supreme law of the land." This part of Article VI is called the **supremacy clause.** The supremacy clause means that all U.S. citizens, as well as state and local governments, grant ultimate authority to federal laws, treaties, and the Constitution. Finally, Article VII indicates that the Constitution was to go into effect after nine states ratified it.

The Amendments

The third part of the Constitution consists of twenty-seven **amendments**—formal changes to the basic document. The first ten amendments, known as the Bill of Rights, were added in 1791. The remaining seventeen amendments have been added since then. The last one, the Twenty-seventh Amendment, was added in 1992.

Later in this chapter, we examine the amendments in more detail, as well as how the amendment process actually works. First though, we look at the major principles of government embodied in the U.S. Constitution.

SECTION 1 REVIEW

1. What are the three major parts of the Constitution?
2. How does the Preamble set the tone of the document?
3. **For Critical Analysis:** This section points out that the rules of government found in the U.S. Constitution are very general in nature. It also points out that the U.S. Constitution is the world's oldest written constitution. What is the relationship between these two facts?

The Major Principles of Government Embodied in the Constitution

Preview Questions:

🌐 What are the basic principles on which the Constitution of the United States is built?

🌐 How does the system of checks and balances operate?

Key Terms:

rule of law, tyranny, Madisonian Model, checks and balances, veto power, judicial review, unconstitutional, federalism

The governmental framework supplied by the Constitution has a number of elements. In general, they fall under six broad principles.

Much of the Constitution seems to focus on how the government should be controlled. As James Madison (1751–1836) once said, after you have given the

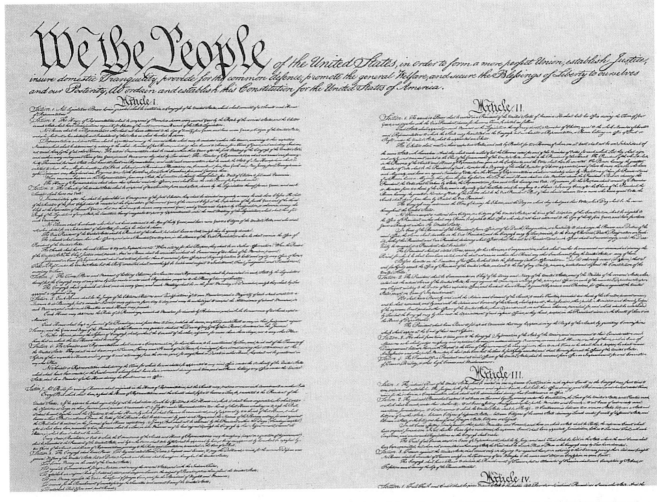

▲ *The U.S. Constitution, including its amendments, is relatively brief—it is only about 7,000 words in length. In contrast, cities, police forces, and schools have thick manuals describing the rules by which they are governed. Why do you suppose it is possible that our entire nation is governed by a document just a few pages long?*

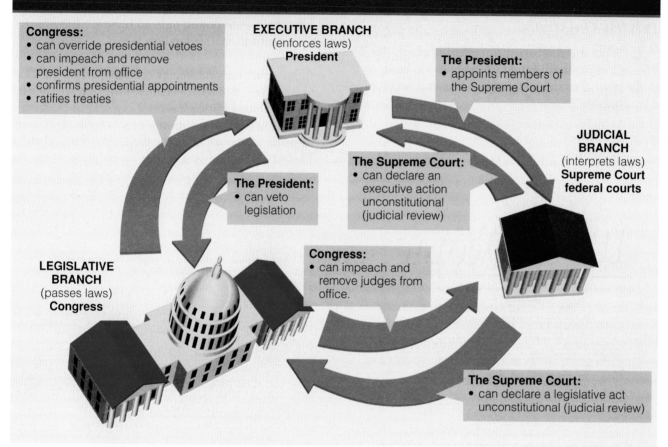

FIGURE 3–2 Checks and Balances Among the Branches of Government The figure below details the system of checks and balances among the branches of the United States government. As you can see, each branch of government has some authority over the actions of each other branch. Why did the framers include a system of checks and balances in the Constitution?

Congress:
- can override presidential vetoes
- can impeach and remove president from office
- confirms presidential appointments
- ratifies treaties

EXECUTIVE BRANCH
(enforces laws)
President

The President:
- appoints members of the Supreme Court

JUDICIAL BRANCH
(interprets laws)
Supreme Court federal courts

The President:
- can veto legislation

The Supreme Court:
- can declare an executive action unconstitutional (judicial review)

LEGISLATIVE BRANCH
(passes laws)
Congress

Congress:
- can impeach and remove judges from office.

The Supreme Court:
- can declare a legislative act unconstitutional (judicial review)

government the ability to control its citizens, you have to "oblige it to control itself." In keeping with the concept of controlling the government, the first basic governing principle of the Constitution is limited government, which was discussed in Chapters 1 and 2. The others are popular sovereignty, separation of powers, checks and balances, judicial review, and federalism.

Limited Government

The framers were fearful of the powerful English monarchy, against which they had so recently rebelled. They therefore included in the Constitution the principle of limited government, which means that the national government created by the Constitution can do only what the people allow it to do. This principle

can be found in many parts of the Constitution. For example, while Articles I, II, and III indicate what the national government *can* do, the first nine amendments to the Constitution list ways that the national government *cannot* limit certain individual freedoms.

Under a limited government, all citizens must live according to the **rule of law.** Like other citizens, those who run the government must always obey the laws found in the Constitution. Otherwise stated, no person—even the president—is above the law.

Popular Sovereignty

Popular sovereignty means that the people are the ultimate source of any power given to the government. Remember that the phrases that frame the Preamble to the Constitution are "We the People of the United States . . . do ordain and establish this Constitution for the United States of America." In other words, it is the people who form the government.

The principle of popular sovereignty is closely linked to the principle of limited government. According to both principles, the people are the ultimate source of governmental authority.

Separation of Powers

The framers of the Constitution wanted to create a government that would prevent the rise of **tyranny**—absolute and unlimited power and authority. To do so, they separated the powers of the government. They distributed governmental powers among three branches: executive, legislative, and judicial. When powers are separated in this way, no one branch has enough power to dominate the others. The plan for separation of powers used in the Constitution is called the **Madisonian Model,** for James Madison, who developed it. The plan is laid out in Articles I, II, and III. Congress, or the legislative branch, passes laws; the president, or the executive branch, carries them out; and the courts, or the judicial branch, interpret them.

Checks and Balances

The separation of powers is part of a system of **checks and balances.** The framers feared that one branch of government could dominate the other two. In order to prevent this, the framers made sure that each branch of government could exercise certain powers over the actions of the other branches. Figure 3–2 on page 68 shows how this is done.

As you can see in the figure, the president checks Congress by holding **veto power,** which is the ability to refuse to sign congressional bills into law. Congress, in turn, controls taxes and spending, and the Senate must approve presidential appointments. For example, the president can appoint justices to the Supreme Court, but only with the approval of the Senate.

Under the system of checks and balances, each branch's independence is protected. At the same time, however, the system calls for cooperation, because in order to take an action, at least two branches must work together. For example, Congress can pass a law, but the executive branch must approve, administer,

and enforce it. Thus, the branches depend on each other, but they also maintain their independence.

Judicial Review

Judicial review refers to the power of the courts to decide whether a law or other governmental action violates the Constitution. In cases that come before the U.S. Supreme Court, if the justices find that a federal or state law violates the U.S. Constitution, that law is declared **unconstitutional.** Such a law no longer has any validity or legitimacy—it is as if it did not exist. For example, suppose your state passed a law that allowed the state police to monitor telephone conversations (called *wiretapping*) without formally obtaining permission from a judge. The U.S. Supreme Court

▼ This is the entrance to the United States Supreme Court building in Washington, D.C. Inside you would find the nine justices of the Supreme Court, who are entrusted with interpreting and applying the Constitution. Why do you think these justices receive a lifetime, rather than a limited, appointment to the bench?

might strike down that law as unconstitutional because it violates the Fourth Amendment to the Constitution.

The Constitution does not specifically mention judicial review. Most constitutional scholars believe, however, that the framers *meant* the federal courts to have that power. For example, in *Federalist Paper* No. 78, Alexander Hamilton made the following statement:

The interpretation of the laws is the proper and peculiar province [specialty] of the courts. A constitution is, in fact, and must be regarded by the judges, as a fundamental law. It therefore belongs to them to ascertain its meaning, as well as the meaning of any particular act proceeding from the legislative body. If there should happen to be an irreconcilable variance between the two, . . . the Constitution ought to be preferred to the statute.

Judicial review became part of the U.S. system in the 1803 case of *Marbury v. Madison.* In this famous case, the Supreme Court ruled for the first time that part of an act passed by Congress was unconstitutional. Chief Justice John Marshall declared that it is "the province and duty of the judicial department to say what the law is." You can read about this case in *Case Study: Government in Action—Marbury v. Madison (1803)* on page 71.

After this important decision, the Supreme Court became part of the checks and balances system. Through the power of judicial review, the Court could declare actions of the other two branches of government unconstitutional.

Federalism

The Constitution set up a form of government based on the principle of **federalism.** In a federal system, some powers belong to the national, or federal, government, while others belong to the states. This division of powers was a compromise between two groups of delegates to the Philadelphia convention: those who had strong nationalist views and those who felt that the states should retain most of their rights. In the next chapter, you will read about the federal system in more detail.

SECTION 2 REVIEW

1. List the basic principles on which the Constitution is built.
2. How do these principles relate to each other?
3. **For Critical Analysis:** How does the inclusion of these principles make the Constitution stronger than the Articles of Confederation (discussed in Chapter 2)?

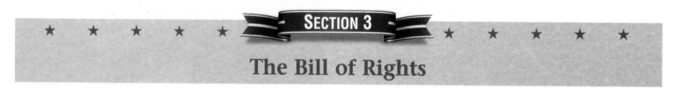

SECTION 3

The Bill of Rights

Preview Questions:

- Why was the Bill of Rights drafted?
- What events led to the ratification of the Bill of Rights?

Key Term:

writ of *mandamus*

As you saw in Figure 3–1, amendments make up a major part of the Constitution. The Bill of Rights, the first ten amendments, became part of the Constitution in 1791, only a few years after the Constitution was ratified. In fact, the Constitution was ratified in several important states only after the Federalists promised that amendments would be added to protect individual liberties. After ratification, Congress turned to the task of drafting the amendments that would be included in the Constitution.

Madison's Difficult Job

At the state ratifying conventions, many proposals for amendments had been made. James Madison, as a member of the new Congress, took on the job of considering all these proposals and drawing up the amendments that would be presented to Congress for approval.

Government in Action

Marbury v. Madison (1803)

John Adams was elected president in 1797. A Federalist, he supported the idea of a strong national government. In 1800, he lost his bid for reelection to Thomas Jefferson. Adams feared that Jefferson's supporters, who were Anti-Federalists, would attempt to weaken the power of the national government. During the final hours of his presidency, he appointed loyal Federalists to fill a number of government positions, hoping in this way to lessen Jefferson's impact.

Documents called *commissions* had to be delivered to the people Adams had appointed in order to make the appointments official. The task of delivering the commissions went to Adams's secretary of state, John Marshall. Out of forty-two last-minute commissions, Marshall managed to deliver only thirty-eight before Jefferson took office. The rest were left to be delivered by Jefferson's administration. Of course, the new president had no interest in delivering Adams's commissions.

William Marbury was a Federalist whose commission was not delivered. With three others, he decided to sue to force the new secretary of state, James Madison, to deliver the commissions. Marbury and the others brought the suit directly to the Supreme Court. They asked the Court to issue a **writ of *mandamus,*** which is an order issued by a court to force a government official to act. The Judiciary Act of 1789 had given the Supreme Court the power to issue such orders to officials of the U.S. government.

As fate would have it, John Marshall—who had failed to deliver Marbury's commission before stepping down as Adams's secretary of state—had by this time become chief justice of the Supreme Court. He was now in a position to decide the case for which he was, in part, responsible. Marshall faced a dilemma. On the one hand, he could

order Madison to deliver the commissions, but the new secretary of state could simply refuse to do so. The Court had no way of enforcing its decisions. On the other hand, Marshall could deny Marbury's request and allow Madison to do as he pleased. But then he would be failing to use the authority that the Court had been given by the Judiciary Act of 1789. The Court's power would be seriously lessened by this failure to act.

Marshall solved the problem by holding that the Supreme Court did not have the authority to hear the case. The section of the Judiciary Act of 1789 giving the Supreme Court the authority to issue writs of *mandamus* was unconstitutional, Marshall stated. Article III of the Constitution, which spells out the Supreme Court's powers, did not mention writs of *mandamus*, and Congress did not have the right to expand the Court's powers. The section of the Judiciary Act of 1789 that expanded the Court's powers was therefore void.

Marshall's decision still stands today as a judicial and political masterpiece. It did not require anyone to do anything, so enforcing it was not a problem. At the same time, it enlarged the power of the Supreme Court by stating that it was "the province and duty of the judicial department to say what the law is." In other words, Marshall made it clear that the courts had the power of judicial review.

THINK ABOUT IT

1. If the Supreme Court has no way to enforce its decisions, then how are its decisions put into practice?
2. What might result if the courts did not have the power of judicial review?

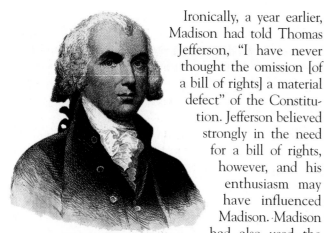

▲ *James Madison played a pivotal role in creating the Constitution and guiding it through the difficult ratification process. He later became our fourth president. He is often remembered as the "Father of the Constitution" and as co-author of the* Federalist Papers.

Ironically, a year earlier, Madison had told Thomas Jefferson, "I have never thought the omission [of a bill of rights] a material defect" of the Constitution. Jefferson believed strongly in the need for a bill of rights, however, and his enthusiasm may have influenced Madison. Madison had also used the issue to gain support for his own election to Congress. He had promised in his campaign letter that if he was elected, he would force Congress to "prepare and recommend to the States for ratification, the most satisfactory provisions for all essential rights."

Madison sorted through more than two hundred state recommendations and finally submitted seventeen amendments. Congress tightened the language of these amendments somewhat and eliminated five of them. Of the remaining twelve, one—dealing with the apportionment of representatives—was rejected by the states. Another—dealing with compensation (payment) of members of Congress—was not ratified at the time but was ratified over two hundred years later, in 1992! The remaining ten are what now form our Bill of Rights.

Just the Facts

In many public opinion polls, over 50 percent of the Americans surveyed have said they do not know what the Bill of Rights is.

The Difference between *Ought* and *Shall*

Madison worked with the proposals that the state ratifying conventions had provided. All of these proposals used the words *ought* and *ought not*. The *oughts*

THE GLOBAL VIEW

Britain's Unwritten Constitution and Lack of a Bill of Rights

Although the founders were strongly influenced by English tradition, they departed from that tradition in two important ways. They created a single, written constitution, and they added the Bill of Rights to that document.

Unlike the United States, Great Britain has no single document that sets forth its constitutional rules. Instead, Britain's "unwritten" constitution consists of various acts passed by Parliament, court decisions, other authoritative documents, and British customs and practices. Also, Britain has no written bill of rights protecting the rights and liberties of British citizens. There is, of course, the English Bill of Rights of 1689. This document, though, deals mainly with the rights of Parliament, not of citizens, and it can also be changed by Parliament. All other Western European nations have a bill of rights protecting their citizens, as the United States does. It is ironic that Britain, the country that invented the concept of a bill of rights—and that first used the phrase—does not have one.

THINKING GLOBALLY

1. Which do you think is more important in determining whether a representative government will endure, a written constitution or a national tradition of liberty?
2. The customary rights of British citizens can be changed by an act of Parliament. Can the constitutional rights of U.S. citizens be changed by an act of Congress?

# of Government

Elizabeth Cady Stanton (1815–1902)

Elizabeth Cady Stanton was a prominent American reformer and feminist. She participated in the first antislavery movement and, in 1848, organized the first women's rights convention. Beginning in 1852, she led the women's movement in the United States with Susan B. Anthony. She was president of the National Woman Suffrage Association from 1869 to 1890 and of the National American Woman Suffrage Association from 1890 to 1892.

HER WORDS

"We hold these truths to be self-evident: That all men and women are created equal."
(*Declaration of Sentiments—Seneca Falls, New York, 1848*)

"We insist that [women] have immediate admission to all the rights and privileges which belong to them as citizens of the United States."
(*Declaration of Sentiments, 1848*)

DEVELOPING
CRITICAL THINKING SKILLS

1. On what document did Stanton base the first quotation?
2. Do you believe that Stanton's demand in the second quotation has become reality in the United States?

and *ought nots* were typical of the language contained in the English Bill of Rights as well. But wishful thinking was not good enough or bold enough for Madison. Madison required the language of *command*.

Consider an example. One constitutional amendment proposed by the state of Virginia's ratifying convention stated that "excessive bail *ought* not to be required, nor excessive fines imposed, nor cruel and unusual punishments inflicted." Madison changed that wording to read: "Excessive bail *shall* not be required, nor excessive fines imposed, nor cruel and unusual punishments inflicted."

Other amendments use this wording, too, in such phrases as, "Congress shall make no law . . . ," "no soldier shall . . . ," and "the accused shall . . . ."

The first ten amendments do not tell the national government what it *should* do. Rather, they tell the national government what it *must* do.

Ten Amendments Are Ratified

On December 15, 1791, the Bill of Rights was adopted when Virginia became the eleventh state to ratify the ten amendments. The basic structure of American government had been established. After 1791, the fundamental rights of individuals were protected, at least in theory, at the *national* level.

The Bill of Rights provides constitutional guarantees, such as freedom of expression and belief. The Tenth Amendment spells out the reserved powers of the states, explained in the next chapter, which describes our federal system of government.

SECTION 3 REVIEW

1. What role did James Madison play in developing the Bill of Rights?
2. Why was the distinction between the words *ought* and *shall* so critical in the final version of the Bill of Rights?
3. **For Critical Analysis:** Look at the first ten amendments to the Constitution (see the Resource Center in the back of this text). Are some of the rights guaranteed by those amendments more important than others?

The Formal Process of Amending the Constitution

Preview Questions:

- What are the processes by which formal changes can be made in the Constitution?
- Why have so few amendments been added to the Constitution?

Key Term:

repealed

The Constitution has endured for over two hundred years with only twenty-seven added amendments. One reason that the number of amendments is small is that the framers, in Article V, made the formal amendment process extremely difficult. There are two ways to introduce an amendment and two ways to ratify one. The result is that there are only four possible ways for an amendment to become law.

Methods of Introducing an Amendment

The two methods of introducing an amendment are as follows:

1. An amendment may be introduced by a two-thirds vote in the Senate and in the House of Representatives. All of the twenty-seven existing amendments have been introduced in this way.
2. Two-thirds of the state legislatures may request that Congress call a national amendment convention. Congress may then call one, and the convention may propose amendments to the states for ratification.

The notion of an amendment convention is exciting to many people. On two separate occasions, calls for a national amendment convention almost became reality. Between 1963 and 1969, thirty-three state legislatures (out of the necessary thirty-four) attempted to call a convention to amend the Constitution to eliminate the Supreme Court's "one person, one vote" decisions in regard to congressional elections (discussed in Chapter 14). Between 1975 and 1998, thirty-two states asked for a national convention to introduce an amendment requiring that the national government balance its budget—that it spend no more than it receives in revenues. (See *Case Study: Government in Action—The Balanced-Budget Amendment* on page 75.)

Methods of Ratifying an Amendment

There are two methods of ratifying an amendment that has been introduced:

1. An amendment is ratified when three-fourths of the state legislatures vote in favor of ratification. This

"I CANNOT TELL A LIE--I DID IT WITH MY LITTLE HATCHET!"
Mrs. Nation's Reform Crusade in Kansas, as the Globe Artist Understands It From the Press Dispatches.

▲ *Carrie Nation, shown here in a 1901 political cartoon, was an early crusader against alcohol. She was famous for storming into taverns and destroying their supplies. Her efforts led to the passing of which amendment to the Constitution?*

Government in Action

The Balanced-Budget Amendment

It sounds simple—make the U.S. Congress balance its budget. In other words, forbid Congress to spend more than it receives in taxes and other fees. Many people believe an amendment to balance the budget is needed. After all, only very recently has the U.S. Congress been able to "live within its means" after decades of deficit spending. As simple as this idea sounds, though, a balanced-budget amendment has yet to be ratified—or even introduced.

Congress Fails to Support the Amendment

As early as 1986, the Senate voted on a balanced-budget amendment. In 1992, there was a vote in the House of Representatives. On January 26, 1995, the House approved a balanced-budget amendment by a vote of 300 to 132. But when the amendment reached the Senate in March, it failed. By the time you read this text, there may well have been additional votes on introducing such an amendment.

What If Two More States Vote for a National Convention?

As mentioned elsewhere, thirty-two of the fifty states have asked for a national convention to introduce a balanced-budget amendment. If two more states vote to have a national convention, what might happen? The Constitution itself does not offer guidelines for such a convention. Congress might provide rules, but once the convention begins, Congress would have little practical way to control it. We can be sure of one thing. The convention would receive great media coverage. No major surprises would be sprung on an unsuspecting nation.

THINK ABOUT IT

1. Who in Congress might be in favor of introducing a balanced-budget amendment?
2. If a national constitutional convention were held to vote on such an amendment, in what ways might it resemble the first national convention, if at all? In what ways might it be different?

method is considered the "traditional" one and has been used twenty-six times.
2. The states can call special conventions to ratify the amendment. If three-fourths of the states approve, the amendment is ratified.

The second method was used only once, in 1933, to ratify the Twenty-first Amendment. That amendment **repealed**—made void—the Eighteenth Amendment, which prohibited the "manufacture, sale, or transportation of intoxicating liquors."

You can see the four methods for introducing and ratifying amendments in Figure 3–3 on page 76.

Why So Few Amendments?

More than eleven thousand amendments to the Constitution have been considered by Congress. Yet only twenty-seven have been ratified. The process, therefore, must be more difficult than Figure 3–3 seems to indicate.

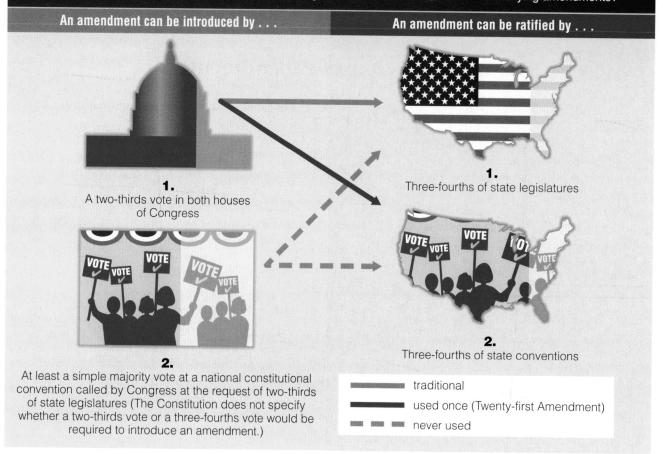

FIGURE 3–3 The Process of Amending the Constitution Amending the constitution is a two-step process of introduction and ratification. What are the two methods for introducing constitutional amendments? For ratifying amendments?

An amendment can be introduced by . . .

1. A two-thirds vote in both houses of Congress

2. At least a simple majority vote at a national constitutional convention called by Congress at the request of two-thirds of state legislatures (The Constitution does not specify whether a two-thirds vote or a three-fourths vote would be required to introduce an amendment.)

An amendment can be ratified by . . .

1. Three-fourths of state legislatures

2. Three-fourths of state conventions

— traditional
— used once (Twenty-first Amendment)
- - - never used

Just the Facts

Since the ratification of the first ten amendments over two hundred years ago, only seventeen more amendments have been approved; but in the 105th Congress alone, over one hundred constitutional amendments were proposed for Congress's consideration.

The competing social and economic interests in this nation guarantee one thing. The two-thirds approval required from both the House and the Senate to introduce an amendment is difficult to achieve. It takes only thirty-four of the one hundred senators to block the introduction of an amendment, for example. That means the senators from seventeen sparsely populated states, voting together, could keep any amendment from being introduced.

The ratification process is even more difficult. Three-fourths (thirty-eight) of the states must approve the amendment in one of the two manners described previously. As you can imagine, to be ratified, any amendment must have wide popular support in both parties and in all regions of the country.

There is also a time-limit problem. The Constitution does not specify a time limit for ratification. In 1917, however, Congress set a seven-year deadline on the ratification of what was to become the Eighteenth Amendment. The Supreme Court later ruled in favor of Congress on the constitutionality of this time limit in the case of *Dillon v. Gloss.* Since then, most amendments have included a seven-year time limit on ratification. Some amendments, after being successfully introduced, have failed because they did not meet this deadline.

To achieve goals and benefit everyone in a society, citizens must work together. Cooperation, the process of working together, involves coping with conflict in a group.

Compromise

In every conflict, there are at least two strong positions. Compromise is the political process through which a conflict between opposing groups is resolved. In order for a compromise to be effective, all sides must agree to certain points. First, each opposing party must be willing to accept less than what it actually wants. One party is usually willing to accept less if the other party or parties will also accept less. Compromise means that no side wins entirely, but no side loses completely, either. A compromise carries with it the promise of some benefit to all parties involved.

Negotiation

Normally, compromises are reached through negotiation. Sometimes, a neutral third party who is not in favor of either side assists in the negotiation

PARTICIPATING IN
YOUR GOVERNMENT

Compromise and Negotiation

process. The negotiation process has four steps:

1. Each side must state what it wants.
2. Each side must state what it views as an unacceptable outcome.
3. Each side must state the minimum that it will accept.
4. Normally, each side must be willing to give up one or more of its goals to achieve a compromise.

TAKING ACTION

1. Choose an issue that is presently dividing your

school, or imagine one that might. Examples could include a difference of opinion between students and faculty regarding a certain rule; differences between groups of students regarding a new dress code; or a requirement that all students learn to use the Internet. Poll your classmates on the issue to find out where they stand. Then divide students into two groups according to their opinions. Form a third group to act as a student task force to mediate between the two opposing groups. Meanwhile, groups should select students to act as their representatives. Use the four steps of the negotiation process to reach a compromise.

2. On one of your local television stations or on C-SPAN, watch a debate in which lawmakers argue the pros and cons of pending legislation. Take notes about the positions of the opposing sides. Then determine where the opponents have decided to compromise in order to get the legislation passed.

In contrast, the newest amendment was ratified 203 years after its introduction. On May 7, 1992, Michigan became the thirtieth state to ratify the Twenty-seventh Amendment, which deals with congressional salaries. This amendment was one of the twelve that were originally sent to the states in 1789. Given the seven-year time limit specified by Congress for most recent amendments, some people questioned whether the amendment would become effective even if the necessary number of states ratified it. Is 203 years too long a lapse of time between the introduction and the final ratification of an amendment? It apparently is not, because the amendment was certified as legitimate on May 18, 1992.

1. By what two methods can amendments to the Constitution be introduced?
2. By what two methods can they be ratified?

3. Why have so few amendments been added to the Constitution?
4. **For Critical Analysis:** What is the essential difference between a constitutional amendment and a law passed by Congress?

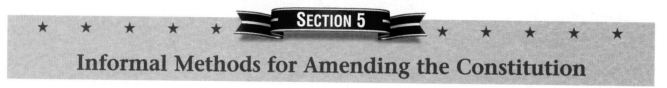

SECTION 5

Informal Methods for Amending the Constitution

Preview Questions:

- What is the difference between the formal and informal amending process?
- By what methods has the Constitution been informally amended?

Key Terms:

commerce clause, executive agreements, cabinet, tenure

For the most part, the Constitution provides the skeleton for our system of government. The details of that system have been fleshed out over the years as the various branches of government have fulfilled their duties. Formal amendments have played an important role in making the Constitution a living document. The Constitution, however, has kept pace with the times and grown as an instrument of government through informal changes as well. It has proved itself to be a remarkably flexible document, adapting itself time and again to new events and concerns.

The methods by which the Constitution has been informally amended are numerous. They include:

- Congressional legislation.
- Presidential actions.
- Judicial review and interpretation.
- Political parties.
- Custom and usage.

Congressional Legislation

We might say that the Constitution gave Congress the ball and Congress carried it. For example, the Con-

stitution gives Congress the power to regulate foreign and interstate commerce (business dealings that cross national and state boundaries) in Article I, Section 8, Clause 3, called the **commerce clause.** But there is no clear definition of what either foreign commerce or interstate commerce includes. Under the commerce clause, Congress has passed thousands of laws, which by their nature have defined the meaning of foreign and interstate commerce. In so doing, Congress has informally added to the Constitution.

Consider another example. In Article III, Section 1, the Constitution says that our national judiciary shall consist of one supreme court and "such inferior courts, as Congress may from time to time ordain and establish." Through a series of acts, Congress has indeed established a federal court system, one that you will study in Chapter 20.

Presidential Actions

Nowhere does the Constitution indicate that the president should propose bills or even budgets to Congress. Yet, since the time of Woodrow Wilson (who served as president from 1913 to 1921), each year the president has proposed hundreds of bills to Congress.

The Constitution states that, although Congress may declare war, the president is commander in chief of the armed forces. At times, our president has sent American forces into conflict without a declaration of war by Congress. President Lincoln did this in the Civil War (1861–1865). President Truman did this during the Korean conflict (1950–1953). Presidents Kennedy and Johnson sent military personnel to

Following is an excerpt from President Bill Clinton's State of the Union address, delivered to Congress and the American people on February 4, 1997:

In two days, I will propose a detailed plan to balance the budget by 2002. This plan will balance the budget and invest in our people while protecting Medicare, Medicaid, education and the environment. It will balance the budget and build on the Vice President's efforts to make our government work better even as it costs less.

It will balance the budget and provide middle class tax relief to pay for education and health care, to help to raise a child, to buy and sell a home.

Balancing the budget requires only your vote and my signature. It does not require us to rewrite our Constitution.

The next excerpt is from a speech given by J. C. Watts, a Republican congressional representative from Oklahoma, on February 4, 1997, in response to President Clinton's State of the Union address:

The Balanced-Budget Amendment will force the government to change its ways, permanently. No longer will a president or a Congress be able to spend money we don't have, on benefits our children will never see.

In a few weeks we will vote on that Amendment. Republicans can't pass it on their own because it takes a two-thirds majority. So, we need Democrat votes and we need your help.

BUILDING
SOCIAL STUDIES SKILLS

Analyzing Primary Sources

The quotations are from *primary sources*. A primary source is an original document, record, or account of an event in history. Speeches are one type of primary source. Others include the following:

- legal documents
- letters
- diaries and journals
- newspapers and magazines
- documentaries
- voting records
- sound recordings
- photographs
- poetry and songs
- political cartoons

Some primary sources are more reliable than others for factual information. For example, a newspaper editorial about someone may be less reliable than a diary or journal written by that person.

Analyzing primary sources is much the same as analyzing information from other sources. Use the following steps:

1. **Determine the reliability of the source.** Consider the background of your source and how the source got the information. Is it direct, first-hand knowledge? Does the information seem to be believable, unbiased, and accurate? Consider how your source is using the information. Is it to inform or to persuade?
2. **Read the information carefully.** Look for the main ideas and the supporting ideas.
3. **Ask yourself questions.** Ask who and what is involved and when and where the action is taking place. Ask how the events occurred, if that question hasn't already been answered. Always ask why the source is making the information available.

PRACTICING YOUR SKILLS

1. What is the purpose of these speeches—to inform or to persuade? Explain your answer.
2. What is the main idea in each excerpt? What are the supporting ideas?
3. What did President Clinton mean when he said that balancing the budget "does not require us to rewrite our Constitution"? What was Representative Watts's response to this statement?

▲ These Marines aboard a LAV-25 (light armored vehicle) keep a sharp watch after their patrol was stopped by supporters of Panamanian general Manuel Noriega. Marines were dispatched to Panama in 1989 by President George Bush. How is this action an example of the informal amending process?

place limits on these practices. Thus the Fourth Amendment protects citizens from such "unreasonable searches and seizures."

The Supreme Court has changed its interpretation of the Constitution in accordance with changing times. A good example has to do with a ruling in 1896. At that time, the Court said that providing separate-but-equal public facilities for African Americans did not violate the equal protection clause of the Fourteenth Amendment. By 1954, times had changed, and the Supreme Court reversed that decision. It ruled that facilities for blacks and whites could never be truly equal if they were separate.

Political Parties

The activities of political parties have had a profound effect on the American political system. Political parties today are responsible for nominating candidates, for organizing campaigns, and for placing employees in our government. Political parties provide the government with policy positions and political direction. Members of both the Senate and the House of Representatives, as well as the president, often base their decisions on the positions of the political parties to which they belong.

We might say the government of the United States is a government organized by political parties. The Constitution does not, however, refer to those parties. The Constitution specifies the requirements a candidate must have to hold office. It says when elections are to be held but does not explain how candidates should be chosen. The national conventions for the Republican and Democratic parties that occur every four years are not mentioned in the Constitution.

Vietnam during the 1960s. President Reagan sent armed forces to the tiny Caribbean island of Grenada in 1983. President Bush sent troops to Panama in 1989 and to the Middle East in 1990. President Clinton made the decision to send troops to Haiti in 1994 and to Bosnia in 1995.

Presidents have also conducted foreign affairs by the use of **executive agreements**—agreements made between the president and foreign chiefs of state. Although these agreements are made without the approval of Congress, they are legally binding.

Judicial Review and Interpretation

Another way of informally changing the Constitution is through the power of judicial review. Through judicial review, the Supreme Court adapts the Constitution to current situations. For example, in recent years, the Court has had to make decisions in cases involving government use of wiretapping and other electronic eavesdropping methods. Although electronic technology did not exist when the Constitution was ratified, the Supreme Court has used the Fourth Amendment to

Custom and Usage

Over time, a certain number of unwritten customs have taken on the strength of written laws. Today, for example, we accept the existence of a presidential **cabinet,** made up of the heads of the departments in the executive branch, as an official organization within the presidency. The Constitution, however, does not mention a cabinet.

The Constitution and Cyberspace

This nation's founders could not have foreseen today's world of communications technology and cyberspace—the Internet, the World Wide Web, and the like. Although our Constitution has been flexible up to now, some Americans are at odds over whether the Constitution can survive the challenges of cyberspace. Will some of our constitutional rights have to be sacrificed in the interest of national security in today's cyberworld?

Some Americans Believe That National Security Should Always Come First

Americans who believe that national security should come first think that the government should be allowed to monitor Internet communications. If the government could learn about possible terrorist activities and criminal conspiracies in advance, it could take steps to prevent them. This group of Americans argues that some of our constitutional rights, such as the right to free speech and the right to privacy, should be sacrificed in the interest of promoting national security.

Another national security concern has to do with the need to prepare for a possible *infowar*, defined by government officials as any effort to seize control of the electronic information systems in the United States. Today, most military communications take place over electronic communications networks, such as the Internet, to which civilians have access. If enemy "hackers" succeeded in jamming or disabling these networks, military operations might come to a standstill. Thus, according to those who are worried about this issue, we need to pass new laws to keep the wrong people from using the Internet.

Others Say That the Electronic Frontier Should Be Left Alone

Other Americans believe that the government should not attempt to control communications technology. These Americans argue that any such attempts would stunt the growth of the Internet and check further expansion into the electronic frontier.

Government attempts to control cyberspace also threatens certain basic constitutional rights of U.S. citizens. The First Amendment guarantees our right to free speech. Does this right include our right to communicate over the Internet? Furthermore, the Fourth Amendment protects us from unreasonable searches and seizures. In controlling electronic communication, would the government find itself conducting "unreasonable searches" of our private communications?

In any event, some believe, it makes little difference what the government tries to do in cyberspace. Terrorists, criminals, and enemy hackers will find ways to overcome any new obstacles created by government regulation of electronic communications. So why bother in the first place?

YOU DECIDE

1. In what situations do you think national security should take priority over constitutional rights?
2. As you learned in the first chapters of this text, politics consists of making compromises. Read this feature carefully, and suggest a reasonable compromise between the two positions that are presented here.

How Our Constitution Has Changed

In the more than two hundred years since the ratification of the Constitution, numerous changes have been made. Here are just a few.

THEN (WHEN THE CONSTITUTION WAS RATIFIED)	NOW
Slavery was permitted.	Slavery was abolished (by the Thirteenth Amendment of 1865 and subsequent laws).
There was no mention of judicial review.	The doctrine of judicial review is well established (first stated by the Supreme Court in *Marbury v. Madison* in 1803).
No limit on presidential terms had been established.	Presidential terms are limited to two elected terms (by the Twenty-second Amendment in 1951).
Voting rights were severely restricted (to property-owning white males).	There are only minimal restrictions, such as age and residency requirements, on voting rights.

Tradition sometimes evolves to become written law. For example, for many years, no president ran for a third term. This tradition was started by George Washington. Franklin D. Roosevelt defied the tradition by running for office and winning a third presidential term in 1940 and then winning a fourth term in 1944. Many politicians and other citizens believed that Roosevelt was creating a permanent presidency, almost as if he were setting himself up as a king. As a result, the Twenty-second Amendment was added to the Constitution. This amendment limits the president's **tenure** (the period of holding office) to two four-year terms.

Until the Twenty-fifth Amendment was passed in 1967, the Constitution did not say that the vice president was to assume the office of president in the event of the president's death. Yet on eight occa-

Just the Facts

Alexander Hamilton believed that the U.S. president should hold office for life.

▲ *Vice President Lyndon B. Johnson was sworn in as president aboard* Air Force One *only hours after the assassination of President John Kennedy on November 22, 1963. Why did the ceremony occur so quickly after Kennedy's death?*

sions, that is exactly what happened. The Constitution, though, gave only the powers and duties of the president to the vice president in such instances. It did not give the vice president the office itself (Article II, Section 1, Clause 6).

SECTION 5 REVIEW

1. How can the Constitution be informally amended?
2. Why is this process important to our understanding of constitutional change?
3. **For Critical Analysis:** Custom and usage can generate informal amendments to the Constitution. Explain how a violation of custom and usage by a president or a congressional committee might lead to a formal change in the Constitution. Give an example.

★ ★ ★ ★ Chapter Summary ★ ★ ★ ★

Section 1: The Structure of Our Constitution

- The Constitution provides the framework for the U.S. system of government. It is made up of three parts: Preamble, articles, and amendments.
- The Preamble sets forth the general purposes of the government.
- The seven articles establish the government's basic organization.
- The twenty-seven amendments are formal changes made in the Constitution since its ratification.

Section 2: The Major Principles of Government Embodied in the Constitution

- A limited government can only do what the people allow it to do. Under a limited government, no person is above the law. Popular sovereignty means that the people are the ultimate source of power.
- Separation of powers among the three branches of government is intended to prevent the rise of tyranny. Checks and balances allow each branch to exercise certain powers over the actions of the other branches.

- With the power of judicial review, which was established in the Supreme Court case of *Marbury v. Madison,* the courts can decide whether a law or other governmental action violates the Constitution.
- Under federalism, some powers belong to the national government, while others belong to the states.

Section 3: The Bill of Rights

- The Bill of Rights, the first ten amendments, became part of the Constitution in 1791.
- The purpose of the Bill of Rights was to protect individual liberties against violations by the national government.

Section 4: The Formal Process of Amending the Constitution

- Article V sets out four possible ways of amending the Constitution.
- An amendment may be introduced by a two-thirds vote in the Senate and the House of Representatives. All twenty-seven existing amendments have been introduced in this way. Alternatively, an amendment may be proposed by a national convention, although such a convention has never been held.
- Once introduced, an amendment is ratified when three-fourths of the state legislatures vote in favor of ratification. This is the traditional ratification method. States may also call state conventions to vote on ratification. Three-fourths of the states must approve for the amendment to be ratified. This method has been used only once.
- The widespread support required for introduction and ratification, together with time limits usually placed on ratification, makes the formal amendment process extremely difficult.

Section 5: Informal Methods for Amending the Constitution

- Informal methods for amending the Constitution have helped it change with the times.
- Informal methods include congressional legislation, presidential actions, judicial review and interpretation, the actions of political parties, and custom and usage.

CHAPTER 3 Review

★ REVIEW QUESTIONS ★

1. Describe the basic structure of the Constitution.
2. What is the supremacy clause, and why is it important?
3. Identify and briefly describe the six basic principles on which the Constitution is based.
4. How does the Constitution provide for limited government?
5. How does the system of checks and balances work?
6. Explain how the Bill of Rights was added to the Constitution.
7. What are the two methods of introducing an amendment to the Constitution?
8. What are the two methods of ratifying an amendment?
9. Why have only twenty-seven amendments been added to the Constitution?
10. What are the methods by which the Constitution has been informally amended? Give an example of each.
11. What are the four steps in the negotiation process outlined in the *Participating in Your Government* feature in this chapter? Why is each step an important part of this process?

★ CRITICAL THINKING ★

1. The principle of checks and balances was built into the American system of government. In what ways do you think this system has created conflict between the branches? In what ways has it avoided conflict?
2. Think of an amendment that you would like to add to the Constitution. Develop and present an argument, in writing, on why your amendment should be added.
3. What characteristics of the Constitution have enabled it to survive and be adapted to the growth and changing conditions of our nation?
4. The Constitution has been amended only twenty-seven times in over two hundred years, although many more amendments have been proposed. Why do you think the founders made the amendment process so difficult?
5. Develop and present arguments either for or against the present amendment process.

★ IMPROVING YOUR SKILLS ★

Communication Skills

Learning from What You Read One of the most common assignments made in high school and college is to study a chapter in a textbook. Yet many students do not know how to read effectively in order to learn. They "read blindly," and when they have finished reading the chapter, they can't remember most of what they read.

Do you want to know how to use your brain for learning? First, you "turn it on" by *wanting* to learn. Second, you become a detective searching for meaning by using the following approach in reading your textbook: You will find that you can become a more efficient reader and a more effective learner.

1. *Survey.* Survey the assigned material so that you gain an overview of the content. Pay attention to the title, the section heads, the first paragraphs of each section, and the last paragraphs of each section. Read the introduction, the preview questions, the chapter summary, and the chapter objectives.
2. *Question.* Questions create curiosity, improve concentration, give purpose to your search, and make important ideas more visible—all of which improve comprehension. Rephrase the main headings and subheadings into questions. Jot down questions that occur to you while surveying the chapter. Read the review questions at the ends of the sections and the chapter.

3. **Read.** Read each section carefully, actively searching for answers to your questions as you read. You are a detective with a purpose and you will absorb ideas more quickly as a result of surveying the chapter and asking questions.

4. **Recite.** At the end of each section, look away from the book for a few seconds. Think about what you've learned and recite it out loud. This makes a deeper impression on your mind. Answer the review questions out loud. Hearing your answers will help you put the information into long-term memory.

5. **Review.** Look at the whole chapter to see how all the parts relate to each other. This total review is the final step for organizing the information so that you will understand and remember it.

This method of learning is called the SQRRR (or SQ3R) approach, which stands for *survey, question, read, recite,* and *review.* This method has been proven to be an easy and effective method for improving study, memory, and learning skills.

Writing

1. Write an explanation of the SQRRR study approach, defining the purpose of each step in your own words.
2. Rephrase, in writing, the main headings and subheadings in this chapter into questions.

Social Studies Skills

Interpreting a Diagram Figure 3–3 (The Process of Amending the Constitution) on page 76 shows ways an amendment can be introduced and ratified. Use this chart to answer the following questions.

1. How do the drawings relate to the words directly underneath them?
2. Which amendment procedure has never been used?

3. Which amendment procedure has been used only once?
4. What is the most traditional method for introducing and ratifying an amendment?

★ ACTIVITIES AND PROJECTS ★

1. With a group of your classmates, make a scrapbook of articles and political cartoons from newspapers and magazines (or the Internet) that illustrate the underlying principles of the Constitution: limited government, popular sovereignty, and so on. As a group, write a brief description for each item, explaining how it shows the Constitution in action.
2. Select and carefully read one of the twenty-seven amendments that you believe is of particular interest or significance. Research and prepare a report on the reasons and events that led to the adoption of that amendment. Present the report in class.

What If . . .

The Bill of Rights Had Never Been Ratified?

The first ten amendments to the Constitution, the Bill of Rights, were ratified in 1791, a few years after the Constitution was ratified. These amendments set forth the basic freedoms that all Americans enjoy today. What might American lives be like if the Bill of Rights had never been ratified?

CHAPTER 4

Our System of Federalism

CHAPTER OBJECTIVES

To learn about and understand . . .

⭐ The three basic types of governmental systems

⭐ The division of governmental powers in the American federal system

⭐ The relations among the states and what the national government must do for the states

⭐ The supremacy of the national government in the American federal system

⭐ How American federalism has changed over the years

*"The object of government . . . is
not the glory of rulers or of races, but
the happiness of the common man."*

Lord William Beveridge
(1879–1963)
British Economist

INTRODUCTION

As pointed out by William Beveridge in the above quotation, any governing situation requires that the rulers worry about the common person— or the people being governed. For example, the principal governs your school with the interests of students and parents in mind. A principal who is only interested in personal "glory" may not last. The school board may remove that person. We might expect that the closer a government is to the people, the more sensitive that government will be to the people's needs. The founders of our nation conceived of a government that had several levels, each one closer to the people than the one above it.

Today, the American federal system of government consists of over 85,000 separate governmental units, as Figure 4–1 on page 88 illustrates. Those governments are run by over half a million elected and appointed government officials.

◀ States and the national government work together to fund and maintain our interstate highway system.

Three Basic Types of Governmental Systems

Preview Questions:

- ⭐ What are the three basic types of governmental systems?
- ⭐ How do these systems differ from one another?
- ⭐ What is the nature of federalism?

Key Terms:

unitary system, confederal system, federal system

The United States started with a *confederal* system under the Articles of Confederation. Today, we have a *federal* system. In most other countries, neither of these systems is used. Most countries have a *unitary* system of government. These three systems of government are discussed in this section and shown graphically in Figure 4–2 on page 89.

Unitary System

A **unitary system** is a centralized system in which state and local governments exercise only those powers given to them by the central, or national, government, which holds ultimate authority. Japan is a nation that uses a unitary system. The Japanese national government, for example, makes the most important decisions for all schools within the nation and even decides the subjects that must be taught nationwide.

France today uses a modified form of the unitary system. Within France, there are regional political units, called departments, as well as municipalities, or local governments. Each of these regional and local governing units has its own elected and appointed officials. But decisions made by those officials can, for the most part, be overruled by the national government. Also, the national government in Paris can cut off the funding of many departmental and municipal government

FIGURE 4–1 Governmental Units in the United States Today There are 85,006 existing governmental units. What percentage of this total do townships form?

The Number of Governments in the United States Today	
Government	**Number**
National Government	1
State Governments	50
Local Governments	
Counties	3,043
Municipalities (mainly cities or towns)	19,279
Townships (less extensive powers)	16,656
Special districts (water, sewer, etc.)	31,555
School districts	14,422
TOTAL	**85,006**

84,955 (grouping of Local Governments)

Each Type of Government As a Percentage of All Governments in the U.S.

- National (0.001%)
- State (0.05%)
- Counties (3.57%)
- School districts (16.96%)
- Townships (19.59%)
- Municipalities (22.67%)
- Special districts (37.12%)

SOURCE: U.S. Department of Commerce, *Statistical Abstract of the United States* 1997 (Washington, D.C.: U.S. Government Printing Office, 1997).

activities. Finally, all policies related to police, land use, welfare, and education are determined by the national government, although they are carried out by the departmental and municipal entities.

Confederal System

A **confederal system,** or confederation, is a league of independent states. The central government handles only those matters of common concern expressly delegated to it by the member states. It cannot pass laws that directly apply to individuals unless the member states explicitly support such laws. Switzerland is a nation that currently uses a confederal system of government. Certain international organizations, such as the United Nations and the North Atlantic Treaty Organization (NATO), also follow a confederal model.

Federal System

The **federal system** is a compromise between the confederal and unitary forms of government. Authority is usually divided between national and state or other regional governments by a written constitution, as in the United States. All levels of government—national, state, and local—have the power to pass laws that directly influence the people. The national government's laws are supreme, but it cannot overrule state and local laws unless they conflict with national laws. This is what makes a federal system different from a unitary system.

Keep in mind that *federalism* and *democracy* do not mean the same thing. Federalism is a system of government in which powers are divided between national and regional governments, such as state governments. Democracy is a system in which the people are involved, either directly or indirectly, in the governing process.

Reasons for Federalism in the United States

Why did the framers of the Constitution choose a federal system? You already know that political compromise

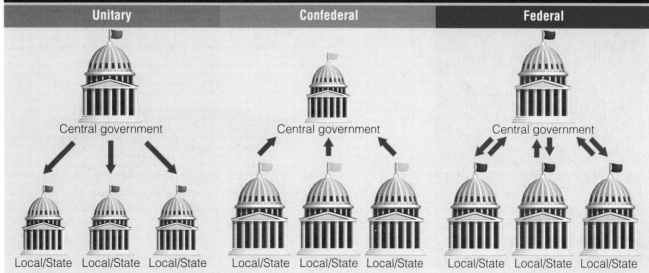

FIGURE 4–2 The Flow of Power in Three Systems of Government As you can see, in a unitary system, power flows from the central government to the local and state governments. In a confederal system, power flows in the opposite direction—from the state and local governments to the central government. Finally, in the federal system, power flows in both directions. Which of these systems is, in essence, a compromise between the other two?

| Unitary | Confederal | Federal |

Central government — Central government — Central government

Local/State Local/State Local/State — Local/State Local/State Local/State — Local/State Local/State Local/State

ARCHITECTS

of Government

Alexander Hamiliton (1755–1804)

Alexander Hamilton was a colleague of George Washington and a delegate to the Constitutional Convention. He served as Washington's first secretary of the treasury from 1789 to 1795. Hamilton, the author of most of the *Federalist Papers*, advocated a strong national government.

HIS WORDS

"The proposed Constitution, so far from implying an abolition of the state governments, makes them constituent parts of the national sovereignty."

(Federalist Paper No. 9, 1787)

"The complete independence of the courts of justice is particularly essential to a Limited Constitution."

(Federalist Paper No. 78, 1788)

DEVELOPING CRITICAL THINKING SKILLS

1. In the first quotation, why was Hamilton stressing that state governments would not be abolished?
2. What did Hamilton mean by a "Limited Constitution"?

played a role. In addition, specific characteristics of the states lent themselves to a federal system.

Political Compromise The Articles of Confederation failed because they did not allow for a strong enough national government. Many of the framers of the Constitution were therefore determined to strengthen the national government. Others, however, still feared that

a strong national government would threaten individual rights. They favored small government close to the people. The natural outcome was a compromise—a federal system. The appeal of federalism was that it retained state traditions and local power while establishing a strong national government capable of handling common problems, such as national defense.

Size and Regional Isolation Even in the days when the United States was made up of only thirteen colonies, its geographic area was larger than that of France or England. Travel was slow, and communication was difficult. Many regions were isolated. The news of any particular political decision might take several weeks to reach everyone. Therefore, even if the framers of the Constitution had wanted a unitary system (and most of them did not), such a system would have been unworkable.

Differences in Political Cultures We have always been a nation of different subcultures. The Pilgrims who founded New England, the people who worked in the agricultural society of the South, and the people who populated the Middle Atlantic states differed greatly from one another. The groups that founded New England were religious in orientation, while the groups that populated the Middle Atlantic states were more business oriented. Those that populated the agricultural society of the South were more individualistic than the other groups; that is, they were less inclined to accept the authority of the national government.

A unitary system of government for a nation composed of numerous political subcultures is difficult to imagine. A federal system of government, in contrast, allows state and local governments to create laws that serve the interests of particular subcultures.

SECTION 1 REVIEW

1. Describe confederal and unitary systems. How do they differ from federal systems?
2. Why doesn't a federal system necessarily have to be democratic?
3. Why did the framers create a federal system of government for the United States?
4. **For Critical Analysis:** Increasingly, the national

government has attempted to influence the states to make uniform laws—laws that are the same in all states. For example, by threatening to withhold federal funding to help rebuild highways, the national government forced all of the states to raise the minimum age for buying and consuming alcoholic beverages to twenty-one. Why do you think the national government is pushing toward more uniformity in state laws?

SECTION 2

The Division of Governmental Powers

Preview Questions:

- What are the three types of powers delegated to the national government?
- What powers are denied to the national government?
- What powers are reserved for the states?
- What powers are denied to the states?
- What are the concurrent powers?

Key Terms:

division of powers, expressed powers, enumerated powers, implied powers, necessary and proper clause, elastic clause, inherent powers, reserved powers, concurrent powers

Although the United States has a federal system, the words *federal system* cannot be found in the U.S. Constitution. Nor can you find a systematic explanation of the **division of powers**—the way in which governmental powers are divided between the national government and state governments. Nonetheless, the original Constitution, along with the Tenth Amendment, tells what the national and state governments can do. The Tenth Amendment states:

The powers not delegated to the United States by the Constitution, nor prohibited by it to the States, are reserved to the States respectively, or to the people.

The key word here is *delegated*, which means "assigned" or "given." Certain powers are delegated to the national government. Others are "reserved to" (retained by) state governments, or the people.

Powers Delegated to the National Government

Three types of powers are delegated to the national government by the Constitution: *expressed* (or *enumerated*) *powers*, *implied powers*, and *inherent powers*.

Expressed, or Enumerated, Powers Most of the powers explicitly delegated to the national government are enumerated—that is, specifically listed—in Article I, Section 8. These are called **expressed powers,** or **enumerated powers.**

Eighteen separate clauses enumerate twenty-seven different powers that are specifically given to Congress. These include:

- Coining money.
- Regulating interstate commerce.
- Levying and collecting taxes.
- Declaring war.
- Establishing post offices.

Some of the amendments to the Constitution give expressed powers, too. The Sixteenth Amendment, for example, gives Congress the power to impose a federal income tax.

Other parts of the Constitution grant expressed powers to the executive branch. Article II, Section 2, enumerates certain powers of the president, which include:

- Making treaties.
- Appointing certain federal officeholders.
- Granting pardons.

Just the Facts

From 1790 to 1800, the seat of the U.S. government was Philadelphia.

BUILDING

SOCIAL STUDIES
SKILLS

Analyzing
Political
Cartoons

Political, or editorial, cartoons have appeared in the editorial sections of newspapers and magazines throughout our nation's history. They are usually funny, but they can also communicate serious messages. Their simplicity, directness, and humor can make them a powerful tool for influencing public opinion. Sometimes they present a positive point of view, but more often they are critical of a person, group, or issue. Cartoons are an effective way to express a point of view on often complex political issues. Although they may present an issue in simple terms, the reader must understand the background of the issues to appreciate the cartoon.

Political cartoons often use two techniques: *symbolism* and *caricature*. Symbols are objects that stand for something else. Some common symbols in political cartoons are the donkey for Democrats, the elephant for Republicans, and Uncle Sam for the government. Caricatures are distortions or exaggerations of the physical features of someone or something. For example, a cartoonist may take a slightly prominent feature, such as big teeth, and enlarge it to make it comical.

Labels are sometimes used to identify the important features in a cartoon. Captions are also used, either to hint at the main idea of the cartoon or to represent the words of the character in the cartoon.

Here is what to do when you read a political cartoon:

1. Examine the entire cartoon to determine the general topic.
2. Identify the symbols or characters used and what they represent.
3. Read all of the labels and captions.
4. Determine the tone of the cartoonist. Are the figures represented in a positive or negative light?
5. Try to determine the quality of the humor. Is it harsh and angry, or is it gently mocking?
6. Determine whose viewpoint is being expressed. Remember that a political cartoon is an editorial in a picture form. The cartoonist is expressing only one point of view.

Implied Powers The national government has certain powers that are not expressly given to it in the Constitution but are *reasonably implied* (suggested or indicated) by the expressed powers. These powers are called **implied powers.** Their constitutional basis is found in Article I, Section 8, Clause 18. This clause states that Congress shall have the power

To make all Laws which shall be necessary and proper for carrying into Execution the foregoing Powers, and all other Powers vested by this Constitution in the Government of the United States, or in any Department or Officer thereof.

The key words in the clause are *necessary and proper*. For this reason, it is often called the **necessary and** **proper clause.** It is also called the **elastic clause** because it adds elasticity to our constitutional system. The necessary and proper clause gives Congress all of those powers that can be reasonably inferred from the brief wording of the Constitution, even though they are not expressly stated. Through exercising the power vested in it by this clause, the national government has broadened the scope of its authority to meet many problems that the founders did not or could not anticipate.

There are thousands of examples of the national government's exercise of implied powers. The Constitution does not expressly state that the national government is responsible for the construction of an interstate highway system. Yet our government has paid money for precisely this purpose. Certainly the

7. Try to imagine what the other side of the issue would look like in cartoon form.

PRACTICING YOUR SKILLS

....

1. Study the cartoon on the right. What is the cartoonist's point of view? What is the tone of the cartoon? Does the cartoonist use symbols or caricatures? If so, try to identify them.
2. Find and clip out a political cartoon. Interpret the cartoon for the class by following the instructions listed above. Then design a cartoon of your own that expresses an alternative point of view.

▲ *Published on July 4, 1976, this political cartoon shows Uncle Sam in the driver's seat, while his rearview mirror reflects the famous John Trumbull painting of the signing of the Declaration of Independence. (See painting on page 42.) Although political cartoons are usually biting and satirical, this one is a reminder of our democratic traditions and history. How might the publication date have affected the tone of the cartoon?*

Constitution does not state that the national government should involve itself in disputes between workers and their managers. But the national government has involved itself in such disputes by establishing laws and regulations concerning worker safety, labor unions, and discrimination in the workplace. Nowhere does the Constitution state that Congress should pass laws prohibiting the manufacture, sale, and consumption of certain drugs. Nonetheless, Congress has done so.

Inherent Powers The final category of powers, known as **inherent powers,** are powers that the national government has simply to ensure the nation's integrity and survival as a political unit.

The inherent powers are few but important. Each nation's government must clearly have the ability to act in its own interest within the community of nations. Therefore, each national government must have the ability to make treaties, to regulate immigration, to acquire territory, to wage war, and to declare peace. Figure 4–3 on page 94 lists the powers delegated to the national government by the Constitution.

Powers Denied to the National Government

The Constitution prohibits, or denies, a number of powers to the national government, as shown in Figure 4–4 on page 95. It does this in several ways.

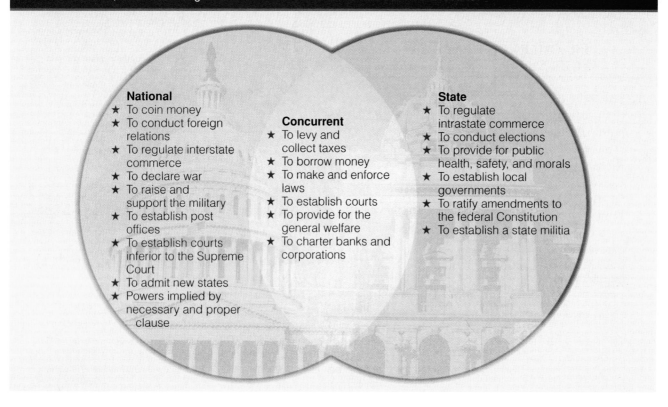

FIGURE 4–3 Powers Granted by the Constitution The figure below outlines the powers granted by the Constitution to the national government, to the state governments, and to both the national and state governments concurrently. According to the Constitution, which level of government is entitled to create and administer courts?

National
★ To coin money
★ To conduct foreign relations
★ To regulate interstate commerce
★ To declare war
★ To raise and support the military
★ To establish post offices
★ To establish courts inferior to the Supreme Court
★ To admit new states
★ Powers implied by necessary and proper clause

Concurrent
★ To levy and collect taxes
★ To borrow money
★ To make and enforce laws
★ To establish courts
★ To provide for the general welfare
★ To charter banks and corporations

State
★ To regulate intrastate commerce
★ To conduct elections
★ To provide for public health, safety, and morals
★ To establish local governments
★ To ratify amendments to the federal Constitution
★ To establish a state militia

Expressly Denied Powers Most of the powers expressly denied to the national government can be found in Article I, Section 9, and in the First through the Eighth Amendments. The national government cannot, for example, impose taxes on goods sold to other countries. Moreover, the national government cannot pass laws that significantly restrain our constitutional rights and liberties, such as freedom of religion, speech, press, or assembly. It cannot conduct illegal searches or seizures.

Powers Not Delegated Our national government has only those powers given to it by the Constitution. Any power not delegated to it, either expressly or implicitly, by the Constitution in one of the ways discussed above is prohibited to it. The Constitution does not, for example, give the national government the power to create a national public school system. As a result, the United States does not have one.

Powers Reserved to the States

Through the Tenth Amendment, the Constitution reserves certain powers to the states. These **reserved powers** include powers that are not given to the national government and that are not denied to the state governments. (See Figure 4–3.) The national government cannot take away these powers from the states.

One reserved power is each state's right to regulate commerce within its borders. Another is the right to provide for a state militia. In essence, states have the authority over all their internal affairs and over the health, safety, and welfare of their people.

Consider a few examples of how states exercise their reserved powers. If you eat out, the restaurant you go to has to meet certain standards of cleanliness. These standards are set by your state government. If you attend a public school, that school is part of a school system created by your state government. The state decides at what age you must attend school and how many hours

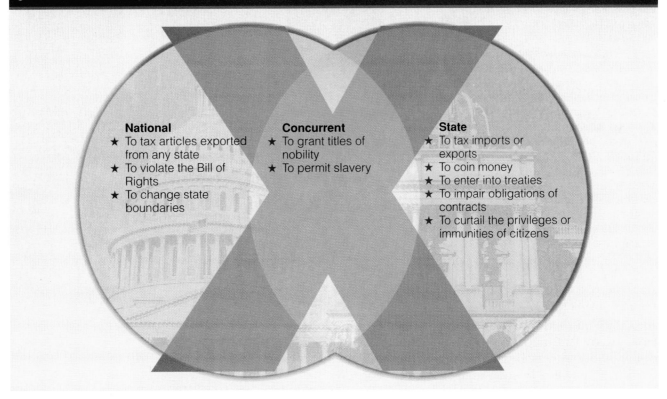

National
★ To tax articles exported from any state
★ To violate the Bill of Rights
★ To change state boundaries

Concurrent
★ To grant titles of nobility
★ To permit slavery

State
★ To tax imports or exports
★ To coin money
★ To enter into treaties
★ To impair obligations of contracts
★ To curtail the privileges or immunities of citizens

you must spend at school. If you are required to take an American government class, that requirement may have been set by your state government. Your state determines at what age you can get married without permission from your parents. The state establishes the requirements for obtaining and for keeping a valid driver's license. Your state government also creates traffic laws that people driving within your state must obey.

Powers Denied to the States

Just as the Constitution denies certain powers to the national government, so it denies some powers to the state governments. Powers that are expressly denied to the states are found in Article I, Section 10, which has three clauses: Treaties and Coinage, Duties and Imposts, and War. Additionally, the Thirteenth, Fourteenth, Fifteenth, Nineteenth, Twenty-fourth, and Twenty-sixth Amendments specifically deny certain powers to the states.

One power expressly denied to the states is the power to tax imports and exports to and from other states or foreign countries. Another denied power concerns treaties. No state is allowed to enter into a treaty on its own with another country.

Because the Constitution lays out a federal system, no state is allowed to endanger that system. Therefore, states are not allowed to tax activities and agencies of the federal government.

What about Local Governments?

As you know by now, the federal system involves a federal government and fifty state governments. But what about the over eighty thousand local government units? How are they governed? We will examine this question in more detail in Chapter 25 of this book. For now, you should understand that the Constitution does not specifically refer to the powers of local government.

▶ Framed by the Manhattan skyline, U.S. Customs agents load bales of marijuana onto a truck after eight tons of the drug, with an estimated street value of $19 million, were seized at a Brooklyn port. Nine individuals, allegedly members of Colombia's Medellin drug cartel, were arrested by the Federal Bureau of Investigation. Although the framers never anticipated problems such as these, the Constitution does, through its necessary and proper clause, give the national government the authority to establish bureaus such as the FBI and to seize illegal substances.

Also, the Constitution does not require states to create local government units, such as counties, municipalities, or school districts. Local governments thus exist at the will of the states. In other words, a state can create local governments when the need arises. A state can also disband local governments.

When local governmental units act, they are acting by the power of the state government. That means local governments cannot constitutionally do anything that state governments cannot constitutionally do.

Concurrent Powers

The Constitution gives certain powers to *both* the national government and the state governments. These are called **concurrent powers.**

For example, both state and national governments have the power to tax. The types of taxation, however, are divided between the levels of government. States may not levy taxes on imported goods, but the national government may. In addition, neither level of government may tax the facilities of the other. For example, Texas cannot tax the national government on the fees the national government charges people to use federal court buildings located in Texas.

Certain concurrent powers are implied rather than stated expressly. They include the power to borrow money, the power to establish courts, and the power to charter banks. The national government and state governments share these powers.

◀ Federal, state, and local government programs depend on taxes collected from citizens. Based on the cartoon shown here, how does the average taxpayer feel about the "tax bite" each April 15?

1. What is meant by the phrase "division of powers"?
2. What are the three types of powers delegated to the national government? Explain and give examples of each one.
3. What is the significance of the necessary and proper clause?
4. What are the two ways in which the Constitution denies powers to the national government?
5. What are some powers that the Constitution reserves to the states?
6. Where do local governments fit into the federal system?
7. What are the concurrent powers?
8. **For Critical Analysis:** The Tenth Amendment reserves to the states all of those powers not delegated to the national government nor prohibited to the state governments. The constitution does not expressly delegate to the national government the power to build an interstate highway system. How, then, can you explain the fact that the national government has built such a system?

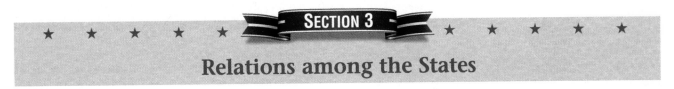

SECTION 3

Relations among the States

Preview Questions:

- What is horizontal federalism?
- What does the Constitution say about relations among the states?
- What duties does the national government owe to the states under the Constitution?

Key Terms:

horizontal federalism, privileges and immunities clause, alien, full faith and credit clause, extradition, *Dennison* rule, republican form of government

We have been discussing the relationship between the national government and the state governments. Federalism also involves interaction among state governments, or **horizontal federalism.** The states have social, commercial, and other dealings among themselves. For example, the citizens of one state travel to other states and buy various items from sellers in other states.

The rules of horizontal federalism laid out in the U.S. Constitution prevent any one state from setting itself apart from the others. The Constitution has three important provisions that relate to horizontal federalism. Each was taken almost directly from the Articles of Confederation.

Privileges and Immunities

Article IV, Section 2, declares the following:

The Citizens of each State shall be entitled to all Privileges and Immunities of Citizens in the several States.

The **privileges and immunities clause** prevents states from discriminating against citizens of other states. A resident of one state cannot be treated as an **alien**—a foreigner—in another state. Each state is required to extend to any U.S. citizen from any other state the protection of that state's laws, the right to work, access to the courts, and any other privileges that it may grant its own citizens. A resident of Texas thus cannot be treated as an alien in New York. She or he must have access to New York courts, the right to travel, and the right to own property.

In certain instances, however, states are allowed to "discriminate" against (treat differently) out-of-state

▶ Though the Constitution prevents states from discriminating against citizens of other states, there are certain situations in which citizens from other states may legally be treated differently. Travelers entering Arizona, for example, must stop at border stations like this so inspectors can verify that certain agricultural products are not brought into the state. Why would a state want to inspect certain agricultural products?

residents. For example, at most state universities, out-of-state residents have to pay higher fees than do in-state residents. Some states require people to be residents for a certain amount of time before they can receive public-assistance benefits, such as welfare.

The Full Faith and Credit Clause

Article IV, Section 1, reads as follows:

Full Faith and Credit shall be given in each State to the public Acts, Records, and judicial Proceedings of every other State.

The **full faith and credit clause** requires states to recognize one another's laws and court decisions. That means that rights established in one state will be honored in other states. For example, if you own property in Florida, your ownership rights are valid in Texas. This is important if you wish to sell the property to a Texas resident. As another example, if you are legally married in the state of Missouri, that marriage will be honored in Montana.

The full faith and credit clause was originally included in the Articles of Confederation to promote mutual friendship among the people of the different colonies. As part of the U.S. Constitution, this clause has contributed to the unity of American citizens because it allows Americans to move from state to state without worrying about losing any rights.

Interstate Extradition

A person who is charged with committing a crime in one state may flee to another state. This person is a fugitive. **Extradition** occurs when the fugitive is caught and returned to the state from which he or she fled. Article IV, Section 2, of the Constitution states the following:

A Person charged in any State with Treason, Felony, or other Crime, who shall flee from Justice, and be found in another State, shall on Demand of the executive Authority of the State from which he fled, be delivered up, to be removed to the State having Jurisdiction [authority] of the Crime.

Although the language of this section seems clear, for many years state governors were not required by law to extradite fugitives. An 1861 ruling by the U.S. Supreme Court, called the **Dennison rule,** upheld the right of the governor of Ohio to refuse an extradition request by the governor of Kentucky for a "free man of

▶ *This poster presents three African American heroes of the Reconstruction period. They are (left to right) Senator Blanche K. Bruce, Frederick Douglass, and Senator Hiram Revels.*

color." The man had been charged in Kentucky with the crime of helping a slave escape to freedom.

The *Dennison* rule stood for 126 years. Then, in 1987, the U.S. Supreme Court reversed itself in a case involving an Iowan, Ron Calder, who was supposed to stand trial in Puerto Rico. The governor of Iowa refused to extradite Calder but was forced to do so after the Supreme Court ruled in favor of the extradition.

In many cases today, the question of extraditing fugitives has little meaning. Congress has made it a federal crime to flee across state lines to avoid prosecution for certain serious crimes. That means that agents of the national government will arrest fugitives regardless of what state they are in. Fugitives are usually turned over to the state from which they fled.

What the National Government Must Do for the States

The national government has certain duties to the fifty states. Most of them are listed in Article IV, Section 4:

The United States shall guarantee to every State in this Union a Republican Form of Government, and shall protect each of them against Invasion; and on Application of the Legislature, or of the Executive (when the Legislature cannot be convened) against domestic Violence.

Guarantee of Republican Form of Government A **republican form of government** is one in which the people are governed by elected representatives. Our national government therefore has had to ensure that

each state government was formed according to the will of the majority of its citizens.

The only time that the republican guarantee became truly important was after the Civil War, when a number of southern states had not ratified the Thirteenth, Fourteenth, and Fifteenth Amendments. These amendments ended slavery, guaranteed due process of law and equal protection under the law for all Americans, and granted citizenship status and voting rights to African Americans (see the Resource Center for the wording of each amendment). In effect, the southern states that had not ratified the amendments were depriving their citizens of a republican form of government. As a result, Congress refused to admit senators and representatives from those states until they had made the appropriate reforms.

Just the Facts

Susan B. Anthony and other advocates of voting rights for women were very dissatisfied with the Fourteenth Amendment because it guaranteed voting rights only for "male citizens."

Protection against Foreign Invasion An attack launched against any one state is an attack against all fifty states. Everybody today takes that concept for granted. It was not so well accepted in the 1780s, though. At that time, the states were not sure whether they would stand together if one of them were attacked. Each state agreed, therefore, to give its war-making powers to the national government, but only if the government pledged in turn to protect each of the states.

Protection against Domestic Violence Each state is obliged to keep the peace within its own geographical boundaries. If for some reason a state cannot do so, the national government may provide help. On a number of occasions, presidents have had to send in federal troops, called the National Guard, to control

Hunger is one of the most heartbreaking and urgent problems facing the world today. Although it may be difficult to believe that every day many people are dying of starvation and malnutrition, hunger haunts us everywhere—in our own nation as well as in faraway countries.

Hunger is being fought on many fronts. Some involve short-term solutions, such as providing a hot meal to someone who doesn't know where to turn. Others involve long-term solutions, such as supporting new legislation to change policies of food distribution. If you would like to aid in these efforts, helping to feed the hungry in your own community is a good starting point.

While most of us would like to help, many of us are not aware of the opportunities available for helping those in need. Following is a list of some actions you might consider, and some organizations that would welcome volunteers.

PARTICIPATING IN YOUR GOVERNMENT

Helping Hungry People

TAKING ACTION

1. Locate groups in your area that help fight hunger. Start by calling your church, your synagogue, or the mayor's office, or look in the Yellow Pages under "Social Service Agencies." If you don't have any luck, there are many national organizations that can help you locate a group.

A few of them are listed below:

National Student Campaign against Hunger
11965 Venice Blvd.
Suite 408
Los Angeles, CA 90066
310-397-5270, Ext. 324

The Salvation Army
613 Slaters Lane
Alexandria, VA 22313
703-684-5500

Seed CDC
1127 Capital Ave., SW
Atlanta, GA 30315
404-523-6722

2. Offer to help out in the office of a local hunger project by answering phones, writing letters, or raising funds.
3. Donate food to a food bank. If you can't locate the food bank nearest you, contact:

Second Harvest
116 South Michigan Ave.,
Suite 4
Chicago, IL 60603
1-800-332-3663

---

upheavals within various states. For example, in 1967, President Lyndon Baines Johnson sent federal troops to Detroit at the request of Michigan's governor, George Romney. Local and state police personnel were unable to stop riots and looting in the inner city. Similarly, President Johnson sent federal troops to the cities of Chicago and Baltimore to help control violent outbreaks that followed the assassination of Dr. Martin Luther King, Jr., in April 1968.

In all three instances, the president sent the National Guard at the request of local and state officials. The president is not legally bound to wait for such a request, however. Whenever federal property is

endangered or a federal law is violated, the president can act. Indeed, in 1894, President Grover Cleveland sent federal troops to Illinois, in spite of the objections of Governor William Altgeld, to stop rioting in the Chicago rail yards. The rioters had threatened federal property and had slowed down the flow of mail and interstate commerce.

President Dwight D. Eisenhower sent federal troops to Little Rock, Arkansas, in 1957, and President John F. Kennedy sent troops to the University of Mississippi in 1962 and to the University of Alabama in 1963. In each of these instances, federal courts had ordered the desegregation of state-run schools. The orders were not

◀ *Making a difference in their community, these teenage volunteers from the Community for Creative Non-Violence serve up Thanksgiving dinner to the homeless and needy of Washington, D.C.*

4. Consider volunteering to work in a food bank warehouse sorting contributed food or assisting with pickups or deliveries.
5. Volunteer two or three hours a week in a soup kitchen that cooks and serves food for homeless people.

If you are interested in starting your own group to fight hunger, order a copy of Seed's *Hunger Action Handbook—What You Can Do and How to Do It*. It's available from Seed at the address given in item 1 above.

If your are interested in volunteering to work on a project to end hunger around the world, order Seed's magazine *Volunteer Opportunities Guide*.

being followed—African American students were being refused admittance to the schools. The president in each case acted to enforce the federal court orders.

Territorial Integrity Under the Constitution, the national government must guarantee the territorial integrity of each state. That is, it must recognize each state's legal existence and physical boundaries. It must also guarantee the number of votes each state has in Congress. Article IV, Section 3, prevents the national government from geographically dividing a state to make a new state or from changing boundaries between states. If the national government wants to do either of these things, the states involved and Congress must agree on the changes.

Some argue that the admission of West Virginia to the United States in 1863 violated this guarantee. West Virginia was formed from thirty-five counties in the predominantly nonslaveholding region of western Virginia. Representatives from these counties refused to follow the Virginia state legislature's decision to secede from the Union during the Civil War. Disregarding the wishes of the majority of Virginia legislators (who opposed the formation of West Virginia), Congress allowed the thirty-five counties to become a separate state.

▶ In 1962, President John F. Kennedy sent federal troops to the University of Mississippi to ensure the safety of James Meredith, the first African American student to enroll at that institution. Why do you think it was necessary to send federal troops to a state university?

SECTION 3 REVIEW

1. What are the constitutional provisions that relate to horizontal federalism?
2. What does the full faith and credit clause require?

3. Under the Constitution, what responsibilities does the federal government have toward the states?
4. **For Critical Analysis:** If the decision had been up to you, would you have allowed the thirty-five counties in western Virginia to form a state?

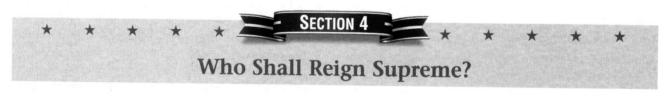

SECTION 4

Who Shall Reign Supreme?

Preview Questions:

- ☢ What is the supremacy clause?
- ☢ What decision did the Supreme Court make in *McCulloch v. Maryland?* Why was it important?
- ☢ What was the issue before the Supreme Court in *Gibbons v. Ogden?*
- ☢ What issue was at the heart of the controversy that led to the Civil War?

Key Terms:

supremacy clause, secession

The **supremacy clause,** which is contained in Article VI, Paragraph 2, of the Constitution, gives the national government supremacy over all state and local governments. The clause implies that states cannot use their reserved or concurrent powers to counter national

◀ Thurgood Marshall, then an attorney for the National Association for the Advancement of Colored People (NAACP), poses on the steps of the Supreme Court with the president of the Little Rock, Arkansas, NAACP and six of the students who integrated the previously all-white Central High in Little Rock. Governor Orval Faubus had used National Guard troops to prevent the court-ordered integration. What bearing did the supremacy clause have on his actions?

policies. Every time a state or local officer, such as a judge or sheriff, takes office, he or she becomes bound by an oath to support the U.S. Constitution.

Much of the legal history of the United States has involved conflicts between the supremacy of the national government and the desires of the states to remain independent. The most extreme example of this conflict was the Civil War. Through the years, because of the Civil War and several key Supreme Court decisions, the national government has increased its power.

McCulloch v. Maryland

The case of McCulloch v. Maryland was decided by the Supreme Court in 1819. It was one of the most significant decisions ever made by the Court. At issue were both the necessary and proper clause and the supremacy clause.

The case began when the state of Maryland imposed a tax on the Baltimore branch of the Second Bank of the United States. This bank had been chartered, or created, by the U.S. Congress. The branch's chief cashier, James McCulloch, decided not to pay the tax. A state court ruled that McCulloch had to pay. The national government appealed to the U.S. Supreme Court.

▲ If you were to travel back in time to the early years of our nation, you would be surprised at how weak the federal government was in comparison to the strong and independent states. In his decision in the case McCulloch v. Maryland (1819), Supreme Court Chief Justice John Marshall opened the door for the creation of the large and powerful central government we have today.

Who Shall Control the Land?

In 1996, President Bill Clinton declared 1.7 million federal acres of Utah desert and rock canyon a national monument. The result? No future development of those areas will be allowed. These lands hold large coal reserves, which will never be mined unless the law is changed. The value of the coal reserves has been estimated to be as high as $1 trillion.

Many Americans do not agree with the national government over land-control issues. The federal government owns nearly 30 percent of the lands in the United States. In the western states, this figure is much higher, as you can see in the chart, *Federally Owned Lands in the Western States* on page 105. Traditionally, the U.S. government has allowed state residents to use federal lands for cattle grazing and other purposes. Recently, however, in the interests of environmental protection, the federal government has tightened the reins on local use of federal land and water resources.

As a result, in many areas of the West, there is growing hostility toward the federal government—and particularly toward the people who enforce federal land-use policies. During the last few years, a number of rebels in the increasingly "wild" West have been defying federal government orders and using federal lands without permits.

Some people suggest that federal lands should be returned to the states. The states could then decide how the lands should be used. Supporters of the movement for state ownership of federal lands argue that state and local governments are in a better position to make environmental decisions affecting their regions. Opponents of state ownership of federal lands point out that among the biggest supporters of state ownership are special-interest groups, such as the mining and timber industries, that would like to put the lands to commercial use. These groups could pressure state governments into allowing mining and logging activities that would damage the environment. Thus, opponents of state control over federal lands claim that the public interest would be better served by national regulation of the environment.

THINK ABOUT IT

1. To what extent do you think the states, particularly in the West, have the right to claim ownership over lands currently owned by the federal government?
2. What role should the federal government play in land management in this country? What role should the state governments play?
3. Should the federal government turn federal lands over to private individuals, such as cattle ranchers and oil drillers? Why or why not?
4. What does the conflict over land use tell us about the problems that are a part of our system of federalism today?

One issue before the Court had to do with whether Congress had the implied power, based on the necessary and proper clause, to create a national bank, such as the Second Bank of the United States. A second constitutional issue was also involved. If Congress's creation of the bank was constitutional, could a state tax the bank? In other words, was a state action that conflicted with a national government action invalid under the supremacy clause? The decision would have far-reaching consequences.

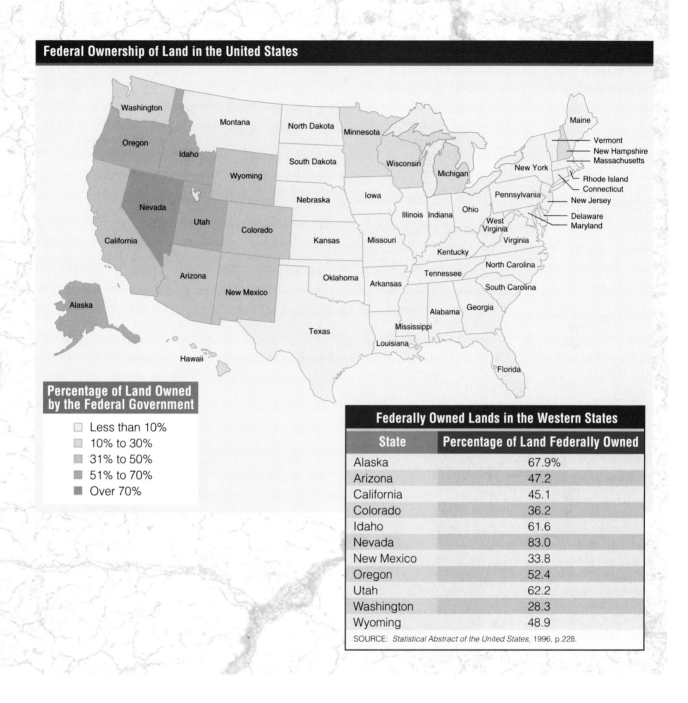

Federal Ownership of Land in the United States

Percentage of Land Owned by the Federal Government

- ☐ Less than 10%
- 10% to 30%
- 31% to 50%
- 51% to 70%
- Over 70%

Federally Owned Lands in the Western States

State	Percentage of Land Federally Owned
Alaska	67.9%
Arizona	47.2
California	45.1
Colorado	36.2
Idaho	61.6
Nevada	83.0
New Mexico	33.8
Oregon	52.4
Utah	62.2
Washington	28.3
Wyoming	48.9

SOURCE: *Statistical Abstract of the United States*, 1996, p.228.

Chief Justice John Marshall announced the decision of the Court. Marshall pointed out that no provision in the Constitution expressly granted the national government the power to form a national bank. Nonetheless, if establishing such a bank helped the national government exercise its expressed powers, then the authority to do so could be implied. Marshall also said that the necessary and proper clause included "all means which are appropriate" to carry out "the legitimate ends" of the Constitution.

Having established this doctrine of implied powers, Marshall then answered the other important constitutional question before the Court and established the doctrine of national supremacy. Marshall argued that no state could use its taxing power to tax an arm of the national government. If it could, the Constitution's declaration that the Constitution "shall be the supreme law of the land" was empty and meaningless. From that day on, Marshall's decision became the basis for strengthening the national government's power.

Just the Facts

During the lengthy case of Gibbons v. Ogden, *Gibbons visited Ogden's home and challenged Ogden to a duel. Ogden instead sued Gibbons for trespassing and won a $5,000 judgment.*

Gibbons v. Ogden

The commerce clause, which is found in Article I, Section 8, of the Constitution, gives Congress the power to regulate commerce "among the several States." The framers of the Constitution, however, did not define the word *commerce*.

How *commerce* should be defined was one issue in the case of *Gibbons v. Ogden*, decided in 1824. Another was whether the national government had the exclusive power to regulate commerce involving more than one state.

The New York legislature had given Aaron Ogden the exclusive right to operate steamboats between New York and New Jersey. Thomas Gibbons, who had a license from the U.S. government to operate boats in interstate waters, decided to compete with Ogden, but he did so without New York's permission. Ogden sued Gibbons in a New York state court and won. Gibbons appealed, and ultimately the case reached the U.S. Supreme Court.

In the Court's decision, Chief Justice Marshall defined *commerce* as including all business dealings, including steamboat travel. Marshall also stated that the power to regulate interstate commerce was an exclusive national power and had no limitations other than those specifically found in the Constitution. Since this 1824 decision, the national government has used the commerce clause numerous times to justify its regulation of virtually all areas of economic activity.

▶ *President Abraham Lincoln meets with Union army officers following the Battle of Antietam in 1862. The Civil War was fought not only over slavery, but also over other issues, including the rights of individual states versus the supremacy of the national government. Did the end of the Civil War result in increased states' rights or increased power for the national government?*

The Battleground of the Civil War

It is easy to think of the Civil War as a fight to free the slaves. The war, however, can also be viewed as a power struggle between the states and the national government. At the heart of the controversy that led to the Civil War was the issue of national versus state supremacy. That debate was brought to a bloody climax between 1860 and 1865.

In 1824, 1828, and 1832 the national government had passed tariff acts, which imposed higher taxes on goods imported into the United States. The southern states believed that such taxes were against their best interests. One southern state, South Carolina, attempted to *nullify* the tariffs, or make them void. It claimed that in cases of conflict between state and national governments, the state should have the ultimate authority to determine the welfare of its citizens.

Supporters of this idea used it to justify the **secession**—withdrawal—of the southern states from the Union. When the South was defeated in the war, however, the idea that a state can successfully claim its right to secede was defeated as well. Although the Civil War occurred because of the South's desire for increased states' rights, the result was just the opposite—an increase in the political power of the national government.

SECTION 4 REVIEW

1. If a state law conflicts with a national law, which side must yield?
2. How did the Supreme Court's decision in *McCulloch v. Maryland* expand the power of the national government?
3. Why was the Supreme Court's decision in *Gibbons v. Ogden* significant?
4. How was the controversy that led to the Civil War related to the concept of federalism?
5. **For Critical Analysis:** The milestone events discussed in this section—*McCulloch v. Maryland*, *Gibbons v. Ogden*, and the Civil War—form part of a trend toward the complete supremacy of the national government. What evidence, if any, do you see today that the trend is changing?

SECTION 5

The Changing Face of American Federalism

Preview Questions:

- What is dual federalism?
- Why has U.S. federalism in the era since 1937 been labeled cooperative federalism?
- What does the phrase *new federalism* mean?

Key Terms:

dual federalism, cooperative federalism, New Deal, new federalism, devolution

Scholars have devised various models, or theories, to describe the relationship between the states and the national government at different times in U.S. history. These models are useful in describing the evolution of federalism.

Dual Federalism

The model of **dual federalism** assumes that the states and the national government are more or less equal, with each level of government having separate and distinct functions and responsibilities. The states exercise sovereign power over certain matters, and the national government exercises sovereign power over others.

For much of this nation's history, this model of federalism prevailed. Some scholars maintain that dual federalism characterized relations between the national government and the states from 1789 to the early 1930s. Others date the beginning of dual federalism to the 1830s or 1840s. In any event, during the era following the Civil War, the courts tended to support each state's right to exercise its powers in regard to the regulation of activities within that state. For example, in 1918, the Supreme Court ruled that a 1916 federal law banning child labor was unconstitutional because it attempted to regulate a local problem. The era of dual federalism came to an end in the 1930s, when the United States was in the depths of the greatest economic depression it had ever experienced.

Cooperative Federalism

The model of **cooperative federalism,** as the term implies, involves cooperation among all levels of government. This model views the national and state governments as complementary parts of a single governmental mechanism. The purpose of this mechanism is to solve problems facing the entire United States. For example, federal law enforcement agencies, such as the Federal Bureau of Investigation (FBI), lend technical help to solve local crimes, and local officials cooperate with federal agencies to help solve serious crimes in their areas.

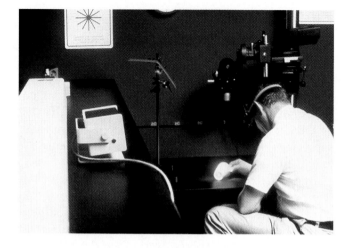

▲ Although most law enforcement is local, this fingerprint specialist works for the Federal Bureau of Investigation, a federal crime-fighting agency. This is cooperative federalism at work today. What are the benefits of a national clearinghouse for fingerprints?

Cooperative federalism grew out of the need to solve the tremendous national problems caused by the Great Depression, which began in 1929. In 1933, President Franklin D. Roosevelt launched his **New Deal.** This program involved many government spending and public-assistance measures aimed at helping to bring the United States out of the Depression. The New Deal legislation of Franklin D. Roosevelt ushered in an era of cooperative federalism, which has continued to some extent until the present day. The New Deal leg-islation also marked the real beginning of an era of national supremacy.

Some scholars argue that even if the Great Depression had not occurred, the power of the national government probably would have expanded because of changes the nation was experiencing. Its population was growing, and it was becoming more industrial. Its interdependence with other countries was increasing. Indeed, it was becoming a world power. Because of these changes, problems and situations that once were treated locally began to have a profound impact on Americans hundreds or even thousands of miles away. Environmental pollution does not respect state borders, for example. Neither do poverty, crime, and violence. National defense, space exploration, and an increasingly global economy also call for action on the national—not state—level. So the growth of national-level powers in the twentieth century had a very logical and very real set of causes.

▲ Designed to give economically deprived young children a "Head Start," this federally sponsored program was begun in the 1960s when it was found that many children were entering kindergarten without the skills they needed to learn. How does Head Start differ from other preschool programs?

How Federalism Has Changed

What federalism means in this country today is different from what it meant during the "New Deal" federalism begun by Franklin D. Roosevelt in the 1930s. Some of the changes are listed below.

THEN (1930s–1970s)	NOW
A positive attitude existed toward national government regulation of the economic affairs of most businesses.	National government overregulation is viewed by many as a problem.
Government was seen as having the solutions to most of the social and economic problems facing the nation.	Government is seen as part of the problem, not a solution, and solutions may be impossible.
Most regulation of business was done by state governments, and state policies varied.	Most regulation of business is done by national government.
National government assumed more responsibilities.	State and local governments are assuming more responsibilities.

The 1960s and 1970s saw an even greater expansion of the national government's role. The "Great Society" programs of Lyndon Johnson's administration (1963–1969) included Medicaid, Medicare, the Job Corps, Operation Head Start, and other programs. The Civil Rights Act of 1964 prohibited discrimination in public accommodations, employment, and other areas on the basis of race, color, national origin, religion, or gender. The economy was regulated further in the 1970s by national laws protecting consumers, employees, and the environment. Today, few activities are beyond the reach of the national government.

The New Federalism—More Power to State Governments

During the 1970s and 1980s, several presidents attempted to revitalize dual federalism, which they renamed the "new federalism." This movement was launched in the early 1970s by President Richard M. Nixon and, to varying degrees, has continued to the present. The **new federalism** involves returning to the states certain powers that have been exercised by the national government since the 1930s. Thus, it involves a shift from *nation-centered* federalism to *state-centered* federalism. An example of the new federalism is the welfare reform legislation of 1996 (discussed in Chapter 22), which gave the states more authority over welfare programs. The term **devolution**—transfer of powers to political subunits—is often used to describe the goals of the new federalism.

Just the Facts

Richard Nixon was the first president in American history who managed to visit every state while in office.

Who Should Control Drug Policy?

In a federal system, there is always conflict between the national government and the state governments. In general, the national government prevails in such conflicts. Nowhere is conflict greater than in the area of drug regulation. Do states have the right to regulate the sale and use of drugs, free from the control of the national government? The answer to this question is that they do, but only to the extent that state laws do not conflict with national drug policy. National drug policy is set forth in the Comprehensive Drug Abuse, Prevention, and Control Act of 1970 and its amendments.

Some Say That the States Should Control Drug Policy

Some Americans believe that drug policies should be formed by the states, cities, and neighborhoods in which people live, rather than by the national government. State and local governments could then tailor drug policies to reflect local views and interests. In this way, Americans could develop drug policies that conform to their wishes and the wishes of their families, friends, and neighbors, rather than having a single policy imposed on them by the national government.

Those who favor state control of drug policy also point out that states now control the use of alcohol—who can sell it, who can buy it, where it can be bought, and when. In addition, the states control the sale of prescription drugs. Why can't states control the sale of other drugs, too? Finally, proponents of state control believe that innovative solutions to the terrible problems of drugs can only be found by different states trying different means.

Others Say That Controlling Drug Policy Is the National Government's Role

Proponents of a strong national policy on drugs believe that the best interests of the country, not just the best interests of each state, should prevail. U.S. citizens, regardless of where they live, should be protected uniformly from the consequences of drug possession and the crimes that result from drug use and distribution. After all, illegal drug use and trafficking are nationwide problems. It is estimated that each year over 25 million Americans violate a drug law at least once.

Of course, some states are more negatively affected by these problems than others. These states—which include California, Florida, Texas, and New York—are the ports of entry for drugs for much of the country. If it were left up to the states to control and implement drug policies, these states would bear a far greater burden than others in terms of the cost of enforcement.

In any event, many state legislators and governors are reluctant to tackle the drug problem themselves. The resources of the national government must therefore be used in the fight against illegal drug manufacturing, importation, shipment, and use.

YOU DECIDE

1. What might happen if using certain drugs was legal in some states but not in others?
2. If the states had total control over drug policy, how could they handle the problem of interstate drug trafficking?

Ethics and the Debate over Federalism

In 1981, President Ronald Reagan made the following statement in an address to state legislators:

The Founding Fathers saw the federalist system as constructed something like a masonry wall. The States are the bricks, the national government is the mortar. . . . Unfortunately, over the years, many people have increasingly come to believe that Washington is the whole wall.

The devolutionary movement recognizes the importance of the "bricks" in the "wall" of government. Proponents of devolution feel that we need to achieve a new balance between national and state powers. But some Americans doubt that control over certain programs should be turned over to the states.

At the heart of the debate over federalism today is a question that clearly has ethical dimensions: Which government—national, state, or local—can best handle certain types of problems? Several pressing political issues today touch on this question. Examples include federal land use, drug policy, and educational standards.

As you have learned, the debate over federalism began even before the Constitution was ratified. It has continued throughout our history and certainly is at the forefront of political debate today. Ultimately, each generation of Americans decides anew on which level of government should exercise which powers to best meet the needs of the citizenry.

SECTION 5 REVIEW

1. What is the national government's role under a dual federalism system?
2. How has the balance of political power between the states and the national government shifted over the years?
3. Briefly describe the doctrine of cooperative federalism.
4. What were some of the new national programs begun by the Lyndon Johnson administration?
5. **For Critical Analysis:** Explain what *devolution* means. Who might be in favor of devolution, and why? Who might be against it, and why?

★ ★ ★ ★ Chapter Summary ★ ★ ★ ★

Section 1: Three Basic Types of Governmental Systems

- In a unitary system, the national government has ultimate authority. In a confederal system, the states have ultimate authority. In a federal system, governmental powers are shared by a national government and political subunits, such as states.
- The framers of the Constitution chose a federal system because it represented a compromise between those who favored a strong national government and those who favored a small government.

Section 2: The Division of Governmental Powers

- The powers of the national government include expressed, implied, and inherent powers.
- Powers not delegated to the national government are reserved to (retained by) the states and the people.
- Concurrent powers can be exercised by both the national government and state governments.

Section 3: Relations among the States

- States may not discriminate against citizens of other states.
- States must recognize one another's laws and court decisions, and states must agree to extradite persons accused of crimes in other states.

Section 4: Who Shall Reign Supreme?

- The supremacy clause states that the national government is the supreme governing body of the land.
- In 1819 the Supreme Court established the doctrine of implied powers and the supremacy of a national government action over a state action.

Section 5: The Changing Face of American Federalism

- Under dual federalism, the national government and the states are more or less equal.
- Under cooperative federalism, the national government and the states are complementary parts of a single government mechanism.
- New federalism involves returning to the states certain powers that have been exercised by the national government since the 1930s.

CHAPTER 4 Review

★ REVIEW QUESTIONS ★

1. Explain the differences among the three basic types of governmental systems, unitary systems, confederal systems, and federal systems.
2. Explain how federalism creates a two-way system of government.
3. Why did the framers of the U.S. Constitution choose a federal framework?
4. What is the source of the national government's expressed powers? What is the source of its implied powers?
5. What is the necessary and proper clause? How has this clause enabled the national government to expand its powers?
6. How does the Constitution limit the powers of the national government?
7. Explain the concept of concurrent powers.
8. What does the privileges and immunities clause prevent?
9. Why is the concept of full faith and credit so important to interstate relationships?
10. What obligations does the Constitution impose on the national government with regard to the states?
11. What is the significance of the supremacy clause in our federal system?
12. Describe the situation that led to the 1819 Supreme Court case *McCulloch v. Maryland*. What was the outcome of this case ?
13. Describe the situation that led to the 1824 Supreme Court case *Gibbons v. Ogden*. Why was this case important?
14. Describe how the balance of political power between the state and national governments has changed over the years.

★ CRITICAL THINKING ★

1. What do you think the U.S. government would be like if powers were not divided between the national government and the states?
2. Should states have more power, less power, or the same amount of power that they currently have?
3. Why do you think the power to wage war and the power to conduct relations with foreign nations belong exclusively to the national government?
4. What factors do you think have been responsible for growth in the national government's power?

★ IMPROVING YOUR SKILLS ★

Communication Skills

Asking Effective Questions Asking questions is one of the most important ways to learn facts and share ideas. Asking pertinent questions in class about material you do not understand will help you become a better student. Asking effective questions will also help you become a better-informed and more responsible citizen. Effective questions are designed to obtain specific information.

To ask effective questions requires preparation. When we don't obtain the information we seek from questions we ask, it is usually because we are asking the wrong source, asking the wrong questions, or asking questions in the wrong way. Before you ask questions, do the following:

1. Determine the exact information you want to obtain.
2. Determine the best sources of that information.
3. Decide what questions will best draw out the information.
4. Decide how you should ask the questions. Remember that questions that can be answered with only a *yes* or a *no* will not give you much information. Word your questions carefully.

Writing Follow the four steps above to plan a class interview with a city or county official concerning a current issue in your community.

1. As a group, discuss the kinds of information you would like to obtain. Write down ideas as they are suggested. Then narrow your ideas to a few specific issues.
2. Decide which city or county official would be the best source for the information you wish to obtain.
3. Using the ideas you generated in Step 1, create a formal list of questions for the interview. Have your teacher approve your questions.
4. Call the official's office, identify yourself, explain the reason for your call, and request an appointment with him or her. You might prefer to write a letter to the official and ask for a written response to your questions.

Social Studies Skills

Map Reading Look at the map on page 105 (Federal Ownership of Land in the United States) and answer the following questions:

1. What do the colors in the map represent?
2. Do most states have federally owned land?
3. Do any states have no federally owned land?
4. In which states does the federal government own 50 percent or more of the land?

★ ACTIVITIES AND PROJECTS ★

1. Prepare for a class debate on the issue of whether the national government or state governments should control drug policies.
2. Call or write the district office of your local school district. Find out how and when the school district was created. Also find out who governs the school district and how school policies are established.
3. Hold a debate on the following issue:

   RESOLVED: That the Constitution be amended to give two-thirds of the states the power to declare null and void an act of Congress.

4. Do some research in your school library on federal land ownership. Prepare written answers for the following questions:

   a. How did the national government acquire ownership of lands in the western states?
   b. Does the national government have ownership rights over any lands in the original thirteen states?
   c. What specific types of environmental regulations have made it difficult for those living in western states to use federally owned lands?
   d. Should federal lands be made available to private concerns? If so, under what conditions? If not, why not?

What If . . .

The States Could Ignore National Laws?

The United States has a federal system of government in which the U.S. Constitution and national laws and regulations reign supreme. Before the Civil War, some states believed they had the power to nullify (declare void) any federal law that they felt conflicted with their rights as states. What might happen today if states could choose to accept only federal laws and regulations that they believed were appropriate?

National Education Standards

Almost every day, we read or hear about the educational crisis in America. Too many students are dropping out of high school, and students who do graduate lack the necessary job skills. State and local governments have begun to tackle the challenge of educational reform. Some attempts have met with success and others have not. Would standards and tests established by the national government help to solve the problem? In this extended case study, we explore this issue.

A Source Document

Following is an excerpt from one of President Bill Clinton's State of the Union addresses.

I have a plan, a Call to Action for American Education. . . .

First, a national crusade for education standards—not federal government standards, but national standards, representing what all our students must know to succeed in the knowledge economy of the twenty-first century. Every state and school must shape the curriculum to reflect these standards and train teachers to lift students up to them. To help schools meet the standards and measure their progress, we will lead an effort over the next two years to develop national tests of student achievement in reading and math.

Tonight, I issue a challenge to the nation: Every state should adopt high national standards, and by 1999, every state should test every fourth grader in reading and every eighth grader in math to make sure these standards are met.

Raising standards will not be easy, and some of our children will not be able to meet them at first. The point is not to put our children down, but to lift them up. Good tests will show us who needs help, what changes in teaching to make, and which schools need to improve. They can help us to end social promotion. For no child should move from grade school to junior high, or junior high to high school until he or she is ready.

Media Reports

President Clinton's call for national education standards and tests became the subject of widespread debate after his address. Here are excerpts from just a few of the articles about Clinton's proposed plan.

On National Testing, the Right Answer Is Yes

San Francisco Chronicle

An unlikely coalition has formed in the House of Representatives against President Clinton's proposal to create voluntary national tests in fourth-grade reading and eighth-grade math.

Conservative Republicans see the tests as an intrusion of the federal government into the sacrosanct realm of local school curriculum. Liberal Democrats view the exams as just one more way to make students in poor school districts look bad while neglecting their education in other respects.

. . . Polls show that the public overwhelmingly supports national standards based on a challenging rigorous curriculum, along with a test to measure whether those standards are being met.

The public has good reason for backing such measurements. Although the United States has made a modest ascent in the last few years from shameful to almost respectable showings in some international educational comparisons, instruction and expectations are woefully uneven across the country.

The setting of standards . . . would offer academic benchmarks to which states and local school districts could aspire. The pressure would be on to turn dumbed-down to smartened-up.

Source: The *San Francisco Chronicle*, September 28, 1997, p. 6. Copyright 1997. Reprinted with permission.

Enough Already: A Standardized Test Is a Cheap, Ineffective Effort to Meet Problems That Already Are Well Documented

Editorial, Syracuse Post-Standard

What's wrong with a new national test to see how students measure up to a uniform proficiency standard? . . .

What's wrong is that such national tests are a cheap, ineffective effort to address problems that already are well documented.

There's no shortage of testing going on in America's schools already. In New York state, kids are subjected to more than a dozen standardized tests during their school careers, starting in kindergarten. . . .

Nearly every other state is also upgrading efforts to measure student and school achievement. What would another set of national tests add? There is a mounting pile of data about individual and systemic performance. What purpose is served by yet another standardized test? As one educator puts it, children can spend their time taking tests— or learning something. . . .

Ask a governor, a mayor or school superintendent anywhere in the country about student achievement and you'll get an earful. You don't have to look far, either, to find successful pilot programs and other promising solutions to what ails schools. What's needed is not more tests to produce results that already are all too well-known. What's needed are the resources and the follow-through to bring the proven remedies to bear on the problems and keep them there until they produce the results that really count.

Source: *Syracuse Post-Standard*, September 26, 1997, p. A18. The Herald Co., Syracuse, NY. © 1997 The *Post-Standard*. All rights reserved. Reprinted with permission.

National Testing Won't Tell a Thing We Don't Know Now

Rocky Mountain News

"Federal intrusion!" cry the conservatives. "Unfair discrimination!" shout the liberals. The subject: national tests for elementary school children, which President Clinton cites as one of the primary aims of his second term. "No to testing," we agree, but for a totally non-ideological reason. We just think it's a dumb idea. . . .

Having watched our own children take standardized test after standardized test in public school, we can't imagine that the problem in American education today comes from too little testing. In fact, the upset over U.S. schools and how they compare to those abroad came about as a result of massive testing.

Decades of parental observation have also taught us that the standardized tests don't do a very good job gauging the performance of either the students or the teachers. . . .

Teachers teach the tests. Not the subject matter—the tests, and how to take them.

Our kids were whizzes at the test game. We had a devil of a time convincing a fourth-grade teacher that one of them didn't have a clue how to multiply 3 times 3 because, as she told us, "he tests out." Multiple-choice exams don't tell you much about what they don't know.

Source: *Rocky Mountain News*, September 28, 1997, p. 3B. Column by Cokie and Steven Roberts. Reprinted by permission of United Feature Syndicate, Inc.

Conclusion

A significant question currently before the American people is how we can revamp our educational system so that American students do succeed in the "knowledge economy of the twenty-first century." Many people believe that establishing national education standards and tests is a step in the right direction. Others are not so sure.

Analysis Questions

1. President Clinton mentioned several benefits of national standards and tests. What are these benefits?
2. Why do some conservative Republicans believe that the national government should not get involved in education?
3. Why are some liberal Democrats also critical of national standards and tests?
4. In the excerpt from the *Rocky Mountain News*, the author gave a "non-ideological" reason for not approving of national tests. What is this reason?

The Rights and Responsibilities of All Citizens

Fireworks explode over the Washington Monument and other buildings of the capitol in an Independence Day celebration.

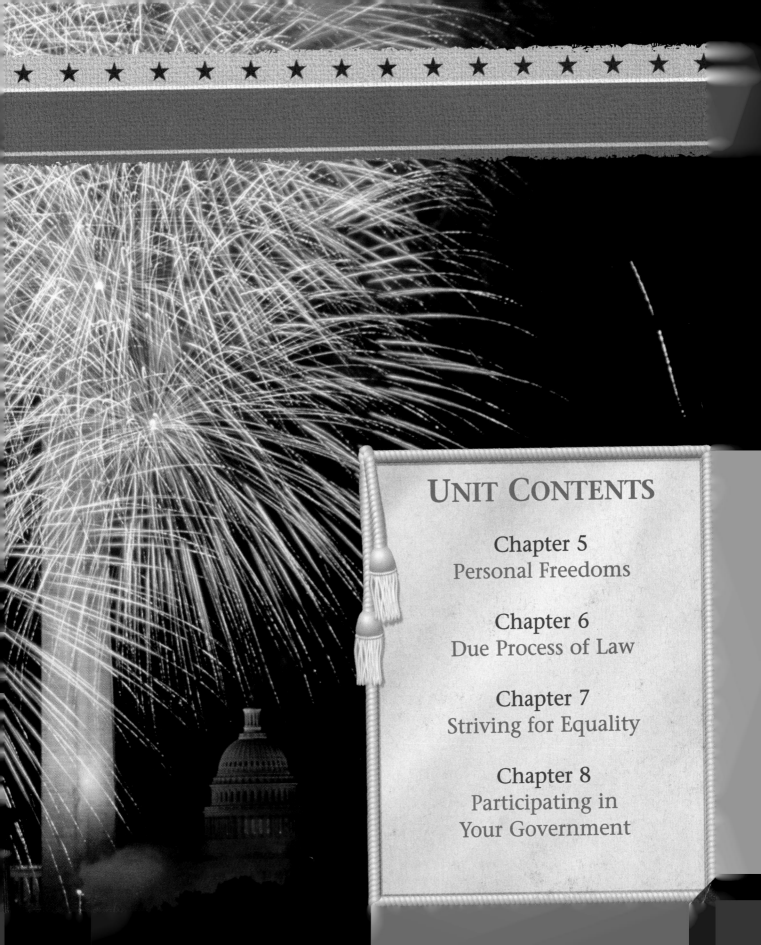

CHAPTER 5

Personal Freedoms

CHAPTER OBJECTIVES

To learn about and understand . . .

- The origins of our system of personal freedoms and how these freedoms are guaranteed under the Bill of Rights

- The First Amendment guarantee of freedom of religion

- How the government protects, as well as limits, freedom of expression under the First Amendment

- The meaning of the right to assemble and petition the government

"If we don't believe in freedom of expression for people we despise, we don't believe in it at all."

Noam Chomsky
(1928–   )
American Linguist and Political Analyst

INTRODUCTION

The freedom to voice one's opinion is a hallmark of democracy. After all, people cannot rule themselves if they are not allowed to express their thoughts on political matters. Over the years, the Supreme Court has carefully guarded the right of individuals to speak their minds, no matter how unpopular their views. As Noam Chomsky points out in the above quotation, the real test of a democracy is providing freedom of expression for *all* persons, including those whom we "despise."

Realize, though, that other people have rights, too. If a student in your class talks continuously, other students cannot exercise *their* right to free speech. Thus, your instructor may limit the time that students can speak or may prohibit speech entirely at certain times. Similarly, our government may place certain restrictions on free speech and on other constitutional rights and liberties to protect the rights of others in society.

◀ American flags decorate the base of the tallest structure in the capital, the Washington Monument.

Our System of Personal Freedoms

Preview Questions:

- ⭐ What protections against government actions were included in the original Constitution?
- ⭐ From what does the Bill of Rights protect us?
- ⭐ Why is the due process clause of the Fourteenth Amendment important?
- ⭐ What does the Supreme Court have to do with the Bill of Rights?

Key Terms:

civil liberties, assembly, petition, abridge, writ of *habeas corpus*, bill of attainder, *ex post facto* law, contract, consideration, due process clause

▲ In his painting Freedom of Speech, *American artist Norman Rockwell shows a man exercising his First Amendment rights. Consider the setting, the way the man is dressed, and the crowd around him. What message do you think Rockwell is trying to convey about free speech?*

Freedom of speech is one of our **civil liberties,** which can be defined as constitutional protections against certain government actions. Some of our civil liberties are set forth in the Constitution itself. Others are provided for in the Bill of Rights—the first ten amendments to the Constitution. In this chapter, we look first at the liberties guaranteed by the Constitution. We then examine the liberties, or freedoms, guaranteed by the First Amendment. These freedoms include the freedoms of religion, speech, press, **assembly** (gathering together for a common purpose), and **petition** (requesting that the government change its policies).

Generally, the government cannot infringe on (restrain) our constitutional liberties, and Congress cannot **abridge** (diminish or reduce) them. As mentioned, though, some limits on our constitutional freedoms are necessary. Additionally, sometimes one constitutional freedom, or right, conflicts with another. For example, the constitutional freedom of the press to publish information about a defendant in a criminal case might interfere with the defendant's constitutional right to have a fair trial. In such a situation, a court will have to decide which right should take priority. In effect, the government (through the federal courts, which constitute the government's judicial branch) is forced to abridge one or the other of these rights.

Constitutional Protections

The founders believed that the constitutions of the individual states included ample protections of citizens' rights. Therefore, few references to individual civil liberties were included in the Constitution until the Bill of Rights was created in 1791. Nonetheless, some safeguards in the original Constitution protected citizens against an overly powerful government.

For example, Article I, Section 9, of the Constitution provides that the **writ of *habeas corpus*** will be available to all citizens, except in times of rebellion or national invasion. *Habeas corpus* is a Latin phrase that roughly means "you should hand over the body." A writ of *habeas corpus* is an order that requires officials to

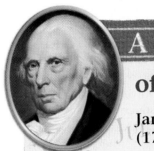

ARCHITECTS

of Government

James Madison
(1751–1836)

James Madison was a member of the Continental Congress from 1780 to 1783. He participated in the Constitutional Convention in 1787 and earned the title "Master Builder of the Constitution." As a principal contributor to the *Federalist Papers*, he also helped to gain ratification for the Constitution. After ratification, he participated in the development of the Bill of Rights. Madison was Thomas Jefferson's secretary of state and later, in 1809, was elected to be the fourth president of the United States.

HIS WORDS

"The proposed Constitution . . . is, in strictness, neither a national nor a federal Constitution, but a composition of both."

(*Federalist Paper No. 39, 1788*)

"I will prepare and recommend to the states for ratification, the most satisfactory provision for all essential rights."

(*Hand-penned letter to voters, 1788*)

DEVELOPING
CRITICAL THINKING SKILLS

1. How does the first quotation relate to the American system of government?
2. What are the essential rights to which Madison was referring in the second quotation?

without giving them the opportunity to plead their cases before a judge. Such opponents might conveniently disappear or be left to rot in prison.

The Constitution also prohibits Congress and state legislatures from passing bills of attainder. A **bill of attainder** is a legislative act that directly punishes a specifically named individual (or a specifically named group or class of individuals) without a trial. No legislature can pass a law that identifies, convicts, or sentences a person or group of people for a real or imagined offense. For example, your legislature cannot pass a law that says students who attend your school and who drive over thirty-five miles per hour will automatically be sentenced to one night in jail.

The Constitution also prohibits Congress from passing *ex post facto* laws. *Ex post facto* roughly means "after the fact." An ***ex post facto* law** punishes an individual for committing an act that has become illegal but that was not illegal when the individual committed it. For example, suppose that you went fishing in a nearby lake last week, when it was legal to fish in that area. This week, a law is passed saying that fishing in that area is illegal. You cannot be prosecuted for fishing there last week, because at that time it was legal to do so.

The *ex post facto* provision also prevents legislatures from increasing the penalty for a crime that was previously committed. A person who has committed a crime is subject only to the penalty that was in effect at the time the crime was committed.

The Bill of Rights

Even though a few individual protections against government were included in the original Constitution, there was no general listing of the rights of the people, or bill of rights. Public demand for a bill of rights was strong, and several states ratified the Constitution only with the promise that a bill of rights would be added.

Just the Facts

The First Amendment freedoms of religion, speech, and the press apply to noncitizens as well as citizens.

The first session of Congress in 1789 lived up to that promise by considering a series of proposed amendments and recommending the amendments to the states for ratification. Ten of these amendments, the

bring a prisoner into court and explain to the judge why the prisoner is being held. If the court finds that the imprisonment is unlawful, the prisoner must be released. If our country did not have such a provision, powerful political leaders could jail their opponents

First Amendment	Guarantees freedom of religion, speech, press, assembly, and petition.
Second Amendment	Guarantees the right to keep and bear arms, because a state requires a well-equipped citizen army for its own security.
Third Amendment	Prohibits the lodging of soldiers in peacetime, without the dweller's consent.
Fourth Amendment	Prohibits unreasonable searches and seizures of persons or property.
Fifth Amendment	Guarantees the rights to trial by jury, due process of law, and fair payment when private property is taken for public use; prohibits compulsory (required) self-incrimination and double jeopardy (trial for the same crime twice).
Sixth Amendment	Guarantees the accused in a criminal case the right to a speedy and public trial by an impartial jury and with counsel; allows the accused to cross-examine witnesses against him or her, and to solicit testimony from witnesses in his or her favor.
Seventh Amendment	Guarantees a trial by jury for the accused in a civil case involving $20 or more.
Eighth Amendment	Prohibits excessive bail and fines, as well as cruel and unusual punishments.
Ninth Amendment	Establishes that the people have rights in addition to those specified in the Constitution.
Tenth Amendment	Establishes that those powers neither delegated to the national government nor denied to the states are reserved to the states or to the people.

Bill of Rights, were ratified by the states and became part of the Constitution on December 15, 1791. The first eight amendments grant the people rights. The Ninth Amendment states that the rights guaranteed in the Constitution are not the only rights the people have. The Tenth Amendment states that if the Constitution does not give a certain power to the federal government, and does not deny it to the state governments, then the power belongs to the states or to the people. The first ten amendments are summarized in Figure 5–1.

The Bill of Rights protects individuals against abuses of power by the national government. Consequently, the Bill of Rights begins with the words, "Congress shall make no law . . . ." According to Justice Hugo Black, who served on the United States Supreme Court from 1937 through 1971, the Bill of Rights is "a collection of 'Thou Shalt Nots' " directed at the government.

In a democracy, government policy tends to reflect the view of the majority. A key role of the Bill of Rights, however, is to protect the rights of minorities against the will of the majority. Justice Robert Jackson, who sat on the Supreme Court from 1941 through 1954, said that "the very purpose of the Bill of Rights was to withdraw certain subjects from the vicissitudes [changes and variations] of political controversy, to place them beyond the reach of majorities." These rights "may not be submitted to a vote." In other words, certain rights should be protected for every citizen, whether the majority agrees on these rights or not.

The Role of the Courts

Needless to say, people may disagree over the meaning of a particular statement. This is certainly true with respect to the Constitution and the Bill of Rights. When people disagree over the meaning of a certain constitutional right, who decides the issue? The courts decide—particularly the United States Supreme Court. The Supreme Court is the ultimate arbiter, or decision maker, when it comes to deciding on the nature and scope of our constitutional rights. The courts also are the major guardians of our civil rights and liberties. All officers and agencies of the government are supposed to protect individual rights. If a person claims that the government has violated his or her civil liberties, he or she turns to the courts to interpret and apply constitutional guarantees.

One of our freedoms not mentioned elsewhere in this chapter is the freedom of contract, a freedom protected by Article I, Section 10, of the Constitution. A **contract** is a legal agreement involving an exchange of promises between two people or groups of people. Each party to the contract promises either to perform or to refrain from performing certain actions. Throughout your life, you will form contracts. If you buy a car, rent an apartment, or even buy an airline ticket, a contract is involved.

Contracts may be written or verbal, although a written contract is easier to enforce. In some cases, such as the purchase of goods worth $500 or more, unwritten contracts are normally not enforceable.

A contract contains several parts. First, the party writing the contract makes an offer, usually involving the exchange of goods or services. For example, a health club offers an individual the use of its facilities. The second part of the contract is the recipient's acceptance of the offer. Most contracts are enforceable only if each party

BUILDING

SOCIAL STUDIES SKILLS

Understanding Contracts

receives something of value, which is called **consideration.** For example, the health club in the contract receives an initiation fee and monthly fees. The customer in turns gets use of the club's facilities. The offer, the acceptance, and the consideration must all be included in the deal. If one or more of these parts is left out, the contract is not legally binding.

Each party must understand and accept the terms of the contract. After the terms of the contract have been fulfilled, the contract is completed. The contract must be agreed to, without

force or bribery, by persons of legal age and sound mind. If all of these conditions are not met, the contract can be canceled.

A breached, or broken, contract is one that has been violated, or one in which one or both parties did not fulfill the terms of the contract. Legal action to enforce a breached contract may be taken by either party. The dispute may be settled out of court, or the injured party can sue for damages.

Always remember that you need to fully understand all parts of any contract that you are asked to sign.

PRACTICING YOUR SKILLS

1. Ask your parents or adult friends to show you a contract, such as a car rental agreement, and identify the main parts discussed above.
2. Write down a summary of the three main parts in the contract.

The Role of the People

Even though the courts stand guard over the rights of Americans, it is important to remember that the ultimate responsibility to protect these rights lies with us, the people. Each generation must learn anew to uphold its rights by voting, expressing opinions to elected representatives, and bringing cases to the attention of the courts when constitutional rights are

threatened. Judge Learned Hand, an often-quoted United States Circuit Court judge, made the point this way:

I often wonder whether we do not rest our hopes too much upon constitutions, upon laws and upon courts. These are false hopes; believe me, these are false hopes. Liberty lies in the hearts of men and women; when it dies there, no constitution, no law, no court can ever do much to help it.

Along with your rights as a citizen, you also have many responsibilities. Fulfilling these responsibilities helps protect your rights and keeps the country running smoothly and democratically. Certain responsibilities are required by law. Some of these include the following:

Attending School. Every state requires that young people attend school until they reach a certain age. In most states, the age is sixteen. Attending school is vital to democracy, for it is through education that every American becomes an informed and effective citizen. An educated population is essential to our strength as a nation.

Obeying Laws. All citizens should know as much about the laws as they can. Obeying these laws is one of our most important responsibilities as Americans. If a law seems unfair or unnecessary, citizens can work through government to change it.

Paying Taxes. All Americans must pay some amount of taxes.

Responsibilities of Citizens

Although we often complain about this duty, it is important to remember that our tax dollars are used for services we rely on every day. These include fire and police protection, education, national defense, and protection of the environment.

Defending the Nation. American citizens have a responsibility to defend the nation. In peacetime, the military is made up of volunteers. Even in peacetime, however, eighteen-year-old males are required to register for the draft (even though there currently is no draft). Registering for the draft involves giving your name, age, and address so that you can be contacted for military service in the event that the country suddenly needs to increase its armed forces.

TAKING ACTION

1. The list presented above is a list of *required* responsibilities. What are some *voluntary* responsibilities of American citizens?

2. What do you think would happen if the four legally required responsibilities listed above became voluntary? Write a paragraph explaining your answers.

3. Do you think women should be drafted for military service? If so, what roles do you think women should play in protecting the nation? Explain your answer.

Making the States Comply with the Bill of Rights

For many years, the Bill of Rights was not applied to state or local governments. For example, the First Amendment guarantees of freedom of religion, speech, press, assembly, and petition did not have to be guaranteed by the states for their citizens. Rather, these guarantees only applied to actions of the *national* government. (State governments, of course, were—and continue to be—bound by their own constitutions, most of which contain bills of rights.)

Beginning in the 1920s, however, the United States Supreme Court began to apply the guarantees of the Bill of Rights to the states. The Court based its actions on the **due process clause** of the Fourteenth Amendment, which reads in part as follows:

No State shall . . . deprive any person of life, liberty, or property, without due process of law.

Due process is simply the right to be treated fairly under the legal system. That system and its officers are responsible for ensuring that "rules of fair play" are

◀ The class of 2001, including thirty-two women, is escorted across the parade grounds on its first day at Virginia Military Institute. Although the state of Virginia battled in court to maintain the school's 158-year all-male tradition, the Supreme Court ruled that women could not be excluded from the taxpayer-supported college.

followed in making decisions, in determining guilt or innocence, and in punishing those who have been found guilty. Thus, "due process" means that the correct procedures have been followed and that everyone has been given an equal right to be heard.

The Supreme Court has interpreted the due process clause to mean that no state may deny any person any right that is "basic or essential to the American concept of ordered liberty." In a long series of cases, starting in 1925, the Supreme Court gradually began using the due process clause to say that states could not abridge a right that the national government could not abridge. For example, in a 1931 Supreme Court case, the Court ruled that the freedom of the press offered by the national Bill of Rights had to be offered by every state as well. In a 1934 case, the Supreme Court ruled that freedom of religion provided for in the First Amendment had to be provided by all states.

Especially during the 1960s, the Supreme Court broadened its interpretations to limit state action in most areas in which national government action is limited. These areas include the Fourth Amendment prohibition against unreasonable searches and seizures, the Fifth Amendment prohibition against compulsory self-incrimination, and the Eighth Amendment prohibition against cruel and unusual punishments.

Many of these decisions, as you will see, have been controversial. For all practical purposes, however, the Bill of Rights now guarantees individual rights against infringement by both state and national governments.

◀ "Our plan has ended welfare as an entitlement." These were the words of Georgia Governor Zell Miller, as he signed into law a state welfare reform bill. Surrounded by Republican and Democratic state leaders, he had the support of both parties. Do you think that an individual who is unable or unwilling to work should be entitled to a minimum income provided by the government?

1. What are civil liberties? List the civil liberties each American is guaranteed under the Bill of Rights.
2. What rights and liberties are protected by the original Constitution?
3. How do the courts serve as the principal guardians of personal freedoms in this country?
4. Does the Bill of Rights protect Americans against actions by *state* governments?
5. **For Critical Analysis:** Reread the quote from Judge Learned Hand on page 123. Explain what you think he means when he says we should not rest our hopes for our personal liberties too much upon constitutions, laws, and courts.

★ ★ ★ ★ ★ **SECTION 2** ★ ★ ★ ★ ★

Freedom of Religion

Preview Questions:

🌐 Why is freedom of religion important in a democracy?

🌐 What does "separation of church and state" mean?

🌐 What is the distinction between the right to believe in a particular religion and the right to practice it as you wish?

Key Terms:

establishment clause, free exercise clause

Imagine for a moment several problems that may face students and administrators at public schools regarding the practice of religion. Joan, a sophomore at Central High School, wants permission to leave school during class hours to attend religious classes at her church. Should she be allowed to leave? At Oak High School, in a neighboring state, administrators have set aside thirty seconds during homeroom period to allow students to engage in silent prayer. Is this legal? Understanding the Constitution and how it has been interpreted by the Supreme Court can help you answer these questions.

It is not surprising that the protection of religious liberty is the first right listed in the Bill of Rights. After all, many of the colonists came here to escape religious persecution. The First Amendment begins with the following words:

Congress shall make no law respecting an establishment of religion, or prohibiting the free exercise thereof. . . .

The first part of the amendment is known as the **establishment clause.** It prohibits the government from establishing an official religion. This constitutional separation of church and state makes the United States different from countries that are ruled by religious governments, such as the Islamic government of Iran. It also makes us different from nations that have in the past strongly discouraged the practice of any religion at all, such as the People's Republic of China.

The second part of the First Amendment's guarantee of freedom of religion is called the **free exercise clause.** This clause protects individuals' rights to worship or believe as they wish without government interference.

Separation of Church and State

In 1802, President Thomas Jefferson referred to the First Amendment's establishment clause as "a wall of separation between church and state." Although church and government are constitutionally separated by the establishment clause in the United States, they have never been enemies or strangers. The establishment clause does not prohibit government from supporting religion in general, and religion remains a part of public life. Most government officials take an oath of office in the name of God, for example, and our coins and paper currency carry the motto "In God We Trust." Clergy of various religions—rabbis, priests, ministers, and others—serve with each branch of the armed forces. The Pledge of Allegiance contains a reference to God. Some public meetings and even sessions of Congress open with prayers.

▼ Displayed at the Allegheny County Courthouse in Pennsylvania, this Nativity scene was found by the Supreme Court to be in violation of the establishment clause of the First Amendment, while this eighteen-foot modernistic Menorah (a religious symbol used in the celebration of Chanukah, a Jewish holiday) was not. The justices reasoned that the Menorah was part of a display that included a Christmas tree and a "Salute to Liberty" banner that linked both symbols, which made it acceptable. Do you agree with the Supreme Court rulings?

The "wall of separation" that Thomas Jefferson referred to, however, does exist and has been upheld by the Supreme Court on many occasions. The first important ruling by the Supreme Court on the establishment clause came in *Everson v. Board of Education* (1947). The case involved a New Jersey law that allowed the state to pay for bus transportation of students who attended parochial schools (schools run by churches or other religious groups). The Court upheld the New Jersey law because the law did not aid the church *directly* but provided for the safety and benefit of the students. The ruling affirmed the importance of separating church and state. At the same time, it made it clear that not *all* forms of state and federal aid to church-related schools are forbidden under the Constitution.

In other words, Jefferson's "wall of separation" has some doors and windows in it. To a certain extent, how large these doors and windows are depends on how the justices of the Supreme Court interpret the establishment clause. Next, we consider some of these Supreme Court interpretations.

Aid to Parochial Schools All property owners, except nonprofit institutions, must pay property taxes. A large part of these taxes goes to support public schools. Private schools, however, receive no public tax support. A high proportion of private schools are parochial schools operated by religious groups. Does giving state aid to parochial schools violate the establishment clause?

Under certain circumstances, parochial schools can constitutionally obtain state aid. Many states have provided aid to church-related schools in the form of textbooks, transportation, and equipment. Other forms of aid, such as providing for teacher's salaries and payment for field trips, have been found unconstitutional.

In 1971, in *Lemon v. Kurtzman*, the Supreme Court stated that to be constitutional, a state's aid to religious schools must meet three requirements:

Just the Facts

At one point in the early 1600s in Virginia, those who failed to attend church were punished with prison terms and forced labor.

1. The purpose of the financial aid must be clearly secular (not religious).
2. The primary effect of the financial aid must neither advance nor inhibit religion.
3. The financial aid must not represent an "excessive government entanglement with religion."

Since 1971, this test of the constitutionality of state aid to parochial schools, often called the *Lemon* test, has been applied in several cases. For example, in *Aguilar v. Felton* (1985), the issue was whether federally funded special educational services for disadvantaged students could be provided on parochial school property. The Supreme Court held that they could not, because providing public services on church property would constitute an "excessive entanglement" of church and state.

Education, Prayer, and the Bible On occasion, some schools have attempted to foster a general sense of spirituality without promoting any particular religion. Whether the states have a right to allow this practice was the main question in *Engel v. Vitale* (1962), sometimes called the "regents' prayer" case. The State Board of Regents in New York had composed a nondenominational prayer (a prayer not associated with any particular religion) and urged school districts to use it in classrooms at the start of each day. It read:

Almighty God, we acknowledge our dependence upon Thee, and we beg Thy blessings upon us, our parents, our teachers, and our country.

Some parents objected to the prayer, saying it was a violation of the establishment clause. The Supreme Court agreed and ruled that the regents' prayer was unconstitutional. Speaking for the majority, Justice Hugo Black wrote that the First Amendment must at least mean "that in this country it is no part of the business of government to compose official prayers for any group of the American people to recite as part of a religious program carried on by government."

In 1980, a Kentucky law requiring that the Ten Commandments be posted in all public schools was found unconstitutional in *Stone v. Graham*. In 1985, in *Wallace v. Jaffree*, the Supreme Court ruled that an Alabama law requiring a daily one-minute period of silence for meditation and voluntary prayer also violated the establishment clause. In deciding the issue, the Court applied the three-part *Lemon* test. The Court concluded that the law violated the establishment clause because it was "an endorsement of religion lacking any clearly secular purpose."

To summarize, the Supreme Court has ruled that public schools, which are agencies of government, cannot sponsor religious activities. It has *not*, however, held that individuals cannot pray, when and as they choose, in schools or in any other place. Nor has it

◀ The line separating church and state is not always clear or sharply defined. Here students gather to pray in front of their public high school. How does this situation differ from a prayer led by a teacher in the classroom?

held that the Bible cannot be studied as a form of literature in the schools.

Evolutionism versus Creationism Certain religious groups believe that the theory of evolution should not be taught in public schools. Evolutionary theory directly counters these groups' religious belief that human beings were created exactly as described in the biblical story of the creation. The Supreme Court, however, has held that state laws forbidding the teaching of evolution are unconstitutional.

For example, in *Epperson v. Arkansas* (1968), the Supreme Court held that an Arkansas law prohibiting the teaching of evolution violated the establishment clause. The Court concluded that the law, in effect, imposed religious beliefs on students. In 1987, in *Edwards v. Aguillard,* the Supreme Court ruled that a Louisiana law requiring that schools teach the biblical story of the creation along with evolution was unconstitutional. The Court said that the law was unconstitutional, in part, because its primary purpose was the promotion of a particular religious belief.

Nevertheless, some groups both at state and local levels continue their efforts to promote the teaching of creationism. Recently, for example, a school district in Georgia adopted a policy that creationism could be taught along with evolution. No doubt, this law and similar laws and policies will eventually be challenged.

The Supreme Court's Current Views on Excessive Entanglement In the 1990s, the Supreme Court seemed to be taking a somewhat different approach to church-state issues. For example, in 1997, the Court decided to review its decision in *Aguilar v. Felton* (1985). In the *Aguilar* case, the Court ruled that federally funded special educational services for disadvantaged students attending parochial schools could not be provided on

◄ *The First Amendment guarantees our right to believe and worship as we wish. The right to practice one's beliefs in certain ways may be limited, however. Why might this girl not be allowed to set up and light devotional candles at school?*

parochial school property. As a result of the Court's decision, the special educational services had to be provided in public school classrooms, in buses or vans parked near religious school property, or by computer. These arrangements were so costly and inconvenient that the school district and the parents asked the Supreme Court to reconsider its decision in *Aguilar.* The Court agreed to do so.

When it reviewed the *Aguilar* decision in 1997, in *Agostini v. Felton,* the Supreme Court reversed its position on the issue. It held that *Aguilar* was "no longer good law." Federally funded special educational services for disadvantaged students could be given on the premises of parochial schools without violating the establishment clause.

The Court's reversal in *Agostini* illustrates an important point. Constitutional provisions, including the establishment clause, can be interpreted differently by different courts and at different times. Why, for example, did the Supreme Court rule one way in 1985 and another way in 1997? What caused the Court to change its mind? Justice Sandra Day O'Connor answered this question in the *Agostini* case. What had changed since *Aguilar,* she said, was "our understanding" of the establishment clause. Now, why did the Court's "understanding" of the establishment clause change? Very likely, the answer is that the Court's make-up had changed significantly since 1985. In fact, six of the nine justices who participated in the 1997 decision were appointed *after* the 1985 decision.

Free Exercise of Religion

An equally important First Amendment guarantee holds that government cannot pass laws "prohibiting the free exercise of religion." As mentioned earlier, this free exercise clause protects individuals' right to worship or believe as they wish.

The Other Side of the Coin—Should Churches Become Entangled in Politics?

The courts have ruled that the First Amendment requires the government to stay out of church affairs. What about the reverse? Is it appropriate for churches to become politically involved? Many religious groups have engaged in political activities. Do such activities violate any laws?

One possible violation is related to taxation. Churches are not required to pay most federal, state, and local taxes. In exchange, churches are forbidden by law from endorsing specific political candidates. The nation's tax collector, the Internal Revenue Service (IRS), would like to enforce this rule, but it can only find violations if it examines a church's records—and it cannot examine, or audit, the records of *all* churches.

Recently, a group called the Americans United for Separation of Church and State (AUSCS) has been trying to get the IRS to enforce the rule more strongly. This group has given information to the IRS about various church-related organizations that it claims have either endorsed or opposed specific political candidates. Members of AUSCS may even report on the activities of their own church leaders if they believe that there is too much entanglement between the church and political activities. AUSCS has not targeted any specific denomination. It has singled out Baptist, Catholic, and even Buddhist churches.

THINK ABOUT IT

1. Why should anyone care if church groups engage in political activities supporting or opposing political candidates?
2. Do you believe it is ever appropriate for churches to engage in political activities? Why or why not?

Belief and Practice Are Distinct The free exercise clause protects religious beliefs but does not necessarily guarantee that individuals can act any way they want on the basis of their beliefs. There is an important distinction between belief and practice. The Supreme Court has ruled consistently that the right to hold any *belief* is absolute. The government has no authority to compel you to accept or reject any particular religious belief. The right to *practice* one's beliefs, however, may have some limitations. As the Court itself once asked, "Suppose one believed that human sacrifice were a necessary part of religious worship?"

The first time the Supreme Court dealt with the issue of belief versus practice was in *Reynolds v.*

> **Just the Facts**
>
> *Members of religious organizations have a right to carry their missionary activities to the front door of a private home.*

United States (1879). Reynolds was a Mormon who had two wives. Polygamy, or the practice of having more than one spouse at a time, was encouraged at that time by the Mormon church but was prohibited by federal law. Reynolds was convicted and appealed the case, arguing that the law violated his constitutional right to freely exercise his religious beliefs. The Court did not agree. It said that polygamy was a crime, and crimes are not protected by the First Amendment.

Through the years, the Supreme Court has followed the general principle that people are free to believe and to practice their religion as they wish, so long as their conduct does not threaten the health, safety, or morals of the community. For example, it has ruled that Christian Scientists cannot prevent their children from accepting medical treatment, such as blood transfusions, if the children's lives are in danger, even though accepting such treatment is against their religion. It has upheld laws forbidding the use of poisonous snakes in religious rites, as well as laws requiring religious groups to obtain permits before holding a parade.

In 1990, in *Oregon v. Smith*, the Supreme Court ruled that the state of Oregon could deny unemployment benefits to two drug counselors who had been fired for using peyote, an illegal drug, in their religious services. The counselors had argued that using peyote was part of the practice of an American Indian religion. Three years later, Congress reacted to this and other Supreme Court decisions by passing the Religious Freedom Restoration Act, which obligated national, state, and local governments to "accommodate religious conduct." The act stayed in effect until 1997, when the Supreme Court ruled that it was unconstitutional.

The Flag-Salute Issue Can children be forced to salute the flag when this practice goes against their religious beliefs? This question was raised when Lillian and William Gobitis, ages ten and twelve, were expelled from school for refusing to salute the American flag at the start of each day. The children and their parents were Jehovah's Witnesses, who believe that saluting a flag violates the Bible's command forbidding the worship of idols. In this case, *Minersville School District v. Gobitis* (1940), the Court stated that the flag was a symbol of national unity and held that schools could require students, including the Gobitis children, to salute the flag.

Three years later, in a remarkable turnaround, the Court reversed that decision. In *West Virginia Board of Education v. Barnette* (1943), it ruled that a legal requirement to salute the flag was unconstitutional. Justice Robert H. Jackson, writing for the majority, said:

> To believe that patriotism will not flourish if patriotic ceremonies are voluntary and spontaneous, instead of a compulsory routine, is to make an unflattering estimate of the appeal of our institutions to free minds.

SECTION 2 REVIEW

1. What is the establishment clause?
2. What is meant by separation of church and state?
3. What is the free exercise clause?
4. What is the distinction between religious beliefs and religious practices, and why is this distinction significant?
5. In exchange for not paying taxes, what activity is forbidden to churches?
6. **For Critical Analysis:** "Our constitutional rights, including the freedom of religion, change over time." Do you agree or disagree with this statement? Explain your answer.

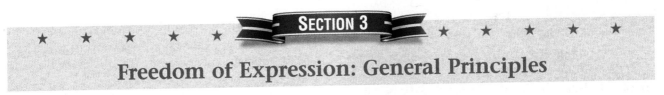

SECTION 3

Freedom of Expression: General Principles

Preview Questions:

- ● Why is freedom of speech important in a democracy?
- ● What types of speech are protected by the First Amendment?
- ● What doctrines has the Supreme Court used in deciding cases concerning freedom of expression?
- ● What types of speech are not protected by the First Amendment?

Key Terms:

pure speech, speech plus, symbolic speech,

espionage, sabotage, treason, seditious speech, doctrine, clear and present danger rule, bad-tendency rule, preferred-position doctrine, prior restraint, censorship, libel, slander, obscenity, "fighting words"

How many times have you heard someone say, "I can say what I want. It's a free country."? This common remark reveals the philosophy underlying our notion of what democracy in America means. We firmly believe in our right to express ourselves freely. The First Amendment guarantees freedom of expression by stating that "Congress shall make no law . . . abridging the freedom of speech, or of the press." We can think of freedom of the press as a special instance of freedom of speech. Thus, in general, the same rules apply to both.

Freedom of Speech and Its Importance

The right to free speech is the cornerstone on which a democracy is built. Every person has the right to speak freely and to question the government's decisions. Citizens in a democracy also must have the chance to hear and judge for themselves what others have to say. Our system depends on people's ability to make sound, clear judgments on matters of public concern. In order to do this, people must be free to learn all the facts of an issue, so they can weigh the various interpretations and opinions. This allows people to help shape the decisions and policies of their government. It also makes it difficult for government to cover up mistakes or injustices. Supreme Court Justice Hugo Black once stated:

▲ *Supreme Court Justice Oliver Wendell Holmes once said that we need to protect "not free thought for those who agree with us, but freedom for the thought that we hate." What did Justice Holmes mean by these words?*

Freedom to speak and write about public questions is as important to the life of our government as is the heart of the human body. In fact, this privilege is the heart of our government! If that heart be weakened, the result is debilitation [lack of strength]; if it be stilled, the result is death.

As mentioned earlier, people in this country do not seem to have a problem protecting the free speech of those with whom they agree. The real challenge is protecting unpopular beliefs. The opinions of the majority, after all, need little constitutional protection. Justice Oliver Wendell Holmes put it simply: What needs protection is "not free thought for those who agree with us, but freedom for the thought that we hate." The First Amendment is designed to especially protect ideas that may be unpopular or different.

Types of Speech

What exactly is free speech? Speech is more than the spoken word. It includes all types of communication, both verbal and nonverbal. Thus, free speech covers a very broad group of behaviors. How far can this freedom go? To what degree are various forms of speech protected? To answer such questions, the Supreme Court has identified three general categories of speech that are protected by the First Amendment: pure speech, speech plus, and symbolic speech.

Pure speech is the peaceful expression of thoughts, ideas, or opinions before a willing audience. This is the neighborly chat or the local candidate's campaign speech. It is your expression of ideas about a political issue or official. This type of speech is generally protected under the First Amendment.

Speech plus is verbal expression combined with some sort of action, such as marching or demonstrating. Because this form of speech involves actions, it may be subject to government restrictions that do not apply to pure speech. The Supreme Court has ruled that although speech plus is protected by the First Amendment, those engaged in it cannot obstruct traffic, block sidewalks, or endanger public safety.

Symbolic speech involves nonverbal expressions using symbols. Picketing in a labor dispute and wearing a black armband to protest a government policy are fairly common examples. The Supreme Court has given symbolic speech substantial protection. For example, in *Texas v. Johnson* (1989), the Supreme Court held that burning the American flag was a form of symbolic speech protected by the First Amendment. In *R.A.V. v. City of St. Paul, Minnesota* (1992), the Court ruled that a city law banning hate-motivated disorderly conduct (in this case, placing a burning cross in another's front yard as a gesture of hate) was an unconstitutional restriction on freedom of speech.

◀ Although he may not match Hollywood's image of a spy, Aldrich Ames is the highest-ranking employee of the Central Intelligence Agency ever convicted of spying. He pleaded guilty to espionage, tax evasion, and conspiracy charges, and is currently serving a life sentence in prison.

Limits on Free Speech

Although Americans have the right to free speech, the Court has also ruled that there are instances when some speech goes too far. Justice Oliver Wendell Holmes argued that "the most stringent protection of free speech would not protect a man in falsely shouting *fire* in a crowded theater."

Supreme Court justices have had different philosophies about what the Constitution means when it says, "Congress shall make no law . . . abridging the freedom of speech." Some justices have argued that the phrase should be taken literally. Most justices, however, have taken a more moderate position, arguing that the rights of free speech must be balanced against the need to keep order and preserve the government. As a result, some types of speech are not protected under First Amendment rights.

Seditious Speech One type of limit on free speech involves individuals who are, in fact, working against the government. U.S. law has established a fine line between legitimate criticism and the expression of ideas that may seriously harm society. Clearly, government may pass laws against violence, espionage, sabotage, and treason. **Espionage** is spying for a foreign power. **Sabotage** involves actions normally intended to hinder or damage the nation's defense or war effort. **Treason** is specifically defined in the Constitution as levying war against the United States or adhering (remaining loyal) to enemies of the United States, giving them aid or comfort (Article III, Section 3). Treason is the only crime that is specifically defined in the Constitution. But what about **seditious speech,** which urges resistance to lawful authority or advocates overthrowing the government?

Laws Dealing with Seditious Speech As early as 1798, Congress took steps to curb seditious speech when it passed the Alien and Sedition Acts. These acts made it a crime to utter "any false, scandalous, and malicious" criticism against the government. The acts were considered unconstitutional by many but were never tested in the courts. Under these acts, several dozen individuals were prosecuted, and some were actually convicted. In 1801, President Thomas Jefferson pardoned those who had been sentenced under the acts, and Congress soon repealed them.

Congress passed another sedition law during World War I as part of the Espionage Act of 1917. The law made it a crime to "willfully utter, print, write, or publish any disloyal, profane, scurrilous [insulting], or abusive language" about the government. More than two thousand persons were tried and convicted under this act, which was terminated at the end of World War I. An important case upholding the constitutionality of the act was *Schenck v. United States* (1919). We will look more closely at this case later in the chapter.

In 1940, Congress passed the Smith Act, which forbade people from advocating the violent overthrow of the U.S. government. According to the act, these activities threatened society's right to a certain national security. The Supreme Court first upheld the constitutionality of the Smith Act in *Dennis v. United States* (1951). In this case, eleven top leaders of the Communist Party had been accused and convicted of violating the Smith Act. The Court found that their activities went beyond the permissible peaceful advocacy of change.

Two justices on the court, Justices Black and Douglas, dissented strongly from the majority opinion. Justice Black closed his dissenting opinion with this observation:

Public opinion being what it now is, few will protest the conviction of these Communist petitioners. There is hope, however, that in calmer times, when present pressures, passions and fears subside, this or some later Court will restore the First Amendment liberties to the high preferred place where they belong in a free society.

Subsequently, the Court did change its position. Since the 1960s, the Court has defined seditious speech to mean only the advocacy of immediate and concrete acts of violence against the government.

Guidelines Used in Free-Speech Cases

Over the years, the Supreme Court has developed guidelines or doctrines to use in deciding cases concerning freedom of expression. A **doctrine** is a theory or set of principles presented to support a belief.

Clear and Present Danger One guideline the Court has used resulted from a case in 1919, *Schenck v. United States*. Charles T. Schenck was convicted of printing and distributing leaflets urging men to resist the draft during World War I. The government claimed that his actions violated the Espionage Act of 1917, which made it a crime to encourage disloyalty to the government or resistance to the draft.

The Supreme Court upheld both the law and the convictions. Justice Holmes, speaking for the Court, stated:

Words can be weapons. . . . The question in every case is whether the words are used in such circumstances and are of such a nature as to create a clear and present danger that they will bring about the substantive evils that Congress has a right to prevent. It is a question of proximity [closeness] and degree. (Emphasis added.)

Thus, according to the **clear and present danger rule,** government should be allowed to restrain speech only when speech clearly presents an immediate threat to public order. It is often hard to say when speech crosses the line between being merely controversial and being a "clear and present danger." Nevertheless, the principle has been used in many cases since 1919.

The Bad-Tendency Rule The clear and present danger principle seemed too permissive to some Supreme Court justices. Several years after the *Schenck* ruling, in the case of *Gitlow v. New York* (1925), the Court held that speech could be permissibly curtailed even if it had only a *tendency* to lead to illegal action. Since the 1920s, however, this guideline, known as the **bad-tendency rule,** has generally not been supported by the Supreme Court.

The Preferred-Position Doctrine Another guideline, called the **preferred-position doctrine,** states that freedom of speech is so essential to a democracy that it holds a preferred position. According to this doctrine, any law that limits this freedom should be presumed unconstitutional unless the government can show that the law is absolutely necessary. Freedom of speech should rarely, if ever, be diminished, because printed and spoken words are the prime tools of the democratic process.

Prior Restraint **Prior restraint** occurs when an activity is stopped before it actually happens. With respect to freedom of expression, prior restraint involves censorship. **Censorship** occurs when an official removes objectionable material from an item before it is published or broadcast. For example, suppose a court rules that two paragraphs in an upcoming article in the local newspaper must be removed before the article can be published. This ruling involves censorship and prior restraint. The Supreme Court has generally ruled against prior restraint. According to the Court, governments cannot try to curb ideas *before* they are expressed.

A case involving this issue was *New York Times v. United States* (1971), also called the *Pentagon Papers* case. The *Times* was about to publish the *Pentagon Papers*, an elaborate secret history of the U.S. government's involvement in the Vietnam War (1964–1975). The secret documents had been obtained illegally by a disillusioned former Pentagon official. The government wanted a court order to bar publication of the documents, arguing that national security was being threatened and that the documents had been stolen. The *Times* argued that the public had a right to know the information contained in the papers and that the press had the right to inform them. The Supreme Court rejected the government's request to bar publication. The Court held that the government had not proved that printing the documents would in fact

After completing an analysis of the Vietnam War, Defense Department official Daniel Ellsberg released portions of the study to the New York Times. The government tried to block its publication, saying that national security would be threatened. This photo was taken in 1971. Why does the poster refer to 1984?

endanger national security. Therefore, the *Times* could publish the papers.

On some occasions, however, the Court has allowed prior restraint. In 1988, in *Hazelwood School District v. Kuhlmeier*, the Court, noting that students below college level have fewer rights than adults, ruled that high school administrators *can* censor school publications. It ruled that school newspapers are part of the school curriculum. Therefore, administrators have the right to censor speech that promotes "conduct inconsistent with the shared values of the civilized social order."

Unprotected Speech—Libel, Slander, Obscenity, and "Fighting Words"

Some forms of expression are not protected at all by the Constitution. For example, no person ever has the right to libel or slander another. **Libel** is a published report of falsehoods that tends to injure a person's reputation or character. **Slander** is the public utterance (speaking) of a statement that holds a person up for contempt, ridicule, or hatred. To prove libel and slander, however, certain requirements must be met. The statements made must be untrue and must have been made with intent to do harm, and actual harm must have occurred. Additionally, the Court has ruled that public officials cannot collect damages for remarks made against them unless they can prove the remarks were made with "reckless" disregard for accuracy.

Obscenity is another form of speech that is not protected under the First Amendment. The dictionary defines *obscenity* as that which is offensive and indecent. Exactly what obscenity is in a certain instance, however, is hard to determine. Supreme Court Justice Potter Stewart once said, "I know it when I see it." One problem in defining obscenity is that people differ in what they consider "offensive and indecent." What seems obscene to one person may seem realistic to another. What one reader considers indecent another reader may see as "colorful." Another problem is that even if a definition were agreed upon, it would change with the times.

After many unsuccessful attempts to define obscenity, the Supreme Court came up with a three-part test in *Miller v. California* (1973). It decided that a book, film, or other piece of material is legally obscene if:

1. The average person applying present-day standards finds that the work taken as a whole appeals to prurient interest—that is, tends to excite unwholesome sexual desire.
2. The work depicts or describes in an obviously offensive way, a form of sexual conduct specifically prohibited by an anti-obscenity law.
3. The work taken as a whole lacks serious literary, artistic, political, or scientific value.

The very fact that the Supreme Court has had to set up such a complicated test shows how difficult it is to define obscenity. The Court went on to state, in effect, that local communities should be allowed to set their own standards for what is obscene. What is obscene to many people in one area of the country might be perfectly acceptable to those in another area.

Just the Facts

The works of Mark Twain were once considered obscene in most of the United States.

Another form of speech not protected by the First Amendment is what the Supreme Court has called **"fighting words."** This is speech that is so inflammatory that it will provoke the average listener to violence. The Court has ruled that fighting words must go beyond merely insulting or controversial language. The words must be a clear invitation to immediate violence or breach of peace.

SECTION 3 REVIEW

1. Why is free speech important in a democracy?
2. What are the three types of protected speech and to what extent is each type protected by the First Amendment?
3. Are there circumstances in which Congress can limit the right to free speech? Explain.
4. What are some of the guidelines the Supreme Court has developed to help it decide what is protected as free expression?
5. What kinds of speech are not protected at all by the First Amendment?
6. **For Critical Analysis:** Would the American public today accept the Alien and Sedition Acts of 1798? Explain your answer.

★ ★ ★ ★ ★ **SECTION 4** ★ ★ ★ ★ ★

Freedom of Expression: Some Additional Issues

Preview Questions:

🌐 How is freedom of the press balanced against the right to a fair trial?

🌐 How does the First Amendment apply to films and other media?

🌐 What is commercial speech?

Key Terms:

gag orders, shield laws, commercial speech

Because our founders believed the press should be free to publish a wide range of opinions and information, they protected the press's right to free expression in the First Amendment. As mentioned earlier, we can think of freedom of the press as a special type of freedom of speech. The guidelines given in the preceding section generally apply to both these types of freedom of expression.

In this section, we discuss some special concerns related to freedom of the press. We also discuss how the First Amendment applies to media the founders could not have foreseen, including films and the Internet.

Freedom of the Press and the Right to a Fair Trial

The First Amendment guarantees freedom of the press. The Sixth Amendment guarantees "the right to a speedy and public trial, by an impartial jury." Where is the line drawn between the right of a free press to comment on criminal cases and the duty of the judiciary to ensure a fair trial? The Supreme Court has tried to balance suspects' rights with the rights of the press and the public's right to know.

This issue surfaced in 1954 when Dr. Samuel H. Sheppard was convicted of murdering his wife. He appealed his conviction to the Supreme Court, arguing that during pre-trial media coverage, so many lurid details about his life and behavior had circulated that it was impossible for him to have a fair trial. Finally, in 1966, the Supreme Court agreed. The Court found that the press had created a virtual "circus" around the case and reversed Sheppard's conviction.

In the 1970s, judges increasingly issued **gag orders,** which restrict publicity about a trial in progress or even a pre-trial hearing. (A *pre-trial hearing* is not a trial.

Rather, it is a preliminary examination by a judge to determine whether there is enough evidence to hold a person accused of a crime.) In 1976, a man was tried and charged with murdering six members of a neighboring family. A judge issued an order prohibiting the press from reporting information about the pre-trial hearing. The Supreme Court ruled against the judge's gag order, stating that it was an unconstitutional prior restraint and thus a violation of the First Amendment.

The Supreme Court ruled in *Gannet Company v. De Pasquale* (1979) that both the press and the public can be excluded from pre-trial hearings if it is likely that publicity will adversely affect the defendant. In *Richmond Newspapers, Inc. v. Virginia* (1980), however, the Supreme Court ruled that judges cannot close trials unless there is some overriding interest at stake.

▲ Stephen Jones, center, attorney for Oklahoma City bombing suspect Timothy McVeigh, talks to reporters outside the federal courthouse in Denver on Friday, March 14, 1997, after he asked a federal judge to dismiss charges against McVeigh or delay the start of the trial because of recent publicity that could affect the outcome of the trial. McVeigh was later found guilty of the bombing that killed 168 and injured hundreds of others.

Confidentiality and the Press

Reporters sometimes have information that may provide essential evidence in a trial. They want to protect the identities of the people who gave them the evidence. Many reporters argue that if they reveal their sources, their informants will no longer trust them and will not give them the information they need in order to keep the public informed. After all, reporters argue, much of what is said to them is said in confidence. The people talking trust that they will not be named. State and federal courts have generally rejected this argument, and more than one reporter has gone to jail because she or he refused to reveal the sources of a story.

The Supreme Court held in *Branzburg v. Hayes* (1972) that reporters have no constitutional right to withhold information from a court. In this case, a reporter had been allowed to watch individuals making hashish from marijuana if he promised to keep their names confidential. He kept his promise and refused to give the names to a grand jury. The Court ruled that *anyone*—including the news media—must give such

information in a case if called upon to do so. If special exemptions are to be given, the Court said, they must come from Congress and the state legislatures.

In response, more than half of the states now have **shield laws** to protect reporters' notes and information from being revealed in court. For the most part, however, reporters have no more right to withhold evidence from police investigators than other citizens do.

▲ Cameras in the courtroom are a relatively recent phenomenon. Contrary to the political cartoon shown here, however, the purpose of televised trials is not ratings. What is the reason for televising trials?

Film, Radio, and Television

In the early days of the movie industry, the Supreme Court held that freedom-of-press protections did not apply to films. By the 1950s, however, the Court had

▶ *Although the government regulates television and radio broadcasts, the Internet remains, for now, unregulated. Do you think the government should establish and enforce standards for the Internet?*

reversed its position. In *Burstyn v. Wilson* (1952), the Court held that expression by means of motion pictures is included under the free speech and free press guarantees of the First Amendment.

Generally, the Court has continued to hold that movies and video productions are a form of artistic endeavor protected by the First Amendment. Yet the Court has held that not all censorship of films is unconstitutional. In *Teitel Film Corporation v. Cusack* (1968), the Court ruled that a state or local government can ban a movie after proving at a judicial hearing that the film is obscene. To avoid problems and in response to public pressure, the movie industry eventually created its own rating system, rating films as G, PG, PG-13, and so on. Today, most audiences rely on these ratings to determine the appropriateness of each film.

Radio and television broadcasters are subject to many regulations because they use electromagnetic airwaves, which are considered public property. To gain access to these airwaves, a broadcaster must have a license issued by the Federal Communications Commission (FCC). The FCC has the authority to regulate and penalize license holders and revoke licenses. The Supreme Court has regularly rejected the argument that the First Amendment prohibits such regulation by the FCC.

The Supreme Court has given the growing cable television industry First Amendment freedoms broader than those it has given traditional television. In *Wilkinson v. Jones* (1987), the Court ruled that the states cannot regulate "indecent" cable programming. It struck down a state law in Utah that prohibited cable broadcast of any sexually explicit or other "indecent material" between 7 A.M. and midnight. The Court argued in part that cable does not use public property (airwaves) to broadcast its material.

Cyberspace

One of the most controversial issues in regard to free speech on the Internet concerns sexually explicit materials. For the most part, anyone of any age anywhere in the world at any time can visit Internet sites that show sexually explicit materials. Many believe that the government should step in to keep such materials off the Internet. Others believe that speech on the Internet should not be regulated.

In 1996, Congress passed the Communications Decency Act. This law made it illegal to transmit indecent material via the Internet. The law was challenged, and the case ultimately went to the Supreme Court. In 1997, in *Reno v. American Civil Liberties Union*, the act was declared unconstitutional. For the time being, at least, speech on the Internet is virtually unregulated by the national government.

Advertising

Does the First Amendment protect the content of advertising, otherwise known as **commercial speech?** Until the 1970s, the Supreme Court held that advertising was not protected under the First Amendment. Then, in *Bigelow v. Virginia* (1975), the Supreme Court said that a state law that prohibited the newspaper advertising of abortion services was unconstitutional. In 1976, it struck down another state law that forbade the advertising of prescription drug prices. According to Justice Harry Blackmun,

> *Advertising, however tasteless and excessive it sometimes may seem, is nonetheless dissemination of information as to who is producing and selling what product for what reason and at what price.*

Blackmun concluded that consumers are entitled to the "free flow of commercial information."

The government does, however, prohibit false and misleading advertisements as well as the advertising of illegal goods and services. The national government has even forbidden the advertising of certain legally sold products. For example, Congress has prohibited the advertising of cigarettes on radio and television. Additionally, the Supreme Court has held that state and local governments can prohibit advertising in certain places, such as on billboards along highways. Generally, commercial speech receives less protection than ordinary speech under the First Amendment.

SECTION 4 REVIEW

1. How might freedom of the press conflict with the right to a fair trial? How has this conflict been resolved?
2. Why do television and radio broadcasters have fewer First Amendment protections than newspaper reporters?
3. How does commercial speech differ from any other type of speech?
4. **For Critical Analysis:** Allowing each community to decide what is and is not obscene leads to diversity in obscenity laws. How can this way of determining what is or is not obscene be applied to the Internet?

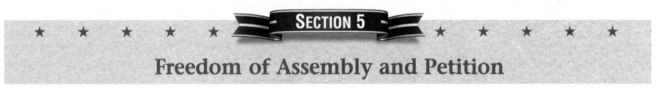

SECTION 5

Freedom of Assembly and Petition

Preview Questions:

- Why are the freedoms of assembly and petition important in a democracy?
- Why are limits placed on the freedoms of assembly and petition?
- What are these limits?

It would be meaningless to guarantee free speech in a democracy if people did not have the right to assemble and to express their beliefs publicly. An assembly is usually a group of people who gather together for a specific purpose. People acting as a group are often more successful in getting their ideas heard than are people acting individually. They are more likely to influence government policies and actions if they organize and collectively display their feelings. Suppose, for example, that there are twenty students who think that the school library should have more books. If they act individually, they can talk to their friends, write letters to their principal, and tell their parents. But what if they join together as the "Committee for School Library Improvement" and create a weekly newsletter, which they distribute to all the parents and school administrators? Certainly, acting as a group, the twenty students have a better chance of improving the library than they would if they acted separately as individuals.

The Freedom of Assembly

The Constitution protects the right of people to assemble, or organize, to influence public policy. It also protects the right of petition—the right of the people to express their views to public officials through petitions, letters, signs in a parade, demonstrations, or marches on a picket line.

In 1937, the Supreme Court first ruled on the right to assembly in *De Jonge v. Oregon*. De Jonge had been convicted for conducting a public meeting sponsored by the Communist Party. The Supreme Court overturned his conviction, saying that under the First Amendment, "peaceable assembly for lawful discussion cannot be made a crime." The Court stated that the rights of free speech, free press, and free assembly represent the "security of the republic." The case established that the right of assembly was as important as the rights of free speech and free press. It also established that the right of assembly was protected by the due process clause of the Fourteenth Amendment.

Limits Placed on the Freedom of Assembly

When, in the name of public peace, does the right to assembly end? The Constitution protects the right to assemble as long as the assembly is *peaceable*. It does not give people the right to riot, to incite violence, to block public streets, or to endanger life, property, or public order. The Supreme Court has also generally agreed that it is reasonable to make and enforce rules covering the time,

▲ A Ku Klux Klan (KKK) leader exercises his constitutional right to freedom of assembly by addressing a small group of KKK members from the steps of the U.S. Capitol. The Constitution guarantees the freedom of assembly to all groups, regardless of how unpopular their views may be.

place, and manner of assembly. These rules can specify when and where assembly may take place.

Demonstrations are intended to bring issues to public attention. This means that they usually happen in highly visible public places. The need for public exposure means that there is a good chance that the demonstration will interfere with other citizens' rights to use the same places. There is also a good chance of conflict. Most demonstrations are held to protest something, and people who support the other side of the issue are likely to be present and to be upset by the demonstration. Therefore, the Supreme Court has often upheld state and local laws that require demonstrators to give advance notice and to obtain permits.

An early case supporting limits on assembly was *Cox v. New Hampshire* (1941). Cox was a member of a group that violated a law requiring a permit for a parade. The Supreme Court voted unanimously to uphold the permit law as constitutional. The Court rejected Cox's argument that the law violated his rights of free speech and assembly.

In 1950, a speaker named Irving Feiner was addressing an outdoor public meeting, where he was inviting the audience to attend a meeting of the Progressive Party. During the speech, he criticized President Harry Truman, the American Legion, and the mayor of Syracuse, New York. He also urged African Americans to fight for civil rights. Feiner's remarks angered the crowd, almost to the point of rioting. Feiner ignored police requests to stop. He was arrested and convicted of disturbing the peace. In *Feiner v. New York* (1951), the Supreme Court upheld his conviction for unlawful assembly. The Court concluded that the police had not acted to suppress his speech but rather had acted to preserve public

Changes in Personal Freedoms

Our personal liberties are in a constant state of change. Listed below are just a few of the changes that have occurred since the Bill of Rights was ratified in 1791.

THEN (1791)	NOW
Religion and values were taught in schools.	Religious teaching in public schools is prohibited by law.
Religious displays and public prayer were common.	There are few publicly supported religious displays, and public prayer is rare.
There were no significant privacy rights, because the Constitution did not specifically mention such rights.	Significant privacy rights exist in many circumstances and jurisdictions because the Supreme Court has held that such rights are implied by the First, Third, Fourth, Fifth, and Ninth amendments to the Constitution.
There were no restrictions on free speech by federal courts.	Federal courts have held that certain forms of speech are not protected under the First Amendment (for example, seditious speech).
The Bill of Rights protected citizens only against national government actions.	Nearly all of the rights listed in the Bill of Rights apply to actions by state governments as well as by the national government.

order. The case set a precedent that police *may* break up assemblies to preserve peace.

Testing the Limits of Freedom of Assembly

Limits on when and where an assembly may take place were tested in 1977 when the American Nazi Party decided to hold a rally and march through the Chicago suburb of Skokie, Illinois. Citizens and city officials objected because of the make-up of the community. About one-half of the residents were Jewish, and about 10 percent were either survivors of the Nazi death camps of World War II or relatives of people who had died in the camps. Those who objected to the Nazis' plans felt that the march would cause these people pain and that it could lead to violence and rioting.

Skokie's city government required the Nazis to post a $300,000 bond to obtain a parade permit. The Nazis claimed that the high-priced bond was meant to prevent their march and that it infringed on their freedoms of speech and assembly. A federal district court agreed that the city of Skokie had violated the Nazis' First Amendment rights, and the Supreme Court let the lower court's ruling stand.

The Right to Die

Americans generally agree about the rights to "life, liberty, and the pursuit of happiness." What about the right to die? Specifically, what about the right to commit assisted suicide? This often unpleasant and highly emotional subject continues to occupy political discussions throughout the United States. In 1997, the Supreme Court upheld a state law banning assisted suicide. The Court stated that there was no "constitutional right" to commit suicide, with or without the assistance of another. That means that in the fifty states, Americans will continue to be at odds about what laws should be passed on this subject.

Many Believe That People Have a "Right to Die"

Some argue that our constitutional right to privacy includes the right of terminally ill persons to commit suicide. Although the Constitution does not mention privacy rights, the Supreme Court has held that such rights are implied by many of the constitutional amendments that make up the Bill of Rights. Supporters of the right to die contend that this implied right to privacy not only allows terminally ill persons to choose to commit suicide but also allows them to secure help from physicians in ending their lives through chemical means.

After all, say those in favor of physician-assisted suicide, turning off a terminally ill patient's life-support system is often legal. What is the difference between that and complying with a terminally ill person's request for assistance in ending his or her own life? The government has no business requiring a person to continue to suffer when there is no hope of recovery. Physicians cannot preserve life at all costs, for that is impossible. They must serve each patient's needs while respecting the patient's dignity.

Others Say That We Have No Such Right

Those who oppose assisted suicide also have a strong case. They ask whether we really ever know for certain that a person who seems terminally ill is beyond recovery. Miracles do happen. In the absence of miracles, modern-day medical technology sometimes saves supposedly terminally ill persons. Our medical knowledge is increasing all the time. Persons who appear terminally ill today may be cured tomorrow.

Others oppose physician-assisted suicide for religious reasons. Some religious beliefs do not allow for any type of suicide, no matter what the situation.

Still others who oppose physician-assisted suicide point out that some persons who have requested physician-assisted suicides are not in a state of unbearable physical suffering. Rather, they are depressed. Under no circumstances should they be allowed to have help in taking their own lives.

What we should be doing, argue those who are against the right to die, is seeking proper care for those who are dying. We should develop better ways of alleviating or reducing pain. We should not abandon the terminally ill, but we should not comply with the wishes of those who would end their own lives.

YOU DECIDE

1. In your opinion, should terminally ill persons have the legal right to end their lives with the assistance of a physician?
2. Reread the first ten amendments to the Constitution. Can you find anything in those amendments that can be used to justify either position on the right to die?

An issue in some communities today is whether gang members can be deprived of their right of assembly in the interests of preserving public order and preventing crime. In 1997, for example, the California Supreme Court ruled that banning gang members from gathering together did not violate the gang members' constitutional rights. According to the court, society's rights to peace and quiet and to freedom from harm outweighed the gang members' First Amendment rights.

SECTION 5 REVIEW

1. Why is the right to assemble peaceably important in a democracy?
2. What limits may government place on the right to assemble?
3. **For Critical Analysis:** Should gang members' First Amendment right to assemble be sacrificed in the interests of keeping others in a community safe from harm?

★ ★ ★ ★ Chapter Summary ★ ★ ★ ★

Section 1: Our System of Personal Freedoms

- Although the original Constitution protects individuals from certain government actions, most of our civil liberties are set forth in the Bill of Rights.
- The courts interpret and apply our civil rights and liberties. The Supreme Court is the ultimate protector of our civil rights and makes final decisions concerning the Constitution.
- Ultimately, the responsibility for protecting the rights and liberties set forth in the Constitution and the Bill of Rights lies with the American people.
- Initially, the Bill of Rights protected individuals only against the actions of the national government. The Supreme Court has interpreted the due process clause of the Fourteenth Amendment (1868) to mean that most provisions in the Bill of Rights apply to actions of state governments as well as the national government.

Section 2: Freedom of Religion

- The establishment clause of the First Amendment provides that the government cannot establish a reli-

gion or impose religious requirements on individuals. The Supreme Court has interpreted the establishment clause to mean that the government must avoid any excessive entanglement with religion.
- The free exercise clause of the First Amendment protects individuals' rights to worship or believe as they see fit.
- The free exercise of religion may be limited when religious practices violate criminal laws or threaten the health, safety, and welfare of others.

Section 3: Freedom of Expression: General Principles

- The First Amendment protects freedom of speech and of the press. Three types of protected speech are pure speech, speech plus, and symbolic speech.
- The Supreme Court has developed several doctrines to use in deciding cases involving freedom of expression.
- Libel, slander, obscenity, and "fighting words" are not protected under the First Amendment.

Section 4: Freedom of Expression: Some Additional Issues

- Freedom of the press may sometimes be restricted when press coverage might interfere with a defendant's right to a fair trial.
- Films are included under the free speech and free press guarantees of the First Amendment. Radio and television broadcasters using the public airwaves, however, are subject to government regulation.
- Generally, commercial speech (advertising) receives less protection than ordinary speech.

Section 5: Freedom of Assembly and Petition

- The Constitution protects the right of assembly as long as the assembly is peaceable, but the government may impose reasonable restrictions on this right to ensure public safety.
- The Supreme Court has generally held that it is reasonable for government to make and enforce rules regarding the time, place, and manner of assembly.

★ REVIEW QUESTIONS ★

1. What is meant by the concept of civil liberties?
2. What safeguards in the original Constitution protect citizens against a too powerful government?
3. What is the Bill of Rights, and why was it added to the Constitution?
4. What effect has the due process clause of the Fourteenth Amendment had on the Bill of Rights?
5. What rights are guaranteed under the First Amendment?
6. What is the establishment clause? What freedom does it provide for the American people?
7. What did Thomas Jefferson mean when he spoke of a "wall of separation between church and state"?
8. Give some examples of laws or policies that, according to the Supreme Court, constitute an "excessive government entanglement" with religion.
9. What does the free exercise clause protect? What doesn't it protect?
10. Describe the three categories of free speech generally protected by the First Amendment.
11. What kinds of speech are not protected under the First Amendment?
12. What guidelines does the Supreme Court use when deciding what limits should be placed on free expression?
13. What is prior restraint? Is it constitutional?
14. How does the First Amendment apply to speech on the Internet?
15. What is the main limitation that the Constitution places on freedom of assembly?
16. Why are the rights guaranteed by the First Amendment essential in a democracy?

★ CRITICAL THINKING ★

1. Should a group or political party that advocates the overthrow of the U.S. government be allowed to enjoy the First Amendment freedoms of speech, press, and assembly? Why or why not?
2. The founders certainly could not have predicted the use of mobile phones, communication satellites, cable television, and the like. At what point do you think that the First Amendment freedom of the press should apply to these and other new forms of communication, such as the Internet?
3. Discuss whether or not the government would violate any First Amendment rights if it regulated videotape rentals to prevent, for example, the spread of obscene materials to minors.
4. Many issues face the Supreme Court when civil liberties are on trial. The justices must balance the rights of individuals with the rights of society as a whole. Under what circumstances do you believe that the individual's rights must be restricted in order to benefit society? Be specific.
5. The use of electronic mail, or e-mail, has become increasingly popular in the United States and elsewhere. As a result of this popularity, advertisers are attempting to use e-mail to send ads. If you were a government official, how might you try to regulate advertising via e-mail?
6. How do you think the First Amendment's guarantee of freedom of the press should be applied during wartime? Should the government be allowed to censor press coverage? Or should the press be allowed to report on what it sees? Give reasons to support your answers.

★ IMPROVING YOUR SKILLS ★

Communication Skills

Summarizing In the early days of television, a program called *Dragnet*, featuring a police officer named Joe Friday, was popular. When trying to get key information from witnesses, Friday often said, "Just the facts, ma'am." He was trying to get to the core of the case.

He did not want every detail and opinion. He wanted the witnesses to *summarize* what they knew.

A summary contains only main ideas. Being able to summarize enables you to communicate more effectively. It is also a useful study skill, because it helps you keep your focus on the main ideas. Here are some guidelines to use when writing a summary.

1. Read the material carefully. If the material is lengthy, skim it first.
2. Determine the author's point of view as you review the material. (This may involve looking for evidence or identifying generalizations, as explained in the feature on reading the newspaper in Chapter 6.)
3. Now rewrite the material in summary style, using your own words.
   a. Be sure to include only the main ideas.
   b. Eliminate all unimportant details.
4. Try to keep your summary brief (no more than 20 percent of the length of the original text).

Writing Turn to the section entitled "Unprotected Speech—Libel, Slander, Obscenity, and 'Fighting Words'" on page 135. Summarize the section. Then review your summary and ask yourself if you followed the four guidelines listed above.

Social Studies Skills

Reading an Information Table Sometimes, lists of information are presented in table form, such as you see in Figure 5–1, "The Bill of Rights," on page 122. Use this figure to answer the following questions.

1. How many freedoms are listed for the First Amendment?
2. Which amendment guarantees the accused person in a criminal case the right to a trial by jury?
3. Which amendment do you think could be named the "reserved powers" amendment?
4. Which amendments imply a right to privacy?

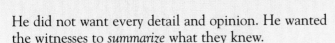

★ ACTIVITIES AND PROJECTS ★

1. Choose one of the Supreme Court cases mentioned in this chapter and conduct additional research on it in your school or local library. Prepare a report that summarizes the arguments presented on both sides. Then write the decision that you would make if you were a justice hearing the case.
2. Invite a newspaper or television reporter to your class to discuss the freedoms and limitations involved in newspaper publishing or television broadcasting. Ask the reporter to discuss how some of the issues mentioned in this chapter, such as libel and slander, are treated in these media.
3. Interview a member of the clergy to find out his or her opinion on the separation of church and state. Prepare a summary of that person's opinion, and present your summary to your class.
4. Write a letter to the editor of your local newspaper, expressing your views on the right of unpopular groups to assemble.
5. Prepare for a class debate on this question: Should the federal government regulate the Internet?
6. Given a written explanation of what you think John F. Kennedy meant when he said, "In giving rights to others which belong to them, we give rights to ourselves and to our country." In your explanation, provide three examples of cases in which this statement has proved true.

What If . . .

There Were No Separation of Church and State?

The First Amendment to the Constitution has been interpreted as requiring that government and religion be kept separate. How would America be different if this requirement were not in effect?

CHAPTER 6

Due Process of Law

CHAPTER OBJECTIVES

To learn about and understand . . .

⭐ The concept of due process of law and its importance in the American system of civil rights

⭐ The rights of persons accused of crimes

⭐ The types of punishments that may be imposed on persons convicted of crimes

Keynote

"It is better that ten guilty persons escape than that one innocent suffer."
Sir William Blackstone
(1723–1780)
English Jurist

INTRODUCTION

The First Amendment rights that you read about in the previous chapter would do you little good if government officials did not enforce them in a fair and reasonable manner. For example, suppose that you were arrested for disturbing the peace during a demonstration. What good would your right of assembly be if you were not allowed to tell your side of the story, to have a lawyer's assistance in doing so, and to be treated fairly and equally?

Sir William Blackstone's statement in the above quotation captures the British-American sense that the government should go to great lengths—even letting some guilty persons go free—to protect the innocent. In the United States, numerous constitutional safeguards and procedural rules protect the innocent.

These safeguards and rules are especially important in criminal cases. The right to *due process of law* then becomes critical.

◄ Under our Constitution, any person accused of criminal activities has the right to a fair and public trial, heard by an impartial jury of his or her peers.

Due Process of Law

Preview Questions:

🌐 What is due process?

🌐 What is the difference between procedural and substantive due process?

Key Terms:

due process of law, procedural due process, substantive due process

The Declaration of Independence proclaims that "all men are created equal." As we all know, this does not mean that everyone is born with the same wealth, intelligence, strength, or ambition. Each of us has a unique combination of qualities and characteristics. The words of the declaration mean that all people should have equal *rights*. That is the cornerstone of the democratic ideal.

The Fifth Amendment declares that the federal government cannot deprive any person of "life, liberty, or property, without due process of law." The Fourteenth Amendment places the same restriction on state and local governments. The key phrase here is *due process of law*. All Americans are entitled to due process by virtue of living in the United States.

Due process of law has come to mean that government may not act unfairly or arbitrarily. It may not act unreasonably, and it may not act in a capricious (unstable and undependable) way. Of course, disagreements over

▲ *In an attempt to keep young offenders out of the criminal justice system, some cities have instituted teen courts. In this Orange County, California, courthouse, teenage prosecutors, the defense attorney, and the defendant rise as the jury is brought back into the courtroom. Do you think teen courts are effective in preventing crime?*

the meaning of these commands have plagued us from the time this nation was founded and will undoubtedly continue to do so.

In order to understand due process, it is important to consider its two types: procedural and substantive.

Procedural Due Process

Procedural due process means that the law must be carried out by a *method* that is fair and orderly. Whenever a person is about to be denied "life, liberty, or property," fair procedures must be followed to make sure that the basic constitutional rights of that person are not violated. At a minimum, the person should have an opportunity to object to the proposed action in a formal hearing before a fair, neutral decision maker, such as a judge. The person must be given the opportunity to confront and cross-examine witnesses and accusers and to present his or her own witnesses.

Substantive Due Process

Fair procedures would obviously be of little use if they were used to administer unfair laws. For example, suppose that you were arrested for violating a criminal law. You were convicted and sentenced to one year in prison. If the law that you were convicted of violating was unfair to begin with, it wouldn't much matter whether the proper procedures were used to convict you.

ARCHITECTS

of Government

Sandra Day O'Connor
(1930–   )

On September 21, 1981, history was made when the U.S. Senate confirmed the appointment of Sandra Day O'Connor as the first woman justice of the United States Supreme Court. A graduate of Stanford Law School, O'Connor served briefly as a deputy county attorney for San Mateo County, California, in the early 1950s. In 1965, she became an assistant attorney general for the state of Arizona. She was a member of the Arizona Senate from 1969 until 1974, when she was elected to the Superior Court for Maricopa County, Arizona. From 1979 to 1981, she served on the Arizona Court of Appeals. As a Supreme Court justice, she has tended to support the view that the Court should play a limited role in making national policy.

HER WORDS

"As the first woman to be nominated as a Supreme Court justice, I am particularly honored, but I happily share the honor with millions of American women of yesterday and today whose abilities and conduct have given me this opportunity for service."
(Senate confirmation hearings, 1981)

"[J]udges should avoid substituting their own views . . . . for those of the legislature."
(Senate confirmation hearings, 1981)

DEVELOPING
CRITICAL THINKING SKILLS

1. In the first quotation, what did Justice O'Connor mean by saying that the "abilities and conduct" of "American women of yesterday and today" had given her "this opportunity for service"?
2. Do you agree with the second quotation? Why or why not?

Substantive due process requires that the *laws themselves* be reasonable. If a law is unfair or unreasonable, even if properly passed by the legislature, it must be declared unconstitutional.

Challenges to Due Process

Most of the due process cases that reach the Supreme Court concern procedural due process. In recent years, many of these cases have involved prisoners' rights to due process. Consider *Young v. Harper*, a case that came before the Supreme Court in 1997. The case involved a "pre-parole" program in Oklahoma that allowed certain prisoners to be released whenever state prisons became overcrowded. A board of prison officials determined who could participate in the program. Ernest Harper, who had served fifteen years of a life sentence for murder, was one of the inmates released under the program. He found a job, established a residence, and complied with the terms of his release.

"What's so great about due process? Due process got me ten years."

▲ Due process guarantees that the accused is treated fairly under the law, but it does not, as the prisoner in this cartoon seems to think, guarantee a happy ending. Is due process equally important for both the innocent and the guilty?

There are still many places in the world where men, women, and children are being illegally imprisoned and tortured. These people aren't guilty of any crime except being born a different color, practicing a different religion, speaking a different language, or having different political views from the people who are imprisoning or torturing them. If you are interested in learning more about struggles for human rights around the world, a good place to start is with Amnesty International.

Amnesty International was founded in 1961 to assist individuals and groups around the world in taking a stand against human rights injustices. In 1977, the organization won the Nobel Peace Prize for "defending human dignity against violence and subjugation." In 1986, Amnesty International enlisted the support of rock musicians to bring the human rights message to American

PARTICIPATING IN YOUR GOVERNMENT

How to Support Human Rights

youth. The resulting "Conspiracy of Hope" tour boosted national action.

Today, Amnesty International has grown into a worldwide network of more than 1.1 million people in over 160 countries and territories. More than a hundred researchers in the organization compile the latest information on state-supported abuses of human rights and torture. By the end of the 1990s, Amnesty International had taken on more than 35,000 individual cases and was a key factor in the release of almost 2,000 political prisoners. Other goals are to ensure prompt and fair trials for political prisoners and to end torture and executions. The organization attempts to achieve these goals through publicity, lobbying, legal aid, and letter-writing campaigns that focus on the cases of specific individuals.

To become a member, send whatever donation you can. The suggested membership fees are $25, or $15 for students and senior citizens. If you are interested, write to Amnesty International USA, 322 Eighth Avenue, New York, NY 10001, or telephone 212-807-8400. To get information about Amnesty International online, use your Internet browser to go to: **www.amnesty.org**

Five months after Harper's release, the governor of Oklahoma ordered him to return to prison. Harper claimed that his right to due process had been violated. After all, he claimed, regular parolees could not be sent back to prison unless certain procedures were followed. These procedures included notifying the parolee of the claimed parole violations and providing the parolee with an opportunity to object to any evidence against him or her at a formal hearing. Harper claimed that "pre-parolees" were entitled to the same due process rights. When the case reached the Supreme Court, the Court agreed.

A recent example of a challenge to substantive due process is *Reno v. American Civil Liberties Union* (1997). That case arose after Congress passed the Communica-

tions Decency Act of 1996. The act made it a crime to transmit "indecent" speech or images over the Internet or to make such speech or images available to minors online. The act defined indecent speech as any communication that depicts or describes sexual activities or organs in a way that is "patently offensive," as measured by current community standards. Those who violated the act could have been fined up to $250,000 or imprisoned for up to two years.

Civil rights groups immediately claimed that the law was unconstitutional. For one thing, it violated free speech rights. For another, it violated the constitutional principle of fairness because it was so vague. It imposed criminal penalties without specifically defining the crime. For example, what community's stan-

•••••••••••••••••••••••••••••••

1. Research three specific cases
   in which Amnesty International has recently been
   involved. Report back to the
   class on your findings and
   your assessment of the
   organization.
2. Research human rights violations in a particular country
   in which you are interested.
3. Research the history of
   apartheid in South Africa,
   and prepare a report on
   recent changes in the South
   African government.

▶ *Forced to leave their homes, these refugee
children are living reminders of the human toll
taken by political instability and war. (Photo-
postcard courtesy of Amnesty International.)*

dards would apply to the Internet, which has no geographic boundaries? The Supreme Court agreed and
held that the law was unconstitutional. It went too far
in restraining freedom of speech. In addition, because
of its vagueness, it was fundamentally unfair and thus
violated substantive due process.

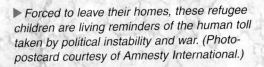
SECTION 1 REVIEW

1. Which two amendments in the Constitution
   contain due process clauses?

2. What does due process of law mean?
3. Explain the difference between procedural and
   substantive due process.
4. **For Critical Analysis:** We often hear about situations in which persons accused of crimes "get off
   on technicalities." These "technicalities" generally involve claims that procedural due process
   requirements were not met. Law enforcement officials sometimes argue that such uses of procedural
   due process hinder their ability to successfully
   prosecute known criminals. This can be seen as
   one of the costs to society of having procedural
   due process. What might be some other costs of
   procedural due process? What are the benefits?

Rights of the Accused: Searching and Wiretapping

Preview Questions:

- What constitutes an unreasonable search and seizure?
- What is the exclusionary rule?

Key Terms:

probable cause, searches and seizures, search warrant, exclusionary rule

Most of the words contained in the Bill of Rights are actually about the rights of persons accused of crimes. The protections of the Fourth, Fifth, Sixth, and Eighth Amendments are mostly applied to criminal cases. The concern for criminals' rights stems from an old fear that in trying to make sure all criminals are apprehended and punished, the government may abuse the rights of innocent people. Much of the work of the Supreme Court has involved assuring that the evidence used against accused persons is constitutionally valid.

Collecting Evidence

Police cannot arrest someone on a whim. They need evidence to justify the arrest, and courts need evidence to justify a conviction. In collecting evidence, law enforcement officers must make sure that they do not violate the Fourth Amendment. That amendment reads as follows:

The right of the people to be secure in their persons, houses, papers, and effects, against unreasonable searches and seizures, shall not be violated, and no Warrants shall issue, but upon probable cause, supported by Oath or affirmation, and particularly describing the place to be searched, and the persons or things to be seized.

Under this amendment, police and the courts need to have **probable cause,** or reasonable grounds, to believe that a suspect has committed a crime before making an arrest. At the same time, the Fourth Amendment is quite specific in forbidding unreasonable **searches and seizures.** Law enforcement personnel use searches and seizures to look for and collect the evidence they need to convict individuals suspected of crimes. To prevent unreasonable searches and seizures, police are usually required to have a **search warrant**—a court order that authorizes police to search the scene of a suspected crime—before conducting a search. The warrant must describe the place to be searched and the person or objects to be seized.

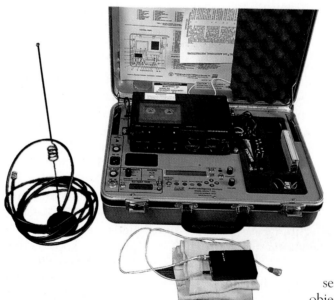

▶ The authors of the Fourth Amendment could hardly have imagined the sophisticated electronic listening devices available today. What legal steps must be taken before law enforcement personnel may use a wiretap like this?

The Supreme Court has held that only in limited circumstances may a lawful search and seizure be made *without* a warrant:

- When police are in "hot pursuit" of a suspect.
- When a lawful arrest is made, provided the area searched is within reach of the person being arrested. The area within reach is defined as the area in which the person might gain possession of a weapon or destroy evidence.
- When an arrest happens in a public place, provided the officer has probable cause to believe that the person has committed a crime or is about to commit one.
- When a crime is committed in the presence of an officer.
- When searching an automobile, a boat, an airplane, or any other vehicle, if the police officer has good reason to believe the vehicle either contains evidence of a crime or is being used to commit one. This is because a "movable scene of crime" could disappear while the warrant is being sought.
- When searching bags of trash left at the curb for regular collection.
- When seizing evidence in plain view.

The Exclusionary Rule

Since 1914, federal courts—the courts of the national government—have used the **exclusionary rule** to prevent the introduction of illegally seized evidence at trials. According to this rule, any evidence obtained in an illegal search is excluded from (cannot be used in) federal criminal trials. Even highly incriminating evidence, such as a knife stained with the victim's blood, cannot usually be introduced into a trial if it was not legally obtained.

The reasoning behind the exclusionary rule is that it forces police to gather evidence properly. If they follow appropriate procedures, they will be rewarded with a conviction. If they are careless or abuse the rights of the suspect, they will not get a conviction. Those who criticize the exclusionary rule, however, argue that its strict application may permit guilty people to go free

'This is a warning – there's a wobbly paving stone right in front of you'

◄ *Safeguarding the rights of the accused is a hallmark of American justice. Some people, however, believe that criminal suspects have too many rights. What does the creator of this political cartoon think?*

because of police carelessness or innocent errors.

For forty years after the exclusionary rule was established, it was applied only in federal courts. Each state was left to decide whether the rule would be applied to proceedings in state courts. This situation changed as a result of a 1961 Supreme Court case.

In 1960, Dollree Mapp, who lived in Cleveland, Ohio, was suspected of illegal gambling activities. The police broke into her home and, while searching the house, found obscene material. She was tried and convicted of possessing obscene material and appealed her case to the Supreme Court. In *Mapp v. Ohio* (1961), the Court ruled that the evidence had been illegally seized and reversed her conviction. Since then, the exclusionary rule has been applied to both state and federal governments.

The exclusionary rule has been under considerable pressure from critics in recent years. Beginning in 1984, opponents of the rule won several important victories in the Supreme Court. The Court first found an "inevitable discovery" exception to the rule. In a case in which a murderer was tricked by Iowa police into leading them to the body of his victim, the Court ruled that the police could use the evidence. It said that tainted evidence (evidence obtained by unlawful search and seizure) could be used if it would eventually have been discovered by lawful means. The Court has also allowed room for honest mistakes by police officers. It allowed the use of evidence seized in a mistaken search of an apartment in Baltimore in a 1987 case.

The Court has also created an exception for "good faith." This happened in a case in which federal agents in Los Angeles had used what they believed was a proper warrant to seize illegal drugs. Later, the warrant was found to be faulty. The Court upheld the agents' actions because the agents had thought the warrant was valid and had therefore acted in good faith.

New Technology, New Questions

The information age raises questions about searches and seizures that the framers of the Constitution could not have begun to imagine. They didn't know that we would enter an era of wiretapping, electronic eavesdropping devices, and videotaping or that we would be communicating by facsimile (fax) machines, computer networks, and cordless and cellular telephones. Increasingly, our communications are transmitted, stored, and shared in ways that were unheard of only a few years ago.

In 1928, the Supreme Court first ruled on wiretapping. The case involved federal agents who had tapped the telephones of bootleggers. (Bootleggers engaged in making or selling alcoholic beverages, which was illegal at that time.) The Court held that intercepting telephone conversations was not a search and seizure, so agents did not need a warrant. In *Katz v. United States* (1967), however, the Court ruled that police could not eavesdrop on telephone conversations without a court warrant, holding that such communications are protected by the Fourth Amendment.

In 1989, when more than nine million cordless phones were in use, the Court let an Iowa ruling

stand that said police can intercept cordless phone conversations without a warrant. Lower courts have ruled that because the phones use a radio transmission, users cannot expect privacy. (Recall that radio transmissions use airways, which belong to the public.) This makes cordless phone conversations fair game for police eavesdropping.

The Constitution does not mention privacy. The Supreme Court, however, has said that the right to privacy is a constitutional right implied by several amendments, especially the Fourth Amendment. As technology makes it more and more possible for government to intrude into private lives, there will be more and more complex cases for the courts to decide.

THINK ABOUT IT

1. Do you think police officials should be able to intercept cordless phone conversations without a warrant? Explain why or why not.
2. What other new forms of communication can you think of that might raise similar questions?

How the courts apply the exclusionary rule has often given rise to controversy. Some argue that the courts in the 1960s and 1970s went too far in the direction of protecting criminal defendants' rights. This group claims that the exceptions to the exclusionary rule made during the 1980s and 1990s are necessary to restore some balance between the rights of criminal defendants and the rights of society. Others believe that the exceptions to the exclusionary rule allow law enforcement personnel to exercise power too arbitrarily. How does the court know, for example, whether a police officer was acting in "good faith" when obtaining evidence against a criminal suspect?

Wiretaps and Congress

When the Fourth Amendment was created, of course, wiretapping was impossible. We can only guess what the writers of the Bill of Rights would have said about this practice. In general, however, the Supreme Court has held that the Fourth Amendment protects telephone communications. (Read about this issue in the *Case Study: Government in Action* on this page.)

In 1968, Congress passed the Omnibus Crime Control and Safe Streets Act. It permits *court-approved* wiretapping by both federal and state law enforcement officials in the investigation of a large number of listed

▲ After serving twenty-seven years in prison for the 1968 robbery-slaying of a teacher, Elmer "Geronimo" Pratt celebrates his release in June of 1997. The conviction of the former Black Panther leader was overturned by a judge because a Federal Bureau of Investigation informant lied under oath during Pratt's murder trial.

crimes. In 1978, Congress passed the Foreign Intelligence Surveillance Act, which requires officials to have warrants for wiretapping or other electronic bugging, even in national security cases.

SECTION 2 REVIEW

1. What does the Fourth Amendment prohibit?
2. Under what circumstances has the Supreme Court ruled that a lawful search and seizure can be made without a warrant?
3. What is the exclusionary rule? What exceptions to the rule have been allowed by the Supreme Court?
4. What has been the Supreme Court position on the right to privacy? Which amendment, in particular, has been cited to justify this position?
5. **For Critical Analysis:** When, if ever, do you believe that it would be acceptable to use illegally obtained evidence in a criminal case?

SECTION 3

Rights of the Accused: A Fair Trial

Preview Questions:

- ★ How does the Constitution set out protections for persons arrested for a crime?
- ★ How has the Supreme Court expanded the protections of accused persons?
- ★ What are the rights of persons arrested by the police?

Key Terms:

burden of proof, self-incrimination, contempt of court, waived, acquitted, *Miranda* warnings, bench trial, no contest, capital cases, grand jury, indictment, hung jury, mistrial, bail

Suppose that evidence against a person suspected of committing a crime has been gathered, and the police

have made an arrest. In our system, the **burden of proof** rests on the prosecution. This means that it is up to the prosecution to prove that the person is guilty of a crime. It is not up to the defense to prove that the person is innocent. Furthermore, the person is not obliged to help the government prove its case. The person has additional rights as well, including the right to counsel and the right to a trial by jury in serious criminal cases. These and other rights of persons accused of crimes are spelled out in the Fifth, Sixth, and Eighth Amendments.

Self-Incrimination

The Fifth Amendment protects persons against forced **self-incrimination.** It says that no one shall be compelled in any criminal case to be a witness against himself or herself. That means you cannot be forced to confess to a crime or to give testimony that is self-incriminating at a trial. This is sometimes called the "right to remain silent."

A person may also claim his or her Fifth Amendment right in any number of noncriminal proceedings. Whether at a divorce proceeding, a congressional hearing, or a disciplinary meeting before a local school board, a person need not provide evidence that may be self-incriminating.

If a judge believes that a defendant in a criminal trial has "taken the Fifth" unreasonably, the judge can hold the person in contempt. **Contempt of court** involves the act of showing disrespect for the court or disobeying a court order. One who is held in contempt of court may be fined, put in jail, or both.

The Fifth Amendment thus protects defendants against use of force or violence to obtain confessions. The Supreme Court has voided a number of state prosecutions because the methods used to obtain criminal confessions involved either the use or the threat of physical or psychological force.

The right to remain silent can be **waived** (given up) by a person at the time he or she is arrested, but it is not lost. If the defendant takes the stand to testify on his or her own behalf, he or she may still claim Fifth Amendment rights when on the witness stand. The Fifth Amendment does not, however, protect a person from being fingerprinted or photographed, submitting a handwriting sample, appearing in a police lineup, or taking a blood test. The courts decide when the Fifth Amendment applies.

The Right to Counsel

The Sixth Amendment guarantees a criminal defendant the right to have the assistance of counsel for his or her defense. This means that people accused of a crime have the right to hire a lawyer to represent their cases in court. If they cannot afford to hire a lawyer, the Court will appoint one for them.

Expansion of Fifth and Sixth Amendment Protections

The Sixth Amendment assures the right to counsel in federal courts, but until relatively recently, people who were tried in state courts did not have this right. In 1932, the Supreme Court ordered the states to provide an attorney for indigent (poor) defendants accused of capital crimes (crimes for which the death penalty could be imposed). Not until 1963, however, did the Supreme Court extend that right to everyone accused of a serious crime. The change occurred in the case of a penniless drifter from Florida named Clarence Earl Gideon.

Gideon v. Wainwright (1963) Gideon was charged with robbing a pool hall in Florida by stealing change from a vending machine. He did not have any money to hire a lawyer, so he asked the court to appoint one. His request was denied. He was convicted of the crime and sentenced to a five-year jail term.

While in jail, Gideon studied law books and concluded that he had been improperly denied his right to counsel. He petitioned the Supreme Court for a retrial in a handwritten petition. The Court accepted his appeal and ruled unanimously that the due process clause of the Fourteenth Amendment required states to give criminal defendants the Sixth Amendment right to counsel. According to Justice Black,

> The right of one charged with crime to counsel may not be deemed fundamental and essential to fair trials in some countries, but it is in ours. From the very beginning, our state and national constitutions and laws have laid great emphasis on procedural and substantive safeguards designed to assure fair trials before impartial tribunals in which every defendant stands equal before the law. This noble ideal cannot be realized if the poor man charged with crime has to face his accusers without a lawyer to assist him.

Gideon was retried with a lawyer to represent him. This time he was **acquitted** (found not guilty). More than a thousand other Florida prisoners and thousands of prisoners in other states who had been convicted without counsel were also released.

As a result of *Gideon v. Wainwright* (1963), today everyone has a right to a lawyer. In addition, the Court has extended the *Gideon* decision to apply not only in felony cases but to all cases in which a jail sentence might be involved.

Escobedo v. Illinois (1964) In the mid-1960s, the Supreme Court decided two more important cases that expanded the protections of persons accused of crimes under the Fifth and Sixth Amendments. The first case was *Escobedo v. Illinois* (1964). Danny Escobedo had been picked up by Chicago police for questioning in the death of his brother-in-law. While he was being questioned, he asked to see his lawyer several times. The requests were refused, even though his lawyer was in the police station waiting to see him. Through a long night of questioning and without the help of his lawyer, Escobedo made several damaging statements. These statements were used in court as part of the evidence that led to his conviction for murder.

Later, the Supreme Court freed him from prison. The Court said that a confession could not be used against a defendant if it was obtained by police who refused to allow him to see his attorney and did not advise him of the right to refuse to answer their questions.

Miranda v. Arizona (1966) In an important decision two years later, *Miranda v. Arizona* (1966), the Court went further and established the procedure that you

◀ *"Read him his rights." A familiar phrase to viewers of police dramas, this order refers to the Miranda rules, which inform a suspect of his or her right to remain silent. What are the other provisions of the Miranda rules?*

might know today as "being read your rights." Ernesto Miranda, a man with mild mental retardation, had been accused of kidnapping and raping an eighteen-year-old woman. Following his arrest, Miranda was selected from a police lineup by the victim, questioned for two hours, and not advised of his rights. He confessed and was convicted. The Supreme Court struck down his conviction. The Court ruled that the Fifth Amendment's protection against self-incrimination requires that suspects be clearly informed of their rights before they are questioned. The Court stated as follows:

[W]hen an individual is taken into custody or otherwise deprived of his freedom by the authorities in any significant way and is subjected to questioning . . . . He must be

```
DEFENDANT                          LOCATION

        SPECIFIC WARNING REGARDING INTERROGATIONS

1. YOU HAVE THE RIGHT TO REMAIN SILENT.

2. ANYTHING YOU SAY CAN AND WILL BE USED AGAINST YOU IN A COURT
   OF LAW.

3. YOU HAVE THE RIGHT TO TALK TO A LAWYER AND HAVE HIM PRESENT
   WITH YOU WHILE YOU ARE BEING QUESTIONED.

4. IF YOU CANNOT AFFORD TO HIRE A LAWYER ONE WILL BE APPOINTED
   TO REPRESENT YOU BEFORE ANY QUESTIONING, IF YOU WISH ONE.

SIGNATURE OF DEFENDANT                    DATE

WITNESS                                   TIME

☐ REFUSED SIGNATURE   SAN FRANCISCO POLICE DEPARTMENT    PR.9.1.4
```

◀ *Police usually read a Miranda card like this to suspects, advising them of their rights upon arrest. Why is it in the best interests of law enforcement to read—instead of repeat from memory or explain—a suspect's Miranda rights?*

warned prior to any questioning that he has the right to remain silent, that anything he says can be used against him in a court of law, that he has the right to the presence of an attorney, and that if he cannot afford an attorney one will be appointed for him prior to any questioning if he so desires. Opportunity to exercise these rights must be afforded to him throughout the interrogation.

The guidelines set by the Court in the *Miranda* case have become widely known as the **Miranda warnings.** Since this case was decided, the Supreme Court and lower courts have enforced the *Miranda* requirements hundreds of times. Police usually read a *Miranda* card to suspects advising them of their rights.

In several cases since *Miranda*, however, the Court has relaxed some of the restrictions of the *Miranda* rules. For example, in 1984, the Court ruled that police do not have to read suspects their rights when "public safety" is at risk. In order to find a loaded gun, for example, the police could question a suspect before advising him of his right to remain silent.

Just the Facts

The person suspected of murdering Ernesto Miranda was read the Miranda *warnings.*

The Right to Trial by Jury

The Sixth Amendment provides criminal defendants the right to be tried by an impartial jury in serious criminal cases. The Supreme Court has defined serious cases as those that could result in the defendant's being sentenced to six or more months in prison.

The jury is supposed to be impartial, which means persons who have made up their minds before the trial should be excluded. It is also supposed to represent a fair cross-section of the community, which means no group can be systematically excluded. No persons can be kept off a jury on the grounds of race, religion, color, national origin, or gender.

The Constitution does not specify the size of a jury. Tradition in England and America has set jury size at twelve persons and has required a unanimous verdict in criminal trials. Some states have experimented with smaller juries and nonunanimous verdicts to save money. The Supreme Court has allowed states to have juries with six members.

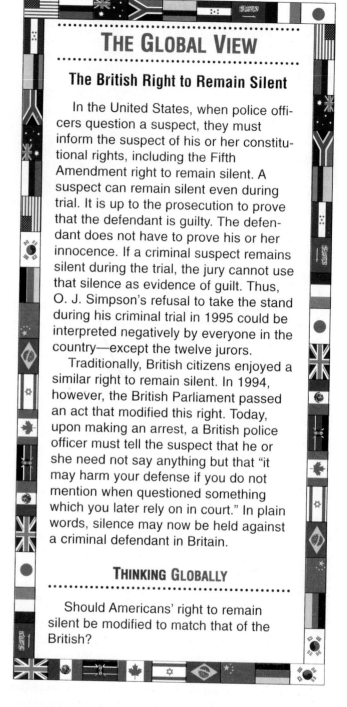

THE GLOBAL VIEW

The British Right to Remain Silent

In the United States, when police officers question a suspect, they must inform the suspect of his or her constitutional rights, including the Fifth Amendment right to remain silent. A suspect can remain silent even during trial. It is up to the prosecution to prove that the defendant is guilty. The defendant does not have to prove his or her innocence. If a criminal suspect remains silent during the trial, the jury cannot use that silence as evidence of guilt. Thus, O. J. Simpson's refusal to take the stand during his criminal trial in 1995 could be interpreted negatively by everyone in the country—except the twelve jurors.

Traditionally, British citizens enjoyed a similar right to remain silent. In 1994, however, the British Parliament passed an act that modified this right. Today, upon making an arrest, a British police officer must tell the suspect that he or she need not say anything but that "it may harm your defense if you do not mention when questioned something which you later rely on in court." In plain words, silence may now be held against a criminal defendant in Britain.

THINKING GLOBALLY

Should Americans' right to remain silent be modified to match that of the British?

Defendants may waive (give up or relinquish) their right to a jury trial. The judge must be satisfied that the defendant is fully aware of his or her rights and understands what that action means. If the right is waived, a **bench trial**—one heard by a judge alone—is held. Furthermore, a defendant may plead guilty—or

Protecting the Rights of Minors

Gerald Gault, aged fifteen, was accused of making an obscene phone call to a neighbor. He was taken into custody while his parents were at work. The police did not bother to notify Mr. and Mrs. Gault of what had happened to their son. Gerald was placed in a detention center. When his frantic parents finally learned that he was in custody, they were simply told that there would be a hearing the next day. No one mentioned the nature of the complaint against Gerald.

The complaining neighbor, Mrs. Cook, did not attend Gerald's hearing. Instead, a police officer testified about what Mrs. Cook told him. Gerald denied making the obscene remarks and blamed the call on a friend. No lawyers were present, and no record was made of what was said at the hearing. (A juvenile court hearing does not have a jury.) The judge ruled that the evidence weighed against Gerald. Gerald was declared a delinquent and sentenced to a state reform school until the age of twenty-one. Any adult found guilty of the same crime would have been sent to a county jail for no longer than sixty days.

The legal process for juveniles is just as complicated as, if not more complicated than, the legal process for adults. But adults have always had the right to a jury trial and the right to a lawyer. Gerald Gault's parents believed that he had been mistreated by being denied the rights an adult would have had. Their case went all the way to the United States Supreme Court, which ruled that juveniles are in fact entitled to many of the same rights as adults. Specifically, the justices held that juveniles charged with a delinquent act are entitled to be informed of the charges against them, to confront and cross-examine witnesses, to remain silent, and to be represented by an attorney.

The *Gault* decision (1967) gave young people accused of crimes many of the same rights as

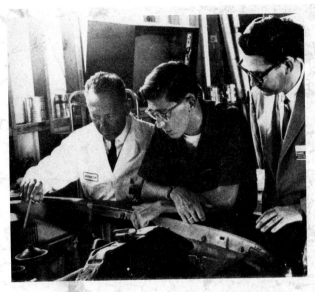

▲ Until the Gault *decision of 1967, young defendants enjoyed few of the rights of adult offenders. Gerald Gault (center), pictured here studying automotive repair, was released from a state reform school after the U.S. Supreme Court ruled that he had been denied due process of law. Should juvenile and adult defendants have the same rights?*

adults, but not all. Not until 1970 did the Supreme Court decide that juveniles charged with criminal acts must be found "delinquent by proof beyond a reasonable doubt," the high standard of proof that applies in criminal cases brought against adults. Juveniles still do not have the right to a jury trial or bail.

THINK ABOUT IT
....

1. How would you have reacted had you been in Gerald Gault's situation?
2. Should juveniles have the right to a trial by jury? If so, should it be a jury of their peers, as it is with adults? What might be the advantages and disadvantages of such jury trials?

no contest, meaning he or she does not wish to contest the charge—and thereby avoid a trial.

The Grand Jury

The Fifth Amendment provides for a grand jury in federal **capital cases** (cases that might involve the death penalty). A grand jury proceeding is the formal process by which a person may be accused of a serious crime.

A **grand jury** is a body made up of twelve to twenty-three citizens that examine the evidence presented against a suspect. The purpose of the grand jury investigation is to see if enough evidence exists to hold a criminal trial. If the jury finds there is enough evidence, an **indictment,** a formal charge of a crime against the accused, is handed down. If the grand jury does not find enough evidence, the charge is dropped.

A grand jury proceeding is not a trial. It does not determine guilt or innocence and is held in secret, unlike normal jury trials. Critics of the grand jury method say that it costs too much in both time and money. Supporters of the system argue that it can prevent an accused person from going through a trial without enough evidence on hand to warrant such a traumatic and expensive undertaking.

Double Jeopardy

The Fifth Amendment says that no person shall be "twice put in jeopardy of life and limb." This means that once a defendant has been acquitted of a crime, he or she is protected from being tried again for the same crime.

A person *can* be retried when a jury trial results in a hung jury. A **hung jury** is one that cannot reach a unanimous verdict. A person can also be retried if there is a **mistrial,** which may occur when there is an error in the proceedings. If the crime violates both state and federal laws, the person can be tried in both a state court and a federal court without a violation of the ban on double jeopardy.

A Speedy and Public Trial

The Sixth Amendment provides that the accused shall enjoy the right to a speedy and public trial. The

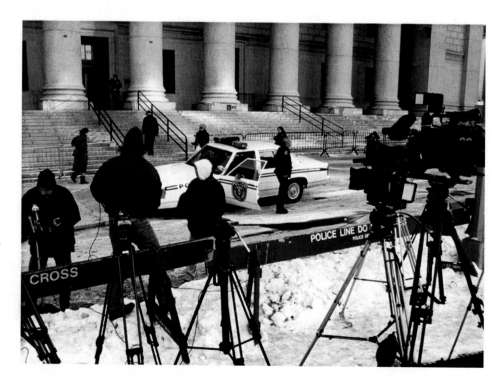

▶ Balancing the public's right to know and the defendant's right to a fair trial can be difficult. Barred from the trial itself, media members wait outside the court to catch a glimpse of Ramzi Ahmed Yousef, who was ultimately found guilty of masterminding the World Trade Center bombing in New York City. Do you think that trial and sentencing procedures for accused terrorists should be different from the trial and sentencing procedures for those accused of other crimes? Why or why not?

Newspapers offer detailed information on what is happening all over the world. When you read newspaper articles, avoid jumping to conclusions. Remember that an article usually gives an overview of a situation and may only present one viewpoint or one aspect of the story. To avoid jumping to conclusions, think about the following as you read an article.

The Evidence A well-presented argument should always be accompanied and reinforced by some evidence. For example, suppose you read an article about the need to ban a certain textbook in your school district because the material in the book would be offensive or harmful to students. The article thoroughly convinces you of its viewpoint. But in reviewing the article, you find that it gives no evidence of the actual contents of the book. It may be that you have been convinced only by a good writer's opinion and an emotional argument. Issues demand evidence, so look for it as you read.

Specificity of the Argument Is it possible that what seems like an argument is only a generalization? A *generalization* is an oversimplification that doesn't hold true in every specific case. Many political arguments are stated in generalizations. For example, you may read an article quoting a politician who says, "Standard test scores continue to fall because of the poor attitudes of high-school students." Could it really be true

BUILDING

SOCIAL STUDIES SKILLS

Reading a Newspaper Article Critically

that the attitudes of *all* high-school students are poor? Could there be other reasons for falling test scores that have little to do with students' attitudes?

Alternative Explanations An argument may sound reasonable and may seem to have evidence to back it up. But other explanations may be equally valid. For example, you may read that stock prices fell yesterday because of a threat of another war in the Middle East. This may be followed by a good explanation with solid evidence that sounds perfectly logical. But there may be hundreds of other reasons why the stock market fell, some of which no one really understands.

Editorials versus News Stories You must always distinguish between an editorial article and a news story. Editorials are typically found on the editorial page of your newspaper, often toward the end of the first section. They present the opin-

ions of the editorial staff of the newspaper. Regular news articles, in principle, report on actual events or on the opinions of the people interviewed. News stories are not supposed to present a point of view, although some do.

By using the guidelines above, you can critically evaluate what you read in newspapers. Thus, you can make good decisions based on the accuracy of the information presented. You might also try to adapt these guidelines for other media, so that you can critically evaluate the news stories presented on television and radio.

PRACTICING YOUR SKILLS

Read one news story about politics and one political editorial. (You can find the latter on the editorial page of your newspaper.) Then compare and contrast the news story with the editorial, asking yourself the following questions:

1. How does each article use evidence to support the story or issue?
2. If the articles are making arguments one way or another, how specific are the arguments? Identify any generalizations you find.
3. Are there any alternative explanations for what's being presented?

right to a speedy trial is meant to prevent prisoners from sitting in jails for unreasonable lengths of time. Since 1980, the suggested time span has been one hundred days. If the criminal trial has not occurred by the end of that period, the defendant should normally be set free.

The guarantee of a public trial is intended to prevent the courtroom from becoming a place of secret persecution. The Supreme Court has also ruled, however, that trials cannot be *too* public. It has reversed convictions when too much press coverage or other publicity prevented the defendant from getting a fair trial.

Excessive Bail

The Eighth Amendment provides that excessive bail shall not be required. **Bail** is the amount of money or property a defendant is required to give to the court as a guarantee that she or he will appear in court at the proper time. In determining the amount of bail, the judge considers the seriousness of the case, the criminal record of the accused, and the ability of the accused to afford bail.

Under a 1984 federal law, a person accused of committing a federal crime can be held without bail if federal judges have good reason to believe the person will commit another serious crime before the trial. In 1987, the Supreme Court upheld that law. More than half the states have adopted similar laws.

SECTION 3 REVIEW

1. What protection does the Fifth Amendment offer?
2. Why does the Constitution guarantee a right to counsel?
3. What are the *Miranda* rules?
4. What is the function of a grand jury? What is double jeopardy?
5. **For Critical Analysis:** Criminal defendants have a constitutional right to a speedy and public trial, but defendants in noncriminal cases do not. Why is the right to a speedy and public trial more important in criminal cases than in noncriminal ones?

SECTION 4

Plea Bargaining and Sentencing

Preview Questions:

- What is plea bargaining? Why is it so common?
- What types of sentences may be imposed on an individual convicted of a crime?
- What is probation? What is parole?

Key Terms:

plea bargaining, sentence, probation, parole, denaturalization

If an accused person pleads guilty to the crime with which that person has been charged (or to a lesser crime, through a plea bargaining process), then no trial is held. If a trial is held and the defendant is found guilty, then the defendant will be sentenced. We look here at the plea bargaining process and at the types of sentences that may be imposed on criminal defendants.

Plea Bargaining

Approximately 90 percent of all cases are settled before or during the trial through a process called plea bargaining.

What Is Plea Bargaining? In a **plea bargaining** arrangement, the defendant agrees to plead guilty, usually to a charge less serious than the charge the prosecutor originally brought. For example, suppose that John Smith has been charged with armed robbery, which carries a maximum sentence of twenty years. Smith's attorney may relate to Smith that the prosecutor will reduce the charge to simple robbery, which carries a maximum of only five years in prison, in exchange for a guilty plea to the reduced charge. Smith knows for certain that he will receive a maximum of only five years in prison if he agrees.

◄ *Because of serious overcrowding, many inmates at this Los Angeles county jail were freed early. Under what constitutional right was this allowed?*

Ethics and Plea Bargaining The practice of plea bargaining has given rise to much criticism. Certainly, plea bargaining raises some significant ethical questions. After all, it allows criminal suspects who are actually guilty to avoid the full consequences of their actions by pleading guilty to (and being sentenced for) lesser crimes.

Why is plea bargaining allowed in our justice system? Generally, prosecutors and the courts argue that it is necessary because it helps to reduce the number of cases that go to trial. When a criminal suspect pleads guilty to a crime, no trial is necessary. Our courts are already strained by heavy caseloads. If plea bargaining were not allowed, the courts could not handle the increased number of criminal trials. And even if they could, it would be very costly to the public, whose tax dollars pay for the costs of courtrooms, judges' salaries, prosecutors' salaries, and the like.

Sentencing

A sentence must be imposed if a defendant's guilt is established, whether through a plea bargain or through a full trial. After a guilty plea is entered or a trial court returns a verdict of "guilty," the judge will pronounce the sentence. A **sentence** is the penalty imposed on a person convicted of a crime. A sentence often involves a specific period of time to be spent in prison. It may also involve an alternative form of punishment.

Determinate and Indeterminate Sentences A determinate sentence is a fixed sentence for a particular crime. A state law may say, for example, that anyone convicted of armed robbery must serve twenty years behind bars. When those twenty years are completed, the offender has to be released.

An indeterminate sentence prescribes a maximum and minimum number of years to be served, depending on whether the convicted criminal demonstrates good behavior and seems rehabilitated and ready to return to society.

The trend today is toward determinate sentencing. For some crimes, this kind of sentencing is mandatory.

Alternatives to Imprisonment **Probation** is an alternative to a jail sentence for some convicted offenders. Under probation, a judge may suspend a convicted criminal's sentence and allow him or her to go free, provided he or she maintains good behavior and is supervised by a probation officer. Historians believe that Massachusetts was the first state to authorize probation. It did so in 1836.

Because of overcrowding in prisons, about one-third of all persons tried and convicted today are placed on

Just the Facts

The average cost of construction per prison cell ranges from $50,000 at a minimum-security site to $100,000 or more at a maximum-security facility.

Just the Facts

The first public execution in the American colonies took place on September 30, 1630, when John Dillington was hanged for murder.

Parole

When individuals are allowed to leave prison before the end of their sentences, they are said to be on **parole.** Historically, parole was used as a reward for good behavior. Today, however, parole may be used to reduce overcrowding in prisons. Parole differs from probation in that parole occurs after imprisonment, whereas probation occurs before or in place of imprisonment. Parole is often used in conjunction with indeterminate sentencing.

Parole, as we know it now, has existed only since the late 1800s, when Ohio, in 1884, became the first state to parole inmates of state prisons. Today, all states have parole as an option. In some states, however, particularly in some southern states, parole is used less often and is more difficult to obtain.

probation. Most individuals placed on probation are juveniles convicted in juvenile court.

There are many other alternatives to imprisonment. For example, a person convicted of a crime may be required to pay a fine, obtain treatment, or spend a certain number of hours each week, month, or year in community service.

Cruel and Unusual Punishment

The Eighth Amendment forbids cruel and unusual punishment. The authors of the Constitution were fearful of certain barbaric punishments such as tarring and feathering and whipping that had occurred during the colonial era.

The Supreme Court has found relatively few punishments to be cruel and unusual. In *Louisiana v. Resweber* (1947), the Court found that it was not unconstitutional to subject a convicted murderer to a second electrocution after the first attempt had failed.

FIGURE 6–1 The Death Penalty At the time the Constitution and Bill of Rights were written and ratified, the death penalty was widely accepted, and many offenses were punishable by death. Today, thirty-eight states impose the death penalty, and virtually all death sentences are for murder. Does your state have the death penalty?

States Imposing the Death Penalty	Method of Execution	States Imposing the Death Penalty	Method of Execution
Alabama	Electrocution	Nebraska	Electrocution
Arizona	Lethal injection or lethal gas	Nevada	Lethal injection
Arkansas	Lethal injection or electrocution	New Hampshire	Lethal injection or hanging
California	Lethal injection or lethal gas	New Jersey	Lethal injection
Colorado	Lethal injection or lethal gas	New Mexico	Lethal injection
Connecticut	Electrocution	New York	Lethal injection
Delaware	Lethal injection or hanging	North Carolina	Lethal injection or lethal gas
Florida	Electrocution	Ohio	Lethal injection or electrocution
Georgia	Electrocution	Oklahoma	Lethal injection
Idaho	Lethal injection	Oregon	Lethal injection
Illinois	Lethal injection	Pennsylvania	Lethal injection
Indiana	Electrocution	South Carolina	Electrocution
Kansas	Lethal injection	South Dakota	Lethal injection
Kentucky	Electrocution	Tennessee	Electrocution
Louisiana	Lethal injection	Texas	Lethal injection
Maryland	Lethal injection or lethal gas	Utah	Lethal injection or firing squad
Mississippi	Lethal injection or lethal gas	Virginia	Electrocution
Missouri	Lethal injection or lethal gas	Washington	Lethal injection or hanging
Montana	Lethal injection or hanging	Wyoming	Lethal injection or lethal gas

SOURCE: *The Book of the States, 1996–1997 Edition* (Lexington, Ky.: The Council of State Governments, 1996)

In *Rhodes v. Chapman* (1980), it found that putting two prisoners in a cell built for one is not cruel and unusual.

The Court has, however, found some punishments to be cruel and unusual. It struck down **denaturalization** (loss of citizenship) as a punishment for leaving the United States in order to avoid the military draft. It has also ruled that a prison inmate cannot be denied proper medical care.

The Death Penalty

One of the most disputed issues involving our criminal justice system has to do with capital punishment—the death penalty. The use of the death penalty in this country dates back to colonial days. At that time, a variety of crimes were punishable by death. Today, the use of the death penalty is largely limited to cases involving first-degree murder.

Supporters of the death penalty maintain that it serves as a deterrent to serious crime. In other words, those who support the death penalty believe that people are less likely to commit murder when they know that the crime is punishable by death. Opponents of the death penalty do not believe that it has any deterrent value. They feel that it constitutes a barbaric act in an otherwise civilized society.

In 1972, in *Furman v. Georgia*, the Supreme Court found that the death penalty was a cruel and unusual form of punishment (and thus unconstitutional) as it was then applied. At the time, it was applied mainly at judges' discretion—that is, the judge in a given case had the power to decide whether or not the death penalty would be imposed. Thirty-five states enacted laws they thought would satisfy the Court's objections. Some made the death penalty mandatory for certain crimes. Others set up a two-stage process with a separate hearing to decide on an appropriate sentence. The mandatory process was found to be unconstitutional, but the two-stage process was found to be constitutional. In 1976, in *Gregg v. Georgia*, the Court ruled that the "punishment of death does not invariably violate the Constitution." It ruled that a well-designed two-stage process could eliminate the possibility that the death penalty would be inflicted in an arbitrary or capricious manner.

The Court ruled on various cases involving the death penalty during the 1980s and 1990s. In essence, it has maintained that, if fairly applied, the death penalty is constitutional.

Today, thirty-eight states provide for the death penalty. (See Figure 6–1 for the methods of execution used by these states.) Recent public opinion polls demonstrate that a large majority of Americans favor using the death penalty more frequently. During the 1990s, increasing numbers of death-row inmates were executed. Figure 6–2 shows the year-by-year numbers of executions that have occurred during the last several decades. Those

Just the Facts

The Virginia Corrections Department decided to install air conditioning in its death chamber so that everybody would be "more comfortable."

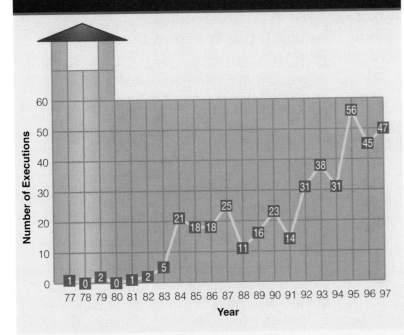

FIGURE 6–2 Executions from 1977 through 1997 Note the change in the number of annual executions from 1977 through 1997. What do you think accounts for the rising number of executions in recent decades?

SOURCE: Death Penalty Information Center, 1997.

Changes in Due Process

The way in which Americans obtain due process of law has changed substantially since the Constitution and the Bill of Rights were adopted in 1791.

THEN (IN 1791)	NOW
Due process guarantees in the national Constitution did not apply to state governments.	Due process guarantees in the national Constitution apply to state governments.
No exclusionary rule excluded the use at trial of evidence obtained illegally.	The exclusionary rule now excludes the use at trial of evidence obtained illegally.
No *Miranda* rules existed to inform persons being taken into custody of their constitutional rights.	*Miranda* rules require law enforcement personnel to inform persons being taken into custody of their constitutional rights.
The death penalty was used for many types of offenses.	The death penalty is used primarily for murder.

numbers may increase in the coming years, in part because of a recent federal law that limits the time period within which prisoners may appeal their cases to federal courts.

SECTION 4 REVIEW

1. What is plea bargaining? What arguments can be made for and against it?
2. What is the difference between determinate and indeterminate sentencing? Currently, which type of sentencing is more often used?
3. What is the difference between probation and parole?
4. **For Critical Analysis:** In your opinion, is the death penalty cruel and unusual punishment? Give reasons for your answer.

★ ★ ★ ★ **Chapter Summary** ★ ★ ★ ★

Section 1: Due Process of Law

- There are two due process clauses in the Constitution, one in the Fifth Amendment and one in the Fourteenth Amendment.
- Procedural due process means that the government must use fair methods when enforcing the law.
- Substantive due process means that the laws themselves must be fair and reasonable.

Section 2: Rights of the Accused: Searching and Wiretapping

- The Fourth Amendment protects persons from unreasonable searches and seizures.
- Police and the courts are required to have probable cause before making an arrest.
- Normally, police are required to have a search warrant before conducting a search. The exclusionary rule requires that any evidence obtained in an illegal search be excluded from trial.

The Rights of Criminal Suspects

Criminal procedures are no longer specialized rules known only to prosecutors, criminal defense attorneys, and judges. Indeed, in the last decade or so, American society has become well acquainted with how procedural requirements can affect the outcome of criminal proceedings. TV crime series and live coverage of criminal trials (such as O. J. Simpson's trial in 1994 and 1995) show us how difficult it is for criminal prosecutors to obtain evidence legally and to make sure that the evidence will be admissible in court.

Do criminal suspects have too many rights? This is an issue over which many Americans are at odds.

Criminal Suspects Have Too Many Rights, According to Some Americans

Many Americans believe that criminal suspects have too many rights. Among this group is a New York state trial court judge, Harold Rothwax. Rothwax contends that the *Miranda* requirements and court interpretations of the Fourth and Fifth Amendments have resulted in the "collapse of criminal justice" in this country. Even individuals who confess their guilt are allowed to go free if they can prove that law enforcement officers violated a procedural requirement, such as by failing to read a criminal suspect his or her *Miranda*

rights at the appropriate moment or obtaining evidence without a valid search warrant. Among other things, Rothwax proposes that the *Miranda* requirements be eliminated.

Others Maintain That the Rights of the Accused Should Not Be Lessened

Other Americans, while they may agree that criminal procedures do sometimes get in the way of criminal justice, emphasize that these procedures play a vital role in securing citizens' rights. Procedural requirements help to ensure that state prosecutors do not infringe on the constitutional rights of defendants, particularly the right to due process of law. After all, a criminal prosecution brings the force of the state, with all its resources, to bear against the individual. The *Miranda* requirements, the exclusionary rule, and other procedural rules are designed to safeguard the rights of individuals against the immense power of the state.

YOU DECIDE

1. If accused persons had fewer rights, how might that affect our society?
2. What might be the relationship between the rights of accused persons and the crime rate?

Section 3: Rights of the Accused: A Fair Trial

- 🌐 The Fifth Amendment protects persons against self-incrimination. The Sixth Amendment guarantees the right to legal counsel and trial by an impartial jury.
- 🌐 The Fifth Amendment protects persons against double jeopardy. The Sixth Amendment provides that the accused have the right to a speedy trial.
- 🌐 The Eighth Amendment provides that excessive bail shall not be required.

Section 4: Plea Bargaining and Sentencing

- ⭐ In a plea bargaining arrangement, the defendant agrees to plead guilty to a less serious charge in return for a less severe sentence.
- ⭐ A sentence may be imprisonment or an alternative. Prisoners may be released on parole before they have served their entire sentences.
- ⭐ The Eighth Amendment forbids cruel and unusual punishment, but the Supreme Court has found relatively few punishments to be cruel and unusual.

★ REVIEW QUESTIONS ★

1. What does "due process of law" mean?
2. What is procedural due process? What is substantive due process?
3. When may police conduct a lawful search without a warrant? What is probable cause?
4. Why is the exclusionary rule important? Are there any exceptions to the rule? If so, when do they apply?
5. What is self-incrimination?
6. What amendment provides that criminal defendants have a right to counsel (an attorney)?
7. Explain the impact of *Miranda v. Arizona* (1966).
8. Explain the concept of double jeopardy.
9. How do the right to trial by jury and the right to a speedy and public trial help ensure a fair trial?
10. What is a grand jury, and what is its function?
11. What is bail? Which amendment protects criminal defendants from excessive bail?
12. Describe the types of sentences that may be imposed on convicted persons.
13. What amendment protects persons against cruel and unusual punishment?
14. How many states allow the use of the death penalty?

★ CRITICAL THINKING ★

1. As you have learned in this chapter, the rights of criminal suspects have been expanded over time. How can this be, given that the Constitution and the Bill of Rights have remained unchanged?
2. Should people who either strongly support or strongly oppose the death penalty be excluded from the jury in a criminal case for which the punishment may be death? Discuss.

3. The Fifth Amendment protects individuals against double jeopardy. How, then, can you explain the fact that both the federal government and a state government may prosecute a person for the same crime?
4. Would justice be better served if more exceptions were made to the exclusionary rule? Would justice be better served if fewer exceptions were made to the rule?

★ IMPROVING YOUR SKILLS ★

Communication Skills

Forming an Opinion Throughout your life, you have been asked, "What do you think?" or "What is your opinion?" If the question is simple, such as "What is your favorite food?" then your answer is simple. But sometimes the question is more complex, and an opinion is difficult to form. In this case, it is better to form your opinion carefully rather than make a quick "snap judgment" that you may regret later.

An opinion is a belief based on what seems to be true or probable. A good opinion is one that is made with *reasoned* judgment. Making a reasoned judgment involves investigating all of the available facts, carefully exploring your own feelings, and forming an opinion based on those facts and feelings. Remember these two guidelines:

1. *Be sure that you use facts to form your opinion.* Facts are evidence that can be proved and that can be used to give your opinion more weight. Take the time to examine all of the evidence.
2. *Consider all sides of an issue with an open mind.* Do not reject the opinions of others without listening first to their reasons.

Writing Choose one of the Supreme Court cases discussed in this chapter and read the entire opinion written by the Court. The cases in this chapter are:

- *Young v. Harper*
- *Reno v. American Civil Liberties Union*
- *Mapp v. Ohio*
- *Gideon v. Wainwright*
- *Escobedo v. Illinois*
- *Miranda v. Arizona*
- *In re Gault*
- *Louisiana v. Resweber*
- *Rhodes v. Chapman*
- *Furman v. Georgia*
- *Gregg v. Georgia*

After you have finished your research, prepare a two-page, typewritten paper summarizing the facts of the case and explaining why the Court decided as it did. In your report, discuss the dissenting opinions as well as the Cout majority opinion. Remember that the dissenting opinion has great value, especially when the Court is divided or the issue is a controversial one. Include at least two quotations containing the Court's own words.

Social Studies Skills

Comparing and Contrasting
1. What is similar about *Gideon v. Wainwright* and *Miranda v. Arizona*?
2. How do these two cases differ?

★ ACTIVITIES AND PROJECTS ★

1. Invite a local police officer to speak to your class. Topics you might ask the officer to discuss include:
   (1) the *Miranda* warnings
   (2) the procedures followed when dealing with criminal suspects
   (3) the rules the police follow when obtaining and handling evidence
   (4) how the police work to protect the rights of individuals and of society in general
   (5) how often police officers are called to testify in court

2. Do some research on your local juvenile justice system. (Call your county courthouse to find out to whom you should talk to get information on this topic, or ask your teacher how to proceed.) Find out what rights and protections a minor is entitled to upon being accused of a crime. What procedures are followed in the prosecution of minors for crimes? Write a summary of what you have learned, and present it in class.

What If . . .

There Were No Exclusionary Rule?

Under the exclusionary rule, evidence obtained by illegal means (without a search warrant, for example) is not admissible at trial. What would happen if there were no exclusionary rule? Would the lack of such a rule substantially affect the rights of criminal defendants?

CHAPTER 7

Striving for Equality

CHAPTER OBJECTIVES

To learn about and understand . . .

⭐ The right to equal protection under the law

⭐ The struggle of African Americans for equal treatment

⭐ The welfare of other groups, including Hispanic Americans, Asian Americans, and Native Americans, with respect to civil rights

⭐ The laws that protect the rights of persons with disabilities

⭐ The historical struggle of women for voting rights and the extent of their political participation today

⭐ The origins and current status of affirmative action programs

> "*I have a dream that one day this nation will rise up and live out the true meaning of its creed: 'We hold these truths to be self-evident: that all men are created equal.'*"
>
> *Martin Luther King, Jr.*
> (1929–1968)
> Civil Rights Leader

INTRODUCTION

On August 28, 1963, Dr. Martin Luther King, Jr., delivered the powerful words quoted above before an audience of almost 250,000 in front of the Lincoln Memorial in Washington, D.C. His voice crossed the boundaries of color and religion that day, delivering the message that all Americans are entitled to equal treatment under the law.

The Fourteenth Amendment, added to the Constitution in 1868, guarantees equal treatment under the law for all persons. Yet, as you will read in this chapter, it was not until nearly a century later that the government took steps to enforce that right—through court decisions and congressional legislation. Even today, various groups in American society continue to struggle to obtain their right to equal protection under the law.

◀ Thousands of people across our nation march to celebrate the life of Martin Luther King, Jr., joining in spirit these citizens of Austin, Texas.

Equal Protection under the Law

Preview Questions:

- ⬤ What is the difference between civil liberties and civil rights?
- ⬤ What is the Fourteenth Amendment's equal protection clause?
- ⬤ What guidelines does the Supreme Court follow when deciding whether a law violates the equal protection clause?

Key Terms:

civil rights, equal protection clause, rational-basis test, suspect classification

Commonly, civil rights are lumped together with civil liberties, which we discussed in Chapters 5 and 6. In other words, many Americans use the terms to mean essentially the same thing. Some scholars, though, make a distinction between the two concepts. They point out that civil liberties are limitations on government action, setting forth what the government *cannot* do. Civil rights, in contrast, specify what the government *must* do to ensure equal protection. Generally, the term **civil rights** refers to the rights of all Americans to equal treatment under the law, as provided for by the Fourteenth Amendment's equal protection clause.

From the beginning of this nation, some groups have not been treated equally. The framers of the Constitution allowed the institution of slavery to continue, thus allowing the unequal treatment of African Americans to go on. The framers also treated other groups unequally. They refused to grant voting rights to women or to Native Americans. In fact, the only persons who were allowed to vote were property-owning white males. In later years, as people from around the globe continued to immigrate to this country, they, too, faced discrimination in one form or another. All of these groups have had to struggle to obtain equal treatment under the law. More recently, others in American society, such as persons with disabilities, have had to struggle to overcome discrimination.

Today, there are numerous minority groups in the United States, and over one hundred different languages

▲ "I have a dream . . ." Martin Luther King, Jr., delivers his famous address at the Lincoln Memorial in August 1963. What was the purpose of King's march on Washington?

are spoken in this country. It would be impossible, in one chapter, to examine the welfare of each and every one of these groups. We thus limit our coverage to a discussion of the welfare of the following large groups with respect to civil rights: African Americans, Hispanic Americans, Asian Americans, Native Americans, women, and persons with disabilities. We begin by examining the basis for our civil rights: the constitutional guarantee of equal protection under the law.

The Equal Protection Clause

Equal in importance to the due process clause of the Fourteenth Amendment is that amendment's **equal**

protection clause. The clause reads as follows: "No State shall . . . deny to any person within its jurisdiction the equal protection of the laws." Another significant clause in the Fourteenth Amendment states that "Congress shall have power to enforce, by appropriate legislation, the provisions of this article." This clause allows the national government to pass laws to enforce the right to equal protection.

The equal protection clause has been interpreted by the courts to mean that the government may not pass laws that discriminate *unreasonably* against a particular group or class of persons. The government can, however, pass laws that *reasonably* discriminate among groups of persons. That is, laws may apply to some groups but not others. Deciding whether a discriminatory law is reasonable or unreasonable is the task of the courts, and ultimately the Supreme Court.

Reasonable versus Unreasonable Discrimination

Over the years, the Supreme Court has developed at least three standards to use when deciding whether a discriminatory law is reasonable or unreasonable. In determining which of these standards apply to a particular case, the Court examines both the nature of the law involved and the nature of the individual rights affected by that law.

Ordinary Scrutiny The standard most often applied by the courts is called *ordinary scrutiny.* Ordinary scrutiny involves the **rational-basis test.** Under this test, a law that treats some persons differently than others will not violate the equal protection clause if the government can show that it had a rational basis for the law. For example, a law providing government benefits to persons with low incomes would probably be viewed as having a rational basis. In contrast, a law providing government benefits to people over six feet tall would not.

Strict Scrutiny When a law is based on a **suspect classification,** such as race or national origin, the rational-basis test is not enough. The law will be subject to a much stricter standard, called strict judicial scrutiny. Very few laws can survive this demanding standard. For example, a law that allows persons of one particular race, but not other races, to receive government benefits will be found unconstitutional.

Intermediate Scrutiny The courts apply a third standard, known as intermediate scrutiny, to laws that treat people differently. Generally, under this standard, a law will not violate the equal protection clause if the government can show that the law is *substantially related* to a legitimate government interest. For example, a legitimate government interest is to protect the safety of citizens. A law prohibiting persons over a certain age from piloting commercial aircraft would be substantially related to that government interest.

Equal Protection and Equality

From the beginning of this nation, equality has been a core American political value. The promise of equality was embedded in the Declaration of Independence's statement that all "men" are created equal. Although equality is a broadly shared political value in this country, there is disagreement over what equality means. Does it mean equality with respect to political rights, such as the right to vote and run for public office? Does it mean that all persons should have equal opportunities—in the job market, for example? Does it mean that all persons have a right to equality with respect to social and economic status? In any of these situations, what, exactly, is the government's responsibility? Clearly, these and similar questions concerning the nature of equality involve policy choices with ethical implications, particularly with respect to affirmative action—a topic explored later in this chapter.

The Constitution does not include the term *equality.* Rather, the Constitution, in the Fourteenth Amendment, speaks only of equal protection under the law. And equal protection under the law, although it may provide for equal opportunities, does not guarantee equal *outcomes.* Indeed, the framers of the Constitution did not envision a nation in which all people had equal social status or equal wealth. For example, in *Federalist Paper* No. 10, James Madison made a distinction between equality in political rights and equality in other respects:

> *Theoretic politicians . . . have erroneously supposed, that by reducing mankind to a perfect equality in their political rights, they would, at the same time, be perfectly equalized . . . in their possessions, their opinions, and their passions.*

Madison, as the above quote indicates, assumed that political equality does not necessarily result in social or economic equality. In *Federalist Paper* No. 10, he elaborates on this idea by stating that there is a "diversity in the faculties of men" that allows some people to be more successful than others in securing such things as property rights. In other words, individual skills and talents vary from one person to the other. Therefore, equal opportunity will result in some people being more successful than others economically and socially.

As you read through the remainder of this chapter, keep in mind that equality means different things to different people. Throughout our history, individual citizens and groups of citizens have challenged the courts on the issue of equality. When the rights of one group are upheld or reinforced, another group may feel that its rights are diminished or challenged. These issues of equality continue to the present and will undoubtedly continue into the future. You will find that conflicting ideas about civil rights often have to do with conflicting ideas about the meaning of equality.

SECTION 1 REVIEW

1. What is the difference between civil rights and civil liberties?
2. How does the equal protection clause of the Fourteenth Amendment relate to civil rights?
3. What standards do the courts use in deciding whether a discriminatory law violates the equal protection clause?
4. **For Critical Analysis:** State laws typically prohibit people under a certain age from purchasing alcoholic beverages or from voting. Clearly, such laws discriminate against a certain class of people—younger persons—yet they have not been held to violate the equal protection clause. Why is this?

SECTION 2

African Americans

Preview Questions:

- What are "Jim Crow" laws?
- What is the separate-but-equal doctrine, and when was it first used by the Supreme Court?
- Why was the Supreme Court's decision in *Brown v. Board of Education of Topeka* (1954) significant?
- What events led to the passage of the Civil Rights Act of 1964?

Key Terms:

separate-but-equal doctrine, *de jure* segregation, *de facto* segregation, busing, boycott, civil rights movement, civil disobedience

The equal protection clause was originally intended to protect the newly freed slaves after the Civil War. In the early years after the war, the U.S. government tried to protect the rights of black people living in the former states of the Confederacy. The Thirteenth Amendment, which had granted the slaves freedom, and the Fourteenth Amendment, which guaranteed equal protection under the law, were part of that effort. By the late 1870s, however, Southern legislatures began to pass laws intended to separate the white community from the black community. Such segregation laws were commonly called "Jim Crow" laws (from a song used in the nineteenth century in minstrel shows). Some of the most common Jim Crow laws involved the use of public facilities, such as schools and buses. They also affected housing, restaurants, hotels, and many other facilities.

The Separate-but-Equal Doctrine

In 1892, a group of Louisiana citizens decided to challenge a state law that required railroads to provide separate railway cars for African Americans. A black man named Homer Plessy boarded a train in New Orleans and sat in the railway car reserved for whites. When he refused to move, he was arrested and convicted of breaking the law.

Four years later, in 1896, the Supreme Court upheld the conviction and provided a constitutional basis for these segregation laws. In *Plessy v. Ferguson*, the Court held that the law did not violate the equal protection clause because *separate* facilities for black people were *equal* to those for white people. The lone dissenter, Justice John Harlan, insisted that "our Constitution is color blind, and neither knows nor tolerates classes among citizens." The majority opinion, however, established the **separate-but-equal doctrine.** This doctrine was used to justify segregation in many areas of American life for the next fifty years.

In the 1870s, southern legislatures began to pass laws designed to separate black and white Americans. Examine this drawing—the people, their positions, and the expressions on their faces. What do you think is happening here?

provided no separate law school for black students.

The major breakthrough, however, did not come until 1954. The case involved an African American girl who lived in Topeka, Kansas.

Departures from the Separate-but-Equal Doctrine

Beginning in the late 1930s, the Supreme Court gradually began to move away from the separate-but-equal doctrine. By 1950, the Court was taking the position that segregated facilities for black students at universities violated the equal protection clause. For example, in *McLaurin v. Oklahoma State Regents for Higher Education* (1950), a black student had been admitted to a doctoral program at the University of Oklahoma, but his admission was subject to certain conditions. He had to sit in a particular row in each classroom, sit at a certain table in the library, and eat at a special table in the cafeteria—all of which had been designated as "colored" areas. The Supreme Court held that these conditions deprived the student of his right to equal protection of the laws.

In another significant 1950 case, *Sweatt v. Painter*, a black student had been denied admission to the University of Texas Law School solely because of his race. At that time, no law school in Texas admitted blacks. The Supreme Court held that the equal protection clause required that the applicant be admitted to the law school. The Court concluded that "separate" was not "equal" in this situation, because the state

The *Brown* Decision and Its Aftermath

In the 1950s, schools in Topeka, Kansas, like those in many cities, were segregated. Mr. and Mrs. Oliver Brown wanted their daughter, Linda Carol Brown, to attend a white school a few blocks from their home instead of an all-black school that was twenty-one blocks away. With the help of lawyers from the National Association for the Advancement of Colored People (NAACP), Linda's family sued the Board of Education.

In *Brown v. Board of Education of Topeka* (1954), the Supreme Court reversed *Plessy v. Ferguson*. The Court unanimously held that segregation by race in public education is unconstitutional. Chief Justice Earl Warren wrote as follows:

Does segregation of children in public schools solely on the basis of race, even though the physical facilities and other tangible factors may be equal, deprive children of the minority groups of equal educational opportunities? We believe that it does. . . . [Segregation generates in children] a feeling of inferiority as to their status in the community that may affect their hearts and minds in a way unlikely ever to be undone. . . . In the field of education the doctrine of "separate but equal" has no place. Separate educational facilities are inherently unequal.

The Court ordered desegregation to begin "with all deliberate speed." The federal courts later took an active role in supervising the process.

▲ White students and adults hurl abuse at Elizabeth Eckford as she passes through the lines of National Guard troops during the first day of integration at Central High School in Little Rock, Arkansas.

▲ Forty years later . . . Elizabeth Eckford, left, one of the "Little Rock Nine," talks with Hazel Massery in front of Central High School in September 1997. Massery was one of the students heckling Eckford on the first day of school, as they were all captured in historic photos of the event.

Reactions to School Integration The Supreme Court ruling did not go unchallenged. Bureaucratic loopholes were used by the states to delay desegregation. Another reaction was "white flight." Many white parents sent their children to newly established private schools or moved to "white" suburbs. As a result, some public schools in the inner cities became 100 percent black. Governor Orval Faubus of Arkansas used the state's National Guard to block the integration of Central High School in Little Rock, Arkansas, in 1957. The action led to increasing violence in the area. The federal court demanded that the troops be withdrawn. President Dwight Eisenhower had to step in to stop the violence before Central High finally became integrated. Eisenhower federalized the Arkansas National Guard—that is, placed it in the service of the national government—and ordered the troops to keep the peace as integration went forward.

Just the Facts

In 1967, interracial marriage was still forbidden in seventeen states. Violators could be fined up to $1,000 and imprisoned for up to five years.

De Facto Segregation and Busing By 1970, school systems no longer practiced **de jure segregation**—segregation that is legally permitted. That is not to say that segregation had been eliminated. It meant only that no public school could legally identify itself as one serving only white students or only black students.

The process of achieving complete desegregation, in fact, is still underway. It will continue wherever **de facto segregation** exists—that is, wherever circumstances produce segregation even though no law requires it. Housing patterns are one of the major reasons for school segregation. In your community, for example, many members of a single ethnic group may live in a certain geographical area. This kind of pattern creates school districts that are largely all black or all Hispanic or all white.

Attempts to eliminate *de facto* segregation have included redrawing school district lines and reassigning pupils. Some public school systems have tried to

◄ Rosa Parks sits near the front of a city bus in Montgomery, Alabama. In 1955, Parks, who was a seamstress, refused to give up her seat on a city bus to a white person. Parks was arrested even though the Supreme Court had that day banned segregation in the city's public transit vehicles. What significant event in the civil rights movement occurred as a result?

achieve racial desegregation through **busing**—transporting students by bus to schools physically outside their neighborhoods. The Supreme Court first sanctioned busing in Charlotte, North Carolina, in 1971. Following this decision, the Court upheld busing in several Northern cities—Columbus, Ohio; Dayton, Ohio; and Denver, Colorado. In 1974, however, the Supreme Court rejected the idea of busing black children from the city to the suburbs and white children from the suburbs to the city. In 1976, the Court allowed the Norfolk, Virginia, public school system to end fifteen years of court-ordered busing of elementary schoolchildren.

Busing has been unpopular with many groups in both the white community and the black community. It is criticized for a number of reasons. It causes many parents and children to lose the convenience of neighborhood schools, and it forces children to endure long bus rides. Local governments often resent being told what to do by the federal courts. Some black parents have criticized busing because it disrupts their children's lives and because of the hostility of white students in the new schools. Some also resent the implication that black children can learn only if they sit next to white children. Others, however, have favored busing as a way of improving black children's education and career opportunities. They also believe that busing gives children of both races an opportunity to learn how to get along together.

The Civil Rights Movement

In 1955, one year after the *Brown* decision, an African American woman named Rosa Parks boarded a public bus in Montgomery, Alabama. When it became crowded, she refused to move to the "colored section" at the rear of the bus. She was arrested and fined for violating Alabama's segregation laws. Her arrest spurred the local African American community to organize a year-long boycott of the entire Montgomery bus system. A **boycott** occurs when many people agree to not buy or use a particular product or service. The protest was led by a twenty-seven-year-old Baptist minister, Dr. Martin Luther King, Jr. During the protest period, he was jailed, and his house was bombed. Despite the hostility and the overwhelming odds, the protesters were triumphant.

In 1956, a federal district court prohibited the segregation of public transit buses in Montgomery. The era

Just the Facts

In 1963, more than ten thousand demonstrations for racial equality were held.

Each of us has a set of values, whether or not we are consciously aware of what our values are. Our parents, our friends, our teachers, the books we read, and the movies and TV programs we watch all influence our values. Out of those values arise value judgments about everything we consider.

As a citizen, you must be able to examine issues, laws, court decisions, and the like. It is important to be aware of your values before you form an opinion. For example, if you are serving on a jury, your values may enter very strongly into your assessment of the testimony you hear. Be aware of how your religious beliefs and other personal convictions affect your views about what you hear and learn.

Biases are personal inclinations or preferences that may interfere with the ability to make impartial judgments. Biases and values are closely linked. Our biases result from our values, and they affect the choices and judgments we make. If you have a bias against a par-

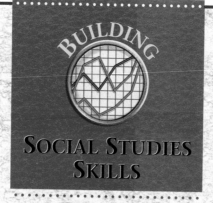

Identifying Your Values and Biases

ticular group of people, for example, you may resent a law favoring them even before you know anything about the law. If you have a bias against rich people or poor people, you may form an opinion about a court case concerning public-welfare payments before you know the facts of the case. It is important that you try to conquer your biases when looking at political issues. If you succeed, you will form a more objective picture of the arguments presented.

PRACTICING YOUR SKILLS

Read a magazine or newspaper article that concerns a civil rights issue, such as immigration, housing for the poor, equal pay for women, or busing in public schools. After you read the article, ask yourself the following questions:

- To which groups of people mentioned in the article do I automatically react positively? To which groups do I react negatively? Why do I respond that way?
- How do my past experiences with a person or persons from a particular group make me feel about that group as a whole?
- What have my parents and teachers taught me about relating to different groups of people?
- To what groups of people have I not been exposed? Do I understand these groups? How does this influence my opinion regarding their civil rights?

of the **civil rights movement,** the movement to end racial segregation, had begun. The movement was led by a number of diverse groups and individuals. Dr. Martin Luther King, Jr., and his Southern Christian Leadership Conference (SCLC) were among the leaders. Other groups, such as the Congress of Racial Equality (CORE) and the National Association for the Advancement of Colored People (NAACP), also sought to secure equal rights for African Americans.

Civil disobedience, which is the deliberate and public disobedience of laws thought to be unjust, was one tactic used to gain civil rights. For example, in 1960, in Greensboro, North Carolina, four African American students sat at the lunch counter at Woolworth's and ordered food. The store's policy was to serve only whites, and this policy was upheld by state segregation laws. The waitress refused to serve the four African Americans, but they refused to leave and were eventu-

ARCHITECTS

of Government

Martin Luther King, Jr. (1929–1968)

Martin Luther King, Jr., was the chief architect of the civil rights movement in the United States. A Baptist minister, King led numerous nonviolent marches, protests, and demonstrations for African American rights, including the historic civil rights march to Washington, D.C., in 1963. He was awarded the Nobel Peace Prize, at age 35, in 1964—he was the youngest person ever to receive this distinction. He was assassinated four years later in Memphis, Tennessee.

HIS WORDS

"[T]he goal of America is freedom. Abused and scorned tho' we may be, our destiny is tied up with America's destiny."

(Letter from jail in Birmingham, Alabama, April 1963)

"So let freedom ring . . . from every mountain side, let freedom ring . . . to speed up that day when all God's children, black men and white men, Jews and Gentiles, Protestants and Catholics, will be able to join hands and sing in the words of that old Negro spiritual, 'free at last, free at last. Thank God almighty, we are free at last!'"

(Speech, March on Washington, D.C., August 28, 1963)

DEVELOPING CRITICAL THINKING SKILLS

1. In the first quotation, why did King link the destiny of African Americans to the destiny of America?
2. In the second quotation, what did King mean when he talked about letting freedom ring?

ally arrested. Such nonviolent sit-ins, along with freedom marches, freedom rides, boycotts, lawsuits, and occasional violent confrontations, were all tactics used during the civil rights movement to create awareness of the plight of African Americans and to bring about change.

The Civil Rights Act of 1964

As the civil rights movement demonstrated its strength, Congress began to pass civil rights laws. The Civil Rights Act of 1964 was the most comprehensive of all the civil rights laws. It forbade specific forms of discrimination on the basis of race, color, national origin, religion, and gender. It also did the following:

- It outlawed discrimination in public places of accommodation, such as hotels, restaurants, snack bars, movie theaters, and public transportation.
- It cut off federal funds for any federal or state government project or facility that practiced any form of discrimination.
- It banned discrimination in employment.
- It outlawed arbitrary discrimination in voter registration.
- It authorized the federal government to sue to desegregate public schools and facilities.

SECTION 2 REVIEW

1. What was the separate-but-equal doctrine?
2. What was the Supreme Court's decision in *Brown v. Board of Education of Topeka*?
3. What is the difference between *de jure* and *de facto* segregation?
4. What is the Civil Rights Act of 1964, and how does it protect Americans against discrimination?
5. **For Critical Analysis:** How could the Supreme Court, in *Plessy v. Ferguson*, decide that separate-but-equal facilities for white and black Americans did not constitute discrimination? What changed between 1896, when the Court made that decision, and 1954, when the Court reversed itself? Why did the Court conclude, in 1954, that separate is never truly equal?

Other Groups, Other Demands

Preview Questions:

⊙ What are the major Hispanic groups in the United States?

⊙ How have immigrants from Japan, China, and other Asian nations fared in the United States?

⊙ How has U.S. government policy relating to Native Americans changed over the years?

Key Terms:

quotas, relocation camps, assimilation

In addition to African Americans, other racial and ethnic groups in American society have had to struggle for equal treatment. These groups include Hispanic Americans, Native Americans, and Asian Americans.

Hispanic Americans

Hispanic Americans, or Latinos, now make up the second-largest minority group in the United States, representing 10 percent of the U.S. population. If cur-

rent growth rates continue, this figure will rise to over 15 percent by the year 2030 (see Figure 7–1). It is expected that by the year 2050, Hispanic Americans will overtake African Americans as the nation's largest minority. Each year, the Hispanic population grows by 870,000 people. One-third of these people are newly arrived legal immigrants, most of them from Mexico.

Hispanic Groups To classify all Hispanic people in the United States as one minority group is misleading. Spanish-speaking individuals do not necessarily refer to themselves as Hispanic. Rather, they often identify themselves by their countries of origin. The largest Hispanic group consists of Mexican Americans, who constitute slightly over 60 percent of the Hispanic population living in America. Approximately 15 percent of Hispanic Americans are Puerto Ricans, and nearly 6 percent are Cuban Americans. Other, smaller groups consist of individuals who have fled from various Latin American countries for political reasons, hoping to find refuge in the United States.

Political Participation Taken as a group, Hispanic people in the United States have a comparatively low level of political participation. When we compare citizens of equal incomes and educational backgrounds, however, Hispanic citizens' participation rate is higher than average. For example, poor Hispanic Americans are more likely to vote than poor non-Hispanic whites. Given their increasing numbers, the electoral importance of Hispanic Americans cannot be denied. Their political power is, according to one observer, "a sleeping giant."

Hispanic Americans are already gaining power in some states. By the late 1990s, over 5 percent of the members of the state legislatures of Arizona, California, Colorado, Florida, New Mexico, and Texas were of Hispanic ancestry. Their numbers are also increasing in Congress. In the 1970s, five representatives in the U.S. Congress were Hispanic. In the 105th Congress (1997–1999), the number of Hispanic legislators was eighteen. President Bill Clinton appointed two Hispanic Americans to his cabinet, Henry Cisneros and Federico

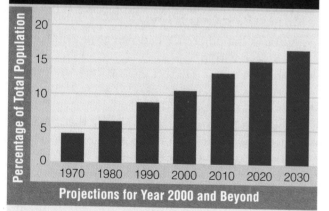

FIGURE 7–1 Hispanic Population, 1970–2030
This chart illustrates the growth of the Hispanic population in the United States. What groups of Americans fall into the broad category of Hispanic Americans?

Percentage of Total Population

Projections for Year 2000 and Beyond

SOURCE: Census Bureau; Bureau of Labor Statistics, 1997.

ARCHITECTS

of Government

César E. Chávez
(1927–1993)

César Chávez, a Mexican American, was an early labor organizer of Hispanic immigrants, most of whom worked in California vineyards and lettuce fields. In 1962, he organized farm workers into a labor union called the United Farm Workers. He started a five-year campaign against California grape growers to force them to recognize the union. In 1965, he launched a strike that led to a nationwide boycott of produce not bearing the seal of the United Farm Workers Union. Until the end of his life in 1993, Chávez continued his attempts to improve the welfare of farm workers in California.

HIS WORDS

"Our workers labor for many hours every day under the hot sun, often without safe drinking water or toilet facilities. Our workers are constantly subjected to incredible pressures and intimidation to meet excessive quotas. . . . When our workers complain, or try to organize, they are fired, assaulted, and even murdered."

(Speech, January 12, 1990)

"The stench of injustice in California should offend every American. Some people, especially those who just don't care, or don't understand, like to think that the government can take care of these problems. The government should, but won't."

(Speech, January 12, 1990)

DEVELOPING
CRITICAL THINKING SKILLS

1. Why would workers continue to work under the conditions described in the first quotation?
2. What did Chávez mean when he said, in the second quotation, "The government should, but won't."?

▲ *Hispanic Americans unite for their first major march in Washington, D.C., in October 1996. One man holds a Peruvian flag as tens of thousands of Hispanic Americans protest welfare and immigration reform legislation. Why would these issues be of concern to the Latino population?*

Peña, although Cisneros did not continue into Clinton's second term and Peña resigned in 1998.

Cuban Americans have been particularly successful in gaining political power at the local level, particularly in Dade County, Florida. Mexican Americans have also gained some power in local politics. Puerto Ricans have had fewer political successes, however. Generally, voting turnout by Puerto Ricans is low (only about 30 percent are registered to vote). Although they represent 10 percent of New York City's population, only a small percentage of that city's administrators are Puerto Rican.

Hispanic Americans conducted their first large public march on Washington (*La Marcha*) on Saturday, October 12, 1996. The rally was organized in an attempt to unify Hispanic groups so that they could more effectively combat recent anti-immigration efforts undertaken by national and local politicians.

Asian Americans

Because Asian Americans are seen as relatively successful economically, they are typically not thought of as being victims of discrimination. Yet they have suffered, at times severely, from discriminatory treatment. The Chinese Exclusion Act of 1882 prevented persons from China and Japan from coming to the United States to prospect for gold or to work on the railroads

▶ When Japan bombed Pearl Harbor on December 7, 1941, signaling America's entry into World War II, the sentiment against Japanese American citizens was strong, especially on the West Coast. Japanese Americans living in the western United States were sent to internment camps, such as this one in Puyallup, Washington.

or in factories in the West. After 1900, immigration continued to be restricted by **quotas.** Only limited numbers of persons from China and Japan were allowed into the United States. Those who were allowed into the country faced widespread racial prejudice. Many Americans had little respect for Chinese or Japanese customs and culture.

The courts could do little to prevent discrimination in the private sector against Chinese and Japanese immigrants. But when government officials discriminated against these groups, the equal protection clause came into play. For example, in *Yick Wo v. Hopkins* (1886), Yick Wo and about two hundred other Chinese laundry owners claimed that San Francisco's board of supervisors had discriminated against them. The board had refused to allow them to continue their laundry operations, but it had allowed eighty other laundries, which were not owned by Chinese persons, to continue operating. The Supreme Court squarely addressed the discriminatory nature of the board's action:

The fact of this discrimination is admitted. No reason for it is shown, and the conclusion cannot be resisted that no reason for it exists except hostility to the race and nationality to which the petitioners belong, and which, in the eye of the law, is not justified. The discrimination is therefore illegal, and . . . a denial of the equal protection of the law.

The Japanese bombing of Pearl Harbor in 1941, which launched America's entry into World War II, increased many Americans' concern about the Japanese. In 1942, President Franklin Roosevelt signed an executive order requiring the establishment of special **relocation camps** for virtually all Japanese Americans living in the United States. These Japanese Americans were required to dispose of their property, usually at below-market prices. They were subjected to a curfew and excluded from certain "military areas." Finally, they were ordered to report to assembly centers, from which they were transported to camps that came to be known as internment camps. The Supreme Court upheld these actions in *Hirabayashi v. United States* (1943) and *Korematsu v. United States* (1944). Finally in 1944 and 1945 the internment camps were closed after the Supreme Court ruled in late 1944 that the government's actions were illegal. In 1988, Congress provided funds to compensate former camp inhabitants and their survivors—$1.25 billion for 65,000 people.

Both Japanese Americans and Chinese Americans have overcome initial prejudice to lead America's ethnic groups with respect to income and education. Japanese and Chinese persons who moved to the United States after 1965 represent the most highly skilled immigrant group in American history. Of all Asian Americans in the United States, about 40 per-

◀ *These Vietnamese girls perform a traditional New Year's dance celebrating the Year of the Rat. Like many other ethnic groups living in the United States, these Vietnamese have tried to retain some of their traditional holidays and customs.*

cent of those over the age of twenty-five have college degrees.

New groups from Asia, particularly those from Southeast Asia, have also had to fight discrimination. More than a million Southeast Asian war refugees, most of them from Vietnam, have come into the United States in the last twenty-five years. Like their Chinese and Japanese predecessors, the newer Asian immigrants have quickly increased their median income. Only about one-third of all such households receive welfare assistance. Most have come with families and have been sponsored by American families or organizations, so they have had good support systems to help them get started.

Native Americans

Of all the groups that have suffered discriminatory treatment in the United States, Native Americans stand out because of the unique nature of their treatment. In the 1600s, there were about ten million Native Americans, or Indians, living in the New World. Today, fewer than two million people in the United States identify themselves as Native Americans. Most Native Americans live in Oklahoma, New Mexico, Arizona, and California. About half of them live on reservations.

In 1789, Congress designated the Native American tribes as foreign nations to enable the government to sign land and boundary treaties with them. As members of foreign nations, Native Americans had no U.S. citizenship rights. It was not until Congress passed the Citizenship Act of 1924 that citizenship rights were extended to all persons born in the United States, including Native Americans.

Early Policies toward Native Americans The Northwest Ordinance, passed by the Congress of the Confederation in 1787, stated that "the utmost good faith shall always be observed towards the Indians; their lands and property shall never be taken from them without their consent; and in their property, rights, and liberty, they shall never be invaded or disturbed, unless in just and lawful wars authorized by Congress." Over the next hundred years, many agreements were made with the Indian tribes. Many were also

Just the Facts

The number of North American Indian languages and dialects once exceeded two thousand.

▶ *As the white population expanded in the United States, Native Americans were forced from their lands. This painting shows the forced march of the Cherokees as they were moved to western lands over the "Trail of Tears." During this march, thousands of tribe members died. How did the government justify this action?*

broken—both by Congress and by individuals who wanted Indian lands for settlement or exploration.

In 1830, Congress instructed the Bureau of Indian Affairs (BIA) to remove all tribes to lands west of the Mississippi River in order to free lands east of the Mississippi for white settlement. (The BIA had been established in 1824 as part of the War Department.) Native Americans who refused to be "removed" to whatever lands were designated for them (reservations) were moved forcibly. During the resettlement of the Cherokee tribe in 1838 and 1839, on a forced march known as the "Trail of Tears," nearly four thousand out of fifteen thousand Cherokees died.

The government had been following a policy of separation. To prevent conflicts, boundaries had been set between lands occupied by Native Americans and lands occupied by whites. But as white settlers continued to push westward, beyond the Mississippi, it became clear that the policy of separation could no longer effectively separate Native Americans from whites. There simply wasn't enough room on the continent for both groups to have separate lands. Thus, in the late 1880s, the U.S. government changed its policy. The goal became the **assimilation** of Native Americans into American society. Each family was given acreage within the reservation to farm. The rest of the reservation land was sold to whites. The number of acres in reservation status was

reduced from 140 million to about 47 million. Tribes that refused to cooperate with this plan lost their reservations altogether. To further the goal of cultural assimilation, the BIA set up Native American boarding schools for the children to remove them from their parents' influence. In these schools, Native American children were taught how to speak the English language, instructed in the Christian religion, and encouraged to dress like white Americans.

Native Americans Strike Back Native Americans have always found it difficult to gain political power. In part, this is because the tribes are small and scattered. Also, many of their members do not live on the reservations, making organized political movements difficult. Today, they remain a fragmented political group. Nonetheless, by the 1960s, Native Americans were succeeding in forming organizations to strike back at the U.S. government and to reclaim their heritage, including their lands.

The first group to become identified with the new Native American movement was the National Indian Youth Council (NIYC). At the end of the 1960s, a small group of persons identifying themselves as Indians occupied Alcatraz Island, in San Francisco Bay, California, claiming that the island was part of their ancestral lands. In 1972, several hundred Native Americans marched to Washington and occupied the

▲ *Leaders of the American Indian Movement (AIM) confer with the Reverend Ralph Abernathy, a civil rights leader, at Wounded Knee, South Dakota. Why did the American Indian Movement choose this site for its demonstration?*

BIA. They arrived in a caravan labeled "The Trail of Broken Treaties." In 1973, supporters of the American Indian Movement (AIM) seized hostages at Wounded Knee, South Dakota. Wounded Knee had been the site of the massacre of at least 150 Sioux Indians by the U.S. Army in 1890. The goal of these demonstrations was to protest federal policy toward Native Americans and to dramatize the injustices they had suffered.

Compensation for Past Injustices As more people became aware of the concerns of Native Americans, Congress began to compensate them for past injustices. In 1990, Congress passed the Native American Languages Act. This act declared that Native American languages

are unique and serve an important role in maintaining Indian culture and continuity. Under the act, the government and the Indian community share responsibility for the survival of native languages and native cultures. Courts, too, have shown a greater willingness to recognize Native American treaty rights. For example, in 1985, the Supreme Court ruled that three tribes of Oneida Indians could claim damages for the use of tribal land that had been unlawfully transferred in 1795.

Native Americans have also begun to make some economic progress. In 1988, Congress passed the Indian Gaming Regulatory Act, which allows Native Americans to have profit-making gambling operations on their lands. Gambling on Native American property is now a multibillion-dollar industry, providing jobs and incomes for many tribes. In addition, many tribes have begun to develop other industries based on the land and mineral rights they hold.

SECTION 3 REVIEW

1. What is the largest Hispanic group in the United States? How have Hispanic Americans fared economically and politically?
2. What are some early examples of discrimination against Asian Americans?
3. Describe the policy of the U.S. government toward Native Americans. How has that policy changed in recent years?
4. **For Critical Analysis:** Why did it take so many years for Native Americans to begin organizing demonstrations to protest federal policies?

★ ★ ★ ★ ★ **SECTION 4** ★ ★ ★ ★ ★

Securing Rights for Persons with Disabilities

Preview Questions:

🌑 When did Congress first pass legislation protecting persons with disabilities?

🌑 What are the basic requirements of the Americans with Disabilities Act of 1990?

🌑 When must employers accommodate the needs of job applicants or employees with disabilities?

Key Terms:

disability, Equal Employment Opportunity Commission (EEOC)

Discrimination based on disability is a special form of discrimination. It crosses the boundaries of race, ethnicity, gender, religion, and age. Persons with

Most people have never had to try to enter a building in a wheelchair, only to find steps or a revolving door blocking the way. Most people have not experienced what it feels like to be prevented from entering an aisle or a fitting room or a rest room. Most people have never tried to enter a store without their sight. Most people have never been turned down for a job because of a disability. Yet more than forty million Americans do have some kind of disability, and their disabilities hinder their enjoyment of many of the privileges most of us take for granted every day.

Whether you have some type of disability, have a friend or relative who does, or are just concerned about the problems of disability, there are steps you can take as a responsible citizen. This may mean many things, from respecting handicapped parking spaces, to becoming familiar with laws passed to help people who have disabilities, to taking action in your own community.

Equal Access for *All* Individuals

What you do as a concerned citizen in your community may make a big difference in quite a few lives. Here are some suggestions for taking action if you find that those with disabilities are denied equal access to transportation, shopping, recreation, or employment in your community.

- Write a letter or call the mayor's office detailing your complaint.
- Write a letter to the editor of your newspaper. Encourage friends to write letters.
- Attend meetings at which decisions are being made by public agencies and private companies that would affect people with disabilities.
- Write a letter or make a personal visit to the manager of an inaccessible store and discuss the problem. Encourage others to write letters.
- Some cities publish booklets listing information about the accessibility of buildings in the city. Find out if your hometown has one. If not, organize a group of volunteers to compile one.
- If you, or someone you know, has been discriminated against by a place of employment, file a written complaint. If you are not satisfied by the response to your complaint, write to:

---

disabilities, especially physical deformities or severe mental impairments, have to face social bias against them simply because they are "different." Attitudes toward people who have disabilities have changed considerably in the last several decades. This group, however, continues to suffer from discrimination in all its forms.

In 1973, Congress passed the Rehabilitation Act—the first legislation protecting the rights of persons with disabilities. The act prohibited discrimination against people with disabilities in programs receiving federal aid. In 1975, Congress passed the Education for All Handicapped Children Act, which guarantees that all children with disabilities will receive a "free and appro-priate" public education. Further legislation in 1978 led to regulations requiring that ramps, elevators, and other accommodations be installed in all federal buildings. The Americans with Disabilities Act (ADA) of 1990, however, is by far the most significant legislation protecting the rights of this group of Americans.

The Americans with Disabilities Act of 1990

The ADA requires that all public buildings and public services be accessible to persons with disabilities. The act also requires that employers "reasonably

Two beachgoers fly a kite at the beach. Parking spaces for handicapped patrons, Braille on elevator buttons, sidewalk cutouts, and accessible bathrooms all came about as a result of efforts by activists for rights for persons with disabilities. What is the most significant federal law protecting persons with disabilities?

Office of Civil Rights
Department of Health and
Human Services
330 Independence Ave., SW
Washington, DC 20201

- Ask family members or friends to join in your campaign.
- Communicate your concerns to your state senators and representatives.

TAKING ACTION

1. Take a tour of a government building, and take notes regarding every feature designed to provide equal access for people who have disabilities. Report your findings to the class.
2. Make a list of five buildings in your community that

would provide barriers for any people who have special needs due to their disabilities. Devise a plan of action to remedy the problems.

accommodate" the needs of otherwise-qualified workers or job applicants who have disabilities, unless doing so would cause the employer to suffer an "undue hardship." The ADA defines the term **disability** as a physical or mental impairment that "substantially limits" a person's everyday activities. Health conditions that have been considered disabilities under federal law include blindness, alcoholism, heart disease, cancer, muscular dystrophy, cerebral palsy, paraplegia, diabetes, and acquired immune deficiency syndrome (AIDS). The ADA, however, does not require employers to hire or retain workers who, because of their disabilities, pose a "direct threat to the health or safety" of their co-workers.

Accommodating Workers with Disabilities

Few Americans today would object to laws protecting persons with disabilities from discrimination. Yet the Americans with Disabilities Act (ADA) of 1990 has presented problems for both employers and those employees who are protected by the act.

Employers are often at odds with employees with disabilities who seek accommodation. They are also often at odds with the courts, whose decisions remain somewhat unpredictable because there are few precedents to guide them. For example, many employers have been held liable under the ADA simply because

► *A guide dog accompanies a blind employee to work at her office at Southern California Edison, a power company.*

they asked the wrong questions when interviewing job applicants with disabilities. The **Equal Employment Opportunity Commission (EEOC),** which administers federal laws prohibiting employment discrimination, has specific guidelines indicating the kinds of questions that employers may—and may not—ask job applicants who have disabilities. Often, the line between a permissible question and an impermissible question is a fine one, indeed. For example, an employer may ask a job applicant, "Can you do the job?" But the employer may not ask, "How would you do the job?" without facing potential liability for violating the ADA.

An employer cannot require a prospective employee to take a medical examination before being offered a job. The employer can, however, condition the job offer on passing a medical examination, but only if all employees for that job category have to take the same exam. The results of all medical examinations must be kept confidential and must be maintained in separate medical files, not the employee's personnel file.

Many employers have also been held liable under the ADA because they concluded, mistakenly, that job applicants or employees with disabilities were not otherwise qualified to perform the jobs in question or that it would constitute an undue hardship to accommodate their needs. For example, in one case, a federal employee

was qualified as being disabled under the ADA because he had frequent bouts of severe depression. His medication caused drowsiness, and he routinely fell asleep on the job. The employer assumed that it would cause undue hardship to accommodate the worker's on-the-job naps. A federal appellate court, however, held that the government "may presumably require its employees to stay awake as a matter of decorum. But that is not necessarily to say that an occasional nap would make any federal employee unfit."

Persons with disabilities sometimes find it difficult to pursue suits for disability-based discrimination. Under most federal laws protecting against employment discrimination, persons covered by the laws have little difficulty establishing the fact that they are members of the protected classes. For example, a woman claiming that she has been discriminated against on the basis of gender does not have to establish the fact that she is a woman. In contrast, a person with a disability, before coming under the protection of the ADA, must prove that he or she does, in fact, have a disability. Additionally, the person must demonstrate that he or she was otherwise qualified for the job in question. Finally, the person must show that the employer refused to employ him or her solely because of the disability. Each of these three requirements may be difficult to meet.

1. Summarize the major federal laws that protect people with disabilities.
2. Under the Americans with Disabilities Act (ADA) of 1990, what is a disability? Give some examples of health conditions that have been considered disabilities under federal law.
3. Why do employers find it difficult to comply with the requirements of the ADA?
4. What are some of the obstacles that must be overcome by those who bring lawsuits for disability-based discrimination?
5. **For Critical Analysis:** Do you think that the Americans with Disabilities Act has gone too far in protecting the needs of job applicants and employees with disabilities? Has it gone far enough?

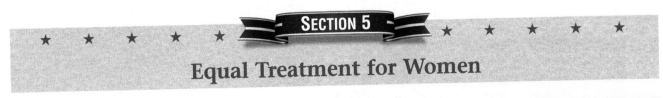

SECTION 5

Equal Treatment for Women

Preview Questions:

⭐ When and where was the first women's rights convention held in this country?

⭐ What amendment to the Constitution gave women the right to vote? When was this amendment ratified?

Key Term:

suffrage

In 1776, Abigail Adams wrote to her husband, John Adams, the following words, anticipating that new laws would probably be necessary if a Declaration of Independence was issued:

> *I desire you would remember the ladies. . . . If particular care and attention is not paid to the ladies, we are determined to foment a rebellion and will not hold ourselves bound by any laws in which we have no voice or representation.*

Despite this request, women, although considered citizens in the early years of the nation, had no political rights. Of course, neither did women in other countries—but America was different. Americans were not bound as tightly to age-old traditions and laws that allowed only men to participate fully in the political arena. In fact, in the New World "frontier," women had assumed far more responsibilities than their European counterparts. And during the Revolutionary era, women had played a significant political role, particularly in organizing boycotts against British imports and making substitute goods.

In this context, Abigail Adams's request is not all that surprising. The failure of the framers of the Constitution to give women political rights was viewed by many early Americans as an act of betrayal. Not only did the Constitution betray the Declaration of Independence's promise of equality; it also betrayed the women who had contributed to the making of that independence during the Revolutionary War. Nonetheless, it was not until the 1840s that women's rights groups began to form.

Just the Facts

A carved statue of Susan B. Anthony, Lucretia Mott, and Elizabeth Cady Stanton stayed in the downstairs storeroom of Congress for three-fourths of a century. Now it is in the sunlight of the Capitol Rotunda.

The Struggle for Voting Rights

In 1848, Lucretia Mott and Elizabeth Cady Stanton organized the first women's rights convention, held in Seneca Falls, New York. The three hundred people who attended approved a Declaration of Sentiments: "We hold these truths to be self-evident: that all men *and women* are created equal." In the following years, other women's groups held conventions in various cities in the Midwest and the East. With the outbreak of the Civil War, though, women's rights advocates focused on supporting the war effort.

The Political Participation of Women in Europe

The figure below shows the percentage of women in parliament and in government in various countries. As you can see, women's political participation in some European nations is quite high.

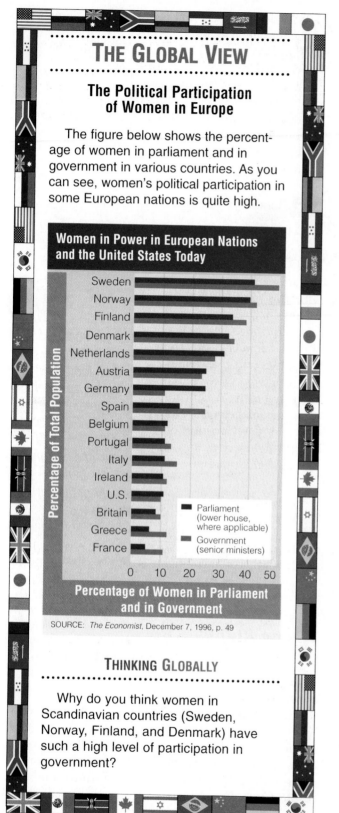

Women in Power in European Nations and the United States Today

Percentage of Total Population

Sweden
Norway
Finland
Denmark
Netherlands
Austria
Germany
Spain
Belgium
Portugal
Italy
Ireland
U.S.
Britain
Greece
France

■ Parliament (lower house, where applicable)
■ Government (senior ministers)

0 10 20 30 40 50

Percentage of Women in Parliament and in Government

SOURCE: *The Economist*, December 7, 1996, p. 49

THINKING GLOBALLY

Why do you think women in Scandinavian countries (Sweden, Norway, Finland, and Denmark) have such a high level of participation in government?

FIGURE 7–2   Years, by Country, in Which Women Gained the Right to Vote

Year	Country	Year	Country
1893	New Zealand	1945	Italy
1902	Australia	1945	Japan
1913	Norway	1947	Argentina
1918	Britain	1950	India
1918	Canada	1952	Greece
1919	Germany	1953	Mexico
1920	United States	1956	Egypt
1930	South Africa	1963	Kenya
1932	Brazil	1971	Switzerland
1944	France	1984	Yemen

The movement for political rights again gained momentum in the late 1860s. Women's **suffrage**—the right of women to vote—became a major goal. Two organizations were formed to work toward this goal. The National Woman Suffrage Association, headed by Susan B. Anthony and Elizabeth Cady Stanton, considered suffrage to be only one step on the road toward greater social and political equality for women. In contrast, the American Woman Suffrage Association, founded by Lucy Stone and other women, considered the right to vote its only goal.

By 1890, the two organizations had joined forces. The resulting organization, the National American Woman Suffrage Association, focused solely on one goal—gaining for women the right to vote. When little progress was made, small, radical splinter groups took to the streets. There were parades, hunger strikes, arrests, and jailings. Finally, in 1920, seventy-two years after the Seneca Falls convention, the Nineteenth Amendment to the Constitution was passed: "The right of citizens of the United States to vote shall not be denied or abridged by the United States or by any State on account of sex." Although it may seem that the United States was slow to give women the vote, it was really not too far behind the rest of the world (see Figure 7–2).

Women in American Politics Today

More than ten thousand individuals have served in the U.S. House of Representatives. Only 1 percent of

◀ "Votes for Women!" was the rallying cry of the women's suffrage movement. These "suffragettes" marching in 1912 paved the way for the ratification of the Nineteenth Amendment in 1920, which gave women the right to vote.

them have been women. No woman has yet held a major leadership position in either the House or the Senate. Women continue to face a "men's club" atmosphere in Congress, although elections during the 1990s brought more women to Congress than ever before. Following the national elections in 1996, 49 of the 435 members of the House of Representatives and 9 of the 100 members of the Senate were women. Considering that there are 97.1 million eligible women voters, compared with 88.6 million eligible male voters, women are vastly underrepresented in the U.S. Congress.

The same can be said for women presidential appointments to federal offices. Franklin Roosevelt appointed the first woman to a cabinet post—Frances

◀ Female members of the House of Representatives march to the Senate side of Capitol Hill in a show of gender solidarity after female senators voted against allowing Admiral Frank Kelso to retire at the four-star rank. Admiral Kelso was held ultimately responsible for the "Tailhook" scandal, in which women were harassed by naval officers.

Perkins, who was secretary of labor from 1933 to 1945. Jimmy Carter (1977–1981) named three women to his cabinet and appointed many female judges. Ronald Reagan (1981–1989) also appointed women to two major cabinet posts and to head the U.S. delegation to the United Nations. He also appointed the first woman ever to sit on the Supreme Court, Sandra Day O'Connor. George Bush (1989–1993) appointed two women to cabinet posts, and a woman served as his international trade negotiator. President Bill Clinton appointed three women to cabinet posts in his first term and appointed Ruth Bader Ginsburg to the Supreme Court. In his second term, he appointed a woman, Madeleine Albright, to be secretary of state, the first woman to hold this position.

SECTION 5 REVIEW

1. What convention marks the beginning of the movement for women's suffrage in the United States?
2. When and how were women given the right to vote?
3. Give some examples of political offices held by women today.
4. **For Critical Analysis:** Why was the original Constitution silent on the issue of women's suffrage?

SECTION 6

Beyond Equal Protection

Preview Questions:

⭐ What is equal employment opportunity?
⭐ What is affirmative action?
⭐ What are the arguments for and against affirmative action?
⭐ How does the Constitution allow for laws that treat men and women differently?

Key Terms:

equal employment opportunity (EEO), affirmative action, reverse discrimination

Part of the Civil Rights Act of 1964 prohibited discrimination in employment. In connection with this part of the act, the government launched efforts to ensure **equal employment opportunity (EEO).** Under EEO guidelines, employers were required to make sure that their hiring and promotion practices guaranteed the same opportunities to all individuals, regardless of race, color, national origin, religion, or gender.

Experience soon showed, however, that members of certain groups were still excluded from many jobs and promotions. Because they had often had less opportunity for education and relevant work experience than white males, they were not as well qualified. Because of this problem, a new strategy was developed. This strategy, initiated by President Lyndon Johnson, involved the concept of *affirmative action*. Over the years, affirmative action has caused a great deal of controversy— a controversy that continues today.

Affirmative Action

Affirmative action can be defined as remedial steps taken to improve work opportunities for persons considered to have been deprived of job opportunities in the past on the basis of race, color, national origin, religion, or gender. The idea is that even though new laws make discrimination illegal, they cannot make up for the consequences of discriminatory practices of the past.

Affirmative action programs require employers to take positive steps to remedy *past* discrimination. This means that preference in jobs and college admissions may be given to members of groups that have been discriminated against in the past. All public and private employers who receive federal funds have been required to adopt and implement these programs. Thus, the policy of affirmative action has been applied to all agencies of the federal, state, and local governments and to all private employers who sell goods or services to any agency of the federal government. In short, it covers nearly all the nation's major employers and many of its smaller ones.

Affirmative Action Is Tested The Supreme Court's first major affirmative action case was *Regents of the University of California v. Bakke* (1978). Allan Bakke, a white male, had been denied admission to the university's medical school at Davis. The school set aside sixteen of the one hundred seats in each year's entering class for nonwhite students. A specific number of positions set aside in this way is known as a quota. In filling the quota, the school had admitted several nonwhites who were less qualified than Bakke. He charged the university with **reverse discrimination—** discrimination against whites.

The Supreme Court was divided on the case. In a five-to-four decision, the Court held that Bakke had been denied equal protection and should be admitted. The majority on the Court said that the Constitution does not allow race to be used as the *only* factor in making affirmative action decisions. The majority also said, however, that both the Constitution and the Civil Rights Act of 1964 do allow its use as *one among several* factors in such situations.

One year later, a major test of affirmative action programs in private employment came in *United Steelworkers of America v. Weber* (1979). The company had created training programs and had reserved half the positions for members of minority groups. On three occasions, Brian Weber, a white

◄ Allan Bakke sued the regents of the University of California for "reverse discrimination" after being denied entry to the medical school at UC Davis. Did the Supreme Court overturn the doctrine of affirmative action as a result of this case?

How Civil Rights Have Changed

In the past half century, particularly as a result of legislation in the 1960s, there have been many changes in civil rights in the United States. Here are some of them.

THEN (ABOUT 1950)	NOW
There were no affirmative action programs to give preferences in hiring and college admissions decisions to groups that were discriminated against in the past.	Affirmative action programs exist, but they are under attack.
Little protection was provided to prevent discrimination against minorities and women.	Federal laws prohibit discrimination based on race, color, national origin, religion, gender, age, and disability.
There were no equal employment opportunity guarantees for minorities and women.	Equal employment opportunity is required by law.
Few civil and political rights were guaranteed for minority groups.	Equal rights for minority groups are mandated by federal laws.
Segregation in public schools was legal.	Segregation in public schools cannot be required by law; some *de facto* segregation continues to exist.

worker, was not selected for the training even though he had more seniority than several of the African American employees chosen. The Supreme Court upheld the company's affirmative action program. The Court ruled that such programs did not violate the Civil Rights Act of 1964.

Rejecting Some Affirmative Action In the late 1980s, the Supreme Court issued a series of rulings that rejected some affirmative action programs. In *Richmond v. Croson Co.* (1989), for example, the Court rejected a minority set-aside program for city government contracts in Richmond, Virginia. The city had provided that any company awarded a construction contract by the city had to subcontract, or set aside, at least 30 per-

cent of the work for minority businesses. The Court ruled that the set-aside program denied white contractors their Fourteenth Amendment right to equal protection. In several subsequent cases, the Supreme Court rejected other affirmative action programs.

In response to these decisions, courts across the country began reopening old civil rights cases and allowing white men to challenge the hiring and promotion of members of minority groups under court decrees issued up to twenty years earlier. In response, civil rights activists pressured Congress to take action to protect discrimination victims from the Supreme Court's recent rulings. The result was the Civil Rights Act of 1991, which effectively overturned the rulings and made it easier for workers to sue their employers.

Government in Action

California Bans Affirmative Action

On November 5, 1996, the citizens of California voted in favor of a civil rights initiative to amend their state constitution. That initiative, which appeared on the ballot as Proposition 209, read in part as follows:

The state shall not discriminate against, or grant preferential treatment to, any individual or group on the basis of race, sex, color, ethnicity, or national origin in the operation of public employment, public education, or public contracting.

The ink was barely dry on the new state constitutional amendment when several groups and individuals filed a lawsuit in a federal court to prevent the amendment from being enforced. These groups claimed that the law was unconstitutional because, among other things, it denied to racial minorities and women the equal protection of the laws guaranteed by the Fourteenth Amendment. The federal judge granted the groups' request for a temporary restraining order—which meant that the law could not be enforced until further proceedings. On appeal, however, the federal appellate court reversed the lower court's decision, and the Supreme Court refused to hear the case. In effect, this means that state-sponsored affirmative action programs are now illegal in California.

In 1997, the leader of the movement to pass Proposition 209, Ward Connerly, launched the American Civil Rights Institute. Its purpose is to lobby for federal legislation to ban affirmative action and to help gain support for measures similar to Proposition 209 that are on other states' ballots. Soon after the organization was started, a dozen states, including Colorado, Florida, Oregon, and Washington, asked Connerly for help in putting anti–affirmative action propositions on their ballots.

THINK ABOUT IT

1. Those who challenged the constitutionality of California's Proposition 209 claimed that it would deny to racial minorities and women the equal protection of the law. What arguments could you make to support this claim? What arguments could you make against it?

2. "Affirmative action is not a workable solution to discrimination because affirmative action itself involves discrimination—against majority groups, particularly white males." Do you agree with this statement? Why or why not?

The act also broadened the remedies available for employment discrimination. The act did *not*, however, decide on the constitutionality of affirmative action programs. That is the Supreme Court's job.

The End of Affirmative Action?

Since the passage of the Civil Rights Act of 1991, the courts seem to have gone even further in questioning the constitutional validity of affirmative action.

In 1995, the Supreme Court issued a landmark decision in *Adarand Constructors, Inc. v. Peña*. The Court held that any federal, state, or local affirmative action program that uses racial or ethnic classifications as the basis for making decisions is subject to strict scrutiny by the courts. This means that, to be constitutional, a discriminatory law or action can be justified only by a *compelling* government interest.

As mentioned earlier in this chapter, the strict scrutiny standard is difficult to meet. Some doubted,

THAT FIRST STEP WAS THE HARDEST

EQUALITY

JOBS

HOUSING

SOUTHERN
INTEGRATION

SCHOOLS

▲ *What is the irony of the title of this political cartoon, "That First Step Was the Hardest"?*

in a 1996 case, *Hopwood v. State of Texas*, two white law school applicants sued the University of Texas School of Law in Austin, claiming that they had been denied admission because of the school's affirmative action program. The program allowed admissions officials to take racial and other factors into consideration when determining which students would be admitted. A federal court held that the program violated the equal protection clause because it discriminated in favor of minority applicants. In its decision, the court directly challenged the *Bakke* decision by stating that the use of race even as a means of achieving diversity on college campuses "undercuts the Fourteenth Amendment." In other words, race could never be a factor in such decisions, even if it was not the sole factor. The Supreme Court declined to hear the case, thus letting the lower court's decision stand.

▲ *The backlash to affirmative action has been felt in different ways and to different degrees throughout the nation. The Supreme Court let stand a ruling that struck down the law school's affirmative action admissions plan at this University of Texas campus in Austin.*

after the Court's *Adarand* decision, whether any affirmative action would survive strict scrutiny. Justice Sandra Day O'Connor tried to ease these doubts by stating in the *Adarand* opinion that the government "is not disqualified from acting in response to . . . the unhappy persistence of both the practice and the lingering effects of racial discrimination." In effect, though, the *Adarand* decision severely narrowed the application of affirmative action programs. An affirmative action program can no longer make use of quotas or preferences for unqualified persons and cannot be maintained simply to remedy past discrimination by society in general. It must be narrowly tailored to remedy actual discrimination that has occurred. Once the program has succeeded, it must be changed or dropped.

Lower courts have followed the Supreme Court's lead—and some have even gone further. For example,

Affirmative Action

Since the passage of the Civil Rights Act of 1964, the federal government and some state and local governments have applied the concept of affirmative action to areas such as employment, college admissions, and the awarding of government contracts. Behind the idea of affirmative action is the assumption that society should make a special effort to counter the effects of past discrimination by giving preferences to members of certain groups. Today, affirmative action is supported by some but opposed by others.

Affirmative Action Has Run Its Course, According to Some

Opponents of affirmative action argue that it gives different groups different legal rights. Therefore, it violates the equal protection clause of the Constitution. When employment and college admission policies are based on preferences rather than merit, all of society suffers, according to these people.

Critics of affirmative action stress that racial and gender preferences do not necessarily equate to more power for members of racial minorities and women in general. Well-qualified women and members of racial minorities may actually suffer because of affirmative action preferences. Why? Because, once they are on the job or in the classroom, others will tend to put them in the same classification as less qualified persons who were hired or admitted simply to fill the requirements of affirmative action programs. In other words, the more highly qualified women and members of racial minorities will not get credit for their personal qualifications.

Opponents of affirmative action also claim that it has not worked. Black male college graduates still earn less than their white counterparts, for example, and the gap has increased since 1980. Racial and gender bias continues to exist in

society. This is a social problem that government cannot handle.

Others Believe That Affirmative Action Is Still Justified

Others believe that affirmative action programs are still necessary to combat the effects of past discrimination. Minorities and women have made great strides in both education and the workforce in the last thirty years. In part, this is because of the effectiveness of affirmative action programs.

Proponents of affirmative action acknowledge that racial and gender bias still exists. But they claim that this is not a reason to abandon affirmative action. Rather, it is a reason to continue it. If affirmative action were eliminated, we would destroy everything that has been accomplished in the last several decades. We would never attain the goal of equal opportunity. Thus, we must continue to require government agencies, employers, and college administrators to give preferences to minority applicants and to women. When certain law schools were required to eliminate affirmative action programs, the percentage of African Americans and Hispanics in the entering classes dropped dramatically. This should not be happening.

To be sure, affirmative action programs should be redesigned to minimize unwanted side effects. But they should not be eliminated.

YOU DECIDE

1. How is it possible that well-qualified women and members of minority groups might suffer because of affirmative action preferences?
2. If the government, through affirmative action, cannot end racial and gender bias in America, who can?

► *These young people, who are celebrating a school victory, represent the multicultural diversity of our schools and of our nation. How might these students be affected in the future by changes in current affirmative action programs?*

Affirmative action programs face other threats as well. In 1996, state-sponsored affirmative action programs were entirely banned in California. (See the *Government in Action* feature on page 195.) Other states may follow suit. The era of affirmative action, according to some observers, may be ending.

Court decisions and California's Proposition 209 reflect the growing backlash across the country against affirmative action. In part, criticism of affirmative action programs stems from the immense cost of these programs—primarily administrative expenses—to both the government and private businesses. Additionally, as America becomes more culturally diverse, affirmative action programs that give preferences to specific minorities discriminate against other minorities. As a result, they may defeat the purpose of affirmative action.

SECTION 6 REVIEW

1. What are affirmative action programs?
2. What is reverse discrimination?
3. **For Critical Analysis:** Do affirmative action programs help or hinder efforts to achieve equal employment opportunity?

★ ★ ★ ★ **Chapter Summary** ★ ★ ★ ★

Section 1: Equal Protection under the Law

🌑 The basis for civil rights laws is the Fourteenth Amendment to the U.S. Constitution. The Fourteenth Amendment provides that all persons are entitled to the equal protection of the laws and that Congress has the power to enforce the amendment's provisions.

🌑 The equal protection clause has been interpreted by the courts to mean that the government may not pass laws that discriminate unreasonably against a particular group of persons.

Section 2: African Americans

🌑 Although the Fourteenth Amendment was ratified in 1868, African Americans were denied equal treatment as a result of segregation laws passed by the southern states. Segregation laws were upheld by the Supreme Court in *Plessy v. Ferguson* (1896), in which the Court established the separate-but-equal doctrine.

🌑 In *Brown v. Board of Education of Topeka* (1954), the Supreme Court held that racial segregation in the public schools was unconstitutional.

🌑 The civil rights movement began in the mid-1950s under the leadership of Martin Luther King, Jr. The movement used a variety of nonviolent techniques to focus the country's attention on the plight of African Americans.

⭐ The Civil Rights Act of 1964 prohibited discrimination based on race, color, national origin, religion, or gender.

Section 3: Other Groups, Other Demands

⭐ It is expected that by the year 2050, Hispanic Americans will become the nation's largest minority group. Hispanic Americans are gaining political power in several states.

⭐ Japanese Americans and Chinese Americans lead America's ethnic groups in terms of income and education. Asian Americans have suffered from discriminatory treatment, however.

⭐ Native Americans stand out among groups that have suffered discriminatory treatment in this country because of the unique nature of their treatment. Only in recent years have Congress and the courts begun to compensate Native Americans for past injustices and to recognize their claims to tribal lands.

Section 4: Securing Rights for Persons with Disabilities

⭐ Federal laws protecting people who have disabilities include the Rehabilitation Act of 1973, the Education for All Handicapped Children Act of 1975, and the Americans with Disabilities Act (ADA) of 1990.

⭐ The ADA requires that all public buildings and services be accessible to persons with disabilities and that employers "reasonably accommodate" the needs of otherwise-qualified workers or job applicants who have disabilities.

Section 5: Equal Treatment for Women

⭐ In 1848, Lucretia Mott and Elizabeth Cady Stanton organized the first women's rights convention, held in Seneca Falls, New York.

⭐ By the 1890s, the two major women's organizations in the United States had joined to become the National American Woman Suffrage Association. Its sole goal was gaining the right to vote for women.

⭐ In 1920, with the ratification of the Nineteenth Amendment, women gained the right to vote.

⭐ Although more women hold political office today than ever before, women are still vastly underrepresented in government.

Section 6: Beyond Equal Protection

⭐ Affirmative action programs attempt to make up for past discrimination against certain groups by giving preference to members of those groups.

⭐ In *Regents of the University of California v. Bakke* (1978), the Supreme Court held that affirmative action programs did not violate the equal protection clause of the Fourteenth Amendment so long as race was not the only factor used when making affirmative action decisions.

⭐ In the late 1980s, the Supreme Court issued a series of decisions holding various affirmative action programs unconstitutional. Congress countered by passing the Civil Rights Act of 1991, which overturned the Court's decisions.

⭐ In the 1990s, there has been a backlash against affirmative action, reflected both in court decisions and in California's Proposition 209, which banned state-sponsored affirmative action in that state.

★ REVIEW QUESTIONS ★

1. What is the constitutional basis for civil rights laws?
2. How do the courts decide whether discriminatory laws are reasonable or unreasonable?
3. What are Jim Crow laws? When and where were they enacted?
4. What is the separate-but-equal doctrine? When was this doctrine established?
5. Explain the significance of the Supreme Court's decision in *Brown v. Board of Education of Topeka* (1954).
6. What was the civil rights movement, and when did it begin?
7. Identify the most comprehensive of the civil rights laws passed during the 1960s. What were some of the provisions of this law?
8. African Americans are the nation's largest minority group. What is the second-largest minority group?
9. Describe some of the types of discrimination that Asian Americans have experienced.
10. When were the first Native American political organizations formed? How has federal policy toward Native Americans changed in recent years?
11. What federal laws protect persons with disabilities?
12. Name three significant leaders of the women's rights movement in the United States. When did women gain the right to vote?
13. What is affirmative action? For what purpose were affirmative action programs initiated?
14. In what case did the Supreme Court first uphold the constitutionality of affirmative action programs? In what case did the Court decide that such programs should be subject to strict scrutiny?
15. What did California's Proposition 209 call for? What was its effect?

★ CRITICAL THINKING ★

1. Can laws that treat men and women differently ever be justified?
2. Is it possible to eliminate *de facto* segregation?
3. Should parents be prohibited from sending their children to all-black schools, all-Hispanic schools, and so on, even though the parents wish to do so?
4. This chapter stated that women are "vastly underrepresented" in Congress. Does this mean that women cannot be "represented" by men? Explain.
5. Affirmative action programs were widely supported in the 1960s and 1970s, but now they are under attack. How can you explain this development?

★ IMPROVING YOUR SKILLS ★

Communication Skills

Resolving Conflicts Resolving conflicts between different groups in society is the essence of politics. Conflicts arise daily, and learning how to resolve them is a skill that will serve you well in the years to come.

When attempting to resolve a conflict, your goal should be to reach a compromise that is agreeable to everybody involved. Often, it requires patience and good negotiating skills. Here are some techniques that you might find helpful for resolving conflicts.

1. Talk with each party separately to get a clear idea of the nature of the dispute.
2. Try to understand each party's position and what the parties' *real* interests are.
3. Identify and compare the parties' perceptions of the issues involved in the dispute.
4. Realistically assess the alternative ways in which the dispute might be settled.
5. Devise realistic solutions and see if any of the solutions are agreeable to both parties.

Writing Review this chapter's section on affirmative action and the *America at Odds* feature, also on affirmative action. Then prepare a one-page questionnaire to distribute to your classmates on this topic. Begin with a one-paragraph summary of what affirmative action is, when it was initiated, and why it has been controversial. Include as many questions as you like, but phrase your questions carefully. Follow these helpful guidelines:

1. Do not ask respondents to give their names or any other personal information on the questionnaires.
2. Indicate when and where the questionnaires should be returned. (Do not have respondents return questionnaires to you in person. They need to be confident that their responses will remain anonymous.)
3. Make sure that each question can be answered by a simple "yes" or "no."
4. In asking questions, avoid double negatives. They cause confusion.
5. Keep your questions brief and to the point.

Distribute your finished questionnaire to your classmates. When the results are in, prepare a report on your findings, and present it to your class.

Social Studies Skills

Creating Pie Charts Presenting data in graphic form, such as in a pie chart, makes the data clearer for others to understand. Assume that you created and distributed the questionnaire on affirmative action. One of the questions on your questionnaire was the following: "Do you believe that all affirmative action programs should be abolished?", with possible answers to the question "Yes," "No," and "No opinion." You have been asked to present the responses to this survey question to your classmates in the form of a pie chart.

1. Assume that out of a total of 112 respondents, 53 responded with a yes, 52 with a no, and the remainder had no opinion. What percentage of the respondents answered yes? What percentage answered no? What percentage had no opinion?
2. Now, draw a circle to represent a "pie." Calculate how large each "wedge" of the pie should be to show your survey results in terms of percentages, and draw the wedges appropriately.

★ ACTIVITIES AND PROJECTS ★

1. Call the office of the Equal Employment Opportunity Commission (EEOC), using the number listed in the U.S. government pages of your local telephone directory. (If you cannot find the number, call 1-800-669-4000.) Ask the EEOC representative to send you information on how to file a claim of employment discrimination with the agency. When you receive the information, share it with your classmates.
2. Research the treatment of Japanese Americans during World War II. Find out where the internment camps were located, how Japanese Americans were transported to the camps, and what life was like in the camps. If possible, find and read a copy of the Supreme Court's decision in *Korematsu v. United States* (1944). Analyze the Court's reasons for concluding that the discriminatory actions against Japanese Americans did not violate the Constitution. Write a summary of the results of your research.
3. Debate the topic of affirmative action in class. Two students should argue the position that affirmative action should be continued, two students should argue the opposite position, and one student should act as a moderator. (More students can participate, but the numbers of students on the two sides of the debate should be equal.)

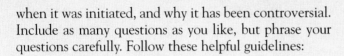

What If . . .

Affirmative Action Programs Were Banned?

The backlash against affirmative action programs in recent years has stirred a national debate over the value and effectiveness of these programs. What might happen if Congress passed a law prohibiting all affirmative action programs? What effects might such a law have on American society?

CHAPTER 8

Participating in Your Government

CHAPTER OBJECTIVES

To learn about and understand . . .

⭐ What it means to be a citizen

⭐ America's policies concerning immigration and the history of these policies

⭐ The rights and responsibilities of citizens

⭐ Why tolerance and open-mindedness are important

"Our citizenship in the United States is our national character. Our great title is AMERICANS."

Thomas Paine
(1737–1809)
Anglo-American Political Theorist and Writer

INTRODUCTION

If you live in a city that has one or more professional sports teams, you may know how enthusiastic the city can become when the team is winning. People are proud to be associated with that team and that city. The same is true for your school. When the school is doing well—for example, in sports—students are proud to be going to that school. Thomas Paine, in the opening quotation, obviously thought that Americans should be proud to be citizens of the United States.

The United States is the first modern nation in which citizens deliberately took governmental power into their own hands. They created a governmental system in which the people, rather than a monarch, a dictator, or a ruling party, have ultimate power. With citizenship comes responsibilities and the necessity of participating in government. In this chapter, you will read about what some of those responsibilities are.

◀ Newly sworn-in citizens wave U.S. flags following their naturalization ceremony.

Who Is a Citizen?

Preview Questions:

- 🌐 When did citizenship in the United States become a national issue?
- 🌐 What is the significance of the decision in *Dred Scott v. Sandford* (1857)?
- 🌐 What is the purpose of the Fourteenth Amendment?
- 🌐 How may American citizenship be lost?

Key Terms:

jus soli, wards, *jus sanguinis*, naturalization, naturalized citizens, expatriation, denaturalization

When the United States first became a nation, the concept of citizenship was not an issue of national concern. Indeed, the Constitution, including the first ten amendments, does not define citizenship. The framers of the Constitution left it up to state governments, rather than the national government, to decide who was a citizen. Any citizen of a state was automatically assumed to be a citizen of the United States, at least in the minds of the framers. Today, citizenship is decided by the national government.

The *Dred Scott* Case

The issue of state versus national citizenship became critical in a famous Supreme Court case, *Dred Scott v. Sandford* (1857). A slave named Dred Scott had been moved by his owner to Illinois, where slavery was illegal under state law. Dred Scott sued in court for his freedom. The Supreme Court, which at that time was dominated by southern judges, ruled that Scott could not be a citizen of the United States. He

▲ *Dred Scott, a slave, was moved by his owner to Illinois, where slavery was illegal. Scott then claimed that his residence there made him and his family free. Did the U.S. Supreme Court agree with him?*

was a slave, and therefore he had no right to sue in court at all. The Supreme Court applied this ruling to Scott while he was in Illinois even though slavery was illegal there and African Americans had long been considered citizens in that state (as well as in most other northern states).

The reasoning of the Court was that at the time the Constitution was adopted, African Americans were not recognized as citizens of the states. It did not matter whether they were slaves or free. According to the logic of the Court, the only individuals who were U.S. citizens were those who were directly descended either from persons who were state citizens in 1787 or from immigrants who became citizens through legal means. Slaves, who fell into neither of these categories, were therefore not citizens.

The Thirteenth and Fourteenth Amendments

Many individuals in the northern states did not agree with the *Dred Scott* decision. Some historians believe that the ruling in that case was one of the major causes of the Civil War. The Thirteenth Amendment, which abolished slavery, was passed at the close of the Civil War in 1865. But in passing this amendment, the nation was faced with the need to define who was a citizen. This question was finally answered in 1868 with the Fourteenth Amendment, which begins with the following words:

> *All persons born or naturalized in the United States, and subject to the jurisdiction thereof, are citizens of the United States and of the State wherein they reside.*

In essence, the Fourteenth Amendment reversed the *Dred Scott* decision by making state citizenship an automatic result of national citizenship. The Fourteenth Amendment created the two most common ways to become an American citizen: (1) by birth anywhere on land considered American soil and (2) by the legal process called *naturalization*. There is a third way as well—by being born of a parent who is a citizen of the United States.

ARCHITECTS

of Government

Abraham Lincoln (1809–1865)

A former store operator, surveyor, and postmaster in New Salem, Illinois, Abraham Lincoln became a lawyer and was elected to the Illinois state legislature in 1834. After he was elected president in 1860, he saw seven states secede from the Union by 1861. He wrote the Emancipation Proclamation in September 1862 and easily won reelection in 1864. He was the first chief executive to be assassinated. On April 14, 1864, he was shot and killed in Ford's Theater in Washington, D.C., by John Wilkes Booth, a deranged actor who sympathized with the southern cause.

HIS WORDS

"[W]e here highly resolve that these dead shall not have died in vain; that this nation, under God, shall have a new birth of freedom; and that government of the people, by the people, for the people, shall not perish from the earth."
(*Gettysburg Address, November 19, 1863*)

"The ballot is stronger than the bullet."
(*Speech, Bloomington, Illinois, May 19, 1856*)

DEVELOPING CRITICAL THINKING SKILLS

1. In the first quotation, what did Lincoln mean when he resolved that those who died "shall not have died in vain"?
2. How has modern history confirmed Lincoln's remark in the second quotation?

Citizenship by Birth

Most Americans are citizens simply because they were born in the United States. There are, however, a number of other ways to acquire U.S. citizenship.

Location of Birth—*Jus Soli* The Fourteenth Amendment states that all persons born in the United States are American citizens. This is called citizenship by location. In legal terms, it is called citizenship by **jus soli.** *Jus soli* is a Latin phrase that translates as "the law of the soil."

What is considered American soil? Today, the United States includes not only the fifty states but also the District of Columbia, Guam, Puerto Rico, the Virgin Islands, the Northern Mariana Islands, and American Samoa. Additionally, American embassies in foreign countries and any ship or aircraft operated by agencies of the U.S. government are considered U.S. soil. Individuals who are born in the United States but are not subject to the jurisdiction, or control, of the U.S. government are not considered to be born on U.S. soil. These individuals are usually children born to foreign diplomats stationed in the United States.

Significantly, at the time the Fourteenth Amendment was passed, Native Americans—who were considered **wards,** or persons under the legal guardianship, of the U.S. government—were not granted citizenship under the Fourteenth Amendment. In 1924, Congress remedied this situation by passing the Citizenship Act, which granted citizenship to all Native Americans who did not already possess it.

Law of the Blood—*Jus Sanguinis* Since 1790, Congress has included the so-called "law of the blood," or *jus sanguinis,* as grounds for American citizenship. Under this law, a child born on foreign soil becomes an American citizen at birth if at least one of the parents is a U.S. citizen. In addition, that U.S. citizen must have lived in the United States (or in an American possession) for at least ten years, five of them after the age of fourteen.

Just the Facts

For a small charge, you can own a U.S. flag that has flown over the Capitol, along with an appropriate certificate. (Send your request to your U.S. representative or senator.)

► Unlike many other countries, the United States offers citizenship to people born in foreign lands. Upon meeting the requirements, immigrants are granted a certificate of citizenship in ceremonies held throughout the U.S., in places such as Ellis Island, New York. Why is Ellis Island an appropriate location for a citizenship ceremony?

Citizenship by Choice—Naturalization

The U.S. Constitution, in Article I, Section 8, declares that Congress shall have the power to "establish a uniform Rule of Naturalization." **Naturalization** is the process by which individuals who are not yet U.S. citizens become citizens. These individuals are then called **naturalized citizens.** Naturalization can occur in three ways: (1) by act of Congress, (2) by treaty, and (3) by individual action.

By Act of Congress On rare occasions, Congress has passed laws naturalizing entire groups of people. As already mentioned, this was done in 1924 with respect to Native Americans who were not yet citizens. Before that, inhabitants of Hawaii and Puerto Rico were granted citizenship by Congress in 1900 and 1917, respectively. The same thing occurred for residents of the Virgin Islands (1927), Guam (1950), and the Northern Marianas (1977). We have already mentioned the collective naturalization of African Americans and others by the Fourteenth Amendment to the U.S. Constitution in 1868.

By Acquisition of Territory Large groups of people have also been naturalized when the United States has acquired new territory. Those living in the areas involved were naturalized by a treaty or by an act of Congress. For example, when the Louisiana Purchase Treaty was signed in 1803, the United States purchased the Louisiana Territory from France. That treaty said that people living in the territory became U.S. citizens. The same provision was made in the treaties in which the United States acquired Florida (1819) and Alaska (1867). Additionally, an act of Congress gave citizenship to all inhabitants of Texas in 1845.

By Individual Action Today, naturalization most often occurs through individual action. Every year, hundreds of thousands of people apply for citizenship in the United States. The process is outlined in Figure 8–1. Candidates for naturalization must have the following qualifications:

● They must be eighteen years of age or older (except minors who become citizens when their parents are naturalized).

FIGURE 8–1 How Noncitizens Become Naturalized Citizens of the United States As you can see, naturalization is a three-step process. The process may appear simple, but it normally is not. Why do you think the process usually takes a long time?

Step 1: Application	Step 2: Examination	Step 3: Final Hearing
Candidates for citizenship must submit an application form, a card of fingerprints, and certain autobiographical data, such as where they were born and who their parents were.	Each candidate appears before an officer at an Immigration and Naturalization Service office. The candidate must bring along two U.S. citizens to serve as witnesses. Every candidate must prove his or her qualifications, consistent with those presented previously with the application. Candidates must also demonstrate a basic knowledge of American history and an understanding of our form of government.	The Immigration and Naturalization Service takes a minimum of thirty days to process an application. During that time, it may seek additional information about the candidate. The information is presented to a judge in a citizenship court with the recommendation that the candidate be granted citizenship. If the judge agrees, then the applicant appears before a judge, takes the oath of allegiance, and receives a certificate of citizenship. He or she has become a naturalized citizen of the United States.

- They must have entered the United States legally and have lived in the United States for at least five years.
- They must demonstrate an understanding of basic English words and phrases.
- They must be able to prove, if necessary, their high moral character.
- They must understand the basic concepts of American government and history.
- They must not have advocated the overthrow of the U.S. government by force or violence within the past ten years.
- They must not have belonged to any subversive organization within the past ten years.
- They must not be draft evaders, military deserters, anarchists, or polygamists. (A polygamist is a person with more than one spouse.)

How Citizenship Can Be Lost

The federal government is the *only* entity that can take away citizenship. The three basic ways in which Americans can lose citizenship are through expatriation, punishment for a crime, and denaturalization.

Expatriation The word **expatriation** is made up of the prefix *ex-*, meaning "from," and the Latin word *patria*, which means "native country, or fatherland." To expatriate someone is to banish that person from his or her native country. An individual can voluntarily become an expatriate by becoming a naturalized citizen of another country or by renouncing American citizenship to a representative of the U.S. government. Once renounced, citizenship cannot easily be regained.

Punishment for a Crime The federal government can take away citizenship if a person is convicted of treason, of inciting rebellion, or of conspiring to overthrow the government by violent means.

Just the Facts

In ancient Greece, exile (expatriation) was often the penalty for homicide.

Denaturalization In rare cases, a naturalized citizen may lose his or her citizenship through a process called **denaturalization.** Denaturalization occurs if the federal government learns that a naturalized citizen obtained his or her citizenship through fraudulent means.

SECTION 1 REVIEW

1. What did the Supreme Court rule in the *Dred Scott* case?
2. According to the Fourteenth Amendment, who is a citizen of the United States?
3. In what three ways can American citizenship be lost?
4. **For Critical Analysis:** Former Supreme Court Justice Earl Warren believed that loss of citizenship as punishment for any crime, even treason, was a "cruel and unusual" punishment, which is unconstitutional. Do you agree or disagree? Explain your answer. For what reasons, if any, do you think citizens should lose their citizenship? Explain your answer.

SECTION 2

Immigration and the Noncitizen

Preview Questions:

- What is the difference between an immigrant and an alien?
- According to U.S. laws, what are the different types of aliens?
- How has the nation's policy on immigration changed over the years?

Key Terms:

immigrants, aliens, resident aliens, nonresident aliens, enemy aliens, refugees, illegal aliens, visa, deported, undocumented aliens, amnesty

Not everybody living in the United States, of course, is a citizen of this country. Various words have

In 1997, over five million persons were eligible to apply for U.S. citizenship.

been used to describe people who are not citizens. The two most common are immigrants and aliens. The difference between the two is important. **Immigrants** are individuals who live in the United States with the intention of becoming naturalized citizens and remaining here permanently. During the last decade, immigrants have made up more than one-third of the nation's population growth. **Aliens,** in contrast, are individuals living in this country who are not citizens.

Types of Aliens

According to U.S. law, there are five different categories of aliens. Each category includes important legal distinctions.

▲ *These Cuban refugees huddle together after being rescued from their makeshift raft off the coast of Florida. Why would some Cubans be willing to risk their lives to escape their island nation?*

1. **Resident aliens** are individuals who have come to the United States to establish permanent residence. They are immigrants and are called resident aliens until they become naturalized citizens. Resident aliens may stay in the United States as long as they desire and are not required to seek American citizenship.

2. **Nonresident aliens** are individuals who expect to stay in the United States for a specified period of time. A journalist from Britain who has come to cover the presidential election is a nonresident alien. A Japanese tourist from Tokyo visiting San Francisco for the month of June is a nonresident alien. The head salesperson for a Swiss watch company who is in New York to promote a new line of watches is a nonresident alien.

3. **Enemy aliens** are citizens of nations with which America is at war. During World War I, when our nation was at war with Germany, German citizens who resided in the continental United States were considered to be enemy aliens. During World War II, when our nation was at war with Japan, U.S. residents of Japanese descent living on the West Coast were considered, as a group, enemy aliens.

4. **Refugees** are immigrants to the United States who are granted entry because they are unsafe or unwelcome in their own countries for political reasons. In recent years, the United States has accepted refugees from Southeast Asia, Cuba, El Salvador, Nicaragua, Haiti, and Poland. Refugees are allowed to apply for permanent resident status one year after they arrive in the United States.

5. **Illegal aliens** are individuals who enter the United States without a legal permit or who enter as tourists or students (nonresident aliens) and stay longer then their status legally allows. Everyone entering the United States is supposed to have a valid passport, visa, or entry permit. A **visa** is an authorization that allows someone to enter another country legally. Usually, a visa is an official stamp placed on the inside of an individual's passport. Most visas for nonimmigrants are granted for a specific time period. A tourist, for example, may be allowed to travel legally in the United States for six months. Staying past that period is illegal.

Illegal aliens can be **deported,** or forced to leave the United States. Over one million illegal aliens are deported each year.

The Rights of Aliens

American citizens have many rights under their state constitutions and the U.S. Constitution. In particular, the Bill of Rights guarantees the freedom of speech, assembly, and religion. These rights apply equally to legal aliens, whether resident or nonresident. In certain circumstances, many of these rights also apply to illegal aliens. In general, legal (resident) aliens can legally own real estate and send their children to public schools. They cannot, however, vote in any election, be it local, state, or federal. Legal aliens normally are not required to serve in the military, nor are they called for jury duty. In exchange for their privileges, resident aliens must pay taxes and obey all laws.

A Nation of Immigrants

According to the latest statistics, Native Americans (American Indians, Eskimos, and Aleuts) make up less than 1 percent of the total U.S. population. This means that almost everyone in the United States can trace his or her roots to another country. The study of immigration in America is therefore a large part of the study of America itself.

As you can see from the figure in the *Building Social Studies Skills* feature on page 214, immigration was greatest in absolute numbers from 1901 to 1910. The 1970s and the 1980s were also high periods of immigration. Relative to the percentage of the total population, though, immigration has been low in the last quarter century. Since 1821, in total, over 65 million people have immigrated to the United States.

Policies on Immigration

In the early days of our country, small numbers of people inhabited vast areas of land. It is not surprising, then, that most early Americans wanted to encourage immigration. During the constitutional debates in Philadelphia, Alexander Hamilton pointed out that immigrants could make an important contribution to the nation and should be treated as "first-class citizens."

The states believed that there was strength in large numbers. They wanted more people to move to their states, so they set up advertising campaigns to lure prospective citizens. By the time the Civil War broke out, more than thirty states and territorial governments had immigration offices whose purpose was to attract immigrants. Some states passed laws requiring that new immigrants be inspected, particularly for diseases. In New York, for example, sick immigrants were not allowed to enter the state.

The legality of the states' regulation of immigration was upheld in *Mayor of New York v. Miln* (1837). In *Henderson v. Mayor of New York* (1875), however, the Supreme Court declared that state legislation on immigration was unconstitutional. These state laws infringed on the exclusive power of Congress to regulate interstate and foreign commerce.

Restricting Immigration The 1880s saw the first true restrictions on immigration. Before that time, most immigrants had come from northern and western Europe and had blended in easily with the existing population in the United States. Most of these immigrants were Protestants, except for the Irish and a few Germans, who were Catholic. In contrast, the immigrants who arrived from the 1880s onward were from eastern and southern Europe. Their languages were different, and most were not Protestant but Jewish, Catholic, or Eastern Orthodox. Their customs seemed strange and foreign to the earlier immigrants. During the same period, Chinese immigrants started entering the western states, particularly to help build the new railroads.

Congress responded to the influx of Asians with the Chinese Exclusion Act of 1882, which stopped entry of Chinese immigrants into the United States for ten years. That act was the first to establish the federal government's right to restrict immigration based on nationalities. More restrictive acts were passed in 1888 and 1891. They allowed the national government not only to exclude certain individuals—convicts, prostitutes, and insane persons, for example—but also to deport aliens who entered the country in violation of these immigration laws.

Quotas The concept of limiting the rights of certain nationalities to immigrate resulted in the Quota Act of 1921. This act limited the annual number of immigrants from each nationality to 3 percent of the number of foreign-born persons of that nationality who were

Government in Action

Taking the Census

The U.S. Constitution, in Article I, Section 2, requires that the federal government take an "enumeration," or census, every ten years. The census is required because the number of representatives each state can elect to the House of Representatives depends on the state's population. The census results are also used to determine where to build highways, schools, restaurants, and banks, as well as how much money in federal grants should be given to local government institutions such as hospitals. Inorder to be as accurate as possible, the Bureau of the Census made a significant effort to include homeless persons and illegal aliens in the 1990 count.

The Bureau of the Census, which is part of the Department of Commerce, operates within the executive branch of the government. All the census forms gathered are processed by sophisticated optical scanners at lightning speeds. The Census Bureau, in 1890, became the first major institution to use machine-readable punch cards. (Their inventor, Herman Hollerith, later started the company that became International Business Machines, otherwise known as IBM.)

To get information for the latest census, almost half a million part-time employees were hired, in addition to the Bureau's normal staff of almost ten thousand. Two hundred thousand of these part-time workers surveyed their home neighborhoods, talking to people from door to door.

Here are some of the questions that were asked in the latest census:

"Boy, did I have an afternoon! The census man was here."

▲ Every ten years, the Census Bureau undertakes the huge task of counting everyone in the United States. As you can see from the cartoon, some census takers—and families—face a greater challenge than others.

- What is your age, date of birth, and marital status?
- How many years of schooling have you completed?
- How many years' active duty military service have you completed?
- What was your income last year?
- Are you of Spanish/Hispanic origin?
- Do you have complete plumbing facilities?
- Do you have complete kitchen facilities?

living in the United States in 1910. For example, assume that there were 100,000 Polish persons living in the United States in 1910. Under the 1921 Quota Act, 3 percent of 100,000—or 3,000 persons—would be allowed to immigrate from Poland to the United States

each year. Most Asian groups were not included in the list of nationalities. Therefore, they could not legally immigrate to the United States for some time. The law did not apply to certain categories of educated people, such as professors, ministers, doctors, and lawyers.

U.S. Households by Type, 1990

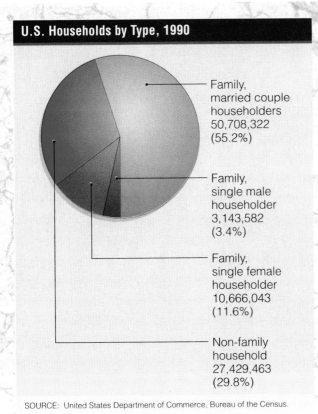

Family, married couple householders 50,708,322 (55.2%)

Family, single male householder 3,143,582 (3.4%)

Family, single female householder 10,666,043 (11.6%)

Non-family household 27,429,463 (29.8%)

SOURCE: United States Department of Commerce, Bureau of the Census.

U.S. Cities with Greatest Populations, 1990

Size Rank	City and State	1990 Population
1	New York, NY	7,322,564
2	Los Angeles, CA	3,485,398
3	Chicago, IL	2,783,726
4	Houston, TX	1,630,553
5	Philadelphia, PA	1,585,577
6	San Diego, CA	1,110,549
7	Detroit, MI	1,027,974
8	Dallas, TX	1,006,877
9	Phoenix, AZ	983,403
10	San Antonio, TX	935,933
11	San Jose, CA	782,248
12	Indianapolis, IN	741,952
13	Baltimore, MD	736,014
14	San Francisco, CA	723,959
15	Jacksonville, FL	672,971
16	Columbus, OH	632,910
17	Milwaukee, WI	628,088
18	Memphis, TN	610,337
19	Washington, DC	606,900
20	Boston, MA	574,283
21	Seattle, WA	516,259
22	El Paso, TX	515,342
23	Nashville–Davidson, TN	510,784
24	Cleveland, OH	505,616
25	New Orleans, LA	496,938

SOURCE: United States Department of Commerce, Bureau of the Census.

- Do you have a telephone?
- Which fuel is used most for heating your house or apartment?

All of the people who collect or handle census information are sworn to secrecy—they can only reveal the information they gather to authorized personnel. But if you are curious about census statistics, you can contact the Public Information Office at the Bureau of the Census, Washington, D.C., 20233, 301-457-2804. The Census Bureau also offers information on census statistics on its Web site. Go to **www.census.gov/** to find this data.

THINK ABOUT IT

1. Do you think the Census Bureau is invading Americans' privacy by asking so many questions about how they live, even though the bureau keeps all files secret? Explain why or why not.
2. Some cities claim that the Census Bureau undercounted the number of city residents. Why would this be a concern?

Immigration from the Western Hemisphere was also unrestricted. The world responded, with 700,000 immigrants entering the United States in 1924.

The Immigration Act of 1924 and the National Origins Act of 1929 established a new quota system for each nationality and set a limit on the total number of immigrants to be allowed entry at all (150,000 per year). The quota system that resulted from these acts served as the basis for U.S. immigration policy for more than thirty-five years.

▶ *Thousands of immigrants entered the United States through Ellis Island. Can you identify the famous person in this group? (© 1996 Estate of Ben Shahn/Licensed by VAGA, New York, New York)*

Current Immigration Policy Today's immigration policy is based largely on the Immigration Act of 1990, which revised several other acts, including an act passed in 1965.

The 1965 law had eliminated quotas based on national origin. As many as 270,000 immigrants could be admitted each year without regard to nationality, country of origin, or race. No more than 20,000 persons could come from any one country, however. Close relatives of American citizens were given special status, as were aliens with specialized occupational talents.

An important change in immigration law occurred with the passage of the Immigration Act of 1990. This act raised legal immigration levels by about 40 percent, to 700,000 per year. It stressed family reunification, provided legal status for certain illegal immigrants, and struck down barriers blocking people with certain political beliefs from entry. The 1990 act's most significant feature was a tripling of the number of visas (to about 140,000 a year) granted to highly skilled professionals, such as engineers, researchers, and scientists.

During the 1990s, public pressure to curb immigration, particularly illegal immigration, grew. In response, Congress passed the Immigration Reform Act of 1996. The act put into effect a number of provisions to stem illegal immigration, some of which are listed in Figure 8–2 on page 213.

One provision of the act would have forced hundreds of thousands of illegal immigrants and refugees to leave the United States. In addition, the Welfare Reform Act of 1996 prohibited immigrants, including legal immigrants who are not yet citizens, from receiving most forms of public assistance, including welfare benefits.

Many Americans thought that this new policy toward immigrants was too harsh. In response, Congress revised its policy in 1997. Under the new policy, many refugees automatically became eligible for permanent legal residence. Other illegal immigrants were allowed to remain in the United States while the government processed their applications for permanent legal residence. Additionally, immigrants were again made eligible for public-assistance benefits.

The Immigration Controversy

The number of immigrants legally allowed into the United States does not necessarily represent the actual number of immigrants who come here. This nation has a large flow of illegal aliens, also known as **undocumented aliens.** Many of these individuals are tourists who overstay their visas and start working. Many are from Mexico and other Latin American countries. No one knows for sure how many illegal aliens arrive each year, but the estimate is two million. The number of illegal aliens who permanently live in the United States is estimated to be between five million and twelve million.

Periodically, the federal government has attempted to remedy the problem of illegal immigration. The Immigration Reform and Control Act of 1986, for example, imposed severe penalties on employers who willfully hired illegal aliens (fines range from $250 to $10,000 for each offense). Employers who repeatedly violate this law can be jailed for up to six months.

The 1986 law also included an **amnesty** program. (Amnesty is a general pardon for past offenses—in this case, illegally residing in the United States.) From the summer of 1987 to the summer of 1988, illegal aliens who could prove that they had been in this country continuously for at least five years could apply to obtain temporary legal residency status. Eighteen months later, they could apply for permanent residency. Eventually, they could apply for citizenship.

FIGURE 8–2 Highlights of the 1996 Immigration Reform Act The figure below outlines some of the important provisions of the 1996 Immigration Reform Act. What major problems were addressed by the act?

✔ Doubled the number of border patrol agents

✔ Increased penalties for immigrant smuggling and document fraud

✔ Authorized a speeded-up process for returning illegal aliens to their countries of origin

✔ Barred illegal aliens from reentering the United States for up to ten years

✔ Provided for the establishment in five states of pilot programs to assist employers in verifying workers' immigrant status

✔ Provided that any person who "sponsors" an immigrant, such as a family member, must have an income equal to at least 125 percent of the official poverty level.

◀ Chinese workers complete the last mile of the Pacific Railroad. Although Chinese people were at first encouraged to come to America, as their numbers increased they were officially discouraged from immigrating to this country by the passing of the Chinese Exclusion Act of 1882. (Sketch by Waud, 1869)

A bar graph is a convenient way of showing large amounts of information at a glance. Bar graphs are often used to show changes in trends over time or to compare data.

When reading a bar graph, first read the title to find out what information it contains. Then consider the contents of the graph. Bars in a graph can run vertically or horizontally. One part of the information—ages, dates, percentages, or the like—is usually presented on the vertical axis. Another part of the information is presented on the horizontal axis. Sometimes, additional information, often indicated

BUILDING
SOCIAL STUDIES SKILLS

Reading Bar Graphs

with different colors or shading, is presented within the bars themselves.

PRACTICING YOUR SKILLS

Use the bar graph below to answer the following questions:

1. In which period did the fewest immigrants come to the United States?
2. In which period did the most immigrants come to the United States?
3. During what decades was immigration decreasing?
4. During what decades was immigration increasing?

Immigration to the United States, 1821–1996

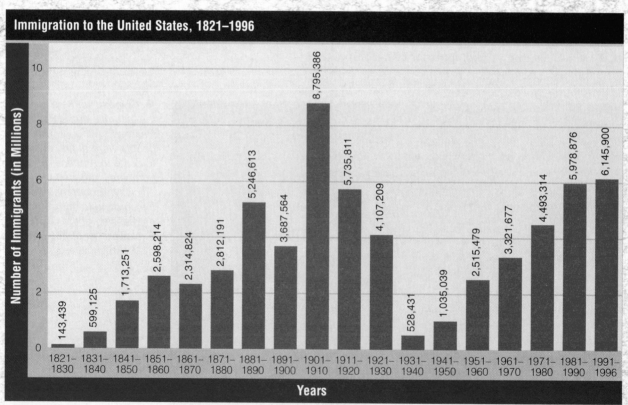

Number of Immigrants (in Millions)

Years	Number
1821–1830	143,439
1831–1840	599,125
1841–1850	1,713,251
1851–1860	2,598,214
1861–1870	2,314,824
1871–1880	2,812,191
1881–1890	5,246,613
1891–1900	3,687,564
1901–1910	8,795,386
1911–1920	5,735,811
1921–1930	4,107,209
1931–1940	528,431
1941–1950	1,035,039
1951–1960	2,515,479
1961–1970	3,321,677
1971–1980	4,493,314
1981–1990	5,978,876
1991–1996	6,145,900

Years

SOURCE: U.S. Immigration and Naturalization Service.

◄ Except for Native Americans, the United States is made up entirely of immigrants and descendants of immigrants. The national attitude toward immigration, however, has shifted throughout our history—sometimes encouraging, sometimes limiting immigration. According to this cartoon, what is the impact of unlimited immigration?

The most recent attempt to stem illegal immigration was the 1996 Immigration Reform Act. As we have already discussed, this act had many provisions aimed at curbing illegal immigration into the United States.

Immigration policy is the focus of a continuing debate in the United States. Many Americans strongly believe that immigrants, especially illegal immigrants, take jobs that American citizens would otherwise have and lower Americans' wages. These critics also fear that new waves of immigrants will have difficulty fitting in with present-day American society.

Anti-immigration sentiments were clearly evident in California in 1994. In that year, Proposition 187 was put on the ballot. It denied public social services, publicly funded health care, and public education to people who were suspected of being illegal aliens. It required that individuals who were suspected of being illegal aliens be interviewed, questioned, and forced to produce legal residency documents. It required all law enforcement agencies in California to report anyone suspected of being in the United States illegally. Voters passed the proposition, but it was challenged in the courts. A federal court later held that the state could not deny children of illegal immigrants a public education.

Supporters of immigration point out the obvious—at one time or another, all of us, except Native Americans, were immigrants. Therefore, ask immigration advocates, how can we arbitrarily decide that today immigration is "bad" for America? Additionally, many new immigrants to America take low-paying jobs that Americans leave unfilled. Furthermore, most immigrants pay taxes and adjust rapidly to the requirements of life in their new country.

SECTION 2 REVIEW

1. List and briefly describe the five types of aliens identified under U.S. law.
2. What are the rights of aliens?
3. What were the first true restrictions placed on immigration in the United States?
4. **For Critical Analysis:** A 1986 amnesty program allowed many illegal aliens to obtain legal residency in this country. How do you think such a program might influence other foreigners who want to immigrate illegally to the United States? Give reasons for your answer.

Citizenship Rights and Responsibilities

Preview Questions:

🌐 What is meant by the nationalization of the Bill of Rights?

🌐 What are some of the rights and responsibilities of American citizenship?

Key Terms:

allegiance, dual citizenship, incorporation theory, political patronage, spoils system, civil service examinations, merit

Citizenship involves both rights and responsibilities. A citizen owes **allegiance,** or loyalty, to her or his nation. In turn, the nation owes the citizen all the rights and protections of the law. Thus, American citizenship is an implied contract between the nation and the individual for mutual support and assistance.

Rights of Citizens

Citizens' rights are spelled out in the Constitution and in federal and state laws. One right that all citizens have is simply to live on American soil. Citizens also have the right to vote, to hold public office, and to travel freely throughout the United States. Our major rights are guaranteed by the Bill of Rights and by several additional amendments to the Constitution.

The Bill of Rights If you reread the First Amendment to the Bill of Rights, you will notice that it starts with the words "*Congress* shall make no law." Most citizens do not realize that, originally, the Bill of Rights limited only the power of the national government, not the power of the states. In other words, a citizen

in the state of Virginia in 1795 could not successfully sue in federal court to overturn a law passed in Virginia that violated one of the amendments in the Bill of Rights. Each state had (and still has) its own constitution, normally with its own bill of rights.

The states' bills of rights were similar to the national Bill of Rights. There were some differences in content, however. Perhaps more important, there were differences in interpretation. A citizen in one state therefore effectively had a different set of civil liberties than a citizen in another state. It was not until the Fourteenth Amendment was ratified in 1868 that the Constitution explicitly guaranteed due process of law to people in all states.

The Fourteenth Amendment You have already read about the due process clause of the Fourteenth Amendment in Chapters 5 and 6. Here, we examine that clause once again and discuss in more detail how the Bill of Rights came to be applied to actions of state governments.

Section 1 of the Fourteenth Amendment, ratified in 1868, provides as follows:

No State shall make or enforce any law which shall abridge the privileges or immunities of citizens of the United States; nor shall any State deprive any person of life, liberty, or property, without due process of law; nor deny to any person within its jurisdiction the equal protection of the laws.

◀ *A shadow of a hand holding a candle falls across a bronze casting of the Bill of Rights. Although each state has its own constitution and bill of rights, all Americans are protected by the national Bill of Rights.*

FIGURE 8–3 Incorporating the Bill of Rights into the Fourteenth Amendment The court cases listed below extended the protections of the Bill of Rights to apply to the citizens of states as well as the national government. Why do you think the Bill of Rights originally applied only to the national government?

Year	Issue	Amendment Involved	Court Case
1925	Freedom of speech	I	*Gitlow v. New York*, 268 U.S. 652
1931	Freedom of the press	I	*Near v. Minnesota*, 283 U.S. 697
1932	Right to a lawyer in capital punishment cases	VI	*Powell v. Alabama*, 287 U.S. 45
1937	Freedom of assembly and a right to petition	I	*De Jonge v. Oregon*, 299 U.S. 353
1940	Freedom of religion	I	*Cantwell v. Connecticut*, 310 U.S. 296
1947	Separation of church and state	I	*Everson v. Board of Education*, 330 U.S. 1
1948	Right to public trial	VI	*In re Oliver*, 333 U.S. 257
1949	No unreasonable searches	IV	*Wolf v. Colorado*, 338 U.S. 25
1961	Exclusionary rule	IV	*Mapp v. Ohio*, 367 U.S. 643
1962	No cruel and unusual punishment	VIII	*Robinson v. California*, 370 U.S. 660
1963	Right to a lawyer in all criminal cases	VI	*Gideon v. Wainwright*, 372 U.S. 335
1964	No compulsory self-incrimination	V	*Malloy v. Hogan*, 378 U.S. 1
1965	Right to privacy	various	*Griswold v. Connecticut*, 381 U.S. 479
1966	Right to an impartial jury	VI	*Parker v. Gladden*, 385 U.S. 363
1967	Right to a speedy trial	VI	*Klopfer v. North Carolina*, 386 U.S. 213
1969	No double jeopardy	V	*Benton v. Maryland*, 395 U.S. 784

Section 5 of the amendment gives Congress the power to enforce these provisions through appropriate legislation.

Note the use of the terms *citizens* and *person*. *Citizens* have political rights, such as the right to vote and to run for office. But no *person*, citizen or alien, can be denied civil liberties (speech, press, and religion) nor have his or her property taken without equal access to the legal system.

The Nationalization, or Incorporation, of the Bill of Rights The Fourteenth Amendment was to be a national standard that would guarantee both due process and equal protection under the law for all persons throughout the nation. The courts did not immediately agree that the amendment should apply to the states, however. Many jurists still believed, as John Marshall had stated in the *Barron v. Mayor of Baltimore* (1833) decision, that the states were "distinct governments framed by different persons and for different purposes." Marshall's statement in the *Barron* decision was plain. The Bill of Rights limited only the national government and not the state governments.

In 1873, in the *Slaughter-House* cases, the Supreme Court upheld the principle of **dual citizenship.** According to this principle, one is a citizen both of a state and of the United States. The Court argued that to deprive states of their authority and their identity would "fetter and degrade state governments." The *Slaughter-House* cases involved a Louisiana law that banned livestock yards and slaughterhouses within New Orleans, except the Crescent City Company's operation. Butchers and others harmed by the law sought to have it declared void, in part under the Fourteenth Amendment. The Supreme Court held that the Fourteenth Amendment created two types of citizenship—federal and state. The amendment extended federal constitutional protection only to the privileges and immunities of national citizenship. The Court reasoned that the Louisiana statute did not infringe on any of the privileges and immunities of national citizenship. Therefore, it did not conflict with the Constitution.

Only gradually did the Supreme Court accept the **incorporation theory,** which held that no state could act in violation of the U.S. Bill of Rights. Figure 8–3 shows the rights that the Court has incorporated into the Fourteenth Amendment and the cases in which the Court first applied these rights. The process of incorporation, as you can see, has taken place relatively slowly.

How Citizenship and Immigration Laws Have Changed

There have been many changes in citizenship and immigration laws since the early 1800s. We look at some of those changes here.

Then (Early 1800s)	Now
State governments decided who could be citizens of the United States.	The national government decides who can be citizens of the United States (since the passage of the Fourteenth Amendment to the Constitution in 1868).
The freedoms and guarantees contained in the national Bill of Rights did not protect citizens against actions by state governments.	Most of the freedoms and guarantees contained in the national Bill of Rights protect citizens against state actions.
Immigration was controlled by state governments.	Immigration is controlled solely by the national government.
Generally, there were few restrictions on immigration.	There are numerous restrictions on immigration, as established by federal laws.

The last hundred years of Supreme Court decisions have bound the fifty states to observe most of the provisions in the U.S. Bill of Rights. The exceptions have usually involved the right to bear arms, the right to refuse to quarter soldiers (to provide them shelter), and the right to a grand jury hearing. Thus, for all intents and purposes, the Bill of Rights of the federal Constitution must be uniformly applied by all state governments.

Responsibilities of Citizens

American citizens have the legal duty to support the government by obeying its laws, paying taxes, serving on juries, and defending the nation whenever necessary. But good citizenship does not depend on doing *only* what is required by law. Rather, good citizenship means becoming a *participant* in this country's democratic system. We look here at some ways in which citizens participate.

Voting The most common, and the easiest, way for Americans to participate in their democracy is by voting. For most Americans, voting is the single most effective way to affect the course of political events in their country. Votes for or against particular candidates determine who will represent the people's interests at the various levels of government.

Some people do not vote because they believe that their votes do not count. That is not necessarily true. In 1948, Lyndon Johnson won the Texas Democratic primary election for U.S. senator by 87 votes out of 940,000 cast. If those 87 people had not voted, Texas would have had a different senator. John F. Kennedy won the popular vote for the presidency in 1960 by a margin of only 120,000 votes, less than one-fifth of 1 percent, over Richard Nixon. In 1976, Jimmy Carter won over Gerald Ford in the popular vote for the presidency by a margin of only 2 percent. In local elections, these types of close results occur often.

Voting trends in the United States are not encouraging. In the last few presidential elections, less than half of all eligible voters actually voted. Voter turnout is generally even lower in state and local elections.

Defending Civil Rights American citizens have a duty to defend not only their own civil liberties but also those of their fellow Americans. That means that as a citizen you have a responsibility to allow others the same liberties that you have been granted, even when their beliefs are different from your own. This is especially true with respect to religion. You may not agree with the religious preferences of others, but you have a duty as an American citizen to accept each person's right to worship in her or his own way. Good citizenship requires that each of us extends to others the rights guaranteed to all of us by the Constitution.

Paying Taxes Through federal, state, and local taxes, the government raises funds to pay for the services that citizens demand. It is every citizen's responsibility to pay his or her share of taxes.

Attending School Our society depends on our schools to give young people the skills and knowledge they need to become contributing members of society. A good education prepares citizens to support themselves and to contribute to the economy. A well-educated citizen can also make informed voting choices. Such individuals are often well equipped to face our diverse and rapidly changing society. Moreover, education fosters an understanding and appreciation of all peoples and cultures.

Defending the Nation It is also a citizen's responsibility to help defend the nation against threats to its peace and security. All young men must register for military service when they turn eighteen years of age. This does not mean they will have to serve in the military, but it does mean they can be called in the event of a national emergency. Citizens may also volunteer to serve in the

◀ *These eighteen-year-old citizens exercise their right to vote for the first time. The Twenty-sixth Amendment, ratified on July 1, 1971, lowered the legal voting age from twenty-one to eighteen.*

Army, Navy, Marines, Air Force, or Coast Guard.

Serving on a Jury or as a Witness All citizens have the right to a fair trial. To ensure this right, our Constitution guarantees that anyone accused of a crime has a right to a trial by a jury of peers. This means that citizens may be called upon to serve on juries. During a trial, witnesses are often needed to help prove guilt or innocence. At some time in your life, you may see or hear something that could help determine the guilt or innocence of a person accused of a crime. If you do, you have the responsibility to serve as a witness in court if you are called on to do so.

Contributing to the Well-Being of Society What would our country be like if everyone were willing to vote but not willing to participate in other ways? We would have no political parties, no help during election campaigns, no neighborhood improvement projects, no community service projects, and no political action groups. There would be no letters to the editor or to elected representatives. In fact, there would be no representatives, because no one would ever run for public office. If this were the situation, our representative government would not last very long. American democracy needs citizens to take interest and get involved in our democracy in order to survive.

To get students involved in their communities, an increasing number of school districts are requiring that students perform some type of community service. A number of parents have gone to court to fight such requirements. So far, however, the courts have upheld them. Students in school districts that have these

Applying for a job with the national government is actually quite simple. For information about job openings and application procedures, you can contact the nearest office of the U.S. Office of Personnel Management (OPM), or you can contact the OPM in Washington, D.C. The OPM has also developed the "Federal Employment Information System" to help in your job search. Using this system, you have access to federal and some state and local government job listings. Each federal agency lists its job openings on the system, and you can receive information via telephone, postal mail, and e-mail. The system provides current and complete information about job opportunities, job requirements, salaries, and employee benefits. It also includes access to application forms. The information is updated daily, and it is available twenty-four hours a day, seven days a week. The national office of the OPM is at the following address:

U.S. Office of Personnel
  Management
1900 E St., NW
Washington, DC 20415
Telephone: 202-606-1800

PARTICIPATING IN YOUR GOVERNMENT

Applying for a Government Job

Many people find it easier to access the system online. The World Wide Web site for the system is **www.usajobs.opm.gov/**.

The Federal Employment Information System makes it very easy to identify jobs in particular geographic areas or in particular government agencies. After you have identified jobs that are of interest to you, you should follow these steps:

1. **Obtain a job announcement.** You should obtain a copy of the vacancy announcement for those positions that interest you. These are available upon request. Most of the questions that you may have about a particular position will be answered by the information in the announcement. Announcements include such information as the closing date for application, where the position is located, the specific duties of the position, the educational requirements, and whether or not a written test is required. Read the information carefully to determine if you are qualified for the job.

2. **Fill out the application.** You can obtain an application at the same time you obtain the job announcement. Read the form carefully, and fill it out neatly and accurately.

3. **Take the civil service test.** A test is required for some, but not all, government jobs. If a test is required, after the information center receives your application, it will notify you of the time and place of the test. You can also obtain sample tests to use for practice and preparation. Some time after taking the test, you will receive your score and be told whether you qualified for the job.

requirements must contribute to the community, or they will not receive their diplomas. Mandatory community service of this kind is viewed as positive by many, but not all. Some argue that community service should always be voluntary.

At various times, it has been suggested that *all* Americans be required to engage in national community service, perhaps after graduation from high school. Those who argue in favor of domestic national service believe that many of the nation's needs are unmet. Young Americans could help fill these needs. There is strong opposition to such a program, however. Opponents argue that no one should be forced to work in any job.

A group of job applicants in Washington, D.C., takes one of the first steps toward qualifying for a job in government service by taking the civil service examination. Will these jobs be granted by patronage, or under the merit system?

In addition to the Federal Employment Information System, almost every government agency has its own written and online information about jobs within the agency. Thus, if you are only interested in jobs within a particular agency, you might wish to contact it directly. In addition, you might wish to consult the *Federal Career Directory: A Guide for College Students*, which is available in libraries or from the Superintendent of Documents, Government Printing Office,

Washington, DC, 20402. You can also request a free pamphlet called *Working for the USA* from the OPM. Another excellent source of information about careers and summer jobs in Washington, D.C., is the *Washington Information Directory*, published by Congressional Quarterly, Inc., 1414 Twenty-second St., NW, Washington, DC 20037.

TAKING ACTION

One of the best ways to find out if you would like to work for the government is by getting a summer job or an internship with a local, state, or national agency. The national government has many summer staff positions available, such as congressional aide and legislative assistant. At the state level, jobs

are available in state capitals and in regional offices. Summer jobs at the local government level may involve working at the county courthouse or the town recreation center. If you are interested, you should contact the following:

- Local and county government offices.
- Governors' offices and state agencies.
- Individual members of Congress.
- Individual members of your state legislature.
- Agencies of the U.S. government, such as the OPM.

You might also wish to interview government employees, at both the local and national levels, in career areas that are of interest to you. They can discuss with you the many kinds of positions available within the government and what their responsibilities include.

Careers in Public and Community Service

Making sure that rights, privileges, and services are extended to all citizens is the job of the men and women who work in public and community service. Nearly three million people are employed by the national gov-

ernment in civilian positions ranging from letter carrier to judge. Over two million more are employed by the nation's armed services. About four million are employed by state governments in positions that include state troopers and fish and wildlife department employees. More than ten million other people are employed at local levels as school administrators, firefighters, town

▲ *The nature of volunteering in America has changed as each generation—from Revolutionary-era militia men to 1960s Peace Corps members to today's young people—decide what form their service will take. Here a student from Berea College in Kentucky works on a quilt with an elderly hospital patient.*

clerks, park maintenance employees, and in many other positions. The range of public service jobs is incredibly varied, but all involve helping people.

Jobs with the National Government National government employees run the gamut from foreign service workers to agents of the Federal Bureau of Investigation and the Central Intelligence Agency. National government workers are employed by the Immigration and Naturalization Service, the Internal Revenue Service, the Department of Agriculture, the U.S. Postal Service, and the federal court system. Men and women involved in space exploration are employees of the national government. The national government also hires zookeepers, his-

torians, engineers, nurses, secretaries, public relations representatives, computer programmers, and people in many other positions.

Jobs with State and Local Governments While the number of national government employees has declined recently, the number of state and local government employees has increased dramatically. The increase is partly due to cutbacks in national government programs and partly due to the continued growth of the nation's cities and suburbs. State services include tax collection, law enforcement, highway safety and maintenance, motor vehicle licensing and registration, and the administration of such assistance programs as welfare, unemployment insurance, and workers' compensation.

Civil Service Until the 1880s, the national government was staffed according to a system politely known as **political patronage.** It was also called the **spoils system.** Under the spoils system, those elected to national office would appoint their own friends and political allies to national government jobs after discharging the previous officeholder's appointees. This system failed to meet the need for qualified, trained government employees. Every time a new party was elected to office, an entirely new group of employees took over. Obviously, this made it very difficult for the national government to undertake long-range programs.

The abuses of the spoils system became serious enough to merit congressional attention. In 1883, a bi-partisan commission, the Civil Service Commission, was established by Congress to prepare and administer competitive examinations for government jobs. The examinations are known as **civil service examinations.** Several states also passed civil service laws and began to fill jobs through civil service examinations. These laws put into effect the idea that **merit,** or suitability, is the reason to hire someone for public service. Currently, under the Office of Per-

◀ *Astronauts represent just one of the many diverse, and often exciting, career opportunities in government.*

sonnel Management, merit remains the primary criterion for government employment, especially at the national level.

Military Service Those who join a branch of military service may choose from many career options. Training is available in such areas as electronics, aviation, aircraft mechanics, computer programming, and ship navigation. Because the military must staff its ranks with volunteer enlistees, it finds that it is competing with civilian employers for workers. As a result, the military now offers benefits and training programs that encourage people to enlist and to stay in the service once their initial enlistment period has expired. New recruits also receive good starting salaries, free room and board or a housing allowance, free medical care, paid vacations, and access to tax-free goods at military stores.

SECTION 3 REVIEW

1. What are the rights of a U.S. citizen?
2. What is the incorporation theory?
3. What are the responsibilities of a U.S. citizen?
4. What is the procedure for getting a job with the national government?
5. **For Critical Analysis:** Voting is the most common way for citizens to participate in our democracy, but not all of us vote. Does not voting reduce a person's effectiveness as a citizen?

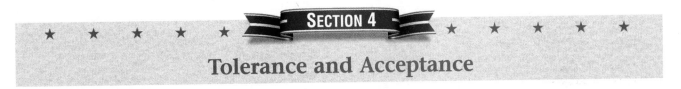

SECTION 4

Tolerance and Acceptance

Preview Questions:

🌐 How is the ethnic make-up of America, especially its school-age population, changing?

🌐 What does tolerance really mean?

🌐 What are some ways in which Americans can become more familiar with our country's diverse cultures?

Key Term:

tolerance

Census data make it clear that America is truly a multicultural society. In 1980, for example, non-Hispanic whites represented a majority in six of the ten largest cities in America. In the 1990s, non-Hispanic whites were a majority in only three. The combined numbers of African Americans, Hispanic Americans, Asian Americans, and others now constitute the majority population in Chicago, Dallas, Detroit, Houston, Los Angeles, New York, and San Antonio. Today, members of minorities account for one out of every four Americans. In the past, African Americans were the majority among minorities. That is no longer true in many areas. In California, for example, African Americans are now outnumbered by Asian Americans and Hispanic Americans.

The School-Age Population Is Changing

Public schools are increasingly faced with the challenge of educating children with many different backgrounds. In one high school in a Los Angeles suburb, for example, more than thirty languages are spoken.

This trend toward cultural diversity will continue. In 1990, there were 45 million non-Hispanic white children under the age of eighteen; in 2000, there is an estimated 43 million, and by 2010, there will be 38 million. During the same twenty-year time span, the number of minority children is expected to grow from 19 million to 23 million.

Perhaps the most difficult challenge facing educators today is how to best educate children who do not speak English or who do not speak it very well. Should attempts be made to educate these children in their native languages through bilingual education programs? Or should students be taught only in English? These questions are explored in the *Extended Case Study* beginning on page 230.

English-Only Laws

English has never been legally declared the "official" language of the United States, even though the majority of Americans speak English. In other words, there are no national laws that require government officials and employees to speak only English on the job. Some states, however, have passed laws making English the official language. Should there be a similar national law? Americans are at odds over this issue.

Make English Official, Argue Some Americans

Some Americans believe that English should be made the official language of the United States. Proponents of English-only laws argue that what made this country great was its ability to assimilate large numbers of foreigners—all speaking different languages—very quickly. This group argues that becoming part of this society and economy requires learning to understand and speak English. So learning English should be encouraged or required, not discouraged. Without English-only laws, say these proponents, immigrants remain isolated and are unable to fully participate in the "American dream."

English-only legislation, according to its proponents, should therefore be applied to public schooling. They argue that bilingual programs, particularly those for Spanish-speaking children, have been a failure. Studies show that the longer students remain in such programs, the less successful they are in school. For example, the dropout rate for Hispanic students remains the highest in the country despite the nearly thirty-year history of bilingual education programs. (For more information on bilingual education, see the *Extended Case Study* on this topic beginning on page 230.)

English Already Predominates, Others Reply

Those who oppose English-only laws say that we simply do not need them. The English language will continue to be the dominant language without such laws. In fact, English is fast becoming the universal language of the modern world. It is already the language of choice in finance, trade, technology, diplomacy, and mass entertainment. One-third of all books printed in the world are in English. Three-quarters of the world's secondary school students study English. Understanding English is the key to understanding most of today's movies and pop music—a fact particularly important among the young people of this earth.

Furthermore, the Internet is quickly making English its dominant language. According to the opponents of "official" English, given the dominance of English, it is almost ridiculous to think that there is any need for a policy to protect it.

YOU DECIDE

1. Can you think of other arguments for or against English-only laws?
2. Describe how the following persons might feel about English-only laws and why their feelings about such laws might differ: (a) an immigrant who has recently arrived in the United States from a non-English-speaking country, (b) a person born in the United States whose parents immigrated from a non-English-speaking country, and (c) a person whose family has lived in the United States for many generations.

◄ As America's racial and ethnic make-up continues to change, teenagers such as these will find themselves living in a nation quite different from the one in which their parents grew up. What are the benefits and challenges of a diverse society?

The Need for Tolerance

Many of our forebears came to North America to escape religious, ethnic, and economic persecution. One of the enduring assets that the United States has developed from this history is its ability to accept and appreciate diversity. Part of being a good citizen is acknowledging and respecting the views, customs, appearances, actions, languages, and religions of others. The *Random House Dictionary* defines **tolerance** as follows:

> A fair, objective, and permissive attitude toward those whose opinions, practices, race, religion, nationality, etc., differ from one's own.

Just the Facts

University codes designed to prohibit "hate speech"—hostile verbal exchanges among different racial or ethnic groups—have been struck down by the Supreme Court as unconstitutional restraints on the freedom of speech.

A further definition of *tolerance* includes "interest in and concern for the ideas, opinions, and practices that are foreign to one's own." Thus, tolerance can be taken to mean not only getting along with people who may be different from us but also taking an active interest in their ideas, practices, and ways of life. An American practicing good citizenship therefore is involved in the cultural diversity of this nation. Here are some ways in which this can be done:

- Maintaining friendships with people from various ethnic, cultural, national, or religious backgrounds.
- Reading and studying about the origins of prejudice.
- Experimenting with cuisine and music from various cultures.
- Participating in multicultural conferences, forums, and discussions.
- Respecting religious and cultural customs and beliefs that are different from your own.

Ethics and Tolerance

Nothing in the Constitution or in any law specifically requires Americans to be tolerant. Rather, these qualities are part of the ethical, or moral, heritage of this nation. Our First Amendment rights—to freedom of speech and freedom of religion, for example—would mean little if these rights were not respected throughout society. As the French social philosopher Alexis de Tocqueville (1805–1859) said in *Democracy in America* (1835):

> The best laws cannot make a constitution work in spite of morals; morals can turn the worst laws to advantage. That

◀ *The Statue of Liberty, a huge copper monument, stands as a symbol to the world that we welcome immigrants. The statue, located on Liberty Island, dominates the New York Harbor scene. A gift from the French people to the United States, the statue was unveiled in 1886 to honor the first U.S. centennial.*

is a commonplace truth, but one to which my studies are always bringing me back. It is the central point in my conception. I see it at the end of all my reflections.

The point here is that laws alone cannot make a constitution work. Rather, for a constitution to endure, citizens must be morally committed to its principles. Our rights under the First Amendment form the *legal* basis of tolerance, but not the *moral* basis. That comes from a conscientious effort to understand and respect the ideas and customs of others.

SECTION 4 REVIEW

1. About what percent of the U.S. population consists of members of minority groups?
2. Why does our increasingly diverse population create new challenges for educators?
3. What does *tolerance* mean?
4. **For Critical Analysis:** How do you explain the attitudes of Americans who are intolerant toward members of other ethnic groups?

★ ★ ★ ★ **Chapter Summary** ★ ★ ★ ★

Section 1: Who Is a Citizen?

- When slavery was abolished in 1865 at the end of the Civil War, the nation realized it needed to define who is a U.S. citizen.
- The Fourteenth Amendment sets forth the two basic sources of American citizenship. The first, and most common, is by birth on American soil. The second is by a legal process called naturalization.
- There is also a third source—by being born of a parent who is a U.S. citizen.
- Citizenship may be lost by expatriation, punishment for a crime, or denaturalization.

Section 2: Immigration and the Noncitizen

- Although the United States is a "nation of immigrants," not everyone who lives here falls into that category.
- Immigrants are those persons living in the United States who intend to become naturalized citizens and remain in the country permanently.

- People who reside in the United States but are not U.S. citizens and have not stated an intention to become U.S. citizens are considered to be aliens.
- According to the U.S. law, there are five categories of aliens: (1) resident alien, (2) nonresident alien, (3) enemy alien, (4) refugees, and (5) illegal aliens.
- American policies on immigration have gone through many changes.
- Immigration policies and the number of people that should be allowed to immigrate each year are a source of ongoing controversy.

Section 3: Citizenship Rights and Responsibilities

- Americans have both rights and responsibilities.
- The last hundred years of Supreme Court decisions have bound the fifty states to observe most of the guarantees in the U.S. Bill of Rights.
- Responsible citizens should obey the law and participate in political life by voting, defending civil rights, paying taxes, attending school, defending the nation, serving on juries or as witnesses when necessary, and contributing to the well-being of society.
- Making sure that rights, privileges, and services are extended to all citizens is the job of the men and women who choose careers in public and community service.
- Careers in public service are incredibly varied, and include a diversity of occupations from zookeeper to accountant to astronaut.
- Under the Office of Personnel Management, merit remains the primary criterion for government employment.

Section 4: Tolerance and Acceptance

- The numbers of African Americans, Hispanic Americans, Asian Americans, and other members of minority groups are increasing as a proportion of the U.S. population.
- Public schools face the challenge of educating children with many different backgrounds and different languages.
- Americans are at odds over the issue of requiring that English be the official language of the United States.
- Tolerance is necessary in a multicultural society. Tolerance includes having an interest in and concern for ideas, opinions, and practices that are different from one's own.

CHAPTER 8 Review

★ REVIEW QUESTIONS ★

1. What was the significance of the decision in *Dred Scott v. Sandford* (1857)?
2. What are the two basic sources of American citizenship according to the Fourteenth Amendment?
3. What are the three methods by which an individual can become a naturalized citizen?
4. How can a person lose his or her citizenship?
5. According to U.S. law, what are the five categories of aliens, and how are they defined?
6. How have U.S. policies concerning immigration changed over the years?
7. How did the Fourteenth Amendment lead to the standardization of U.S. citizens' rights?
8. What are some of the responsibilities of U.S. citizens?
9. Until the 1880s, how was the federal government staffed? How did civil service examinations change this system?
10. What does tolerance mean?

★ CRITICAL THINKING ★

1. Some countries are concerned that their own highly skilled citizens are leaving to come to the United States—a situation often referred to as "brain drain." What do you think the U.S. government should do about the immigration of such people?
2. Which groups, if any, do you feel should *not* be allowed to immigrate to the United States? Explain your answer.
3. The United States gives its citizens the freedom to vote or not vote as they see fit. In some countries, it is illegal not to vote, except for medical reasons. Those who are caught not voting must pay a fine. How do you think such a law would affect the system of government in the United States?
4. Many homeowners, particularly in the Southwest, employ illegal Hispanic immigrants as housekeepers. On the one hand, these homeowners are helping the illegal aliens violate U.S. immigration law. On the other hand, they are allowing the illegal aliens to live better lives. What do you think are the pros and cons of homeowners' hiring illegal aliens?

★ IMPROVING YOUR SKILLS ★

Communication Skills

Expressing Your Opinion Effectively When you express your opinion, you usually are trying to inform or persuade others. Expressing your opinion effectively involves gathering convincing evidence and presenting it as clearly and forcefully as possible. Use the following guidelines to help you express your opinion to the best of your ability.

1. *Define your audience.* Knowing your audience is critical. Expressing your opinion to your friends, for example, calls for a different style of presentation than expressing your opinion to the city council. Knowing your audience helps you tailor your presentation. The audience can determine how serious or humorous you should be, whether spontaneous conversation would be more effective than a memorized speech, and other factors.
2. *Define your goals.* Decide what you wish to accomplish by expressing your opinion. Do you want to persuade your audience or to inform them?
3. *Gather convincing factual evidence and organize your ideas.* Make sure you have the facts to back up your opinion and to answer any questions that might come up. Try to think of potential opposing arguments, and plan your responses to them. Organize your ideas according to which ones are most important.

UNIT II: The Rights and Responsibilities of All Citizens

4. *Rehearse your presentation with family or friends.* This will help you anticipate how an audience will respond.

Writing Suppose your state legislature is considering raising the highway speed limit. You have the opportunity to express your opinion on the proposed measure. First, decide whether you are for or against the new limit. Then write an outline of the speech you will give to present your opinion.

Social Studies Skills

Reading a Pie Chart Look at the pie chart below and answer these questions.

U.S. Households by Type, 1990

Family, married couple householders
50,708,322
(55.2%)

Family, single male householder
3,143,582
(3.4%)

Family, single female householder
10,666,043
(11.6%)

Non-family household
27,429,463
(29.8%)

SOURCE: United States Department of Commerce, Bureau of the Census.

1. Which type of household represents the smallest percentage of all households? The largest percentage?

2. What does the term *non-family household* mean?

★ ACTIVITIES AND PROJECTS ★

1. Stage a debate on one of the following statements:
   (a) Immigrants are taking away the jobs of Americans.
   (b) Americans should be required by law to vote.
   (c) Any person or business firm caught hiring illegal aliens should be fined $10,000.
2. Many people feel that for every right, there is a responsibility. Make a chart to show this relationship. List all the rights of American citizens on one side of a sheet of paper. For every right, list a corresponding responsibility on the other side.
3. Gather information on the 1986, 1990, and 1996 immigration acts. Make a table showing how each act changed immigration policy.
4. Research the requirements for naturalization in some country other than the United States, and present your findings to the class.

What If . . .

Immigration Were Entirely Banned?

On a regular basis, the United States offers citizenship to legal immigrants. What might happen to America in years to come if immigration were entirely banned?

Bilingual Education

Part of the controversy over English-only laws, described in Chapter 8, involves bilingual education programs. Bilingual education, at least in theory, gives children instruction in their native language while also teaching them English. Bilingual education programs were authorized by the Bilingual Education Act of 1968, which was primarily intended to help Hispanic children learn English. Such programs have always been controversial, and today they are increasingly coming under attack. Recently, a ballot measure was proposed in California called "English for the Children." The measure, if passed by California voters, would all but eliminate bilingual education programs in that state.

A Source Document

Excerpts from the California "English for the Children" ballot initiative.

[A]ll children in California public schools shall be taught English by being taught in English. In particular, this shall require that all children be placed in English language classrooms. Children who are English learners shall be educated through sheltered English immersion during a temporary transition period not normally intended to exceed one year. Local schools shall be permitted to place in the same classroom English learners of different ages but whose degree of English proficiency is similar. Local schools shall be encouraged to mix together in the same classroom English learners from different native-language groups but with the same degree of English fluency. Once English learners have acquired a good working knowledge of English, they shall be transferred to English language mainstream classrooms.

Media Reports

Debate over the "English for the Children" measure extends beyond California, because the measure, if it passes, will have implications for the way English is taught in schools throughout the United States. Here are some excerpts from arguments presented in the news media on the California measure.

Is It Hasta la Vista for Bilingual Ed?

U.S. News & World Report

Like other recent ballot measures, this one seems to have all the makings of a California classic: a racially divisive, inflammatory issue that pits the state's testy white electorate against its growing immigrant population. But so far the politics have played out quite differently. The initiative is expected to be strongly supported by Latinos and other immigrants—if not by the activists who say they represent them. In a recent Los Angeles Times poll that incited editorial writers and talk-radio hosts, 84 percent of Latinos said they would support the bilingual-education initiative, surpassing even the 80 percent of white voters who said they would back it. Immigrants tend to regard English as the language of upward mobility and want their children to learn it as quickly as possible. And bilingual education, many believe, isn't working.

Source: U.S. News & World Report, November 21, 1997. Copyright U.S. News & World Report.

Out of a Linguistic Ghetto

Washington Post

Twenty-three percent of California's pupils—1.3 million children—are classified as limited [in English proficiency].

Most parents whose children are assigned to bilingual education and are often taught for all but 30 minutes a day in a language other than English believe their children are being shunted onto a slow academic track.

Compulsory bilingual education is not simply another case of compassion that cripples—of misguided government solicitousness that weakens the social competence of the intended beneficiaries. Precious little real compassion enters into this grab for government money. This is a matter of perverse incentives: School districts get extra jobs and government payments totaling more than $320 million for bilingual education. . . .

America has long been, in the words of the Hispanic-American writer Richard Rodriguez, "a marinade of sounds." But as Rodriguez wrote in Hunger of Memory, *his brilliant meditation on language and the immigrant experience, those who are not proficient in English risk "being lured into a linguistic nursery." Next June Californians can empower parents to rescue their children from confinement in that nursery.*

Source: *The Washington Post*, October 26, 1997. © 1997, Washington Post Writers Group. Reprinted with permission.

Double Talk?

Transcript of a PBS *NewsHour* Debate

JAMES LYONS, EXECUTIVE DIRECTOR OF THE NATIONAL ASSOCIATION OF BILINGUAL EDUCATION: *It is not the case that bilingual education is failing children. There are poor bilingual education programs, just as there are poor programs of every type in our schools today. But bilingual education has made it possible for children to have continuous development in their native language, while they're in the process of learning English, something that doesn't happen overnight, and it's made it possible for children to learn math and science at a rate equal to English-speaking children while they're in the process of acquiring English. . . .*

We have children who are graduating today after 13 years in public schooling unable to read, unable to write. Is bilingual education to blame? No, it's not. It can't be, because these children were never in a bilingual education program, and, in fact, they're native English speakers. I think we're confusing what is the cause of the problem. We have poor schools throughout this country in virtually every state of the union. Bilingual education is part of the poor schools in some places; in other places they're allowing

children to achieve everything that they need to achieve and to excel, go to college.

Source: Transcript of *The NewsHour* with Jim Lehrer on PBS, September 21, 1997.

Conclusion

Bilingual education programs are the result of policies favoring multiculturalism. These policies date back to the 1960s. The controversy over bilingual education is thus, to some extent, part of a larger debate over the merits of multiculturalism. Multiculturalism involves the belief that the government should accommodate the needs of different cultural groups and should protect and encourage ethnic and cultural differences. Critics of multiculturalism believe that government policies should emphasize the unity, not the diversity, of American culture. One way to do this is by helping the children of immigrants learn, as quickly as possible, the English language—a basic unifying element in American culture.

The primary focus of the movement against bilingual education in California, though, is education. Do bilingual education programs hinder Hispanic children's chances of success in the world dominated by the English language? Voters in states that have large Hispanic populations will eventually decide this question at the polls.

Analysis Questions

1. Should students in "English immersion" programs be encouraged to speak English, instead of their native languages, in their homes? Why or why not?
2. In the final excerpt above, James Lyons points out that even some native English speakers are graduating from high school without knowing how to read and write. Does this really have any bearing on the bilingual education issue, as Lyons contends? Explain.
3. Some people have argued that English-only policies reflect a bias against minority groups, especially Hispanic Americans. Analyze this argument with respect to the bilingual education issue in California.
4. How would you argue in support of bilingual education? How would you argue against it?

The Politics of Democracy

The Lincoln Memorial stands in honor of one of this country's greatest presidents.

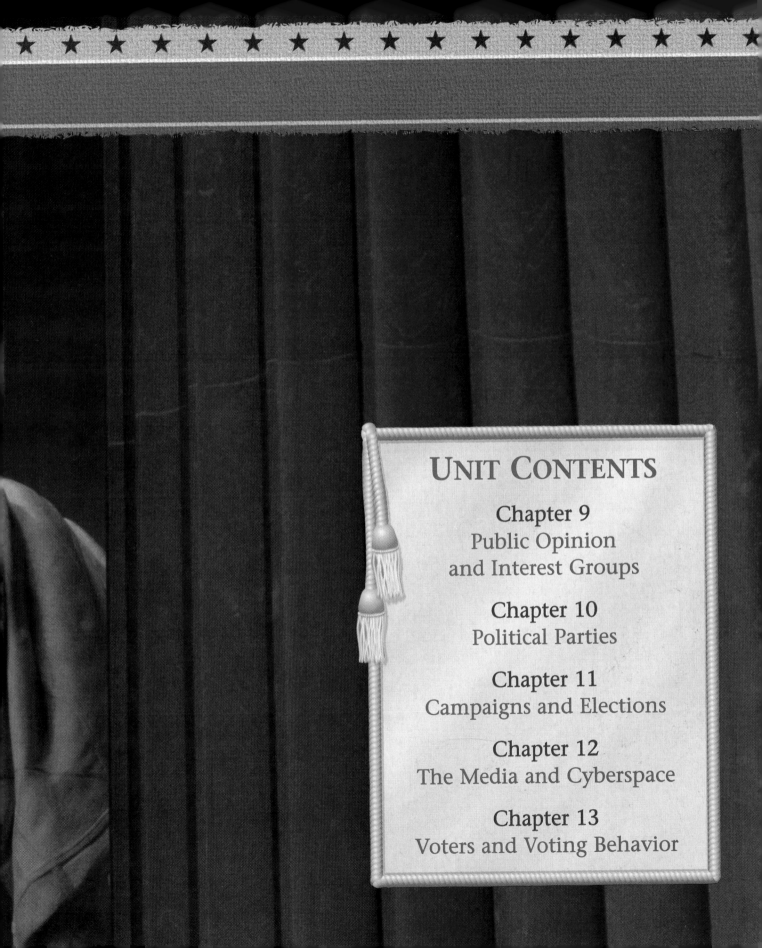

CHAPTER 9

Public Opinion and Interest Groups

CHAPTER OBJECTIVES

To learn about and understand . . .

⭐ What public opinion is and how it is measured

⭐ The many factors that affect public opinion

⭐ How political attitudes are categorized

⭐ The many different types of interest groups and how they function in American politics

⭐ The various strategies used by interest groups to affect public policy

"A government can be no better than the public opinion that sustains it."

Franklin D. Roosevelt
(1882–1945)
Thirty-second President of the United States

INTRODUCTION

Suppose for a moment that your school is governed democratically. In this democracy, the students have the final say in determining school policies and procedures. But what if a significant number of students did not have an opinion on what school policies and procedures should be? What if many students had opinions but did not clearly communicate those opinions to school officials? In this situation, there could be no true democracy.

This example, when applied to our democratic nation, tells you something about how government works. Above all else, the aim of a democratic government is to convert the will of the people into public policy. In the above quotation, President Roosevelt was reminding the people of their responsibility to make our democratic system work by forming opinions and openly expressing them to public officials. Otherwise, these officials will never know what the people want.

◀ The purpose of the NAMES Project was to heighten public awareness of AIDS sufferers. The names embroidered onto quilts were of people who had died of the disease.

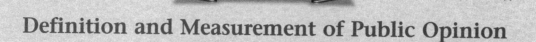
Definition and Measurement of Public Opinion

Preview Questions:

- 🌐 What is public opinion, and why is it important in American politics?
- 🌐 What is a public opinion poll, and how does it work?

Key Terms:

public opinion, public opinion poll, samples, straw poll, biased sample, random sample, sampling error

People hold opinions—sometimes very strong ones—about a range of issues, from the ethics of the death penalty to the appearance of the latest fashion. In this chapter, however, we are concerned with **public opinion,** which is made up of individual attitudes or beliefs shared by a significant portion of adults about politics, public issues, and public policy.

Public opinion is important in American politics because opinions can determine how government handles such issues as the environment and the death penalty. You may hear a news report stating that "a significant number of Americans" feel a certain way about an issue. This probably means that a particular opinion is held by a large enough number of people to make government officials turn their heads and listen. Public opinion is most often cast in terms of percentages: 62 percent feel this way, 27 percent do not, and 11 percent have no opinion.

Public opinion is limited to those issues that are in the public arena, such as taxes, health care, Social Security, clean-air legislation, unemployment, and so on. The issue must be of interest to a significant number of people, and must be cause for some kind of political action, social action, or media coverage.

When does *private* opinion become *public* opinion? After all, you and your friends probably have private opinions about many people and issues. You may think your school principal is a great person. You may dislike the way your neighbor painted the house next door. Private opinion becomes public opinion only when it is *publicly* expressed and concerns *public* issues. Whenever your private opinion becomes so strong that you are willing to go to the polls to vote for or against a candidate or an issue, your private opinion has become public opinion. If you feel so intensely about an issue you are willing to speak out on a radio talk show, your private opinion has become public opinion.

Measuring Public Opinion

If public opinion is to affect public policy, then public officials must be made aware of it. They must know how strongly people feel about the issues. They must also know when public opinion changes. The most common ways public officials learn about public opinion are through election results, personal contacts, interest groups, and media reports. A somewhat more

▲ *Polling by phone is one way of of measuring public opinion. While most respondents give straight answers, statisticians adjust their numbers for the occasional nonstandard answer, like Sally's.*

precise way to measure public opinion is through public opinion polls.

A **public opinion poll** is a survey of the public's opinion on a particular topic. A poll cannot include the entire population. Instead, polls are based on scientific polling techniques that use **samples**—groups of people who are representative of the population being studied.

◀ *The data for opinion polls are gathered from only a small portion of the population, and therefore might not represent the majority. For example, opinions gathered at a yacht club might differ greatly from opinions gathered at a neighborhood shopping center.*

Early Polling Efforts During the 1800s, writers often spiced up a magazine or newspaper article by doing a **straw poll,** or mail survey, of readers' opinions. Straw polls try to read the public's collective mind simply by asking a large number of people the same question. Straw polls are still used today. Some newspapers, for example, have interviewers ask adults in shopping centers and other central locations to "vote" on certain issues. More and more of this type of polling, however, makes use of telephone technology and "900" telephone numbers.

The major problem with straw polls is that there is no way to ensure that the opinions expressed are representative of the population being studied. Generally speaking, such opinions represent only a small portion of that population. The most famous of all straw-polling errors took place in 1936. A magazine called *Literary Digest* sent out millions of postcard ballots for the purpose of predicting the outcome of a presidential election. The *Digest* predicted that Alfred Landon would easily defeat incumbent Franklin D. Roosevelt. Instead, Roosevelt won by a landslide.

How did the magazine go so wrong? The *Digest* had drawn a **biased sample,** one that did not accurately represent the population. The magazine's editors had sent mail-in cards to citizens whose names appeared in telephone directories, to its own subscribers, and to automobile owners—in all, a staggering 2,376,000 people. In 1936, however, in the middle of the Great Depression, people who owned a car or a telephone or who subscribed to the *Digest* were not representative of the majority of Americans. The vast majority of Americans were far less prosperous than this group. Despite the enormous number of people surveyed, the sample was unrepresentative. Thus, the results of the survey were inaccurate.

Several newcomers to the public opinion poll industry, however, did predict the Roosevelt landslide victory. They were the Gallup poll of George Gallup and the Roper poll of Elmo Roper. The Gallup and Roper organizations are still at the forefront of the poll-taking industry.

Sampling How can interviewing a small sample of 1,500 to 2,000 voters possibly indicate what *millions* of voters think? Clearly, the sample must be representative of all the voters in the population being studied. A sample must consist of a group of people who are *typical* of that general population. If the sample is properly selected, the opinions of those in the sample will be representative of the opinions held by the larger population. If the sample is not properly chosen, then the results of the poll may not reflect the ideas of the general population under study.

Just the Facts

In numerous Gallup polls, less than half of the respondents can correctly name their congressional representatives.

The most important principle in sampling is randomness. In a **random sample,** every person in the population being polled has an equal chance of being chosen. Suppose that a polling organization wants to measure women's opinions on an issue. In order to have a truly representative random sample, the sample should have the same characteristics, in the same proportions, as the entire female population. For example, if 25 percent of the female population is between the ages of 25 and 40, then 25 percent of the sample must be in this age group.

Polls can be surprisingly accurate when they are conducted properly. Politicians, the news media, and the public place a great deal of faith in the accuracy of poll results. Policymakers use polls to determine where the majority stands on particular issues.

Writing a Letter to the Editor

One of the many ways in which public opinion is expressed in this country is through letters to the editors of newspapers and magazines. Letters to the editor are usually printed on the opinion and editorial (op-ed) page of the newspaper and on the pages immediately following the table of contents in a magazine. Usually, newspapers and magazines print letters that best represent a variety of their readers' opinions. Use the following guidelines when you write a letter to the editor:

- **Know your purpose for writing.** Before you begin writing, be sure to know whether you are trying to inform, persuade, inquire, or complain.
- **Know your subject.** Research your subject before you write your letter so you can back up your opinions with facts.
- **Make sure your letter is neat and well organized.**
- **Use precise language.** Don't try to impress anybody with your vocabulary. Avoid harsh or sarcastic language. The

important thing is to convey your message.
- **Be brief and to the point.** Newspapers and magazines do not have the space to print long-winded introductions or explanations. Plan your opening sentence carefully so that your letter will make a strong initial impact. Deal with only one topic.
- **Use correct grammar and spelling.**
- **Appeal to your readers' sense of fair play and justice.** Challenge them to think

about and respond to the issue.
- **Try to be optimistic and practical.** If your letter is pointing out a problem, offer potential solutions.

For the final draft, type your letter on one side of the paper using double spacing. Sign your name and give your address and telephone number. You can use a pen name or initials if you wish.

TAKING ACTION

1. Select an issue affecting your school that you would like to write about for a local newspaper. Write a draft of your letter, and read it to the class. Ask for constructive criticism from students and teachers.
2. Obtain a copy of the newspaper, and read its instructions on submitting letters to the editor. Then send the editor a neatly typed copy of your finished letter.

Supporters of polling argue that it is a tool for democracy. In contrast, critics of polling think that it makes politicians reactors rather than leaders. Critics also argue that election polls can discourage voters from voting when the polls predict that their candidates will lose.

Problems with Polls Although the methods used by public opinion pollsters have improved since the days of *Literary Digest*, polls have limitations and faults.

One criticism of polls is that the wording of questions can affect responses to the questions. Consider a question about building a new town library. One way to gather opinions about this issue is to ask, "Do you believe the town should have a new library?" Another way is to ask, "Are you willing to pay higher property taxes so that the town can build a new library?" Very likely, the poll results will differ depending on how the question is phrased.

The Changing Face of Public Opinion Polling

Before the 1930s, public opinion polling was much less sophisticated than it is today.

THEN (BEFORE THE 1930S)	NOW
Public opinion polls were sponsored by the media.	Public opinion polls are sponsored by interest groups, political parties, and candidates, as well as the media.
Public opinion polls did not predict election results very well.	Public opinion polls consistently predict election results very well (at least with respect to who is going to win or lose).
Most opinion polls were "straw polls" that did not use scientific sampling techniques.	Opinion polls are now based on random, representative samples and are therefore more reliable measures of public opinion.
Opinion pollsters typically relied on personal interviews to gather information.	Opinion pollsters use a variety of techniques to gather information, including call-in surveys, telephone or computer-assisted polls, and talk shows.

Polls often reduce complex issues to simple "yes" or "no" questions. For example, suppose respondents are asked to answer "yes" or "no" to the question, "Do you favor aid to foreign countries?" Opinions could vary according to the recipient country or the purpose or the type of aid. The poll would nonetheless force respondents to answer "yes" or "no." These answers would not necessarily reflect respondents' true feelings.

Public opinion polls can also be misused. Instead of measuring public opinion, they can end up creating it. For example, a candidate might claim that all the polls show that he or she is ahead. People who want to vote for the winner may support this person.

Some people also question polls' reliability. Drawing accurate random samples is difficult. Any opinion poll contains a **sampling error,** the difference between what the sample results show and what the true result would be if everybody in the country had been polled.

Furthermore, the answers given to pollsters may not be reliable. Those interviewed may be influenced by the interviewer's personality and give an answer that they think will please the interviewer. They may answer without having any information on the issue. Finally, opinion polls cannot reflect rapid shifts in public opinion unless they are taken frequently. This can be especially important in voting polls taken before elections.

SECTION 1 REVIEW

1. What is public opinion?
2. What were some problems with early polling efforts?
3. What is sampling? What is random sampling?

4. What are some problems with public opinion polls?
5. What does the sampling error of a poll represent?
6. **For Critical Analysis:** Explain why supporters of polling argue that it is a tool for democracy and why critics of polling think that it makes politicians reactors rather than leaders. Then explain which opinion you agree with and why.

SECTION 2

Factors That Affect Public Opinion

Preview Questions:

- ⭐ What is political socialization?
- ⭐ What is the difference between informal and formal political socialization?
- ⭐ What are agents of political socialization, and how do these agents and other factors affect public opinion?

Key Terms:

political socialization, mass media, peer group

When asked, most Americans are willing to express an opinion on political issues. Not one of us, however, was born with these opinions. Most of the attitudes and beliefs that are expressed as political opinions are acquired through a learning process called **political socialization.** This complex process begins in early childhood and continues through a person's life.

Political socialization can be informal or formal. Informal political socialization usually begins with the family. Although parents do not normally sit down and say, "Let us explain to you the virtues of becoming a Republican," children nevertheless come to know their parents' feelings, beliefs, and attitudes. Words such as *acquire*, *absorb*, and *pick up* perhaps best describe the informal process of political socialization. In contrast, formal political socialization involves activities such as taking a government class in high school.

> **Just the Facts**
>
> The authors of the Federalist Papers believed that public opinion was potentially dangerous and that this danger could be reduced by having a large republic.

Studies have shown that most political socialization is informal. There is little evidence that formally learning about political views has a lasting impact on people's political opinions. Rather, the strong early influence of the family later gives way to the multiple influences of school, peers, television, co-workers, and so on. We look here at the major agents of political socialization—groups that influence our political views—as well as at some other factors that affect public opinion.

The Importance of Family

Most parents do not deliberately set out to form their children's political ideas and beliefs. They are usually more concerned with the moral, religious, and ethical values of their offspring. Yet children first see the political world through the eyes of their families—

▲ One shift in public opinion that has surprised many observers is the rise in home schooling. What changes in American society may have caused some parents to decide to teach their children "the old-fashioned way"?

the most important force in political socialization. Children do not "learn" political attitudes the same way they learn to ride a bike. Rather, they learn by absorbing everyday conversations and stories about politicians and issues and by watching the actions of their family members. Families play such a crucial role in political socialization because they dominate a child's early years in terms of time and emotional commitment. The powerful influence of family is not easily broken.

The family's influence is strongest when children clearly perceive their parents' attitudes. In one study, more high-school students could identify their parents' political party affiliation than any other of their parents' attitudes or beliefs. It is no wonder, then, that in most cases, the political party of the parents becomes the political party of the child.

Educational Influence

Education is a powerful influence on an individual's political attitudes. From their earliest days in school, children learn about the U.S. political system. They say the Pledge of Allegiance and sing patriotic songs. They celebrate national holidays such as Presidents' Day and Veterans Day and learn the history and symbols associated with them. In the upper grades, children learn more about government and democratic procedures through civic education classes and through student government and clubs. They also learn citizenship skills through school rules and regulations.

The level of education a person has influences his or her political knowledge and participation. For example, more highly educated men and women tend to show more knowledge about politics and policy. They also tend to vote and participate more often in politics.

The Mass Media

The **mass media**—newspapers, magazines, television, and radio—also have an impact on political socialization. The most influential of these media is television. Grade-school children spend an average of thirty-two hours per week watching television, more time than they spend in academic classes. Television is the leading source of political and public affairs information for most people.

▲ Reaching across racial, social, and economic lines, television finds its way into the homes of almost every American. Have television programs influenced your political views in any way?

The media can also determine what issues, events, and personalities are in the public eye. When people hear the evening's top stories, they usually assume that these stories concern the most important issues facing the nation. But by publicizing some issues and ignoring others, and by giving some stories high priority and others low priority, the media decide the relative importance of issues. They help determine what people will talk and think about. This, in turn, helps determine on which issues politicians will act.

For example, television played a significant role in shaping public opinion about the Vietnam War, which has been called the first "television war." Part of the public opposition to the war in the late 1960s came from the scenes and narrative accounts of destruction, death, and suffering that were televised daily. The war to free Kuwait from Iraqi occupation in 1991 also had extensive media coverage, though some critics feel that this coverage may have shown only the better side of U.S. efforts.

Clearly, the media play an important role in shaping public opinion. The *extent* of that role, however, is often debated. Some studies have suggested that the media may be as influential as the family in shaping

Public opinion polls claim to tell us a variety of things: whether the president's popularity is up or down, or who is ahead in the race for the next presidential nomination.

When you see this information, keep in mind that poll results are not equally reliable. Before you believe what a poll is leading you to conclude, ask the following questions:

1. **Who paid for the poll?** If a poll was sponsored by a particular candidate or interest group the results may be presented in a misleading way. Take this into account and look carefully at how the poll results are worded.
2. **Who was interviewed?** A poll should reveal something about the population sampled. The best samples are random samples, in which everyone has an equal chance of being interviewed. You should be skeptical of the person-in-the-shopping-mall interviews. Almost certainly, the people in the mall are not representative of all the people in the community.
3. **How were the interviews obtained?** Were the interviews conducted by telephone? By mail? In person? Many pollsters think that people are less honest over the telephone than in person. Because telephone

BUILDING
SOCIAL STUDIES SKILLS

How to Read a Public Opinion Poll

surveys cost less than person-to-person interviews, however, they are often used. Also be wary of the results of mail questionnaires. Only a small percentage of people tend to complete and return them. These people may not be representative of the general population.

4. **When were the interviews conducted?** If the interviews were conducted a year ago or more, the results may be outdated. This is particularly true if a change has taken place that would cause people to feel differently.
5. **How were the questions worded?** Elmo Roper, a famous pollster, once said:

If you ask people about any subject that they've got very strong opinions on, how you word

the question really doesn't matter. When they don't have convictions, how you ask questions and in what sequence you ask them are critical. You can flip-flop the answers ten points one way or the other just because of a relatively subtle phraseology difference or the context in which you ask the questions.

PRACTICING YOUR SKILLS

1. Look through at least three news or business magazines. Make photocopies of all of the opinion polls and then analyze them in terms of the following questions:
   a. How many individuals were included in each poll?
   b. What percentage of the population being studied does this number represent?
2. Watch the TV news for seven consecutive days. Write down the number of times the newscasters refer to the results of opinion polls. Can you tell by the statements concerning the polls whether the number of individuals polled was small or large? Can you determine whether the polls were done over the phone or in person? After answering these questions, decide how much credibility you wish to give to each poll result.

opinion. Other studies have shown that the media may not have as much power to influence opinion as has been thought. Generally, people already have ideas about issues they see or hear about in the mass media. These ideas act as a screen to block out any information that does not fit with them. For example, if you are already firmly convinced that being a vegetarian is beneficial to your health, you probably will not change your mind if you watch a TV show that asserts that vegetarians live no longer on average than people who eat meat. Apparently, the media are most influential with those persons who have not yet formed an opinion about the issue being discussed.

Opinion Leaders

Every state and community has leaders who can influence the opinions of their fellow citizens. These people may be public officials, religious leaders, teachers, or celebrities. They are persons to whom others listen and from whom others draw ideas and convictions about various issues of public concern. These leaders play a significant role in the formation of public opinion. Martin Luther King, Jr., was a powerful opinion leader during the civil rights movements, for example.

Peer Groups

The influence of peer groups is another factor in political socialization. A **peer group** is a group of people who share a number of social characteristics—for example, close friends, classmates, co-workers, club members, or church group members. Most political socialization occurs when the peer group is involved in political activities. For example, your political beliefs might be influenced by peers with whom you are working on a common political cause, such as controlling pollution in your neighborhood or saving an endangered species. Your political beliefs probably would not be as highly influenced by peers with whom you collected stamps or made pottery.

Economic Status and Occupation

A person's economic status may influence his or her political views. For example, poorer people are more likely to favor government-assistance programs than are wealthier people.

Where a person works may also affect her or his opinion. For example, individuals working for a non-profit corporation that depends on government funds will tend to support governmental spending in that area. Business managers are more likely to favor tax shelters and aid to businesses than are people who work in factories. People who work in factories are more likely to favor a national health-care program.

Age

Age does not appear to play a central role in determining political preferences. There are, however, some age differences. Young adults are a bit more liberal than older Americans are on most issues. Young adults tend to be more progressive than older persons on such issues as racial and gender equality.

If older Americans are a little more conservative than younger Americans, it may be because individuals tend to maintain the values they learn when they first became politically aware. Forty years later those values may be considered relatively conservative. Additionally, people's attitudes are sometimes shaped by the events that unfold as they grow up. Individuals who grew up during an era of Democratic Party dominance will likely remain Democrats throughout their lives. The same holds true for those who grew up during an era of Republican Party dominance.

SECTION 2 REVIEW

1. What is political socialization?
2. Name four agents of political socialization.
3. What is the strongest influence on a person's political attitudes?
4. How do economic status, occupation, and age affect a person's political attitudes?
5. **For Critical Analysis:** Every year, events occur in other countries that would never occur in the United States. Yet only a small percentage of these events are ever publicized in this country. What do you think determines which world events receive widespread media coverage?

Categorizing Political Attitudes

Preview Questions:

- What is a liberal?
- What is a conservative?
- What is an ideologue?

Key Terms:

liberals, conservatives, moderates, radical left, radical right, reactionaries, ideologues

Political attitudes are often labeled as either conservative or liberal. Indeed, political officeholders and candidates frequently identify themselves as either liberal or conservative, or they are identified as such by the media. These terms refer to parts of a political spectrum that goes from the left (extremely liberal) to the right (extremely conservative). The terms *liberal* and *conservative* have changed in meaning over the years and will continue to change as political attitudes and ideologies evolve.

Liberal versus Conservative

As just mentioned, the two most commonly used labels with respect to political and social ideals are liberal and conservative. **Liberals** generally support the idea that the national government should take an *active* role in solving the nation's domestic problems. Liberals generally believe that more needs to be done to close the gap between the rich and the poor in this country. Liberals tend to view change in a positive light.

Conservatives tend to value tradition and to promote public policies that *conserve* tradition and the

▶ In the depths of the Great Depression, assistance for poor people was broadly supported by the American people. Sixty-one years later, President Bill Clinton signed into law a bill reforming welfare, thereby ending the guarantee of federal financial assistance to poor people. He is surrounded by several state governors, Vice President Al Gore, and former welfare mothers.

A New Beginning

Welfare to Work

ways of the past. Conservatives place a high value on the principles of community, continuity, and law and order. Conservatives believe that the national government is already too big and should not be expanded further. They think that the nongovernmental sector of society—businesses and consumers—should be left alone to a greater extent than it has been in the past few decades.

Liberals generally support social welfare programs that assist poor and disadvantaged persons, whereas conservatives tend to favor limiting such programs. Liberals generally accept the notion of expanding the role of the national government, whereas conservatives favor giving state and local governments more control over their own citizens and finances. Liberals generally favor decreasing defense spending, whereas conservatives generally favor maintaining or increasing it.

The Left, the Center, and the Right

Look at the diagram of the political spectrum shown in Figure 9–1. As you can see, liberals are on the left side of the spectrum, and conservatives are on the right. Generally, Democrats tend to be liberal and Republicans conservative. There are, however, Democrats who are more conservative than certain liberal Republicans.

People whose political views are in between the liberal and conservative camps are generally called **moderates.** Moderates rarely classify themselves as either liberal or conservative.

On the extreme left of the political spectrum is the **radical left**—radicals (including Communists and socialists) whose followers are willing to work against the established political agencies to reach their goals. They may even accept or advocate using violence or overthrowing the government in order to achieve those goals.

On the extreme right is the **radical right**—radicals (including **reactionaries** and fascists) who resist change much more strongly than do either moderates or conservatives. Reactionaries and fascists are willing to actively fight against social change in order to return to the values and social systems they believe existed in the past. Like the radical left, those on the radical right may even resort to violence to achieve their goals.

The Average American versus the Ideologues

Most Americans, when asked, can identify themselves as liberal, conservative, or something in between. More people identify themselves as moderates than as either liberals or conservatives, however. The Gallup polling organization, the *New York Times*, and CBS News routinely ask individuals to identify themselves in these terms. During the last two decades, between 35 and 50 percent of those polled have said they considered themselves moderate, between 17 and 21 percent have said they considered themselves liberal, and between 26 and 33 percent have said they considered themselves conservative. (The remainder held no opinion.)

> ### Just the Facts
>
> *People with more education tend to be relatively liberal on social issues but relatively conservative on economic issues.*

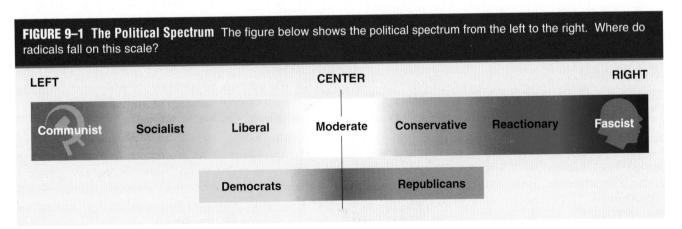

FIGURE 9–1 The Political Spectrum The figure below shows the political spectrum from the left to the right. Where do radicals fall on this scale?

LEFT   CENTER   RIGHT

Communist   Socialist   Liberal   Moderate   Conservative   Reactionary   Fascist

Democrats   Republicans

Some people hold a set of strong political opinions that are well thought out and relatively consistent with one another. These people are often called **ideologues.** Either liberals or conservatives may be ideologues. Most Americans, however, are not interested in *all* political issues and have a mixed set of opinions that do not fit under a conservative or a liberal label. Research shows that only about 10 percent of Americans could be identified as ideologues. The rest of the population looks at politics more in terms of party lines—Democratic or Republican—or from the viewpoint of their own economic well-being.

Ideology versus Self-Interest

Public opinion polls suggest that the majority of Americans hold the strongest political convictions about issues that directly affect their own lives. For example, a poor person would be more likely to support aid to the poor than a wealthy person would be. An elderly person with serious health problems would be more likely to support government funding for long-term medical care than would a young person in good health.

Some researchers have determined that self-interest is a great motivator of public opinion. Individuals who have suffered at the hands of a criminal often express harsh opinions about issues such as capital punishment or building more prisons. People who have been suddenly laid off frequently express negative opinions about the current president's ability to manage the economy.

SECTION 3 REVIEW

1. How do liberals differ from conservatives?
2. What kinds of people are considered ideologues?
3. **For Critical Analysis:** Of what use are the labels *conservative* and *liberal*?

SECTION 4

Interest Groups

Preview Questions:

- What is an interest group?
- What purposes do interest groups serve in American politics?
- How do interest groups differ from political parties?
- What are the various types of interest groups?

Key Terms:

interest group, public interest groups, trade organizations, labor force

All of us have interests that we want represented in government. Farmers want higher prices for their products. Young people want good educational and job opportunities. Environmentalists want clean air and water. Homeless people want programs for food and shelter. Throughout our nation's history, organizing to promote and protect such interests has been a natural part of democracy. As the French political observer Alexis de Tocqueville wrote in his often-cited book *Democracy in America* (1835), Americans have a tendency to form "associations" and have perfected "the art of pursuing in common the object of their common desires." According to de Tocqueville:

[I]n no country in the world has the principle of association been more successfully used or applied to a greater multitude of objectives than in America.

The old adage "there is strength in numbers" is true in American politics. The right to organize groups is protected by the Constitution, which guarantees people the right "peaceably to assemble, and to petition the Government for redress of grievances." The

◀ *Senior citizens in America are a large, vocal, and powerful group. Here a proud member of the American Association of Retired Persons (AARP) looks on as others lobby on behalf of older Americans. What issues might be of particular interest to senior citizens?*

Supreme Court has defended this important right over the years.

What Is an Interest Group?

Defining the term *interest group* seems simple enough. *Interest* in this sense refers to objectives and policy goals. A *group* is an accumulation of people with something in common. An **interest group** is an organization made up of people who share common objectives and who actively attempt to influence government policymakers through direct and indirect methods.

Whatever their goals—more or fewer social services, higher or lower prices—interest groups pursue them on every level and in every branch of government. On any given day in Washington, you can find national interest groups in action. If you eat breakfast in the Senate dining room, you might see congressional committee staffers reviewing testimony with representatives from women's groups. Later that morning, you might visit the Supreme Court and watch a lawyer from a civil rights group arguing on behalf of a client in a discrimination suit. Lunch in a popular Washington restaurant might find you listening in on a conversation between an agricultural lobbyist and a representative. That afternoon you might visit the Department of Labor, and watch

bureaucrats working out rules and regulations with representatives from a labor interest group. Then you might stroll past the headquarters of Common Cause, the American Association of Retired Persons (AARP), and the National Wildlife Federation (NWF).

Interest groups are often criticized in the United States, but they do serve several purposes in American politics:

- Interest groups help bridge the gap between citizens and government and enable citizens to explain their views on policies to public officials.
- Interest groups help raise public awareness and inspire action on various issues.
- Interest groups often give specialized and detailed information to public officials that might be difficult to obtain otherwise. This information may be useful in making public policy choices.
- Interest groups serve as another check on public officials to make sure that they are carrying out their duties responsibly.

Just the Facts

Interest groups often concentrate on preventing legislation, rather than promoting it.

How Do Interest Groups Differ from Political Parties?

Realize that although both interest groups and political parties are groups of people joined together for political purposes, they differ in several important ways:

- Interest groups are often policy *specialists*, whereas political parties are policy *generalists*. Political parties are broad-based organizations that must attract the support of many opposing groups and consider a large number of issues. Interest groups, in contrast, focus on only a handful of key policies. An environmental group is not as concerned about the problems of the homeless as it is about polluters. An agricultural group is more involved with promoting farm programs than it is with crime in the cities.

- Interest groups are usually more tightly organized than political parties. They are often financed through contributions or dues-paying memberships. Organizers communicate through conferences, mailings, newsletters, and electronic formats, such as e-mail.
- A political party's main sphere of influence is the electoral system. That is, parties run candidates for political office. Interest groups try to influence the outcome of elections; but unlike parties, they do not compete for public office. Although candidates for office may be sympathetic to or even be members of certain groups, they do not run for election as candidates of that group.

Types of Interest Groups

American democracy embraces almost every conceivable type of interest group, and the number is increasing rapidly. A look at your telephone directory—or even better, the Washington, D.C., directory—will give you an idea of the number and variety of groups. No one has ever compiled a *Who's Who* of interest groups, but you can get an idea of the number and variety by looking through the annual *Encyclopedia of Associations*.

Some interest groups have large memberships, such as the American Association of Retired Persons (AARP), with 33 million members. Others, such as the Tulip Growers Association, have only a few members. Some are familiar groups that have been in existence for many years, such as the National Rifle Association, while others crop up overnight. Some are highly structured and run by a professional full-time staff, while others are loosely structured and informal. Figure 9–2 shows profiles of some important interest groups.

The most common interest groups are private interest groups. These groups seek public policies that benefit the economic interests of their members and work against policies that threaten those interests. Other groups, sometimes called **public interest groups,** are formed with the broader goal of working for the "public good."

Business Business has long been well organized for effective action. Hundreds of business groups now operate in Washington, D.C., in the fifty state capitals, and at the local level across the country. Two umbrella organizations that include most businesses are the Chamber of Commerce of the United States and the National Association of Manufacturers (NAM). More than 200,000 individual businesses belong to the Chamber of Commerce, which also has 4,000 local, state, and regional affiliates. It has become a major voice for the nation's thousands of small businesses. The NAM chiefly represents big business and has thirteen thousand members.

The hundreds of **trade organizations** are far less visible than the Chamber of Commerce and the NAM, but they are also important in seeking policy goals for their members. Trade associations cover a range of areas, from the aerospace industry to angora goat producers, through builders and pickle makers, to truckers and theater owners. Trade organizations usually support policies that benefit business in general. They may not agree on specific issues, however. For example, people in the oil industry work for policies that favor the development of oil as an energy resource. Other business groups have worked for policies that favor the development of coal, solar power, and nuclear power. Trucking companies work for policies that would result in the construction of more highways. Railroad com-

AARP

Name: American Association of Retired Persons (AARP)
Founded: 1958
Membership: 33,000,000 working or retired persons fifty years of age or older
Description: The AARP strives to better the lives of older people, especially in the areas of health care, worker equity, and minority affairs. The AARP sponsors community crime prevention programs, research on the problems associated with aging, and a mail-order pharmacy.
Budget: $322,000,000
Address: 601 E. St. N.W., Washington, D.C. 20049
Contact: (202) 434–3741; **www.aarp.org**/

LWVUS

Name: League of Women Voters of the United States (LWVUS)
Founded: 1920
Membership: 120,000 volunteer women and men eighteen years of age or older
Description: The LWVUS promotes active and informed political participation. It distributes candidate information, encourages voter registration and voting, and takes action on issues of public policy. The group's national interests include international relations, natural resources, and social policy.
Budget: $3,000,000
Address: 1730 M. St. N.W., Washington, D.C. 20036
Contact: (202) 429–1965; **www.lwv.org**/

NEA

Name: National Education Association (NEA)
Founded: 1857
Membership: 2,300,000 elementary and secondary school teachers, college and university professors, academic administrators, and others concerned with education.
Description: The NEA's committees investigate and take action in the areas of benefits, civil rights educational support, personnel, higher education, human relations, legislation, minority affairs, and women's concerns.
Budget: $147,500,000
Address: 1201 16th St. N.W., Washington, D.C. 20036
Contact: (202) 833–4000; **www.nea.org**/

MADD

Name: Mothers Against Drunk Driving (MADD)
Founded: 1980
Membership: 3,200,000 members and supporters
Description: MADD looks for effective solutions to problems related to drunk driving and underage drinking. The organization also supports those who have been victims of drunk driving.
Budget: $53,000,000
Address: 511 E. John Carpenter Freeway, No. 700, Irving, TX 75062
Contact: (214) 744–6233; (800) GET MADD; **www.madd.org**/

SC

Name: Sierra Club (SC)
Founded: 1892
Membership: 650,000 persons concerned with the interrelationship between nature and humankind
Description: The Sierra Club endeavors to protect and conserve natural resources, save endangered areas, and resolve problems associated with wilderness, clean air, energy conservation, and land use. Its committees are concerned with agriculture, economics, environmental education, hazardous materials, the international environment, Native American sites, political education, and water resources.
Budget: $45,000,000
Address: 85 2d St., 2d Floor, San Francisco, CA 94105
Contact: (415) 977–5500; **www.sierraclub.org**/

panies do not, of course, want more highways built, because that would hurt their business.

Labor Interest groups representing labor have been some of the most influential groups in the country. Nationwide labor groups date back as far as 1886, when the American Federation of Labor (AFL) was formed.

The largest and most powerful labor group today is the AFL-CIO (the American Federation of Labor–Congress of Industrial Organizations), an organization consisting of nearly ninety unions representing more than thirteen million workers. Several million other workers are members of non–AFL-CIO unions such as the International Brotherhood of Teamsters, the

United Mine Workers, the International Longshoremen's Union, and the Warehousemen's Union.

Like labor unions everywhere, American unions press for policies to improve working conditions and pay for their members, but there are also issues on which they compete with or oppose each other. For example, a bricklayers' union might try to change building codes to benefit its own members even though such changes might hurt the carpenters' union. Labor groups may also compete for new members. For example, in California, the Teamsters, the AFL-CIO, and the United Mine Workers have competed to organize farm workers. Today, these unions are competing to organize farm workers in Texas, Florida, and other states.

Note that organized labor does not represent all of America's workers. It represents only 15 percent of the **labor force**—the total of those over the age of sixteen who are working or who are actively looking for a job. The interests of workers who do not belong to labor unions sometimes differ from the interests of unions and their members.

Although unions had great strength and political power in the late 1800s and the early 1900s, their strength and power have waned in the last two decades. They are still a powerful lobbying force, however.

Agricultural Groups Many groups work for general agricultural interests at all levels of government. Several broad-based agricultural groups represent over five million American farmers, from peanut farmers to dairy producers to tobacco growers. They are the American Farm Bureau Federation, the National Grange, and the National Farmers' Union. The Farm Bureau, with over 4.7 million members, is the largest and generally the most effective of the three mentioned. The Grange, founded in 1867, is the oldest and has a membership of about 290,000 farm families. The National Farmers' Union consists of approximately 300,000 smaller farmers. Specialized groups, such as the Associated Milk Producers, Inc. (AMPI), also have a strong influence on farm legislation.

THE GLOBAL VIEW

Gun Control in Britain and the United States—A Tale of Two Lobbies

The British have had a long history of strict gun-control laws. Recent British laws are said to be the toughest gun-control measures in the world. Under these laws, almost all handguns are banned, and the small guns currently permitted are expected to be banned soon. British residents face the prospect of spending up to ten years in prison if they fail to give up their weapons.

Gun-control laws in the United States are far less strict than those of Britain. In public opinion polls, a majority of U.S. citizens (routinely over 60 percent) say they would like stricter gun-control laws, but such laws have not been passed in this country. Why not? The answer to this question, at least in part, has to do with the effective lobbying efforts of the National Rifle Association, which strongly opposes any gun-control legislation. In contrast, the most important gun lobby in Britain is primarily concerned with protecting sport shooting, and it has been effective in protecting the use of shotguns in the countryside.

THINKING GLOBALLY

Opponents of the British handgun ban argued that in 1996, 41 percent of homicides in Britain were committed with knives; 29 percent resulted from the use of blunt objects, hitting, or kicking; and 18 percent were the result of strangulation. Only 12 percent were committed with guns. Do these statistics represent a valid argument against the British handgun ban? Explain.

◀ Striking United Parcel Service (UPS) employees picket as a truck leaves a downtown Chicago shipping center. More than 185,000 members of the Teamsters Union were involved in the 1997 nationwide strike against UPS. Why are strikes an effective tool of labor unions?

People in many product areas of agriculture have formed their own organizations. Groups have been formed around specific farm commodities such as dairy products, soybeans, grain, fruit, corn, cotton, beef, sugar beets, and so on. Like business and labor groups, farm organizations sometimes find themselves in competition. In some western states, for example, barley farmers, cattle ranchers, and orchard owners may compete to influence laws concerning water rights. Different groups also often disagree over the extent to which the government should regulate farmers.

Consumer Groups Groups organized to promote consumers' rights were very active in the 1960s and 1970s. Some are active today. The most well known and perhaps the most effective are the public interest consumer groups organized under the leadership of consumer activist Ralph Nader. (See the *Architects of Government* feature on page 252.) Another well-known consumer group is Consumers Union, a nonprofit organization started in 1936. In addition to publishing *Consumer Reports,* Consumers Union has been influential in fighting for the removal of phosphates in detergents, lead in gasoline, and pesticides in food. Consumers Union strongly criticizes government agencies when they act against consumer interests. Recently, members of several leading policy groups formed the National Consumer Coalition (NCC). The

NCC's goal is to promote consumer choice in several issue areas, including housing, transportation, health and safety, and telecommunications. In each city, consumer groups have been organized to deal with such problems as poor housing, discrimination against minorities and women, and business inaction on consumer complaints.

Older Americans While the population of the nation as a whole has tripled since 1900, the number of older Americans has increased eightfold. Persons over the age of sixty-five account for 13 percent of the population. Many of these people have united to call attention to their special needs and concerns. Interest groups formed to promote the interests of older Americans have been very outspoken and persuasive. As pointed out before, the large membership of the American Association of Retired Persons has enabled it to become a potent political force. The Gray Panthers is another organization formed to promote the interests of older people.

Environmental Groups Concern for the environment has led to growth in the membership of established environmental groups and formation of new groups. Indeed, environmental groups are some of the most powerful interest groups in Washington. The National

of Government

Ralph Nader
(1934–   )

Ralph Nader is one of the nation's most well-known consumer activists. Nader's book *Unsafe at Any Speed*, which was published in 1965, influenced Congress to bring automobile safety design under the control of the national government. Nader founded the Center for the Study of Responsive Law, the Center for Auto Safety, and the Public Interest Research Group. He also formed Essential Information, a nonprofit organization dedicated to encouraging all citizens to become active and engaged in their communities. In 1996, he was the Green Party's candidate for president.

HIS WORDS

"The time has not come to discipline the automobile for safety; that time came over four decades ago. But that is not cause to delay any longer what should have been accomplished in the nineteen-twenties."

(*Unsafe at Any Speed, p. xi*)

"For almost 70 years the life insurance industry has been a smug sacred cow feeding the public a steady line of sacred bologna."

(*Testimony to U.S. Senate Committee*, May 18, 1974)

DEVELOPING
CRITICAL THINKING SKILLS

1. In the first quotation above, what did Nader mean by the phrase "discipline the automobile for safety"? Why should this have been accomplished in the 1920s?
2. Regarding the second quotation, why do you think Nader had such a negative view of the insurance industry?

Wildlife Federation now has 5.6 million members. Other major environmental groups include the Sierra Club, the National Audubon Society, and the Nature Conservancy.

These groups have organized to support pollution reduction and control, wilderness protection, and natural resource and wildlife conservation. They have organized to oppose strip mining, nuclear power plants, logging activities, chemical waste dumping, and many other environmental hazards.

Professional Groups Most professions that require advanced education or specialized training have organizations to protect and promote their interests. These groups are concerned mainly with the standards of their professions, but they also work to influence government policy.

Four major professional groups are the American Medical Association (AMA), representing physicians; the American Bar Association (ABA), representing lawyers; and the National Education Association (NEA) and the American Federation of Teachers (AFT), both representing teachers. Each has an impact on public policy in its own area. In addition, there are dozens of less well-known and less politically active professional groups, such as the Screen Actors Guild,

▲ *The Gray Panthers is a group dedicated to promoting the interest of older Americans. What clues do you have from the photo that the Gray Panthers may be more militant than the AARP?*

the National Association of Social Workers, and the American Political Science Association.

Women's Groups Groups concerned with women's interests swelled with the women's rights movement. The National Organization for Women (NOW) is the largest women's group, having about 250,000 members. It has a national board made up of salaried officers and regional representatives. NOW has established the Legal Defense and Education Fund, which focuses on education and public information concerning women's rights.

Church-Related Organizations Many church-related organizations try to influence public policy in several important areas. The National Council of Churches, for example, has spoken out on civil rights, human rights, and other social issues.

Ethnic Organizations A number of ethnic groups in the United States have formed organizations to influence public policy at all levels of government. The National Association for the Advancement of Colored People (NAACP) works for improvement in the political, social, and economic status of African Americans.

Hispanic Americans have a number of organizations that work for their interests. They include the Mexican American Legal Defense and Education Fund and the League of United Latin American Citizens. Asian Americans have the Organization of Chinese Americans and the National Asian Pacific American Legal Consortium.

As America becomes more culturally diverse and economically complex, we will most likely see an even greater array of interest groups.

SECTION 4 REVIEW

1. How do interest groups fit into American politics?
2. How does an interest group differ from a political party?
3. Name four different types of interest groups.
4. **For Critical Analysis:** One individual may belong to several different interest groups. Might the goals of one of these groups conflict with those of another? Explain.

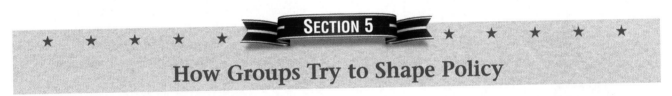

SECTION 5

How Groups Try to Shape Policy

Preview Questions:

- At what level or levels of government do interest groups operate?
- What are some of the methods used by lobbyists to influence public policymakers?
- What is the difference between the direct and the indirect techniques used by lobbyists?
- What are some of the indirect techniques that interest groups employ?
- How have government regulations affected lobbyists?

Key Terms:

lobbying, lobbyist, political action committees (PACs), ratings systems

Interest groups operate at all levels of government, and they use a variety of strategies to steer policies their way. Sometimes, they attempt to directly influence the policymakers themselves. At other times, they try to shape public opinion, which indirectly influences policymakers. The extent and nature of their activities depend on their goals and their resources.

Direct Techniques

Lobbying and providing election support are two important direct techniques used by interest groups.

Lobbying Today, **lobbying** refers to all attempts by organizations or individuals to influence the passage, defeat, or contents of legislation and the administrative decisions of government. A **lobbyist** is a representative of an organized lobby who handles the group's lobbying efforts. Lobbying takes its name from the foyer, or lobby, of the legislature itself, where petitioners used to corner legislators to speak about their concerns. The use of the term *lobbying* dates back at least to the 1830s. By 1841, according to an English visitor to the United States, it was a well-established practice, at least in state capitals:

> *A practice exists in the State capitals, called* lobbying. *. . . A certain number of agents, selected for their skill and experience in the arts of . . . persuading . . . members, are employed by public companies and private individuals, who have bills before the legislature which they are anxious to get passed. These persons attend the lobby of the House daily, talk with the members, . . . invite them to dinners and suppers, etc.*

Most of the larger interest groups have lobbyists in Washington, D.C. These lobbyists often include former members of Congress or former employees of executive bureaucracies who are experienced in the methods of political influence and who "know people." Many lobbyists also work at the state and local levels of government. In fact, lobbying at the state level has increased in recent years as states have begun to play a more significant role in policymaking.

▲ *This Washington lobbyist for the health-care industry uses the latest technology to make his client's case to legislators. Why does an organization hire a lobbyist?*

While lobbying can be directed at the legislative branch of government, it is also directed at administrative agencies and even at the courts. For example, individuals concerned over the suffering caused by acquired immune deficiency syndrome (AIDS) formed a strong lobby in the early 1990s. Their goal was to force the Food and Drug Administration to allow patients to use experimental anti-AIDS drugs before the drugs were fully tested.

Lobbyists use several methods to achieve their goals:

1. *Making personal contact with key legislators.* This is one of the most effective direct lobbying techniques. A competent lobbyist must be persuasive, have a good understanding of human nature, and present a strong case with accurate information.

   It is to the lobbyist's advantage to provide accurate information so that the legislator will rely on the individual or interest group in the future. For example, a lobbyist from the Sierra Club lobbying for clean-air legislation must be familiar with all aspects of the problem before contacting a congressional staff member. If the lobbyist does not present accurate information, the club's credibility and effectiveness will be damaged, if not destroyed.

2. *Providing expertise to legislators or other government officials.* Members of Congress cannot be experts on every issue, so they eagerly seek information to help them make up their minds. Some lobbying groups do research and present their findings to these legislators, as well as to other officials.

3. *Offering "expert" testimony before congressional committees for or against proposed legislation.* A bill to prohibit logging in a certain forested area, for example, might concern several interest groups. The timber industry would probably oppose the bill, and representatives from that interest group might be asked to testify before a congressional committee. Groups that would probably support the bill, such as wildlife conservationists and other environmental groups, might also be asked to testify. Each side would offer as much evidence as possible to support its position on the bill.

4. *Assisting legislators or bureaucrats in drafting legislation.* Lobbyists often have knowledge or expertise that is useful in drafting legislation, and that is a major strength for an interest group. Lobbyists also are a source of ideas and sometimes offer legal advice on specific details.

5. *Following up.* Even after a lobbying group wins a legislative victory, the battle is not over. Executive agencies responsible for carrying out legislation can often increase or decrease the power of the new law. Lobbyists often try to influence the government officials who implement the policy. For example, beginning in the early 1960s, laws outlawing gender-based discrimination were broadly outlined by Congress. Both women's rights groups favoring the laws and interest groups opposing the laws lobbied for years to influence how the laws would be implemented by executive agencies.

Providing Election Support Interest groups often become directly involved in the election process. Many interest group members join and work within political parties in order to influence party platforms and the nomination of candidates. They provide campaign support for legislators who favor their policies and sometimes urge their own members to try to win posts in party organizations. Most important, interest groups urge their members to vote for the candidates that support the views of the group. They can also threaten legislators with the withdrawal of their votes. No candidate can expect to have support from *all* interest groups. If a candidate expects to win, however, he or she often needs support (or little opposition) from powerful interest groups.

Today, interest groups often provide money to campaigns through **political action committees (PACs),** which are groups organized to collect money and provide financial support for political candidates. Interest groups funnel money through PACs to the candidates whom they think will benefit them the most. (PACs are discussed in greater depth in Chapter 11.) The number of PACs has grown significantly, along with the amounts of money they spend on elections. Campaign contributions do not guarantee that officials will vote the way the groups wish. Rather, groups make these contributions to ensure that they will have access to the public officials they have helped to elect.

Indirect Techniques

Interest groups also try to influence public policy indirectly through third parties or the general public.

YOU JUST CALLED FOR REPEAL OF THE BILL OF RIGHTS, WHATEVER THAT IS...

◀ *Interest groups encourage voters to vote for their issues, and they also encourage voters to sign petitions so that issues can be placed on state ballots as voter-sponsored initiatives. Today, some groups hire individuals to gather signatures for specific ballot initiatives. What is the attitude of the voters in this cartoon?*

Mothers Against Drunk Driving (MADD)

The formation of Mothers Against Drunk Driving (MADD) began with a tragedy. On May 3, 1980, Cari Lightner, aged thirteen, was walking in a bicycle lane near her home in Fair Oaks, California, on her way to a church carnival. She was struck from behind by a swerving car and hit so hard that she was hurled 120 feet down the road. The driver of the car never stopped, but he was arrested four days later.

The driver was drunk at the time of the accident. In fact, when he killed Cari, he had been out of jail on bail for only two days because of another hit-and-run drunk-driving accident. Although he had been convicted of drunk driving and related offenses three times in four years, he had served only forty-eight hours in jail. The police told Candy Lightner, Cari's mother, that the driver would probably never go to jail, because drunk driving was not considered a serious crime in California. The driver, in fact, never did go to prison, though he did serve eleven months in a work camp and halfway house.

Candy Lightner was shocked and angry. After extensive research, she found out that nothing effective was being done to keep drunk drivers off the road. Drunk drivers could literally "get away with murder" without fear of being punished. "Death caused by drunk driving is the only socially acceptable form of homicide," she concluded.

Candy Lightner decided to do all she could to help other victims and to prevent such tragedies from happening again. She quit her job to form an interest group called Mothers Against Drunk Driving, or MADD. She began her campaign by convincing the California governor and legislature that stiffer penalties were needed for drunk-driving offenses. She quickly gained the support of other parents who had experienced similar tragedies.

Once launched, MADD proved to be a powerful force. Members wrote letters, gave speeches, and issued press releases. MADD members sponsored community-awareness meetings and educational seminars. They circulated petitions calling for state and national action. They applied for corporate and foundation grants. They took their fight to Washington, D.C., where they held

---

Indirect techniques may appear to be spontaneous, but they are normally well planned. Interest groups use indirect techniques in part because public officials are often more impressed by contacts from voters than by contacts from lobbyists.

Shaping Public Opinion Public opinion ultimately puts pressure on policymakers, so interest groups pay careful attention to their public images. If public opinion favors a certain group's interests, then public officials will be more likely to listen to that group and more willing to pass legislation favoring its interests. Using public opinion in this way is often referred to as bringing grassroots pressure to bear on officials or mounting campaigns for the people back home. Such efforts may include television publicity, newspaper and magazine advertisements, mass mailings, and public relations techniques to improve the group's or industry's public image. For example, environmental groups run television ads to dramatize threats to the environment. Oil companies respond to criticism about high profits with advertising showing their concern about public welfare. The goal of all these activities is to convince both the public and the policymakers that the public overwhelmingly supports the interest group's position.

Some interest groups try to influence legislators through **ratings systems.** They select legislative issues that are important to their groups' goals and rate legislators on the percentage of times the legislators vote

press conferences, lobbied, and urged stronger legislative action on drunk driving, such as raising the legal minimum drinking age to twenty-one.

Now headquartered near Dallas, the organization has more than 600 chapters and 3,200,000 members. Since the founding of MADD, all fifty states have tightened their drunk-driving laws. Media coverage, stiffer penalties and laws, and commissions and task forces to study the problem are all accomplishments of which MADD can be proud.

THINK ABOUT IT

1. Drunk driving has been a problem for many years in the United States. Why do you think no organizations such as MADD were formed prior to 1980?
2. Who might be in favor of *not* passing harsher legislation against drunk drivers? Why?

favorably on those issues. For example, one environmental group identifies twelve members of Congress whose voting record on environmental issues is unacceptable and labels them the "Dirty Dozen." The Communication Workers of America (CWA) labels policymakers who take positions consistent with its own as "heroes" and those who take the opposite position as "zeroes." Needless to say, legislators do not want to earn membership on the "Dirty Dozen" or "zeroes" lists of these groups.

Mobilizing Constituents Interest groups sometimes urge members and others to write letters or call government officials to show their support for or opposition to certain policies. Large interest groups can generate hundreds of thousands of letters, calls, and e-mail messages. They often provide form letters or postcards for people to fill out and mail. For example, consider the American Association of Retired Persons (AARP). The AARP has mobilized many of its 33 million constituents on a number of occasions to oppose legislation that might adversely affect the interests of older Americans. Such campaigns make the policymakers more aware of issues important to the groups.

Bringing Lawsuits Achieving policy goals through the legal system offers another avenue for influencing the political process. Civil rights groups paved the way for using lawsuits to achieve policy goals with major victories in cases concerning equal housing, school

How Lobbying Has Changed

Interest groups have always tried to lobby government. Before the twentieth century, however, lobbying was much different than it is today.

THEN (BEFORE THE TWENTIETH CENTURY)	NOW
Lobbying occurred mainly in the halls and offices of legislators.	Lobbying occurs in regulatory agencies and executive offices as well as the halls and offices of legislators.
Lobbying was always done in person.	Lobbying is still done in person, but lobbyists also use telephones, mail, faxes, and e-mail.
Lobbying was not regulated by the government.	Lobbying is regulated by the government through registration requirements.

desegregation, and labor market equality in the 1950s and 1960s. Lawsuits are also used by environmental groups. For example, an environmental group, such as the Sierra Club, might legally challenge developers who threaten to pollute the environment. The legal challenge will force the developers to bear the costs of defending themselves and possibly delay the project. The next time, developers might be more willing to make concessions and avoid lengthy and costly legal battles. In fact, much of the success of environmental groups has been linked to their use of lawsuits.

Influencing Judicial Appointments Groups also try to influence courts indirectly by lobbying the Senate to support or oppose judicial nominees. For example, in 1987, nearly two hundred groups mobilized to support or oppose Robert Bork, who had been nominated to the Supreme Court by President Ronald Reagan. As a result of their actions, the Senate rejected Bork's nomination. (Judicial nominations are discussed in detail in Chapter 20.)

Staging Demonstrations Some interest groups stage protests to make a statement in a dramatic way. The Boston Tea Party of 1773, in which American colonists dressed as Native Americans threw tea into the Boston

Harbor to protest British taxes, is testimony to the fact that the tactic has been around for a long time.

In recent years, many groups have generated protest marches and rallies to support or oppose issues such as legalized abortion, busing, government assistance to farmers, and the increased restrictions on the use of western lands owned by the national government.

Why Do Interest Groups Get Bad Press?

Despite their importance to democratic government, interest groups, like political parties, are sometimes criticized by both the public and the press. Our image of interest groups and their special interests is not very favorable.

You may have seen political cartoons depicting lobbyists prowling the hallways of Congress, briefcases stuffed with money, waiting to lure representatives into a waiting limousine. These cartoons are not entirely factual, but neither are they entirely fictitious. In 1977, "Koreagate"—a scandal in which a South Korean businessman was accused of offering lavish "gifts" to several members of Congress—added to the view that politicians were too susceptible to special interests. In the

GUN LOBBY

OH NO... NOW THEY WANT A FIVE-DAY WAITING PERIOD BEFORE WE CAN PURCHASE A CONGRESSMAN!

◀ In the aftermath of the 1982 assassination attempt on the life of President Ronald Reagan, a mandatory five-day waiting period to purchase a handgun went into effect. This cartoon refers to that law while taking a stab at another political problem—corruption.

early 1990s, it was revealed that a number of senators who had received generous contributions from a particular savings and loan association later supported a "hands-off" policy on the part of savings and loan regulators. This meant less government regulation of savings and loan institutions. The savings and loan association in question later got into financial trouble, costing the federal government billions of dollars. In the wake of numerous scandals over the years, Congress passed a set of rules in 1996 banning members of Congress from accepting free trips, meals, and gifts from interest group lobbyists.

Despite incidents of this kind, a few bad apples do not spoil the whole interest group barrel. For every dishonest action, there are hundreds of honest transactions between interest group leaders and public officials. For every lobbyist who attempts to bribe a public official, there are hundreds who try only to provide public officials with solid facts that support the goals of their groups.

The Regulation of Interest Groups

Interest groups are not free to do whatever they choose. In 1946, Congress passed the Federal Regulation of Lobbying Act in an attempt to control lobbying. It is the only major law regulating interest groups,

and it applies only to those persons or organizations that lobby Congress. The act includes the following requirements:

1. Any person or organization that receives money to be used principally to influence legislation before Congress must register with the clerk of the House and the secretary of the Senate.
2. Any groups or persons registering must identify their employers, salary, amount and purpose of expenses, and duration of employment.
3. Every registered lobbyist must give quarterly reports on his or her activities, which are published in the *Congressional Quarterly*.
4. Anyone failing to satisfy the specific provisions of this act can be fined up to $10,000 and receive a five-year prison term.

The act is very limited and has not regulated lobbying to any great degree. First, the Supreme Court has restricted the application of the law to lobbyists who *directly* seek to influence federal legislation. Any lobbyist indirectly seeking to influence legislation through efforts to shape public opinion does not fall within the scope of the law. Second, only persons or organizations whose principal purpose is to influence legislation are required to register. Interest groups or individuals claiming that their principal function is something else need

AMERICA AT ODDS

Gun Control

The National Rifle Association (NRA) has been a successful interest group in the United States for many years. The NRA has worked hard to prevent the government from passing gun-control legislation. The NRA argues that the right to bear arms is protected by the Second Amendment to the Constitution and that Congress has no authority to limit this right. Many Americans are at odds with the views of the NRA, however. In fact, polls suggest that a majority of Americans want gun-control laws tightened up—through increased registration and licensing requirements, for example.

It's Time for More Gun Control, Some Say

According to those who favor more gun-control laws, the United States has the most heavily armed population in the world. As a result, it has the highest murder rate. Proponents of gun-control laws do not believe that the Second Amendment was intended to allow private citizens to bear firearms in their homes. Rather, they argue that the Second Amendment was intended to allow citizens to bear firearms in the event they are called upon to be part of a state-sponsored militia.

In any event, say members of this group, under what circumstances would an American ever need a semiautomatic weapon to protect himself or herself? Certainly, no one needs these sophisticated weapons for sport shooting.

Finally, a gun in the home is many times more likely to kill a family member than to stop a criminal. Armed citizens are simply not a deterrent to crime.

The NRA and Others Say No to Gun Control

Opponents of stricter gun-control laws, including the nearly three million members of the NRA, have strong beliefs. Specifically, they contend that the Second Amendment contains no qualifiers—no "buts" or "excepts." In other words, the government has *no* authority to restrict gun ownership.

In addition, this group argues that increased registration and licensing of guns will have no effect on crime. After all, criminals, by definition, do not obey laws.

Finally, more than 99 percent of all handguns are used for no criminal purpose. At least one-half of handgun owners in the United States own them for protection and security. According to the NRA, a handgun at home is an insurance policy.

YOU DECIDE

1. "If guns are outlawed, only outlaws will have guns." Do you accept this reasoning? Explain.
2. Read the Second Amendment. How do you interpret it?

---

not register. Many groups can avoid registration in this way. Third, the act does not cover lobbying directed at agencies in the executive branch or lobbyists who testify before congressional committees. Fourth, the public is almost totally unaware of the information in the quarterly reports, and Congress has not created an agency to oversee interest group activities.

One problem with strengthening the regulation of lobbying is that any stricter regulation may run into constitutional problems, particularly with respect to the First Amendment freedoms of speech and assembly. Additionally, as long as the Supreme Court does not view indirect lobbying as falling within the scope of the law, lobbying will be difficult to control.

SECTION 5 REVIEW

1. Name two methods used by interest groups to influence policymakers directly.
2. How do lobbyists attempt to influence policymakers through the electoral process?
3. Describe some of the techniques by which lobbyists indirectly influence legislators.
4. What federal regulation of interest groups exists?
5. **For Critical Analysis:** What additional restrictions, if any, do you think should be placed on interest groups? Explain how the First Amendment rights of these groups might be violated by further restrictions.

★ ★ ★ ★ **Chapter Summary** ★ ★ ★ ★

Section 1: Definition and Measurement of Public Opinion

- Public opinion consists of beliefs and attitudes about politics and public policy shared by a large portion of the population.
- The most common ways in which public officials learn about public opinion are through election results, personal contacts, interest groups, and media reports.
- One way to measure public opinion is through the use of scientific public opinion polls.

Section 2: Factors That Affect Public Opinion

- Most views that are expressed as political opinions are acquired through a learning process called political socialization.
- Some of the agents of political socialization include the family, the educational establishment, the mass media, opinion leaders, and peer groups.
- Economic status and age can also influence the political socialization process.

Section 3: Categorizing Political Attitudes

- Liberals have a viewpoint toward public policy that almost always favors change. Liberals also believe in expanding the role of the national government.
- Conservatives believe that public policy should protect tradition and that state and local governments should rely less on the national government.
- Most Americans consider themselves moderates—neither liberals nor conservatives.

Section 4: Interest Groups

- Interest groups are organizations made up of people who share common objectives and who actively attempt to influence government policymakers through direct and indirect methods.
- Although both interest groups and political parties are made up of people who join together for political purposes, they are very different. Most interest groups focus on specific issues, whereas political parties must support a wide range of causes.
- Private interest groups primarily seek economic benefit for their own members. Public interest groups are formed with the broader goal of working for the "public good."

Section 5: How Groups Try to Shape Policy

- Interest groups operate at all levels of government and use a variety of strategies to affect public policy.
- Direct techniques used by interest groups include lobbying and providing election support.
- Interest groups also try to influence public policy through indirect methods, such as shaping public opinion, mobilizing constituents, bringing lawsuits, influencing judicial appointments, and mounting demonstrations.
- Although lobbying is regulated by the Federal Regulation of Lobbying Act of 1946, the act is very limited.

★ REVIEW QUESTIONS ★

1. What is public opinion?
2. How is public opinion measured?
3. Explain the problems of early polling efforts.
4. What are some criticisms of opinion polls?
5. Describe the factors that help explain how public opinion is formed.
6. Explain how various agents of political socialization influence our political opinions.
7. What distinguishes a conservative from a liberal?
8. What groups are on the extreme left and right sides of the political spectrum?
9. What purposes do interest groups serve in American politics, and how do they operate?
10. Briefly describe three types of private interest groups.
11. In what ways do interest groups directly try to influence policymakers?
12. Describe five methods used by lobbyists to indirectly influence policymakers.
13. What are the requirements of the Federal Regulation of Lobbying Act of 1946?
14. Briefly describe the guidelines for writing a letter to a newspaper or magazine editor.

★ CRITICAL THINKING ★

1. What individuals have most influenced your political perspectives? In what ways have they influenced you?
2. Name some interest groups that you think could be seen as public interest groups. Name some interest groups that could be seen as private interest groups. What led you to classify these groups as you did?
3. Why might stricter regulation of lobbying endanger First Amendment rights?
4. How might one's personal experiences (with crime, for example) affect one's views on national policies (such as crime policies)?

★ IMPROVING YOUR SKILLS ★

Communication Skills

Formulating a Thesis Statement Many times throughout your studies, you will be asked to write about your ideas or about what you have learned. Before writing an essay, you should write a thesis statement, which should explain the main idea of your essay. Here is a sample thesis statement from Section 3 of this chapter:

Political attitudes are often labeled as either conservative or liberal.

The following steps will help you formulate a thesis statement:

1. *Choose a general topic that interests you.* Begin to gather and list facts and information about the general topic.
2. *Gradually narrow the topic in stages.* As you gather more information and facts, look for related facts and make choices about which facts are really important.
3. *Organize the facts.* Discard information that has no bearing on your topic, keeping only information that is directly related.
4. *Decide what you believe the facts mean.*
5. *Formulate a thesis statement that can be fully proved by the collected facts.*

Writing The following thesis statements were taken from this chapter. Using your own words, rewrite each of them.

1. Above all else, the aim of a democratic government is to convert the will of the people into public policy.
2. Public opinion is important in American politics because opinions can determine how government

handles such issues as environmental pollution and the death penalty.

3. Education is a powerful influence on an individual's political attitudes.

4. The media can also determine what issues, events, and personalities are in the public eye.

Social Studies Skills

Understanding a Pictogram Look at the pictogram below. Why does it have a right side, a left side, and a center? According to the pictogram, are there any moderates who are Democrats? Are there any moderates who are Republicans? Which groups on the spectrum represent the radical left and the radical right? Do the groups on the radical right and the radical left share any characteristics? If so, what are they? What does the pictogram tell you about the party affiliation of those who occupy the political center?

★ ACTIVITIES AND PROJECTS ★

1. Develop your own schoolwide "straw poll" on three issues facing high-school students in the United States today. Report to the class on your findings, and describe the polling techniques you used.

2. Identify an important national issue that is currently under debate. Research two interest groups that are involved with the issue. Write a one-page summary on each group's position.

What If . . .

Lobbying Were Made Illegal?

Today, lobbyists representing thousands of interest groups try to influence government at all levels. How would elected representatives make decisions if there were no lobbying?

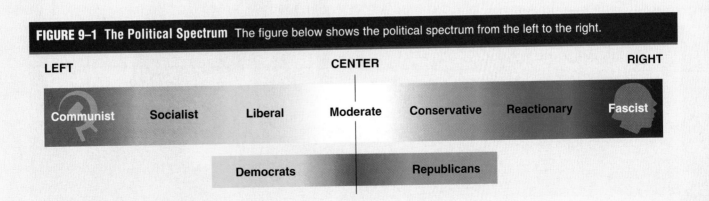

FIGURE 9–1 The Political Spectrum The figure below shows the political spectrum from the left to the right.

LEFT   CENTER   RIGHT

Communist   Socialist   Liberal   Moderate   Conservative   Reactionary   Fascist

Democrats   Republicans

Political Parties

CHAPTER OBJECTIVES

To learn about and understand . . .

⭐ The nature and functions of political parties and the reasons for the two-party system in the United States

⭐ The development of the two-party tradition in America

⭐ The nature and impact of third parties in American politics

⭐ The organization and structure of the two major political parties

"If I could not go to heaven but with a party, I would not go there at all."

Thomas Jefferson
(1743–1826)
Third President of the United States

INTRODUCTION

Political parties were an unforeseen development in American political history. The founders defined many other important institutions, such as the presidency and Congress, and described their functions in the Constitution. Political parties, however, are not even mentioned.

As you can see from Thomas Jefferson's quotation above, he expressed a critical view of political parties. In fact, most of the founders viewed parties as a threat to both the concept of popular government and the unity of the nation. Yet when popular elections were established, some method of organizing and mobilizing supporters of political candidates was needed. That is why political parties came into existence. They provide a way for the public to choose who will serve in government and which policies will be carried out.

◀ Delegates celebrate at the Democratic National Convention, hoping for a victory for their presidential candidate.

The Nature and Functions of Political Parties

Preview Questions:

- What is a political party?
- What roles do political parties play?
- Why does America have a two-party system?
- Why do people join political parties?

Key Terms:

political party, electorate, two-party system, minor parties, third parties, one-party system, multiparty system, consensus, single-member district system, plurality, run-off election, nomination, primary, canvasses, minority party, majority party, coalitions, party identifiers, solidarity, independents, party platform, planks

Many citizens would like to be involved in helping government make decisions. Many of us, in fact, demand to have a say in the decisions that affect us. Political parties help meet this demand. A **political party** is a group of individuals outside of government who organize to win elections, to operate the government, and to determine public policy. Political parties are one of the major vehicles of participation in our political system, and they form an important link between citizens and the government. In fact, some people think that democracy would be impossible without

◀ *What campaign themes are suggested by the buttons on this hat?*

them. Remember that democracy is defined as a system in which the people rule and are the only source of political authority. A democratic government is one in which the people can and do participate in national politics. By working together, citizens who share similar political views can often have a greater impact on the government.

The definition of a political party applies to political parties in the United States as well as to parties in most modern democratic nations. The exact roles that parties play in politics differ from nation to nation, however.

The Three Dimensions of American Political Parties

American political parties are sometimes described as three-dimensional. Each party consists of (1) the party in the electorate, (2) the party organization, and (3) the party in government.

The Party in the Electorate The party in the electorate is the largest component. The **electorate** is made up of the nation's voters, and the party in the electorate consists of all those eligible voters who describe themselves as Democrats or Republicans. There are no dues, no membership cards, and no obligatory duties. Members of the party in the electorate need never work on a campaign or attend a party meeting. They may register as Democrats or Republicans, but registration is not legally binding and can be changed at will.

The Party Organization Each major party has a national organization with national, state, and local offices. The party organizations are made up of people who maintain the party's strength between elections, make its rules, raise money, organize conventions, help with elections, and seek candidates.

The Party in Government The party in government consists of all the candidates who won elections and hold public office. Members of Congress, state legislators, and presidents usually run for office as either Democrats or Republicans. The party in government helps to organize the government's agenda by convincing its own party members to vote for the party's stated policies. If the party is to translate its promises into public policy, the job must be done by the party in government.

Reasons for America's Two-Party System

In the United States, we have a **two-party system.** Two major parties dominate national politics—the Democrats and the Republicans. Smaller parties, often called **minor parties** or **third parties,** also play a role in the U.S. system. They do not play a dominant role, however.

In contrast, in a **one-party system,** a single party monopolizes the organization of governmental power and the positions of authority. The single party's functions are controlled by party leaders. Even if elections are held, party members, once on the ballot, have no competition. In most dictatorships, such as Iraq and the People's Republic of China, only one party is officially allowed to exist. Until recently, this was also true of many countries of Eastern and Central Europe, including the former Soviet Union.

Another alternative is a **multiparty system,** in which more than two political parties compete for power and electoral offices. This type of system exists in most European democracies, including France and Germany. In a multiparty system, parties are usually organized around different beliefs or interests, such as religion, occupation, or political ideology. For example, Italy has nine national parties and several regional parties, including the Christian Democrats, the Socialists, the Radicals, the Liberals, and the Proletarian Unity Party. Israel has more than twenty parties. In one recent election, the Czech Republic had twenty-two political parties, including the Communist Party, the Socialist Party, and the Alliance of Farmers and the Countryside.

Why has the two-party system become so firmly entrenched in America? A number of factors help to explain this phenomenon.

WHAT MANNER OF BEAST IS THIS?

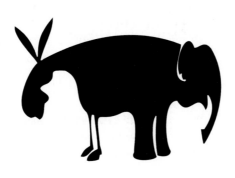

HUCK

▲ *You probably recognize the symbols for the two major political parties—the Democrats' donkey and the Republicans' elephant. What is the artist of this political cartoon trying to say about the nature of the two parties?*

National Consensus and Moderate Views A **consensus** is a general agreement. A consensus on public policy is sometimes defined as agreement among 75 percent or more of the people. In the United States, most citizens generally agree on certain broad social and economic issues. Most of us believe in the basic principles of government outlined in the U.S. Constitution. For example, most of us believe that people have the right to own private property and the right to freedom of religion. We also believe that people should be free to choose where they live and work. Our differences usually lie more in *how* to attain the goals than in the goals themselves.

Because of the general political consensus in the United States, conditions have not lent themselves to the formation of numerous strong rival parties. Americans have been deeply divided during such times as the Civil War in the 1860s and the Great Depression in the 1930s. We have disagreed strongly over certain issues, such as civil rights and the war in Vietnam during the 1960s and 1970s. We have not, however, had long-lasting divisions based on religious beliefs such as those that have occurred in the Middle East. Nor have we had long-lasting differences based on national origin, language, class, or social status, such as those that have occurred in some other countries.

In many European democracies, various radical political parties have strong support. In contrast, American politics tend more toward center, or moderate, positions. There are no large, long-lasting groups that support radical governmental policies.

Political consensus and moderation in the United States have given us two parties that look very much alike. Both tend to be middle-of-the-road parties built on compromise. For this, they have often been criticized. Their sternest critics think of them as "tweedledum" and "tweedledee"—two things that have different names but are practically the same.

Tradition The first major political division among Americans was between the Federalists and the Anti-Federalists over the ratification of the Constitution.

ARCHITECTS

of Government

Jesse Jackson
(1941–   )

An important leader in the civil rights struggles of the 1960s, Jesse Jackson joined Martin Luther King, Jr., in the Southern Christian Leadership Conference (SCLC) and became a close adviser and field organizer. After King was assassinated in 1968, Jackson founded Operation PUSH (People United to Save Humanity), a Chicago-based civil rights and economic development organization. In 1983, Jackson became the first African American to be a serious candidate for a major party's presidential nomination. While competing for the Democratic Party's presidential nomination, he won two primary elections and obtained more than 10 percent of the vote in many others. He continues to be a leading spokesperson for civil rights.

HIS WORDS

"Our flag is red, white, and blue, but our nation is a rainbow—red, yellow, brown, black, and white—and we're all precious in God's sight."
(*Speech, July 16, 1984*)

"We've removed the ceiling above our dreams. There are no more impossible dreams."
(Independent [London], June 9, 1988)

DEVELOPING
CRITICAL THINKING SKILLS

1. In the first quotation, what is Jackson saying about the inherent value of each individual?
2. In the second quotation, do you think that Jackson really means that there are *no* impossible dreams?

Some people believe that this two-sided political battle established the domination of the two-party system in this country. In addition, today's established institutions do not encourage third parties. The news media, for example, do not typically spend much time covering third-party activities. Rather, they tend to focus exclusively on the Democrats and Republicans.

Our Elective Process Our elective process also lends itself to the two-party system. Under what is called the **single-member district system,** the candidate who gets the most votes obtains a **plurality** (the largest number) and wins the election. This means that a candidate who receives less than 50 percent of the total vote cast can sometimes win. For example, suppose that you vote in a local election. A total of 1,000 votes are available, and three candidates are running for mayor: Gomez, Rosenfield, and Gladstone. Gomez receives 450 votes, Rosenfield receives 250 votes, and Gladstone receives 300 votes. Gomez wins the election even though he has received less than 50 percent of the total votes cast. (If a majority vote is required, then sometimes a **run-off election** must take place between the two candidates who received the highest number of votes.)

What Do Political Parties Do?

Historically, political parties have played a vital role in our democratic system. The main function that political parties perform in a large democracy is linking the people to the government. Political parties link the people's policy preferences to actual government policies. Political parties also perform many other functions that no other body or institution of government performs.

Selecting Candidates One of the most important functions of the two political parties is to recruit and nominate candidates for political office. A party's endorsement for a candidate is called a **nomination.** By nominating candidates, the political parties simplify voting choices for the electorate. Political parties narrow the field from a large number of people who want to run for office to one candidate. They accomplish this by the use of primaries. A **primary** is a preliminary election to choose a party's final candidate. In theory, the party chooses the best-qualified member to be its candidate. In the final election, it is much easier for voters to choose between two candidates who have been selected by established political parties than to choose among many candidates. In effect, parties structure elections.

Informing the Public Political parties help educate the public about important political issues. In recent years, these issues have included welfare reform, immigration, environmental policies, and taxes. Each party presents its views on the issues through television, newspapers, campaign speeches, rallies, debates, and pamphlets. These activities help citizens learn about the issues, consider proposed solutions, and form opinions.

Through these activities, political parties also help to stimulate citizens' interest and participation in public affairs. Political parties ask people to work at party headquarters and to help with door-to-door **canvasses,** in which they distribute campaign literature and ask people to vote for their candidates. They seek volunteers to work at polling places where people actually cast their votes and to drive voters to the polling places. These party functions provide important ways for citizens to participate in the political process and serve their communities.

Coordinating Policymaking In our complex government, parties are essential for coordinating policymaking among the various branches of government. The president, cabinet members, and members of Congress are also normally members of a political party. The political party is usually the major institution through which the executive and legislative branches cooperate with each other. The president works through party leaders in Congress to promote the administration's legislative program. Parties unify government and organize it. This is particularly true in Congress, where virtually all committees are structured according to which party is in power and which party is not. Parties also act as the glue of our federal structure by connecting the various levels of government with a common bond.

The party that does not control Congress or a state legislature or has not elected its candidate to the presidency also acts as a "watchdog" and keeps an eye on the activities of the party in power. Such monitoring by the "loyal opposition" encourages the party in power to heed the public's wishes and to remain responsive. The party with fewer members in the legislature is the **minority party.** The party with the most members is the **majority party.**

Balancing Competing Interests Clinton Rossiter, a political scientist, described parties as "vast, gaudy,

▼ *Phoning voters and encouraging them to vote for party candidates is just one of the small but important tasks party members perform. Here teenagers work the phones during the Texas governor's race. What other tasks could politically motivated young people perform?*

friendly umbrellas under which all Americans, whoever and wherever and however-minded they may be, are invited to stand for the sake of being counted in the next election." Political parties are **coalitions**—individuals and groups with a variety of interests and opinions that are drawn together. For example, each party includes many groups that disagree with one another about controversial issues, such as illegal immigration and affirmative action. The role of party leaders in this situation is to adopt a broad enough view on these issues so that no groups will be alienated. In this way, different groups can hold their own views and still come together under the umbrella of the Republican or the Democratic Party. Leaders of both the Democratic Party and the Republican Party modify the conflicting views of different groups and arrive at compromises. In so doing, they help to unify their party members and determine the party position on the issues.

Joining a Political Party

In the United States, the ideas and actions of each individual are important. One person can make a difference, even in a country as large and varied as ours. But there are also great advantages in working with an organized group. Actively participating in a political party is one of the most important ways citizens can affect government decision making.

You may already think of yourself as a Democrat or a Republican. If not, you may soon find yourself drawn to one party or another. You may be drawn to a party because your family or friends support it, because you admire one of its leaders, or because you feel its candidates will act according to your views and beliefs.

If you are interested in becoming involved in a political party, local party organizations are often the easiest places to get started. You can volunteer to do various kinds of work for the local party. You can register new voters and distribute information, answer phones or conduct door-to-door canvasses, provide transportation for voters on election day, or become a member of the state party organization. Many national leaders have gained valuable experience this way.

You can find the state and local offices of both major parties in the telephone directory or through newspapers. You can also contact the two major parties' national offices at these addresses:

Democratic Party
430 Capital St. SE
Washington, DC 20003
202-863-8000
www.democrats.org/

Republican Party
Republican National Committee
310 First St. SE
Washington, DC 20003
202-863-8500
www.rnc.org/

Running Campaigns Through their national, state, and local organizations, parties coordinate campaigns. Political parties take care of many routine tasks that are essential to the smooth functioning of the electoral process. They work at getting party members registered and at conducting drives for new voters. They sometimes staff the polling places. Without parties, campaigns as we know them could not exist.

Raising Money for Candidates The major parties raise millions of dollars during each election cycle. Party leaders use this money to support specific party candidates in both the presidential and the congressional elections.

Party Membership

What does it mean to belong to a political party? To be a member of a political party in the United States, you need only claim to be a member. Generally, in the United States, people belong to a political party because they agree with many of its main ideas and support some of its candidates. In other countries, such as the People's Republic of China, people belong to a political party because they are required to do so, whether they agree with the ideas and candidates or not.

What Do Party Members Do? In many European countries, being a party member means actually joining a political party. You get a membership card to carry around in your wallet or purse, you pay dues, and you vote to select your local and national party leaders. In the United States, becoming a member of a political party is far less involved. American citizens have only to think of themselves as a Democrat, a Republican, or a member of a third party, such as the Libertarian Party or the Green Party. Members of parties do not have to

You can contact minor parties at the following addresses:

- *Libertarian Party* (2600 Virginia Ave. NW, Suite 100, Washington, DC 20037, 1-800-682-1776). This party was founded in 1971 with the goal of forming a voluntary society of free markets and free enterprise in which the role of government is severely limited. Its presidential candidate is consistently included on virtually every state ballot. You can access the Libertarian Party's Web site at **www.lp.org/**.

- *Prohibition National Committee* (P.O. Box 2635, Denver, CO 80201, 303-572-0646). This party was founded in 1869 and still occasionally runs presidential candidates. It advocates the repeal of all laws that legalize the manu-

facture and sale of alcoholic beverages.

- *Social Democrats, U.S.A.* (815 15th St. NW, Washington, DC 20005, 202-638-1515). Founded at the turn of the century, this is a moderate socialist party. It was important during the Great Depression of the 1930s. You can access this party's Web site at **www.socialdemocrats. org/sdusa/**.

- *Socialist Labor Party* (P.O. Box 218, Mountain View, CA 94042, 650-938-8359). This party, established in 1891, seeks the abolition of capitalism peacefully through the election process. The party's Web site address is **www.slp.org/#anchor642079**.

- *The Greens/Green Party USA* (P.O. Box 100, Blodgett Mills, NY 13738, 607-756-4211).

Founded in 1972, this party emphasizes ecological issues. Its slogan is, "We do not inherit the earth from our parents; we borrow it from our children." To access the Green Party's Web site, go to **www.greens.org/usa/**.

TAKING ACTION

1. Do any minor parties have offices in your state or locality? If so, contact one and ask for information about its goals, policies, and opportunities for volunteering.

2. Locate the state or local offices of the two major political parties in your area. Contact one of them, and ask for a copy of the party platform. Write a summary of that platform, and present it to your class.

---

pay dues, work for the party, attend party meetings, or support the party platform. In fact, they may do nothing more than occasionally vote for some of the party's candidates. People who think of themselves as party members but do not actively participate in party efforts are sometimes known as **party identifiers.**

Other individuals—active members—choose to work for the party and even become candidates for office. Political parties need year-round support from these people to survive. During election campaigns in particular, candidates depend on party volunteers to mail literature, answer phones, conduct door-to-door canvasses, organize speeches and appearances, and, of course, donate money. Between elections, parties also need active members to plan upcoming elections, organize fund-raisers, and keep in touch with party leaders in other communities to keep the party strong.

Clearly, political party members in the United States have very different ideas about what it means to belong to a political party. There are diverse levels of interest and activity, but all members "belong."

People and Parties People join political parties for different reasons. According to one political scientist, James Q. Wilson, one reason is to express **solidarity,** or mutual agreement with the views of friends, loved ones, and other like-minded people. They also join because they enjoy the excitement of politics. In addition, many believe they will benefit materially, through better employment or personal advancement, from joining a party. Finally, some join political parties because they wish to work for a set of ideals and principles that they feel are important in American politics and society.

▶ Delegates to the 1996 Republican National Convention in San Diego listen as Jack Kemp, presidential candidate Bob Dole's choice for running mate, gives his acceptance speech. Both parties knew who their nominees would be before their conventions, so why were these events even held?

Another political scientist, V. O. Key, believes that "people tend to have a broad image of parties. They see a party as generally dedicated to the interests of a particular set of groups within society." Thus, when interviewed, people may make the following remarks when asked why they support the Democratic Party: "It seems like the economy is better when the Democrats are in control." "The Democrats are for the working people." People might say about the Republican Party: "The Republicans help small-business owners more than the Democrats." "The Republicans deal better with foreign policy issues."

Regardless of how accurate these stereotypes are, individuals with similar characteristics do tend to align themselves more often with a particular major party. Family, age, occupation, education, and income all influence party choice. (See Figure 10–1 on page 273.) Yet never have all members of any one group tied themselves *permanently* to either party. Something that causes a person to favor a certain party in one election may not hold true in the next.

Persons may choose to belong to one of the major political parties because that party's position on various issues is, *on the whole*, preferable to that of the other party. In his book *Why I Am a Democrat* (1996), Theodore Sorenson, a well-known Democrat during the Kennedy-Johnson years (1961–1969), stresses this point:

I am a Democrat . . . because of my basic values and beliefs. . . . I am simply one of the millions who find the Democratic Party's candidates, principles, and positions consistently preferable to those of the Republicans.

No doubt, many other party members—of either major party—would give similar reasons for their party affiliation.

In the last few decades, the number of people who identify with either of the major parties has dropped sharply. Today, nearly 40 percent of voters classify themselves as **independents.**

Comparing Parties One way to compare today's Democratic and Republican parties is to study their party platforms. A **party platform** is a declaration of the party's beliefs and positions on major issues. The party's statement of its beliefs is called a platform because the candidates of the party "stand" on it. The platform is made up of **planks,** which are the party's official positions on specific issues, such as crime, drug abuse, and education. Each party adopts a platform every four years at its national convention.

SECTION 1 REVIEW

1. What are the three dimensions, or components, of American political parties?
2. What factors help to explain why we have a two-party system in the United States?

FIGURE 10–1 Party Affiliation by Group—1997 This table shows political party affiliation among members of various groups. Those who identify themselves as independents are not affiliated with either major party. What can you determine about the relationship between household income and party affiliation?

	Republican	Democrat	Independent
Total Sample	30 %	31 %	39 %
By Sex			
Male	31	26	43
Female	28	37	35
By Race			
White	33	28	39
Nonwhite	9	56	35
Black	6	64	30
Hispanic	21	37	42
By Age			
Under 30	29	26	45
30–49	30	29	41
50–64	30	33	37
65+	29	42	29
By Education			
College Graduate	35	28	37
Some College	31	29	40
High School Graduate	29	32	39
Less than High School Graduate	22	38	40
By Family Income			
$75,000+	42	24	34
$50,000–$74,999	37	27	36
$30,000–$49,999	32	29	39
$20,000–$29,999	27	33	40
Less than $20,000	22	38	40
By Religious Preference			
Total Protestant	38	25	37
Protestant Evangelical	42	25	33
Protestant Non-Evangelical	34	26	41
Catholic	30	32	38
By Marital Status			
Married	33	29	38
Divorced/Separated	22	35	43
Widowed	27	44	29
Never Married	26	30	44

SOURCE: The Pew Research Center for People and the Press, 1997.

3. Describe the important functions performed by political parties.
4. Why do people identify with political parties?
5. **For Critical Analysis:** Today, an increasing percentage of the voters (nearly 40 percent) classify themselves as "independent"—that is, they do not identify with either of the two major parties. In view of this trend, why is there no political party to represent the views of these voters?

The Development of the Two-Party Tradition

Preview Questions:

- Why were the first political parties formed?
- What was the first American political party to go out of existence?
- What great economic event brought the Democrats to power in the twentieth century?

Key Term:

realigning election

As we pointed out at the beginning of this chapter, Thomas Jefferson reacted negatively to the idea of political parties. So did many of the other founders. In his farewell address, George Washington warned against the "baneful [very harmful] effects of the spirit of the party." Benjamin Franklin worried about the "infinite mutual abuse of parties, tearing to pieces the best of characters." John Adams, the second president, stated, "There is nothing I dread so much as the division of the Republic into two great parties, each under its own leader." James Madison was particularly concerned over the conflicts that could arise between parties that represented local or regional interests. In 1819, Madison made the following observation in a letter to Richard Bland Lee:

> Political parties intermingled throughout the community unite as well as divide every Section of it. Parties founded on local distinctions and fixed peculiarities which Separate the whole into great conflicting masses are far more to be dreaded in their tendency.

Generally, the founders thought the power struggles that would arise between economic and political groups would eventually topple the balanced democracy they wanted to create. Even though the founders viewed political parties as dangerous, the first political *factions* in America—Federalists and Anti-Federalists—were formed around the issue of supporting or opposing the Constitution. Once the Constitution was ratified, these two national factions continued, but in a somewhat altered form.

▼ Disagreements between political parties arose almost as soon as the first parties were created. This 1798 cartoon depicts an actual fight that took place in Congress between Democratic Republican Matthew Lyon and Federalist Roger Griswold.

Alexander Hamilton, the first secretary of the Treasury, became the leader of the Federalist Party. Its supporters believed that a democracy should be ruled by wealthy and well-educated citizens. They favored a strong executive branch and a strong central government that would encourage the development of commerce and manufacturing.

Those who opposed the Federalists and Hamilton's policies referred to themselves not as Anti-Federalists but as Democratic Republicans. Led by Thomas Jefferson, they were sympathetic to the "common man" and favored a limited role for government. They believed that the nation's welfare would be best served if the states had more power than the central government. In their view, Congress should dominate the government, and its policies should help the nation's

The respected leader of the Whig Party, Henry Clay, speaks to an attentive U.S. Senate in 1850. Although the Whigs later dissolved, most members found an ideological home in a party that still exists today, the Republican Party.

shopkeepers, farmers, and laborers. The party, also known as the Jeffersonians, became the Democratic Party in the 1820s.

Once formed, political parties continued to be a part of American politics. Through the years, some parties have disappeared, some have been transformed, and new parties have appeared.

From 1796 to 1860

The nation's first two parties clashed openly in the elections of 1796, in which John Adams, the Federalists' candidate to succeed Washington as president, defeated Thomas Jefferson. Over the next four years, Thomas Jefferson and James Madison worked to build the Democratic Republican Party. In the elections of 1800 and 1804, Thomas Jefferson won the presidency under the Democratic Republican banner. His party also won control of Congress. The Federalists never returned to power and became the first (but not the last) American party to go out of existence. (See the time line in Figure 10–2 on page 278.)

The Democratic Republicans dominated American politics for the next twenty years. Jefferson was succeeded in the White House by two more Democratic Republicans, James Madison and James Monroe.

By the mid-1820s, the Democratic Republicans had split into two groups. Andrew Jackson, who was elected president in 1828, aligned himself with the group that called themselves the Democrats. Most of the Democrats were small farmers, debtors, frontiersmen, and slaveholders.

The other group, the National Republican Party (later the Whig Party), was led by Henry Clay and John Quincy Adams. It was a coalition of bankers, businesspersons, and southern planters. As the Whigs and Democrats competed for the White House throughout the 1840s and 1850s, the two-party system as we know it today emerged. Both parties were large, with supporters across the nation and with well-known leaders. Both had grassroots organizations of party workers committed to winning as many political offices (at all levels of government) for the party as possible. On the issue of slavery, both the Whigs and the Democrats remained vague.

By the 1850s, both parties were split by the growing problem of slavery. The Democrats were divided into northern and southern camps. The Whig coalition fell apart, and most Whigs were absorbed into the new

Just the Facts

The Democratic Party in the United States is the oldest continuing political party in the Western world.

What kinds of people vote for Democrats? What kinds of people vote for Republicans? The answers to such questions are frequently presented in table form. Tables can effectively present a great deal of information in a limited space. By examining a table, you can compare information and detect trends over time.

Follow these steps when reading a table:

- **Step 1.** *Read the title of the table.*

Interpreting Tables

- **Step 2.** *Notice how the table uses vertical and horizontal headings to present information.*
- **Step 3.** *Note whether the numerical information is stated as whole numbers or percentages. If it is stated as percentages, of what are the percentages a part? If it is stated as whole numbers, see if the numbers are expressed in tens, hundreds, thousands, or larger multiples.*
- **Step 4.** *Analyze the meaning of the percentages or other*

Vote by Groups in Presidential Elections, 1964–1996

| | 1964 | | 1968 | | | 1972 | | 1976 | | |
	Johnson D	Goldwater R	Humphrey D	Nixon R	Wallace I	McGovern D	Nixon R	Carter D	Ford R	McCarthy I
National	61.3%	38.7%	43.0%	43.4%	13.6%	38%	62%	50%	48%	1%
Sex										
Male	60	40	41	43	16	37	63	53	45	1
Female	62	38	45	43	12	38	62	48	51	*
Race										
White	59	41	38	47	15	32	68	46	52	1
Nonwhite	94	6	85	12	3	87	13	85	15	*
Age										
Under 30	64	36	47	38	15	48	52	53	45	1
30–49 years	63	37	44	41	15	33	67	48	49	2
50 years and older	59	41	41	47	12	36	64	52	48	*
Politics										
Republican	20	80	9	86	5	5	95	9	91	*
Democrat	87	13	74	12	14	67	33	82	18	*
Independent	56	44	31	44	25	31	69	38	57	4
Education										
College	52	48	37	54	9	37	63	42	55	2
High school	62	38	42	43	15	34	66	54	46	*
Grade school	66	34	52	33	15	49	51	58	41	1

*Less than 1 percent

numbers by comparing the various sets of figures.

- **Step 5.** *Read the source to determine where the data came from.*

When reading a table such as the one below, remember that the statistics presented in the table do not describe individuals. Rather, they describe behavior trends in various groups. By looking at the tables on these pages, you can conclude that most people with college educations vote for Republican

presidential candidates. You cannot conclude, however, that *all* people with college educations vote for the Republican candidate. In other words, you cannot assume that just because a person has a particular trait, he or she will vote for a particular candidate or particular party.

PRACTICING YOUR SKILLS

Look at the table and answer the following questions:

1. What percentage of women voted for the Democratic candidate in 1984?
2. Decide whether the table supports this statement: College graduates have supported Republican presidential candidates since 1968.
3. Does it appear that voters under thirty years of age always support Democrats?

Vote by Groups in Presidential Elections, 1964–1996 (continued)												
1980			1984		1988		1992			1996		
Carter D	Reagan R	Anderson I	Mondale D	Reagan R	Dukakis D	Bush R	Clinton D	Bush R	Perot I	Clinton D	Dole R	Perot I
41%	51%	7%	41%	59%	45%	53%	43%	38%	19%	49%	41%	8%
38	53	7	36	64	41	57	41	38	21	43	44	10
44	49	6	45	55	49	50	46	37	17	54	38	7
36	56	7	34	66	40	59	39	41	20	43	46	9
86	10	2	87	13	86	12	NA	NA	NA	NA	NA	NA
47	41	11	40	60	47	52	44	34	22	54	34	10
38	52	8	40	60	45	54	42	38	20	48	41	9
41	54	4	41	59	49	50	50	38	12	48	44	7
8	86	5	4	96	8	91	10	73	17	13	80	6
69	26	4	79	21	82	17	77	10	13	84	10	5
29	55	14	33	67	43	55	38	32	30	43	35	17
35	53	10	39	61	43	56	44	39	18	44	46	8
43	51	5	43	57	49	50	43	36	20	51	35	13
54	42	3	51	49	56	43	56	28	NA	59	28	11

SOURCE: *Gallup Report*, November 1984, p. 32; *New York Times*, November 15, 1992, p. B9; *New York Times*, November 10, 1996.

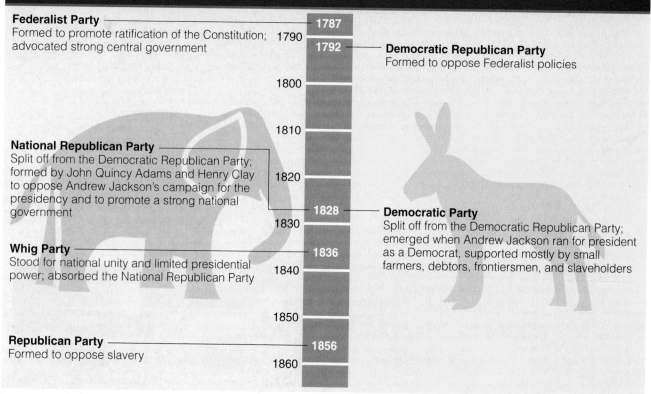

FIGURE 10–2 The Evolution of the Major American Political Parties The figure below shows the historical development that led to the Democratic and Republican parties as we know them today. When did the modern Democratic Party begin?

Federalist Party
Formed to promote ratification of the Constitution; advocated strong central government

1787
1790
1792

Democratic Republican Party
Formed to oppose Federalist policies

1800

1810

National Republican Party
Split off from the Democratic Republican Party; formed by John Quincy Adams and Henry Clay to oppose Andrew Jackson's campaign for the presidency and to promote a strong national government

1820

1828
1830

Democratic Party
Split off from the Democratic Republican Party; emerged when Andrew Jackson ran for president as a Democrat, supported mostly by small farmers, debtors, frontiersmen, and slaveholders

Whig Party
Stood for national unity and limited presidential power; absorbed the National Republican Party

1836
1840

1850

Republican Party
Formed to oppose slavery

1856
1860

Republican Party, which opposed the extension of slavery into new territories. Campaigning on this platform, they succeeded in electing Abraham Lincoln as the first Republican president in 1860.

From the 1860s to the Present

By the end of the Civil War in 1865, the Republicans and the Democrats were the most prominent political parties. From the election of Abraham Lincoln in 1860 until the election of Franklin Roosevelt in 1932, the Republican Party, sometimes referred to as the Grand Old Party, or GOP, remained the majority party in national politics, winning all but four presidential elections.

The social and economic impact of the Great Depression of the 1930s destroyed the majority support that Republicans had enjoyed for so long and contributed to a realignment in the two-party system.

A **realigning election** shows a long-lasting shift in fundamental party loyalties among a large portion of voters, so that what was the weaker party emerges as the dominant party. The landmark realigning election of 1932 brought Franklin Delano Roosevelt to the presidency and the Democrats to power at the national level.

Roosevelt was reelected three times, for a total of four terms. When he died, his vice president, Harry S Truman, assumed the presidency. Truman also won the 1948 election. The Republicans, under Dwight David Eisenhower, won the 1952 and 1956 presidential elections. From 1960 through 1968, the Democrats, headed by John F. Kennedy and Lyndon Baines Johnson, held the presidency. The Republicans came back to win the presidential election under Richard M. Nixon in 1968. Jimmy Carter, a Democrat, served a single term as president after winning the election in 1976. After that, Republicans held the presidency until Bill Clinton was elected in 1992.

In Congress, the Democrats remained the dominant party from the Great Depression until 1994. The 1994 elections resulted in a Republican majority in Congress. The Republicans retained this position in the 1996 elections.

SECTION 2 REVIEW

1. Which party dominated American politics at the beginning of the 1800s?

2. What national problem destroyed the Whig Party in the 1850s?

3. When did a realigning election bring the Democratic Party into power? What was the reason for the realignment?

4. **For Critical Analysis:** Although debate among Republicans and Democrats is often heated, some critics of our two-party system claim that the two parties are essentially the same. If these critics are right, then why do some Americans become loyal members of one party or the other?

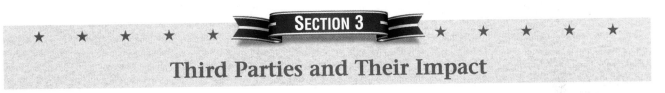

SECTION 3

Third Parties and Their Impact

Preview Questions:

- What are the different types of third parties and why are they formed?
- How do third parties influence American politics?
- Why do third parties have problems winning elections?

Key Terms:

ideology, minimum wage, old-age pensions

As mentioned earlier, throughout American history, minor parties, or third parties, have competed for power in the nation's two-party system. Indeed, third parties have been represented in most of our national elections. Third parties find it difficult, if not impossible, to gain credibility within the two-party–dominated American system. Nonetheless, they play an important role in our political life.

Third Parties Come in Several Varieties

Third, or minor, parties are as varied as the causes they represent, but they all have one thing in common. They believe that certain needs and values are not being properly addressed by the major parties. Third parties name candidates who propose to remedy the situation. The four parties and their candidates listed in Figure 10–3 on page 280 are only a few of the minor parties that ran candidates in the 1996 presidential elections.

Some third parties have tried to appeal to the entire nation. Others have focused on particular regions, states, or locales. Most have been short lived, but a few have lasted for a long time. Enduring third parties include the Socialist Labor Party, founded in 1891, and the Social Democrats, founded in 1901. The number and variety of third parties make them difficult to classify, but most fall into one of the three general categories discussed here.

Issue-Oriented Parties An issue-oriented third party is formed to promote a particularly timely issue. For example, the Free Soil Party was organized in the years before the Civil War in 1860 to oppose the expansion of slavery into the western territories. The Prohibition Party was formed in 1869 to convince the government to prohibit the manufacture and use of alcoholic beverages. The U.S.A. Green Party was

Just the Facts

Millard Fillmore, a former Whig president, ran for president in 1856 as the candidate of the Know-Nothing Party.

FIGURE 10–3 Selected Third Parties and Their Candidates in the 1996 Presidential Elections
This figure shows four of the many third parties that fielded candidates in the 1996 elections. Why do third-party candidates fail to win elections?

John Hagelin (Candidate for the Natural Law Party)	Ralph Nader (Candidate for the Green Party)	Howard Phillips (Candidate for the U.S. Taxpayers Party)	Harry Browne (Candidate for the Libertarian Party)

Advocated transcendental meditation and "yoga flying" for all American voters; supported government-provided health care as long as alternative medicine was used	Fought against the self-perpetuation of the two-party system; advocated environmentalist positions	Called for the elimination of all direct taxes, the elimination of the civil service, and the end of U.S. participation in the United Nations, NATO, and the International Monetary Fund	Supported the elimination of the Central Intelligence Agency, the Environmental Protection Agency, the Internal Revenue Service, and the Federal Bureau of Investigation, along with less government control over individual enterprises.

founded in 1972 to raise awareness of environmental issues. The Reform Party was formed in 1996, mainly to provide a campaign vehicle for H. Ross Perot, who wished to run for president. Perot's primary campaign issue concerned the rising national debt. Most issue-oriented parties fade into history as the issue that brought them into existence fades from public attention, is taken up by a major party, or is resolved.

Ideological Parties An **ideology** is a comprehensive set of beliefs about human nature and government institutions. Ideological parties are those that support a particular set of beliefs or a particular political doctrine. For example, a party such as the Socialist Workers Party may hold that the U.S. free-enterprise system should be replaced by a system in which government or workers own all of the factories in the economy. The party may support the idea that competition should be replaced by cooperation and social responsibility in order to secure a fair distribution of income. In contrast, an ideological party such as the Libertarian Party may

◀ *This lapel pin promotes the presidential candidacy of Theodore ("Teddy") Roosevelt of the Bull Moose Party in 1912. Why did Roosevelt, a Republican, create a third party?*

oppose government interference in private enterprise.

Splinter or Personality Parties A splinter party develops out of a split within a major party. Often, this split involves the formation of a party to elect a specific person. Theodore Roosevelt's Bull Moose Party of 1912 (also called the Progressive Party) is an example of a splinter party formed from the Republican Party. When Roosevelt did not receive the Republican Party's nomination, he created the Bull Moose Party to promote his platform. From the Democrats have come Henry Wallace's Progressive Party and the States' Rights (Dixiecrat) Party, both formed in 1948. In 1968, the American Independent Party was formed to support George Wallace's campaign for president. In 1996, as mentioned, the Reform Party was formed around H. Ross Perot.

Most splinter parties have been formed around a leader with a strong personality, which is why they are sometimes called personality parties. When that person steps aside, the parties usually collapse.

Third Parties' Impact on American Politics

Even though most Americans do not support third parties or vote for their candidates, third parties have influenced American politics in several important ways. First, third parties have brought many important political issues to the public's attention. They have focused on unpopular or highly debated issues that major parties have preferred to ignore. Third parties are in a position to take bold stands on issues avoided by the major parties because they are not trying to be all things to all people. Generally, third parties can bring substantial pressure to bear on the major parties.

Progressive social reforms such as the **minimum wage** (the lowest legal wage), women's right to vote, railroad and banking regulations, and **old-age pensions** (retirement plans that give people income after they stop working) were first proposed by third parties. The Free Soil Party of the 1850s was the first true anti-slavery party, and the Populists and Progressives put many social reforms on the political agenda. Ralph Nader's Green Party in California was created in an effort to push the Democrats to the left. In 1992, H. Ross Perot succeeded in arousing real concern about the federal budget deficit, and Perot received about 19 percent of the vote. (Support for Perot's Reform Party fell to 8.5 percent of the vote in the 1996 elections, however.)

It is sometimes argued that third parties are the unsung heroes of American politics, bringing new issues to the public forefront. Some of the ideas proposed by third parties were never accepted, but others were taken up by the major parties as the ideas became more popular.

Third parties have also influenced some election outcomes. They have taken victory from one major party and given it to another, thus playing the "spoiler role." For example, in 1912, when the Progressive Party split off from the Republican Party, the presidential race consisted of Woodrow Wilson as the Democratic candidate, William Howard Taft as the regular Republican candidate, and Theodore Roosevelt as the Progressive candidate. The presence of the new Progressive Party "spoiled" the Republicans' chances for victory and gave the election to Wilson, the Democrat. Without third-party action by Roosevelt, Taft might have won.

Finally, third parties provide a voice for voters who are frustrated with and alienated from the Republican and Democratic parties. In 1992, H. Ross Perot received a great deal of support from voters who were dissatisfied with the politics of both of the major parties.

▲ *What point do you think the editorial cartoonist was making with this portrayal of 1912 presidential candidates Theodore Roosevelt and William Howard Taft?*

▶ *Although third-party presidential candidate H. Ross Perot had little chance of actually winning, his candidacy garnered attention and support throughout the country. What was Perot's main campaign issue?*

Why Do Third Parties Fail to Win Elections?

Third parties fail to win elections for many reasons. One is the public's traditional habit of voting within the major parties. The American people have always had a two-party system and are accustomed to selecting only from the nominees of those parties.

Another major problem for third parties is raising enough funds for a modern campaign. Most Americans have come to believe that third-party candidates could never win, and they are unwilling to contribute to an underdog candidate's campaign. A 1974 law does, however, decrease the severity of this problem for third-party candidates in presidential elections. The law states that presidential candidates who receive over 5 percent of the votes will be partially repaid for their campaign expenses by the national government.

Another problem for third parties is getting candidates on the ballot in all fifty states. Before 1968, some state laws required candidates to gather a considerable number of signatures in a short period of time in order to be listed on the state ballot. In 1968, a third-party candidate, George Wallace, challenged such a law in Ohio, and the Supreme Court ruled that the law was unconstitutional. States have since relaxed these requirements. Election laws in some states still favor the two major parties, however, and thereby work against minor parties.

Finally, any third party that succeeds in winning the support of a significant number of voters will soon fall victim to its own success. After all, the two major parties can easily adopt additional planks in their platforms to attract individuals who are supporting the third party. In this way, the two major parties undermine any successful third-party campaign. Suppose, for example, that a third party favors a federal tax on all businesses, to be used for cleaning up air pollution. If that third party succeeds in gaining considerable voter support, then either of the major parties can simply support the tax in its own party platform—or both parties can support it.

SECTION 3 REVIEW

1. Name the three types of third parties, and explain why they are formed.
2. What important influences do third parties have on the American political system?
3. What are some problems that third parties face?
4. **For Critical Analysis:** Based on past experience, it is unlikely that a third party's presidential candidate will ever win a national election. What, then, do you think motivates millions of Americans to join third parties?

The Structure of Political Parties

Preview Questions:

- ⭐ How are the two major parties structured?
- ⭐ In general, how are state and local party organizations structured?
- ⭐ What are the four major elements in the structures of both major national organizations?

Key Terms:

patronage, ward, precinct, national convention, party ticket, national party committee, national party chairperson

In theory, each of the major American political parties has a standard, pyramid-shaped organization much like that of a large company, with the bosses at the top and the employees at various lower levels. Actually, neither party has a closely knit or highly organized structure. Both are fragmented and *decentralized*. There is no direct chain of command by which orders come from the top of the organization to those in lower positions. If there were, the national chairperson of the Democratic or Republican Party, along with the national committee, could simply dictate how the organization was to be run, just as if it were Microsoft or Netscape. Instead, state party organizations are all very different and are only loosely tied to the party's national structure. Local party organizations are often quite independent from the state organization. There is no individual or group whom everyone in the party obeys. Rather, there are a number of personalities, frequently at odds with one another, who form a loosely identifiable leadership group.

◀ *U.S. senator Carol Moseley-Braun addresses by video a fund-raising dinner where President Bill Clinton and First Lady Hillary Rodham Clinton also spoke. What kind of people might you find in the audience at this event?*

Machine Politics

Today, political party organizations in large cities are fairly quiet, except in a few places. This was not always the case. At one time in history, big-city political parties were *the* party organizations in America. From the last years of the nineteenth century through the 1930s, many cities were operated by what was known as a "machine." In this system within a party, each city block had its organizer, each neighborhood had its political club, each district or ward had its leader, and the whole machine had its "boss." **Patronage,** the practice of rewarding faithful party members with jobs or contracts, held the machine together.

The machine was especially helpful to immigrants and the poor, who often needed help to overcome language barriers and to obtain social services and jobs. These people, in exchange for this assistance, gave the machine their loyalty. Politically, machines linked neighborhoods and ethnic groups into a strong political power base that could elect and reelect a mayor—or boss.

However helpful they were at times, some machines turned out to be quite corrupt. The Tammany Society, which dominated New York City politics for more than a century, was especially notorious. One of its most infamous leaders was William "Boss" Tweed, whose scandalous behavior was exposed by the *New York Times* in 1871. Readers were entertained and shocked by stories describing how politicians received millions of dollars in kickbacks from businesses that sought government contracts. The stories also

shed light on civil and criminal violations that were not punished, as well as phony leases and padded bills that were paid to members of the Tweed machine. Tweed was imprisoned, but many other members fled the country with their wealth intact.

The years of the great machines, in places such as New York City, Jersey City, Kansas City, and Philadelphia, are now over. Mayor Richard Daley of Chicago, often called the last of the big-city bosses, died in 1976.

Big-city machines died mostly because their function of providing social services was taken over by state and national agencies. Reformers claimed that local government should focus on administration rather than politics. They argued that human services and jobs should be provided in an efficient and honest manner—without the payoffs, kickbacks, and graft that long characterized machine politics. They sought to break up the centralized power of machines and were largely successful.

THINK ABOUT IT
....

1. What advantages, if any, could machine politics have in a big city?
2. What other reasons can you think of for the breakup of machine politics?

State and Local Party Organizations

In both the Democratic Party and the Republican Party, state and local organizations are separate from the national organizations. Most state and local organ-

izations work closely with the national organizations only during major elections.

State Organizations The powers and duties of state party organizations vary from state to state. In general, the state party organization is built around a central

How Political Parties Have Changed

Although we still have only two major political parties in the United States, there have been many changes in the party system. Here are some of the changes that have occurred since the 1930s.

THEN (1930S)	NOW
Strong party machines dominated local politics in many large cities.	The era of city political machines has ended.
About 20 percent of American voters classified themselves as independents.	Nearly 40 percent of American voters classify themselves as independents.
Campaign funds for political candidates were raised by parties.	Campaign funds for political candidates are raised by parties *and* candidates.

committee and a chairperson. The committee works to raise funds, recruit new party members, maintain a strong party organization, and help members running for state offices.

The state chairperson is usually a powerful party member chosen by the committee. In some cases, however, the chairperson is selected by the governor or a senator from the state.

Local Organizations Local party organizations differ greatly. Generally, there is a party unit for each district in which elective offices are to be filled. These include congressional and legislative districts, counties, cities and towns, wards, and precincts. A **ward** is a political division or district within a city designated for electing members of a city council. A **precinct** is the basic unit of party organization and of election polling. The local, grassroots foundations of politics are formed within voting precincts. Polling places—where people vote on election day—are located within precincts. Political parties elect or appoint precinct captains or chairpersons who organize their precincts, assist new members, register voters, and take care of party business.

National Party Organization

On the national level, the president is considered to be the official party leader. In some cases, well-known members of Congress are viewed as national party leaders. In addition, there are four major elements in the national structure of both major parties: the national convention, the national committee, the national chairperson, and the congressional campaign committees.

The National Convention

Most of the public attention that the party receives comes during the party's **national convention,** which is held every four years during the summer before the presidential election. The media cover these conventions extensively, and as a result, they have become quite extravagant. They are often described as the party's national voice and are usually held in major cities such as New York, Chicago, Miami, or San Francisco.

The national conventions are attended by delegates chosen by the states in various ways. The delegates write the party platform, which sets forth the party's positions on national issues and makes promises to initiate certain policies if the party wins the presidency. Once they have decided on the party platform, the delegates turn to their most important job—choosing the

Just the Facts

The first Democratic National Convention was held in 1832 in Baltimore, and the first Republican National Convention was held in 1856 in Philadelphia.

Political Parties

The United States has a two-party system. Candidates who want to be elected have little choice but to run as Democrats or Republicans. Among voters, though, party identification has been slipping. Fewer and fewer voters are willing to identify themselves with one of the major parties. Rather, they identify themselves simply as independents. Fifty years ago, only 20 percent of voters were independents. Today, almost 40 percent of voters identify themselves as independents. This percentage is higher than the percentage of voters that identify with either of the major parties.

Some Americans Are Worried about the Weakening of the Two Major Parties

The "old guards" of the two major political parties are not happy. Increases in the number of independents have weakened the effectiveness of the two major parties. Voters no longer want to vote a *straight ticket*. That is, they do not want to vote for all of the candidates of one party during any election. Often, for example, people vote for a Democrat for president and a Republican for Congress, or vice versa. This is called split-ticket voting.

Those in favor of maintaining the strength of the two major parties have an important argument on their side. They contend that only a strong party has a chance of creating significant policy changes. The party in power, according to these people, needs a strong show of support by Americans. Only then can it deal from a position of strength when it has to make new policies in response to changes in America and abroad. If the parties continue to lose the loyalty of the voters, perhaps fewer and fewer important policy changes will occur.

Others Welcome the Weakening of the Two Major Parties

Some people welcome the rising number of independents and the weakening of the two major political parties. This group argues that the major parties have not kept up with changing times. They also contend that there is no longer any clear-cut distinction between the two parties. Therefore, there are no compelling reasons for voters to identify with one or the other of these parties. Increasingly, claim these individuals, both parties seem to be dominated by interest groups.

In any event, candidates running for office at any level no longer have to depend on their parties to the extent they did in the past. They can now make their own arrangements for campaign advertising and fund-raising. They can, and do, hire professional campaign managers. If candidates do not really need political parties to help them get elected, why do voters need the parties?

In spite of the growing number of independents, the Democrats and Republicans are not about to disappear. The parties may become weaker, but all that means is that working for major political parties may not guarantee the rewards that existed in the past.

YOU DECIDE

1. Give some reasons for belonging to a major political party today.
2. Do you think that people in government today are less committed to their parties than officeholders were in the past? Why or why not?

party's presidential and vice presidential candidates, who make up the **party ticket.**

The National Committee Each state elects a number of delegates to the **national party committee.** These committees direct party business during the four years between national conventions. Their most important duty, however, is to plan the next national convention and ways to obtain a party victory in the next presidential election.

The National Chairperson Each party's national committee selects a **national party chairperson** to serve as head of the national party committee. The chairperson is chosen by the party's presidential candidate at a meeting of the national committee right after the national convention. The national chairperson directs the work of the national committee from party headquarters in Washington, D.C. This leader is involved in fund-raising, publicity, promoting party unity, recruiting new voters, and other activities. During presidential election years, the committee and the chairperson focus on the national convention and the presidential campaign.

The Congressional Campaign Committees Each party has a campaign committee in each house of Congress that works to help reelect party members to Congress. Chosen by their colleagues, members serve two-year terms.

SECTION 4 REVIEW

1. What is the structure of most state and local party organizations?
2. What are the main elements of the national party organization?
3. What are the purposes of a national party convention?
4. **For Critical Analysis:** How does the structure of the major political parties differ from the structure of a typical big business?

★ ★ ★ ★ **Chapter Summary** ★ ★ ★ ★

Section 1: The Nature and Functions of Political Parties

- Political parties are groups who organize to win elections, operate the government, and determine public policy. The three components of American political parties are the party in the electorate, the party organization, and the party in government.
- The United States has a two-party system. The two-party system is the result of national consensus and moderate views, political tradition, and the elective process.
- Political parties select candidates, inform the public, coordinate policymaking, run campaigns, and raise money for candidates.
- In the last few decades, an increasing number of voters have classified themselves as independents—not members of either major party.

Section 2: The Development of the Two-Party Tradition

- The first political factions in America were formed to support or oppose the Constitution.
- The Federalists became the first actual U.S. political party. Those who opposed them became the Democratic Republicans.
- The Democratic Republicans split into two parties. The Whig Party was absorbed into the new Republican Party in the 1850s.
- By the end of the Civil War, the Republicans and the Democrats were the most prominent political parties.

Section 3: Third Parties and Their Impact

- There are three general types of third parties: (1) issue-oriented parties; (2) ideological parties, and (3) splinter or personality parties.
- Many important issues in American politics have been brought to the public's attention by third parties. These parties have also influenced some election outcomes.
- Third parties fail to win elections due to a variety of reasons.

Section 4: The Structure of Political Parties

- In theory, the two major political parties in the United States have pyramid-shaped organizations. In actuality, each is fragmented and decentralized.
- The four major elements in the national structure of both major parties are the convention, the committee, the chairperson, and the congressional campaign committees.

CHAPTER 10 Review

★ REVIEW QUESTIONS ★

1. Explain what a political party is, and describe the roles that parties play in American politics.
2. What factors help to explain America's two-party system? How is this system different from those of other nations?
3. What are the main functions of political parties, and why are these functions important?
4. What do party members do, and why do people join political parties?
5. Why do individuals identify with political parties?
6. Why did the founders react negatively to the idea of political parties?
7. What were the first political parties in the United States, and why were they formed?
8. By the end of the Civil War, what were the dominant parties in the United States?
9. Name the three different types of third parties.
10. What effects have third parties had on American politics?
11. Name three minor parties in the United States.
12. Is it likely that a widely supported third party will emerge in the future?
13. Describe the structure of party organizations.
14. What function do national party committees perform?
15. Why do some people argue that the two major parties are no longer as necessary as they have been in the past?

★ CRITICAL THINKING ★

1. Some commentators argue that political parties are no longer necessary because candidates have their own campaign organizations to raise funds and arrange for campaign advertising. Analyze this argument.
2. Although both the Democrats and the Republicans have national party structures, most of the power of political parties lies at the county and state levels. Discuss why the national party organizations cannot control local politics.
3. Discuss what you believe to be the major differences between the platforms of the Republican Party and the Democratic Party.
4. On several occasions, both the Democrats and the Republicans have asked the same individual to run as their presidential candidate. This occurred, for example, with Dwight D. Eisenhower. Explain how such a phenomenon could occur.

★ IMPROVING YOUR SKILLS ★

Communication Skills

Skimming for Information You learned about the SQ3R reading strategy on pages 84–85. This strategy will help you to understand and remember details as you read a textbook. At times, though, you must read material quickly, such as when deciding which newspaper articles to use in a research project. *Skimming* is a technique that allows you to assess the key concepts of an article or chapter without reading the entire selection. When skimming for information, look at headings, topic sentences (usually the topic sentence is the first or second sentence in a paragraph), and conclusions. Know what information you are looking for ahead of time.

Writing Practice your skimming techniques by going to the library and researching one of the political parties listed on the time line shown in Figure 10–2 on page 278. Find three books on U.S. political parties and skim them quickly until you find the main facts about the party you have chosen. Then write down five facts you learned about the party.

Social Studies Skills

Reading a Time Line Information and data are often organized in chronological order—that is, according to

the dates on which events occurred. The battles of the Civil War, World War I, and World War II can be organized in this fashion, for example. When information in a chart is organized in chronological order, the chart is called a time line. Look at the time line on the formation of political parties on page 278 and answer the following questions:

1. Over what period does the time line extend?
2. How many years does the distance between horizontal lines on the time line represent?
3. Which was started earlier, the Republican Party or the Democratic Party?

★ ACTIVITIES AND PROJECTS ★

1. Research a political party organization in your state or city. Visit the party's headquarters, if possible, and find out about the party's structure and activities and about how the state or city organization coordinates its activities with the national party organization. Ask about the main problems the party faces in your area and about activities in which you and your classmates could become involved. Write a short report, and present your findings to your class.
2. Determine through research whether your state government is predominantly controlled by Democrats or by Republicans. To do this, find out what party has controlled the state legislature and what party has controlled the governorship in each of the last twenty-five years. Write a short report describing your findings.
3. Try to determine whether the city (or county) in which you live is controlled by Democrats or Republicans. List the reasons for your conclusion.
4. Invite an election official to discuss political party participation in your county, or plan a panel presentation in which local party leaders discuss community issues.
5. Investigate what you must do and what documentation you must provide in order to register to vote. What is the most convenient means of registering to vote for you? Write a brief report describing your findings.

What If . . .

A Third-Party Candidate Won a Presidential Election?

For many years, the president of the United States has been either a Democrat or a Republican. These presidents have usually enjoyed the full backing of their political party. We have, however, had presidential candidates from third parties. What might happen if a third party candidate actually became president? How might Congress react?

CHAPTER 11

Campaigns and Elections

CHAPTER OBJECTIVES

To learn about and understand . . .

⭐ The nominating process and the various methods of nomination used in the United States

⭐ How campaigns are organized and financed

⭐ Some of the problems associated with campaign financing

⭐ How elections are organized and carried out

"Elections are won by men and women chiefly because most people vote against somebody rather than for somebody."

Franklin P. Adams
(1881–1960)
American Journalist and Humorist

INTRODUCTION

Every year, in virtually every high school in America, elections for class officers are held. Each school has a different system, but there are many similarities. Generally, if you meet certain minimal requirements, it is not difficult to get your name on the ballot. Candidates normally campaign for some period of time prior to the election. If what Franklin Adams claimed in the above quotation is true, one way to get elected is to campaign *against* your opponents. That means that you point out what is wrong with them, rather than what is right about you.

When you participate in campaigns and elections for class officers, you are participating in a democratic process. In this chapter, we look at two very important parts of our representative democracy: campaigns and elections.

◀ Balloons fall on the celebrating crowd at the Republican National Convention as the delegates cheer for their presidential and vice presidential candidates.

The Nomination

Preview Questions:

- 🌐 What are the methods by which candidates are nominated in the United States?
- 🌐 What are direct primaries, and what different forms do they take?
- 🌐 How are presidential candidates nominated?

Key Terms:

nomination, self-nomination, ballot, petition, write-in candidate, caucuses, nominating convention, delegates, direct primary, closed primary, open primary, blanket primary, plurality, nonpartisan elections

American political campaigns are usually long, complicated, and expensive events. They produce hours of film, volumes of newsprint, thousands of posters and buttons, and finally a winning candidate who becomes a public official for the next few years. The first step in this long process is **nomination,** the choosing of candidates within each party. These candidates will then seek office by running against the candidates chosen by the other party.

Nomination is a critical step in the election process because it narrows the field of possible candidates. The methods by which candidates are nominated have varied from time to time and from state to state. They can, however, be grouped in the general categories discussed in this section.

Just the Facts

All seven Democrats in a 1995 local election in Rhode Island missed the deadline for nominating themselves to run for office.

Self-Nomination and Petition

Until the early 1800s, **self-nomination,** or simply announcing one's desire to run for public office, was the most common way of becoming a candidate. This method is still used in small towns and rural areas in many parts of the country.

Self-nomination does not mean that a person's name will automatically appear on the **ballot**—the card or other object on which voters indicate their choices in the election. The candidate must first file a **petition,** a formal request to be listed on the ballot. The petition must have a certain number of signatures—the number required is determined by the state—to show that the candidate has some public support.

A self-nominated candidate may not be able to gather enough signatures to win a place on the ballot. In this situation, she or he may decide to run as a **write-in candidate,** someone who will campaign without being listed on the ballot and who will ask voters to write his or her name on the ballot on election day. For these votes to count, most states require the write-in candidate to register with the local board of elections. Write-in candidates have rarely been successful at winning public office.

Party Caucus

The Constitution gives no instructions for nominating candidates for the presidency and vice presidency. Thus, in 1797, the leaders of the two par-

◀ *A high-school election is an example of democracy on a small scale. What similarities exist between electing a class president and electing a country's president?*

ties decided to keep political power in their hands by holding conferences later called **caucuses.** In these early meetings, the party leaders, who were wealthy and influential members of the community, would choose the candidates in secret. The voters at large would have no part in choosing those who were nominated.

By the presidential race of 1820, the caucus method of nomination had become controversial. The system was called "King Caucus" by Andrew Jackson and other presidential candidates who felt it was undemocratic and too powerful. Party leaders were faced with rising opposition and were forced to find other methods of nominating candidates. As the caucus system faded away in presidential politics, its use soon diminished at the state and local levels as well.

The caucus is still used for some local nominations, especially in New England. These modern caucuses, however, are open to the general public and bear little resemblance to the original caucus.

▲ This 1824 cartoon shows Andrew Jackson being attacked by dogs. The dogs represent supporters of the caucus system. Why did Jackson protest the caucus system?

Party Nominating Convention

As the caucus method lost favor around the country, caucuses were replaced in many states by party conventions. A **nominating convention** is an official meeting of a political party in which candidates and delegates are chosen. **Delegates** are persons sent to a higher-level convention to represent the people of a geographical area. For example, delegates at a local party convention nominate candidates for local office and also choose delegates to represent the party at the state convention. By 1840, the convention system had become the most common way of nominating candidates for government offices at every level.

Party conventions were intended to be more democratic than party caucuses because more people were allowed to take part. Yet, like the caucus method, the convention method was abused. One historian, Charles Beard, described the corruption of party leaders in the late 1840s:

They packed [conventions] with their henchmen, who drove out or overwhelmed dangerous opponents. They padded the rolls of party members with the names of dead men. . . . They stuffed the ballot boxes, and they prepared the slates

which were forced through the nominating convention in the face of opposition.

These practices soon came to the attention of the public. As criticism grew, state legislatures turned away from conventions as a means of nominating local and state party candidates. The convention is still used, however, in some states, including Connecticut, Delaware, Michigan, and Utah. At the national level, the party convention is used to select the presidential candidates of the two major parties from the winners of the state primaries and conventions.

The Direct Primary

In most states, the convention method was gradually replaced by the **direct primary**—an election held *within* each party to pick candidates for the general election. The direct primary is the method most commonly used today to nominate candidates for office.

Although the primaries are *party* nominating elections, they are now closely regulated by the states. The states usually set the dates and conduct the primaries. The states also provide polling places, election officials, registration lists, and ballots, in addition to counting the votes.

Most state laws require that the major parties use the primary to choose their candidates for the U.S. Senate and the House, for the governorship and all other state offices, and for most local offices as well. In a few states, however, combinations of nominating conventions and primaries are used to pick candidates for the top offices.

Because state laws vary, several different kinds of primaries are used throughout the country. They include closed primaries, open primaries, run-off primaries, and nonpartisan elections.

Closed Primaries In a **closed primary,** only party members vote to choose that party's candidates, and they vote only in the primary of their own party. Thus, only Democrats vote in the Democratic primary to select candidates of the Democratic Party. Only Republicans vote for the Republican candidates. A person usually establishes party membership when he or she registers to vote. In some states, such as Illinois, a person may register at the polling place.

Regular party workers favor the closed method because it promotes party loyalty. Independent voters oppose it because it excludes them from the nominating process.

Open Primaries An **open primary** is a direct primary in which voters can vote for a party's candidates regardless of whether they belong to the party. In most open primaries, all voters receive both a Republican ballot and Democratic ballot. Each voter then chooses one of these ballots in the privacy of the voting booth and selects candidates of that party.

A different version of the open primary is used in Alaska and Washington. These states have a "wide-open" primary, or **blanket primary,** in which each voter receives a single large ballot listing each party's candidates for each nomination. Voters may choose candidates from different parties. This means that a

▲ The first state Republican convention was held outdoors on July 6, 1854, in Jackson, Michigan. Party conventions replaced what system of nominating candidates?

voter may choose a Democratic candidate for one office and a Republican candidate for another office.

Run-Off Primaries Candidates for most offices must win only a **plurality** of votes—more votes than any other candidate—to be declared the winner. They do not need to win a majority of the votes. In some states, however, candidates are required to win by a majority. If none of the candidates receives a majority in the primary election, a run-off election is held. In a run-off election the two candidates who won the most votes in the first primary election run against each other. The person who wins the run-off election becomes the party's candidate in the general election.

Nonpartisan Elections In most states, some offices are filled in **nonpartisan elections**—elections in which candidates do not run under party labels. Nonpartisan elections are most often used at the local level to choose, for example, candidates for the school board, hospital board, city council, and other local offices.

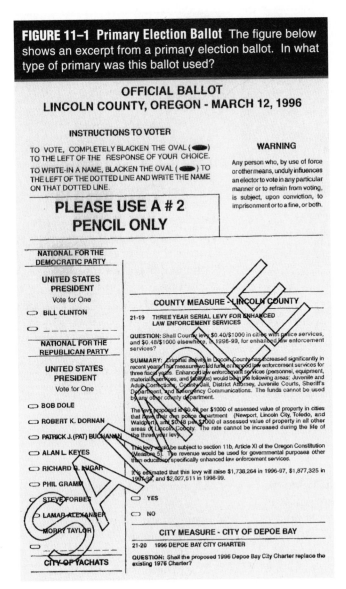

FIGURE 11–1 Primary Election Ballot The figure below shows an excerpt from a primary election ballot. In what type of primary was this ballot used?

Nonpartisan ballots are also often used to elect state judges.

Nominating Presidential Candidates

In some respects, being nominated for president is more difficult than being elected. The nominating process narrows a very large number of hopefuls down to a single candidate from each party.

Choosing presidential candidates is unlike nominating candidates for any other office. One reason for this is that the nomination process combines several different methods. The process begins with state primaries, caucuses, and conventions, which are followed by the national party conventions.

State Primaries About three-fifths of the states hold presidential primaries early in the election year to select delegates to attend the national conventions. For a candidate, a good showing in the early primaries means plenty of media attention as television networks and newspapers report on the results. Because the results of early primaries tend to influence later primaries, many states that once had late primaries have moved the dates of their primaries to earlier in the year. Today, most primaries are held during a five-week period starting in late February.

Laws made by state legislatures and state parties determine how the primaries are set up, who may enter them, and who may vote in them. For example, several different methods of voting are used in presidential primaries. In some states, primary voters only select delegates to a party's national convention and do not know which candidates the delegates intend to vote for at the convention. In other states, the names of the candidates that the delegates support appear on the ballot along with the delegates' names.

State Party Caucuses or Conventions In some states, instead of presidential primaries, delegates to the national conventions are chosen by caucuses or conventions. Iowa, for example, holds caucuses to choose delegates to local conventions. These delegates, in turn, choose those who will attend the state and national conventions. Other states use a combination of caucuses and primaries.

National Party Conventions Presidential nominating conventions have been described as giant pep rallies— "the Fourth of July of American politics." Despite the hats, conga lines, and blaring horns, each convention's task is a serious one. It must adopt the official party

> ## Just the Facts
>
> One candidate for the Republican nomination for president in 1996, Senator Phil Gramm from Texas, spent about $550 in campaign funds for every vote he received in the primaries.

National presidential conventions, staged every four years, are perhaps the most exciting political events in this country. Although it may seem far-fetched, there are opportunities for individual voters, whatever their ages, to become involved in the national conventions.

For both the Republican Party and the Democratic Party, the majority of delegates must be elected at the local level. Generally, there are few requirements. In most situations, a person need only be eighteen years old to qualify, and a number of eighteen-year-old persons have been elected as delegates to national conventions. Elections for convention delegates can occur in one of two ways: (1) at the party primary election, or (2) at a neighborhood or precinct caucus.

What to Do If You Want to Run in the Primary

If you wish to run as a convention delegate in a primary election, you must file a petition with the board of elections before the election. You should

PARTICIPATING IN YOUR GOVERNMENT

Becoming a Presidential Convention Delegate

check with your local county committee or with the party's national committee about the rules that you must follow.

When a Presidential Caucus Is Involved

In some states, delegates to the national conventions are nominated at the local precinct caucus. For example, in Iowa, anyone can participate in a caucus if he or she is eighteen years old, a resident of the precinct, and a registered party

member. You can contact the state or county political party of your choice to find out when the caucus will be held.

TAKING ACTION

For further information about these opportunities, contact the state party office of your local state legislator for specific dates and regulations. You can also contact the national committees of the major parties for informational brochures on how to become a delegate.

Republican National
   Committee
Republican National
   Headquarters
310 First St. SE
Washington, DC 20003
202-863-8500
www.rnc.org/

Democratic National
   Committee
Democratic National
   Headquarters
430 Capital St. SE
Washington, DC 20003
202-863-8000
www.democrats.org/

---

platform and decide who will be the party's vice presidential and presidential candidates.

These tasks are carried out during four days in July or August. At each convention, two or three thousand delegates come together, theoretically representing the wishes of the voters and political leaders of their home states.

On the first day of the convention, delegates hear the reports of the Credentials Committee, which evaluates each prospective delegate's claim to be seated as a

legitimate representative of his or her state. When the eligibility of delegates is in question, the committee decides who will be seated. In the evening, there is usually a keynote speaker—someone of national importance—to whip up enthusiasm among the delegates.

The second day includes committee reports and debates on the party platform. Of course, other things are happening as well. Backers of certain candidates are seeking to influence uncommitted delegates and change the minds of those pledged to other candidates.

Delegates from state caucuses also are meeting to discuss their strategies and how they will vote.

The third day is devoted to nominations and voting. Balloting begins with an alphabetical roll call in which states and territories announce their votes. By midnight, the convention's real work is over, and the presidential candidate has been selected. The vice presidential nominations and the acceptance speeches occupy the fourth day.

Conventions today are not as important in the nominating process as they once were. They still feature the

▲ Keynote speaker Evan Bayh, governor of Indiana, addresses the 1996 Democratic National Convention. A politician the party wishes to spotlight is frequently chosen to give the keynote, or main, convention address.

same extravagance, long speeches, and demonstrations. Because so many delegates are selected by primaries, however, we usually know who will be nominated before the convention begins. Even though conventions may be less important in determining nominations, they are important in developing the party platform and in promoting the party's goals.

SECTION 1 REVIEW

1. Why are nominations an important part of the electoral process?
2. Briefly explain the different methods of nomination used throughout the country.
3. What is the nominating method most commonly used today, and how does it work?
4. What is the process by which a candidate for president is nominated?
5. **For Critical Analysis:** Which nomination method do you think is most appropriate for a representative government? Explain your answer.

★ ★ ★ ★ ★ **SECTION 2** ★ ★ ★ ★ ★

The Campaign

Preview Questions:

🌎 How are campaigns typically organized and planned?

🌎 What are the basic provisions of the Federal Election Campaign Act?

🌎 What is the purpose of PACs, and how do they function?

Key Terms:

campaign manager, political consultant, image building, tracking polls, negative campaign advertising

Once nominated, candidates concentrate on campaigning. The term *campaign* was originally a military

word. Generals mounted campaigns, using their scarce resources (soldiers and materials) to achieve military objectives. In political campaigns, resources are also scarce, and their use must be timed and directed carefully.

There are many different ways to campaign. Which method a candidate uses often depends on the office sought and the amount of competition for that office. A candidate running for the local school board may put up posters, talk to voters door-to-door, and speak at luncheons. In contrast, the campaign of a candidate running for president is much more complicated, much more time consuming, and many times more expensive.

The goal of any campaign is to win the election. To accomplish this, a campaign must be organized and carefully planned. It must also have sufficient funds.

▶ Surrounded by Secret Service agents, President Bill Clinton greets well-wishers as he campaigns at a 1996 reelection rally in Santa Barbara, California.

Campaign Organization

The success of any campaign depends on the people who organize it. In a small local election, a campaign may be handled by a few friends. In a national race, thousands of individuals are involved. A presidential campaign, for example, may have as many as five hundred paid staff members and a million volunteers.

Candidates for major offices set up campaign organizations similar to the one in Figure 11–2 on page 299. As you can see in the figure, the **campaign manager** coordinates and plans the campaign strategy, while other staff members provide leadership in specific areas, such as fund-raising and public opinion polling.

Volunteers, who make up the great majority of campaign workers, are critical to any major campaign. Volunteers handle most of the day-to-day work, such as putting up posters, handing out pamphlets, answering phone calls, helping voters register, and seeing that voters get to the polls on election day.

To run a successful campaign today, the candidate's organization must be able to raise funds, attract media coverage, produce commercials, convey the candidate's position, hire pollsters, research the opposing candidate, schedule the candidate's time effectively, make sure that the candidate's name is well known by the public, and get the voters to the polls. Increasingly, campaigns rely on the expertise of professional political consultants. The **political consultant** devises a campaign strategy, creates a campaign theme, and manages the image building of the candidate. **Image building** is using public and private polls to mold the candidate's image to meet the particular needs of the campaign.

Any serious candidate running for governor, state legislator, U.S. Congress, or the presidency has a paid political consultant who daily suggests new campaign ideas to the candidate and decides what new advertising is needed. Most of these campaign consultants are not politically neutral—they will only work for candidates from a particular party. Some political consultants have become so popular that they choose the candidates they wish to handle.

Some critics of political consultants argue that they are only concerned with personalities, not with issues and philosophies. Other people point out that this is the consultant's job. A professional political consultant is a public relations person who looks at each election as a contest between personalities rather than between

Just the Facts

If you are running for office, you may have to spend around $20,000 a month to hire a political consultant.

FIGURE 11–2 A Typical Presidential Campaign Organization The figure below shows how people involved in a presidential campaign are organized for action. What is the role of the campaign manager?

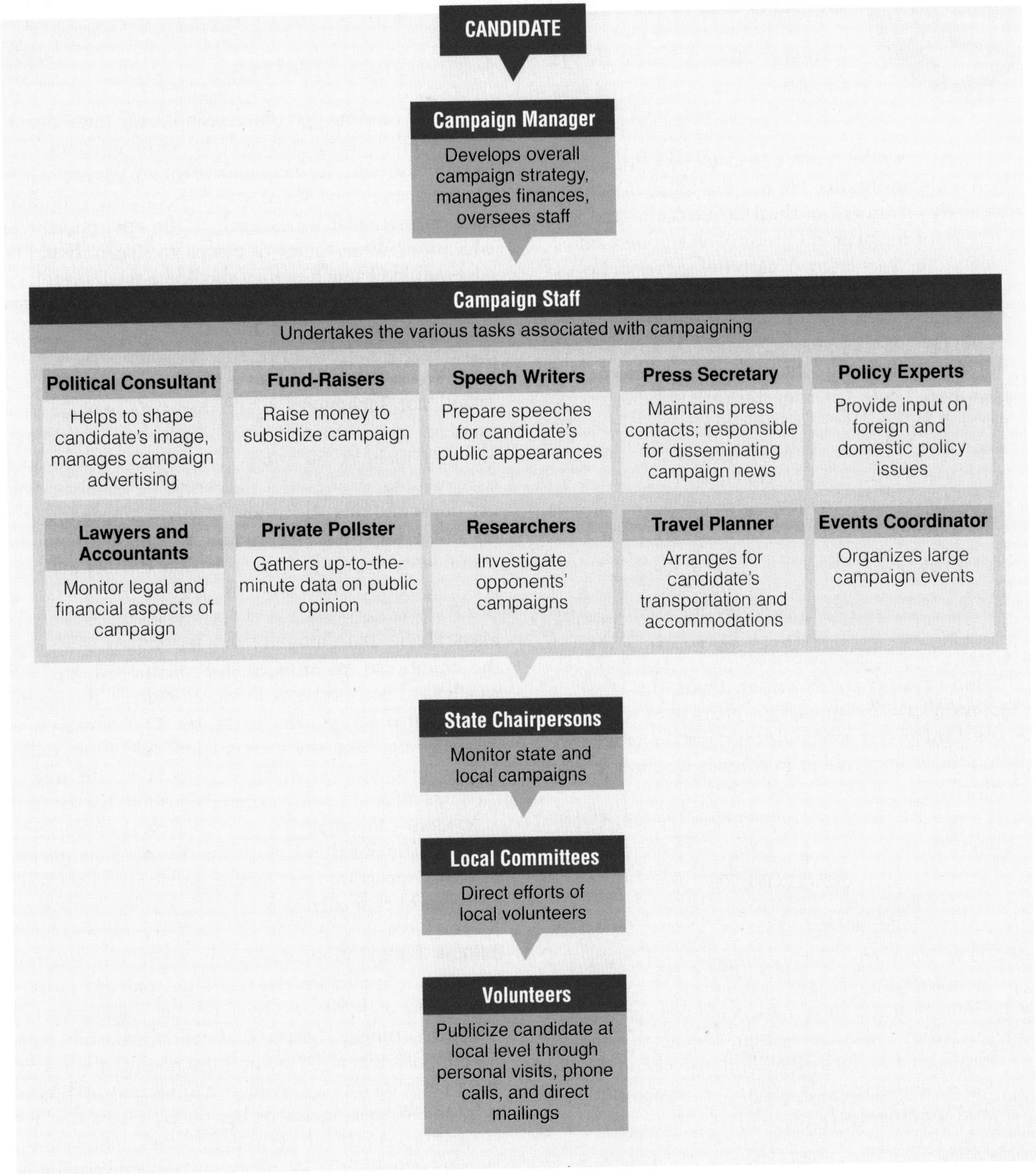

CANDIDATE

Campaign Manager

Develops overall campaign strategy, manages finances, oversees staff

Campaign Staff

Undertakes the various tasks associated with campaigning

Political Consultant	**Fund-Raisers**	**Speech Writers**	**Press Secretary**	**Policy Experts**
Helps to shape candidate's image, manages campaign advertising	Raise money to subsidize campaign	Prepare speeches for candidate's public appearances	Maintains press contacts; responsible for disseminating campaign news	Provide input on foreign and domestic policy issues
Lawyers and Accountants	**Private Pollster**	**Researchers**	**Travel Planner**	**Events Coordinator**
Monitor legal and financial aspects of campaign	Gathers up-to-the-minute data on public opinion	Investigate opponents' campaigns	Arranges for candidate's transportation and accommodations	Organizes large campaign events

State Chairpersons

Monitor state and local campaigns

Local Committees

Direct efforts of local volunteers

Volunteers

Publicize candidate at local level through personal visits, phone calls, and direct mailings

ARCHITECTS

of Government

Chester James Carville, Jr. (1946–)

James Carville is one of today's best-known political consultants. He was Bill Clinton's chief campaign strategist in the 1992 elections and an important member of Clinton's reelection campaign four years later. A native of Georgia, he completed all of his schooling in Louisiana, where he started his political career. After practicing law for six years, he began devoting himself full-time to helping others win office. Before becoming Clinton's chief strategist, he masterminded successful campaigns for the governor of Kentucky (1987), a New Jersey senator (1988), and the governor of Georgia (1990).

HIS WORDS

"When your opponent is drowning, throw him an anvil."

(All's Fair: Love, War, and Running for President, 1994)

"I think that when it's written about, this [Clinton's 1992 campaign] is going to be a kindness campaign that signaled not just a change in the way we govern, but in the way we run for office."

(Interview, July 24, 1992)

DEVELOPING
CRITICAL THINKING SKILLS

1. How would you classify the tone of the first quotation?
2. Some political historians would not agree with Carville's second quotation. Specifically, they argue that he focused too extensively on negative campaigning. Is negative campaigning bad for America?

opposing principles. Critics also argue that political consultants, in their quest to help their candidates win, sometimes reshape a candidate's public image so that it bears little resemblance to reality.

Campaign Strategy

When running for office, candidates must decide what kind of campaign will be most effective. For example, should the candidate wage an aggressive or a low-key campaign? What stand should the candidate take on particular issues, such as the environment or education? What theme or campaign slogan should be adopted? How much money should be spent on television, radio, or newspaper advertising? A campaign strategy is devised to address these and many other issues that will arise during the campaign.

Traditional Techniques Over the years, a variety of standard campaign techniques have been developed and are included in most campaigns. Door-to-door campaigning requires that the candidate knock on voters' doors and talk with them briefly. Campaign workers often use these techniques to talk with voters. Candidates also go to factory gates and shopping centers to seek out voters and talk with them.

Mass Media and Computerized Techniques Although the traditional techniques just mentioned are still widely used, one of the major developments in contemporary American politics is the rise of a new style of campaigning using the mass media—television, radio, and newspapers. You will read more about the role of the mass media in political campaigns in Chapter 12.

Modern campaigns also use computers extensively. Experts estimate that some three hundred companies currently specialize in computer services and software for political campaigns.

Opinion Polls Candidates want to find out what is most important to the voters. Thus, opinion polls—both public and private—have become a major part of campaign strategy. Often, presidential hopefuls have private polls taken. By polling the potential voters in the state or nation, a candidate can identify and try to fix problem areas in his or her public image through advertising. As the election approaches, many candidates use **tracking polls.** These are polls taken almost every day to find out how well the candidates are competing for votes. Information from these polls enables campaign organizations to fine-tune candidates' speeches and advertising in the last critical days.

Campaign Costs

The sophisticated techniques that candidates use have made campaigning very expensive. Huge sums are spent for television and radio time, advertising, travel, and office rent, to list only a few expenses. The more important the office sought, the greater the amount likely to be spent. It is estimated that to win or keep a seat in Congress today, a candidate must be prepared to spend at least $500,000. Presidential campaigns are even costlier. In all, campaign expenditures in the 1996 presidential campaigns were about $600 million. Some candidates are able to use part of their own money to run for office, but most rely on contributions from individuals and organizations.

The connection between money and campaigns gives rise to some of the most difficult problems in American politics. The biggest fear is that some special-interest groups will try to buy favored treatment from those who are elected to office. To prevent these abuses, laws have been passed to regulate campaign finances.

Campaign-Financing Laws

In 1971, Congress passed the Federal Election Campaign Act (FECA) in an attempt to solve problems in the ways political campaigns were financed. The 1971 act placed no limit on candidates' overall spend-

ing, but it restricted the amount that could be spent on advertising in the mass media, including television. It limited the amount that candidates and their families could contribute to their own campaigns. It also required candidates to disclose all contributions and expenditures of over $100. Also in 1971, Congress passed a law that provided for a $1 checkoff on federal income tax returns. Taxpayers could choose to donate $1 of their tax payment for general campaign funds to be used by major-party presidential candidates. This law was first applied in the 1976 campaign. (Since then, the amount of the checkoff has been raised to $3.)

The 1971 act did not go far enough, however, and amendments to the act were made in 1974. The 1974 amendments did the following:

- *Created the Federal Election Commission (FEC) to administer and enforce the act's provisions.*
- *Provided public financing for presidential primaries and general elections.* Presidential candidates who raise some money on their own in at least twenty states can get funds from the U.S. Treasury to help pay for primary campaigns. For the general election campaign, presidential candidates receive federal funding for almost all of their expenses *if* they are willing to accept campaign spending limits.
- *Limited presidential campaign spending.* Any candidate accepting federal support must agree to limit expenditures to amounts set by federal law.
- *Required disclosure.* Candidates must file periodic reports with the FEC that list who contributed to the campaign and how the money was spent.
- *Limited contributions.* Citizens can contribute up to $1,000 to each candidate in each federal election or primary. The total limit for any individual in one

FIGURE 11–3 Congressional Campaign Spending, 1981–1996 (in millions of dollars) As you can see from the figure below, campaigning for a congressional seat has become very expensive in this country. Do you think it would be more expensive to run a presidential campaign? Why?

Summary Financial Activity in All Congressional Campaigns	1981–1982	1983–1984	1985–1986	1987–1988	1989–1990	1991–1992	1993–1994	1995–1996
Raised	$354.7	$397.2	$472.0	$477.6	$471.7	$659.3	$740.5	$790.5
Spent	$342.4	$374.1	$450.9	$459.0	$446.3	$680.2	$725.2	$765.3
Number of Candidates	2240	2036	1873	1792	1759	2950	2376	2605

SOURCE: Federal Election Commission, 1997.

year is $25,000. Groups can contribute a maximum of $5,000 to a candidate in any election.

In a significant 1976 case, *Buckley v. Valeo*, the Supreme Court ruled on one part of the 1971 act. The Court declared unconstitutional the provision that limited the amount each individual could spend on his or her own campaign. The Court stated as follows:

The candidate, no less than any other person, has a First Amendment right to engage in the discussion of public issues and vigorously and tirelessly to advocate his own election and the election of other candidates. Indeed, it is of particular importance that candidates have the . . . opportunity to make their views known so that the electorate may intelligently evaluate the candidates' personal qualities and their positions on vital public issues before choosing among them on election day.

The Growth of PACs

The FECA, as further amended in 1976, allows corporations, labor unions, and interest groups to set up political action committees (PACs) to raise money for candidates. For a PAC to be legitimate, the money must come from at least fifty volunteer donors and must be given to at least five candidates in the national elections. PACs can contribute up to $5,000 per candidate in each election, but there is no limit on the total amount of PAC contributions during an election campaign.

The number of PACs has grown dramatically since the 1970s, as has the amount they spend on elections. In 1976, there were about 1,000 PACs. By the late 1990s, there were more than 4,600. The total amount of spending by PACs grew from $19 million in 1973 to an estimated $550 million in 1998–1999. A sample of PAC contributions to political candidates in a recent period is shown in Figure 11–4.

PACs are not limited to making contributions to candidates' campaigns. They may conduct their own campaigns for presidential and congressional candidates. They also spend hundreds of thousands of dollars for television commercials and other independent efforts to praise or attack candidates they support or oppose. PACs may spend as much money as they

FIGURE 11–4 Top Fifteen PAC Contributions to Congressional Candidates This figure lists the fifteen political action committees that made the largest contributions to congressional campaigns over an eighteen-month period ending in 1996. What was the total contribution of all fifteen of these PACs during that period?

Group	Contribution to Candidates
Democratic-Republican Independent Voter Education Committee	$2,611,140
American Federation of State, County & Municipal Employees	2,505,021
UAW–V–CAP (UAW Voluntary Community Action Program)	2,467,319
Association of Trial Lawyers of America Political Action Committee	2,362,938
Dealers Election Action Committee of the National Automobile Dealers Association (NADA)	2,351,925
National Education Association Political Action Committee	2,326,830
American Medical Association Political Action Committee	2,319,197
Realtors Political Action Committee	2,099,683
International Brotherhood of Electrical Workers Committee on Political Education	2,080,587
Active Ballot Club, A Dept. of United Food & Commercial Workers Int'l Union	2,030,795
Machinists Nonpartisan Political League	1,999,675
Laborers' Political League	1,933,300
United Parcel Service of America Inc., Political Action Committee (UPSPAC)	1,788,147
Committee on Letter Carriers Political Education (Letter Carriers Political Action Fund)	1,715,064
American Institute of Certified Public Accountants Effective Legislation Committee (AICPA)	1,690,925

SOURCE: Federal Election Commission, 1997.

choose on their own campaigns, providing the candidates themselves don't control how the money is spent.

PACs have been criticized for several reasons. One involves the fear, mentioned earlier, that groups that contribute money may try to buy influence with elected officials. Another involves the fact that PACs tend to give more campaign contributions to incumbents—people already in office. This bias in favor of incumbents may make it easier for incumbents to win and more difficult for challengers to compete.

Ethics and Political Campaigns

Several aspects of the modern political campaign give rise to ethical issues. The most important issue is, of course, the close relationship between money and success in gaining public office. Given the increasingly high cost of conducting a campaign, how can the "average person" hope to win a seat in Congress?

Furthermore, the need to raise funds to wage a successful campaign has led to inventive—and ethically (as well as legally) questionable—fund-raising practices, as you will read in the next section. Finally, once in office, how can a successful candidate ignore the interests of the individuals and interest groups whose contributions made it possible for the candidate to be elected?

Another issue has to do with **negative campaign advertising**—advertising that attempts to discredit an opposing candidate in the eyes of the voters. Increasingly, campaign organizations include opposition researchers, people who "dig up dirt" on a candidate's rivals. These people research the public archives to find out about an opposing candidate's past voting records or about embarrassing political events that occurred while an opposing candidate was in office. During the political campaigns prior to the 1996 elections, candidates spent an estimated $30 million on opposition research. We will return to the issue of negative campaign advertising in the *America at Odds* feature at the end of this chapter.

SECTION 2 REVIEW

1. Describe how a typical campaign is structured.
2. What are some of the techniques used in campaigning?
3. What are the provisions of the Federal Election Campaign Act?
4. How do PACs function, and what is their purpose?
5. **For Critical Analysis:** Federal law currently allows individuals to earmark $3 of their federal income tax payment for presidential election campaign funding. This doesn't seem like much, so why would a person choose not to check the $3 box on his or her income tax return?

SECTION 3

Problems with Enforcing Campaign-Financing Rules

Preview Questions:

🌐 How do candidates use loopholes to avoid campaign-financing rules?
🌐 What is "soft money," and why is it significant?
🌐 What are some of the problems surrounding foreign contributions to U.S. campaigns?
🌐 How might campaign-financing rules be reformed?

Key Terms:

loopholes, soft money

Given the restrictions imposed by campaign-financing laws, how is it possible that candidates can raise as much money as they did during the 1996 campaigns? Presidential candidates spent approximately $600 million during the campaigns preceding the 1996

▶ President Bill Clinton takes a break from campaigning against Republican presidential candidate Bob Dole to celebrate his fiftieth birthday. What subtle messages in this photo could hurt Dole?

elections. Only $86 million, or about 14 percent, came from the federal government. What about the remaining $514 million? Where did that money come from? The answer is that individuals and corporations have found **loopholes**—legal ways of evading certain legal requirements—in the federal laws limiting campaign contributions.

Avoiding Campaign-Financing Rules

Two significant loopholes in campaign-financing laws involve so-called soft money and foreign contributions. Candidates are increasingly using these loopholes in order to avoid campaign-financing rules.

Soft Money The biggest loophole in federal campaign laws is that they do not prohibit individuals or corporations from contributing to political *parties*. Contributions to political parties, instead of to particular candidates, are referred to as **soft money.** Many contributors make donations to the national parties to cover various "party-building" costs, such as expenses for voter registration drives, the printing of brochures and fliers, advertising in the media (which often means running

candidate-oriented ads), campaigns to "get out the vote," and fund-raising events, such as the Democratic Party's $10,000-a-ticket fiftieth-birthday dinner for President Bill Clinton in August 1996. Soft money clearly goes to support the candidates, but it is difficult to track exactly where the money goes.

The soft-money loophole has existed since the passage of a 1979 amendment to federal election laws. Until the 1990s, however, it was not widely used. Today, soft-money contributions allow parties to raise millions of dollars from corporations and individuals. It has not been unusual for major corporations to make extremely large contributions. The Walt Disney Company has given more than half a million dollars to the Democratic National Committee, for example, and tobacco companies have given more than a million dollars to the Republican Party. (See Figure 11–5 for a list of the top ten contributors of soft money to each party during the last presidential campaign.)

Soft dollars have become the main source of campaign money in the presidential race, far outpacing PAC contributions and federal campaign funds. In fact, soft-money donations in 1996 were more than twice what they were in the 1992 presidential elections. The Republicans raised close to $300 million in soft dollars, and the Democrats received over $200 million.

Foreign Contributions It is against federal law for political parties or candidates in the United States to accept money from foreign sources. Yet various loopholes in the law allowed tens of millions of dollars to be sent, through various means, from foreign sources to U.S. candidates and political parties during the 1996 election campaigns.

A major loophole in the federal campaign laws permits legal U.S. residents, even if they have foreign citizenship, to make contributions to political parties. Another loophole allows U.S. branches of foreign companies to contribute campaign funds (provided the funds were earned in the United States). In numerous cases, when contributions during the campaigns prior to the 1996 elections were examined, it became obvious that the funds were *not* earned in the United States.

One case, unearthed by *New York Times* columnist William Safire, involved the fundraising activities of John

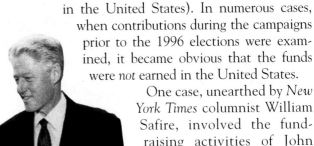

◄ *Although candidates must raise money to survive politically, there are laws limiting their actions. Here President Bill Clinton shakes the hand of Democratic fundraiser John Huang, who was later accused of fund-raising improprieties.*

FIGURE 11–5 Soft Money for the Parties Here we show some of the corporations that made large "soft money" contributions to the two major parties during the last presidential election. Why is it difficult to regulate soft-money contributions?

Democratic Party Contributor	Corporate Interest	Soft-Money Contribution
Joseph E. Seagram & Sons	Beer, wine, liquor	$620,000
Walt Disney Co.	Media, entertainment	547,000
DreamWorks SKG	Media, entertainment	525,000
Goldman, Sachs & Co.	Securities, investment	510,000
MCI Telecommunications Corp.	Phone utilities	486,136
Revlon Group, Inc.	Cosmetics	471,250
Loral Corp.	Defense electronics	465,500
Laborers Union	Building trade union	455,000
Connell Co.	Food importer, processor	407,000
Philip Morris	Tobacco	400,250
Republican Party Contributor	**Corporate Interest**	**Soft-Money Contribution**
Philip Morris	Tobacco	$1,649,683
RJR Nabisco	Tobacco	973,450
Atlantic Richfield	Oil, gas	695,275
Georgia-Pacific	Forestry, forest products	660,000
American Financial Corp.	Insurance	530,000
Joseph E. Seagram & Sons	Beer, wine, liquor	471,600
AT&T	Phone utilities	449,590
US Tobacco	Tobacco	448,768
Chevron Corp.	Oil, gas	442,100
Signet Bank	Commercial banks	431,621

SOURCE: Center for Responsive Politics, 1996.

Why All Those Foreign Contributions?

Republican presidential nominee Bob Dole, when emphasizing the need for campaign reform, said, "We simply cannot allow the political influence of any American to be outweighed by foreign money." Dole was referring to the millions of dollars that found their way from foreign sources to the Democratic Party during the 1996 campaign. Even though federal law prohibits foreign contributions to American campaigns, various loopholes exist. The text describes how Indonesian interests contributed to the Democratic Party in 1996.

According to one study, Japanese interest groups are even more important. Japanese interest groups apparently spend $100 million a year both monitoring and trying to influence U.S. policy, mainly with respect to trade and other business issues. Additionally, British interest groups and companies have donated heavily to American political campaigns. British companies, such as Brown & Williamson Tobacco and British Petroleum, routinely donate to the Republican Party. In general, Europeans spend tens of millions of dollars a year on big-name law firms and consultants to influence such issues as the tax treatment of American subsidiaries of foreign companies.

Why are foreign companies so concerned about influencing U.S. policy? There are two main reasons. First, the United States is a huge market for other countries' exports. Second, the American military can promote stability or cause destruction virtually anywhere. Because the U.S. government influences the lives of foreigners, foreigners have a real stake in U.S. political affairs. Small countries can be dramatically affected by what happens in Washington, D.C. One way these countries can get a hearing in the United States is to "buy their way in."

THINK ABOUT IT

1. To what extent should U.S. subsidiaries of foreign companies be restricted in their lobbying efforts, compared with their U.S.-owned competitors?
2. What problems might result if subsidiaries of foreign companies were banned from making campaign contributions to U.S. candidates? Do you see any way to prevent foreign interests from influencing U.S. politics?

Huang. Huang once worked for the Lippo Group, an Indonesian-based banking and real estate company. Later, he was appointed by President Clinton to a position in the Commerce Department. After that, he became a full-time fund-raiser for the Democratic Party. Huang obtained a contribution of $427,000 from an Indonesian couple living in Virginia. The man, a legal resident but not an American citizen, worked as a landscaper. The woman, though, was connected to Indonesian business interests.

The Democratic Party came under fire after the 1996 elections because of the questionable legality of certain foreign contributions to the Democratic National Committee. As a result, Congress and the Justice Department have been investigating the matter, as well as other possible abuses of laws governing campaign financing.

Can We Reform Campaign Financing?

There is widespread agreement among Americans that we should reform the way in which campaigns are

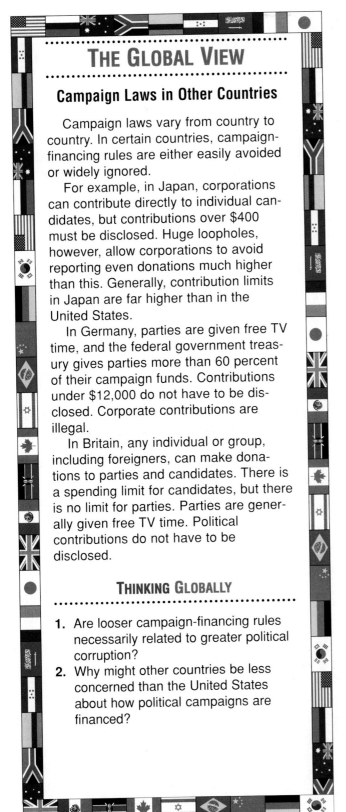

THE GLOBAL VIEW

Campaign Laws in Other Countries

Campaign laws vary from country to country. In certain countries, campaign-financing rules are either easily avoided or widely ignored.

For example, in Japan, corporations can contribute directly to individual candidates, but contributions over $400 must be disclosed. Huge loopholes, however, allow corporations to avoid reporting even donations much higher than this. Generally, contribution limits in Japan are far higher than in the United States.

In Germany, parties are given free TV time, and the federal government treasury gives parties more than 60 percent of their campaign funds. Contributions under $12,000 do not have to be disclosed. Corporate contributions are illegal.

In Britain, any individual or group, including foreigners, can make donations to parties and candidates. There is a spending limit for candidates, but there is no limit for parties. Parties are generally given free TV time. Political contributions do not have to be disclosed.

THINKING GLOBALLY

1. Are looser campaign-financing rules necessarily related to greater political corruption?
2. Why might other countries be less concerned than the United States about how political campaigns are financed?

---

financed. There is no agreement, however on how to do so. Here are few of the many possible options.

Ban or Limit Contributions by PACs Many liberal public interest groups (such as those associated with Ralph Nader) would like to limit strictly or ban completely funds that come from PACs. One of the reasons for limiting or banning PAC funds is the tendency of PAC campaign contributions to favor incumbents, as mentioned earlier.

Critics of limiting or banning PAC contributions argue that such an action would place even more power in the hands of government. Campaign contributions can be viewed as "protection" money, according to these observers. In other words, large campaign contributions may help protect an interest group from legislation that adversely affects the group's interests.

One problem with the elimination of PACs is that they were devised originally as a way to stop campaign-financing abuses. Presumably, PACs can be better regulated than other forms of campaign giving. Indeed, a variety of rules are attached to PAC contributions, all aimed at reducing PAC influence.

Ban or Limit Foreign Contributions We described earlier how foreign contributions were obtained during the 1996 campaigns. Clearly, ethical issues are involved in such practices. Not so clear is how these issues can be resolved.

Is the way out of the foreign-contributions problem simply to ban foreign gifts? The Federal Election Commission considered this possibility as recently as 1991. The commission rejected a proposal to prohibit companies that were more than 50 percent foreign owned from establishing corporate political action committees. The reason it rejected the proposal involved a practical matter. Business has become more and more global, and it is no longer easy to decide whether a company is foreign or domestic. American companies may have ownership rights in a foreign company, and this company may have a U.S. subsidiary. (A subsidiary company is one that is more than 50 percent owned by another company, called the "parent company.") Is this subsidiary a foreign or a domestic company?

Ban or Limit Soft-Money Contributions As we pointed out earlier, soft-money contributions reached all-time

How Campaigns Have Changed

In the early 1900s, campaigns were quite different from what they are today.

THEN (EARLY 1900S)	NOW
Wealthy people made significant contributions to campaigns, and there were no reporting requirements.	Federal campaign laws limit contributions, and there are reporting requirements. Soft money is a way to avoid the limits, though.
Political candidates were usually white males.	Candidates include members of minorities and women.
The major political parties controlled the campaigns.	The parties have little to say about how candidates run their campaigns.

high levels during the 1996 campaigns. At the same time, the Federal Election Commission had its budget cut. It stood by virtually helpless in 1996 as the parties avoided campaign-financing laws. One long-time Washington lobbyist, Michael Lewan, said, "Not so long ago, a Senator or a fund-raiser would call and ask for $1,000. . . . People now call and ask me to get my clients to give $100,000 or $200,000 or $250,000."

A number of politicians and groups have suggested that soft-money contributions be eliminated or strictly limited. Many current members of Congress also favor this type of campaign reform. Those who favor the reform probably do not have enough support to pass strong legislation, however.

Remove All Limits on Private Campaign Spending Another suggested campaign-financing reform involves removing all limits on private campaign spending or contributions. Rather, there should be full disclosure of all funding sources. Politicians would have to document, on a daily basis, the source and size of every contribution, including contributions in the form of labor and equipment.

The Free-Speech Issue Any type of campaign reform would very likely involve a larger issue—freedom of speech. Remember that in *Buckley v. Valeo* (1976), a case mentioned earlier in this chapter, the Supreme Court held that the right to free speech and free expression includes the right to spend

▲ Why is it so difficult to reform campaign financing?

as much money as one wants on one's own political campaign. Several scholars believe that the Supreme Court should overturn its decision in *Buckley v. Valeo*. Otherwise, it may be difficult to reform—to any significant degree—campaign financing.

SECTION 3 REVIEW

1. Explain what is meant by the term *loophole*.
2. What are two major loopholes in campaign-financing rules?
3. In recent presidential elections, what has been the main source of campaign money?
4. List and describe four options for campaign-financing reform.
5. Explain at least one argument in favor of retaining PACs.
6. **For Critical Analysis:** Look at Figure 11–5 on page 305. How can you explain the fact that Philip Morris, the tobacco company, contributed soft money to both the Democratic Party and the Republican Party?

SECTION 4

The Structure of American Elections

Preview Questions:

⭐ What are the various types of elections in the United States, and how do they differ?
⭐ What is a ballot, and what forms do ballots take?
⭐ How does the electoral college system work?

Key Terms:

general election, special election, Australian ballot, office-group ballot, party-column ballot, electoral college, electors, popular vote

There finally comes a time when the last debate has been debated, the last poll has been reported, and the last television reporter has commented. It is time for the elections. Democratic government cannot succeed unless elections are free, honest, and accurate.

Because most of the elective offices in the United States are at the state and local levels, most of the election law in the United States is state law. The Constitution grants the power to fix "the times, places, and manner of holding elections" to the state legislatures, but the Constitution gives Congress the power to alter such regulations. Congress has required the use of secret ballots and has passed several laws to protect the right to vote for certain groups of people. Congress also has the power to regulate certain aspects of the presidential election process, to forbid certain corrupt practices, and to regulate campaign finances.

Kinds of Elections

Two important kinds of elections in the United States are general elections and special elections. In both kinds of elections, voters elect both federal and state officeholders.

General Elections The most familiar kind of election is the **general election,** a regularly scheduled election in which voters choose who will hold many public offices. General elections for national offices are held in even-numbered years on the first Tuesday after the first Monday in November. U.S. congressional representatives, who serve two-year terms, are elected in every general election. U.S. senators serve six-year terms, but the terms are staggered, so that every two years, one-third of the Senate positions are voted on. The president and vice president are elected every four years. General elections are also held to choose state and local government leaders. Often, these elections are held at the same time as elections for national offices.

The U.S. practice of holding general elections at fixed intervals every two years is not common among democracies. In parliamentary systems, elections may be called at irregular intervals. In Great Britain, for example, elections must be called every five years, but they may be called more often if the majority party (the party that controls Parliament) wishes.

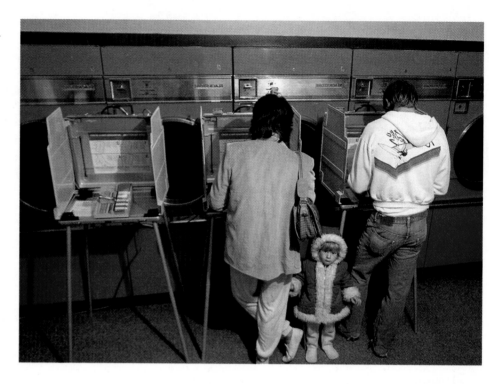

▶ Although most voters find their polling places in schools or libraries, these Santa Cruz, California, voters mark their ballots in this coin-operated laundromat.

Special Elections A **special election** is held when an issue must be decided before the next general election. For example, an important city official might resign or die before the end of his or her term. The city may decide to hold a special election to fill the vacancy. In many states, voters also participate in direct lawmaking through the initiative, referendum, and recall processes described in Chapter 24. These processes involve special elections.

Polling Places Local units of government are divided into voting districts, or precincts. State law usually limits the size of precincts. Within each precinct, voters cast their ballots at one polling place.

A precinct election board supervises the polling place and the voting process in each precinct. The board sets hours for the polls to be open according to the laws of the state and sees that ballots or voting machines are available. In most states, the board provides a list of registered voters and makes certain that only qualified voters cast ballots in that precinct. When the polls close, the board counts the votes and reports the results, usually to the county clerk or board of elections. Representatives from each party, called poll watchers, are allowed at each polling place to make sure the election is run fairly.

Ballots

In the early days of our country, voters gathered in a central place and called out their votes. They could be applauded or booed as they voiced their preferences. Of course, with this method of voting, people were sometimes unduly influenced by others, and many people wanted the system changed.

By the mid-1800s, a new system had come into use. Political parties passed out paper ballots to voters. The ballots were different colors to symbolize different parties, and the ballot box was in public view. Thus, anyone watching still knew who voted for whom. Because voting was not private, voters were subject to vote-buying and political pressure.

Australian Ballot The balloting system was improved in 1888 when a new method of voting was introduced from Australia. The **Australian ballot** had four main features: (1) it was printed by election officials at public expense; (2) it listed the names of all candidates in an election; (3) it was distributed only at the polling places to qualified voters; and (4) the actual voting was done in secret. Two variations of the Australian ballot are used in the United States today.

- **Office-group ballot.** With the **office-group ballot,** all candidates for each office are listed together. For example, all candidates for state senator are listed under that heading along with their party affiliation. Sometimes this ballot is called the *Massachusetts ballot,* because that state first used it in general elections in 1888.
- **Party-column ballot.** The **party-column ballot** lists candidates under party labels. For example, the Republican candidates for senator, representative, governor, state legislator, and local office are listed in the Republican column. There is often a place at the top of the ballot where a voter, with one mark, can vote for all of one party's candidates. This practice is called "straight-ticket" voting. Obviously, the practice is encouraged by the party-column ballot, especially if the party has a strong candidate at the head of the ticket. Straight-ticket voting is losing favor because differences between the two parties seem to be less apparent and voters' identification with party labels appears to be weakening.

Length of Ballots Besides selecting public officials, voters must often decide on a number of local and statewide issues. Because all of these choices must be listed on the ballot, the ballot is typically lengthy. One recent California ballot, for example, had over eight pages. Many people criticize such ballots because of their length. Some say that it is almost impossible to make intelligent and informed decisions on so many candidates and issues. They argue that the smaller the number of elected officials on a ballot, the better the chance that voters will know the candidates' qualifications. Others disagree. They argue that the greater the number of officials elected to office, the more democratic the system. They maintain that the public has the right to get as involved as it can in government decision making.

Voting Machines

Thomas Edison took out the first patent for a voting machine in 1868, and his invention was used for the first time in an election in Lockport, New York, in 1892. Since then, voting machines have steadily replaced paper ballots. Now, over half of all voters in the United States cast ballots on voting machines.

Voting machines differ in some details, but all work in much the same way. By pulling a large lever, the voter closes a curtain so that voting is done in private. The ballot appears on the face of a machine, and the voter makes choices by pulling down small levers over the names of the chosen candidates. The machine is programmed so that the voter can cast only one vote per contest. Once all the levers are in the desired positions, the voter opens the curtain. This action records the votes and clears the machine for the next voter.

> **Just the Facts**
>
> *The Texas legislature recently voted to allow astronauts to receive electronic balloting for any election that takes place while they are orbiting the globe.*

▲ *Using one of the earliest voting machines, this man votes by turning a knob. How is voting conducted in your community?*

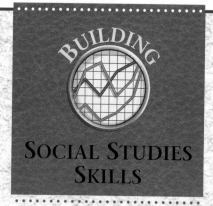
Average, *percent, mean, median*—these are all terms used with statistics. Throughout this textbook, you have been reading and using statistics. Some are mentioned in the text, and some are used in graphs and tables. Statistics can tell us the extent to which various characteristics—such as occupations, income, and amounts of money spent on various budget items—are present in different populations. A population, as statisticians use the term, can be a group of people, businesses, or branches of government.

You may not realize it, but the data that statisticians gather can be helpful to you in making your own decisions. For example, when you are trying to choose a career, you might want to know the average income in the occupations that interest you. You can also turn your own information into statistics. For example,

Understanding Mean and Median

in planning a budget, you might want to learn what your average monthly expenditures for food have been over the past year.

Averages: Mean and Median

Important information is often summarized in averages.

People, however, sometimes use the word *average* when, to be precise, they should use the term *mean* or *median*. Researchers use means and medians to give an overall view of a population or to summarize various statistics.

Mean The mean is the average of a series of items. It is found by adding the items and then dividing by the number of items in the series. The numbers below are the weekly salaries of seven students who have part-time after-school jobs. You can find the mean salary by adding the weekly wages and then dividing by the number of students.

$$
\begin{array}{r}
\$\ 10 \\
41 \\
49 \\
53 \\
\underline{57} \\
\$210 \div 5 = \$42
\end{array}
$$

The mean weekly salary for these students is $42.

Many election districts use computer-readable ballots. The voter marks a square or punches a hole on a card. A computer reads the card and then totals the votes for each candidate and prints out the results. This method speeds up the voting process by doing away with the need for manual counting. It also reduces the number of persons needed to administer elections and increases the number of voters that can be handled per precinct. It can also minimize fraud and counting errors.

Electing the President

We mentioned that *nominating* the presidential and vice presidential candidates is different from nominat-

ing officials for any other office. The same is true of *electing* the president and vice president. The system used is a complex one with its own set of rules.

The Electoral College System The writers of the Constitution argued long and hard about the method of electing the president. Many did not want the president to be directly elected by the people. They did not trust the average person's judgment and feared that citizens scattered all across the new country would have a hard time learning enough about the candidates to make a wise choice. They preferred that the president be chosen by the nation's elite—a small group of wealthy, powerful, and supposedly reasonable leaders—so they devised a system in which those leaders could elect the president. The result was the electoral college

Unemployment Rates in Selected Countries, 1997	
Country	Rate of Unemployment (Percent of Labor Force)
United States	4.9
Canada	9.0
Australia	8.6
Japan	3.4
France	12.7
Germany	7.8
Italy	11.9
Sweden	9.5
United Kingdom	6.9

SOURCE: Department of Labor, Bureau of Labor Statistics, 1997.

Median Sometimes, using the mean to interpret a set of statistics can be misleading. This is especially true if one or two numbers in the series are much larger or smaller than the others. A median can be more useful.

The median is the *midpoint* in any series of numbers arranged in order. For example, in the list of salaries in the right-hand column on page 312, $49 is the median weekly wage. The number of students who earn more than $49 a week is equal to the number who earn less than $49 a week.

In this situation, the mean of the series, $42, is smaller than the median, $49. This is because one of the students earns $10 a week, less than one-fourth of any other student's salary. This one small salary pushes the mean much lower than it would be if only the other four salaries were averaged.

PRACTICING YOUR SKILLS

The table to the left shows the unemployment rates in several countries in 1997.

1. Calculate the mean unemployment rate in countries other than the United States.
2. Calculate the median rate of unemployment in countries other than the United States.
3. Explain the importance of mean and median in using data.

system. The **electoral college** is a group of persons, called **electors,** who officially elect the president and vice president.

Over time, political practice has made the electoral vote more responsive to popular majorities. In the early days, electors could vote any way they chose, but today virtually all electors vote for the candidate who received the most votes in their state. Some states have even made it illegal for electors not to vote this way. These changes have helped democratize the electoral system.

How the System Works The first step in the electoral college process is the general election, in which all registered voters may vote for the president and vice president. This is called a **popular vote,** or the vote of the people.

Most voters today believe that they vote directly for a president or vice president. In fact, however, a slate of electors will cast the official votes for them. These electors are chosen by the states' political parties, subject to the laws of the state. Each state has as many electoral votes as it has U.S. senators and representatives. In addition, there are three electors from the District of Columbia.

The electoral college system is a winner-take-all system. This means that the candidate who receives the most popular votes in a state is credited with *all* that state's electoral votes—one vote per elector. This is true no matter what the margin of victory.

In December, after the general election in November, members of the electoral college meet in their state capitals to cast their votes for president and vice president.

Negative Campaign Advertising

Many people seem to think that negative campaigning is a modern invention. But it is not. In 1796, the supporters of John Adams labeled his opponent, Thomas Jefferson, an "atheist, anarchist, demagogue, coward, [and] trickster." Negative political campaigning, then, has been around for at least two hundred years. Nevertheless, many groups want to put an end to it.

Stop Negative Politicking, Demand Some Americans

During the 1996 presidential and congressional campaigns, negative advertising reached new heights. In 1996 alone, presidential candidates Bill Clinton and Bob Dole spent $130 million on thirty-second TV spots—mostly negative ads.

Opponents of such negative political advertising argue that it explains why, in the 1996 elections, we saw the lowest voter participation in over seven decades. After all, nasty ads discourage people from voting at all.

Furthermore, it is not clear that negative political ads work well. In 1996, organized labor spent over $35 million on negative advertising aimed squarely against Republican candidates. The majority of those candidates won anyway. If negative advertising is not really effective, then it ends up being a waste of resources. Critics think that it is a form of campaigning that should be abandoned.

Negative Campaigning Is Good for Democracy, Argue Others

Some Americans do not agree that negative campaigning is necessarily bad. They point out that negative campaigning has a long history in American politics. They believe, too, that unless a challenger to someone already in office comes up with an attention-getting negative ad, he or she will never be elected. Further, why shouldn't a candidate make the public aware of his or her opponent's broken promises or expose an opposing candidate who really is unethical or dishonest?

To be sure, negative advertising probably "turns off" a small percentage of potential voters and keeps them from voting. On balance, though, negative ads are good for democracy because they educate the voters and make politicians more accountable.

Finally, negative ads get the voters' attention. A well-crafted negative ad campaign brings people into the political process who might otherwise not care.

YOU DECIDE
....

1. Do you think many people believe the messages conveyed by negative political ads? Do you think people believe any political ads?
2. How would it be possible to regulate negative political advertising without reducing freedom of speech?

▶ Negative campaign advertising is deliberately designed to discourage votes for the opponent. Would you vote for a candidate who is presented as being dishonest?

YOU CAN'T TRUST HIS PROMISES.

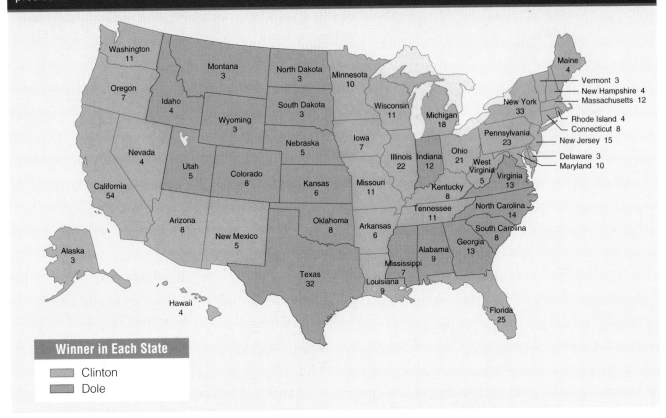

FIGURE 11–6 Electoral Votes for President, 1996 Each state has the same number of electors as it has U.S. senators and representatives. Why did the founders of our country choose to use the electoral college system for electing the president?

Winner in Each State

Clinton
Dole

Although they are not legally bound to do so by Article I, Section 2, of the Constitution, the electors usually vote for the candidate who won popular support in their state. Only on rare occasions has an elector broken a pledge to vote for the party's nominee. It has never affected the outcome of an election.

The votes are sealed and then sent to the Senate. The ballots are counted and certified before a joint session of Congress early in January. The candidates who receive a majority of the electoral votes are officially declared president and vice president.

To be elected, a candidate must receive more than half of the 538 electoral votes available. This means that a candidate needs 270 votes to win. Figure 11–6 shows how electoral votes were cast in the 1996 presidential election.

If no candidate gets an electoral college majority, the House of Representatives votes on the candidates.

Each state's delegation casts only a single vote. (This has happened twice—in 1800 and in 1824.)

The winner-take-all system makes it possible for a candidate who lost the total popular vote to win the electoral vote and thus be elected. This happened three times during the 1800s. Critics of the electoral college point out that it could happen again. In 1960, John F. Kennedy, a Democrat, defeated Richard Nixon, a Republican. If only nine thousand people in Illinois and Missouri had voted for Nixon instead of Kennedy, Nixon would have won the electoral college votes in those two states. As a result, Nixon would have won the election while losing the popular vote by a narrow margin.

The electoral system has been criticized by many as being out of date and undemocratic. Over the years, more than five hundred amendments calling for changes in the system have been brought before Congress.

FIGURE 11–7 Electoral Votes in Close Races As pointed out in this section, some presidential races have been very close, as illustrated in these examples from the 1800s.

Thomas Jefferson	John Quincy Adams	Rutherford Hayes

In 1800, Thomas Jefferson and Aaron Burr received the same number of electoral votes; the House of Representatives voted for Thomas Jefferson as president.

In 1824, no candidate received a majority of the electoral college votes. In accordance with the Twelfth Amendment, the House of Representatives was required to select the president from the top three candidates. Although Andrew Jackson had received more electoral college votes than John Quincy Adams, the House elected Adams president.

In 1876, Rutherford Hayes received less of the popular vote than Samuel Tilden, but Hayes received one more electoral college vote, making him the president.

Proposals have ranged from modifying it to throwing it out completely and electing the president by direct popular vote. All amendments on the subject have failed.

SECTION 4 REVIEW

1. What are the basic types of elections in the United States, and how do they differ?
2. What are local voting units called?
3. What is an Australian ballot? What are the different types of Australian ballots?
4. How does the electoral college system work?
5. **For Critical Analysis:** Should the electoral vote for president be replaced by a direct popular vote? Explain why or why not.

★ ★ ★ ★ **Chapter Summary** ★ ★ ★ ★

Section 1: The Nomination

- The first step in the election process is the nomination—the selection of the candidates from each party who will seek office. Methods of nomination include (1) self-nomination and petition, (2) the party caucus, (3) the party nominating convention, and (4) the direct primary.
- Direct primaries may be closed (in which case only party members can vote to choose that party's candidates) or open (in which case voters can vote for either party's candidates regardless of whether they belong to the party). Run-off primaries may be used in states in which a candidate must receive a majority of votes.
- About three-fifths of the states hold state presidential primaries to choose delegates to attend the national conventions, where presidential candidates are actually nominated.

Section 2: The Campaign

- Election campaigns must be well organized and well planned. The campaign manager coordinates and plans the campaign strategy, and many candidates hire professional political consultants to devise campaign strategies and work on the candidate's public image.

- Campaigns have become very expensive, and the connection between money and campaigns has created difficult problems in American politics.
- The Federal Election Campaign Act of 1971 was passed to regulate campaign financing. Amendments to the act in 1974 established the Federal Election Commission (FEC), provided for public financing for presidential primaries and general elections, limited presidential campaign spending, required disclosure of finances, and limited contributions.
- Political action committees (PACs) may be organized to help finance political campaigns. The number of PACs has grown dramatically since the 1970s.

Section 3: Problems with Enforcing Campaign-Financing Rules

- Increasingly, the parties are skirting federal campaign regulations limiting donations.
- A loophole in campaign-financing laws allows soft-money contributions—contributions to parties rather than particular candidates.

- Foreign contributions to parties and candidates are also a matter of concern and are difficult to regulate.

Section 4: The Structure of American Elections

- A general election is a regularly scheduled election, held in even-numbered years, at which voters choose who will hold public office. Special elections are held when issues must be decided before the next general election.
- Local units of government are divided into precincts. Within each precinct, voters cast their ballots at one polling place.
- In 1888, the Australian (secret) ballot was introduced into the United States. The ballot takes two forms: the office-group ballot (on which all candidates for a given office are listed together, regardless of party affiliation) and the party-column ballot (on which candidates are listed under party labels).
- In the United States, the electoral college, not the popular vote, determines who wins presidential elections.

★ REVIEW QUESTIONS ★

1. What is the purpose of the nominating process?
2. Describe the methods by which candidates can be nominated.
3. What is a direct primary? How does a closed primary differ from an open primary?
4. What other types of primaries are there?
5. What is the purpose of national party conventions?
6. Why is the organization and planning of a campaign important?
7. How has Congress tried to regulate campaign finances?
8. Explain the purpose of PACs.
9. What are loopholes? What are some loopholes in campaign-financing laws?
10. Describe some of the ways in which campaign financing might be reformed.
11. What is a general election?
12. What other types of elections are held in the United States?
13. What is an Australian ballot, and what forms does it take?
14. How did the electoral college system develop, and how does it work today?

★ CRITICAL THINKING ★

1. Find out what kind of primary system is used in your state. If you could choose a primary system for your state that is different from the type currently used, which would you choose? Give reasons for your answer.
2. Why are secret ballots so important to free elections?
3. What factors do you think have led to the growth in the number of PACs? Do you think PACs should be further regulated? Explain.

4. Why is it so difficult to reform campaign-financing rules?
5. How might our presidential elections change if we abolished the electoral college and used the direct popular vote instead?

★ IMPROVING YOUR SKILLS ★

Communication Skills

Comparing and Contrasting Comparing and contrasting is a skill that you will need in order to fully understand and evaluate information, to write and deliver oral reports, and to formulate and express a reasoned opinion. To compare and contrast items means to put them side by side and look for similarities and differences. It may be helpful to look for the similarities first and then go on to search for differences.

Check carefully that the categories you are using to compare and contrast apply to both items. For example, if you are comparing and contrasting two mayoral candidates, your list of categories might include experience in government, leadership abilities, voting record, position on environmental issues, and knowledge of the community, its problems, and its people. Make sure these categories can be applied equally to both candidates. It is often helpful to create a Venn diagram composed of two intersecting circles to show graphically the similarities and differences. Draw large circles on paper, then list all the similarities and differences for candidate A and candidate B in the appropriate portion of the circle.

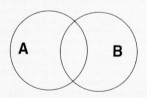

Writing Identify two candidates for any political office from a past or current election. List ten categories that can be used to compare and contrast the candidates. Next, list the similarities between the candidates with respect to these categories. Then list the differences between the candidates. Write a statement summarizing the similarities and differences.

Social Studies Skills

Reading Maps Look at the map of the United States on page 315. Answer the following questions:

1. What does the map show?
2. How is the number of electoral votes determined for each state?
3. Which state has the most electoral votes?
4. What are the fewest possible electoral votes that a state can have?
5. How many states have the minimum number of electoral votes?
6. Do you see any patterns in the regional distribution of electoral votes for presidential candidates Bob Dole and Bill Clinton?
7. A president can be elected with 270 electoral votes. Determine the minimum number of states that the candidate must win in order to obtain 270 votes, and list those states.

★ ACTIVITIES AND PROJECTS ★

1. Interview a candidate who campaigned in a recent election or an aide of that candidate. Ask the candidate or aide how the campaign was organized, planned, and financed. Report your results to the class.
2. Prepare a campaign plan for an imaginary candidate. Invent a campaign theme, and decide how the campaign should be organized and financed. Present your plan to the class.
3. Do some research to find out how much each of the following officeholders spent during his or her campaign to be elected (or reelected) to office:

   - Your representative in the U.S. Congress.
   - A U.S. senator from your state.
   - The governor of your state.
   - A local city councilperson.

   Present your findings to your classmates, making sure that you indicate the sources of your information.
4. Stage a debate on the following statement: Candidates for political office shall not be allowed to spend their own money for their campaigns.

What If . . .

Candidates Could Not Spend Their Own Money on Their Campaigns?

Today, wealthy candidates can spend as much as they want on their own campaigns. Would the type of people who run for political office change if a law was passed (and upheld by the Supreme Court) that prevented individuals from spending their own money on their campaigns?

CHAPTER 12

The Media and Cyberspace

CHAPTER OBJECTIVES

To learn about and understand . . .

- ⭐ The role played by television in political campaigns and elections

- ⭐ The increasing importance of talk radio in the political arena

- ⭐ The current and potential impact of the Internet on American politics and government

Keynote

"The press in America . . . determines what people will think and talk about—an authority that in other nations is reserved for tyrants, priests, parties, and mandarins."

Theodore H. White
(1915–1986)
Political Commentator

INTRODUCTION

Think about how many times you hear rumors at school. Sometimes you take such rumors with a grain of salt. Sometimes you take them more seriously. If you read an article in your school newspaper about an action that the principal is planning, however, you definitely take the information seriously. Whether you like it or not, the printed word in the press has an impact on you. So do the words spoken on radio and TV or transmitted over the Internet.

As illustrated by the above statement by Theodore H. White, who wrote many books on presidential campaigns, the media in the United States have a power equivalent to that held by tyrants in some other countries. In this chapter, you will learn about the importance of the media—and increasingly, the Internet—in American politics.

◀ Newspaper and television reporters fill the White House press briefing room to listen carefully and ask questions of the president's press secretary.

The Role of Television in Campaigns and Elections

Preview Questions:

- In what ways do candidates use television during campaigns?
- What is negative campaign advertising?
- How does TV news coverage differ from news coverage in the print media?

Key Terms:

negative campaign advertising, attack ads, issue ads, managed news coverage, sound bite

The media, especially television, have had a wide-ranging effect on politics in general. Their most immediate and obvious impact, however, is felt during campaigns and elections. Years ago, the biggest expense in a campaign budget might have been the campaign train rental. Today, the biggest expense is unquestionably television advertising, which consumes about half of the total budget for a major campaign.

The Candidates and Television

It is not surprising that political candidates are willing to spend large sums of money for television advertising.

Just the Facts

A study of a recent presidential campaign conducted by the University of Michigan Center for Political Studies revealed that 50 percent of voters paid no attention to newspaper articles about the campaign.

Virtually all American homes (99 percent) now have television sets, and these sets are in use a good deal of the time. According to a study by Nielsen Media Research in 1998, the average American household has the television on for seven hours and forty-eight minutes every day. Additionally, 72 percent of Americans now claim that television is their primary source for news.

Candidates are well aware of the importance of TV coverage during political campaigns. One of the ways that candidates obtain TV coverage is through political advertising. Another is through appearances on news programs. Still another, particularly in presidential campaigns, is through televised debates between the candidates.

Political Advertising The first televised political commercials appeared during the 1952 presidential campaign, along with the first televising of party conventions. At that time in the United States, there were only about 15 million television sets—a total that climbed to about 54 million in 1960, 93 million in 1970, and well over 100 million today.

Making a political commercial is just like making any other type of commercial. The ad writers have thirty or sixty seconds to communicate a message that viewers will remember. Usually, they center the ad around the most positive personality traits of a candidate. That is not always the case, however. Very soon after the first political commercials appeared on television, **negative campaign advertising** began to appear. This type of advertising focuses on negative features of the opponent.

Negative Campaign Advertising The use of negative campaign advertising by political candidates was certainly not a new phenomenon. Indeed, one of the most common forms of negative campaign advertising—**attack ads,** which attack the character of a candidate's opponent—has a long tradition in this country. Consider that in 1800, one of Thomas Jefferson's opponents described Jefferson as having a "weakness of nerves, want of fortitude, and total imbecility of character."

Negative campaign advertising may also take the form of **issue ads**—ads that emphasize the flaws in an opposing candidate's position on important political issues. One of the most effective issue ads was one used in President Lyndon Johnson's campaign against Barry Goldwater in 1964. In this ad, a little girl stood quietly in a field of daisies. She held a daisy and pulled off the petals, counting to herself. Suddenly, when she reached for the last petal, a deep voice was heard counting "10, 9, 8, 7, 6 . . ." When it hit zero, the unmistakable mushroom cloud of an atom bomb filled the screen. Then President Johnson's voice was heard saying, "These are the stakes: To make a world in which all of God's children can live, or to go into the dark. We must either love each other, or we must die." A message then read: "Vote for President Johnson on November 3." The implication, of course, was that Goldwater would lead the country into a nuclear war. Even though the ad was removed within a few days, it remains a classic example of negative advertising.

Other elections provide further examples of negative advertising. In 1988, a negative ad produced for the campaign of George Bush criticized Bush's opponent, Michael Dukakis. As governor of Massachusetts, Dukakis had supported granting prisoners in that state brief working leaves from prison, or *furloughs*. The ad showed a revolving door with men in striped uniforms leaving a prison and then showed a picture of Willie Horton, a convicted murderer who committed another killing while he was on official leave from the penitentiary. The ad was meant to give the impression that Dukakis was "soft" on crime.

Negative political advertising seems to have reached new heights in the 1990s, particularly in the 1996 campaigns. According to some critics, political ads during the 1996 campaigns were so nasty that they turned many viewers against the political process. These critics claim that negative political advertising was one of the reasons for low voter turnout in the 1996 elections.

News Coverage Political advertising is expensive, but coverage by the news media is free. Not surprisingly, candidates try to use the media's interest in campaigns to their advantage. Today's campaign managers and political consultants have become experts in the art of

◀ Candidates work hard to be seen as more than just politicians. What image might Jimmy Carter, shown here campaigning for the presidency he won in 1976, be trying to convey?

creating newsworthy events for TV camera crews and journalists to cover.

Besides becoming aware of how camera angles and timing affect a candidate's appearance, the campaign staff learns to plan its political events to accommodate the press. The staff attempts to make what its candidate is doing appear photogenic and interesting. It also knows that journalists and political reporters compete for stories, and that they can be manipulated through granting favors such as an exclusive personal interview with a candidate. Skillful manipulation of the media to increase the quantity and quality of news coverage is often called **managed news coverage.**

Gaining favorable news coverage is particularly important for presidential candidates. Indeed, political scientist Thomas Patterson contends that the press now performs a role that traditionally was performed by political parties—screening potential nominees for the presidency. In his book *Out of Order* (1993), Patterson emphasizes the important role played by the news media in presidential nominations:

Just the Facts

A thirty-second ad during Super Bowl '98 cost $1.3 million.

Once upon a time, the press occasionally played an important part in the nomination of presidential candidates. Now its function is always a key one. The news media do not entirely determine who will win the nomination, but no candidate can succeed without the press. The road to nomination now runs through the newsrooms.

Most candidates spend large amounts of money on television commercials. The figure on the next page shows the average cost of a single half-minute commercial during prime time in selected markets.

Many people, however, feel that the use of television advertising is draining the content out of campaigns. The issues are often presented in a shortened or overstated form. Complex issues, such as balancing the federal budget, military policy, and cleaning up the environment, are reduced to mere slogans. Commercials frequently use emotional appeals, rather than facts, to persuade voters. Negative advertising, which may involve blaming other candidates for current social problems or attacking their personal lives, is often used.

When you see political commercials, remember that they—like other commercials—are trying to sell you a product. In this case, the product is a

BUILDING
SOCIAL STUDIES SKILLS

Evaluating Political Commercials

political candidate. Knowing how to evaluate television ads during an election campaign will help you learn to evaluate political candidates and issues. Start by asking yourself these questions:

- **Which individual or group paid for the commercial?** All political advertising is required by law to identify who paid for it. Think about

why the ad's sponsor is interested in getting the candidate elected.

- **What forms of communication are used?** Is the message conveyed through urgent music, shocking pictures, soft images, or popular symbols? What is the narrator's tone of voice? What is the story line? Recognizing these elements of an ad will tell you how it is trying to make you feel.

- **Does the ad present facts, or does it appeal directly to your emotions?**

- **Is the ad about the candidate being advertised, or does it only attack her or his opponent?** Does it blame another candidate for current problems? Is it negative or positive advertising?

- **Does the ad deal with issues that are appropriate to the office?** For example, a candidate for governor might take a stand on military spending. Military spending is normally a question for the national

Debates The first great television debate took place in 1960 between Richard M. Nixon, the Republican presidential candidate, and John F. Kennedy, the Democratic candidate. Nixon used a cosmetic product called "Lazy Shave" to hide his five o'clock shadow. As a result, he looked unshaven and drawn. In contrast, Kennedy, who

◀ *Candidates Richard Nixon and John F. Kennedy participate in a televised long-distance debate during the 1960 presidential campaign. Many who listened on the radio considered Nixon the winner, while television viewers gave the victory to Kennedy. Why?*

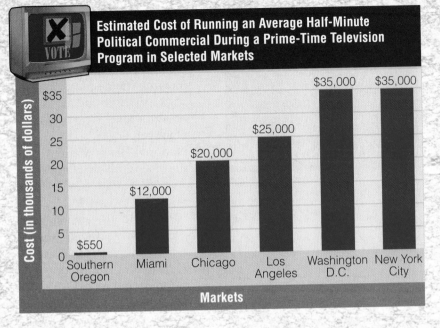

Estimated Cost of Running an Average Half-Minute Political Commercial During a Prime-Time Television Program in Selected Markets

Cost (in thousands of dollars)

- Southern Oregon: $550
- Miami: $12,000
- Chicago: $20,000
- Los Angeles: $25,000
- Washington D.C.: $35,000
- New York City: $35,000

Markets

through the advertising claims and make sound judgments regarding each candidate's qualifications and abilities.

PRACTICING YOUR SKILLS

1. Use the questions in this feature to evaluate a political commercial on local television. If no political commercials are currently running, see if you can view footage of old campaign commercials at a local television station. Then evaluate the ads according to the guidelines presented.

2. Do you think negative advertising about a political opponent is fair? Find examples of ads you consider negative to support your position. Present the examples and your opinions to the class.

government and not the state government. Therefore, it has no real bearing on the race for the governorship.

- **Does the ad tell you anything substantial about the candidate, or does it only seek to boost her or his image?** Look at the propaganda techniques listed on page 342 and 343 to find out if any are used.

Regardless of the strengths or weaknesses of the practice, it seems that political candidates, like laundry detergent and soft drinks, are destined to be sold through television commercials. As voters, it is up to us to sift

wore no make-up, had a fresh appearance. In the debate itself, Nixon answered questions like the college debater he once was, while Kennedy aimed his remarks directly at the television audience. Many believe the debate turned the tide in Kennedy's favor and established the importance of a good television appearance for a presidential candidate.

Since that first debate, many others have helped influence the outcome of elections. Television debates offer a unique opportunity for voters to find out how candidates differ on issues. They also offer a way for candidates to capitalize on the power of television to project a positive image. Candidates view television debates as a chance to

improve their own images or a chance to point out the failings of their opponents. Post-debate commentaries by news analysts also play an important role in determining what the public thinks, even when the commentaries are biased.

Some contend that a candidate's performance in a televised debate may be as important as political

Just the Facts

In 1996 the Federal Election Commission (FEC) ruled that third-party candidate H. Ross Perot could not participate in the presidential debates. Perot sued, but the court ruled in favor of the FEC.

Local television stations have certain obligations to the public because they use public air waves. Citizens sometimes feel their local stations are not living up to these obligations and have objected to problems such as a station's hiring practices, its programming, and the percentage of time it gives to news and public affairs. If you want to find out about your local station's policies, go to the station's headquarters and ask to see its public file.

Stations must keep a public file and make it available to citizens. The file must contain applications filed with the Federal Communications Commission (FCC), data on station ownership, data on employment practices, an FCC manual entitled *The Public and Broadcasting—A Procedure Manual* (if the station is commercial), letters from the audience, and a list of ten problems that need service in the community and how the station's programming serves those needs.

A number of citizens' organizations attempt to monitor or influence television programming in various ways. Some of the organizations are listed below:

- **Accuracy in Media (AIM)** (4455 Connecticut Ave., NW, Suite 330, Washington, DC 20008, 202-364-4401) is a nonprofit educational

PARTICIPATING IN YOUR GOVERNMENT

Talking Back to Your Television

organization dedicated to fighting what it considers distorted news reporting by the major media. AIM's Web site is at **www.aim.org/**.
- **Media Alliance** (814 Mission St., Suite 205, San Francisco, CA 94103, 415-546-6334) has been working for over twenty years to promote fairness and accuracy in the media. Media Alliance also promotes accountability, freedom of the press, ethical news reporting, and equal access to the media. You can access Media Alliance online at **www.media-alliance.org/**.
- **The Center for Educational Priorities** (72025 Hill Road, Covelo, CA 95428, 707-983-8374) believes that education should be a priority in all areas of American life, especially in the media. The

group advocates greater cooperation throughout American culture to assist parents, teachers, and broadcasters in meeting their educational responsibilities. To access this organization's Web site, go to **www.cep.org/**.
- **National Black Media Coalition** (11120 New Hampshire Ave., Suite 204, Silver Spring, MD 20904, 301-593-3600) is made up of over seventy African American organizations that are dedicated to eliminating racism from broadcasting. The Internet address for the coalition is **www.nbmc.org/**.
- **National Organization for Women (NOW)** (1000 Sixteenth St. NW, Suite 700, Washington, DC 20036, 202-331-0066), through its *Media Project,* gives assistance to persons working to promote employment and positive images of women in broadcasting. To reach NOW online, go to **www.now.org/**.

TAKING ACTION

1. Contact one of the organizations listed above and find out more about its activities. Report to the class on what you discover.
2. Think of one way in which you could influence a local media source. Write out the steps you would follow to do so.

◄ *The tables are turned on media tycoon Steve Forbes as he attracts a great deal of press coverage during his brief 1996 run at the presidency.*

advertising in shaping the outcome of the elections. Others doubt that televised debates have ever been taken very seriously. According to one political commentator, William Plass, presidential debates oversimplify the issues in order to reach a wider audience.

The Impact of Television

Before the advent of radio and TV broadcasts, the print media (primarily newspapers and news magazines) were the main news sources. These media continue to be important sources for news. As mentioned earlier, though, television is the primary news source for most Americans. Clearly, news is presented differently on TV than in newspapers or news magazines. But does the difference in news presentation affect the quality of news coverage?

One way to find out is to compare how the same issue is covered by the TV networks and the print media. No doubt, you will find some striking differences. For one thing, the print media, particularly leading newspapers such as the *New York Times* and the *Washington Post*, treat issues in much more detail. Furthermore—in addition to news coverage based on reporters' research—print media often include editori-

als. Editorials take positions on issues and set forth arguments supporting these positions.

In contrast, TV news presentations are usually brief and somewhat superficial. This is to be expected, because time is a critical element in all television programming. News must be reported quickly, in just a few minutes. Occasionally, there is only time for what is called a **sound bite**—a comment lasting a few seconds that captures a thought and has an immediate impact on viewers but that gives little or no relevant information.

Whereas print media reporters rely on words, TV news reporters must rely extensively on visual elements. Critics argue that, to hold viewers' attention, TV news programs focus on showing the candidates' personalities and their exciting activities rather than on explaining the candidates' positions on policy issues. Furthermore, according to the critics, news organizations believe that policy issues are of less interest to voters than the campaign game itself. The result is that TV news coverage is too often devoted not to the issues but to campaign strategies, projections about who is ahead in the "horse race," and poll results.

Today, the nature of television coverage dictates how campaigns are run. Almost every decision that consultants make about a candidate's activities—where to eat

The Media and Citizens' Responsibilities

Wading through the flood of information from the media and from candidates can be tiresome. It is the responsibility of each of us, however, not only to vote but also to make the best possible choices when we do so. This means that we need to be well informed. We need to recognize the strategies behind political advertising and the limitations of television news coverage.

Remember that even if the evening news is not the best source of all the facts, good sources do exist. Public television, in-depth network programs, magazines, and newspapers all provide fairly complete coverage of the news. It may take some work to seek out good information. If being an informed citizen is important, however, seeking out this information is worth the effort.

▲ Left a quadriplegic by a horseback-riding accident, actor Christopher Reeve addresses the 1996 Democratic National Convention on the subject of increased government funding for disability research. Why might Democrats be more receptive than Republicans to such a proposal?

dinner, what to wear, and what to say about the Middle East—is calculated according to its potential television impact. Many observers see the current era of politics as one in which the slick slogan and smooth image will dominate. Overall, television has created a new kind of political candidate—one who must be at ease with the camera. These days, no candidate can ignore this important part of campaigning.

SECTION 1 REVIEW

1. In what ways do candidates use television during campaigns?
2. What is negative campaign advertising?
3. How does news coverage on TV differ from news coverage in the print media?
4. **For Critical Analysis:** If American voters based their political views solely on what they learned from TV news programs, what might result?

SECTION 2

Talk Radio—A New Force in Politics?

Preview Questions:

- When did radio become an important force in politics?
- What is talk radio, and how does it affect politics?
- Why is talk radio sometimes referred to as the new "Wild West" of the media?

Key Term:

talk radio

On November 2, 1920, KDKA-Pittsburgh transmitted the first scheduled radio program in the United States—the presidential election race between Warren G. Harding and James M. Cox. The listeners were a few thousand people tuning in on very primitive radio sets. In the following years, radio quickly became a fixture in American homes. Today, about 100 million homes have radios, and there are about 220 million radios outside of homes, including those in offices and, of course, automobiles.

Politicians have realized the power of radio since 1933, when President Franklin D. Roosevelt (president from 1933 to 1945) delivered his first "fireside chat" over the radio. Today, talk radio is a political force to be reckoned with. The term **talk radio** simply refers to talk shows broadcast over the radio. In 1988, there were two hundred talk-show radio stations. Today, there are over a thousand, and that number is growing. According to recent estimates, one in six Americans listens to talk radio regularly. Over 40 percent of Americans who responded to one poll said they considered talk radio to be their primary source for political news.

Talk Radio's "Arrival" in 1994

When President Bill Clinton called talk-radio station KMOX in St. Louis directly from Air Force One, talk radio had arrived. Clinton's attention showed that even the president recognized the political influence of talk radio. The time was 1994, during the congressional elections. Clinton had placed the call to complain about criticism he had been receiving from the talk-show host Rush Limbaugh. Ever since Clinton's inauguration in 1993, Limbaugh, a conservative Republican and a powerful political force in 1994, had used his syndicated talk-radio program to attack Clinton's policies and those of the Democratic Congress. The president wanted equal time. Limbaugh's show then had an audience of about 20 million listeners

◀ Although this 1930s microphone looks old fashioned, it was revolutionary in its day, allowing politicians to bring their voices into the homes of Americans everywhere.

and was broadcast on 660 radio stations.

Another influential talk-radio personality was "shock jock" announcer Howard Stern. Stern had serious discussions on his talk show with George Pataki when Pataki was running against Mario Cuomo for the governorship of New York in 1994. Stern also hosted Christine Todd Whitman, a candidate for governor of New Jersey, during that campaign. Both Pataki and Whitman were elected, and some political analysts claim that Howard Stern's show had a significant impact on voters' decisions.

Many sitting presidents, including Ronald Reagan and Bill Clinton, have held regularly scheduled radio shows. Ed Koch, former mayor of New York City, has a show on WABC in New York. Mario Cuomo, former governor of New York, Gary Hart, former U.S. senator from Colorado and former presidential candidate, also have shows. Susan Molinari, who represented New York in the U.S. House of Representatives, resigned her seat in 1997 to anchor the radio show *CBS News Saturday Morning*. She was seen as a rising star on the

◀ New York congresswoman Susan Molinari gives the keynote speech at the 1996 Republican National Convention. Although seen as a rising star in her party, Molinari resigned her congressional seat to anchor a radio news show. Which position do you see as more powerful and influential?

ARCHITECTS
of Government

Bill Gates
(1955–)

Bill Gates (William Henry Gates III) was born in Seattle, Washington, on October 28, 1955. In 1977, Gates and Paul Allen founded Microsoft Corporation and produced DOS, the disk operating system used in the majority of the world's computers today. By the 1990s, Gates had become one of the wealthiest men in America. The following quotations are responses by Bill Gates to questions asked via e-mail.

HIS WORDS

"Most classes that seem boring at first can be made interesting if you look at the subject in the right way. This may take some inventiveness on your part, but it's worth it if only so that you learn how to learn."

(The New York Times Syndicate,
September 23, 1997)

"My key messages about the future [are] that everybody will be connected, and that computers will see, listen and learn . . . ."

(The New York Times Syndicate,
September 23, 1997)

DEVELOPING
CRITICAL THINKING SKILLS

1. What did Gates mean by the phrase "learn how to learn" in the first quotation? How might you apply the advice given in this quotation to a class or classes that you are currently taking?
2. Regarding the second quotation, how might computers that can "see, listen and learn" affect our lives in the future?

political scene after giving the keynote address at the 1996 Republican National Convention.

The "Wild West" of the Media?

Talk radio is sometimes characterized as the "Wild West" of the media. Political ranting and raving are common. Journalistic concerns about accurate and unbiased news commentary do not exist.

Some people are uneasy because talk shows allow fringe groups—those on the radical right or radical left of the political spectrum—to air their views to millions of listeners. Clearly, a talk show is not necessarily a democratic forum in which all views are presented. Talk-show hosts such as Limbaugh and Stern do not attempt to hide their political biases. If anything, they exaggerate their biases for effect. People who support the sometimes outrageous remarks broadcast during radio talk shows claim that such shows are simply a response to consumer demand. Furthermore, those who think that talk radio is good for America argue that talk shows, taken together, provide a forum for the common people for political debate.

Those who claim that talk-show hosts go too far in their rantings and ravings ultimately have to deal with the constitutional issue of free speech. After all, as First Amendment scholars contend, there is little the government can do about the forces that shape the media. The courts have always protected freedom of expression to the fullest extent possible.

SECTION 2 REVIEW

1. What U.S. president first used the radio extensively to communicate with Americans?
2. Why is it said that talk radio "arrived" in 1994? What event led to that statement?
3. What are some of the characteristics of radio talk shows?
4. **For Critical Analysis:** How can you explain the popularity of radio talk shows?

The Internet and Political Campaigns

Preview Questions:

- ⬤ How widespread is Internet use in the United States today?
- ⬤ In what ways do political candidates benefit from the Internet?
- ⬤ What role did the Internet play in the 1996 elections?
- ⬤ How can the Internet be used to obtain information on campaign financing?

Key Terms:

Internet, World Wide Web

James Madison once made the following statement:

[K]nowledge will forever govern ignorance, and people who mean to be their own governors must arm themselves with the power which knowledge gives.

Today, much knowledge can be obtained via the **Internet.** By the late 1990s, the Internet connected more than 150 million computers and some eighty thousand networks around the world. Information on just about any topic is available on the **World Wide Web,** the leading information retrieval service of the Internet. The Web gives Internet users access to literally millions of documents, photos, videos, and other information. Whether information on the Web is reliable is another issue, as will be discussed in the chapter-ending *America at Odds* feature.

Will Internet use change politics as we know it? Very likely, but no one can say for certain just *how* the Internet will reshape American politics and political institutions. This is true of any new medium. In the 1950s, for example, few people realized

the extent to which television would affect how news is delivered, how campaigns are run, and so on. Certainly, though, the growth of the Internet, at least in the United States, has been explosive. Polling data indicate that over 20 percent of the U.S. population over the age of sixteen (or thirty-five million Americans) now use the Internet.

Today's political parties and candidates are beginning to realize the benefits of using the Internet to promote their goals. Voters are

Just the Facts

Currently there are more than 120,000 government Web sites offering more than 265 million official documents.

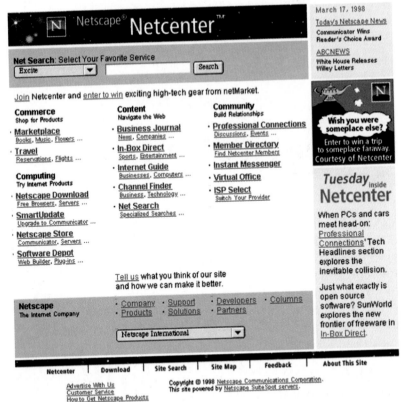

▲ As recently as the early 1990s, only a handful of scientists used the World Wide Web. Now, servers such as Netscape make it easy for the average computer owner to navigate the Internet.

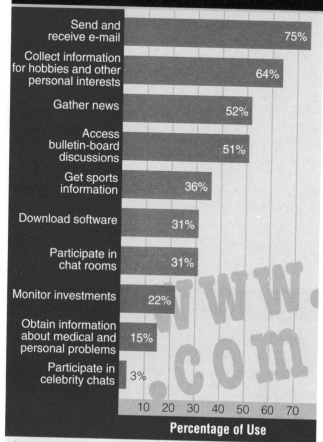

FIGURE 12–1 Online Activities As you can see in this chart, people use the Internet for a variety of purposes. What percentage of Internet users obtain news via the Internet?

Activity	Percentage of Use
Send and receive e-mail	75%
Collect information for hobbies and other personal interests	64%
Gather news	52%
Access bulletin-board discussions	51%
Get sports information	36%
Download software	31%
Participate in chat rooms	31%
Monitor investments	22%
Obtain information about medical and personal problems	15%
Participate in celebrity chats	3%

Percentage of Use

SOURCE: 1996 polls conducted by IntelliQuest, Yankelovich, and Gerogia Institute of Technology.

also provides an inexpensive way for the candidate to let people know how he or she stands on particular issues. In effect, the Internet presents an alternative to brochures, letters, and position papers. For the individual voter, using the Internet is a convenient way to obtain information on a candidate's position. The voter can avoid the need to attend special meetings or to go to campaign sites.

Of course, because creating a Web site is relatively inexpensive, a political candidate's opponents can easily create sites proposing alternative positions on issues. Another problem with using the Internet for campaigning is that the user has to be motivated to access the information. Therefore, the Internet will never completely replace door-to-door campaigning or personalized letters to potential supporters.

The Internet and the 1996 Elections

The growing effect of the Internet on campaigns and elections became clear in 1996. Before the 1996 elections, the Web site for the Democratic National Committee received 50,000 hits a day—that is, it was accessed by users 50,000 times a day. The Republicans' site received 75,000 hits a day. On the night of the election, millions of election watchers turned to the Internet for instant results. Indeed, so many were trying to find out what was happening that traffic at the MSNBC site, a Web site sponsored jointly by Microsoft Corporation and NBC, was five times the usual level. CNN estimated that it had fifty million hits that night on its AllPolitics site, up from its previous record of eighteen million.

also increasingly using the Internet to find information about parties and candidates, as well as political news in general. As you can see in Figure 12–1, while the most common use of the Internet is sending and receiving e-mail messages, over half of the users polled use the Internet to obtain information and news as well.

Campaigns and the Internet

For a political candidate, the Internet provides an inexpensive way to contact, recruit, and mobilize supporters. It

Who Used the Internet to Obtain Campaign News? According to one survey, 26 percent of those eligible to vote were regular users of the Internet in 1996. Of this percentage, the majority (55 percent) were men.

◀ The AllPolitics Web site, identified by its logo shown here, is sponsored by CNN. It is one of the many Internet sites that cover the news.

The Internet users were also younger and a bit richer than the population at large. Another survey revealed that about 10 percent of regular Internet users went to the Internet for political news during the 1996 presidential campaigns and elections. Ninety percent of these users said they sought presidential campaign information, and a third said that they got information on the latest congressional races. In a *Wall Street Journal*/NBC News poll, 34 percent of daily Web users identified themselves as Democrats, 28 percent as Republicans, and the rest as independents.

Did the Internet Influence the Vote? After the 1996 elections, about 9 percent of the voters surveyed in one poll indicated that information on the Internet had influenced their vote. If, in fact, 9 percent of voters were influenced in the 1996 elections by their use of the Internet, that means that about 8.5 million Americans—one out of eleven voters—were affected. When a medium can influence one in eleven voters, that medium has become important. The Internet is now a significant medium for communicating political information.

Tracking Campaign Contributions

The Internet also makes it easy to find out which groups and individuals contributed money to particular candidates. Although campaign contributions do not literally "buy" the support of a candidate, they do give the contributor access to the candidate. And clearly, candidates listen closely to the wishes of those who made it possible for the candidate to be elected.

The Federal Election Commission (FEC) has its own Web site, at **www.fec.gov/**. A more manageable site, however, is FECInfo, developed by Tony Raymond, a former manager at the FEC. FECInfo is a nonpartisan, independent site containing FEC data. The Internet address for the FECInfo Web site is **www.tray.com/FECInfo/**.

If you want to find out what groups and individuals in your zip code area sent contributions to particular candidates, you can do so easily at the FECInfo site. Simply type in your zip code, and you get the list. You can also find out to whom particular individuals or organizations gave contributions and the sizes of those contributions by typing in the names of the individuals or organizations.

Another source of information on campaign financing is Common Cause, which can be accessed at **www.commoncause.org/**. Common Cause describes itself as a nonprofit, nonpartisan citizen's lobbying organization dedicated to promoting honest and accountable government. At its Web site, you can find details on the industries and interest groups that made the largest contributions to the political parties during the 1996 campaigns, the biggest campaign spenders in Congress, and other campaign-financing topics.

▲ Citizens can keep up with state and national campaign finances by checking the Web page of the watchdog group Common Cause. Why do you think Common Cause goes to the effort and expense of maintaining a Web site?

1. What percentage of the U.S. population currently uses the Internet, and what is the most common online activity?
2. What are some benefits of the Internet for political candidates?
3. Discuss how information available on the Internet influenced the vote in the 1996 elections.

4. **For Critical Analysis:** Suppose that you have decided to vote for a candidate because of her pro-environmental stance. Then you learn from an online database that an anti-environmental interest group contributed a large amount of money to her campaign organization. Would this new information affect your decision to vote for the candidate? Should it? How would you determine if the information provided by that particular database was correct? Explain your views.

SECTION 4

The Internet, Interest Groups, and Democracy

Preview Questions:

- How can the Internet benefit interest groups?
- What are some of the advantages of the Internet for labor unions?
- What implications does the Internet have for the future of our democracy?

Key Terms:

information warfare, search engines, cyber strike, electronic democracy

The impact of the Internet is becoming apparent not only in political campaigns and elections but also in many other significant ways. In this final section, we look at how the Internet is currently affecting American democracy. We also consider some of the implications of online communications for the future.

Online Interest Groups

Organizing an interest group and advertising its positions on policy issues have always been very expensive undertakings. It takes money to pay for advertising in the print or broadcast media. It takes money to pay for the travel expenses of those who go from place to place to recruit new members. It takes money to pay for

office space, cover administrative costs, and the like. Typically, it is the members of the group who pay these expenses, through their membership dues. Because many potential supporters of a cause cannot afford these dues, successful interest groups have tended to have a middle-class or upper-class bias.

Enter the Internet. For interest groups with few resources, the Internet offers the possibility of building national or global networks at a very low cost. For example, Earthtrust is a worldwide organization dedicated to resolving environmental problems. Earthtrust was organized as a global network with very few resources. All it did was equip volunteers in remote areas with inexpensive computer hookups and e-mail accounts. The use of e-mail allowed Earthtrust to knit together a widely dispersed but highly effective organization. This task was accomplished in less than two years, something unthinkable prior to inexpensive Internet access. You can access Earthtrust at **www.earthtrust.org/**.

Today, a group of nongovernmental organizations with such diverse missions as saving the wilderness, liberating political prisoners, and stopping hunger have formed the Econ-Net/Peace Net, otherwise known as the Global Civil Society. Through this network, technology-oriented activists provide expertise and training. Similarly, Native American activists have linked themselves together through NativeNet and INDIANnet.

Is an Information War Possible?

Today, there is evidence that Russia, the largest of the fifteen republics of the former Soviet Union, may be trying to figure out a way to "cyber-bury" the United States. Russia is spending millions of dollars on preparing for what we call **information warfare.** It is working on developing high-tech "wrecking" systems that could attack U.S. civilian computers. If Russia, or any other country, waged a successful cyber, or information, war against the United States, our electric utilities, telephone systems, and financial systems could be seriously impaired.

Preparing for an Information War

In preparation for an information war, the U.S. government's National Defense University in Washington, D.C., has been playing cyber games. Some of the games involve seeing what would happen if forces engaged in information warfare started to corrupt files from the Pentagon's military database. Other games examine what would happen if corrupting programs got into the financial computer systems that allow money to be transferred throughout the world.

Do We Really Have to Worry about an Information War?

Today, information warfare is in the game-playing stage. The question is, will it ever become reality? A few high-level defense officials in the United States do not think so, but a growing number think differently. They believe that terrorists and criminal groups already have the capability to mount information warfare on the United States. The director of the Information Technology Office at one of the Defense Department's agencies, Howard Frank, recently said, "A couple years ago, no one took information warfare seriously. But the more you learn about it, the more concerned you become." In 1996, President Clinton created the Commission on Critical Infrastructure Protection. Its goal is to devise a policy to deal with information warfare threats. Additionally, the Central Intelligence Agency (CIA) has created an Information Warfare Center.

THINK ABOUT IT

1. Some people point out that even a very poor country can easily obtain the programmers and computer hardware necessary to conduct information warfare. Do you agree with this statement? Explain your answer.

2. In what way would information warfare resemble real warfare, if at all?

Labor Discovers the Power of the Internet

Labor interest groups have certainly discovered the power of the Internet. In 1996, the Bridgestone-Firestone Tire Company fired and replaced 2,300 striking employees. The employees' union, the International Federation of Chemical Workers Unions, decided to go online to gather support for its cause. The federation sent e-mail messages to all of its members throughout the world requesting that they e-mail their protests to Bridgestone-Firestone management. The federation also had its members send e-mail messages to firms that purchased tires from Bridgestone-Firestone and to banks and other companies that did business with the firm. By spending a few minutes writing a message and clicking "send," union members throughout the world could e-mail their thoughts on the company's action.

In the past, similar campaigns have been conducted using faxes. The difference between the two types of campaigns is remarkable. Sending one fax to 150 unions required several hours and resulted in a huge phone bill. In contrast, sending an e-mail message to almost any number of recipients via the Internet requires about a minute and costs almost nothing.

When unions want to put pressure on a particular employer, they can also engage consumers in their fight.

They can do this by sending individual e-mail messages to those who buy the company's products, as well as by creating special Web sites. For example, in 1997 dock workers went on strike in Liverpool, England. Claiming that the media were indifferent to their cause, the striking workers created their own Web site to let the public know about their problem. They effectively linked the site (provided access from their site) to the various **search engines,** such as Yahoo, WebCrawler, Excite, and Lycos. They also linked the site to discussion forums in numerous other sites dealing with union activities. One result was a sympathy **cyber strike**—a strike organized in cyberspace, using the Internet—against Drake International, one of the two companies that provided replacement workers for the striking dock workers. This cyber strike was organized by Canadian union members.

Unions in the United States also have Web sites. The address for the AFL-CIO's site is **www.aflcio.org/**. This site offers links to related Web sites that contain information on labor-related actions of various major U.S. corporations.

Cyber Politics— What's Ahead?

A few years ago, only a limited number of computer users even knew about the Internet. Today, tens of millions of Americans are online. In a short time, the Internet has become a vital force in business and education. It is now becoming a vital force in politics as well. Although we cannot foresee the future, it is clear that certain developments—made possible by the Internet—will have an impact on politics in the years to come.

Online Interest Groups and Democracy For one thing, as we have seen, it is possible to organize interest groups online at relatively low cost. This may give ordinary citizens the ability to put more pressure on government. In the past, these groups have had little representation in legislative lobbies. Some observers claim that because of the opportunities offered by the Internet, the United States may have a more truly democratic government in the future.

▶ *Although the influence of labor unions has been declining, new life has come into these old organizations through an unexpected source—the Internet. Able to unite far-flung members and inspire them to take action—such as sending an e-mail protest to an offending company—unions are using technology to their advantage.*

America's working families welcome you to their website.

Our mission is to improve the lives of working families and to bring economic justice to the workplace and social justice to the nation. Click here to learn more about today's unions.

What's New:

- Work in Progress
  This week with Today's Unions
- Press Statement - March 11
  Sweeney on H.R. 3246
- Union Dues Initiative in California
  Get the facts on Proposition 226
- On the Web Against Hate
  The Leadership Conference on Civil Rights, a coalition of 180 civil rights groups including the AFL-CIO and several affiliates, set up a website to fight hate speech on the Internet
- Press Statement - March 5
  Decision by National Labor Relations Board General Counsel Fred Feinstein Not to Seek Reappointment
- Remarks by John J. Sweeney

How the Media Have Changed

In the last forty years, there have been great changes in the media, particularly with the growing importance of the Internet.

THEN (FORTY YEARS AGO)	NOW
Radio and newspapers were the primary news sources.	Television is the primary news source, with the Internet becoming increasingly important.
There was no live news coverage of presidential actions.	Practically everything the president does is covered on live TV.
Cable TV did not exist.	About 65 percent of Americans have cable TV, and many others have satellite TV. Eventually, many television programs will be transmitted through the Internet.

◄ With the virtual-reality capabilities of the cyberworld, you should soon be able to attend national political conventions while sitting in your own home. In what other ways will the Internet affect politics in the future?

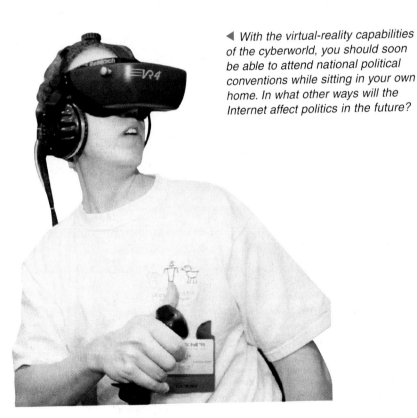

News on the Internet

When TWA Flight 800, carrying 230 people from New York to Paris, exploded shortly after takeoff on July 17, 1996, the world was stunned. Immediately, theories about what had caused the crash started to circulate, particularly on the Internet. A few months later, a former ABC news correspondent, Pierre Salinger, announced that he had evidence that Flight 800 had crashed after a U.S. missile accidentally hit it. The mainstream press carried the story. Salinger's source was, as you may have guessed, the Internet. He had uncovered on the Internet a supposedly secret document from a "foreign intelligence agency." There was just one problem. The document had been published on the World Wide Web months earlier as a joke. Immediately, two groups were at odds, and they continue to be so. One group wants to force news-providing information services on the Internet to be accountable for what they publish. In other words, such services should be able to back up what they publish online with accurate research and data. The other group believes that the Internet should remain free of any restrictions, including the requirement of accountability with respect to news on the Internet.

If a News Story Cannot Be Verified, Don't Use It, Some People Demand

Those who are concerned about Internet-generated news believe that if news cannot be verified, it should not be used. More specifically, these people argue that news must come from reliable, accountable, standard online news sources, such as the *New York Times*, the *Washington Post*, the *Wall Street Journal*, and MSNBC 24-Hour News. Such news sources use standard techniques for checking and verifying facts. Thus, these sources are reliable. In contrast, much that is published as news on the Web is completely unverified—rumors, opinions, even out-and-out lies. Salinger's weak Web sources for his theory regarding the crash of TWA Flight 800 simply represent the tip of an iceberg.

Even the White House is concerned about unsubstantiated news on the Internet. One internal memo issued by the office of the White House Counsel was entitled "Communications Stream of Conspiracy Commerce." The memo reported that some right-wing fringe groups had placed bogus stories on the Internet, which spread rapidly around the world. The stories then resurfaced in mainstream newspapers favoring conservative positions.

Leave the Web Alone, Others Insist

Those who are not concerned about the quality or accuracy of Internet-generated news believe simply that everyone should read what is on the Internet with care. In other words, we cannot accept news stories on the Internet uncritically. We must act as our own editors. After all, there is a big difference between the news we find in tabloids such as the *National Enquirer* and the news reported in the *Washington Post*. Why should it be any different on the Web?

Electronic journalism, to be sure, has no clear authorship. Indeed, many news sites on the Web have multiple authors and are really just editorial perspectives. When the source or credibility of news on the Internet is unclear, we simply have to proceed with care. Furthermore, it is the duty of the mainstream news media to verify any news they obtain from the Web.

YOU DECIDE

1. How might standard news organizations be held accountable for information from the Web that they reuse in their own stories?
2. What constitutional issue might arise if the government attempted to regulate news sources on the Internet?

Are We Moving toward an Electronic Democracy?
Already, citizens and their government officials are communicating with each other electronically. Members of Congress are online, sending and receiving messages daily. Agencies of the national government have Web sites and e-mail addresses. Legislative information can be found online at various sites, including THOMAS (located at **www.thomas.loc.gov/**), a Web site maintained by the Library of Congress. This site contains the texts of all laws, all committee hearings, and the congressional record. At the local level, citizens in many communities are using the Internet to contact their local public officials and representatives, as well as to access library information, civic announcements, and the like.

No doubt, we can look forward to even more electronic interaction between citizens and government. This prospect suggests a future that is characterized by patterns of political behavior very different from those to which we are now accustomed. Some people envision the emergence of an **electronic democracy** at the national level. In this electronic democracy, the entire voting population, via online voting forums, can vote on important policy issues as they arise.

The Independence of the Internet In the past, the power to transmit information via the mass media was concentrated in a small number of locations and institutions. Today, Internet users anywhere who want to obtain specific information about policy issues have easy access to what is happening in Congress. They also have at their fingertips a virtual library that extends around the globe. Significantly, voters can now obtain information directly, before it has been edited by people working in newspaper offices or television studios. Voters can also access information that newspaper editors or TV program managers may decide is not newsworthy enough to cover in their media. In a way, then, the power traditionally possessed by the mass media—the power to set the public agenda by deciding what issues are important—is being passed to the people.

Just the Facts

Although the number of daily newspapers is declining, the number of weekly newspapers is increasing.

Global Implications Today's Internet news forums are almost impossible to shut down. Other news media are subject to at least some government control, but the government has little say in determining what political views are available on the Internet. In the United States, where freedom of speech is a prized right, it would be especially difficult to control speech on the Internet. In some other countries, however, governments strictly control the news media to prevent their citizens from learning about alternative political cultures and philosophies. Even those governments find it difficult to control their citizens' use of the Internet, however. Some scholars claim that because the Internet allows persons living in such countries to learn about democratic beliefs and principles, the Internet is a democratizing force.

Our increasingly electronic world also poses a new kind of risk—the risk of information warfare. After all, virtually all nations are becoming increasingly dependent on electronic communications systems. What if a nation's communications systems were somehow impaired? This question is explored in the *Case Study: Government in Action* feature on page 335.

SECTION 4 REVIEW

1. Why does the Internet make organizing an interest group fairly easy and inexpensive?
2. Cite specific examples of how labor groups have used the Internet to further their goals.
3. Describe some of the ways in which the Internet may change American political activities and institutions.
4. What are the advantages of organizing an interest group online?
5. **For Critical Analysis:** Traditionally, a key role of the mass media has been to select what events are newsworthy and to interpret those events for readers and viewers. What are some of the advantages and disadvantages of this function of the mass media for Americans?

★ ★ ★ ★ **Chapter Summary** ★ ★ ★ ★

Section 1: The Role of Television in Campaigns and Elections

- The media, especially television, have had a wide-ranging effect on politics in general, especially on campaigns and elections.

- Candidates use several types of television coverage during campaigns, including political advertising, news coverage, and debates.
- Negative advertising has a long history and continues to be widely used during political campaigns.
- Television has had an impact on the way people view the candidates, understand the issues, and cast their votes. Gaining favorable coverage has become increasingly important for presidential candidates. Citizens must develop the habit and skills necessary for separating political advertising and a candidate's true position and abilities.

Section 2: Talk Radio—A New Force in Politics?

- Politicians have realized the power of radio ever since President Franklin D. Roosevelt delivered his first "fireside chat" in 1933.
- Talk radio "arrived" in 1994 when President Bill Clinton demanded equal time on a radio talk show to respond to talk-radio host Rush Limbaugh's criticisms of Clinton's policies.
- Many talk-show hosts come from political backgrounds and host well-known political figures and candidates.
- Talk radio is sometimes characterized as the new "Wild West" of the media because the usual journalistic concerns over accuracy and bias in news commentary do not exist, and political ranting and raving are common.

Section 3: The Internet and Political Campaigns

- Internet users have immediate access to millions of documents, photos, videos, and other information. Both historical and contemporary sources are readily available. Over 35 million Americans now use the Internet.
- The Internet provides an inexpensive way for a political candidate to contact, recruit, and mobilize supporters.
- Voters benefit from the Internet because of the ease with which they can obtain and exchange information.
- According to one poll, about 9 percent of the voters in the 1996 elections were influenced by informa-

tion obtained on the Internet. The Internet is now an important medium for communicating political information.

- Through the Internet, voters have access to many unbiased sources of information about political parties, candidates, and campaigns. In addition, the Internet makes it possible to find out which groups and individuals contributed money to particular candidates.

Section 4: The Internet, Interest Groups, and Democracy

- The Internet offers interest groups with few resources an opportunity to organize global networks at a very low cost. Labor interest groups now have the ability to organize "cyber strikes" against employers. The ability to organize interest groups online at relatively low cost may give citizens the ability to put more pressure on government.

- The Internet has become a vital force in business and education. It is becoming a major force in politics, as well.
- When virtually all U.S. citizens are online, electronic democracy on a nationwide level may become a reality.
- The Internet has made it possible for individuals to obtain news directly from online sources, before it has been edited. This brings new challenges as Americans sift through the information to make sure the news is correct and that the sources are verifiable.
- The widespread use of the Internet throughout the world may result in greater democracy on a global level, but growing dependence on electronic information systems in all nations also poses the risk of information warfare.

★ REVIEW QUESTIONS ★

1. Describe the types of television coverage that candidates use in political campaigns.
2. What is negative campaign advertising? What are attack ads? What are issue ads? Give an example of a negative campaign ad.
3. Give some examples of how television has affected political campaigns and candidates.
4. How does news coverage on television differ from news coverage in the print media?
5. When did radio first become a force in politics? When did talk radio "arrive"? Name some politicians who have radio shows.
6. For what reasons is talk radio sometimes called the "Wild West" of the media?
7. How do political candidates use the Internet during their campaigns?
8. How does the Internet benefit voters?
9. What percentage of the electorate were regular users of the Internet during the 1996 campaigns? Did the Internet influence these users' votes in any way in the 1996 elections?
10. How can Internet users obtain information on campaign contributions?
11. What are some of the advantages of the Internet for interest groups? How have labor groups used the Internet to further their aims?
12. How might the ease and low cost with which interest groups can be organized on the Internet affect American political life in the future?
13. What is an electronic democracy? Why might the Internet make a nationwide electronic democracy possible in the future?
14. How might news available from online sources differ from news made available in the traditional media?
15. What are some of the global implications of the increasingly widespread use of the Internet?

★ CRITICAL THINKING ★

1. What is the relationship between the media and political candidates? How do they assist each other?
2. Should the media be required to provide equal coverage for all candidates and for all political parties?
3. A majority of Americans (72 percent) now claim that TV is their primary source for news. Analyze the implications of this development for American democracy.
4. Do you think that cyber warfare is as serious a threat as warfare using traditional weaponry? Why or why not?

★ IMPROVING YOUR SKILLS ★

Communication Skills

Recognizing Propaganda Techniques A message that is meant to influence people's ideas, opinions, or actions in a certain way is called *propaganda*. Propaganda can be either positive or negative. Although it can include lies, it can also contain truthful information. Propaganda, which tells only one side of the story, distorts the truth, or appeals mostly to people's emotions. Commercial advertising is a type of propaganda, and sometimes, political candidates make use of propaganda. Six of the most common propaganda techniques are discussed here. When you read or listen to political messages, ask yourself if these techniques are being used. Recognizing propaganda techniques will help you make wise voter decisions.

1. **Glittering generalities.** Vague phrases that sound exciting but do not really say much are often referred to as "glittering generalities." For example, a candidate might say, "I stand for freedom and a strong America." Almost every American agrees with this statement, but it says nothing specific about the candidate or what he or she will do if elected.

2. **Testimonials.** Using testimonials involves getting a well-known person to endorse (publicly support) a candidate or issue. People admire the endorser and therefore accept his or her judgment about the person or issue being endorsed.

3. **Name calling.** Name calling involves giving people or things a negative label so that they will be rejected or disliked. For example, a candidate trying to gain the votes of moderates might claim that his opponent has "socialist" views or is a "reactionary."

4. **Plain folks.** Candidates often go out of their way to convince voters that they are just "plain folks"— average Americans like the voters to whom they are speaking.

5. **Bandwagon effect.** The bandwagon effect occurs when people join a movement because they believe everyone else is doing so. To make use of this effect, a candidate might, for example, announce that poll results show that she is ahead in the race. This may be enough to convince undecided voters that this candidate will be a winner and that they should "hop on the bandwagon" and vote for her. This method plays on the voters' fears that they are being left out of something.

6. **Transfer.** Transfer occurs when a person associates himself or herself with a respected person, group, or symbol. For example, a candidate might say, "Like Abraham Lincoln, I believe that . . . ."

Social Studies Skills

Analyzing Network News Watch a daily news program broadcast by one of the major networks, such as NBC or CBS. Keep the following questions in mind as you watch the news program.

1. Did the news program show any video clips or photos of specific events? If so, what were these events, and why were the video clips or photos shown?

2. Did you detect any particular slant or bias on the part of the newscasters with respect to the news that they were reporting?

3. If a political candidate was featured or discussed, did that candidate use any of the propaganda techniques just discussed?

4. Identify any "sound bites" used by the newscasters to convey messages.

Summarize the results of your analysis in a one-page report, and read your report to the class.

★ ACTIVITIES AND PROJECTS ★

1. Watch a nightly network news program to find out about a political event that is currently in the news. Then find out how that same event is covered in the print media. Select at least two newspapers or news magazines for comparison purposes. Write a two-page report in which you analyze the similarities and differences between the coverage of the event on TV and the coverage of the event in the print media.

2. Do some research on negative campaign advertising. Try to find out how media experts view the effect of negative ads on the voting population. Does negative political advertising turn voters against the political process?

3. Compose a "letter to the editor" setting forth your views on a topic that is currently being discussed in the national news media. Distribute copies of your letter to your classmates, and ask for feedback.

What If . . .

Voting Were Done via the Internet?

In the not-too-distant future, virtually all Americans may be able to access the Internet. How might voter turnout and voter choices change if all U.S. citizens, using a password, could vote in every election using the Internet?

CHAPTER 13

Voters and Voting Behavior

CHAPTER OBJECTIVES

To learn about and understand . . .

★ The history of the right to vote in the
United States

★ What factors affect voting

★ What factors affect the choices of voters

UNIT CONTENTS

CHAPTER 14

The Organization of Congress

CHAPTER OBJECTIVES

To learn about and understand . . .

✪ The creation and evolution of the U.S. Congress

✪ The terms and qualifications of members of Congress

✪ The characteristics and responsibilities of members of Congress

✪ The structure and organization of Congress

> *"The vote is the most powerful instrument ever devised by man for breaking down injustice."*
>
> *Lyndon Baines Johnson*
> (1908–1973)
> Thirty-sixth President of the United States

INTRODUCTION

Most of you reading this book will turn eighteen in the next year or two. Then you will legally have the right to vote. This was not always true for people your age. Not until July 1, 1971, when the Twenty-sixth Amendment to the Constitution was ratified, did eighteen-year-olds obtain the right to vote.

The importance of the right to vote has been stressed time and again. Susan B. Anthony referred to the right to vote as "pivotal." Abraham Lincoln considered the ballot to be stronger than the bullet. President Lyndon Johnson, as indicated in the keynote quotation above, considered the vote to be the "most powerful instrument ever devised" for "breaking down injustice."

In this chapter, we survey the history of voting in America. We also examine current patterns of voter turnout and voter behavior.

◀ The solemn duty of voting takes on a festive air in George Caleb Bingham's painting *The County Election.*

345

The History of Voting and Current Voting Requirements

Preview Questions:

- ★ What restrictions were placed on voting in the early days of America?
- ★ How did women gain the right to vote?
- ★ How were African Americans denied the vote? What events changed this?
- ★ What are current voting eligibility requirements?

Key Terms:

suffrage, disenfranchise, literacy tests, grandfather clauses, poll tax, registration, residency

In the United States today, all citizens who are at least eighteen years of age have the right to vote. This was not always true, however. Restrictions on **suffrage,** the legal right to vote, have existed since the founding of our nation. Expanding the right to vote has been an important part of the gradual democratization of the American electoral process.

Several of the nation's founders believed that only people who owned property should be allowed to vote. They considered this to be fair and reasonable because many of the government's functions were economic in nature. Few thought about extending the vote to African Americans (most of whom were slaves) or to women. The notion of allowing all citizens to vote was "theoretical nonsense," according to Charles Pinckney, a delegate to the Constitutional Convention from South Carolina. The first Chief Justice of the Supreme Court, John Jay, stated that "the people who own the country ought to govern it." Most states limited suffrage to adult white males who owned property.

In spite of this general agreement, other opinions were offered. The logic behind allowing only property

> **Just the Facts**
>
> *Noncitizens were allowed to vote in some states until the early 1920s.*

owners to vote was challenged by Thomas Paine in his pamphlet *Common Sense:*

> *Here is a man who today owns a jackass, and the jackass is worth $60. Today the man is a voter and goes to the polls and deposits his votes. Tomorrow the jackass dies. The next day the man comes to vote without his jackass and cannot vote at all. Now tell me, which was the voter, the man or the jackass?*

Early Restrictions on Voting

The Constitution left the power to set voter qualifications to the individual states. Some states placed so many restrictions on the right to vote that only 5 to 6 percent of the adult population were eligible. Restrictions were based on property ownership, race, gender, religious beliefs, and payment of taxes.

Religious restrictions were the first to be removed. By 1810, they had been abolished in all states. Next, with the growth of democratic sentiment and the expansion of the western frontier, property ownership and tax-payment requirements began to disappear. Men without property were first given the right to vote in the western states. By 1850, the era of universal white male suffrage had arrived.

Women and the Right to Vote

During the era when the Constitution was written, some women argued for women's rights, but they were largely ignored. Beginning in the 1820s in Tennessee school board elections, women had the right to vote in some places in local elections. A woman first voted in a national election in 1807 in New Jersey. This was only possible because the state constitution did not explicitly prevent women from voting. The state legislature acted quickly to amend the constitution, making it clear that women were not allowed to vote.

In 1869, Susan B. Anthony and Elizabeth Cady Stanton organized the National Woman Suffrage Association, which adopted as its goal an amendment to the Constitution guaranteeing women the right to

▲ *Bearing an American flag, suffragette Mrs. Hervert Carpenter marches in support of voting rights for women. If her picture appeared in a newspaper of today, both her name and description would be different. How would they differ, and why?*

vote. They lobbied Congress and state legislatures for women's voting rights. The first suffrage bill was introduced in Congress in 1868, and a suffrage bill was introduced each year thereafter until 1893.

When Wyoming applied to join the union in 1889, it had already granted women the right to vote. At first, Congress tried to bar Wyoming's admission to the Union for that reason. Congress gave in when the Wyoming territorial legislature declared, "We will remain out of the Union 100 years rather than come in without the women."

Vigorous campaigns by women between 1910 and 1914 led seven other states, all west of the Mississippi, to give women the right to vote. Throughout the early 1900s, however, strong opposition existed to a constitutional amendment granting women the vote. On President Woodrow Wilson's inauguration day in 1913, a group of militant suffragists organized a demonstration that ended in a near riot. Other demonstrations bordered on violence, and leaders were jailed and fined. In 1917, the National Women's Party organized an around-the-clock picket line at the White House. Members of the Party were arrested, and later, when they went on hunger strikes, they were force-fed. This treatment embarrassed the Wilson administration and won some support for the movement. These efforts, along with women's contributions to the war effort during World War I, led Congress in 1919 to introduce the Nineteenth Amendment, which granted the vote to women. The amendment was ratified in 1920.

African Americans and the Right to Vote

The Fifteenth Amendment guaranteed suffrage to African American males in 1870. That amendment read as follows:

The right of citizens to vote shall not be abridged by the United States or by any state on account of race, color, or previous condition of servitude.

Yet for the next century, the gap remained wide between these words and reality.

States seemed to try to outdo each other in finding imaginative ways to prevent African Americans from voting. Certain groups of white southerners used methods ranging from mob violence to economic restrictions to keep black Americans from voting. For example, registrars—officials in charge of registering people to vote—often closed their offices when blacks tried to register. Whites threatened blacks with loss of their homes or jobs if they tried to vote. Other tactics included locating polling places far from African American neighborhoods and moving polling places at the last minute without notifying potential voters.

Legal means were also used to **disenfranchise** blacks—effectively remove their ability to vote. At times, poor whites were also disenfranchised by these means.

Just the Facts

From the end of the Civil War until the 1930s, African American voters generally supported Republicans.

ARCHITECTS

of Government

Susan B. Anthony
(1820–1906)

Raised in a Quaker household, Susan B. Anthony developed a belief in the equality of all men and women. She became a teacher and then engaged in reform activities. She first focused on discouraging the use of alcoholic beverages and then worked toward the abolition of slavery.

Anthony became a key organizer at a series of state and national women's rights conventions in the mid-1800s. Along with Elizabeth Cady Stanton, she formed the National Woman Suffrage Association in 1869. In 1872, she was arrested when she challenged the law by voting in that year's presidential election. She died four-teen years before the Nineteenth Amendment, which gave women the right to vote, was ratified.

HER WORDS

"The true Republic: men, their rights and nothing more; women, their rights and nothing less."

(Motto printed on the front
of her newspaper, Revolution)

"It may be delayed longer than we think; it may be here sooner than we expect; but the day will come when man will recognize women as his peer, not only at the fireside but in the councils of the nation."

(Speech, 1871)

DEVELOPING
CRITICAL THINKING SKILLS

1. What is the relationship between a republican form of government and rights, as indicated in the first quotation?
2. What did Anthony mean, in the second quo-tation, when she said that women would be recognized as peers by men?

▲ African American men make their first visit to the polls in this illustration entitled The First Vote created by A. R. Waud in 1867. Which constitutional amendment gave all African American males the right to vote?

Some states required voters to pass **literacy tests.** Supposedly, the practice ensured that voters could read and write and thus evaluate political information. Literacy tests required those who wished to register to vote to interpret sometimes complicated written passages. Most African Americans, many of whom had been denied an education, were functionally illiterate and so could not pass the tests. Many whites were also illiterate, and poor whites were also kept from voting in this way. Fewer whites than blacks were barred from voting, however. For one thing, local election registrars exercised their own discretion in deciding who had to take the test, how to administer it, and how to evaluate it. Furthermore, under **grandfather clauses,** people whose grandfathers had the right to vote before 1867 did not have to take literacy tests. This was, of course, before African Americans could legally vote in the South. Obviously, literacy tests were used primarily to take away African American voting rights.

◄ African Americans, led by the Reverend Martin Luther King, Jr., line the sidewalk leading to the Dallas County Courthouse in Selma, Alabama, as they wait to register to vote in 1965. Given that African Americans had gained the right to vote almost a hundred years earlier, why was a voter registration drive necessary?

The **poll tax,** a fee of several dollars, was another device used to deny African American voting rights. At the time, this tax was often a sizeable portion of a working person's monthly income. It was a burden not only on most blacks but also on immigrants, many working-class citizens, and poor whites in general.

Early Legislation The civil rights movement of the 1950s and 1960s and subsequent policy changes helped end both formal and informal barriers to African American suffrage. Led by decisions of the Supreme Court, the lower federal courts had begun to strike down many of these discriminatory practices in the 1940s and 1950s. The courts can only act as cases are brought before them, however, so this process was slow. Finally, in response to the civil rights movement led by Martin Luther King, Jr., Congress passed several civil rights laws, beginning in the late 1950s. These laws included the Civil Rights Act of 1957, which set up the United States Civil Rights Commission and gave the U.S. attorney general the power to prevent anyone from interfering with another person's right to vote in national elections. The Civil Rights Act of 1964 was a much broader measure that forbade using any registration requirement in an unfair or discriminatory manner.

As progressive as the legislation was, it was difficult to implement. Dramatic events in Selma, Alabama, in 1964 illustrated this problem. Dr. Martin Luther King, Jr., had begun a voter registration drive in that city, hoping to focus national attention on the issue of African American voting rights. Dr. King and his followers were met with abuse and violence by local whites, city and county police, and state troopers. Witnessing the violence on national television, the nation was horrified, and many demanded action. President Lyndon Johnson urged Congress to pass new and stronger legislation to ensure African American voting rights. Congress acted quickly.

The Voting Rights Act of 1965 The Voting Rights Act of 1965 finally made the Fifteenth Amendment an effective part of the Constitution. The act made it illegal to interfere with anyone's right to vote in any election held in this country, whether national, state, or local. It suspended the use of literacy tests and sent federal voter registrars into states and counties where less than 50 percent of the people eligible to vote were registered. These registrars supervised the voter registration process to ensure that African Americans were not prevented from registering. All of Mississippi, Alabama, Louisiana, and South Carolina, large parts of

FIGURE 13–1 African American Voter Registration in Eleven Southern States before and after the Voting Rights Act of 1965

This table illustrates the change in African American voter registration after passage of the Voting Rights Act of 1965. Which of these states showed the most dramatic increase in the number of African Americans registered to vote?

State	Number of Registered Voters in:		Percent Increase
	1960	1966	
Alabama	66,000	250,000	278.8%
Arkansas	73,000	115,000	57.5
Florida	183,000	303,000	65.6
Georgia	180,000	300,000	66.7
Louisiana	159,000	243,000	52.8
Mississippi	22,000	175,000	695.5
North Carolina	210,000	282,000	34.3
South Carolina	58,000	191,000	229.3
Tennessee	185,000	225,000	21.6
Texas	227,000	400,000	76.2
Virginia	100,000	205,000	105.0

SOURCE: U.S. Bureau of the Census, *Statistical Abstract of the United States 1982–83* (Washington, D.C.: Government Printing Office, 1982).

North Carolina, and some counties in five northern states were covered by registrars. The Voting Rights Act also provided that new state election laws could not go into effect without the approval of the U.S. Department of Justice. As a result of the Voting Rights Act of 1965, African American voter registration increased dramatically in several states, as shown in Figure 13–1.

The constitutionality of the Voting Rights Act was upheld in *South Carolina v. Katzenbach* (1966), and the act has been amended and extended several times. The act now covers other groups, including Hispanic Americans, Asian Americans, Native Americans, and Native Alaskans, and thus serves as a basic protection for minority voting rights. States must now provide bilingual ballots in all counties in which 5 percent or more of the people speak a language other than English.

Current Eligibility Requirements

In 1961, the Twenty-third Amendment included the voters of the District of Columbia in the presidential electorate. In 1964, the Twenty-fourth Amendment eliminated the poll tax (and any other tax) as a condition for voting in any national election. This left people under the age of twenty-one as the remaining group of citizens who could not vote. Many thought it strange that men could be sent to war when they were eighteen years old but could not vote in most states until they were twenty-one.

During World War II, Georgia had lowered its minimum voting age. By the time the Vietnam War was at its peak in the 1960s and the argument for the eighteen-year-old vote was at its strongest, Kentucky and Alaska had lowered the minimum age as well. In the 1970 elections, voters in Maine, Massachusetts, Montana, and Nebraska approved the eighteen-year-old vote. In 1971, the Twenty-sixth Amendment gave all eighteen-year-olds the right to vote.

Legal restraints on the right to vote are now largely a thing of the past for all citizens over the age of eighteen. Figure 13–2 on page 351 summarizes the major amendments, Supreme Court decisions, and laws that have brought this about. There are still, however, legal requirements for voting.

One requirement, in every state except North Dakota, is **registration,** which is the act of informing voting officials of your name, address, and other important information. In general, a person must register well in advance of an election, but in some states people are allowed to register up to and on election day. Registration provides officials with lists of eligible voters and is intended to prevent fraudulent voting.

Another state voting requirement is **residency,** which requires that a person live within a state for a specified period of time in order to qualify to vote. The length of time a person must reside in the state or district varies widely from state to state. In 1972, the Supreme Court declared lengthy residency requirements unconstitutional for voting in state and local elections and suggested that thirty days was an ample residency period. Most states have changed their residency requirements to comply with that ruling.

Another requirement is citizenship. Aliens may not vote in any public election held anywhere in the United States.

The right to vote is now widely held. Most states do, however, disqualify prison inmates, mentally ill people, convicted felons, and election-law violators from voting.

FIGURE 13–2 Extension of the Right to Vote The table below shows the major landmarks in the effort to grant all Americans the right to vote. Which of the landmarks below reduced the minimum voting age to eighteen for all elections?

Year	Action	Impact
1870	Fifteenth Amendment	Discrimination based on race outlawed
1920	Nineteenth Amendment	Discrimination based on gender outlawed
1924	Citizenship Act	All Native Americans given citizenship
1944	*Smith v. Allwright*	Supreme Court prohibits the whites-only primary
1957	Civil Rights Act of 1957	Justice Department can sue to protect voting rights in various states
1960	Civil Rights Act of 1960	Courts authorized to appoint referees to assist in voter registration procedures
1961	Twenty-third Amendment	Residents of the District of Columbia given right to vote
1964	Twenty-fourth Amendment	Poll tax in national elections outlawed
1965	Voting Rights Act of 1965	Literacy test prohibited; federal voter registrars authorized in several states
1970	Voting Rights Act Amendment of 1970	Voting age for federal elections reduced to eighteen years; maximum thirty-day residency requirement for presidential elections; state literacy test abolished
1971	Twenty-sixth Amendment	Minimum voting age reduced to eighteen in all elections
1975	Voting Rights Act Amendments of 1975	Federal voter registrars authorized in ten more states; bilingual ballots to be printed if 5 percent or more of state population does not speak English
1982	Voting Rights Act Amendment of 1982	Extended provisions of two previous voting rights act amendments; allows private parties to sue for violations

SECTION 1 REVIEW

1. What did many of the nation's founders believe about who should and should not be allowed to vote?
2. How did women gain the right to vote?
3. How have the voting rights of African Americans evolved since 1870?
4. What are the current eligibility requirements for voting?
5. **For Critical Analysis:** Although most voting restrictions have been eliminated, there are still differences in registration requirements among the various states. If these differences were eliminated, would more people vote? Why or why not?
6. **For Critical Analysis:** Carefully examine Figure 13–2 above. The time from the ratification of the Fifteenth Amendment to the passage of the Voting Rights Act Amendment of 1982 is a span of over one hundred years. Why do you think it took so long for voting rights to be extended to male and female citizens of all races? Do you think that it ever occurred to the founders that voting rights would be extended to all American citizens over eighteen years of age, regardless of race or gender? Why or why not? Support your answer with historical evidence.

More Suffrage, Less Participation

Preview Questions:

- What are the reasons some U.S. citizens do not vote?
- What types of people are most likely to vote in the United States?

Key Terms:

voter turnout, absentee ballots

William Bennett Munro, a historian, once made the following comment:

It all goes to prove what a strangely perverse creature the American citizen is. Refuse him the right to vote, and he would take up arms to wrest it from his rulers. But give this right to him freely, and he tucks it away in moth balls.

One by one, the barriers to voting have fallen away. Struggles over the extension of suffrage have given more Americans the right to vote than ever before. Yet millions of Americans, for one reason or another, do not vote. **Voter turnout** is the percentage of citizens eligible to vote who take part in the election process—the citizens who actually "turn out" to cast a ballot on election day. Compared with other countries, the level of voter turnout in the United States is very low. Only in Switzerland is the turnout lower than in the United States.

In 1988, slightly more than 50 percent of persons of voting age voted in the presidential election. In 1992, voter turnout in the presidential election increased to 55.2 percent, but it dropped to 49 percent in the 1996 election. Turnout had not been below 50 percent since 1924, when voting was still new to women.

Voter turnout is even lower at the state and local levels. It may seem as if people would vote more often in elections that directly affect them. The figures do not confirm this assumption, however. In local elections for such offices as mayor, city council, and county attorney, it is fairly common for 25 percent or less of the electorate to vote.

Voters are more likely to participate in elections for higher office, especially the presidency. That means that, on average, more people participate in congressional elections in years when the president is also being elected. The same thing is true at the state level. When the governor is also being elected, there is more participation in the election of state representatives.

Why Some People Do Not Vote

Why are there so many nonvoters when Americans have struggled so hard for the right to vote? Why, even in a presidential election, do about half of all those who could vote stay away from the polls? There are a number of possible reasons why more Americans do not vote.

Inability to Vote A certain percentage of voters simply cannot vote on any given election day. In each of the past few presidential elections, five to six million citizens could not go out and vote because they were too ill or suffered from disabilities. Another two to three

▲ *What if they held an election and nobody came? These Dallas, Texas, precinct workers wonder where the voters are as they survey their empty polling place.*

Government in Action

The Motor Voter Law and Mail-In Voting

One of the most important pieces of legislation that President Clinton signed into law after taking office in 1993 was the Voter Registration Act. Popularly known as the Motor Voter Law, this 1993 legislation requires states to provide all eligible citizens with the opportunity to register to vote when they apply for or renew a driver's license. The law also requires that states allow mail-in registration, with forms to be made available at certain public-assistance agencies. The law, which took effect on January 1, 1995, has made it easier for millions of Americans to register.

Republican Opposition to the New Law

Republicans in Congress fought to prevent the passage of the Motor Voter Law. They believed that the majority of individuals who would register to vote under the new law would vote for Democratic candidates. In particular, the mail-in registration forms provided at public-assistance agencies appeared to promote biases against Republicans. Why? Because those receiving public-assistance benefits typically vote for Democrats and for an expanded role of government in our economy.

Even when the new law was passed, Republican Governor Pete Wilson of California refused to implement it. He argued that it was unconstitutional and would cost the state $18 million. Ultimately, the federal courts forced California to put the new law into effect.

How Effective Has the Motor Voter Law Been?

Supporters of the Motor Voter Law point out that between January 1, 1995, when the law went into effect, and the 1996 elections, new registrants were signed up at a rate of about 680,000 per month. All in all, prior to the 1996 elections, about fifteen million new voters were registered.

So, did voter participation increase in the United States? The answer is no. Fewer voters went to the polls in 1996 than in 1992. Indeed, as already mentioned, voter turnout in 1996 was the lowest it had been in any U.S. presidential election since 1924.

Is Mail-In Voting a Solution?

One way of increasing voter turnout is to use mail-in ballots. Oregon has taken the lead in using mail-in voting. In many Oregon elections, there are no polling places. Registered voters receive ballots in the mail prior to an election and have three weeks to mail them back. Vote-by-mail returns are counted on election night. In a special election held in January 1996, 68 percent of the registered voters in Oregon participated—all by mail.

Mail-in voting has at least two benefits. One benefit is that the state saves money. Oregon officials estimated that the state was able to save one dollar per vote through mail-in voting. The other benefit is that fewer last-minute negative campaign ads are broadcast on TV. By the time election day nears, most people have mailed their ballots. There is little point in spending money on TV ads when most voters' choices have already been made.

THINK ABOUT IT

1. Why shouldn't all voters in all states be able to register to vote at polling places on election day?
2. What disadvantages, if any, might result from allowing mail-in voting many days before the actual election date?

million were away from their home precincts at the time of the election. **Absentee ballots** (ballots that can be mailed in prior to an election) are generally available for those who know in advance that they will be unable to vote at their polling places, but not all eligible voters take advantage of this option.

Residency and Registration Requirements

Some people do not vote because they do not meet the residency or registration requirements of their states. One problem with residency requirements is that American society is highly mobile. When a citizen moves to a new state, he or she must wait out the required period before becoming eligible to vote in that state. Absentee ballots remedy this problem somewhat. For many Americans, though, residency requirements remain an inconvenience.

Registration requirements have been relaxed over the years. In the past, people could register only at an official building and only during normal working hours. In recent years, more and more states have added mobile registrars, who open booths in shopping centers, schools, and neighborhoods that are open evenings and weekends. Since 1995, a federal law has helped to simplify the voter registration process. For a discussion of this law, see the *Case Study: Government in Action* feature on page 353. Almost half the states now allow registration by mail. Nonetheless, the very fact that Americans must register—often well in advance—is thought by some experts to be one reason for low voter turnout.

No Sense of Political Effectiveness

More and more Americans seem to believe that political participation is not worthwhile because their participation will have no influence on the course of events. They simply do not believe that their votes can have an impact on how government is run. They do not vote because they believe it "won't make any difference."

Being "Turned Off" by Political Campaigns

Some people are simply "turned off" by the negative advertising and superficial treatment of issues during campaigns. Others are dissatisfied with the candidates. A woman once interviewed by CBS News expressed it this way: "I never vote. It only encourages 'them.'"

People are also put off by the excessively long campaigns and the large number of officeholders they are expected to elect, from members of Congress to local county assessors. The problem is compounded because elections for different offices may be held at different times.

Time-Consuming Election Procedures

Some people are discouraged by long ballots and long lines at the polls. Given these inconveniences, some people do not want to bother to vote. To some, voting is too costly in time and effort, especially if they attempt to be well informed on the issues before voting.

Lack of Interest

Some people lack sufficient interest to vote. They are indifferent, or apathetic.

Satisfaction with the Status Quo

Others are not interested in voting because they approve of the way in which the nation's business is being handled. They

"I am totally turned off by political campaigns."

"All the name-calling, the back-stabbing, the fighting, and the deception."

"If I wanted to see that kind of behavior ..."

"... I would watch the daytime soaps!"

GLICK

▲ *Although the struggle to gain voting rights for all American citizens was hard fought, many eligible voters today do not take advantage of this opportunity. According to this political cartoon, what is one reason?*

Voting

In most democratic countries, people are automatically registered to vote when they reach voting age. In the United States, however, in every state but North Dakota you must register to vote before you are allowed to cast a ballot in an election. This means you must go to a local election board or temporary registration office set up at a school, a shopping center, or some other public place several weeks or even several months before the election. Check to find out the deadlines for registering to vote in your state, since specific registration laws vary considerably from state to state.

When you register, you will need to fill out a form with information such as your birth date, current address, and signature. From these registration forms, election officials draw up a list of eligible voters. Registration is used as a means of preventing voters from voting more than once.

Most states require that you meet minimum residency requirements in order to register. You must have lived in the state in which you plan to register for a certain period of time, which can vary from a few days to as long as fifty days.

On election day, as a registered voter, you will enter the polling place and check with an election official, who will look up your name to see that you are registered. In some places, the official will give you a printed ballot or punch card that lists the candidates and measures on which you will vote. Many polling places have voting machines as described in Chapter 11. When you finish voting, the machine automatically registers your vote.

Suppose that you will not be able to go to your polling place to vote. Perhaps you will be away from home for some reason. Perhaps you will have gone away to college. Or perhaps you will be moving to a new state and will not meet its residency requirements in time to vote there in the next election. In these situations, you can use an absentee ballot—a ballot that you fill out and send to your place of voting. You must contact voting officials, usually at the local board of elections, within a certain number of days before the election to get an absentee ballot.

TAKING ACTION

1. Find out about the voting requirements in your state and compare them with the requirements in two other states.
2. Write a letter to a state legislator indicating why you believe your state voting requirements are too strict, too lenient, or appropriate.

---

believe that no matter who is elected, things will continue to go well for them and for the country.

Ineligibility or Inability to Vote In any given election, some people cannot vote because they are resident aliens. Others are confined to mental institutions or prisons. Still others do not or cannot vote because of personal religious beliefs.

Indecision Some people fail to vote because they cannot make up their minds. They are undecided about which candidate to support. Sometimes this indecision does not result from lack of information. Rather, voters are confused because they received *too much* information from dozens of candidates.

Why Some People Do Vote

Having looked at why some people do not vote, let's examine what types of people do vote.

Education The more education a person has, the more likely it is that she or he is a regular voter. People who graduated from high school vote more regularly than those who finished only grade school, and college graduates vote more often than high-school graduates. Among factors affecting turnout, this one is the most important.

Age Voter turnout increases with age until age sixty-five, at which point there is a slight decline. Greater participation with age is likely due to the fact that older people are more settled, are already registered, and have had more experience with voting than when they were younger.

Marital Status Married people vote more frequently than single people.

Income The higher a person's income, the greater the likelihood that she or he will vote.

Minority Status Racial and ethnic minorities are underrepresented among the ranks of voters. In several recent elections, however, participation by minority groups has increased.

Government Employees The twenty million people who work for the government and therefore depend on government and government programs tend to vote more than other groups. These people also tend to know more about how government operates.

These factors are all cumulative. That is, the more of these traits a person has, the higher the likelihood that he or she will vote. For example, a well-educated, married, well-to-do person is far more likely to vote than a less-educated, lower-income, single, twenty-year-old citizen.

The Effect of Low Voter Turnout

There are two points of view about low voter turnout. To some people, low voter turnout endangers our representative democracy because fewer individuals are actually participating in the decisions of government. Low turnout is a sign that people are not interested in our system or that they feel alienated from

▶ Candidates work hard to attract interest and, they hope, votes. Why do you suppose some voters respond to election campaigns as this cartoon character does?

or angry with the way government is run. It may also be a sign that people are not concerned about the issues.

To others, low voter turnout is not a cause for concern. They believe the decline in voter participation is simply a sign that people are satisfied with the status quo. Nonvoters are obtaining the type of government they want without voting. Those who are not concerned about voter turnout believe that representative democracy is a reality even when many eligible voters do not take part in elections. We return to this topic in the *America at Odds* feature at the end of this chapter.

Nevertheless, the fact remains that voting is an essential component of our representative democracy. As President Grover Cleveland pointed out to the nation in his inaugural address, "Your every voter, as surely as your chief magistrate [the president], exercises a public trust."

Ideas for Reform

Voter turnout might be increased by a number of techniques. One is increased voting by mail, a subject discussed in the *Case Study: Government in Action* feature on page 353. Another possibility is allowing people to vote electronically via television or the Internet. The technology to do so is available, but it is still too costly for widespread use. In the future, though, when the cost is lower, voting electronically may become a reality. Because so many Americans spend so much time in front of their television sets and an increasing number of citizens are online, perhaps electronic elections will reverse the low voting record of this nation's citizens.

SECTION 2 REVIEW

1. What is voter turnout? How high have recent voter turnout levels been in the United States?
2. Explain five reasons for low voter turnout in the United States.
3. What are the characteristics of those persons most likely to vote?
4. **For Critical Analysis:** Why is it that the more education a person has, the more likely it is that he or she will be a regular voter?

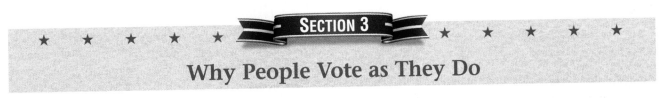

SECTION 3

Why People Vote as They Do

Preview Questions:

⭐ How does party identification affect voters' choices?
⭐ How does the image of the candidate affect voters' choices?
⭐ What is policy voting?
⭐ What socioeconomic factors affect voters' choices?

Key Terms

party identification, policy voting, green vote, socioeconomic factors, gender gap, Solid South

How do people develop attitudes about voting? What prompts some people to vote Republican and others to vote Democratic? What persuades voters to choose certain kinds of candidates? Clearly, questions about how voters make choices cannot be answered with absolute certainty. Particularly because of the technology of opinion polling, however, researchers have collected more information on voting than on any other form of political participation in the United States. The information sheds light on why people decide to vote for particular candidates. Some of their reasons are explored here.

Party Identification

Many voters have a standing allegiance to a political party, or a **party identification.** These identifications can be a general guide to voters' choices. People choose the party with which they generally agree so they do not have to concern themselves with every issue that comes along. They can generally rely on their party identification to guide them. Of course, party identification is influenced by family, age, peer groups, and other factors. Regardless of how it is developed, it is one of the most prominent and lasting predictors of how a person will vote.

◀ *This 1988 campaign button shows presidential candidate George Bush in the company of some previous Republican presidents. Why do you suppose these particular presidents were selected?*

There are indications, however, that party identification has lost some of its impact. As we saw in Chapter 10, a large number of voters now classify themselves as independents. Additionally, there has been an increase in split-ticket voting—voting for candidates of both parties in the same election.

Many contend that the increase in split-ticket voting indicates that the voters generally do not trust either party to run the government. Today's voters seem to be comfortable with divided government, in which the president is from one political party and the majority in Congress are from the other party.

Candidates' Images

All candidates, of course, try to portray an image of honesty, decisiveness, leadership, and integrity. Nevertheless, all have very different backgrounds, personalities, appearances, and levels of knowledge and experience. Voters often base their decisions more on their *impression* of candidates than on the candidates' *actual* qualifications.

Adlai Stevenson, a Democratic presidential candidate who lost to Republican Dwight D. Eisenhower in 1952 and 1956, was perceived by many people as being too intellectual and sophisticated. Republican Barry Goldwater, who lost to Lyndon Johnson in 1964, was viewed as more willing than Johnson to lead the nation

Just the Facts

In 1920, Socialist presidential candidate Eugene Debs received 920,000 votes—even though he ran his entire campaign from jail.

into war. Richard Nixon's positive image in 1968 and 1972 allowed him to win over negatively evaluated opponents. Many voters turned against President Jimmy Carter in 1980 because they felt he was weak in the face of events that confronted his administration. One of the keys to George Bush's victory in 1988 was his ability to raise his image during the campaign while the ratings of his Democratic opponent, Michael Dukakis, fell.

Policy Choices

Policy voting occurs when people vote for candidates who share their stand on the issues. If a candidate supports a strong defense program and opposes gun-control laws, and you agree and vote for her for those reasons, you have engaged in policy voting. If a candidate believes in lowering the public debt by raising taxes, and you agree and vote for him for that reason, then you have engaged in policy voting. In order to engage in true policy voting, persons must have a clear view of their own policy positions and must know where the candidates stand on important policies.

Usually, economic issues have had the greatest influence on voters' choices. When the economy is doing well, it is very difficult for a challenger, particularly at the presidential level, to defeat the incumbent—the person already in office. When the economy is doing poorly—inflation is increasing or unemployment is rising—the incumbent is at a disadvantage.

At times, particularly when the United States is involved in a war, foreign-policy issues have an important effect on voters' choices. Environmental issues have also come to the forefront in American politics. As a result, many candidates attempt to capture the **green vote**—the vote from those who favor stronger laws to protect and preserve the environment.

UNIT III: The Politics of Democracy

Photographers have documented much of the nation's political history, and their work has become an important part of the American historical record. Government textbooks, newspapers, and magazines are all filled with photographs of political events. Pictures can often help you visualize events much more vividly than the written word. They can tell a story, give important details, or express a certain mood.

Remember, however, that a photograph can also be misleading. It captures only one moment—it does not show the events that precede or follow that moment. Sometimes, a photographer poses or frames a subject, which can create a certain viewpoint, or leaves out important details. In short, a photograph may present only what the photographer wishes to record.

To analyze a picture, use these tips:

- **Determine the main subject of the photograph.** Read the caption or title if there is one.
- **Study the details of the photograph.** Look beyond the main subject to the background. Ask yourself what the details tell you about the context of the photo.
- **Try to decide what the photographer's viewpoint is.** Is he or she trying to present the subject in a positive or negative light?

BUILDING

SOCIAL STUDIES SKILLS

Analyzing a Photograph

- **Try to determine whether the photograph is an accurate depiction of the event.** Read about the event and look at other pictures to help you decide.

PRACTICING YOUR SKILLS

1. What is the subject of the photograph in this feature? Where was the photograph taken?
2. What details in the photograph give you information?
3. What generalizations about voter participation can you draw from this photograph?
4. What is the photographer's point of view?

▲ To reach a generation of people who feel disconnected from politics and vote in very small numbers, MTV successfully encouraged viewers to "Rock the Vote" in 1992. Back with their "Choose or Lose" campaign in 1996, MTV volunteers register voters on the campus of Michigan State University in East Lansing.

▶ These college-age voters mark their ballots in the 1996 presidential election. Many of these young people are voting for the first time—a distinct privilege for every American.

Some of the most heated debates in campaigns take place over social issues, such as women's rights, the death penalty, prayer in the schools, and public benefits for immigrants. Generally, presidential candidates try to avoid taking a stand on these issues. A candidate who takes a stand on such issues risks offending voters who have strong opinions on one side or the other.

Socioeconomic Factors

As mentioned earlier, many things determine how a person votes. Some are related to **socioeconomic factors,** which are all of the social and economic circumstances of a person's life. These factors include a person's age, education, income level, religion, occupation, and geographic location. Some have to do with the family and circumstances into which a person is born. Others have to do with choices the person makes throughout his or her lifetime. The difficulty in identifying socioeconomic factors in voting behavior is that voters may not be aware of these factors or the ways in which they influence political views.

Age We might expect that a person's age would determine his or her voting choices. In fact, age is not too significant a factor. Some differences can be identified,

however. For one thing, young adults tend to be more liberal than older Americans on most issues. For example, young adults tend to hold more progressive views than older persons on such issues as racial equality.

Older Americans tend to be somewhat more conservative than younger groups, but their greater conservatism may be explained simply by the fact that people retain the values they learn when they first become politically aware. Forty years later, those values may be considered relatively conservative. Also, people's attitudes are sometimes shaped by the events that occurred while they were growing up. People who grew up during an era when the Democratic Party was dominant will likely remain Democrats throughout their lives. The same holds true for those who grew up during an era of Republican Party dominance.

In elections from 1952 through 1980, voters under the age of thirty clearly favored the Democratic presidential candidates. This trend reversed itself in 1984, when voters under thirty voted heavily for Ronald Reagan. George Bush maintained that support in 1988. In 1992, however, Democrat Bill Clinton won back the young voters by 10 percentage points, a margin that expanded to 20 percentage points in 1996.

Gender Until relatively recently, no strong relationship between voter preferences and gender was seen in

Changes in How We Vote

Voting requirements and behavior have changed considerably since the beginning of the twentieth century.

THEN (ABOUT 1900)	NOW
Citizens registering to vote normally had to appear at an official building during working hours.	States must provide eligible citizens with the opportunity to register to vote when they apply for or renew a driver's license. Some states allow voters to register by mail.
Party identification was a major determinant of how people voted.	Party identification is still an important determinant of how people vote, but its importance appears to have declined.
Only male citizens over the age of twenty-one could vote.	Almost every U.S. citizen over the age of eighteen can vote.
Voter turnout regularly exceeded 60 percent.	The last time voter turnout exceeded 60 percent was in 1968. In the 1996 presidential elections, turnout was less than 50 percent.

presidential elections. Some analysts claim that a **gender gap**—a difference between the percentage of votes a candidate receives from women and the percentage of votes the candidate receives from men—became a determinant in the 1980 presidential elections. In that election, male voters favored Ronald Reagan over Jimmy Carter by 16 percentage points, whereas women gave about an equal number of votes to the two candidates.

Although the gender gap has varied in elections since 1980, it reappeared in force in 1996. In the 1996 elections, President Clinton received 54 percent of women's votes and only 43 percent of men's votes. The gender gap was particularly wide among single and divorced women, who gave Clinton 60 percent of their votes and the other presidential candidate, Bob Dole, 28 percent.

Education We saw earlier that education affects the likelihood that a person will vote. There is also a rela-

tionship between the level of a voter's education and *how* she or he votes. As a general rule, people with more formal education are more likely to vote Republican, while those with less are more likely to vote Democratic.

Occupation and Income Americans, men and women alike, spend many of their waking hours at work. Thus it is not surprising that occupation can influence voting decisions. Professionals, businesspeople, and white-collar workers tend to vote for Republican Party candidates. Factory workers, laborers, and union members are likely to vote for Democratic Party candidates. Voters in the middle- to upper-income brackets are likely to vote Republican, while those with lower incomes tend to vote Democratic. But there are no hard and fast rules. Some very poor individuals are devoted Republicans, just as some extremely wealthy persons support the Democratic Party.

Voter Apathy

Less than 50 percent of the voting-age population participated in the 1996 presidential election. Only 77 percent of those eligible actually registered to vote. Such a dismal showing had not occurred since 1924, when voting was still new to women. Some Americans are worried that voters are becoming apathetic and that this apathy, or indifference, may mean the end of democracy as we know it.

Citizens Who Don't Care May Destroy Our Democratic System, Some People Warn

Those who worry about the low degree of voter participation in our elections make a good point. Democracy depends on people electing political candidates who will represent their views. If fewer Americans participate in elections, how can we be sure that the wishes of the people are carried out? When fewer people vote, policy will be determined by powerful interest groups. The "intensely interested" will dominate politics. They will go to the polls more often than others and elect the candidates they want.

Older Americans, in fact, have done exactly that. Congress often passes legislation in their favor. Not surprisingly, two-thirds of those aged sixty-five and older vote. Only one-third of those between the ages of eighteen and twenty-five go to the polls on election day. Some young people complain that too many government benefits go to older Americans. Yet unless greater numbers of young people start voting, older citizens will continue to get Congress to do what they want.

Voter apathy is the enemy of a representative democracy.

Things May Not Be So Bad, After All, Others Respond

Some political scholars do not express the same concern about voter apathy. They argue that when fewer people vote, it simply means that people are generally satisfied with the way things are going. When citizens are employed, loan interest rates are low, the economy is doing well, and there are no threats from foreign nations, why bother to vote? Nothing that important will be decided by our representatives, anyway.

This group of scholars believes that people who stay home from the polls have about the same set of ideas as those who vote. They contend that even if 90 percent of eligible citizens voted, the election results would be the same.

In any event, this group of political scientists does not believe that only the "intensely interested" get what they want. After all, they point out, poor people tend to have statistically low voter turnout rates. Nonetheless, the government has spent huge sums of money to eliminate poverty.

When all is said and done, voting is voluntary. Whatever Americans choose to do, according to some, is acceptable, because they are exercising their right to do what they wish. Is this not the essence of a democracy? The alternative would be forcing people to vote, and that is a bad idea.

YOU DECIDE

1. In 1876, 82.4 percent of adult men voted. In 1996, 49.2 percent of Americans over the age of eighteen voted. Does this mean that the United States was a more democratic society in 1876 than it is today?
2. Should American citizens be required to vote? Why or why not?

Religion and Ethnic Background Traditionally, the majority of Protestants have voted Republican, while Catholics and Jews have tended to be Democrats. Italian, Irish, Polish, Eastern European, and Slavic voters have generally supported Democrats, while those of Scandinavian, British, and French descent have voted Republican.

African Americans voted principally for Republicans until Roosevelt's New Deal in the 1930s. Since then, they have identified with the Democratic Party. They have given the Democratic presidential candidate a clear majority of their votes in every election since 1952, although this majority began to weaken in the 1980s.

Geographic Region For more than a hundred years after the Civil War, most southerners, regardless of background or socioeconomic status, were Democrats. This strong coalition, known as the **Solid South,** has recently crumbled in the presidential elections, but the rural vote in the South still tends to be Democratic. The Democrats also draw much of their strength from large northern and eastern cities. Rural areas, except in the South, tend to be Republican. Republicans also receive strong support from the western states.

SECTION 3 REVIEW

1. What influence does party identification have on how a person votes?
2. How do candidates' images and policies affect voters' choices?
3. What socioeconomic factors can influence voters' choices?
4. **For Critical Analysis:** What are some of the advantages of having a "divided government"? Are there any disadvantages? Explain.

★ ★ ★ ★ **Chapter Summary** ★ ★ ★ ★

Section 1: The History of Voting and Current Voting Requirements

- In the United States today, all citizens who are at least eighteen years of age have the right to vote, but many restrictions on suffrage existed in the nation's past.
- The Nineteenth Amendment, ratified in 1920, granted women the right to vote.
- The Fifteenth Amendment guaranteed suffrage to African American males in 1870, but various methods were used for the next century to restrict their ability to vote. The civil rights movement, the Civil Rights Act of 1964, and the Voting Rights Act of 1965 finally made the Fifteenth Amendment an effective part of the Constitution.
- In 1971, the Twenty-sixth Amendment gave eighteen-year-olds the right to vote.

Section 2: More Suffrage, Less Participation

- Reasons for the low voter turnout in this country include inability to vote due to illness or disability, inability to meet residency and registration requirements, lack of a sense of political effectiveness, being "turned off" by political campaigns, time-consuming election procedures, lack of interest, satisfaction with the status quo, and indecision.
- A certain number of people cannot vote because they are confined to mental institutions or prisons.
- The characteristics that influence whether or not a person votes include education, age, marital status, income, minority status, and government employment.
- Some people view low voter turnout as a threat to representative democracy, while others view it as a sign that people are satisfied with the way things are.

Section 3: Why People Vote as They Do

- Party identification is an important indicator of how a person will vote, although it has become less important in recent elections.
- Voters are also influenced by the image they have of a candidate.
- Policy voting occurs when people vote for candidates who reflect their own views on the issues.
- Voters are also influenced by socioeconomic factors such as age, gender, education, occupation and income, religion and ethnic background, and geographic region.

CHAPTER 13 Review

★ REVIEW QUESTIONS ★

1. What were some of the early restrictions placed on the right to vote in the United States?
2. What does the Nineteenth Amendment prohibit? What events led to its passage?
3. What did the passage of the Fifteenth Amendment guarantee? How did many states respond to this amendment?
4. Explain some of the early tactics used to prevent African Americans from voting.
5. What events led to the passage of the Voting Rights Act of 1965?
6. What are the typical voting requirements today?
7. List and explain five possible reasons for not voting.
8. What are the characteristics that indicate that people are likely to vote?
9. What are two views about the effects of low voter turnout?
10. How do party identification, candidates' images, and policy choices affect voters' choices?
11. How do socioeconomic factors influence voters' choices?
12. What is the Motor Voter Law? Did this law increase the number of registered voters? Did the law increase voter turnout in 1996?

★ CRITICAL THINKING ★

1. Historical struggles over the extension of suffrage have given more Americans the right to vote than ever before, yet only about half of those eligible to vote do so. How would you explain this phenomenon? Do you think it is a problem? Why or why not?
2. Absentee ballots account for almost 8 percent of all votes cast in the United States in any one election year. Some commentators believe, nonetheless, that election results would not be any different if absentee ballots were not allowed. Do you agree? Why or why not?

3. Some argue that low voter turnout is not a problem if those who do not go to the polls believe the government is being run correctly. Do you agree or disagree with this statement? Give reasons for your answer.
4. Review the *Case Study: Government in Action* feature on page 353, which discusses the Motor Voter Law passed in 1993. At that time, Congress was controlled by the Democratic Party. If it is true, as Republicans claim, that the law favors the Democratic Party, was it ethical of Congress to pass the law? Or does ethics enter into this decision in any way?

★ IMPROVING YOUR SKILLS ★

Communication Skills

Using Library Resources To prepare a report for this class or any others you are taking, you will need to do research in the library. Knowing how to use library resources will help you to find the information you need.

- **The Online Library Catalog.** Most students are familiar with the Online Library Catalog, which lists all of the books and periodicals (journals and magazines) in the library. This catalog, often called OPAC (Online Public Access Catalog), offers many benefits that the old card-catalog system could not provide. You can carry out a complete library search just by using OPAC.
- **Subject Headings, Key Words, and Title Words.** In the card-catalog system items were arranged by author, title, and subject. In the OPAC system, items are arranged by author, title, and subject and under "title words" (words in titles of books and periodicals) and sometimes "key words" (words in titles and the text of books or articles).

  When you want to do research on a particular subject, try to determine what key words would call up books and articles on the subject. You must narrow your search so that you do not come up with thousands of books or articles. For example, suppose that

you wanted to research campaign financing during the 1996 elections. If you used "campaign financing" as key words, you might find thousands of articles on the topic. If, however, you keyed in "campaign financing, 1996," you would narrow your search results. Learning how to narrow the field of your inquiry is an important part of the research process.

- **An Often-Overlooked Resource: The Reference Librarian.** Many library patrons are unaware of the expertise of reference, or research, librarians. Reference librarians have a master's degree in library science. They are familiar with the basic resources in all areas of study and can guide you to sources relevant to your research topic. If you are ever uncertain about how to find information on a topic, ask the librarian for advice. If you are using a college library, ask any library employee how you can find the reference librarian. Reference librarians usually know exactly what sources you should consult for certain types of information.

Writing Think about a major topic related to politics that you would like to learn more about, such as the latest presidential campaign, the life of an important political figure, or a congressional ethics scandal. Using the resources listed in this feature, develop a list of at least four books or articles related to that topic that are in your library. Write a one-paragraph summary of what is included in each book or article. You can obtain information for the summary by reading the preface and the table of contents of a book, or the first few paragraphs of a magazine or newspaper article.

Social Studies Skills

Reading Political Cartoons

Study the cartoon on page 356 and answer the following questions.

1. Who is the man slumped in the chair supposed to represent?

2. Why do you think the man changes channels?
3. Do you think the man's attitudes are representative of the attitudes of most voters?
4. Do you think the cartoonist is sympathetic to the feelings of the man in the chair?

★ ACTIVITIES AND PROJECTS ★

1. Use library resources to gather information about voter turnout in European nations and in the United States. Prepare a report that explains the similarities and differences. Present the report to the class.
2. Interview an election official in your state to find out about registration and residency requirements. Prepare a bulletin board display that shows the procedures in your area.
3. Create a voter's brochure that could be used for new residents in your state. Include voter requirements and procedures for your state and a brief message urging citizens to vote.
4. Stage a debate on one of these statements:
   a. The United States should enact a compulsory voting law.
   b. No registration or residency requirements should be placed on voting.

What If . . .

Voting Were Compulsory?

Some nations require every eligible voter to vote. Eligible voters who do not vote are fined and may even go to jail. How would compulsory voting affect the outcome of elections in the United States?

Campaign Financing

It has always cost money to conduct a political campaign, and there is nothing new about the connection between money and politics. But the sums raised and spent during the 1996 campaigns, about $2 billion, seemed so staggering that a cry for campaign-financing reform was heard throughout the nation. The following articles discuss campaign-financing practices and why Americans want reform.

U.S. Media Reports

The two following articles were taken from U.S. media sources.

The Dirtiest Election Ever

By Fred Wertheimer, President, Democracy 21
The Washington Post, National Weekly Edition

In 25 years of following political money, I have seen campaign finance abuses, and I have seen campaign finance abuses. And I say without hesitation that this election will go down as the worst in modern times, if not in our history. In important ways, the abuses involving hundreds of millions of dollars are worse even than the illegal contributions gathered by Richard Nixon's men during the Watergate era.

This year we've seen a record-shattering $200 million in contributions made outside the federal law, mostly from business interests. We've seen huge amounts of foreign money raised by the elusive Democratic operative John Huang from an Indonesian conglomerate and others, hundreds of six-figure checks from corporation and business executives to the Democrats and Republicans, a first-ever $20-million-plus advertising blitz funded by union dues to win back Democratic control of Congress, Senator Dole's

finance vice chairman convicted for laundering contributions, President Clinton personally involved in a $35 million ad campaign circumventing the campaign finance laws, Philip Morris contributing more than $3 million primarily to Republicans to help protect its tobacco interests, and even the spectacle of Vice President Gore participating in a fundraiser at a Buddhist temple.

When you add it all up—the illegality, the cheating, the evasion, as well as the arrogance and cynicism—what we have is a collapse of the system on a scale we simply haven't seen before.

Source: *The Washington Post,* National Weekly Edition, November 11–17, 1996 (pp. 29–30). © 1996 *The Washington Post.*

Watergate Campaign-Finance Reforms Collapse as Money Trucks Drive through the Loopholes

By David Rogers and Phil Kuntz
Wall Street Journal

The Democratic National Committee's attempt this week to avoid filing an official pre-election spending report is just the latest example of how both parties and their interest-group allies have gone to great lengths to evade the laws now on the books.

While most attention has focused on the Democrats and foreign donations to President Clinton's campaign, U.S. corporations and unions are flooding the political market with unprecedented sums. Both Mr. Clinton and Robert Dole have shifted millions of dollars about in order to circumvent spending limits, and the Federal Election Commission—its budget cut by Congress—has been left to stand by helplessly. . . .

After decades in public life, both Mr. Dole and President Clinton are now calling for reform. But without a stronger enforcement agency, new rules may only lead to new loopholes. And the political system—paralyzed by self-preservation and limited by the First Amendment—has failed in recent years to follow through. Campaign-finance-overhaul bills were defeated in both houses earlier this year, just as they were in the past several Congresses.

A Foreign Media Source

Sometimes, we can get a different "slant" on a problem by reading media reports generated in other countries. The following excerpt is from *The Economist*, a magazine published in London. As you read the excerpt, compare the writer's approach with those in the articles you just read.

Politicians for Rent

The Economist

Last year in the United States, at least $660 million was spent by candidates and parties in search of seats in the House or the Senate . . . . It has been calculated that, if the average Senate campaign now costs $4.5 million, each senator must raise at least $14,000 every week of his or her six-year term to pay for it.

Such costs are exceptional: The only other democracy in which candidates spend so much seeking office is Japan. . . . [M]ost Americans are not flattered to have money of this order spent on getting their attention. On the contrary, they feel the present campaign-spending system is out of control. Politicians, many think, are spending most of their working hours raising funds for the next campaign; governing America is done in their spare time. The huge sums needed to run for office also raise the entry barrier into politics and confer unfair advantages on incumbents. . . .

A basic question, which sometimes goes unasked, is why so much money is needed in American campaigns. The one-word answer is television. In Britain, parties may not buy television time and most political advertising goes on relatively cheap billboards. In America, with its television-hungry audience and huge electoral districts, candidates take to the airwaves to broadcast their message.

Television is not the only culprit. America is unusual in that its political parties play a relatively small role in financing candidates' campaigns. In European countries, party machines—often subsidized by the taxpayer—bear much of the cost of an election. In America, candidates have to raise most of the money themselves.

The explosion of costs also comes from the fees of political consultants, now considered essential to campaigns, and from fundraising, a relentlessly rising spiral of lavishing money in order to raise more. What does the money go on? Broadcast time. Thirty-second attack ads must be answered by more thirty-second attack ads, whatever the cost. This suggests that candidates are not so much corrupt, as trapped: they dare not be outspent.

Conclusion

Most Americans agree that campaign-financing reform is needed. Getting reform legislation passed, however, will not be easy. Congress has considered many reform measures, yet campaign-financing laws remain unchanged. Currently, President Clinton and congressional leaders claim that they are committed to enacting campaign-financing reforms. Whether they do so remains to be seen.

Analysis Questions

1. In the excerpt from the *Wall Street Journal*, the authors stated that the political system is "paralyzed by self-preservation and limited by the First Amendment." Analyze this statement.
2. Do you agree with the author of the article from *The Economist* that U.S. candidates for political office are "not so much corrupt, as trapped"? Give reasons for your answer.
3. Why is television advertising so important in American political campaigns? Is there any way a candidate can realistically compete for political office without advertising his or her position on TV?
4. Does *The Economist* view campaign financing differently than the U.S. media do? Explain.

The Federal Legislative Branch

Elected to serve the interests of Americans across the fifty states, senators and representatives come here, to the U.S. Capitol Building in Washington, D.C., to debate and legislate.

"It is the duty of the President to propose and it is the privilege of the Congress to dispose."

Franklin D. Roosevelt
(1882–1945)

Thirty-second President of the United States

INTRODUCTION

As a student, you are certainly familiar with the concept of having someone else propose that you do something. Your teachers propose that you read certain pages in your textbook as homework, that you write specific essays, and that you take final exams. In your student life, though, it is not your privilege to "dispose." If you do not do what your teachers propose, your grades will suffer. That is not necessarily the case with the U.S. Congress and the president, as indicated in Franklin Roosevelt's statement in the keynote quotation above. The president may propose new laws, but it is up to Congress to decide whether to pass them.

In this chapter, you will read about the creation and development of the U.S. Congress. You will also learn about the men and women who make up Congress and the structure and organization of its two chambers.

◄ Joint sessions of Congress, as shown here, are held on special occasions, including the evening of the president's annual State of the Union address.

The Creation and Evolution of Congress

Preview Questions:

- ✪ What is a bicameral legislature? Why did the founders create a bicameral legislature in this country?
- ✪ How is the total number of seats in the House of Representatives apportioned? How is the House reapportioned every ten years?
- ✪ What are congressional districts? What methods have been used over the years to draw them?

Key Terms:

legislative power, bicameral legislature, term, convening, sessions, recesses, special sessions, apportioned, census, reapportionment, congressional district, single-member districts, at large, gerrymandering

The founders of the American republic believed that a central legislature should hold most of the power exercised by a national government. Their experience with King George III of England and his royal governors had left them with a deep suspicion of strong executive authority.

For this reason, the founders made Congress the central institution of American government and gave it more powers than any other branch. As James Madison said, Congress is "the first branch of the government." The founders granted Congress the most critical function of a democracy—translating the public will into public policy. They devoted the first article of the Constitution to Congress. That article reads:

All legislative powers herein granted shall be vested in a Congress of the United States, which shall consist of a Senate and House of Representatives.

Congress is thus charged under the Constitution with the **legislative power**—the power to make laws.

Congress is often considered to be the branch of government that is closest to the people. That is because members of Congress are elected directly by the people. In contrast, the president and vice presi-

▶ *President Franklin Roosevelt delivers a State of the Union address before a joint session of Congress. Why is it important for a president to have the support of Congress?*

dent are elected through the electoral college, and Supreme Court members are appointed by the president with the approval of the Senate. Thus, among this nation's leaders, members of Congress are most directly accountable to its citizens. Because of this, Congress is sometimes called "the voice of the people."

Bicameral Legislature

The founders of this nation did not agree about the organization of Congress. In fact, one of the most serious conflicts at the Constitutional Convention was a long and heated debate between the large and small states over congressional representation. After a month of struggle, the delegates finally adopted the Great Compromise, which you read about in Chapter 2.

By a narrow margin, the Convention voted for a **bicameral legislature,** a Congress of two chambers. The chambers were to be called the Senate and the House of Representatives. Each American state, large or small, would be represented by two senators, so all states would have equal power in the Senate. In the House, however, the number of representatives from each state would be determined by the size of each state's population. The larger a state's population, the more representatives it would have. The Constitution requires that each state, no matter how small, have at least one representative.

Besides providing the needed compromise, the bicameral legislature had another advantage. With this structure, the two chambers could serve as checks on each other's power and activity. The House was to represent the people as a whole—the will of the majority—since its members would be distributed according to population. Because the House was to be elected directly by the people, it was to be the "common person's" chamber. The Senate was to represent the states, and the interests of the small states would be protected because they would have the same number of representatives as the larger states. The Senate, originally to be chosen by the elected representatives sitting in state legislatures, was to protect the elite interests against the tendencies of the House to protect the masses. (This was similar to the division between the House of Commons and the House of Lords in the English Parliament, with which the founders were familiar.) The Senate was to be a safeguard against the passage of "emotional" legislation by the House. As George Washington was said to have remarked, "We shall pour House legislation into the Senatorial saucer to cool it."

Congressional Meetings

Each Congress lasts for a meeting period, or a **term,** of two years. The terms are numbered consecutively, with the first term dating back to March 4, 1789. The date for the **convening,** or formal opening, of each term was reset by the Twentieth Amendment in 1993, and the terms now begin on January 3 of odd-numbered years unless Congress sets another date.

Each term of Congress is divided into two regular **sessions,** or meetings—one for each year. Until about 1940, Congress remained in session for only four or five months, but the complicated legislation and increased demand for services from the public in recent years have forced Congress to remain in session through most of each year. Both chambers, however, schedule short **recesses,** or breaks, for holidays and vacations.

Congress remains in session until its members vote to adjourn. Neither chamber may adjourn a session without the consent of the other. Only the president may call Congress to meet during a scheduled recess. Such meetings are called **special sessions,** and only twenty-six of them have ever been held. The fact that Congress now meets nearly year-round makes the need for a special session unlikely.

Apportionment of the House of Representatives

The Constitution provides that the total number of House seats shall be **apportioned,** or distributed, among the states on the basis of population. Because representation in the House is based on population, the more people a state has, the more representatives it sends to the House. California, for example, with an estimated population of over 34 million in 2000, has fifty-two representatives. Georgia, with a population of

The Structure of the Russian Legislature

Russia, like the United States, has a bicameral legislature. The lower chamber is the State Duma. The upper chamber is the Federation Council.

The State Duma The State Duma is the more powerful of the two chambers, and it bears most of the responsibility for passing laws. The Duma has 450 seats. Half of these seats are divided proportionately among members of political parties that received at least 5 percent of the vote. The other half go to representatives, or deputies, who are elected in contests among candidates in Russia's 225 local voting districts—similar to the way in which members of the U.S. Congress are elected.

The Federation Council The upper chamber of Russia's legislature, the Federation Council, is the weaker of the two chambers but still has considerable authority. For example, the council has the authority to schedule presidential elections, to impeach the president, and to approve the appointment of Supreme Court judges. Most laws passed by the Duma do not need to be approved by the council before being sent to the president. Some laws must be approved by both chambers, however, such as laws concerning international treaties, declarations of war and peace, taxes and the budget, and certain financial matters.

THINKING GLOBALLY

In what ways does the Russian legislature differ from the U.S. Congress?

over 6.5 million, has eleven representatives. In contrast, Wyoming, with an estimated population of 522,000 in 2000, has one representative. Each state is guaranteed at least one seat, no matter what its population. Today, seven states have only one representative. In addition, the District of Columbia, American Samoa, Guam, and the American Virgin Islands each send nonvoting delegates to the House. Puerto Rico, a self-governing possession of the United States, is represented by a nonvoting resident commissioner.

If representation in the House is to be based on population, it is necessary to know what the population is. The Constitution directs Congress to take a **census,** or official count of the population, every ten years. This was originally meant to allow Congress to increase the number of House seats according to changes in the population. For a time, the number of representatives in the House grew with each census. By 1910, the number had reached 435.

In the census year of 1920, as the population swelled, House leaders and many Americans expressed concern about the size of the House. Many thought the House was growing too big for effective action. When the official census figures were revealed in 1921, the House waited for eight years before taking any action concerning its membership.

In 1929, President Herbert Hoover called a special session of Congress to address the situation and urged Congress to provide apportionment guidelines for the upcoming 1930 census. As a result, Congress passed the Reapportionment Act of 1929. The act provided that the number of representatives would remain fixed at 435. It also established a permanent system for **reapportionment,** or redistribution, of the 435 House seats following each census. The law provides the following:

1. The size of the House remains stable at 435.
2. After each census, the Census Bureau determines the number of seats each state should receive according to the census results.
3. The Census Bureau presents a plan to the president that shows the distribution of seats.
4. The president submits this information in a message to Congress. If Congress does not voice its opposition within sixty days, the plan goes into effect.

Thus, shifts in the U.S. population greatly affect the distribution of House seats. In the last few decades, increasing numbers of Americans have moved from northeastern and midwestern states to states in the South and the West. The map in Figure 14–1 below illustrates this trend by showing the changes made in each state's House seats after the last census.

◀ *Every ten years, the Census Bureau takes an official count of the U.S. population using data processing equipment such as this. How does the census affect congressional representation?*

Congressional Districting

Senators are elected to represent all of the people in the state. In contrast, representatives are elected by the voters of a particular area known as a **congressional district.** The 435 members of the House are chosen by the voters in 435 separate congressional districts across the country. If a state's population allows it to have only one representative, such as in Wyoming and Vermont, the entire

FIGURE 14–1 Reapportionment of House Seats Following the 1990 Census The map below shows the apportionment of House seats for each state based on the population figures from the 1990 census. Based on this map, what region of the country lost the most seats?

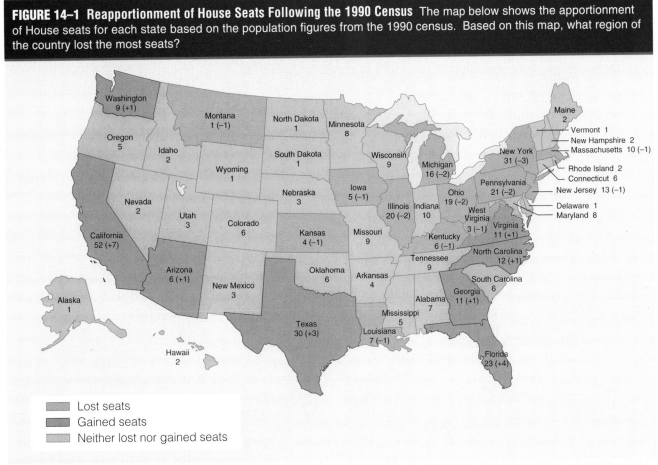

SOURCE: United States Department of Commerce, Bureau of the Census.

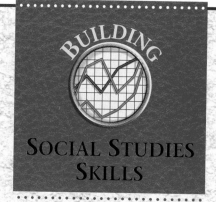

A good source for finding information, including political information, is a map. To effectively gather information from a map, follow these guidelines:

1. **Study the map's title.** The title gives such information as the subject and purpose of the map, and the area that the map represents.
2. **Study the map legend, or key.** The legend, or key, contains information that explains special symbols used on the map. Before trying to interpret the map, study the legend to make sure that you know what all the colors, shadings, and lines represent.
3. **Check the map's directions.** Some maps have a compass or direction indicator. If not, it is always assumed that north is at the top of the map.

Using a Political Map

4. **Study the distance scales.** Maps may present distance scales in miles or kilometers. A scale is used to determine the distance between two points on the map.

Many types of special-purpose maps are used to study government and politics. These maps relate specific data to a geographic area.

PRACTICING YOUR SKILLS

Study the map on page 377 and answer the following questions:

1. How many states lost population between 1980 and 1990? What was the average population loss in these states?
2. What was the average population gain in the states that gained population?
3. Is it possible to tell from this map what the population size is in any state?

---

state is one congressional district. Florida, in contrast, has twenty-three representatives and hence twenty-three congressional districts. Texas has thirty congressional districts and thirty representatives. The boundaries of the congressional districts are drawn by state legislatures.

Congressional districts have not always been used by all the states. The Constitution makes no provisions for congressional districts. In the early 1800s, each state was given the right to decide whether or not to have districts at all. Most states set up **single-member districts.** Voters in each of these districts elected one of the state's representatives. In states that chose not to have districts, representatives were chosen **at large,** from the state as a whole. In these states, voters could cast votes for all of that state's representatives. If one party's candidate won a plurality of votes, all of a state's representatives in Congress would be from that party.

Over the years, many people became dissatisfied with this system. Critics claimed that it was unfair for a political party whose candidates won the congressional election by a slight margin to win all of the House seats for the state. In 1842, Congress responded by passing an act that required all states to send representatives to Congress from single-member districts. The act gave each state legislature the responsibility of drawing its own district lines. It required, however, that each district have adjoining boundaries. Later revisions of the law required that districts contain, as nearly as possible, equal numbers of people. This requirement is important because it means each House

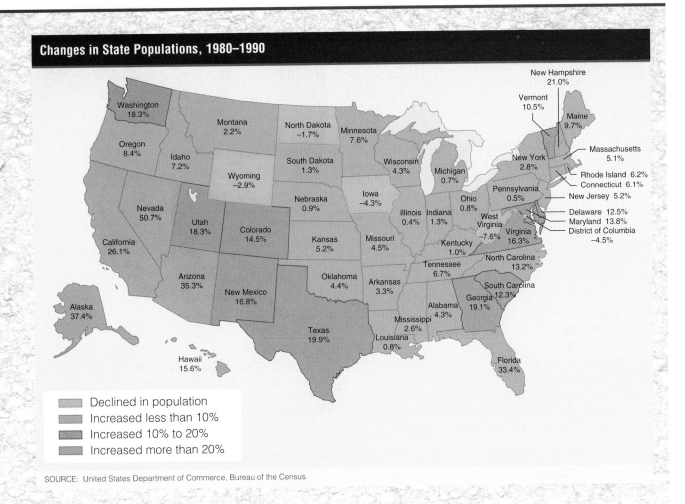

Changes in State Populations, 1980–1990

New Hampshire 21.0%
Vermont 10.5%
Maine 9.7%
Washington 18.3%
Montana 2.2%
North Dakota −1.7%
Minnesota 7.6%
Massachusetts 5.1%
New York 2.8%
Oregon 8.4%
Idaho 7.2%
Wisconsin 4.3%
Michigan 0.7%
Rhode Island 6.2%
Connecticut 6.1%
Wyoming −2.9%
South Dakota 1.3%
Pennsylvania 0.5%
New Jersey 5.2%
Nevada 50.7%
Utah 18.3%
Colorado 14.5%
Nebraska 0.9%
Iowa −4.3%
Ohio 0.8%
Illinois 0.4%
Indiana 1.3%
West Virginia −7.6%
Delaware 12.5%
Maryland 13.8%
District of Columbia −4.5%
California 26.1%
Kansas 5.2%
Missouri 4.5%
Kentucky 1.0%
Virginia 16.3%
North Carolina 13.2%
Arizona 35.3%
New Mexico 16.8%
Oklahoma 4.4%
Arkansas 3.3%
Tennessee 6.7%
South Carolina 12.3%
Georgia 19.1%
Alaska 37.4%
Alabama 4.3%
Mississippi 2.6%
Texas 19.9%
Louisiana 0.8%
Hawaii 15.6%
Florida 33.4%

Declined in population
Increased less than 10%
Increased 10% to 20%
Increased more than 20%

SOURCE: United States Department of Commerce, Bureau of the Census.

member represents approximately the same number of people, so the people are equally represented in the House. Districts were also required to be of compact territory, which meant that states could not draw boundaries that spread one district into parts over the state.

The requirements of the 1842 act were largely ignored by states. Many state legislatures continued to seek advantages for their own political parties. They did so in two ways, as discussed below.

Congressional Districts of Unequal Population Legislatures sometimes attempted to retain power by creating districts with unequal populations. For example, at one point during the 1960s, in many states the largest district had twice the population of the smallest dis-

trict. Because all districts have equal representation, a person's vote in the largest congressional district had only half the value of a person's vote in the smallest district.

The Supreme Court finally addressed this issue. In *Baker v. Carr* (1962), the Court ruled that the Tennessee state legislature's reapportionment scheme violated the constitutional requirement of equal protection under the law. In 1964, it ruled in *Wesberry v. Sanders* that congressional districts must have equal populations. This principle has come to be known as the "one person–one vote" rule. That is, one person's vote has to count as much as another's vote. The long-standing tendency of state legislatures to apportion in ways that overrepresented rural voters began to change.

Gerrymandering Since the early 1800s, the practice of drawing district boundaries to benefit a certain party, group, or candidate has been called **gerrymandering.** Gerrymandering often results in very oddly shaped election districts. This practice took its name from Elbridge Gerry, governor of Massachusetts. In 1812, the Massachusetts state legislature carved up Essex County in a way that favored Gerry's party. A cartoonist, observing a map that detailed the strange shape of the district, penciled in a head, wings, and claws and commented that the map now resembled a salamander. A news editor replied, "Better say a *gerrymander!*"

Two different methods of gerrymandering have been used. One way, called "packing" by politicians, involves drawing congressional district boundaries so that districts include as many of the political party's voters as possible. The other method, called "cracking," involves drawing the boundaries so that the opponent's strength is divided among two or more districts. In this way, the opponent has a more difficult time getting enough votes to win an election.

Because gerrymandering has not been specifically outlawed, it is still used today, although much less frequently. The "compact and contiguous" requirements, combined with the one person–one vote ruling, usually have prevented the worst forms of gerrymandering.

Racial Gerrymandering In the early 1990s, the U.S. Department of Justice required all of the states to draw the boundaries of congressional districts in a special way. Specifically, the districts were to be drawn to maximize the voting power of minority groups. The result was often bizarre. North Carolina's newly drawn Twelfth Congressional District was 165 miles long. It was a narrow strip that followed Interstate 85. Georgia's new Eleventh District stretched from Atlanta to the Atlantic Ocean, splitting eight counties and five municipalities.

Many of these districts were challenged in court. In a series of cases, the United States Supreme Court sided with the opponents of what came to be called "racial gerrymandering." For example, in 1995, the Court attacked the concept of race-based redistricting by declaring that Georgia's Eleventh District was unconstitutional. The Court stated that assigning voters on the basis of race was offensive and demeaning to racial minorities. In two cases decided in 1996, the Supreme Court ruled that the Twelfth District of

▲ In 1812, Elbridge Gerry redrew the boundaries of this Massachusetts district to ensure the election of a Republican. A cartoonist added a head, wings, and claws to the drawing of the new district, commenting that it resembled a salamander. *What term is still used to describe the drawing of electoral boundaries to the advantage of one political party?*

North Carolina and three Texas districts were also unconstitutional for this reason.

SECTION 1 REVIEW

1. With what basic governmental power is Congress charged?
2. Why did the founders create a bicameral legislature?
3. What is apportionment? What was the significance of the Reapportionment Act of 1929?
4. How have congressional districts been determined in the past? How are they determined today?
5. **For Critical Analysis:** Does the fact that a census is only taken every ten years cause problems of unfair representation for those states whose populations are growing rapidly? Explain.

House and Senate Terms and Qualifications

Preview Questions:

- 🌐 What are the terms of office for members of the House of Representatives?
- 🌐 What are the terms of office and qualifications for members of the Senate?
- 🌐 Why are incumbents so successful in getting reelected?

Key Terms:

franking privilege, casework, pork barrel

There are several differences between the two chambers of the U.S. Congress. (See Figure 14–2 on page 380.) Here we look at some of those differences, including those relating to terms of office and qualifications.

The House of Representatives

With its 435 members, the House of Representatives is over four times larger than the Senate. Still, it is referred to as the lower chamber of Congress.

Term of Office Members of the House of Representatives are elected for two-year terms. The framers believed that such a short term of office would make representatives more responsive to the people. Many people still believe this. Others argue that a two-year term is impractical because representatives spend too much time during the second year campaigning for the next election. A constitutional amendment to lengthen the term for House membership has been proposed several times but has never been successful.

Congressional elections are held in November of even-numbered years, and representatives begin their terms of office on January 3 following the November election. This means that all 435 members must run for reelection at the same time, and the House begins anew following each election.

Despite the short terms of office, there is still a great deal of continuity among members of the House. In the past decade, well over 90 percent of all House incumbents have been reelected. In 1996, 93.4 percent of the incumbents who ran were reelected. Some representatives have been reelected over a dozen times. There is no limit on the number of terms a representative may be reelected to the same office. Many people believe, however, that the number

> **Just the Facts**
>
> *The dome of the Capitol is topped by a bronze statue representing freedom. The statue was installed on December 2, 1863.*

◄ *Feeling that congressional members had too much of a built-in advantage when it came time for reelection, many citizens joined the wave of anti-incumbent sentiment that swept the nation in the early 1990s. Based on the cartoon, what protects incumbents from political challengers?*

of terms a representative can serve should be limited. (This issue is discussed further in the *America at Odds* feature on page 395.)

Qualifications The Constitution sets forth the qualifications for election to the House of Representatives. Members of the House must be at least twenty-five years of age, citizens of the United States for at least seven years prior to the election, and legal residents of the state from which they are elected.

Although not required to do so by the Constitution, representatives have traditionally lived in the districts they represent. This practice is rooted in the belief that representatives should be familiar with the needs of the people they represent in Congress.

The Constitution also gives the House the power to judge the qualifications of its members and to refuse a seat to an elected member. From 1823 to 1967, the House refused to recognize nine members as legitimate lawmakers and denied them their seats. This power, however, was limited by the Supreme Court in 1969 in *Powell v. McCormack.* In that decision, the Court ruled that Congress cannot exclude any member-elect who meets the Constitution's requirements relating to age, citizenship, and residence.

The Senate

The Senate is known as the upper chamber of Congress. The Constitution calls for each state to have two senators, regardless of the state's size or population. Article V of the Constitution specifies that "no state without its consent shall be deprived of its equal suffrage in the Senate." This provision guarantees that the states' equal representation in the Senate cannot be changed by amendment. Thus, as long as the original Constitution is in effect, each state will always have two senators to represent it.

Before the adoption of the Seventeenth Amendment in 1913, senators were chosen by state legislatures. Since that time, senators have been chosen by the people at large in the November general elections of even-numbered years.

Term of Office Senators are elected for six-year terms. The terms are staggered, so that the terms of one-third of the senators end every two years. In addition, the two senators from each state never run for election in the same year unless a vacancy occurs because of death, retirement, or resignation. If such a vacancy does occur, the governor of the state may call a special election to choose a replacement, or the state legislature may allow the governor to appoint a replacement until an election is held.

The founders designed the Senate as they did to give stability to the legislative branch. Because Senate seats do not all come up for election at the same time, the Senate is considered a "continuous body." Because

FIGURE 14–2 Differences between the House and the Senate* This table lists the differences between the United States House of Representatives and the Senate. In which of these two chambers of Congress would most politicians prefer to serve? Why?

House	Senate
Members chosen from local districts	Members chosen from entire state
Two-year term	Six-year term
Always elected by voters	Originally (until 1913) elected by state legislatures
May impeach (indict) federal officials	May convict federal officials of impeachable offenses
Larger (435 voting members)	Smaller (100 members)
More formal rules	Fewer rules and restrictions
Debate limited	Debate extended
Floor action controlled	Unanimous consent rules
Less prestige and individual notice	More prestige and media attention
Originates bills for raising revenues	Power of "advice and consent" on presidential appointments and treaties
Local or narrow leadership	National leadership

*Some of these differences, such as term of office, are provided for in the Constitution. Others, such as debate rules, are not.

Government in Action

Getting the Best Offices in Congress

What happens every two years in Washington, D.C., that can be compared to the National Football League's college draft? The answer is room draw—the competition for offices on Capitol Hill. Among members of the House of Representatives, the newly elected members have last pick. They fight over cramped offices that are sometimes about the size of large broom closets. In general, selection is based on seniority—who has been in office longer. Members who have been in office the same amount of time use a lottery system. (The Senate also has a room draw, but because it has fewer members, the process is much less formal.)

Before the first day of room draw, scouts—that is, office managers for the various representatives—develop reports that include the probabilities of obtaining particular offices. During the first day of room draw, office managers use their cellular phones frequently to confer with their bosses. Each representative has twenty minutes to decide (measured to the second with a digital clock). Some legislators end up running at the last minute to make an office inspection within that twenty-minute period.

Some etiquette is involved in this process. For example, it is considered bad form to survey a retiring legislator's office before election day. If a member of Congress dies in office, though, according to one observer, "it's vulture city, with everyone looking over the office. It gets a little morbid when people come by to look."

THINK ABOUT IT
....

1. If you were a member of Congress, would you be worried about what office you had? Why or why not?
2. Why is the Senate procedure for allocating offices much less formal than that of the House?

senators serve six-year terms, they have more time than representatives to understand and deal with issues before they must think about the next election. The six-year term is supposed to make senators less subject to the pressures of public opinion and the pleas of special interests. The longer term in office gives senators more time to act as national leaders before facing the electorate again.

Qualifications The qualifications senators must meet are somewhat different from those for representatives. Members of the Senate must be at least thirty years of age, citizens of the United States for at least nine years, and legal residents of the states from which they are elected. The Constitution allows the Senate to judge the qualifications of its members and to exclude a member-elect by a majority vote.

The Power of Incumbency

There are several possible explanations for the repeated successes of incumbents. One explanation, although the least likely one, is that voters know how their representatives vote on important policy issues, agree with their positions, and want to send them back to Washington. The more likely source of incumbents' success, however, is visibility. Incumbents work very hard at making themselves known throughout their districts so that, in the voting booth, voters will at least recognize their names on the ballot. Incumbents frequently travel back to their home districts (on the average members visit their home districts about thirty-five times a year). They also enjoy the **franking privilege,** which is a free mail service designed to keep voters informed about current issues and the representative's voting record. Instead of postage, they use their printed signatures, called franks, on official correspondence.

Additionally, incumbents win friends and votes by servicing "the folks back home." They do this in two ways. One is **casework,** which involves helping individual constituents cut through bureaucratic red tape to get what they want. The other is **pork barrel,** which involves bringing federal funds to their districts in the form of federal projects, contracts, or grants available to cities, colleges, businesses, and other organizations.

Just the Facts

The terms pork *and* pork barrel *were not used to describe legislation until the 1880s.*

Another explanation for an incumbent's success is that a current member of the House (or Senate) is usually in a better position to raise campaign funds than an opponent. Incumbent representatives raise, on average, six times more for their reelection campaigns than do challengers.

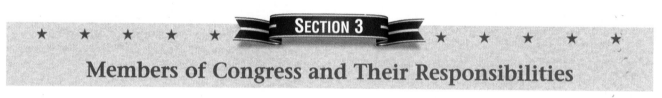

SECTION 2 REVIEW

1. What is the term of office for representatives? For senators?
2. What are the constitutional requirements for election to the House of Representatives? For election to the Senate?
3. What are two possible reasons why incumbents are frequently reelected?
4. **For Critical Analysis:** Do you believe that the constitutional requirements to serve as a representative or a senator should be changed? Why or why not?

SECTION 3

Members of Congress and Their Responsibilities

Preview Questions:

- What are the general characteristics of members of Congress?
- Who sets the salary for members of Congress?
- What are some of the special benefits and privileges members of Congress receive?
- What roles does a member of Congress play?
- How does the Constitution allow the House and Senate to judge the conduct of their members?

Key Terms:

congressional immunity, censure, expulsion, reprimand

Although members of Congress act as the people's representatives, by no stretch of the imagination are they a representative cross section of the American people. The process of recruiting, nominating, and selecting congressional candidates ensures that only certain types of individuals serve in Congress.

Profile of Members

If we look at a collective portrait of the members of Congress, we can quickly see that they are not a typical collection of Americans. Members tend to have very high levels of income, education, and occupational status compared with the rest of the population. Nearly all have college degrees, and most have graduate or professional degrees. Law is the dominant occupation. Other "elite" occupations, such as business and banking, are also well represented.

An overwhelming number of those elected to Congress have been white, Protestant males of Western European descent. A profile of the 105th Congress

FIGURE 14–3 Profile of the 105th Congress This table looks at the make-up of the 105th Congress in terms of ethnicity, gender, and educational background as compared with the general population. What conclusions can you draw about the differences between the 105th Congress and the general population from this table?

Characteristic	House	Senate	U.S. Population 1990
Age (Median)	50.9	58.4	33.0
Male	89.0%	91.0%	49.1%
Female	11.0%	9.0%	51.9%
Minority	13.5%	4.0%	33.0%
College Educated	98.0%	99.0%	21.4%
Not College Educated	2.0%	1.0%	78.6%

in terms of gender and ethnic background, as well as other features, appears in Figure 14–3 above.

Compensation and Benefits

Congress sets its own pay and compensation. The members of both houses are now paid an annual salary of $136,700. The Speaker of the House receives the same pay as the vice president, $175,400 a year. The Senate's president *pro tempore* and the majority and minority leaders in each chamber earn $151,800 a year. (We will discuss these leadership positions in Section 4 of this chapter.)

The salaries of members of Congress are high compared with the average American family income of about $45,000, but they are low compared with the salaries of people in the upper ranks of business, law, and other professions. The presidents of some large corporations make millions of dollars per year, as do some professional athletes and entertainers. The annual salaries of many lawyers and doctors amount to hundreds of thousands of dollars. Congressional salaries are even low compared with the salaries of top officials of the interest groups that lobby Congress.

In addition to their salaries, members of Congress enjoy a number of benefits and special privileges. Each member is allowed a tax deduction to help keep up two residences, one in Washington and the other at home. Members receive allowances to pay office staff and to pay for trips home, telephone expenses, telegrams, newsletters, and so on.

Each member pays a small amount for generous life and health insurance policies. A medical staff offers free outpatient care at the Capitol, and military hospitals provide full care at low rates. Also, each member has a generous pension plan. Other benefits include free parking, subsidized meals in the Senate and House dining rooms, free recreational facilities, plants for the office, and research help from the Library of Congress. Members of Congress also are granted franking privileges, as mentioned earlier.

Privileges of Members

Members of Congress have certain special constitutional privileges to protect them as they carry out their legislative duties. Article I, Section 6, commands that senators and representatives

shall in all Cases, except Treason, Felony and Breach of the Peace, be privileged from Arrest during their Attendance at the Session of their respective Houses, and in going to, and returning from the same.

Originally, this clause was designed to protect the legislative branch against interference from the executive branch. Before the colonies became independent, British officials often harassed colonial legislators and kept them from performing their duties. American leaders wanted to prevent such occurrences. The provision applies to arrests in civil cases but does not protect members from criminal arrests. It has been of little importance in our national history.

A more important privilege set out in the Constitution is the speech and debate clause. This clause guarantees freedom of speech to members while they are conducting congressional business. This form of

> **Just the Facts**
>
> The franking privilege (free use of the U.S. Postal Service) for senators and representatives costs American taxpayers several hundred million dollars a year.

PARTICIPATING IN YOUR GOVERNMENT

How to Find Out What's Going On in Congress

Who Is in Congress? If you want to find out who is in Congress or who your representative or senators are, you can look in the *Congressional Directory*, available in most libraries. It includes biographies of lawmakers, lists of committees and staff members, and maps of districts. You can also access the Web site for the Clerk of the House of Representatives, which provides a state-by-state listing of representatives. Go to **clerkweb.house.gov/**. For a complete listing of senators, you may wish to access **www.senate.gov/**. Additionally, the *Almanac of American Politics* can help you learn more about your members' views. Another resource that summarizes and evaluates each member's performance and describes each district is *Politics in America: Members of Congress in Washington and at Home* (Washington, D.C.: Congressional Quarterly Press).

Your representative and senators have telephone numbers in both Washington, D.C., and your state. You can also contact members of Congress via e-mail. You can find the e-mail addresses for all members of Congress at the following Web site: **www.lib.umich.edu/libhome/Documents.center/congress/conemail.txt**.

What Is Happening in Congress? To get information about bills being considered in Congress, call the Legislative Status Office at 202-225-1772. To find out whether a bill has been passed, call 202-456-2226. To learn what legislation is currently being considered in Congress, call 202-225-7400 for the House or 202-224-8601 for the Senate. You can obtain a copy of a bill from the House or Senate Document Room. Both the Democratic and Republican parties prepare tapes to provide accounts of proceedings on the floors of both houses. To listen to these tapes call:

Senate Democratic:
202-224-8541
Senate Republican:
202-224-8601
House Democratic:
202-225-7400
House Republican:
202-225-7430

TAKING ACTION

1. Find an article in a local or national newspaper or a national news magazine that mentions a proposed bill in Congress. Determine the

---

protection is called **congressional immunity.** The goal is to protect the freedom of legislative debate. The provision allows members to address their colleagues in open debate without fear of being sued for making harmful or false statements. Normally, a member may make any statements he or she wishes in connection with official duties and not be sued for libel or slander or be otherwise subject to legal action. This privilege does not cover speeches, articles, or conversations made in public apart from legislative business.

Roles of Members

In 1899, one senator said, "God made a day twenty-four hours long for the ordinary man. After a man becomes a United States senator, he requires a day forty-eight hours long." These words still ring true for senators as well as for representatives. Studies show that national legislators work almost sixty-hour weeks while Congress is in session. They must spend a great deal of time learning about the issues on which they

U.S. House of Representatives
105th Congress, 2nd session

[text version]

What's New

House Operations

House Directory

House Office Web Sites

Member Offices

Committee Offices

Leadership Offices

Other House Organizations, Commissions, and Task Forces

Media Galleries **NEW**

This Week on the House Floor
The schedule the House intends to consider this week.

Currently on the House Floor
Up-to-date events on the House floor as they happen.

Today in Committee
Up-to-the-hour Committee hearing schedules.

Annual Congressional Schedule **NEW**

The Legislative Process
Access to information about bills and resolutions being

Roll Call Votes **NEW**
As compiled through the electronic voting machine by the House Tally Clerks under the direction of Robin H. Carle, Clerk of the House.

House Committee Hearing Schedules and Oversight Plans
Each committee maintains its own schedule of hearings on the web. A committee's oversight plan describes its agenda for the 105th Congress, based on the jurisdiction of the committee. The public can attend any open committee meeting listed, and some hearings are televised by C-SPAN.

THOMAS Legislative Information on the Internet

In the spirit of THOMAS Jefferson, the Library of Congress provides you with searchable information about the U.S. Congress and the legislative process. Search bills by topic, bill number, or title. Search through and read the text of the Congressional Record for the 104th and 105th Congress. Search and find committee reports by topic or committee name.

Write Your Representative

Constituents may identify and/or contact their elected Member to the U.S. House of Representatives.

◀ *As you can see by this excerpt from its Web site, the House of Representatives has joined the information age. To find out what your representatives are working on in Washington, D.C., and to let them know what you think about it, access the site at* **www.house.gov**.

status of the bill in Congress. Contact the office of your senator or representative to find out his or her views on the bill. Follow the progress of the bill over the next few weeks as it passes through the chambers.

2. Use one of the references listed on page 384 to help you make a profile of the representative for your district or one of the senators for your state. In the profile, include what committees the member is on, how many staff members he or she has, what bills he or she has introduced recently, and what political action committees (PACs) support him or her.

will vote, reviewing bills introduced by other legislators, and getting support for their own bills. Committee and subcommittee work occupies a great deal of time. Legislators also try to be present on the floor of the House or Senate chambers as much as possible to listen to speeches, give speeches, and vote on bills. Every day, dozens of people ask to see them—a fellow member with questions about a bill, a lobbyist with arguments against a bill, a constituent visiting the Capitol. Between meetings, members prepare bills,

study reports, attend political party functions, and write speeches and articles.

In carrying out all their duties, the 535 members of Congress play several different but closely related roles. We explore some of these roles below.

Policymaker The Constitution requires that policymaking be the primary role of Congress and its members. Congress is the highest elected body in the country charged with making the legal rules that

► *A powerful Republican chairman of a powerful committee, Senator Jesse Helms singlehandedly thwarted President Bill Clinton's desire for William Weld (foreground), a former Democratic governor of Massachusetts, to serve as U.S. ambassador to Mexico. As chairman of the Senate Foreign Relations Committee, Helms refused to consider Weld's nomination for the post and appears to be showing him the way out.*

govern our society. Policymaking includes conducting investigations to identify problems, researching and deciding on bills, and voting intelligently for policies in the national interest. Policymakers decide many important matters, such as establishing the rate of federal taxes and the size of the federal budget.

Representative A member of Congress is also a representative, expected by "the folks back home" to represent their views in Washington. Members of Congress are supposed to reflect and translate into action the interests and concerns of constituents. Some political philosophers argue that representatives should vote exactly as their constituents would vote if the constituents themselves were present. This is the view of representative as an *instructed delegate*, where *delegate* means "agent of the people." Others argue that representatives should vote according to their own best judgment and evaluation of the issues. This is the view of representative as a *trustee*, someone who manages the affairs of another.

Servant of Constituents Representatives and senators not only represent the voting decisions of their constituents but also act as the servants of the constituents. In this role, they work as intermediaries between their constituents and the imposing and complicated federal

bureaucracy. Helping constituents with problems is part of the casework of a member of Congress.

Generally, members of Congress are flooded with constituents' requests from the moment they take office. These requests range from appearing in a local parade with the mayor of a city, to helping a student to secure an appointment to a service academy such as West Point, to helping with Social Security benefits, to helping with an immigration or passport problem. These small but time-consuming concerns take up hours of a legislator's day, even though routine tasks are delegated to the staff. This is time spent away from the main responsibility of policymaking, but a constituency well served is a constituency well satisfied, especially at the next election.

Committee Member The typical senator is a member of eleven committees and subcommittees. The average representative is a member of six. If a member is on a committee long enough, he or she will become a policy expert whose advice is sought by other members.

Politician and Party Member All of the roles that members of Congress play are related to their roles as politicians and party members. In order to continue to serve in Congress, legislators must be reelected, and reelection campaigns take time and energy. Every

ARCHITECTS of Government

Ben Nighthorse Campbell (1933–)

Ben Nighthorse Campbell was the seventh Native American ever to serve in the U.S. Congress. Campbell is the son of a Cheyenne jeweler and a Portuguese immigrant. He earned a gold medal for judo in the 1964 Olympics. When he was elected to serve as a U.S. senator from Colorado in 1992, he became the first Native American to serve in the Senate in more than sixty years.

HIS WORDS

"Sometimes I think there ought to be more Indians in Congress, or else no Indians, because it is very tough being the only Indian."

(*Interview, July 1991*)

"I am tired of plastic politicians—professional politicians who have nothing to do with their lives."

(*"Business People in Congress," The Nation's Business, March 1989, p. 58R*)

DEVELOPING CRITICAL THINKING SKILLS

1. How serious do you believe Campbell's first statement was?
2. In the second quotation, what did Campbell mean when he talked about "professional" politicians?

Conduct of Members

The Constitution gives the House and the Senate the power to punish the misconduct of their members through **censure** (condemnation) or **expulsion** (forcing the member from office). In its two-hundred-year history, the House has expelled four members—three for treason during the Civil War and one for corruption in 1980. Twenty-three representatives and nine senators have been formally censured for misconduct. In a censure proceeding, the member must stand in the well (the lowest part) of the chamber and face his or her colleagues as the misconduct charges are read.

Since the 1970s, both the House and the Senate have been faced with frequent cases of misconduct by members, but they have not wanted to punish them by expulsion or censure. For this reason, Congress devised a less severe form of censure called **reprimand.** The member need not be present when the House or Senate votes on this action. After the House or Senate has voted to reprimand one of its members for misconduct, no additional action is taken against the member. Several members of the House have been reprimanded since the 1970s.

In 1989, Speaker of the House Jim Wright resigned his seat under charges of unethical behavior. The House Ethics Committee charged him with a number of violations of House rules, most of which involved

▲ *Although Speaker of the House Jim Wright was not expelled from the House of Representatives, he resigned under a cloud of charges. According to this political cartoon, did his "You can't fire me, I quit" approach save his dignity?*

action that legislators take as policymakers, representatives, and servants of constituents affects votes in the next election. Even if members of Congress dislike politics, they must be politicians. Otherwise, they will not be around long enough to shape policy.

Wright's financial dealings with individuals and companies that had an interest in legislation before the House.

SECTION 3 REVIEW

1. How would you describe the average congressperson?
2. What are some of the benefits received by members of Congress?
3. What is the speech and debate clause?
4. Briefly describe each of the roles that a congressperson plays.
5. How do the House and the Senate punish the misconduct of their members?
6. **For Critical Analysis:** Should members of Congress always vote the way their constituents want, or should they vote according to their own best judgment? Give reasons for your answer.

SECTION 4

The Structure of Congress

Preview Questions:

- How is the Speaker of the House chosen, and what are his or her powers?
- Who are the other House leaders, and what are their functions?
- Who presides over the Senate, and what is his or her role?
- Why has the committee system evolved in Congress?
- What are the various types of committees?
- What are the various types of congressional support?

Key Terms:

majority party, Speaker of the House, caucus, presidential succession, majority leader, minority leader, minority party, whips, president *pro tem*, standing committees, seniority rule, subcommittees, select committees, joint committees, conference committee, administrative assistant, legislative director, legislative assistants, caseworkers, legislative correspondents

The organization of Congress is based on political party lines. The **majority party** in each chamber is the one with the greatest number of members. Being the majority party is quite important. That party chooses the major officers of each chamber of Congress, controls debate on the floor, selects all committee chairpersons, and has a majority on all committees.

House Leadership

Each term, before Congress begins its work, members of each party in each chamber meet to choose their leaders. The Constitution provides for the presiding officers of the House and Senate. Congress may choose other leaders as required.

Speaker of the House Chief among leaders in the House of Representatives is the **Speaker of the House.** This office is mandated by the Constitution to be filled by majority vote at the beginning of each congressional term. The Speaker has traditionally been a long-time member of the majority party who has risen in rank and influence through years of service in the House. The candidate for Speaker is selected by the majority party conference, or **caucus.** All the rest of the House must do is approve the selection.

As the presiding officer of the House and the leader of the majority party, the Speaker has a great deal of power. In the early nineteenth century, the Speaker had even more power and was known as the "king of the congressional mountain." Speakers known by such names as "Uncle Joe Cannon" and "Czar Reed" ruled the House with almost absolute control. A revolt in 1910 reduced the Speaker's powers and gave more powers to some of the committees. Nevertheless, today, the Speaker still has many important powers, including the following:

- Controlling, to a significant extent, which bills are assigned to which committees.
- Presiding over the sessions of the House and recognizing or ignoring members who wish to speak.
- Voting in the event of a tie, interpreting and applying the rules, ruling on points of order (questions about procedures asked by members), and putting questions to a vote.
- Playing a major role in making important committee assignments.
- Scheduling bills for action.

The Speaker may choose whether to vote on any measure but does not often vote. If the Speaker chooses to vote, he or she appoints a temporary presiding officer (called the Speaker *pro tempore*), who then occupies the Speaker's chair. The House rules say that the only time the Speaker *must* vote is to break a tie because a tie automatically defeats a measure. By choosing not to vote in some cases, the Speaker can actually cause a tie and defeat a proposal that is unpopular with the majority party.

The Speaker of the House is second in the line of **presidential succession.** That is, in the event that the president and vice president cannot serve, the Speaker becomes president of the United States.

The Speaker also has a good deal of political clout inside and outside Congress. If the Speaker belongs to the same party as the president, he or she often acts as the administration's spokesperson in the House. When the Speaker's party is different from the president's, the Speaker is often a national spokesperson for his or her party. The Speaker also derives power from the fact

◄ *Newt Gingrich's position as Speaker of the House gave him high visibility and political power.*

▲ *As majority whip of the House of Representatives in 1998, Tom DeLay rallies fellow representatives, encouraging them to support the Republican agenda with their votes on the floor.*

that he or she has a good deal of control over the information and communications channels in the House.

Majority Leader The **majority leader** is elected by the caucus of party members to act as spokesperson for the majority party and to keep the party together. The majority leader's job is to help plan the party's legislative program, to organize other party members to support legislation favored by their party, and to make sure the chairpersons of the many committees finish work on bills important to the party. He or she makes speeches on important bills, stating the majority party position.

Minority Leader The **minority leader,** as the name suggests, is the leader of the **minority party.** Although not as powerful as the majority leader, the minority leader has similar responsibilities. The primary duty of the minority leader is to maintain cohesion within the party. He or she persuades influential minority party leaders to follow the party's position and organize fellow party members in constructive criticism of the majority party's policies and programs.

Whips The leadership of the parties includes assistants to the majority and minority leaders known as **whips.** Whips originated in the British House of Commons. They were named after the "whipper in," the rider who keeps the hounds together in a fox hunt, because their job is to keep party members in line with the party's positions. Whips try to determine how each member is going to vote on certain issues. They then advise the leaders on the strength of party support. Whips also try to see that members are present when important votes are to be taken and that members vote with the party leadership. For example, if the Democratic Party strongly supports a child-care bill, the Democratic Party whip might meet with other Democratic members individually and in small groups to try to persuade them to vote with the party.

Senate Leadership

The Constitution makes the vice president of the United States the president of the Senate. As presiding officer, the vice president may call on members to speak and put questions to a vote. The vice president, however, is not an elected member of the Senate and may not take part in Senate debates. He or she may cast a vote in the Senate only in the event of a tie. In practice, the vice president has little influence in the Senate and is rarely even present.

Although their role in the Senate is limited, a few vice presidents have been able to influence legislative matters, largely because of their personal abilities. The most successful have been those who were once senators themselves and thus had close personal relationships with their former colleagues.

Because vice presidents are rarely available to preside over the Senate, senators also elect another presiding officer, the president *pro tempore* (usually shortened to **president *pro tem***), who serves in the absence of the vice president. The president *pro tem* is elected by the whole Senate and is ordinarily the member of the majority party with the longest continuous term of service in the Senate. In the absence of both the president *pro tem* and the vice president, a temporary presiding officer is selected from the ranks of the Senate. Usually, this person is a junior member of the majority party.

The real power in the Senate is held by the majority leader, the minority leader, and their whips. The majority leader in the Senate, as in the House, is the most powerful officer and chief spokesperson of the majority party. He or she directs the legislative program and party strategy. The minority leader commands the Senate minority party's opposition to the policies of the majority party and directs the legislative strategy of his or her party. The role of the Senate majority and minority whips is the same as the House whips.

◀ Senate majority leader Trent Lott makes a point to his fellow Republicans in July 1997. How would Lott's job be different if a Republican, instead of a Democrat held the presidency?

Committees and Subcommittees

Members of Congress spend much of their time on committee work, because most of the actual work of legislating is performed by committees and subcommittees within Congress. The committee system was not created by the Constitution, and Congress was not always made up of committees. Both chambers got along fine without permanent committees in the early years of the republic. The House began to slowly establish the committee system in 1795, and the Senate began to follow suit in 1816. Through the years, committees and subcommittees have gained responsibility and power.

This evolution has taken place for several reasons. First, as many as twenty thousand bills are introduced in Congress each year. If the entire Congress considered each of these bills, the process would be endless. It would obviously be impossible for senators and representatives to study and research the specific content of each one. Breaking up into committees allows members to split up the bills among smaller groups of representatives and senators who can specialize in the few issues considered by the committees on which they serve. Committee members often become experts on the kinds of bills that come before their committees and can therefore make informed judgments about them.

Second, the committee system allows committees to screen the thousands of bills that are introduced into Congress during every term. Committees decide which bills are ready to go through the system and which deserve further examination. Members of the committees listen to experts, lobbyists, and citizens who support and oppose the bills. Ultimately, committees decide which bills have a chance to become law. Committees are supposed to serve as filters to ensure that only the

House	Senate
Agriculture	Agriculture, Nutrition, and Forestry
Appropriations	Appropriations
Banking and Financial Services	Armed Services
Budget	Banking, Housing, and Urban Affairs
Commerce	Budget
Education and the Workforce	Commerce, Science, and Transportation
Government Reform and Oversight	Energy and Natural Resources
House Oversight	Environment and Public Works
International Relations	Finance
Judiciary	Foreign Relations
National Security	Governmental Affairs
Resources	Indian Affairs
Rules	Judiciary
Science	Labor and Human Resources
Small Business	Rules and Administration
Standards of Official Conduct	Small Business
Transportation and Infrastructure	Veterans' Affairs
Veterans' Affairs	
Ways and Means	

most important and responsible legislation is permitted to reach the House and Senate floors for a vote.

Standing Committees The most powerful committees of Congress are the permanent committees, called **standing committees.** Before any bill can be considered by the entire House or Senate, it must be approved by a majority vote in the standing committee to which it was assigned. Each standing committee deals with a certain policy area, such as agriculture or foreign affairs, and approves the bills related to that area.

The number of standing committees has varied over the years. Today, there are nineteen standing committees in the House and seventeen in the Senate. The names of these committees are listed in Figure 14–4 above. The size of the committees has varied from twelve to fifty-seven members in the House and from ten to twenty-eight members in the Senate.

Standing committees in each chamber are controlled by the majority party in that chamber. The committee chairperson is chosen by the majority party caucus and is almost always the majority member who has served for the longest period of time on that particular committee. This is known as the **seniority rule.**

Most of the members of each standing committee are also members of the majority party. Committee membership is generally divided between the parties according to the number of members in the chamber. For example, if the Democrats hold 40 percent of the seats in the House and the Republicans hold 60 percent, a ten-member committee will have four Democrats and six Republicans.

Most House and Senate standing committees are divided into **subcommittees**—smaller groups of committee members that study one aspect of the subject handled by the committee. The number and power of subcommittees has grown in recent years. Today, there are more than two hundred subcommittees in Congress. Since the early 1970s, the role of subcommittees in the lawmaking process has increased, and there is evidence that subcommittees are sometimes more powerful than the standing committees themselves.

Select Committees In addition to standing committees, Congress has a number of special committees, called **select committees.** These committees are set up to investigate specific problems or issues, such as drug abuse or hunger. Select committees may be either permanent or temporary.

Joint Committees Congress also has **joint committees,** whose membership is drawn from both the Senate and the House. A few joint committees are permanent. Joint committees are created to give a full congressional overview of a complex subject. For example, the Joint Economic Committee (JEC) studies complex questions relating to the U.S. economy as a whole and issues its findings to Congress and to the public. Other joint committees have been set up to study matters such as atomic energy and defense. When they are

▶ *Members of the Senate Armed Services Committee listen to a panel of Navy personnel during a fact-finding hearing. What is the purpose of a standing committee such as this one?*

appointed for a specific purpose—for example, to investigate alleged wrongdoing—these committees are usually referred to as select or special committees.

Conference Committees The Constitution requires that, in order for a bill to become a law, it must be passed in identical form by both chambers of Congress. In many instances, however, the two chambers pass different versions. A **conference committee** is a temporary joint body created to iron out the differences between the House and Senate versions of the bill. The committee must work out a final bill that is written in language agreeable to both chambers before the bill can be sent to the president. The strategic role of conference committees is discussed in Chapter 16.

Congressional Support

When the first Congress met, the United States population was around 4 million. Today, it is over 270 million. This dramatic increase in population has brought an equally dramatic increase in the workload of congressional members. Furthermore, constituents are demanding more services, and members of Congress are providing them. As more citizens turn to Congress for help, Congress hires more staff members to take care of them.

Along with the increase in workload has come an increase in the complexity of legislation. Legislators could not possibly have the specialized background to understand all the details of every piece of legislation, so they must rely on help from staff members. Congress now employs over 32,000 people to assist legislators.

Personal Staff Personal staff includes people working directly for the individual senators and representatives in their Washington and district offices. The average House member has about twenty personal staff members, and the average senator has about twice that number.

Lawmakers have several types of personal staff members in their offices. Staff titles and positions vary from staff to staff. Figure 14–5 on page 393 provides an overview of the typical positions in each senator's and representative's office.

The **administrative assistant,** called the AA, runs the lawmaker's office, supervises the lawmaker's schedule, and gives advice on political matters. She or he is responsible for directing and supervising the member's staff. The AA is typically a close personal and political friend or adviser of the member of Congress.

The **legislative director,** called the LD, often decides which staff member should do what. The legislative director has one or more **legislative assistants,**

FIGURE 14–5 Typical Staff of a Member of Congress

The chart below represents the organization of a typical lawmaker's staff. Who is the most powerful member of the lawmaker's staff? How do you know?

Lawmaker
U.S. senator or representative

Administrative Assistant (AA)
Runs office, maintains schedule, advises lawmaker on political matters, supervises staff

Legislative Correspondents (LCs)
Handle mail, report to AA

Caseworkers (CWs)
Help constituents with requests, report to AA

Legislative Director (LD)
Delegates work among staff members

Press Aides
Prepare press releases

Interns and General Office Help
Assume clerical and various other tasks

Legislative Assistants (LAs)
Research and present information on bills, write speeches, assist in committee meetings, monitor important work on floor

called LAs, who make sure that the lawmaker has all the necessary information about bills for which the member is responsible. An LA studies and does background research on bills in Congress, drafts bills, and writes speeches and articles for the lawmaker. LAs also assist in committee meetings and keep track of the work taking place on the floor of Congress.

Caseworkers manage the numerous requests for help from constituents. For example, a caseworker might help a major university through the steps involved in obtaining a federal grant. Or a caseworker might simply arrange for a citizen to take a tour of Capitol Hill. Lawmakers typically have offices in key cities in their states or districts. Many caseworkers work in these offices.

Lawmakers also have **legislative correspondents** (LCs) to handle mail, aides to prepare press releases, general office help, and interns.

Committee Staff Besides the personal staffs of lawmakers, every committee and subcommittee in Congress has staff members who work for that committee. The larger and more important the committee, the larger the staff. A committee staff collects and analyzes information on issues, identifies and researches problems, suggests policies, schedules committee hearings, and prepares reports. Because the essential work of Congress depends on the committee system, committee staffs have grown even faster than personal staffs.

Support Agencies Several agencies provide services that help Congress and are a part of the legislative branch of the government.

1. *General Accounting Office.* The largest of these support agencies is the General Accounting Office (GAO). It reviews the financial management of government programs created by Congress to see that spending is proper and reasonable and to assure that federal funds are spent for the purposes that Congress intended. The GAO is headed by the *comptroller general*, a person appointed by the president, with the Senate's approval, to a fifteen-year term. You can learn more about the GAO by accessing its Web site. Go to **www.gao.gov/**.

2. *The Library of Congress.* The Library of Congress was established in 1800 by Congress to "purchase such books as may be necessary for the use of Congress." It now contains over twenty million items and is an information and fact-finding center for legislators and their assistants. The library includes the Congressional Research Service (CRS), which every year answers some 250,000 requests for information from lawmakers, congressional staff, and committees. CRS workers research topics ranging from the crime rate in Bulgaria to the number of spotted owls in Oregon. The Library of Congress's Web address is **www.loc.gov/**.

3. *The Congressional Budget Office.* The Congressional Budget Office (CBO) serves Congress by providing technical and computer services and coordinating budget-making work. It also studies the budget proposals put forward by the president each year and predicts the economic consequences of proposed

How Congress Has Changed

Congress is a traditional institution, but nonetheless it has changed over time, particularly over the past fifty years.

THEN (FIFTY YEARS AGO)	NOW
Junior members rarely were full participants.	Junior members are full participants.
There were virtually no minority or female members in either chamber.	There are several minority and female members in both chambers.
The way members voted was controlled by their parties.	Members often act independently of their parties.

and actual legislation. The CBO prepares a report on the budget each April. To reach the CBO's Web site, go to **www.cbo.gov/**.

4. *The Government Printing Office.* The Government Printing Office (GPO) prints the *Congressional Record*, which is a daily record of all the bills intro-

duced in both chambers and of the speeches and testimony presented in Congress. A voter can write to the GPO asking about a particular lawmaker's position on an issue, such as prayer in schools or gun control. The GPO staff will send the voter a copy of the *Record* containing a speech by the

▶ *The gracious interior of the Jefferson building, one of three buildings on Capitol Hill that house the Library of Congress, is shown here. The Library was established in 1800 and quickly grew into a national institution. Today the Library of Congress is one of the largest and most important research centers in the world.*

Term Limits

A hundred years ago, the average length of service in the House of Representatives was four years. Today, in contrast, many representatives in Congress see congressional service as a career. And, once elected, their chances for reelection are good. Over 90 percent of House incumbents who run are reelected. Should the terms of members of Congress be limited? This is not a new question. Members of the first Congress suggested term limitations, but the idea was rejected. By 1995, twenty-three states had passed laws limiting the number of terms that senators and representatives from those states could serve in Congress. The Supreme Court, however, in *U.S. Term Limits, Inc. v. Thornton* (1995), declared that such laws were unconstitutional. Clearly, given the number of states that have already voted on term limits, a sizeable number of Americans favor them. Others do not.

The System We Have Works Very Well, Argue Some Americans

Opponents of limiting terms in Congress point out that if such limits existed, we would have less-experienced legislators running the business of government. Opponents also argue that limits might place even more legislative power in the hands of unelected committee staffs, who would often keep their positions much longer than elected members of Congress. "Power would flow from elected to unelected officials," says Thomas Mann of the Brookings Institution in Washington, D.C.

Opponents of term limits believe that limiting terms would enhance the power of interest groups. Members, knowing that they would need new careers in a few years, might cater to interest groups that could provide them with jobs.

Imposing term limits also limits the right of voters to continue to choose whom they elect, which infringes on democracy. Finally, opponents of term limits argue that limits would make members of Congress less responsive to the wishes

of their constituents. Voters would have no way of punishing any bad behavior in which these officials engaged during their last term.

Members of Congress Should Not Stay around Forever, Others Argue

Perhaps equally convincing are the arguments of those in favor of term limits. They point out that limiting congressional terms could free members of Congress from their concern over being reelected. Senators and representatives could tackle the business of government more objectively and with less concern over their reelection. Of course, if more than one term is allowed, this argument applies only to legislators serving their final terms in Congress.

The main argument in favor of term limits is that they would eliminate the professional politician. The power of incumbency is so great that most incumbents win, and career politicians dominate public policy. We end up with individuals who are out of touch with the nongovernmental world in which most of us live. Those who favor term limits believe that what members of Congress learn—putting deals together and other political activities—is something that we could well do without. As Thomas Jefferson once said, "Whenever a man has cast a longing eye on [political office], a rottenness begins in his conduct." After all, power and influence tend to corrupt, and with seniority in Congress come too much power and influence.

YOU DECIDE

1. Do you think that limiting terms would make members of Congress more responsive to the people? Why or why not?
2. Why would limiting terms limit the right of voters to choose whom they elect? Is this an infringement on democracy?

► The Library of Congress home page provides access to a wealth of information to any user, ranging from history and special exhibitions to the special research tools available over the Internet.

lawmaker on the issue. The GPO also does all the national government's printing and provides copies of many government publications to the public free or at a low cost. You can access the GPO online at **www.access.gpo.gov/**.

As you have learned, Congress was established as the first branch of the national government. It was meant to be the branch closest to the people. Through the years, the growth of Congress and its ever-increasing workload have forced upon this branch of government

► Working from the online home page of the U.S. Government Printing Office, you can order individual government publications, find out about working at the printing office, or simply find out what's new at the GPO.

many changes that the framers of the Constitution could not have predicted. Today, Congress is larger and busier than ever before, and its membership has begun to reflect the ethnic and cultural diversity of our nation. Additionally, its work is increasingly done in the meeting rooms of its committees and subcommittees. Despite these changes, however, Congress remains the "voice of the people."

SECTION 4 REVIEW

1. What is the role of the Speaker of the House?
2. Who are the other leaders in the House, and what are their functions?
3. How is Senate leadership organized?
4. What purposes do committees serve?
5. Describe the functions of the various types of committees in Congress.
6. What types of support do members of Congress receive?
7. **For Critical Analysis:** Each member of Congress has an extensive staff. Does this make it easier for incumbents to be reelected?

★ ★ ★ ★ **Chapter Summary** ★ ★ ★ ★

Section 1: The Creation and Evolution of Congress

- Congress is the legislative (lawmaking) branch of government. The two chambers of Congress are the Senate and the House of Representatives.
- A term of Congress lasts for two years, and there are two regular sessions per term. Only the president may call a special session of Congress.
- Seats in the House are apportioned among the states on the basis of their population. A census to determine population is taken every ten years. The Reapportionment Act of 1929 permanently set the number of House members at 435 and established a system of reapportionment based on population.

- Congressional districts for the House are drawn by state legislatures.

Section 2: House and Senate Terms and Qualifications

- Members of the House are elected for two-year terms, while senators are elected for six-year terms.
- The Constitution sets forth basic qualifications for both senators and representatives.

Section 3: Members of Congress and Their Responsibilities

- Congress is not a cross section of the American public. Members tend to have a higher-than-average level of income, education, and occupational status, and they have traditionally been predominantly white, Protestant males of Western European descent.
- Congress sets its own pay and compensation and its members enjoy many privileges and benefits.
- The roles congressional members play include those of policymaker, representative, servant of constituents, committee member, and politician.
- Both the House and the Senate have the constitutional power to punish their members for misconduct.

Section 4: The Structure of Congress

- Congress is organized along political party lines. Chief among the leaders in the House is the Speaker of the House. Other leaders in the House include the majority leader, the minority leader, and whips.
- The Constitution makes the vice president of the United States the president of the Senate. The president *pro tempore* serves in the absence of the vice president. The Senate also has a majority leader, a minority leader, and whips.
- Four kinds of committees do the basic work of Congress: standing committees, select committees, joint committees, and conference committees.
- Congressional staff and support agencies assist lawmakers in carrying out the work of Congress.

CHAPTER 14 Review

★ REVIEW QUESTIONS ★

1. Why did the founders create a bicameral legislature?
2. On what date does a new term of Congress begin? How long does a term last?
3. How are House seats divided among the states?
4. What is gerrymandering? What events have reduced its use?
5. What is "racial gerrymandering"? What is the Supreme Court's position on race-based redistricting?
6. Despite the fact that representatives serve short terms, why is there a great deal of continuity in the House?
7. How did the Constitution ensure that the Senate would be a continuous body?
8. How does Congress punish the misconduct of its members?
9. What are some typical characteristics of members of Congress?
10. What special privileges do members of Congress have to protect them as they carry out their duties?
11. List and briefly explain the five roles of a member of Congress.
12. What is the role of the Speaker of the House?
13. Who are the leaders in each political party in both chambers, and what are some of their duties?
14. What purposes do committees serve in Congress?
15. Briefly describe the four types of committees in Congress.
16. What kinds of activities are performed by the personal staff of a member of Congress?
17. What agencies perform support services for Congress?
18. Describe two ways to find out what is going on in Congress.
19. What are the arguments for and against term limits for members of Congress?

★ CRITICAL THINKING ★

1. Can you think of any situations in which one role of a member of Congress might conflict with another role? If so, describe these situations, and present possible ways to resolve them.
2. How would Congress be different if it were an exact cross section of the American public?
3. Do you think members of Congress are ever offered bribes in return for favors? Do you think this practice is common? Give evidence to support your answer.
4. Should members of Congress vote according to what they think is best for the country, or should they always vote as their constituents want them to? Give reasons for your answer.

★ IMPROVING YOUR SKILLS ★

Communication Skills

Continuity in Writing: Transitional Terms and Phrases
When you are writing an essay or a report, it is important that you know how to connect your ideas to make your writing more readable and clear. Continuity in writing is strengthened by the use of transitional terms and phrases—bridges that carry the reader from one sentence to the next.

Compare these two paragraphs:

1.

Incumbent representatives are more visible than opponents. They are better able to keep constituents informed. They win friends by servicing constituents. They are in a better position to raise campaign funds. They are reelected over 90 percent of the time.

2.

Incumbent representatives are more visible than opponents. They are better able to keep constituents informed. They

win friends by servicing constituents. They are in a better position to raise campaign funds. For these reasons, they are reelected over 90 percent of the time.

The difference between the two paragraphs is the phrase, *For these reasons*. Without this transitional phrase, the relationship of the last sentence to the preceding sentences is unclear. The transitional phrase links the last sentence to the list of statements supporting it.

Use the following tips to strengthen the continuity of your writing.

1. **Use logic.** Organize your sentences so that ideas progress naturally and logically.
2. **Use transitional terms and phrases to show relationships between ideas.** Study the list of suggested terms below.
   - **Result:** consequently, thus, as a result, therefore
   - **Summary:** in conclusion, in summary, in short
   - **Sequence:** first, second, then, finally, meanwhile
   - **Emphasis:** especially, particularly
   - **Addition:** also, furthermore, further, moreover, including

Writing Select two topics from this chapter. For each topic, write two separate, short paragraphs. In the first paragraph, do not use any transitional terms or phrases. In the second, use one or more of the transitional terms and phrases listed above. Finally, write a brief explanation of how the use of transitional terms and phrases made a difference between the two paragraphs.

Social Studies Skills

Reading Political Maps Look at the map on page 375. It shows the reapportionment of seats in the House of Representatives following the last census.

1. How is color used in this map?
2. When were the data collected to make this map?
3. How many states saw no change in their number of representatives?
4. How many states lost seats in the House of Representatives?
5. Among the states that gained seats, what was the average size of the gain?

★ ACTIVITIES AND PROJECTS ★

1. Prepare a biography of your representative or one of your senators using the resources listed on page 384, your library, and information you obtain from the office of the representative or senator. Present your report to the class.
2. Make a list of the committees and subcommittees on which your senators have served or are now serving. Establish whether these committees and subcommittees have been particularly important for your state or region. For example, if you live in an area where there is a military base, has your senator been named to a committee or subcommittee that determines spending in the area of national defense? Write a short report that summarizes your research findings.
3. Describe the job of a member of the House or the Senate by creating a want ad for a congressperson. In the ad, include qualifications, benefits and salary, and required skills. Also include the typical responsibilities of members.

What If . . .

The Reapportionment Act of 1929 Had Never Been Passed?

The Reapportionment Act of 1929 fixes the maximum number of House members at 435. Without it, the Constitution would allow over one thousand House members. How might Congress be run then?

CHAPTER 15

The Powers of Congress

CHAPTER OBJECTIVES

To learn about and understand . . .

⭐ The legislative powers of Congress, including expressed and implied powers

⭐ The nonlegislative powers of Congress

"The accumulation of all powers, legislative, executive, and judiciary, in the same hands, whether one, a few, or many . . . may justly be pronounced the very definition of tyranny."

James Madison
(1751–1836)
Fourth President of the United States

INTRODUCTION

The power to make laws for an entire nation carries with it a tremendous responsibility. The founders recognized this fact. It is perhaps why they devoted the first and lengthiest article of the Constitution to carefully defining the powers of Congress. It is also why they reserved certain powers to the states, denied large areas of power to Congress, gave other powers to the judicial and executive branches, and provided that some powers would be shared. They believed, as illustrated by James Madison's statement above, that powers must be divided among the three branches of government. This sharing and division of powers is part of the system of checks and balances they created to avoid what James Madison called "the very definition of tyranny."

◀ Much of the work of Congress is done by committees in hearings such as this one, held by the Senate Governmental Affairs Committee.

Legislative Powers

Preview Questions:

- What are expressed powers?
- What powers does Congress exercise over the nation's budget and economy?
- What powers does Congress exercise over foreign affairs?
- What other expressed powers does Congress possess?
- What is the necessary and proper clause, and how has it been applied?

Key Terms:

expressed powers, direct tax, indirect tax, revenue bills, appropriation, government bonds, national debt, federal budget, currency power, bankruptcy, interstate commerce, copyright, patent, implied powers, necessary and proper clause, elastic clause, strict constructionists, loose constructionists, impoundment

As you learned in Chapter 14, Congress is the "first branch of government." It is the only one of the three branches of the national government that has the power to make laws. In Article I, Section 1, of the Constitution, the founders granted "All legislative powers herein" to Congress.

Yet Congress is not free to pass whatever laws it pleases. If that were the case, we would not have a limited government. The founders wanted a strong central legislature, but they did not want one with unlimited powers. For that reason, they set forth in the Constitution the powers that Congress could exercise. They also limited the powers of Congress by denying Congress certain powers and by stating, in the Tenth Amendment, that all powers not delegated to Congress were reserved to the states, or to the people.

Expressed Powers

Article I of the Constitution expressly gives certain powers to Congress. These powers, because they are listed, or enumerated, in the Constitution, are referred to as the **expressed powers** of Congress. They are also called *delegated powers* or *enumerated powers*. (See Figure 15–1 on page 403.)

Although the expressed powers of Congress are spelled out in the Constitution, the actual scope of these powers is not. The wording is brief and general. The scope and content of the expressed powers have been defined by how Congress has used these powers over the years and by the interpretations handed down by the Supreme Court.

The Power to Tax and Spend The first power listed in Article I, Section 8, gives Congress the power to do the following:

[levy] and collect taxes, duties, imports, and excises, to pay the debts, and provide for the common defense and general welfare of the United States.

This clause gives Congress the power to collect and to spend money. This "power of the purse" is among the most important powers of Congress. The main purpose of the power to tax is to raise the money needed to finance the operations of government. Under the Articles of Confederation, Congress had no power of taxation. As a result, the government never had enough money to function well. To remedy this, the Constitution granted Congress such power.

Originally, Congress was not allowed by the Constitution to impose a direct tax except in proportion to each state's population. A **direct tax** is any tax that must be paid directly to the government by the taxpayer. (In contrast, an **indirect tax** is paid to another party, who in turn pays it to the government. For example, a sales tax is paid to a merchant, who then pays the tax to the government.) This rule prevented the federal government from levying taxes on personal or corporate income.

The Sixteenth Amendment, which was ratified in 1913, changed this situation. This amendment states:

The Congress shall have the power to lay and collect taxes on incomes, from whatever source derived, without apportionment among several States, and without regard to any census or enumeration.

FIGURE 15–1 Powers Granted to Congress by Article I, Section 8, of the Constitution This table lists both the expressed powers and the implied powers granted to Congress by the Constitution. How would you describe the difference between the expressed powers and the implied powers?

Expressed Powers

Taxation of goods	Congress can set and collect taxes on goods as they are manufactured, sold, used, or imported [Clause1].
Borrowing money	Congress can borrow money on the credit of the United States [Clause 2].
Regulation of commerce	Congress can regulate interstate and foreign trade [Clause 3].
Bankruptcy	Congress can make laws with respect to bankruptcy [Clause 4].
Naturalization	Congress can determine how aliens can become U.S. citizens [Clause 4].
Money	Congress can mint coins and can print and circulate paper money [Clause 5].
Standards	Congress can establish uniform weights and measures [Clause 5].
Punishment of counterfeiters	Congress can punish counterfeiters of American currency [Clause 6].
Post offices and roads	Congress can establish post offices and routes over which mail can be carried [Clause 7].
Copyrights and patents	Congress can grant copyrights to authors and composers and patents to inventors [Clause 8].
Lower courts	Congress can set up all federal courts except the Supreme Court [Clause 9].
Punishment for certain acts in international waters	Congress can prohibit acts of piracy outside U.S. territory and can punish certain other acts that all nations prohibit [Clause 10].
Declaration of war 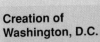	Congress can declare war. Until international law banned such action in the mid-nineteenth century, it could also authorize private parties to capture and destroy enemy ships in wartime [Clause 11].
The army 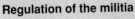	Congress can raise and maintain an army [Clause 12].
The navy	Congress can create and maintain a navy [Clause 13].
Regulation of the armed forces	Congress can set rules for military forces [Clause14].
The militia	Congress can call into service the militia (the National Guard) [Clause 15].
Regulation of the militia	Congress can organize, arm, and discipline the militia and can govern it when it is in the service of the United States [Clause 16].
Creation of Washington, D.C.	Congress can govern Washington, D.C., and can erect buildings there that seem necessary for the seat of the U.S. government [Clause 17].

Implied Powers

The necessary and proper (elastic) clause	Congress can make all laws necessary and proper for executing the foregoing expressed powers [Clause 18].

▶ *Surrounded by scaffolding, the Statue of Liberty undergoes repairs and renovations. Who would have appropriated (or authorized) this expenditure of federal funds?*

The Sixteenth Amendment provided for the collection of income taxes without regard to a state's population. Income taxes have since become a major source of revenue for the national government.

Congress also has the power to levy taxes to regulate the growth and strength of the U.S. economy. For example, tariffs on imported goods raise the price of foreign goods. Congress sometimes uses tariffs to protect American companies from foreign competition. Congress also uses its taxation power to regulate the economy by decreasing or increasing tax rates. For example, Congress may try to stimulate the economy by lowering individual income taxes, thus giving taxpayers more income to spend.

All **revenue bills**—bills proposed to raise money—must start in the House of Representatives, and almost all important work on tax laws occurs in the House Ways and Means Committee. The Senate, however, also must vote in favor of a revenue bill in order for it to become law.

Congress also has the power of **appropriation.** That is, it has the power to authorize government spending. Article I, Section 9, of the Constitution states, "No money shall be drawn from the Treasury, but in Consequence of [except by] Appropriations made by Law." Thus, before the national government can spend money, Congress must pass a law authorizing the government to do so. For example, Congress must approve spending before the Department of Defense or the Environmental Protection Agency can carry out their programs.

The powers to raise and spend funds are vitally important. They allow Congress to determine national policy in many different areas, because government agencies cannot operate without funds. They need funds to carry out their programs and services, such as national defense, highway construction, maintenance of national parks, and public assistance.

The Power to Borrow
When the government spends more than it collects in taxes and other revenues, it has to borrow money. The Constitution gives Congress the power to borrow. One method of borrowing is by authorizing the sale of **government bonds.** These bonds are government "IOU's" bought by individuals or companies. The government promises to repay the buyers of bonds at a later time and also to pay interest.

Of course, the debt incurred does not just disappear. The borrowed money makes up the **national debt**—the amount of money the government owes at any given time. Decades of borrowing during the twentieth century caused the national debt to rise to about $4 trillion, the amount it is today. In the last several years, however, the government has had to borrow less money. By 1998, it appeared that future government budgets would be balanced for a time, meaning that the national debt would not be increased further.

Control of spending is not entirely up to Congress. It is directly related to the national economy and to the **federal budget,** which is the national government's financial plan for how it will operate. The federal budget lays out in detail how much the government will spend, how the spending will be divided among agencies and programs, and what the sources of the funds will be. Since 1921, the executive branch has prepared a federal budget proposal every year and submitted it to Congress every January. The House and Senate budget committees and the Congressional Budget Office can then adjust the budget by adding or eliminating programs. The final budget agreement is usually a compromise between what the executive branch wants and what Congress wants.

Coining Money and Establishing Bankruptcy Laws The Constitution gives Congress the power "to coin Money [and] regulate the Value thereof." This **currency power** was given to Congress to prevent the problems and confusion created when each state issued its own money under the Articles of Confederation. The uniform value of coins and paper money is fixed by Congress and is the same in any state or territory. All of the currency issued by the federal government is considered legal tender and must be accepted as payment for debts. In relation to its currency power, Congress has the power to punish *counterfeiters*—people who print false paper money or other government notes or who make coins illegally.

Congress also has the power to set uniform laws for dealing with bankruptcy throughout the United States. **Bankruptcy** occurs when one is legally declared unable to pay one's debts. Congress can establish the legal proceedings by which the belongings of the person filing for bankruptcy are distributed among those to whom the debt is owed.

Commerce Power Article I, Section 8, of the Constitution gives Congress the power to "regulate Commerce with foreign Nations, and among the several States, and with the Indian Tribes." Commerce involves the buying and selling of goods on a large scale.

Trade between states is known as **interstate commerce.** Under the Articles of Confederation, Congress had no power to regulate interstate commerce and very little authority over foreign trade. This lack of control led to intense rivalries and economic wars among the states. States began taxing each other's goods and

"TIMBERRRRRRRRR!"

THE GROWING DEFICIT

SPENDING CUTS

◄ *Although 1992 presidential candidate Ross Perot made the federal budget deficit his main campaign issue, you can see from this 1966 political cartoon that concern over government spending is not a new issue. Considering budget developments in the late 1990s, how might you redraw this cartoon today?*

restricting the flow of products across their borders. The result was chaos.

In order to give the nation a stable economy, the writers of the Constitution gave Congress broad powers to regulate both foreign and interstate commerce. Exactly what "commerce" includes, however, has not always been clear. The first case involving the commerce clause to reach the Supreme Court was decided in 1824. In that case, *Gibbons v. Ogden,* Chief Justice John Marshall interpreted commerce to include not only the buying and selling of goods and services but nearly all commercial and business activities. Today, these activities include banking and finance, radio and television broadcasting, labor-management relations, and railroad and airline transportation. Marshall also declared that Congress had the *exclusive* power to regulate interstate commerce— that is, the states did not share this power.

Marshall's broad interpretation of commerce has given Congress powers far beyond what the framers originally envisioned. For example, Congress used the commerce clause to pass the Civil Rights Act of 1964. The act prohibits discrimination based on race, color, national origin, religion, or gender in places of public accommodations, such as restaurants, motels, and hotels. It also prohibits discrimination in employment. The commerce clause has also been used as a basis for minimum wage laws and laws protecting workers' rights. It has been used to pass laws prohibiting the transportation of explosives, diseased livestock, narcotics, and falsely labeled drugs across state borders.

> **Just the Facts**
>
> *The government prints over 8 billion one-dollar bills annually. The average "life" of a one-dollar bill is seventeen months.*

► *Whether you are buying a pack of gum at a convenience store or shipping freight worldwide, you are probably involved in interstate commerce. Defined by the Supreme Court to include virtually any business activity, interstate commerce is regulated by Congress.*

Power in Foreign Relations Congress shares powers concerning foreign relations with the president, who is primarily responsible for American foreign policy. Congress's authority in foreign relations comes from many of its other powers, including the power to approve treaties, to declare war, to approve appointments of diplomatic officers made by the president, and to regulate foreign commerce. Through its spending power, Congress also has control over funding for national defense and foreign aid.

The War Powers The Constitution grants war powers to both the legislative branch and the executive branch. Only Congress has the power to declare war. In addition, Congress is responsible for raising and maintaining the armed forces of the United States. The president, however, is commander in chief of the armed forces. The framers almost overwhelmingly rejected a proposal to give the president the power to initiate war. They believed that Congress would not rush into war as quickly as a president would.

Congress has declared war only five times in our history. American forces have, however, been involved in combat on foreign soil many times without a declaration of war by Congress. Most of these military actions were ordered by presidents who claimed that military force was needed to protect American lives, interests,

or property abroad. The Korean War (1950–1953), the Vietnam War (1964–1975), and the Persian Gulf War (1991) were all fought without formal declarations of war by Congress.

During the Vietnam War, many members of Congress came to believe that the president's power to involve the nation in undeclared wars must be checked. In an effort to regain its constitutional war-making power and to limit the president's power, Congress passed the War Powers Resolution in 1973. This law requires the president to inform Congress of the circumstances and scope of a proposed military action within forty-eight hours of sending American troops abroad. If Congress does not approve the action within sixty days or extend the sixty-day limit, the president must withdraw the troops.

Judicial Powers Congress has the power to create federal courts below the level of the Supreme Court. In addition, the Senate must approve the appointment of judges to these courts and to the Supreme Court. Congress also has the power to impeach any civil officer of the United States. The power of impeachment is a nonlegislative power that we will discuss shortly.

Powers to Establish Post Offices, Copyrights, and Patents The Constitution gives Congress the power to "establish Post Offices and post Roads." Thus, Congress can pass laws concerning the carrying and protection of the mails. Based on this power, Congress has passed laws to prevent the use of the mails for fraud (deception or trickery, usually to cheat someone out of money) and for the carrying of outlawed materials.

Granting copyrights and patents is also a congressional power. A **copyright** is the exclusive right of a person to publish, print, or sell his or her literary, musical, or artistic work for a definite period of time. Copyrights cover a wide variety of creative works, such as books, plays, paintings, sculptures, musical compositions, song lyrics, motion pictures, photographs, and computer software. Under the present law, a copyright is in effect for the lifetime of the person who created the work plus fifty years. A **patent** is the exclusive right of an inventor to use or sell his or her invention for a definite number of years. Currently, a patent is in force for twenty years.

Powers of Naturalization and Dominion over Territories

The exclusive power "to establish a uniform Rule of Naturalization" belongs to Congress. Naturalization is the process by which people from foreign countries become American citizens. It was discussed in Chapter 8.

Congress also has the power to acquire, manage, and dispose of various U.S. territories. Thus, Congress has passed laws to govern territories such as the Virgin Islands, Guam, Puerto Rico, and other areas that are not states.

Implied Powers

Not all of the powers of Congress are specifically listed in the Constitution. Other powers, known as **implied powers,** are based on the last clause in Article I, Section 8. This clause gives Congress the power to do the following:

To make all laws which shall be necessary and proper for carrying into Execution the foregoing Powers, and all other

◄ A postal worker processes mail at a busy Texas post office. Why do you think the Constitution gave Congress the power to establish "Post Offices and post Roads"?

Powers vested by this Constitution in the Government of the United States, or in any Department or Officer thereof.

This clause, called the **necessary and proper clause,** is also referred to as the **elastic clause** because it has allowed Congress to stretch and greatly expand its powers. Much of the adaptability of the Constitution can be traced to this provision.

Strict or Loose Interpretation? What do the words of the necessary and proper clause mean? How far can Congress stretch its powers? Almost from the time the words were written, their meaning has been debated. The first dispute erupted in 1789 when Alexander Hamilton, as secretary of the Treasury, urged Congress to set up a national bank.

A group opposing the idea, led by Secretary of State Thomas Jefferson, argued that the Constitution gave Congress no such power. Members of this group were known as **strict constructionists.** They maintained that Congress could do only the things absolutely necessary to carry out its expressed powers.

Alexander Hamilton and his followers looked at the Constitution a little differently. These people, known as **loose constructionists,** believed that the necessary and proper clause gave Congress the power to do anything that might be reasonably "implied" by an expressly delegated power. They argued that a national bank was necessary to carry out Congress's express powers of making currency, taxing, regulating commerce, and borrowing money.

President Washington was persuaded by Hamilton's argument and signed the bill authorizing the establishment of the First Bank of the United States. For the next twenty years, the bank's existence went unchallenged in the courts.

Government in Action

Who Controls the Federal Budget?

For more than a century after the creation of the American republic, Congress, with few exceptions, controlled the nation's purse strings. The increasing complexity of the American economy, however, has led to fragmented congressional control over the budget, and the president's role has grown. In 1921, when Congress created the Bureau of the Budget, it authorized the president to keep funds from being spent in order to save money if "excess" funds had been authorized by Congress. The process by which the president refuses to spend money appropriated by Congress is known as **impoundment.**

During the next half-century, funds appropriated by Congress for various purposes were withheld by presidents, but no major confrontations between Congress and a president erupted. Then Richard Nixon arrived in the White House. President Nixon believed that Congress was spending too much, so he extended the impoundment power to new levels. By some estimates, he impounded as much as $2.5 billion that had been appropriated by Congress for various purposes. In 1974, Congress acted to restore its "power of the purse" by passing the Budget and Impoundment Control Act. The act established a permanent budget committee for each house of Congress and put severe limits on the president's ability to impound funds. It also created the Congressional Budget Office (CBO). Financial experts in the CBO were to help members of Congress plan the budget. The act requires that appropriated funds be spent unless both houses vote in favor of a presidential request that they not be spent.

The size and content of the federal budget seem to fuel endless debate between Congress and the president. This debate may reflect a built-in conflict between the two branches. Congress has always been more inclined to focus on local constituencies and pressures. Members of Congress

hesitate to make difficult decisions about cutting programs that benefit their districts or states. The presidency, in contrast, is seen as a forum for national interests. As long as this is the case, the two branches will probably disagree over taxing and spending.

Additionally, for many of the years since World War II, the president and the majority of Congress have belonged to different parties. Conflicts over the budget are bound to arise with a Republican president and a Democratic Congress or a Democratic president and a Republican Congress. In fact, in 1995, the government partially "shut down" twice over a three-month period because Congress and the president could not reach agreement on the federal budget. The Republican-dominated Congress tried to force a Democratic president, Bill Clinton, to accept a budget that included cuts in domestic spending. By the time an acceptable budget was reached, it was seven months overdue.

THINK ABOUT IT
....

1. Should the president have the power of impoundment? Explain.
2. Why would members of Congress want to control the president's power of impoundment?
3. Who would be likely to spend more for domestic programs, Congress or the president? Explain.
4. Which do you think is more likely to cause a budget conflict: the differing priorities of the presidency and Congress, or the fact that the president is not a member of the majority party in Congress? Give reasons for your answer.

Cause and Effect versus Correlation

The world is full of correlations, or relationships. It is important to remember that correlation is not the same as causation. Causation occurs when a change in one variable *causes* a change in another. There are scientific ways to prove causation.

Many correlations can be discovered in American politics. At election time, analysts might expect to find correlations between being poor and voting Democratic, being wealthy and voting Republican, and being young and not voting at all. Certain demographic traits, then, are correlated, or associated, with voting patterns. The demographic traits cannot be assumed to *cause* the voting patterns, however. Being under thirty does not cause people not to vote. Rather, younger Americans tend to move frequently and to lack attachment to a community and family. These characteristics, in turn, tend to keep them away from the polls.

Consider another example. Every president elected in a year ending in zero from William H. Harrison in 1840 to John F. Kennedy in 1960 died in office. The correlation is between years ending in zero and presidential death. It seems quite obvious, however, that presidential death was not *caused* by the years ending in zero. Instead, this is simply a strange coincidence (called a *spurious correlation* by social scientists) in American politics.

These and many other correlations have nothing to do with causation. In reading and hearing about American politics, it is important not to assume that causation exists in a relationship that is simply correlational.

PRACTICING YOUR SKILLS

1. Write a brief essay describing a cause-and-effect relationship with which you are familiar. Explain why this is a cause-and-effect relationship and not merely a correlation.

2. Read an article concerning the stock market. You can find such an article in the business section of your local newspaper or in a national newspaper such as the *Wall Street Journal*. Try to determine whether the writer's assessment of why the stock market went up or down involves a correlation between two events or a true cause-and-effect relationship.

McCulloch v. Maryland In 1816, however, with the chartering of the Second Bank of the United States, the debate was reopened. This time, the question of strict or loose construction of the Constitution was ruled on by the Supreme Court. In *McCulloch v. Maryland* (1819), the Court found the creation of the Second Bank to be necessary to carry out the national government's monetary powers. Far more importantly, by its ruling, the Court supported the loose constructionists' idea that the necessary and proper clause gave Congress the right to make any laws necessary to carry out its other powers.

The Scope of Implied Powers The doctrine of implied powers has been used to improve rivers, canals, and other waterways; to create the United States Air Force; to define and provide punishment for federal crimes; and to fix minimum wages. Over the years, however, the Supreme Court has held that Congress cannot take an action based on the necessary and proper clause unless the action is linked with one or more of the expressed powers. The basis for an implied power must always be found among the expressed powers. The expressed and implied powers of Congress are listed in Figure 15–1 on page 403.

1. What part of the Constitution sets out the expressed powers?
2. Why are commerce and money powers important?
3. What are the other expressed powers of Congress?
4. Why is the necessary and proper clause also called the elastic clause?

5. What is the significance of the Supreme Court's decision in *McCulloch v. Maryland?*
6. What is impoundment? How does it lead to conflict between the president and Congress?
7. **For Critical Analysis:** It has been said that the necessary and proper clause, when liberally interpreted, allows the national government to involve itself in virtually any aspect of American life. Do you agree? Why or why not?

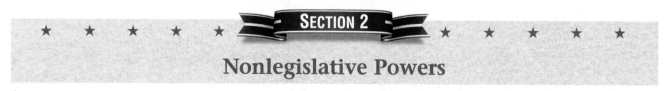

★ ★ ★ ★ ★ **SECTION 2** ★ ★ ★ ★ ★

Nonlegislative Powers

Preview Questions:

- ✪ What role does Congress play in the impeachment process?
- ✪ What role has Congress played in the constitutional amendment process?
- ✪ What advice and consent must Congress give to the president as part of its nonlegislative powers?
- ✪ What powers of investigation does Congress have?
- ✪ What is the oversight function of Congress, and what methods are used in this process?

Key Terms:

impeach, senatorial courtesy, subpoena, contempt of Congress, immunity, oversight function

Congress's most important duty is to make laws, but the Constitution also gives Congress a number of nonlegislative duties. Some nonlegislative functions are to be carried out by both houses of Congress, others are to be carried out by only the House, and others are to be carried out by only the Senate. Some of these functions involve Congress with the other two branches of government.

The Power of Impeachment

One of the most important but least used judicial powers of Congress is the power of impeachment.

Article 1, Section 2, of the Constitution grants Congress the power to **impeach,** or bring formal charges against, any member of the executive or judicial branch of government accused of misconduct or wrongdoing. *Impeachment is not, however, a determination of guilt.*

The House of Representatives has the exclusive power to bring charges of impeachment. Bringing such charges requires a majority vote. Then the case goes before the Senate for a trial to determine the guilt or innocence of the person charged. If the impeachment involves the president, the Chief Justice of the Supreme Court presides over the trial. Conviction requires the approval of two-thirds of the senators. If convicted, the official may be removed from office and

▲ *In the days before television, the only way to view an event such as the impeachment trial of President Andrew Johnson was to obtain a ticket like this.*

"He says he's from the phone company..."

▲ *What is illegal about the activity pictured in the cartoon above?*

prohibited from ever holding office again. Once the proceedings are over, the person can be tried, convicted, and punished in a regular court.

Only thirteen officials have ever been impeached by the House—one president, one senator, one Supreme Court justice, and ten federal judges. The Senate convicted five of these officials. All five were federal judges. The only president to be impeached, Andrew Johnson, was acquitted by the Senate. In 1974, the House Judiciary Committee recommended impeaching President Richard Nixon, but Nixon resigned from office before the case came to a vote in the full House.

The Power to Propose Constitutional Amendments

Congress shares with the states the power to propose constitutional amendments (see Chapter 3). The Constitution provides that amendments may be proposed by a two-thirds vote of both chambers of Congress. Alternatively, at the request of two-thirds of the state legislatures, Congress can call for a national convention to propose amendments. Proposed constitutional amendments of recent years have included amendments guaranteeing women equal rights (Equal Rights Amendment, or ERA), limiting the terms of members of Congress, balancing the federal budget, making it illegal to damage the American flag, and allowing prayer in schools.

So far, all constitutional amendments have been initiated by Congress. The states have approved twenty-seven of the proposed amendments and have failed to ratify only six. To be adopted, an amendment must be ratified by three-fourths of the state legislatures (thirty-eight states) or by a majority vote in conventions in three-fourths of the states. Congress decides which of these procedures is to be used.

The Power to Choose a President

Congress has two responsibilities related to the election of presidents. First, in a joint session of Congress, the president of the Senate is authorized to count the electoral votes and declare the winner. This process has become largely ceremonial. Second, if no person has a majority of the electoral votes, the House of Representatives chooses the president, and the Senate chooses the vice president. The House has used this electoral power only twice, to choose Thomas Jefferson in 1801 and John Quincy Adams in 1825.

Under the Twenty-fifth Amendment, both the Senate and the House must confirm the president's choice for vice president when that post is vacant due to illness, death, or resignation. That process has been used twice. Gerald Ford was confirmed as vice president in 1973, and Nelson Rockefeller was confirmed as vice president in 1974.

Just the Facts

James Madison predicted that in five out of every six presidential elections, no candidate would receive a majority of the electoral votes—thus leaving the decision to the House of Representatives.

Giving Advice and Consent

According to the Constitution, the Senate must approve presidential appointments to many important

Members of Congress get hundreds of letters, calls, and visits weekly. They cannot possibly handle every request personally. If you want your views heard, you need to know what to do. There are certain steps you can take to make your communication with congressional representatives more effective.

Write Follow these guidelines for effective written communication:

- Address the person properly, using his or her full title.
- Make your letter as brief as possible. Get straight to the point.
- If the subject of the letter is a bill or issue, mention it in the first paragraph.
- Make sure the issue is current.
- Give reasons for supporting your position. Be specific and constructive.
- Refer to any personal contact you (or your family) have had with the member or the member's family, friends, or staff.
- Avoid using a form letter. Compose one in your own words.
- Compliment the member for a job well done if you feel he or she is serving your district or state well.

You can also use the above guidelines to write an e-mail

PARTICIPATING IN YOUR GOVERNMENT

How to Communicate with Members of Congress

message to your congressional representatives. The e-mail addresses of all members of Congress can be found at the following URL:

www.lib.umich.edu/libhome/ Documents.center/congress/ conemail.txt

Visit If you go to Washington, D.C., you may be able to visit your legislator there. If you cannot go to Washington, you can visit your legislator when he or she is in your home district. Call the legislator's office ahead of time and arrange an appointment. During your visit, use the guidelines presented for writing a letter. Be brief, give reasons for your position, be specific and

constructive, and give credit where it is due.

Call Phone calls can be made to 202-224-3121, the number for both the House and the Senate. Ask the person who answers to connect you with the member's office. Identify yourself and explain the reason for your call. You will be given the opportunity to speak with a staff member who handles the subjects about which you are concerned.

Invite One of the best ways to see your legislator is to invite him or her to speak to a group. Legislators are sometimes interested in speaking to student groups. Remember, your legislators are more likely to listen to you in the future if their contacts with you are positive.

TAKING ACTION

1. Compose a letter to one of your legislators voicing a concern you have about a current issue.
2. Arrange a visit to a legislator's office when he or she is in your district. Carefully prepare what you will say ahead of time. Report to the class after your visit.

positions in the executive and judicial branches. Most such appointments involve the promotion of military officers, and Senate action is only a formality. The Senate looks more closely at nominations to major posts, however. These include appointments to the cabinet (see Chapter 17), independent boards and agencies, major foreign service posts, and all federal judicial posts, including the Supreme Court.

How the Powers of Congress Have Changed

The scope of the constitutional powers of Congress has been defined over time through congressional actions and Supreme Court decisions. Here are just a few examples of how the powers of Congress have changed since the early years of this nation.

THEN (1790s)	NOW
Congress did not have the power to tax personal income.	Congress was given the power to tax personal income by the Sixteenth Amendment (1913).
Congress had few powers under the commerce clause because it was unclear what the term *commerce* meant and whether Congress had the exclusive power to regulate interstate commerce.	In *Gibbons v. Ogden* (1824), the Supreme Court defined commerce broadly and held that Congress had the exclusive power to regulate interstate commerce. Eventually, the commerce clause was used to justify Congress's extensive regulation of the nation's commercial activities.
It was uncertain whether Congress had the authority to conduct investigations.	The constitutionality of congressional investigations was upheld by the Supreme Court in 1927. Today, Congress routinely conducts investigations for a number of purposes.

Executive and Judicial Appointments Over the years, the Senate has approved most presidential choices of cabinet officers. Of the more than six hundred cabinet appointments made, only twelve have been rejected. In the last twenty years, however, senators have examined the appointees more closely and have tended to raise more questions about the candidates' finances, personal backgrounds, and private lives. For example, when President George Bush nominated John Tower, a former Texas senator, to be his secretary of defense, lengthy hearings were held, and Tower's private life became an issue. The Senate finally voted to reject the Tower appointment. In 1997, after President Bill Clinton had appointed Anthony Lake to be the new director of the Central Intelligence Agency, Lake withdrew from the process as Senate hearings were being conducted to approve his appointment. Lake said that he had nothing to hide. He simply wanted to end what was becoming an exhausting ordeal and protect his privacy.

Presidential choices of federal officials who serve in the various states as federal judges, U.S. attorneys, and regional directors of federal agencies are also often debated. By the long-standing practice of **senatorial courtesy,** the Senate usually rejects a nominee for a state appointment to federal office if senators from that state are opposed to the nomination.

The Senate is most selective in the approval of Supreme Court nominations. About 20 percent of the names submitted for Court membership have been rejected by the Senate.

Treaties The Senate also has the responsibility to give advice and consent in relation to treaties made by the

Just the Facts

Before the 1830s, party caucuses in Congress nominated presidential candidates.

CHAPTER 15: The Powers of Congress **413**

▶ President Reagan introduces the members of the special investigation committee that became known as the Tower Commission, named for its chairman, former Senator John Tower. Later, President Bush nominated him to be his secretary of defense. Although Tower had been a senator and had held various responsible positions, the Senate held lengthy hearings and finally rejected his appointment.

president. This is done by a process of ratification, in which two-thirds of the members present must vote in favor of the treaty. During the years following the adoption of the Constitution, the Senate as a whole advised the president before the treaty was signed. Today, the president usually consults with the Senate Foreign Relations Committee and certain influential senators. When a treaty comes up for a vote, the Senate can approve, reject, or amend it.

The most controversial battle in the twentieth century over Senate ratification of a treaty occurred in 1919, when the Senate rejected the Treaty of Versailles, the general peace agreement to end World War I. The treaty included provisions for the League of Nations. Forty-nine senators voted for the pact and thirty-five against, but the vote was seven short of the necessary two-thirds. More recently, in 1980, Senate opposition to the second Strategic Arms Limitations Treaty (SALT II) between the United States and the former Soviet Union was so strong that the treaty was never submitted for ratification.

Even though the House does not have the right under the Constitution to ratify treaties, it does control the funding needed to put some treaties into effect. For this reason, the president usually finds it politically beneficial to consult with influential House members on most treaty matters.

In recent years, presidents have often bypassed the Senate by entering into executive agreements with other countries. We consider this practice in Chapter 18.

Investigative Powers

Through its investigative committees, Congress determines what new laws are needed, reviews the effectiveness of existing laws, and checks whether the executive branch is carrying out programs as they were intended to be carried out. Subjects of investigations may range from foreign policy to the influence of organized crime to the collapse of the savings and loan industry.

The power to conduct investigations is not specifically granted in the Constitution. Nevertheless, congressional investigations have a long history. The first was held in 1792 to look into the slaughter of six hundred American soldiers led by General Arthur St. Clair on the Ohio frontier. In 1927, the Supreme Court upheld the constitutionality of congressional investigations, and Congress has conducted investigations ever since.

GULLIVER

CONGRESSIONAL VETO POWERS

FOREIGN POLICY

◀ Foreign policy, which can be one of the most difficult challenges facing a president, offers the potential for disaster or international acclaim. Why is foreign policy an area especially susceptible to "congressional meddling"?

Most congressional investigations are conducted by standing committees or their subcommittees. Investigations may last for a few days or go on for months. Committee staff members may travel around the country as well as to other nations to collect evidence and find witnesses. Fact-finding trips have helped Congress make laws concerning such issues as crime prevention, farm-price supports, and aid to African famine victims.

Congressional committees have the power to issue a **subpoena,** which is a legal order requiring a person to appear before a congressional committee (or a court of law). Sometimes, dozens of witnesses are called to testify. Committees can also require witnesses to testify under oath and can prosecute witnesses for perjury (lying under oath). If a person refuses to testify or cooperate, he or she can be held in **contempt of Congress** and can be arrested and jailed.

Committees can also grant witnesses **immunity,** or freedom from prosecution, if the witnesses provide certain information that helps to solve crimes. Witnesses granted immunity can give testimony about activities in which they were involved without fear of prosecution.

Despite these powers, a congressional committee is not a court of law. A congressional investigation, however, may uncover evidence that results in criminal indictments of individuals in state or federal courts. It may also mean changes in government programs, the

Just the Facts

Bob Dole, former Senate majority leader and presidential candidate, entered Washington politics with no savings at all but left with several million dollars—all obtained perfectly legally from speaking fees and payments for similar activities.

▲ James Brady, seated in his wheelchair and accompanied by his wife Sarah, gave a "thumbs up" sign to photographers just prior to his testimony before a 1989 Senate judiciary subcommittee hearing about handgun legislation. Brady became concerned about controlling handguns after he was shot during an attempt on President Reagan's life in 1981.

ARCHITECTS
of Government

Daniel K. Inouye
(1924–   )

After Hawaii was admitted to statehood in 1959, Daniel K. Inouye was the first member of Congress elected from the new state. Of Japanese origin, Inouye served in the U.S. Army during World War II and lost his right arm in an attack against a German bunker in northern Italy. Senator Inouye has chaired numerous special investigations in the Senate and continues to be a top-ranking Senate Democrat.

HIS WORDS

"Our native Hawaiian neighbors have asked for the opportunity to express themselves [about] sovereignty. They have spoken and I am prepared to support their decision, and if called upon, will work with them towards their goal for sovereignty."
(*Press release, September 13, 1996*)

"The Internet is constantly evolving, and these new technologies can keep the people of Hawaii better informed about the federal government, the issues and their importance to our state. One of the most important responsibilities that I have to my constituents is staying in touch with them."
(*Announcement on Senator Inouye's Home Page,
May 13, 1997*)

DEVELOPING
CRITICAL THINKING SKILLS

1. Regarding the first quotation, does any group living within the United States have sovereign status?
2. Regarding the second quotation, do improvements in communications technology mean that members of Congress will be more responsive to their constituents' needs and interests than they were in the past?

loss of government contracts for businesses, or the passage of new laws and regulations.

The Oversight Function

Congress exercises its power to examine how effectively the executive branch and its officials carry out the laws through its **oversight function.** The term *oversight* has two opposing meanings. An oversight can be something that was accidentally missed or ignored. In the context of this chapter, however, *oversight* means careful supervision. The oversight function of Congress is sometimes referred to as its "watchdog function."

Congress has defined its oversight function in several laws. The Legislative Reorganization Act of 1946 calls for Congress to exercise "continuous watchfulness" over executive agencies. The Reorganization Act of 1970 states, "Each standing committee shall review and study, on a continuing basis, the application, administration, and execution" of laws relating to its interests.

Methods of Oversight Congress exercises its oversight function in several ways. One method is to hold committee hearings and investigations. A second technique is to require agencies to submit reports to Congress on their activities. During any one term, Congress may receive more than a thousand such reports from various agencies.

Congress also exercises oversight by controlling the budget. The House and Senate review the budgets of all executive agencies every year. If Congress evaluates an agency positively, it may reward the agency by increasing its budget. Other agencies may have their budgets cut or kept at present levels.

Lawmakers often have one of the congressional support agencies, such as the General Accounting Office (GAO), undertake a study of an executive agency's work. In fact, nearly every important law passed by Congress directs the GAO to study how the law has been implemented by the relevant executive agency.

Limits of Oversight For several reasons, Congress is limited in its ability to perform the oversight function. For one thing, the actions of the executive branch are not reviewed on a regular basis. For another, the complexity, size, and number of federal programs make oversight difficult. There are dozens of executive agencies, and many of them have large numbers of employees.

Limiting Congress's Power to Investigate

Nowhere does the Constitution specifically mention Congress's investigative power. Nonetheless, Congress, over many decades, has given itself the authority to conduct investigations. Many Americans believe that Congress has rightfully assumed and exercised investigatory powers. Others, though, feel that Congress has sometimes "gone too far" in exercising investigatory powers, and therefore these powers should be limited.

Congress Cannot Operate without Investigations, Some Say

Americans who are in favor of the way Congress uses its investigative powers argue that Congress must have the ability to obtain factual information on which to base its legislative decisions. Otherwise, it could not effectively exercise its constitutional powers.

Indeed, in 1885 Woodrow Wilson said, "The investigative function of Congress should be preferred even to its legislative function."

Certainly, groups within the Senate and the House believe that Congress must have the power to investigate violations of its rules of ethics. They also point out that when a president has committed a serious breach of duty or acted in an improper way, only through congressional investigations can needed information be found. This was true in the 1970s when Congress investigated the Watergate cover-up, in which President Richard M. Nixon was apparently deeply involved. It has been true with the congressional investigations of ethical issues surrounding the presidency of Bill Clinton in the 1990s. Other presidents will undoubtedly present other issues and problems. Congress must be able to investigate.

Investigate, but Not without Checks, Others Caution

Few Americans would argue that Congress should have *no* investigative powers. Many believe that limits should be placed on these powers, however. A well-known journalist, Walter Lippmann, once characterized a congressional investigation as "that legalized atrocity in which congressmen, starved of their legitimate food-for-thought, go on a wild and feverish manhunt and do not stop at cannibalism."

Perhaps Lippman was referring to one of the blackest periods in Congress's history, which began in the late 1940s and continued into the 1950s. At issue then was the perceived spread of communism throughout the world. The head of a Senate investigative committee, Senator Joseph McCarthy, repeatedly made unprovable charges against public and private individuals whom he and his committee members suspected of being Communist sympathizers. He set in motion background checks of many of the most famous scientists, screenwriters, movie directors, and professors in America. Finally, at the end of 1954, McCarthy was censured by the Senate. This, however, did little to help the ruined reputations and lives of those whom he had destroyed. There were many calls for reform in the congressional investigation process to prevent the recurrence of such abuses.

YOU DECIDE

1. In a court of law, the accused has many more rights and guarantees than individuals who come under the investigation of congressional committees. Do you think that the same rules that apply to court trials should be applied to congressional investigations? Why or why not?

2. Some have argued that many senators and representatives have started congressional investigations in order to put themselves in the public limelight. Is there any way to determine whether a congressional investigation is valid? Explain.

Overseeing the work of all these people would be almost impossible.

Political considerations can also influence how seriously oversight functions are carried out. In the 1980s, for example, it became known that some of President Ronald Reagan's staff had allowed arms to be sold to Iran in exchange for Iran's help in releasing American hostages held in the Middle East. The profits from those arms sales were then funneled to rebels in Nicaragua. Both of these actions were in violation of U.S. law. A year before this scandal was publicized, two congressional committees had begun investigating fund-raising efforts for the Nicaraguan rebels undertaken by a member of the president's staff, Colonel Oliver North. The investigations were dropped, however, because some key members of the congressional committees did not wish to challenge a popular president.

Constitutional Limits on the Powers of Congress

There are important limits on the seemingly sweeping powers of Congress. One is the system of checks and balances. The president, as head of the executive branch, can veto legislation passed by Congress. The judicial branch can declare laws passed by Congress unconstitutional.

Congress is limited by the fact that the Constitution does not give it certain powers. Thus, Congress may not create a national school system, establish units of local government, require that all eligible persons vote on election day, or pass a national divorce law. Congress cannot do these and a great many other things because it has not been given the constitutional authority to do them.

The Constitution also explicitly places certain limits on Congress. The purpose of the Bill of Rights, after all, was to limit or deny certain powers to the national government, such as the power to restrict freedom of speech.

Article I, Section 9, of the Constitution places specific limits on Congress as well. The most important of these limits protect the rights of citizens. The Constitution says that Congress shall not take away a citizen's right to a writ of *habeas corpus,* except in times of invasion or civil war. (As explained in Chapter 5, a writ of *habeas corpus* is the paper that orders the police to bring a citizen charged with a crime before a judge. The court then decides if there is enough evidence to hold the citizen. If not, the citizen must be released.)

The Constitution also prevents Congress from passing bills of attainder. (As mentioned in Chapter 5, a

► Colonel Oliver North, shown here, was called to testify before a special oversight committee concerning his role in the Iran-Contra arms deal.

bill of attainder is a law that convicts a person of a crime without a trial.) In addition, Congress may not pass *ex post facto* laws—laws that make a particular act a crime and then punish people who committed the act *before* the law was passed.

Furthermore, the Constitution does not allow Congress to grant titles of nobility to any person. Nor is Congress allowed to pass laws regulating commerce that are more favorable to one state than to another.

These limits on the powers of Congress are in place so that the legislative branch does not come to exemplify James Madison's "very definition of tyranny." As you have learned, Congress still possesses the powers needed to perform its immense job. Through the powers expressed in the Constitution and implied by the necessary and proper clause, Congress is able to act as an effective legislative body. Congress also wields nonlegislative powers in such areas as impeachment, the constitutional amendment process, investigation, and oversight.

SECTION 2 REVIEW

1. Which chamber of Congress has the exclusive power to impeach?
2. What is Congress's role in the constitutional amendment process?
3. What are Congress's responsibilities concerning the election of the president?
4. What are the major methods of oversight that Congress may use?
5. How are Congress's powers limited by the Constitution?
6. **For Critical Analysis:** Are Congress's current powers to oversee the president's actions sufficient to prevent the president from becoming too powerful? Explain your answer.

★ ★ ★ ★ **Chapter Summary** ★ ★ ★ ★

Section 1: Legislative Powers

- Article I, Section 1, of the Constitution grants all power to make laws to Congress.
- The powers that are specifically provided for in Article I of the Constitution—the expressed powers—include the powers to:

- tax and spend
- borrow (the Constitution places no limit on the amount of money that Congress may borrow)
- coin money, including paper money and coins
- set bankruptcy laws
- regulate commerce, including both interstate commerce and foreign trade
- approve treaties
- declare war
- create federal courts below the level of the Supreme Court
- establish post offices and post roads (including highways, railways, waterways, and airways needed to deliver the mail)
- grant copyrights and patents (Copyrights protect the original works of authors and composers, while patents protect the rights of inventors and engineers.)
- establish rules for naturalization, the process by which individuals from other countries become citizens of the United States (This process must be uniform in all states.)
- acquire, manage, and dispose of territories.

- The implied powers are based on the necessary and proper clause. In *McCulloch v. Maryland* (1819), the Supreme Court ruled that the necessary and proper clause gave Congress the right to make any laws necessary to carry out its other powers.

Section 2: Nonlegislative Powers

- The Constitution gives Congress a number of nonlegislative duties, including the powers to:

- impeach government officials
- propose constitutional amendments
- choose the president if no candidate receives a majority of the electoral votes.

- The Senate must approve presidential appointments to many important positions in the executive and judicial branches. The Senate must also give advice and consent in relation to treaties made by the president.
- Through its investigative committees, Congress has the power to hold hearings to investigate important issues and problems.
- The power to examine how effectively the executive branch and its officials carry out the laws passed by Congress is called the oversight function.

CHAPTER 15 Review

★ REVIEW QUESTIONS ★

1. What are expressed powers?
2. Why is the congressional power to tax and spend important?
3. Why does the United States have a national debt?
4. Explain the commerce power of Congress and how the definition of *commerce* has expanded.
5. How does Congress share war powers with the president?
6. Why is the necessary and proper clause also called the elastic clause? How has this clause been used?
7. How was the main issue in *McCulloch v. Maryland* resolved? Why is this case important?
8. What are Congress's nonlegislative powers?
9. How has Congress used its investigative powers?
10. How has the congressional power to investigate evolved, and how is it limited?

★ CRITICAL THINKING ★

1. Do you agree with the War Powers Resolution of 1973, which limits the president's power to send troops into combat without congressional approval? Why or why not?
2. The framers of the Constitution wanted to ensure that Congress could not involve itself in the states' internal affairs. Nonetheless, the Supreme Court's expansive interpretation of the commerce clause has allowed Congress to control virtually all economic activities, even those carried out strictly within each state's borders. Do you think this is a fair exercise of congressional power? Give reasons for your answer.
3. Should partisanship (loyalty to a political party) ever be a factor in the Senate's decision to consent to—or reject—a presidential appointee? Why or why not?

★ IMPROVING YOUR SKILLS ★

Communication Skills

Common Considerations in Writing Whether you are writing a letter, a report, or an essay, you must consider three things before you begin: the reader, the purpose, and the subject matter.

Know Your Reader: Before you begin writing, think about who the reader will be. A letter you write to a friend, for example, will be very different from a letter you write to a member of Congress. When you understand the needs of your reader, you will be able to write a more meaningful message. Understanding your reader will also help determine the tone of your letter. If you are writing an informal note to a friend, your approach and vocabulary will be quite different than if you were writing a letter to your school principal or your congressperson.

Know Your Purpose: Before you begin writing, you should also think about the purpose of your writing. Most writing is done for one of the following reasons:

- to inform
- to request
- to inquire
- to confirm
- to persuade
- to entertain

For example, if you are writing to apply for a job, you want to inform your potential employer of your capabilities; you also want to persuade the personnel representative that you are the best candidate for the job.

Know Your Subject: Finally, you should know as much as possible about your subject before you begin writing. Use the research guidelines on page 364 and the interview techniques on page 112, if necessary, to

get information. Think of innovative ways to learn about your subject. There are many sources for you to use. These include newspapers, magazines, reference books, and online research sites.

Writing Think of an issue about which you are concerned. Compose one letter to a friend and one letter to a congressional representative expressing your views. Compare the two letters. Describe your purpose in writing the letters. Make a list of any information you could obtain that would improve your letters. Identify where the information could be located.

Social Studies Skills

Understanding Symbols Many charts and graphs use symbols to help illustrate key points and to make the diagrams easy to read and understand. Look at Figure 15–1 on page 403.

1. What is the focus of this figure?
2. Make a list of all of the symbols that are used.
3. How does the topmost symbol relate to the first power of Congress?
4. To which power does the Statue of Liberty relate, and why?
5. What symbol relates to Congress's copyright powers?

★ ACTIVITIES AND PROJECTS ★

1. Divide into groups of five or six. Each group member is to collect articles that describe congressional actions from current newspapers and magazines. Create a bulletin board display, grouping the articles according to the types of congressional power—expressed, implied, or nonlegislative—they describe. Discuss how the articles illustrate those powers.
2. Research how often the War Powers Resolution of 1973 has been effectively used. Write a short report detailing your findings.
3. Research a recent Congressional investigation. What was the purpose of the investigation? Which committee was responsible for the investigation? Who was called to testify, and what were the professional positions of those who testified? What was the outcome of the investigation? If possible, watch some of these hearings on C-SPAN.

What If . . .

Congress Could Not Regulate Interstate Commerce?

Commerce among the fifty states is regulated solely by Congress. What might happen if the states could do whatever they wanted with respect to how they regulated and taxed goods and services leaving and entering their borders?

How Congress Makes Laws

CHAPTER OBJECTIVES

To learn about and understand . . .

⭐ The ways in which the House and the Senate organize to begin a new term

⭐ The steps involved in the lawmaking process from the introduction of a bill to the vote

⭐ The final stages of the process in which a bill becomes law

"Congress in its committee rooms is Congress at work."

Woodrow Wilson
(1856–1924)
Twenty-eighth President of the United States

INTRODUCTION

The ritual is the same every year in virtually every high school in America. A prom is organized sometime during the year to honor seniors who are graduating. Usually, the junior class is in charge. Imagine several hundred juniors trying to decide on the theme, the budget, the music, the decorations, and all the other details for the senior prom. You can imagine how difficult and time-consuming it would be to get all of the juniors to agree on every detail of the prom plan. To avoid these problems, a prom committee is formed. It is the committee—perhaps with the approval of the whole class—that does the work needed to put on the prom.

Congress is not much different. As reflected in Woodrow Wilson's words quoted above, however, much of Congress's work takes place in committees.

◀ This woodcut from the 1880s captures the Senate as it gathers for its morning session.

Congress Begins Its Work

Preview Questions:

- 🌎 What roles do political caucuses play during the congressional term?
- 🌎 How are the opening days of the House and Senate different?
- 🌎 What various types of legislation are considered by Congress?

Key Terms:

clerk of the House, State of the Union address, bill, public bills, private bills, joint resolution, concurrent resolutions, simple resolutions, rider

You have seen how Congress is organized to carry out its functions, and you have learned about the powers of Congress. You will now take a look at how Congress performs its most important function— lawmaking. The laws enacted by Congress have helped shape this country into the nation it is today, and laws will continue to guide the nation in the future.

> **Just the Facts**
>
> *In 1950, there were only four caucuses in Congress. Today, there are over one hundred.*

This chapter explores how the lawmaking process works. It describes the opening of a congressional session and the various forms new legislation takes. Then it explains the steps that a bill must go through to become a law.

As you have learned, a new term of Congress begins on January 3 of every odd-numbered year. During each term, thousands of bills are introduced. The legislative process that each bill undergoes is complicated. Consequently, Congress must organize itself so that its members can consider all of these bills.

The process of organization begins with the political parties to which members of Congress belong. After all, those political parties are often responsible for getting the members elected. It is not surprising, then, that the chambers of Congress include political

groups. These groups begin work even before each term begins.

Political Caucuses

Before a new term begins, Democratic and Republican members of the House and Senate meet in separate, private party conferences called caucuses. Both the Senate and the House hold two party caucuses—one for Republicans and one for Democrats. These caucuses meet in order to reach agreement among themselves about key issues so they can act as a unified force. They also plan the party's strategy for the upcoming term. In addition, they choose the party leaders who will organize and direct party activities during the term. These choices are often made on the basis of seniority.

The major parties are not the only groups to hold caucuses. Indeed, the number of caucuses has grown in recent years. Caucuses have generally been organized on the basis of regions and special interests. Examples are the Congressional Sunbelt Council and the Congressional Steel Caucus. They have also been organized on the basis of gender and ethnicity. The Black Caucus, the Congressional Women's Caucus, and the Hispanic Caucus are examples of such groups. The activities of these caucuses are directed toward fellow members of Congress and toward administrative agencies. Within Congress, they press for committees to hold hearings on issues of interest to them, push particular legislation, and lobby for votes on bills they favor. Thus, even before the term begins, members of Congress have set the legislative process in motion.

Since the 104th Congress (1995–1997), there has been significant reduction in funds for financing some caucuses. They may become less influential in the future.

The Opening Day of Congress

On the opening day of Congress, each chamber meets in its own wing of the Capitol building, shown in Figure 16–1 on page 425.

Rooms on Second Floor of the Capitol

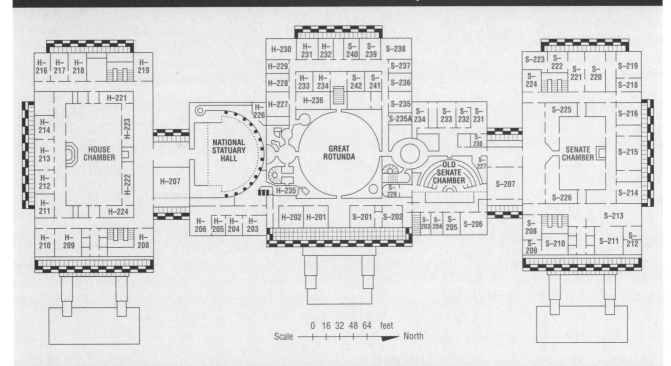

House Side	**Senate Side**

House Side

H–201, 202, 203, 204, 205, 206. Speaker
H–207. House reception room (Sam Rayburn Room)
H–208. Committee on Ways and Means
H–209, 210. Speaker's rooms
H–211. Parliamentarian
H–212, 213, 214. Representatives' retiring rooms
H–216, 217, 218. Committee on Appropriations
H–219. Minority whip
H–221, 223. Republican cloakrooms
H–222, 224. Democratic cloakrooms
H–226. House document room
H–227, 228, 229, 230, 231, 232, 233, 236. Minority leader
H–234. Prayer room
H–235. Congresswomen's suite

Senate Side

S–201, 202, 203, 204, 205, 237, 238, 239, 240, 241, 242. Senators' offices
S–206. President *pro tempore*
S–207. Senators' conference room (Mike Mansfield Room)
S–208, 209. Secretary of the Senate
S–210. Secretary of the Senate (John F. Kennedy Room)
S–211. Secretary of the Senate (Lyndon B. Johnson Room)
S–212. Vice president
S–213. Senators' reception room
S–214. Ceremonial office of the vice president
S–215. Senators' retiring room (Marble Room)
S–216. President's room
S–218, 219. Official reporters of debates
S–220. Bill clerk and journal clerk
S–221, 222, 223, 224. Majority leader (Robert C. Byrd Rooms)
S–225. Democratic cloakroom
S–226. Republican cloakroom
S–227. Executive clerk
S–229, 243. Assistant Republican leader
S–230, 231, 232, 233, 234, 235, 235A, 236. Republican leader (Howard H. Baker, Jr., Rooms)

Opening Day in the House Every House member is up for election every two years, so each term begins anew. All members have to be sworn in, whether it is their first term or their tenth. In addition, rules must be made, and organization must be decided upon.

The **clerk of the House** (a staff officer of the House of Representatives) from the previous session presides at the beginning of the first day's session. The chamber is called to order, and a roll call is taken. The members then *officially* elect a Speaker of the House. This election is only a formality, because the Speaker has already been chosen by the majority party caucus. The Speaker of the House is sworn in by the member of the House who has served the longest. The Speaker then swears in the rest of the representatives.

Next the House *officially* elects its nonmember, or staff, officers. These include the clerk, the sergeant at arms, and the postmaster. Again, these choices have already been decided by the majority party caucus. Then the rules that will govern how the House proceeds throughout the term are adopted. The rules of the House have been evolving for over two hundred years, and they are usually readopted with little or no change. Finally, members are appointed to permanent committees, and committee chairpersons, also determined previously by majority party caucus, are formally selected. The opening day of the House ends with a message in which the House informs the Senate that it is ready for the president's annual message to Congress.

Opening Day in the Senate On opening day in the Senate, only one-third of the Senate's members are beginning new terms, which makes the Senate a continuous body. This means its members have less organizational business to attend to than do members of the House. The Senate swears in its recently elected members and fills vacancies in its organizations and com-

▶ *President Woodrow Wilson addresses the Sixty-third Congress in 1913.*

mittees. The Senate then informs the House that it is ready for the president's annual address.

State of the Union Address

After both houses have organized, a joint committee of the two officially notifies the president that Congress is in session and ready to begin work. Within a few weeks, the president delivers his annual **State of the Union address.**

Article II, Section 3, of the Constitution, states as follows:

He [the president] shall from time to time give to the Congress Information on the State of the Union, and recommend to their Consideration such Measures as he shall judge necessary and expedient; . . .

Members of Congress, together with members of the cabinet, the Supreme Court, the foreign service corps, and other dignitaries, assemble in the large chamber of the House of Representatives to hear the address.

The State of the Union address was originally a long and often boring speech. Our third president, Thomas Jefferson, started a precedent when he submitted the speech in writing. He claimed that a speech before Congress was too much like a British monarch's opening speech to Parliament. In 1913, Woodrow Wilson broke Jefferson's precedent by personally delivering his first State of the Union address. He used the speech as a chance to outline his administration's overall agenda and to urge the passage of certain programs.

The media, especially television, have added to the importance of the speech over the years. Today, presidents use it as a ceremonial way of reporting on the "health" of the nation and its concerns, both domestic and foreign. The president also lays out the administration's broad policies and makes legislative recommendations in the speech.

Bills, Resolutions, and Riders

Congress considers several kinds of legislation each year. Most legislation is in the form of bills. Some legislation takes the form of resolutions and riders.

Bills A **bill** is a draft of a law presented to the House or the Senate for enactment. There are two kinds of bills: public and private.

ARCHITECTS

of Government
Carol Moseley-Braun (1947–)

In 1992, Carol Moseley-Braun became the first African American woman ever elected to the U.S. Senate. Before her election, she was an assistant U.S. attorney and a member of the state legislature in Illinois. In the Senate, she was the first permanent woman member of the Senate Finance Committee. She also served on the Banking, Housing, and Urban Affairs Committee, as well as the Special Committee on Aging.

HER WORDS

"In order to compete in a global economy, America will need a workforce even smarter than it is now."

(Press release, March 18, 1997)

"Chicago is a perfect example of what legislation can accomplish on a national level. Environmental protection can be and is good business."

(Press release, January 30, 1997)

DEVELOPING
CRITICAL THINKING SKILLS
....

1. In her first quotation, what did Senator Moseley-Braun mean when she referred to a "global economy"?
2. How could environmental protection be "good business"?

Public bills involve matters of national interest. For example, a bill proposing a federal tax increase, health-care guidelines, a ban on assault-style automatic weapons, clean-air measures, or an appropriation of funds for a military program would be a public bill. Public bills are often controversial, and those that are

Many Laws Proposed, Few Passed

In principle, Congress serves all Americans who want government to pass legislation in their favor. Business groups, farmers, labor unions, various other interest groups, federal agencies, the president, and many others look to Congress to pass laws favorable to their interests. Consequently, thousands of bills are introduced in Congress each term. Yet only about one in ten of these bills becomes a law. As President John F. Kennedy once noted, "It is very easy to defeat a bill in Congress. It is much more difficult to pass one." Why do so few of the bills introduced become law?

One reason is that the lawmaking process is long and complex. The steps involved in passing a new law leave many opportunities for members of Congress to delay, alter, or kill a bill. These legislative hurdles give opponents of the bill numerous advantages. If their efforts to stop the bill fall short at one step along the way, they can always try again further down the line.

Bills that are opposed by important interest groups are not likely to be passed. Because members of Congress depend on money from interest groups to get reelected, they are reluctant to antagonize these groups. For example, in every Congress since 1978, the House and Senate banking committees have tried to restructure the financial industry by attempting to overhaul a 1933 law. But reform has been hopelessly deadlocked because of the conflicting interests of big banks, small banks, insurance companies, and securities firms.

With the rise of negative campaigning, many members have concluded that it is safer to duck hard issues than to make choices and risk losing favor with one side or the other. They increasingly appoint outside commissions and task forces to study controversial problems. This process often takes many months and does not produce a solution. For example, the Bipartisan Commission on Comprehensive Health Care devoted nine months and $1.5 million to an examination of the health needs of uninsured older Americans. The proposed solution would have cost the government $66 billion a year. The proposal was immediately abandoned because it failed to explain how the program was to be funded.

A plan designed to protect older persons from the high costs of health care for major illnesses had strong support from both parties. The plan was dropped when a small but vocal group of well-off older Americans objected to the tax-rate increases that would have been required. "Five percent of the elderly swung us around like a dead cat," said Senator Alan Simpson, a Republican from Wyoming.

Another reason so few bills become law is that lawmakers sometimes introduce bills knowing they have no chance of passing. They introduce such bills for various reasons. They may want to draw public attention to legislation in such areas as crime control or education. They may want to go on record in support of a certain idea. They may simply wish to satisfy a group of voters from their district or an important interest group. This can help them avoid criticism during election time, because they can report that they have taken "action" on the issue. They can blame committees and other lawmakers for the bill's failure to become law.

THINK ABOUT IT

1. Why do opponents of a bill have an advantage over supporters?
2. Should lawmakers be able to introduce bills that they know have no chance of becoming law? Explain.
3. Should lawmakers be able to introduce bills for the benefit of interest groups? Why or why not?

FIGURE 16–2 Selected Bills from the 105th Congress

Congress considers numerous bills during each congressional term. Some bills have riders attached to them (see page 430). Why is this?

Bill	Subject
H.R. 9	To waive certain prohibitions with respect to nationals of Cuba coming to the United States to play organized professional baseball
H.R. 16	To provide a program of national health insurance
H.R. 207	Hate Group Public Funding Exclusion Act
H.R. 1401	To amend the Internal Revenue Code of 1986 to provide a five-year extension of the credit for producing electricity from wind
H.R. 2404	Stop the Theft of Our Social Security Numbers Act
H.R. 2408	After School Education and Safety Act of 1997
H.R. 3002	Postsecondary Adult Vocational Education Act
H.R. 3009	Health Care Consumer Protection Act of 1997
H.R. 3012	Dakota Water Resources Act of 1997
H.R. 3049	To adjust the immigration status of certain Haitian nationals who were provided refuge in the United States
S. 104	Nuclear Waste Policy Act of 1997
S. 601	To amend federal law to prohibit taking a child hostage in order to evade arrest
S. 1009	American Family Fair Minimum Wage Act of 1997
S. 1503	Voting Rights of Homeless Citizens Act of 1997

▲ *During a recent visit to the United States, Jiang Zemin, the president of the People's Republic of China, met with Speaker of the House Newt Gingrich, Senate Majority Leader Trent Lott, and other congressional leaders.*

seriously considered by Congress may be debated for months or possibly years before they become law.

Private bills are bills that apply to certain persons or places rather than to the nation as a whole. A private bill might pay a settlement to a woman whose car was demolished by a U.S. Postal Service truck, for example, or might grant the right to enter the United States to a certain group of refugees. Figure 16–2 lists selected bills from the 105th Congress (1997–1999).

Resolutions There are three basic types of resolutions. These are joint resolutions, concurrent resolutions, and simple resolutions.

A **joint resolution** is a formal declaration of opinion that is voted on by both chambers of Congress and sent to the president for his approval. Joint resolutions are very similar to bills. They must go through the same steps as bills to become law. When they are passed, they have the force of law. Joint resolutions often deal with temporary or unusual matters or correct an error in an earlier law. For example, funds for a special military action overseas might be authorized by a joint resolution. Joint resolutions are also used to propose constitutional amendments.

Concurrent resolutions deal with matters that require the action of the House and Senate but that do not require a law. They are measures intended to express an opinion or an official policy. For example, a concurrent resolution might commemorate the anniversary of a successful space exploration or the welcoming of an important visitor, such as the head of the People's Republic of China. A concurrent resolution might set the date for the adjournment of Congress. Concurrent resolutions must be passed by both chambers of Congress but do not require the president's signature and do not have the force of law.

Simple resolutions deal with matters affecting only one chamber of Congress and are passed by that chamber alone. Simple resolutions are regularly used to adopt new rules or procedures or to amend existing ones. These resolutions may also be used to express opinions. For example, the Senate may pass a resolution in support of an action taken by the president toward the People's Republic of China. Like concurrent resolutions, simple resolutions are not sent to the president for approval and do not have the force of law.

Riders A bill or resolution usually deals with only one subject. Sometimes, however, a provision called a **rider** is attached to a bill. A rider is unlikely to pass on its own, so it is attached to an important bill that is likely to pass into law. The rider's sponsors hope it will "ride" through the legislative process on the strength of the bill. Riders become law if the bill to which they are attached is passed. Riders often deal with controversial issues and sometimes lead to the defeat of the bill to which they are attached.

1. What is the purpose of holding party caucuses prior to the convening of Congress?
2. How do the opening days of the House and Senate differ?
3. What does the president discuss in the State of the Union address in modern times?
4. What are bills, resolutions, and riders?
5. Why might a member of Congress introduce a bill that has little chance of passing into law?
6. What is the difference between a joint resolution and a concurrent resolution?
7. **For Critical Analysis:** If the Speaker of the House, the clerk, the sergeant at arms, and other officials have already been chosen by the majority party caucus, why do you think the House continues to *officially* elect its officers on opening day?

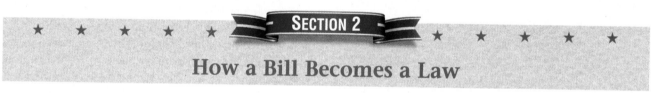

SECTION 2

How a Bill Becomes a Law

Preview Questions:

- How is a bill introduced in Congress?
- How are bills assigned to committees? What happens within the committees?
- How does the House act on a bill when the bill reaches the floor? What methods are used for taking votes?
- How does the Senate act on a bill when it reaches the floor? How does this action differ from action taken in the House?

Key Terms:

hopper, sponsors, pigeonhole, markup session, calendar, House Rules Committee, quorum, committee of the whole, voice vote, standing vote, teller vote, roll-call vote, record vote, filibuster, cloture, cloture rule

As you know, Congress is the legislative branch of our national government. This means that the job of Congress is to make laws. The lawmaking process begins when a bill is introduced into Congress and ends when the president signs the bill into law. Here we look at each of the steps involved in the lawmaking procedure. These steps are summarized in Figure 16–3 on page 431.

Introducing Legislation

Ideas for legislation come from various sources. An idea might be suggested by a constituent or a lobbyist, a federal agency, or a member of Congress or one of his or her staff. Many bills are proposed by the executive branch. Although almost anyone may suggest legislation, only a member of Congress can formally introduce it.

FIGURE 16–3 How a Bill Becomes a Law This figure shows the steps in the process of enacting laws. At what stage in the process do members from both chambers work together to create a compromise bill?

| H.R. 100 A BILL | **House** | | **Senate** | S. 100 A BILL |

Introduction
A member of the House drafts the bill and puts it into the legislative "hopper." It is then assigned to the appropriate House committee.

Introduction
A member of the Senate drafts the bill and introduces it by presenting it to the clerk or to the Senate floor. It is then assigned to the appropriate Senate committee.

House Committee
The committee, if it decides to consider the bill, may refer it to the appropriate House subcommittee.

Senate Committee
The committee, if it decides to consider the bill, may refer it to the appropriate Senate subcommittee.

House Subcommittee
The House subcommittee examines, discusses, and revises the bill. If the subcommittee recommends passage, it returns the bill to the full committee.

Senate Subcommittee
The Senate subcommittee examines, discusses, and revises the bill. If the subcommittee recommends passage, it returns the bill to the full committee.

House Committee
The full House committee amends and rewrites the bill.

Senate Committee
The full Senate committee amends and rewrites the bill.

House Rules Committee
The House Rules Committee grants a rule governing floor debate.

Floor
Members of the House debate the bill, present amendments, and vote on passage. If the bill is passed in different versions by the House and the Senate, it goes to a conference committee.

Floor
Members of the Senate debate the bill, present amendments, and vote on passage. If the bill is passed in different versions by the House and the Senate, it goes to a conference committee.

Conference Committee
A conference committee composed of members from both chambers confers to work out differences between the two versions of the bill. The proposed compromise bill is then returned to both chambers for approval. If both chambers approve the compromise bill in identical form, it goes to the president for action.

President
The president can: (1) sign the bill into law; (2) hold the bill without signing or vetoing it for ten days (excluding Sundays), after which time it automatically becomes law; (3) veto and return the bill to Congress with objections, after which Congress can override the president's veto with a two-thirds vote in both chambers; (4) make use of a "pocket veto,"—that is, hold a bill that comes up for decision less than ten days before Congress adjourns, which prevents the bill from becoming law; or (5) if the Supreme Court determines that the line-item veto is not unconstitutional, use the line-item veto to veto part of the bill and sign the rest of the bill into law.

Bills may be initiated in either chamber of Congress—except for revenue bills. According to Article I, Section 7, of the Constitution,

All Bills for raising Revenue shall originate in the House of Representatives; but the Senate may propose or concur with Amendments as on other Bills.

A representative introduces a bill by simply dropping the written proposal into the **hopper,** a box near the clerk's desk. A senator may introduce a bill by presenting it to the clerk at the presiding officer's desk or by formally presenting the bill from the floor of the Senate. Those who draft and propose bills are called **sponsors.**

Once they have been introduced, bills are printed and distributed. Bills are numbered according to where and when they were introduced. For example, bill H.R. 288 would be the 288th measure introduced in the House of Representatives during the congressional term. Having received a number, the bill is entered in the House *Journal* and the *Congressional Record* for the day. The House *Journal* and the *Congressional Record* are official publications of Congress.

When the number of a bill is printed in the *Congressional Record*, the bill has been placed at *first reading*. For a bill to become law, it must have *three* readings at various stages of its progress. The second reading usually occurs when floor debate begins. The third takes place after any amendments have been added to the bill and a final vote is about to be taken.

Study by a Committee

As soon as a bill is introduced and assigned a number, it is sent to the appropriate standing committee. For example, a farm bill would be sent to the Agriculture Committee, and a gun-control bill would be sent to the Judiciary Committee. In the House, the Speaker assigns the bill to the appropriate committee. In the Senate, the presiding officer assigns the bill to a committee. Committee chairpersons may, in turn, send the bill on to a subcommittee. For example, a Senate bill concerning conventional military weapons in Europe would be sent to the Senate Foreign Relations Subcommittee on European Affairs. Each committee sorts the bills it receives and considers only those it deems important. The chairperson may decide to **pigeonhole** a bill—that is, put it aside and ignore it. Most bills are pigeonholed and thus die in committee.

If a bill is not pigeonholed, it is placed on the committee's agenda or assigned to a subcommittee. Committee or subcommittee staff members go to work researching the bill and sometimes hold public hearings. During such hearings, people who support or oppose the bill may express their views. Committees (and subcommittees) also have the power to order witnesses to testify at public hearings. Witnesses may be executive agency officials, experts on the subject, or representatives of interest groups concerned about the bill. Depending on the level of interest in the subject, the hearings may be attended by only a few people or by a large group.

Sometimes a committee or subcommittee member takes a fact-finding trip to gather information on a bill. These trips are made to locations affected by the proposed measure. For example, if proposed legislation concerns an urban housing project, a member of the Senate Committee on Banking, Housing, and Urban Affairs may visit an inner-city area. If proposed legislation concerns wolves in a national park, a member of the National Parks and Public Lands Subcommittee of the House Committee on Interior and Insular Affairs may visit the national park in question.

If the bill is being studied by a subcommittee, the subcommittee, after gathering information on the bill, meets to approve the bill as is, add new amendments, or draft a new bill. This meeting is known as the **markup session.** If members cannot agree on changes, a vote is taken. When a subcommittee has completed its work on a bill, the bill goes to full committee. The full committee then meets for its own markup session. It may hold its own hearings, amend the subcommittee's version, or simply approve the subcommittee's recommendations.

Finally, the committee reports the bill back to the full House or Senate. It can report the bill favorably, report the bill with amendments, or report a newly written bill. It can also report a bill unfavorably, but usually such a bill will have been pigeonholed earlier instead. Along with the bill, the committee sends to

Informed citizens know about the voting records of their representatives and senators. You can obtain this information from several sources. All record, or roll-call, votes are printed in the *Congressional Record* (online at **www.access.gpo.gov/su_docs/aces/aces150.html**) and in the *Congressional Quarterly Weekly Report* (online at **pathfinder.com/CQ/**). Some large newspapers, such as the *Washington Post* (online at **www.washingtonpost.com/**) and the *New York Times* (online at **www.nytimes.com/**), print weekly summaries of how local members voted on key issues. Another source for voting records is Project Vote Smart, which gives the voting records (and much other information) for each member of Congress. You can reach this organization at:

Project Vote Smart
129 NW Fourth St., Suite 204,
Corvallis, OR 97330
Phone: 541-754-2746
www.vote-smart.org/

Reading these final votes, however, does not give you the full picture. A member of Congress may have voted one way in committee proceedings and the other way in the final voting process. She may have wanted to go on record as voting according to public opinion in the final stage of passage. Members may also have changed

Locating and Interpreting Congressional Voting Records

their votes after the voting was completed.

One way of examining a member's voting behavior throughout the lawmaking process is by reading studies prepared by interest groups. Dozens of groups prepare studies and rate congressional members' voting records. (Remember that these groups have their own sets of standards. You need to find out what these standards are in order to understand the basis of the ratings.) Some of these groups include:

Consumer Federation of
   America
1424 Sixteenth St., NW
Suite 604
Washington, DC 20036
Phone: 202-387-6121

Sierra Club
85 Second St., Second Floor
San Francisco, CA 94105
Phone: 415-977-5500
www.sierraclub.com/

Voter Information Services
P.O. Box 649
Reading, MA 01867
Phone: 781-944-6406
www.vis.org/

TAKING ACTION

1. Contact one of the groups listed above. Ask for information about the organization and its ratings of the senators and representatives in your state. Decide whether you think the group would be considered liberal, middle-of-the-road, or conservative.

2. Obtain the voting record of one of your state's senators. The record should show how the senator voted on various bills over the past year. Determine where on the political spectrum that senator's views lie. Compare your determination with the evaluation you obtained from one of the groups listed above. How would you explain the differences, if there are any, between its evaluation and yours?

the House or Senate a written report that explains the committee's actions, describes the bill, lists the major changes made by the committee, and gives opinions on the bill.

Scheduling Legislation

Next, the bill is placed on a calendar and scheduled for debate. A congressional **calendar** is a schedule of the order in which bills will be taken up on the floor.

There are five calendars in the House, and bills are assigned to one or another of them depending on nature and subject matter. These calendars are as follows:

1. **The Union Calendar.** Formally called the Calendar of the Committee of the Whole House on the State of the Union, this calendar includes all government property, revenue, and appropriations bills.
2. **The House Calendar.** All other public bills go on this calendar.
3. **The Private Calendar.** Formally known as the Calendar of the Committee of the Whole House, this calendar includes almost all private bills.
4. **The Consent Calendar.** This calendar is for bills removed from the first two calendars mentioned above and agreed to by unanimous consent. These are typically minor bills.
5. **The Discharge Calendar.** All requests to discharge bills from committees are placed on this calendar.

The **House Rules Committee** plays a major role in the scheduling process. This committee, along with the House leaders, regulates the flow of bills through the House. The Rules Committee can move bills ahead quickly, hold them back, or stop them completely. It can also set up special rules that limit the time for debate and the number of amendments that can be suggested for the bill.

The Senate is much smaller, and a few leading members control the flow of bills to committees and to the floor. The Senate has only one calendar, the Calendar of General Orders, which lists all bills to be considered by the Senate. The Senate brings bills to the floor by "unanimous consent." This is a motion by which all members present on the floor decide to consider a bill from the calendar.

The Constitution requires that before any action can take place on the floor of either chamber, a certain number of members must be present. This number, known as a **quorum,** is a majority of the full House (218 members) or a majority of the Senate (51 members).

Action in the House

When a bill reaches the House floor, it receives its second reading as the clerk reads the bill through. After each paragraph is read, amendments may be offered and debate may take place. Many bills are minor and pass with little or no opposition. Because of its large size and the number of bills introduced, the House has developed several procedures to speed up the legislative process for some of the more important matters.

Committee of the Whole To speed along the passage of an important bill, the entire House may sit as a **committee of the whole.** In this committee, a temporary chairperson is appointed by the Speaker of the House, and the usual formal House rules do not apply. At least 100 members must be present in order to conduct business, instead of the official quorum of 218. The measure is debated or amended, with votes on amendments as needed. The committee of the whole can approve or reject bills by a majority vote. The committee adjourns when it completes its action, and the House returns to its normal session and procedures. The Speaker presides once again. The full House hears the chairperson report the committee's recommendations, and it formally adopts them.

Debate Because of its large size, the House places severe limitations on floor debate. The Speaker of the House recognizes those who may speak and can force any member who does not "stick to the subject" to give up the floor.

Normally, the chairperson of the standing committee reporting a bill takes charge of the session during which it is debated. You can often watch such debates on C-SPAN (a cable television service that covers congressional activities, among other things).

Any member may propose an amendment to a bill during floor debate. At any time, any member may "move the previous question." This motion is a demand for a vote on the issue before the House. If the motion passes, only forty minutes of further debate are allowed before a vote is taken.

This vote tabulating machine was used at the majority leader's table to monitor votes taken in the House of Representatives from 1973 to 1980.

3. A **teller vote** may be conducted at the request of one-fifth of a quorum. The Speaker appoints two tellers, one from each party. The members pass between them and are counted, for and against. Teller votes are rare today and have largely been replaced by electronic voting.

4. A **roll-call vote,** also known as a **record vote,** is recorded electronically. In 1973, the House installed a computerized voting system. To use it, members insert a plastic card and press a button in one of forty-eight voting stations around the floor. Their votes are flashed on large display panels above the Speaker's desk, on other walls of the House, and on consoles located on the leadership tables. The board shows which members have voted as well as how they voted.

If a bill is approved by a majority, it is signed by the Speaker. A page then carries it to the Senate and places it on the desk of the Senate president (the president *pro tem*). (There are usually about one hundred pages at any given time. They run errands between offices, work on the floors of the two chambers of Congress, and answer phones in the cloakrooms.)

Just the Facts

Congressional pages are juniors in high school. Normally, pages spend one school year living in Washington, D.C., and working for a senator or representative.

Vote After a House bill has been fully debated and amended, it is ready for a vote. The bill now has its third reading, and a vote on the entire floor is taken. The House uses four methods for taking floor votes:

1. Voice votes are the most common method of taking a floor vote. In a **voice vote,** the presiding officer asks those members in favor to say "aye" and those opposed to say "no." The Speaker of the House determines which side has the most voice votes.

2. If a member questions the results of the voice vote, a **standing vote** may be demanded. First, those in favor of the bill stand and are counted. Then, those opposed stand and are counted.

Action in the Senate

The steps in the lawmaking process are similar in both chambers. There are differences, however. Most involve floor debates.

Debate Whereas floor debates are strictly limited in the House, debates are usually unlimited in the Senate. Generally, senators may speak on the floor for as long as they wish. Furthermore, they are not restricted to speaking only about the measure under consideration.

▲ *During a filibuster of the Civil Rights Act of 1957, cots were set up in the old Supreme Court chamber so senators could rest. This filibuster, by Senator Strom Thurmond of South Carolina, was a record-setting twenty-four hours and eighteen minutes long. What is the point of a filibuster?*

about any topic they want or even read a book aloud. Even the threat of a filibuster has resulted in the Senate's failure to consider a number of bills and in the amendment of many more.

Cloture is a parliamentary rule by which debate is ended and an immediate vote is taken on the matter under discussion. The Senate can end filibusters by using the **cloture rule.** For the cloture rule to go into effect, a minimum of sixteen senators must move that debate be limited. If the motion is approved by three-fifths of the entire Senate (sixty senators), no senator may speak for more than one hour on the bill being considered. After that time, the bill under consideration must be brought to a vote.

Obtaining a vote in favor of cloture is usually difficult. Many senators hesitate to support cloture motions because of the Senate tradition of open debate and because they know they may want to filibuster a bill in the future.

Vote Voting in the Senate is very similar to voting in the House. Voting is done by voice vote, by standing vote, or by roll-call, or record vote. Teller votes are not used in the Senate, however.

There is no routine motion to call for a vote. The Senate's dedication to freedom of debate is intended to encourage the fullest possible discussion of matters on the floor.

One way for a single senator or a group of senators to defeat a bill they oppose is to filibuster against it. To **filibuster** means to keep talking until a majority of the Senate either abandons the bill or agrees to modify the bill's most controversial provisions. Essentially, filibustering is a tactic to delay or block action by "talking a bill to death."

All that senators need do to filibuster is stay on their feet and keep talking. After three hours, they may talk

Ethics and Congressional Voting Behavior

Sooner or later, every member of Congress faces the dilemma of how to vote on a particular bill. Should the member vote according to his or her conscience—that is, according to his or her personal assessment of what is in the country's best interests? Or should the member of Congress vote as his or her constituents want their representative to vote, which may or may not be in the best interests of the nation as a whole?

Consider an example. Since the end of the Cold War with the Soviet Union in the early 1990s (see Chapter 23), the government has sought to reduce the number of military bases in the United States. Yet what

The British Parliament

The national legislature in Great Britain is known as Parliament. Like the U.S. Congress, Parliament is bicameral, made up of the House of Commons and the House of Lords. The British Parliament manages both the legislative and the executive powers of the nation. Parliament's legislative powers include passing and changing laws. Its executive powers include choosing the prime minister, who is the leader of the majority party in the House of Commons, and the cabinet that will serve the prime minister.

The lower chamber is the House of Commons, or simply, "the Commons." It is the more powerful of the two chambers. Its 635 members of Parliament, or MPs, are popularly elected from geographic districts. Any MP is allowed to introduce legislation. Most measures, however, are introduced by the prime minister and the cabinet. Once introduced, a bill is debated and sent to one of eight standing committees, which reviews and prepares it for final consideration by the full chamber.

The upper chamber of Parliament, the House of Lords, consists of seven hundred hereditary peers (members of the nobility) and members who are appointed for life by the queen.

The House of Lords was once powerful, but today it has little real authority over legislation. If the House of Lords defeats a bill passed in the Commons, the Commons need only pass it in the next session to make the bill become law.

THINKING GLOBALLY

What is a key difference between the House of Lords and the U.S. Senate?

---

state wants to see its military bases closed? After all, these bases offer employment for many state citizens, and the personnel on the bases buy numerous goods from businesses located within the state. In short, from an economic perspective, a state stands only to lose from the closing of one (or more) of its military bases. Therefore, a senator or representative from that state will be pressured by his or her constituents to keep the base or bases open, even though it may not be in the national interest to do so.

Whether members of Congress should vote as their constituents wish or in the public interest, as the members perceive it, is a question that dates back to the early years of the nation. Consider a debate that took place in Congress in 1790. In that debate, James Madison clearly sided with the latter view—that congressional representatives should act in the public interest:

> *Their ideas [those of the voters of a particular district] may contradict the sense of the whole people; hence the consequence that instructions are binding on the representative is of a doubtful, if not a dangerous nature.*

Elbridge Gerry, an Anti-Federalist, was among those who took the opposite position. In the 1790 debate, Gerry stated as follows:

> *To say that sovereignty vests with the people, and that they have not a right to instruct and control their representative is absurd to the last degree.*

The debate over the proper function of congresspersons has never been resolved in favor of one view or the other. Rather, members of Congress today tend to reflect a combination of these views.

Congressional choices are also complicated by the need to consider the interests of campaign contributors. A senator or representative who wants to be reelected to Congress must pay attention to the wishes of the various individuals and interest groups that contributed to his or her campaign. A disturbing question for many Americans today is whether interest groups, through their campaign contributions, wield too much influence in Congress. This issue will be explored further in the *America at Odds* feature on page 440 at the end of this chapter.

SECTION 2 REVIEW

1. How are bills introduced in the House? How are bills introduced in the Senate?
2. What happens to a bill when it is assigned to a committee?

3. How are bills scheduled for debate in the House?
4. What is the committee of the whole?
5. How does debate in the House differ from debate in the Senate?
6. **For Critical Analysis:** Why do you think the Senate allows unlimited debate in the form of a filibuster?

SECTION 3

The Final Stages

Preview Questions:

⭐ When is a conference committee formed, and what is its purpose?
⭐ What options does a president have on receiving a bill passed by Congress?

Key Terms:

conference committee, conferees, conference report, veto, pocket veto, line-item veto

Bills passed in one chamber are sent to the other chamber, where the legislative process begins again. To become law, a bill must be passed in *identical* form by both chambers of Congress. When the two chambers pass different versions of the bill, the bill is sent to a conference committee.

Conference Committees

A **conference committee** is a temporary joint committee of the House and the Senate that is set up when a bill is passed in different forms by the two chambers. The members of the conference committee try to work out the differences between the two versions of the bill

▶ *The majority of bills signed by the president do not attract as much attention as this one did. Here, President Lyndon B. Johnson signs the historic Civil Rights Act of 1964 into law in the presence of civil rights leaders, government dignitaries, and the press.*

Analyzing Information

When you research any topic in government or political science, as well as any other social studies subject, you will read books, articles, biographies, and primary source documents such as laws and constitutions. You must be able to analyze this information.

When you analyze information, you must break it apart and decide such things as whether the relationships you are reading about are causal and whether the information presented represents fact or opinion. After you take the information apart, you must put it back together and draw your own conclusions. Here are the steps you should follow when you analyze information in social studies.

1. **Carefully read the material.** If you don't understand what you are reading, you cannot analyze it correctly. When you read the material, look for the main ideas and supporting details.
2. **Keep asking yourself questions.** While you read, ask yourself who is involved and why, when the main events occurred, and other key questions. The main question to keep asking yourself is, "Why?"
3. **Determine whether there is bias.** If you are reading a speech by a political candidate, the bias may be easy to find. If you are reading an analysis written by a researcher, identifying bias may be more difficult. In your examination of bias, you need to separate fact from opinion. A fact is something that can be proved or verified. An opinion is a subjective viewpoint that cannot be confirmed.
4. **Reach a conclusion.** After you have analyzed the information, you need to reach a conclusion. For example, after reading an article on one of your state's senators, you might conclude that he or she supports a certain position, such as gun control.

PRACTICING YOUR SKILLS

Look in a daily newspaper and select an article from the first page to analyze. For the article you choose, list the facts presented in one column and the opinions in another column. Then determine whether you can detect any bias in what you have read.

---

and come up with an acceptable compromise bill. Most of the members of the committee, called **conferees** or managers, are members of the standing committees that handled the bill in the House and the Senate.

In theory, the conference committee can only consider those points in a bill on which the two chambers disagree. No new proposals may be added. In reality, however, the conference committee sometimes makes important changes in the bill or adds new provisions.

Once the conferees agree on the final compromise bill, they submit a **conference report** to both chambers of Congress. The bill must be accepted or rejected by both chambers as it was submitted by the committee, with no further amendments made. If the bill is approved by both chambers, it is ready for action by the president.

Presidential Action

The Constitution requires that all bills passed by Congress be submitted to the president for approval. The president has five choices in handling a bill:

1. The president can approve the legislation by signing it, at which point the bill becomes law.
2. The president can refuse to act on the bill for ten days, excluding Sundays. If the president does not

Are Members of Congress Responding to the Wrong Signals?

▶ *Friends of the Earth, which has a registered political action committee, celebrates Earth Day with a festive hot-air balloon. Compared to the tobacco or entertainment industries, Friends of the Earth's political contributions are very small. Yet, they do provide some campaign funds for individual congressional candidates.*

FRIENDS OF THE EARTH

If you were elected to Congress, either as a senator or a representative, you would have come a long way up the political ladder. How did you make this climb? Typically, you had to accept contributions from various interest groups. Once you are in office, these interest groups expect you to give them something in return. If they support certain legislation, you must consider their views when voting on that legislation. If they oppose a certain bill, you must take their views into account. This is particularly true if you want to be reelected. If you do not act in a manner that these groups consider appropriate, you may find that they will not help to finance your reelection campaign.

sign the bill while Congress is in session, the bill becomes law after the ten-day lapse. A president may use this procedure if he generally approves of the bill but objects to some of its provisions. By letting the bill become law without his signature, the president indicates his dissatisfaction with these provisions. This procedure is rarely used.

3. The president may **veto,** or reject, the bill. (*Veto* is Latin for "I forbid.") The bill must then be returned to the chamber in which it originated, together with the president's objections to the bill. Congress may try to amend the bill to suit the president and then pass the amended bill. Alternatively, it may try to override the president's veto by a two-thirds vote of the members present in each chamber. Although it seldom happens, an override passes the bill over the president's veto. The president who holds the record for the greatest number of vetoes is

But what about the people? Aren't you elected to represent the people from your district or state? Certainly you are. They are the ones who elected you. There is clearly a conflict here. If you look only to those who elected you for signals on how to vote on particular issues, the next time you are up for election, you may not receive enough campaign financing to get reelected.

Are senators and representatives responding to the wrong signals because of their worries about being reelected? Americans are at odds over this issue.

Our Current System Is Just Fine, Some Say

One group of political researchers and politicians believe that our current system is just fine. They argue that, after all, interest groups do represent Americans. If the National Rifle Association (NRA) or labor groups represented by the AFL-CIO are effective in helping members of the House get elected and reelected, why shouldn't those members take some of their signals from these groups? If the Friends of the Earth and the Sierra Club raise a lot of money to keep a senator in office, why shouldn't that senator give them special attention?

What is the alternative, anyway? Should senators and representatives listen only to the dictates of political parties? A party does not always have a "finger on the pulse" of America. Moreover, suppose that a Republican senator strongly supports labor-union views even if the party does not. To whom should that senator listen?

Perhaps the president could tell a senator or representative how to vote. But this would be a direct violation of the spirit of the separation of powers. Those who favor the current system simply say, "Leave it as is."

We Have the Best Congress Money Can Buy, Others Complain

Other Americans believe that interest groups are spending entirely too much money on the election and reelection campaigns of members of Congress. They say that special-interest groups are just that—specialized. They do not represent Americans as a whole but rather represent very tight, well-defined groups of Americans. As a result, according to these critics of the current system, legislation favors only the most vocal— and richest—groups in America. Members of Congress are supposed to represent the people. To represent the people, they must pay attention to the people and not just to money. They should vote for legislation that they think is best for all Americans.

YOU DECIDE

1. How do you think members of Congress should make decisions? Which factor should have the greatest influence on their decision making?
2. What groups or individuals, if any, do you believe have too much influence on members of Congress?

Franklin D. Roosevelt, who vetoed 631 bills during his thirteen years in office. Congress overrode only nine of those vetoes.

4. The president may kill a bill passed during the last ten days Congress is in session by refusing to act on it. This is called a **pocket veto.** The president simply does not sign the bill, and because Congress is no longer in session after ten days have passed, it does not have the opportunity to override the pocket veto.

5. Under the Line-Item Veto Act of 1996, the president can exercise a **line-item veto.** This means the president can veto one or more provisions in a bill before signing it. President Bill Clinton first exercised the line-item veto power in August 1997. Critics claim that the 1996 act upset the constitutional balance of powers by transferring too much power to the president. The issue is now before the Supreme Court. If the Court agrees that the 1996 act is unconstitutional,

The Way in Which Laws Are Made Has Changed

Although Congress is a very traditional institution, the way in which laws are made has changed over the years, particularly since World War II (1941–1945).

THEN (1945)	Now
The power of the Speaker of the House was decreasing.	The power of the Speaker of the House is increasing.
The House Rules Committee had independent power.	The House Rules Committee is controlled by the Speaker.
The budget was the president's responsibility.	Congress takes more responsibility in the budgeting process.
The president did not have line-item veto power.	The president has line-item veto power, although the line-item veto has been challenged as unconstitutional.

then by the time you read this book, the president will no longer be able to exercise the line-item veto.

Each time a bill makes it through all these stages and becomes law, it stands as an example of the legislative process in action. This process has continued for over two hundred years, but it also begins anew with each congressional term, when both the House and Senate organize for action. As the nation has evolved and become more complex, so, too, has this process. Today, committees and subcommittees play an ever-increasing role. Regardless of these changes, the legislative process remains a vital part of our representative democracy.

SECTION 3 REVIEW

1. What happens when the two chambers of Congress pass two different versions of the same bill?

2. What are the president's options once Congress has passed a bill?
3. **For Critical Analysis:** Do you think it is necessary for a bill to go through so many steps to become a law? Why or why not?

★ ★ ★ ★ **Chapter Summary** ★ ★ ★ ★

Section 1: Congress Begins Its Work

🌐 Before a new term begins, Democratic and Republican members of the House and Senate meet in separate party caucuses to reach agreement on key issues and to plan the party's strategy for the upcoming term. They also choose party leaders to organize and direct party activities during the term.

🌐 The House of Representatives is reorganized and begins anew every two years, while the Senate is a continuous body. After both chambers are organized, the president delivers the State of the Union

▲ This political cartoon explains the presidential line-item veto by using a simple comparison. Consider how the cook in the example might feel about a diner's line-item veto. Now, how might Congress feel about the presidential version?

address, which outlines the administration's broad policies and makes legislative recommendations.

⚫ Bills are proposed laws and are either public (concerning matters of national interest) or private (concerning specific persons or places). Joint resolutions are formal declarations of opinion that are voted on by both chambers and sent to the president. When passed, bills and joint resolutions have the force of law.

⚫ Concurrent resolutions are measures passed by both chambers and intended to express an opinion or a policy. Simple resolutions deal with matters affecting only one chamber and are passed by that chamber alone. These types of resolutions do not have the force of law.

Section 2: How a Bill Becomes a Law

⚫ Although almost anyone can suggest legislation, only a member of Congress can formally introduce it.

⚫ Bills introduced in either chamber are referred to standing committees and from there (usually) to subcommittees.

⚫ Once they have been reported out of committees, bills are debated on the floor of the House or Senate. Debate is severely limited in the House but is unlimited in the Senate. Filibustering is a technique used to kill a bill in the Senate.

⚫ After a bill has been debated and perhaps amended, it comes up for a vote on the floor.

Section 3: The Final Stages

⚫ To become a law, a bill must be passed in identical form by both chambers of Congress.

⚫ When the two chambers do not agree, a conference committee attempts to iron out differences and produce a compromise version acceptable to both chambers.

⚫ A bill that has passed both chambers in identical form is sent to the president, who has the choice of signing it, letting it become law without signing it, vetoing it, or letting it die by use of a pocket veto, or by exercising the line-item veto unless the Supreme Court finds that the line-item veto is unconstitutional.

CHAPTER 16 Review

★ REVIEW QUESTIONS ★

1. When does each new term of Congress begin?
2. What are the purposes of political party caucuses?
3. What happens in the House and the Senate on the opening day of Congress? Why are their opening days different?
4. What is the purpose of the State of the Union address?
5. Briefly describe the two types of bills that may be introduced and the three types of resolutions that may be passed in Congress.
6. Who can propose legislation for Congress to consider? How is a bill formally introduced?
7. Describe what happens when a committee considers a bill.
8. Describe the five congressional calendars used in the House, and explain how they differ from each other.
9. What procedure has the House developed to speed up the legislative process?
10. How does debate in the Senate differ from debate in the House?
11. What is a filibuster, and what is the cloture rule?
12. When is a conference committee formed, and what is its purpose?
13. What options does the president have upon receiving a bill passed by both houses?

★ CRITICAL THINKING ★

1. The sessions of the House and Senate are broadcast on cable stations around the country. How, if at all, do you think this affects the operation of Congress and the behavior of individual members? Do you think committee sessions should be broadcast?
2. Is the process of lawmaking too complicated? Does it give too many opportunities for interest groups to block needed legislation? Explain.
3. What, if any, reforms do you think should be made in congressional lawmaking procedures?
4. With the ease of using e-mail to contact one's senator or member of the House, do you think members of Congress will become more responsive to the wishes of their constituents? Why or why not?

★ IMPROVING YOUR SKILLS ★

Communication Skills

Composing an Essay An essay is a short report written on a specific topic. When writing an essay, follow these guidelines:

1. *Read the instructor's directions carefully.* Look for terms that will help you identify what information is asked for. Words such as *purpose, reasons, details,* and *objectives* are examples of such terms. Look also for performance terms that will tell you what to write. Performance clues include the following:
   - *Discuss:* tell in some detail.
   - *Describe or show:* create a picture with actions and examples.
   - *State:* Make a complete formal statement.

2. *Make a short outline.* To know where you are going with your essay, you need to create an outline. The more detailed your outline, the smoother the writing of your essay will be. Be sure to include your thesis statement and supporting evidence in your outline.

3. *Write the first draft.* Using the logical flow of information written in your outline, start your first draft. The more detailed your outline, the simpler this task will be. Make sure that in your first paragraph you include your topic, or thesis, statement. Be precise in your writing, and stay with your topic.

Include examples to support your statements. Remember that each paragraph must have an introduction and a conclusion. The essay itself must have a concluding paragraph as well.

4. *Edit your first draft.* When you edit your first draft, ask yourself the following questions:
   - Does my essay stay on the topic?
   - Does it contain any unnecessary information?
   - Is it missing any information?
   - Is it interesting and informative?
   - Do I support my thesis statement?

   Keep these questions in mind as you edit your draft. Make sure that you have used correct grammar and spelling. If you are using a computer, you may be able to use a spell checker and a grammar checker.

5. *Make a polished draft.* The final draft of your essay should look like a final draft. It should not contain spelling or grammatical errors, nor should it wander from the central topic. Read your final draft carefully. Is it addressed to the appropriate audience? Have you used vocabulary suitable for that audience? If you notice any errors, make sure they are corrected.

Writing Following the five steps given above, write an essay on one of the following topics:

   - Filibustering
   - How a bill becomes a law
   - The difference between the opening day of the House and of the Senate

Social Studies Skills

Understanding Flow Charts Examine the flow chart *How a Bill Becomes a Law* on page 431. What differ- ences are there, if any, between the flow on the right-hand side and the flow on the left-hand side of the chart?

★ ACTIVITIES AND PROJECTS ★

1. Gather information on a problem related to a current issue. Use the guidelines presented in the *Communication Skills* section of this review to write a bill that proposes a solution.
2. Stage a class debate on the following statement: Filibustering should be eliminated from the Senate.
3. Stage a mock committee hearing on an issue currently being debated in Congress.
4. Obtain a videotape of Senate proceedings during its last filibuster. As you watch it, make a list of who spoke, for how long they spoke, and the topics the speakers covered. What were the results of this filibuster?

What If . . .

A Total of Only One Hundred Bills Could Be Introduced in Congress Each Year?

Today, thousands of bills are introduced in the House and Senate each term. Fewer than 10 percent of these bills become public law. A rule (or even a constitutional amendment) could prohibit members of Congress from introducing more than, say, one hundred bills each year. How might this affect the behavior of members of Congress?

The Senate Confirmation Process

The Twentieth Century Fund, a nonpartisan group that analyzes various policy issues, recently released a report on the process by which the Senate confirms presidential appointments for various government positions. The report, entitled *Obstacle Course*, concluded that the confirmation process is slow, cumbersome, overly intrusive, and demeaning to nominees. It also concluded that presidential nominees are not provided with a "zone of privacy." During President Bill Clinton's second term, he nominated Anthony Lake for the post of director of the Central Intelligence Agency (CIA). Lake had served as Assistant to the President for National Security Affairs and as a senior foreign policy adviser to the Clinton/Gore campaign. During the subsequent Senate confirmation proceedings, Lake requested that his nomination be withdrawn. Even though the general consensus was that Lake had sufficient votes for confirmation in both the Intelligence Committee and in the full Senate, he made this formal request because he could no longer tolerate the way the confirmation process was being conducted. Increasingly, the Senate confirmation process has become a controversial topic.

Source Documents

The first excerpt is from Anthony Lake's letter to the president requesting his withdrawal as a nominee and giving the reasons for his request. The second excerpt is from a statement made by President Clinton on the issue.

Letter to the President from Anthony Lake

While we have made great progress in the nomination process over the past month and during last week's hearings, I have learned over the weekend that the process is once again faced by endless delay. It is a political football in a game with constantly moving goal posts. . . .

I have believed all my life in public service. I still do. But Washington has gone haywire.

I hope that, sooner rather than later, people of all political views beyond our city limits will demand that Washington give priority to policy over partisanship, to governing over "gotcha."

March 18, 1997

Statement by President Bill Clinton

White House press release

This episode says a lot about how so much work is done in our nation's Capital. For too long, we have allowed ordinary political processes and honest disagreements among honorable people to degenerate first into political sniping, then into political revenge. And too often, that results in political destruction that absolutely builds nothing for the American people and is not worthy of our responsibilities to them.

March 18, 1997.

Media Reports

Lake's withdrawal as a candidate for the post of CIA director focused the nation's attention on the Senate confirmation process. Here are two examples of how the media treated the issue.

Senators Gunning for Lake from the Start

by Walter Shapiro, *USA Today*

Were it not for the poignancy of the outcome, there would be something drolly amusing about the flabbergasted Republican response to Anthony Lake's sudden withdrawal as CIA nominee.

Senate Intelligence Committee Chairman Richard Shelby was reduced to insisting, despite ample contrary evidence, "I was never out to get Mr. Lake. It was not personal with me." Veteran Utah Sen. Orrin Hatch, who had proudly saddled up with the GOP posse, now said of Lake, "I personally liked him, wanted to vote for him and in the end probably would have."

Comments like those are reminiscent of small boys who can't comprehend why a playmate, whom they dangled upside down from a jungle gym, no longer wants to hang out with them. You can hear them telling their parents, "We were just funning with him. And we would have given him his lunch money back, honest." . . .

Not only is Senate confirmation slow and cumbersome (Lake dangled before the Intelligence Committee for almost four months), but the process has become harsh and demeaning.

Source: USA Today, March 19, 1997 (p. 2A). Copyright 1997, USA Today. Reprinted with permission.

Advice and Consent

Editorial, *Christian Science Monitor*

For all its abuses, the confirmation process—like a tough primary campaign—is a test of candidates' mettle. A word of realism comes from Robert M. Gates, who went through the Senate wringer before being confirmed as President Bush's CIA director: "If you can't fight your way through the process . . . my guess is you might not just do a hot job as director."

Source: Christian Science Monitor, March 20, 1997. Reprinted with permission.

Conclusion

Twenty years ago, the Senate confirmation process was often regarded as a "rubber stamp machine" in which the Senate routinely gave its stamp of approval to presidential appointees. Today, it has been called by various observers a "bed of nails," "nasty and brutal," "despotic," and even a "chamber of horrors." Many of the recommendations in the Twentieth Century Fund's report mentioned earlier would streamline the appointment process. For example, one recommendation is to stop requiring Senate confirmation for certain nominees, such as candidates for noncontroversial and lower-level appointments. According to many observers, however, Congress would not likely agree to give up any of its "advice and consent" power.

Analysis Questions

1. Do you believe that presidential nominees should be entitled to a "zone of privacy"? In other words, should some questions be out of bounds in the Senate confirmation process? Why or why not?
2. "Noncontroversial and lower-level presidential nominees should not require Senate approval." How would you argue in support of this statement? How would you argue against it?
3. Analyze the argument, suggested in the final excerpt above, that the Senate confirmation process is a test of candidates' mettle, or courage, and that candidates who cannot endure the process would probably not succeed in their jobs.
4. Are delays in confirming presidential appointments harmful to the government? Explain.

The Federal Executive Branch

Four U.S. presidents—George Washington, Thomas Jefferson, Theodore Roosevelt, and Abraham Lincoln—look out thoughtfully from their vantage point on Mount Rushmore in the Black Hills of South Dakota.

CHAPTER 17

The Presidency

CHAPTER OBJECTIVES

To learn about and understand . . .

⭐ How the office of the president was created and how it is structured according to the Constitution

⭐ The role of the vice president and how it has changed over time

⭐ The role of the cabinet in the executive branch of government

⭐ The agencies within the Executive Office of the President and their functions

> "No one who has not had the responsibility can really understand what it is like to be president. . . . There is no end to the chain of responsibility that binds him, and he is never allowed to forget that he is president."
>
> *Harry S Truman*
> (1884–1972)
> Thirty-third President of the United States

INTRODUCTION

If you are the president of your junior or senior class, you may sometimes forget the fact that you hold that office. After all, as president, you are not expected to solve all your classmate's problems. If you are the captain of one of your school's sports teams, the same is true. While you are playing, your teammates look to you for leadership. When you are not playing, though, they do not demand your constant attention. Being president of the United States is an entirely different matter.

No one except the president understands what it really means to be president. The responsibility of leading one of the greatest military and economic powers in the world is enormous. As Harry Truman pointed out in the above quotation, the president never for a moment forgets this responsibility.

◀ President Jimmy Carter and his wife, Rosalynn, celebrate his 1977 inauguration by walking from the Capitol to the White House.

451

Preview Questions:

- How was the office of the presidency created?
- What are the formal and informal qualifications for becoming president?
- What are the conditions of a presidential term?
- What kinds of compensation does the president receive?
- What is presidential succession?

Key Terms:

chief executive, succession

As the head of the executive branch of the U.S. government, the president holds one of the most powerful and important elective offices in the world. Yet when the founders created the presidency in 1787, the United States was a new nation of only four million people.

Just the Facts

John Adams and John Quincy Adams were the only father and son who both served as presidents of the United States.

The past two centuries have seen the office formed and expanded by the personalities and policies of the various occupants, as well as by custom and tradition. Over the years, the office has evolved to meet changing needs and circumstances.

Creating the Presidency

Creating the executive branch of the national government was one of the most important tasks faced by the delegates to the Constitutional Convention of 1787. Given their previous experience with kings and royal governors, most delegates did not want a monarchy—not even an elected monarchy, which Alexander Hamilton once argued for in a two-hour-long speech. The delegates wanted the ultimate source of power to rest with the people. They also recognized, from watching the Articles of Confederation in action, the need

for an executive branch. In order to determine how the executive branch would be formed, the founders analyzed the British monarchy and the roles of governors in American colonial and state governments. They also studied the writings of European thinkers, such as Locke and Montesquieu.

For weeks, delegates quarreled over how much power the executive branch should have and what the relationship of the executive to the legislative branch should be. Some delegates, such as James Madison and Gouverneur Morris, argued for a strong, independent executive that would be a "check" on an overly ambitious legislature. Others wanted a weak executive appointed by Congress and subject to its will. Everyone was seeking a proper balance of power. Morris summed up the problem as follows:

> *Make him too weak: the legislature will usurp [take for itself] his power. Make him too strong: he will usurp on the legislature.*

Some liked the idea of a *committee executive*—a group of several persons, each holding executive power in a particular area. In the end, they rejected the committee arrangement. A single official, according to one political scientist, James Q. Wilson, could act with "energy, dispatch, and responsibility."

The delegates' debates resulted in the creation of the office of the president—a uniquely American institution. Nowhere else in the world at that time was there a democratically elected executive. On April 30, 1789, George Washington, with his left hand on the Bible, raised his right hand and swore to "preserve, protect, and defend the Constitution of the United States." Since that time, over forty Americans have repeated these same words and have held the office of president.

The source of the president's authority is Article II of the Constitution, which says that "the executive power shall be vested in the president of the United States of America." This makes the president of the United States the nation's **chief executive,** or head of the executive branch. The Constitution then sets out the president's relatively limited constitutional responsibilities.

◀ *This painting depicts George Washington's inauguration of April 30, 1789. Have the responsibilities and powers of the office of the presidency increased or decreased over the years? (Collection of the New-York Historical Society)*

Because the Constitution defined presidential powers in broad general statements, the founders were uncertain as to just how the president would perform the various roles. Only experience would tell.

Qualifications

The Constitution lists only three formal qualifications for becoming president. Other, informal qualifications are personal qualities that Americans, over time, have come to expect their presidents to have.

Formal Qualifications The Constitution says that the president must (1) be a "natural-born citizen," (2) be at least thirty-five years old, and (3) be a resident of the United States at least fourteen years before taking office.

One element of the American dream is the idea that anybody can be president. Indeed, millions of Americans meet the three constitutional requirements. Like members of Congress, however, most presidents thus far in history have not been typical of the population as a whole. Rather, they have shared certain characteristics. In reality, then, there seem to be important *informal* requirements for becoming president of the United States.

Informal Qualifications Political experience has become an unwritten but important qualification for the presidency. One of only two presidents in this century without such experience was Dwight D. Eisenhower, whose success as a general in the U.S. Army during World War II led to his election as president. Presidential candidates have commonly been U.S. senators or state governors. Experience in government and politics allows these individuals not only to form the political alliances necessary to obtain the nomination but also to become known to the public. Those who currently hold public office have the resources to build a political following and to campaign.

Another informal qualification is political acceptability. Candidates with a *moderate* position reflect the views of the majority of Americans and are more likely to be nominated and elected. Usually, candidates with extremely liberal or extremely conservative political views have little chance of winning a nomination, much less an election. There are exceptions, however,

> ### Just the Facts
>
> *Franklin Roosevelt was remotely related to eleven former presidents, five by blood and six by marriage. He was a fifth cousin of Theodore Roosevelt.*

▶ General Dwight D. Eisenhower encourages U.S. Army paratroopers as they prepare to invade continental Europe in June 1944. Although lacking political experience, Eisenhower was later elected to the presidency on the strength of his leadership and victory in World War II.

such as the election of conservative Republican Ronald Reagan over the moderate incumbent President Jimmy Carter in 1980.

Presidents have also shared several common characteristics. All have been white and male. Most have been descendants of immigrants from northern Europe. Most have been lawyers, members of Congress, or state governors. Traditionally, presidents have been married, Protestant, and financially successful. A few, such as Harry S Truman, have come from poor families; others, such as Theodore and Franklin Roosevelt and John F. Kennedy, have come from wealthy families. Most, however, have come from more modest circumstances and have been self-made men. All modern presidents except Harry Truman have had college educations.

Term

The Constitution states that a president "shall hold his office during the term of four years." The framers of the Constitution agreed that four years was long enough for a president to gain experience, demonstrate abilities, and establish stable policies.

The Constitution placed no limit on the number of terms a president might serve. George Washington served two terms as president but declined to seek a third. He established a tradition followed by all presidents well into the twentieth century. Franklin D. Roosevelt, however, broke with this tradition in 1940, when he ran for a third term and won. In 1944 he ran for a fourth term and won again. In 1951 the Twenty-second Amendment was added to the Constitution. Section 1 of that amendment begins as follows:

No person shall be elected to the office of the President more than twice, and no person who has held the office of President, or acted as President, for more than two years of a term to which some other person was elected President shall be elected to the office of President more than once.

Compensation

A president receives a salary, determined by Congress, which cannot be increased or decreased during a given term of office. Currently, the president receives $200,000 a year in salary and $50,000 a year for travel, entertainment, and other official expenses.

Of course, the president receives many other special benefits. One is the right to live in the White House, a luxurious 132-room mansion on 18.3 acres of land in the heart of the nation's capital. The White House is equipped with a staff of more than eighty persons, including chefs, gardeners, maids, butlers, and a personal tailor. It has a tennis court, a swimming pool,

▲ One of the benefits of holding the highest office in the land is the use of the presidential jet, Air Force One.

bowling lanes, and a private movie theater. The president is also provided with a special fleet of automobiles, jetliners, and helicopters, including the presidential jet, *Air Force One*. In addition, the president has the use of Camp David, a resort hideaway in the Catoctin Mountains of Maryland; medical and dental care; a large suite of offices, including the Oval Office; a large staff; and Secret Service protection for his family. The president does, of course, pay taxes, just like other citizens of the United States.

Presidential Succession

Eight presidents have died in office. Four died of natural causes, and another four died from assassins' bullets. One president, Richard Nixon, was forced to resign (Nixon resigned on August 9, 1974). Because of the possibility that a president will not be able to serve a full term, it is very important that an order of **succession** to the office of president be established. An order of succession is a legal procedure by which government leaders will succeed to the presidency should the president die, become disabled, or be removed from office.

Order of Succession The Constitution originally said only that if the president died or could no longer serve in office, the "powers and duties" of the office were to be carried out by the vice president. It did not indicate that the vice president would actually become president. In 1841, however, after the death of President William Henry Harrison, Vice President John Tyler not only took over Harrison's duties but also became president. Thus began a tradition of vice presidents' assuming the presidency.

In 1967, a few years after the assassination of President John F. Kennedy, the Twenty-fifth Amendment was passed to officially settle the question of presidential succession. The amendment says that the vice president does indeed become president when the office is vacant. Because the vice presidency is then vacant, the new president chooses a new vice

Just the Facts

The tenth president, John Tyler, had fifteen children.

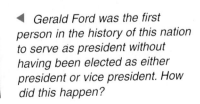

◀ Gerald Ford was the first person in the history of this nation to serve as president without having been elected as either president or vice president. How did this happen?

Political debates have long been a part of American campaigning. Ever since the famous Lincoln-Douglas debates in the late 1850s, American voters have enjoyed seeing their candidates face off in a one-to-one battle of words. The presidential debate between John F. Kennedy and Richard Nixon in 1960 was the first televised presidential debate. Since that historic debate, many presidential debates have been shown on television. Political debates also occur among congressional candidates at the state and local levels.

When you watch a political debate, there are a number of points you should keep in mind.

1. **The setting.** Kennedy's victory in the 1960 debate showed the world the importance of looking good on television. This lesson has not been lost on today's politicians. Candidates and their advisers go to great lengths to look good during televised debates. For example, in the 1976 debate between incumbent President Gerald Ford and the challenger, Jimmy Carter, campaign staff workers for both candidates engaged in heated negotiations regarding the size of the podium to be used during the debate. The handlers of Ford, who was tall, wanted both candidates to use tall podiums so that Carter would appear even shorter than he was. Carter's people, in contrast, wanted

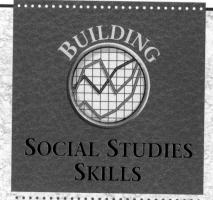

BUILDING
SOCIAL STUDIES SKILLS

Analyzing a Political Debate

short podiums so that he would appear taller than he was. After much discussion, medium-sized podiums were chosen as a compromise.

2. **The candidates' strengths and weaknesses.** Going into a debate, each candidate seeks to highlight his or her perceived strengths and to minimize his or her weaknesses. For example, in 1984, the age of the incumbent president, Ronald Reagan, was perceived as a weakness. Most political commentators agreed that after a poor showing in the first of two presidential debates, it was important that Reagan appear forceful and energetic in the next debate. The president's campaign staff coached him to look relaxed and robust for the next debate. Reagan's success in doing so helped push him toward a landslide victory in the election.

3. **The issues.** Although debates are supposed to center on the important political issues of the day, it is important to understand that the candidates themselves do everything they can to avoid any specific discussion of issues. Rather, candidates prepare short, catchy speeches about various topics to be delivered in response to issue questions. These speeches are generally superficial.

Given these points, it is easy to see why some commentators believe that political debates are not really useful. Much, however, can be learned from political debates. These debates are highly charged with risk for the candidates. When watching a political debate, we can get a glimpse of the candidates' ability to deal with high-pressure situations.

PRACTICING YOUR SKILLS

Obtain either a transcript or a videotape of an important political debate. After reading or viewing the debate, answer the following questions:

1. What aspects of the setting might have favored one of the candidates? Why?
2. How specific were the candidates in responding to issue-related questions?
3. In your opinion, which candidate won the debate?

1	Vice President
2	Speaker of the House of Representatives
3	President *Pro Tempore* of the Senate
4	Secretary of State
5	Secretary of the Treasury
6	Secretary of Defense
7	Attorney General
8	Secretary of the Interior
9	Secretary of Agriculture
10	Secretary of Commerce
11	Secretary of Labor
12	Secretary of Health and Human Services
13	Secretary of Housing and Urban Development
14	Secretary of Transportation
15	Secretary of Energy
16	Secretary of Education
17	Secretary of Veterans Affairs

different from that of the president. A change in parties would weaken continuity in the office. For this reason, some argue that the heads of the cabinet departments, who were appointed by the president, should follow the vice president in the order of succession.

Presidential Disability The Twenty-fifth Amendment also describes the steps to be followed should a president become disabled while in office. The amendment provides that the vice president shall become acting president under one of two conditions: (1) if the president informs Congress of an inability to perform in office or (2) if the vice president and a majority of the cabinet inform Congress, in writing, that the president is disabled. In either situation, the president may resume the powers and duties of the office by informing Congress that no disability exists. If, however, the vice president and a majority of the cabinet contend that the president has not recovered, Congress has twenty-one days to decide the issue by a two-thirds vote in the House and Senate.

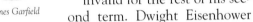
James Garfield

Presidents have become disabled in office on a few occasions. James Garfield lingered for eighty days before he died from an assassin's bullet in 1881. Woodrow Wilson suffered a paralytic stroke in 1919 and was an invalid for the rest of his second term. Dwight Eisenhower had several temporary but serious illnesses while in office, including a heart attack in 1955 and a mild stroke in 1957.

When President Ronald Reagan underwent surgery for removal of a cancerous growth on July 13, 1985, he informally followed the provisions of the Twenty-fifth Amendment when he temporarily transferred power to Vice President George Bush. Just before the operation began, Reagan signed letters to the Speaker of the House and the president *pro tem* of the Senate indicating that the vice president "shall discharge those powers and duties in my stead commencing with the administration of anesthesia to me." When he recovered from surgery later in the day, Reagan transmitted another letter to both officials announcing that he was

president, subject to a majority vote of both chambers of Congress.

The Twenty-fifth Amendment was used for the first time in 1973 when Vice President Spiro Agnew resigned from office. President Richard Nixon named Gerald Ford as his new vice president, and Ford's nomination was approved by Congress. A year later, when President Nixon resigned from office, Vice President Ford became president, and Ford nominated Nelson Rockefeller to be vice president. Congress again approved the nomination. Gerald Ford thereby became the first person in the history of the republic to become president without having been elected as either vice president or president.

The order of succession following the vice president was fixed by Congress in the Presidential Succession Act of 1947. The order is shown in Figure 17–1.

Not everyone agrees with the current order of succession after the vice president. The next in line is the Speaker of the House, whose political party could be again in charge. Most legal experts saw Reagan's acts as the first *official* use of this provision of the Twenty-fifth Amendment.

SECTION 1 REVIEW

1. What three qualifications for being president are required by the Constitution?

2. What informal qualifications have Americans come to expect in presidents?
3. How many terms can a president serve?
4. What is defined by the Twenty-fifth Amendment?
5. **For Critical Analysis:** The informal qualifications for being president have much more significance than the formal qualifications, which are few and easy to meet. What do you think really determines who can and cannot become president?

SECTION 2

The Office of Vice President

Preview Questions:

- What are the duties of the vice president?
- What are the qualifications and compensation for the vice president?
- How are vice presidential candidates selected?

Key Term:

balance the ticket

During most of American history, the office of vice president has been seen as a fairly insignificant position. Indeed, it has been avoided by some ambitious politicians. In 1848, Daniel Webster declined the Whig Party's nomination as vice presidential candidate by saying, "I do not propose to be buried until I am dead."

Obviously, the vice presidency has been the subject of many jokes. Thomas Marshall, vice president under Woodrow Wilson (1913–1921), once told the following story:

Once there were two brothers. One ran away to sea, the other was elected Vice President, and nothing was ever heard from either of them again.

Despite the slighting of the vice presidency, the office is important. As John Adams also said, "I am vice president. In this I am nothing, but I may be everything." If the president should die, become dis-

abled, or be removed from office, the vice president becomes our new national leader.

Duties

The vice president is given only two duties by the Constitution. The first duty is to preside over the Senate. Aside from casting a tie-breaking vote, however, this responsibility is mainly ceremonial. Recent vice presidents have usually turned much of this job over to the president *pro tem* of the Senate.

As you have learned, another vice-presidential duty under the Twenty-fifth Amendment is to help decide whether the president is disabled and to assume the duties of the presidency if necessary.

Qualifications and Compensation

The official qualifications for vice president are the same as those for president. A vice president must be a natural-born citizen, at least thirty-five years of age, and a resident of the United States for at least fourteen years. The vice president receives a salary of $175,400 a year, plus a yearly expense allowance. The official residence of the vice president is a mansion on the grounds of the Washington Naval Observatory. The vice president has an office in the White House and in the Capitol, each with a large staff; special transporta-

An *ideology* is a collection of political, economic, and social beliefs and opinions. In Chapter 9, you learned about political socialization and the many factors that affect your political ideology. Among them were family, school, friends, and co-workers. The process begins early in your childhood and continues throughout adulthood.

Throughout your life as a citizen, you will be called on to express your political ideology in many ways: by voting, joining interest groups, participating in community projects, and possibly running for public office. Even your actions in day-to-day life reflect your political ideology.

Try to gain a good understanding of what you believe in and why. If you do, you will be more confident of your beliefs when confronted with questions and decisions. Start by exploring the roots of the political you. Begin by asking yourself the following questions:

- Who is the first president I remember? What do I remember about him?

PARTICIPATING IN YOUR GOVERNMENT

Discovering the Political You

- What characteristics and qualifications do I believe the president should have? Why?
- How do I feel about the current president's policies and actions?
- How would I describe the political beliefs of my parents or other adult friends? Who did they vote for in the last presidential election? Do they belong to a political party? Are they active in public affairs and politics? Do I agree or disagree with their views?
- How would I describe the political beliefs of my best friends? Which political issues

do I discuss with them? How do my beliefs differ from theirs?
- How would I describe the political attitude of most people in my community?
- What impact have school and teachers had on my political views?
- How have the media—television, newspapers, magazines, or radio—influenced my views? Which publications do I enjoy reading?
- What influences have other groups or individuals had on my political views?
- What personal experiences have affected my feelings about social issues?

TAKING ACTION

1. Write an autobiographical account of your political roots, using the above questions as guidelines.
2. Interview a parent, a relative, or a friend in your parents' generation. Use the questions given in this feature as guidelines for your interview questions. How do the views of the person you interviewed differ from your own?

tion, including the official vice-presidential plane, *Air Force Two*; and protection by the Secret Service.

Selection of the Vice President

The selection process normally begins at the parties' national conventions when the presidential nominees

name their running mates. Often, the choice of a running mate is influenced by the need to **balance the ticket** in order to improve the presidential candidate's prospects of winning. Thus, the vice-presidential candidate often comes from a region of the country or a wing of the party that is different from that of the presidential candidate. If the presidential nominee is from the South, the vice-presidential nominee may be from the North or West. If the presidential nominee comes

▶ Vice President Al Gore consoles the family of Commerce Secretary Ron Brown, who was killed in an airplane crash. Vice presidents frequently represent the United States at the funerals of foreign dignitaries as well. Why do you suppose that is?

from an urban background, the vice-presidential nominee may come from a rural background.

Like the president, the vice president is officially elected by the electoral college (see Chapter 11) and serves a four-year term. Unlike the president, however, the vice president has no limits on the number of terms he or she may serve. The vice president is not subject to removal from office by the president.

More Involvement?

The assassination of President John F. Kennedy in 1963 and attempts on the lives of President Gerald Ford and President Ronald Reagan have focused more public attention on the office of vice president. Since the time of President Eisenhower, presidents have begun to take their vice presidents more seriously, involving them in some pol-

icy discussions and diplomacy. Vice presidents often represent the president overseas, take part in cabinet meetings, and serve on the National Security Council and on various commissions. By becoming more involved, the vice president assumes a slightly more influential role in the administration and is more qualified to take over the presidency if necessary.

Vice presidents become much more visible to the public during a president's second term. The reason is obvious. The president usually wants the vice president to become the next president and so starts giving the vice president more responsibilities. During the next presidential campaign, the vice president can point to this experience as a qualification for election.

◀ His rather loose constitutional job description allows Vice President Al Gore to promote President Bill Clinton's policies abroad. Gore waves to the crowd during a 1995 conference in South Africa.

SECTION 2 REVIEW

1. What has been the historical attitude toward the vice presidency? How has this attitude changed?
2. What are the constitutional duties of the vice president?

3. How is the vice president selected? What are the constitutional qualifications for becoming vice president?
4. **For Critical Analysis:** Do you think the vice president should automatically attend all cabinet meetings and receive all intelligence information that crosses the president's desk? Why or why not?

SECTION 3

The Cabinet

Preview Questions:

⭐ How was the cabinet developed? What is its role today?

⭐ What factors does the president take into account when choosing cabinet members?

Key Terms:

cabinet, kitchen cabinet

▲ *George Washington poses with members of the first presidential cabinet. How many cabinet members are there today?*

The **cabinet** is an advisory group chosen by the president to help accomplish the work of the executive branch. Although the cabinet is not mentioned in the Constitution, every president has had one. The cabinet has evolved since 1789, when Congress set up four executive departments. President George Washington met regularly on policy matters with Thomas Jefferson, head of the State Department; Henry Knox, head of the War Department; Alexander Hamilton, head of the Treasury Department; and Edmund Randolph, head of the office of the attorney general (which later became the Justice Department). Newspaper writers of the day called this group Washington's "cabinet." Every president since Washington has relied to some degree on the advice and work of the cabinet.

Today, the cabinet is made up of the heads of the fourteen executive departments, the vice president, and other key officials chosen by the president. The fourteen departments of the executive branch are:

- State
- Treasury
- Defense
- Commerce
- Labor
- Health and Human Services
- Housing and Urban Development
- Justice
- Interior
- Agriculture
- Education
- Energy
- Transportation
- Veterans Affairs

Who Are the Cabinet Members?

The president appoints the heads of the executive departments, thereby appointing the cabinet members.

Government in Action

The Conflicting Roles of Cabinet Heads

Cabinet members play two major, and sometimes conflicting, roles. First, as cabinet members, they are appointed by the president and serve as advisers to the president. The extent to which a president uses the cabinet for advice depends on the president's view of the cabinet. Cabinet members, nevertheless, represent the president's policies to the rest of the executive branch, to Congress, and to the employees in their departments.

The second role that cabinet members play is as the administrative heads of their executive departments. This role can sometimes conflict with the role of presidential adviser and supporter. For example, as department heads they must push for their departments' programs and ensure that the departments' goals and activities respond to the needs of the citizens that the departments serve. This means that cabinet members must be responsive to various interest groups. Departments such as the Department of Labor and the Department of Health and Human Services deliver services to various organized interest groups, which expect the departments and the secretaries to respond to their requests. Secretaries cannot ignore such interest groups, particularly if these groups have supporters in Congress.

Secretaries must also answer to members of Congress. Powerful legislators with interests in the departments' activities and policies may try to influence cabinet members. Their ideas may differ from those of the president. Because these legislators have the power to approve the programs within the departments and to appropriate money to run the departments, secretaries cannot ignore these members of Congress. Finally, even though secretaries of departments hold office at the discretion of the president, they have large bureaucracies to manage. They must rely on the career officials in their departments, who remain on the job from one administration to the next and who run the departments on a day-to-day basis. These career officials are usually dedicated to the interests that the departments have developed over the years. They may push secretaries in directions that are not always in accord with the president's own plans and policies.

THINK ABOUT IT

1. In what way do cabinet members have to answer to Congress?
2. In the event of a conflict, should a cabinet member's first loyalties be to the president or to the department that he or she heads? Give reasons for your answer.

Each of these appointments is subject to confirmation by the Senate. The cabinet is viewed as part of the president's official "family," and the Senate gives the president considerable freedom in selecting cabinet members. Rejections have been rare. Out of hundreds of such appointments, only a few have been turned down.

Presidents choose cabinet members for several reasons. Political party affiliation plays an obvious role. Republican presidents usually choose Republicans, and Democrats usually choose Democrats. Usually, presidents award a few cabinet posts to important party members who supported their presidential campaigns.

The president also tries to balance the nominees geographically according to their backgrounds. For example, the secretary of the interior is usually someone from a western state who has experience dealing with land policy and conservation issues. This is because of the large store of natural resources in the West and federal ownership of large portions of western land. The secretary of housing and urban development is usually someone with an urban background. The secretary of agriculture is usually from one of the farming states.

Presidents sometimes take into account the desires of interest groups that are affected by a cabinet department's policies. For example, the secretary of labor is generally someone acceptable to labor unions. The secretary of the treasury could be a well-known banker or someone with close ties to the financial community.

Recent presidents have also considered gender, race, ethnic backgrounds, and other personal characteristics when choosing department heads. Public pressure has forced presidents to try to create a cabinet that reflects the ethnic and cultural diversity of the nation.

By custom, cabinet members resign after a new president is elected. In this way, the new president can create a new cabinet.

The Role of the Cabinet

The cabinet has no power as a body. The president alone determines the extent of the cabinet's power and influence. Presidents are not required by law even to form a cabinet or to hold regular meetings. Therefore, meetings may be held frequently or infrequently, depending on the individual president. Meetings are held in the Cabinet Room of the White House and are usually closed to the public and the media. Frequently, they are attended by other government officials, such as the director of the Office of Management and Budget.

Changing Roles Presidents have never been obliged to follow the advice of their cabinets. How much presidents use the cabinet as a whole is strictly up to them. Some presidents, such as George Washington, James Buchanan, and Dwight Eisenhower, relied on their cabinets often for advice and assistance. Other presidents relied on their cabinets very little. On one famous occasion, when President Abraham Lincoln convened his cabinet to read them the draft of the Emancipation Proclamation, he started off by saying: "I have gotten you together to hear what I have written down. I do not wish your advice about the matter, for that I have determined myself." On another occasion, Lincoln is reported to have rejected a unanimous negative vote of his cabinet, saying, "seven nays, one aye—the ayes have it." Lincoln's vote was, of course, the one aye (or "yes" vote). Woodrow Wilson went even further—he held no cabinet meetings at all during World War I (1914–1918).

Other presidents have bypassed their official cabinet altogether and have relied on informal groups of political friends for advice. Andrew Jackson, for example, began meeting with a small group of friends and minor government officials to discuss important matters. Because they often met in the White House kitchen, they came to be called the **kitchen cabinet.** Franklin Roosevelt created a famous group of advisers called the "brain trust." These business executives, professors, research specialists, and other special advisers, includ-

▶ *President Andrew Jackson (1829–1837) relied on a small group of friends and minor government officials for advice, instead of the men of wealth and influence who traditionally had advised presidents. This political cartoon pokes fun at Jackson and his "kitchen cabinet."*

"JACKSON CLEARING HIS KITCHEN."

ing the chief justice of the Supreme Court, helped him construct many of the New Deal programs of the 1930s.

Some recent presidents have tried to make effective use of the cabinet as an advisory body. Usually, such attempts have failed. Most recent presidents have tended to seek advice from a very select number of individuals outside the cabinet.

SECTION 3 REVIEW

1. How was the cabinet created?
2. Who serves on the cabinet?
3. What factors does the president consider when choosing cabinet members?

4. Since the president can appoint whomever he or she wishes to serve on the cabinet, subject to Senate confirmation, the cabinet can be composed of the president's closest friends and advisers. Why then, would some presidents, choose to bypass their official cabinet and rely on an unofficial group for advice? Why did President Franklin D. Roosevelt, in particular, create a separate group of advisers, his "brain trust"?
5. **For Critical Analysis:** Although the president picks the department heads, they do not always agree with the president's policies. Why do you think this is so? (*Hint:* The president's constituency is the entire American public. Who makes up the constituency of a particular executive department?)

SECTION 4

The Executive Office of the President

Preview Questions:

🌐 What are the agencies within the Executive Office of the President?

🌐 What are the duties of these agencies?

Key Terms:

Executive Office of the President (EOP), chief of staff, press secretary, Office of Management and Budget (OMB), fiscal year, National Security Council (NSC), Council of Economic Advisers (CEA)

Around 1900, the White House Office consisted of a few presidential assistants, secretaries, bookkeepers, and household staff members. By 1932, it included thirty-seven people. In 1939, President Franklin D. Roosevelt set up the **Executive Office of the President (EOP)** to cope with the increased responsibilities brought on by the Great Depression. Since then, the EOP has grown rapidly, along with the rest of the government.

The EOP is made up of the top advisers and assistants who help the president carry out major duties. Over the years, the executive office has changed according to the needs and leadership styles of the presidents. It has become an increasingly influential and important part of presidential government. Figure 17–2 on page 465 shows the administrative units within the Executive Office of the President.

White House Office

Of all the executive staff agencies in the EOP, the White House Office has the most direct contact with the president. The White House Office consists of the president's key aides, whom the president sees daily, as well as several hundred professional and clerical staff members. The most important advisers occupy the West Wing, where the president's Oval Office and the Cabinet Room are located. (Some staff members work in the East Wing as well.)

Administrative Unit	Year Established
White House Office	1939
Office of the Vice President of the United States	1939
Council of Economic Advisers	1946
National Security Council	1947
Office of the U.S. Trade Representative	1963
Council on Environmental Quality	1969
Office of Management and Budget	1970
Office of Science and Technology	1976
Office of Administration	1977
Office of Policy Development	1977
Office of National Drug Control Policy	1989

The Staff The White House Office is led by the **chief of staff,** who advises the president on important matters and directs the operations of the presidential staff. The chief of staff, who is often a close personal friend of the president, has been one of the most influential of the presidential aides in recent years.

A number of other top officials, assistants, and special assistants to the president also aid in areas such as national security, the economy, and political affairs. A **press secretary** meets with reporters and makes public statements for the president. The counsel to the president serves as the White House lawyer and handles the president's legal matters. The White House staff also includes speechwriters, researchers, the president's physician, the director of the staff for the first lady, and a correspondence secretary. Altogether, over four hundred men and women work in the White House Office and make up the White House staff.

Duties of White House Staff The White House staff has several duties. First, the staff investigates and analyzes problems that require the president's attention. Staff members who are specialists in a specific area, such as diplomatic relations or foreign trade, gather information for the president and suggest solutions. White House staff members also screen the questions, issues, and problems that people present to the presi-

ARCHITECTS
of Government
Michael McCurry
(1954–   )

Michael (Mike) McCurry was appointed by President Bill Clinton as the White House press secretary in January 1995. Born in 1954, McCurry received his A.B. degree from Princeton University in 1976. McCurry is no stranger to Washington, D.C. He served as press secretary to various organizations during the twenty years prior to his appointment as press secretary to President Clinton. He was the press secretary for, among others, the Democratic National Committee, the 1988 presidential campaign of Bruce Babbitt (who later became secretary of the interior), and the 1992 presidential campaign of Democratic senator Bob Kerrey of Nebraska.

HIS WORDS

"I want to serve the President well. . . . He's laid out a very ambitious and challenging program for the country, and I want to tell that story and help him tell that story well."
 (*White House press release, January 5, 1995*)

"It's an honor to serve the President of the United States, but I work for you [the press], too. . . . I think at least since Thomas Jefferson said it, the press has been an indispensable element of our form of self-government."
 (*White House press release, January 5, 1995*)

DEVELOPING CRITICAL THINKING SKILLS

1. Regarding the first quotation, how does the White House press secretary "tell" the president's "story"?
2. In the second quotation, what did McCurry mean when he said that he works for the press, too?

► The federal government sometimes engages in creative accounting to balance its budget. How does this cartoon contradict its statement that the budget is balanced?

THERE..... NOW THE BUDGET'S BALANCED TOO!

Distributed by King Features Syndicate 6-13-80

©1980 THE CINCINNATI ENQUIRER JIM BORGMAN

dent, so matters that can be handled by other officials do not reach the president's desk. The staff provides public relations support as well. For example, the press staff handles the president's relations with the White House press corps and sets up press conferences. Finally, the White House staff makes sure the president's decisions are carried out. Several staff members are usually assigned to work directly with members of Congress for this purpose.

Office of Management and Budget

The **Office of Management and Budget (OMB)** was originally called the Bureau of the Budget. Under recent presidents, the OMB has become an important and influential unit of the executive office. The main function of the OMB is to assist the president in preparing the proposed annual budget, which the president must submit to Congress in January of each year. The **fiscal year** (official accounting period) for the national government runs from October 1 to September 30.

The budget of the national government lists the revenues and expenditures expected for the coming year. It indicates which programs the national government will pay for and how much they will cost. Thus, the budget is an annual statement of the public policies of

the United States translated into dollars and cents. Making changes in the budget is a key way for presidents to try to influence the direction and policies of the government.

Preparing the budget is a long, complicated process similar to the process of preparing a budget for a business firm or municipal government. First, each government agency estimates the amount of funds it needs for the coming year. Then, the OMB sets objectives for each federal program. It reviews all estimates at a series of budget hearings. At the hearings, agencies must defend their dollar requests. The figures for each department are then revised and fitted into the president's overall program. They become part of the budget document the chief executive submits to Congress. After the budgets of the various agencies have been resolved, the next step is to work to get the administration budget passed by Congress, which has budget proposals of its own.

The president appoints the director of the OMB with the consent of the Senate. The director of the OMB has become at least as important as cabinet members and is often included in cabinet meetings. He or she oversees the OMB's work and argues the administration's position before Congress. The director also lobbies members of Congress to support the president's budget or to accept key features of it. Once the budget is approved by Congress, the OMB has the responsibil-

The Presidency Then and Now

During the first one hundred years or so of this nation's history, the office of the president was quite a small affair, compared with what it is today.

THEN (FROM 1789 TO 1900)	NOW
Presidents lived a rather simple life.	While they are in office, presidents live as well as many of the richest people in America.
Presidents often answered their own mail.	So many layers separate the president from the public that almost no one has direct access to the president.
Until 1900, the White House Office consisted of a few presidential assistants, secretaries, bookkeepers, and household staff members.	Currently, the White House Office has a large staff, and this staff is an important part of the executive branch of government.
The president was elected after a relatively low-level campaign.	The president never stops campaigning, even while in office.

ity of putting it into practice. It oversees the execution of the budget, checking the federal agencies to ensure that they use funds efficiently.

Beyond its budget duties, the OMB also reviews new bills prepared by the executive branch. It checks these bills to be certain that they agree with the president's own positions.

National Security Council

The **National Security Council (NSC)** was created in 1947 to provide advice on and managerial assistance with matters concerning American military and foreign policy, as well as national security. The NSC members are the president, the vice president, and the secretaries of state and defense. A national security adviser appointed by the president directs the staff of the NSC. The director of the Central Intelligence Agency (CIA) and the chairperson of the Joint Chiefs of Staff have

also become members. The Joint Chiefs of Staff is a group made up of the commanding officers of the four branches of the armed services, plus a chairperson.

When serious world crises have developed, most presidents have immediately called the NSC into session. Many have used the council as a regular working group to discuss foreign policy. The role of the NSC is largely decided by each president, and each president uses it differently.

Office of Policy Development

The Office of Policy Development advises the president on domestic policy matters, such as trade, energy, housing, and farming. The office studies the nation's needs and makes domestic policy suggestions to the president. Once the policies have been formed, this office helps the president put the government's programs into effect.

The Vice President's Abilities

As pointed out in this chapter, the Constitution establishes the same qualifications for the vice president as for the president. The actual duties the Constitution gives the vice president are very limited, however. It is possible, and has actually been the case, for a vice president to do virtually nothing during his or her term in office. This means that if the president dies or cannot serve for some other reason, the nation may end up with a leader who has not spent much time learning about what the president does. Consequently, some people argue that we should amend the Constitution to broaden the duties of the vice president. Others disagree.

Leave Well Enough Alone, Say Some Americans

Those who oppose a constitutional amendment to broaden the vice president's duties have history on their side. After all, the United States has survived and indeed thrived in its more than two hundred years of existence with its current system. The framers of the Constitution chose not to give the vice president many powers or duties for a very good reason. The president alone is to lead the nation. If the presidency is to be strong, the president should not have to worry about a

"strong" vice president who might have a different governing philosophy. Not surprisingly, presidents prefer to have their vice presidents stay in the background, leaving the limelight to the presidents themselves.

In any event, too much fuss is made about the lack of vice-presidential experience. After all, how many presidents had extensive experience in national politics before being elected to the presidency or vice presidency? Harry Truman started out as a men's clothing merchant and Jimmy Carter as a peanut farmer. Ronald Reagan had a career as an actor. None of these men had extensive experience in national politics. It would be difficult to prove that there is a definite relationship between our presidents' backgrounds and how well they performed in office.

Give the Vice President More Duties, Say Others

Those in favor of giving the vice president more duties and powers point out that Americans need a vice president who is tested and experienced because, after all, the vice president might take over the most important job in the world.

In addition, if the Constitution gave the vice president more powers and duties, then the

Council of Economic Advisers

The **Council of Economic Advisers (CEA)** was created by Congress in 1946 to advise the president on economic matters. It analyzes the national economy, advises the president on how the economy is doing, and recommends measures to maintain economic stability in the nation. The council also helps the president prepare the annual *Economic Report of the President*. The council usually includes three leading economists, appointed by the president with the consent of the Senate, and a small staff of persons who prepare statistics.

Other Units in the Executive Office

The Office of the Vice President, which we have already discussed, is part of the Executive Office of the

American electorate would pay more attention to vice-presidential candidates. Currently, voters really care only about the presidential candidate's qualifications. If they knew that the vice president was actually going to carry out some policy actions while in office, then they would be much more concerned about the vice-presidential candidate's past experience.

In the private sector, vice presidents of major corporations are active participants in the governing of the business. That way, if they are "tapped" to become president of the company, they know

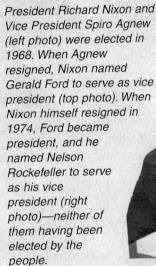

President Richard Nixon and Vice President Spiro Agnew (left photo) were elected in 1968. When Agnew resigned, Nixon named Gerald Ford to serve as vice president (top photo). When Nixon himself resigned in 1974, Ford became president, and he named Nelson Rockefeller to serve as his vice president (right photo)—neither of them having been elected by the people.

what to do. The same should be true of the vice president of the United States.

YOU DECIDE

1. Why do you think presidents allow their vice presidents to remain in the background?
2. Gerald Ford became president after having been appointed vice president, thereby becoming our only unelected president. Do you think there should be a change in the Constitution to prevent this? If so, why?

President. Several other agencies in the executive office assist the president with the many other responsibilities of the executive branch.

Council on Environmental Quality The Council on Environmental Quality (CEQ) was created in 1969 to assist the president with matters of environmental policy. It studies government programs designed to protect the environment and helps the president to prepare a

yearly report on the environment to Congress. The council is made up of three members appointed by the president with Senate approval.

Office of Science and Technology The Office of Science and Technology advises the president on scientific, engineering, and other technological matters that have a bearing on national policies and programs. It reviews the national government's contributions to science and technology. The director, chosen by the president with Senate approval, is drawn from the nation's scientific community.

Office of the U.S. Trade Representative The Office of the U.S. Trade Representative establishes and carries out U.S. trade policy. The trade representative, appointed by the president and approved by the Senate, speaks for the United States at international trade meetings and directs negotiations and trade agreements with foreign governments.

Office of National Drug Control Policy The Office of National Drug Control Policy was established in 1989. The director is appointed by the president with Senate approval and is regularly identified by the press as the nation's "drug czar." The office is responsible for drafting continuing plans to wage the national government's war on drugs. It also coordinates the efforts of the more than fifty federal agencies that deal with drug control.

Office of Administration The Office of Administration is the general housekeeping agency for all the other units of the executive office. It provides them with support services such as information gathering, financial management, data processing, library services, record keeping, and general office help.

All of the offices and agencies covered in this section form just a part of the "chain of responsibility" that, according to Harry Truman, "binds" the president. From the time that George Washington took the oath of office and stepped into the newly created executive branch, each person to hold the position has helped to define the office of president in our government.

▲ *While airlines are privately funded and administered, the National Aeronautics and Space Administration (NASA) is operated by federal employees with tax dollars. Why is it necessary for a government agency to run the space program?*

4. **For Critical Analysis:** Seventy years ago, the White House staff consisted of fewer than forty people. Today, its numbers are in the hundreds. Why do you think it has grown so much over the years? What advantages and disadvantages can you see in having such a large White House staff?

SECTION 4 REVIEW

1. What is the White House Office, and what are its functions?
2. What are the duties of the Office of Management and Budget?
3. What is the function of the National Security Council?

★ ★ ★ ★ **Chapter Summary** ★ ★ ★ ★

Section 1: The Office of President

🌐 Article II of the Constitution states that the president shall hold the nation's executive power.
🌐 The Constitution requires the president to be (1) a natural-born citizen, (2) at least thirty-five years old, and (3) a resident of the United States

at least fourteen years before taking office. Informal qualifications include political experience and political acceptability.

- ✪ The president may serve a maximum of two four-year terms, is paid an annual salary, and receives many other benefits.
- ✪ The vice president assumes the presidency should the president become unable to serve. The order of succession following the vice president was fixed by Congress in the Presidential Succession Act of 1947.

Section 2: The Office of Vice President

- ✪ The vice presidency has historically been seen as an insignificant position but has become more important in recent years.
- ✪ The vice president's constitutional duties are to preside over the Senate, to help decide whether a president is disabled, and to assume the duties of the presidency if necessary.
- ✪ The official qualifications for vice president are the same as those for president.
- ✪ Persons chosen by their parties to run for president usually name their own running mates. Often, the choice is influenced by the need to pick someone to balance the ticket.

Section 3: The Cabinet

- ✪ The cabinet is an advisory group chosen by the president to help accomplish the work of the executive

branch. The cabinet is not mentioned in the Constitution but has evolved out of tradition.

- ✪ The president appoints the heads of executive departments, thereby appointing the cabinet members.
- ✪ In choosing cabinet members, the president takes several factors into consideration, including political party affiliation, experience in a given area, geographic background, and the desires of interest groups.
- ✪ The cabinet has no official power as a body. Individual presidents determine how much power and influence their cabinets will have.

Section 4: The Executive Office of the President

- ✪ The Executive Office of the President (EOP) is made up of the top advisers and assistants who help the president carry out major duties.
- ✪ The White House Office is led by the chief of staff, who in recent years has been one of the most influential of presidential aides.
- ✪ Other EOP agencies include the Office of Management and Budget, the National Security Council, the Office of Policy Development, and the Council of Economic Advisers.

CHAPTER 17 Review

★ REVIEW QUESTIONS ★

1. What qualifications must a president have, according to the Constitution?
2. According to the Twenty-second Amendment, which was ratified on February 27, 1951, how many terms may a president serve?
3. What did the Twenty-fifth Amendment, which was ratified on February 10, 1967, establish?
4. What are the constitutional duties of the vice president?
5. How is the vice president elected?
6. How is the cabinet chosen?
7. What role does the cabinet play?
8. How is the White House Office organized?
9. What is the function of the Office of Management and Budget?
10. Who are the members of the National Security Council?
11. What are the arguments for and against giving the vice president greater political responsibility during his or her term?

★ CRITICAL THINKING ★

1. What qualifications or characteristics do you think a president should have? Which of the recent presidents, if any, have had these qualifications or characteristics?
2. Do you think the role of the vice president will expand or diminish in the future? What factors do you think will have a bearing on his or her role and influence?
3. Which cabinet members currently have the most influence on the president? Give evidence to support your answer.
4. Why do you think the Executive Office of the President has grown so dramatically? Do the numerous agencies and staff members really assist the president in carrying out presidential duties? Do you believe the Executive Office will continue to grow, or do you think its number of assistants will decrease?

★ IMPROVING YOUR SKILLS ★

Communication Skills

Paraphrasing In doing homework, answering questions, and writing reports, you will sometimes be asked to *paraphrase*. Paraphrasing is restating someone else's writing or ideas in your own words. Paraphrasing will help you recognize the main idea, condense information, and organize material. Paraphrasing might be useful in answering such questions as, "What were the president's views on the new budget?" or "What were the instructions for completing this assignment?"

Follow these guidelines when paraphrasing:

- Read the material carefully. Make sure you understand what the author is saying.
- Review the information. While retaining the author's point of view, rewrite the information in your own words. Do not include any ideas of your own. Include all of the ideas in the original material, but reword them using your own writing style, tone, and vocabulary.

Writing Turn to the *America at Odds* feature on page 468. Paraphrase the arguments for and against a constitutional amendment giving the vice president more duties. You might wish to add to your account by doing some research on the topic and paraphrasing other arguments as well.

Social Studies Skills

Identifying Similarities and Differences The ability to make comparisons in order to identify the similarities and differences in political systems, political parties,

interest groups, political documents, and, of course, politicians and world leaders is a key social studies skill. In order to make such comparisons accurately, you must choose specific issues on which to base your analysis. For example, when you compare the two major political parties, you should decide in advance which points you will examine. You might compare the parties' stands on immigration, health care, research funds for AIDS, or other pertinent issues. The same system should be used for comparing leaders, such as current and past presidents or political candidates.

Use the above ideas to compare the members of one or more of the following pairs, identifying their similarities and differences.

1. The Republican Party and the Libertarian Party.
2. Direct democracy and representative democracy.
3. The two senators from your state.
4. The two major presidential candidates in the last election.
5. President Herbert Hoover and President Franklin D. Roosevelt.
6. The National Rifle Association and the American Medical Association.
7. *Federalist Paper* No. 10 and *Federalist Paper* No. 51.
8. The president of the United States and the prime minister of Britain.

★ ACTIVITIES AND PROJECTS ★

1. Choose a current cabinet member and research his or her political and professional background, experience, and influence on the president. Write a biographical account of this cabinet member that includes a discussion of his or her qualifications to head his or her department. Include the duties and responsibilities of that particular cabinet member, as well as the scope of responsibilities of the department that she or he serves.

2. Conduct a class debate on the following statement: The president shall hold office for a single term of six years.

3. Select a vice president from the 1900s who never became president of the United States. Conduct outside research and prepare a biography of this person. Include information about his political accomplishments that led to his appointment as vice president, his accomplishments while in office, and information about his subsequent professional and political life.

What If . . .

The President Could Be Elected to Only One Six-Year Term?

Some scholars have suggested that a constitutional amendment be added to create a single six-year term for the presidency. What effects might such a change have on the presidency?

CHAPTER 18

The President at Work

CHAPTER OBJECTIVES

To learn about and understand . . .

⭐ The powers of the president as they are outlined in the Constitution and as they have developed with the office

⭐ The many interrelated roles of the president

⭐ The limits placed on presidential powers

"In our brief national history we have shot four of our presidents, worried five of them to death, and impeached one and hounded another out of office."

P. J. O'Rourke
(1947–   )
U.S. Journalist and Humorist

INTRODUCTION

As you can probably imagine, your school principal's job is a difficult one. The principal has to follow rules and guidelines set down by national and state legislatures as well as by the school district. Your principal has to worry about not spending more money than the budget allows. He or she must sometimes face angry parents, angry students, and even angry teachers. The president of the United States is in a similar position but on a national—and even an international—scale.

The humorist P. J. O'Rourke was only half joking in the opening quotation. Many presidents have suffered disastrously under the burden of their work. President Harry S Truman once said, "The pressures and complexities of the presidency have grown to a state where they are almost too much for one man to endure."

◀ President Ronald Reagan waves to the crowd as he boards the presidential helicopter.

475

Presidential Powers

Preview Questions:

- What powers does the Constitution give to the president?
- What are the other sources of presidential powers?
- How have strong presidents contributed to the growth of presidential powers?
- How have the media enhanced the power of the presidency?

Key Terms:

executive order, White House press corps

The president heads the largest organization in the nation, a government that has nearly three million civilian and one million military employees. The president is entrusted with carrying out the laws of the land. In addition, the president is the chief architect of American foreign policy, an increasingly difficult task in our rapidly changing world. The president is the head of the world's most powerful military arsenal, the negotiator of treaties with other nations, the chief collector of taxes, and the leading speaker for our nation. With a multitude of powers and duties that have increased greatly over time, the presidency has become ever more powerful and more complex.

What is the basis for such extensive presidential powers? The Constitution is the first place to look for the answer to this question. Article II of the Constitution outlines the powers of the president. The president's powers are, of course, limited by the checks and balances of the other two branches of government.

Constitutional Powers

Article II begins by simply stating that "the Executive Power shall be vested in the President of the United States of America." As you have learned, the founders wanted a strong president, but they had difficulty agreeing on how much strength and power the president should have. As a result, Article II grants the president

▶ *President Bill Clinton addresses the 105th Congress. Seated behind the president are Vice President Al Gore, president of the Senate (on the left) and Speaker of the House Newt Gingrich (on the right).*

broad but vaguely described powers. From the very beginning, there were differing views as to what exactly the "executive power" clause enabled the president to do. Because this power is not precisely defined, it can change with differing circumstances.

Sections 2 and 3 of Article II go on to list specific presidential powers. You will see what these powers mean in practice later in the chapter, when the president's many roles are discussed. According to Sections 2 and 3, the president has the power to do the following:

1. Serve as commander in chief of the armed forces and the state militias.
2. Appoint heads of executive departments with Senate approval.
3. Grant reprieves and pardons, except in cases of impeachment.
4. Make treaties, with the advice and consent of the Senate.
5. Appoint ambassadors, federal court judges, justices of the Supreme Court, and other top officials with Senate consent.
6. Deliver the annual State of the Union address to Congress and send other messages to Congress from time to time.
7. Call either or both chambers of Congress into special session.
8. Receive ambassadors and other representatives from foreign countries.
9. Commission all military officers of the United States.
10. Ensure that all laws passed by Congress are carried out.

Inherent Powers

Certain presidential powers, often called inherent powers, are not spelled out in the Constitution but seem to be attached to the office itself. These powers have simply been assumed by strong presidents and then carried on by their successors. Indeed, the greatest growth in presidential powers has come about in this way.

Since the birth of the republic in 1787, many presidents have strengthened the executive branch by their actions. Most experts agree that the strongest presidents have been George Washington, Thomas Jefferson,

Andrew Jackson, Abraham Lincoln, Theodore Roosevelt, Woodrow Wilson, and Franklin D. Roosevelt. Each one ruled in difficult times and acted decisively, and each set a precedent for a certain activity.

For example, George Washington took the liberty of removing officials from office even though he was not given this authority in the Constitution. He also established the practice of meeting regularly with the heads of the four departments that then existed. He began the practice of submitting proposed legislation to Congress. This practice set a precedent for the president to act as chief legislator. He also began the practice of vetoing legislation. As commander in chief, he used troops to put down a rebellion in Pennsylvania. As chief diplomat, he made foreign policy without consulting Congress. This latter action took Congress by surprise and laid the groundwork for our long history of active presidential involvement in the making of foreign policy.

President Lincoln, confronting the problems of the Civil War, took important actions while Congress was not in session. He suspended certain constitutional liberties, spent funds that Congress had not appropriated, blockaded Southern ports, and banned "treasonable correspondence" from the U.S. mails. All of these acts were done in the name of his powers as commander in chief and his responsibility to "take care that the laws be faithfully executed."

Theodore Roosevelt defined his position for a strong presidency in what he called the "stewardship theory." He said:

> My belief was that it was not only [the president's] right but his duty to do anything that the needs of the Nation demanded unless such action was forbidden by the Constitution or by the laws. . . . I did not usurp power [seize power without legal authority], but I did greatly broaden the use of executive power. In other words, I acted for the public welfare, I acted for the common well-being of all our people, whenever and in whatever manner was necessary, unless prevented by direct constitutional or legislative prohibition.

Franklin D. Roosevelt expanded the presidential power over the economy during the Great Depression

Just the Facts

One president, Grover Cleveland, served two nonconsecutive terms (1885–1889, and 1893–1897).

in the 1930s. Since that time, Americans have expected the president to be actively involved in economic matters and social programs.

Other Presidential Powers

Presidents are in a position of power simply because they have access to important information sources that are beyond the reach of most people. Presidents also have access to almost anyone they wish to see. They can determine who gets a certain job, and they can guide how federal funds are spent. These factors, and others, make people highly responsive to presidents' wishes.

The president's political skills and ability to persuade others also play a significant role in determining presidential powers. After three years on the job, Harry Truman made this remark about the powers of the president:

The president may have a great many powers given to him in the Constitution and may have certain powers under certain laws which are given to him by the Congress of the United States; but the principal power that the president has is to bring people in and try to persuade them to do what they ought to do without persuasion. That's what the powers of the president amount to.

Other presidential powers include military powers and the power to issue executive orders.

SHOULD THE GAME GET ROUGH!

Copyright 1947, by The Chicago Tribune

▲ To contain the spread of communism after World War II (1941–1945), President Harry Truman launched a policy (the Truman Doctrine) of lending economic assistance to countries in which a communist takeover seemed likely. What potential result of the Truman Doctrine worries the cartoonist?

Military Powers Often, a president has exercised military powers that Congress has argued were outside the president's authority. The United States has been involved in over two hundred activities involving the armed services, but Congress has declared war only five times. In 1846, President James K. Polk provoked Mexico into a war. Before the United States entered World War II,

Franklin D. Roosevelt ordered the Navy to "shoot on sight" any German submarine that appeared in the Western Hemisphere security zone. Harry S Truman ordered, without congressional approval, American armed forces into the conflict between North and South Korea. The United States also entered the Vietnam War without congressional approval. No congressional vote was taken before President George Bush sent troops into Panama in 1989, into the Middle East in 1990, or into Somalia in 1992. (He did, however, obtain congressional approval to use American troops to expel, with the use of force, Iraq from Kuwait in 1991.) President Bill Clinton made the decision to send troops to Haiti in 1994 and to Bosnia in 1995.

Executive Orders Another presidential power is the power to issue executive orders. An **executive order** is

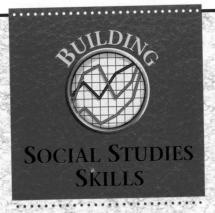

BUILDING SOCIAL STUDIES SKILLS

Reading Biographies

As you study American government, you will often find yourself studying people and the roles they played in shaping and influencing our nation's history. One way to learn about these people is through biographical accounts. A biography is the story of a person's life. Information for biographies is usually derived from both primary and secondary sources. A biography normally presents the details of the person's life, including his or her beliefs, ideals, and personality. It tells of the person's accomplishments and importance.

Use the following guidelines when reading a historical or political biography:

- Determine and track the most important events in the person's life.
- Identify the person's personality traits, ideals, motivations, attitudes, and values. Try to determine how these factors influenced historical events surrounding the person's life.
- Try to determine what effects the person's upbringing had on his or her personal development.
- Track the person's accomplishments and assess their impact and significance.
- Determine any author bias. Does the author generally agree or disagree with the philosophies and actions of the person about whom he or she is writing?
- Read biographies that offer opposing views of the person.

PRACTICING YOUR SKILLS

1. At your school or local library, skim three separate biographies of one American president. Make a list of how those biographies differ. For example, one may be anecdotal, relating minor events in the president's life. Another might emphasize the president's early years. Yet another might examine only the political factors that influenced that president.

2. Read the concluding chapter in two of the biographies. Can you get a sense from your reading whether the author of the biography liked or disliked the president about whom he or she was writing? Write a short analysis of your reasoning.

---

an order issued by the president to carry out policies described in laws that have been passed by Congress. Executive orders have the force of law. Presidential executive orders have been issued since the time of George Washington. They have been used to restructure the White House bureaucracy, to ration consumer goods and establish wage and price controls under emergency conditions, to implement affirmative action policies, and for many other purposes. Some presidents have issued as many as one hundred executive orders a year. In all, U.S. presidents have issued about thirteen thousand executive orders.

The Media and the Presidency

The presidency was the first institution of American government to use the vast power of the media to enhance its own power. Franklin D. Roosevelt first used the power of the media in his series of "fireside chats." During these radio broadcasts, he talked informally about the nation's problems and his ideas for solving them. Roosevelt was a skillful communicator, and listeners felt he was speaking to them personally. He consequently had a powerful influence on millions of people.

All presidents since Franklin D. Roosevelt have used the media to gain public support for their policies. Ronald Reagan (1981–1989), called "the great communicator," was particularly successful in using the media to his great advantage.

The broadcast media, especially television, give presidents the opportunity to talk directly to the people whenever they wish to do so. Unlike other politicians, presidents can get air time whenever they want and reach millions of Americans. When President George Bush went on television for the first time after ordering American troops to bomb Iraq on January 16, 1991, more than 100 million Americans were watching. At that time, this was the largest U.S. television audience for a single program in history. Fred W. Friendly, an influential television producer, once made the following observation:

▲ President Ronald Reagan prepares his last State of the Union address at his desk in the Oval Office. As you can see, the event was made into a "photo op" (photo opportunity) for the media. Why do you suppose the White House encourages photo ops such as these?

[N]o mighty king, no ambitious emperor, no pope or prophet, even dreamt of such awesome a pulpit, so potent a magic wand. . . . The president, in his ability to command the national attention, has diminished the power of all other politicians.

President Bill Clinton used the broadcast media extensively to appeal to different groups of Americans. He held regularly scheduled radio shows and appeared on MTV, *Larry King Live*, as well as other television shows.

Newspapers and magazines are other powerful media sources that provide ways for presidents to bring their ideas to the public's attention. One two-year study of *Time* and *Newsweek* magazine coverage found that more than half of the lead stories dealt with the American president and his activities. President-watching, one of our favorite American pastimes, actually gives the president more power.

The prominence of the president in the media is fostered by the **White House press corps,** a group of reporters from different news organizations assigned to cover the presidency full-time. They spend most of their time waiting (often in a White House

lounge reserved especially for them) for a story to break and for their twice-daily briefing by the president's press secretary. Consequently, the president can do very little without making news. No other nation allows the press such access to its highest government official.

SECTION 1 REVIEW

1. What are the powers of the president as expressed in the Constitution?
2. What other factors have enhanced presidential power?
3. Explain the role strong presidents have had in the historical growth of presidential power.
4. How does the media's role contribute to presidential power?
5. **For Critical Analysis:** Do you think that immediate access to the media gives the president an unfair advantage over other policy- and opinion-makers in the United States? Why or why not?

The Many Presidential Roles

Preview Questions:

- What is the president's function as chief of state?
- What are the president's powers as chief executive?
- What is the president's role as commander in chief? How has this role been disputed?
- By whom are treaties made? What role does the Senate play in making treaties?
- How does the president play the role of chief legislator?

Key Terms:

reprieve, pardon, amnesty, armistice, cease-fire, diplomat, chief diplomat, treaty, executive agreements, power of recognition, ambassador, veto power, patronage

The presidency is, of course, a single office. The individual in that office, however, must play a number of different roles simultaneously. Each of these roles is closely interrelated with the others.

The framers did not describe exactly how the president should fulfill these roles. Expecting that George Washington would be the nation's first leader, they trusted that he would serve as a model for future presidents. As Washington himself stated:

My station is new . . . I walk on untrodden ground [ground on which nobody has ever walked]. There is scarcely any part of my conduct that may not hereafter be drawn into precedent.

Through George Washington's examples and the examples of the presidents who have followed, presidential roles have become more clearly defined over the years. Six basic roles performed by the president are those of chief of state, chief executive, commander in chief, chief diplomat, chief legislator, and political party leader. In addition, there are other, less well-defined presidential roles, including those of economic leader and chief citizen. The way in which presidents carry out their roles depends on many factors, such as the domestic and international issues of the time, the president's personality, and the people the president has working in the executive branch.

Chief of State

Every nation has at least one person who is the ceremonial chief of state. In most democratic countries, the jobs of chief of state and head of government are occupied by different people. In Britain, for example, the queen acts as the ceremonial leader and chief of state, while the real head of government is the prime minister. In the United States, those roles are fused into the presidency. As Theodore Roosevelt put it, the president is both "a king and a prime minister."

Just the Facts

The first African American to be nominated for vice president was Frederick Douglass, who was the candidate of the People's Party in 1872.

As chief of state, the president represents the nation to the rest of the world and engages in a number of activities that are largely symbolic or ceremonial in nature. These include the following:

- Throwing out the first baseball to open the baseball season.
- Turning on the lights on the national Christmas tree.
- Dedicating parks and post offices.
- Launching charity drives.
- Making personal phone calls to congratulate the country's heroines and heroes.

In performing the role of chief of state, the president becomes the personal symbol of the nation. The president and the president's family are in the public eye almost every day. Some have argued that having the president perform these ceremonial functions makes less time available to do "real work." Others believe this role is uniquely American and is important in conveying that presidents are more than just politicians.

Having a Separate Chief of State

In the seven Western European countries headed by royalty, the monarch is considered the chief of state and plays a ceremonial role. In the United Kingdom, for example, Queen Elizabeth represents the state at ceremonial occasions, such as the opening sessions of Parliament, the christening of ships, and receptions for foreign ambassadors.

In the monarchies of the Netherlands and Norway, the king or queen initiates the process of forming a government after national elections by determining which parties can combine to rule in a coalition. This process really depends on the results of the election and the desires of the political parties—yet the monarch must certify the results.

The majority of European states are not monarchies, but they nonetheless split the duties of government between a prime minister and a president. In Switzerland, for example, the president is elected indirectly by the legislature and assumes purely ceremonial duties.

Throughout Western Europe, the pattern is the same: presidents have ceremonial powers only. The single exception to this rule occurs in France. In that nation's presidential system, the head of state has real political power, particularly in foreign affairs.

THINKING GLOBALLY

What are the benefits of having a monarch or president to perform only chief-of-state activities? Are there any benefits to the American system, in which the duties of chief executive and chief of state are combined?

Chief Executive

Executive power is the ability to carry out and enforce the laws. The president is the nation's chief executive, constitutionally bound to enforce the acts of Congress, the decisions of the federal courts, and treaties the United States has signed.

Two constitutional provisions refer to this power. The first is the oath of office the president must take:

I do solemnly swear [or affirm] that I will faithfully execute the Office of President of the United States, and will, to the best of my Ability, preserve, protect, and defend the Constitution of the United States.

The other provision is the Constitution's command that the president "shall take Care that the Laws be faithfully executed." These laws apply to many areas of public concern, such as taxes, civil rights, Social Security, immigration, environmental welfare, and any activities involving interstate commerce.

An important power of the chief executive is the power to appoint and remove national government officers. Another significant power is the power to grant reprieves, pardons, and amnesty. To assist in the various tasks of the chief executive role, the president has a federal bureaucracy, which you will read about in the next chapter.

The Powers of Appointment and Removal With Senate consent, the president names most of the top-ranking officers of the national government. Among them are ambassadors and other diplomats, cabinet members and their top aides, the heads of independent agencies, and all federal judges, attorneys, and marshalls. The president also appoints, with Senate approval, the justices of the Supreme Court. This is a formidable power that can shape the course of government. For example, during the administration of President Richard Nixon (1969–1974), the seats of four Supreme Court justices became vacant. Nixon appointed four justices to the Court who had more conservative views than their predecessors, President Reagan appointed three more conservative justices in the 1980s, and President Bush appointed two during his term (1989–1993). President Clinton was able to check somewhat the increasingly conservative make-up of the Court by appointing Ruth Bader Ginsburg

At the opening of the Ronald Reagan Presidential Library in Simi Valley, California, five U.S. presidents appear together. Can you name them?

and Stephen Breyer to the Court. Because Supreme Court justices are appointed for life, the power to appoint Supreme Court justices represents lasting influence for any president.

The Constitution does not comment on the president's power to remove appointed officials from office. This power has been assumed by presidents since George Washington. It has been contested by Congress only occasionally. In *Myers v. United States* (1926), the Supreme Court ruled that the president had the right to fire executive branch officials, including those who had been appointed with Senate approval. In addition, the president can remove any head of a cabinet department and any individual in the Executive Office of the President.

Reprieves, Pardons, and Amnesty The president has the power to grant reprieves and pardons for offenses against the United States, except in cases of impeachment. A **reprieve** is a postponement of legal punishment. A **pardon** is a release from legal punishment. A pardon is granted in order to remedy a mistake made in a conviction or is given to an offender who presumably has been rehabilitated. In 1925, the Supreme Court upheld this power, stating that the president could reprieve or pardon all offenses "either before trial, during trial, or after trial, by individuals, or by classes, conditionally or absolutely, and this without modification or regulation by Congress." In one controversial case, for example, President Gerald Ford granted "a full, free, and absolute pardon" to Richard Nixon for any crimes the former president might have committed in connection with the Watergate scandal, which

occurred in 1972 during Nixon's presidential reelection campaign.

The president also has the power to grant **amnesty**, which is a special pardon given to a group of people who have committed an offense against the government. In 1977, for instance, President Jimmy Carter granted limited amnesty to the young men who had evaded the draft of the armed forces during the Vietnam War.

Just the Facts

Thomas Jefferson, John Adams, and James Monroe all died on the Fourth of July.

Commander in Chief

Partly because the presidency was tailored for George Washington, the Constitution made the president commander in chief of the nation's armed forces. As Alexander Hamilton wrote in the *Federalist Papers*:

> [O]f all the cares and concerns of the government, the direction of war most peculiarly demands those qualities which distinguish the use of power by a single hand.

As president, George Washington actually led troops to crush the Whiskey Rebellion in 1794. More recent presidents have not taken the power quite so literally, but their military decisions have changed the course of history. Although the president shares war powers with Congress, the president's position in military affairs is dominant.

ARCHITECTS of Government

Franklin Delano Roosevelt (1882–1945)

Franklin Delano Roosevelt was the thirty-second president of the United States and the only president to be elected four times. He was an attorney who entered state politics in New York. Later, he served as assistant secretary of the Navy (1913–1920). Roosevelt governed during the Great Depression of the 1930s and during World War II (1941–1945). His "fireside chats" marked the first use of radio by a president. He oversaw the transformation of the executive branch into today's modern bureaucracy.

HIS WORDS

"No democracy can long survive which does not accept as fundamental to its very existence the recognition of the rights of minorities."

(Letter to the National Association for the Advancement of Colored People, June 25, 1938)

"The United States Constitution has proved itself the most marvelously elastic compilation of rules of government ever written."

(Radio broadcast, March 2, 1930)

DEVELOPING CRITICAL THINKING SKILLS

1. Regarding the first quotation, what are some laws that have been passed in the United States to further the rights of minorities?
2. Regarding the second quotation, how can a constitution be "elastic"?

War Powers

Under the Constitution, war powers are divided between Congress and the president. As you know, Congress is given the power to declare war and the power to raise and maintain the country's armed forces. The president is given the power to lead the armed forces as commander in chief.

Over the years, the president has gathered an enormous amount of power as commander in chief. Many times in our history, presidents have sent American soldiers to troublesome spots on the globe, even though Congress has not declared war.

As commander in chief, the president must also take responsibility for the most difficult of all military decisions—if and when to use nuclear weapons. Harry Truman made the decision to drop the atomic bomb on the Japanese cities of Hiroshima and Nagasaki. "The final decision on where and when to use the atomic bomb was up to me," he said. "Let there be no mistake about it." Today, wherever the president goes, an aide is always nearby carrying the computer-coded device that contains all the codes necessary to order a nuclear attack. This device is an ever-present reminder of the world-threatening consequences of nuclear war and the awesome responsibilities of the president.

The War Powers Resolution

As commander in chief, the president can respond to a military threat quickly without waiting for congressional action. This power to commit troops and involve the nation in a war upset more and more members of Congress as the undeclared war in Vietnam dragged on for many years from the 1960s into the early 1970s. Criticism of the president's role in Vietnam led to the War Powers Resolution of 1973, which limited the president's war-making powers. The law, passed over President Nixon's veto, limited the president's ability to commit troops abroad to a period of sixty days. If Congress does not authorize a longer period, the troops must be removed.

Other War Powers

Presidents also have other war powers. They can make secret agreements with other countries. They can set up military governments in conquered lands. They can also end fighting by calling an **armistice,** or a **cease-fire,** which is a temporary end to battle.

Presidents have a good deal of control over domestic affairs in times of war. During World War II (1941–1945), President Roosevelt introduced gasoline and food rationing, wage and price controls, and government control of industries producing products needed for the war.

Emergency Powers The president's powers as commander in chief go beyond war powers. The president has the power to deal with national emergencies during peacetime. For example, after the assassination of Dr. Martin Luther King, Jr., in 1968, riots broke out in many cities. At the request of several state governors, President Lyndon Johnson dispatched the National Guard to control the rioting. Furthermore, if there is a natural disaster, such as a flood or a hurricane, the president can respond by sending needed supplies or troops to help keep order.

Chief Diplomat

A **diplomat** is a person who represents one country in dealing with representatives of another country. According to the Constitution, the president is the nation's **chief diplomat.** As such, the president directs the foreign policy of the United States and is the most important representative of the United States in relations with other nations.

Proposal and Ratification of Treaties A **treaty** is a formal agreement between two or more sovereign states. The president has the sole power to negotiate and sign treaties with other countries. The Senate, however, must approve the treaty by a two-thirds vote of the members present before it becomes effective. If the treaty is approved by the Senate and signed by the president, it then becomes law.

▲ *This photo shows the mushroom cloud that resulted from the atomic blast at Nagasaki on August 9, 1945. Who made the decision to bomb the Japanese cities of Nagasaki and Hiroshima?*

Woodrow Wilson lost his effort to persuade the Senate to approve the Treaty of Versailles, the general peace agreement to end World War I (1914–1918). The treaty would have made the United States a member of the League of Nations. In contrast, President Clinton, during his first term, convinced the Senate to approve the North American Free Trade Agreement (NAFTA) of 1993 and the international agreement that established the World Trade Organization, which came into existence in 1995.

The Power to Make Executive Agreements Presidential power in foreign affairs is enhanced by the ability to make **executive agreements,** which are pacts between the president and other heads of state. Such agreements have the same legal status as treaties. They do not, however, require the approval of the Senate, although Congress may refuse to appropriate the necessary funds to carry out such an agreement.

Executive agreements vary in their purposes. Some involve routine matters, such as promises of trade or assistance to other countries. Others concern matters of great importance. In 1940, for example, President Franklin D. Roosevelt established an important executive agreement with Prime Minister Winston Churchill of Great Britain. The agreement provided for the United States to loan American destroyers to Great Britain to help protect its land and shipping during World War II, which started in Europe in 1939. In return, the British allowed the United States to use military and naval bases on British territories in the Western Hemisphere.

► Credited with leading the nation out of the Great Depression, President Franklin Delano Roosevelt later witnessed the spread of communism in Eastern Europe. Based on the quote inscribed on the wall of the FDR Memorial in Washington, D.C., what is his opinion of such a form of government?

Some have charged that presidents have kept executive agreements secret that involved matters of importance. Congress passed a law in 1950 requiring that all executive agreements be made public. Some executive agreements were still kept secret, however, by presidents who believed the secrecy of the agreements was important to national security. For example, in 1969, Congress discovered that several presidents had not made public a number of executive agreements that involved giving American military support to South Vietnam, Thailand, and Laos. To prevent such occurrences, Congress passed a law in 1972 that requires the president to inform Congress within sixty days of making any executive agreement.

Presidents have sometimes avoided the Senate confirmation process by titling what is essentially a treaty or an executive agreement by some other name, such as a "memorandum of understanding" or a "political agreement." Recently, for example, President Clinton formed an agreement with Russia that allows that country to have a voice in NATO (North Atlantic Treaty Organization) decisions. Clinton termed the agreement a "founding act" rather than a treaty or executive agreement to bypass the Senate approval requirement.

Power of Recognition The president has the power to accept the legal existence of another country's government. This is called the **power of recognition.** Recognition of another country's government is required before diplomatic relations or negotiations between that country and the United States can be undertaken.

Withholding recognition can be a way of showing disapproval for a national government. Presidents have not, for example, given diplomatic recognition to the Communist government of Cuba. In this way, they have expressed disapproval of the policies of the Cuban government. The government of the People's Republic of China was not recognized until 1979, thirty years after it was established. President Bush withheld recognition of the Baltic nations when they declared their independence in 1991. He gave it only after the European community had already recognized these nations.

Recognition can also be withdrawn as a way of expressing disapproval of a government's actions or policies. In 1979, for example, President Carter formally broke diplomatic ties with the revolutionary Khomeini government in Iran after American citizens were taken and held as hostages in that country.

The president can recognize a foreign government by receiving a foreign diplomat from that country or by

Just the Facts

Lyndon Baines Johnson is the only president to have taken the oath of office in an airplane.

◄ President Bill Clinton, surrounded by members of Congress, signs the Comprehensive Methamphetamine Control Act to regulate the sale and use of an illegal drug.

sending an **ambassador**—an official government representative—to that country. If the United States disapproves of the conduct of a nation that has already been recognized, the president may recall the American ambassador to that country or may ask the country to recall its ambassador from the United States.

Chief Legislator

Nowhere does the Constitution use the words *chief legislator*. It does, however, instruct the president to "from time to time, give to the Congress information of the state of the Union, and recommend to their consideration such measures as he shall judge necessary and expedient." The president has in fact become a major shaper of the nation's political agenda—the set of proposed policies that are actually discussed and acted on by Congress.

Legislative Programs Congress has come to expect the president as chief legislator to develop a legislative program. Woodrow Wilson began the tradition of using the State of the Union address as a chance to outline the administration's legislative programs and urge their passage. Each year since then, the president has used the address to present a legislative program to Congress. Especially since the advent of radio and television, the State of the Union address is as much a message to the American people and to the world as it is a message to Congress. Its impact on public opinion can determine the way Congress responds to the president's agenda.

Congress also receives from the president a suggested budget, along with the annual *Economic Report of the President*. The budget message suggests the amounts of funds the government will need for its programs. The *Economic Report of the President* talks about the state of the nation's economy and recommends ways to improve it. From time to time, the president also submits special messages on certain subjects. These messages call on Congress to enact the laws the president thinks are necessary. For example, President Clinton sent special messages to Congress urging Congress to consider proposed legislation or resolutions regarding health care, national education standards, the Iraq crisis, and a number of other matters.

Besides using these formal avenues, the president also works closely with members of Congress to gain their support for particular programs. The president writes, telephones, and meets with various congressional leaders to discuss pending bills and sends aides to lobby on Capitol Hill. The president uses press conferences, public appearances, and televised events to persuade the public to support the administration's legislative programs. The public may in turn persuade legislators.

One study of the political agenda found that "no other single actor in the political system has quite the capability of the president to set agendas in given policy areas." As one lobbyist told a researcher,

Obviously, when a president sends up a bill [to Congress], it takes first place in the queue. All other bills take second place.

Veto Power The Constitution gives the president another, more direct, power over legislation—the **veto power.** As you learned in Chapter 16, each bill passed by both chambers of Congress is sent to the president for approval. The president's options upon receiving the bill are (1) to sign it and make it law; (2) to veto it and return it to Congress; (3) to take no action, permitting the bill to become law without signing it; (4) if Congress is due to adjourn within ten working days, to kill the bill by simply not acting on it (the so-called "pocket veto"); or (5) by using the line-item veto (if the Supreme Court finds that it is not unconstitutional), to veto part of the bill and sign the rest into law.

Veto power allows the president to act as a check on Congress. Congress has overridden only a very small percentage of presidential vetoes, as you can see in Figure 18–1. Sometimes, just the threat of a veto will force Congress to stop a bill or change it to fit the president's wishes.

Special Sessions As you have learned, only the president has the power to call special sessions of Congress. Should an important issue arise while Congress is not in session, the president can call a special session to deal with it. Today, such sessions are almost never needed, because Congress meets throughout most of the year.

FIGURE 18–1 Presidential Vetoes This table demonstrates the use of presidential vetoes by each president from 1901 through 1997. Which president during this period exercised the most vetoes? What do you know about this president that helps to explain these numbers?

Years	President	Regular Vetoes	Vetoes Overridden	Pocket Vetoes	Total Vetoes
1789–1901	All presidents	489	35	387	876
1901–1909	T. Roosevelt	42	1	40	82
1909–1913	Taft	30	1	9	39
1913–1921	Wilson	33	6	11	44
1921–1923	Harding	5	0	1	6
1923–1929	Coolidge	20	4	30	50
1929–1933	Hoover	21	3	16	37
1933–1945	F. Roosevelt	372	9	263	635
1945–1953	Truman	180	12	70	250
1953–1961	Eisenhower	73	2	108	181
1961–1963	Kennedy	12	0	9	21
1963–1969	Johnson	16	0	14	30
1969–1974	Nixon	26*	7	17	43
1974–1977	Ford	48	12	18	66
1977–1981	Carter	13	2	18	31
1981–1989	Reagan	39	9	28	67
1989–1993	Bush	37	1	0	37
1993–1997	Clinton	18	0	0	18
Total		**1,474**	**104**	**1,039**	**2,513**

*Two pocket vetoes, overruled in the courts, are counted here as regular vetoes.
SOURCE: Louis Fisher, *The Politics of Shared Power; Congress and the Executive,* 2nd ed. (Washington, D.C.: Congressional Quarterly Press, 1987), p.30; *Congressional Quarterly Weekly Report,* October 17, 1992; and author's update.

Political Party Leader and Politician

The last of the six basic roles of president, shown in Figure 18–2, is that of political party leader. Presidents head their political parties by tradition and practical necessity. George Washington was the only president elected without the backing of a political party. All other presidents have been elected with the help of political parties and have become the national leaders of the parties that nominated them.

As party leader, the president has a number of major duties. These include choosing a vice president after receiving the presidential nomination; making several thousand high-level government appointments, mainly to faithful party members (a system known as **patronage**); and working to fulfill the party platform. The successes and failures of the president in these

FIGURE 18–2 The Six Basic Roles of the President This table lists the major roles of the president and cites examples of the actions and functions associated with each role. Can you think of any instances in which these roles might overlap?

Role	Description	Specific Functions
Chief of State	Performs certain ceremonial functions as personal symbol of the nation	★ Throws out first baseball of baseball season ★ Lights national Christmas tree ★ Decorates war heroes ★ Dedicates parks and post offices
Chief Executive	Enforces laws, federal court decisions, and treaties signed by the United States	★ Can appoint, with Senate approval, high-ranking officials of the federal government ★ Can dismiss presidential appointees from the executive branch without Senate approval ★ Can grant reprieves, pardons, and amnesty
Commander in Chief	Leads the nation's armed forces	★ Can commit troops for up to ninety days in response to a military threat (War Powers Resolution) ★ Can make secret agreements with other countries ★ Can set up military governments in conquered lands ★ Can end fighting by calling a cease-fire (armistice) ★ Can handle national emergencies, such as riots and natural disasters, during peacetime
Chief Diplomat	Directs U.S. foreign policy and is the nation's most important representative in dealing with foreign countries	★ Can negotiate and sign treaties with other nations with Senate approval ★ Can make executive agreements with other heads of state without Senate approval ★ Can accept the legal existence of another country's government (power of recognition) ★ Receives foreign chiefs of state
Chief Legislator	Informs Congress about the condition of the country and recommends legislative measures	★ Proposes legislative program to Congress in traditional State of the Union address ★ Suggests budget to Congress and submits annual economic report ★ Can veto a bill passed by Congress ★ Can call special sessions of Congress
Political Party Leader	Heads political party	★ Chooses a vice president ★ Makes several thousand top-level government appointments, often to faithful party members (patronage) ★ Tries to execute the party's platform ★ May attend party fund-raisers ★ May help elect party members running for office as mayors, governors, or members of Congress

▲ President Bill Clinton and First Lady Hillary Clinton show support for their party at this Democratic National Committee conference. What is a president's official role in his party?

Congress, and the business and labor communities increasingly look to the president to lower unemployment, fight inflation, keep taxes down, and promote economic growth.

The Employment Act of 1946 directed the president to submit an annual economic report to Congress and declared for the first time that the federal government had the responsibility to promote productivity, high employment, and stable purchasing power. The law created the Council of Economic Advisers (CEA) to give the president economic advice. In 1993, the National Economic Council (NEC) was created to coordinate the economic policymaking process.

We give our presidents numerous tools with which to manage the economy. One is the duty of preparing the budget, which gives the president the opportunity to determine the government's spending priorities for the coming year.

Chief Citizen and Moral Leader

The presidency is not merely an administrative office. It is also a place of moral leadership.

Most Americans would probably agree with this statement, which was made by Franklin D. Roosevelt (1933–1945). The office of the presidency automatically makes its occupant the nation's chief citizen. The president is expected to represent all of the people and to work in the public interest.

Presidents must be extremely careful and judicious in the way they conduct themselves because, as already mentioned, their actions are closely scrutinized by the media. During the Clinton administration, many Americans questioned the moral integrity of President Clinton and his ability to fulfill the role of chief citizen. Perhaps no other president—including Richard Nixon (see the *Case Study: Government in Action* feature on page 493)—faced more ethical and legal challenges than Bill Clinton.

areas are reflected in the party's future election campaigns. Presidents may support the party by attending party fund raisers or by sending assistants to help elect or reelect party members running for office as mayors, governors, or members of Congress.

As discussed in the chapters on Congress, members of Congress are politicians as well as lawmakers, always concerned about their constituencies and the next election. The president is in the same position. Like all politicians, the president wants to win elections and battles in Congress and to maintain a high level of public approval.

Economic Leader

In recent years, the president has taken on the role of being the nation's economic leader. A president's popularity, measured in the polls, often rises and falls with the nation's economic well-being. The public,

SECTION 2 REVIEW

1. What are the functions of the president as chief of state and chief executive?

2. As commander in chief, what are the president's powers?
3. What are the president's powers as chief diplomat?
4. How does the president perform the role of chief legislator?

5. Explain why the president is the leader of a political party.
6. **For Critical Analysis:** Do you think the president's role as political party leader is in conflict with any of the other presidential roles? Explain why or why not.

Checks on the President's Powers

Preview Questions:

⭐ How can Congress check presidential powers?
⭐ How can the judiciary check presidential powers?

Key Term:

executive privilege

The framers of the Constitution were well aware that an overly strong chief executive would be able to abuse the office of president. To avoid such abuses, they built in a system of checks and balances. Both Congress and the judiciary have powers that restrict the president. The president is also checked to some degree by certain unwritten limitations.

Congressional Limitations

Although the president has the power to veto legislation, Congress can override the president's veto with a two-thirds vote by the members present in each chamber. Even though it is not often used, the override remains a powerful check by Congress on presidential powers. Since George Washington's presidency, only about 7 percent of all presidential vetoes have been

◄ *Although the president has many powers, both constitutional and by tradition, he is still held in check by the legislative and judicial branches of government. Here, a congressional committee discusses the grounds for impeachment of President Andrew Johnson. Was Johnson ultimately impeached?*

American citizens have a right and sometimes a duty to let the president know directly about their opinions on important public policy matters. Each president receives thousands of communications every day. Of course, no president actually reads all of these communications, but assistants often use them to tally up public opinion for and against a particular issue.

The president's decisions are often affected by direct communications from the public. For example, when President Reagan started sending advisers and military aid to the Central American country of El Salvador in 1981, he immediately began to receive a flood of letters, which ran ten-to-one against his policy. After that, his decisions on this matter were partly molded by the strong public opposition shown in the letters. The opposite occurred when President Bush sent troops to the Middle East after Iraq invaded Kuwait in 1990. Bush's actions were widely supported by the American public.

Your views can, and should, be brought to the president's attention. Whenever you strongly agree with or oppose the actions taken by the presi-

PARTICIPATING IN YOUR GOVERNMENT

How to Contact the President

dent, you can contact the White House directly. Address your letter in the following way:

The President of the
    United States
The White House
1600 Pennsylvania Ave. NW
Washington, DC 20500

You can also contact the White House by telephone at 202-456-1414, by fax at 202-456-2883, or by e-mail at **President@whitehouse.gov/**.

A less well-known, but perhaps equally effective, way to express your views to the president is by writing a letter to the editor of a major newspaper. The president's aides in the White House clip letters from newspapers across the country. These letters provide a digest of public opinion for the president and the president's staff to review on a regular basis.

Whether you choose to write the president directly or to write to the editor of a major newspaper, it is important to remember that your views are more likely to be given serious consideration (your letter is more likely to be printed) if your letter is well written, clearly organized, and neatly prepared. A letter that is well thought out and neatly typed can be a very effective tool for communicating your feelings to the president.

TAKING ACTION

1. As a class, choose a policy issue that concerns you today. Compose a letter to the president, and send it directly to the White House.
2. Write a letter to the editor of a major newspaper about the same issue, remembering that it might be made part of a digest of letters given to the president by aides.

overridden by Congress. The most overrides—fifteen—occurred during the administration of Andrew Johnson (1865–1869). Both Harry Truman and Gerald Ford saw twelve of their presidential vetoes overridden.

Congress can also use its "power of the purse" to check the president. For example, Richard Nixon tried to restrict government spending because of a worsening economy in the early 1970s by cutting domestic programs while at the same time increasing some areas of military spending. Congress undermined these plans by appropriating funds for welfare programs that the president did not want and by cutting appropriations for the weapons programs he favored.

Government in Action

Watergate and the Presidential Abuse of Power

On June 17, 1972, police officers caught five intruders inside the offices of the Democratic National Committee at the Watergate, a complex of business offices and apartment buildings in Washington, D.C. The break-in was quickly dismissed as a "third-rate burglary" and seemed destined to be forgotten. But it soon became clear that there was more to the story. First, the Federal Bureau of Investigation (FBI) began investigating the incident, and later the Senate formed a special committee to investigate the Watergate case. The press, especially the *Washington Post*, followed up on clues. These investigations turned up the following:

- Crisp $100 bills found on the burglars were traced to CREEP, the Committee for the Reelection of the President, a pro-Nixon campaign group. About $420,000 (taken mainly from Nixon campaign contributions) was used as "hush money" to keep the burglars quiet about who had hired them and what they were doing.
- CREEP solicited big contributions from people being investigated by government agencies and sought illegal contributions from corporations.
- CREEP collected money from the dairy industry at about the same time the president approved an increase in the federal price supports for milk.
- The president approved the formation of a special investigations unit in the White House to stop security leaks. This unit tapped the phones of administration officials, poked through private files, and broke into private offices.
- The acting director of the FBI destroyed vital Watergate evidence at the instigation of two of the president's top assistants.
- An "enemies list" of people who opposed Nixon was compiled by the president's staff. The income-tax forms of people on the enemies list were singled out for investigation by the Internal Revenue Service.

President Nixon blocked many efforts by Congress and the courts to find out if the White House had ordered the Watergate break-in. Nixon did so by invoking the doctrine of **executive privilege**—the special right to withhold information, usually in affairs dealing with national security and foreign affairs. The Supreme Court finally ruled that neither the president nor members of the executive branch could use executive privilege to withhold information about a crime.

Thus, the president was forced to surrender tape recordings that had been made by concealed microphones in White House offices and in the Executive Office Building. On the tape for June 23, 1972, Nixon was heard approving a plan to use the Central Intelligence Agency (CIA) to block the FBI investigation of the break-in.

In July 1974, the House Judiciary Committee recommended that the House of Representatives impeach President Richard Nixon on the grounds that he had obstructed justice, abused presidential powers, and obstructed the impeachment process. It appeared likely that, for the first time since 1868, the president of the United States would be impeached. President Nixon resigned and was later pardoned by his successor, President Gerald Ford.

The president of the United States is never above the law. The American form of democracy is one in which laws rule rather than men and women.

THINK ABOUT IT

1. Should Richard Nixon have gone to trial for any criminal activities for which he was responsible?
2. Is there any way for Congress to ensure that no similar scandals occur in the future?

The President at Work, Then and Now

Since the early 1900s, the way the president works has changed. This is not surprising, because over that period the president has become a world leader.

THEN (EARLY 1900S)	NOW
Congress proposed most legislation.	The president proposes most major legislation, but all legislation must be introduced by members of Congress.
The president had little control over the budget, except for the veto power.	The Office of Management and Budget, an executive agency, prepares the budget.
The president's responsibilities in domestic and foreign affairs were limited.	The president takes responsibility for maintaining peace and involves himself in the economic well-being of the nation.
The president rarely left the United States.	The president travels to foreign lands frequently.

The power of impeachment is considered the ultimate congressional check on the presidency. The Constitution says that Congress may impeach the president for "treason, bribery, or other high crimes or misdemeanors." Congress has only used this power once. In 1868, the House of Representatives voted to impeach President Andrew Johnson. He was charged with violating the Tenure Office Act, which prohibited him from removing executive officials without the consent of the Senate. The Senate, which tries cases of impeachment, found Johnson not guilty. In 1974, a House committee voted to recommend the impeachment of President Nixon because of his part in the 1972 Watergate break-in scandal, but he resigned from the presidency before the recommendation reached the full House.

During the 1970s, several laws limiting presidential power were passed by Congress. American involvement in Vietnam and the Watergate scandal led in 1972 to a limitation on the president's use of secret executive agreements. The 1973 War Powers Resolution required the president to consult with Congress before committing American troops to war. As you learned in Chapter 15, the 1974 Budget and Impoundment Control Act limited the president's power to impound, or withhold, funds appropriated by Congress.

Congress can also exercise other checks on the president's power. The Senate, for example, must approve major appointments and treaties made by the president.

Judicial Limitations

As discussed in Chapter 3, the Supreme Court, in *Marbury v. Madison* (1803), affirmed the Supreme Court's right to review a president's actions. The president and the Supreme Court, however, are not as closely involved in the day-to-day operations of each other's affairs as are the president and Congress. In most instances, Supreme Court justices are inclined to respect the president's decisions and viewpoints.

The Supreme Court, however, has imposed some limits on the president's domestic power. In 1936, the Court declared several laws unconstitutional that had

Suing the President

In 1994, Paula Corbin Jones filed a sexual harassment lawsuit against President Bill Clinton. A constitutional question immediately arose. Can a sitting president be sued for conduct that allegedly occurred before he took office? In 1997, the Supreme Court said yes. The president had argued *executive privilege*. This is a doctrine that grants presidents *immunity* from lawsuits by people who are adversely affected by presidential decisions. The Court said that this doctrine only applies to official actions. A lawsuit against a president involving unofficial conduct had never gone to trial in the history of this nation. (Presidents Theodore Roosevelt, Harry Truman, and John Kennedy were subjected to lawsuits for their private actions, but in each case, the lawsuit was settled or dismissed after the defendant assumed the presidency.)

Leave the President Alone, at Least While in Office, Some Say

Many Americans do not agree with the Supreme Court's decision. They believe that a sitting president should be left alone. The public interest demands that presidents use their undivided time and attention to carry out their public duties.

Also, lawsuits against sitting presidents involving their behavior before taking office could be politically motivated. Given that Americans are suing more often, we may find future presidents routinely being bothered by lawsuits based on unofficial conduct prior to taking office. Many of these lawsuits could be started by political opponents simply to harm or to destroy a president's reputation. Even if the lawsuits are later shown to be without merit, the damage would already be done.

Finally, such lawsuits subject the head of the executive branch to the orders and schedules of the judicial branch. This is contrary to the constitutional separation of powers.

No Person Is above the Law, Others Insist

Those who agree with the Supreme Court's 1997 decision argue that the president is not above the law, even with respect to private conduct. Presidents, like everyone else, should be accountable for their actions.

Furthermore, if a private lawsuit had to wait until a president was no longer in office, the suit could be delayed as long as eight years. By then, the plaintiff's chances of proving the case could be severely weakened. Key witnesses could forget important details. Witnesses might even die before the suit could go forward.

In any event, the constitutional separation of powers is not an issue. The courts routinely use the power of judicial review to invalidate official actions of presidents. If *official* presidential actions are subject to judicial review, then the courts can determine the legality of a president's *unofficial* conduct as well. Courts can always manage a case so as to minimize the demands on the president's time.

YOU DECIDE

1. How does the doctrine of executive privilege further the interests of the nation? What might happen if this doctrine did not exist?
2. Suppose that you had been harmed by a person who later became president. Would you be willing to sue the president while the president was in office, or would you wait until the person stepped down from the presidency to bring the suit? Give reasons for your answer.

been passed by Congress as part of President Franklin Roosevelt's New Deal Program. In 1952, the Court held that President Harry Truman could not issue an executive order unless it was provided for by the Constitution or by an act of Congress. In 1975, the Court upheld limits on the power of the president to impound funds appropriated by Congress.

The Court has also set limits on a president's claim to executive privilege—the special right to withhold information. Presidents usually claim executive privilege based on the need for secrecy in carrying out foreign affairs or in matters of national security. George Washington first invoked the right of executive privilege when he refused to turn over to the House of Representatives his own papers and documents on a matter of diplomacy on the grounds that Congress was not constitutionally entitled to them. In 1974, in the Watergate scandal, President Richard Nixon claimed that executive privilege entitled him to keep his White House tapes and other materials from Congress and even to prevent his officials from testifying before Congress. In *United States v. Nixon* that same year, the Court ruled that the president could not use the doctrine of executive privilege to withhold evidence in a criminal trial.

In 1997, President Bill Clinton argued that executive privilege should make him immune from lawsuits brought against him for conduct alleged to have occurred before he became president. In *Clinton v. Jones* (1997), the Supreme Court held that executive privilege only applies to *official* presidential actions—actions that the president undertakes while in office—and that the lawsuit could go forward.

The fact that the Senate must approve judicial appointments made by the president limits the president's ability to shape the Supreme Court. Usually, presidents nominate justices who are acceptable to congressional leaders and to their supporters. Also, the justices chosen for the Court are not bound to follow the policies of the president who appointed them. Because the Supreme Court is an independent body, the justices may follow their own interpretations of the law. In fact, sometimes,

"The constitutional process has been served... I shall resign"

Ford Takes Office Today.

▲ This headline quotes Richard M. Nixon as he resigns the presidency under the shadow of Watergate. Do you think that Nixon would have been impeached had he stayed in office?

the persons appointed to the Supreme Court disappoint the presidents who chose them by taking opposing views. For example, President Dwight D. Eisenhower appointed Earl Warren as chief justice in 1953. Warren soon moved away from Eisenhower's conservative stand on social issues and led the Court in many liberal decisions that were disliked by the Eisenhower administration.

Political Limitations

One of the most severe restraints on the president is not legal but political. Public opinion and media attention put pressure on the president and can greatly influence how power is exercised. Without favorable public opinion, a president cannot succeed in carrying out a political program, especially if the president would like to run for a second term of office.

A good example concerns President Clinton's desire to change the health-care system in the United States. During his first term in office, he made health-care reform a major policy goal. He discovered, however, that many Americans did not favor the changes that he was proposing. He decided to abandon the issue.

The president's party also imposes political limitations on presidential actions. This is particularly true during a president's first term. Presidents who want to be renominated for second terms cannot turn their backs on their political parties. Thus, if a president's policy actions reduce the effectiveness of senators and representatives who belong to the president's party, then the party may not support the president in the next election cycle. But suppose the president is serving a second term. In that case, the party may not support the president's choice (often the current vice president) as the party's next presidential candidate.

Despite congressional, judicial, and political limitations, the office of president of the United States remains the most powerful one in the world. This power is derived from the Constitution, from institutional sources, and from the actions of strong presidents in the past. The president uses this power to perform many functions and fulfill many roles. As you can see, along with these powers comes the burden of enormous responsibility.

SECTION 3 REVIEW

1. How can Congress limit the president's powers?
2. Which U.S. president has been impeached? What was the result of the impeachment trial in the Senate?
3. How can the Supreme Court limit the president's powers?
4. **For Critical Analysis:** Historically, Congress has only overridden presidential vetoes 7 percent of the time. Does this mean that Congress is not

sufficiently checking the president's power? Why or why not?

★ ★ ★ ★ **Chapter Summary** ★ ★ ★ ★

Section 1: Presidential Powers

⭐ The Constitution grants broad powers to the president.
⭐ The presidency has derived additional powers from the fact that the president has access to persons and control over many resources, such as jobs.
⭐ Certain presidential powers that are today considered part of the rights of the office were simply assumed by strong presidents and then carried on by their successors.
⭐ The media have also enhanced the power of the president.

Section 2: The Many Presidential Roles

⭐ The president serves the dual roles of chief of state and chief executive.
⭐ The president is commander in chief of the armed services and, as such, has certain war powers.
⭐ As chief diplomat, the president has the power to negotiate and sign treaties with other countries, but the Senate must approve the treaties by a two-thirds vote. The president also has the power to recognize the governments of other countries.
⭐ As chief legislator, the president has become a major shaper of the congressional agenda. The president is also a political party leader and politician.

Section 3: Checks on the President's Powers

⭐ To avoid any misuse of power, the framers of the Constitution built in a system of checks and balances.
⭐ Congress has the power to override the president's veto.
⭐ Congress also has the "power of the purse" and the ultimate power of impeachment.
⭐ The Supreme Court has the right to review the president's actions.
⭐ Because the Senate must approve judicial appointments, the president's ability to shape the Supreme Court is limited.
⭐ Public opinion and media attention also serve as a check on presidential power.

CHAPTER 18 Review

★ REVIEW QUESTIONS ★

1. What basic power is granted to the president in the Constitution? In what part of the Constitution is this power established?
2. What are some other sources of presidential power?
3. How have strong presidents, such as Abraham Lincoln and Franklin D. Roosevelt, contributed to the powers of the presidency?
4. What effect have the media had on the presidency?
5. What is the president's role as chief of state?
6. What are the powers of the president as chief executive?
7. How are the war powers divided between the president and Congress? How does the War Powers Resolution of 1973 attempt to limit the president's war powers?
8. As chief diplomat, what are the powers and duties of the president?
9. How does a treaty differ from an executive agreement?
10. How does the president recognize the legal existence of another country's government? Can the president withdraw that recognition? If so, how does the president withdraw recognition?
11. Explain the president's role as chief legislator.
12. Why is the president a political party leader?
13. How can Congress check the powers of the president?
14. How can the Supreme Court restrain the president's powers?
15. Briefly describe how President Nixon's actions in the Watergate scandal were abuses of presidential power.
16. What are some arguments for and against the Supreme Court's ruling that a sitting president may be sued for conduct that allegedly took place before the president took office?

★ CRITICAL THINKING ★

1. In your opinion, what is the most important role that the president plays? Why do you think that role is so important?
2. Do you think that the power of the presidency has increased or decreased in recent years? Give some examples to support your answer.
3. What do you think the president should do if Congress passed a law that violated the president's party platform?
4. The roles of the president are sometimes in conflict. Describe some instances in which the political needs of the president may not be consistent with the needs of the nation.
5. How has television changed the relationship between the president and the American people? How has it affected the president's power?

★ IMPROVING YOUR SKILLS ★

Communication Skills

Synthesizing Synthesizing means combining two or more sources of information into a single, unified whole. Learning to synthesize information will help you answer questions, make decisions, take notes, do research, and write reports. Synthesizing is necessary whenever you have to take two or more sources of information and blend the ideas in a clear way that reflects your own writing or speaking style. When synthesizing, follow these guidelines:

● Read the materials carefully and decide on your point of view, opinion, and approach.
● Select the ideas or examples that support your ideas. Think about how your ideas and the ideas in the sources relate to each other.
● Combine these ideas into a synthesized whole.

Writing Find three articles about a recent presidential decision or issue. Write a synthesis of the articles based on your view of how the ideas presented are interrelated.

Social Studies Skills

Evaluating a Policy Decision As a student of American government, you must be able to evaluate policy decisions. The following guidelines will help you evaluate decisions made by government officials at every level.

- Determine the nature of the decision and the surrounding circumstances at the time the decision was made.
- List other choices and alternatives that were available at the time. Remember that some alternatives that are apparent now may not have been apparent at the time.
- Determine the risks and benefits of each alternative. Each probably had several potential short-term and long-term effects. Remember that some long-term effects may not have been evident at the time.
- Analyze the results of the decision. Determine whether or not, in your opinion, a good decision was made.

1. Choose a recent policy decision made in your school or community. Evaluate the policy decision by using the steps above. Report your evaluation to the class.
2. As a group, discuss and evaluate a national policy decision using the steps above.

★ ACTIVITIES AND PROJECTS ★

1. Collect cartoons that refer to a current issue that the president is addressing. Paste the cartoons on a posterboard or in a booklet, and write a summary of each one. In your summary, discuss whether the messages the cartoonists are trying to convey are positive or negative. Indicate whether or not you agree with the cartoonists' depictions of the president's actions. Then try to determine the president's actual position on the issue, and draw your own editorial cartoon in which you express your views on that position.

2. Keep close track of the president's activities for three weeks by watching TV news programs, reading newspapers and magazines, or accessing news sources on the Internet. Notice how closely you can keep track of the president's daily life. Keep notes on what you learn. Report your results to the class, and explain why you think the media are so interested in what the president does. Try to evaluate if the president and his or her family are able to retain privacy while living in the White House.

3. Make a list of ten executive orders made during one president's administration. In addition, list the public response and consequences of these orders.

4. Make a list of ten executive agreements made during one president's administration. In addition, list the public response and consequences of these agreements.

What If . . .

The President Did Not Have to Spend All of the Funds Congress Appropriated?

Until 1975 the president had the authority to impound funds that Congress had appropriated for various programs. Currently, however, the president must spend all of the funds appropriated by Congress. How might presidents be able to act if they were not obligated to do so?

The Bureaucracy in Action

CHAPTER OBJECTIVES

To learn about and understand . . .

- ⭐ The nature, size, and growth of the U.S. government bureaucracy

- ⭐ The make-up of the various executive departments

- ⭐ The purposes and functions of independent agencies and government corporations

- ⭐ How the civil service works

- ⭐ How bureaucrats make policy

An aerial view of our capital city—Washington, D.C.
Can you find the White House?

501

★ **Keynote** ★

"Bureaucracy is not an obstacle to democracy but an inevitable complement to it."

Joseph A. Schumpeter
(1883–1950)
Austrian American Economist

INTRODUCTION

Did you eat breakfast this morning? If you did, government bureaucrats—individuals who work in the offices of government—had a lot to do with what you ate. If you had bacon, the meat was inspected by federal agents. If you drank milk, the price was affected by rules and regulations of the Department of Agriculture. If you looked at a cereal box, you saw fine print about nutrition that was provided as a result of regulations made by other federal agencies and implemented by bureaucrats.

A bureaucrat is a member of a large administrative organization—a bureaucracy. The job of government bureaucrats is to carry out government policies. Bureaucrats deliver our mail, clean our streets, and run our national parks. As Joseph Schumpeter indicated in the opening quotation, only with the help of bureaucrats can a democracy function.

The Bureaucracy: Its Nature and Size

Preview Questions:

⭐ What is a bureaucracy, and how is a bureaucracy organized?

⭐ How much has the government bureaucracy in our country grown?

Key Terms:

bureaucrat, bureaucracy

The term *bureaucracy* does not refer only to the national government. Any large-scale organization has to have a bureaucracy. Even small businesses may operate as bureaucracies. A **bureaucracy** is simply an organization that is structured in a pyramid-like fashion and in which everybody (except the person at the top of the "pyramid"—the head of the bureaucracy) reports to at least one other person. For the national government, the head of the bureaucracy is the president of the United States.

Just the Facts

The national government issues over four billion copies of various books, pamphlets, fliers, reports, and other publications annually.

A bureaucratic organization allows each person to concentrate on his or her area of knowledge and expertise. In your school, for example, you do not expect the school nurse to solve the problems of the principal. You do not expect the football coach to solve the problems of the finance department.

Another key aspect of a bureaucracy is that the power to act resides in the *position* rather than in the *person*. In your school, the person who is currently the principal has about the same authority as previous principals.

The Growth of the Bureaucracy

Today, the word *bureaucracy* generally evokes a negative reaction. During election time, throughout the nation, there are calls from politicians to "cut big government and red tape," and "get rid of overlapping and wasteful bureaucracies." No one campaigns for office on a platform calling for a bigger bureaucracy. Candidates do, however, promise to establish programs that would require many new employees—which means the bureaucracy would have to grow. Americans constantly demand more services. With each new service comes a new group of bureaucrats.

The U.S. government bureaucracy that was created in 1789 was small. There were only a few employees in each cabinet department. For example, the Department of State had only nine employees. The Department of War had two employees, and the Department of the Treasury had thirty-nine employees.

▲ *These soldiers, marching through the desert on a training mission, are part of the U.S. Department of Defense. The Department of War, as it was formerly known, has grown from a staff of two civilians to a staff of thousands. Like all other departments, Defense is headed by a civilian cabinet member who is appointed by the president.*

Organization charts are used to illustrate how organizations are structured and how they operate. Each position or segment in the organization is represented by a symbol, often a box, which is usually labeled with the title of the position or segment. In most organization charts, the position or segment with the most power and authority is shown at the top. Organization charts also show lines of authority in the organization. Typically, these are lines going from the position or segment with the most authority down to lower and lower levels. Each lower level reports to a higher level, and the lines of authority show these reporting relationships.

An example of an organization chart is shown here. This chart represents the organization of the U.S. Sentencing Commission, an agency in the U.S. Department of Justice. The lines on the chart show that the bureaucrats who head each of the offices at the bottom of the Sentencing Commission's organization chart all report to the staff director. The staff director, in turn, reports to the chairperson of the nine commissioners who head the agency. Ultimately, the commis-

Reading an Organization Chart

sioners are responsible to the head of the Department of Justice, the attorney general of the United States. The attorney general, as one of the president's cabinet members, reports to the president (see Figure 19–1 on page 504).

PRACTICING YOUR SKILLS

1. Describe the flow of power and authority from the various offices to the chairperson.
2. How are decisions arrived at in this agency? How can you tell?
3. Which positions have the same authority as the chairperson?

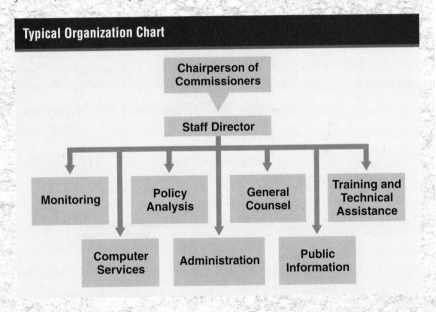

Typical Organization Chart

Chairperson of Commissioners

Staff Director

Monitoring · Policy Analysis · General Counsel · Training and Technical Assistance

Computer Services · Administration · Public Information

By 1798, the government bureaucracy was still tiny. The secretary of state had seven clerks. His total expenditures on stationery and printing amounted to $500, or about $5,000 by today's standards. The Department of War spent a grand total of $1.4 million each year, or about $13 million in today's terms.

Times have changed. The U.S. government bureaucracy has grown to nearly three million employees. State governments employ another four million civilians, and local governments employ more than ten million. (You'll find out more about state and local governments in Chapters 24, 25, and 26.) In total,

FIGURE 19-1 Organization of the Government of the United States The table below outlines the organization of the U.S. government, including the most important executive departments, independent executive agencies, independent regulatory agencies, and government corporations. Approximately how many people are employed by the U.S. government?

THE CONSTITUTION

Legislative Branch

The Congress

Senate   House

Architect of the Capitol
United States Botanic Garden
General Accounting Office
Government Printing Office
Library of Congress
Congressional Budget Office

Executive Branch

The President
The Vice President
Executive Office of the President

White House Office
Office of the Vice President
Council of Economic Advisers
Council on Environmental Quality
National Security Council
Office of Administration
Office of Policy Development

Office of Management and Budget
Office of National Drug Control Policy
Office of Science and Technology Policy
Office of the U.S. Trade Representative

Judicial Branch

The Supreme Court of the United States

United States Courts of Appeals
United States District Courts
Territorial Courts
United States Court of International Trade
United States Court of Federal Claims
United States Court of Appeals for the Armed Forces
United States Tax Court
United States Court of Veterans Appeals
Administrative Office of the United States Courts
Federal Judicial Center
United States Sentencing Commission

Department of Agriculture
Department of Commerce
Department of Defense
Department of Education
Department of Energy

Department of Health and Human Services
Department of the Interior
Department of Justice
Department of Labor
Department of State

Department of Housing and Urban Development
Department of the Treasury
Department of Transportation
Department of Veterans Affairs

Independent Establishments and Government Corporations

African Development Foundation
Central Intelligence Agency
Commodity Futures Trading Commission
Consumer Product Safety Commission
Corporation for National and Community Service
Defense Nuclear Facilities Safety Board
Environmental Protection Agency
Equal Employment Opportunity Commission
Export-Import Bank of the United States
Farm Credit Administration
Federal Communications Commission
Federal Deposit Insurance Corporation
Federal Election Commission
Federal Emergency Management Agency
Federal Housing Finance Board
Federal Labor Relations Authority
Federal Maritime Commission
Federal Mediation and Conciliation Service
Federal Mine Safety and Health Review Commission

Federal Reserve System
Federal Retirement Thrift Investment Board
Federal Trade Commission
General Services Administration
Inter-American Foundation
Merit Systems Protection Board
National Aeronautics and Space Administration
National Archives and Records Administration
National Capital Planning Commission
National Credit Union Administration
National Foundation for the Arts and the Humanities
National Labor Relations Board
National Mediation Board
National Railroad Passenger Corporation (Amtrak)
National Science Foundation
National Transportation Safety Board
Nuclear Regulatory Commission
Occupational Safety and Health Review Commission

Office of Government Ethics
Office of Personnel Management
Office of Special Counsel
Panama Canal Commission
Peace Corps
Pension Benefit Guaranty Corporation
Postal Rate Commission
Railroad Retirement Board
Securities and Exchange Commission
Selective Service System
Small Business Administration
Social Security Administration
Tennessee Valley Authority
Trade and Development Agency
U.S. Arms Control and Disarmament Agency
U.S. Commission on Civil Rights
U.S. Information Agency
U.S. International Development Cooperation Agency
U.S. International Trade Commission
U.S. Postal Service

SOURCE: *U.S. Government Manual, 1997/98.*

about 15 percent of the entire labor force is employed directly by national, state, and local governments, including the military.

Spending has, of course, increased as well. The national government spends over $1.7 trillion each year. Expenditures by all levels of government are about 40 percent of the total value of the goods and services produced in the nation in a year. In 1929, by comparison, that percentage was 8.5 percent. The government's expenditures are financed in part by fees and borrowing. The greatest single source of government revenue is the taxes paid by the average citizen.

How the U.S. Government Bureaucracy Is Organized

A complete organization chart of the U.S. government would be large enough to cover an entire wall. A simplified version is provided in Figure 19–1 on page 504. The executive branch consists of a number of bureaucracies that provide services to Congress, to the federal courts, and to the president directly.

There are four major types of bureaucratic structures within the executive branch of the national government:

- Executive departments
- Independent executive agencies
- Independent regulatory agencies
- Government corporations

We will look at these structures in the following sections. Each type of bureaucratic structure has its own relationship to the president and its own internal workings.

SECTION 1 REVIEW

1. What is a bureaucracy?
2. Describe the growth of government bureaucracy in historical terms.
3. **For Critical Analysis:** Why do you think that state and local bureaucracies (in total) are so much larger than the federal bureaucracy?

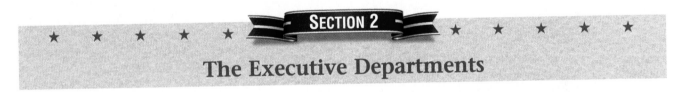

SECTION 2

The Executive Departments

Preview Questions:

- What are some of the major executive departments and their duties?
- How are the departments organized?
- Which departments primarily serve the president?

You were introduced to the various executive departments in Chapter 17, which discussed the president's cabinet and other close advisers. The fourteen executive departments are the major service organizations of the national government. They are directly

▶ *An inspector for the Bureau of Engraving and Printing examines a sheet of paper money for flaws. Under what U.S. government department's authority does this bureau print money? (See Figure 19–2 on page 506.)*

FIGURE 19–2 Executive Departments This table lists and describes the fourteen executive departments, their principal duties, and their most important subagencies. Which of these departments is responsible for the maintenance and care of lands and parks owned by the U.S. government?

Department (Year Established)	Principal Duties	Most Important Subagencies
State (1789)	Negotiates treaties; develops our foreign policy; protects citizens abroad	Passport Agency; Bureau of Diplomatic Security; Foreign Service; Bureau of Human Rights and Humanitarian Affairs; Bureau of Consular Affairs; Bureau of Intelligence and Research
Treasury (1789)	Pays all U.S. government bills; borrows money; collects federal taxes; mints coins and prints paper currency; operates the Secret Service; supervises national banks	Internal Revenue Service; Bureau of Alcohol, Tobacco, and Firearms; U.S. Secret Service; U.S. Mint; Bureau of Engraving and Printing; Customs Service
Interior (1849)	Supervises lands and parks owned by the U.S. government; operates hydroelectric power facilities owned by the U.S. government; supervises Native American affairs	U.S. Fish and Wildlife Service; National Park Service; Bureau of Indian Affairs; Bureau of Mines; Bureau of Land Management
Justice (1870)	Furnishes legal advice to the president; enforces national criminal laws; supervises the U.S. corrections system (prisons)	Federal Bureau of Investigation; Drug Enforcement Administration; Bureau of Prisons; U.S. Marshals Services; Immigration and Naturalization Service
Agriculture (1889)	Provides assistance to farmers and ranchers; conducts research to improve agricultural activity and to prevent plant disease; works to protect forests from fires and disease	Oil Conservation Service; Agricultural Research Service; Food and Safety Inspection Service; Federal Crop Insurance Corporation; Farmers Home Administration
Commerce (1903)	Grants patents and trademarks; conducts the national census; monitors the weather; protects the interests of businesses	Bureau of the Census; Bureau of Economic Analysis; Minority Business Development Agency; Patent and Trademark Office; National Oceanic and Atmospheric Administration; U.S. Travel and Tourism Administration
Labor (1913)	Administers national labor laws; promotes the interests of workers	Occupational Safety and Health Administration; Bureau of Labor Statistics; Employment Standards Administration; Office of Labor-Management Standards; Employment and Training Administration

accountable to the president and are responsible for performing such government functions as training troops (Department of Defense), printing money (Department of the Treasury), and enforcing federal laws setting minimum safety and health standards for workers (Department of Labor).

Each department was created by Congress as the need arose, and each manages a specific policy area. The head of each department is known as the secretary. For the Department of Justice, the head is called the attorney general. Each department head is appointed by the president and confirmed by the Senate. Figure 19–2 above provides an overview of the departments in the executive branch and their main duties.

Organization within Departments

Although there are organizational differences between the departments, each department generally

FIGURE 19–2 Executive Departments (continued)

Department (Year Established)	Principal Duties	Most Important Subagencies
Defense (1949)[1]	Manages the armed forces (Army, Navy, Air Force, Marines); operates military bases; is responsible for civil defense	National Guard; Defense Investigation Service; National Security Agency; Joint Chiefs of Staff; Departments of the Air Force, Navy, Army
Housing and Urban Development (1965)	Concerned with the nation's housing needs; develops and rehabilitates urban communities; promotes improvements in city streets and parks	Office of Block Grant Assistance; Emergency Shelter Grants Program; Office of Urban Development Action Grants; Office of Fair Housing and Equal Opportunity
Transportation (1967)	Finances improvements in mass transit; develops and administers programs for highways, railroads, and aviation; is involved with offshore maritime safety	Federal Aviation Administration; Federal Highway Administration; National Highway Traffic Safety Administration; U.S. Coast Guard; Federal Transit Administration
Energy (1977)	Is involved in conservation of energy and resources; analyzes energy data; conducts research and development	Office of Civilian Radioactive Waste Management; Bonneville Power Administration; Office of Nuclear Energy, Science, and Technology; Energy Information Administration; Office of Conservation and Renewable Energy
Health and Human Services (1979)[2]	Administers the Social Security and Medicare programs; promotes public health; enforces pure food and drug laws; is involved in health-related research	Food and Drug Administration; Public Health Service; Administration for Children and Families; Health Care Financing Administration
Education (1979)[2]	Coordinates national programs and policies for education; administers aid to education; promotes educational research	Office of Special Education and Rehabilitation Services; Office of Elementary and Secondary Education; Office of Postsecondary Education; Office of Vocational and Adult Education
Veterans Affairs (1989)	Promotes the welfare of veterans of the U.S. armed forces	Veterans Health Administration; Veterans Benefits Administration; National Cemetery System

[1] Formed from the Department of War (1789) and the Department of the Navy (1798).
[2] Formed from the Department of Health, Education, and Welfare (1953).

uses a typical bureaucratic structure. The organization of the Department of Agriculture provides a model for how an executive department is organized.

The head of the Department of Agriculture is, of course, the secretary of agriculture. One aspect of the secretary's job is to carry out the president's agricultural policies. Another aspect, however, is to promote and protect the department. The secretary spends time ensuring that Congress allocates enough funds for the department to work effectively. The secretary also makes sure that the department's constituents—the people the department serves—are happy. Most of the constituents of the Department of Agriculture are owners of major farming corporations. In general, the secretary tries to maintain or improve the status of the department with respect to all the other departments and units of the national government.

The secretary of agriculture is assisted by a deputy secretary and several assistant secretaries. All of these are nominated by the president and put into office with Senate approval. Staff members help the secretary and assistants with numerous jobs, such as hiring new

ARCHITECTS

of Government

Donna E. Shalala
(1941–   )

Appointed secretary of the Health and Human Services Department by President Bill Clinton in 1993, Donna Shalala has been a leader all her life. As a political science teacher at Columbia University, she became an expert in urban affairs. She was a director and officer of the Municipal Assistance Corporation, formed to rescue New York City from economic collapse. From 1977 to 1980, she worked as assistant secretary for policy development and research in the Department of Housing and Urban Development. In 1978, she became the youngest woman college president in history when she was named president of Hunter College. Later, when she was made chancellor of the University of Wisconsin, she became the first woman to head a Big Ten university. Before joining the Clinton administration, she was director of the Children's Defense Fund.

HER WORDS

"The real test of welfare reform hasn't come. Getting people in jobs is a piece of cake. Ask me two or three years from now where people are."
(The Wall Street Journal, *August 25, 1997*)

"You must tell young people early on that if they use drugs, you have absolutely no interest in hiring them."
(*Speech, April 12, 1996*)

DEVELOPING
CRITICAL THINKING SKILLS
....
1. Why might Shalala believe that former welfare recipients can easily get jobs but may have trouble keeping them?
2. To whom do you think Shalala was addressing the remarks in the second quotation?

▲ *Combines harvest wheat in Yuma County, Colorado, while far away in Washington, D.C., the secretary of agriculture promotes farming interests. How has agriculture in America changed in the last hundred years?*

people and generating positive public relations for the department.

Closeness to the Chief Executive

Some observers of the executive departments group them according to their closeness to the chief executive. The so-called "inner" departments—State, Defense, Justice, and Treasury—are there primarily to serve the president. The heads of these departments are typically those who are closest politically and personally to the president. The rest of the departments—known as the "outer" departments—are so called because their functions deal primarily with their own constituencies.

The goals of the outer departments often differ markedly from the president's. For example, the president may want to reduce an anticipated budget deficit by reducing spending. The president may ask the secretary of agriculture to cut back on programs that help certain farmers. The secretary of agriculture, who probably wants to please the department's constituents, may resist the president's suggestion to cut back. In his book *What Government Agencies Do and Why They Do It*, political scientist James Q. Wilson emphasized this point when he made the following observation:

> Government organizations are especially risk averse [desirous of avoiding any risks] because they are caught up in a web of constraints so complex that any change is likely to rouse the ire of some important constituency.

SECTION 2 REVIEW

1. Name some of the major executive departments and their duties.
2. Briefly describe the organization within an executive department.
3. **For Critical Analysis:** Describe a situation in which an executive department might have goals that differ from those of the president. How could this situation be resolved?

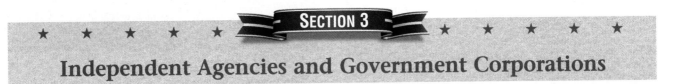

SECTION 3

Independent Agencies and Government Corporations

Preview Questions:

- Why were independent executive agencies created?
- What are the purposes and functions of independent regulatory agencies?
- What are government corporations?

Key Terms:

independent executive agency, partisan politics, independent regulatory agency, government corporation

The three remaining major parts of the U.S. government bureaucracy are the independent executive agencies, independent regulatory agencies, and government corporations. This section discusses the most important aspects of each of these three parts of the bureaucracy.

Independent Executive Agencies

An **independent executive agency** is a bureaucratic organization that is not part of a cabinet department but that reports directly to the president. The president appoints the agency's chief officials. An independent executive agency focuses on a single area—for example, the environment or the space program. The presi-

dent and Congress cooperate in creating new independent executive agencies and deciding where in the executive branch the agencies will be located.

The Reasons for Independent Agencies Prior to the twentieth century, the national government did almost all of its work through the executive departments. In the twentieth century, by contrast, presidents have asked for executive agencies to be kept separate, or independent, from existing departments. Today there are more than two hundred independent executive agencies.

Sometimes, agencies are kept independent because of the sensitive nature of their functions. At other times, Congress has made agencies independent to protect them from **partisan politics**—politics in support of a particular party's ideology. The Civil Rights Commission is a case in point. Congress wanted to protect the work of the Civil Rights Commission not only from the influences of its own political pressure groups but also from the influence of the president. The Central Intelligence Agency (CIA) is another good example. Both Congress and the president know that the intelligence activities of the CIA could be abused if it were not politically independent. Finally, the General Services Administration (GSA) was created as an independent executive agency in 1949 to monitor federal government spending. It needed to be independent of Congress, whose spending it is supposed to oversee.

▲ *An aerial view of the headquarters of the Central Intelligence Agency (CIA). The CIA operates independently of partisan politics because of its sensitive work. How might independence be a problem in such an organization?*

The Most Important Independent Executive Agencies

Among the many independent executive agencies, a few stand out in importance either because of the mission they were established to accomplish or because of their large size. Figure 19–3 on page 511 lists some of the major independent executive agencies.

The agencies listed in Figure 19–3 are often in the news. In contrast, the majority of the independent executive agencies, which have few employees and very small budgets, are relatively unknown. Among them are:

- The Migratory Bird Conservation Commission
- The American Battle Monuments Commission
- The Citizens' Stamp Advisory Committee
- The East-West Foreign Trade Board
- The Susquehanna River Basin Commission

Independent Regulatory Agencies

An **independent regulatory agency** is an agency outside the major executive departments that is

Name	Date Formed	Principal Duties
Central Intelligence Agency (CIA)	1947	Gathers and analyzes political and military information about foreign countries so that the United States can improve its own political and military status; conducts activities outside the United States, with the goal of countering the work of intelligence services operated by other nations whose political philosophies are inconsistent with that of the United States
General Services Administration (GSA)	1949	Purchases and manages all property of the U.S. government, acts as the business arm of the U.S. government, overseeing government spending projects; discovers overcharges in government programs
National Science Foundation (NSF)	1950	Promotes scientific research; provides grants to all levels of schools for instructional programs in the sciences
Small Business Administration (SBA)	1953	Protects the interests of small businesses; provides low-cost loans and management information to small businesses
National Aeronautics and Space Administration (NASA)	1958	Is responsible for the U.S. space program, including building, testing, and operating space vehicles
Federal Election Commission	1974	Ensures that candidates and states follow the rules established by the Federal Election Campaign Act of 1971, as amended

▲ *Traders buy and sell on the floor of the New York Stock Exchange. The actions of the nation's stock exchanges are supervised by the Securities and Exchange Commission.*

charged with creating and implementing rules to regulate private activity and protect the public interest in a specific area. These agencies are sometimes called the "alphabet soup" of government, because most such agencies are known in Washington by their initials.

One of the earliest regulatory agencies was the Interstate Commerce Commission (ICC), established in 1887 (and eliminated under President Clinton in 1995). At the time the ICC was founded, Americans were beginning to seek some form of government control over business and industries. The goal of the ICC was to make technical, non-political decisions about what rates and profits would

> **Just the Facts**
>
> *The U.S. government paid more than $11 million to psychics to discover whether the psychics could offer insights into foreign threats to the United States.*

The Freedom of Information Act, passed in 1966 and amended in 1974, allows people to obtain information from national government agencies. The act does not give people access to information that is classified or concerned with sensitive issues. You cannot, for example, obtain criminal investigation files or information on anyone's private financial transactions. Nor can you obtain interoffice memoranda or letters used in internal decision making within any government agency. You can, however, obtain many kinds of information.

When you request information under the Freedom of Information Act, you must describe the information for which you are asking. If an agency does not comply promptly with your request for information, you can sue that agency and expect a speedy judicial hearing. The agency must then explain why it has refused to supply the requested information. If the judge decides against the government, the government has to pay your legal fees.

Currently, federal agencies receive about 500,000 requests for information every year. More than 90 percent of these requests are completely filled.

Using the Freedom of Information Act

The Freedom of Information Act gives real meaning to each citizen's right to know.

Why do people request information under the Freedom of Information Act? Many times, individuals are simply curious to know whether the Federal Bureau of Investigation (FBI) has files on them. Reporters often use the act to obtain background information in order to write stories about federal actions and policies.

If you wish to request information from an executive department or agency, use the form letter on the next page. To find an agency's street address or e-mail address, check with your local librarian. Alternatively, you can go online and find this information at the Federal Web Locator site. You can access this site at **www.law.vill.edu/Fed-Agency/fedwebloc.html**.

Congress has exempted itself from the Freedom of Information Act. Thus, it is not obligated to provide information.

TAKING ACTION

1. Make a request to a specific agency, such as the FBI, for information related to you or one of your parents (or some other family member). Use the form letter presented to make such a request. Ask, for example, for any information about you that the agency has on file.
2. Access the Federal Web Locator site listed above. Make a list of the departments and commissions that are linked to that site. Select one and prepare a brief report on the information that is available to you online.

---

be allowed for various transportation and shipping businesses. These decisions were to benefit the entire public. The agency had the power to make and change the rules regarding rates and profits. Therefore, congressional legislation would not be required every time a new rule was proposed.

After the ICC was formed, other agencies were created to regulate aviation (the Civil Aeronautics Board, or CAB, no longer in existence), communication (the Federal Communications Commission, or FCC), the stock market (the Securities and Exchange Commission, or SEC), and many other areas of busi-

Sample Letter for Requesting Information from an Executive Department or Agency

Agency Head or FOIA Officer
Title
Name of Agency
Address of Agency
City, State, Zip

Re: Freedom of Information Act Request.

Dear ____________:

Under the provisions of the Freedom of Information Act, 5 U.S.C. 552, I am requesting access to (identify the records as clearly and specifically as possible).

If there are any fees for searching for, or copying of the records I have requested, please inform me before you fill the request. (Or: . . . please supply the records without informing me if the fees do not exceed $______.)

(Optional) I am requesting this information (state the reason for your request if you think it will assist you in obtaining the information.)

(Optional) As you know, the act permits you to reduce or waive fees when the release of the information is considered as "primarily benefiting the public." I believe that this request fits that category and I therefore ask that you waive any fees.

If all or any part of this request is denied, please cite the specific exemption(s) that you think justifies your refusal to release the information, and inform me of the appeal procedures available to me under the law.

I would appreciate your handling this request as quickly as possible, and I look forward to hearing from you within 10 days, as the law stipulates.

Sincerely,

Signature
Name
Address
City, State, Zip

SOURCE: U.S. Congress. House Committee on Government Operations. *A Citizen's Guide on How to Use the Freedom of Information Act and the Privacy Act Requesting Government Documents*, 95th Congress, 1st session (1977).

ness. Figure 19–4 on page 514 lists the major independent regulatory agencies.

Administration of Regulatory Agencies Regulatory agencies combine some functions of all three branches of government. They are legislative in that they make rules that have the force of law. For example, the Federal Trade Commission (FTC) enacted a three-day "cooling-off" rule with respect to door-to-door sales. Anytime you sign a contract or buy something from a door-to-door salesperson, you have three days in which to decide whether or not you like the deal. If you

FIGURE 19–4 Selected Independent Regulatory Agencies The table below lists the major independent regulatory agencies, the date each was formed, and the principal duties of each. Which branch of the national government is responsible for administering these agencies?

Name	Date Formed	Principal Duties
Federal Reserve System Board of Governors (Fed)	1913	Responsible for determining policy on interest rates, credit availability, and the money supply
Federal Trade Commission (FTC)	1914	Responsible for preventing businesses from engaging in unfair trade practices, for stopping the formation of monopolies in the business sector, and for protecting consumer rights
Securities and Exchange Commission (SEC)	1934	Responsible for regulating the nation's stock exchanges, in which shares of stocks are bought and sold; requires full disclosure of the financial profiles of companies that wish to sell stocks and bonds to the public
Federal Communications Commission (FCC)	1934	Responsible for regulating all communications by telegraph, cable, telephone, radio, and television
National Labor Relations Board (NLRB)	1935	Responsible for protecting employees' rights to join unions and to bargain collectively with employers; attempts to prevent unfair labor practices by both employers and unions
Equal Employment Opportunity Commission (EEOC)	1964	Responsible for working to eliminate discrimination based on religion, gender, race, national origin, or age; examines claims of discrimination
Environmental Protection Agency (EPA)	1970	Responsible for undertaking programs aimed at reducing air and water pollution; works with state and local agencies to help fight environmental hazards
Nuclear Regulatory Commission (NRC)	1974	Responsible for ensuring that electricity-generating nuclear reactors in the United States are built and operated safely; regularly inspects operations of such reactors
Defense Nuclear Facilities Safety Board	1988	Responsible for reviewing and evaluating the construction and operation of defense-related nuclear facilities; investigates any practices at these facilities that may harm public health and safety

decide against the purchase, the seller must refund all your money.

Regulatory agencies are executive in that they provide for the enforcement of the rules they make. If, for example, a door-to-door sales company does not abide by the three-day cooling-off rule, the FTC can shut down its business.

Regulatory agencies are also judicial in that they decide disputes involving the rules that they have made. For example, the Environmental Protection Agency (EPA) which was established in 1970 to reduce air and water pollution, issues rules, or standards, pertaining to pollution with which businesses must comply. If a business challenges the fairness or applicability of a rule, the EPA is authorized to hold judicial proceedings to hear and decide the matter. (The business may be allowed to appeal the EPA's final decision to a federal court, however.)

Government in Action

Improving Efficiency and Getting Results

Critics of the government bureaucracy often claim that government workers are inefficient and unproductive. Bureaucrats are not held accountable for results, these critics claim. They are paid no matter how productive—or unproductive—they are. The U.S. government has recently launched several efforts to meet such criticisms.

The Government Performance and Results Act, which went into effect in 1997, is one such effort. Under the act, beginning in October 1997 virtually every agency (except for the intelligence agencies) must describe its goals and its methods for evaluating how well those goals are met. A results-oriented goal could be as broad as lowering the number of highway traffic deaths or as narrow as reducing the number of times the phone rings before it is answered.

As one example, consider the National Oceanic and Atmospheric Administration, which is part of the Department of Commerce. It improved the effectiveness of its short-term forecasting services, particularly in issuing warnings of tornadoes. The warning time has increased from seven to nine minutes. This may seem insignificant, but it provides critical additional time for those in the path of a tornado.

The government has also been experimenting with pay-for-performance systems. For some time, the private sector has used pay-for-performance plans as a means to increase employee productivity and efficiency. These plans link a person's pay in some way with the person's or the organization's performance. About one-third of the major firms in this country use some kind of pay-for-performance system, such as team-based pay, skill-based pay, a profit-sharing plan, or individual bonuses. In contrast, workers for the federal government traditionally have received fixed salaries, and all promotions, salary increases, and the like have normally been based on seniority, not output.

In 1996, though, the U.S. Postal Service implemented its Economic Value Added program, in which bonuses are tied to performance. In 1997, as part of a five-year test of a new pay system, three thousand scientists working in Air Force laboratories began getting salaries based on results. Also in 1997, the Department of Veterans Affairs launched a skill-based pay project at its New York regional office.

Many hope that by offering such incentives, the government will be able to compete more effectively with the private sector for skilled and talented employees. Additionally, according to some, pay-for-performance plans will go a long way toward countering the "job for life" mentality that has traditionally characterized employment in the government bureaucracy.

Certainly there will always be a need for our federal bureaucracy to carry out the laws and policies of our government. Just as certainly, however, the efforts to reform the system and to make employees more responsive to the needs of all U.S. citizens will continue.

THINK ABOUT IT

1. Why might workers act differently if they are paid for performance rather than being paid a fixed salary?
2. What might be some difficulties in trying to measure the performance of a government bureaucrat?
3. Why does the government, which offers employees benefits and job security usually unavailable in the private sector, believe that it has to compete with the private sector for employees?

FIGURE 19–5 Selected Government Corporations This table lists some of the major government corporations, the date each was formed, and the principal duties. Four of these corporations were formed in 1933 during the Great Depression. How might these corporations have helped to stimulate the economy at that time?

Name	Date Formed	Principal Duties
Tennessee Valley Authority (TVA)	1933	Operates Tennessee River control system and generates power for a seven-state region and for U.S. aeronautics and space programs; promotes the economic development of the Tennessee Valley region; controls floods and promotes the navigability of the Tennessee River
Federal Deposit Insurance Corporation (FDIC)	1933	Insures individuals' bank deposits up to $100,000; oversees the business activities of banks
Commodity Credit Corporation (CCC)	1933	Attempts to stabilize farm prices and protect farmers' incomes by purchasing designated farm products at prices above what they would get in the marketplace
Export/Import Bank of the United States (Ex/Im Bank)	1933	Promotes American-made goods abroad; grants loans to foreign purchasers of American products
National Railway Passenger Corporation (AMTRAK)	1970	Provides a national and intercity rail passenger service network
U.S. Postal Service (formed from the Postmaster General of the Treasury Department [1789])	1971	Delivers mail throughout the United States and its territories; is the largest government corporation, with almost 800,000 employees
Corporation for National and Community Service	1993	Engages Americans of all backgrounds in community-based services that address the nation's educational, public safety, human, and environmental needs

Agency Members Members of the regulatory agencies are appointed by the president with the consent of the Senate. These agencies do not, however, report to the president, which is why they are called independent. By law, the members of a regulatory agency cannot all belong to the same political party.

Government Corporations

The newest form of federal bureaucracy is the **government corporation,** a business that is owned by the government. Government corporations are not like the private corporations in which you buy stock, become a shareholder, and collect dividends. The U.S. Postal Service is a government corporation, but it sells no shares. If a government corporation loses money in the course of doing business, it is not shareholders but taxpayers who foot the bill.

Government corporations are like private corporations in that they provide a service that could be handled by the private sector. They are also like private corporations in that they charge for their services, although sometimes they charge less than a private-sector corporation would. Some of the major government corporations are listed in Figure 19–5.

Although government corporations are independent, each is attached to some executive department and is therefore subject to the control of the secretary of that department. For example, the Commodity Credit Corporation (CCC)—a lending bank for farmers—is located within the Department of Agriculture. The secretary of agriculture chairs its seven-member board.

◄ *This U.S. Postal Service Web site shows the Post Office acting more like a business than a government agency. What has forced the Post Office to become more competitive?*

SECTION 3 REVIEW

1. Briefly describe two independent executive agencies and their functions.
2. Why were independent regulatory agencies created? What powers do they have?
3. What is a cooling-off period? How does it affect consumers? Businesses?
4. What is the Government Performance and Results Act of 1997? Why was it enacted?
5. What are government corporations?
6. **For Critical Analysis:** An independent executive agency of the U.S. government may be changed into a government corporation. That occurred in 1971, when the U.S. Post Office was transformed into the U.S. Postal Service. What difference, if any, might this change make in the way the organization operates?

SECTION 4

★ ★ ★ ★ ★ ★ ★ ★ ★ ★

How the Civil Service Works

Preview Questions:

⊛ How has the civil service changed during our history?
⊛ In what ways has Congress attempted to reform the civil service?
⊛ What reforms of the civil service were enacted by President Jimmy Carter?

Key Terms:

civil service, spoils system, merit system, whistle-blower

Every bureaucratic institution has two groups: political appointees and civil servants. It is usually the president who makes political appointments to most of the top jobs in the U.S. government bureaucracy. These jobs are considered "political plums." Descriptions of eight thousand of these positions can be found in a book called *Policy and Supporting Positions*, also known as the "plum book," published by the U.S. Government Printing Office in Washington, D.C. The remaining individuals who work for the U.S. government belong to the **civil service.** They are not appointed but go through a formal application process.

One would think that the president, by appointing the top-ranking bureaucrats in the executive branch, could exercise substantial control over the bureaucracy. In fact, this is not necessarily the case. Political appointees, like the president, typically occupy their positions for a comparatively brief time. As a result, the professional civil servants in a particular department or agency are often slow to accept changes in their traditional routines suggested by their new bosses. They know that the political appointees may not be around for very long (on average, political appointees hold their positions for less than two years). The following words of President Franklin D. Roosevelt (1933–1945) describe the difficulties facing any president who wants to change the policies or practices of a government department or agency:

The Treasury is so large and farflung and ingrained in its practices that I find it almost impossible to get the actions and results I want. But the Treasury is not to be compared to the State Department. You should go through the experience of trying to get any changes in the thinking, policy, and action of the career diplomats, and then you'd know what a real problem was.

The people Roosevelt was referring to—career diplomats—were civil servants who were not appointed by the president. Rather, they became government employees as a result of a formal application process involving competitive examinations.

A Short History of the Civil Service

When the U.S. government was formed in 1789, it had no career public servants. Rather, it consisted of nonprofessional bureaucrats, and almost all of them were Federalists. When Jefferson became president in

1801, he found that few members of his Democratic Republican Party were holding federal administrative jobs. He fired more than a hundred officials and replaced them with Democratic Republicans.

For the next twenty-five years, a growing body of federal administrators gained experience and expertise, becoming in the process professional public servants. These administrators stayed in office regardless of who was elected president. The bureaucracy had become a self-maintaining element within government.

To the Victor Belong the Spoils When Andrew Jackson took over the White House in 1828, he found that many officials who had been appointed before he took office were openly hostile toward him and his Democratic Party. The bureaucracy considered itself the only group fit to rule. Because the bureaucracy was reluctant to carry out his programs, Jackson did the obvious. He fired more government officials than any president before him. The **spoils system**—an application of the principle that to the victor of a battle or war belong the spoils (the goods or property of the loser)—became associated with the new Jackson administration. In the political context, the "spoils" are public offices, which are awarded to the loyal supporters of the victorious candidate.

In addition to putting his own people on the government payroll, Jackson decided to reorganize the bureaucracy to ensure that his policies were carried out. During his eight years in office, almost every department and bureau was restructured.

The Civil Service Reform Act of 1883 Jackson's spoils system survived for a number of decades, but over time it became increasingly corrupt. In addition, the size of the bureaucracy increased by 300 percent between 1851 and 1881. Reformers began to examine the professional civil service systems that had been established in several European countries. These systems operated under a **merit system** in which job appointments were based on competitive examinations. The cry for civil service reform grew louder.

The ruling Republican Party was divided in its attitude toward reform. A faction of the party, called the "stalwarts," opposed reform of any sort. In 1881 Charles J. Guiteau was denied a bureaucratic position and assassinated President James A. Garfield, a moderate reformer. Guiteau was heard to shout, "I am a stalwart,

◄ President James A. Garfield was assassinated by Charles J. Guiteau in 1881 after Guiteau was denied a civil service position. How did Garfield's assassination help bring about civil service reform?

and Arthur is president now!" After Garfield's assassination, Chester A. Arthur, the vice president and a stalwart, became president. Ironically, it was under the Arthur administration that civil service reform actually occurred, partly as a result of public outrage over Garfield's assassination. The movement to replace the spoils system with a permanent career civil service had found the cause that would carry it to victory.

Finally, in 1883, the Civil Service Reform Act (also known as the Pendleton Act) was passed, bringing the Jacksonian spoils system to an end. The act established the principle of employment on the basis of open competitive examinations and created the Civil Service Commission to administer the personnel service. Only 10 percent of federal employees, however, were covered by the system. Later laws, amendments, and executive orders increased the coverage to more than 90 percent of the federal civil service.

The Hatch Act of 1939 In principle, a civil servant is politically neutral. But in reality, civil servants know that politicians are the ones who appropriate funds and determine the growth of their agencies. In 1933, when Franklin D. Roosevelt established the New Deal, a virtual army of civil servants was hired to staff the numerous new agencies that were created to cope with the problems of the Great Depression. Because the Democratic Party provided jobs for these individuals, it

seemed natural for those persons to campaign for Democratic candidates. The Democrats controlling Congress in the mid-1930s did not object to this campaigning. But in 1938, a coalition of conservative Democrats and Republicans took control of Congress and passed the Political Activities Act of 1939, also known as the Hatch Act.

The main provision of the act prohibited civil service employees from taking an active part in partisan political campaigns. U.S. government employees could not run for public office or raise funds for political candidates. The act also prohibited those who held government positions from using their authority to influence nominations and elections or to pressure government employees into making political contributions. The intention of Congress in passing this act was to ensure a politically "neutral" civil service.

The Federal Employees Political Activities Act of 1993
The fact that civil service employees could not participate in partisan political campaigns led to concerns over the First Amendment freedoms of speech and association. Eventually, Congress modified the Hatch Act to meet these concerns. In 1993, Congress passed the Federal Employees Political Activities Act. This act permitted U.S. government employees to participate in partisan campaigns (by contributing money to candidates, for example, or by attending political

▶ *A wealth of information is available online through the Web site of the Office of Personnel Management. You can apply for a job, find out about current salaries, or simply discover "What's New" at the OPM.*

rallies or assisting in voter registration drives). The act also allowed government employees to run for public office in *nonpartisan* elections. The act made it clear, however, that government employees are not allowed to engage in political activity *while conducting official duties*. The act did not change the Hatch Act provision that prohibited members of the civil service from using their rank or authority to influence nominations and elections or to pressure government employees into making political contributions.

Today's Civil Service System

The Civil Service Commission worked well, according to those who observed the bureaucracy. But a persistent group of reformers felt that the commission had taken on too many tasks. President Jimmy Carter, a particularly concerned critic, worked out a series of reforms that were adopted by Congress on October 13, 1978. One of the reforms was to split the Civil Service Commission into the Office of Personnel Management (OPM) and the Merit Systems Protection Board (MSPB).

The Office of Personnel Management (OPM) The OPM is in charge of hiring most of the employees of U.S. government agencies. Members of the OPM are appointed by the president and confirmed by the Senate. The OPM has elaborate rules for hiring, promoting, and firing. One rule requires potential employees to take competitive examinations for most civil

FIGURE 19-6 General Schedule (GS) Ratings and Minimum Salaries
This table shows each of the GS ratings and its minimum salary for a recent year. Which civil service employees are assigned GS ratings?

Rating	1997 Minimum Salary
GS–1	$13,278
GS–2	14,928
GS–3	16,290
GS–4	18,286
GS–5	20,459
GS–6	22,805
GS–7	25,341
GS–8	28,065
GS–9	31,000
GS–10	34,138
GS–11	37,507
GS–12	44,953
GS–13	53,456
GS–14	63,169
GS–15	74,304

service jobs. An applicant who passes the examination is sent to an agency that has a job opening that requires skills that the applicant has. For each agency job that is open, the OPM sends three names to the agency for consideration (this is called the "rule of three"). In general, the agency has to hire someone on the list.

Within the civil service, each individual hired is assigned a general schedule, or GS, rating. Figure 19–6 shows the recent minimum salary for each GS rating.

The Merit Systems Protection Board (MSPB)
The MSPB was created as an independent agency with an independent staff. Its goal is to protect the integrity of the merit system. It accomplishes this goal by undertaking studies of the merit system and by hearing charges of wrongdoing and appeals of adverse agency actions against civil servants. The MSPB can order corrective and disciplinary action against executive agencies and, in rare cases, against employees. The MSPB also has an independent legal staff, which investigates illegal personnel practices and can prosecute officials who violate civil service rules and regulations.

Protection for Whistle-blowers
The term **whistle-blower,** with respect to the U.S. government bureaucracy, has a special meaning. It is someone who "blows the whistle" on (reports to a higher official about) an illegal or wrongful action being carried on by a government agency or organization. The Merit Systems Protection Board provides some protection for whistle-blowers. The Whistle-Blower Protection Act of 1989 provided further protection. That act authorized the Office of Special Counsel (OSC), an independent agency, to investigate complaints of actions taken to punish whistle-blowers for reporting wrongdoing. Many U.S. government agencies also have toll-free hotlines that employees can use to anonymously report bureaucratic waste and inappropriate behavior.

Just the Facts

The Department of Agriculture once spent $46,000 to calculate how long it takes to cook eggs.

In spite of these laws, many people claim whistle-blowers are not adequately protected. According to a study conducted by the General Accounting Office, 41 percent of the whistle-blowers who turned to the OSC for protection during a recent three-year period said that they were no longer employed by the agencies on which they filed complaints. Many other government employees who have blown the whistle say that they would not do so again because it is so difficult to get help. The basic problem, of course, is that no organization, including a U.S. government agency, wants to have its wrongdoing exposed, especially by "insiders."

SECTION 4 REVIEW

1. What events led to the Civil Service Reform Act of 1883?
2. What are the main provisions of the Hatch Act of 1939? How was this act modified by 1993 legislation?
3. What changes did President Jimmy Carter make in the civil service?
4. What help is available for "whistle-blowers"?
5. **For Critical Analysis:** Out of the nearly three million U.S. government jobs, a new president can appoint individuals to only about eight thousand. Does this mean that presidential policies may be thwarted by an established government bureaucracy whose goals may differ from the president's? Explain.

Bureaucrats as Policymakers

Preview Questions:

- How do departments and agencies act as politicians?
- What is the iron triangle?

Key Terms:

neutral competency, iron triangle

Bureaucrats in the national government are expected to exhibit **neutral competency,** which means that they are supposed to apply their technical skills to their jobs without regard to political issues. They should not be swayed by the thought of personal or political gain. For example, a bureaucrat in the Department of Defense is not supposed to look the other way if she sees a company doing shoddy work on building a fighter jet. Even if this bureaucrat is hoping that the same company might offer her a job after she retires from her government job, she is supposed to apply her skills to solve the problem without letting that hope interfere.

In reality, each independent agency and each executive department is interested in its own survival and expansion. Each is constantly battling the others for a larger share of the budget. All agencies and departments wish to retain or expand their functions and staff. In order to do this, they must gain the goodwill of the White House and of Congress.

How Bureaucrats Act as Politicians

Bureaucratic agencies of the national government are prohibited from directly lobbying Congress. Departments and agencies, nonetheless, have developed techniques to help them gain congressional support. Each organization maintains a congressional information office, which specializes in helping members of Congress by supplying any requested information and solving casework problems. For example, if a member of the House of Representatives gets a complaint from a constituent that her Social Security checks are not arriving on time, that member of Congress can go to the Social Security Administration

▶ Farmers drive tractors in the streets of Washington, D.C., to alert the government and the nation to the plight of the American farmer. Who authorizes expenditures for agricultural programs?

THROUGH THE *Years*

The Bureaucracy Has Indeed Changed

The government bureaucracy that existed in the United States at the beginning of this nation bears little resemblance to the bureaucracy that exists today.

THEN (EARLY 1800S)	NOW
The few bureaucrats in office at the time stayed on until Andrew Jackson fired most of them and the "spoils system" took hold.	Since the passage of the Civil Service Reform Act of 1883 and other acts, the federal civil service has been based on a merit system involving open, competitive exams.
Government employees could be pressured by their superiors to make campaign contributions.	Pressuring government employees to make political contributions is strictly prohibited by the Hatch Act and subsequent legislation.
Government bureaucrats were few in number and had little effect on Americans' daily lives.	There are nearly three million government bureaucrats, and they affect the daily lives of many Americans.
There was no protection for whistle-blowers.	There is protection for whistle-blowers, but some claim that it is inadequate.

and ask that something be done. Typically, requests from members of Congress are acted on quickly.

Bureaucrats as Policymakers— The Iron Triangle

Analysts have determined that one way to understand the bureaucracy's role in policymaking is to examine the policy communities, or iron triangles, that exist in Washington, D.C. A policy community, or **iron triangle,** is defined as a three-way alliance among legislators (members of Congress), bureaucrats, and interest groups. The concept of an iron triangle presumes that laws are passed and policies are established to benefit the interests of all three sides of the triangle.

Consider the bureaucracy within the Department of Agriculture. It consists of about 100,000 individuals working directly for the government and thousands of other individuals working indirectly for the department

as contractors, subcontractors, and consultants. Now consider that various interest groups are concerned with what the government does for farmers. Some of these are the American Farm Bureau Federation, the National Cattleman's Association, the National Milk Producers Association, the Corn Growers Association, and the Citrus Growers Association. Finally, take a close look at Congress and you will see that there are two major committees concerned with agriculture: the House Committee on Agriculture and the Senate Committee on Agriculture, Nutrition, and Forestry. Each of these committees has several subcommittees. The Department of Agriculture employees, the interest groups concerned with the department's activities, and the congressional committees that make decisions about agriculture make up an iron triangle that is an alliance of mutual benefit.

The workings of iron triangles are complicated but well established in almost every part of the bureaucracy. Consider again the Department of Agriculture.

The Government Bureaucracy

The U.S. government bureaucracy will always have its critics. Those who are part of it believe that, although improvements could be made, the bureaucracy is functioning quite well. But critics believe that U.S. government bureaucrats are out of control. They argue that citizens' rights are being endangered.

Government Bureaucrats Have Lost Touch, Critics Claim

Critics of the current U.S. government bureaucracy believe that bureaucrats have lost touch with ordinary citizens. There is a sense that "they" can do whatever they want.

Just consider the FBI. In 1992, agents of the FBI shot and killed the wife and child of a suspected white supremacist, Randy Weaver, at Ruby Ridge, Idaho. In 1993, the FBI, along with the Bureau of Alcohol, Tobacco, and Firearms, raided a compound in Waco, Texas, which was occupied by members of a religious sect called the Branch Davidians. The raid, which was conducted to seize suspected illegal weapons, may have resulted in the fiery death of many members of that sect.

Critics also argue that government bureaucrats are insensitive to the needs of local land users. The bureaucracy is instituting more restrictions on the use of government-owned lands, mostly for environmental-protection purposes, but many ranchers and other users of government-owned lands in the West complain about how bureaucrats implement these new rules.

The bureaucracy is also slow, say its critics. In 1972, Congress told the Environmental Protection Agency to research six hundred existing pesticides. The goal was to determine which ones should be banned because they might pose health risks. By the end of the twentieth century, however, only about thirty of these pesticides had been evaluated. In addition, these critics claim, the bureaucracy is overly concerned with details. Agency rules fill thousands of pages each year.

For All Its Faults, the Bureaucracy Is Doing a Great Job, Others Maintain

According to supporters of the U.S. government bureaucracy, it is doing a great job. We must have bureaucrats to make sure that the laws passed by Congress are carried out.

Today, citizens benefit from the existence of the government bureaucracy. Just compare life today with life in the nineteenth century. Bureaucrats in the U.S. Food and Drug Administration make sure that the food we eat and the drugs we take will not kill us. The Occupational Safety and Health Administration attempts to ensure safe working conditions. The National Highway Traffic Safety Administration tries to reduce the dangers associated with driving on our highways.

Compared with government bureaucracies elsewhere in the world, the U.S. bureaucracy is pleasant to deal with and efficient. Moreover, bureaucrats in the United States do not expect "side payments," or "bribes," to get their jobs done. We have a truly neutral bureaucracy compared with bureaucracies in many other countries.

Finally, bureaucrats may be slow and overly concerned with details, but they have to be. If they did not generate detailed regulations, endless disputes (and legal proceedings) would occur.

YOU DECIDE

1. High-ranking bureaucrats are appointed. Does that mean that the bureaucracy is a threat to democracy?
2. Does it make sense to try to determine whether there are any problems with the U.S. bureaucracy by comparing it with bureaucracies in other countries? Explain your answer.

The secretary of agriculture is nominated by the president (and confirmed by the Senate) and is head of the department. But that secretary cannot even buy a desk lamp if Congress does not approve the appropriations for the department's budget. Within Congress, the responsibility for considering the Department of Agriculture's request for funding belongs first to the House and Senate appropriations committees and then to the agricultural subcommittees under them. The members of those committees, most of whom represent agricultural states, have their own ideas about what is appropriate for the Agriculture Department's budget. They carefully scrutinize the ideas of the president and the secretary of agriculture.

Finally, the various interest groups—including producers of farm chemicals and farm machinery, agricultural cooperatives, grain dealers, and exporters—have vested interests in whatever the Department of Agriculture does and in whatever Congress lets the Department of Agriculture do. Those interests are well represented by the lobbyists who crowd the halls of Congress. Many lobbyists have been working for agricultural interest groups for decades. They know the congressional committee members and Agriculture Department staff and routinely meet with them.

SECTION 5 REVIEW

1. How do bureaucrats act as politicians?
2. What groups do the three sides of the iron triangle represent?
3. **For Critical Analysis:** The effectiveness of the iron triangle could presumably be reduced if interest groups were not allowed to lobby in Congress. What problems would a restriction on lobbying pose?

★ ★ ★ ★ Chapter Summary ★ ★ ★ ★

Section 1: The Bureaucracy: Its Nature and Size

- A bureaucracy is an organization that is structured in a pyramid-like fashion.
- The U.S. government bureaucracy has grown from a few employees to nearly three million today.
- The national bureaucracy is made up of executive departments, independent executive agencies, independent regulatory agencies, and government corporations.

Section 2: The Executive Departments

- The fourteen executive departments are directly accountable to the president.
- Each department was created by Congress as the need arose, and each manages a specific policy area.
- Each department head is appointed by the president and must be confirmed by the Senate.

Section 3: Independent Agencies and Government Corporations

- Independent executive agencies were created to be independent because of the sensitive nature of their functions and to protect them from partisan politics.
- An independent regulatory agency implements rules to protect the public interest in its particular sector.
- A government corporation is a business that is owned by the government.

Section 4: How the Civil Service Works

- In our nation's early history, government workers were appointed on the basis of the president's political party preferences.
- In 1883, the Civil Service Reform Act established the principle of government employment on the basis of open competitive examinations.
- The Hatch Act of 1939 attempted to ensure a "neutral" civil service by prohibiting U.S. government employees from participating in partisan political campaigns.
- In 1978, the Civil Service Commission was divided into the Office of Personnel Management and the Merit Systems Protection Board.
- The Merit Systems Protection Board and the Whistle-Blower Protection Act of 1989 provide some protection for whistle-blowers.

Section 5: Bureaucrats as Policymakers:

- Bureaucratic agencies are prohibited from lobbying Congress, but they have developed techniques to help them gain congressional support.
- The so-called iron triangle is a three-way alliance among legislators, bureaucrats, and interest groups.

CHAPTER 19 Review

★ REVIEW QUESTIONS ★

1. What is the U.S. government bureaucracy?
2. Describe how the bureaucracy has grown.
3. Name three executive departments and describe the policy area served by each.
4. Which executive departments make up the "inner" departments?
5. Why has Congress created independent executive agencies?
6. What are independent regulatory agencies responsible for, and how are they administered?
7. What is a government corporation?
8. How did the Civil Service Reform Act of 1883 change the way in which government employees are hired?
9. What rule did the Hatch Act establish? How was this act modified in 1993?
10. What are the main functions of the Office of Personnel Management and the Merit Systems Protection Board?
11. What protections exist for whistle-blowers?
12. How does the federal bureaucracy help to shape public policy?
13. How does an iron triangle work?

★ CRITICAL THINKING ★

1. The bureaucracy has often been called the "fourth branch of government." Do you agree with this assessment? Why or why not?
2. What steps, if any, do you think should be taken to make the bureaucracy more open, efficient, and responsive to citizens' needs?
3. Many presidents have sought to reduce the confusion, size, and complexity of the bureaucracy. Why do you think their attempts have generally not succeeded?
4. How might the U.S. government make civil service careers more appealing to you and other young people?
5. You may have heard news stories about $5,000 screwdrivers and $500 nails purchased by the Department of Defense. Who do you think is responsible for such waste and inefficiency?

★ IMPROVING YOUR SKILLS ★

Communication Skills

Giving an Oral Report Oral reports are a way of sharing information with your classmates. If you are well prepared and know the information, you will most likely feel confident. Begin with a written report that you have researched and created according to earlier exercises in this text. Having researched the topic yourself, you will be prepared to discuss the subject and answer questions that might come up. The more you have researched the topic, the more sure of yourself you will be. Follow these suggestions:

- Reread your written report several times. Review some of your most significant sources of information.
- Write an outline from your report that covers the most important points. Include examples and details you think are particularly important and illustrative.
- Transfer your outline to index cards, which you can use while giving your oral report. Use abbreviations that will help trigger your memory. Use some type of mark—a star or check, for instance—to indicate points at which you want to elaborate on examples or details.
- Practice delivering your oral report as often as you can to friends and family members. Ask them for criticism and helpful tips. Practice maintaining eye contact with them, which will help make your speech more interesting. Also practice in front of the mirror so you can improve your presentation. Pay close attention to your tone of voice, how loud you are speaking, how fast you are speaking, and how convincing you sound.

Writing an Abstract An abstract is a concise summary. If you ever submit a research paper for publication in a journal in your field of study, you will probably be asked to submit an abstract of the article as well. But even if you never publish an article, knowing how to write an abstract is a helpful skill. This is because, in writing an abstract, you are forced to condense your report to its bare essentials. You are forced to stand back for a moment and look at what point you are making in your paper, what data support that point, and make sure that your conclusion clearly supports it.

In order to gain practice condensing your thoughts and your words, write an abstract summarizing the oral report prepared for the *Giving an Oral Report* section on page 526. Your abstract should be no longer than a paragraph or two. This means that you will have to be very careful to emphasize only the major points, data, and conclusions in your abstract. Give a final draft of your abstract to your teacher for review. Read it carefully to make sure there are no spelling or grammatical errors. Then, distribute copies of your abstract to your class before or after giving your oral report.

Social Studies Skills

Working with Organization Charts Look at Figure 19–1, Organization of the Government of the United States, on page 504. Answer the following questions:

1. Does the chart show all of the U.S. government agencies that exist today?
2. Is the U.S. Information Agency part of the judicial branch? If it is not, to what branch of government does it belong?
3. In this chart, does the fact that the Department of State is listed below the Department of Education mean that one department has a higher ranking within the executive branch than the other?

★ ACTIVITIES AND PROJECTS ★

1. Learn the details of the hiring process for U.S. government jobs and find out how to apply for one of these jobs by contacting the federal job center in your state. Look under Federal Information Center in your telephone directory, or contact the Office of Personnel Management, OPM, 1900 E Street NW, Washington, DC 20415, telephone 202-606-1800. You can also look up the OPM's regional office in your area in the *United States Government Manual*, found in most libraries. The OPM's Web site can be accessed at **www.opm.gov/**.
2. Do a research project on the Freedom of Information Act. How many of the thousands of requests received each year come from private citizens like yourself, as opposed to businesspeople?
3. Do a research project on either the U.S. Postal Service or AMTRAK. In particular, determine to what extent over the years those government corporations have been funded by the fees collected and to what extent they have been subsidized by American taxpayers.
4. Stage a class debate on the following statement: The size of the U.S. government bureaucracy shall be frozen at its current level.

What If . . .

All Government Agencies Had to Be Profitable?

Right now, most government agencies do not even consider profitability. Select a government agency or an independent corporation, such as NASA (the National Aeronautics and Space Administration) or AMTRAK, and explain what changes would occur if it had to be profitable.

Presidential Inaugural Addresses

Americans have always looked to their presidents for leadership. In their inaugural addresses, presidents try to speak to the most pressing concerns of Americans and explain how they will tackle these concerns. We have selected for study in this section excerpts from two inaugural addresses: one given in 1933 by Franklin D. Roosevelt and the other given in 1997 by Bill Clinton. As you read these selections, try to determine how the problems facing Americans in 1933 differed from those facing the nation in 1997.

Source Documents

The First Inaugural Address of Franklin D. Roosevelt

I am certain that my fellow Americans expect that on my induction into the Presidency I will address them with candor and a decision which the present situation of our Nation impels. This is preeminently the time to speak the truth, the whole truth, frankly and boldly. Nor need we shrink from honestly facing conditions in our country today. This great Nation will endure as it has endured, will revive and will prosper. So, first of all, let me assert my firm belief that the only thing we have to fear is fear itself. . . .

In such a spirit on my part and on yours we face our common difficulties. . . . Values have shrunken to fantastic levels; taxes have risen; our ability to pay has fallen; government of all kinds is faced by serious curtailment of income; the means of exchange are frozen in the currents of trade; the withered leaves of industrial enterprise lie on every side; farmers find no markets for their produce; the savings of many years in thousands of families are gone.

More important, a host of unemployed citizens face the grim problem of existence, and an equally great number toil with little return. Only a foolish optimist can deny the dark realities of the moment.

. . . I shall presently urge upon a new Congress in special session detailed measures for their fulfillment, and I shall seek the immediate assistance of the several States.

. . . If I read the temper of our people correctly, we now realize as we have never realized before our interdependence on each other; that we can not merely take but we must give as well; that if we are to go forward, we must move as a trained and loyal army willing to sacrifice for the good of a common discipline, because without such discipline no progress is made, no leadership becomes effective.

. . . It is to be hoped that the normal balance of executive and legislative authority may be wholly adequate to meet the unprecedented task before us. But it may be that an unprecedented demand and need for undelayed action may call for temporary departure from that normal balance of public procedure.

I am prepared under my constitutional duty to recommend the measures that a stricken nation in the midst of a stricken world may require. These measures, or such other measures as the Congress may build out of its experience and wisdom, I shall seek, within my constitutional authority, to bring to speedy adoption. . . .

We do not distrust the future of essential democracy. The people of the United States have not failed. In their need they have registered a mandate that they want direct, vigorous action. They have asked for discipline and direction under leadership. They have made me the present instrument of their wishes. In the spirit of the gift I take it.

March 4, 1933

The Second Inaugural Address of William J. Clinton

My fellow citizens: At this last presidential inauguration of the 20th century, let us lift our eyes toward the challenges that await us in the next century. . . .

528

The promise of America was born in the 18th century out of the bold conviction that we are all created equal. It was extended and preserved in the 19th century, when our nation spread across the continent, saved the union, and abolished the awful scourge of slavery.

Then, in turmoil, and triumph, that promise exploded onto the world stage to make this the American Century.

And what a century it has been. America became the world's mightiest industrial power; saved the world from tyranny in two world wars and a long cold war; and time and again, reached out across the globe to millions who, like us, longed for the blessings of liberty.

Along the way, Americans produced a great middle class and security in old age; built unrivaled centers of learning and opened public schools to all; split the atom and explored the heavens; invented the computer and the microchip; and deepened the wellspring of justice by making a revolution in civil rights for African Americans and all minorities, and extending the circle of citizenship, opportunity and dignity to women.

Now, for the third time, a new century is upon us, and another time to choose. . . . At the dawn of the 21st century a free people must now choose to shape the forces of the Information Age and the global society, to unleash the limitless potential of all our people, and, yes, to form a more perfect union. . . .

As times change, so government must change. We need a new government for a new century—humble enough not to try to solve all our problems for us, but strong enough to give us the tools to solve our problems for ourselves; a government that is smaller, lives within its means, and does more with less. Yet where it can stand up for our values and interests in the world, and where it can give Americans the power to make a real difference in their everyday lives, government should do more, not less. The preeminent mission of our new government is to give all Americans an opportunity—not a guarantee, but a real opportunity—to build better lives.

Beyond that, my fellow citizens, the future is up to us. Our founders taught us that the preservation of our liberty and our union depends upon responsible citizenship. And we need a new sense of responsibility for a new century. There is work to do, work that government alone cannot do: teaching children to read; hiring people off welfare rolls; coming out from behind locked doors and shuttered windows to help reclaim our streets from drugs and gangs and crime; taking time out of our own lives to serve others.

Each and every one of us, in our own way, must assume personal responsibility—not only for ourselves and our families, but for our neighbors and our nation. Our greatest responsibility is to embrace a new spirit of community for a new century. For any one of us to succeed, we must succeed as one America.

January 20, 1997

Conclusion

When Franklin D. Roosevelt delivered his first inaugural address in 1933, this country was in the throes of the Great Depression. The nation's financial markets had collapsed, banks were failing, and many companies had closed their doors. Many people were without jobs, homeless, and hungry. The major challenge was to get the nation back on its feet economically. When Bill Clinton delivered his second inaugural address in 1997, the economy was doing well, and the nation was prospering. The problems facing the nation had to do with such issues as what the role of government should be in the coming century, how to cure social ills such as high crime rates and poverty, how to overcome racial divisiveness and work peaceably with others on both a national and a global level, and how to use the potential of information technology in accomplishing national goals.

Analysis Questions

1. Compare and contrast the two presidents' views concerning what role the government should play in solving the nation's problems.
2. What did each president think that citizens could or should do to help solve the nation's problems?
3. Consider these statements: "For any one of us to succeed, we must succeed as one America" (President Clinton). "[W]e now realize as we have never realized before our interdependence on each other" (President Roosevelt). What are the implications of these statements for citizenship responsibilities?
4. Leadership involves, among other things, the ability to both define a group's goals and take steps to help achieve those goals. Given that Congress is the lawmaking branch of government, how can a president take steps to achieve national goals?

The Federal Judicial Branch

If you decide to "make a federal case" out of something, you just might end up here, in the United States Supreme Court.

CHAPTER 20

The Federal Courts

CHAPTER OBJECTIVES

To learn about and understand . . .

⭐ The law in the United States and its origins

⭐ The organization of the federal court system

⭐ The process by which cases reach the Supreme Court

⭐ The way Supreme Court justices are chosen and the characteristics they share

⭐ The policymaking role of the federal courts

"The peace, the prosperity, and the very existence of the Union are nestled in the hands of . . . federal judges. Without them the Constitution would be a dead letter."

Alexis de Tocqueville
(1805–1859)
French Political Writer

INTRODUCTION

At some time or another, you might feel that one of your constitutional rights has been violated. If that happens, you might eventually find yourself in a federal court. The federal court system is the judicial branch of the national government. In the federal court, you would stand before a federal judge, who would interpret the U.S. Constitution. It is federal judges who bring the Constitution to bear on the lives of all Americans.

The judges in the federal courts examine and re-examine the Constitution and their own decisions so that justice and the Constitution are well served. Thus, the Supreme Court may overrule its earlier decisions as it protects what Alexis de Tocqueville described as "the peace, the prosperity, and the very existence of the Union."

◀ Although we often hear about the Supreme Court "bench," the nine justices actually sit in the high-backed chairs shown here.

533

Sources of American Law

Preview Questions:

- What is the difference between the common law and statutory law?
- What is constitutional law?
- What is the difference between civil law and criminal law?

Key Terms:

common law, case law, precedent, statutory law, civil law, criminal law

The federal court system was established by the founders in Article III of the Constitution. Section 1 of that article reads as follows:

The judicial Power of the United States, shall be vested in one supreme Court, and in such inferior Courts as the Congress may from time to time ordain and establish.

Congress was thus given the power to control the number and kind of "inferior" courts, which include all courts other than the Supreme Court. Since the Constitution was ratified, Congress has created an extensive network of federal courts.

The federal courts interpret not only the Constitution but all federal laws, including acts passed by Congress. When Congress passes a new law, the law necessarily must be phrased in rather broad terms. It is up to the courts to decide how the law should apply to specific situations when disputes arise over the meaning of the law. The federal courts thus play a prominent role in our legal system.

Because of our English heritage, our legal system is similar to that of England. In this section, we look first at the origins and development of the English (and American) common law tradition. We then discuss some basic classifications of law.

Common Law

In 1066, the Normans conquered England, and William the Conqueror and his successors began the process of unifying the country under Norman rule. One of the means they used to do this was the establishment of the king's court, or *curia regis*. Before the Norman conquest, disputes had been settled according to local customs. The king's court sought to establish a

▶ The American criminal justice system is designed to safeguard the rights of the accused and to punish the guilty. What is the difference between civil and criminal law?

Legal Systems in Other Countries

Each country has its own legal system, just as it has its own type of government. Basically, though, most of the world's legal systems fall into two categories: common law systems and civil law systems. England, the United States, and most of the countries that were once colonies of England have common law systems. Civil law systems predominate in Europe and in the Latin American, African, and Asian countries that were colonized by European nations. Japan and South Africa also have civil law systems, and elements of the civil law system are found in the Islamic courts of Muslim countries. In the United States, the state of Louisiana, because of its historical ties to France, has in part a civil law system.

A civil law system is based on Roman civil law, or "code law." The term *civil law,* as used here, does not refer to civil as opposed to criminal law. Rather, it refers to *codified* law—an ordered grouping of legal principles enacted into law by a legislature or governing body. In a civil law system, the primary source of law is a statutory code, and case precedents are not judicially binding, as they normally are in a common law system. Although judges in a civil law system often refer to previous decisions as sources of legal guidance, they are not required to follow precedents.

THINKING GLOBALLY

Would judges be likely to have more power to influence policy in a common law system or a civil law system? Explain.

common, or uniform, set of customs for the whole country. As the number of courts and cases increased, the most important decisions of each year were gathered together and recorded in *Year Books.*

Judges, in settling disputes similar to ones that had been decided before, used the *Year Books* as the basis for their decisions. For cases that were unique, judges had to create new laws. Whenever possible, though, they based their decisions on the general principles suggested by earlier cases.

The body of judicial law that developed under this system is still used today and is known as the **common law**—the law that developed from custom and court decisions in England and the United States.

The common law, then, began centuries ago in England. The English colonists, of course, brought the common law with them to America.

An important part of the common law that has developed in the United States since the American Revolution is the case law that has been decided in our nation over that period. **Case law** consists of rules of law announced in court decisions. It includes all reported court cases that interpret statutes, regulations, and constitutional provisions. These interpretations become part of the official law on the subject and serve as a **precedent,** or an example for future cases.

Constitutional Law

Constitutions are important sources of law. The national government and each state government have constitutions that set forth their general organization, powers, and limits. The U.S. Constitution is the supreme law of the land. A law in violation of the U.S. Constitution, no matter what its source, will be declared unconstitutional and will not be enforced. Similarly, unless it conflicts with the U.S. Constitution, a state constitution is supreme within the state's borders. The U.S. Constitution defines the powers and limitations of the national government. All powers not granted to the national government are retained by the states or by the people.

Statutory Law

Statutes enacted by the U.S. Congress and the various state legislative bodies make up yet another source of law. This type of law is generally referred to as **statutory law.** Statutory law also includes laws passed by cities and counties, none of which can violate the U.S. Constitution or the relevant state constitutions. Today, legislative bodies and regulatory agencies assume an ever-increasing share of lawmaking. Much of the work of modern courts consists of interpreting what the legislators meant when the law was passed and applying it to a present set of circumstances.

Civil versus Criminal Law

Laws can generally be classified as either civil or criminal. **Civil law** spells out the duties that exist between persons or between citizens and their governments. Law concerning contracts for business transactions, for example, is part of civil law. If you sign a contract to purchase a car on credit, the law governing that transaction is civil law. The object of a civil lawsuit is to obtain compensation (such as money damages) for harms suffered because of another's wrongful action.

Criminal law, in contrast, has to do with wrongs committed against the public as a whole. Criminal acts are prohibited by local, state, or national government statutes. In a criminal case, the government seeks to impose a penalty (fines and/or imprisonment) on a person suspected of having violated a criminal law. When someone robs a convenience store, that person has committed a crime and, if caught and proven guilty, will normally spend time in prison.

SECTION 1 REVIEW

1. What is the common law, and what are the origins of the common law tradition?
2. How does statutory law differ from case law? How does statutory law differ from constitutional law?
3. What are some differences between civil law and criminal law?
4. **For Critical Analysis:** Do traffic laws fall into the category of civil law or criminal law? Explain.

SECTION 2

The Federal Court System

Preview Questions:

- 🌎 How is the federal court system organized?
- 🌎 What is the difference between a trial court and an appellate court?
- 🌎 What does the term *jurisdiction* mean, and in what circumstances can a federal court exercise jurisdiction?

Key Terms:

trial courts, appellate court, judicial circuit, jury duty, hung jury, jurisdiction, original jurisdiction, appellate jurisdiction, federal question, diversity of citizenship, concurrent jurisdiction, exclusive jurisdiction

The Structure of the Federal Court System

The federal court system is basically a three-tiered structure that consists of U.S. districts courts, U.S. courts of appeals, and the U.S. Supreme Court. There are also specialized federal courts that handle only certain types of claims, such as tax claims. Figure 20–1 on page 537 shows how the federal court system is organized.

U.S. District Courts On the bottom tier of the federal court system are the U.S. district courts. The district courts are **trial courts.** As the term implies, these are courts in which trials are held. At a trial, each party (or usually, each party's attorney) submits evidence to support its side and to convince the court to rule in its

FIGURE 20–1 The Federal Court System This chart shows the organization of the federal court system. From looking at the table, what do you know about the relationship of the United States Court of Federal Claims to the United States Court of Appeals for the Federal Circuit?

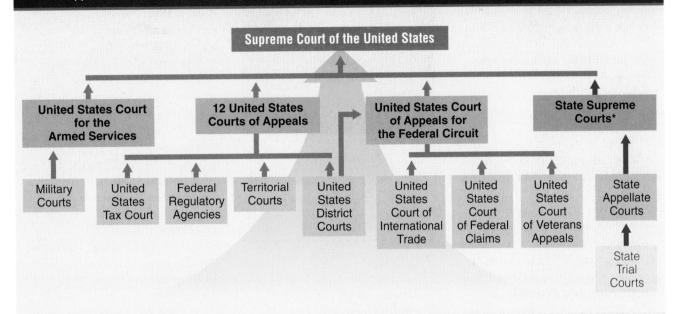

*The state supreme court is usually the court of last resort, but this is not the case in every state. When an issue based on the federal Constitution, a treaty, or a federal statute is involved, it might be possible to take the appeal of a state supreme court decision to the Supreme Court of the United States.

favor. Evidence may take the form of testimony, exhibits, videos, or other demonstrations. After the trial concludes, the jury (if it is a jury trial) decides on the facts of the case—that is, on what conclusion should be reached based on the evidence. If it is not a jury trial, the judge makes this decision.

There is at least one federal district court in every state. The number of districts can vary over time, according to population changes and the size of case-loads. Currently, there are ninety-four judicial districts.

U.S. Courts of Appeals A party who loses his or her case in a district court normally can appeal the decision to a federal court of appeals, or **appellate court.** The U.S. courts of appeals are *intermediate* appellate courts. They are located on the middle tier of the system, between the district courts and the Supreme Court. These courts are also known as circuit courts of appeals because each appellate court is located in a **judicial circuit.** Over time, Congress has established thirteen judicial circuits. The appellate court in each circuit

hears appeals from the district courts located within that circuit. Figure 20–2 on page 540 shows the geographical boundaries of the U.S. district courts and the courts of appeals.

Unlike the federal district (trial) courts, appellate courts do not hear testimony or examine other evidence. Rather, an appellate court reviews the record of the lower court's proceedings and other records relating to the case to determine whether the lower court made any mistake. Appellate courts are thus *reviewing* courts.

The U.S. Supreme Court The U.S. Supreme Court is the highest level of the three-tiered federal court system. The Supreme Court consists of nine justices, who are nominated by the president and confirmed by the

If you are an American citizen of sound mind and have never committed a serious crime, you may one day be summoned by a state or federal court for **jury duty.** Names of jurors are usually chosen from tax assessor's rolls, lists of registered voters, and driver's license registrations.

In most states, if your name is chosen, the clerk of the court will send you a jury qualification form, which you must fill out and return. You will then receive a summons requiring you to appear in court at a particular time and place. If for some reason you cannot be there, you must explain this to the court. There are few valid reasons for being excused. Being employed is not a valid excuse to be exempted from jury duty. The law protects you from being fired from your job or penalized in any way for the time you spend serving on a jury.

When you appear in court, you may be asked to wait in a room with other prospective jurors until you are called. Then you will be escorted to the courtroom. You will be asked to take an oath that you will answer questions truthfully. Lawyers on both sides, the pros-

ecution and the defense, will ask you questions. If one of the lawyers finds a reason why you may be biased in the case, you will be disqualified by the judge.

If you are accepted to serve on the jury, you will take another oath in court along with the other jurors. Then you will be told when you are to reappear for the trial.

When the trial begins, you must listen carefully to all of the testimony. When both sides have presented their cases, the judge will instruct you about the law to be applied. Then you and the other jurors will be asked to decide the facts of the case.

You and the other jurors will be taken to a private room. You will have the opportunity to share your views about the evidence you have heard. You must listen to the other jurors' views and may try to persuade the others to take your position.

Senate. We will examine the Supreme Court in more detail shortly.

Jurisdiction of the Federal Courts

In Latin, *juris* means "law," and *diction* means "to speak." Thus, *jurisdiction* literally refers to the power "to speak the law." In other words, **jurisdiction** is the authority of a court to decide a certain case. Before any court can hear a case, it must have jurisdiction over the persons, property, or subject matter of the dispute. A court has **original jurisdiction** when it can hear a case for the first time. Trial courts, for

example, have original jurisdiction. A court has **appellate jurisdiction** when it functions as a reviewing court. Courts of appeals normally only have appellate jurisdiction.

Each state maintains its own court system, which is separate from the federal court system. Generally, a state court's jurisdiction is limited to the geographical boundaries of the state in which it is located. (See Chapter 24 for a discussion of other situations in which state courts can exercise jurisdiction.)

Because the national government is a government of limited powers, the jurisdiction of the federal courts is also limited. Basically, the federal courts can only decide cases involving federal questions or diversity of citizenship.

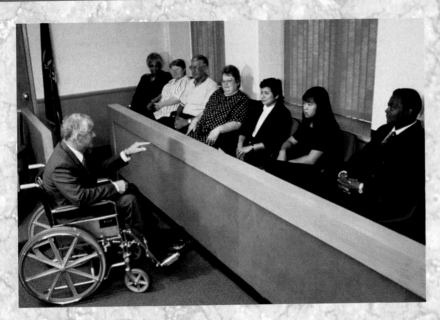

▲ *A jury listens attentively as a lawyer makes his point. How are juries selected?*

room. They will announce their decision. This decision is final, and the trial is ended. Generally, the judge thanks the jury and dismisses it.

Serving on a jury can be interesting and educational. It is also an opportunity to participate in our system of equal justice under the law.

TAKING ACTION

1. Stage a mock trial in your class. Choose a prosecuting attorney, a defense attorney, a defendant, a judge, and a jury.
2. Attend a jury trial. Listen to the evidence presented, and determine what your verdict would be if you were on the jury.

A jury that cannot agree on a verdict is called a **hung jury.** In that case, either another trial is held with a different jury or the matter is dropped.

Most juries are able to come to a unanimous decision. When all of the jurors agree on the verdict, the jury members will be ushered back into the court-

Federal Questions Article III, Section 2, of the Constitution states as follows:

The judicial Power shall extend to all Cases, in Law and Equity, arising under this Constitution, the Laws of the United States, and Treaties made, or which shall be made, under their Authority.

Whenever a case involves a claim based on the Constitution, a treaty, or a federal law, a **federal question** arises. Any lawsuit involving a federal question can originate in a federal court. A person who claims that his or her constitutional rights have been violated can bring a lawsuit in a federal court. So can a person who claims that some person or firm has vio-

lated his or her rights under a federal law, such as a law protecting employees from discrimination.

Diversity of Citizenship Federal courts can also hear cases involving **diversity of citizenship.** Such cases may arise when the parties in a lawsuit live in different states or when one of the parties is a foreign government or a foreign citizen. Before a federal court can take jurisdiction in a diversity case, however, the amount in controversy must be more than $75,000.

For example, suppose that you are a California resident. While you are traveling in Texas, a car driven by a New York resident crashes into your vehicle. You could sue the New York driver in a federal court on the

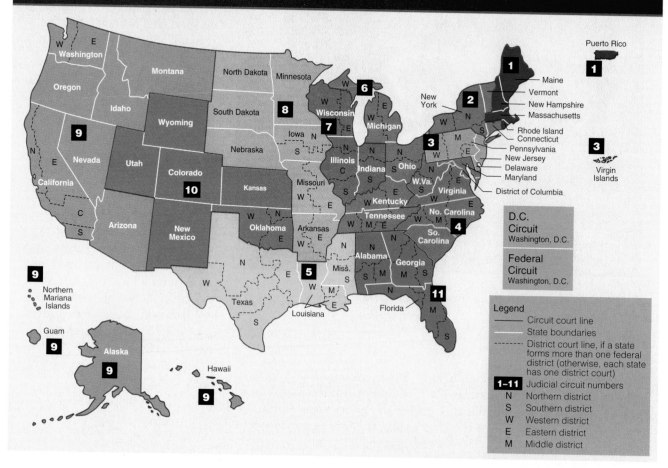

FIGURE 20–2 Boundaries of the Judicial Districts and Circuits The map shows the U.S. district courts and the U.S. courts of appeals, or circuit courts. How many judicial circuits make up the U.S. circuit courts?

Legend

———	Circuit court line
———	State boundaries
- - - - -	District court line, if a state forms more than one federal district (otherwise, each state has one district court)
1–11	Judicial circuit numbers
N	Northern district
S	Southern district
W	Western district
E	Eastern district
M	Middle district

basis of diversity jurisdiction—*if* the harms you sustained were valued at more than $75,000. Otherwise, the suit normally must be brought in a state court.

Concurrent and Exclusive Jurisdiction When both federal and state courts have the power to hear a case, as is true in suits involving diversity of citizenship, **concurrent jurisdiction** exists. **Exclusive jurisdiction,** in contrast, exists when a case can be tried only in a state court or only in a federal court. Federal courts have exclusive jurisdiction in cases involving federal crimes, bankruptcy, patents, and copyrights. Federal courts also have exclusive jurisdiction in certain other circumstances, such as in suits against the United States. States have exclusive jurisdiction in such areas as divorce and adoptions.

SECTION 2 REVIEW

1. Describe the basic structure and organization of the federal court system.
2. What is the constitutional basis of the federal court system?
3. What is jurisdiction? Over what kinds of cases can the federal courts exercise jurisdiction?
4. **For Critical Analysis:** If you are involved in an auto accident in another state, you may have to undergo a trial in that state. You might prefer to bring your suit in a federal court located nearer to your home. But unless the amount in controversy is over $75,000, you cannot ask for a federal trial. Is this fair? Why or why not?

The Supreme Court

Preview Questions:

🌐 What is a writ of *certiorari*, and in what situations may the Supreme Court issue one?

🌐 What are the four types of opinions issued by the Supreme Court?

🌐 What procedures are followed by the Supreme Court in performing its work?

Key Terms:

writ of *certiorari*, oral arguments, opinion, unanimous opinion, majority opinion, concurring opinion, dissenting opinion

Because of its importance in the federal court system, the United States Supreme Court deserves special attention. Here we look at how cases reach the Supreme Court, how the decisions of the Court are put into written form, and how the Court performs its work.

How Cases Reach the Supreme Court

Many people are surprised to learn that there is no absolute right of appeal to the United States Supreme Court. The Supreme Court is given original

▲ *In 1998, the justices of the U.S. Supreme Court included (seated, left to right) Antonin Scalia, John Paul Stevens, Chief Justice William Rehnquist, Sandra Day O'Connor, and Anthony Kennedy; (standing, left to right) Ruth Bader Ginsburg, David H. Souter, Clarence Thomas, and Stephen Breyer.*

Students and the First Amendment

In May 1983, Robert Reynolds, the principal of Hazelwood East High School, near St. Louis, Missouri, ordered that two articles scheduled to appear in the school-sponsored student newspaper, the *Spectrum*, be deleted. One article dealt with student pregnancy. The other discussed the effects of parents' divorces on Hazelwood High students. The principal argued that the articles didn't properly protect student identities and dealt with subjects not suitable for younger students. He also asserted his right to censor the paper.

Three students working on the paper sued the school district, arguing that their First Amendment right to freedom of expression had been violated. The U.S. District Court for the Eastern District of

◀ *After her high-school principal refused to allow several controversial articles to appear in the student newspaper,* Spectrum, *editor Cathy Kuhlmeier took her case to court. What law did Kuhlmeier claim her school district had violated?*

Missouri decided that the students' First Amendment rights had not been violated. The court held that school officials may restrain students' speech when this seems "reasonable" and when it is related directly to a school activity.

The case was appealed. The U.S. Court of Appeals for the Eighth Circuit disagreed with the district court judge's decision. The appellate court held that the newspaper was a public forum because it was intended as a "conduit for student viewpoint" and

jurisdiction in a small number of situations. In all others, it acts as an appeals court. Thousands of cases are filed with the Supreme Court each year. On average, though—at least in recent years—it hears fewer than one hundred cases each year.

To bring a case before the Supreme Court, a party must request the Court to issue a writ of *certiorari*. A **writ of *certiorari*** [pronounced sur-shee-uh-*rah*-ree] is an order sent by the Supreme Court to a lower court requesting the record of the case in question. Parties can petition the Supreme Court to issue a writ of

certiorari, but whether the Court will do so is entirely within its discretion. In no instance is the Court required to issue a writ of *certiorari.*

Most petitions for writs of *certiorari* are, in fact, denied. A denial is not a decision on the merits of a case, nor is it an indication of agreement with a lower court's opinion. The Court will not issue a writ unless at least four justices approve of it. This is called the "rule of four."

Typically, the Court grants writs only in cases that raise important policy issues that need to be addressed.

that school officials were entitled to censor only if the publication could have resulted in a lawsuit.

In January 1988, the United States Supreme Court, in *Hazelwood School District v. Cathy Kuhlmeier*, reversed the lower court's ruling by a vote of five to three. Justice Byron White, writing for the majority, argued that "school officials may impose reasonable restrictions on the speech of students, teachers, and other members of the school community." The majority also noted that students' rights "are not automatically coextensive with the rights of adults in other settings."

In his dissent, Justice William Brennan (joined by Justices Thurgood Marshall and Harry Blackmun) said that the decision might make public schools into "enclaves of totalitarianism."

This Supreme Court decision prompted several state legislatures to consider writing specific state laws to spell out students' rights and, in some cases, to grant student publications specific privileges against censorship.

THINK ABOUT IT

1. Do you think that the principal's action violated the student-editors' rights?
2. To what extent does a school principal have the obligation to prevent students from publishing material that may be offensive to other students or harmful to school policy?

Hazelwood School District v. Cathy Kuhlmeier The figure below shows the decision of each court that heard *Hazelwood School District v. Cathy Kuhlmeier*. The scales of justice indicate which side of the dispute outweighed the other in the eyes of each court involved.

U.S. District Court
Hazelwood School District v. Cathy Kuhlmeier

U.S. Court of Appeals

U.S. Supreme Court

For example, in a recent term, the Court heard a case involving the pressing issue of whether the constitutional right to privacy includes a right to commit assisted suicide. It also heard a case concerning indecent speech on the Internet and whether a law passed by Congress to curb such speech violated the right to free speech. Also, if the lower federal courts are issuing conflicting opinions on an important issue, the Supreme Court may review a case involving that issue to define the law on the matter. It is in this way that current legal issues undergo constitutional scrutiny.

Decisions and Opinions

The Supreme Court normally does not hear any evidence. As mentioned, this is generally true in all appellate courts. The Court's decision is based on the written records of a case. The attorneys, however, can present **oral arguments**—arguments presented in person rather than on paper. The case is then privately examined by the justices.

After reaching a decision, the Court writes an opinion. The **opinion** sets forth the Court's reasons for its

▶ When the Supreme Court reaches a decision, final opinions are quickly printed and handed to the press by the Supreme Court's public information officer. As shown here, members of the press eagerly wait to receive and then to read their copies of the decisions. Supreme Court opinions are also published almost immediately on the Internet.

decision, the rules of law that apply, and the judgment. There are four types of written opinions. When all of the justices agree on an opinion, the opinion is written for the entire Court and can be deemed a **unanimous opinion.** When there is not a unanimous opinion, a **majority opinion** is written. This opinion outlines the views of the majority of the justices involved in the case. Often, a justice who feels strongly about making or emphasizing a particular point that was not made or emphasized in the majority opinion writes a **concurring opinion.** The justice writing the concurring opinion concurs (agrees) with the conclusion given in the majority opinion but for reasons that are different from those stated in the majority opinion. Finally, dissenting opinions are usually written by justices who did not agree with the majority. The **dissenting opinion** is important because it often forms the basis of arguments used years later that cause the Court to reverse the previous decision and establish a new precedent.

The Supreme Court at Work

The Supreme Court begins its regular annual term on the first Monday in October and usually adjourns in late June or early July of the following year. Special sessions may be held after the regular term is over, but

only a few cases are decided in this way. More commonly, cases not heard in one term are carried into the next term.

Cases that are appealed to the Court are scheduled for oral argument or denied a hearing in a written "orders list." Orders lists are released on Mondays. Generally, arguments are heard during seven two-week sessions scattered from October to April or May. The justices hear oral arguments on Monday, Tuesday, Wednesday, and sometimes Thursday. Recesses are held between periods of oral arguments to allow the justices to consider the cases and handle other Court business. Oral arguments run from 10 A.M. to noon and again from 1 to 3 P.M., with thirty minutes allowed for each side's argument, unless special exceptions are granted. All statements and the justices' questions are tape-recorded during these sessions. Lawyers addressing the Supreme Court can be questioned by the justices at any time during oral argument, a practice not followed in most courts.

Each Wednesday and Friday during the annual Court term, the justices meet in conference to discuss cases under consideration and to decide which new appeals and petitions the Court will accept. These conferences take place in an oak-paneled chamber and are strictly private—no secretaries, tape recorders, or video cameras are allowed.

When each conference is over, the chief justice, if in the majority, will assign the writing of opinions. When the chief justice is not in the majority, the most senior justice in the majority assigns the writing.

After the necessary editing and the publication of preliminary prints, the official Court decision is placed in the *United States Reports*, the official record of the Court's decisions, which is available in many libraries. The decisions are also printed in West Publishing Company's *Supreme Court Reporter*, which is available about a year sooner. Additionally, Supreme Court decisions are now released immediately for online publication. You can access these decisions at **www.ssctplus.com/online/index.htm**.

SECTION 3 REVIEW

1. Explain writ of *certiorari* and how it is used.
2. What is an opinion of the Court? What four types of opinions may the court issue?
3. **For Critical Analysis:** As noted, no one has the unconditional right to have his or her case heard before the Supreme Court. Do you think this means that our judicial system is flawed? Why or why not?

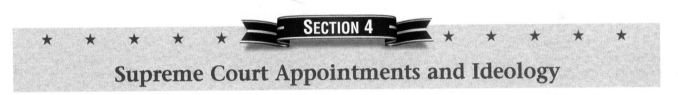

SECTION 4

Supreme Court Appointments and Ideology

Preview Questions:

- How are Supreme Court justices appointed?
- Once appointed, how long does a Supreme Court justice remain in office?
- How are federal judges paid?
- What characteristics do most Supreme Court justices share?
- Are the judges nominated by the president always confirmed by the Senate?

All federal judges, including the justices of the Supreme Court, are appointed. (In contrast, state court judges are often elected.) Article II, Section 2, of the Constitution authorizes the president to appoint the justices of the Supreme Court with the advice and consent of the Senate. Laws passed by Congress provide that the same procedure be used for appointing judges to the lower federal courts as well.

According to Article III, Section 1, "The Judges, both of the supreme and inferior Courts, shall hold their Offices during good Behavior." This means that, in effect, Supreme Court justices—and all federal judges—are appointed for life. Federal judges who engage in clearly illegal conduct, such as bribery, may be removed from office through impeachment, but this

rarely occurs. Normally, federal judges serve in their positions until they resign, retire, or die.

Article III, Section 1, also states that judges "shall, at stated Times, receive for their Services a Compensation, which shall not be diminished during their Continuance in Office." In other words, federal judges, while in office, cannot have their salaries lowered. Congress determines the salaries for the judges of the federal court system, including the salaries of the justices of the Supreme Court. Current salaries are shown in Figure 20–3 on page 546. In addition, federal judges receive retirement benefits.

Just the Facts

Six of the nine current Supreme Court justices reported assets of around $1 million on recent financial disclosure forms.

Who Becomes a Supreme Court Justice?

Although the Constitution sets no specific qualifications for those who serve on the Supreme Court, all who

Court	Salary
Supreme Court	$167,900 (except for the chief justice, who receives $175,400)
Court of Appeals	$145,000
District Court	$136,700
Other Special Federal Courts	From $145,000 to $136,700

Occupational Position before Appointment	Number of Justices (108 Total)
Private legal practice	25
State judgeship	21
Federal judgeship	28
U.S. attorney general	7
Deputy or assistant U.S. attorney general	2
U.S. solicitor general	2
U.S. senator	6
U.S. representative	2
State governor	3
Federal executive post	9
Other	3

Religious Background	Number of Justices
Protestant	83
Roman Catholic	11
Jewish	6
Unitarian	7
No religious affiliation	1

Age on Appointment	Number of Justices
Under 40	5
41–50	31
51–60	58
61–70	14

Political Party Affiliation	Number of Justices
Federalist (to 1835)	13
Democratic-Republican (to 1826)	7
Whig (to 1861)	1
Democrat	44
Republican	42
Independent	1

Educational Background	Number of Justices
College graduate	92
Not college graduate	16

Sex	Number of Justices
Male	106
Female	2

Race	Number of Justices
Caucasian	106
Other	2

have served share certain characteristics. The make-up of the federal judiciary is far from typical of the American public. Figure 20–4 summarizes the backgrounds of all of the 108 Supreme Court justices to 1998.

As you can see in this table, the majority of the justices were in private legal practice or state or federal judgeships at the time of their appointment. Most justices were in their fifties when they assumed office, although two were as young as thirty-two and one as old as sixty-six. The average age of newly sworn justices is about fifty-three. In general, the justices have belonged to the same political parties as the presidents who appointed them.

Just the Facts

George Washington appointed more Supreme Court justices (ten) than any other president.

Note that the great majority of justices have had a college education. By and large, those who did not attend college or receive a degree lived in the late eighteenth and early nineteenth centuries, when a college education was much less common than it is today. In recent years, justices have typically had degrees from such prestigious institutions as Yale, Harvard, and Columbia.

The religious background of Supreme Court justices is strikingly atypical of that of the American population as a whole, even making allowances for changes over time in the religious composition of the nation.

ARCHITECTS

of Government

Ruth Bader Ginsburg
(1933–   )

A native of Brooklyn, New York, Ruth Bader Ginsburg attended Cornell University as well as Harvard and Columbia Law School. She taught law at Columbia, Rutgers, and Stanford, among others. On August 10, 1993, she became the second woman to serve on the United States Supreme Court.

HER WORDS

"A prime part of the history of our Constitution is the story of the extension of constitutional rights and protections to help people once ignored or excluded."

(From the decision in United States v. Virginia, *June 26, 1996)*

"[A] sovereign may tax the entire income of its residents."

(From the decision in Oklahoma Tax Commission v. Chickasaw Nation, *June 14, 1995)*

DEVELOPING
CRITICAL THINKING SKILLS

1. In the first quotation, to what "history" was Justice Ginsburg referring?
2. What does the word *sovereign* mean in the second quotation?

Catholics, Baptists, and Lutherans have been underrepresented compared with their numbers in the population as a whole. Episcopalians, Presbyterians, and Methodists have been overrepresented among the justices, as have Unitarians. Typically, there have been one Catholic justice and one Jewish justice on the Court.

Ideology and Judicial Appointments

The power to nominate Supreme Court justices belongs solely to the president. This is not to say, however, that the president's nominations are always confirmed. In fact, almost 20 percent of presidential nominations to the Supreme Court have been either rejected or not acted upon by the Senate. Many bitter battles over Supreme Court appointments have occurred when the Senate and the president have not seen eye to eye about political matters.

From the beginning of Andrew Jackson's presidency in 1829 to the end of Ulysses S. Grant's presidency in 1877, the U.S. Senate often refused to confirm the president's judicial nominations. During the long period from 1893 until 1968, the Senate rejected only three Court nominees. From 1968 through 1986, however, there were two rejections of presidential nominees to the highest court. These persons had been nominated by President Richard Nixon.

President Ronald Reagan had two of his nominees for a Supreme Court vacancy rejected by the Senate. Both were then judges in the courts of appeals. In 1987, he nominated Robert Bork, who faced sometimes hostile questioning by the Senate on his views of the Constitution. Next, Reagan nominated Douglas Ginsburg. Ginsburg ultimately withdrew his nomination when the press leaked information about his alleged use of marijuana during the 1970s. Finally, the Senate approved Reagan's third choice, Anthony Kennedy.

President George Bush nominated two justices to the Supreme Court—David Souter and Clarence Thomas. Both were confirmed. In 1993, the Senate confirmed President Bill Clinton's nomination

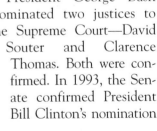

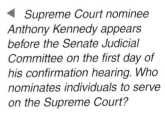

◄ *Supreme Court nominee Anthony Kennedy appears before the Senate Judicial Committee on the first day of his confirmation hearing. Who nominates individuals to serve on the Supreme Court?*

of Ruth Bader Ginsburg, who became the second woman to sit on the Supreme Court (the first was Sandra Day O'Connor, who was appointed by President Reagan in 1981). In 1994, Clinton nominated Stephen Breyer, who was also confirmed without significant opposition.

Ideology plays an important role in the president's choices for the Supreme Court. It also plays a large role in whether or not the Senate confirms those choices. Political party affiliation is an important part of ideology where presidential appointments are concerned. In the long history of the U.S. Supreme Court, fewer than 14 percent of the justices nominated by a president have been from an opposing political party.

SECTION 4 REVIEW

1. Name some common characteristics of the people who have served on the Supreme Court.
2. Why might the Senate reject a presidential nomination for the Supreme Court?
3. **For Critical Analysis:** If Supreme Court justices are supposed to make decisions that are free from political bias, why has the Senate confirmation of justices become such an ideological battle?

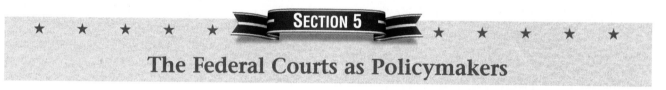

SECTION 5

The Federal Courts as Policymakers

Preview Questions:

- How do the courts make policy?
- What is the power of judicial review, and why is this power significant with respect to policymaking?
- What is judicial activism? What is judicial restraint?
- What checks the power of the federal courts?

Key Terms:

judicial review, judicial activism, judicial restraint

The framers probably expected the Supreme Court to play an important role in the national government. Yet they surely did not expect the federal courts to play such a large role in public policymaking. Indeed, in *Federalist Paper* Number 78, Alexander Hamilton stated that "the judiciary is beyond comparison the weakest of the three departments of power." Certainly, during its first decade, the Supreme Court handled few important matters. In 1800, John Jay refused to serve a second term as chief justice. He explained why in a letter to President John Adams:

I left the [Supreme Court] perfectly convinced that under a system so defective it [the Court] could not obtain the energy, weight, and dignity which are essential to its afford-

ing due support to the national government; nor acquire the public confidence and respect which, as a last resort of the justice of a nation, it should possess.

Clearly, things have changed since then. Today, the courts play a significant policymaking role in government.

How Do the Courts Make Policy?

The function of the courts, of course, is to interpret and apply the law, not to make the laws—that is what the legislative branch of government does. Yet judges do make law. At times, this is unavoidable. For example, sometimes courts hear cases that are not covered by any law that currently exists. This may happen when new technology, such as the Internet, leads to disputes that are not covered by existing law. In such cases, a Supreme Court decision may become the law until Congress passes legislation to cover the matter. Perhaps the most important policymaking tool of the courts, however, is the power of judicial review. This is particularly true of the Supreme Court.

Judicial review is the process by which a court determines whether or not a law is contrary to the mandates of the Constitution. The courts have the authority and power to determine whether a particular law violates the Constitution.

The Constitution did not specifically provide for judicial review. Most constitutional scholars, however, believe that the framers intended the federal courts to have this power. In *Federalist Paper* Number 78, for example, Alexander Hamilton stressed the importance of the "complete independence" of federal judges and their special duty to "invalidate all acts contrary to the manifest tenor of the Constitution." Hamilton thought that without judicial review, there would be nothing to ensure that the other branches of government stayed within their constitutional limits when exercising their powers.

Chief Justice John Marshall shared these views. In 1803, Marshall claimed this power for the Courts. In *Marbury v. Madison*, Marshall wrote the following words:

> *It is emphatically the province and duty of the Judicial Department to say what the law is. . . . If two laws conflict with each other, the courts must decide on the operation of each. . . . So if the law be in opposition to the Constitution . . . [t]he Court must determine which of these conflicting rules governs the case. This is the very essence of judicial duty.*

With these words, Marshall established the power of the federal courts to determine whether a law passed by Congress violates the Constitution.

Judicial Activism and Judicial Restraint

Judicial scholars like to characterize Supreme Court justices as being either activist or restraintist. Justices who practice **judicial activism** believe that the Court should use its power of judicial review to alter the direction of the activities of Congress, state legislatures, and administrative agencies, such as the Federal Trade Commission. Justices who practice **judicial restraint** believe that the Court should only rarely use its powers of judicial review. In other words, decisions made by popularly elected legislators should not be changed by the Supreme Court, so long as the legislative actions are clearly not unconstitutional.

Just the Facts

The Liberty Bell cracked when it was rung at the funeral of John Marshall in 1835.

◄ As government steps in to rescue a nation suffering from the effects of the Great Depression, the resulting increase in federal powers appears to make this 1930s cartoonist nervous. Do you think the man in the cartoon represents business interests or the common person?

Distinguishing between Fact and Opinion

When investigating issues, it is important to distinguish between statements of fact and statements of opinion. It is also important to recognize that statements of fact that appear to be true may be based on inaccurate or false information. A *fact* is a statement that can be proved by evidence, such as records, documents, and unbiased historical sources. An *opinion* contains value-based statements that cannot be proved.

Consider the following statement: "The State Endowment for Humanities provides state funds to artists and writers." This statement is factual because it can be easily verified by state government records. Now consider this statement: "The State Endowment for Humanities funds ugly art." Whether or not the art is ugly is an opinion based on personal values. It cannot be proved with facts and leaves room for disagreement.

Use these guidelines when distinguishing between fact and opinion:

- Ask yourself what idea the writer or speaker wants you to accept.
- Pinpoint the statements being used to communicate or support the idea.
- Ask yourself if and how these statements can be verified or proved.

PRACTICING YOUR SKILLS

Find a copy of a speech made by a politician. (Look in *Vital Speeches of the Day*, which you can find in your school or local library or on the Internet. You can also find excerpts from speeches in the *New York Times*.) Read at least two pages of the speech. Make a list of statements of fact and statements of opinion, and tell why you identified each statement as you did. Finally, explain why you agree or disagree with the view presented.

Judicial activism can take either a liberal or a conservative direction. In the early 1930s, for example, the Supreme Court was activist and conservative, ruling that extensive regulation of business was unconstitutional. In the 1950s and 1960s, the Court was activist and liberal. Many of the Court's critics believed it should exercise more restraint. They criticized the 1954 *Brown v. Board of Education of Topeka* decision (see Chapter 7) on the grounds that the highest court settled a problem of school racial segregation that should have been resolved by Congress or left to the states.

In the 1980s and 1990s, the pendulum seemed to swing again in the other direction. Some contend that the Supreme Court of the 1990s was an activist conservative Court, especially with respect to issues concerning states' rights. In *United States v. Lopez* (1995), for example, the Court ruled that Congress had exceeded its constitutional authority under the commerce clause when it passed the Gun-Free School Zones Act in 1990. This was the first time in sixty years that the Supreme Court had limited the national government's regulatory authority under the commerce clause.

In several later cases, the Court similarly placed limits on Congress's powers. In *City of Boerne v. Flores* (1997), for example, the Court declared that Congress had exceeded its power when it passed the Religious Freedom Restoration Act of 1993. In *Printz v. United States* (1997), the Court ruled that certain sections of the Brady Handgun Violence Prevention Act of 1993 unconstitutionally burdened state governments.

Today's courts are sometimes referred to as "mini-legislatures" because of their policymaking powers. The power of the federal courts to shape law is not limited to the Supreme Court. In particular, the federal appellate courts exercise a good deal of policymaking power

How the Supreme Court Applies the Constitution

The Supreme Court of the 1950s and 1960s took a different view of what the Constitution means than the Supreme Court of the 1990s.

THEN (1950s–1960s)	Now
The Supreme Court decided around 150 cases per year.	The Supreme Court decides between 75 and 90 cases per year.
The Supreme Court exercised judicial activism to promote civil rights.	The Court is more restrained with respect to civil rights and criminal procedures but more activist with respect to states' rights.
Virtually all affirmative action programs were considered constitutional.	Some affirmative action programs are subject to strict scrutiny, and many have been held to violate the equal protection clause.

because their decisions are often final. Unless the Supreme Court overturns an appellate court's decision, the appellate court's decision becomes the law in that judicial circuit. As discussed in Section 3 of this chapter, the Supreme Court does not—and cannot—review all appellate court decisions.

Critics contend that the powers of the federal courts should be checked. Currently, there is a movement in Congress to rein in the power of the federal courts, particularly judicial activism. Others, however, believe that there are already enough checks on the power of the courts.

What Checks Our Courts?

Our judicial system is probably the most independent in the world. But the courts do not have absolute independence, for they are part of the political

◄ *The Supreme Court made headlines with the* Dred Scott *decision of 1857, which outraged many Americans in the North. What checks exist to limit the power of the highest court in the land?*

process. Political checks limit the extent to which courts can exercise judicial review and make activist changes.

These checks are exercised by the legislature, the executive branch, other courts, and the public.

Legislative Checks Courts may make rulings, but often the funds to carry out those rulings must be appropriated by legislatures at the local, state, and federal levels. When such funds are not appropriated, the courts in effect have been checked. A court, for example, may decide that prison conditions must be

The Rights of the Accused

The rights of persons accused of crimes have been expanded by Supreme Court decisions, particularly in the 1960s. For example, in 1963 the Court ruled that criminal defendants have the right to an attorney, even if the government must pay the attorney's fees. In 1966, the Court held that all suspects in criminal cases have the right to be informed of their constitutional rights, including the right to be silent. This is known as the *Miranda* ruling. In 1968, the Court granted the right to a jury trial in all criminal cases in which the penalty for conviction is more than six months' imprisonment.

Some believe that the Supreme Court has gone too far in defending the constitutional rights of the accused. Has it?

Yes, the Supreme Court Has Gone Too Far, Say Some

Those who believe that the Supreme Court has gone too far in protecting the rights of the accused point out that the increase in crime in the United States since World War II has paralleled the increase in the rights of the accused. They argue that protecting these rights ties the hands of the police and public prosecutors, thereby reducing the effectiveness of the government's war against crime.

Furthermore, they argue that because the rights of the accused have been so well publicized, actual and potential criminals are aware of their ability to get off on a "technicality" (such as a procedural error). Thus, they are on the watch for any improper action on the part of law enforcement personnel. Consequently, the expected punishment of those committing crimes has fallen, leading to more crime.

No, the Supreme Court Has Not Gone Too Far, Say Others

Others argue that the Supreme Court has not gone too far in protecting the rights of accused persons. In fact, claim these people, Court decisions during the 1980s have threatened the rights of the accused, particularly under the exclusionary rule. (Remember from Chapter 6 that under this rule, any evidence obtained illegally—such as without a search warrant if one is required—will not be admitted at trial.) For example, in an important case in 1984, *United States v. Leon,* the Supreme Court allowed a conviction to stand even though a judge had issued a warrant without firmly establishing probable cause. In this case, the Court created the *good faith exception* to the exclusionary rule. As long as the police are acting in good faith, they may not have violated the rights of the accused.

improved, but if a legislature does not find the funds to carry out the ruling, the decision has little effect.

Court rulings can also be overturned by constitutional amendments at both the federal and state levels. Many amendments to the U.S. Constitution check the state courts' ability to allow discrimination, for example. Recently, however, proposals to amend the Constitution in order to reverse court decisions on school prayer, flag burning, and abortion have failed.

Finally, legislatures can pass new laws that overturn court rulings. This may happen when a court interprets a statute in a way that Congress did not intend. The legislature can pass a new statute to counter the court's ruling.

Executive Checks The president has the power to change the direction of the Supreme Court and the federal judiciary by appointing new justices and judges whose ideologies are more in line with those of the current administration. Furthermore, a president,

A police sergeant guards the intersection near a private residence in Detroit after three officers were shot and hospitalized during an attempted search for illegal narcotics. In an effort to obtain evidence legally, the officers had brought a search warrant, issued by the judge after they had firmly established probable cause. One person in the house came out firing a gun. Were the gunman's rights being violated?

Additionally, the Supreme Court has slowly eroded the *Miranda* ruling. Today, confessions are admissible even without clear evidence that they were voluntary. Confessions by criminal suspects who have not been fully informed of their legal rights may be taken into consideration. The Court has also ruled that when "public safety" requires action, police can question a suspect before advising that person of his or her right to remain silent.

YOU DECIDE

1. In your opinion, has the Supreme Court gone too far in protecting the rights of accused persons?
2. Who would suffer the most if the Supreme Court were to reverse the decisions of previous Courts with respect to the rights of the accused?

governor, or mayor can refuse to enforce a court's rulings. As President Andrew Jackson once said, in response to a ruling by Chief Justice Marshall concerning Native Americans, "John Marshall has made his decision. Now let him enforce it."

The Rest of the Judiciary Higher courts can reverse the decisions of lower courts, but lower courts can also put a check on higher courts. The Supreme Court, for example, cannot possibly hear all of the cases that go through the lower courts. Lower courts can directly or indirectly ignore Supreme Court decisions by deciding in the other direction in particular cases. Only if a case goes to the Supreme Court can the Court correct such a situation.

Public Checks History has shown members of the

Just the Facts

The Supreme Court originally had just six members and has had as many as ten.

▲ *Chief Justice Roger B. Taney wrote the majority opinion in the* Dred Scott *decision. How did the southern loyalties of the justices influence the decision in this case?*

1. How do the courts make policy?
2. Briefly describe the practices of judicial activism and judicial restraint.
3. What checks are placed on the courts?
4. **For Critical Analysis:** What type of president normally wants to nominate a Supreme Court justice who exercises judicial restraint?

★ ★ ★ ★ Chapter Summary ★ ★ ★ ★

Section 1: Sources of American Law

⬟ The common law began centuries ago in England and today, in the United States, includes the case law made in this country since the Revolution.

⬟ Constitutions are another source of law. In the United States, the Constitution is the supreme law of the land.

⬟ Another source of American law is statutory law—law enacted by state legislatures and the U.S. Congress.

⬟ Civil law spells out the duties that exist between persons or between citizens and their governments. Criminal law has to do with wrongs committed against the public as a whole.

Section 2: The Federal Court System

⬟ The federal court system is a three-tiered structure that consists of district courts, courts of appeals, and the Supreme Court.

⬟ U.S. district courts are trial courts. Decisions of district courts may be appealed to U.S. courts of appeals. Each of these is located in a judicial circuit, and there are thirteen circuits.

⬟ Jurisdiction refers to the authority of a court to decide a certain case. Federal courts have jurisdiction in cases involving federal questions or diversity of citizenship.

⬟ Concurrent jurisdiction exists when a case can be heard in either a federal or a state court. Exclusive jurisdiction exists when a case can be heard only in a federal court or only in a state court.

Supreme Court that if their decisions are noticeably at odds with public opinion, the Court will lose its support and some of its power. Perhaps the best example was the *Dred Scott* decision of 1857. In that decision, the Supreme Court held that slaves were not citizens of the United States and were not entitled to the rights and privileges of citizenship. The Court ruled, in addition, that the Missouri Compromise banning slavery in the territories was unconstitutional. Most observers contend that the *Dred Scott* ruling contributed to making the Civil War inevitable.

Observers of the court system believe that the judges' sense of self-preservation forces them to develop self-restraint. Some observers even argue that this self-restraint is more important than the other checks previously discussed.

Section 3: The Supreme Court

- Thousands of cases are filed with the Supreme Court each year, yet on average, it hears less than one hundred.
- To bring a case before the Supreme Court, a party requests the Court to issue a writ of *certiorari*, which is an order issued to a lower court requiring it to send the record of the case in question. Whether the Court will issue the writ is entirely within its discretion.
- The Court's decisions are written in opinions. When all justices agree, the opinion is unanimous. If there is no unanimous opinion, concurring and dissenting opinions may be written.
- During the Court's annual term, the justices meet regularly in conference to discuss cases under consideration and to decide which new appeals and petitions the Court will accept.

Section 4: Supreme Court Appointments and Ideology

- Supreme Court justices are nominated by the president and confirmed by the Senate.
- Ideology plays an important role in the president's choices and in the Senate's confirmation.

Section 5: The Federal Courts as Policymakers

- Today's courts play a significant policymaking role in government, particularly by exercising the power of judicial review, which allows the courts to determine whether a law or presidential action is constitutional.
- Those practicing judicial activism believe the Court should use its power to alter the direction of the activities of Congress, state legislatures, and administrative agencies.
- Those practicing judicial restraint believe the Court should only rarely use its powers of judicial review.
- Political checks limit the extent to which courts can exercise judicial review. The legislature, the executive branch, other courts, and the public all place checks on the courts.

★ REVIEW QUESTIONS ★

1. What is the common law?
2. What is the difference between civil law and criminal law?
3. Briefly describe the three-tiered structure of the federal court system.
4. What is the role of the courts of appeals in the federal court system?
5. What is meant by *jurisdiction*?
6. What was the significance of *Marbury v. Madison*?
7. How do cases reach the Supreme Court?
8. In what general situations will the Supreme Court typically issue a writ of *certiorari*?
9. Describe the four types of written opinions that can be presented by the Supreme Court.
10. Briefly describe the procedures the Supreme Court justices follow when deciding a case.
11. How are federal judges appointed? For how long do they hold office?
12. Name some common characteristics of Supreme Court justices.
13. How does ideology come into play when Supreme Court justices are appointed?
14. How do the federal courts make policy?
15. What is judicial review?
16. Define the practices of judicial activism and judicial restraint.
17. What political checks limit the extent to which the courts can exercise judicial review and make activist changes?

★ CRITICAL THINKING ★

1. Do you think it is a good idea that Supreme Court justices are appointed for life? What are the advantages and disadvantages of this arrangement?
2. Do you think federal judges should be popularly elected? What qualifications would you like to see in a federal judge?
3. Some analysts argue that the federal courts often make the law instead of interpreting it. Do you agree or disagree with this statement? Give reasons for your answer.
4. Sometimes a case arises for which there is no precedent. How do you think a judge should decide such a case?

★ IMPROVING YOUR SKILLS ★

Communication Skills

Conducting an Interview Interviewing people who have worked in and around government is an excellent way of learning more about how our government works. These people can often offer insights and first-hand information that is difficult to obtain by reading newspapers and watching the news.

To conduct a successful interview, you will need to be well prepared and organized. With careful preparation and a sound strategy, you can present yourself effectively and obtain the information you want. Follow these guidelines:

- **Arrange the details, in person or by telephone, with the person to be interviewed.** Politely and clearly identify yourself, your school, and your teacher. Tell the person why you would like the interview. If the person agrees, suggest a few different times and dates that might be convenient for the person. Try to arrange a setting that is convenient for both of you, but also try to choose a location where you will not be interrupted. You want to have your subject's undivided attention. Interruptions, such as telephone calls, will distract the subject, break the rapport you are developing, and stretch out the time the interview takes.
- **Decide in advance what information you want to obtain from the interview.** Think about what questions you could ask to get that information. Prioritize the questions, taking into consideration the amount of

time you will have with that person. Avoid questions that the person can answer with a simple "yes" or "no." Try to ask questions that will encourage the person to go into detail about the subject matter. In addition, gather some background information on the person you intend to interview. If you do this research, it may keep you from asking an ignorant or offensive question that could derail your entire interview.

- **Write down a formal list of questions.** If you are working in a group, decide who will ask which questions and in what order. Ask your teacher to review the questions.
- **Practice asking the questions of classmates.**
- **During the interview, try to make the person feel welcome and comfortable.** Don't just be on time for your interview. Plan to arrive early. In this way, you can size up the subject's environment, and sometimes you can get more time with your subject than would have been possible otherwise. If you are late, you may find that your subject has decided to cancel the interview or will not give you as much time as originally planned. When you arrive, remind your subject who you are, and why you wanted the interview. Encourage the person to use examples and stories. If possible, use each answer as a springboard for the next question. If you listen carefully and respond appropriately, you can lead your subject smoothly into the next question you had planned to ask.
- **After the interview, thank the person.** When you have finished asking all the questions on your list, give your subject an opportunity to speak. You might ask, "Is there anything else you would like to say?" Often, there is. Then, thank the person and leave. Send a thank-you note as a final follow-up. Write up your notes that you took during the interview as soon as possible, while you still remember exactly what the subject said.

Writing Suppose you have the opportunity to interview a Supreme Court justice. Decide what information you would most like to obtain from this person. Create a formal list of ten questions, written down in order of priority. Give a brief explanation of why you think each of these questions is important.

Social Studies Skills

Map Reading Carefully examine Figure 20–2 on page 540. How does the size of the judicial districts in the East compare with the size of those in the West? How would you explain this difference?

★ ACTIVITIES AND PROJECTS ★

1. Research a presidential appointee to the Supreme Court who has been rejected by the Senate. In your research, try to find out why the Senate opposed the nominee. Then decide whether you think the Senate's decision was correct. Report your findings to the class.
2. Sit in on a jury trial, taking note of what the issue is, who the accused is, and what arguments are made by the two opposing sides. Write a summary of what happened during the time you spent at the trial.
3. Stage a debate in class on the following statement: "The make-up of the federal judiciary should better reflect the make-up of the nation in terms of gender, ethnicity, and race."
4. With your teacher's assistance, prepare for and stage a mock trial within your classroom. Students should serve as the prosecuting and defense attorneys, and other students as the jury. Your teacher could serve as the judge.

What If . . .

Supreme Court Justices Were Elected?

Currently, Supreme Court justices are appointed for life. Is it possible that they might act differently if they were elected? Explain.

The Power of the Federal Courts

Recently, many Americans have criticized federal court judges for using their power of judicial review to overturn laws enacted by legislatures. They argue that the Constitution authorizes Congress, not the courts, to make laws. They contend that is inappropriate for federal judges, who are not elected and therefore not "accountable" to the people, to decide on important policy matters. Several legislators in the 105th Congress introduced bills that would limit the policy-making powers of the federal courts. These attempts, in turn, have been criticized by those who maintain that Congress should leave the courts alone. Here are some media reports dealing with this controversy.

Source Documents

To Some, It's the Most Dangerous Branch

by Harvey Berkman and Marcia Coyle,
National Law Journal

Limiting the power of the judiciary, the branch that the Founding Fathers considered the least dangerous, was the subject of hearings by Congress, the branch that worried the Founders most.

The House Judiciary Subcommittee on Courts and Intellectual Property held hearings May 14 and 15 on the suggestion that judicial activism be considered an impeachable offense and on a bill to constrain the authority of federal judges.

Rep. Tom DeLay, R-Texas, the leading congressional voice for impeaching activists, told the committee: "The system of checks and balances so carefully crafted by our Founding Fathers is in serious disrepair" due to the assumption by activist judges of the legislature's law-making power.

Source: *The National Law Journal*, May 26, 1997. © 1998, The New York Law Publishing Company. Reprinted with permission. All rights reserved.

"Activist" Label Actively Applied

by Richard Willing, *USA Today*

Coming up with a definition of "judicial activism" that all can agree on may be Orrin Hatch's toughest task.

The Utah [Republican] senator has his own definition: a judge who does not "appreciate the inherent limits on judicial authority under the Constitution" but who seeks to "legislate from the bench." . . .

In practice, "activists" often turn out to be judges who make decisions conservatives or liberals oppose.

Says Joel Grossman, professor of history and law at Johns Hopkins University: "Judicial activism is not the property of the left. . . . Basically, judicial activism is what the other guy does that you don't like."

Source: *USA Today*, March 10, 1997 (p. 3A). © 1997 USA Today. Reprinted with permission.

Clinton Accuses GOP of Crippling Judiciary

Associated Press, *The Chicago Tribune*

Warning of a crisis in the nation's courthouses, President Clinton accused Republicans of resorting to "the worst of partisan politics" to block his nominations of dozens of federal judges.

With 100 vacant judicial seats across America, Clinton declared, "We can't let partisan politics shut down our courts and gut our judicial system."

In his weekly radio address Saturday, Clinton joined in a rancorous congressional debate between Democrats and Republicans over lifetime judicial appointments. Clinton said the resulting impasse poses "a very real threat to our judicial system" by leaving courts clogged with unheard cases.

Clinton . . . said he has sent the Senate 70 nominations this year to cut back on the 100 vacant federal judgeships, but lawmakers have acted on only 18. . . .

Republicans contend they simply are trying to assure the judges are well qualified and won't devote themselves to politically motivated activist decisions.

Source: *The Chicago Tribune*, September 28, 1997 (p. 8). Reprinted with the permission of The Associated Press.

A Case of High Regard for the High Court

by Robert Marquand, *The Christian Science Monitor*, as quoted in *The Sunday Oregonian*

These days, in marked contrast to a White House nagged by scandal and a Congress often locked in partisan bickering, the Supreme Court is riding high in terms of its public image and esteem.

The court does not have the power of the purse or sword, but Americans continue to trust it as a fair arbiter of the nation's business—more so than other branches of government, recent surveys say. . . .

The justices don't need to campaign for office every few years; they were selected for life. They don't need speech writers or have to check the polls. The current justices, unlike earlier courts, generally write their own opinions. They are free to dissent. Their rulings are not tied to interest-group pressure.

Source: *The Christian Science Monitor*, quoted in *The Sunday Oregonian*, June 29, 1997 (pp. E1 and E2). Reprinted with permission.

Conclusion

To date, Congress has not passed any laws that would significantly restrain the power of the federal courts, particularly the power of judicial review. As is evident, one problem lies in how to define judicial activism. If judges could be impeached for activist decisions, who would decide what constitutes an activist decision? In the meantime, as the final reading above indicates, the Supreme Court is held in high regard by the American public. There are many who would not like to see its power to check the actions of Congress diminished.

Analysis Questions

1. Why is it difficult to determine which judicial decisions are activist?
2. Suppose that the federal courts could not exercise the power of judicial review. How would this affect our democracy?
3. In a democracy, should unelected court judges have the power to overrule decisions made by the elected representatives of the people?
4. If the decision were yours to make, would you curb the federal courts' powers in any way? Explain.

American Policy in a Changing World

The nation's most famous address—1600 Pennsylvania Avenue—officially is known as the Executive Mansion. This mansion is much more commonly referred to as the White House.

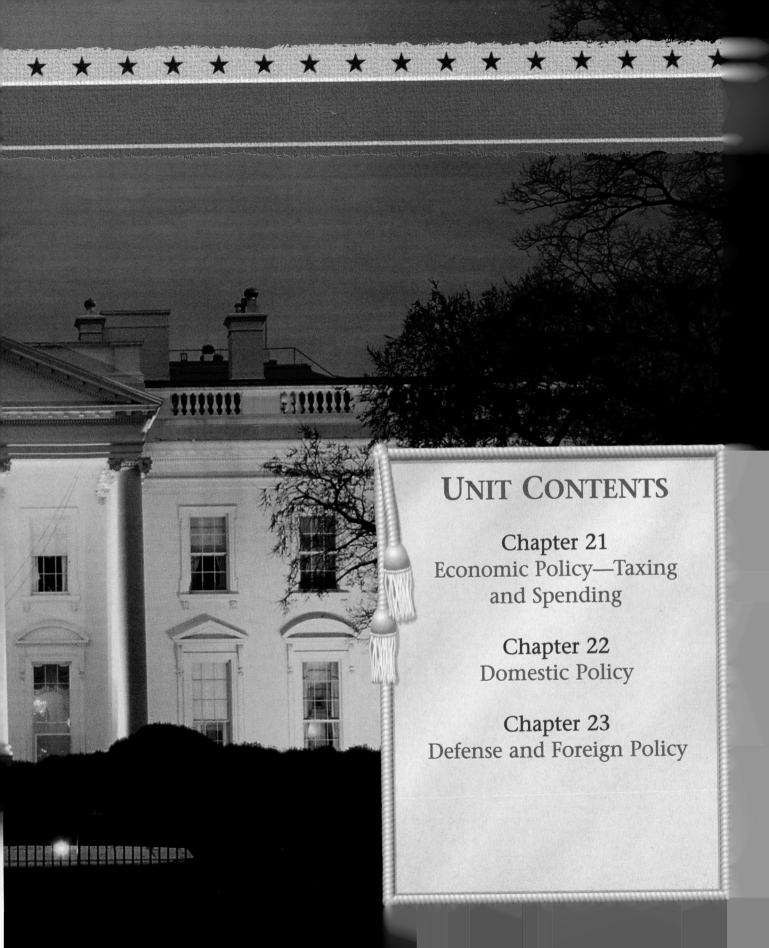

CHAPTER 21

Economic Policy—Taxing and Spending

CHAPTER OBJECTIVES

To learn about and understand . . .

⭐ The basic principles and types of taxation

⭐ U.S. government spending and why it has grown

⭐ Monetary policy and how it is used as a tool for managing the economy

⭐ Fiscal policy and the growth of the public debt

"Nothing is so well calculated to produce a death-like torpor in the country as an extended system of taxation and a great national debt."

William Cobbett

(1762–1835)
English Journalist and Reformer

INTRODUCTION

You pay taxes on many of the goods and services you buy and use every day. The taxes we pay create revenues for various local, state, and federal governments. Those revenues allow governments to provide important public services, such as the school you attend and the roads on which you drive. The U.S. government has typically spent more than it has received in taxes. The result has been a "great national debt" such as the one referred to in William Cobbett's quotation above. Cobbett believed that an extended taxation system, plus a large national debt, would prevent a nation from making progress. Yet we have one of the strongest economies on earth in spite of our taxes and in spite of our national debt.

In this chapter, we look at how the national government taxes and how it spends. In addition, we examine how the national government tries to keep the economy on an even keel.

◀ Our tax dollars are at work as road crews repair the Oakland Bay Bridge in California.

563

Preview Questions:

- What is the benefits-received principle of taxation?
- What is the ability-to-pay principle of taxation?
- What are the major types of taxes?
- What is the difference between proportional, progressive, and regressive tax systems?
- How do taxes direct economic activity?

Key Terms:

benefits-received principle, ability-to-pay principle, sacrifice principle, proportional taxation, progressive taxation, marginal tax rate, regressive taxation

Governments—national, state, and local—have various methods of taxation at their disposal. The best known of these is the federal personal income tax system. At the state and local levels, property taxes make up the bulk of the taxes collected. In addition to these taxes, there are corporate income taxes, sales taxes, excise taxes, inheritance taxes, and gift taxes. About 85 percent of all national, state, and local government revenues come from taxation.

Principles of Taxation

Different levels of taxation can be justified according to three major principles.

Benefits-Received Principle Under the **benefits-received principle,** those who use a particular government service support it with taxes in proportion to the benefits they receive. Those who do not use the service do not pay taxes for it. For example, a gasoline tax to pay for highway construction and repair is based on this principle. Those who use the highways usually buy more gasoline and therefore pay more in gasoline taxes.

A tax based on the benefits-received principle is useful in raising funds to pay for a service used only by certain individuals. Many government services, however, such as national defense, benefit everyone equally. Furthermore, sometimes those who most need certain services, such as older people and poor people, are the ones least able to pay taxes for them.

Ability-to-Pay Principle Under the **ability-to-pay principle,** those with higher incomes pay more in taxes than those with lower incomes, regardless of the number of government services they use.

The Sacrifice Principle The third principle of taxation, the **sacrifice principle,** holds that the sacrifices people make to pay their taxes should be equitable, or fair. In its effects, this principle is similar to the ability-to-pay principle. This is because it is generally assumed that the sacrifices people make when paying taxes to the government become smaller as their incomes become larger. A millionaire paying a $100 tax is surely sacrificing less than a person who earns $10,000 a year and pays the same tax. The problem with this principle is determining how to make everyone's sacrifice equitable.

Forms of Taxation

Taxes can be classified in three ways, depending on their effects on those who are taxed. Figure 21–1 on page 565 shows the major types of taxes in this country and indicates the form of each type.

Proportional Taxation **Proportional taxation** is a system by which taxpayers pay a fixed percentage of every dollar of income. When their incomes increase or decrease, the taxes they pay increase or decrease, accordingly. If the proportional tax rate is 10 percent, you pay ten cents in taxes out of every dollar you earn. If you earn $1,000, you pay $100 in taxes; if you earn $1,000,000, you pay $100,000 in taxes. Figure 21–2 on page 565 illustrates the principle of proportional taxation.

Progressive Taxation With **progressive taxation,** the actual *percentage* of taxes paid—the tax rate—rises as income rises. The progressive system can be described as a system in which the marginal tax rate increases. The **marginal tax rate** is the rate paid on *additional*

Tax	Description	Type (Progressive, Regressive, or Proportional)
Personal income	Tax paid as a percentage of income. This is the major source of revenue for the national government. Many states and some local governments also levy personal income taxes.	Progressive at the national level but sometimes proportional at the state level
Social insurance (Social Security)	Tax covered by the Federal Insurance Contributions Act (FICA). This is the second largest source of U.S. government revenue.	Proportional up to $68,400 in 1998, regressive above that
Corporate income	Tax paid to the national government as a percentage of corporate profits. Some states also levy corporate income taxes.	At the national level, progressive up to $100,000, proportional above that
Excise	Tax paid by the consumer on the manufacture, use, or consumption of certain goods. The major national excise taxes are on alcohol, tobacco, and gasoline. Some states also levy excise taxes.	Generally regressive
Estate	U.S. government tax on the property of someone who has died. Some states also levy an estate tax.	Progressive; percentage of tax increases with the value of the estate
Inheritance	Tax paid by those who inherit property from someone who has died. This is a state tax only.	Varies by state
Gift	Tax paid by the person who gives a gift. This is a tax of the national government only.	Progressive; percentage increases with the value of the gift
Sales	Tax paid on purchases. Almost all states, as well as many local governments, levy a sales tax. The rate varies from state to state and within states. Items that are taxed also vary from state to state. Some states tax clothing, but many states do not.	Generally regressive
Property	State and local taxation on the value of property. Both real property, such as buildings and land, and personal property, such as stocks, bonds, and home furnishings, may be taxed.	Proportional; percentage is set by state and local governments
Custom duties	Tax on imports that is paid by the importer.	Proportional

FIGURE 21–2 Proportional Tax System This table illustrates the principle of proportional taxation. At the same proportional tax rate, how much tax would be paid on total income of $650?

Income	Proportional Rate	Tax
First $100	10%	$10
Second $100	10%	$10
Third $100	10%	$10
Total Income: $300	Total Tax: $30	

amounts of income. Figure 21–3 on page 566 illustrates the principle of progressive taxation.

Regressive Taxation As you might expect, **regressive taxation** is the opposite of progressive taxation. In a regressive tax system, the rate of taxation decreases as income rises. For example, imagine that all government revenues are obtained from a 50 percent tax on food. Generally, the percentage of income spent on food falls as the total income rises. Therefore, the percentage of total income paid in taxes under such a

FIGURE 21–3 Progressive Tax System This table illustrates the principle of progressive taxation. Which individuals in a society are most likely to feel that a progressive tax system is unfair?

Income	Marginal Rate	Tax
First $100	10%	$10
Second $100	20%	$20
Third $100	30%	$30
Total Income: $300		Total Tax: $60

How Our Progressive National Income Tax System Evolved

The Constitution, in Article I, Section 8, gives Congress the authority "to lay and collect taxes, duties, imposts and excises." No reference was made to an income tax at the time the Constitution was drafted. In 1894, however, the Wilson-Gorman Tariff Act was passed. It provided for individual income taxes of 2 percent on incomes above $4,000. The country knew about income taxes from the period during the Civil War, when taxes amounting to $4.4 million had been collected. Nonetheless, the concept of income taxation set forth by the Wilson-Gorman Tariff Act was aggressively challenged, and in 1895 the Supreme Court ruled that it was unconstitutional.

system would likewise fall as income rises. This would be a regressive taxation plan. Some examples of regressive taxes are sales taxes on food and clothing, the Social Security tax, and the excise tax on gasoline.

▶ Although it may be hard to believe, there were actually celebrations in the street when the Sixteenth Amendment, which instituted the income tax, was adopted. At that time, Thomas Woodrow Wilson was president of the United States. Not everyone was cheering, however, as you can see by this 1913 political cartoon. What is the cartoonist's point about income tax?

"OH TOMMY!"

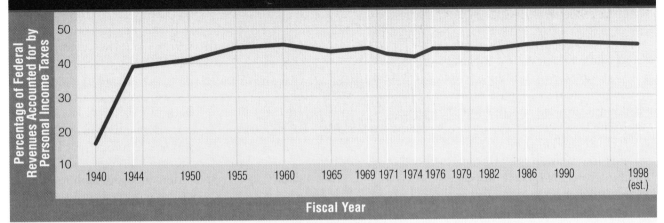

FIGURE 21–4 Federal Revenues Accounted for by Personal Income Taxes, 1940 to Present This graph shows the percentage of national government revenues that are accounted for by personal income taxes. During which period of time did this percentage show its most dramatic increase?

SOURCE: U.S. Department of the Treasury.

Finally, in 1913, the Sixteenth Amendment was passed. It reads as follows:

The Congress shall have power to lay and collect taxes on incomes, from whatever source derived, without apportionment among the several states, and without regard to any census or enumeration.

Congress responded by passing the Underwood-Simmons Tariff Act of 1913. Section 2 of the act provided for a 1 percent rate on taxable income with an exemption of $3,000 plus an additional exemption of $1,000 for a married head of household. The concept of exempting the first several thousand dollars of income from taxes has continued to the present time in the form of personal exemptions and standard deductions.

The Underwood-Simmons Tariff Act also provided for a surtax (an additional tax). This tax was levied progressively on incomes over $20,000, with a maximum total tax rate of 7 percent on incomes over $500,000. These taxes may seem paltry in comparison to today's rates, but they were considered quite large in those times. The concept of progressiveness introduced in 1913 met with considerable debate, which continued for several years thereafter.

Undoubtedly, progressiveness is here to stay, at least in principle. The progressive nature of our personal income tax system is much less obvious than it once was, however. For some time prior to 1961, the maximum marginal tax rate was over 90 percent. Various tax reform measures over the years since then have reduced the maximum tax rate. Today, it is 39.6 percent.

Personal income taxes are the largest and the most important source of tax revenues for the national government. In 1940, individual income taxes accounted for 15.5 percent of U.S. government revenues. Now, individual income taxes account for 44 percent of U.S. government revenues, as shown in Figure 21–4 above.

Just the Facts

The average American worked until May 9 in 1998 to pay for all the federal, state, and local taxes due that year.

Taxation as a Way of Directing Economic Activity

Taxation is more than a way for government to raise revenues. It is also a way for government to direct how businesses and individuals use resources, as well as a way to regulate economic activity.

Taxes are commonly used to encourage certain activities by businesses and individuals. Often, cities and states temporarily reduce or eliminate business taxes for companies as a way of persuading them to locate in a particular area. Governments at all levels

Economic information encompasses a wide variety of subjects including international trade, distribution of resources, business, transportation, agriculture, and manufacturing. It can also include data relating to unemployment rates, rates of economic growth, and the cost of living.

One method of finding economic information is by reading and interpreting special-purpose maps, such as economic maps. These maps communicate specific sets of economic data.

To accurately read an economic map, you need to determine what kind of economic information the map

Reading Maps for Economic Information

provides and then use the map to help you draw conclusions about the topic.

Study the map presented in this feature, and then answer the following questions.

1. What percentage of states qualify as having "low taxes"?
2. What percentage of states qualify as having "very high taxes"?
3. Is there any geographic pattern with respect to where the low-tax states are concentrated?

Estimated Total Tax Bill for Middle-Class Families in the Fifty States, 1998

- Very high taxes (annual taxes of $4,000 and over)
- High taxes (annual taxes of $3,500–3,999)
- Medium taxes (annual taxes of $2,500–3,499)
- Low taxes (annual taxes of less than $2,495)

Participating in YOUR GOVERNMENT

Responsible Driving and Traffic-Law Violations

Contrary to one old saying, laws—particularly when they are traffic laws—are *not* meant to be broken. Traffic laws are created for one purpose only: to make driving a safe experience. As a responsible citizen, you have a duty to obey all traffic laws in your community and in any other location whenever you are driving. If individuals didn't follow traffic laws, driving would be much more dangerous. Indeed, deaths on the highway remain a serious problem in this country; but many more deaths per passenger miles driven occur in countries in which the citizens do not obey traffic laws as well as we do.

If you do violate a traffic law and are pulled over by a police officer, you may get a traffic ticket. Traffic tickets are issued by state and local authorities to motorists who ignore or abuse their responsibilities and violate traffic laws. The ticket usually indicates the type, location, and date of the offense and when the offender should appear in court. Ignoring a traffic ticket can result in an increase in the fine or even in arrest.

If you receive a traffic ticket, you have a duty to follow your state's procedures. Essentially, you have two choices. Usually, you can mail in a check or a money order in the amount specified on the ticket (if your state allows this). If you feel you were unfairly ticketed, however, you can choose to appear in court at the time and location specified on the ticket. You may plead not guilty, or you may plead guilty and explain the special circumstances that influenced your action. For example, you might protest a ticket for an illegal left turn if the "No Left Turn" sign was painted over with graffiti. The judge will listen to your argument and then make a decision, which may be no penalty, a reduced penalty, or the full penalty.

TAKING ACTION

1. Obtain a listing of the fines for various traffic-law violations in your state. Write a paragraph describing why the most expensive fines are so costly.
2. Write a description of what might occur if there were no traffic laws.

---

encourage investment in their bonds by offering tax-free interest. Taxes are also used to direct resources toward investments that are desirable but costly. For example, many states encourage homeowners to insulate their homes by allowing homeowners to deduct insulation costs from their income before calculating their state income taxes.

Taxes can also be used to discourage certain activities. Excise taxes, for example, are supposed to discourage the use of such items as cigarettes and gasoline. Customs duties are supposed to reduce sales of imported goods. Other taxes are used as penalties for certain actions. For example, people who withdraw money from certain types of individual retirement accounts (IRAs) before the age of 59½ must pay 10 percent of the amount withdrawn as a federal tax penalty.

Government officials must keep in mind that individuals and businesses may react to changes in tax rates. For example, raising taxes in a state or city can actually decrease revenues if businesses and homeowners move away to escape the higher taxes. In contrast, a city can find itself short of funds if it grants too many tax reductions to try to attract businesses. As you can imagine, this forces cities to make difficult decisions. Thus, government officials must try to strike a balance between too many and too few taxes.

THE GLOBAL VIEW

Comparing the Tax Burden across Countries

It may seem that the U.S. taxpayer is overburdened with taxes. After all, the average American worker works well into the month of May before having earned enough to pay all national, state, and local taxes for that year. Nonetheless, income and Social Security taxes are lower for U.S. workers than for workers in many other countries, as you can see in the bar graph below. Note, though, that many of the countries listed in the chart provide their citizens with a greater array of expensive social services—such as health care, child care, elder care, and higher education—than does the United States.

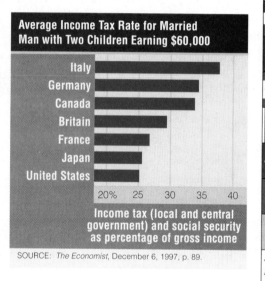

Average Income Tax Rate for Married Man with Two Children Earning $60,000

Italy
Germany
Canada
Britain
France
Japan
United States

20%   25   30   35   40

Income tax (local and central government) and social security as percentage of gross income

SOURCE: *The Economist*, December 6, 1997, p. 89.

THINKING GLOBALLY

Would you be willing to pay more in taxes to obtain the greater array of government-provided services characteristic of many European countries?

▲ *One of the ways in which government promotes citizen behavior it wants to encourage is to reward it financially. Some states allow homeowners to deduct from their taxable income the cost of insulating their homes. Why would the government care if homes are adequately insulated?*

SECTION 1 REVIEW

1. What is the difference between the benefits-received principle and the ability-to-pay principle of taxation?
2. What is the sacrifice principle of taxation?
3. How do progressive, regressive, and proportional tax systems differ?
4. What type of system is the personal income tax system used by the U.S. government?
5. How can taxes be used to direct economic activity?
6. **For Critical Analysis:** How might people's behavior change if they were subjected to higher and higher tax rates on their income?

Government Spending

Preview Questions:

- Why has government spending grown since the Great Depression?
- What is the true size of government spending today?
- How does the national government spend its revenues?

As you already know, government is involved in virtually every aspect of your life. Government has grown considerably in size since the Great Depression. Just prior to the Great Depression, civilian government employees at all levels of government totaled about three million. During the Depression, a need for more government services arose. Today, almost three million people work for the national government alone. If you add local and state levels, government employs nearly twenty million civilian workers. This figure represents more than a sixfold increase during a period in which the population only doubled.

Now consider how much the government actually spends on salaries and benefits for its workers, plus national defense, public works, and other projects. Look at Figure 21–5 on page 572. There you can see what has happened with respect to government spending on goods and services from 1959 to the present.

As you can see from the figure, different levels of government have grown at different rates. Up to the mid-1960s, state and local governments spent less than the national government. Since the mid-1960s, however, state and local governments have spent more than the national government. Today, total government spending on goods and services represents a little more than 20 percent of all of the income earned in the nation each year.

Why Has Government Grown?

Researchers have tried to explain the rapid growth in total government spending since the Great Depression. One theory is that, especially in the late 1960s and early 1970s, people demanded more government services to even out certain income inequalities. Although the

▲ *No matter how small or how large the town or city is, residents have come to expect many kinds of municipal services, from trash collection to medical services. Here, a woman visits City Hall to inquire about the various city services that are available to her.*

nation as a whole was becoming richer, certain groups were suffering from poverty. During the 1960s, the national government launched several new programs to help these groups. The Medicare program, for example, was created to help older Americans obtain medical care. Operation Head Start was launched to help educate disadvantaged children.

These and numerous other government projects and programs all required government employees to administer them. The result was a vastly expanded federal bureaucracy and workforce.

In the late 1970s and early 1980s, however, the economy suffered a series of slowdowns. Americans began to feel that maintaining all the programs they wanted was too costly. To remedy this situation, politicians began to think of ways to cut government spending. In fact, the rate of growth of government

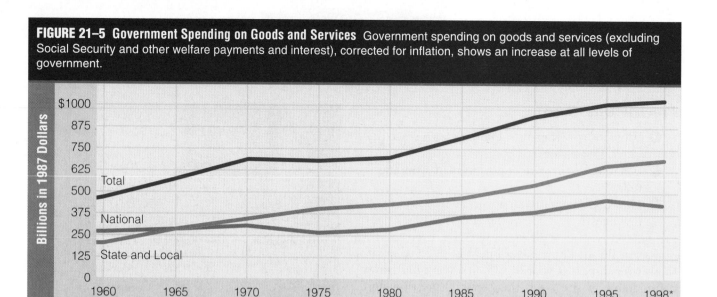

FIGURE 21–5 Government Spending on Goods and Services Government spending on goods and services (excluding Social Security and other welfare payments and interest), corrected for inflation, shows an increase at all levels of government.

Billions in 1987 Dollars

Total

National

State and Local

$1000, 875, 750, 625, 500, 375, 250, 125, 0

1960 1965 1970 1975 1980 1985 1990 1995 1998*

Year

* Author's estimate.
SOURCE: *Economic Report of the President.*

spending—at the national level, at least—has slowed down for a while.

The True Size of Government

The true size of government is not indicated by government spending on public goods and services alone. To understand the true size of government, we need to consider spending on programs such as welfare and interest payments on the national debt. Look at Figure 21–6 on page 573. There you see the size of government spending on all programs. Since 1890, national government spending on all items has grown from about 8 percent of annual total national income to about 40 percent of annual total national income.

The spending reflected in Figure 21–6 may still fall short of real government spending. In order to avoid increasing obvious national government spending, Congress has passed laws requiring states, municipalities, and even private businesses to engage in certain actions. For example, when Congress passed laws requiring private businesses to accommodate workers

▲ *Workers at this training facility for disabled citizens learn skills that will help them find and keep jobs. To give these workers and others like them a chance for success, Congress requires that employers make accommodations for workers with disabilities.*

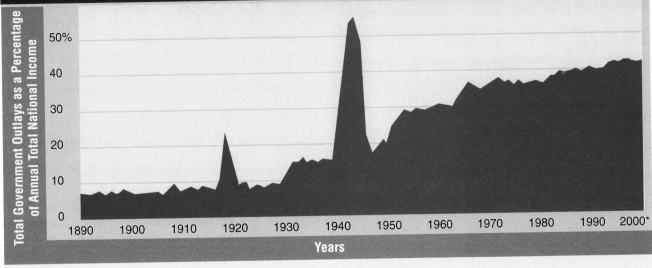

FIGURE 21–6 Total Government Outlays over Time Here you see that total government outlays (national, state, and local combined) remained small until the 1930s, except during World War I. Since World War II, government outlays have not fallen back to their historical average. Why is that?

*Author's estimate.
SOURCES: *Facts and Figures on Government Finance* and *Economic Indicators,* various issues.

with disabilities, this did not show up as an increase in government spending. Nonetheless, as a result of this law, individual businesses, as well as state and local governments, now incur extra costs in order to help persons with disabilities. These costs are properly a part of total national government spending, yet they do not show up in the statistics. That means that the true size of government may be even greater than government estimates show.

How the National Government Spends Its Revenues

Look at Figure 21–7. There you see a pie chart of how the national government spends its revenues. Two of the most important spending items are income security and Social Security. These programs are designed to keep peoples' incomes at certain levels when they are ill, unable to work, or retired.

National defense is also an important part of the U.S. government budget, but a declining one. Since the Cold War with the Soviet Union ended in the

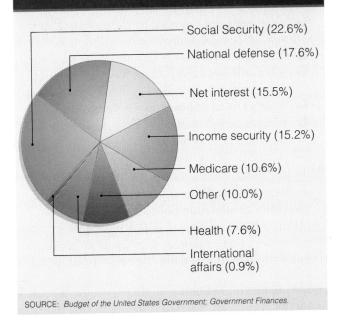

FIGURE 21–7 U.S. Government Spending Here you can see that the categories of most importance in the budget of the U.S. government are Social Security, national defense, and net interest. What types of projects and programs might the "other" category cover?

- Social Security (22.6%)
- National defense (17.6%)
- Net interest (15.5%)
- Income security (15.2%)
- Medicare (10.6%)
- Other (10.0%)
- Health (7.6%)
- International affairs (0.9%)

SOURCE: *Budget of the United States Government; Government Finances.*

early 1990s, U.S. government spending on defense has declined regularly. It probably will continue to do so in the foreseeable future.

Interest on the government debt (which you will read about later) is an item of importance in the national budget. This is similar to the interest you would pay if you borrowed funds—to buy a house, for example. These interest payments would constitute a real part of your budget. They constitute a real part of the U.S. government budget, too.

You can see that health-care expenditures, mainly in the form of Medicare, are another important part of the U.S. government budget. According to current projections, a rising share of the budget in years to come will go toward health care.

Expenditures on education, training, and employment make up a relatively small part of U.S. government spending. So, too, does the amount spent on veterans. Given that we have not had any major wars in recent years, spending on veterans should decline in the future.

SECTION 2 REVIEW

1. About how much did each level of government (national, state, and local) spend on goods and services in 1959? About how much does each of these levels of government spend today?
2. Why has the size of government spending increased so dramatically since the Great Depression of the 1930s?
3. Why might the true size of government be greater than government estimates show?
4. On what programs does the national government spend its revenues?
5. **For Critical Analysis:** Could we do without some of the programs administered and paid for by the national government? If so, which ones should be retained? Which ones should be eliminated? Give reasons for your answers.

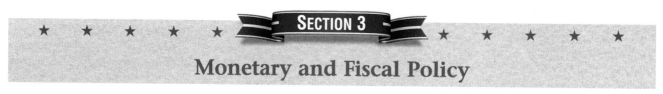

SECTION 3

Monetary and Fiscal Policy

Preview Questions:

- What are the tools used by the government to manage the economy?
- How does monetary policy affect the economy?
- What role does the Federal Reserve System play in the nation's economy?
- What is fiscal policy, and who determines it?
- What is deficit spending? How does the public debt affect the economy?

Key Terms:

monetary policy, Federal Reserve System, fiscal policy, loose monetary policy, tight monetary policy, inflation, business cycles, recession, depression, budget deficit, U.S. Treasury bonds, public debt, national debt, flat tax, off-budget items

Managing the economy is an important aspect of economic policy. In managing the economy, the U.S.

government uses two basic tools: monetary policy and fiscal policy. **Monetary policy** involves regulating the amount of money in circulation in order to control the economy. This is the responsibility of the **Federal Reserve System** (also known as "the Fed"), an independent regulatory agency that acts as the nation's central bank. **Fiscal policy,** which is the responsibility of the president and Congress, involves adjusting taxes and spending in an attempt to control the nation's economy.

Monetary Policy

Congress established the Federal Reserve System in 1913. It is led by a board of governors that consists of seven individuals, including the powerful chair. The Federal Reserve System is divided into twelve geographic districts. The Fed is an independent regulatory agency, which means that it is free from the direct political control of either Congress or the president. It has the vital responsibility of determining the nation's monetary and credit policies. All members of the Federal Reserve System's board of governors are appointed by the president, with the approval of the Senate. Each member can serve up to fourteen years on the board.

"Tight" versus "Loose" Monetary Policy

You may have read or heard a news report in which a business executive or public official complained that money was "too tight." Or you may have run across a story in which an economist warned that money was "too loose." In these cases, the terms *tight* and *loose* refer to the monetary policy of the Federal Reserve System, also known as the Fed. Monetary policy involves monitoring and adjusting how much money is in circulation. The amount of money in circulation affects the amount of credit available, which in turn affects business activity in the economy.

Credit allows individuals and businesses to buy goods and services with promise of payment later. Like any other good or service, credit has a cost. For people who want to buy items on credit, the cost is interest—the amount the creditor charges for use of the loaned funds. As interest rates (the cost of credit) increase, the extent to which businesses and consumers want to use credit decreases. In contrast, when the cost of credit drops, the amount of credit businesses and consumers want to use rises.

If the Fed is following a **loose monetary policy,** it is increasing the money supply—the amount of money in circulation. Credit is abundant and inexpensive to use, and people are usually willing to borrow more. Consumers will take out loans to buy new cars, new homes, and other items. Businesses will borrow to expand or to start new plants and hire more workers. These workers will have more income to spend. This, in turn, will stimulate further production.

If, in contrast, the Fed is following a **tight monetary policy,** it is decreasing the money supply. Credit is expensive and in short supply. Consumers may not buy as many new cars and homes. Business executives may postpone or cancel plans for expansion. Workers who become unemployed because of the business slowdown will have less income to spend. As a result, businesses may cut back even more. A weakening of the economy—perhaps even a serious decline—may follow.

Striking the Right Balance

Why would any nation want a tight money policy? The answer is that if money becomes too plentiful too quickly under a loose monetary policy, inflation may result. **Inflation** occurs when all prices increase, and the purchasing power of the dollar decreases. For example, during the Revolutionary War,

◀ Much of the federal government's financial activities take place in the U.S. Treasury Building.

the supply of Continental currency grew so rapidly that the notes became almost worthless. An expression that came out of the era was, "Not worth a Continental." The goal of monetary policy is to strike a balance between tight and loose money. It is the Federal Reserve's responsibility to ensure that money and credit are plentiful enough to allow the economy to expand. The Fed cannot, however, let the money supply become so plentiful that rapid inflation results.

The Federal Reserve System's Record In principle, the Federal Reserve's monetary policy is supposed to be countercyclical. To explain what this means, we need to consider that the economy regularly goes through

▶ This 1939 mural by Works Progress Administration (WPA) artists honors the concert given by African American opera singer Marian Anderson at the Lincoln Memorial. Why did the government pay artists to create such works as these?

ARCHITECTS

of Government

Alan Greenspan
(1926–   )

Alan Greenspan has served as chair of the board of governors of the Federal Reserve System since 1987. Born on March 6, 1926, Greenspan grew up in New York City. After attending the Juilliard School of Music in New York City and playing with a swing band for a year, he entered New York University to study economics. He received a Ph.D. from that institution in 1977. Before becoming chairman of the Fed's board of governors, he worked as an economic consultant, preparing forecasts and doing research for large firms and banking institutions.

HIS WORDS

"In any action—including leaving policy unchanged—we seek to assure ourselves that the expected benefits are large enough to risk the cost of a mistake."

(Testimony before the Joint Economic Committee in Congress, March 20, 1997)

"The information revolution, which lies behind so much of the rapid technological change that makes prices difficult to measure, may also play an important role in helping our statistical agencies acquire the necessary speed and agility to better capture the changes taking place in our economies."

(Address to the Center for Financial Studies, Frankfurt, Germany, November 7, 1997)

DEVELOPING
CRITICAL THINKING SKILLS

1. With respect to the first quotation, describe what benefits and costs might be involved in a Federal Reserve action.
2. With respect to the second quotation, why is it important for the Federal Reserve to capture the changes taking place in our economy?

up-and-down swings called **business cycles.** At one extreme of a business cycle is a **recession,** when unemployment is high and businesses are not working at full capacity. (Sometimes, this extreme is represented by a **depression,** which is a very bad recession.) At the other extreme is a boom time, when unemployment is low and businesses are operating at peak capacity. Booms often result in inflation.

In order for its policy to be countercyclical, the Federal Reserve must take actions that counter the trend of national business activity. Thus, during a boom, the Federal Reserve System might follow a tight monetary policy to prevent inflation. During a recession, it might use a loose monetary policy to stimulate business activity. Researchers who have watched the Fed since 1914, however, have concluded that often its actions have not been countercyclical because of the time it has taken the Federal Reserve System to act. By the time the Federal Reserve System started pumping money into the economy, for example, it was time to withdraw it. By the time it started reducing the rate of growth of the money supply, it was time to start increasing it.

Fiscal Policy

Monetary policy is carried out by the independent Federal Reserve System. Fiscal policy, in contrast, is determined by Congress and the president.

Traditionally, fiscal policy has involved lowering taxes during times of recession and raising them during times of inflation. Alternatively, fiscal policy may involve increasing government spending during times of recession and decreasing government spending during times of inflation. The goal of these activities is to manage the total demand for goods and services in the economy.

Fiscal policy can also include targeting specific aspects of society that are malfunctioning. For example, public works programs have been designed to use tax dollars directly to employ unemployed individuals.

Making Sense of Dollars and Cents

Every year, the U.S. Mint produces approximately twelve *billion* new pennies, and Americans promptly lose, store, mutilate, or otherwise dispose of half of them. That's six billion pennies rattling around people's dressers, jackets, car floors, and penny jars. These days, there is serious debate in Washington, D.C., over the fate of this coin.

The penny has its supporters and opponents. James Benfield, the founder and only paid employee of the Coin Coalition, an organization intent on getting rid of the penny, claims that "the penny's a nuisance." Michael Brown, in contrast, opposes the abolition of the smallest U.S. currency unit. He argues that rounding off prices (for example, charging $4.00 instead of $3.98) would cost U.S. consumers over half a billion dollars each year. Brown is a spokesman for Americans for Common Cents, an organization backed by the zinc industry (the penny is 97 percent zinc), the manufacturers of the blanks that are stamped out as pennies, and U.S. coin collectors.

The controversy about pennies was stimulated by the Senate Banking Committee's "coinage reform," an effort to pinpoint needed changes in U.S. currency. This reform also brought about the movement to create a one-dollar coin and do away with the one-dollar bill. This idea is supported by the U.S. vending machine industry (including video machine manufacturers), the American Council for the Blind, the copper industry, the convenience store industry, and mass-transit businesses. This idea is opposed by the ink and paper producers that supply these ingredients for the printing of paper currency.

Opponents of the paper dollar bill claim that handling such bills manually—including straightening and unfolding them, arranging them right side up, and counting them—is a very expensive and time-consuming process. Also, the U.S. Treasury spends over $300 million each year shredding and replacing worn-out dollar bills. The paper dollar bill is difficult for visually impaired people to identify. Using dollar coins—for example, in vending machines and mass-transit turnstiles—would be more convenient and would reduce both the handling of smaller coins and the

Examples include the Civilian Conservation Corps (CCC) and the Works Progress Administration (WPA) during the Great Depression in the 1930s and the Comprehensive Employment and Training Act (CETA) in the 1970s.

It is important to realize that no single governmental body designs and implements fiscal policy. The president, with the aid of the director of the Office of Management and Budget (OMB), the secretary of the treasury, and the Council of Economic Advisers, recommends the desired mix of taxes and government expenditures. Congress, with the aid of its many committees (the House Ways and Means Committee, the Senate Finance Committee, and the Senate Budget Committee, to name a few), enacts fiscal policy. The

president has veto power over what Congress enacts. Disagreement as to proper fiscal policy can—and often does—emerge among members of Congress and between Congress and the president. Resolving these conflicts is often a tedious and time-consuming process, during which numerous hearings may be called and many experts may give testimony.

Fiscal Policy and Employment The government formally took on the responsibility of reducing unemployment when it passed the Employment Act of 1946, which reads as follows:

The Congress hereby declares that it is the continuing policy and responsibility of the federal government to use all

need to make change. The copper industry supports a proposed copper dollar, for obvious reasons.

In 1979, a one-dollar coin, called the Susan B. Anthony dollar, was introduced but failed to gain public acceptance. So as not to repeat this failure, the new strategy would introduce a new coin dollar and phase out entirely the paper dollar, thus forcing Americans to use the coin. This was successfully done in Canada in 1987. A recent Gallup poll, however, showed that while 62 percent of the American population favor abolishing the penny, 85 percent oppose abolishing the dollar bill in favor of a dollar coin.

THINK ABOUT IT

1. Who do you think would lose if the penny were eliminated? Who would gain?
2. Who would lose and who would gain if the one-dollar bill were replaced with a one-dollar coin?

▲ *Employees of the U.S. Bureau of Engraving and Printing make the nation's money. Their job security is assured as millions of worn-out bills must by replaced each year. Are you in favor of replacing the dollar bill with a coin?*

practicable means consistent with its needs and obligations . . . to promote maximum employment, production, and purchasing power.

The effect of this legislation was to require the government to monitor the unemployment rate and the overall state of the national economy and adjust fiscal policy as needed.

Federal Budget Deficits and the Public Debt

Whenever the U.S. government spends more than it receives in tax revenues, it runs a **budget deficit.** As you learned in Chapter 15, the Constitution gives Congress the power to borrow money. Every time a budget deficit occurs, the government borrows money by issuing **U.S. Treasury bonds.** The government sells these bonds to corporations, private individuals, pension plans, foreign governments, foreign businesses, and foreign individuals. The bonds represent a promise that the U.S. government will repay these buyers the purchase price of the bonds, plus interest, in the future. Thus, each bond sale adds to the **public debt** (also called the **national debt**), defined as the total amount the government owes. The government has run a deficit nearly every year since 1960. Each time, the amount of the deficit is *added* to the public debt. Figure 21–8 on page 580 shows what has happened to the public debt over time. Politicians and the public alike are concerned about this problem.

▶ Inflation was a crippling economic problem in 1980, the year this cartoon was drawn. Why is too much inflation harmful?

FATSO

Is the Public Debt a Burden to the Public?

We often hear about the burden of the public debt. Some argue that the government is eventually going to go bankrupt. As long as the government can collect taxes to pay for interest on its public debt, however, that will not happen. What does happen is that, when Treasury bonds come due, they are simply "rolled over," or refinanced. That is, if a $1 million Treasury bond comes due today, the U.S. Treasury pays it off with the money its gets from selling another $1 million bond.

As for the interest payments on these bonds, they are paid with tax revenues. Not all of the interest payments are paid to Americans. Corporations, governments, and private citizens in other countries can and do legally purchase U.S. Treasury bonds. About 38 percent of our national debt is owed to foreigners. Some fear that if foreigners own too large a percentage of our national debt, they may have too much influence over our government.

There is another factor to consider as well. Through the years, as the government has paid more interest on a rising net public debt, it has by necessity spent less on other government activities such as transportation and housing programs.

Times have changed, for toward the end of the 1990s, there seemed to be less concern over the public debt because the federal budget deficit was extremely small (or did not exist at all). This lack of public concern may be a mistake. The budget deficit is never as small as it looks. The official budget has categories called

Just the Facts

President Ronald Reagan (1981–1989), used the following example to help people comprehend the $1 trillion public debt at that time: A million dollars' worth of $1,000 bills would be four inches high; a trillion dollars' worth of $1,000 bills would be sixty-seven miles high.

FIGURE 21–8 Public Debt of the U.S. Government
By looking at this table, you can see how the public debt has grown. What is the source of the money used to pay the interest on this debt?

Year	Net Public Debt* (billions of dollars)
1940	$ 42.7
1945	235.2
1950	219.0
1955	226.6
1960	237.2
1965	261.6
1970	284.9
1975	396.9
1980	709.3
1983	1,141.8
1986	1,736.2
1989	2,190.3
1990	2,410.3
1991	2,717.6
1992	2,998.6
1995	3,603.3
1996	3,733.0
1997	3,760.1
2000 (est.)	3,888.0

* In current dollars.

UNIT VII: American Policy in a Changing World

The Flat Tax

As we mentioned earlier in this chapter, the U.S. personal income tax is a progressive tax. That is to say, the higher your income, the higher your taxes. The highest marginal income-tax rate that Americans have paid was 94 percent in 1944. This dropped to 92 percent in 1952, then to 91 percent in 1954. Starting in 1982, it was 50 percent, and today it is around 40 percent.

Some Americans have argued that we should simplify our income-tax system by using a single rate for all—a **flat tax** rate. The flat tax rate—say, 17 percent—would apply only after some initial amount of yearly income had been earned—say, $20,000 or $30,000 per family. There would be absolutely no deductions from taxable income. In contrast, in today's system, deductions are allowed for home-mortgage interest payments, charitable contributions, and other expenditures. Those in favor of simplifying our tax code have some important arguments.

Yes, Opt for Simplicity, Some Say

We need to get rid of our current tax code because it is so complicated. It is estimated that American taxpayers spend $70 billion in valuable time each year figuring out how to file their taxes. In addition, lawyers and accountants who specialize in helping individuals "do their taxes" every year take about $20 billion from Americans in fees.

Under a flat tax system, individuals would not be able to deduct anything from their taxable incomes. Therefore, accountants, lawyers, and specialty tax firms such as H & R Block would not be helping taxpayers to find deductions. Moreover, individuals would have fewer incentives to pay such specialists to reduce their taxable incomes. Under current tax laws, high-income individuals save over $4,000 for every $10,000 reduction in taxable income. Under the simplified system, they would save only $1,700, or 17 percent. The incentive to seek out ways to reduce taxable income would therefore be reduced.

Others Ask, What about Fairness?

Those opposed to a flat tax are worried about several things. They argue that the U.S. government would end up collecting insufficient tax revenues with this new system. In that case, the government would have a budget deficit.

On a more basic level, opponents raise an issue of fairness. Is it fair that everyone should pay the same tax rate, no matter how much he or she earns? Shouldn't individuals who make more money give more back to the country? After all, these individuals have plenty of income. When they give some of it back in the form of taxes, it can be redistributed to the poorer members of our society.

Finally, who is to say that a flat tax would remain flat for very long? Congress seems to "fiddle" with the tax code virtually every year. Even if in one year Congress made all tax rates the same, in the next year it might change the system again.

YOU DECIDE

1. Do you think you would be better off or worse off now or in the future if the U.S. government used a flat income tax rate?
2. Would the nation as a whole benefit from a flat tax?

How Government Spending Has Changed

The spending patterns of the national government have changed significantly over the years. Consider how these spending patterns have changed just since the 1960s.

THEN (1960s)	NOW
Spending by state and local governments was, in all, less than national government spending.	Spending by state and local governments is more than national government spending.
The rate of growth in the size of national government spending was increasing.	The rate of growth in the size of national government spending is decreasing.
In the early 1960s, marginal tax rates exceeded 90 percent.	The highest marginal tax rate is 39.6 percent.
Annual national budget deficits were typical, and the national debt was increasing.	The national government has succeeded, at least for a while, in balancing its budget. A balanced budget means that the national debt will not increase.

off-budget items. For many years, when the U.S. Postal Service was operating at a loss, those losses were removed from the official federal budget. Taxpayers ended up paying for them anyway. More important, increased expenditures on Medicare and Social Security in the future will certainly cause the government to again face a serious deficit problem.

In past years, critics of excessive government spending have argued in favor of a constitutional amendment requiring a balanced budget. When the federal government budget started to balance, calls for such an amendment disappeared. In future years, they may return, however.

SECTION 3 REVIEW

1. What are the two basic tools used to manage the U.S. economy?
2. What is monetary policy? Who is responsible for the nation's monetary policy?
3. How does the Federal Reserve System regulate monetary policy?
4. Explain what inflation is and how it occurs.
5. How is fiscal policy carried out?
6. Briefly describe how the national debt has grown.
7. How much of our national debt is owed to

foreigners? How might this create a problem for the United States?

8. **For Critical Analysis:** Why has it been difficult for our government to reduce the public debt?

★ ★ ★ ★ **Chapter Summary** ★ ★ ★ ★

Section 1: Systems of Taxation

- Most government revenues are raised through taxation. Three principles used to justify different levels of taxation are the benefits-received principle, the ability-to-pay principle, and the sacrifice principle.
- Taxes can be imposed according to proportional, progressive, or regressive systems. The personal income tax system of the U.S. government is progressive.
- Governments sometimes use taxes to direct economic activity. For example, excise taxes on cigarettes and alcohol are meant to discourage their purchase and use.

Section 2: Government Spending

- Since just before the Great Depression to today, the total number of civilian government employees has increased by about sixfold.
- Government spending on goods and services has more than doubled since 1959 and today represents a little more than 20 percent of annual total national income. Since the mid-1960s, state and local governments have spent more than the national government.
- Government spending increased dramatically in the late 1960s and early 1970s. Since the late 1970s and

early 1980s, however, the growth of government has slowed down. The true size of government includes payments on programs such as welfare, interest payments on the national debt, and the costs of accommodating laws requiring certain actions to be undertaken.

- The largest U.S. government expenditures are for Social Security, national defense, and income security programs.
- Net interest on the public debt has become an item of concern in the national budget.

Section 3: Monetary and Fiscal Policy

- The basic tools that the U.S. government uses to manage the national economy are monetary policy and fiscal policy.
- Monetary policy is the responsibility of the Federal Reserve System and involves regulating the amount of money in circulation.
- If the Fed is following a loose monetary policy, it increases the amount of money in circulation. If the Fed is following a tight monetary policy, it decreases the amount of money in circulation.
- When the economy is in a recession, unemployment is high and businesses are not working at full capacity. In a boom economy, unemployment is low and businesses are operating at peak capacity.
- Fiscal policy, which is the responsibility of the president and Congress, consists of adjusting federal taxes and spending to manage the total demand for goods and services in the economy.
- When the government spends more money than it receives in revenues, it runs a budget deficit and must borrow money. The total amount of money owed by the federal government is the public debt.

★ REVIEW QUESTIONS ★

1. What are the three principles of taxation?
2. What are the three types of tax systems, and how do they differ?
3. What is the most important source of U.S. government revenues?
4. Describe one theory explaining government growth during the 1960s and 1970s.
5. Why did politicians want to cut back on government spending in the late 1970s and early 1980s? What effect did this have on the growth of government?
6. Is national government spending on goods and services higher or lower than spending by state and local governments?
7. Does the U.S. government spend more on Social Security than on national defense? On which three items in the budget are expenditures highest?
8. What is monetary policy? What is the difference between a tight and a loose monetary policy?
9. Briefly describe the Federal Reserve System.
10. What is fiscal policy?
11. How does the government accumulate a public debt?

★ CRITICAL THINKING ★

1. Our government has in the past provided loans to large businesses to save them from bankruptcy. For example, in 1979 the national government loaned Chrysler Corporation 1.5 billion dollars. Chrysler was, at that time, the third largest automobile manufacturer in the United States. Chrysler, and other companies, argue that these loans keep them operating and save thousands of jobs. What do you think are the pros and cons of such a policy?
2. Do you think that the U.S. government should be required to have a balanced budget? Why or why not?

3. If the government were forced to reduce its spending, which groups in America would likely see reduced government-provided benefits?
4. A household that does not balance its budget will eventually go bankrupt. How can the national government continue to run a budget deficit and still survive? How can it function efficiently when a large portion of its revenues are used just to pay interest on the debt?

★ IMPROVING YOUR SKILLS ★

Communication Skills

Seeing Both Sides of an Issue Whether you are doing research, writing a report, debating a question, or discussing a problem, it is often important to see both sides of an issue. It is easy to become blind to other points of view after you have firmly made up your mind. Sometimes it is difficult to admit that there is another side to an issue. Usually, however, there is at least one other side, and it never hurts to find out as much as you can about it. You have nothing to lose by listening to your opponent. Doing so will either cause you to change your position or help you to strengthen your own arguments. In either event, you will understand the other side more clearly.

Writing Choose an issue on which you have taken a strong position. That issue may be gun control, capital punishment, or a state or local issue that is currently in the news. Research an opposing view of the issue as thoroughly as possible, and write a report on that position. When you have finished, evaluate how you now feel about the issue. Has your position remained unchanged? Do you feel even more strongly than before that your position is correct? Have you gained a clearer understanding of the other side? Include your impressions in your report.

Social Studies Skills

Working with Percentages and Averages Look at Figure 21–2 and Figure 21–3 below. Answer the following questions:

1. In Figure 21–2, what is the difference between the percentage income tax rate on the first $100 earned and on the third $100 earned?
2. In Figure 21–3, what is the difference between the percentage income tax rate on the first $100 earned and on the third $100 earned?
3. What is the average rate of taxation for $300 of income earned in Figure 21–3?

★ ACTIVITIES AND PROJECTS ★

1. Organize and prepare for a class debate on the following statement: The U.S. government should abolish the current tax system and impose a flat tax, exempting the first $25,000 of income from taxation.
2. Write to your U.S. congressional representative or one of your state's U.S. senators. Ask the representative or senator to explain his or her views on the current tax system. Write a one-page, typewritten report on these views, and present it to your class.

3. Do some research on your state's budget. Find out what the major sources of state revenues are and how they are spent. Report your findings to your classmates.
4. Conduct a survey of your classmates (or of the students in your school). Find out how many are in favor of and how many are opposed to the following statement: The government should be forced to balance its budget.

What If . . .

The U.S. Government Were Not Allowed to Run a Deficit?

Currently, it is possible for the U.S. government to spend more than it receives. Suppose that a constitutional amendment requiring a balanced budget made it illegal for the government to do this. How would Congress and the president have to react?

FIGURE 21–2 Proportional Tax System This table illustrates the principle of proportional taxation.

Income	Proportional Rate	Tax
First $100	10%	$10
Second $100	10%	$10
Third $100	10%	$10
Total Income: $300		Total Tax: $30

FIGURE 21–3 Progressive Tax System This table illustrates the principle of progressive taxation.

Income	Marginal Rate	Tax
First $100	10%	$10
Second $100	20%	$20
Third $100	30%	$30
Total Income: $300		Total Tax: $60

CHAPTER 22

Domestic Policy

CHAPTER OBJECTIVES

To learn about and understand . . .

⭐ The problem of crime in America, especially among teenagers, and the true cost of crime for our society

⭐ Some of the methods the government has used to fight crime

⭐ The steps taken by the government to reduce poverty in the United States

⭐ Environmental pollution and governmental policies designed to control it

> "A policy is a temporary creed liable to be changed, but while it holds good it has got to be pursued with apostolic zeal."
>
> *Mohandas K. Gandhi*
> (1869–1948)
> Political and Spiritual Leader of India

INTRODUCTION

Sometimes, a school participates in one of the "adopt a highway" programs around the country. When this happens, members of a particular class are given the responsibility of keeping a certain section of highway clean. Now, if the class members follow Gandhi's prescription given in the above quotation, they will follow this policy religiously. That is to say, their section of the highway will be absolutely spotless.

Notice, though, that Gandhi refers to a policy as "a temporary creed liable to be changed." This is certainly true with U.S. domestic policy—public policy concerning issues within a national unit, as opposed to foreign policy. In this chapter, you will read about a variety of domestic policy issues. Because many Americans are concerned about crime, we turn to this domestic policy issue first.

◄ Crowds stand in awe at the majestic scene before them at the Grand Canyon National Park in Arizona.

The Problem of Crime

Preview Questions

- 🌎 Have crime rates been rising or dropping in the last decade?
- 🌎 What is the true cost of crime for our society?
- 🌎 What are three-strikes-and-you're-out laws?

Key Terms:

domestic policy, felony

Crime is the subject we all love to hate. In the last decade, the American public has ranked crime as either the most serious problem or the second most serious problem facing the United States. Traditionally, dealing with crime was a function of state governments. Increasingly, though, it has been placed on the *national* domestic policy agenda. Crime committed by career criminals is especially likely to be viewed as a problem for the national government to solve.

Worries about crime are certainly not new in this nation. According to some researchers in the field, crime was probably as frequent around the time of the American Revolution as it is now. The President's Commission on Law Enforcement and Administration of Justice, during the time of the Civil War, had this to say about San Francisco:

No decent man is in safety to walk the streets after dark; while at all hours, both night and day, his property is jeopardized by [fires] and burglary.

How Bad Is Crime in America?

Americans today are most worried about violent crime. And indeed, violent crime in the United States showed a long and steady increase over a very recent

period of history. Look at the bottom part of the graph in Figure 22–1 below. There you can see the number of violent crimes per hundred thousand Americans from 1960 to the present. In 1960, that number was 161. Thirty-one years later, in 1991, it had risen to more than 758—an increase of almost 500 percent! If you examine the top line in Figure 22–1, you will see the total of all crimes per one hundred thousand inhabitants. In 1960, that figure was 1,887. In 1991, it was nearly 5,898—an increase of over 300 percent.

During the 1990s, though, crime data were somewhat encouraging. If you look at the bottom portion of Figure 22–1, you will see that violent crimes started to decrease in 1992 and has continued to decrease since then.

What has caused crime levels to drop since the early 1990s? According to some experts in criminal justice, several factors are responsible. One of them is the expansion of the police forces in many communities. Others include the increased use of imprisonment, more crime-prevention programs directed at teenagers, and the waning use of crack cocaine.

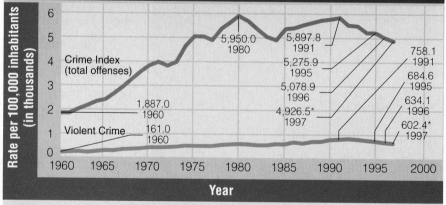

FIGURE 22–1 Crime Rates in the United States since 1960 Here you can see two aspects of how the U.S. crime rate has changed over time. The line at the top of the graph reflects the changes in the overall crime rate from 1960 to 1997. The bottom part of the graph reflects the changes in the violent crime rate over that time period. Which type of crime rate shows a more significant decrease from 1991 to 1997?

Rate per 100,000 inhabitants (in thousands)

Crime Index (total offenses)

5,950.0 1980
5,897.8 1991
5,275.9 1995
5,078.9 1996
4,926.5* 1997

1,887.0 1960

Violent Crime 161.0 1960

758.1 1991
684.6 1995
634.1 1996
602.4* 1997

Year

*Projections based on crimes reported during the first six months of 1997.
SOURCE: U.S. Department of Justice.

Although crime rates are decreasing, crime levels remain disturbingly high. Of particular concern is a startling development of the last few decades: a large increase in the number of murders committed by teenagers. In 1976, the number of murders committed by persons aged fourteen to seventeen was six per 100,000. By the mid-1990s, that number had increased to more than nineteen per 100,000.

Most of the persons in this age group who commit crimes are males. The number of males aged fourteen to sixteen, as a percentage of the population, started to increase in the late 1990s. Consequently, some researchers believe that overall crime rates may start to rise again in the future.

◀ This handcuffed teenager hides his face after being arrested. Do you agree with the relatively recent trend of trying teenagers as adults when they are accused of serious crimes?

the 1990s, the total U.S. prison population had risen to nearly 1.7 million—more than twice what it was a decade earlier. As the number of prisoners increases, so does the cost of building and operating prisons. Each week, an estimated 1,500 new prison beds are needed. The cost of sentencing one person to one year in jail now averages between $25,000 and $40,000. All in all, the annual nationwide cost of building, maintaining, and operating prisons is over $35 billion.

The Cost of Crime to Americans

If you are robbed, you know what crime costs you. If someone burns your house down on purpose, you know what crime costs you. But there is more to crime than meets the eye. Look at Figure 22–2. Property loss accounts for only about 10 percent of the total cost of crime. The other costs are as follows:

- Funds spent on the criminal justice system, including prison construction and maintenance
- Private protection in the form of alarms, private security guards, and related expenses
- Urban decay
- Destroyed lives
- Medical care

One cost of crime that is certain to rise is the cost of building and maintaining prisons. By the end of

FIGURE 22–2 The Total Cost of Crime in the United States Here we show the total dollar cost of crime per year in the United States. Is it ever possible to put a dollar value on the "destroyed lives" of crime victims?

Expenditure	Explanation	Total Cost (for year)
Criminal justice	Spending on police, courts, and prisons at the national, state, and local levels	$95 billion
Private protection	Spending on private guards, security systems, alarms, and related expenses	$70 billion
Urban decay	The cost of jobs lost and residents fleeing because of excessive crime in inner cities	$50 billion
Property loss	The value of stolen goods and vandalized buildings	$50 billion
Destoyed lives	The economic value of lives lost or broken as a result of robberies, rapes, and other crimes	$175 billion
Medical care	The cost of treating victims	$10 billion
TOTAL		$450 billion

SOURCE: Federal Bureau of Investigation.

▶ Because of overcrowding, prisoners are sometimes housed in tents, as shown in this photograph taken in Huntsville, Texas. Today, over 1.7 million people in the United States are incarcerated, causing overcrowding in many prisons and jails.

One of the major reasons we need more prisons is that we continue to arrest more people for the sale or use of illegal drugs. More than a million people a year are arrested for drug offenses. It is estimated that over twenty million Americans violate one or more drug laws each year. Therefore, the potential "supply" of prisoners seems virtually without limit.

Cracking Down on Crime— Three Strikes and You're Out

In the mid-1980s, politicians began to respond to increasing crime rates by passing new sentencing laws, typically called three-strikes-and-you're-out laws. Basically, these laws require that judges sentence any individual who is convicted of a third felony to life in prison. A **felony** is a serious criminal offense punishable by imprisonment for at least one year or by death. "Three strikes" laws exist at the national level as well as in several states. Proponents of three-strikes legislation point out that California, one of the first to pass three-strikes laws, has seen reduced crime rates as a result. Because 7 percent of all criminals commit between 50 and 70 percent of all crimes, the three-strikes legislation may be striking at the heart of our crime problem.

These laws present some problems, however. Here is what one career criminal, Frank Schweickert, said in a *New York Times* interview:

Before, if I was doing a robbery and getting chased by cops, I'd lay my gun down. . . . But now you are talking about a life sentence. Why isn't it worth doing whatever it takes to get away? If that meant shooting a cop, if that meant shooting a store clerk, if that meant shooting someone innocent in my way, well they'd have gotten shot. Because what is the worst thing that could happen to me: life imprisonment? If I'm getting a murder sentence anyway, I might as well do whatever it takes to maybe get away.

Essentially, as Schweickert suggests, for those who have two prior felony convictions, three-strikes legislation may be perceived as having reduced the cost of committing murder while engaging in another criminal activity.

Additionally, the criminals who have been "put away" under such laws may not be the ones we need to worry about. In California, for example, of 2,750 felons who were imprisoned for twenty-five years to life,

85 percent had committed nonviolent crimes. Indeed, marijuana possession was four times more likely to be the cause of the "third strike" than violent crimes, such as murder, rape, and kidnapping.

SECTION 1 REVIEW

1. Are crime rates currently rising or dropping?
2. What is the "cost" of crime for Americans?

3. What are three-strikes-and-you're-out laws, and how have they affected crime rates?
4. **For Critical Analysis:** Some people argue that current governmental responses to crime—passing tougher laws, building more prisons, and the like—take the wrong approach to the problem. Rather, the government should pay more attention to the causes of crime, such as poverty, broken homes, and the lack of educational and employment opportunities. Do you agree with this argument? Why or why not?

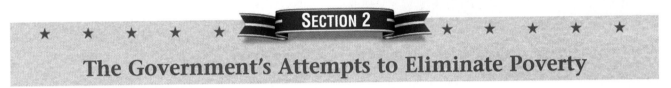

SECTION 2

The Government's Attempts to Eliminate Poverty

Preview Questions:

- How is poverty defined?
- What are the major income-maintenance programs that the government has designed to help poor people?

Key Terms:

in-kind subsidy, income transfer, Social Security, Supplemental Security Income (SSI), Temporary Assistance to Needy Families (TANF), food stamps, earned-income tax credit (EITC)

Throughout the history of the world, mass poverty has existed. This nation and others, however, particularly in the Western world, have sustained enough economic growth in the past several hundred years so that mass poverty can no longer be said to be a problem. As a matter of fact, the existence of poverty in the United States today is often seen as puzzling. How can there still be so much poverty in a nation of so much abundance?

Defining Poverty

The income level that is used to determine who falls into the poverty category is called the poverty threshold, or poverty line. It was originally based on the cost of a nutritionally adequate food plan designed by the U.S. Department of Agriculture. The threshold was determined by multiplying the cost of the food plan by three, on the assumption that food expenses take approximately one-third of a poor family's income. In 1969, a governmental interagency committee decided to set new standards. Until then, annual revisions of the threshold were based only on price changes in the food budget. After 1969, the adjustments were made on the basis of changes in the average of all prices.

The poverty threshold thus represents the amount of income needed to maintain a specified standard of living as of 1963, with the value increased yearly in relation to general price increases. For 1997, for example, the official poverty level for a family of four was about $16,000. It has increased since then in proportion to price increases. As the example above indicates, the poverty threshold varies with family size. It also varies with location.

Poverty over Time

The official poverty level is based on gross income (income before taxes), including cash but not including in-kind subsidies. A subsidy is a benefit, such as money, given by the government to a specific group of people for a specific purpose. An **in-kind subsidy** is a subsidy that takes the form of real things instead of

▲ *These children pose next to a chain-link fence in their Los Angeles, California, neighborhood. Children form the largest group of poor people in the United States today.*

money. For example, food stamps and housing vouchers are in-kind subsidies. If we adjust poverty levels for such benefits, the percentage of the population that is below the poverty line drops dramatically.

The New Poor

Traditionally, the poorer segments of our population have been minorities, older people, and women. These groups have recently experienced minor increases in income levels. Poverty rates among people in particular subgroups, however, show an alarming increase. These new groups are women who head households and children.

The poverty rate for single females who head households has increased significantly in recent years. In the early 1960s, about 10 percent of all families were headed by single mothers. By the 1990s, about 25 percent of all families were headed by single mothers. Today, nearly 33 percent of female householders without husbands are living in poverty. For female householders who are African American, this figure is about 44 per-

cent. For Hispanic Americans in this group, it is over 50 percent.

Many of our nation's children are also poor. Today, children are 50 percent more likely than the rest of the population to be living in poverty. In part, this is because of the increasing number of single-parent homes. Although in the last two decades the poverty rate for children living in two-parent families has been dropping, the poverty rate for children living in female-headed families has been rising.

The Homeless

Recent years have brought a new awareness of the plight of homeless people in the United States. With this awareness has come a debate about how many homeless people there are and how they should be helped. Lack of information about these people has led to conflicting claims. Some government officials claim that the total number of homeless people is small and that most of these people are mentally ill. Organizations that work to help homeless people, however, claim they number from two to three million.

▲ *Scenes such as this one of a homeless man lying on a park bench have become increasingly common in most of America's large cities. What is ironic about this particular photograph?*

BUILDING

SOCIAL STUDIES SKILLS

Reading Line Graphs

Line graphs are used to show changes in trends over a period of time. The U.S. government's budget deficit, a president's popularity, or a student's grades over a period of years could easily be shown on a line graph, for example.

To read a line graph, begin by reading the title, then read the axes. The horizontal axis usually shows time on a scale of days, months, or years. The vertical axis usually gives a scale for measuring quantities.

In the graph below, one curve shows the official poverty rate in the United States. The other curve shows welfare spending. Study the graph, and then answer the following questions.

PRACTICING YOUR SKILLS

1. When did welfare spending start to rise sharply in the United States?
2. What happened to the poverty rate after welfare spending started to rise in this way?
3. What is the highest poverty rate shown on the graph, and when did it occur?
4. Approximately how much was spent on welfare in 1950? In the mid-1990s?
5. Why did spending on welfare increase in the late 1930s? What accounted for the decline in the mid-1940s?

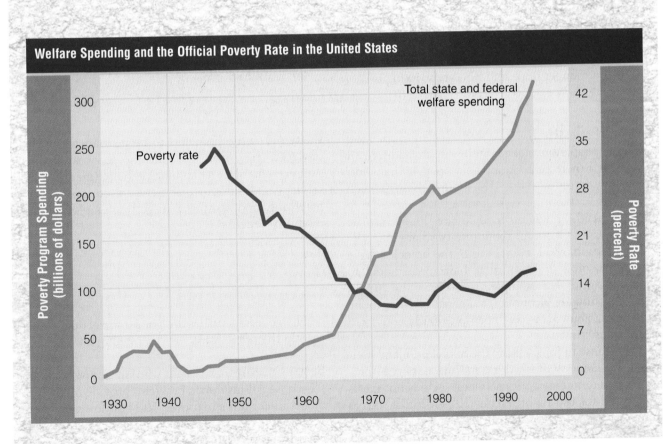

Welfare Spending and the Official Poverty Rate in the United States

Social Security in Trouble

Social Security was originally designed as a social insurance program that workers paid for themselves. The benefits a worker received were determined by the size of the worker's past contributions. Today, Social Security is not really an insurance program, because the benefits people receive may not correspond with the contributions they have made. The benefits are legislated by Congress, and there is no guarantee that Congress will continue to legislate the same amount of benefits in the future as it does today. Congress could (and probably will have to) legislate for lower levels of benefits instead of higher ones. In essence, Social Security is an intergenerational **income transfer.** That is, it transfers income from Americans who work—the young through the middle-aged—to older, retired persons who no longer work.

The problem with the Social Security system is that the number of people who are working is declining relative to the number of people who are retiring. This means that workers will have to pay more of their income in Social Security taxes to provide retirement benefits for older, retired workers. Today, Social Security benefits cost about 15 percent of all wage earners' income in the economy. By the year 2025, this figure is projected to be almost 23 percent. Clearly, increasing or even maintaining the current level of Social Security benefits will create a financial strain for the government.

THINK ABOUT IT
....

1. Why should you worry about Social Security now?
2. If you are worried about receiving Social Security benefits, what should you do during your working life?

Recent research has revealed that in fact most homeless people are *not* mentally ill. In addition, it appears that there are fewer homeless people than most homeless advocates claim. The nonpartisan research group Urban Institute estimated after a survey that about 600,000 homeless people are living in the United States. Of those, about one-third are mentally ill. In addition, about two-thirds of the homeless have serious personal problems that have contributed to their difficulties. For example, studies have shown that over one-third are alcoholics and about one-fourth are either drug abusers or have been previously convicted of a serious crime.

In response to the plight of the homeless, many shelters have been established around the nation to provide short-term emergency services, such as hot meals and a bed for the night. About 20 percent of today's homeless are families, most of them young single women with children, who are housed in temporary shelters. For the homeless to be permanently helped, however, they need not only the services offered by shelters but also rehabilitative help (mental health services and substance-abuse counseling), classes in parenting, and assistance in getting employment and disability benefits.

Attacks on Poverty: Major Income-Maintenance Programs

The government has designed a variety of programs to help the poor. A few are discussed below.

Social Security For people who are retired or unemployed, social insurance programs provide income payments in certain situations. The best known is **Social Security,** a program created in 1935 when Congress passed the Social Security Act. Social Security is

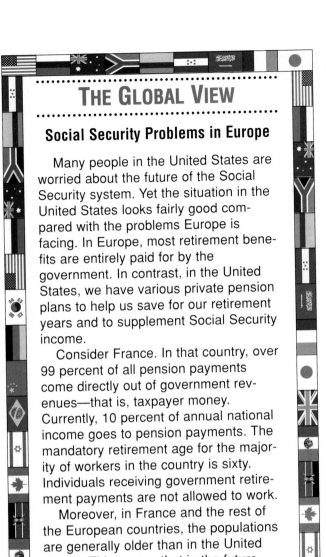

Social Security Problems in Europe

Many people in the United States are worried about the future of the Social Security system. Yet the situation in the United States looks fairly good compared with the problems Europe is facing. In Europe, most retirement benefits are entirely paid for by the government. In contrast, in the United States, we have various private pension plans to help us save for our retirement years and to supplement Social Security income.

Consider France. In that country, over 99 percent of all pension payments come directly out of government revenues—that is, taxpayer money. Currently, 10 percent of annual national income goes to pension payments. The mandatory retirement age for the majority of workers in the country is sixty. Individuals receiving government retirement payments are not allowed to work.

Moreover, in France and the rest of the European countries, the populations are generally older than in the United States. This means that in the future, there will be fewer working individuals to support the elderly population. In other words, those who are working will have to turn over more and more of their incomes to pay for the retirement benefits of older persons. Over the next thirty years, European countries must decide how to handle this challenge.

THINKING GLOBALLY

Often, it is illegal to work while receiving government-paid pensions in Europe. Why do you think this is so?

essentially a government program of required saving financed from payroll taxes imposed on both employers and employees. Workers pay for Social Security while working and receive the benefits after retirement. When the insured worker dies before retirement, benefits go to the survivors, including widows and children. Special benefits provide for disabled workers. Over 90 percent of all employed persons in the United States are covered by Social Security.

Supplemental Security Income (SSI) Many people who are poor do not qualify for Social Security benefits. They are assisted through other programs. In 1974, the **Supplemental Security Income (SSI)** program was instituted. The purpose of SSI was to establish a nationwide minimum income for older persons and persons with disabilities. SSI is financed and administered by the U.S. government. It has become one of the fastest-growing programs in the United States. When it started, less than $8 billion was spent on it annually. Today that figure is close to $40 billion.

Welfare—Temporary Assistance to Needy Families Until 1996, the basic welfare program in the United States was known as Aid to Families with Dependent Children (AFDC). AFDC was a state-administered program financed in part by grants from the national government. The program provided aid to families in which the children did not have the financial support of the father because of desertion, disability, or death. Under the AFDC

Just the Facts

In Hawaii, in 1996, a working mother with two children would have had to earn $36,400 per year to match the purchasing power of welfare benefits.

program, the federal government largely set the requirements that had to be met before a welfare applicant could receive welfare payments.

With the passage of the 1996 Welfare Reform Act, the states gained more responsibility for establishing welfare rules and managing the welfare program. The U.S. government turns over to the states, in the form of grants, funds targeted for a program called **Temporary Assistance to Needy Families (TANF).** If a state wishes to increase the amount of payments to individuals for TANF over what the national government gives it, the state has to pay for the additional costs.

▶ In Phoenix, Arizona, Elsie Wilkes looks for a job online with the assistance of "empowerment center" employee Carol Vallejo. Why do you think this former welfare office was renamed an empowerment center?

funding food stamps jumped from $860,000 in 1964 to more than $25.8 billion in 1998.

Since the 1960s, the food-stamp program has become a major part of the welfare system in the United States. In retrospect, it seems to have been started mainly for the benefit of the nation's agricultural workers by increasing their food-buying ability. The program has since become a method of promoting better nutrition among the poor, however, both urban and rural.

The U.S. government has placed several restrictions on those who receive TANF benefits. After two years, welfare recipients may continue to receive benefits only if they are working either in a public service job or in the private sector. Also, TANF benefits can be paid for a maximum of five years. States are allowed to deny TANF benefits to unmarried teenage mothers.

Food Stamps Food stamps are government-issued coupons that can be used to purchase food. Food stamps are available for low-income individuals and families. Workers who are on strike and even some college students are eligible to receive food stamps. Recipients must prove that they qualify by showing that they earn little or no money.

The food-stamp program has grown a great deal since it began in 1964. At that time, about 367,000 Americans were receiving food stamps. In 1998, the U.S. budget called for giving food stamps to 23.4 million recipients. The annual cost of

The Earned-Income Tax Credit (EITC) Program A program created in 1975, the **earned-income tax credit (EITC)** program gives back to low-income workers part or all of their Social Security taxes. Currently, over one-fifth of all taxpayers claim an earned-income tax credit. In some states, such as Mississippi, as well as in the District of Columbia, nearly half of all families are eligible for the EITC. One of the effects of this program has been to discourage low-income earners from taking on a sec-

▶ While many Americans believe that welfare reform will encourage unemployed citizens to find work, they may not realize that workers in low-wage jobs also qualify for some forms of assistance. Do you believe that welfare reform will ultimately hurt or help the poor?

"WELL THEN, YOU'LL JUST HAVE TO TIGHTEN YOUR BELTS A LITTLE MORE...."

ond job. The reason is that when they do so, they earn more money and lose all or part of their EITC benefits.

The Effects of Government Programs In spite of the programs just mentioned and the hundreds of billions of dollars transferred to the poor, the officially defined rate of poverty in the United States has shown no long-run tendency to decline. It reached a low of around 11 percent in 1973 and a peak of over 15 percent in 1983. It fell in the late 1980s but started to rise in 1991 and 1992. Today, it is about 13 percent.

▲ The federal food stamp program, in which eligible individuals and families receive coupons to buy food, has grown significantly since its inception in 1964. Food stamps like these may soon become obsolete, however, as the government moves toward using a system similar to the debit cards that many banks offer their customers.

SECTION 2 REVIEW

1. How is poverty defined for government purposes?
2. Which groups in society show the highest poverty rates?
3. What are the major income-maintenance programs designed by the government to help the poor?
4. Explain the differences between Social Security and Supplemental Security Income.
5. **For Critical Analysis:** Is the policy of allowing states to deny welfare benefits to unwed mothers a sound one? Why or why not?

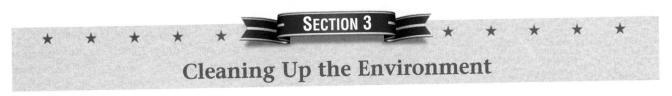
SECTION 3

Cleaning Up the Environment

Preview Questions:

🌟 What are some of the major federal environmental laws? What did they set out to accomplish?

🌟 What were the major provisions of the National Environmental Policy Act of 1969?

🌟 What are global warming and the greenhouse effect? What has been the U.S. government's response to these problems?

Key Terms:

environmental impact statement, global warming, greenhouse effect, Kyoto Protocol

When the Exxon supertanker *Valdez* struck Bligh Reef in the clear and frigid waters of Prince William Sound in Alaska in 1989, it spilled a quarter of a million barrels (more than ten million gallons) of crude oil into the water. The result was the worst oil spill in North American history. Within a week, the oil slick covered almost 1,000 square miles, killing many marine animals, fish, and migratory birds and harming many others. Within four weeks, the slick had grown to 1,600 square miles and threatened wildlife living hundreds of miles to the southwest of the accident site. By the end of the summer of 1989, Exxon Corporation had already spent more than $1 billion on cleanup efforts but had

Just the Facts

American businesses invest billions of dollars a year in reducing pollution.

ARCHITECTS
of Government

Carol M. Browner
(1955–   )

Born in 1955, Carol M. Browner graduated from the University of Florida at Gainesville in 1977. In 1979, she received her law degree from the University of Florida Law School. Later, she worked first as a legislative aide to Senator Lawton Chiles of Florida and then as legislative director for Senator Al Gore. She became the director of Florida's Department of Environmental Regulation in 1991. In 1993, President Bill Clinton appointed her to the position of administrator of the Environmental Protection Agency (EPA). Browner's mission is to promote public health by protecting the nation's air, water, and soil.

HER WORDS

"We are now at a crossroads. Everyone in this country shares the idea of a clean environment for future generations, and they want to achieve that. We are, however, going to have to be mindful of the consequences of environmental protection."

(*Interview*, E.P.A. Journal, January–March 1993)

"A healthy environment and a healthy economy go hand-in-hand."

(Super Fund Week, February 24, 1995)

DEVELOPING
CRITICAL THINKING SKILLS

1. What does Browner mean, in the first quotation, when she refers to a "crossroads"?
2. Regarding the second quotation, how is the environment related to the economy?

▲ Domestic policies dealing with pollution attempt to keep the nation's air, water, and earth clean and safe. In the aftermath of the Exxon Valdez *disaster, workers used high-pressure hoses to clean oil-covered rocks along this Alaska shoreline.*

probably recovered less than one-fourth of the crude oil that had escaped from the hold of the *Valdez.*

Two years later, in the winter of 1991, the world saw an oil spill ten to twenty times worse than the one that occurred in Alaska. This spill, however, was not an accident. It was created during the Persian Gulf War when Iraqi troops released oil from a Kuwaiti super-tanker loading platform.

Oil-spill disasters in the United States and elsewhere serve as constant reminders that human actions often result in unwanted side effects—serious damage to our environment and the organisms that live in it. Industries emit pollutants into the air and the water every day. Each year, the atmosphere of our planet receives twenty million metric tons of sulfur dioxide, eighteen million metric tons of ozone pollutants, and sixty million metric tons of carbon monoxide. (One metric ton is about 2,200 pounds.)

Just the Facts

A visitor to Chicago in the late 1800s commented that the pollution was so stifling that during his one week's stay he "did not see in Chicago anything but darkness, smoke, [or] clouds of dirt."

How the Government Has Addressed the Pollution Problem

Our country's government has been responding to pollution problems since before the American Revolution, when the Massachusetts Bay Colony issued regulations to try to stop the pollution of Boston Harbor. In the nineteenth century, states passed laws controlling water pollution after scientists and medical researchers had convinced most policymakers that dumping sewage into drinking and bathing water caused disease. Today, there are numerous laws designed to control environmental pollution. Figure 22–3 on pages 600 and 601 lists the major landmarks of environmental legislation in the United States.

The National Environmental Policy Act The year 1969 marks perhaps the true start of U.S. government involvement in pollution control. In that year, a Union Oil Company oil well exploded six miles off the coast of Santa Barbara, California, releasing 235,000 gallons of crude oil. The result was an oil slick that covered an area of eight hundred square miles, washing up on the city's beaches and killing plant life, birds, and fish.

Congress responded by passing the National Environmental Policy Act (NEPA) in 1969. This landmark legislation required that an **environmental impact statement** be prepared for every major federal action, showing the extent to which the action would affect the quality of the environment. The NEPA therefore gave citizens and public interest groups concerned with the environment a weapon against unnecessary and inappropriate use of our resources by government. The act also created the Council on Environmental Quality (CEQ) and authorized the establishment of the Environmental Protection Agency (EPA) to implement CEQ policies.

The Clean Air Act Amendments of 1990 In 1990, amendments to the 1963 Clean Air Act were passed. These amendments consisted of over a thousand pages of regulations on American industry.

One innovative aspect of these amendments was that they required that certain gasoline formulas be used in cars in the smoggiest cities. The amendments also stated that if, by the year 2003, certain cities still

FIGURE 22–3 Major Federal Environmental Legislation The figure below lists and describes important environmental laws at the national level. When was the first of these acts passed? With what was it concerned?

Legislation	Description
1899 Refuse Act	Made it unlawful to dump refuse into navigable waters without a permit. A 1966 court decision made all industrial wastes subject to this act.
1955 Federal Water Pollution Control Act	Set standards for treatment of municipal water waste before discharge. Revisions of this act were passed in 1965 and 1967.
1963 Clean Air Act	Coordinated research and assisted state and local governments in establishing control programs.
1965 Clean Air Act Amendments	Authorized establishment of national standards for automobile exhaust emissions, beginning with 1968 models.
1965 Solid Waste Disposal Act	Provided assistance to state and local governments for control programs and authorized research in this area.
1965 Water Quality Act	Authorized the setting of standards for discharges into waters.
1967 Air Quality Act	Established air quality regions and acceptable regional pollution levels. Required local and state governments to implement approved control programs or be subject to U.S. government controls.
1969 National Environmental Policy Act	Established Council for Environmental Quality (CEQ) to coordinate all national pollution-control programs. Authorized the establishment of the Environmental Protection Agency to implement CEQ policies.
1970 Clean Air Act Amendments	Authorized the Environmental Protection Agency to set national air-pollution standards. Periodically, the agency revises or creates new standards to control polluting emissions by factories, automobiles, aircraft, and other sources of air pollution.
1972 Federal Water Pollution Control Act Amendments	Set national goal of restoring polluted waters to swimmable, fishable conditions by 1983.

experienced dangerous levels of pollution, automobile emissions standards for cars driven in those cities would be drastically increased. Severe restrictions on potential cancer-causing air toxins and total emissions of sulfur dioxide from electric utilities were imposed.

Global Warming

One of the most widely publicized environmental concerns in the world today is the possibility of **global warming**—a gradual increase in average temperature throughout the world due to the so-called greenhouse effect. The **greenhouse effect** is the trapping of heat inside the earth's atmosphere. The effect has always existed and is not a problem in itself. The concern is

that the effect may be growing stronger in modern times. One important cause of the greenhouse effect is carbon dioxide (CO_2). Carbon dioxide is produced when fossil fuels, such as coal and gasoline, are burned. In theory, then, the more fossil fuels we burn, the more CO_2 in the atmosphere.

Not too many years ago, ironically, most environmental observers and concerned scientists were worried about a new ice age. In the June 24, 1974, issue of *Time* magazine, for example, the editor said that "the atmosphere has been growing gradually cooler for the past three decades. The trend shows no indication of reversing." Dr. Reid Bryson, a specialist in climatology, stated in 1980 that "the overall cooling trend is unmistakable, and in coming years it will profoundly affect agriculture, geopolitics, and human survival world-

FIGURE 22–3 Major Federal Environmental Legislation (continued)

Legislation	Description
1972 Pesticide Control Act	Required that all pesticides used in interstate commerce be approved and certified as effective for their stated purposes. Required certification that they were harmless to humans, animal life, animal feed, and crops.
1974 Clean Water Act	Originally called the Safe Water Drinking Act, this law set (for the first time) federal standards for water suppliers serving more than twenty-five people, having more than fifteen service connections, or operating more than sixty days per year.
1976 Resource Conservation and Recovery Act	Encouraged conservation and recovery of resources. Put hazardous waste under government control. Disallowed the opening of new dumping sites. Required that all existing open dumps be closed or upgraded to sanitary landfills by 1983. Set standards for providing technical, financial, and marketing assistance to encourage solid-waste management.
1977 Clean Air Act Amendments	Pushed deadline for automobile emission requirements ahead to 1981.
1980 Comprehensive Environmental Response, Compensation and Liability Act	Established a "superfund" to clean up toxic waste dumps.
1990 Clean Air Act Amendments	The most comprehensive legislation to date. This act required the following. The oldest coal-burning power plants were to cut emissions by 40 percent to reduce acid rain. Industrial emissions of 189 toxic chemicals were to be reduced by 90 percent by the year 2000. Production of CFCs was to stop by the year 2002. Controls were placed on other factories and businesses intended to reduce smog in ninety-six cities to healthful levels by 2005. Utilities were granted "credits" to emit certain amounts of sulfur dioxide. Those that emit less than the maximum allowed sell their credits to other polluters.

wide." As late as May 12, 1983, the editors of *Rolling Stone* magazine stated the following:

> For years now, climatologists have foreseen a trend toward colder weather—long range, to be sure, but a trend as inevitable as death. . . . According to one theory, all it would take is a single cold summer to plunge the earth into a sudden apocalypse of ice.

By the 1990s, however, some scientists were claiming that the earth was getting warmer. According to the National Academy of Sciences, "global environmental change [global warming] may well be the most pressing international issue of the next century . . . the future welfare of human society is . . . at risk."

Scientists deeply disagree over the extent and nature of global warming and the greenhouse effect, however. Nevertheless, some of the most complex computer models of the world's climate, such as one at the National Center for Atmospheric Research, suggest that if the current rate of global warming continues, by the year 2050 the earth's temperature will rise by four degrees Fahrenheit. This would be an enormous change in temperature and would cause ecological changes that would result in dramatic social, economic, and political upheavals. The ice caps on mountain peaks would melt. Coastal water levels would rise, which might flood some cities.

Some scientists and policymakers believe that the problem of global warming must be addressed on a global scale. A significant step was made in December

1997 at a summit meeting held in Kyoto, Japan. At that meeting, leaders of the world's industrialized nations agreed to reduce emissions of "greenhouse" gases in their respective countries. The global warming treaty, called the **Kyoto Protocol,** establishes different rates of reduction for different countries or regions. For example, the United States is to reduce emissions to 7 percent below 1990 levels between the years 2008 and 2012. Japan is to reduce emissions by 6 percent, and the European Union by 8 percent.

Remember that no treaty can become binding on the United States until the Senate ratifies it. As of early 1998, it was not certain whether the Senate would ratify the Kyoto agreement. (For media reports on the controversy over global warming and the Kyoto Protocol, see the *Extended Case Study* following Chapter 23.)

Ethics and Environmental Policy

Virtually everyone values a clean and healthy environment. There is little disagreement among Americans on the basic goal of environmental protection and preservation. Yet when it comes down to the question of who will make what sacrifices to achieve this goal, there is much disagreement.

▲ Many people benefit when one person volunteers to help. A teenager may spend time with senior citizens, reading aloud, running errands, or simply providing welcome companionship. Meanwhile, regular caretakers can take a needed break and the teen makes new friends and gains an increased sense of self-worth.

Some types of volunteer work can be done from your home, if you have a computer available that is connected to the Internet. For example, an online organization called Lost Child needs volunteers to send notices to usenet news groups about missing children. You can reach this organization at the following Web site:

www.icc-911.com/ lostchild/

TAKING ACTION

1. Contact two of the organizations listed on page 602 and find out how volunteers function in those organizations and what requirements volunteers must meet. Write a one-page paper summarizing what you learned.
2. Interview a parent, a relative, or a friend on the topic of volunteering. Specifically, find out if that person has ever volunteered their time and efforts to help others in need and, if so, how he or she did so. Take notes during the interview, and use these notes to write a brief paper presenting the results of your interview.

Consider the spotted owl controversy. The spotted owl is on the government's list of endangered species, and regulations require that its habitat be protected. Protecting endangered species, including the spotted owl, is a national goal and one that is considered to be in the nation's interest. Yet the nation as a whole does not bear the economic burden imposed by habitat-preserving regulations. Rather, private industries and individuals do. The economic well-being of the timber industry in the northwestern United States, for example, has suffered significantly from regulations

◄ This little spotted owl is not only an endangered species, it has also been the center of a nationwide controversy between environmentalists and industry.

Welfare Reform

Each year, the government spends thousands of dollars on every family of four whose income is below the official poverty line. Nonetheless, the poverty rate is remaining about the same or falling only slightly. For years, people complained that our welfare system did not work. Finally, in response, Congress made changes in welfare policy in 1996 and again in 1997.

Under the current system, states play a much greater role than they did in the past in establishing welfare rules, such as determining who is eligible to receive what benefits. Some of the financial burden of the welfare system has also been shifted from the national government to state governments. The most important change in welfare policy is that current law requires the states to limit welfare assistance to two years. After two years, welfare recipients may continue receiving benefits, but only if they are working.

Americans are at odds over the 1996 welfare reform. Some say it will just lead to more poverty. Others feel that, in the long run, those currently on welfare will be better off.

Welfare Reform Means More Poor People, Say Some

According to the critics of these welfare reform measures, the new provisions are doing a disservice to America's poor people. After all, according to these critics, getting off welfare is a process, not an event. It is not realistic to believe that people ill equipped for the job market can simply "go off welfare" and get a job in two years. The problem is typically not a lack of available jobs. It is preparing welfare recipients for the world of work. The politics of welfare reform has never been related to real people. Rather, it has been driven by political considerations, particularly the need to balance the budget.

To be sure, the previous welfare system had become relatively inflexible and bureaucratically complex. But it should be fixed, not abandoned. Otherwise, we will see a worsening of the plight of poor people in the United States.

designed to preserve the natural habitat of the spotted owl and other endangered species. The question here—and in many similar situations—is ethical in nature because it concerns an issue of fairness: Why should one individual or group have to sacrifice more than others to preserve our environment?

Even if the United States found a way to solve its many environmental problems, it would still face the question of how to deal with polluting activities in other countries. Countries have, of course, made significant steps toward the global coordination of environmental-protection efforts. But problems arise when one country has to pay a higher "price" than others to implement global environmental standards. One of the difficulties faced by world leaders at the Kyoto meeting on global warming, for example, was

how to induce developing countries to agree to reduce carbon dioxide emissions. These nations rely more extensively on the burning of fossil fuels for energy than the developed countries do. Therefore, if the developing nations had to comply with strict standards regulating carbon dioxide emissions, their rate of industrial development would be slowed and their economies threatened.

A similar problem arises with respect to the goal of preserving the world's rain forests. It has been argued that because green vegetation helps to produce the right mix of gases in the air that we breathe, we will suffer in the future if we continue to destroy the rain forests. Yet any global agreement to preserve rain forests necessarily imposes a disproportionate burden on countries that have large concentrations of these

Changes Had to Be Made in Our Welfare System, Say Others

According to the supporters of welfare reform, the welfare system was destined for continued failure. In addition, allowing the states to impose work requirements on welfare recipients creates new incentives for those recipients to get jobs.

It may be true, according to these supporters of reform, that some poor people will suffer in the short term. But in the long run, everyone will be better off. Fewer individuals will become dependent on welfare payments. Evidence shows that long periods on welfare reduce work skills. Welfare recipients develop the habit of receiving government assistance. Individual self-confidence and the incentive to earn income are thereby destroyed.

Those in favor of welfare reform argue that children from poor families will also ultimately be better off. Welfare payments to their parents may help such children in the short run. In the long run, though, dependence on government payments corrupts the family's values. Children of families living on welfare for a long time come to believe that it is normal to be supported by the government. They become emotionally incapable of seeking financial independence.

▲ Pam Johnson is a former welfare recipient for whom the system was successful. She received financial assistance and worked her way off welfare and into a full-time job where she is now helping other people in need.

YOU DECIDE

1. If you were a state governor or legislator, how would you view the increased flexibility given to states in administering the welfare program?
2. From the perspective of people living in poverty, will state management of the welfare system better serve their interests than management at the national level? Explain.

forests, such as Brazil, where, unfortunately, vast areas of rain forest are being cleared. The wood is used as an industrial fuel source, and the cleared land is used as pasture for cattle and for farming, although rain forest soil is typically poor. During the planting season, satellite photographs have recorded as many as 7,000 fires a day in Amazonia. The forests may never recover.

To preserve their forests, those countries would have to forgo the profits that can be made by clearing the land to sell the timber or to grow commercially profitable crops. In sum, the difficulty with environmental policy, both on a national and a global level, is how to create and implement a policy that is not only effective but also as fair as possible to those who must comply with it.

◀ Clear-cutting in the Amazon rain forest is causing worldwide concern. This photo shows the destruction left when a forest is clear-cut. What worldwide environmental problems are caused by clear-cutting in the South American rain forests?

Changes in Domestic Policy

Changing social conditions have led to many changes in domestic policy over just the last fifty years. Here we list some of the ways in which domestic policy has changed since the 1950s.

THEN (1950s)	Now
Crime rates were lower than they are now, and there was less concern over stiffening sentences for criminal acts.	Crime rates are much higher than in the 1950s, and stiff sentencing laws, including "three strikes and you're out" laws, have been passed to curb crime.
Homelessness was not perceived as a significant problem.	Homelessness is perceived as a significant problem; it has been estimated that about 600,000 Americans are homeless.
The national government determined who was eligible for welfare assistance.	State governments determine who is eligible for welfare assistance.
There was little concern about global warming.	Global warming is perceived by many as a major threat to our environment.

SECTION 3 REVIEW

1. What was the Exxon *Valdez* incident?
2. What did the National Environmental Policy Act of 1969 establish?
3. What were the major provisions of the Clean Air Act Amendments of 1990?
4. What is meant by *the greenhouse effect*? Why might it be a serious problem?
5. What is the Kyoto Protocol? What environmental problem does it address?
6. **For Critical Analysis:** Can we expect poor countries to have the same environmental concerns as the United States? Explain.

★ ★ ★ ★ Chapter Summary ★ ★ ★ ★

Section 1: The Problem of Crime

- In the last decade, Americans have ranked crime as either the most serious or second most serious problem facing the United States.
- Crime levels for all crimes, including violent crimes, rose dramatically during the period from 1960 to the early 1990s. Since 1992, crime rates have been dropping.
- The true cost of crime includes the money spent on the criminal justice system, such as on prison construction and maintenance; private protection in the form of alarms and other security protections; urban decay; property loss; destroyed lives; and medical care.

New sentencing laws, called three-strikes-and-you're-out laws, require judges to imprison for life a person who is convicted of a third felony. Evidence indicates that these laws may help to reduce crime rates.

Section 2: The Government's Attempts to Eliminate Poverty

The poverty threshold (about $16,000 in 1997) is the income level that is used to determine who falls into the poverty category. The official poverty level does not take into account in-kind subsidies, such as food stamps and housing vouchers.

The poorer segments of our population include single females who head households and children. Additionally, there may be about 600,000 homeless people in the United States.

Major government programs attacking poverty include Social Security, Supplemental Security Income (SSI), Temporary Assistance to Needy Families (TANF), food stamps, and the earned-income tax credit (EITC) program.

In spite of government attempts to eliminate poverty, it has climbed from about 11 percent in 1973 to about 13 percent today.

Section 3: Cleaning Up the Environment

Attempts to control pollution problems in America date back to before the American Revolution. At the national level, the National Environmental Policy Act (NEPA) of 1969 marks the beginning of truly significant government involvement in pollution controls.

The NEPA (1) required that an environmental impact statement be prepared for federal actions that would significantly affect the quality of the environment, (2) created the Council on Environmental Quality (CEQ), and (3) authorized the establishment of the Environmental Protection Agency (EPA) to implement CEQ policies.

The 1990 Clean Air Act Amendments set standards to regulate automobile emissions, gasoline content, potential cancer-causing air toxins, and total emissions of sulfur dioxide from electric utilities.

A widely publicized concern today is the possibility of global warming due to the greenhouse effect (the trapping of heat inside the earth's atmosphere). Scientists disagree over the extent and nature of this development, however.

CHAPTER 22 Review

★ REVIEW QUESTIONS ★

1. How have crime rates changed over the past several decades? Are they currently increasing or decreasing?
2. What is the true cost of crime in the United States? What factors are considered in determining the true cost of crime?
3. What are "three strikes" laws? Are they effective in fighting crime? What are their disadvantages?
4. How is the poverty level determined?
5. Among what groups in society is poverty increasing?
6. Name five government programs designed to reduce poverty.
7. In what basic way did the government change the welfare system in 1996?
8. Describe some major efforts on the part of the U.S. government to help solve the problem of environmental pollution.
9. What is global warming? What is the greenhouse effect? Why are scientists and policymakers concerned with these phenomena?
10. How are world leaders addressing the problem of global warming?
11. Briefly describe the arguments for and against the welfare reforms begun in 1996.

★ CRITICAL THINKING ★

1. Do you see any relationship between the higher crime rates of today (compared with those of a few decades ago) and the increasing support among Americans for the death penalty?
2. Are "three strikes" laws really a deterrent to crime? Explain your response.
3. Should the U.S. government let state and local governments have complete control over welfare? Why or why not?
4. In your opinion, who should be responsible for cleaning up the environment—businesses, state governments, or the U.S. government? Give reasons for your answer.
5. What steps should the international community, including the United States, be taking to ensure a worldwide reduction in pollution and to protect the Earth's remaining natural resources?

★ IMPROVING YOUR SKILLS ★

Communication Skills

Recognizing Your Own Value Judgments Students of government are often called upon to express their opinions. This book has included many features on how to think critically before expressing an opinion. Underlying this need to think critically is the need to recognize your own value judgments.

Whether we are aware of it or not, we all make value judgments about everything that we consider. Our values are influenced by our parents and other family members, peers, schools and teachers, books we read, movies we see, religious beliefs, and countless other variables.

Even though you may not be able to pinpoint or change these past influences, you should try to become aware of how your values affect your thinking. Not recognizing your own values and value judgments can close your mind to facts and reasoning.

The next time you find yourself reacting very positively or very negatively to an issue about which you do not have all the facts, stop and examine your value judgments. Ask yourself if they are preventing you from evaluating the issue objectively.

Writing Reread the section on the new poor on page 592. Make a list of your value judgments concerning this issue.

Social Studies Skills

Identifying Similarities and Differences When you examine various laws, you will find similarities and differences among them. Look again at the information in Figure 22–3 on pages 600 and 601. What are the similarities between the 1970 Clean Air Act Amendments and the 1990 Clean Air Act Amendments? What are the differences?

★ ACTIVITIES AND PROJECTS ★

1. Contact your local police department to find out what is being done in your community to curb crime. Are there more police officers today than there were a year ago, two years ago, or ten years ago? What kinds of preventive programs, such as teenage drug counseling programs, exist in your community? Write a report on your findings, and present it to your class.

2. Invite a police officer to your classroom to discuss crime-related problems in your community. Ask that officer what high-school students can do to help in the effort to reduce crime.

3. Invite a local government official to your class to discuss local efforts to help those in need. Or, you might interview the leader of a homeless shelter within your community to find out what kinds of assistance are available to the homeless. You might find it very worthwhile to volunteer to serve a meal at a local shelter or food bank.

4. Contact the department in your state that regulates environmental pollution. Find out how the state and the national government cooperate in dealing with environmental problems. Write a summary of what you learned, and present it to your class.

5. Stage a classroom debate on the topic of global warming. Students on one side of the debate should present research results indicating that the global temperature is rising. Students on the other side should present research results indicating the opposite.

6. Invite either a local community official who is in charge of environmental affairs for your community or a local leader of the Sierra Club to visit the class to discuss local environmental problems and what is being done to solve them.

What If . . .

There Were No Welfare Programs?

For much of the early history of the United States, there were no welfare programs. What might happen today if federal, state, and local governments eliminated all welfare programs?

CHAPTER 23

Defense and Foreign Policy

CHAPTER OBJECTIVES

To learn about and understand . . .

⭐ The development of American foreign policy

⭐ The involvement of the president and Congress in making foreign and defense policy

⭐ The processes by which foreign and defense policy are made

⭐ The structure and functions of the Department of Defense and the Department of State

⭐ The goals of American foreign policy and the methods used to achieve them

⭐ The organization and functions of the United Nations

"*Americans think of themselves collectively as a huge rescue squad on twenty-four-hour call to any spot on the globe where dispute and conflict may erupt.*"

Eldridge Cleaver
(1935–1998)
U.S. African American Leader

INTRODUCTION

Some families have a family doctor. In an emergency, that doctor can usually be reached through his or her answering service. To some extent, Americans today look at their government as the family physician to the world. This is certainly the view of Eldridge Cleaver, as indicated in the quotation above.

It is not surprising that people around the globe look to the United States for assistance. After all, the United States is the only remaining superpower in the world. With this dominant position has come an even greater responsibility. Our foreign policy today is not focused on a single enemy. Rather, it is focused on keeping the world moving toward freedom, peace, and prosperity everywhere. The United States has not always been in this position, though, as you will learn in this chapter.

◀ U.S. Air Force troops ready this military jet for take-off from its perch on an aircraft carrier.

611

The Development of American Foreign Policy

Preview Questions:

- What is isolationism? Why was this policy abandoned by the United States?
- What was the Cold War?
- What have been some historical approaches of American foreign policy? How were these approaches developed?

Key Terms:

foreign policy, national security, defense policy, isolationism, Monroe Doctrine, interventionism, colonial empire, neutrality, superpowers, Marshall Plan, communism, Communist bloc, containment, collective security, Western bloc, iron curtain, Cold War, deterrence, mutual-assured destruction (MAD)

Every nation has a **foreign policy**—a systematic and general plan that guides the nation's attitudes and actions toward the rest of the world. Foreign policy includes all the economic, military, commercial, and diplomatic positions and actions a nation takes in its relationships with other countries.

The basic purpose of American foreign policy has always been to protect the national security of the United States. **National security** refers to the nation's independence and freedom from unwanted interference, threat, or takeover by other nations. **Defense policy**—protecting the nation through military preparedness—is thus an integral part of foreign policy. Over the years, our nation has worked to preserve national security in many ways. A brief look at the history of American foreign policy will help to explain how several approaches to foreign policy have evolved.

The Formative Years

The nation's founders and our early presidents believed that **isolationism**—avoiding political involvement with other nations—was the best way to protect American interests. The young United States tried to stay out of other nations' conflicts, particularly European wars. The reason was not that America was uninterested in the fate of Europe. Rather, the reason was that Americans were focused on building a new nation at home. We had many problems of our own, a huge continent to explore and settle, and two oceans separating us from most of the world. Furthermore, the United States was not yet strong enough to directly influence European developments. The young nation instead set an example for a new political system that was so attractive it might naturally lead Europe to political reform.

When George Washington became president, the United States was still small, weak, and struggling to thrive and develop. In his farewell address in 1796, President Washington urged Americans "to steer clear of permanent alliances with any portion of the foreign world." President Thomas Jefferson later echoed this sentiment when he stated that what Americans wanted were the following:

Peace, commerce, and honest friendship with all nations, entangling alliances with none.

During the 1700s and 1800s, the United States generally stayed out of conflicts and political issues in the rest of the world. From the beginning, however, the United States developed ties abroad through trade treaties and exchanges of diplomatic representatives with other nations.

Of course, staying completely isolated, even in that day and age, was not an easy thing to do. In the 1820s, many European nations were expanding into Latin America. The United States saw Central and South America as its own backyard and viewed European expansion as a threat to its economic and security interests. In a historic message to Congress in 1823, President James Monroe proclaimed what has become known as the **Monroe Doctrine.** In his message, President Monroe stated that the United States would not accept foreign intervention in the Western Hemisphere. He declared that the United States would look on "any attempt on [the part of other nations] to extend their system to any portion of this hemisphere as dangerous to our peace and security." In return, the United States would not meddle in European affairs.

Expansionism and the Beginning of Interventionism

While Americans were trying to avoid involvement in European affairs, they were also expanding westward across the North American continent. This expansion led the United States into conflicts with other nations—such as Mexico, France, Spain, and Great Britain—that held claims to lands to the south and west of the original colonies. Meanwhile, American traders were roaming the world in search of new markets, and American businesses were expanding across the Pacific, beginning trade with Japan, China, and other Asian countries in the mid-1800s. Isolationism no longer seemed to fit America's role in a fast-changing world. The United States built up its military forces and began to take a greater role in international affairs.

The first real step toward **interventionism,** or direct involvement in foreign affairs, came with the Spanish-American War of 1898, when the United States fought to free Cuba from Spanish rule. The United States defeated Spain and gained control of several Spanish island possessions, including Puerto Rico, Guam, and the Philippines. As a result, the United States now had a **colonial empire** and was acknowledged as a world power. (A colonial empire consists of numerous colonies—dependent countries or people who are not allowed to govern themselves.)

To protect American interests in Asia, Secretary of State John Hay announced the Open Door Policy of 1899. For years, Japan and many European powers had struggled to gain trade advantages in Asia. The new policy opened Chinese markets to the world's leading trading nations. It allowed all countries, including the United States, equal access to the region.

In the early 1900s, President Theodore Roosevelt adopted a policy that shifted the emphasis of the Monroe Doctrine. He proposed that the United States be allowed to invade Latin American countries when doing so was necessary to guarantee our country's own political and economic stability. Under what came to be known as the *Roosevelt Corollary* to the Monroe

Just the Facts

American troops occupied Haiti from 1915 to 1934.

◄ *In the early 1900s, President Theodore Roosevelt backed up the soft talk of diplomacy with the big stick of military might. Under what circumstances was an invasion of Latin America allowed under the Roosevelt Corollary to the Monroe Doctrine?*

Doctrine, the United States began to police Latin America in the early 1900s. U.S. troops went into several Latin American countries to help prevent domestic uprisings.

World Wars

As World War I raged in Europe in 1914, isolationism was still a strong sentiment in the United States. For three years, the United States stayed out of the war. President Woodrow Wilson urged a policy of **neutrality,** or refusal to take sides in an armed conflict. When American ships in international waters were attacked without reason by German submarines, however, the United States entered the war. President Wilson believed the United States had to enter—and win—the war to preserve our democratic system. It was the first time the United States had taken part in a full-scale war that arose from European disputes.

World War I ended in 1918, and during the 1920s and 1930s, most Americans did not want the United States to be involved in European affairs. The United States refused to join the League of Nations, the new international diplomatic body proposed by President Wilson. Most Americans seemed to favor a return to a policy of isolationism.

This return to isolationism, however, was only temporary. The United States initially tried to stay out of World War II and officially sought to remain neutral. When the Japanese attacked Pearl Harbor in 1941, the United States entered the war. The United States, in alliance with Australia, Great Britain, Canada, China, France, and the Soviet Union (the Allies), eventually fought Germany, Italy, and Japan (the Axis countries). The war ended four years and millions of lives later, after the United States dropped atomic bombs on the Japanese cities of Hiroshima and Nagasaki.

After World War II, the United States began to play a dramatically different role in world affairs. The United States and the Soviet Union emerged as **superpowers,** countries so strong that their actions determined the status of international peace and security.

The United States decided to participate actively in the postwar resettlement of Europe. The **Marshall Plan,** named after Secretary of State George Marshall, was a massive program of economic assistance to help the war-torn countries of Europe recover from the war. This foreign aid program was started in 1948 and helped Europe recover rapidly.

The Cold War

The World War II alliance between the United States and the Soviet Union began to deteriorate quickly. The Soviet Union opposed American political and economic values. The government of that nation was controlled by the Communist Party. **Communism,** as it was practiced in the Soviet Union, was a totalitarian system in which the government owned all property and controlled all production. Many Americans

▲ Smoke and flames pour from the U.S.S. West Virginia and the U.S.S. Tennessee after the Japanese attack on the U.S. Pacific Fleet stationed at Pearl Harbor, Hawaii. What was the immediate result of this act of aggression?

thought that the Soviet Union and the spread of communism were primary threats to democracy.

Between 1945 and 1949, one after another, the countries of Eastern Europe—Hungary, Poland, Bulgaria, Romania, and Czechoslovakia—fell under Soviet domination, forming what became known as the **Communist bloc.** When communists, backed by the Soviets, tried to take over in Greece and Turkey, President Harry Truman sent American troops to help those countries. These actions were the beginning of a new foreign policy called **containment.** This policy was aimed at preventing the spread of communism by offering threatened nations U.S. military and economic aid.

In order to make the policy of containment effective, it was necessary to form alliances of countries that needed protection. The United States initiated a policy of **collective security** involving the formation of mutual defense alliances with other nations. (This policy is discussed later in this chapter.) President Truman pledged military aid to any European nation threatened by Communist expansion. Thus, the United States became the leader of the **Western bloc** of democratic nations. This bloc included France, Great Britain, Australia, Canada, Japan, the Philippines, and other countries in Western Europe and Latin America.

Britain's prime minister, Winston Churchill, established the tone for a new relationship between the Soviet Union and the Western allies in his famous "iron curtain" speech in Fulton, Missouri, on March 5, 1946:

> An iron curtain has descended across the Continent. Behind that line all are subject in one form or another, not only to Soviet influence but to a very high . . . measure of control from Moscow.

The reference to an **iron curtain** described the political boundaries between the democratic countries in Western Europe and the Soviet-controlled communist countries in Eastern Europe. The term *iron curtain* became even more appropriate in 1961. In that year, the Soviets constructed the Berlin Wall to separate East Berlin, which was controlled by the Soviet Union, from West Berlin, which was not.

The tensions between the Soviet Union and the Western allies came to be known as the **Cold War.** The Cold War was a war of words, warnings, and ideologies backed up by a constant readiness for military conflict. The Western allies and the Soviet Union did not take up arms against each other during the Cold War.

▲ The world's two superpowers, the United States and the Soviet Union, each amassed huge stockpiles of nuclear weapons during the Cold War. As the two countries negotiated an end to the arms race, whom does the cartoonist see as the biggest loser?

Nevertheless, several violent confrontations grew out of the effort to contain communism. The wars in Korea and Vietnam are examples.

The Arms Race and Deterrence The tensions created by the Cold War led the Soviet Union and the United States to try to surpass each other militarily. They began competing for more and better weapons with greater destructive power. This phenomenon was commonly known as the arms race. The arms race was based on a policy of **deterrence**—that is, each side wanted to make itself so strong militarily that its very strength would deter, or discourage, any attack on it. Out of deterrence came the theory of **mutual-assured destruction (MAD).** This theory held that if the forces of both nations were

Just the Facts

Since 1963, the United States has conducted underground tests of more than four hundred nuclear weapons.

How to Watch
TV News

Watching the news on television is usually the easiest (though not always the best) way to learn about important world events. As you watch the news, think about what you are seeing and hearing. Remember that by the time a news story reaches you, it has been "processed" several times. For example, suppose tonight's feature story is about the Pentagon (the building in Washington, D.C., that houses the Defense Department). First, information on the event was issued by a Pentagon spokesperson. Then, a reporter wrote his or her version of the story. After that, network editors went over the story. Only then could the on-camera newscaster deliver the story to the American public.

Keep a few points and guidelines in mind as you watch and listen to TV news:

● Every day, thousands of events occur throughout the world. News programs are relatively short, and editors must choose a small number of these stories to report. The time they have to deliver the story is limited, and decisions have to be made about what to include and what to leave out.

● The day of the week often influences how the news is reported. Sunday is often a slow news day—a day when not much happens. Thus, a story reported on a Sunday may be discussed at greater length than the same story reported on a different day. On a slow Monday morning, reporters may exaggerate statements made by officials so that there is something to report. This is sometimes called a "Monday morning plant." On Friday nights, less will likely be reported, because fewer people watch the news at that time.

● Sometimes a *trial balloon* is released. This occurs when an official "leaks" information about a proposal to find out what public reaction to the proposal will be. A "hostile leak" occurs when an opponent of a proposal leaks information to the press to encourage hostile reactions.

● Sometimes, an event is not as bad as a news story makes it seem when it is initially reported. Reporters, of course, want every story to seem important so they will get more credit. In contrast, sometimes the worst news is worse than reporters initially suggest. Experienced reporters are sometimes reluctant to

---

equally capable of destroying each other, neither would take a chance on war.

The End of the Cold War Beginning in the mid-1980s, the stranglehold that the Soviet Union had maintained for forty years over both the Communist bloc and its own people started to loosen. The major event that signaled the end of the Communist era occurred on November 9, 1989, when the Berlin Wall was torn down. Within a relatively short period of time, democracies were introduced in a number of Eastern European countries, such as Poland and Czechoslovakia. The Soviet Union stopped trying to control that part of the world. Instead, it focused its efforts on maintaining unity at home in the face of a massive independence movement among the majority of the fifteen Soviet republics.

In August 1991, a number of dissatisfied Communist Party leaders took illegal control of the Soviet Union's central government. Russian citizens raised up in revolt and defied those leaders. The democratically elected president of the Russian Republic (the largest of the

◀ *ABC anchor Peter Jennings delivers the evening news. How does TV news coverage differ from news coverage in printed news sources?*

fully discuss a problem on the air because they fear they will lose access to important public officials.

PRACTICING YOUR SKILLS

1. Decide on one important topic to investigate. Watch one in-depth news program on the topic. You can find such programs on the Public Broadcasting System (PBS) channel in your area or on a commercial network channel on a weekend. Then watch news about the same topic on a regular news program. Note any differences that you observe.

2. Try to listen to a news commentary on the same subject on a radio station, again probably your local PBS affiliate. Note any differences between the radio presentation and the TV presentation.

3. Choose an important issue that is likely to remain in the news for several days. Take notes on the first news story you hear. Record the time given to the story, the importance the news program seems to attach to the story, and your impression of the nature and seriousness of the event. For the next several days, listen to as many other news stories as you can concerning that same issue. After several days, note how your opinion has changed, if at all.

Soviet republics), Boris Yeltsin, openly defied military troops in Moscow. Within three days, Yeltsin and his supporters had succeeded in regaining control in Moscow. Within weeks, the Communist Party in the Soviet Union had lost virtually all of its power. Most of the fifteen former Soviet republics declared their independence, and the Soviet Union was, in effect, no more.

Without question, the year 1991 will go down in history books as one of the most significant in modern times. That year saw the total collapse of communism in the Soviet Union and the true end of the Cold War.

Foreign Policy in the Post–Cold War Era

The Cold War has ended, but that does not necessarily mean that all is well and that foreign policy decision making is simpler. Indeed, some argue that foreign policymaking is now more complex. During the Cold War, we knew who our "enemies" were. To a great extent, U.S. foreign policy was fashioned in response to actions taken by the Soviet Union and the Communist bloc. Today, the United States is grappling with the

▲ *Two young Germans chip away at the Berlin Wall, which for almost thirty years stood between Communist East Berlin and free West Berlin. As the wall crumbled, so did the Soviet Union's control of Eastern Europe. What ultimately brought about the end of the Cold War?*

question of how to develop a foreign policy appropriate to the new world situation brought about by the demise of the Soviet Union. How can we best protect our national interests? How can we promote democracy—and human rights—throughout the world? Should the United States play the role of the world's "peacekeeper"? Should economic considerations (such as profiting by favorable trading arrangements with other nations) take priority over human rights issues in foreign policymaking? These are just a few of the questions that face foreign policymakers today.

SECTION 1 REVIEW

1. Why did the United States develop a policy of isolationism in its early years? Why was this policy abandoned?
2. What is the Monroe Doctrine, and why is it significant?
3. When and why did the United States initiate a policy of collective security?
4. **For Critical Analysis:** Some of the factors that influence U.S. foreign policymaking include (1) national security, (2) favorable trading arrangements, and (3) human rights issues. How should these factors be ranked, in terms of priority, with respect to foreign policymaking? Why?

SECTION 2

The Makers of Foreign Policy

Preview Questions:

⭐ In the area of foreign policy, what powers does the Constitution give to the president? What other presidential foreign policy powers have developed over time?

⭐ What role do cabinet members play in the making of foreign policy and defense policy?

⭐ What other agencies are involved in shaping foreign policy?

⭐ What are Congress's constitutional powers in the area of foreign policy?

Key Term:

intelligence

The Constitution provides for a partnership between Congress and the president in developing American foreign policy. The roles of each partner in

Could a False Alarm Start a Nuclear War?

On January 25, 1995, President Boris Yeltsin of Russia saw a warning light on the "nuclear briefcase" that his aide was carrying. This briefcase, like the one that accompanies the president of the United States at all times, is actually a computer that contains the top-secret codes and warning systems for nuclear attacks. When the case was opened, the computer was tracking a missile coming over the Norwegian Sea apparently toward Russia. On the computer was an array of keys that would authorize the firing of the 4,700 nuclear warheads that are on permanent alert in Russia.

Yeltsin's choice was not easy. If the warning was a false alarm, and Yeltsin gave the launch order, he could start World War III. If the warning was not a false alarm, and Yeltsin did nothing, a nuclear warhead could explode over Russia, crippling the nation. Yeltsin had four minutes to decide. Fortunately for all of us, he did not panic. A quick investigation showed that the blip on his computer screen had been triggered by a meteorological rocket fired from Norway to obtain information about the *aurora borealis* (or Northern Lights).

The scenario just described was not an isolated event. In 1979, for example, training data were slipped into the U.S. early-warning system to mimic a large Soviet attack. U.S. military decision makers fortunately figured out what had happened before any damage was done. In 1983, a solar storm caused an early-warning system in the Soviet Union to indicate a massive U.S. attack.

The point is that even though the Cold War has ended, both the United States and Russia are still concerned with nuclear arsenals and possible nuclear attacks. And both countries rely on extraordinarily rapid decision making to defend against such attacks. In the United States, from the time assessment of a possible attack occurs to the time of launch and preparation, only twenty-two minutes pass. In Russia, the process takes thirteen minutes. There is little time for a critical, detailed analysis of the situation.

THINK ABOUT IT

1. Why, if the United States and Russia are no longer enemies, do both countries still worry about nuclear war?
2. Does the United States still need an early-warning system to detect nuclear attack? Why or why not?

this partnership were not, however, clearly spelled out. As one constitutional expert observed, the Constitution created "an invitation to struggle for the privilege of directing American foreign policy" for the president and Congress. On many occasions, the president and Congress have in fact struggled over power in this area.

The president has become chief policymaker of foreign policy and has assumed much of the decision-making power in this area. But the president is not alone in shaping foreign policy. Congress, various officials, and a vast national security bureaucracy assist in shaping and checking the president's decisions. It is also important to remember that foreign policy is the sum of an entire country's attitudes and actions toward the rest of the world.

The Executive Branch

The president is granted specific powers by the Constitution in the area of foreign policy. Article II,

Section 1, names the president commander in chief of the armed forces. As commander in chief, the president oversees the military and guides defense policies. Starting with Abraham Lincoln, presidents have interpreted this role broadly and have sent American troops, ships, and weapons to trouble spots at home and around the world.

The Constitution also gives the president the power to make treaties, provided that two-thirds of the Senate approve. In addition to treaty-making powers, the president has the power to make executive agreements—pacts between the president and the heads of other nations. These agreements do not require Senate approval. Furthermore, the Constitution gives the president certain diplomatic powers. These include the power to appoint ambassadors to represent our country in other nations and the power to recognize foreign governments by receiving their ambassadors.

The president also influences foreign policy as head of state. As a national symbol, the president represents the United States to the rest of the world. When a foreign policy issue or international question arises, the nation expects the president to make a formal statement.

The president can also influence foreign policy through many informal techniques. The president, for example, has access to more information than any other governmental authority. A strong, centralized administration enables the president to act quickly and decisively in an emergency. In addition, the president has budget-making powers and can influence the amounts allocated for various programs. The president can also influence public opinion to a greater extent than any other public official. The president's foreign policy responsibilities take on special significance because the president has ultimate control over the use of nuclear weapons.

The Cabinet Members All members of the president's cabinet concern themselves with international problems and recommend policies to deal with these problems. The secretary of state and the secretary of defense, however, are the only cabinet members who concern themselves with foreign policy matters on a full-time basis.

Most presidents have relied heavily on the advice of their secretaries of state in foreign policy matters. The secretary of state participates in the development of U.S. policies to respond to international events. The secretary meets with foreign ministers and heads of other governments. He or she also represents the United States at international meetings and negotiations.

The secretary of defense advises the president on all aspects of U.S. defense policy. The defense secretary also supervises all of the military activities of the American government and works to see that the decisions of the president as commander in chief are carried out. The secretary advises and informs the president on the nation's military forces, weapons, and bases. In addition, the secretary works closely with the American military, especially the Joint Chiefs of Staff, in gathering and studying defense information.

> **Just the Facts**
>
> *Thomas Jefferson was the first U.S. secretary of state.*

▶ *Former secretary of state James Baker is shown here shaking hands with Iraqi Foreign Minister Tariq Aziz at this January 1991 meeting. They met to discuss possible solutions to the crisis caused by Iraq's invasion of Kuwait in 1990.*

You can try to influence foreign policy by communicating with your congressional representatives or with the White House. You can also lobby, demonstrate, and join with others who share your views. Some organizations in which you might find such people include the following:

● American Friends Service Committee
Peace Education Division
1501 Cherry St.
Philadelphia, PA 19102
215-241-7000
www.afsc.org/

This group works for peace, justice, equality, and nonviolent solutions to worldwide problems.

● Amnesty International USA
National Office
322 Eighth Avenue
New York, NY 10001
212-807-8400
www.amnesty-usa.org/ home.html

Amnesty International investigates human rights abuses and lobbies for the release of political prisoners throughout the world.

● The Center for Defense Information
1500 Massachusetts Ave. NW
Washington, DC 20005
202-862-0700
www.cdi.org/

This organization studies the defense budget, weapons

How to Influence American Foreign Policy

systems, and troop levels to educate the public.

● The Brookings Institution
1775 Massachusetts Ave. NW
Washington, DC 20036
202-797-6000
www.brook.edu/

This group conducts research on public policy issues in the social sciences, particularly economics, government, and foreign affairs.

● Committee for National Security
1901 Pennsylvania Ave. NW
Suite 802
Washington, DC 20006
202-745-2450

This committee informs Americans about national security and arms control issues and encourages citizen participation in the debate on U.S. military and foreign policy.

● The Fellowship of Reconciliation
P.O. Box 271
Upper Nyack, NY 10960
914-358-4601
www.nonviolence.org/for/ history.htm

This group fosters public education and nonpartisan discussion of foreign policy issues by publishing books and pamphlets.

TAKING ACTION

1. Contact three of the organizations listed above and ask for information about their objectives and activities. Write a one-paragraph summary of what each organization does and how it operates.
2. Pick a foreign policy issue that interests you, and write a letter to the organization listed above that seems most appropriate to the issue. Ask what the organization is doing in this area and how you can help.
3. Review recent news magazines and newspapers for information on a specific foreign policy issue. Access one of these organizations online to see how the issue is treated by the organization. Then, write a short compare-and-contrast essay showing the (possibly) differing viewpoints.

The Department of State and the Department of Defense will be discussed in greater detail later in this chapter.

National Security Council The National Security Council (NSC) was established by the National Security Act of 1947. Its official function is "to advise the president with respect to the integration of domestic, foreign, and military policies relating to the national security."

The formal members of the NSC include the president, the vice president, the secretary of state, and the secretary of defense. In addition, NSC meetings are often attended by the chairperson of the Joint Chiefs of Staff, the director of the Central Intelligence Agency, and representatives of other departments. The special assistant for national security affairs, who is a member of the president's White House staff, is the director of the NSC. The special assistant coordinates advice and information on foreign policy and serves as a liaison with other officials.

Presidents use the NSC and its members in different ways, and it can be as important and powerful as each president wants it to be. Some presidents have made frequent use of the NSC, whereas others have convened it infrequently and on an informal basis.

Central Intelligence Agency The Central Intelligence Agency (CIA) was created after World War II to coordinate American intelligence activities abroad. The CIA provides the president and his advisers with up-to-date information about the political, military, and economic activities of foreign governments. Such information is called **intelligence.**

The CIA gathers much of its intelligence from overt (open) sources, such as foreign radio broadcasts and newspapers, people who travel abroad, and satellite photographs. Other information is gathered through covert (secret) activities. The CIA has tended to operate autonomously, and the nature of its work, methods, and operating funds have been kept secret.

Historically, the CIA focused its efforts on the Soviet Union and its allies. Since the collapse of the Soviet Union, the CIA has been, to some extent, without a specific mission. It has attempted to engage in economic intelligence gathering but without much

success. It has also been used to fight the war on drugs in other countries, again with little effectiveness.

Other Agencies Several other government groups help shape American foreign policy. The Arms Control and Disarmament Agency was formed in 1961 to study and develop policies to deal with the nuclear arms race. The United States Information Agency (USIA) works to strengthen communications and understanding between the United States and other nations. It is best known for Voice of America, a round-the-clock radio program that is translated into approximately forty languages. The Agency for International Development (AID) gives financial and technical help to other countries. The Peace Corps sends American volunteers to work on development and education projects in other countries.

Congressional Powers

Although the executive branch takes the lead in foreign policy matters, Congress also has some power over foreign policy. Remember that Congress alone has the power to declare war. It also has the power to appropriate funds to build new weapons systems and to equip American armed forces. The Senate has the power to approve or reject treaties and appointments of ambassadors.

In 1973, Congress passed the War Powers Resolution, which limits the president's use of troops in military actions without congressional approval. Presidents since then, however, have not interpreted the act to mean that they must consult Congress before taking military action. Presidents Ford, Carter, Reagan, and Bush all ordered military action and then informed Congress after the fact.

Several congressional committees are directly concerned with foreign affairs. The most important are the Armed Services Committee and the International Relations Committee in the House of Representatives and the Armed Services Committee and the Foreign Relations Committee in the Senate. Other committees in Congress deal with matters—such as oil, agriculture, imports, and others—that indirectly influence foreign policy.

◀ In 1989, the national elections in the Central American country of Panama were believed to be fraudulent, and the Organization of American States (OAS) declared the newly elected government to be illegitimate. Shortly afterward, the United States sent armed military forces to restore the constitutional government in Panama. Under what treaty was this action taken?

SECTION 2 REVIEW

1. What are the constitutional powers of the president in the area of foreign policy?
2. What individuals and agencies in the executive branch are involved in foreign policy matters?

3. What constitutional powers does Congress have in the area of foreign policy?
4. **For Critical Analysis:** If Congress has the sole right to declare war, how is it possible for presidents to involve American armed forces in military actions without congressional approval?

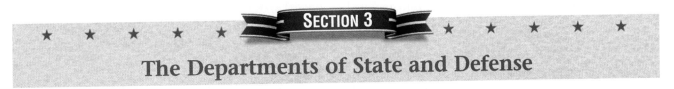

SECTION 3

The Departments of State and Defense

Preview Questions:

⭐ What is the structure of the Department of State? What are its functions?
⭐ What are the responsibilities of the foreign service?
⭐ What is the basic job of the Department of Defense?

Key Terms:

foreign service, embassy, ambassador, chargé d'affaires, attachés, consulate, consul, passports, visa, draft, conscription

Although the president and Congress have the ultimate power to make foreign policy, two departments in the executive branch are primarily responsible for carrying out foreign policy. One is the Department of State, which is the oldest and largest of the executive departments. The other is the Department of Defense.

Department of State

The Department of State is, in principle, the agency most directly concerned with foreign affairs. The overall goal of the department is to ensure the security and well-being of the United States. The Department of State maintains diplomatic relations with nearly two hundred independent nations around the world and with the United Nations. It informs the president about international issues, negotiates treaties with foreign

◀ *The flag of Venezuela flies outside its embassy in Washington, D.C. What is the purpose of an embassy?*

governments, and protects the interests of Americans who are traveling or conducting business abroad.

Structure The department is organized into regional bureaus, one for each of the five major geographic regions of the world: the Middle East, Africa, Latin America, Asia, and Europe. Other bureaus, such as the Bureau of Human Rights and Humanitarian Affairs, the Bureau of Intelligence and Research, and the Bureau of Economic and Business Affairs, have more broadly defined responsibilities. The department employs over 24,000 individuals.

The head of the department is, of course, the secretary of state. The secretary has several assistants. The most important is the deputy secretary of state, who directs the department when the secretary is not present. Various undersecretaries advise the secretary on such issues as foreign economic policy, relations with developing nations, educational and cultural affairs, and military arms exports.

The Foreign Service A part of the Department of State called the **foreign service** conducts most of the country's relations with other nations. The responsibilities of the foreign service include maintaining

embassies, consulates, and other U.S. offices around the world; negotiating agreements with nations; and maintaining cordial relations with foreign governments and people. Thousands of men and women employed in the foreign service represent the United States in hundreds of locations throughout the world.

To become a foreign service officer (FSO), college graduates must first perform well on the civil service exam. They are then trained in special government schools in the skills of diplomacy. In their service abroad, foreign service officers are assigned to either an American embassy or an American consulate.

An **embassy** is the office of an ambassador to a foreign nation. Embassies are located in the capital cities of foreign countries. The primary purpose of an embassy is to facilitate diplomatic communications between governments. The embassy keeps the U.S. State Department informed about the internal politics and foreign policies of the host government (the government of the nation in which the embassy is located). It also keeps the host government informed about the official policies of the American government.

The **ambassador** who heads each embassy is a personal representative of the president of the United States. He or she reports to the president through the

ARCHITECTS

of Government

Madeleine K. Albright
(1933–   )

Madeleine K. Albright was sworn in as U.S. secretary of state on January 23, 1997. She became not only the first woman to hold that post but also the highest-ranking woman ever in the U.S. government's executive branch. Previously, she had been the permanent U.S. representative to the United Nations. Albright also served as president of the Center for National Policy and as a research professor of international affairs at Georgetown University. She was responsible for foreign policy legislation as chief legislative assistant to Senator Edmund Muskie from 1978 to 1981.

HER WORDS

"Because we are entering a century in which there will be many interconnected centers of population, power, and wealth, we cannot limit our focus to the devastated battleground of a prior war. Our vision must encompass not one, but every continent."

(Commencement speech, Harvard University, June 1997)

"Although we seem always to be living in the moment, our challenges are easier because of what others did in the past, and our choices more weighty because of what they will mean to those who come after."

(Speech, Commonwealth Club, June 1997)

DEVELOPING
CRITICAL THINKING SKILLS

1. What "devastated battleground of a prior war" do you think Albright was referring to in the first quotation?
2. In the second quotation, Albright referred to things that others did in the past. What might those things include?

secretary of state. If the ambassador is absent from the embassy, the **chargé d'affaires,** a lower-ranking foreign service official, may temporarily assume the ambassador's duties. Ambassadors are assisted by one or more diplomatic secretaries and a counselor, a high-ranking foreign service officer who advises the ambassador on matters of international law and diplomatic practice. An embassy staff usually includes political, military, and economic **attachés,** or aides, as well as interpreters, clerks, and intelligence officials, among others.

An American **consulate** is the office of the **consul,** an official who is assigned to promote American business interests in foreign cities. The consul and his or her staff handle questions and problems about business requirements, transportation, and interpretation of foreign laws. Consuls also protect the welfare of U.S. citizens living or traveling abroad. In addition, they issue **passports,** certificates that entitle their holders to leave and re-enter their own country and receive certain protections while traveling in foreign countries. No American citizen can legally leave the country without a passport, except when traveling to Canada, Mexico, and a few other nearby countries.

In some cases, to travel abroad, it is necessary to obtain another document called a **visa.** The visa is a special document of admission issued by the consulate of the country the person wishes to enter.

Department of Defense

The Department of Defense (DOD) is the principal executive department that establishes and carries out defense policy and protects our national security. The Department of Defense was established by the National Security Act of 1947 to bring all of the various activities of the American military under the jurisdiction of a single department headed by a civilian. It replaced two older cabinet-level military departments, the War Department and the Navy Department.

The Department of Defense supervises the armed forces of the United States and gives advice to the president on military and defense matters. The DOD also works to ensure that the decisions of the president as commander in chief are carried out.

Structure There are three military departments within the DOD: the departments of the Army, Navy, and Air Force. Each of these branches is headed by a civilian

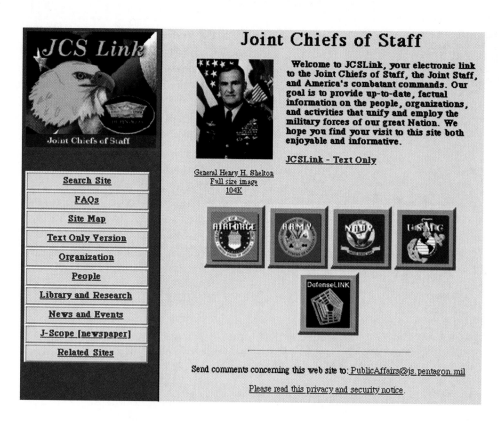

Joint Chiefs of Staff

JCS Link

Joint Chiefs of Staff

Welcome to JCSLink, your electronic link to the Joint Chiefs of Staff, the Joint Staff, and America's combatant commands. Our goal is to provide up-to-date, factual information on the people, organizations, and activities that unify and employ the military forces of our great Nation. We hope you find your visit to this site both enjoyable and informative.

JCSLink - Text Only

General Henry H. Shelton
Full size image
104K

Search Site
FAQs
Site Map
Text Only Version
Organization
People
Library and Research
News and Events
J-Scope [newspaper]
Related Sites

DefenseLINK

Send comments concerning this web site to: PublicAffairs@js.pentagon.mil

Please read this privacy and security notice.

◀ *This Web site of the Joint Chiefs of Staff shows the Chairperson of the Joint Chiefs, General Henry H. Shelton. Who are the Joint Chiefs and what is their job?*

secretary, who is assisted by senior military officers. The U.S. Marine Corps, which is under the jurisdiction of the Navy, maintains its own leadership and identity. Congress determines how each branch of the armed forces will be organized and governed. Moreover, the top leaders of the Department of Defense, including the secretary of defense, are required to be civilians.

Joint Chiefs of Staff

The top-ranking officers of each of the armed forces are known together as the Joint Chiefs of Staff. The Joint Chiefs of Staff include the chief of staff of the Army, the chief of staff of the Air Force, the chief of naval operations, and the commandant of the Marine Corps. The chairperson of the Joint Chiefs of Staff is appointed by the president for a four-year term.

The Joint Chiefs of Staff serve as key military advisers to the president, the secretary of defense, and the National Security Council. They are responsible for handing down the president's orders to the nation's military units, preparing strategic plans, and recommending military actions. They also propose military budgets, new weapons systems, and military regulations. For example, the Joint Chiefs of Staff may propose developing a new missile or forming a special military unit.

Selective Service System

Two methods are used to recruit citizens to serve in the armed forces. The first method is the volunteer enlistment system. Any person who has a high-school diploma may choose to enlist after fulfilling the requirements. The second method, known as the **draft,** is the selection of persons for compulsory military duty. Drafting people to serve in the military is also known as **conscription.** The draft was used from 1940 until 1973 in the United States. The official name for this compulsory system is the Selective Service System.

Although the draft was suspended in 1973, it was not repealed. This means that all males between the ages of eighteen and twenty-six are still eligible for the draft. Each male citizen must register with the Selective Service upon reaching his eighteenth birthday in case a military draft is needed during a national emergency.

Defense Spending

As Figure 23–1 on page 627 illustrates, over the years defense spending has accounted for a large portion of U.S. government expenditures.

Defense spending as a percentage of total expenditures of the United States reached its highest point during World War II (1941–1945) and again climbed

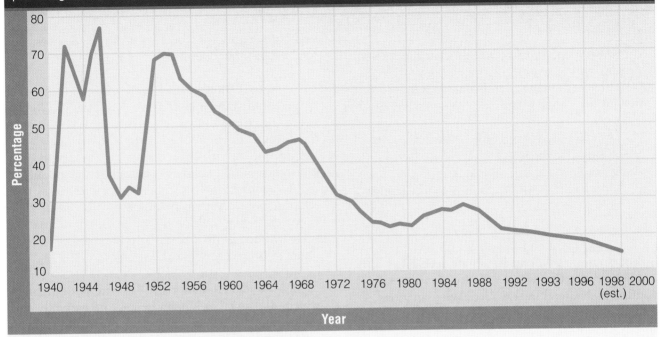

SOURCE: Office of Management and Budget, 1998.

▲ *Soldiers carrying assault rifles run through a wooded area of Fort Jackson, South Carolina. What executive department supervises the Army and all other branches of the military?*

rapidly during the Korean War (1950–1953). Defense spending started growing under the Carter administration (1977–1981) and increased rapidly under the Reagan administration (1981–1989). During the Bush administration (1989–1993), the end of the Cold War brought about a call for decreased military spending on the part of the United States. Since then, there have been substantial cutbacks in defense spending.

SECTION 3 REVIEW

1. What is the primary responsibility of the Department of State?
2. What is the foreign service?
3. Who are the persons that make up the Joint Chiefs of Staff, and what is their function?
4. **For Critical Analysis:** Why do you think the founders made sure that the military would always be subordinate to civilian leaders?

American Foreign Policy Goals and Tools

Preview Questions:

🌐 What are the main goals of American foreign policy?

🌐 What is diplomacy, and what does it involve?

🌐 Why has the United States provided foreign aid to other countries?

🌐 Why has the United States built alliances throughout the world?

🌐 What are the major alliances?

🌐 How can trade measures be used as a foreign policy tool?

Key Terms:

human rights, diplomacy, summit meeting, alliance, mutual defense alliance, multilateral treaties, bilateral treaties, economic sanctions

U.S. foreign policy includes the goals our nation wants to achieve in the world and the techniques and strategies used to achieve them. The specifics of American foreign policy may change with new situations and new administrations, but the fundamental objectives and goals have remained fixed.

Goals of American Foreign Policy

American foreign policy as a whole is guided by the overall purpose of promoting national security, or keeping the nation safe from attack or harm. Most aspects of our foreign policy are related to the need to maintain the United States as a free and independent nation, secure from unwanted external influence. The United States has worked toward this overall purpose by setting policies to achieve several goals.

World Peace One of the most important foreign policy goals of the United States is world peace. The security of the United States, as well as that of other nations, is best protected when nations stay out of wars. Alternatives to military conflict offer the best hope for maintaining true peace. In working toward the goal of world peace, U.S. leaders cooperate and

negotiate with other countries, form alliances, and send aid to other countries when needed.

Economic Prosperity Economic prosperity for the United States is an important goal of American foreign policy. A nation must be economically strong in order to be secure. Economic prosperity also depends on free and open trade with other countries. Our nation is not self-sufficient in a number of natural resources, such as oil. We must be able to obtain those resources from other nations. American businesses also need other countries to buy their products. Because other nations trade with the United States, it is important that those nations also be economically strong.

Human Rights **Human rights** are the basic rights to which all people, as human beings, are naturally entitled. History is full of examples of how violations of human rights have threatened world peace. Revolutions often break out when governments deny human rights to their own people. Often, other nations are

▲ This grain was provided to the people of Sarnath, a state in India suffering from famine, as part of U.S. foreign policy. Why is it in our nation's best interest to promote peace, prosperity, human rights, and democracy in other nations?

drawn in to help resolve the conflicts. The United States supports human rights by publicly criticizing human rights violations committed by other nations. It also provides food, medical supplies, and other types of aid to people of other nations in times of emergency, such as famine or earthquake. Such help is provided for humanitarian reasons, although it also contributes to maintaining political stability throughout the world.

Democracy Another American foreign policy goal has been to encourage democratic forms of government. American foreign policy has supported the democratic rights of people in other nations and has lent support to nations striving toward democracy, such as Romania, Hungary, and Poland in the late 1980s. In 1994, the United States went so far as to send troops to Haiti to reinstate Haiti's democratically elected president, Jean-Bertrand Aristide, who had been forced from power by military leaders. Promoting democratic ideals is another way of protecting American security.

Tools of American Foreign Policy

As you have seen, the major goal of American foreign policy is to protect national security. The United States uses several tools to achieve this and other foreign policy goals. These tools include diplomacy, foreign aid, alliances and pacts, trade agreements, and military force.

Diplomacy Diplomacy is the total process of conducting political relations with other countries, including settling differences and conflicts through peaceful means. It is the most important tool of American foreign policy. Many other foreign policy tools, such as alliances and trade agreements, result from diplomatic negotiations with other countries.

True diplomacy involves working with people through various forms of compromise and negotiation. When disagreements between nations arise, each nation usually sends representatives, known as diplomats, to speak with diplomats from other nations about the issues.

Diplomatic relations are often carried out by the Department of State. Sometimes, though, the president meets with other heads of state in a **summit meeting.** For example, a summit meeting between President George Bush, President Mikhail Gorbachev of the

Soviet Union, and other European leaders in Paris in 1990 led to the signing of an agreement to cut military arsenals in Europe. In 1996, leaders of seven of the world's most powerful nations held a summit meeting in Paris to discuss the problem of terrorism. In 1997, leaders of the world's industrialized nations met in Kyoto, Japan, and formed an agreement on how to deal with the perceived problem of global warming.

Foreign Aid Economic aid to other countries has been an American foreign policy tool for over fifty years. It began with the Lend-Lease Program of the early 1940s, in which the United States gave nearly $50 billion in food, munitions, and other supplies to our allies in World War II. After World War II, the Marshall Plan promoted economic recovery in Europe. Under the Marshall Plan, the United States gave billions of dollars to sixteen Western European nations between 1948 and 1952. This aid helped with Western Europe's postwar economic recovery and increased its ability to trade with the United States.

Over the years, as shown in Figure 23–2 on page 630, the United States has given billions of dollars to other countries in the form of foreign aid. Most aid is in the form of grants, not loans that must be repaid. In total dollars, the United States supplies more foreign aid than any other nation. As a percentage of our national budget, however, we give less foreign aid than some other industrialized nations, such as Japan.

American foreign aid goes primarily to nations that support U.S. foreign policy goals. Aid has been given to prevent the establishment of governments with political ideals contrary to our own and to help countries fight against aggression. The United States also gives economic aid to establish friendly relations with nations.

Most U.S. economic aid programs are administered by the Agency for International Development (AID), an executive agency, in close cooperation with the Department of State and the Department of Agriculture. Military aid is channeled through the Defense Department.

Alliances and Pacts American foreign policy also seeks security through alliances and pacts. An **alliance** is a group of nations or individuals joined together for a common purpose, which may be military, economic, or political. To form alliances, nations sign pacts, or treaties.

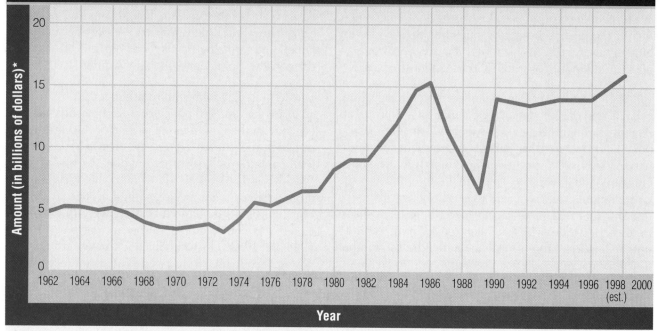

FIGURE 23–2 U.S. Expenditures for Foreign Aid, 1962–1998 The line graph below depicts U.S. expenditures for foreign aid in billions of dollars since 1962. From looking at this graph, how would you describe the 1980s in terms of foreign aid expenditures?

* Includes outlays for international development, humanitarian assistance, and international security assistance.
SOURCE: Office of Management and Budget.

A **mutual defense alliance** is a military alliance formed among countries to protect against a common threat to their security. Under such an alliance, nations become allies and pledge to support each other in case of an attack by enemy forces. The United States has signed mutual defense treaties with at least forty-two nations in various regions. These treaties are **multilateral treaties** in that they are signed by a group of several nations. Major multilateral treaties include the following:

● *North Atlantic Treaty Organization (NATO)*. After World War II, the United States and leaders of Western European nations gathered in Washington to create the North Atlantic Treaty Organization (NATO). NATO was originally composed of the United States, Canada, Great Britain, France, Italy, Portugal, the Netherlands, Belgium, Luxembourg, Denmark, Norway, and Iceland. Greece and Turkey joined the alliance in 1952, West Germany in 1955, and Spain in 1982.

The chief objective of NATO was the collective defense of Western Europe, particularly against

Soviet aggression. NATO's military forces were set up to be the first line of defense for Western Europe. By the 1990s, as relations between the Western nations and the republics of the former Soviet Union improved, NATO members agreed that NATO must redefine its role in broader terms to make it more meaningful in today's world. Further, in July 1998, NATO's sixteen heads of state and governments met to invite certain new democracies in Central and Eastern Europe to begin the process necessary to join the alliance.

● *The Organization of American States (OAS)*. The Inter-American Treaty of Reciprocal Assistance, also called the Rio Pact, was signed in 1947. This pact formalized the long-standing cooperation among the nations of the Western Hemisphere. It committed the United States to defend thirty-two countries of Latin America.

In 1948, the nations that had signed the Rio Pact established the Organization of American States (OAS). The goals of the OAS are to promote economic development and strengthen peace and secu-

◄ When the North Atlantic Treaty Organization (NATO) was formed after World War II with the goal of protecting Western Europe from Soviet aggression, few could have foreseen this day in 1997—the signing of the NATO-Russia accord.

rity in the Western Hemisphere, to prevent conflicts or to settle them peacefully through negotiation, and to seek solutions for political, judicial, and economic problems.

- *Anzus Pact.* The Anzus Pact of 1951 is a defense pact that unites Australia, New Zealand, and the United States. It commits these countries to come to one another's aid in case of attack.

In addition to these multilateral agreements, the United States has entered into many **bilateral treaties,** which are treaties between two nations. The United States has signed bilateral treaties with Spain, Japan, the Philippines, and the Republic of Korea, for example.

Trade Measures Another foreign policy tool involves the terms under which the United States trades with other countries. Two aims of American trade policies are to increase sales of American goods to other countries, which promotes economic prosperity, and to persuade trading partners to support our other foreign policy goals. Trade terms include how much of a foreign product will be allowed into the United States and which tariffs, or taxes, will be levied on the products. Agreements between nations may set trade terms.

Not surprisingly, the United States has been at the forefront in pushing for freer world trade. The United States was a leading member of the General Agreement on Tariffs and Trade (GATT), which formed the World Trade Organization. The United States also opened up trade with Canada and Mexico after the North American Free Trade Agreement was signed in 1993.

Sometimes the United States punishes other nations by withdrawing trade benefits. **Economic sanctions** are measures by which the government withholds trade benefits, supplies, or economic aid to pressure a foreign government to cease certain activities. For example, in 1986, Congress initiated and passed a bill instituting economic sanctions against South Africa to pressure that nation into ending apartheid, its legal system of racial segregation. In 1990, President Bush imposed severe economic sanctions against Iraq in an effort to force Iraq's leader, Saddam Hussein, to withdraw his forces from Kuwait. In the 1990s, the U.S. government imposed trading sanctions on Latin American nations whose governments would not take serious steps to control drug trafficking.

Military Force On a number of occasions, the United States has used military force to achieve foreign policy goals. On five of these occasions, the United States has declared war. American troops have been used abroad without declarations of war many times, however (see Chapter 18).

► *After the protracted disaster of the Vietnam War (1964–1975), the Bush administration felt the American people would not support a war unless they could see both a clearly defined purpose for it and an end of it in sight. Here soldiers of the 101st Infantry Division prepare for battle in the Persian Gulf War of 1991, which, in contrast to the Vietnam War, lasted only one hundred days. What caused the Persian Gulf War?*

SECTION 4 REVIEW

1. What are the major U.S. foreign policy goals?
2. What is diplomacy?
3. Why does the United States provide foreign aid to other nations?
4. Why has the United States built a network of alliances?

5. How are trade measures used as a tool of foreign policy?
6. **For Critical Analysis:** In 1991, the U.S. government claimed that it needed to wage war against Iraq in order to liberate Kuwait. Do you think the United States should be concerned with the internal politics of a Middle Eastern country—or of any other country in the world? Give reasons for your answer.

★ ★ ★ ★ ★ SECTION 5 ★ ★ ★ ★ ★

The United Nations

Preview Questions:

🌐 When and why was the United Nations formed?

🌐 What are the purposes and principles outlined in the U.N. Charter?

🌐 What are the functions of the General Assembly and the Security Council?

Key Terms:

super-majority vote, deliberative organ

The United Nations (U.N.) is a name that was first adopted by those nations allied in opposition against Germany, Italy, and Japan during World War II. The name became prominent worldwide when the

Changes in U.S. Foreign Policy

At the end of World War II in 1945, the United States faced the "Evil Empire," which was the Soviet Union and the Communist bloc of nations. The Cold War was waged until the early 1990s. Today, much has changed.

THEN (DURING THE COLD WAR)	NOW
The most important consideration was the development of nuclear weapons and defense against nuclear attacks.	Nuclear disarmament efforts are under way.
The major threat to American security was the Soviet Union and the Communist bloc.	There is no one major threat to American security.
The United States and the Soviet Union were the world's two superpowers.	The United States is the world's only superpower.

Declaration of the United Nations was signed by twenty-six countries on January 4, 1942. In the late summer and the fall of 1944, diplomats from the United States, the United Kingdom, the Soviet Union, and China held talks in Washington, D.C., with the goal of forming a permanent organization. In April 1945, fifty-one nations attended the United Nations Conference on International Organization in San Francisco. Those countries plus five others became the original members of the United Nations and signed the Charter of the United Nations on June 26 of that year. (The Resource Center at the end of the text contains the text of the preamble to this charter.)

The U.N. Charter

The Charter of the United Nations consists of a preamble and articles similar to the preamble and articles of the United States Constitution. (It differs from the U.S. Constitution in that it has 111 articles, compared with the Constitution's 7 articles, however.) The charter outlines the purposes, structure, and powers of the United Nations. The charter lists the following four purposes and seven principles:

The Four Purposes
1. To preserve world peace.
2. To encourage nations to be just in their actions toward each other.
3. To help nations to cooperate in solving their problems.
4. To serve as an agency through which nations can work toward these three goals.

The Seven Principles
1. All members have equal rights.
2. Each member is expected to carry out its duties under the charter.
3. Each member agrees to the principle of settling disputes peacefully.
4. Each member agrees not to use force or the threat of force against other nations except in self-defense.
5. Each member agrees to help the U.N. in every action it takes to carry out the purposes of the charter.
6. The U.N. agrees to act on the principle that

► *A vote is taken at the United Nations Security Council. Although the goal of this body is to maintain international peace, in cases of clear-cut aggression the council has recommended military action. Can you name a relatively recent event that caused the Security Council to vote to allow the use of force by a coalition of member countries? (If not, see page 637.)*

nonmember states have the same duties as member states to preserve world peace and security.

7. The U.N. accepts the principle of not interfering in the internal affairs—domestic problems—of member nations, so long as these actions do not harm other nations.

The Organization of the U.N.

The United Nations has a complex structure built around six principal organs, or bodies:

1. The General Assembly
2. The Security Council
3. The Economic and Social Council
4. The Trusteeship Council
5. The International Court of Justice
6. The Secretariat

Figure 23–3 on page 635 shows the basic organizational structure of the United Nations.

The General Assembly The General Assembly is the organ within the U.N. in which all members are represented. Each member has one vote but may send as many as five representatives. Important questions are decided by a majority vote or by a **super-majority vote** of two-thirds, depending on the importance of the matter.

The General Assembly is a **deliberative organ,** which means it deliberates on, or discusses and decides, important issues. A General Assembly meeting is, in a sense, a town meeting in which the participants are the member nations of the world. This international town meeting is held once a year at the U.N. permanent headquarters in New York City, on the East River in midtown Manhattan. Regular assembly meetings last for three months, beginning on the third Tuesday in September. Special sessions may be called, usually to discuss important world issues, such as peacekeeping operations.

The Security Council The Security Council has the primary responsibility for maintaining international peace. Originally, the council consisted of eleven members. Five of these were permanent members: France, the United Kingdom, the Soviet Union (now Russia), the United States, and China. Six were nonpermanent members elected by the General Assembly for two-year terms. In 1965, the charter was amended to enlarge the council by adding four more nonpermanent members. Currently, five nonpermanent members must come from African and Asian countries, one from

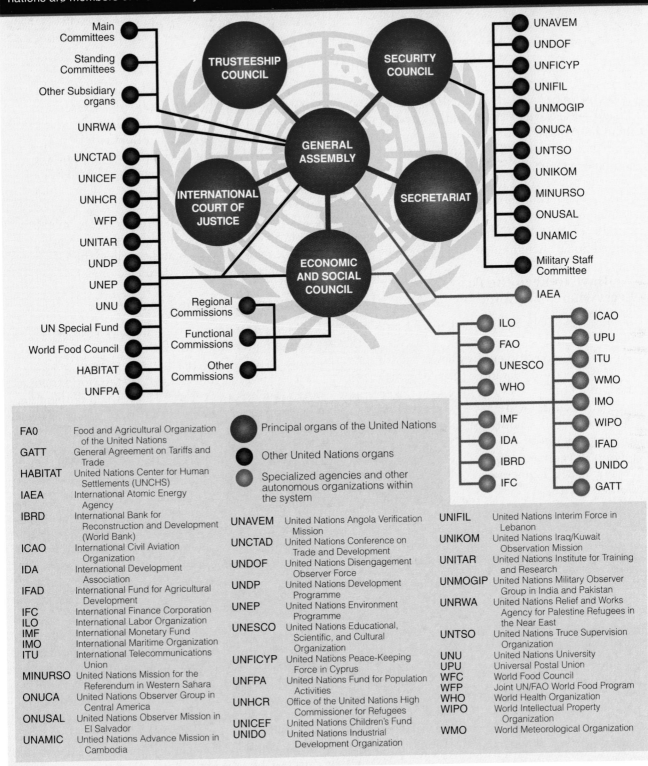

FIGURE 23–3 The United Nations System This chart shows the basic structure of the United Nations. How many nations are members of the Security Council?

Main Committees
Standing Committees
Other Subsidiary organs
UNRWA
UNCTAD
UNICEF
UNHCR
WFP
UNITAR
UNDP
UNEP
UNU
UN Special Fund
World Food Council
HABITAT
UNFPA

TRUSTEESHIP COUNCIL
SECURITY COUNCIL
GENERAL ASSEMBLY
INTERNATIONAL COURT OF JUSTICE
SECRETARIAT
ECONOMIC AND SOCIAL COUNCIL

Regional Commissions
Functional Commissions
Other Commissions

UNAVEM
UNDOF
UNFICYP
UNIFIL
UNMOGIP
ONUCA
UNTSO
UNIKOM
MINURSO
ONUSAL
UNAMIC
Military Staff Committee
IAEA

ILO
FAO
UNESCO
WHO
IMF
IDA
IBRD
IFC

ICAO
UPU
ITU
WMO
IMO
WIPO
IFAD
UNIDO
GATT

● Principal organs of the United Nations

● Other United Nations organs

● Specialized agencies and other autonomous organizations within the system

FA0	Food and Agricultural Organization of the United Nations	
GATT	General Agreement on Tariffs and Trade	
HABITAT	United Nations Center for Human Settlements (UNCHS)	
IAEA	International Atomic Energy Agency	
IBRD	International Bank for Reconstruction and Development (World Bank)	
ICAO	International Civil Aviation Organization	
IDA	International Development Association	
IFAD	International Fund for Agricultural Development	
IFC	International Finance Corporation	
ILO	International Labor Organization	
IMF	International Monetary Fund	
IMO	International Maritime Organization	
ITU	International Telecommunications Union	
MINURSO	United Nations Mission for the Referendum in Western Sahara	
ONUCA	United Nations Observer Group in Central America	
ONUSAL	United Nations Observer Mission in El Salvador	
UNAMIC	Untied Nations Advance Mission in Cambodia	

UNAVEM United Nations Angola Verification Mission
UNCTAD United Nations Conference on Trade and Development
UNDOF United Nations Disengagement Observer Force
UNDP United Nations Development Programme
UNEP United Nations Environment Programme
UNESCO United Nations Educational, Scientific, and Cultural Organization
UNFICYP United Nations Peace-Keeping Force in Cyprus
UNFPA United Nations Fund for Population Activities
UNHCR Office of the United Nations High Commissioner for Refugees
UNICEF United Nations Children's Fund
UNIDO United Nations Industrial Development Organization

UNIFIL United Nations Interim Force in Lebanon
UNIKOM United Nations Iraq/Kuwait Observation Mission
UNITAR United Nations Institute for Training and Research
UNMOGIP United Nations Military Observer Group in India and Pakistan
UNRWA United Nations Relief and Works Agency for Palestine Refugees in the Near East
UNTSO United Nations Truce Supervision Organization
UNU United Nations University
UPU Universal Postal Union
WFC World Food Council
WFP Joint UN/FAO World Food Program
WHO World Health Organization
WIPO World Intellectual Property Organization
WMO World Meteorological Organization

The Role of the United States as the World's Police Officer

It used to be "us"—the United States—against "them"—the Soviet Union and the forces of communism. At least for the time being, though, the United States is the only superpower, both militarily and economically. Some people believe that with this power come moral and ethical responsibilities. These people think that the United States should prevent injustice everywhere and act as the world's police officer. Others believe that the United States should simply mind its own business.

We Have to Keep the Peace Everywhere, Say Some

Those who believe that the United States should play the peacekeeper role say that only the United States has the military power and the economic strength to guarantee peace everywhere. If the United States does not intervene to keep the peace, no country will.

As the world's leading commercial power, these people point out, the United States has a strong interest in economic development everywhere. Economic development can only happen in a world of peace.

Moreover, every time we leave things alone, disaster occurs. Look what happened before the United States intervened in Bosnia. Tens of thousands of innocent civilians were killed. When extremists from the Hutu tribe took over in the African nation of Rwanda, the United States did nothing. The result was that hundreds of thousands of members of a rival tribe, the Tutsi, were slaughtered. The fact is, when the United States has not stepped in to stop ethnic violence, thousands have died.

The United Nations has not yet been able to ensure world stability. Some parts of the world will never experience stability unless the United States becomes the world's police officer.

Yankees, Stay Home, Say Others

Many Americans favor a more isolationist foreign policy. They think that U.S. troops should stay at home. After all, they say, so many ethnic battles are occurring throughout the world that the United States cannot deal with all of them. The United Nations exists for that purpose, so let the United Nations handle these problems.

Besides, argue these critics, every time the United States intervenes, it encounters unmanageable problems, and often violent situations. For example, U.S. troops were in Somalia, Africa, in the early 1990s in an attempt to alleviate famine. Yet that country is no better off today.

Furthermore, the United States has better things to spend its money on than serving as the

Eastern European countries, two from Latin American countries, and two from Western European and other countries.

Members of the U.N. agree to carry out the decisions of the Security Council, which in effect can determine the course of action that the U.N. should take in settling an international dispute. Any one of the five permanent members, though, can veto a Security Council decision.

Under certain circumstances, when clear-cut aggression has occurred, the Security Council may call for military action by asking U.N. members to contribute military personnel to a U.N. peacekeeping force. Such an event occurred in the 1950s, when North Korean military forces attacked South Korea. The resulting Korean War (1950–1953) is now often considered a U.N. peacekeeping mission. Actually, however, the war was led and carried out by the United States and its allies.

◄ Two Somali dock-hands sit atop sacks of food sent to Somalia in 1992 by the United States to help alleviate starvation in that country. Relief agencies that tried to feed Somalia's starving people were often frustrated as food was stolen or left to sit in warehouses.

world's police officer. For example, within our own borders, there are still people who are hungry, children who are at risk, and illiterate adults. Numerous other social and economic problems need to be solved right here at home. Why should we focus on problems in other countries?

If we want a stronger police officer for the world, we should strengthen the United Nations. The United Nations can form an army of mercenaries (hired soldiers) willing to risk their lives at a moment's notice. This suggestion has already been made by a former British prime minister.

Perhaps now is the time to act on it.

In any event, the world's fighting should be left to someone other than the United States, these people argue.

YOU DECIDE

1. Should any nation have the right to intervene in other nations' affairs to protect human rights?
2. Is it ever correct to spend money on foreign aid when domestic problems still exist?

Recent important actions of the United Nations and the Security Council involved the severe economic sanctions imposed on Iraq after its invasion of Kuwait in August 1990. When those economic sanctions did not force Iraq's president, Saddam Hussein, to withdraw his occupational forces from Kuwait, the Security Council voted to allow the use of force by coalition countries. Led by the United States, these countries, with the backing of the United Nations,

proceeded to bomb Iraqi targets in and out of Kuwait beginning in January 1991. The result was the complete defeat of the Iraqi military one hundred days later and the withdrawal of Iraqi forces from Kuwait. The U.N. has made further efforts to oversee the destruction of Iraq's chemical, biological, and nuclear weapon stockpiles.

Other U.N. missions during the 1990s have been sent to Somalia, Haiti, Bosnia-Herzegovina, and

▶ During the Persian Gulf War of 1991, Iraq used such tactics as igniting Kuwaiti oil wells.

several other countries. The U.N.'s peacekeeping efforts in the 1990s, though, met with less success than they did in earlier decades. In the past, U.N. intervention often was undertaken to help resolve disputes between nations that welcomed the U.N.'s assistance. Today, in contrast, the disputes involved are often conflicts between factions or ethnic groups within nations that do not necessarily welcome U.N. assistance.

SECTION 5 REVIEW

1. For what purposes was the United Nations established?
2. Name the seven principles of the United Nations.
3. What is the main purpose of the General Assembly?
4. What is the main responsibility of the Security Council?
5. **For Critical Analysis:** Every member nation of the U.N. has an equal vote in the General Assembly. Do you think this one-nation–one-vote system is fair? Give reasons for your answer.

▲ South Korean refugees fled the combat zone as U.S. Army troops moved forward to engage the North Koreans during the Korean War (1950–1953). Many Americans viewed our presence in Korea as a U.N. peacekeeping mission.

▲ *The civilian casualties in the Bosnian war were heartbreaking. Here two brothers in Sarajevo weep following the funeral of another brother. In the 1990s, the U.S. sent troops into Bosnia-Herzegovina as part of a U.N. peacekeeping mission.*

★ ★ ★ ★ **Chapter Summary** ★ ★ ★ ★

Section 1: The Development of American Foreign Policy

- A foreign policy is a systematic and general plan that guides a nation's attitudes and actions toward the rest of the world.
- The nation's founders and early presidents believed that isolationism was the best way to protect American interests. As America expanded and became more involved in world events, it moved away from isolationism and toward interventionism.
- After World War II, the United States emerged as a superpower, as did the Soviet Union. The World War II alliance between the Soviet Union and the United States deteriorated into the Cold War and an arms race in which each superpower tried to outdo the other in terms of nuclear weapons and power.
- The political collapse of the Soviet Union effectively ended the Cold War in the 1990s.

Section 2: The Makers of Foreign Policy

- The Constitution provides for a partnership between Congress and the president in developing foreign policy, but on many occasions the president and Congress have struggled over power in this area.

- The president's constitutional powers in foreign affairs involve serving as commander in chief of military forces, making treaties with other nations, and appointing ambassadors. The president relies on the secretary of state, the secretary of defense, and other members of the National Security Council for advice.
- The constitutional powers given to Congress in the area of foreign policy include the power of the Senate to confirm the president's diplomatic appointments and to ratify all treaties. Only Congress has the power to declare war.

Section 3: The Departments of State and Defense

- The departments of state and defense are responsible for carrying out foreign and defense policy.
- The Department of State maintains diplomatic relations with nations around the world, advises the president on international issues, negotiates treaties, and protects the interests of Americans traveling or conducting business abroad.
- The Department of Defense is the principal executive department that establishes and carries out defense policy and protects national security.

Section 4: American Foreign Policy Goals and Tools

- The overall purpose of U.S. foreign policy is to protect national security.
- The United States works to achieve this purpose through specific policy goals, including world peace, economic prosperity, human rights, and democracy.
- The tools of American foreign policy include diplomacy, foreign aid, alliances, trade measures, and military force.

Section 5: The United Nations

- The United Nations was established in 1945.
- The stated purposes of the U.N. are to preserve world peace, encourage just actions between nations, help nations solve their problems, and serve as an agency through which nations can work toward these goals.
- The U.N. has seven guiding principles, including equal rights for all members, agreement of members to settle disputes peacefully, and noninterference in the internal affairs of member nations.
- The principal organs of the United Nations are the General Assembly and the Security Council.

★ REVIEW QUESTIONS ★

1. What is the basic purpose of American foreign policy?
2. Describe the policy of isolationism as it was practiced in the early years of U.S. history, and explain why it was abandoned later.
3. Briefly describe U.S. involvement in world affairs since 1898.
4. What was the Cold War?
5. What are the president's foreign policymaking powers as granted by the Constitution? Who assists the president in this area?
6. What are the constitutional powers given to Congress in the area of foreign policy?
7. What responsibilities do the Department of State and the Department of Defense have in foreign policy? What other agencies are involved in foreign policy decisions?
8. What two methods have been used to recruit citizens to serve in the armed forces?
9. What are the main foreign policy goals of the United States?
10. What is diplomacy?
11. Why has the United States provided foreign aid to other nations?
12. How are alliances used to achieve American foreign policy goals?
13. How are trade measures used to achieve foreign policy goals?
14. Why was the United Nations formed?
15. What are the seven principles of the United Nations as listed in the charter?
16. What are the two most important bodies within the United Nations?
17. Who are the members of the Security Council of the United Nations?
18. Name two ways in which you can attempt to influence American foreign policy.

★ CRITICAL THINKING ★

1. Think of at least one foreign policy issue on which the president and Congress might hold different views. Which branch do you think would be most influential in determining policy for that particular issue? Why?
2. Do you think the president or Congress should have a more dominant role in foreign policy? Give reasons for your answer.
3. The United States may use economic sanctions to punish another nation for its political activities. For example, the United States might refuse to trade with a nation whose government does not respect human rights. Do you think economic policy should be used to serve foreign policy goals? Why or why not?
4. It has been said that the United States is the only superpower left in the world. Explain your reasons for agreeing or disagreeing with this statement.
5. Antiwar demonstrators have often argued that the United States has too many pressing problems at home—inadequate health care for the poor, a failing educational system, and urban deterioration—to be spending billions of dollars to fight in other countries. Do you believe that this is a valid argument against U.S. military involvement elsewhere? Explain why or why not.

★ IMPROVING YOUR SKILLS ★

Communication Skills

Determining Fallacies in Reasoning Students of government must often analyze or evaluate statements and viewpoints. Part of this skill involves recognizing fallacies in reasoning. A *fallacy* is a false idea or an error. It can take the form of an unsound or unsupported argument, an error in facts, or an inaccurate conclusion.

When analyzing a statement to detect fallacies, follow these guidelines:

- **Read or listen to the statement carefully.** Try to identify the main idea and the conclusion.
- **Ask yourself how the conclusion was reached.** The following list describes some of the most common fallacies.
  1. No real connection between the information presented and the conclusion.
  2. Only one cause is identified when there are many.
  3. Correlation is mistaken for causation.
  4. More information is needed to support the conclusion.
  5. The conclusion is not based on facts but on the argument that "everyone thinks so."

Writing Read the statements below. Using the list above, write a short description of which fallacies apply to each statement.

- It is wrong for the United States to intervene in the affairs of troubled countries. We have too many problems with crime, education, and poverty in our own country.
- The reason for intervention in the Persian Gulf in 1990 and 1991 was the danger that the world price of oil would be controlled by Iraq.

Social Studies Skills

Sequencing Data and Information Part of understanding the world around you is putting information in some kind of logical order. This is called *sequencing*. When dealing with numbers, you have to be able to sequence them in a way that tells you something. Often this is done in the form of a graph. For example, Figure 23–1 on page 627 shows how defense spending, expressed as a percentage of total government expenditures, has changed through the years. These data are sequenced in *chronological order*, starting from 1940.

Data can be sequenced in many different ways.

1. Assume that you have a table with data on average household income for each of the fifty states. One way to sequence the data is by state in alphabetical order. What are at least two other ways the data could be sequenced?
2. Now look at Figure 23–2 on page 630 and answer these questions:
   a. In what way is the data sequenced on the graph?
   b. Would the sequencing be different if the horizontal axis showed only five-year intervals?

★ ACTIVITIES AND PROJECTS ★

1. Choose one of the last five presidents and write a report on his major foreign policy accomplishments and mistakes. Include a list and brief description of each of his closest foreign policy advisers.
2. Prepare a poster of pictures and articles that illustrate the nation working toward one of its major foreign policy goals.
3. List all of the qualifications you think an ambassador to a Middle Eastern country should have. Prepare a script of the questions you would ask the individual if you were the president and were considering his or her appointment.
4. Choose a goal of U.S. foreign policy and show with historical evidence what the United States has done in the last twenty years to achieve that goal.

What If . . .

The United States Spent Nothing on Foreign and Defense Policy?

Assume that the United States decided to ignore the rest of the world and eliminated the State Department, the Defense Department, and all of the armed forces. What might happen?

Global Warming

One of the major policy issues of our time has to do with the phenomenon of global warming. To deal with this issue, delegates from 160 nations met in Kyoto, Japan, in December 1997. The result was the Kyoto Protocol—an agreement, or treaty, among the industrial nations to reduce their emissions of so-called greenhouse gases, such as carbon dioxide. It has been claimed that emissions of these gases contribute to global warming and other climate changes.

The agreement becomes legally binding on the nations that signed it only when these nations ratify the treaty. In the United States, the Senate must ratify, or approve, any treaty by a two-thirds vote. Some observers doubt whether the Senate will ratify the treaty, at least for several years. Some observers also doubt that global warming is actually occurring.

Source Documents

Nicholson to Gore: Don't Sell Out U.S. Economy

Republican National Committee press release (prior to the Kyoto agreement)

Republican National Committee Chairman Jim Nicholson urged Vice President Al Gore not to cave in to radical environmentalists and international bureaucrats following Gore's speech earlier today in which the Vice President ordered U.S. negotiators in Kyoto to show "new flexibility" in response to demands that Americans agree to new energy taxes and slow economic growth in an effort to stop "global warming."

Nicholson said, "Americans will not support a new international treaty that costs American workers their jobs, lowers American families' standard of living, deprives dis-advantaged Americans of needed opportunities and compromises U.S. sovereignty—all without achieving any genuine environmental progress.

"There is no scientific consensus on global warming. Is it happening? If so, is the cause natural climate variation or human activity? Will the 'solutions' being proposed in Kyoto help or hinder the environment? And will the burden be shared fairly or will Americans make all the sacrifices?

"Until we have reliable answers to these questions, the Clinton/Gore administration should refrain from signing new international treaties wth goals to be enforced by international bureaucracies.

"Republicans support efforts to improve the global environment," Nicholson added. "But there is no scientific justification for giving radical environmentalists and bureaucrats more power over the U.S. economy."

Nicholson also noted [that] the most reliable data show little evidence of global warming over the past 14 years. . . . According to one study, the treaty would add 60 cents to the cost of a gallon of gas, double the price of heating oil, boost the price of food and transportation while killing off more than 1.6 million jobs over the next 9 years. . . .

Nicholson concluded: "I call on the Vice President to exercise caution, and not to cave in to the pressures being exerted by those who—for ideological reasons—want to constrain American economic growth and limit Americans' opportunities and freedoms."

December 8, 1997

Statement by the President

White House press release

I am very pleased that the United States has reached an historic agreement with other nations of the world to take unprecedented action to address global warming. This agreement is environmentally strong and economically sound. It reflects a commitment by our generation to act in the interests of future generations.

No nation is more committed to this effort than the United States. In Kyoto, our mission was to persuade other nations to find common ground so we could make realistic and achievable commitments to reduce greenhouse gas emissions. That mission was accomplished. The United States delegation, at the direction of Vice President Gore, and with the skilled leadership of Under Secretary Stuart Eizenstat, showed the way. The momentum generated by Vice President Gore's visit helped move the negotiation to a successful conclusion and I thank him. . . .

There are still hard challenges ahead, particularly in the area of involvement by developing nations. It is essential that these nations participate in a meaningful way if we are to truly tackle this global environmental challenge. But the industrialized nations have come together, taken a strong step, and that is real progress.

December 10, 1997

Media Report

The decision of world leaders to take joint action against global warming was applauded by some Americans and criticized by others. Here is an excerpt from a media report written in late 1997.

Treaty Isn't Perfect, but It's a Landmark First Step

Editorial, *USA Today*

Even before negotiators had finished their work in Kyoto this week, angry members of the U.S. Senate were vowing that the treaty to control the gases that contribute to global warming would never be ratified. Bring it right on, they told the White House. We'll knock it right out.

Sure. Some industries—cars, coal, steel—fear the treaty's costs. And politicians representing the status quo are not always receptive to new priorities, even those as clear as the need to control greenhouse gases. But critics misread the treaty's worth and overstate its flaws.

As negotiated in the final, ragged hours, the treaty binds industrialized nations to cut greenhouse gases such as car-

bon dioxide. The United States must cut emissions to 7 percent below 1990 levels, on average, between 2008 and 2012. The treaty also creates a system for trading pollution credits. A country exceeding its limit can buy credits from those doing better.

So far, so good. Tight targets benefit the environment, and trading schemes can effectively control both costs and pollution. Still, critics say that because the treaty excludes developing nations, their economies will out-compete ours.

But two-thirds of our trade is with nations that also bear Kyoto's burdens. If our reductions are achieved through new efficiencies, we come out ahead. And if those efficiencies come from marketable new technologies, we attain some new economic benefits.

Source: *USA Today*, December 12, 1997 (p. 13A). Copyright 1997, *USA Today*. Reprinted with permission.

Conclusion

Some critics maintain that policymakers should refrain from taking action on global warming until scientists have more time to study the issue. Proponents of setting caps on greenhouse gases think that policymakers must act immediately, based on the claims of some scientists who believe that global warming is occurring at a dangerous rate. Even though the Senate may not ratify the Kyoto Protocol for some time, the agreement is a "historic step," as President Clinton said, toward global action on an issue that affects all nations of the world.

Analysis Questions

1. Why would the automobile, coal, and steel industries "fear the treaty's costs," as indicated in the excerpt from *USA Today*?
2. Can you think of any reasons why the delegates at Kyoto did not require developing nations to reduce their greenhouse gas emissions? Why should just the industrialized nations do so?
3. From a political perspective, does the Kyoto Protocol benefit President Clinton and Vice President Gore in any way? Explain.
4. To what extent should the costs of protecting the environment be taken into consideration when developing environmental policies?

State and Local Governments

The Iowa State Capitol, a grand, traditional building, lights up the Des Moines night.

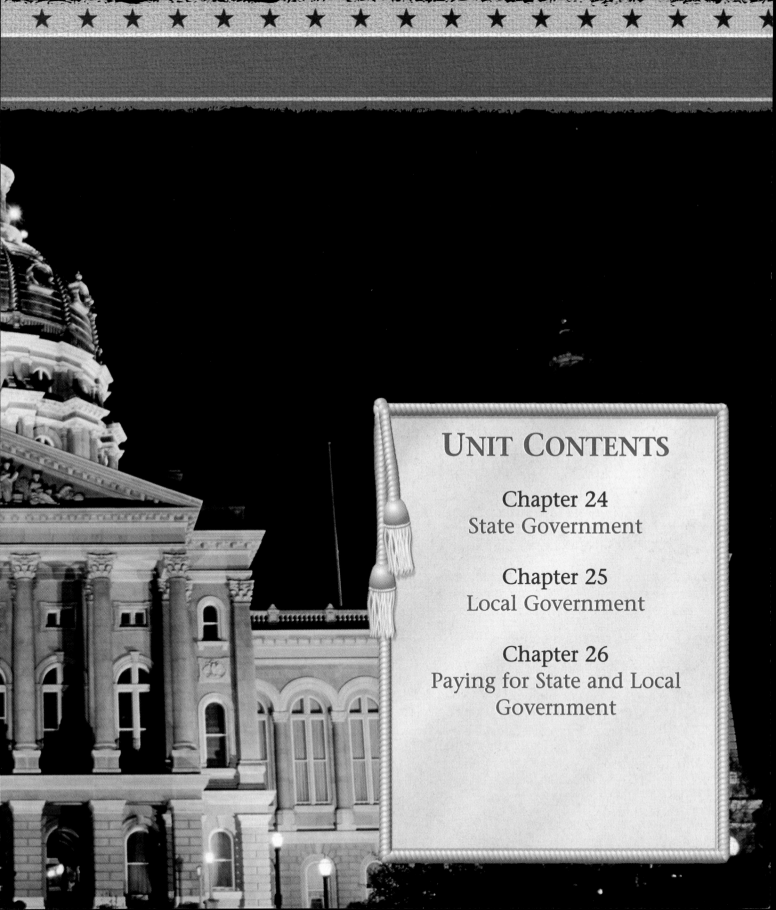

UNIT CONTENTS

CHAPTER 24

State Government

CHAPTER OBJECTIVES

To learn about and understand . . .

⭐ The nature of state constitutions

⭐ State forms of direct democracy—the initiative, the referendum, and the recall

⭐ Modern governors and their powers

⭐ The typical state court system

⭐ The prosecution of offenders

"Yesterday, the greatest question was decided which ever was debated in America. . . . A resolution was passed without one dissenting colony, 'that these United Colonies are, and of right ought to be, free and independent States.' "

John Adams
(1735–1826)
Second President of the United States

INTRODUCTION

In the opening quotation, John Adams used key words from the Resolution of Independence passed on July 2, 1776. His reference to independent states is still accurate today, for the fifty states in this nation are in many ways independent. Each has its own constitution, its own executive, its own judiciary system, and its own legislature.

In this chapter, you will look at some general features of state constitutions. You will also find out about the office of the governor in the various states, as well as the state court systems. Finally, you will find out about how the states typically prosecute those accused of committing crimes.

◄ Although our nation has a strong national government, the nation's fifty states play a prominent role in our federal system. The Michigan state legislature, shown here, conducts its state legislative business.

The U.S. Constitution and the State Constitutions

Preview Questions:

- What powers does the U.S. Constitution give to state governments?
- Why are state constitutions typically longer and more detailed than the U.S. Constitution?
- How can a state constitution be revised?

Key Terms:

intrastate commerce, police power, extraordinary majority, constitutional initiative

We live in a federal system made up of fifty separate state governments and one national government. The U.S. Constitution gives a broad range of powers to state governments. It also prohibits state governments from engaging in certain activities. The U.S. Constitution never explicitly defines the powers of the states. Rather, state powers are simply reserved, which means that states may do anything that the Constitution does not prohibit them from doing or that is not expressly delegated to the national government.

Just the Facts

An Oregon state law requires Oregonians, when operating a bike, to ride only "upon or astride a permanent and regular seat attached to the bicycle."

The major reserved powers of the states include the power to spend and the power to regulate **intrastate commerce**—that is, commerce within a given state. The states also have general **police power.** That means they can protect their citizens by passing and enforcing laws in the areas of public safety (through traffic laws, for example), health and welfare (through immunization and child-abuse laws, for instance), and morality (through laws against pornography, for example). Police powers include such actions as regulating sanitation in restaurants and setting the minimum legal age for drinking.

Restrictions on state and local governmental activity are implied by the Constitution in Article VI, Paragraph 2:

> *This Constitution, and the Laws of the United States, which shall be made in Pursuance thereof; and all Treaties made, or which shall be made, under the Authority of the United States, shall be the Supreme Law of the Land; and the Judges in every State shall be bound thereby, any Thing in the Constitution or Laws of any State to the Contrary notwithstanding.*

This paragraph states that the Constitution is the supreme law of the land. No state or local law can conflict with the Constitution, with laws made by the U.S. Congress, or with treaties entered into by the national government. The U.S. Supreme Court has been the final judge of conflicts arising between the national and state governments.

State Constitutions

The U.S. Constitution is a model of brevity. State constitutions, in contrast, are typically long and detailed. Furthermore, for over two hundred years, the U.S. Constitution has endured as a binding body of law, with only twenty-seven amendments thus far. Such is not the case with state constitutions. Texas has had five constitutions; Louisiana has had eleven; Georgia has had nine; South Carolina has had seven; and Alabama, Florida, and Virginia have had six each. Many state constitutions have been amended numerous times. For example, the Texas constitution has been amended 364 times. The South Carolina constitution has 465 amendments. The Alabama constitution tops the list with 582 amendments. Voters may be asked to approve hundreds of amendments to their state constitution in a single election.

One reason for the length and detail of state constitutions is that constitution framers at the state level have often had a difficult time distinguishing between constitutional law and statutory law. (Remember from

Chapter 20 that statutory law is law made by legislatures, such as the Congress of the United States and the legislatures of the various states.) Many laws that are clearly statutory in nature have been put into state constitutions. For example, South Dakota has in its state constitution the authorization for a cordage and twine plant at the state penitentiary. The Texas constitution includes a pay schedule for state legislators. When legislators want a raise, the constitution must be amended. The Alabama constitution includes a fourteen-page amendment establishing the "Alabama Heritage Trust Fund." An article of the California constitution discusses the tax-exempt status of the Huntington Library and Art Gallery. Obviously, the U.S. Constitution contains no such details. It leaves to the Congress the nuts-and-bolts activity of making specific statutory laws.

Amending State Constitutions

Amendments to state constitutions may be proposed in three ways: by constitutional convention, by legislative activity, or by popular demand. The most commonly used method has been by convention.

State Constitutional Conventions By the end of the 1990s, about 250 state constitutional conventions had been called to write an entirely new constitution or to attempt to amend an existing one. This is not surprising, because four-fifths of all state constitutions expressly allow for such conventions. Some states, such as Illinois, New York, Ohio, and Michigan, require that such conventions be called periodically to consider whether changes are needed and, if so, to propose them. Figure 24–1 on page 650 shows how a constitutional convention is called in each of the states.

Legislative Action All states authorize legislatures to propose constitutional amendments. Usually, an **extraordinary majority** of votes—typically, two-thirds or three-fifths of the total number of legislators—is required to propose an amendment. In some states, a proposed amendment has to be passed in two successive sessions of the legislature.

Constitutional Initiative Eighteen states (Arizona, Arkansas, California, Colorado, Florida, Illinois, Massachusetts, Michigan, Mississippi, Missouri, Montana, Nebraska, Nevada, North Dakota, Ohio, Oklahoma, Oregon, and South Dakota) provide in their constitutions for the **constitutional initiative.** This provision allows citizens to propose constitutional amendments through petitions signed by a certain number of registered voters. Citizens may thus place a proposed amendment on the ballot without the need for a constitutional convention. The number of signatures required to get a constitutional initiative on the ballot varies from state to state. Usually, the number must equal 5 to 10 percent of the total number of votes cast in the last gubernatorial (governor's) election. The states

Just the Facts

In all, the state constitutions in the United States have been amended more than five thousand times.

▲ Oregon is one of several states that allow for the initiative process. If this petitioner and others like him are successful in persuading enough voters to sign, what is the next step for the initiative?

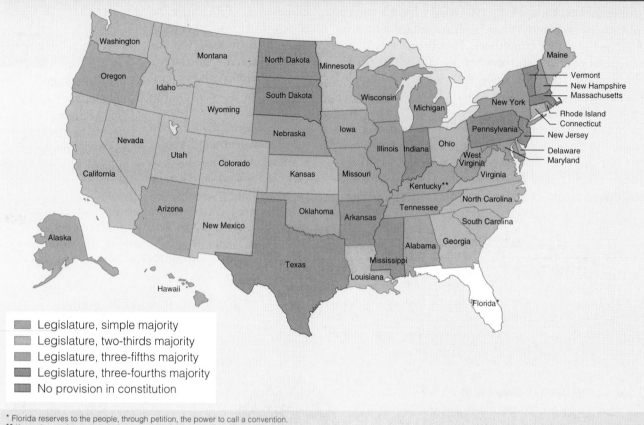

FIGURE 24–1 Provisions for Calling State Constitutional Conventions As you can see from the map below, the states use a variety of methods to call state constitutional conventions. What is the most common method? Which method does your state use?

Legislature, simple majority
Legislature, two-thirds majority
Legislature, three-fifths majority
Legislature, three-fourths majority
No provision in constitution

* Florida reserves to the people, through petition, the power to call a convention.
** Kentucky requires a majority in two successive sessions.
SOURCE: Adapted from *Book of the States*, 1996–97 (Lexington, Kentucky: Council of State Governments, 1996).

that have used the initiative process most often are California and Oregon.

Ratification No matter which method of proposal is used, all states except Delaware require an amendment to be ratified by a majority of voters in a general election. (In Delaware, a constitutional amendment must be approved by a two-thirds vote of the state legislature in two consecutive sessions.) In the states in which voter approval is required, proposals coming from the legislature are adopted far more often than those originated by initiative.

SECTION 1 REVIEW

1. What are some powers reserved to the states?
2. What are some differences between the U.S. Constitution and most state constitutions?
3. How are state constitutions amended?
4. **For Critical Analysis:** Why do you think so many state constitutions contain provisions on matters that might better be dealt with directly by the state legislatures?

Preview Questions:

- ⭐ What is an initiative?
- ⭐ What is a referendum? How is it different from an initiative?
- ⭐ For what purpose is the recall used?

Key Terms:

initiative, referendum, recall

Many states exercise a type of direct democracy through the initiative, the referendum, and the recall. These procedures allow voters to influence the government directly.

The Initiative

The **initiative** lets citizens bypass legislatures by proposing new statutes or changes in government for voter approval. It is similar to the constitutional initiative discussed previously but is used for proposing new laws, rather than changing the state constitution. Most states that allow for citizen initiatives require that an initiative's backers circulate a petition to place the issue on the ballot. A certain percentage of the registered voters in the last gubernatorial election must sign the petition. If enough signatures are obtained, the issue is put on the ballot.

Twenty-two states use the initiative. Typically, they are states in which political parties are relatively weak and nonpartisan groups are strong. Some major initiatives that have been passed in recent years include an Oregon initiative to make physician-assisted suicide legal in that state, a California initiative to end state-sponsored affirmative

action, and initiatives in both California and Arizona authorizing the use of marijuana for medical purposes.

The Referendum

The **referendum** is similar to the initiative, except that the matter to be decided is first proposed by the legislature and then directed to the voters for their approval. The referendum is most often used at the local level to approve local school bond issues. It is also used to amend state constitutions, and all states except Alabama currently provide for the referendum for constitutional changes. Only twenty-three states, however, allow changes to statutory law through referendums. In a number of states, voters can "put on hold" a bill passed by the legislature by obtaining petitions with the required number of signatures from voters who oppose it. A statewide referendum election is then held. If the majority of the voters disapprove of the bill, it is no longer valid.

The referendum was not initially intended for regular use. Indeed, it was used infrequently in the past. Its opponents argue that it is an unnecessary check on representative government and that it weakens legislative responsibility. In recent years, the referendum has become increasingly popular as citizens have attempted to control their state and local governments. Interest groups have been active in sponsoring the petition drives necessary to force a referendum.

◀ *Representative Frank Fitzgerald, right, of Michigan, listens as his attorney, Peter Ellsworth, discusses the pending recall election (see section on the recall on page 652) against Fitztgerald in January 1996.*

The Voter Initiative

The voter initiative first made its appearance in politics in the nineteenth century. Today, over twenty states allow citizens to propose initiatives. In a typical election year, about one hundred initiatives appear on state ballots throughout the country. In California, which has allowed the initiative since 1911, voters were recently faced with a total of over twenty initiatives in two separate elections. Citizens' initiatives often deal with some of the most controversial issues of the day, such as gun control, assisted suicide, affirmative action, and the medical use of marijuana.

Some argue that the voter initiative, as a form of direct democracy, is a good thing. After all, the initiative allows citizens in a state to directly affect the lawmaking process. It is also sometimes assumed that the initiative allows citizens to bypass the usual political process, including the influence of money and interest groups. Yet a closer examination of the initiative process reveals that it is not really immune from the politics of money. In fact, initiatives have become a big business.

For example, proponents of some recent California initiatives have faced costs of up to $40 million. Typically, it costs at least a million dollars to gather the signatures necessary for an initiative to be put on the ballot. About half of each initiative's budget goes to TV advertising. A significant portion of the budget goes to fund raising. Indeed, in California and other states that use the initiative regularly, the process has become a business, with money playing a dominant role.

THINK ABOUT IT

1. Should all states allow citizens to propose new laws (or amend or repeal existing laws) through the initiative process?
2. "Citizens should leave lawmaking up to their state legislators, who were elected for that purpose and who have more political experience." How would you argue in support of this statement? How would you argue against it?

The Recall

A **recall** is a vote to dismiss a public official. The recall is authorized in eighteen states, mainly in the western part of the nation. Recalls are directed at public officials who are deemed incompetent or grossly unethical in their conduct. Voters may circulate a petition calling for the removal of such an official. If the voters circulating the petition obtain a sufficient number of signatures, then a recall election is held. Usually, the number of signatures required is quite high—it may be, for example, 25 percent of the number of votes cast in the last gubernatorial election.

Being placed on a recall ballot does not necessarily mean an elected person is guilty of anything, although charges of criminal activity are often a reason for recalling an official.

Although the recall is rarely used, it functions as a threat to legislators. Proponents of the recall in the eighteen states in which it exists argue that the possibility of recall prevents outrageously inappropriate official behavior. Opponents of the recall argue that it makes officeholders prey to well-financed interest groups.

SECTION 2 REVIEW

1. What is an initiative?
2. What is a referendum?
3. When is a recall used?
4. **For Critical Analysis:** How do you think the existence of the initiative, the referendum, and the recall affects the political behavior of state officials?

The Modern Governor

Preview Questions:

- What are the formal and informal qualifications for being a governor?
- What is the selection process and the typical term of office for governors?
- How may a governor be removed from office?

Key Term:

plurality

Today, a governor is the chief executive officer in each of the fifty states. The most populous states have given their governors great control over the state executive branch. Even a few less-populated states, such as Alaska and Hawaii, have made provisions for strong governors.

Qualifications

In most states, the formal qualifications a person must meet to be governor are simple. He or she must be an American citizen and be of a certain age. The minimum age in most states is twenty-five or thirty, although in some states, such as California, Massachusetts, Ohio, and Wisconsin, one can become governor at age eighteen. Most states require that the governor have lived in the state for at least five years. Finally, a candidate for governor must be a qualified voter, which means he or she must have satisfied certain age and residency requirements. Even these formal qualifications for governor do not exist in Kansas and Ohio.

Clearly, millions of men and women satisfy the formal requirements to become governor. The *informal* requirements are what truly determine who will be elected. No handbook is available to outline such qualifications, but they include name familiarity, political experience, skill in relating to the media, and voter appeal. To become governor, a person must first win a major party's nomination and then win the general election. The combination of personal characteristics that allows such events to occur can be summed up as the informal qualifications for governor.

Just the Facts

The first woman to become governor of a state was Nellie Taylor Ross, who became governor of Wyoming in 1925.

The Selection Process

Today, every state selects its governor by popular vote. In forty-six states, a candidate can be elected with a **plurality** of the votes cast. That is, a candidate can win by receiving one more vote than any other candidate, whether or not this number represents a majority (more than 50 percent) of the total vote. In Arizona, Georgia, and Louisiana, if no candidate obtains a majority of votes, there is a run-off election between the two candidates with the most votes. In the absence of a majority in Mississippi, the winner is chosen by the lower chamber of the legislature. In Vermont, in a similar

◀ *Eleven-year-old Molly Shaheen watches as Steve Landry places a bug in the hand of her mother, New Hampshire governor Jeanne Shaheen. Molly joined her mother during a recent "Take Your Child to Work" day, as Shaheen visited with volunteers who check water samples and insect life in a local river. What message does this photo give to New Hampshire voters?*

▶ *Making headlines for his conviction on seven felony counts, Arizona governor Fife Symington quickly resigned. Perhaps he is mindful of another Arizona governor who was convicted of misusing campaign funds, but who refused to resign. What happened to him?*

situation, the choice is made by both chambers. Major party candidates are usually nominated in primaries, although conventions and caucuses are used in a few states.

The Length of Service

Gone are the one-year terms of office that were so popular in the early days of this nation. In all but two states, the governor now serves a four-year term. The two exceptions are New Hampshire and Vermont, in which the governors serve two-year terms.

Thirty-four states have constitutional or statutory provisions establishing limits on the number of terms that a governor may serve. Typically, such limits prevent governors from serving more than two terms. Some of these states provide that a governor may serve an additional term (that is, a third term) but only after a wait of four years. Sixteen states have no provisions at all about the number of terms a governor may serve.

Governors who choose to run for a second term very often win. The power of incumbency is great at virtually all levels of government. The all-time record for gubernatorial service is held by Governor George Clinton of New York, who held office from 1777 to 1795 and from 1801 to 1804. He did this by winning seven three-year terms.

In the Event of Death or Removal

The governorship may become vacant because of the death or incapacity of the governor. In addition, a gover-

nor may resign to take a cabinet position at the request of the president or to become a U.S. senator. Some governors have been removed legally by either impeachment or recall.

Every state's constitution provides for a successor if the governorship becomes vacant. In forty-three states, the second in command—the lieutenant governor—takes over. In a few states, such as Maine, New Hampshire, New Jersey, and West Virginia, the president of the state senate takes over. In three states—Arizona, Oregon, and Wyoming—the state secretary of state becomes governor.

Impeachment As with impeachment proceedings at the national level, removing the governor by impeachment usually requires an indictment by the lower chamber, a trial by the upper chamber (in which the senators are the jury members and the state supreme court justices are the judges), and conviction. Often the chief justice of the state supreme court presides at the trial. Only Oregon does not allow the removal of the governor by impeachment.

Impeachment is not impossible, but it is infrequent. Governor Evan Mecham of Arizona was impeached and removed from office in 1988 when he was convicted on criminal charges of campaign-finance mishandling and lending $80,000 of state funds to his car dealership. (He was later acquitted of felony charges.) In the twentieth century, only four other governors have been removed in such a manner. Governor J. Fife Symington III of Arizona resigned in 1997 after he was convicted of bank and wire fraud. Had he not resigned, he probably would have been impeached.

Recall About 25 percent of the states provide for removal of the governor by recall. By signing petitions, voters in these states can require a special election to determine whether or not the governor can be removed before his or her term expires.

The ability to remember facts, dates, and comments accurately is important for success in school and in most careers. Whether you are speaking, writing, taking a test, or studying, a good memory is beneficial. You can improve your memory, much as you can improve any other skill. The following guidelines can help you remember better:

- **Search for the organization of ideas.** Use summaries, headings, and categories to synthesize and group ideas.
- **Personalize the information.** Try to relate the information to something in your life.
- **Quiz yourself.** Recite the material from memory immediately after reading or hearing it, or simply ask yourself about what you just read or heard.
- **Reinforce learning and remembering.** Use note-taking, discussing with friends, drawing, and reciting out loud to help you remember what you just learned.
- **Study in twenty- to forty-minute intervals.** Take short breaks between study periods. This helps keep comprehension and memory at peak levels.
- **Use mnemonics.** Special memorizing systems called *mnemonics* (pronounced nee-*mahn*-iks) can help you memorize long lists. For

Improving Your Memory

example, if you needed to memorize a list of four states—Florida, Arizona, California, and Texas—you could create a mnemonic by using the first letters of the states to spell FACT. Just remembering FACT can help you remember the names of those states.

PRACTICING YOUR SKILLS

1. On two successive weekends, watch the same political talk show on TV. The first week, just watch the program the way you normally would. The next day, write a paragraph describing the topic of the program.
2. During the following week's show, use several of the tips provided above as you watch. The next day, again write a summarizing paragraph.
3. Compare the two paragraphs. Which is a more accurate representation of the information?

◀ *As a student, you know that taking in information is just the beginning. Being able to organize, understand, retain, and retrieve what you learn is critical to success in school and beyond.*

The Question of Pay

The annual salaries paid to governors range from a low of $59,310 in Montana to a high of $130,000 in New York. A governor's salary is not his or her only compensation. Governors in most states are provided with an official residence. Additionally, all governors are given generous expense accounts so that, in fact, most of their daily expenditures are paid for by state taxpayers.

Dollars and cents, however, are not what lure great Americans to the office of governor. Honor, prestige, and a sense of public duty are what propel some of the nation's greatest leaders into governorships.

SECTION 3 REVIEW

1. What are the formal and informal qualifications one must meet in order to become governor?
2. What is the typical term of office for governors?
3. What are the ways in which a governor can be removed from office?
4. **For Critical Analysis:** What do you think is the most important informal qualification for becoming governor? What makes that qualification more important than the others?

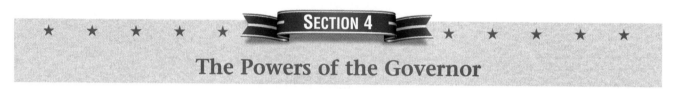

SECTION 4

The Powers of the Governor

Preview Questions:

🌐 What are the most important executive powers of governors?
🌐 What budgetary powers do governors possess?
🌐 What are governors' legislative and judicial powers?

Key Terms:

appropriation bills, clemency proceedings, pardon, commute, reprieve, parole

Each state's constitution explicitly gives certain powers to the governor, just as the U.S. Constitution gives certain powers to the president. The specific executive, legislative, and judicial powers of the governor are all part of a system of checks and balances.

State Executive Powers

The U.S. Constitution states that the president of the United States is "the executive" of the federal government. Most state constitutions, in contrast, describe their governors as the "chief executive" in state government. The difference between *the* and *chief* may not seem like much, but it is. No one legally shares supreme executive power with the president of the United States. In many states, though, the governor shares executive power with other executive officers, such as the lieutenant governor—the equivalent of the vice president. These officials are often also popularly elected.

No popularly elected executive in the state government can be directly controlled by the governor, at least not easily. This may be especially true with the lieutenant governor. In some particularly trying cases, a governor from one political party and a lieutenant governor from the opposing political party are voted into office.

◀ *Governor Gray Davis poses in his Sacramento, California, office. What significant difference exists in the pairing of the president and vice president of the United States and the governor and lieutenant governor of most states?*

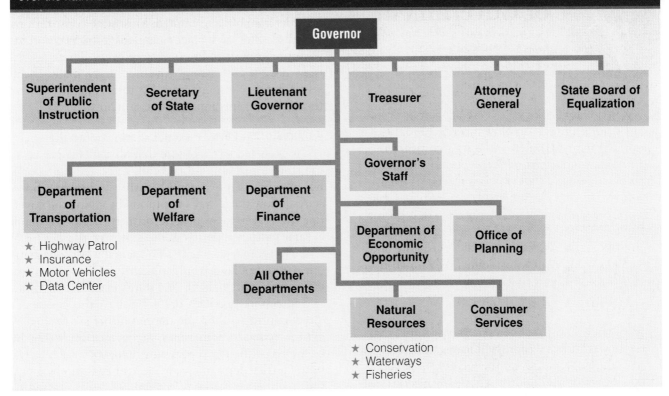

FIGURE 24–2 A Typical State Executive Branch This organizational chart depicts a typical state executive branch. How does the authority of a state governor over the state's executive branch compare to the authority of the U.S. president over the national executive branch?

In such situations, the governor may be unwilling to travel out of the state, fearing that the lieutenant governor will seize power during the governor's absence. In 1990, for example, Governor Michael Dukakis of Massachusetts postponed a trip abroad because he feared his lieutenant governor would use her power too much in his absence.

A state's chief executive must seek cooperation whenever the executive branch is divided. Cooperation is certainly more difficult when important state officials, such as the attorney general and the secretary of state, are not of the same political party as the governor. Figure 24–2 shows the executive branch of a typical state.

Appointment and Removal Powers One of the most important executive powers of the governor is the power to appoint and remove state officials. A governor who can appoint her or his own department and agency heads is more likely to be able to coordinate policies and have more power. A governor who can

reward supporters by appointing them to important department and agency positions will have a greater chance of success in carrying out her or his policies. One way to judge a governor's power is by whether that governor can in fact select and appoint loyal and competent assistants.

One factor that can reduce a governor's ability to appoint loyal followers is the requirement in most states that major appointees be confirmed by the state senate as part of the system of checks and balances. Some state legislatures also set qualifications that appointees must meet in order to assume office. In some states, legislatures require that a specified number of members of each commission or board be from each party. The result is that the governor must appoint members of the opposing party to serve in her or his administration.

The reality is that fewer than one-fifth of state constitutions allow governors to appoint secretaries of state, attorneys general, auditors, treasurers, controllers, and superintendents of public instruction.

ARCHITECTS

of Government

Gary Locke
(1950–   )

When Gary Locke was elected governor of the state of Washington on November 5, 1996, he became the first Chinese American governor in U.S. history and the first Asian American governor of a mainland state. Locke's mother is from Hong Kong, and his father is from Toishan, China. Locke is a graduate of Yale University and Boston University Law School. He has served as a representative in the Washington state legislature and as chief executive of King County, Washington.

HIS WORDS

"We already know that computers will think, that telephones and televisions will merge, and that bio-technology will reveal the secrets of our genetic code. Many of our children will produce goods and services that haven't been invented yet."

(Inaugural Speech, January 15, 1997)

"This is the new world of learning: it is a world where learning is a way of life."

(Speech to the State Labor Council,
July 10, 1997)

DEVELOPING
CRITICAL THINKING SKILLS

1. Regarding the first quotation, what goods and services are people producing today that did not exist when they were children?
2. In the second quotation, what does Locke mean when he refers to learning as "a way of life"?

Additionally, some states have hundreds of state agencies. Even with strong appointment powers, no governor could administer so many agencies effectively.

The governor's ability to remove appointed administrators from office is limited. Most state constitutions, as well as state laws, place numerous restrictions on the governor's power to fire state employees. These restrictions have a cost. Many governors have found themselves rendered ineffective by their inability to rid themselves of incompetent subordinates.

Administering Laws As chief administrator, the governor is expected to make sure that all the laws passed by the state legislature are faithfully executed. Of course, no governor can accomplish such a task alone. Some states follow the U.S. Constitution by giving the governor the power to require department heads to submit annual written reports on the status of the laws that relate to their departments. The actual work of carrying out the state's laws is undertaken by the thousands of individuals who make up the state's executive branch.

Some state agencies are subject to the governor's direct control. Others are not but rather are headed by elected officials. Sometimes, a governor finds that he or she has difficulty supervising an agency, such as the state's justice department, if the agency is run by a person, such as an attorney general, who was elected by the voters and is from another party.

Power of the Purse In the early years of this nation, governors had virtually no budgetary powers. In most states today, in contrast, planning and carrying out the budget is a significant responsibility for the governor. Just as the president of the United States prepares an annual budget, so, too, do the governors of many states prepare annual budgets. In other states, governors prepare biennial budgets, which are drawn up every two years. After the governor finishes the budget, it is sent to the legislature for approval.

The governor's budget can be seen as a political plan of action. The governor clearly emphasizes which programs have high priority by how much money is allocated to those programs. When the governor and the majority in the legislature are of different political parties, disputes often arise about the governor's proposed budget.

Many astute governors use their budget-making powers to effectively control state administration. Imagine, for example, that a governor is having trouble with the head of the Department of Public Instruction. That department head has been popularly elected and is from the opposing political party. The governor cannot fire that person and cannot control that person very easily. The governor, however, can use the budget-making power of the office to reduce the funds going to that department. The "power of the purse" often has profound effects on a department head's attitude.

Once a budget is authorized by the legislature, almost all governors possess the power to control the pattern of expenditures through executive agencies and departments. Governors often have the power to decide which expenditures will be made in a particular year. A governor may withhold the funding for a particular project if she or he is not satisfied with the way in which the project is progressing.

Power over the Militia The governor is the commander in chief of the armed forces of the state, which used to be called the state militia. Legislation at the close of World War I created the National Guard, which is made up of state units under the control of the governor. When there is a national emergency or a war, the president of the United States can "federalize" the National Guard and put it under the power of the U.S. armed forces.

Except in times of national emergency, the governor appoints officers in the National Guard and has the authority to call out the guard to suppress riots or to help in emergencies, such as floods, earthquakes, and other natural disasters.

Most governors delegate military matters to others and place little importance on their role as commander in chief. Sometimes, governors have filled National Guard units with officers selected on a political basis. If those selected are trained, no harm is necessarily done. If they are untrained, some National Guard units may be ineffective during state emergencies.

A member of the National Guard stands watch near a still-smoldering building, set afire during the riots that occurred in Los Angeles in April 1992. Rioting broke out after it was announced that the police officers accused of beating motorist Rodney King had been acquitted. Under what power was California governor Pete Wilson able to call out the National Guard?

Legislative Powers

The governor is the chief legislator of the state. As such, the governor has specific legislative powers. These include the power to call special legislative sessions, to veto legislation, and to recommend legislation.

Calling Special Legislative Sessions In the 1990s, a number of governors had to call special legislative sessions (unscheduled sessions) to solve state budget-deficit problems. In calling the special legislative sessions, the governors were exercising one of their legislative powers.

Every state gives the governor the power to call a special session of the legislature. This power is usually exclusively held by the governor. In those few states that allow the legislature to call itself into special session, the power is rarely exercised.

About half of the states allow the governor to specify the matters that may be taken up by the legislature at the special session. In some states, constitutions forbid the legislature to consider any matters other than those for which the session was called.

Power to Veto Legislation At the national level, veto power gives the president of the United States

> ### Just the Facts
>
> *Operating on the assumption that listening to classical music boosts a baby's "brain power," Georgia governor Zell Miller requested that state's legislature to pay for cassettes of classical music to give to all of Georgia's new parents.*

immense leverage. The simple threat of a presidential veto often prevents Congress from passing the legislation in question. The threat of a governor's veto is not necessarily as effective.

Every state except North Carolina has given the governor the power to veto legislation. In some states, however, the governor has only a short time to veto a bill after the legislature passes it. The time is three days in Iowa, Minnesota, New Mexico, North Dakota, and Wyoming. In a number of other states, it is six or seven days. If the governor does not veto a measure during the designated period, it normally becomes law.

The president of the United States can also use the pocket veto. If the president refuses to sign a bill and Congress adjourns within ten working days after the bill has been submitted, the bill is killed for that session of Congress. In most states, the opposite is true—bills that the governor neither signs nor vetoes become law without her or his signature after the legislature has adjourned. Thirteen states do have some form of pocket veto, however. The time periods are usually longer than the ten days given to the president. In Oklahoma, the pocket veto applies when the governor refuses to sign a bill and the legislature adjourns within fifteen days of when the bill is submitted. In Florida, the period is also fifteen days, and in Michigan, it is fourteen days.

No governor has absolute veto power. In all states, a governor's veto can be overridden by the legislature, usually with a two-thirds vote of the full membership of each chamber. (Of course, a legislature cannot override a pocket veto, because the legislature is no longer in session when the veto takes effect.) About 5 percent of all state bills are vetoed by governors. Less than 10 percent of such vetoes are overridden.

Line-Item Veto Forty-three states make some provision for a line-item veto, which allows the governor to veto a particular item in a bill while signing the rest of the bill into law.

In most states, the line-item veto is restricted to items in **appropriation bills.** Such bills set aside funds to be spent in specific areas, such as public housing and highways. Governors use line-item vetoes by eliminating certain appropriations and letting others stand. In twelve states, the governor can reduce the amount of an appropriation but cannot completely eliminate it. Nineteen states give the governor the ability to use the line-item veto on more than just appropriations.

Line-item vetoes are typically used to reduce appropriations the governor considers to be too high. They also can be used by a governor who wishes to punish lawmakers who have opposed his or her programs.

Judicial Powers

The governor's judicial powers are usually restricted to **clemency proceedings,** which involve showing mercy toward those convicted of crimes. In this area, most governors can grant pardons and reprieves, or request paroles for prisoners.

Pardon The governor of a state has the judicial power to grant pardons. A **pardon** is a release from the penalty for a criminal offense.

Today's busy governors rarely examine more than the most notorious criminal cases. When a governor believes that a conviction is wrongful or a penalty too harsh, the governor may grant a full or conditional pardon. Some states require that the governor work with a state pardon board. Others require that a governor's pardon be ratified by a council or by the state senate. Even in states in which the governor has sole pardoning power, there are state advisory pardon boards that investigate the cases and make recommendations.

The record for the highest number of pardons is held by Governor Miriam "Ma" Ferguson of Texas, who during her term from 1925 to 1927 pardoned almost four thousand convicted felons—about five a day!

Similar to the pardon is the governor's power to **commute,** or reduce in severity, the sentence imposed by a court. Governors have commuted many death sentences to lesser sentences of life imprisonment.

Reprieve A **reprieve** is a postponement of the carrying out of a criminal sentence. The postponement is typically for a specified short period of time. Criminals sentenced to die can often obtain a governor's reprieve to allow their lawyers more time to appeal their cases—for example, when new evidence that may prove their innocence has been discovered.

Parole If a governor believes that a convicted felon has served enough prison time, the governor may request early parole. **Parole** is the release of a prisoner before the end of his or her court-determined sentence.

◀ This cartoon criminal avoided execution by using the appeals process until he died a natural death. What powers do governors have that could help a convicted criminal?

Few governors enjoy exercising their clemency powers. Applications for pardons, reprieves, and paroles are numerous. In recent years, a governor who exercises such powers may be accused of being "soft on crime." This is exactly what happened to Michael Dukakis, governor of Massachusetts, when he ran for president against George Bush in 1988. Dukakis had approved a program in which some convicted criminals could leave jail on weekends for the purpose of getting work experience. One of them committed a murder while out of jail. In publicity campaigns, Bush exploited the image of Dukakis being too lenient on convicted criminals. It is not surprising that most states have full-time boards or committees to handle these problems, instead of directly involving the governor in each one of them.

SECTION 4 REVIEW

1. What are the executive powers of the governor?
2. What are some potential difficulties that the governor faces if the lieutenant governor belongs to a different political party?
3. How can a governor use budget-making powers to control state administration?
4. What are the legislative powers of the governor?
5. What are the judicial powers of the governor?
6. **For Critical Analysis:** What do you think are the advantages and disadvantages of having a governor and lieutenant governor from different political parties?

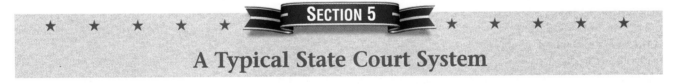

SECTION 5

A Typical State Court System

Preview Questions:

🌐 How are state court systems organized?
🌐 What are the various types of state courts?
🌐 What types of cases does each type of state court hear?

Key Terms:

jurisdiction, limited jurisdiction, general jurisdiction, justice court, justice of the peace, magistrate, magistrate courts

State court systems vary, but most systems are organized around three levels of courts. A person involved in a lawsuit typically first pleads the case before a trial court. That is the first level. If that person loses the case, he or she has the opportunity to appeal the decision to an appellate court (also called a *reviewing court* or an *appeals court*). Appellate courts review the decisions of trial courts. Most states have two levels of appellate courts—an intermediate level and the highest level, which is usually called the state supreme court. In most states, a case proceeds through a trial court with an automatic right to review by the state's intermediate appellate court. Then, if further appeal is granted, the case goes to the state's highest review court. Figure 24–3 shows the three tiers of a typical state court system.

Each court has a particular **jurisdiction,** which, as you may remember from Chapter 20, means that each court has the power to decide certain cases. Courts with **limited jurisdiction** can only hear cases in a very limited subject area. Courts with **general jurisdiction** can hear a much broader range of cases.

Trial Courts of Limited Jurisdiction

Every state has trial courts that have limited jurisdiction in certain subject areas. They are often called special inferior trial courts or minor judiciary courts. Typical courts of limited jurisdiction are domestic relations courts, which handle only divorces and child custody cases; local municipal courts, which mainly handle traffic cases; probate courts, which handle the administration of wills and estate-settlement problems; and small claims and justice courts. Typically, these courts do not keep complete written records of trial proceedings.

Justice Courts One of the earliest courts of limited jurisdiction was the **justice court,** presided over by a **justice of the peace,** or JP. In the earlier days of this nation, JPs were found everywhere in the country. One of the most famous JPs was Judge Roy Bean, the "hanging judge" of Langtry, Texas, who presided over his court at the turn of this century.

Today, in more than half the states, justice courts no longer exist. JPs still serve a useful function in some largely rural areas, where they are usually popularly elected. JP courts, for example, still exist in Texas counties. The subject matter that can be brought before JPs is limited to minor disputes between private individuals or companies and to crimes punishable by small fines or short jail terms.

◀ If you were accused of a crime in Langry County, Texas, at the turn of the century, your chances for acquittal would be slim if you found yourself in the court of famed justice of the peace "Hanging" Judge Roy Bean. What is the primary function of the justices of the peace who preside in the mostly rural areas of the United States today?

FIGURE 24–3 A Typical State Court System As you can see from this organizational chart, a typical state court system is similar to the federal court system discussed in Chapter 20. What is meant by the term *jurisdiction* as it is used in this figure?

State Supreme Court

State Intermediate Appellate Court(s)

State Trial Courts of General Jurisdiction

State Trial Courts of Limited Jurisdiction (for example, Probate Courts and Divorce Courts)

◄ *This historic building in the New England town of Concord, New Hampshire, continues to serve today as both a courthouse and a post office.*

JPs are best known, however, for conducting marriage ceremonies.

Magistrate Courts The equivalent of a county JP in the city is a **magistrate. Magistrate courts** have the same limited jurisdiction as do justice courts in rural settings. Magistrates are often popularly elected for short terms.

Trial Courts of General Jurisdiction

Trial courts that have general jurisdiction may be called county courts, district courts, superior courts, or circuit courts. The name in Ohio is Court of Common Pleas; the name in New York is Supreme Court; the name in Massachusetts is Trial Court. (The court names sometimes do not correspond with what the court does.) General jurisdiction trial courts have the authority to hear and decide cases involving many types of subject matter.

In trial courts, the parties to a controversy may dispute the facts of the case, which law should be applied to those facts, and how that law should be applied. If a party is entitled to and requests a trial by jury, the case will be tried before a jury in the trial courts.

▶ *What point is this political cartoonist trying to make about lawsuits?*

Courts of Appeal and Review

Every state has at least one appellate court. Appellate courts normally only review the records of the trial courts and determine whether the judgments of the trial courts were correct. No jury and no witnesses are present during an appeal.

Intermediate appellate courts are often called courts of appeals. The highest court of the state is usually called the supreme court, but there are several exceptions. For example, in New York, the state supreme court is called the Court of Appeals. In Texas and Oklahoma, there are two "highest" appellate courts. In Texas, for example, state district court decisions can be appealed to either the Texas Supreme Court or the Texas Court of Criminal Appeals.

The decisions of each state's highest court on all questions of state law are final unless overruled by the Supreme Court of the United States.

1. What are the three tiers of the typical state court system?
2. What are courts of limited jurisdiction?
3. Over which type of court does a justice of the peace preside?
4. What are courts of general jurisdiction?
5. How does the procedure for a case heard in an appeals court differ from the procedure in a trial court?
6. **For Critical Analysis:** How do you think the right of appeal might interfere with guarantees of a fair and speedy trial?

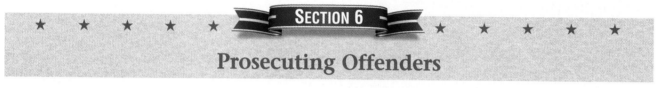

★ ★ ★ ★ ★ **SECTION 6** ★ ★ ★ ★ ★

Prosecuting Offenders

Preview Questions:

- Who presides over state departments of justice?
- What is the job of a prosecuting attorney?
- What is the typical process by which individuals suspected of committing crimes are prosecuted?

Key Terms:

prosecuting attorney, district attorney, warrant, probable cause, indictment, grand jury, information, arraignment, public defender, preliminary hearing, bail, bench trial, trial jury, petit jury, *voir dire*, plea bargaining

State laws are created by the legislature and enforced by state and local law enforcement personnel. When state laws have been violated and the suspected violator is apprehended, prosecution follows. Prosecuting offenders is the job of the state's justice department, the prosecuting attorneys, and others.

The State Department of Justice

Every state has an attorney general, usually popularly elected, who presides over some type of justice department. During the time the attorney general is in office, he or she cannot engage in private legal practice. The attorney general handles lawsuits involving the state and its officials and also deals with local prosecutors.

The Prosecuting Attorney

Those who are suspected of violating a state criminal law are normally arrested by local police. The prosecution of those suspects is then handled by a local **prosecuting attorney** (PA), often called the **district attorney (DA)** or county attorney.

▶ San Francisco district attorney Terrence Hallinan, left, consults with Maria Bee, an assistant district attorney. What is the main task of the district attorney and his or her staff?

How State Government Has Changed

In the last two hundred years, state governments have retained many basic structural features, but they have also changed in several ways. Here are just a few ways in which state governments today differ from those of the early 1800s.

THEN (EARLY 1800s)	NOW
The term of office for state governors was typically one year.	The term of office for state governors is typically four years.
There was little, if any, plea bargaining between prosecutors and defendants in criminal cases.	About 90 percent of criminal cases are plea bargained so that the state can avoid the time and expense of trials.
The national Bill of Rights was not applicable to criminal proceedings brought against individuals by state governments.	Most of the provisions of the national Bill of Rights apply to proceedings against individuals by state governments as well as by the national government.

The PA or DA works for the government and acts on behalf of the people.

District or county attorneys prosecute accused violators of state law, which means that they institute and carry out legal proceedings against these persons. They also assist police personnel in uncovering crimes, defend officials in the counties in which they work, and advise county officials and the minor court judges on legal issues. The major job of the district attorney is to determine which individuals arrested by the police should be charged with crimes.

District attorneys wield great power during all stages of criminal proceedings. They even confer with judges about what the sentencing should be if there is a conviction.

The position of district attorney is political and is normally an elective office. District attorneys are highly visible individuals. DAs who engage in effective anticrime campaigns often go on to launch political careers.

The Criminal Process

Criminal proceedings include numerous safeguards designed to guarantee the rights of individuals against the power of the state. Criminal proceedings may vary somewhat, but the following steps generally occur in criminal cases.

Arrest Unless an individual is caught while actually committing a crime, a **warrant** must be issued for his or her arrest. An arrest warrant is an order issued by a magistrate that authorizes a police officer to make an arrest. Before a warrant may be issued, there must be **probable cause** for suspecting that the individual in question has in fact committed a crime. For example, a police officer must have some evidence—such as fingerprints or the statements of witnesses—that a particular person may have committed a crime before an arrest warrant will be issued. An officer may sometimes make an arrest without a warrant if there is no time to

Witnessing a Crime

Witnessing a crime can be a frightening and intimidating experience. The first reaction is often to run away and forget about it. As a citizen, however, you have a responsibility to help enforce law and order in your community, which may involve identifying yourself as a witness to a crime. If you run away from this responsibility, it may be more difficult to prosecute the criminal, leaving him or her free to commit more crimes and harm more victims in your community. Offering your account as a witness can help make your community and neighborhood a safer place to live.

If you witness a crime, find the nearest phone and call the police immediately. You can usually do this by dialing 911. If the victim needs medical attention, call an ambulance first (also usually by dialing 911). Give the time, the place, and the nature of the crime. While you wait for the police or ambulance to arrive, try to remember as many specific details as possible about the crime, the person who committed the crime, and any vehicle involved. When the police arrive, answer all of their questions as accurately as you can. Do not leave out any details, even if you think they are not important. Also, do not exaggerate or add any personal commentary. If you are asked to sign a written account of your testimony, be sure to read what the officer has written and check it for accuracy before you sign it.

Chances are, you will not be contacted again. You may, however, be called to testify in court. Answer the questions as completely and honestly as possible. Do not leave out details, and do not exaggerate. The attorney for the defendant will probably cross-examine you. Remember that you are not on trial and do not need to defend yourself. The attorney may ask you questions that sound confusing or accusatory, but remember that she or he is only trying to do a job and is probably trying to bring out any inconsistencies or weaknesses in your testimony. If you answer honestly, directly, briefly, and to the point, you should have no problem.

After testifying, you will have fulfilled your responsibility as a citizen. Remember that crime affects all of us and that all of us are responsible for doing what

---

get one, but the action of the arresting officer is still judged by the standard of probable cause.

Indictment Individuals must be formally charged with having committed specific crimes before they can be brought to trial. Such a charge is called an **indictment** if it is issued by a grand jury. A **grand jury** is a group,

▶ Law enforcement agents escort a suspect to an awaiting car following his indictment on a $15 million fraud charge. Who must issue such a charge?

◀ *Police officers in Imperial Beach, California, interview a witness to a crime. What should be your first response if you witness a crime?*

we can to help keep our communities safe.

TAKING ACTION

1. Is there is a "crime alert" or "crime watch" program in your neighborhood? If there is, obtain information on how it works and how you and your household can participate.

2. Many newspapers have a local section that lists reported crimes in the area. If your newspaper has this regular section, read it for several weeks. Note what percentage of the crimes reported were actually witnessed by someone.

3. The next time you attend a school sporting event with a friend, try an experiment. Each of you should spend ten minutes observing what is happening in the crowd around you. The following morning, write down what you observed. Compare your observations with those of your friend. Try to determine why differences might exist in your observations.

consisting of from twelve to twenty-three citizens, that hears evidence and decides whether persons suspected of crimes should be charged. During a grand jury hearing, the prosecutor—perhaps the district attorney or one of the assistant district attorneys—will attempt to show the grand jury that the evidence is sufficient to indict the individual in question. The grand jury then weighs the evidence. If the majority of the jurors believe that the evidence is sufficient to hold the person for trial, it votes for the formal indictment.

Even though the grand jury is intended to act as a check on the power of the prosecutor, it usually does whatever the prosecutor recommends. Ninety-eight percent of all cases brought before grand juries result in formal indictments. The average grand jury spends no more than five to ten minutes reviewing each case.

States are not required to use grand juries, and about half of the states do not use them. In those states, the prosecutor brings the evidence before a magistrate. If the magistrate agrees, she or he issues an **information,** a formal accusation that results in the suspect's arraignment.

Arraignment After being charged, the suspect, or defendant, is arraigned. **Arraignment** is a procedure in which a defendant comes before a judge, who reads the formal charges listed in the indictment or information. The defendant, or his or her lawyer, then enters a plea of guilty or not guilty.

Off-Year Gubernatorial Elections

Increasingly, state elected officials, including governors, are isolating themselves from national politics. This isolation has resulted from a change in when state officials are elected. It is common today for governors and other state executive officers to be chosen in off-year elections—elections in years that are not presidential election years. In 1920, a presidential election year, only twelve states did *not* have gubernatorial elections. In 1996, also a presidential election year, thirty-eight states did not have gubernatorial elections.

Americans who are at odds over this trend know why it has happened. The purpose behind the shifts has been to weaken the influence of national politics over state politics. Consider an example. A Republican candidate is running for governor during a presidential election year. It looks as if the Republican presidential candidate is going to achieve a landslide victory. Under such circumstances, a Republican gubernatorial candidate will have a much better chance of winning. This is called the coattail effect. If the governor's race, in contrast, is held two years later, the presidential election will have little influence. That is, there would be much less of a coattail effect.

Governors Should Be Elected at the Same Time as Presidents, Say Some

Those who are against this system believe that states should not remain isolated. They want state elections to be influenced by the national trend of voters' sentiments. They do not want states to "go their own way." They believe that state governments all too often have been immune to national forces. For example, they point to how some state governments effectively countered the national trend toward racial equality during the 1950s and 1960s.

There is also another problem with off-year elections of governors and other state officials.

Voter participation is much lower. On average, only 75 percent of the voters who vote in presidential elections vote in off-year elections.

Let the States Go Their Own Way, Say Others

Americans who agree with the trend toward off-year election of governors offer several arguments to support their position. They believe that state politics should be isolated from national politics. After all, they say, we live in a system of federalism. State governments are coequal with the national government. Hence, state officials should be elected on their own merits, not on the popularity of a presidential candidate.

These individuals further believe that it is important for states to "go their own way," because it gives Americans choices. In other words, if different states have different policies, then Americans can migrate to the states that have policies that please them. If we become one big "nation," then this choice will no longer exist.

People in this group are not convinced that reduced voter participation is an issue. If reduced voter participation is the price we have to pay for federalism, they say, then so be it.

YOU DECIDE
....

1. What effect, if any, might the increase in split-ticket voting in recent years have on the coattail effect?
2. "Reduced voter participation in off-year elections is the price we have to pay for federalism." Analyze this statement.
3. Can you think of any other arguments for or against the proposition that governors should be elected in presidential election years?

The defendant has the right to an attorney of his or her own choosing. If the defendant cannot obtain an attorney, a court-appointed lawyer, usually called a **public defender,** is assigned to the case.

In a criminal case, a **preliminary hearing** is typically held by a magistrate to ensure that the defendant has been informed of and understands his or her rights and why the arrest was made. Once the magistrate has determined that the defendant has been given "due process" (see Chapter 6), then the magistrate will set **bail,** the amount of money a criminal defendant must pay to be released from custody until a jury renders its verdict.

The Trial Every accused person has a right to a speedy and public trial by an impartial jury. This right is guaranteed by the Sixth Amendment to the U.S. Constitution, which begins with the following words:

> In all criminal prosecutions, the accused shall enjoy the right to a speedy and public trial, by an impartial jury of the State and district wherein the crime shall have been committed.

Not every accused person wants a jury trial, however. The alternative is a **bench trial,** in which the judge hears the evidence and decides whether the defendant is guilty or not guilty.

If a jury trial is requested, the case is heard by a **trial jury**—also called a **petit jury,** as opposed to a grand jury. Whereas a grand jury decides whether an accused person will be charged, a trial jury determines whether the person is guilty or not guilty. Trial juries normally consist of twelve persons, but budget considerations have forced many states to reduce jury size to as few as six members.

Jury Selection The names of potential jurors are usually selected from voter registration lists, home ownership lists, or driver's license lists in a particular location. Once a group of potential jurors has been assembled, the judge, prosecutor, and defense attorneys examine the prospective jurors to ensure that their judgment will be impartial. This process is called *voir dire* (pronounced *vwahr-deer*), a French phrase that means, in the judicial context, "to speak the truth." Usually, *voir dire* consists of questions asked orally to individual prospective jurors to determine whether they could render a fair judgment.

▲ *Jillian Robbins, left, is escorted from her arraignment on charges of murder, attempted murder, and aggravated assault. Charges were made as a result of an alleged random shooting spree on the Pennsylvania State University campus on September 17, 1996.*

The Jury's Verdict In most states, the jury's verdict must be unanimous. That is, everyone on the jury must agree that the accused person is guilty. Exceptions are sometimes made for minor criminal cases, in which only a majority vote is required.

When a jury cannot agree on a verdict, it is called a hung jury, and the judge declares a mistrial. A new trial with a new jury may be held, or the prosecutor may simply drop the charges against the defendant.

The current trend is toward fewer and fewer jury trials. The large number of crimes committed in the United States has made it virtually impossible for everyone accused of a crime to obtain a jury trial because of the cost and time involved. Therefore, more

◀ *A defendant listens as the judge in this Austin, Texas, courtroom reads the formal charges against him. The defendant then enters a plea of guilty or not guilty. What is this procedure called?*

and more prosecuting attorneys are making deals with accused persons, who agree to plead guilty to a lesser crime and avoid going to trial altogether. Making such deals is called **plea bargaining.** Plea bargaining, a practice that arose in the nineteenth century, has become commonplace in the past several decades. Today, about 90 percent of all criminal cases are plea bargained.

SECTION 6 REVIEW

1. Whom does a prosecuting attorney represent?
2. What are the steps involved in a typical criminal proceeding?
3. What is the job of the grand jury? Why is it important?
4. **For Critical Analysis:** Do you think the practice of plea bargaining should be prohibited? Why or why not?

★ ★ ★ ★ **Chapter Summary** ★ ★ ★ ★

Section 1: The U.S. Constitution and the State Constitutions

● The U.S. Constitution reserves to the states all powers not delegated to the national government. This means that the states may do anything that the Constitution does not prohibit them from doing or that is not expressly reserved for the national government. No state or local law may be in conflict with the U.S. Constitution, with laws made by the U.S. Congress, or with treaties entered into by the U.S. government.
● State constitutions are typically lengthy and detailed.
● Amendments to state constitutions may be proposed by constitutional convention, by legislative activity, or by popular demand.

Section 2: Direct Democracy

● Many states exercise direct democracy through initiatives, referendums, and recalls.

- The initiative lets citizens bypass legislatures by proposing new statutes or changes in government.
- The referendum is proposed by the legislature and then directed to the voters for their approval.
- The recall is a petition by citizens calling for the removal of a public official deemed incompetent or grossly unethical in conduct.

Section 3: The Modern Governor

- A governor is the chief executive officer in each of the fifty states.
- Every state selects its governor by popular vote. Most governors serve four-year terms, while a few serve two-year terms.
- The governor may be removed by impeachment in every state but Oregon and by recall in eighteen of the states.

Section 4: The Powers of the Governor

- In most states, executive power is shared by several state officials. Important executive powers of the governor include appointing and removing officials, administering laws, planning and carrying out the budget, and commanding the National Guard.
- The specific legislative powers of the governor include the ability to call special legislative sessions, the power to veto legislation, and the power to recommend legislation.
- The governor's judicial powers are restricted to conducting clemency proceedings.

Section 5: A Typical State Court System

- State court systems vary, but most systems are organized around three levels of courts: the trial courts of general and limited jurisdiction, the courts of appeals, and the state supreme court.
- Courts of limited jurisdiction can hear cases only in a very limited subject area. Courts of general jurisdiction can hear many types of cases.
- Every state has at least one court of appeals, or appellate (reviewing) court.

Section 6: Prosecuting Offenders

- State laws are created by state legislatures and enforced by state and local law enforcement personnel.
- A person who violates a state criminal law normally is arrested by local police and prosecuted by a local prosecuting attorney, often called a district attorney. The district attorney plays an important role in criminal proceedings.
- Criminal proceedings, which include numerous safeguards to protect the rights of individuals, normally involve the following steps: arrest, indictment, arraignment, and trial. A criminal defendant who cannot obtain an attorney is entitled to a state-appointed attorney, or public defender.
- Prior to trial, a jury is selected through a process called *voir dire*. At the end of a jury trial, the jury renders its verdict.

★ REVIEW QUESTIONS ★

1. What are the major powers reserved to the states?
2. Why are most state constitutions long and detailed?
3. What are the three ways in which a state constitution can be amended?
4. What functions do the initiative, the referendum, and the recall serve?
5. How do governors assume their office?
6. What is the normal term for a governor?
7. What is the difference between impeachment and recall?
8. Briefly describe each of the roles performed by a governor.
9. What are the governor's executive powers?
10. Why are the governor's powers of appointment and removal important?
11. Briefly describe the legislative and judicial powers of the governor.
12. What are the three tiers of the typical state court system?
13. What is meant by limited jurisdiction?
14. What is meant by general jurisdiction?
15. What is the job of the prosecuting attorney?
16. Briefly describe the steps involved in a criminal proceeding.
17. What actions should you take if you witness a crime?

★ CRITICAL THINKING ★

1. Do you think every state needs its own constitution? Why or why not?
2. Does your state use the constitutional initiative? If so, how often has it been used? What have been some recent initiatives? Do you think that the initiative process is truly a form of direct democracy?
3. The governorship is considered by many to be an excellent preparation for the presidency. In what ways do you think it would prepare someone for the presidency? In what ways do you think it would not?
4. Why is the right to appeal a case important?

★ IMPROVING YOUR SKILLS ★

Communication Skills

Determining the Reliability of Information Learning to judge the reliability of information is important to your lifelong learning. As you learned in Chapter 12, the information you hear on the radio, watch on television, or gather from Internet sources can be biased or simply incorrect. Information that is reliable is accurate. When trying to assess the reliability of written or spoken information, ask yourself the following questions:

- What are the background and qualifications of the person presenting the information? Is he or she an expert in a particular area?
- What are the biases or value judgments of the writer or speaker?
- Is the information based on primary or secondary sources?
- What fallacies, if any, are present in the reasoning?
- Is the person confusing correlation with causation?
- What evidence is presented to support the argument? Were unbiased, legitimate sources used as evidence? Are there alternative explanations that are being ignored? Is the information oversimplified?

When you have answered these questions about the material, you should be able to evaluate whether or not the information is reliable and correct.

Social Studies Skills

Decision Making and Predicting the Consequences of Decisions Policymakers, government officials, and indeed all types of bureaucrats must make decisions. The consequences of these decisions may be important

for many individuals. At the national level, the consequences may affect millions of people in many countries. Before you can make proper decisions yourself, you should be aware of the steps in decision making:

1. Define what you need, want, or must do.
2. Examine all of the resources you have available to help you make the decision.
3. Identify the choices you actually have.
4. Gather as much information as you can effectively use.
5. Evaluate and compare your decision options and probable consequences of each option.
6. Make your decision.

Predicting the consequences of your own decisions is often quite easy. If you choose to study more for one course than for another, you'll be able to see if the extra studying pays off. But policymakers in government cannot so easily predict the consequences of many of their decisions, because a government policy may affect many different people and activities. Thus, it is hard to predict all of the consequences of a particular policy decision. Write down the possible consequences of the following decisions:

1. The U.S. Postal Service decides to raise the price of sending a first-class letter by 50 percent.
2. The governor of your state asks the state legislature to cut 15 percent of all state spending by next year.
3. The lieutenant governor starts publicly criticizing the governor.

Discuss your responses with other students in your class, and compile a large class list of possible consequences.

★ ACTIVITIES AND PROJECTS ★

1. Write a brief description of your state constitution, including its main principles and its history.
2. Think of a state-sponsored program that is important to you. Imagine that funds for the program are going to be cut and that you are a lobbyist who must convince a state legislator to oppose the funding cut. Write a script that spells out the argument you will present to the legislator.
3. Prepare a biography of your state governor that tells his or her life history, political background, and accomplishments in office.
4. Prepare a biography of your state lieutenant governor that tells his or her life history, political background, and accomplishments in office. In addition, conduct research to determine how many of your state's lieutenant governors have been elected to the position of governor.
5. Prepare a bulletin board display to illustrate the state court system in your state.
6. Invite one of the district attorneys or a judge in your area to speak to your class about the trial process within your community.

What If . . .

There Were No State Court Systems?

In some countries, all courts are, in essence, national. All accused criminals are tried under exactly the same laws, rules, and procedures. How would our system of justice in the United States be different if this became a reality here?

CHAPTER 25

Local Government

CHAPTER OBJECTIVES

To learn about and understand . . .

⭐ The origins and basic functions of local governments

⭐ The operation and organization of local governmental units

⭐ The governing of municipalities

★ *Keynote* ★

"That is the best government which desires to make the people happy, and knows how to make them happy."

Lord Thomas Babington Macaulay
(1800–1859)
English Historian and Politician

INTRODUCTION

How would you feel if once a week you received a sheet of paper from Washington, D.C., that told you what subjects you would be studying for the next five days in each of your classes? That is not what happens, though. Your local school district may set out broad guidelines for what you are supposed to learn. It is those who govern closest to home—your school administrators and your teachers—who decide on your specific classroom duties and assignments.

According to the English historian Lord Macaulay, in the opening quotation, the best governments are the ones that work to make the people happy. For most individuals, the best government is the government closest to home, which is their local government.

◀ Citizens gather to discuss their concerns at a city council meeting in Huntington Beach, California.

675

The Functions of Local Government

Preview Questions:

- What are the major functions of local government?
- What is the largest expense for most local governments?

Key Term:

zoning

Some of the oldest governments in our country are local governments. Long before the states were formed, cities and towns provided government services to their residents. Then, after each state adopted its own constitution, certain powers and responsibilities were formally granted to local government units.

British scholar James Bryce, in his book *Modern Democracies* (1921), described the "business" of local government in the early 1900s as follows:

It is the business of a local authority to mend the roads, to clean out the village well or to provide a new pump, to see that there is a place where straying beasts may be kept till the owner reclaims them, to fix the number of cattle each villager may turn out on the common pasture, [and] to give each his share of timber cut in the common woodland.

To get an idea of the business of local government today, take a ride through your local community. As you look around, think about how much of what you see is provided by your local government. You may pass schools, police cars, fire stations, libraries, parks, golf courses, parking lots, sports arenas, garbage

▶ *Children enjoy playing in neighborhood parks where they have access to playground equipment and large sand boxes that usually aren't available at their homes. Who pays for these items?*

trucks, hospitals, and other facilities that are maintained and operated by local governmental units. The services that cities and counties provide are so extensive that it is difficult to catalog all of them.

Education

Schools are one service provided by local government with which you've probably become quite familiar. Education is the single largest expense of most local governments. Typically, about 45 percent of the local government budget goes toward funding for public schools.

You've probably heard people in your community talking about problems or issues in the schools. Maybe you have some concerns and opinions of your own about how your local government runs the school system. Many local citizens are concerned about public schools because the schools affect the whole community. The school system is responsible for educating young people who will one day work in the community and become its leaders. Usually, state and federal taxes pay some educational costs, but local taxpayers often provide most of the money and make the key decisions regarding the operation of the public schools.

Police and Fire Protection

Police protection is the second largest expense of most American cities, and fire protection is third. Most local communities are very concerned about how crime is being controlled by the local police force. Local governments must decide how many police officers a community needs, how these officers will be armed, and which areas they will patrol.

Fire protection varies with the size of the community. If you live in a small town, your fire department may be staffed by volunteers. If you live in a large city,

▶ A kneeling firefighter points a hose into a burning house while his partner braces him against the force of the water pressure. Although the firefighters pictured are professionals, where might you find a fire department staffed by volunteers?

your fire department is probably staffed by full-time professionals.

Public Welfare

Although the national government and state governments pay part of the cost of public welfare, the share that local governments pay continues to rise. Public welfare includes payments to the poor and needy. For big cities, public welfare is one of the largest expenditures.

One obstacle to local government funding of welfare programs is that city expenditures are growing faster than revenues. That means that the cities are spending more funds than they take in. Furthermore, cities are finding that the number of people needing public assistance is increasing, and that this is happening at ever higher costs.

City Planning and Zoning

Without planning, cities could develop haphazardly. Industrial plants could be built downtown, railroads could run through the heart of the city, skyscrapers could shut out sunlight on narrow streets, main roads could be built too far apart or too close together, and public buildings could be inaccessible to those who need them. Maybe you live in a city, or have visited one, that seems disorganized or run down or in which it is difficult to find your way around. To avoid such problems, most cities have seen the need to establish planning agencies or commissions to plan how cities will grow.

Washington, D.C., is one of the few cities that began as and has remained a planned city. In 1790, Congress decided to build the nation's capital along the Potomac River. President Washington assigned the job of laying out the city to a French engineer named Major Pierre-Charles L'Enfant (1754–1825). L'Enfant designed the city in a grid, with streets running east to west named according to the alphabet and streets running north to south named by number. He also planned for wide streets, scenic parks, graceful turning circles, and large areas to be reserved for public buildings. At first, both L'Enfant and his plan were dismissed as being too extravagant. Later, his original plan was restudied, and it has been followed fairly closely through the years. Today, the National Capital Planning Commission guides the development of our nation's capital city. A map of Washington, D.C., appears in Figure 25–1 on pages 678 and 679.

In almost every community, there are certain areas in which only residential homes are located, or only retail stores, or only warehouses. Signs and billboards are normally located only in certain areas of the community and are similar in size. These aspects of the community are often regulated by zoning boards or planning agencies. **Zoning** is the method that cities use to regulate the way property, such as land and buildings, is used. Through zoning practices, a city strives for order.

Generally, a zoning ordinance places all land in the city into one of three classifications: residential, commercial, or industrial. Residential, commercial, and industrial zones are further divided into subclassifications, or subzones. For example, one residential zone might be designated for single-family houses, while another might allow apartment buildings. Zoning ordinances also place other restrictions on land use, such as limits on the height and area of structures and the distances they must be set back from other property lines. Nearly every major city in the United States is zoned today.

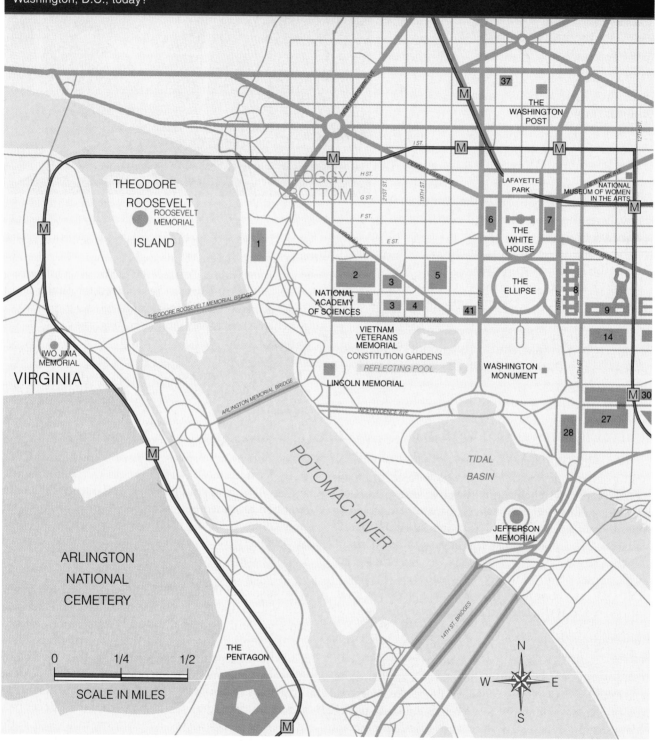

FIGURE 25–1 Map of Washington, D.C. Washington, D.C., was planned by a French engineer, Major Pierre-Charles L'Enfant, who designed the city in a grid with streets running east to west named according to the alphabet and streets running north to south named by number. Washington, D.C., remains a planned city. Who guides the development of Washington, D.C., today?

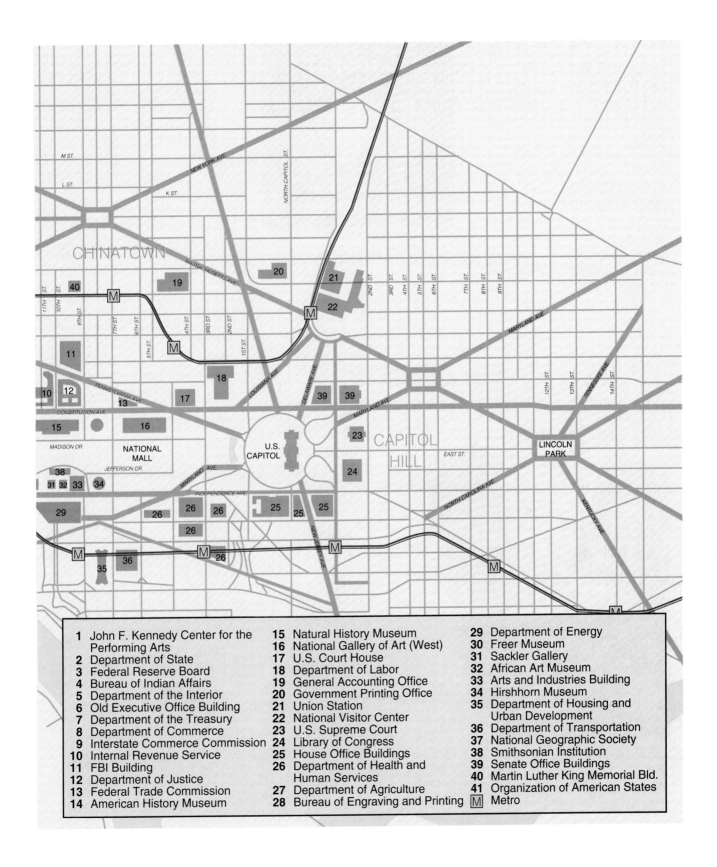

1 John F. Kennedy Center for the Performing Arts
2 Department of State
3 Federal Reserve Board
4 Bureau of Indian Affairs
5 Department of the Interior
6 Old Executive Office Building
7 Department of the Treasury
8 Department of Commerce
9 Interstate Commerce Commission
10 Internal Revenue Service
11 FBI Building
12 Department of Justice
13 Federal Trade Commission
14 American History Museum
15 Natural History Museum
16 National Gallery of Art (West)
17 U.S. Court House
18 Department of Labor
19 General Accounting Office
20 Government Printing Office
21 Union Station
22 National Visitor Center
23 U.S. Supreme Court
24 Library of Congress
25 House Office Buildings
26 Department of Health and Human Services
27 Department of Agriculture
28 Bureau of Engraving and Printing
29 Department of Energy
30 Freer Museum
31 Sackler Gallery
32 African Art Museum
33 Arts and Industries Building
34 Hirshhorn Museum
35 Department of Housing and Urban Development
36 Department of Transportation
37 National Geographic Society
38 Smithsonian Institution
39 Senate Office Buildings
40 Martin Luther King Memorial Bld.
41 Organization of American States
Ⓜ Metro

We are fast becoming a nation of city dwellers. As people move to the cities, they bring their garbage with them. The amount of waste generated by U.S. residences and businesses today is nearly three times what it was in 1960. This places a demanding and costly burden on city governments, as well as on other local government units.

Most cities have chosen to bury or burn their garbage in landfills. Landfill space is becoming more expensive, however, and rising costs are straining municipal budgets.

One option that local governments have turned to is

▲ When officials of the city of Kirkland, Washington, provided bins and offered curbside recycling to residents, cooperation with the city's recycling plan soared.

PARTICIPATING IN YOUR GOVERNMENT

Recycling in Your Community

recycling—the reprocessing of waste, such as newspapers, aluminum, and glass, into usable materials. Some experts believe that recycling could reduce the amount of our nation's trash by at least 30 percent.

One good way of promoting recycling in your community is by starting a curbside recycling program. In such a program, homeowners set out buckets of sorted recyclable material along with the garbage. City workers pick up the materials and see that they are recycled. In Marin County, California, a woman named Gloria Duncan rallied volunteers in her community, met with local garbage collectors, and started a curbside program.

If you want to start a recycling program in your area, here

are some guidelines based on the strategies Duncan used:

1. **Find your allies.** You will need to look for volunteers and experts in your community who are willing to help you in your efforts.
2. **Let the media know.** Contact newspapers, radio stations, television stations, and city magazines. Be sure the public knows about your concerns and what you are trying to accomplish.
3. **Consult with local political leaders.** Explain your goals and ask for advice on how to achieve them. Come up with a plan, and present it.

For help in starting a recycling program, you can call the National Recycling Coalition at 703-683-9025 or check its Web page at **www.recycle.net/**. You can also contact the Environmental Protection Agency Hotline at 800-424-9346 (**www.epa.gov/**) or the Environmental Defense Fund at 800-CALL-EDF (**edf.org/**).

TAKING ACTION

1. Divide your class into groups. Have each group devise specific steps to start a recycling program in your area.
2. If there is a curbside recycling program in your community, find out why, how, and by whom it was started.

◀ *Cities are more than buildings and streets. Framed by the Manhattan skyline, Central Park draws even busy New Yorkers to its ice skating rink. What is unique about your city or town?*

Recreational and Cultural Activities

Americans today have more leisure time than Americans of the nineteenth century. Cities have responded with recreational and cultural programs for residents of all ages, from infants to the elderly. Local governments offer community programs such as football, baseball, swimming, ice skating, and dancing. They also maintain neighborhood parks, playgrounds, and municipal swimming pools. They help build, sponsor, and maintain city zoos and museums. They also help build arenas, sports facilities, and convention centers.

SECTION 1 REVIEW

1. What services do local governments provide?
2. Do local governments pay for the entire cost of public education?
3. **For Critical Analysis:** What might happen in a city without any zoning laws?

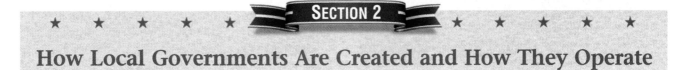

SECTION 2

★ ★ ★ ★ ★ ★ ★ ★ ★ ★

How Local Governments Are Created and How They Operate

Preview Questions:

🌏 What is the relationship between state and local governments?

🌏 What are the typical functions of county governments?

🌏 How are county governments organized?

🌏 What are the major problems of county governments?

🌏 How are municipalities created?

🌏 What are special districts?

Key Terms:

county, parishes, boroughs, county board, county-manager plan, chief administrator plan, elected chief executive plan, urban areas, municipalities, incorporation, Dillon's rule, Cooley's rule, municipal home rule, home-rule city, general-law city, New England town, town meeting, town manager system, selectmen, townships, unincorporated areas

The U.S. Constitution does not mention local governments. States have full authority in establishing local governments, such as counties and cities, and in defining their powers and responsibilities. Consequently, every local government is a creation of its parent state. The state can create a local government, and the state can terminate the right of a local government to exist. Indeed, states have often abolished entire counties, school districts, cities, and special districts. Since World War II, almost 20,000 school districts have gone out of existence or have been consolidated with other school districts.

Local governmental units can be placed in the following major categories: counties, municipalities, New England towns, townships, and special districts. As you can see in Figure 25–2 below, most local governments are special districts.

Counties

If you look at a map of your state, you can see that it is divided into counties of different sizes and shapes. A **county** is a major local government unit that typically administers community services such as roads, schools, and law enforcement. State governments created counties to assist them in carrying out state laws. Organized county governments are found in every state except Connecticut and Rhode Island. In Louisiana, counties are called **parishes.** In Alaska, they are called **boroughs.**

There are over three thousand counties in the United States, which vary greatly in both size and population. San Bernardino County in California is the largest geographically, with 20,102 square miles. New York County in New York is the smallest, with less than 22 square miles. County populations can vary from millions of residents, as in Los Angeles County, to one hundred or fewer residents, as in Loving County, Texas.

County governments also vary a great deal in importance. In rural areas and in the South, county governments have become major providers of services. In these areas, early settlements were spread over large areas with few towns and villages. One town in the county became the county seat, where the county government resided. In the New England states, in contrast, people settled in towns and townships, which became the important units of local government.

Recently, in some metropolitan areas, county governments have taken over some of the functions once handled by city governments. The government of Dade County, Florida, for example, administers water, transportation, and other services in Miami. In many other areas, however, the importance of counties has declined, and there have even been attempts to abolish them.

Functions of County Government The responsibilities and functions of a county are usually determined by the state constitution and state laws. Typically, counties provide record-keeping services for their communities. They maintain records of births, deaths, marriages, and property ownership. They also register voters, prepare ballots, supervise elections, and keep election records on behalf of state governments.

Most counties also provide a number of police and regulatory services. Some counties have a county sheriff's department that maintains jails and other correctional facilities. Many counties have their own court systems. Counties may issue permits and licenses, such as for hunting, fishing, and marriage. Other services might include operating airports, hospitals, and transportation systems; collecting taxes; and maintaining parks and libraries.

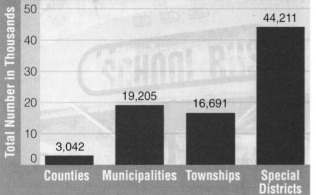

FIGURE 25–2 Local Governments in the United States Today As you can see from this figure, most local government units take the form of special districts. Nearly half of these are school districts. How many schools make up your school district?

Category	Total Number in Thousands
Counties	3,042
Municipalities	19,205
Townships	16,691
Special Districts	44,211

◀ *A bride and groom take advantage of a county service— a civil marriage ceremony.*

levels of those who work for the county. Executive powers may involve the appointment of certain county officers and employees, as well as the administration of courts, jails, hospitals, roadways, welfare programs, and elections.

Most boards share their powers and responsibilities with other elected officials. These officials and their duties include the following:

- *Sheriff*—maintains the jail and serves as the police official in areas of the county that are outside city limits.
- *District attorney*—prosecutes criminal cases on behalf of the state and county.
- *Superintendent of schools*—acts as chief administrator for the county's elementary and secondary schools. (In some states, superintendents are appointed by a school board.)
- *County clerk*—registers and records documents such as deeds, mortgages, birth and death certificates, and divorce decrees.
- *Auditor*—keeps financial records and authorizes payments to meet county obligations.
- *Treasurer*—keeps county funds and authorizes payments from these funds.
- *Assessor*—sets value on taxable property in the county.
- *Coroner*—investigates violent deaths and deaths not witnessed by a doctor.

In some counties, special boards may be elected or appointed to perform specific tasks. They commonly include the school board, the board of health, the hospital board, the library board, and the planning board.

Organization of County Government Because state laws differ, the organization of county governments differs from one state to another. Most counties are governed by a **county board,** which may also be known as a board of commissioners, a board of supervisors, or a board of chosen freeholders. The men and women of these boards are almost always elected. They are usually chosen from districts in the county. Their term of office is usually four years but can run as long as eight. County boards range in size from a few members to over fifty.

The smaller county boards are usually known as boards of commissioners. They have from three to seven members who generally serve full time and hold no other public office during the time they are on the board. These officials may be elected at-large or by districts.

Another kind of county board is a board of supervisors, which typically has about fifteen members. County supervisors are elected from townships and are often supervisors for their respective townships as well.

The powers of these boards are generally both legislative and executive. Legislative powers may include the passing of health and zoning ordinances. The most important legislative functions, however, are those dealing with finances, such as the collection of taxes, appropriation of funds, and setting of salary

► *Sheriff's Department officers in Ulster County, New York, aided by New York state troopers, search the Hudson River for a missing person. Why do you think search and rescue operations generally are handled by county governments instead of city governments?*

Changing County Government Counties have developed in diverse ways through our nation's history. Some of their unusual characteristics have come to be seen as problems. Some politicians and citizens believe that county governments are outmoded and need to change. According to these people, reform is needed in several problem areas.

One of the biggest problems is the absence of real executive leadership. Because there are so many elected county officials, it is difficult for the average citizen to learn which county official is responsible for what. Inefficiency, waste, inaction, and an unresponsive government are often the result. In an effort to provide more effective leadership, some larger counties have reorganized themselves and now have a county manager, chief administrator, or chief executive.

- Under the **county-manager plan,** the elected county board remains the legislative, policymaking arm of county government. The county manager, who is hired by and responsible to the county board, is the board's chief executive. The board makes laws and decides policy, and the manager administers these laws and executes these policies. More than fifty counties around the country have adopted this plan.
- The **chief administrator plan** is a limited version of the county manager plan. The chief administrative officer (CAO) differs from the county manager because he or she shares responsibilities in certain key areas with the county board or with other individuals. In some areas, such as budgets and appointments, the CAO has little or no power. Perhaps because it is a less radical change, this plan is more popular than the county manager plan. Over five hundred counties currently use it.
- Another variation on the county manager plan is the **elected chief executive plan.** The executive officer is elected directly by the voters and works with the county board. Nearly sixty counties today have this kind of system.

The relative weakness of the counties in relation to the states is another problem. Most state constitutions severely restrict the powers of county boards. County officials often cannot respond effectively to modern problems because they have limited abilities to tax, spend, and legislate.

Recognizing the need for more local independence, over half the states have now provided for home rule. In these states, counties can decide the details of their own governmental structures, subject to the approval of the local voters.

Municipalities

When the first census was taken in 1790, only 5.1 percent of the 3,929,214 people living in the United States lived in **urban areas**—areas that are densely populated. In the early 1800s, with the advent of large-scale manufacturing and the invention of farming machines that reduced the need for manual labor, people began to move to the new urban industrial and transportation centers. Cities grew rapidly. By 1860, the urban population was thirty times larger than it had been in 1790. By 1900, 39.7 percent of the population lived in cities. In 1998, this figure reached 78 percent, and it is still rising.

Urban areas with their own units of government are called municipalities. Depending on local custom or state law, **municipalities** may be known as cities, towns, boroughs, or villages. Each municipality is created by the state, and the state has complete authority and control over all local government within the municipal borders. State constitutions and statutes contain a large number of provisions relating to municipal government.

Incorporation Cities and towns develop local governments when they are granted special legal status by the state legislature through **incorporation.** When a city becomes incorporated, it becomes a legal municipal corporation, or a municipality. Each state sets out in its constitution or statutes what a community must do to become a municipal corporation. Most states require that a certain number of persons live in an area before incorporation can take place.

A state does not choose which cities or towns to incorporate. Rather, the citizens of the city or town must submit a petition with a certain number of signatures to a public official, usually a judge. In most states, an election is held to obtain voter approval for the city to be declared a municipal corporation.

The difference between counties and municipalities is in how and why they are created. Counties are established by the state to serve the state's administrative needs. Municipalities, in contrast, are established at the request of their residents, largely because of concentrations of population and the services they need.

Dillon's Rule Because municipalities are legal creations of the state, for many years it seemed that the state government could dictate everything these local governments did. The narrowest possible view of the legal status of municipalities follows **Dillon's rule,** outlined by John F. Dillon in his *Commentaries on the Law of Municipal Corporations,* published in 1811. Dillon stated that municipal corporations—called municipalities—possess only those powers that the states expressly grant to them. Cities governed under Dillon's rule have thus been dominated by the state legislature.

The Home-Rule Movement In a revolt against state legislative power over municipalities, the home-rule movement began. The movement was based on **Cooley's rule,** derived from an 1871 decision (*People v. Hurlbut*) by a Michigan judge, Thomas Cooley. According to this rule, cities should be able to rule from home, or to govern themselves. Since 1900, about four-fifths of all states have allowed this **municipal home rule,** but only on issues in which no state interests are involved.

A municipality must choose to become a **home-rule city.** Otherwise, it operates as a **general-law city** under state rule. The state passes certain general laws relating to cities of different sizes, which are designated as first-class cities, second-class cities, or towns. Once a city, by virtue of its population, receives such a ranking, it follows the general law put down by the state for that city size. Only if a city chooses to be a home-rule city can it avoid such state government restrictions. In most states, only cities with populations of 2,500 or more can choose home rule.

> ### Just the Facts
>
> In 1980, the Supreme Court ruled, by a close vote, that this nation's cities and counties enjoy no legal immunity when they violate someone's civil rights.

New England Towns and Townships

New England towns and townships are not quite the same thing, although they can be grouped together.

The New England Town The term **New England town** is not to be confused with the term *town* used as another word for *city.* A New England town typically consists of one or more urban settlements and the surrounding rural areas. In Maine, Massachusetts, New Hampshire,

▶ This sculpture adorns the City-County Building in Detroit, Michigan. The Renaissance Center appears in the background. Why might both city and county services be located in the same building?

Vermont, and Connecticut, city and county governments in a particular area are combined into one town government. Consequently, counties have little importance in New England. In Connecticut, counties are simply a way to mark geographical boundaries.

From the New England town comes the tradition of the annual **town meeting,** at which direct democracy is practiced. Town meetings in Vermont date back to 1749, forty-two years before it became a state. Each resident of a town is summoned to the annual meeting at the town hall. Those who attend the meeting levy taxes, pass laws, elect town officials, and appropriate money for different activities.

Normally, few residents show up for town meetings today unless a high-interest item is on the agenda. The town meeting takes a full day or longer, and few citizens can set aside such a large amount of time. Because of the declining interest in town meetings,

▶ Town meetings have traditionally been held in historic buildings such as the Stafford Meeting House in Vermont. How is this tradition changing in modern times?

many New England towns have adopted a **town manager system.** Where such systems are used, the voters elect three **selectmen** who then appoint a professional town manager. Selectmen take care of overseeing the town manager's work. The town manager in turn appoints other officials.

Townships Townships are somewhat similar to counties in that they perform functions that counties would otherwise perform. Several dozen townships may exist within a county. Indiana, Iowa, Kansas, Michigan, Minnesota, New Jersey, New York, Ohio, Pennsylvania, and Wisconsin all have numerous townships.

The boundaries of most townships are based on federal land surveys of the 1780s. These surveys mapped land into six-mile squares (townships), which were then subdivided into thirty-six blocks of one square mile each called sections. Along the boundaries of sections, roads were built.

A township differs from a New England town in that it is meant to be a rural government rather than a city government.

Waging the War on Drugs

The problem of illegal drugs is widespread in the United States. Headlines generally focus on legislation and spending on the war against illegal drugs at the national level. Most of the costs associated with the war on drugs are faced at the local level, however. It is local police forces that are involved in upholding state laws against illegal drugs.

The numbers of robberies, violent acts, and murders associated with illegal drugs are hard to calculate. In some major cities, authorities estimate that over half of all homicides are drug related, typically due to "turf" wars and drug deals gone awry. In many cities, drug users steal and commit assaults to obtain money to satisfy their expensive drug habits.

Current attempts at stopping drug sales and use have resulted in over a million drug-related arrests per year. The courts have found themselves increasingly overworked by this high level of police activity. Court calendars are overflowing. Because of speedy-trial statutes for criminal cases, virtually all drug cases are placed on the docket (the court schedule) before civil cases. As a result, civil lawsuits—those involving private parties rather than the state—may take two, three, four, and sometimes five years to get to court.

There are three major views of how the United States should regulate illegal drugs. The most liberal view argues for complete legalization. The most conservative view is that even harsher penalties and a higher degree of law enforcement are needed to eliminate illegal drug use. The middle view advocates increased education and regulation, perhaps along with making certain drugs, such as marijuana, legal. Several states have decriminalized (made legal) the possession of small amounts of marijuana for personal use.

Evidence does not indicate that the current drug war has reduced the amount of criminal

▲ *Police officers and other emergency workers tend to a victim of drug abuse found under a San Francisco freeway overpass.*

activity associated with illegal drugs. On a more promising note, however, the use of all mind-altering drugs, including alcohol and nicotine, is currently on a downward trend for the population as a whole. More Americans seem to be realizing that the human body cannot consume mind-altering drugs and remain healthy.

THINK ABOUT IT
· ·

1. What difficulties arise when the government attempts to make certain activities or goods illegal?
2. What kind of advice would you give to a new mayor in your city with respect to the war on drugs?

▶ *In some cities, garbage collection and other services are coordinated by single-function governing bodies called special districts. What is another example of a special district?*

Moreover, townships are never the principal unit of local government, as are New England towns.

Although townships have few functions left to perform in many parts of the nation, they are still politically important in others. In some metropolitan areas, townships are the political units that provide most public services to residents who live in **unincorporated areas**—areas outside the geographical boundaries of a municipality.

Special Districts

The most numerous type of local governmental unit is the special district, which includes school districts. There are more than 44,000 special districts. Almost half of these are school districts.

Special districts are single-function governmental units. Usually, they are created by the state legislature and governed by a board of directors. In addition to school districts, there are districts for fire protection (the second most common kind of district), as well as for mosquito control, cemeteries, sewers, garbage collection, and numerous other concerns. Special districts may also be referred to as authorities, boards, or corporations.

One important feature of special districts is that they cut across geographical and governmental boundaries. A mosquito-control district may cut across both municipal lines and county lines. A metropolitan transit district may provide bus service to dozens of municipalities and to several counties. Sometimes, special districts even cut across state lines. An example is the Port of New York Authority, which was established by an interstate agreement between New Jersey and New York.

Except for school districts, the typical citizen is not highly aware of special districts. Indeed, most citizens do not know what governmental unit provides their weed control, mosquito control, water supply, or sewage services. Part of the reason for the low profile of special districts is that most of their administrators are appointed, not elected, and therefore receive little public attention.

1. How are the functions of county governments determined? What do county governments typically do?
2. What are some problems with county governments?
3. Describe and explain the differences between the county-manager plan, the chief administrator plan, and the elected chief executive plan of county government. Why have counties adopted these new plans of government?
4. What are municipalities? What does incorporation mean?
5. What are special districts?
6. **For Critical Analysis:** What do you think would be the advantages and disadvantages of incorporation for a city?

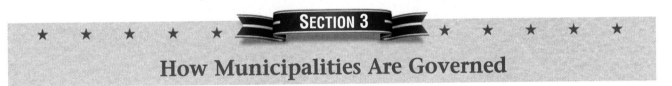

How Municipalities Are Governed

Preview Questions:

- What are the major types of municipal government?
- What are the important features of each type of municipal government?
- What factors brought about the end of patronage and "city machine" politics?

Key Terms:

commission plan, council-manager plan, city manager, mayor-administrator plan, mayor-council plan

Just as cities differ, so do their governments. Municipal governments take many forms, but most can be fit into four classifications: the commission plan, the council-manager plan, the mayor-administrator plan, and the mayor-council plan.

The Commission Plan

When the **commission plan** of municipal government is used, voters elect a commission of three to nine members who have both legislative and executive powers. A commission plan of municipal government is organized as follows:

1. Commission members are elected at large, usually on a nonpartisan ballot.

2. Executive and legislative powers are concentrated in the hands of this small group of individuals.
3. Each commissioner is individually responsible for heading a particular municipal department, such as the department of public safety.
4. The commission is collectively responsible for passing ordinances and controlling spending.
5. The mayor is selected from the members of the commission. The mayoral position is only ceremonial.

The commission plan originated in Galveston, Texas, in 1901, and had its greatest popularity during the first twenty years of the twentieth century. It appealed to municipal government reformers, who believed it would eliminate what they saw as built-in problems with long ballots and partisan municipal politics.

Unfortunately, giving both legislative and executive power to a small group of individuals means that there are no checks and balances on administration and spending. Also, since the mayoral office is ceremonial, there is no provision for strong leadership.

Not surprisingly, only about one hundred cities today use the commission plan. Figure 25–3 on page 690 shows a typical commission plan.

The Council-Manager Plan

In the **council-manager plan** of municipal government, an elected city council appoints a professional

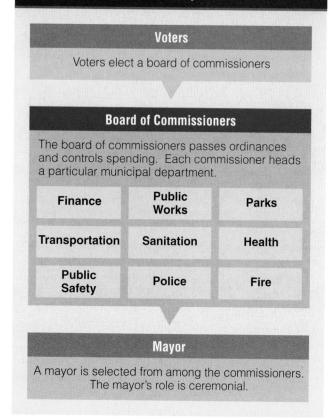

Voters

Voters elect a board of commissioners

Board of Commissioners

The board of commissioners passes ordinances and controls spending. Each commissioner heads a particular municipal department.

Finance	Public Works	Parks
Transportation	Sanitation	Health
Public Safety	Police	Fire

Mayor

A mayor is selected from among the commissioners. The mayor's role is ceremonial.

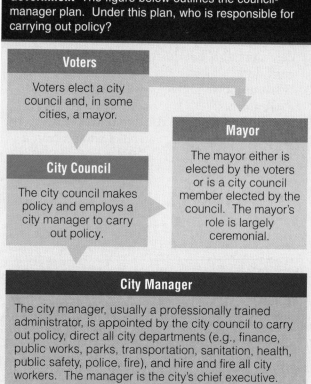

Voters

Voters elect a city council and, in some cities, a mayor.

City Council

The city council makes policy and employs a city manager to carry out policy.

Mayor

The mayor either is elected by the voters or is a city council member elected by the council. The mayor's role is largely ceremonial.

City Manager

The city manager, usually a professionally trained administrator, is appointed by the city council to carry out policy, direct all city departments (e.g., finance, public works, parks, transportation, sanitation, health, public safety, police, fire), and hire and fire all city workers. The manager is the city's chief executive.

manager, who acts as the chief executive. He or she is typically called the **city manager.** In principal, the manager is simply there to see that the general directions of the city council are carried out. In practice, he or she often makes many decisions and policies. The important features of the council-manager plan are as follows:

1. The council (or commission) consists of five to seven members, elected at large on a nonpartisan ballot.
2. The council chooses a professionally trained manager to act as city manager. The city manager can hire and fire subordinates and is responsible to the council.
3. The mayor may be chosen from within the council

or from outside. He or she has no executive function. As in the commission plan, the mayor's position is largely ceremonial.

Figure 25–4 above shows the council-manager plan of government.

Today, about two thousand cities use the council-manager plan. About one-third of cities with populations above 5,000 and about one-half of cities with populations above 25,000 use this type of plan. Only four cities of more than 500,000 people—Cincinnati, Dallas, San Antonio, and San Diego—have adopted the plan.

The major defect of the council-manager plan, as with the commission plan, is that there is no strong executive leadership. It is therefore not surprising that large cities rarely use such a plan. The council-manager plan is also considered undemocratic because the executive—the city manager—is not elected by the people.

Changes in Local Government

Many changes in local government have taken place during the twentieth century. We look here at some of these changes.

THEN (1900)	NOW
Only 39.7 percent of the population lived in urban areas.	About 78 percent of the population lives in urban areas.
Machine politics controlled the government in many of the nation's large cities.	For the most part, machine politics no longer exists.
The patronage system was used extensively in larger cities as part of machine politics.	The use of the patronage system declined as city machines disappeared.
State legislatures exercised significant control over municipal decisions.	Many municipalities opt for municipal home rule to avoid state government restrictions.

The Mayor-Administrator Plan

The **mayor-administrator plan** is often used in large cities where there is a strong mayor. It is similar to the council-manager plan, except that the mayor is an elected chief executive and as such has powers of political leadership. The mayor appoints an administrative officer whose function is to free the mayor from routine administrative tasks, such as personnel and budget supervision.

The Mayor-Council Plan

The **mayor-council plan** of municipal government is the oldest and most widely used. The mayor is the elected chief executive, and the council is the legisla-tive body. A council typically has five to nine members. In very large cities, however, the councils may be much larger. For example, the Los Angeles city council has fifteen members, while the Chicago city council has fifty members. Council members are popularly elected for four- to six-year terms.

▶ *A mayor presides over a meeting of the city council. Do all municipal governments have mayors?*

FIGURE 25–5 Strong Mayor–Council Plan As you can see from this organizational chart, under the strong mayor–council plan, the voters elect both the mayor and the city council. In what type of city is the strong mayor–council system most often found?

Voters

Voters elect a mayor and a city council.

Mayor

The mayor is the city's executive. The mayor can hire and fire city workers, prepare a budget, usually veto measures passed by the council, and often act without council approval. The mayor also appoints department directors.

City Council

The city council makes policy, although the mayor usually has veto power.

Department Directors

Appointed by the mayor, department directors administer city departments.

Finance	Public Works	Parks
Transportation	Sanitation	Health
Public Safety	Police	Fire

▲ *In addition to their many administrative duties, mayors are present at many public events. Rudy Giuliani (left), mayor of New York, is shown here with Tom Freston, chairman and Chief Executive Officer of MTV, as they attend the MTV Music Awards nominations at the Bryant Park Grill in New York.*

Generally, mayor-council plans may be classified as the strong-mayor type or the weak-mayor type. Figure 25–5, above, and Figure 25–6 on page 693 show these two forms of mayor-council plan.

● In the strong mayor–council plan, the mayor is the chief executive and has almost complete control over hiring and firing employees and preparing the budget. The mayor plays a strong role in the formation of city policies and usually serves a four-year term. The strong-mayor system is most often

found in large cities, such as New York and San Francisco.

● The weak mayor–council plan completely separates executive and legislative functions. The mayor is elected as the chief executive officer, and the council is elected as the legislative body. This traditional separation of powers allows for checks and balances on spending and administration. The mayor has limited powers and little control over staffing and budget and is often elected for a two-year term. This plan is often found in small or medium-sized cities. In some small cities, in fact, the office of mayor is only a part-time position.

Many American cities use some form of the mayor-council plan. Recently, however, the mayor-council plan has lost ground to the council-manager plan in small and medium-sized cities.

Patronage and City Machines

In the late nineteenth and early twentieth centuries, many major cities were run by "machines." In these political organizations, each city block had an organizer, each neighborhood had a political club, and each district had a leader. The machine as a whole also had a leader—the boss (usually the mayor).

ARCHITECTS of Government

Harvey Johnson, Jr.
(1947–)

On June 3, 1997, Harvey Johnson became the first African American to be elected as mayor of Jackson, Mississippi, a small southern town that is still racially divided. Johnson was a teenager during the 1960s when civil rights activists in Jackson were murdered, beaten, and falsely arrested. Johnson attended Tennessee State University and later the University of Cincinnati Graduate School. He served in the Air Force as a captain and has also served as the executive director of the Mississippi Institute of Small Towns.

HIS WORDS

"As mayor, I want to be known as a man of integrity who conducts his affairs in a dignified way. . . . There can't be a lot of rhetoric. There has to be more than just talk from a Black guy in a suit calling himself mayor."

(Ebony, *August 1997*)

"We were able to put together a coalition that represented a number of diverse interests in this city."

(Jet, *June 23, 1997*)

DEVELOPING CRITICAL THINKING SKILLS

1. In the first quotation, what did Johnson mean by "rhetoric"?
2. What did Johnson mean when he talked about a "coalition" in the second quotation?

FIGURE 25–6 Weak Mayor–Council Plan This organization chart illustrates the weak mayor–council plan. Under this system, who is responsible for appointing department directors?

Voters
Voters elect a city council and, in some cities, a mayor.

Mayor
The mayor (elected by the voters or appointed by the city council) has limited policy-making power and little control over the budget or city employees.

City Council
The city council makes most policy decisions and appoints department directors. In some cities, the council appoints a mayor.

Department Directors
Appointed by the city council, department directors administer city departments.

Finance	Public Works	Parks
Transportation	Sanitation	Health
Public Safety	Police	Fire

The machine emerged in the 1840s, when the first waves of European immigrants came to the United States to work in urban factories. When those individuals, who often lacked the ability to communicate in English, needed help, the machine was there to help them. The urban machine became a strong political institution by relying on the support of the dominant ethnic groups. In this way, the machine could keep its boss in office year after year.

The machine was oiled by patronage—the practice of awarding jobs and contracts to the party faithful. In fact, the party in power was often referred to as the patronage party. The power of the machine lay in its

AMERICA 🇺🇸 AT ODDS

School Choice

Recent comparisons of average scores on math and science tests put the achievement of U.S. schoolchildren below that of students in Japan, Korea, the Czech Republic, Bulgaria, Russia, and Germany. These findings confirmed what many American educators already know—that our public school system needs improvements. A significant and apparently growing number of Americans believe that the only solution to the "school problem" is to allow educational choice. This could be achieved through the use of vouchers. School vouchers, provided by the state and paid for with tax dollars, could be used by all families with children at any school, private or public.

Some Say, Why Not Give More Choice to Parents?

According to the proponents of school choice through vouchers, simply spending more money on schools has accomplished nothing. Annual per-student expenditures (corrected for inflation) have quintupled about every fifty years since 1890. Just since 1970, annual expenditures per student, on average, have increased from $3,550 to well over $6,000. In many districts, per-pupil annual expenditures exceed $11,000. Yet the pupil-staff ratio was fifteen to one in 1890 and hovers at about thirty-five to one today. Critics of

the current system often complain that a high percentage of educational expenditures goes to school administration, rather than to teachers or new educational resources (buildings, computers, and the like).

Critics of the current system also contend that many schools fail because of poor curriculum, lack of personal safety, and few incentives to discipline disruptive students. With school vouchers, parents could send their children to any school of their choice. Some schools could attract more students by offering more discipline, parental involvement, and more homework. Because the majority of public school teachers are dedicated to teaching, the ensuing competition would cause districts to change their ways to attract better students with vouchers. Proponents of this system point to the example of the U.S. Postal Service, which was forced to improve its service because of competition from private companies, such as Federal Express and UPS.

The System Is Good, So Just Improve What We Have, Say Others

Opponents of school choice through vouchers argue that such a system would create little incentive for school reform. Parents who are dissatisfied with the performance of public schools would use

---

ability to control votes, and the votes of new urban immigrants from Europe or from rural America were especially crucial.

Civil service reform and the concept that jobs should be doled out on the basis of merit, not party, gradually eroded the patronage system. Even as early as 1900, the effects of civil service reform were being felt. George Washington Plunkitt, a powerful figure in New York's political machine, had this to say about civil service reform:

This civil service law is the biggest fraud of the age. It is the curse of the nation. There can't be no real patriotism while it lasts. How are you goin' to interest our young men in their country if you have no offices to give them when they work for their party?

When the last of the big-city bosses, Mayor Richard J. Daley of Chicago, died in December 1976, an era that had lasted well over one hundred years died with him. Over time, a government of administrators began

◀ These second-grade students attend a parochial school in Philadelphia, Pennsylvania. How would they and their families be affected by school vouchers?

the vouchers to send their children to private schools. The public schools would be emptied and their resources depleted.

Additionally, according to these critics, the very students who need school alternatives would have none. No new private schools would be built in the inner cities. Moreover, existing private schools would not be obligated to take students with vouchers, just as private universities are not obligated to take applicants simply because they can pay.

Finally, critics of school choice through vouchers argue that there are other ways to reform the current system. They point to how Chicago's public schools are being improved after reform measures were implemented in 1995. Reading test scores went up in fifty-two of Chicago's seventy-four high schools, and math scores improved in sixty-one schools. Critics of school vouchers also contend that a curriculum established in Washington, D.C., and monitored in every town and city through achievement tests would help to solve our educational problems.

YOU DECIDE

1. Do you agree or disagree with the argument that school vouchers are the solution to today's educational problems?
2. What might be some additional arguments both for and against the use of school vouchers?

◀ In an example of the power sometimes held by mayors of large cities, Mayor Richard J. Daley of Chicago (right) is shown here with President John F. Kennedy in 1962 in the White House. They were discussing "the great need for a Department of Urban Affairs" at the federal level.

In any text on American government, you are presented with many statistics. Percentages, for example, are often used to indicate how much of the American population is living in poverty or how many people voted for a particular candidate.

A percentage indicates a certain number of parts per hundred. Certain expenses, such as tax rates, are determined in percentages. For example, when you buy a $20 book with a 7 percent sales tax, you have to add 7 cents in tax for every dollar you pay for the book. The calculation for this would be .07 × $20 = $1.40, which makes the total cost of the book $21.40.

Percentages can be expressed either as percentages, using the percent sign (%) or the word "percent," or as decimals. In the calculation above, 7 percent was changed to .07. Both mean 7 parts out of 100. The decimal equivalent of a percent is found by moving the decimal point two places to the left and dropping the percent sign. To change decimals to percentages, move the decimal point two places to the right and add the percent sign.

Percentages are used to indicate proportional relationships between numbers. How are percentages calculated? Say you are told that of the 400 people who voted in a recent local election, 300 voted for the Democratic candidate. You can calculate the percentage of people who voted

BUILDING

SOCIAL STUDIES SKILLS

Figuring and Using Percentages

for the Democrat in the following way. Divide the number of those who voted Democratic by the total number of those who voted. The calculation would be 300 ÷ 400 = .75, or 75 percent.

In the same example, if you were told that 75 percent of the voters voted for the Democratic candidate, you can determine how many votes that candidate

got if you know the total number who voted. In this case, you would multiply .75 by 400 to get 300.

PRACTICING YOUR SKILLS

The table below gives the values of stolen property and the amounts recovered in a recent year. On a separate sheet of paper, calculate the percentages of the total amounts that were recovered. Then answer the questions below.

1. Which category of stolen property had the highest recovery rate?
2. Which category had the lowest?
3. How much greater is the highest recovery rate than the lowest recovery rate?

Property Stolen and Recovered

Type of Property	Value Stolen	Amount Recovered	Percentage Recovered
Motor Vehicles	$6 billion	$4 billion	
Firearms	$100 million	$10 million	
Currency	$1 billion	$40 million	
Televisions and Stereos	$1 billion	$50 million	

to appear. Fewer offices were elective, and more were appointive—presumably filled by professionals who had no political axes to grind, payoffs to make, or patrons to please.

SECTION 3 REVIEW

1. What are the major types of municipal government?
2. Which types of municipal government are most common, and why?
3. What is patronage? How did the "machine" use patronage in city politics?
4. **For Critical Analysis:** Which type of municipal government do you think would be most effective in dealing with the problems of a large city with serious social and economic problems? Explain your answer.

★ ★ ★ ★ **Chapter Summary** ★ ★ ★ ★

Section 1: The Functions of Local Government

- Local governments provide many important services, including education, police and fire protection, and public welfare.
- City and county planners use several strategies to ensure orderly growth, including zoning.
- Local governments also provide many recreational and cultural activities for residents of all ages.

Section 2: How Local Governments Are Created and How They Operate

- The major types of local governmental units are counties, municipalities, New England towns, townships, and special districts. Every local government is a creation of the state.
- Organized county governments are found in every state except Connecticut and Rhode Island. The responsibilities and functions of a county are usually determined by the state constitution and state laws.
- Cities and towns develop local governments when they are granted special legal status by the state legislature through incorporation. New England towns are governmental units typically consisting of one or more urban areas and the surrounding rural areas. In some parts of the country, townships perform the functions that counties would perform elsewhere.
- Special districts are units of government created to perform special functions, such as maintaining public schools and providing for garbage collection.

Section 3: How Municipalities Are Governed

- The major types of municipal government are the commission plan, the council-manager plan, the mayor-administrator plan, and the mayor-council plan.
- During the late nineteenth and early twentieth centuries many major cities were run by "machines." Machine politics involved patronage—rewarding the party faithful with jobs and contracts.

★ REVIEW QUESTIONS ★

1. What is zoning? Why is it important to a city?
2. What are the major functions of local government?
3. Name several functions of counties.
4. What is the difference between Dillon's rule and Cooley's rule?
5. What are some problems with county governments? How have some counties attempted to deal with these problems?
6. How is a municipality formed? From where does the authority to form a municipality come?
7. How do New England towns differ from townships?
8. Why are special districts created?
9. Briefly describe the types of municipal government. What are the disadvantages and advantages of each?
10. What is machine politics?
11. What are some arguments for and against the use of school vouchers?

★ CRITICAL THINKING ★

1. What important issue in your community would you like to bring before the city council for action? What kind of action would you recommend that the council take?
2. Do you think that the New England style of direct democracy would work in your community? Why or why not?
3. Do you think that reducing the size of local governments would affect those governments' ability to serve the people? Explain your answer.
4. Which plan of government does your city or town use? How well do you think that plan works? If you do not think it works well, which plan would you recommend?

5. Compare and contrast the various types of municipal government outlined in this chapter. Choose the one you believe to be the most effective and explain your choice.

★ IMPROVING YOUR SKILLS ★

Communication Skills

Working in Groups You will often be in situations in which you are working with a group of other people. You may join a group working to fight pollution in your community, serve on a student council or government board, or collaborate with others on a group project for school. Keep the following tips in mind when you work with a group:

- The ideal group member interacts with other group members in a cooperative, not competitive, way, and keeps an open mind to the opinions of others in the group.
- Remember that you are only one member of the group. Do not dominate the group, but do not be afraid to contribute your opinion.
- Remember that discussion requires patience. Every member of the group deserves the opportunity to speak and to be heard.
- Listen to everything others have to say. Distinguish in your mind between fact and opinion and between the important and the unimportant. Ask questions if you do not understand or if you need more information.
- Stay focused on the goals of the group.
- When it is your turn to speak, speak clearly, with proper pronunciation and grammar. Do not speak too quickly or too slowly.
- If people do not seem to understand each other, it may be because words sometimes mean different

things to different people. It could also be that people are perceiving the situation differently. Be sure to clarify for everyone exactly what the issue under discussion is.

● Discussion is the basis of our democratic system. Each member of the group has a responsibility to listen, to think, and to reason with the other group members.

Writing Write a script about a group working together whose members ignore all of the above tips. Role-play the script with other members of your class.

Social Studies Skills

Working with Charts and Percentages Look at the chart in Figure 25–2 below. Answer these questions:

1. What percentage of the total number of local governments consists of counties?
2. What percentage of the total number of local governments consists of special districts?

★ ACTIVITIES AND PROJECTS ★

1. Imagine that you are in charge of developing a form of government for a city of 25,000 people. Prepare a plan that tells which form of government you would use and what responsibilities would be given to each government official. Present the plan to the class.
2. Choose an issue in your community about which you are concerned. Research the issue, and write a letter to a top city official asking him or her how the city government is addressing the issue.
3. Attend a city council or county board meeting. Take notes on the procedures, and report back to the class.
4. Attend a school board meeting. Write an outline of the major issues in your school district.
5. Invite a city official to your class to speak about his or her responsibilities and roles in the community. Prepare a list of questions in advance so that you will be prepared for the meeting.

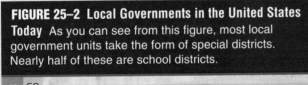

FIGURE 25–2 Local Governments in the United States Today As you can see from this figure, most local government units take the form of special districts. Nearly half of these are school districts.

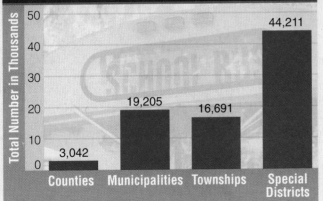

What If . . .

City Governments Were Not Allowed?

Because the Constitution makes no mention of local governments, each is a creation of the state. Theoretically, the states could abolish city governments. How would cities be governed then?

Paying for State and Local Government

CHAPTER OBJECTIVES

To learn about and understand . . .

⭐ The limitations on state and local taxation

⭐ How the national government contributes financially to state and local governments

⭐ The priorities and patterns of state and local spending

"We don't have New Federalism, we have New Feudalism, where every community fends for itself with a hodgepodge of responsibilities and taxing powers."

George Sternlieb
(1923–   )
Urban Specialist and Professor Emeritus of Public Policy at Rutgers University

INTRODUCTION

George Sternlieb's words above echo the frustrations many state and local officials have felt in recent years as the national government has shifted a heavier financial burden to the cities and states. At the same time, public demands for better city and state services have become enormous.

State and local governments spend over one trillion dollars per year. The money for such budgets has to come from somewhere. State governments have many sources of revenue. Local governments have fewer. In both cases, one of the most important sources of revenue is the taxes all of us pay in one form or another. There are limitations, however, on the types of taxes that state and local governments can assess.

◀ This magnificent building is the State House, the state capitol building in Annapolis, Maryland.

Limitations on State and Local Taxation

Preview Questions:

🌐 What limits does the Constitution place on the taxing powers of state and local governments?

🌐 What other limitations are placed on state and local taxing powers?

There are two types of limitations on state and local powers of taxation—those that come from the national government and those that come from the state governments themselves.

U.S. Constitutional Limitations

The U.S. Constitution places only a few limitations on state and local taxing powers. These limitations apply to taxation of agencies of the national government, taxation of interstate commerce, and due process.

Agencies of the National Government U.S. Supreme Court Chief Justice John Marshall said that "the power to tax involves the power to destroy." In his famous 1819 decision, *McCulloch v. Maryland* (discussed in Chapter 4), Marshall put to rest any hope that state governments would be able to tax an agency of the national government. That Supreme Court decision still stands today and prevents states from taxing the operations, land, buildings, or any other aspect of the U.S. government.

Interstate Commerce Article I, Section 10, Clause 2, of the Constitution states as follows:

No State shall . . . lay any Imposts [taxes] or Duties on Imports or Exports, except what may be absolutely necessary for exercising its inspection Laws.

Clause 3 states that "no State shall . . . lay any Duty of Tonnage." Clause 2 prevents the states from taxing both imports into the United States and exports to other countries. Clause 3 prevents the states from taxing ships according to their cargo capacity.

The Supreme Court has said that the U.S. Constitution gives Congress, not the states, the power to regulate interstate and foreign trade. Therefore, no state can pass laws that prevent imports from being brought into the state. The states cannot tax such imports, either.

Due Process The due process clause of the Fourteenth Amendment to the U.S. Constitution can be used to limit the power of state and local governments to impose taxes. Under the due process clause, taxes must be imposed and administered fairly. Furthermore, they may not be so great as to be the equivalent of

▲ *One way states raise money is through taxes on products such as the gasoline being pumped here. State and local governments often have a more difficult time generating revenues than the federal government does.*

seizing property. For example, your local government could not pass a property tax that was so high that only a few people could afford to pay it and the rest would therefore have to give up their property to the government.

The due process clause also forbids unreasonable classifications for the purpose of collecting taxes. It is reasonable to collect a tax on smokers by taxing cigarettes. It is reasonable to collect a tax on the users of automobiles by taxing gasoline. It is unreasonable, however, to make only blond-haired citizens pay a state income tax and to let everyone else live tax free.

State Constitutional Limitations

Each state has placed constitutional limitations on its own taxing power. Additionally, state constitutions limit the taxing power of local governments. Virtually all state constitutions indicate that taxes must be uniformly applied and applied for public purposes only.

States normally exempt religious organizations, museums, operas, and cemeteries from taxation. (This means that these organizations do not have to pay state and local taxes.) Some state constitutions set maximum rates for various taxes, such as those on cigarettes. Others prohibit certain kinds of taxes, such as taxes on personal income.

SECTION 1 REVIEW

1. What are the two basic sources of limitations on state and local taxation powers?
2. What restrictions does the U.S. Constitution place on state and local taxing powers?
3. **For Critical Analysis:** What did John Marshall mean when he said, "the power to tax involves the power to destroy"? Explain your answer.

SECTION 2

Sources of State and Local Revenues

Preview Questions:

- ⭐ What are the major types of taxes used at the state and local levels?
- ⭐ Which tax produces the largest amount of revenue in most states?
- ⭐ Which tax produces the largest amount of revenue for local governments?
- ⭐ From what principal nontax sources do state and local governments receive revenues?

Key Terms:

excise taxes, death taxes, debt financing

State and local revenues come from three sources: taxes, nontax revenues, and intergovernmental transfers.

Types of Taxes

A variety of taxes are assessed at all levels of government. In Chapter 21, you read about some of these taxes, which include the following:

- Personal income tax
- Corporate income tax
- Excise tax
- Estate tax
- Inheritance tax
- Sales tax
- Property tax

Personal Income Tax Most states assess taxes on individuals' personal income each year. Seven states have no personal income tax system: Florida, Nevada, South

Dakota, Texas, Washington, Wyoming, and Alaska. The other forty-three states assess taxes on personal income at rates that vary from state to state.

Corporate Income Tax Corporations pay taxes on their profits in all but five states—Nevada, South Dakota, Texas, Washington, and Wyoming. Like the personal income tax rate, the corporate income tax rate varies from state to state.

Excise Tax Special taxes paid by consumers for the use and consumption of certain goods are called **excise taxes.** A number of states collect excise taxes on cigarettes, gasoline, alcoholic beverages, and telephone use.

There is little uniformity in how much states collect in excise taxes on cigarettes and gasoline. Cigarette taxes per pack of twenty are the lowest in tobacco-growing states—North Carolina (5 cents),

JUST ABOUT DRY

THE TAX SQUEEZE

PROPERTY OWNER

◀ Most municipalities impose a tax on the value of property, or real estate. Why might a property tax be a hardship on taxpayers, as indicated in the cartoon?

South Carolina (7 cents), Virginia (2.5 cents), and Kentucky (3 cents). The states with the highest cigarette taxes are California, Connecticut, Illinois, Iowa, Minnesota, Nevada, New Jersey, New York, North Dakota, Washington, and Wisconsin.

Estate and Inheritance Taxes Some states levy an estate tax on the value of the property (estate) that a person leaves behind when he or she dies. Some states, either in addition to or instead of the estate tax, assess an inheritance tax on those who inherit property from someone who has died. The inheritance tax does not exist at the national level, but the estate tax does. All such taxes are called **death taxes.**

Sales Tax A general sales tax is a tax levied as a proportion of the retail price of any good when it is sold. There is no sales tax at the national level, but most states use this form of taxation. Only five states have no general sales tax: Alaska, Delaware, Montana, New Hampshire, and Oregon. Sales taxes in other states range from 3 percent to over 8 percent. Local sales taxes are added to state sales taxes in many cities, including New York City.

Property Tax In virtually all states, taxes are imposed on the value of property. In addition, virtually every municipality uses the property tax to raise most of its revenues. The best-known property tax is that levied on the value of real estate—land and the houses or buildings on it. A number of states collect taxes on personal property, such as motor vehicles, business machines, boats, trailers, and trucks.

The Relative Importance of Various Taxes The pie chart in Figure 26–1 shows the various sources of rev-

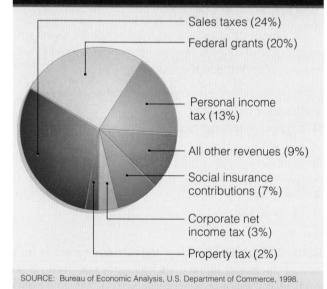

FIGURE 26–1 The Importance of Taxes at the State and Local Levels The pie chart below shows the various sources of revenue for state and local governments. Which type of tax generates the most revenues?

- Sales taxes (24%)
- Federal grants (20%)
- Personal income tax (13%)
- All other revenues (9%)
- Social insurance contributions (7%)
- Corporate net income tax (3%)
- Property tax (2%)

SOURCE: Bureau of Economic Analysis, U.S. Department of Commerce, 1998.

Government in Action

The Little-Known Truth about State Budgets

Both the popular press and politicians often insist that the national government should be forced to balance its budget. In their arguments, they frequently give the distinct impression that the states are required to have balanced budgets. During the 1996 presidential campaign, for example, one of Bob Dole's campaign documents, called "A Plan for Economic Growth," stated as follows: "Most states are required to balance their books. . . . The federal government should be required to do so as well."

The view that the states are required to balance their budgets has been around for a long time. After all, states cannot effectively print money the way the national government can. Most state constitutions, do, in fact, require that state budgets be balanced or show a surplus. Indeed, depending on how one interprets such laws, the number of states forced to balance their budgets ranges from a dozen to forty-nine.

It is true that most states balance their *operating budgets* most of the time. Unlike the national government, however, the states make a distinction between operating budgets and capital budgets.

Capital budgets include expenditures for new airports, airport improvements, heavy machinery, highway construction, and so on. Almost all of the states permit **debt financing**—the sale of bonds to finance long-term improvements. Additionally, most states use special authorities to finance these outlays, which sometimes include operating costs. We really can't tell to what extent operating expenses are hidden in capital budgets, but they certainly are.

THINK ABOUT IT
....

1. Does it really matter whether your state government has a budget deficit?
2. Why would a state government make a distinction between funds spent on paying salaries (an operating expenditure) and funds spent on road projects (a capital expenditure)?

---

enues. As you can see, the majority of revenues are raised through taxes.

By far the most important tax for most states is the general sales tax. The most important tax at the local level is the property tax, which accounts for over three-fourths of all local taxes raised.

Whereas the national government obtains more than 44 percent of its total revenues from personal income taxes, states obtain only about 13 percent from this type of tax. There is tremendous variation in the amounts of state and local taxes collected. The highest taxes are paid by residents of Connecticut, the District of Columbia, Massachusetts, and New Jersey. The lowest taxes are paid by residents of Mississippi and Utah.

State Nontax Revenues

Some state and local governments operate businesses from which they receive revenues. Like the national government, states also borrow. Less important nontax sources of revenue include fines assessed by state and local courts, as well as interest on investments.

Just the Facts

The California state budget exceeds $85 million.

Government-Operated Businesses State and local governments operate toll bridges and toll roads. Some states—Washington, for example—operate ferries.

Every week, decisions are made in your community that directly affect your local environment and your daily life. Getting involved in local government is a good way to learn where you stand on certain political issues and a good place to develop skills for community action.

Suppose you read in the newspaper that the city planning board has decided to demolish the oldest neighborhood in town, where your grandparents' Victorian-style house still stands, to make room for a fish cannery. Suppose you hear that the city plans to cut down all the trees lining your street to widen the road. Suppose you see on the news that the police department has decided to reduce police patrols in your neighborhood, even though burglaries and violent crimes have risen dramatically and you feel unsafe.

Some decisions may be difficult to fight because of the many demands placed on local government. Even so, if enough citizens are in opposition, government officials can be persuaded. After all, in a democracy, government officials are responsible to everyone.

Here are some steps you can take to influence the decisions of your local government.

1. **Form a group.** Gather together other people in your community who also oppose the government action. Start

PARTICIPATING IN YOUR GOVERNMENT

Organizing for Community Action

with your friends, and plan a meeting. Tell them to talk with their friends and neighbors and invite them all to come. Also invite anyone who can speak knowledgeably about your cause. Conduct the meeting as an open forum, and let all who attend express their opinions.

2. **Get organized.** Decide what your goals are, and come up with a plan of action. Give your group a name, and appoint a leader. Announce the purpose of your group to appropriate public officials. Organize activities to express your views.

3. **Attend public hearings.** Urge all the members of your group to attend public meetings where issues of interest are being discussed. Present your opinions in a clear, straightforward manner.

4. **Attract attention.** Write press releases and send them to local TV stations, radio stations, and newspapers. Be direct, and give good reasons for your opinions. Be sure to emphasize the importance of your cause to the community.

5. **Start a petition drive.** Have group members circulate petitions showing support for your position, and get as many signatures as possible. Submit the petitions to the appropriate public officials.

TAKING ACTION

1. Choose a local problem in which you have a strong interest. Follow newspaper reports on this problem for two weeks. Then describe, in writing, the way you would organize community action to solve this problem.

2. Put at least one of your steps into action.

◄ Some state and local governments set up business-like operations such as this collection system on a New Jersey toll road. Why would a government want to take on such a responsibility?

Expenses have risen, and they continue to grow. In many cases, however, tax revenues have failed to keep pace with these growing needs and expenses. Thus states have not been able to meet their financial obligations. In recent years, many states have had to borrow on a grand scale as their expenditures have greatly exceeded their revenues. States that ran into fiscal trouble in the 1990s include California, Connecticut, Florida, Michigan, Maryland, Massachusetts, New Jersey, Pennsylvania, and Virginia.

Alaska has operated many businesses, including a slaughterhouse and a phone company. The state of North Dakota markets Dakota-made flour. The state of California operates a railroad line in San Francisco. Eighteen states, including Idaho, Maine, Utah, West Virginia, and Montana, operate liquor stores.

A number of cities own and operate their own water systems, bus systems, and electric power companies. Cities also operate warehouses, office buildings, and wharfs.

Whenever these government-operated businesses make a profit, the profits constitute a source of revenue that can be used for other state and local expenditures.

Borrowing Sometimes, to cover their expenditures, states and cities are forced to borrow by issuing state and municipal bonds. These bonds are often easy to sell to investors because the interest earned is exempt from U.S. income taxes. State and local governments sell bonds to complete many large projects. The building of highways, bridges, dams, schools, and government buildings is often paid for through this kind of borrowing.

Intergovernmental Transfers

Funds from the national government, in the form of federal grants, represent an important source of revenue for state and local governments. In the next section, you will read about how the U.S. government gives money back to the states.

SECTION 2 REVIEW

1. What are the major taxes used at the state and local levels?
2. Which tax produces the most revenue for the states? For local governments?
3. What are the major sources of nontax revenues?
4. **For Critical Analysis:** Some people argue that some items, such as food and prescription drugs, should be exempt from sales tax because they are necessities. Others argue that sales taxes on such items are important sources of revenue and that everyone should contribute to the government's revenue base. With which side do you agree? Give reasons for your answer.

Funds from Uncle Sam

Preview Questions:

🌐 What are the methods by which the national government distributes funds to state and local governments?

🌐 How do these methods differ?

Key Terms:

categorical grants, matching funds, equalization, project grant, block grants

As part of our system of cooperative federalism, the national government gives back to the states a significant amount of the funds it collects through taxes. The states, in turn, give some of these funds to local governments. Currently, the national government distributes about $245 billion to the states in federal grants. Figure 26–2 on page 709 shows the pattern of U.S. government grants to state and local governments since 1970. The two most important methods used by the national government to return tax dollars to state and local governments are categorical grants and block grants.

Categorical Grants

The concept of a government grant was derived from a 1902 law providing that revenues from the sale of lands owned by the U.S. government were to be shared with certain states and territories for irri-

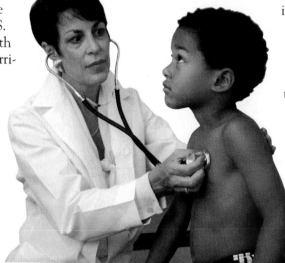

▶ This little boy probably isn't wondering where the money comes from to pay for this office visit, but his doctor knows that some federal dollars help provide for health care and other local services for citizens. What three methods are used most often to distribute federal funds to state and local governments?

gation and land reclamation. Because the grants were tied to specific categories of government spending, they were called **categorical grants.** Today, categorical grants are also given to the states for the establishment of agricultural extension programs, highway construction, vocational education, and maternal and child health.

During Franklin D. Roosevelt's first two terms in office (1933–1941), Congress increased the amount given to the states in the form of categorical grants from $200 million to $3 billion per year. The number and scope of categorical grants expanded further as part of the Great Society program of President Lyndon Johnson during the 1960s. Grants became available in the fields of education, pollution control, conservation, recreation, and highway construction and maintenance.

For some categorical grant programs, state and local governments must contribute **matching funds.** That is, they must provide funding equal to the funding offered by the national government. For other types of programs, funds are awarded according to a formula that takes into account the relative wealth of the state. This is a process known as **equalization.**

Although state and local officials, as well as congressional representatives, enjoy taking credit for the results of projects funded by categorical grants, many would prefer to get the funds with fewer restrictions. For example, a categorical grant for highway construction might include restrictions in the form of specifications for the materials to be used. These specifications would apply to all states receiving a grant. It can be argued that such specifications are necessary to raise local standards and practices to a uniform level. Local officials, however, might argue that the materials suitable for roads in the South are not the best ones for roads in the North.

In general, Congress has kept categorical grants under fairly tight

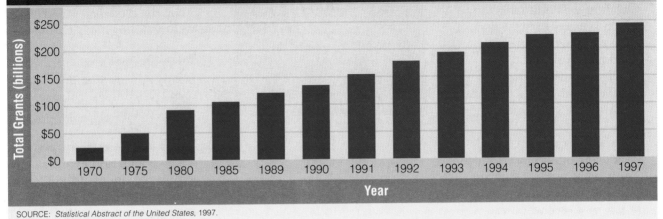

FIGURE 26–2 U.S. Government Grants to State and Local Governments since 1970 As you can see from looking at this bar graph, the amount of funds contributed by the national government to the states, in the form of federal grants, has increased significantly since 1970. Does the national government place any restrictions on how these funds are used by state and local governments?

SOURCE: *Statistical Abstract of the United States, 1997.*

control. Indeed, in a move to bypass state governments, Congress established the **project grant** approach, which allows state and local agencies to apply directly for assistance to local offices that administer U.S. government funds. In this way, funds can be directly placed where—in the eyes of Congress—they are most needed.

Block Grants

Block grants are funds that are transferred to state and local governments from the national government to provide broad support in areas such as health care and criminal justice. Block grants, because they are given for a broad purpose, have fewer strings attached. Governors and mayors generally prefer block grants because they give the states and cities more flexibility in determining how the funds will be spent.

Although they did not originate with him, block grants were an important part of President Ronald Reagan's "new federalism" program, which he outlined in his first State of the Union address in 1982. Before Reagan's election in 1980, only five block grants had been legislated by Congress. During the Reagan administration (1981–1989), Congress increased the number of block grants to

nine. During the 1990s, block grants have become increasingly used as a vehicle for *devolution*—the transfer of power to state and local governments from the national government (see the *America at Odds* feature on page 713).

Ethics and the Politics of Federal Grants

The Tenth Amendment to the Constitution states that those powers not delegated to the national government are reserved to the states, or to the people. Yet even when the power to regulate a certain activity is clearly reserved to the states, Congress has been able to influence state policy by attaching conditions to federal grants.

Consider an example. In 1974, Congress passed the Emergency Highway Conservation Act. This act prohibited national funding for highway construction in states that

◄ *Although no state was required to enact the fifty-five-miles-per-hour speed limit, all fifty states did. Why? (See page 710.)*

Tables help organize large amounts of statistical data so that they can be analyzed easily. Organizing data in table form makes it easier to make comparisons and see relationships. Reading statistical tables involves scanning groups of numbers in rows and columns. Follow these guidelines:

- Read the title and subtitle and any other labels to identify what types of data are being presented.
- Check to see whether numbers are meant to indicate thousands, millions, tons, dollars, or other units.
- Examine the numbers in each row and column and look for comparisons and relationships. Note differences and similarities.

BUILDING
SOCIAL STUDIES SKILLS

Reading Statistical Tables

- A blank space usually means that no figures were available or no activity took place.
- Read footnotes, if any are presented.

PRACTICING YOUR SKILLS

Study the table below and answer the following questions:

1. What does *conterminous* mean? (Check your dictionary.) What does "balance of the conterminous United States" mean?
2. What was the total increase in the population living within fifty miles of the coastal shoreline in the United States from 1940 to 1990? What percentage change did that represent?
3. When you add the total population in coastal areas and the "balance of the conterminous United States," what is the result?

Population in Coastal Areas, 1940–1990

Year	Population of the Conterminous United States (in millions)	Total Population within 50 miles of U.S. Coasts (in millions)	Resident Populations of Counties within 50 Miles of U.S. Shorelines (in millions)				Population of the Balance of the Conterminous United States (in millions)
			Atlantic Ocean	Pacific Ocean	Great Lakes	Gulf of Mexico	
1940	131.7	60.5	29.9	7.5	18.9	4.2	71.2
1950	150.7	73.5	34.6	11.5	21.8	5.6	77.2
1960	178.5	92.7	41.7	16.8	26.4	7.8	85.7
1970	202.3	108.5	48.2	21.5	29.3	9.5	93.8
1980	225.2	118.5	50.7	25.4	29.8	12.6	106.7
1990	250.4	132.5	56.4	30.7	30.3	15.1	117.9

SOURCE: *Statistical Abstract of the United States* (Washington, D.C.: U.S. Government Printing Office, 1991).

had a speed limit greater than fifty-five miles per hour. In effect, the act forced state governments to comply with a national goal (traffic safety) if they wanted to receive federal grants. A similar tactic was used in 1984 to impose a nationwide minimum drinking age of twenty-one. Congress passed a law to withhold up to 15 percent of federal highway funding from any state that did not raise its drinking age to twenty-one by the end of 1987.

The use of federal grants to influence state policy decisions raises questions of fairness, and thus ultimately involves ethical issues. Is it right that the national government, which receives tax revenues from state citizens, should use those revenues to pressure the states to do something they might not choose to do on their own? After all, the Constitution did not delegate the power to regulate traffic laws or the drinking age to the national government. Thus, the regulation of these activities are part of the states' reserved powers.

Although the use of block grants is supported by many citizens and by government officials at both national and local levels, the increasing use of block grants also raises some ethically problematic issues. Because block grants have fewer strings attached than categorical grants, state governments have broader decision-making authority over how the funds are spent. Proponents of devolution—transferring more power to the states—have favored the use of block grants for this reason. Yet what if state governments are not as responsive as the national government has been to the needs of certain groups of Americans? For example, the Welfare Reform Act of 1996 (discussed in Chapter 22) allows the states to have more say in determining who is eligible to receive welfare assistance and how long they can receive it. The national government contributes to the program through block grants. If a state's welfare program exceeds the amount of the grant, the state—and not the national government, as in the past—must pay the excess amount. It is then up to the states to decide whether to curb welfare benefits or pick up the extra costs. In other words, there are no longer any guarantees that the poor and needy will receive public benefits.

SECTION 3 REVIEW

1. By what methods does the national government return tax dollars to state and local governments?
2. Briefly describe each of these methods.
3. Why do some people question the use of block grants?
4. **For Critical Analysis:** How do you think that U.S. government revenues affect your city or town, if at all?

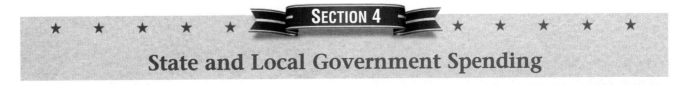

SECTION 4

State and Local Government Spending

Preview Questions:

- What are the three largest categories of state expenditures?
- What are the three largest categories of local expenditures?
- What are two important areas of concern in state and local budgets?

Figure 26–3 shows the major categories of state expenditures as percentages of total spending for a recent year. Figure 26–4 on page 712 shows the same data for local governments. If you look at the tables carefully, you will notice a clear pattern. Both state and local expenditures are concentrated in the areas of education, public welfare, highways, and health and hospitals. Education represents the greatest expenditure, particularly at the local level. This expenditure pattern stands in sharp contrast to the spending of the national

FIGURE 26–3 State Expenditures The table below shows the major categories of state expenditures as percentages of total spending. What is the percentage of state funds spent on highways?

Spending Category	Percentage of Total Spending
Public welfare	32.9
Education	20.7
Health and hospitals	10.2
Highways	9.5
Interest on general debt	5.1
Governmental administration	4.8
Corrections	4.6
Natural resources	2.4
Police	1.1
Housing and Community Development	.4
Other	8.3

Spending Category	Percentage of Total Spending
Education	41.9
Health and hospitals	8.6
Governmental administration	5.4
Police	5.4
Public welfare	5.1
Interest on general debt	5.0
Highways	4.5
Sewerage	3.2
Housing and community development	2.8
Fire protection	2.6
Parks and recreation	2.2
Solid waste management	2.0
Corrections	1.7
Natural resources	0.4
Other	9.2

government, which allocates only about 4 percent of its budget to education.

Several areas of state and local spending have become causes for growing concern. Among these areas are prisons and education.

Just the Facts

The El Paso, Texas, city council approved $112,000 to hire a security firm to guard the city's police station.

The High Cost of Prisons

State and local governments are almost entirely responsible for housing our prison population (over one million Americans). In recent years, the total annual cost of building, operating, and maintaining prisons has been about $35 billion. Although prison maintenance represents an average of less than 5 percent of state spending, some states spend considerably more. For example, Michigan spends over 7 percent of its budget on prisons.

THE GLOBAL VIEW

State and Local Government Spending across Countries

The table below indicates the percentage of total government spending accounted for by state and local governments in seven countries throughout the world, including the United States. As you can see in the table, only in Canada does state and local government spending account for more than 50 percent of total government spending. In the United States, the figure is about 45 percent, whereas in France it is less than 20 percent.

Total Government Spending Accounted for by State and Local Government Spending	
Country	**Percentage**
Canada	56
United States	45
Germany	39
Japan	32
United Kingdom	25
Italy	23
France	18

THINKING GLOBALLY

1. What are the benefits and drawbacks of having a high percentage of total government funds spent at the state and local levels?
2. What factors might account for the differences between state and local government spending in France (18 percent) and Canada (56 percent)?

Giving More Power to the States

A trend toward shifting power from the national government to the states began in the 1980s. This shift in power has been called devolution. The idea behind devolution is that the government in Washington, D.C., is not close enough to the problems of state and local governments to effectively solve those problems. But Americans are at odds over this issue. Some prefer to have state and local governments exercise more control over government programs, such as welfare. Others want the national government to exercise greater control over how state and local governments spend money from U.S. government grants.

It's Time for the States to Take Back Their Powers, Say Some

Some Americans strongly support the concept of devolution. Generally, they believe that many social and economic programs are better handled by state and local governments. They argue that the national government is "out of touch" and does not know how to address local issues or solve local problems. Local governments can tailor the programs to fit the needs of their citizens—something that national programs, because they are applied across the country, cannot do. Many Americans who support devolution also believe that certain programs, such as welfare, can be run more efficiently and cost-effectively at the state and local levels.

Furthermore, many supporters of devolution argue that some presidential administrations (particularly those of Franklin Roosevelt and Lyndon Johnson), by expanding the regulatory role of the national government, diminished the powers of state governments to control activities within their own state boundaries. Such powers, they contend, rightfully belong to the states as part of their reserved powers under the Tenth Amendment.

Devolution Will Not Work, Others Argue

Those who are opposed to devolution worry that it may harm society in the long run. Will state and local governments faced with budget constraints abandon certain protections for disadvantaged groups? If more responsibility for environmental protection is turned over to state and local governments, will those governments be able to withstand the temptation of profiting financially from the development of areas now protected by U.S. environmental laws?

One of the reasons this group of Americans has typically looked to the national government to solve certain problems is that national government officials are more impartial and less likely to be swayed by politics than government officials at the state and local levels. Thus, solutions to certain types of problems are best created and implemented by the national government.

YOU DECIDE

1. When the national government gives more responsibilities to state and local governments, should it also give more funds to these governments?
2. What groups might be most opposed to the concept of devolution? What groups might be most in favor of it?
3. Who is rightfully most responsible for problems such as managing the environment and providing welfare assistance, the national government or the state governments? Why?

▶ This class in world geography doesn't look expensive, but it is. From the first day of kindergarten through high school graduation day, educating America's children costs hundreds of billions of dollars per year.

On the whole, spending on prisons has grown between 13 and 15 percent per year since 1986.

Even though the number of reported crimes is actually declining, public opinion on how criminals should be treated is shifting away from rehabilitation and toward punishment, which means longer prison terms. Prison expansion is expensive—housing an inmate in a new prison costs between $25,000 and $40,000 a year.

Just the Facts

Over 1,500 new inmates are put in prison every week.

Growth in Education Spending

As mentioned earlier, one of the biggest items in every state and local budget is education. During the 1980s and 1990s, there was an emphasis on improving education, particularly in low-income districts. Consequently, state and local spending on elementary and secondary schools doubled in the 1980s from less than $100 billion to almost $200 billion per year. Today, state and local government spending on these public schools is more than $250 billion a year.

SECTION 4 REVIEW

1. List three major spending categories at the state level.
2. List three major spending categories at the local level.
3. What is the largest expenditure in state government budgets?
4. What is the largest expenditure in local government budgets?
5. **For Critical Analysis:** Today, the national government pays about 6 percent of the total cost of public education in the United States. Do you think the national government should pay a higher percentage of this cost? Why or why not?

★ ★ ★ ★ Chapter Summary ★ ★ ★ ★

Section 1: Limitations on State and Local Taxation

- The U.S. Constitution prevents states from taxing the operations, land, buildings, or any activity of the U.S. government. The Constitution prohibits states from regulating and taxing interstate and foreign trade.
- The due process clause of the Fourteenth Amendment requires state and local governments to impose and administer taxes fairly and forbids unreasonable classifications for the purpose of collecting taxes.
- Each state has placed constitutional limitations on its own taxing power and the taxing powers of its local governments.

Section 2: Sources of State and Local Revenues

- Major state and local taxes include the personal income tax, corporate income tax, excise tax, estate tax, inheritance tax, sales tax, and property tax.
- The most important tax at the state level is sales tax. There are, however, five states that have no general sales tax.
- The most important tax at the local level is property tax.
- Some state and local governments operate businesses from which they receive revenues. These include toll bridges, toll roads, ferries, and in some states, liquor stores.
- States and cities also borrow by issuing state and municipal bonds. Almost every state permits this type of debt financing.

Section 3: Funds from Uncle Sam

- The U.S. government returns tax dollars to state and local governments in two main ways: through categorical grants and through block grants.
- Categorical grants provide funds for specific purposes or programs. For some categorical grants, state and local governments must contribute matching funds.
- Block grants provide broad support in areas such as health care and criminal justice.
- Block grants give the states more flexibility in determining how funds are spent and have been used as a vehicle for devolution—the transfer of power from the national government to state and local governments.

Section 4: State and Local Government Spending

- The top spending categories for state governments are education, public welfare, highways, and health and hospitals.
- At the local level, education is by far the greatest expenditure.
- Spending on both prisons and education has increased substantially in recent years, causing concern at the state and local levels. State and local expenditures on public schools now exceed $250 billion per year.

CHAPTER 26 Review

★ REVIEW QUESTIONS ★

1. What limits does the U.S. Constitution place on the taxing abilities of state and local governments?
2. What are the two major taxes used at the state level?
3. What is the most important tax at the local level?
4. What types of nontax revenues do state and local governments receive?
5. What methods does the U.S. government use to return tax dollars to the states?
6. What is the largest single category of government spending at the state level?
7. What is the largest single category of government spending at the local level?
8. What are some of the pros and cons of giving state and local governments more authority to determine how grant funds will be used?

★ CRITICAL THINKING ★

1. Many people argue that the nation's future is at risk because schools are performing poorly. Thus, schools must be improved. If state fiscal conditions worsen in the years ahead, however, school budgets are unlikely to escape without cutbacks. How do you think this conflict can be solved? What do you think are some of the causes for the problems facing the school system?
2. In what areas, if any, do you think your local government spends too much money? Too little money? Give reasons for your answers.
3. Do you think state and local governments should depend on the national government for a significant share of their revenues? Why or why not?
4. Why do you think states rely so heavily on sales taxes? Why do you think cities rely so heavily on property taxes? What kinds of alternatives would you propose to reduce the heavy reliance by state and local governments on these taxes?

5. Do you think that state and local governments should be allowed to raise money through business enterprises? Why or why not?

★ IMPROVING YOUR SKILLS ★

Communication Skills

Using Context Clues to Determine Word Meanings In your reading and studies, you will occasionally come across words that you do not recognize. One way to find the meaning of an unfamiliar word, of course, is to look it up in the dictionary. Another way is to carefully examine the way the word is used in context. If you read carefully, you may find many clues to the meaning of the word in the surrounding words and sentences and in the main topic being discussed.

Writing Read the following sentences. Use context clues to determine the meanings of the underlined words. Then write your own definition of each of the words. Compare your definitions with those of a classmate. Then, check your definitions against the dictionary to see how accurate they are.

> The conventional view is that the <u>burgeoning</u> of the American nation-state occurred hand in hand with the shrinkage in the role and power of the individual American states. Certainly from the 1930s to the 1960s state governments declined in <u>relative</u> importance. Governors and state legislatures wallowed in <u>mediocrity.</u> Social and economic problems seemed to be <u>susceptible</u> only to national solutions. The states came to be widely regarded as historical <u>anomalies,</u> of no particular significance in a new, thoroughly nationalized society.

Finally, write your own sentences with these new words that you have now added to your vocabulary.

Social Studies Skills

Working with Sequencing Data and Statistical Tables

Statistical tables are one of the many ways to sequence data. The way in which the data are sequenced is often up to the person who is presenting the data. For example, the data on state and local expenditures presented in Figure 26–3 on page 711 and Figure 26–4 on page 712 are sequenced in *decreasing* order of expenditures (except for the last, catchall category of "Other"). The data could instead have been presented in *increasing* order of expenditures.

1. Describe at least one other way in which the data could have been presented. (Hint: Look at the other figures in this chapter.)
2. Once you have chosen another way of presenting the same data, prepare a sketch showing how this other presentation would look.
3. Do you have choices in how you order the data when you use this other way of presentation?
4. If your answer to question 3 is yes, give reasons why you would want the data presented in one order rather than another.

★ ACTIVITIES AND PROJECTS ★

1. Imagine that you are a lobbyist for a particular state program whose funds have been cut. Develop an oral argument to present to the state legislature that will convince state legislators to restore the program's funding. Create a videotape or an audio cas-sette tape of your speech and share it with your class. As an alternative, you might wish to create your own Web page with the persuasive argument that you prepared.
2. Obtain a copy of your state's budget. Analyze the budget to determine the items on which your state spends the most money. Write a paragraph on each of the top three items that tells why you think your state spends so much money in that area.
3. If your state has a lottery, obtain statistics showing the growth in revenues collected since the lottery began. Then find out what percentage of these revenues has gone to finance public education.
4. Write a paragraph or two comparing your state with other states with respect to the amount of state and local taxes collected and the manner in which revenues are spent.
5. Invite a local elected city council representative to your class to discuss how your city budget is prepared and how it is adopted.

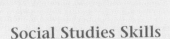

What If . . .

State Governments Could Tax U.S. Government Activities?

Currently, the U.S. government cannot be taxed by state governments. If state governments had this power, how might they use it, and what activities of the U.S. government might they tax?

The Controversy over Term Limits

The U.S. Supreme Court has held that states cannot impose term limits on senators and representatives serving in the U.S. Congress, because the U.S. Constitution does not provide for such limits. The Supreme Court, however, has not invalidated state laws imposing term limits on state legislators. Many states now have laws establishing such limits. These laws have been controversial, however, and legislators and citizens in some states have challenged the laws on constitutional grounds. An example involves California's Proposition 140—a constitutional initiative establishing term limits for California legislators. When Proposition 140 became law, it was challenged in the courts and judged to be invalid. In this *Extended Case Study*, we look at the federal appellate court's decision invalidating Proposition 140 and at some responses to that decision.

A Source Document

Excerpts from *Jones v. Bates,* a case decided by the Court of Appeals for the Ninth Circuit in 1997.

REINHARDT, Circuit Judge:
This case involves a deep and seemingly intractable conflict between principles at the heart of our representative government: the right of the people to choose whom they please to govern them, and the authority of a state to determine the structure of its political system. It also raises the novel question whether, when the people vote on an initiative measure that, if enacted, would severely limit a fundamental, constitutional right, they must be given adequate notice of the measure's effect. . . .

. . . *We do not decide whether a state may adopt lifetime term limits for its legislators without violating the Constitution. We recognize that the state has a compelling interest as a sovereign in choosing the structure of its institutions and the qualifications of its officials—an interest that may suffice to render lifetime term limits constitutional, although we do not decide that question here. Instead, we invalidate the challenged lifetime ban because we hold as a matter of federal constitutional law that a state initiative measure cannot impose a severe limitation on the people's fundamental rights when the issue of whether to impose such a limitation on those rights is put to the voters in a measure that is ambiguous on its face and that fails to mention in its text, the proponents' ballot arguments, or the state's official descriptions, the severe limitation to be imposed. Neither Proposition 140, the proponents' ballot arguments, nor the material prepared by the state mentioned "lifetime" term limits; thus, the voters were not afforded adequate notice of the severity of the limitation involved.*

Media Reports

The federal appellate court's decision that Proposition 140 was invalid for procedural reasons was hailed as a novel decision and has led to significant controversy. The excerpts that follow provide examples of the media's response to the decision.

Judicial Folly: Term Limits Are Flawed, but 9th Circuit Overreaches

Editorial, *The Sacramento Bee*

California's term limits are a bad idea and maybe even unconstitutional. But Judge Stephen Reinhardt's 9th U.S.

Circuit Court of Appeals decision knocking down term limits is a caricature of constitutional judging. . . .

The [court's] novel and fanciful reading of the law states that when voters are asked in an initiative to consider reforms burdening their fundamental rights as citizens, the Constitution requires that the state spell out the effect of the reform without ambiguity. . . .

Did all voters understand what the measure meant? Of course not. Millions of voters have not known what they are voting on as they punched out their ballots for the dozens of complicated and ambiguous fundamental reforms over the last several decades. But that's a policy indictment of the initiative process, not some disqualifying flaw unique to Proposition 140 and the campaign surrounding it.

. . . If the Constitution's requirement of due process requires initiatives to be crystal clear when touching on citizens' fundamental civil rights, then almost no reform measure of the last generation, from those on campaign spending to last year's open primary measure, would stand up to scrutiny.

Source: *The Sacramento Bee*, October 9, 1997 (p. B8). © 1997 *The Sacramento Bee*.

Novel Decision with Broad Impact Assessment

By Henry Weinstein, *Los Angeles Times*

Did California voters know what they were doing when they passed a groundbreaking term limits law in 1990?

Maybe not, according to an unprecedented U.S. 9th Circuit Court of Appeals decision Tuesday that found the measure was incurably defective because it did not explicitly say that its passage would mean lifetime term limits for state legislators. . . .

A broad array of legal experts said the decision . . . was novel and could potentially affect a host of ballot measures.

"I can't think of any other instance where a court struck down a ballot initiative on grounds that the voters didn't know what it said," observed Stanford University law professor Kathleen Sullivan. . . .

Other legal experts said it was very much an open question as to whether a court ought to even be poking into that issue. UCLA law professor Daniel Lowenstein . . . said he was very troubled by the rationale.

"The initiative is provided to every voter in California," Lowenstein said. "They can read it for themselves. There are ballot arguments, newspaper stories about it, voters have a lot of ways of informing themselves. I don't see how a court can make a determination as to whether voters are adequately informed. . . . The very basis of democracy is that voters decide how much information they need."

Source: *Los Angeles Times*, October 8, 1997 (p. A16). © 1997 *Los Angeles Times*.

Conclusion

There are strong arguments both for and against term limits. On the one hand, as the backers of Proposition 140 pointed out, the power of incumbency does discourage qualified candidates who are not incumbents from seeking public office. It also tends to foster a class of career politicians. On the other hand, as James Madison once said, "The people are the best judges of who ought to represent them" and that "to dictate and control them, to tell them who they shall not elect, is to abridge their natural rights." Whether term limits do, in fact, abridge voters' rights to choose whomever they please as their representatives—including experienced incumbents—is the question Americans must decide.

Analysis Questions

1. Assume that you are about to vote on a state constitutional initiative that establishes limits on the number of terms your state's legislators can serve. How would you vote on the issue? Give reasons for your answer.
2. In theory, by passing an initiative, the citizens of a state express their wishes about a certain issue, such as term limits. Do you think that unelected judges in the federal courts should have the power to override these wishes? Why or why not?
3. What arguments for and against term limits, other than the ones stated or implied in the above excerpts, can you think of?
4. Should citizen initiatives be used to establish policy on important issues? Explain.

The Resource Center

CONTENTS

Original Source Documents

DOCUMENT 1

Constitution of the United States of America*

The Preamble

We the People of the United States, in Order to form a more perfect Union, establish Justice, insure domestic Tranquility, provide for the common defence, promote the general Welfare, and secure the Blessings of Liberty to ourselves and our Posterity, do ordain and establish this Constitution for the United States of America.

The Preamble declares that "We the People" are the authority for the Constitution (unlike the Articles of Confederation, which derived their authority from the states). The Preamble also sets out the purposes of the Constitution.

Article I. (Legislative Branch)

The first part of the Constitution is called Article 1; it deals with the organization and powers of the lawmaking branch of the national government, the Congress.

Section 1. Legislative Powers

All legislative Powers herein granted shall be vested in a Congress of the United States, which shall consist of a Senate and House of Representatives.

Section 2. House of Representatives
Clause 1: Composition and Election of Members. The House of Representatives shall be composed of Members chosen every second Year by the People of the several States, and the Electors in each State shall have the Qualifications

requisite for Electors of the most numerous Branch of the State Legislature.

Each state has the power to decide who may vote for members of Congress. Within each state, those who may vote for state legislators may also vote for members of the House of Representatives (and, under the Seventeenth Amendment, for U.S. senators). When the Constitution was written, nearly all states limited voting rights to white male property owners or taxpayers at least twenty-one years old. Subsequent amendments granted voting power to African-American men, all women, and eighteen-year-olds.

Clause 2: Qualifications. No Person shall be a Representative who shall not have attained to the Age of twenty five Years, and been seven Years a Citizen of the United States, and who shall not, when elected, be an Inhabitant of that State in which he shall be chosen.

Each member of the House must (1) be at least twenty-five years old, (2) have been a U.S. citizen for at least seven years, and (3) be a resident of the state in which she or he is elected.

Clause 3: Apportionment of Representatives and Direct Taxes. Representatives [and direct Taxes][1] shall be apportioned among the several States which may be included within this Union, according to their respective Numbers [which shall be determined by adding to the whole Number of free Persons, including those bound to Service for a Term of Years, and excluding Indians not taxed, three fifths of all other Persons].[2] The actual Enumeration shall be made

---

*The spelling, capitalization, and punctuation of the original have been retained here. Brackets indicate passages that have been altered by amendments to the Constitution.

[1]Modified by the Sixteenth Amendment.
[2]Modified by the fourteenth Amendment.

within three Years after the first Meeting of the Congress of the United States, and within every subsequent Term of ten Years, in such Manner as they shall by Law direct. The Number of Representatives shall not exceed one for every thirty Thousand, but each State shall have at Least one Representative; and until such enumeration shall be made, the State of New Hampshire shall be entitled to chuse three, Massachusetts eight, Rhode Island and Providence Plantations one, Connecticut five, New York six, New Jersey four, Pennsylvania eight, Delaware one, Maryland six, Virginia ten, North Carolina five, South Carolina five, and Georgia three.

A state's representation in the House is based on the size of its population. Population is counted in each decade's census, after which Congress reapportions House seats. Since early in this century, the number of seats has been limited to 435.

Clause 4: Vacancies.   When vacancies happen in the Representation from any State, the Executive Authority thereof shall issue Writs of Election to fill such Vacancies.

The "Executive Authority" is the state's governor. When a vacancy occurs in the House, the governor calls a special election to fill it.

Clause 5: Officers and Impeachment.   The House of Representatives shall chuse their Speaker and other Officers; and shall have the sole Power of Impeachment.

The power to impeach is the power to accuse. In this case, it is the power to accuse members of the executive or judicial branch of wrongdoing or abuse of power. Once a bill of impeachment is issued, the Senate holds the trial.

Section 3. The Senate
Clause 1: Term and Number of Members.   The Senate of the United States shall be composed of two Senators from each State [chosen by the Legislature thereof],[3] for six Years; and each Senator shall have one Vote.

Every state has two senators, each of whom serves for six years, and has one vote in the upper chamber. Since the Seventeenth Amendment in 1913, all senators are elected directly by voters of the state during the regular election.

Clause 2: Classification of Senators.   Immediately after they shall be assembled in Consequence of the first Election,

they shall be divided as equally as may be into three Classes. The Seats of the Senators of the first Class shall be vacated at the Expiration of the second Year, of the second Class at the Expiration of the fourth Year, and of the third Class at the Expiration of the sixth Year, so that one third may be chosen every second Year; [and if Vacancies happen by Resignation, or otherwise, during the Recess of the Legislature of any State, the Executive thereof may make temporary Appointments until the next Meeting of the Legislature, which shall then fill such Vacancies].[4]

One-third of the Senate's seats are open to election every two years (unlike the House, all of whose members are elected simultaneously).

Clause 3: Qualifications.   No Person shall be a Senator who shall not have attained to the Age of thirty Years, and been nine Years a Citizen of the United States, and who shall not, when elected, be an Inhabitant of that State for which he shall be chosen.

Every senator must be at least thirty years old, a citizen of the United States for a minimum of nine years, and a resident of the state in which he or she is elected.

Clause 4: The Role of the Vice President.   The Vice President of the United States shall be President of the Senate, but shall have no Vote, unless they be equally divided.

The vice-president presides over meetings of the Senate but cannot vote unless there is a tie. The Constitution gives no other official duties to the vice-president.

Clause 5: Other Officers.   The Senate shall chuse their other Officers, and also a President pro tempore, in the Absence of the Vice President, or when he shall exercise the Office of President of the United States.

When the vice-president is absent, the Senate votes for one of its members to preside; this person is usually called the president pro tempore because of the temporary situation of the position.

Clause 6: Impeachment Trials.   The Senate shall have the sole Power to try all Impeachments. When sitting for that Purpose, they shall be on Oath or Affirmation. When the President of the United States is tried, the Chief Justice shall preside: And no Person shall be convicted without the Concurrence of two thirds of the Members present.

---

[3]Repealed by the Seventeenth Amendment.

[4]Modified by the Seventeenth Amendment.

The Senate conducts trials of officials that the House impeaches. The Senate sits as a jury, with the vice-president presiding if the president is not on trial.

Clause 7: Penalties for Conviction. Judgment in Cases of Impeachment shall not extend further than to removal from Office, and disqualification to hold and enjoy any Office of honor, Trust, or Profit under the United States: but the Party convicted shall nevertheless be liable and subject to Indictment, Trial, Judgment, and Punishment, according to Law.

On conviction on impeachment charges, the Senate can only force an official to leave office and prevent him or her from holding another office in the federal government. The individual, however, can still be tried in a regular court.

Section 4. Congressional Elections: Times, Manner, and Places

Clause 1: Elections. The Times, Places and Manner of holding Elections for Senators and Representatives, shall be prescribed in each State by the Legislature thereof; but the Congress may at any time by Law make or alter such Regulations, except as to the Places of chusing Senators.

Congress set the Tuesday after the first Monday in November in even-numbered years as the date for congressional elections. In states with more than one seat in the House, Congress requires that representatives be elected from districts within each state. Under the Seventeenth Amendment, senators are elected at the same places as other officials.

Clause 2: Sessions of Congress. [The Congress shall assemble at least once in every Year, and such Meeting shall be on the first Monday in December, unless they shall by Law appoint a different Day.][5]

Congress has to meet every year at least once. The regular session now begins at noon on January 3 of each year, subsequent to the Twentieth Amendment, unless Congress passes a law to fix a different date. Congress stays in session until its members vote to adjourn. Additionally, the president may call a special session.

Section 5. Powers and Duties of the Houses

Clause 1: Admitting Members and Quorum. Each House shall be the Judge of the Elections, Returns, and Qualifications of its own Members, and a Majority of each shall constitute a Quorum to do Business; but a smaller Number may

---

[5]Changed by the Twentieth Amendment.

adjourn from day to day, and may be authorized to compel the Attendance of absent Members, in such Manner, and under such Penalties as each House may provide.

Each chamber may exclude or refuse to seat a member-elect.
   The quorum rule requires that 218 members of the House and 51 members of the Senate be present in order to conduct business. This rule is normally not enforced in the handling of routine matters.

Clause 2: Rules and Discipline of Members. Each House may determine the Rules of its Proceedings, punish its Members for disorderly Behaviour, and, with the Concurrence of two thirds, expel a Member.

The House and the Senate may adopt their own rules to guide their proceedings. Each may also discipline its members for conduct that is deemed unacceptable. No member may be expelled without a two-thirds majority.

Clause 3: Keeping a Record. Each House shall keep a Journal of its Proceedings, and from time to time publish the same, excepting such Parts as may in their Judgment require Secrecy; and the Yeas and Nays of the Members of either House on any question shall, at the Desire of one fifth of those Present, be entered on the Journal.

The journals of the two houses are published at the end of each session of Congress.

Clause 4: Adjournment. Neither House, during the Session of Congress, shall, without the Consent of the other, adjourn for more than three days, nor to any other Place than that in which the two Houses shall be sitting.

Congress has the power to determine when and where to meet, provided, however, that both houses meet in the same city. Neither house may recess in excess of three days without the consent of the other.

Section 6. Rights of Members

Clause 1: Compensation and Privileges. The Senators and Representatives shall receive a Compensation for their services, to be ascertained by Law, and paid out of the Treasury of the United States. They shall in all Cases, except Treason, Felony and Breach of the Peace, be privileged from Arrest during their Attendance at the Session of their respective Houses, and in going to and returning from the same; and for any Speech or Debate in either House, they shall not be questioned in any other Place.

Congressional salaries are to be paid by the U.S. Treasury rather than by the members' respective states. The original salaries were $6 per day; in 1857 they were $3,000 per year. Both representatives and senators currently are paid $125,100 each year.

Members cannot be arrested for things they say during speeches and debates in Congress. This immunity applies to the Capitol Building itself and not to their private lives.

Treason is defined in Article III, Section 3. A felony is any serious crime. A breach of the peace is any indictable offense less than treason or a felony. Members cannot be arrested for anything they say in speeches or debates in Congress.

Clause 2: Restrictions.   No Senator or Representative shall, during the Time for which he was elected, be appointed to any civil Office under the Authority of the United States, which shall have been created, or the Emoluments whereof shall have been encreased during such time; and no Person holding any Office under the United States, shall be a Member of either House during his Continuance in Office.

During the term for which a member was elected, he or she cannot concurrently accept another federal government position.

Section 7. Legislative Powers: Bills and Resolutions
Clause 1: Revenue Bills.   All Bills for raising Revenue shall originate in the House of Representatives; but the Senate may propose or concur with Amendments as on other Bills.

All tax and appropriation bills for raising money have to originate in the House of Representatives. The Senate, though, often amends such bills and may even substitute an entirely different bill.

Clause 2: The Presidential Veto.   Every Bill which shall have passed the House of Representatives and the Senate, shall, before it becomes a Law, be presented to the President of the United States; If he approve he shall sign it, but if not he shall return it, with his Objections to the House in which it shall have originated, who shall enter the Objections at large on their Journal, and proceed to reconsider it. If after such Reconsideration two thirds of that House shall agree to pass the Bill, it shall be sent together with the Objections, to the other House, by which it shall likewise be reconsidered, and if approved by two thirds of that House, it shall become a Law. But in all such Cases the Votes of both Houses shall be determined by Yeas and Nays, and the Names of the Per-

sons voting for and against the Bill shall be entered on the Journal of each House respectively. If any Bill shall not be returned by the President within ten Days (Sundays excepted) after it shall have been presented to him, the Same shall be a Law, in like Manner as if he had signed it, unless the Congress by their Adjournment prevent its Return in which Case it shall not be a Law.

When Congress sends the president a bill, he or she can sign it (in which case it becomes law) or send it back to the house in which it originated. If it is sent back, a two-thirds majority of each house must pass it again for it to become law. If the president neither signs it nor sends it back within ten days, it becomes law anyway, unless Congress adjourns in the meantime.

Clause 3: Actions on Other Matters.   Every Order, Resolution, or Vote to which the Concurrence of the Senate and House of Representatives may be necessary (except on a question of Adjournment) shall be presented to the President of the United States; and before the Same shall take Effect, shall be approved by him, or being disapproved by him, shall be repassed by two thirds of the Senate and House of Representatives, according to the Rules and Limitations prescribed in the Case of a Bill.

The president must either sign or veto everything that Congress passes, except votes to adjourn and resolutions not having the force of law.

Section 8. The Powers of Congress
Clause 1: Taxing.   The Congress shall have Power To lay and collect Taxes, Duties, Imposts and Excises, to pay the Debts and provide for the common Defence and general Welfare of the United States; but all Duties, Imposts and Excises shall be uniform throughout the United States;

Duties are taxes on imports and exports. Impost is a generic term for tax. Excises are taxes on the manufacture, sale, or use of goods.

Clause 2: Borrowing.   To borrow Money on the credit of the United States;

Congress has the power to borrow money, which is normally carried out through the sale of U.S. treasury bonds on which interest is paid. Note that the Constitution places no limit on the amount of government borrowing.

Clause 3: Regulation of Commerce.   To regulate Commerce with foreign Nations, and among the several States, and with the Indian Tribes;

This is the Commerce Clause, which gives to the Congress the power to regulate interstate and foreign trade. Much of the activity of Congress is based on this clause.

Clause 4: Naturalization and Bankruptcy.   To establish a uniform Rule of Naturalization, and uniform Laws on the subject of Bankruptcies throughout the United States;

Only Congress may determine how aliens can become citizens of the United States. Congress may make laws with respect to bankruptcy.

Clause 5: Money and Standards.   To coin Money, regulate the Value thereof, and of foreign Coin, and fix the Standard of Weights and Measures;

Congress mints coins and prints and circulates paper money. Congress can establish uniform measures of time, distance, weight, etc. In 1838 Congress adopted the English system of weights and measurements as our national standard.

Clause 6: Punishing Counterfeiters.   To provide for the Punishment of counterfeiting the Securities and current Coin of the United States;

Congress has the power to punish those who copy American money and pass it off as real. Currently, the fine is up to $5,000 and/or imprisonment for up to fifteen years.

Clause 7: Roads and Post Offices.   To establish Post Offices and post Roads;

Post roads include all routes over which mail is carried—highways, railways, waterways, and airways.

Clause 8: Patents and Copyrights.   To promote the Progress of Science and useful Arts, by securing for limited Times to Authors and Inventors the exclusive Right to their respective Writings and Discoveries;

Authors' and composers' works are protected by copyrights established by copyright law, which currently is the 1978 Copyright Act. Copyrights are valid for the life of the author or composer plus fifty years. Inventors' works are protected by patents, which vary in length of protection from three and a half to seventeen years. A patent gives a person the exclusive right to control the manufacture or sale of her or his invention.

Clause 9: Lower Courts.   To constitute Tribunals inferior to the supreme Court;

Congress has the authority to set up all federal courts, except the Supreme Court, and to decide what cases those courts will hear.

Clause 10: Punishment for Piracy.   To define and punish Piracies and Felonies committed on the high Seas, and Offences against the Law of Nations;

Congress has the authority to prohibit the commission of certain acts outside U.S. territory and to punish certain violations of international law.

Clause 11: Declaration of War.   To declare War, grant Letters of Marque and Reprisal, and make Rules concerning Captures on Land and Water;

Only Congress can declare war, although the president, as commander in chief, can make war without Congress's formal declaration. Letters of marque and reprisal authorized private parties to capture and destroy enemy ships in wartime. Since the mid-nineteenth century, international law has prohibited letters of marque and reprisal, and the United States has honored the ban.

Clause 12: The Army.   To raise and support Armies, but no Appropriation of Money to that Use shall be for a longer Term than two Years;

Congress has the power to create an army; the money used to pay for it must be appropriated for no more than two-year intervals. This latter restriction gives ultimate control of the army to civilians.

Clause 13: Creation of a Navy.   To provide and maintain a Navy;

This clause allows for the maintenance of a navy. In 1947 Congress created the air force.

Clause 14: Regulation of the Armed Forces.   To make Rules for the Government and Regulation of the land and naval Forces;

Congress sets the rules for the military mainly by way of the Uniform Code of Military Justice, which was enacted in 1950 by Congress.

Clause 15: The Militia.   To provide for calling forth the Militia to execute the Laws of the Union, suppress Insurrections and repel Invasions;

The militia is known today as the National Guard. Both Congress and the president have the authority to call the National Guard into federal service.

Clause 16: How the Militia is Organized. To provide for organizing, arming, and disciplining the Militia, and for governing such Part of them as may be employed in the Service of the United States, reserving to the States respectively, the Appointment of the Officers, and the Authority of training the Militia according to the discipline prescribed by Congress;

This clause gives Congress the power to "federalize" state militia (National Guard). When called into such service, the National Guard is subject to the same rules that Congress has set forth for the regular armed services.

Clause 17: Creation of the District of Columbia. To exercise exclusive Legislation in all Cases whatsoever, over such District (not exceeding ten Miles square) as may, by Cession of particular States, and the Acceptance of Congress, become the Seat of the Government of the United States, and to exercise like Authority over all Places purchased by the Consent of the Legislature of the State in which the Same shall be, for the Erection of Forts, Magazines, Arsenals, dock-Yards, and other needful Buildings;—And

Congress established the District of Columbia as the national capital in 1791. Virginia and Maryland had granted land for the District, but Virginia's grant was returned because it was believed it would not be needed. Today, the District is sixty-nine miles square.

Clause 18: The Elastic Clause. To make all Laws which shall be necessary and proper for carrying into Execution the foregoing Powers, and all other Powers vested by this Constitution in the Government of the United States, or in any Department or Officer thereof.

This clause—the Necessary and Proper Clause, or the Elastic Clause—grants no specific powers, and thus it can be stretched to fit different circumstances. It has allowed Congress to adapt the government to changing needs and times.

Section 9. The Powers Denied to Congress
Clause 1: Question of Slavery. The Migration or Importation of such Persons as any of the States now existing shall think proper to admit, shall not be prohibited by the Congress prior to the Year one thousand eight hundred and eight, but a Tax or duty may be imposed on such Importation, not exceeding ten dollars for each Person.

"Persons" referred to slaves. Congress outlawed the slave trade in 1808.

Clause 2: Habeas Corpus. The privilege of the Writ of Habeas Corpus shall not be suspended, unless when in Cases of Rebellion or Invasion the public Safety may require it.

A writ of habeas corpus is a court order directing a sheriff or other public officer who is detaining another person to "produce the body" of the detainee so the court can assess the legality of the detention.

Clause 3: Special Bills. No Bill of Attainder or ex post facto Law shall be passed.

A bill of attainder is a law that inflicts punishment without a trial. An ex post facto law is a law that inflicts punishment for an act that was not illegal when it was committed.

Clause 4: Direct Taxes. [No Capitation, or other direct, Tax shall be laid, unless in Proportion to the Census or Enumeration herein before directed to be taken.][6]

A capitation is a tax on a person. A direct tax is a tax paid directly to the government, such as a property tax. This clause was intended to prevent Congress from levying a tax on slaves per person and thereby taxing slavery out of existence.

Clause 5: Export Taxes. No Tax or Duty shall be laid on Articles exported from any State.

Congress may not tax any goods sold from one state to another or from one state to a foreign country. (Congress does have the power to tax goods that are bought from other countries, however.)

Clause 6: Interstate Commerce. No Preference shall be given by any Regulation of Commerce or Revenue to the Ports of one State over those of another: nor shall Vessels bound to, or from, one State, be obliged to enter, clear, or pay Duties in another.

Congress may not treat different ports within the United States differently in terms of taxing and commerce powers. Congress

---

[6]Modified by the Sixteenth Amendment.

may not tax goods sent from one state to another. Finally, Congress may not give one state's port a legal advantage over those of another state.

Clause 7: Treasury Withdrawals. No Money shall be drawn from the Treasury, but in Consequence of Appropriations made by Law; and a regular Statement and Account of the Receipts and Expenditures of all public Money shall be published from time to time.

Federal funds can be spent only as Congress authorizes. This is a significant check on the president's power.

Clause 8: Titles of Nobility. No Title of Nobility shall be granted by the United States: And no Person holding any Office of Profit or Trust under them, shall, without the Consent of the Congress, accept of any present, Emolument, Office, or Title, of any kind whatever, from any King, Prince, or foreign State.

No person in the United States may be bestowed a title of nobility such as a duke or duchess. This clause also discourages bribery of American officials by foreign governments.

Section 10. Those Powers Denied to the States

Clause 1: Treaties and Coinage. No State shall enter into any Treaty, Alliance, or Confederation; grant Letters of Marque and Reprisal; coin Money; emit Bills of Credit; make any Thing but gold and silver Coin a Tender in Payment of Debts; pass any Bill of Attainder, ex post facto Law, or Law impairing the Obligation of Contracts, or grant any Title of Nobility.

Prohibiting state laws "impairing the Obligation of Contracts" was intended to protect creditors. (Shays's Rebellion—an attempt to prevent courts from giving effect to creditors' legal actions against debtors—occurred only one year before the Constitution was written.)

Clause 2: Duties and Imposts. No State shall, without the Consent of the Congress, lay any Imports or Duties on Imports or Exports, except what may be absolutely necessary for executing its inspection Laws; and the net Produce of all Duties and Imposts, laid by any State on Imports or Exports, shall be for the Use of the Treasury of the United States; and all such Laws shall be subject to the Revision and Controul of the Congress.

Only Congress can tax imports. Further, the states cannot tax exports.

Clause 3: War. No State shall, without the Consent of Congress, lay any Duty of Tonnage, keep Troops, or Ships of War in time of Peace, enter into any Agreement or Compact with another State, or with a foreign Power or engage in War, unless actually invaded, or in such imminent Danger as will not admit of delay.

A duty of tonnage is a tax on ships according to their cargo capacity. No states may effectively tax ships according to their cargo unless Congress agrees. Additionally, this clause forbids any state to keep troops or warships during peacetime or to make a compact with another state or foreign nation unless Congress so agrees. States can, in contrast, maintain a militia, but its use has to be limited to internal disorders that occur within a state— unless, of course, the militia is called into federal service.

Article II. (Executive Branch)

Section 1. The Nature and Scope of Presidential Power
Clause 1: Four-Year Term. The executive Power shall be vested in a President of the United States of America. He shall hold his Office during the Term of four Years, and, together with the Vice President, chosen for the same Term, be elected, as follows.

The president has the power to carry out laws made by Congress, called the executive power. He or she serves in office for a four-year term after election. The Twenty-second Amendment limits the number of times a person may be elected president.

Clause 2: Choosing Electors From Each State. Each State shall appoint, in such Manner as the Legislature thereof may direct, a Number of Electors, equal to the whole Number of Senators and Representatives to which the State may be entitled in the Congress; but no Senator or Representative, or Person holding an Office of Trust or Profit under the United States, shall be appointed an Elector.

The "Electors" are more commonly known as the "electoral college." The president is elected by electors—that is, representatives chosen by the people—rather than by the people directly.

Clause 3: The Former System of Elections. [The Electors shall meet in their respective States, and vote by Ballot for two Persons, of whom one at least shall not be an Inhabitant of the same State with themselves. And they shall make a List of all the Persons voted for, and of the Number of Votes for each; which List they shall sign and certify, and transmit sealed to the Seat of the Government of the United States, directed to the President of the Senate. The President of the Senate shall, in the Presence of the Senate and House of Representatives, open all the Certificates, and the Votes shall then be counted. The Person having the greatest Number of Votes shall be the President, if such Number be a Majority of the whole Number of Electors appointed; and if there be more than one who have such Majority, and have an equal Number of Votes, then the House of Representatives shall immediately chuse by Ballot one of them for President; and if no Person have a Majority, then from the five highest on the List the said House shall in like Manner chuse the President. But in chusing the President, the Votes shall be taken by States, the Representation from each State having one Vote; A quorum for this Purpose shall consist of a Member or Members from two thirds of the States, and a Majority of all the States shall be necessary to a Choice. In every Case, after the Choice of the President, the Person having the greater Number of Votes of the Electors shall be the Vice President. But if there should remain two or more who have equal Votes, the Senate shall chuse from them by Ballot the Vice President.][7]

The original method of selecting the president and vice-president was replaced by the Twelfth Amendment. Apparently, the framers did not anticipate the rise of political parties and the development of primaries and conventions.

Clause 4: The Time of Elections.   The Congress may determine the Time of chusing the Electors, and the Day on which they shall give their Votes; which Day shall be the same throughout the United States.

Congress set the Tuesday after the first Monday in November every fourth year as the date for choosing electors. The electors cast their votes on the Monday after the second Wednesday in December of that year.

Clause 5: Qualifications for President.   No person except a natural born Citizen, or a Citizen of the United States, at the time of the Adoption of this Constitution, shall be eligible to the Office of President; neither shall any Person be eligible to that Office who shall not have attained to the Age of thirty five Years, and been fourteen Years a Resident within the United States.

The president must be a natural-born citizen, be at least thirty-five years of age when taking office, and have been a resident within the United States for at least fourteen years.

Clause 6: Succession of the Vice President.   [In Case of the Removal of the President from Office, or of his Death, Resignation or Inability to discharge the Powers and Duties of the said Office, the same shall devolve on the Vice President, and the Congress may by Law provide for the Case of Removal, Death, Resignation or Inability, both of the President and Vice President, declaring what Officer shall then act as President, and such Officer shall act accordingly, until the Disability be removed, or a President shall be elected.][8]

This former provision provided for the method by which the vice-president was to succeed to the presidency, but its wording is ambiguous. It was replaced by the Twenty-fifth Amendment.

Clause 7: The President's Salary.   The President shall, at stated Times, receive for his Services, a Compensation, which shall neither be encreased nor diminished during the Period for which he shall have been elected, and he shall not receive within that Period any other Emolument from the United States, or any of them.

The president maintains the same salary during each four-year term. Moreover, she or he may not receive additional cash payments from the government. Originally set at $25,000 per year, it is currently $200,000 a year plus a $50,000 taxable expense account.

Clause 8: The Oath of Office.   Before he enter on the Execution of his Office, he shall take the following Oath or Affirmation: "I do solemnly swear (or affirm) that I will faithfully execute the Office of President of the United States, and will to the best of my Ability, preserve, protect and defend the Constitution of the United States."

The president is "sworn in" prior to beginning the duties of the office. Currently, the taking of the oath of office occurs on January 20, following the November election. The ceremony is called the inauguration. The oath of office is administered by the chief justice of the United States Supreme Court.

Section 2. Powers of the President
Clause 1: Commander in Chief.   The President shall be Commander in Chief of the Army and Navy of the United

---

[7]Changed by the Twelfth amendment

[8]Modified by the Twenty-fifth amendment

States, and of the Militia of the several States, when called into the actual Service of the United States; he may require the Opinion, in writing, of the principal Officer in each of the executive Departments, upon any Subject relating to the Duties of their respective Offices, and he shall have Power to grant Reprieves and Pardons for Offences against the United States, except in Cases of Impeachment.

The armed forces are placed under civilian control because the president is a civilian, but still commander in chief of the military. The president may ask for the help of the heads of each of the executive departments (thereby creating the Cabinet). The Cabinet members are chosen by the president with the consent of the Senate, but they can be removed without Senate approval.

The president's clemency powers extend only to federal cases. In those cases, he or she may grant a full or conditional pardon, or reduce a prison term or fine.

Clause 2: Treaties and Appointment.
He shall have Power, by and with the Advice and Consent of the Senate, to make Treaties, provided two thirds of the Senators present concur; and he shall nominate, and by and with the Advice and Consent of the Senate, shall appoint Ambassadors, other public Ministers and Consuls, Judges of the supreme Court, and all other Officers of the United States, whose Appointments are not herein otherwise provided for, and which shall be established by Law; but the Congress may by Law vest the Appointment of such inferior Officers, as they think proper, in the President alone, in the Courts of Law, or in the Heads of Departments.

Many of the major powers of the president are identified in this clause, including the power to make treaties with foreign governments (with the approval of the Senate by a two-thirds vote) and the power to appoint ambassadors, Supreme Court justices, and other government officials. Most such appointments require Senate approval.

Clause 3: Vacancies.
The President shall have Power to fill up all Vacancies that may happen during the Recess of the Senate, by granting Commissions which shall expire at the end of their next Session.

The president has the power to appoint temporary officials to fill vacant federal offices without Senate approval if the Congress is not in session. Such appointments expire automatically at the end of Congress's next term.

Section 3. Duties of the President
He shall from time to time give to the Congress Information of the State of the Union, and recommend to their Consideration such Measures as he shall judge necessary and expedient; he may, on extraordinary Occasions, convene both Houses, or either of them, and in Case of Disagreement between them, with Respect to the Time of Adjournment, he may adjourn them to such Time as he shall think proper; he shall receive Ambassadors and other public Ministers; he shall take Care that the Laws be faithfully executed, and shall Commission all the Officers of the United States.

Annually, the president reports on the state of the union to Congress, recommends legislative measures, and proposes a federal budget. The State of the Union speech is a statement not only to Congress but also to the American people. After it is given, the president proposes a federal budget and presents an economic report. At any time he or she so chooses, the president may send special messages to Congress while it is in session. The president has the power to call special sessions, to adjourn Congress when its two houses do not agree for that purpose, to receive diplomatic representatives of other governments, and to ensure the proper execution of all federal laws. The president further has the ability to empower federal officers to hold their positions and to perform their duties.

Section 4. Impeachment
The President, Vice President and all civil Officers of the United States, shall be removed from Office on Impeachment for, and Conviction of, Treason, Bribery, or other high Crimes and Misdemeanors.

Treason denotes giving aid to the nation's enemies. The definition of high crimes and misdemeanors is usually given as serious abuses of political power. In either case, the president or vice-president may be accused by the House (called an impeachment) and then removed from office if convicted by the Senate. (Note that impeachment does not mean removal, but rather the state of being accused of treason or high crimes and misdemeanors.)

Article III. (Judicial Branch)

Section 1. Judicial Powers, Courts, and Judges
The judicial Power of the United States, shall be vested in one supreme Court, and in such inferior Courts as the Congress may from time to time ordain and establish. The

Judges, both of the supreme and inferior Courts, shall hold their Offices during good Behaviour, and shall, at stated Times, receive for their Services a Compensation, which shall not be diminished during their Continuance in Office.

The Supreme Court is vested with judicial power, as are the lower federal courts that Congress creates. Federal judges serve in their offices for life unless they are impeached and convicted by Congress. The payment of federal judges may not be reduced during their time in office.

Section 2. Jurisdiction
Clause 1: Cases Under Federal Jurisdiction.   The judicial Power shall extend to all Cases, in Law and Equity, arising under this Constitution, the Laws of the United States, and Treaties made, or which shall be made, under their Authority;—to all Cases affecting Ambassadors, other public Ministers and Consuls;—to all Cases of admiralty and maritime Jurisdiction;—to Controversies to which the United States shall be a Party;—to Controversies between two or more States; [—between a State and Citizens of another State;—]⁹ between Citizens of different States;—between Citizens of the same State claiming Lands under Grants of different States, [and between a State, or the Citizens thereof, and foreign States, Citizens or Subjects.]¹⁰

The federal courts take on cases that concern the meaning of the U.S. Constitution, all federal laws, and treaties. They also can take on cases involving citizens of different states and citizens of foreign nations.

Clause 2: Cases for the Supreme Court.   In all Cases affecting Ambassadors, other public Ministers and Consuls, and those in which a State shall be a Party, the supreme Court shall have original Jurisdiction. In all the other Cases before mentioned, the supreme Court shall have appellate Jurisdiction, both as to Law and Fact, with such Exceptions, and under such Regulations as the Congress shall make.

In a limited number of situations, the Supreme Court acts as a trial court and has original jurisdiction. These cases involve a representative from another country or involve a state. In all other situations, the cases must first be tried in the lower courts

---

⁹Modified by the twenty-fifth Amendment.
¹⁰Modified by the eleventh Amendment.

and then can be appealed to the Supreme Court. Congress may, however, make exceptions. Today the Supreme Court acts as a trial court of first instance on rare occasions.

Clause 3: The Conduct of Trials.   The Trial of all Crimes, except in Cases of Impeachment, shall be by Jury; and such Trial shall be held in the State where the said Crimes shall have been committed; but when not committed within any State, the Trial shall be at such Place or Places as the Congress may by Law have directed.

Any person accused of a federal crime is granted the right to a trial by jury in a federal court in that state in which the crime was committed. Trials of impeachment are an exception.

Section 3. Treason
Clause 1: The Definition of Treason.   Treason against the United States, shall consist only in levying War against them, or, in adhering to their Enemies, giving them Aid and Comfort. No Person shall be convicted of Treason unless on the Testimony of two Witnesses to the same overt Act, or on Confession in open Court.

Treason is the making of war against the United States or giving aid to its enemies.

Clause 2: Punishment.   The Congress shall have Power to declare the Punishment of Treason, but no Attainder of Treason shall work Corruption of Blood, or Forfeiture except during the Life of the Person attainted.

Congress has provided that the punishment for treason range from a minimum of five years in prison and/or a $10,000 fine to a maximum of death. "No Attainder of Treason shall work Corruption of Blood" prohibits punishment of the traitor's heirs.

Article IV. (Relations Among the States)

Section 1. Full Faith and Credit
Full Faith and Credit shall be given in each State to the public Acts, Records, and judicial Proceedings of every other State. And the Congress may by general Laws prescribe the Manner in which such Acts, Records and Proceedings shall be proved, and the Effect thereof.

All states are required to respect one another's laws, records, and lawful decisions. There are exceptions, however. A state does not have to enforce another state's criminal code. Nor does it have to recognize another state's grant of a divorce if the person obtaining the divorce did not establish legal residence in the state in which it was given.

Section 2. Treatment of Citizens
Clause 1: Privileges and Immunities.   The Citizens of each State shall be entitled to all Privileges and Immunities of Citizens in the several States.

A citizen of a state has the same rights and privileges as the citizens of another state in which he or she happens to be.

Clause 2: Extradition.   A Person charged in any State with Treason, Felony, or other Crime, who shall flee from Justice, and be found in another State, shall on Demand of the executive Authority of the State from which he fled, be delivered up, to be removed to the State having Jurisdiction of the Crime.

Any person accused of a crime who flees to another state must be returned to the state in which the crime occurred.

Clause 3: Fugitive Slaves.   [No Person held to Service or Labour in one State, under the Laws thereof, escaping into another, shall, in Consequence of any Law or Regulation therein, be discharged from such Service or Labour, but shall be delivered up on Claim of the Party to whom such Service or Labour may be due.][11]

This clause was struck down by the Thirteenth Amendment, which abolished slavery in 1865.

Section 3. Admission of States
Clause 1: The Process.   New States may be admitted by the Congress into this Union; but no new State shall be formed or erected within the Jurisdiction of any other State; nor any State be formed by the Junction of two or more States, or Parts of States, without the Consent of the Legislatures of the States concerned as well as of the Congress.

Only Congress has the power to admit new states to the union. No state may be created by taking territory from an existing state unless the state's legislature so consents.

Clause 2: Public Land.   The Congress shall have Power to dispose of and make all needful Rules and Regulations

---

[11]Repealed by the thirteenth Amendment.

respecting the Territory or other Property belonging to the United States; and nothing in this Constitution shall be so construed as to Prejudice any Claims of the United States, or of any particular State.

The federal government has the exclusive right to administer federal government public lands.

Section 4. Republican Form of Government
The United States shall guarantee to every State in this Union a Republican Form of Government, and shall protect each of them against Invasion; and on Application of the Legislature, or of the Executive (when the Legislature cannot be convened) against domestic Violence.

Each state is promised a form of government in which the people elect their representatives, called a republican form. The federal government is bound to protect states against any attack by foreigners or during times of trouble within a state.

Article V. (Methods of Amendment)
The Congress, whenever two thirds of both Houses shall deem it necessary, shall propose Amendments to this Constitution, or on the Application of the Legislatures of two thirds of the several States, shall call a Convention for proposing Amendments, which, in either Case, shall be valid to all Intents and Purposes, as Part of this Constitution, when ratified by the Legislatures of three fourths of the several States, or by Conventions in three fourths thereof, as the one or the other Mode of Ratification may be proposed by the Congress; Provided that no Amendment which may be made prior to the Year One thousand eight hundred and eight shall in any Manner affect the first and fourth Clauses in the Ninth Section of the First Article; and that no State, without its Consent, shall be deprived of its equal Suffrage in the Senate.

Constitutional Amendments may be proposed by either of two ways: a two-thirds vote of each house (Congress) or by majority vote at a convention called by Congress at the request of two-thirds of the states. Ratification of amendments may be carried out in two ways: by the legislatures of three-fourths of the states or by the voters in three-fourths of the states. No state may be denied equal representation in the Senate.

Article VI. (National Supremacy)
Clause 1: Existing Obligations.   All Debts contracted and Engagements entered into, before the Adoption of this Con-

stitution shall be as valid against the United States under this Constitution, as under the Confederation.

During the Revolutionary War and the years of the Confederation, Congress borrowed large sums. This clause pledged that the new federal government would assume those financial obligations.

Clause 2: Supreme Law of the Land. This Constitution, and the Laws of the United States which shall be made in Pursuance thereof; and all Treaties made, or which shall be made, under the Authority of the United States, shall be the supreme Law of the Land; and the Judges in every State shall be bound thereby, any Thing in the Constitution or Laws of any State to the Contrary notwithstanding.

This is typically called the Supremacy Clause; it declares that federal law takes precedence over all forms of state law. No government, at the local or state level, may make or enforce any law that conflicts with any provision of the Constitution, acts of Congress, treaties, or other rules and regulations issued by the president and his or her subordinates in the executive branch of the federal government.

Clause 3: Oath of Office. The Senators and Representatives before mentioned, and the Members of the several State Legislatures, and all executive and judicial Officers, both of the United States and of the several States, shall be bound by Oath or Affirmation, to support this Constitution; but no religious Test shall ever be required as a Qualification to any Office or public Trust under the United States.

Every federal and state official must take an oath of office promising to support the U.S. Constitution. Religion may not be used as a qualification to serve in any federal office.

Article VII. (Ratification)

The Ratification of the Conventions of nine States shall, be sufficient for the Establishment of this Constitution between the States so ratifying the Same.

Nine states were required to ratify the Constitution. Delaware was the first and New Hampshire the ninth.

Done in Convention by the Unanimous Consent of the States present the Seventeenth Day of September in the Year of our Lord one thousand seven hundred and Eighty seven and of the Independence of the United States of America the Twelfth. In witness whereof we have hereunto subscribed our Names,

Go. WASHINGTON
Presid't. and deputy from Virginia

Attest
WILLIAM JACKSON
Secretary

DELAWARE
Geo. Read
Gunning Bedfordjun
John Dickinson
Richard Basset
Jaco. Broom

MASSACHUSETTS
Nathaniel Gorham
Rufus King

CONNECTICUT
Wm. Saml. Johnson
Roger Sherman

NEW YORK
Alexander Hamilton

NEW JERSEY
Wh. Livingston
David Brearley.
Wm. Paterson.
Jona. Dayton

PENNSYLVANIA
B. Franklin
Thomas Mifflin
Robt. Morris
Geo. Clymer
Thos. FitzSimons
Jared Ingersoll
James Wilson.
Gouv. Morris

NEW HAMPSHIRE
John Langdon
Nicholas Gilman

MARYLAND
James McHenry
Dan of St. Thos. Jenifer
Danl. Carroll.

VIRGINIA
John Blair
James Madison Jr.

NORTH CAROLINA
Wm. Blount
Richd. Dobbs Spaight.
Hu. Williamson

SOUTH CAROLINA
J. Rutledge
Charles Cotesworth
    Pinckney
Charles Pinckney
Pierce Butler.

GEORGIA
William Few
Abr. Baldwin

Articles in addition to, and amendment of the Constitution of the United States of America, proposed by Congress and ratified by the Legislatures of the several states, pursuant to the Fifth Article of the original Constitution.

Amendments to the Constitution of the United States

The Bill of Rights[12]

Amendment I.
Religion, Speech, Assembly, and Politics

Congress shall make no law respecting an establishment of religion, or prohibiting the free exercise thereof; or abridging the freedom of speech, or of the press; or the right of the people peaceably to assembly, and to petition the Government for a redress of grievances.

Congress may not create an official church or enact laws limiting the freedom of religion, speech, the press, assembly, and petition. These guarantees, like the others in the Bill of Rights (the first ten amendments), are not absolute—each may be exercised only with regard to the rights of other persons.

Amendment II.
Militia and the Right to Bear Arms

A well regulated Militia, being necessary to the security of a free State, the right of the people to keep and bear Arms, shall not be infringed.

To protect itself, each state has the right to maintain a volunteer armed force. States and the federal government regulate the possession and use of firearms by individuals.

Amendment III.
The Quartering of Soldiers

No Soldier shall, in time of peace be quartered in any house, without the consent of the Owner, nor in time of war, but in a manner to be prescribed by law.

Before the Revolutionary War, it had been common British practice to quarter soldiers in colonists' homes. Military troops do not have the power to take over private houses during peacetime.

---

[12]On September 25, 1789, Congress transmitted to the state legislatures twelve proposed amendments, two of which, having to do with Congressional representation and Congressional pay, were not adopted. The remaining ten amendments became the Bill of Rights.

Amendment IV.
Searches and Seizures

The right of the people to be secure in their persons, houses, papers, and effects, against unreasonable searches and seizures, shall not be violated, and no Warrants shall issue, but upon probable cause, supported by Oath or affirmation, and particularly describing the place to be searched, and the persons or things to be seized.

Here the word warrant means "justification" and refers to a document issued by a magistrate or judge indicating the name, address, and possible offense committed. Anyone asking for the warrant, such as a police officer, must be able to convince the magistrate or judge that an offense probably has been committed.

Amendment V.
Grand Juries, Self-incrimination, Double Jeopardy, Due Process, and Eminent Domain

No person shall be held to answer for a capital, or otherwise infamous crime, unless on a presentment or indictment of a Grand Jury, except in cases arising in the land or naval forces, or in the Militia, when in actual service in time of War or public danger; nor shall any person be subject for the same offence to be twice put in jeopardy of life or limb; nor shall be compelled in any criminal case to be a witness against himself, nor be deprived of life, liberty, or property, without due process of law; nor shall private property be taken for public use, without just compensation.

There are two types of juries. A grand jury considers physical evidence and the testimony of witnesses, and decides whether there is sufficient reason to bring a case to trial. A petit jury hears the case at trial and decides it. "For the same offence to be twice put in jeopardy of life or limb" means to be tried twice for the same crime. A person may not be tried for the same crime twice or forced to give evidence against herself or himself. No person's right to life, liberty, or property may be taken away except by lawful means, called the due process of law. Private property taken for use in public purposes must be paid for by the government.

Amendment VI.
Criminal Court Procedures

In all criminal prosecutions, the accused shall enjoy the right to a speedy and public trial, by an impartial jury of the State and district wherein the crime shall have been committed, which district shall have been previously ascertained by law, and to be informed of the nature and cause of the accusation; to be confronted with the witnesses against him; to have compulsory process for obtaining witnesses in his favor, and to have the assistance of counsel for his defence.

Any person accused of a crime has the right to a fair and public trial by a jury in the state in which the crime took place. The charges against that person must be so indicated. Any accused person has the right to a lawyer to defend him or her and to question those who testify against him or her, as well as the right to call people to speak in his or her favor at trial.

Amendment VII.
Trial by Jury in Civil Cases

In Suits at common law, where the value in controversy shall exceed twenty dollars, the right of trial by jury shall be preserved, and no fact tried by jury, shall be otherwise re-examined in any Court of the United States, than according to the rules of the common law.

A jury trial may be requested by either party in a dispute in any case involving more than $20. If both parties agree to a trial by a judge without a jury, the right to a jury trial may be put aside.

Amendment VIII.
Bail, Cruel and Unusual Punishment

Excessive bail shall not be required, nor excessive fines imposed, nor cruel and unusual punishments inflicted.

Bail is that amount of money that a person accused of a crime may be required to deposit with the court as a guarantee that she or he will appear in court when requested. The amount of bail required or the fine imposed as punishment for a crime must be reasonable compared with the seriousness of the crime involved. Any punishment judged to be too harsh or too severe for a crime shall be prohibited.

Amendment IX.
The Rights Retained by the People

The enumeration in the Constitution, of certain rights, shall not be construed to deny or disparage others retained by the people.

Many civil rights that are not explicitly enumerated in the Constitution are still hailed by the people.

Amendment X.
Reserved Powers of the States

The powers not delegated to the United States by the Constitution, nor prohibited by it to the States, are reserved to the States respectively, or to the people.

Those powers not delegated by the Constitution to the federal government or expressly denied to the states belong to the states and to the people. This clause in essence allows the states to pass laws under its "police powers."

Amendment XI
(Ratified on February 7, 1795).
Suits Against States

The Judicial power of the United States shall not be construed to extend to any suit in law or equity, commenced or prosecuted against one of the United States by Citizens of another State, or by Citizens or Subjects of any Foreign State.

This amendment has been interpreted to mean that a state cannot be sued in federal court by one of its citizens, by a citizen of another state, or by a foreign country.

Amendment XII
(Ratified on June 15, 1804).
Election of the President

The Electors shall meet in their respective states, and vote by ballot for President and Vice-President, one of whom, at least, shall not be an inhabitant of the same State with themselves; they shall name in their ballots the person voted for as President, and in distinct ballots the person voted for as Vice-President, and they shall make distinct lists of all persons voted for as President, and of all persons voted for as Vice-President, and of the number of votes for each, which lists they shall sign and certify, and transmit sealed to the seat of the government of the United States, directed to the President of the Senate;—The President of the Senate shall, in the presence of the Senate and House of Representatives, open all the certificates and the votes shall then be counted;—The person having the greatest number of votes for President, shall be the President, if such number be a majority of the whole number of Electors appointed; and if no person have such majority, then from the persons having the highest numbers not exceeding three on the list of those voted for as President, the House of Representatives shall choose immediately, by ballot, the President. But in choosing the President, the votes shall be taken by States, the representation from each State having one vote; a quorum for this purpose shall consist of a member or members from two-thirds of the States, and a majority of all States shall be necessary to a choice. [And if the House of Representatives shall not choose a President whenever the right of choice shall devolve upon them, before the fourth day of March next following, then the Vice-President shall act as President, as in the case of the death or other constitutional disability of the President.][13]—The person having the greatest number of votes as Vice-President, shall be the Vice-President, if such number be a majority of the whole number of Electors appointed, and if no person have a majority, then from the two highest numbers on the list, the Senate shall choose the Vice President; a quorum for the purpose shall consist of two-thirds of the whole number of Senators, and a majority of the whole number shall be necessary to a choice. But no person constitutionally ineligible to the office of President shall be eligible to that of Vice-President of the United States.

The original procedure set out for the election of president and vice-president in Article II, Section 1, resulted in a tie in 1800 between Thomas Jefferson and Aaron Burr. It was not until the next year that the House of Representatives chose Jefferson to be president. This amendment changed the procedure by providing for separate ballots for president and vice-president.

Amendment XIII
(Ratified on December 6, 1865).
Prohibition of Slavery

Section 1.
Neither slavery nor involuntary servitude, except as a punishment for crime whereof the party shall have been duly convicted, shall exist within the United States, or any place subject to their jurisdiction.

Some slaves had been freed during the Civil War. This amendment freed the others and abolished slavery.

Section 2.
Congress shall have power to enforce this article by appropriate legislation.

---

[13]Changed by the Twentieth Amendment.

Amendment XIV
(Ratified on July 9, 1868).
Citizenship, Due Process, and Equal
Protection of the Laws

Section 1.
All persons born or naturalized in the United States, and subject to the jurisdiction thereof, are citizens of the United States and of the State wherein they reside. No State shall make or enforce any law which shall abridge the privileges or immunities of citizens of the United States; nor shall any State deprive any person of life, liberty, or property, without due process of law; nor deny to any person within its jurisdiction the equal protection of the laws.

Under this provision, states cannot make or enforce laws that take away rights given to all citizens by the federal government. States cannot act unfairly or arbitrarily toward, or discriminate against, any person.

Section 2.
Representatives shall be apportioned among the several States according to their respective numbers, counting the whole number of persons in each State, excluding Indians not taxed. But when the right to vote at any election for the choice of electors for President and Vice President of the United States, Representatives in Congress, the Executive and Judicial officers of a State, or the members of the Legislature thereof, is denied to any of the male inhabitants of such State, being [twenty-one][14] years of age, and citizens of the United States, or in any way abridged, except for participation in rebellion, or other crime, the basis of representation therein shall be reduced in the proportion which the number of such male citizens shall bear to the whole number of male citizens twenty-one years of age in such State.

Section 3.
No person shall be a Senator or Representative in Congress, or elector of President and Vice President, or hold any office, civil or military, under the United States, or under any State, who having previously taken an oath, as a member of Congress, or as an officer of the United States, or as a member of any State legislature, or as an executive or judicial officer of any State, to support the Constitution of the United States, shall have engaged in insurrection or rebellion against the same, or given aid or comfort to the enemies thereof. But Congress may by a vote of two-thirds of each House, remove such disability.

---

[14]Changed by the Twenty-sixth Amendment.

Section 4.
The validity of the public debt of the United States, authorized by law, including debts incurred for payment of pensions and bounties for services in suppressing insurrection or rebellion, shall not be questioned. But neither the United States nor any State shall assume or pay any debt or obligation incurred in aid of insurrection or rebellion against the United States, or any claim for the loss or emancipation of any slave, but all such debts, obligations and claims shall be held illegal and void.

Section 5.
The Congress shall have power to enforce, by appropriate legislation, the provisions of this article.

Amendment XV
(Ratified on February 3, 1870).
The Right to Vote

Section 1.
The right of citizens of the United States to vote shall not be denied or abridged by the United States or by any State on account of race, color, or previous condition of servitude.

Section 2.
The Congress shall have power to enforce this article by appropriate legislation.

Amendment XVI
(Ratified on February 3, 1913).
Income Taxes

The Congress shall have power to lay and collect taxes on incomes, from whatever source derived, without apportionment among the several States, and without regard to any census or enumeration.

Amendment XVII
(Ratified on April 8, 1913).
The Popular Election of Senators

The Senate of the United States shall be composed of two Senators from each State, elected by the people thereof, for six years; and each Senator shall have one vote. The electors in each State shall have the qualifications requisite for electors of the most numerous branch of the State legislatures.

When vacancies happen in the representation of any State in the Senate, the executive authority of such State shall issue writs of election to fill such vacancies: *Provided*, That the legislature of any State may empower the executive thereof to make temporary appointments until the people fill the vacancies by election as the legislature may direct.

This amendment shall not be so construed as to affect the election or term of any Senator chosen before it becomes valid as part of the Constitution.

Amendment XVIII
(Ratified on January 16, 1919).
Prohibition.

Section 1.
After one year from the ratification of this article the manufacture, sale, or transportation of intoxicating liquors within, the importation thereof into, or the exportation thereof from the United States and all territory subject to the jurisdiction thereof for beverage purposes is hereby prohibited.

Section 2.
The Congress and the several States shall have concurrent power to enforce this article by appropriate legislation.

Section 3.
This article shall be inoperative unless it shall have been ratified as an amendment to the Constitution by the legislatures of the several States, as provided in the Constitution,

within seven years from the date of the submission hereof to the States by the Congress.[15]

This amendment made it illegal to manufacture, sell, and transport alcoholic beverages in the United States. It was ended by the Twenty-first Amendment.

Amendment XIX
(Ratified on August 18, 1920).
Women's Right to Vote.

The right of citizens of the United States to vote shall not be denied or abridged by the United States or by any State on account of sex.

Congress shall have power to enforce this article by appropriate legislation.

Women were given the right to vote by this amendment, and Congress was given the power to enforce this right.

Amendment XX
(Ratified on January 23, 1933).
The Lame Duck Amendment

Section 1.
The terms of the President and Vice President shall end at noon on the 20th day of January, and the terms of Senators and Representatives at noon on the 3d day of January, of the years in which such terms would have ended if this article had not been ratified; and the terms of their successors shall then begin.

This amendment modified Article I, Section 4, Clause 2, and other provisions relating to the president in the Twelfth Amendment. The taking of the Oath of Office was moved from March 4 to January 20.

Section 2.
The Congress shall assemble at least once in every year, and such meeting shall begin at noon on the 3d day of January, unless they shall by law appoint a different day.

Congress changed the beginning of its term to January 3. The reason the Twentieth Amendment is called the Lame Duck Amendment is because it shortens the time between when a

---

[15]The Eighteenth Amendment was repealed by the Twenty-first Amendment.

member of Congress is defeated for reelection and when he or she leaves office.

Section 3.
If, at the time fixed for the beginning of the term of the President, the President elect shall have died, the Vice President elect shall become President. If a President shall not have been chosen before the time fixed for the beginning of his term, or if the President elect shall have failed to qualify, then the Vice President elect shall act as President until a President shall have qualified; and the Congress may by law provide for the case wherein neither a President elect nor a Vice President elect shall have qualified, declaring who shall then act as President, or the manner in which one who is to act shall be selected, and such person shall act accordingly until a President or Vice President shall have qualified.

This part of the amendment deals with problem areas left ambiguous by Article II and the Twelfth Amendment. If the president dies before January 20 or fails to qualify for office, the presidency is to be filled in the order given in this section.

Section 4.
The Congress may by law provide for the case of the death of any of the persons from whom the House of Representatives may choose a President whenever the rights of choice shall have devolved upon them, and for the case of the death of any of the persons from whom the Senate may choose a Vice President whenever the right of choice shall have devolved upon them.

Congress has never created legislation subsequent to this section.

Section 5.
Sections 1 and 2 shall take effect on the 15th day of October following the ratification of this article.

Section 6.
This article shall be inoperative unless it shall have been ratified as an amendment to the Constitution by the legislatures of three-fourths of the several States within seven years from the date of its submission.

Amendment XXI
(Ratified on December 5, 1933).
The Repeal of Prohibition.

Section 1.
The eighteenth article of amendment to the Constitution of the United States is hereby repealed.

Section 2.
The transportation or importation into any State, Territory, or possession of the United States for delivery or use therein of intoxicating liquors, in violation of the laws thereof, is hereby prohibited.

Section 3.
This article shall be inoperative unless it shall have been ratified as an amendment to the Constitution by conventions in the several States, as provided in the Constitution, within seven years from the date of the submission hereof to the States by the Congress.

The amendment repealed the Eighteenth Amendment but did not make alcoholic beverages legal everywhere. Rather, they remained illegal in any state that so designated them. Many such "dry" states existed for a number of years after 1933. Today, there are still "dry" counties within the United States, in which alcoholic beverages are illegal.

Amendment XXII
(Ratified on February 27, 1951).
Limitation of Presidential Terms.

Section 1.
No person shall be elected to the office of the President more than twice, and no person who has held the office of President, or acted as President, for more than two years of a term to which some other person was elected President shall be elected to the office of President more than once. But this Article shall not apply to any person holding the office of President when this Article was proposed by the Congress, and shall not prevent any person who may be holding the office of President, or acting as President, during the term within which this Article becomes operative from holding the office of President or acting as President during the remainder of such term.

Section 2.
This article shall be inoperative unless it shall have been ratified as an amendment to the Constitution by the legislatures of three-fourths of the several States within seven years from the date of its submission to the States by the Congress.

No president may serve more than two elected terms. If, however, a president has succeeded to the office after the halfway point of a term in which another president was originally elected, then that president may serve for more than eight years, but not to exceed ten years.

Amendment XXIII
(Ratified on March 29, 1961).
Presidential Electors for
the District of Columbia.

Section 1.
The District constituting the seat of Government of the United States shall appoint in such manner as the Congress may direct:

A number of electors of President and Vice President equal to the whole number of Senators and Representatives in Congress to which the District would be entitled if it were a State, but in no event more than the least populous State; they shall be in addition to those appointed by the States, but they shall be considered, for the purposes of the election of President and Vice President, to be electors appointed by a State; and they shall meet in the District and perform such duties as provided by the twelfth article of amendment.

Section 2.
The Congress shall have power to enforce this article by appropriate legislation.

Citizens living in the District of Columbia have the right to vote in elections for president and vice-president. The District of Columbia has three presidential electors, whereas before this amendment it had none.

Amendment XXIV
(Ratified on January 23, 1964).
The Anti-Poll Tax Amendment.

Section 1.
The right of citizens of the United States to vote in any primary or other election for President or Vice President, for electors for President or Vice President, or for Senator or Representative in Congress, shall not be denied or abridged by the United States, or any State by reason of failure to pay any poll tax or other tax.

Section 2.
The Congress shall have power to enforce this article by appropriate legislation.

No government shall require a person to pay a poll tax in order to vote in any federal election.

Amendment XXV
(Ratified on February 10, 1967).
A Presidential Disability and Vice Presidential Vacancies.

Section 1.
In case of the removal of the President from office or of his death or resignation, the Vice President shall become President.

Whenever a president dies or resigns from office, the vice-president becomes president.

Section 2.
Whenever there is a vacancy in the office of the Vice President, the President shall nominate a Vice President who shall take office upon confirmation by a majority vote of both Houses of Congress.

Whenever the office of the vice-presidency becomes vacant, the president may appoint someone to fill this office, provided Congress consents.

Section 3.
Whenever the President transmits to the President pro tempore of the Senate and the Speaker of the House of Representatives his written declaration that he is unable to discharge the powers and duties of his office, and until he transmits to them a written declaration to the contrary, such powers and duties shall be discharged by the Vice President as Acting President.

Whenever the president believes she or he is unable to carry out the duties of the office, she or he shall so indicate to Congress in writing. The vice-president then acts as president until the president declares that she or he is again able to properly carry out the duties of the office.

Section 4.
Whenever the Vice President and a majority of either the principal officers of the executive departments or of such other body as Congress may by law provide, transmit to the President pro tempore of the Senate and the Speaker of the House of Representatives their written declaration that the President is unable to discharge the powers and duties of his office, the Vice President shall immediately assume the powers and duties of the office as Acting President.

Thereafter, when the President transmits to the President pro tempore of the Senate and the Speaker of the House of Representatives his written declaration that no inability exists, he shall resume the powers and duties of his office unless the Vice President and a majority of either the principal officers of the executive department or of such other body as Congress may by law provide, transmit within four days to the President pro tempore of the Senate and the Speaker of the House of Representatives their written declaration that the President is unable to discharge the powers and duties of his office. Thereupon Congress shall decide the issue, assembling within forty-eight hours for that purpose if not in session. If the Congress, within twenty-one days after receipt of the latter written declaration, or, if Congress is not in session, within twenty-one days after Congress is required to assemble, determines by two-thirds vote of both Houses that the President is unable to discharge the powers and duties of his office, the Vice President shall continue to discharge the same as Acting President; otherwise, the President shall resume the powers and duties of his office.

Whenever the vice president and a majority of the members of the Cabinet believe that the president cannot carry out his or her duties, they shall so indicate in writing to Congress. The vice president shall then act as president. When the president believes that she or he is able to carry out her or his duties again, she or he shall so indicate to the Congress. If, though, the vice president and a majority of the Cabinet do not agree, Congress must decide by a two-thirds vote within three weeks who shall act as president.

Amendment XXVI
(Ratified on July 1, 1971).
The Eighteen Year Old Vote.

Section 1.
The right of citizens of the United States, who are eighteen years of age or older, to vote shall not be denied or abridged by the United States or by any State on account of age.

No one over eighteen years of age can be denied the right to vote in federal or state elections by virtue of age.

Section 2.
The Congress shall have power to enforce this article by appropriate legislation.

Amendment XXVII
(Ratified on May 7, 1992).
Congressional Compensation Changes.

No law, varying the compensation for the services of the Senators and Representatives, shall take effect, until an election of Representatives shall have intervened.

An intervening congressional election is required before any changes in congressional compensation may be instituted.

The Magna Carta (1215)

The Magna Carta is the "great charter" of English civil liberties. King John signed it at Runnymede on June 15, 1215. His barons forced him to do so. The document, which is excerpted below, consists of sixty-three clauses, which protect the rights of the church, the feudal lords, the lords' subtenants, and the merchants. Royal privileges, the administration of justice, and the behavior of royal officials are also covered in the document.

John, by the grace of God, king of England, lord of Ireland, duke of Normandy and Aquitaine, count of Anjou, to all his archbishops, bishops, abbots, earls, barons, justiciars, foresters, sheriffs, stewards, servants, and all bailiffs and faithful men, health. * * *

Chapter 1

First, we grant to God, and by this our present charter we confirm, for us and our heirs forever, that the English church be free, and have its rights whole and its liberties unimpaired; * * * We have granted to all free men of our realm, for ourself and our heirs forever, all these underwritten liberties to have and to hold, for themselves and their heirs, from us and our heirs.

Chapter 20

A free man shall not be amerced for a small offense unless according to the measure of the offense, and for a great offense he shall be amerced according to the greatness of the offense, saving his tenement, and the merchant in the same manner, saving his merchandise, and the villein shall be amerced in the same manner, saving his tools of husbandry, if they fall into our mercy, and none of the aforenamed mercies shall be imposed except by the oath of reputable men of the vicinage.

Chapter 21

Earls and barons shall not be amerced but by their equals, and only according to the measure of the offense.

Chapter 28

No constable, or other bailiff of ours, shall take the corn or chattels of anyone, unless he forthwith pays money for them, or can have any respite by the good will of the seller.

Chapter 30

No sheriff or bailiff of ours, or any other, shall take horses and carts of any free man for carrying, except by the will of the free man.[1]

Chapter 31

Neither we nor our bailiffs will take any wood for our castles, or other of our works, except by consent of the man whose wood it is.

---

1. In 1216 the chapter was modified to say that the horses and carts should not be taken unless the owner received a specified amount of money. In 1217 a chapter was inserted that prohibited bailiffs from taking carts from the demesne of a cleric, a knight, or a lady. In 1225 chapters 30 and 31 from the Charter of 1215 and the new chapter were combined into a single chapter.

Chapter 32

We will not hold the lands of those who are convict of felony, except for one year and one day, and then the lands shall be returned to the lords of the fees.

Chapter 38

No bailiff in future shall put anyone to law by his mere word, without trustworthy witnesses brought forward for it.

Chapter 39

No free man shall be seized, or imprisoned, or disseised, or outlawed, or exiled, or injured in any way, nor will we enter on him or send against him except by the lawful judgment of his peers, or by the law of the land.

Chapter 40

We will sell to no one, or deny to no one, or put off right or justice.

Chapter 41

All merchants shall have safe conduct and security to go out of England or come into England, and to stay in, and go through England, both by land and water, for buying or selling, without any evil tolls, by old and right customs, except in time of war; and if they be of the land at war against us, and if such shall be found in our land, at the beginning of war, they shall be attached without loss of person or property, until it be known by us or our chief justiciar how the merchants of our land are treated who are found then in the land at war with us; and if ours be safe there, others shall be safe here.[2]

Chapter 46

All barons who have founded abbeys, whence they have charters of the kings of England, or ancient tenure, shall have their custody while vacant, as they ought to have it.

Chapter 53

We will have the same respite, and in the same way, about exhibiting justice of deforesting or maintaining the forests, which Henry our father, or Richard our brother afforested, and of the wardship of the lands which are of another's fee, of which thing we have hitherto had the wardship, by reason of the fee, because someone held of us by military service, and of the abbeys which were founded on the fee of another than our own, in which the lord of the fee says he has the right; and when we return, or if we stay from our journey, we will afford full justice to those who complain of these things.

Chapter 54

No one shall be seized or imprisoned for the appeal of a woman about the death of any other man but her husband.

Chapter 60

All these aforesaid customs and liberties which we have granted to be held in our realm, as far as belongs to us, towards our own, all in our realm, both clergy and lay, shall observe, as far as belongs to them, towards their own.

Chapter 63

Wherefore we will and firmly order that the English church should be free, and that the men of our realm should have and hold all the aforenamed liberties, rights, and grants, well and in peace, freely and quietly, fully and completely, for them and their heirs, from us and our heirs, in all things and places, forever, as is aforesaid. It is sworn both by us, and on the part of the barons, that all these aforesaid shall be kept in good faith and without ill meaning. Witnesses, the above-named and many others. Given by our hand, in the meadow which is called Runnymede, between Windsor and Staines, on the fifteenth day of June, in the seventeenth year of our reign.

Source: William Stubbs, ed., *A Translation of Such Documents as Are Unpublished in Dr. Stubbs' Select Charters* (n.d.), pp. 187–197.

---

2. In 1216 the words "unless formerly they have been publicly prohibited" were inserted after "All merchants."

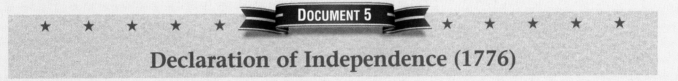

DOCUMENT 4

Mayflower Compact (1620)

The Mayflower Compact was entered into by the adult male Pilgrims in the cabin of the Mayflower on November 11, 1620. The forty-one men who signed it agreed to establish a preliminary government. The compact bound the signers to a government by majority rule during the time they knew they had to wait for a royal charter. Many view this compact as the first step in the development of democracy in America.

In the name of God, Amen. We, whose names are underwritten, the loyal subjects of our dread sovereign lord King James, by the grace of God, of Great Britain, France, and Ireland, king, defender of the faith, &c. Having undertaken for the glory of God, and advancement of the Christian faith, and the honor of our king and country, a voyage to plant the first colony in the northern parts of Virginia, do by these presents, solemnly and mutually, in the presence of God and one another, covenant and combine ourselves together into a civil body politic, for our better ordering and preservation and furtherance of the ends aforesaid; and by virtue hereof do enact, constitute, and frame such just and equal laws, ordinances, acts, constitutions, and officers, from time to time, as shall be thought most meet and convenient for the general good of the colony; unto which we promise all due submission and obedience. In witness whereof we have hereunto subscribed our names at Cape Cod the eleventh of November, in the reign of our sovereign lord King James, of England, France, and Ireland, the eighteenth, and of Scotland, the fifty-fourth, anno Domini, 1620.

Mr. John Carver	Digery Priest
Mr. William Bradford	Thomas Williams
Mr. Edward Winslow	Gilbert Winslow
Mr. William Brewster	Edmund Margesson
Isaac Allerton	Peter Brown
Miles Standish	Richard Bitteridge
John Alden	George Soule
John Turner	Edward Tilly
Francis Eaton	John Tilly
James Chilton	Francis Cooke
John Craxton	Thomas Rogers
John Billington	Thomas Tinker
Joses Fletcher	John Ridgdale
John Goodman	Edward Fuller
Mr. Samuel Fuller	Richard Clark
Mr. Christopher Martin	Richard Gardiner
Mr. William Mullins	Mr. John Allerton
Mr. William White	Thomas English
Mr. Richard Warren	Edward Doten
John Howland	Edward Liester
Mr. Steven Hopkins	

Source: Ben Perley Poore, ed., *The Federal and State Constitutions, Colonial Charters, and Other Organic Laws of the United States*, vol. 1 (1878), p. 931.

DOCUMENT 5

Declaration of Independence (1776)

The Declaration of Independence was adopted by the Second Continental Congress on July 4, 1776. It was the formal mechanism by which the thirteen American colonies justified their separation from Britain. The formal signing of the declaration took place on August 2, 1776.

IN CONGRESS, JULY 4, 1776
THE UNANIMOUS DECLARATION of the thirteen united STATES OF AMERICA

WHEN in the Course of human events, it becomes necessary for one people to dissolve the political bands which have connected them with another, and to assume among the powers of the earth, the separate and equal station to which the Laws of Nature and of Nature's God entitle them, a decent respect to the opinions of mankind requires that they should declare the causes which impel them to the separation.

We hold these truths to be self-evident, that all men are created equal, that they are endowed by their Creator with certain unalienable Rights, that among these are Life, Liberty and the pursuit of Happiness. That to secure these rights, Governments are instituted among Men, deriving their just powers from the consent of the governed; That whenever any Form of Government becomes destructive of these ends, it is the Right of the People to alter or to abolish it, and to institute new Government, laying its foundation on such principles and organizing its powers in such form, as to them shall seem most likely to effect their Safety and Happiness. Prudence, indeed, will dictate that Governments long established should not be changed for light and transient causes; and accordingly all experience hath shown, that mankind are more disposed to suffer, while evils are sufferable, than to right themselves by abolishing the forms to which they are accustomed. But when a long train of abuses and usurpations, pursuing invariably the same Object evinces a design to reduce them under absolute Despotism, it is their right, it is their duty, to throw off such Government, and to provide new Guards for their future security.

Such has been the patient sufferance of these Colonies; and such is now the necessity which constrains them to alter their former Systems of Government. The history of the present King of Great Britain is a history of repeated injuries and usurpations, all having in direct object the establishment of an absolute Tyranny over these States. To prove this, let Facts be submitted to a candid world.

He has refused his Assent to Laws, the most wholesome and necessary for the public good.

He has forbidden his Governors to pass Laws of immediate and pressing importance, unless suspended in their operation till his Assent should be obtained; and when so suspended, he has utterly neglected to attend to them.

He has refused to pass other Laws for the accommodation of large districts of people, unless those people would relinquish the right of Representation in the Legislature, a right inestimable to them and formidable to tyrants only.

He has called together legislative bodies at places unusual, uncomfortable, and distant from the depository or their public records, for the sole purpose of fatiguing them into compliance with his measures.

He has dissolved Representative Houses repeatedly, for opposing with manly firmness his invasions on the rights of the people.

He has refused for a long time, after such dissolutions, to cause others to be elected; whereby the Legislative powers, incapable of Annihilation, have returned to the People at large for their exercise; the State remaining in the mean time exposed to all the dangers of invasion from without, and convulsions within.

He has endeavored to prevent the population of these States; for that purpose obstructing the Laws for Naturalization of Foreigners; refusing to pass others to encourage their migration hither, and raising the conditions of new Appropriations of Lands.

He has obstructed the Administration of Justice, by refusing his Assent to Laws for establishing Judiciary powers.

He has made Judges dependent on his Will alone, for the tenure of their offices, and the amount and payment of their salaries.

He has erected a multitude of New Offices, and sent hither swarms of Officers to harrass our people, and eat out their substance.

He has kept among us, in times of peace, Standing Armies, without the Consent of our legislatures.

He has affected to render the Military independent of and superior to the Civil power.

He has combined with others to subject us to a jurisdiction foreign to our constitution, and unacknowledged by our laws; giving his Assent to their Acts of pretended Legislation:

For quartering large bodies of armed troops among us;

For protecting them, by a mock Trial, from punishment for any Murders which they should commit on the Inhabitants of these States;

For cutting off our Trade with all parts of the world;

For imposing Taxes on us without our Consent;

For depriving us in many cases, of the benefits of Trial by Jury;

For transporting us beyond Seas to be tried for pretended offences;

For abolishing the free System of English Laws in a neighbouring Province, establishing therein an Arbitrary government, and enlarging its Boundaries so as to render it at once an example and fit instrument for introducing the same absolute rule into these Colonies;

For taking away our Charters, abolishing our most valuable Laws, and altering fundamentally the Forms of our Governments;

For suspending our own Legislatures, and declaring themselves invested with power to legislate for us in all cases whatsoever.

He has abdicated Government here, by declaring us out of his Protection and waging War against us.

He has plundered our seas, ravaged our Coasts, burnt our towns, and destroyed the lives of our people.

He is at this time transporting large Armies of foreign Mercenaries to complete the works of death, desolation and tyranny, already begun with circumstances of Cruelty and perfidy scarcely paralleled in the most barbarous ages, and totally unworthy the Head of a civilized nation.

He has constrained our fellow Citizens taken Captive on the high Seas to bear Arms against their Country, to become the executioners of their friends and Brethren, or to fall themselves by their Hands.

He has excited domestic insurrections amongst us, and has endeavored to bring on the inhabitants of our frontiers, the merciless Indian Savages, whose known rule of warfare, is an undistinguished destruction of all ages, sexes and conditions.

In every state of these Oppressions We have Petitioned for Redress in the most humble terms. Our repeated Petitions have been answered only by repeated injury. A Prince, whose character is thus marked by every act which may define a Tyrant, is unfit to be the ruler of a free people.

Nor have We been wanting in attentions to our British brethren. We have warned them from time to time of attempts by their legislature to extend an unwarrantable jurisdiction over us. We have reminded them of the circumstances of our emigration and settlement here. We have appealed to their native justice and magnanimity, and we have conjured them by the ties of our common kindred to disavow these usurpations, which would inevitably interrupt our connections and correspondence. They too have been deaf to the voice of justice and consanguinity. We must, therefore, acquiesce in the necessity, which denounces our Separation, and hold them, as we hold the rest of mankind, Enemies in War, in Peace Friends.—

WE, THEREFORE, the REPRESENTATIVES of the UNITED STATES OF AMERICA, in General Congress, Assembled, appealing to the Supreme Judge of the world for the rectitude of our intentions, do, in the Name, and by Authority of the good People of these Colonies, solemnly publish and declare, That these United Colonies are, and of Right ought to be FREE AND INDEPENDENT STATES; that they are Absolved from all Allegiance to the British Crown, and that all political connection between them and the State of Great Britain, is and ought to be totally dissolved; and that as Free and Independent States, they have full Power to levy War, conclude Peace, contract Alliances, establish Commerce, and to do all other Acts and Things which Independent States may of right do. And for the support of this Declaration, with a firm reliance on the protection of Divine Providence, we mutually pledge to each other our Lives, our Fortunes and our sacred Honor.

John Hancock	Benj. Franklin
Button Gwinnett	John Morton
Lyman Hall	Geo. Clymer
Geo. Walton	Jas. Smith
Benj. Harrison	Geo. Taylor
Thos. Nelson, Jr.	James Wilson
Francis Lightfoot Lee	Geo. Ross
Carter Braxton	Caesar Rodney
Lewis Morris	Geo. Read
Richd. Stockton	Tho. M: Kean
Jno. Witherspoon	Wm. Floyd
Fras. Hopkinson	Phil. Livingston
Wm. Hooper	Frans. Lewis
Joseph Hewes	John Hart
John Penn	Abra. Clark
Edward Rutledge	Josiah Bartlett
Thos. Heyward, Jr.	Wm. Whipple
Thomas Lynch, Jr.	Saml. Adams
Arthur Middleton	John Adams
Samuel Chase	Robt. Treat Paine
Wm. Paca	Elbridge Gerry
Thos. Stone	Step. Hopkins
Charles Carroll of Carrollton	William Ellery
George Wythe	Roger Sherman
Richard Henry Lee	Sam. Huntington
Th. Jefferson	Wm. Williams
Robt. Morris	Oliver Wolcott
Benjamin Rush	Matthew Thornton

★ ★ ★ ★ ★ **DOCUMENT 6** ★ ★ ★ ★ ★

Articles of Confederation (1781–1789)

The Articles of Confederation were in effect the first constitution of the United States, formally joining all the colonies under a centralized government. They were submitted to the Continental Congress in 1776, adopted the next year, but not ratified by all the states until 1781. They remained in force until the ratification of the U.S. Constitution in 1788.

To all to whom these Presents shall come, we the undersigned Delegates of the States affixed to our Names send greeting

Whereas the Delegates of the United States of America in Congress assembled did on the fifteenth day of November in the Year of our Lord One Thousand Seven Hundred and

Seventy-seven, and in the Second Year of the Independence of America agree to certain articles of Confederation and perpetual Union between the States of Newhampshire, Massachusetts-bay, Rhode-island, and Providence Plantations, Connecticut, New York, New Jersey, Pennsylvania, Delaware, Maryland, Virginia, North-Carolina, South-Carolina and Georgia in the Words following, viz.

Articles of Confederation and perpetual Union between the States of Newhampshire, Massachusetts-bay, Rhodeisland and Providence Plantations, Connecticut, New-York, New-Jersey, Pennsylvania, Delaware, Maryland, Virginia, North-Carolina, South-Carolina and Georgia.

Article I

The stile of this confederacy shall be "The United States of America."

Article II

Each State retains its sovereignty, freedom and independence, and every power, jurisdiction and right, which is not by this confederation expressly delegated to the United States, in Congress assembled.

Article III

The said States hereby severally enter into a firm league of friendship with each other, for their common defense, the security of their liberties, and their mutual and general welfare, binding themselves to assist each other, against all force offered to, or attacks made upon them, or any of them, on account of religion, sovereignty trade or any other pretence whatever.

Article IV

The better to secure and perpetuate mutual friendship and intercourse among the people of the different States in this Union, the free inhabitants of each of these States, paupers, vagabonds and fugitives from justice excepted, shall be entitled to all privileges and immunities of free citizens in the several States; and the people of each State shall have free ingress and regress to and from any other State, and shall enjoy therein all the privileges of trade and commerce, subject to the same duties, impositions and restrictions as the inhabitants thereof respectively, provided that such restrictions shall not exceed so far as to prevent the removal of property imported into any State, to any other State of which the owner is an inhabitant; provided also that no imposition, duties or restriction shall be laid by any State, on the property of the United States, or either of them.

If any person guilty of, or charged with treason, felony, or other high misdemeanor in any State, shall flee from justice, and be found in any of the United States, he shall upon demand of the Governor or Executive power, of the State from which he fled, be delivered up and removed to the State having jurisdiction of his offense.

Full faith and credit shall be given in each of these States to the records, acts and judicial proceedings to the courts and magistrates of every other State.

Article V

For the more convenient management of the general interests of the United States, delegates shall be annually appointed in such manner as the legislature of each State shall direct, to meet in Congress on the first Monday in November, in every year, with a power reserved to each State, to recall its delegates, or any of them, at any time within the year, and to send others in their stead, for the remainder of the year.

No State shall be represented in Congress by less than two, nor by more than seven members; and no person shall be capable of being a delegate for more than three years in any term of six years; nor shall any person, being a delegate, be capable of holding any office under the United States, for which he, or another for his benefit receives any salary, fees or emolument of any kind.

Each state shall maintain its own delegates in a meeting of the States, and while they act as members of the committee of the States.

In determining questions in the United States, in Congress assembled, each State shall have one vote.

Freedom of speech and debate in Congress shall not be impeached or questioned in any court, or place out of Congress, and the members of Congress shall be protected in their persons from arrests and imprisonments, during the time of their going to and from, and attendance on Congress, except for treason, felony, or breach of the peace.

Article VI

No State without the consent of the United States in Congress assembled, shall send any embassy to, or receive any embassy from, or enter into any conference, agreement, alliance or treaty with any king, prince or state; nor shall any person holding any office or profit or trust under the United States, or any of them, accept of any present, emolument, office or title of any kind whatever from any king, prince or foreign state; nor shall the United States in Congress assembled or any of them, grant any title of nobility.

No two or more States shall enter into any treaty, confederation or alliance whatever between them, without the consent of the United States in Congress assembled, specifying accurately the purposes for which the same is to be entered into, and how long it shall continue.

No State shall lay any imposts or duties, which may interfere with any stipulations in treaties, entered into by the United States in Congress assembled, with any king, prince or state, in pursuance of any treaties already proposed by Congress, to the courts of France and Spain.

No vessels of war shall be kept up in time of peace by any State, except such number only, as shall be deemed necessary by the United States in Congress assembled, for the defence of such State, or its trade; nor shall any body of forces be kept up by any State, in time of peace, except such number only, as in the judgement of the United States, in Congress assembled, shall be deemed requisite to garrison the forts necessary for the defence of such State; but every State shall always keep up a well regulated and disciplined militia, sufficiently armed and accoutered, and shall provide and constantly have ready for use, in public stores, a due number of field pieces and tents, and a proper quantity of arms, ammunition and camp equipage.

No State shall engage in any way without the consent of the United States in Congress assembled, unless such State be actually invaded by enemies, or shall have received certain advice of a resolution being formed by some nation of Indians to invade such State, and the danger is so imminent as not to admit of a delay, till the United States in Congress assembled can be consulted: nor shall any State grant commissions to any ships or vessels of war, nor letters of marque or reprisal, except it be after a declaration of war by the United States in Congress assembled, and then only against the kingdom or state and the subject thereof, against which war has been so declared and under such regulations as shall be established by the United States in Congress assembled, unless such State be infested by pirates, in which case vessels of war may be fitted out for that occasion, and kept so long as the danger shall continue, or until the United States in Congress assembled shall determine otherwise.

Article VII

When land-forces are raised by any State for the common defence, all officers of or under the rank of colonel, shall be appointed by the Legislature of each State respectively by whom such forces shall be raised, or in such manner as such State shall direct, and all vacancies shall be filled up by the State which first made the appointment.

Article VIII

All charges of war, and all other expenses that shall be incurred for the common defence or general welfare, and allowed by the United States in Congress assembled, shall be defrayed out of a common treasury, which shall be supplied by the several States, in proportion to the value of all land within each State, granted to or surveyed for any person, as such land and the buildings and improvements thereon shall be estimated according to such mode as the United States in Congress assembled, shall from time to time direct and appoint.

The taxes for paying that proportion shall be laid and levied by the authority and direction of the Legislatures of the several States within the time agreed upon by the United States in Congress Assembled.

Article IX

The United States in Congress assembled, shall have the sole and exclusive right and power of determining on peace and war, except in the cases mentioned in the sixth article—of sending and receiving ambassadors—entering into treaties and alliances, provided that no treaty of commerce shall be made whereby the legislative power of the respective States shall be restrained from imposing such imposts and duties on foreigners, as their own people are subjected to, or from prohibiting the exportation or importation of any species of goods or commodities whatsoever—of establishing rules for deciding in all cases, what captures on land or water shall be legal, and in what manner prizes taken by land or naval forces in the service of the United States shall be divided or appropriated—of granting letters of marque and reprisal in times of peace—appointing courts for trial of piracies and felonies committed on the high seas and establishing courts for receiving and determining finally appeals in all cases of captures, provided that no member of Congress shall be appointed a judge of any of the said courts.

The United States in Congress assembled shall also be the last resort on appeal in all disputes and differences now subsisting or that hereafter may arise between two or more States concerning boundary, jurisdiction or any other cause whatever; which authority shall always be exercised in the manner following. Whenever the legislative or executive authority or lawful agent of any State in controversy with another shall present a petition to Congress, stating the matter in question and praying for a hearing, notice thereof shall be given by order of Congress to the legislative or executive authority of the other State in controversy, and a day assigned for the appearance of the parties by their lawful agents, who shall then be directed to appoint by joint consent, commissioners or judges to constitute a court for hearing and determining the matter in question: but if they cannot agree, Congress shall name three persons out of each of the United States, and from the list of such persons each party shall alternately strike out one, the petitioners beginning, until the number shall be reduced to thirteen; and from that number not less than seven, nor more than nine names as Congress shall direct, shall, in the presence of Congress be drawn out by lot, and the persons whose names shall be so drawn or any five of them, shall be commissioners or judges, to hear and finally determine the controversy, so always as a major part of the judges who shall hear the cause shall agree in the determination: and if either party shall neglect to attend at the day appointed, without showing reasons, which Congress shall judge sufficient, or being present shall refuse to strike, the Congress shall proceed to nominate three persons out of each State, and the Secretary of Congress shall strike in behalf of such party absent or refusing; and the judgment and sentence of the court to be appointed, in the manner before prescribed, shall be final and conclusive; and if any of the parties shall refuse to submit to the authority of such court, or to appear or defend their claim or cause, the court shall nevertheless proceed to pronounce sentence, or judgment, which shall in like manner be final and decisive, the judgment or sentence and other proceedings being in either case transmitted to Congress, and lodged among the acts of Congress for the security of the parties concerned: provided that every commissioner, before he sits in judgment, shall take an oath to be administered by one of the judges of the supreme court of the State where the cause shall be tried, "well and truly to hear and determine the matter in question, according to the best of his judgment, without favour, affection or hope of reward:" provided also that no State shall be deprived of territory for the benefit of the United States.

All controversies concerning the private right of soil claimed under different grants of two or more States, whose jurisdiction as they may respect such lands, and the States which passed such grants are adjusted, the said grants or either of them being at the same time claimed to have originated antecedent to such settlement of jurisdiction, shall on the petition of either party to the Congress of the United States, be finally determined as near as may be in the same manner as is before prescribed for deciding disputes respecting territorial jurisdiction between different States.

The United States in Congress assembled shall also have the sole and exclusive right and power of regulating the alloy and value of coin struck by their own authority, or by that of the respective States.—fixing the standard of weights and measures throughout the United States.—regulating the trade and managing all affairs with the Indians, not members of any of the States, provided that the legislative right of any State within its own limits be not infringed or violated—establishing and regulating post-offices from one State to another, throughout all the United States, and exacting such postage on the papers passing thro' the same as may be requisite to defray the expenses of the said office—appointing all officers of the land forces, in the service of the United States, excepting regimental officers—appointing all the officers of the naval forces, and commissioning all officers whatever in the service of the United States—making rules for the government and regulation of the said land and naval forces, and directing their operations.

The United States in Congress assembled shall have authority to appoint a committee, to sit in the recess of Congress, to be denominated "a Committee of the States," and to consist of one delegate from each State; and to appoint such other committees and civil officers as may be necessary for managing the general affairs of the United States under their direction—to appoint one of their number to preside, provided that no person be allowed to serve in the office of president more than one year in any term of three years; to ascertain the necessary sums of money to be raised for the service of the United States, and to appropriate and apply the same for defraying the public expenses—to borrow money or emit bills on the credit of the United States transmitting every half year to the respective States an account of the sums of money so borrowed or emitted,—to build and equip a navy—to agree upon the number of land forces, and to make requisitions from each State for its quota, in proportion to the number of white inhabitants in such State; which requisition shall be binding, and thereupon the Legislature of each State shall appoint the regimental officers, raise the men and cloath, arm and equip them in a soldier like manner, at the expense of the United States; and the officers and men so cloathed, armed and equipped shall march to the place appointed, and within the time agreed on by the United States in Congress assembled; but if the United States in Congress assembled shall, on consideration of circumstances judge proper that any State should not raise men, or should raise a smaller number than its quota, and that any other State should raise a greater number of men than the quota thereof, such extra number shall be raised, officered, cloathed, armed and equipped in the same manner as the quota of such State, unless the legislature of such State shall judge that such extra number cannot be safely spared out of the same, in which case they shall raise officer, cloath, arm and equip as many of such extra number as they judge can be safely spared. And the officers and men so cloathed, armed, and equipped, shall march to the place appointed, and within the time agreed on by the United States in Congress assembled.

The United States in Congress assembled shall never engage in a war, nor grant letters of marque and reprisal in time of peace, nor enter into any treaties or alliances, nor coin money, nor regulate the value thereof, nor ascertain the sums and expenses necessary for the defence and welfare of the United States, or any of them, nor emit bills, nor borrow money on the credit of the United States, nor appropriate money, nor agree upon the number of vessels of war, to be built or purchased, or the number of land or sea forces to be raised, nor appoint a commander in chief of the army or navy, unless nine States assent to the same: nor shall a question on any other point, except for adjourning from day to day be determined, unless by the votes of a majority of the United States in Congress assembled.

The Congress of the United States shall have power to adjourn to any time within the year, and to any place within the United States, so that no period of adjournment be for a longer duration than the space of six months, and shall publish the journal of their proceedings monthly, except such parts thereof relating to treaties, alliances or military operations, as in their judgment require secresy; and the yeas and nays of the delegates of each State on any question shall be entered on the journal, when it is desired by any delegate; and the delegates of a State, or any of them, at his or her request shall be furnished with a transcript of the said Journal, except such parts as are above excepted, to lay before the Legislatures of the several States.

Article X

The committee of the States, or any nine of them, shall be authorized to execute in the recess of Congress, such of the powers of Congress as the United States in Congress assembled, by the consent of nine States, shall from time to time think expedient to vest them with; provided that no power be delegated to the said committee, for the exercise of which, by the articles of confederation, the voice of nine States in the Congress of the United States assembled is requisite.

Article XI

Canada acceding to this confederation, and joining in the measures of the United States, shall be admitted into, and entitled to all the advantages of this Union: but no other colony shall be admitted into the same, unless such admission be agreed to by nine States.

Article XII

All bills of credit emitted, monies borrowed and debts contracted by, or under the authority of Congress, before the assembling of the United States, in pursuance of the present confederation, shall be deemed and considered as a charge against the United States, for payment and satisfaction whereof the said United States, and the public faith are hereby solemnly pledged.

Article XIII

Every State shall abide by the determinations of the United States in Congress assembled, on all questions which by this confederation are submitted to them. And the articles of this confederation shall be inviolably observed by every State, and the Union shall be perpetual; nor shall any alteration at any time hereafter be made in any of them; unless such alteration be agreed to in a Congress of the United States, and be afterwards confirmed by the Legislatures of every State.

And whereas it has pleased the Great Governor of the world to incline the hearts of the Legislatures we respectively represent in Congress, to approve of, and to authorize us to ratify the said articles of confederation and perpetual union. Know ye that we the undersigned delegates, by virtue of the power and authority to us given for that purpose, do by these presents, in the name and in behalf of our respective constituents, fully and entirely ratify and confirm each and every of the said articles of confederation and perpetual union, and all and singular the matters and things therein contained: and we do further solemnly plight and engage the faith of our respective constituents, that they shall abide by the determinations of the United States in Congress assembled, on all questions, which by the said confederation are submitted to them. And that the articles thereof shall be inviolably observed by the States we re[s]pectively represent, and that the Union shall be perpetual.

In witness whereof we have hereunto set our hands in Congress.

Done at Philadelphia in the State of Pennsylvania the ninth day of July in the year of our Lord one thousand seven hundred and seventy-eight, and in the third year of the independence of America.

On the part and behalf of the State of New Hampshire

| JOSIAH BARTLETT, | JOHN WENTWORTH, Junr., August 8th, 1778. |

On the part and behalf of the State of Massachusetts Bay

JOHN HANCOCK,	FRANCIS DANA,
SAMUEL ADAMS,	JAMES LOVELL,
ELBRIDGE GERRY,	SAMUEL HOLTEN.

On the part and behalf of the State of Rhode Island and Providence Plantations

WILLIAM ELLERY,   JOHN COLLINS.
HENRY MARCHANT,

On the part and behalf of the State of Connecticut

ROGER SHERMAN,   TITUS HOSMER,
SAMUEL HUNTINGTON, ANDREW ADAMS.
OLIVER WOLCOTT,

On the part and behalf of the State of New York

JAS. DUANE,   WM. DUER,
FRA. LEWIS,   GOUV. MORRIS.

On the part and in behalf of the State of New Jersey,
Novr. 26, 1778

JNO. WITHERSPOON,   NATHL. SCUDDER.

On the part and behalf of the State of Pennsylvania

ROBT. MORRIS,   WILLIAM CLINGAN,
DANIEL ROBERDEAU, JOSEPH REED,
JONA. BAYARD SMITH, 22d July, 1778.

On the part & behalf of the State of Delaware

THO. M'KEAN,   NICHOLAS VAN DYKE.
Feby. 12, 1779.
JOHN DICKINSON,
May 5th, 1779

On the part and behalf of the State of Maryland

JOHN HANSON,   DANIEL CARROLL,
March 1, 1781.   Mar. 1, 1781.

On the part and behalf of the State of Virginia

RICHARD HENRY LEE, JNO. HARVIE,
JOHN BANISTER,   FRANCIS LIGHTFOOT
THOMAS ADAMS,   LEE.

On the part and behalf of the State of No. Carolina

JOHN PENN,   JNO. WILLIAMS.
 July 21st, 1778.
CORNS. HARNETT,
JNO. WILLIAMS.

On the part & behalf of the State of South Carolina

HENRY LAURENS,   RICHD. HUTSON,
WILLIAM HENRY   THOS. HEYWARD, Junr.
 DRAYTON,
JNO. MATHEWS,

On the part & behalf of the State of Georgia

JNO. WALTON,   EDWD. LANGWORTHY.
 24th July, 1778.
EDWD. TELFAIR,

DOCUMENT 7

Federalist Papers No. 10 and No. 51 (1787/1788)

During the battle over ratification of the U.S. Constitution in 1787 and 1788, Alexander Hamilton, James Madison, and John Jay wrote a series of eighty-five political essays favoring the adoption of the document. James Madison wrote, among others, two of the most famous—Number 10 and Number 51. Number 10, considered a classic in political theory, deals with the nature of groups, or factions, as he called them. His view, favoring a large republic, is presented in Number 51.

The Federalist No. 10

James Madison, November 22, 1787
TO THE PEOPLE OF THE STATE OF NEW YORK.
Among the numerous advantages promised by a well constructed Union, none deserves to be more accurately developed than its tendency to break and control the violence of faction. The friend of popular governments, never finds

himself so much alarmed for their character and fate, as when he contemplates their propensity to this dangerous vice. He will not fail therefore to set a due value on any plan which, without violating the principles to which he is attached, provides a proper cure for it. The instability, injustice and confusion introduced into the public councils, have in truth been the mortal diseases under which popular governments have every where perished; as they continue to be the favorite and fruitful topics from which the adversaries to liberty derive their most specious declamations. The valuable improvements made by the American Constitutions on the popular models, both ancient and modern, cannot certainly be too much admired; but it would be an unwarrantable partiality, to contend that they have as effectually obviated the danger on this side as was wished and expected. Complaints are every where heard from our most considerate and virtuous citizens, equally the friends of public and private faith, and of public and personal liberty; that our governments are too unstable; that the public good is disregarded in the conflicts of rival parties; and that measures are too often decided, not according to the rules of justice, and the rights of the minor party; but by the superior force of an interested and over-bearing majority. However anxiously we may wish that these complaints had no foundation, the evidence of known facts will not permit us to deny that they are in some degree true. It will be found indeed, on a candid review of our situation, that some of the distresses under which we labor, have been erroneously charged on the operation of our governments; but it will be found, at the same time, that other causes will not alone account for many of our heaviest misfortunes; and particularly, for that prevailing and increasing distrust of public engagements, and alarm for private rights, which are echoed from one end of the continent to the other. These must be chiefly, if not wholly, effects of the unsteadiness and injustice, with which a factious spirit has tainted our public administrations.

By a faction I understand a number of citizens, whether amounting to a majority or minority of the whole, who are united and actuated by some common impulse of passion, or of interest, adverse to the rights of other citizens, or to the permanent and aggregate interests of the community.

There are two methods of curing the mischiefs of faction: the one, by removing its causes; the other, by controlling its effects.

There are again two methods of removing the causes of faction: the one by destroying the liberty which is essential to its existence; the other, by giving to every citizen the same opinions, the same passions, and the same interests.

It could never be more truly said than of the first remedy, that it is worse than the disease. Liberty is to faction, what air is to fire, an aliment without which it instantly expires. But it could not be a less folly to abolish liberty, which is essential to political life, because it nourishes faction, than it would be to wish the annihilation of air, which is essential to animal life, because it imparts to fire its destructive agency.

The second expedient is as impracticable, as the first would be unwise. As long as the reason of man continues fallible, and he is at liberty to exercise it, different opinions will be formed. As long as the connection subsists between his reason and his self-love, his opinions and his passions will have a reciprocal influence on each other; and the former will be objects to which the latter will attach themselves. The diversity in the faculties of men from which the rights of property originate, is not less an insuperable obstacle to a uniformity of interests. The protection of these faculties is the first object of Government. From the protection of different and unequal faculties of acquiring property, the possession of different degrees and kinds of property immediately results: and from the influence of these on the sentiments and views of the respective proprietors, ensues a division of the society into different interests and parties.

The latent causes of faction are thus sown in the nature of man; and we see them every where brought into different degrees of activity, according to the different circumstances of civil society. A zeal for different opinions concerning religion, concerning Government and many other points, as well of speculation as of practice; an attachment to different leaders ambitiously contending for pre-eminence and power; or to persons of other descriptions whose fortunes have been interesting to the human passions, have in turn divided mankind into parties, inflamed them with mutual animosity, and rendered them much more disposed to vex and oppress each other, than to co-operate for their common good. So strong is this propensity of mankind to fall into mutual animosities, that where no substantial occasion presents itself, the most frivolous and fanciful distinctions have been sufficient to kindle their unfriendly passions, and excite their most violent conflicts. But the most common and durable source of factions, has been the various and unequal distribution of property. Those who hold, and those who are without property, have ever formed distinct interests in society. Those who are creditors, and those who are debtors, fall under a like discrimination. A landed interest, a manufacturing interest, a mercantile interest, a monied interest, with many lesser interests, grow up of necessity in civilized nations, and divide them into different classes, actuated by different sentiments and views. The regulation of these various and interfering interests forms the principal task of modern Legislation, and involves the spirit of party and faction in the necessary and ordinary operations of Government.

No man is allowed to be a judge in his own cause; because his interest would certainly bias his judgment, and, not improbably, corrupt his integrity. With equal, nay with greater reason, a body of men, are unfit to be both judges and parties, at the same time; yet, what are many of the most important acts of legislation, but so many judicial determinations, not indeed concerning the rights of single persons, but concerning the rights of large bodies of citizens, and what are the different classes of legislators, but advocates and parties to the causes which they determine? Is a law proposed concerning private debts? It is a question to which the creditors are parties on one side, and the debtors on the other. Justice ought to hold the balance between them. Yet the parties are and must be themselves the judges; and the most numerous party, or, in other words, the most powerful faction must be expected to prevail. Shall domestic manufactures be encouraged, and in what degree, by restrictions on foreign manufactures? are questions which would be differently decided by the landed and the manufacturing classes; and probably by neither, with a sole regard to justice and the public good. The apportionment of taxes on the various descriptions of property, is an act which seems to require the most exact impartiality; yet, there is perhaps no legislative act in which greater opportunity and temptation are given to a predominant party, to trample on the rules of justice. Every shilling with which they over-burden the inferior number, is a shilling saved to their own pockets.

It is in vain to say, that enlightened statesmen will be able to adjust these clashing interests, and render them all subservient to the public good. Enlightened statesmen will not always be at the helm: Nor, in many cases, can such an adjustment be made at all, without taking into view indirect and remote considerations, which will rarely prevail over the immediate interest which one party may find in disregarding the rights of another, or the good of the whole.

The inference to which we are brought, is, that the *causes* of faction cannot be removed; and that relief is only to be sought in the means of controlling its *effects*.

If a faction consists of less than a majority, relief is supplied by the republican principle, which enables the majority to defeat its sinister views by regular vote: It may clog the administration, it may convulse the society; but it will be unable to execute and mask its violence under the forms of the Constitution. When a majority is included in a faction, the form of popular government on the other hand enables it to sacrifice to its ruling passion or interest, both the public good and the rights of other citizens. To secure the public good, and private rights, against the danger of such a faction, and at the same time to preserve the spirit and the form of popular government, is then the great object to which our enquiries are directed: Let me add that it is the great desideratum, by which alone this form of government can be rescued from the opprobrium under which it has so long labored, and be recommended to the esteem and adoption of mankind.

By what means is this object attainable? Evidently by one of two only. Either the existence of the same passion or interest in a majority at the same time, must be prevented; or the majority, having such co-existent passion or interest, must be rendered, by their number and local situation, unable to concert and carry into effect schemes of oppression. If the impulse and the opportunity be suffered to coincide, we well know that neither moral nor religious motives can be relied on as an adequate control. They are not found to be such on the injustice and violence of individuals, and lose their efficacy in proportion to the number combined together; that is, in proportion as their efficacy becomes needful.

From this view of the subject, it may be concluded, that a pure Democracy, by which I mean, a Society, consisting of a small number of citizens, who assemble and administer the Government in person, can admit of no cure for the mischiefs of faction. A common passion or interest will, in almost every case, be felt by a majority of the whole; a communication and concert results from the form of Government itself; and there is nothing to check the inducements to sacrifice the weaker party, or an obnoxious individual. Hence it is, that such Democracies have ever been spectacles of turbulence and contention; have ever been found incompatible with personal security, or the rights of property; and have in general been as short in their lives, as they have been violent in their deaths. Theoretic politicians, who have patronized this species of Government, have erroneously supposed, that by reducing mankind to a perfect equality in their political rights, they would, at the same time, be perfectly equalized and assimilated in their possessions, their opinions, and their passions.

A republic, by which I mean a government in which the scheme of representation takes place, opens a different prospect, and promises the cure for which we are seeking. Let us examine the points in which it varies from pure democracy, and we shall comprehend both the nature of the cure and the efficacy which it must derive from the union.

The two great points of difference, between a democracy and a republic, are, first, the delegation of the government, in the latter, to a small number of citizens, elected by the rest; secondly, the greater number of citizens, and greater sphere of country, over which the latter may be extended.

The effect of the first difference is, on the one hand, to refine and enlarge the public views, by passing them through the medium of a chosen body of citizens, whose wisdom may best discern the true interest of their country, and whose patriotism and love of justice, will be least likely to sacrifice it to temporary or partial considerations. Under such a regulation, it may well happen, that the public voice, pronounced by the representatives of the people, will be more consonant to the public good, than if pronounced by the people themselves, convened for the purpose. On the other hand the effect may be inverted. Men of factious tempers, of local prejudices, or of sinister designs, may by intrigue, by corruption, or by other means, first obtain the suffrages, and then betray the interest of the people. The question resulting is, whether small or extensive republics are most favorable to the election of proper guardians of the public weal, and it is clearly decided in favor of the latter by two obvious considerations.

In the first place, it is to be remarked that, however small the republic may be, the representatives must be raised to a certain number, in order to guard against the cabals of a few; and that however large it may be, they must be limited to a certain number, in order to guard against the confusion of a multitude. Hence, the number of representatives in the two cases not being in proportion to that of the constituents, and being proportionally greatest in the small republic, it follows, that if the proportion of fit characters be not less in the large than in the small republic, the former will present a greater option, and consequently a greater probability of a fit choice.

In the next place, as each Representative will be chosen by a greater number of citizens in the large than in the small Republic, it will be more difficult for unworthy candidates to practise with success the vicious arts, by which elections are too often carried; and the suffrages of the people being more free, will be more likely to center on men who possess the most attractive merit, and the most diffusive and established characters.

It must be confessed, that in this, as in most other cases, there is a mean, on both sides of which inconveniences will be found to lie. By enlarging too much the number of electors, you render the representative too little acquainted with all their local circumstances and lesser interests; as by reducing it too much, you render him unduly attached to these, and too little fit to comprehend and pursue great and national objects. The Federal Constitution forms a happy combination in this respect; the great and aggregate interests being referred to the national, the local and particular, to the state legislatures.

The other point of difference is, the greater number of citizens and extent of territory which may be brought within the compass of Republican, than of Democratic Government; and it is this circumstance principally which renders factious combinations less to be dreaded in the former, than in the latter. The smaller the society, the fewer probably will be the distinct parties and interests composing it; the fewer the distinct parties and interests, the more frequently will a majority be found of the same party; and the smaller the

number of individuals composing a majority, and the smaller the compass within which they are placed, the more easily will they concert and execute their plans of oppression. Extend the sphere, and you take in a greater variety of parties and interests; you make it less probable that a majority of the whole will have a common motive to invade the rights of other citizens; or if such a common motive exists, it will be more difficult for all who feel it to discover their own strength, and to act in unison with each other. Besides other impediments, it may be remarked, that where there is a consciousness of unjust or dishonorable purposes, communication is always checked by distrust, in proportion to the number whose concurrence is necessary.

Hence it clearly appears, that the same advantage, which a Republic has over a Democracy, in controlling the effects of faction, is enjoyed by a large over a small Republic—is enjoyed by the Union over the States composing it. Does this advantage consist in the substitution of Representatives, whose enlightened views and virtuous sentiments render them superior to local prejudices, and to schemes of injustice? It will not be denied, that the Representation of the Union will be most likely to possess these requisite endowments. Does it consist in the greater security afforded by a greater variety of parties, against the event of any one party being able to outnumber and oppress the rest? In an equal degree does the increased variety of parties, comprised within the Union, increase this security? Does it, in fine, consist in the greater obstacles opposed to the concert and accomplishment of the secret wishes of an unjust and interested majority? Here, again, the extent of the Union gives it the most palpable advantage.

The influence of factious leaders may kindle a flame within their particular States, but will be unable to spread a general conflagration through the other States: a religious sect, may degenerate into a political faction in a part of the Confederacy but the variety of sects dispersed over the entire face of it, must secure the national Councils against any danger from that source: a rage for paper money, for an abolition of debts, for an equal division of property, or for any other improper or wicked project, will be less apt to pervade the whole body of the Union, than a particular member of it; in the same proportion as such a malady is more likely to taint a particular county or district, than an entire State.

In the extent and proper structure of the Union, therefore, we behold a Republican remedy for the diseases most incident to Republican Government. And according to the degree of pleasure and pride, we feel in being Republicans, ought to be our zeal in cherishing the spirit, and supporting the character of Federalists.

Publius

The Federalist No. 51

James Madison, February 6, 1788

TO THE PEOPLE OF THE STATE OF NEW YORK.

To what expedient then shall we finally resort for maintaining in practice the necessary partition of power among the several departments, as laid down in the constitution? The only answer that can be given is, that as all these exterior provisions are found to be inadequate, the defect must be supplied, by so contriving the interior structure of the government, as that its several constituent parts may, by their mutual relations, be the means of keeping each other in their proper places. Without presuming to undertake a full development of this important idea, I will hazard a few general observations, which may perhaps place it in a clearer light, and enable us to form a more correct judgment of the principles and structure of the government planned by the convention.

In order to lay a due foundation for that separate and distinct exercise of the different powers of government, which to a certain extent, is admitted on all hands to be essential to the preservation of liberty, it is evident that each department should have a will of its own; and consequently should be so constituted, that the members of each should have as little agency as possible in the appointment of the members of the others. Were this principle rigorously adhered to, it would require that all the appointments for the supreme executive, legislative, and judiciary magistracies, should be drawn from the same fountain of authority, the people, through channels, having no communication whatever with one another. Perhaps such a plan of constructing the several departments would be less difficult in practice than it may in contemplation appear. Some difficulties however, and some additional expense, would attend the execution of it. Some deviations therefore from the principle must be admitted. In the constitution of the judiciary department in particular, it might be inexpedient to insist rigorously on the principle; first, because peculiar qualifications being essential in the members, the primary consideration ought to be to select that mode of choice, which best secures these qualifications; secondly, because the permanent tenure by which the appointments are held in that department, must soon destroy all sense of dependence on the authority conferring them.

It is equally evident that the members of each department should be as little dependent as possible on those of the others, for the emoluments annexed to their offices. Were the executive magistrate, or the judges, not independent of the legislature in this particular, their independence in every other would be merely nominal.

But the great security against a gradual concentration of the several powers in the same department, consists in giving to those who administer each department, the necessary constitutional means, and personal motives, to resist encroachments of the others. The provision for defense must in this, as in all other cases, be made commensurate to the danger of attack. Ambition must be made to counteract ambition. The interest of the man must be connected with the constitutional rights of the place. It may be a reflection on human nature, that such devices should be necessary to control the abuses of government. But what is government itself but the greatest of all reflections on human nature? If men were angels, no government would be necessary. If angels were to govern men, neither external nor internal controls on government would be necessary. In framing a government which is to be administered by men over men, the great difficulty lies in this: You must first enable the government to control the governed; and in the next place oblige it to control itself. A dependence on the people is no doubt the primary control on the government; but experience has taught mankind the necessity of auxiliary precautions.

This policy of supplying by opposite and rival interests, the defect of better motives, might be traced through the whole system of human affairs, private as well as public. We see it particularly displayed in all the subordinate distributions of power; where the constant aim is to divide and arrange the several offices in such a manner as that each may be a check on the other; that the private interest of every individual, may be a sentinel over the public rights. These inventions of prudence cannot be less requisite in the distribution of the supreme powers of the state.

But it is not possible to give to each department an equal power of self defense. In republican government the legislative authority, necessarily, predominates. The remedy for this inconveniency is, to divide the legislature into different branches; and to render them by different modes of election, and different principles of action, as little connected with each other, as the nature of their common functions, and their common dependence on the society, will admit. It may even be necessary to guard against dangerous encroachments by still further precautions. As the weight of the legislative authority requires that it should be thus divided, the weakness of the executive may require, on the other hand, that it should be fortified. An absolute negative, on the legislature, appears at first view to be the natural defense with which the executive magistrate should be armed. But perhaps it would be neither altogether safe, nor alone sufficient. On ordinary occasions, it might not be exerted with the requisite firmness; and on extraordinary occasions, it might be prefidiously abused. May not this defect of an absolute negative be supplied, by some qualified connection between this weaker department, and the weaker branch of the stronger department, by which the latter may be led to support the constitutional rights of the former, without being too much detached from the rights of its own department?

If the principles on which these observations are founded be just, as I persuade myself they are, and they be applied as a criterion, to the several state constitutions, and to the federal constitution, it will be found, that if the latter does not perfectly correspond with them, the former are infinitely less able to bear such a test.

There are moreover two considerations particularly applicable to the federal system of America, which place that system in a very interesting point of view.

First. In a single republic, all the power surrendered by the people, is submitted to the administration of a single government; and usurpations are guarded against by a division of the government into distinct and separate departments. In the compound republic of America, the power surrendered by the people, is first divided between two distinct governments, and then the portion allotted to each, subdivided among distinct and separate departments. Hence a double security rises to the rights of the people. The different governments will control each other; at the same time that each will be controlled by itself.

Second. It is of great importance in a republic, not only to guard the society against the oppression of its rulers; but to guard one part of the society against the injustice of the other part. Different interests necessarily exist in different classes of citizens. If a majority be united by a common interest, the rights of the minority will be insecure. There are but two methods of providing against this evil: The one by creating a will in the community independent of the majority, that is, of the society itself, the other by comprehending in the society so many separate descriptions of citizens, as will render an unjust combination of a majority of the whole, very improbable, if not impracticable. The first method prevails in all governments possessing an hereditary or self appointed authority. This at best is but a precarious security; because a power independent of the society may as well espouse the unjust views of the major, as the rightful interests, of the minor party, and may possibly be turned against both parties. The second method will be exemplified in the federal republic of the United States. While all authority in it will be derived from and dependent on the society, the society itself will be broken into so many parts, interests and classes of citizens, that the rights of individuals or of the minority, will be in little danger from interested combinations of the majority. In a free government, the security for civil rights must be the same as for religious rights. It consists in the one case in the multiplicity of interests, and in the other, in the multiplicity of sects. The degree of security in both cases will depend on the number of interests and sects; and this may be presumed to depend on the extent of country and number of people comprehended under the same government. This view of the subject must particularly recommend a proper federal system to all the sincere and considerate friends of republican government: Since it shows that in exact proportion as the territory of the union may be formed into more circumscribed confederacies or states, oppressive combinations of a majority will be facilitated, the best security under the republican form, for the rights of every class of citizens, will be diminished; and consequently, the stability and independence of some member of the government, the only other security, must be proportionally increased. Justice is the end of government. It is the end of civil society. It ever has been, and ever will be pursued, until it be obtained, or until liberty be lost in the pursuit. In a society under the forms of which the stronger faction can readily unite and oppress the weaker, anarchy may as truly be said to reign, as in a state of nature where the weaker individual is not secured against the violence of the stronger: And as in the latter state even the stronger individuals are prompted by the uncertainty of their condition, to submit to a government which may protect the weak as well as themselves: So in the former state, will the more powerful factions or parties be gradually induced by a like motive, to wish for a government which will protect all parties, the weaker as well as the more powerful. It can be little doubted, that if the state of Rhode Island was separated from the confederacy, and left to itself, the insecurity of rights under the popular form of government within such narrow limits, would be displayed by such reiterated oppressions of factious majorities, that some power altogether independent of the people would soon be called for by the voice of the very factions whose misrule had proved the necessity of it. In the extended republic of the United States, and among the great variety of interests, parties and sects which it embraces, a coalition of a majority of the whole society could seldom take place on any other principles than those of justice and the general good; and there being thus less danger to a minor from the will of the major party, there must be less pretext also, to provide for the security of the former, by introducing into the government a will not dependent on the latter; or in other words, a will independent of the society itself. It is no less certain than it is important, notwithstanding the contrary opinions which have been entertained, that the larger the society, provided it lie within a practicable sphere, the more duly capable it will be of self government. And happily for the *republican cause*, the practicable sphere may be carried to a very great extent, by a judicious modification and mixture of the *federal principle*.

Publius

DOCUMENT 8

Anti-Federalist Writings (1787-1788)

Those who opposed the ratification of the United States Constitution were called the Anti-Federalists to show their opposition to the Federalists, who were in favor of the Constitution's ratification. Many of the Anti-Federalists' writings were published under pen names, just as were some of the writings of the Federalists.

Because the original Constitution (without its amendments) did not contain a bill of rights, many Anti-Federalist writers were opposed to ratification as is evidenced by the excerpt below, written by an unknown Anti-Federalist.

The truth is, that the rights of individuals are frequently opposed to the apparent interests of the majority—For this reason the greater the portion of political freedom in a form of government the greater the necessity of a bill of rights— Often the natural rights of an individual are opposed to the presumed interests or heated passions of a large majority of democratic government; if these rights are not clearly and expressly ascertained, the individual must be lost; and for the truth of this I appeal to every man who has borne a part in the legislative councils of America. In such government the tyranny of the legislative is most to be dreaded.

—A (Maryland) Farmer in the Maryland Gazette,
April 1788.

Because the United States was so large a territory, many Anti-Federalists did not believe that it could be governed by one national government. They believed that it would not be a government by the will of the people and, therefore, it would become arbitrary. Robert Yates of New York, using the pen name Brutus, presented these ideas in the following excerpt:

In every free government, the people must give their assent to the laws by which they are governed. This is the true criterion between a free government and an arbitrary one. The former are ruled by the will of the whole [the people], expressed in any manner they may agree upon; the latter by the will of one, or a few. If the people are to give their assent to the laws, by persons chosen and appointed by them, the manner of the choice and the number chosen must be such, as to possess, be disposed, and consequently qualified to declare the sentiments of the people; for if they do not know, or are not disposed to speak the sentiments of the people, the people do not govern, but the sovereignty is in a few. Now, in a large-extended country, it is impossible to have a representation, possessing the sentiments, and of integrity, to declare the minds of the people . . . .

—Brutus, October 1787

DOCUMENT 9

Monroe Doctrine (1823)

The Monroe Doctrine is a statement about U.S. foreign policy prepared by John Quincy Adams, and presented by President James Monroe to the Congress on December 2, 1823. The goal of the doctrine was to prevent European involvement in Latin America's new republics.

Fellow citizens of the Senate and House of Representatives:

Many important subjects will claim your attention during the present session, of which I shall endeavor to give, in aid of your deliberations, a just idea in this communication. I undertake this duty with diffidence, from the vast extent of

the interests on which I have to treat and of their great importance to every portion of our Union. I enter on it with zeal from a thorough conviction that there never was a period since the establishment of our revolution when, regarding the condition of the civilized world and its bearing on us, there was greater necessity for devotion in the public servants to their respective duties, or for virtue, patriotism, and union in our constituents.

Meeting in you a new Congress, I deem it proper to present this view of public affairs in greater detail than might otherwise be necessary. I do it, however, with peculiar satisfaction, from a knowledge that in this respect I shall comply more fully with the sound principles of our government. The people being with us exclusively the sovereign, it is indispensable that full information be laid before them on all important subjects, to enable them to exercise that high power with complete effect. If kept in the dark, they must be incompetent to it. We are all liable to error, and those who are engaged in the management of public affairs are more subject to excitement and to be led astray by their particular interests and passions than the great body of our constituents, who, living at home in the pursuit of their ordinary avocations, are calm but deeply interested spectators of events and of the conduct of those who are parties to them. To the people every department of the government and every individual in each are responsible, and the more full their information the better they can judge of the wisdom of the policy pursued and of the conduct of each in regard to it. From their dispassionate judgment much aid may always be obtained, while their approbation will form the greatest incentive and most gratifying reward for virtuous actions and the dread of their censure the best security against the abuse of their confidence. Their interests in all vital questions are the same, and the bond, by sentiment as well as by interest, will be proportionably strengthened as they are better informed of the real state of public affairs, especially in difficult conjunctures. It is by such knowledge that local prejudices and jealousies are surmounted, and that a national policy, extending its fostering care and protection to all the great interests of our Union, is formed and steadily adhered to. . . .

At the proposal of the Russian imperial government, made through the minister of the emperor residing here, a full power and instructions have been transmitted to the minister of the United States at St. Petersburg to arrange by amicable negotiation the respective rights and interests of the two nations on the northwest coast of this continent. A similar proposal had been made by his imperial Majesty to the government of Great Britain, which has likewise been acceded to. The government of the United States has been desirous by this friendly proceeding of manifesting the great value which they have invariably attached to the friendship of the emperor and their solicitude to cultivate the best understanding with his government. In the discussions to which this interest has given rise and in the arrangements by which they may terminate the occasion has been judged proper for asserting, as a principle in which the rights and interests of the United States are involved, that the American continents, by the free and independent condition which they have assumed and maintain, are henceforth not to be considered as subjects for future colonization by any European powers. . . .

It was stated at the commencement of the last session that a great effort was then making in Spain and Portugal to improve the condition of the people of those countries, and that it appeared to be conducted with extraordinary moderation. It need scarcely be remarked that the result has been so far very different from what was then anticipated. Of events in that quarter of the globe, with which we have so much intercourse and from which we derive our origin, we have always been anxious and interested spectators. The citizens of the United States cherish sentiments the most friendly in favor of the liberty and happiness of their fellow men on that side of the Atlantic. In the wars of the European powers in matters relating to themselves, we have never taken any part, nor does it comport with our policy so to do. It is only when our rights are invaded or seriously menaced that we resent injuries or make preparation for our defense. With the movements in this hemisphere we are of necessity more immediately connected, and by causes which must be obvious to all enlightened and impartial observers. The political system of the allied powers is essentially different in this respect from that of America. This difference proceeds from that which exists in their respective governments; and to the defense of our own, which has been achieved by the loss of so much blood and treasure, and matured by the wisdom of their most enlightened citizens, and under which we have enjoyed unexampled felicity, this whole nation is devoted. We owe it, therefore, to candor and to the amicable relations existing between the United States and those powers to declare that we should consider any attempt on their part to extend their system to any portion of this hemisphere as dangerous to our peace and safety. With the existing colonies or dependencies of any European power, we have not interfered and shall not interfere. But with the governments who have declared their independence and maintained it, and whose independence we have, on great consideration and on just principles, acknowledged, we could not view any interposition for the purpose of oppressing them, or controlling in any other manner their destiny, by any European power in any other light than as the manifestation of an unfriendly disposition toward the United States. In the war between those new governments and Spain, we declared our neutrality at the time of their recognition, and to this we have adhered, and shall continue to adhere, provided no change shall occur which, in the judgment of the competent authorities of this government, shall make a corresponding change on the part of the United States indispensable to their security.

The late events in Spain and Portugal show that Europe is still unsettled. Of this important fact no stronger proof can be adduced than that the allied powers should have thought it proper, on any principle satisfactory to themselves, to have interposed by force in the internal concerns of Spain. To what extent such interposition may be carried, on the same principle, is a question in which all independent powers whose governments differ from theirs are interested, even those most remote, and surely none more so than the United States. Our policy in regard to Europe, which was adopted at an early stage of the wars which have so long agitated that quarter of the globe, nevertheless remains the same, which is, not to interfere in the internal concerns of any of its powers; to consider the government *de facto* as the legitimate government for us; to cultivate friendly relations with it, and to preserve those relations by a frank, firm, and manly policy, meeting in all instances the just claims of every power, submitting to injuries from none. But in regard to those continents, circumstances are eminently and conspicuously different. It is impossible that the allied powers should extend their political system to any portion of either continent without endangering our peace and happiness; nor can anyone believe that our southern brethren, if left to themselves, would adopt it of their own accord. It is equally impossible, therefore, that we should behold such interposition in any form with indifference. If we look to the comparative strength and resources of Spain and those new governments, and their distance from each other, it must be obvious that she can never subdue them. It is still the true policy of the United States to leave the parties to themselves in the hope that other powers will pursue the same course.

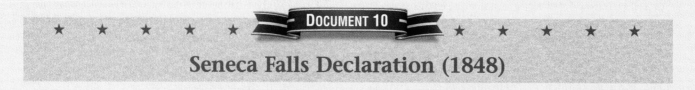

DOCUMENT 10

Seneca Falls Declaration (1848)

The Seneca Falls Declaration, a "declaration of sentiments," was issued at an important women's rights convention held at Seneca Falls, New York in July, 1848. The convention was organized by Elizabeth Cady Stanton and Lucretia Mott.

We hold these truths to be self-evident; that all men and women are created equal; that they are endowed by their Creator with certain inalienable rights; that among these are life, liberty, and the pursuit of happiness; that to secure these rights governments are instituted, deriving their just powers from the consent of the governed. . . .

Now, in view of this entire disfranchisement of one-half the people of this country, their social and religious degradation, in view of the unjust laws above mentioned, and because women do feel themselves aggrieved, oppressed, and fraudulently deprived of their most sacred rights, we insist that they have immediate admission to all the rights and privileges which belong to them as citizens of the United States.

[Excerpt]

DOCUMENT 11

Emancipation Proclamation (1862)

President Abraham Lincoln issued the Emancipation Proclamation on September 23, 1862, in order to gain world support for the Union cause. The document stated that after January 1, 1863, all slaves in the rebel states would be free. The proclamation did not apply to the border states of Delaware, Kentucky, Maryland, and Missouri, nor to that part of the Confederacy already occupied by Northern troops, such as Tennessee and parts of Virginia and Louisiana.

By the President of the United States of America:
A PROCLAMATION

Whereas, on the twenty-second day of September, in the year of our Lord one thousand eight hundred and sixty-two, a proclamation was issued by the president of the United States, containing, among other things, the following, to wit:

"That on the first day of January, in the year of our Lord one thousand eight hundred and sixty-three, all persons held as slaves within any state or designated part of a state, the people whereof shall then be in rebellion against the United States, shall be then, thenceforward and forever, free; and the executive government of the United States, including the military and naval authority thereof, will recognize and maintain the freedom of such persons and will do no act or acts to repress such persons, or any of them, in any efforts they may make for their actual freedom.

"That the executive will, on the first day of January aforesaid, by proclamation, designate the states and parts of states, if any, in which the people thereof, respectively, shall then be in rebellion against the United States; and the fact that any state, or the people thereof, shall on that day be in good faith represented in the Congress of the United States, by members chosen thereto at elections wherein a majority of the qualified voters of such states shall have participated, shall, in the absence of strong countervailing testimony, be deemed conclusive evidence that such state, and the people thereof, are not then in rebellion against the United States."

Now, therefore, I, Abraham Lincoln, president of the United States, by virtue of the power in me vested as commander in chief of the army and navy of the United States, in time of actual armed rebellion against the authority and government of the United States, and as a fit and necessary war measure for suppressing said rebellion, do, on this first day of January, in the year of our Lord one thousand eight hundred and sixty-three, and in accordance with my purpose so to do, publicly proclaimed for the full period of one hundred days from the day first above mentioned, order and designate as the states and parts of states wherein the people thereof, respectively, are this day in rebellion against the United States, the following, to wit:

Arkansas, Texas, Louisiana (except the parishes of St. Bernard, Plaquemines, Jefferson, St. John, St. Charles, St. James, Ascension, Assumption, Terre Bonne, Lafourche, St. Mary, St. Martin, and Orleans, including the city of New Orleans), Mississippi, Alabama, Florida, Georgia, South Carolina, North Carolina, and Virginia (except the forty-eight counties designated as West Virginia, and also the counties of Berkeley, Accomac, Northampton, Elizabeth City, York, Princess Ann, and Norfolk, including the cities of Norfolk and Portsmouth), and which excepted parts are for the present left precisely as if this proclamation were not issued.

And by virtue of the power and for the purpose aforesaid, I do order and declare that all persons held as slaves within said designated states and parts of states are, and henceforward shall be, free; and that the executive government of the United States, including the military and naval authorities thereof, will recognize and maintain the freedom of said persons.

And I hereby enjoin upon the people so declared to be free to abstain from all violence, unless in necessary self-defense; and I recommend to them that, in all cases when allowed, they labor faithfully for reasonable wages.

And I further declare and make known that such persons, of suitable condition will be received into the armed service of the United States to garrison forts, positions, stations, and other places and to man vessels of all sorts in said service.

And upon this act, sincerely believed to be an act of justice, warranted by the Constitution upon military necessity, I invoke the considerate judgment of mankind and the gracious favor of Almighty God.

In witness whereof, I have hereunto set my hand and caused the seal of the United States to be affixed.

Done at the city of Washington this first day of January, in the year of our Lord one thousand eight hundred and sixty-three, and of the independence of the United States of America the eighty-seventh.

By the President: William H. Seward,
Abraham Lincoln   Secretary of State.

★ ★ ★ ★ ★ **DOCUMENT 12** ★ ★ ★ ★ ★

Pledge of Allegiance (1892)

The Pledge of Allegiance, a solemn oath of allegiance to the United States, has been attributed to Francis Bellamy, a Baptist minister.

I pledge allegiance to the Flag of the United States of America and to the Republic for which it stands, one Nation under God,* indivisible, with liberty and justice for all.

---

*The words "under God" were added in 1954.

DOCUMENT 13

The American's Creed (1917)

The American's Creed, composed by William Tyler Page in 1917, is a statement of our common political values. It is a set of beliefs about the proper role of government and the dignity of the individual. It attempts to show the consensus of Americans' values and beliefs. The values expressed are individualistic, democratic, and egalitarian.

Composed in 1917 by William Tyler Page (1868–1942).
"I believe in the United States of America as a government of the people, by the people, for the people; whose just pow- ers are derived from the consent of the governed; a democ- racy in a Republic; a sovereign Nation of many sovereign States; a perfect Union, one and inseparable; established upon those principles of freedom, equality, justice, and humanity for which American patriots sacrificed their lives and fortunes.

"I therefore believe it is my duty to my country to love it; to support its Constitution; to obey its laws; to respect its flag; and to defend it against all enemies."

DOCUMENT 14

Brown v. *Board of Education of Topeka (1954)*

The landmark Supreme Court case Brown v. Board of Educa- tion of Topeka overturned the "separate but equal doctrine" established by the 1896 case of Plessy v. Ferguson. At the time of this decision, the Supreme Court was led by Chief Justice Earl Warren.

In approaching this problem, [w]e must consider public edu- cation in the light of its full development and its present place in American life throughout the Nation. Only in this way can it be determined if segregation in public schools deprives these plaintiffs of the equal protection of the laws.

Today, education is perhaps the most important function of state and local governments. Compulsory school atten- dance laws and the great expenditures for education both demonstrate our recognition of the importance of education to our democratic society. It is required in the performance of our most basic public responsibilities, even service in the armed forces. It is the very foundation of good citizenship. Today it is a principal instrument in awakening the child to cultural values, in preparing him for later professional train- ing, and in helping him to adjust normally to his environ- ment. In these days, it is doubtful that any child may reasonably be expected to succeed in life if he is denied the opportunity of an education. Such an opportunity, where the state has undertaken to provide it, is a right which must be made available to all on equal terms.

We come then to the question presented: Does segrega- tion of children in public schools solely on the basis of race, even though the physical facilities and other `tangible' fac- tors may be equal, deprive the children of the minority group of equal educational opportunities? We believe that it does.

To separate [African Americans] from others of similar age and qualifications solely because of their race generates a feeling of inferiority as to their status in the community that may affect their hearts and minds in a way unlikely ever to be undone.

We conclude that in the field of public education the doctrine of `separate but equal' has no place. Separate edu- cational facilities are inherently unequal. Therefore, we hold that the plaintiffs and others similarly situated for whom the actions have been brought are, by reason of the segregation complained of, deprived of the equal protection of the laws guaranteed by the Fourteenth Amendment. This disposition makes unnecessary any discussion whether such segregation also violates the Due Process Clause of the Fourteenth Amendment.

Because these are class actions, because of the wide applicability of this decision, and because of the great variety of local conditions, the formulation of decrees in these cases presents problems of considerable complexity. On reargument, the consideration of appropriate relief was necessarily subordinated to the primary question—the constitutionality of segregation in public education. We have now announced that such segregation is a denial of the equal protection of the laws.

[Excerpts]

DOCUMENT 15

The Preamble to the Charter of the United Nations

Just as the United States is governed by the rules set forth in the Constitution, so too is the United Nations governed by the rules set forth in the Charter of the United Nations drafted and put into force in 1945. The U.N. Charter, like the Constitution, begins with a preamble that expresses the spirit of the organization.

We the peoples of the United Nations determined

to save succeeding generations from the scourge of war, which twice in our lifetime has brought untold sorrow to mankind, and

to reaffirm faith in fundamental human rights, in the dignity and worth of the human person, in the equal rights of men and women and of nations large and small, and

to establish conditions under which justice and respect for the obligations arising from treaties and other sources of international law can be maintained, and

to promote social progress and better standards of life in larger freedom,

and for these ends

to practice tolerance and live together in peace with one another as good neighbors, and

to unite our strength to maintain international peace and security, and

to ensure, by the acceptance of principles and the institution of methods, that armed force shall not be used, save in the common interest, and

to employ international machinery for the promotion of the economic and social advancement of all peoples,

have resolved to combine our efforts to accomplish these aims.

Accordingly, our respective governments, through representatives assembled in the city of San Francisco, who have exhibited their full powers found to be in good and due form, have agreed to the present Charter of the United Nations and do hereby establish an international organization to be known as the United Nations.

Annotated Table of Legal Cases

How to Read Legal Case Citations and Find Court Decisions

Court decisions are recorded and published in various places. When a court case is mentioned, the notation used to refer to, or to cite, it denotes where the published decision can be found.

State courts of appeal decisions are usually published in two places, the state reports of that particular state and the more widely used *National Reporter System* published by West Publishing Company. Some states no longer publish their own reports. The *National Reporter System* divides the states into the following geographic areas: Atlantic (A. or A.2d, where 2d refers to second series), South Eastern (S.E. or S.E.2d), South Western (S.W. or S.W.2d), North Western (N.W. or N.W.2d), North Eastern (N.E. or N.E.2d), Southern (So. or So.2d), and Pacific (P. or P.2d).

Federal trial court decisions are published unofficially in West's *Federal Supplement* (F.Supp.), and opinions from the circuit courts of appeal are reported unofficially in West's *Federal Reporter* (F. or F.2d). Opinions from the United States Supreme Court are reported in the *United States Reports* (U.S.), the *Lawyer's Edition of the Supreme Court*

Reports (L.Ed.), West's *Supreme Court Reporter* (S. Ct.), and other publications. The *United States Reports* is the official edition of the United States Supreme Court decisions published by the federal government. Many early decisions are missing from these volumes. An unofficial and more complete edition of Supreme Court decisions, the *Lawyer's Edition of the Supreme Court Reports*, is published by the Lawyers Cooperative Publishing Company of Rochester, New York. West's *Supreme Court Reporter* is an unofficial edition of decisions dating from October 1882. These volumes contain headnotes and brief editorial statements of the law involved in the case.

State courts of appeal decisions are cited by giving the name of the case; the volume, name, and page number of the state's official report (if the state publishes its own reports); the volume, unit, and page number of the *National Reporter*; and the volume, name, and page number of any other selected reporter. Federal court citations are also listed by giving the name of the case and the volume, name, and page number of the reports.

Table of Court Cases

***Adarand Constructors* v. *Peña* (1995)**	An affirmative action case in which the Court held that any race-based classification by any government is subject to strict judicial scrutiny. Under this standard, racial classifications are constitutional only if they are narrowly tailored measures that further compelling governmental interests.
***Afroyim* v. *Rusk* (1967)**	A civil rights/citizenship case in which the Court ruled that all citizens have "a constitutional right to remain a citizen in a free country unless [they] voluntarily relinquish that citizenship." Part of the Nationality Act of 1940 was declared unconstitutional because it provided for the automatic expatriation of any American citizen who voted in a foreign election.

Baker v. **Carr (1962)**	A Fourteenth Amendment/apportionment case in which the Court ruled that state legislatures had to be apportioned to provide equal protection under the law.
Barron v. **Mayor of Baltimore (1833)**	A civil rights/Bill of Rights case in which the Court ruled that the Bill of Rights applied only to the national government, not to the state governments.
Betts v. **Brady (1942)**	A rights of the accused/right to an attorney case in which the Court held that criminal defendants were not automatically guaranteed the right to have a lawyer present when they were tried in court, except in capital cases (overturned in *Gideon v. Wainright*).
Bigelow v. **Virginia (1975)**	A freedom of speech/advertising case involving so-called commercial speech in which the Court held that the state cannot prohibit newspaper advertising of abortion services.
Board of Education of Westside Community Schools v. **Mergens (1990)**	A separation of church and state case in which the Court ruled in favor of a Christian Bible club that wanted to meet on school grounds after regular school hours in Omaha, Nebraska.
Brandenburg v. **Ohio (1969)**	A free speech/national security decision in which the Court narrowed its definition of seditious speech so that advocating the use of force is legal unless such advocacy "is directed to inciting or producing imminent lawless action and is likely to produce such action."
Branzburg v. **Hayes (1972)**	A freedom of speech/confidentiality case in which the Court held that the First Amendment grants no special privileges to reporters. They must therefore respond to questioning during a valid criminal trial or investigation.
Brown v. **Board of Education (1955)**	A civil rights case in which the Court asked for rearguments concerning the way in which the states should implement civil rights decisions including its 1954 decision *Brown v. Board of Education of Topeka*. The Court indicated that the lower courts must ensure that African Americans be admitted to schools on a nondiscriminatory basis "with all deliberate speed."
Brown v. **Board of Education of Topeka (1954)**	A civil rights case that established that public schools' segregation of races violated the equal protection clause of the Fourteenth Amendment.
Burstyn v. **Wilson (1952)**	A freedom of press case involving the motion picture industry in which the Court held that "liberty of expression by means of motion pictures is guaranteed by the First and Fourteenth Amendments." Nonetheless, the Court held that prior censorship of films by local and state authorities may be constitutional under certain circumstances, usually involving obscenity.
Cox v. **New Hampshire (1941)**	A freedom of assembly case in which the Court ruled that sixty-eight Jehovah's Witnesses had violated the statute prohibiting parading without a permit and further upheld the right of a municipality to control its public streets.

De Jonge v. Oregon (1937)	A freedom of assembly case involving a man convicted for holding a public meeting that was sponsored by the Communist Party. The Court overturned his conviction, ruling that the Oregon law restricted too much the rights of free speech and assembly. This case put the right of assembly on equal footing with the rights of free speech and press.
Dennis v. United States (1951)	A free speech and national security case in which the Court ruled that the Smith Act—a law against seditious speech—could be applied to members of the Communist Party.
Dillon v. Gloss (1921)	A case ruling that allows Congress to place a "reasonable time limit" on the ratification process for amendments to the United States Constitution.
Dred Scott v. Sandford (1857)	A civil rights/citizenship case in which the Court declared that slaves were not citizens of any state or of the United States. (The Court also declared unconstitutional the Missouri Compromise because it deprived a person of his property [his slave] without due process of law.)
Engel v. Vitale (1962)	The so-called Regents' Prayer Case, in which the Court outlawed even the voluntary saying of a nondenominational prayer written by the New York State Board of Regents. An important separation of church and state case.
Escobedo v. Illinois (1964)	A rights of the accused/right to counsel case in which the Court overturned the conviction of Danny Escobedo, who had been arrested by Chicago police in connection with the murder of his brother-in-law. Escobedo's request to see his lawyer had been refused even though the lawyer was in the police station trying to see Escobedo during his questioning.
Everson v. Board of Education (1947)	A First Amendment/establishment clause case in which the Court ruled in favor of tax-supported busing of students who attended parochial schools.
Feiner v. New York (1951)	A freedom of assembly case in which the Court upheld a conviction for unlawful assembly because the police had acted to preserve public order. Feiner, during a speech in Syracuse, New York, verbally attacked President Harry S Truman and the mayor of Syracuse. When the police were called, the crowd was on the verge of attempting to stop Feiner from speaking.
Ford v. Wainwright (1986)	An Eighth Amendment/capital punishment case in which the Court ruled that the U.S. Constitution bars states from executing convicted killers who have become insane while waiting on death row.
Frontiero v. Richardson (1973)	A civil liberties/gender classification case in which the Court ruled against any sex discrimination based on "romantic paternalism."
Furman v. Georgia (1972)	An Eighth Amendment/capital punishment case in which the Court struck down Georgia's laws allowing the death penalty because the laws gave too much discretion to juries and judges in deciding whether capital punishment should be imposed.

Table of Court Cases—*Continued*

***Gannet Company* v. *Pasquale* (1979)**	A freedom of press/gag order case in which the Court held that if a judge found a reasonable probability that news publicity would harm a defendant's right to a fair trial, the court could impose a gag rule: "Members of the public have no constitutional right under the Sixth and Fourteenth Amendments to attend criminal trials."
***Gibbons* v. *Ogden* (1824)**	For the first time, the national government's power over commerce was defined in an expansive way. In effect, the power of the national government to regulate commerce has no limitations other than those specifically found in the Constitution.
***Gideon* v. *Wainwright* (1963)**	A rights of the accused/right to counsel case in which the Court said that persons who can demonstrate that they are unable to afford to have a lawyer present and are accused of felonies must be given a lawyer at the expense of the government.
***Gitlow* v. *New York* (1925)**	A free speech/bad-tendency rule case that allows First Amendment freedoms to be curtailed if there is a possibility that such expression might lead to some evil. In this case, a member of a left-wing group was convicted of violating New York State's criminal anarchy statute when he published and distributed materials urging the violent overthrow of the U.S. government.
***Gregg* v. *Georgia* (1976)**	An Eighth Amendment/capital punishment case in which the Court indicated for the first time that the death penalty does not "invariably violate the Constitution."
***Griswold* v. *Connecticut* (1965)**	A civil liberties/right to privacy case in which the Court overthrew a Connecticut law that effectively prohibited the distribution of contraceptives. In the case Justice William O. Douglas claimed that the First, Third, Fourth, Fifth, and Ninth Amendments created "penumbras, formed by emanations from those guarantees that help give them life and substance," and went on to talk about zones for privacy that are guaranteed by these rights.
***Hazelwood School District* v. *Cathy Kuhlmeier* (1988)**	A First Amendment/freedom of speech and press case in which the Court held that school officials may impose reasonable restrictions on the students, speeches of teachers, and other members of the school community.
***Hoyt* v. *Florida* (1961)**	A civil rights/gender classification case in which the Court ruled as constitutional a law that required men to serve on juries, but allowed women to choose whether or not they wished to serve.
***Kaiser Aluminum and Chemical Co. (United Steelworkers of America)* v. *Weber* (1979)**	A civil rights/reverse discrimination case in which a union apprenticeship program that used a racial quota was deemed legal even if it violated the words of the Civil Rights Act of 1964 because it did not violate the spirit. Essentially, any form of reverse discrimination—even explicit quotas—is permissible provided that it is the result of legislative, executive, or judicial findings of past discrimination.

Katz v. *United States* (1967)	A Fourth Amendment/wiretapping case in which the Court overturned Katz's conviction for transmitting betting information across state lines from a public phone booth in Los Angeles. The FBI had placed recording devices outside the booth without a warrant.
Klopfer v. *North Carolina* (1967)	A Sixth Amendment/right to a speedy trial case in which the Court first held that the Sixth Amendment's guarantee applies to the states because of the Fourteenth Amendment.
Lemon v. *Kurtzman* (1971)	An excessive entanglement case in which the Court held that the establishment clause was designed to prevent sponsorship, financial support, and active involvement of the government in religious activity. The Court did not allow a Pennsylvania law that provided for financial payments to private schools to cover their costs for textbooks, some teachers' salaries, and other teaching materials for nonreligious courses only.
Louisiana v. *Resweber* (1947)	An Eighth Amendment cruel and unusual punishment case in which the Court held that a convicted murderer could be subjected to a second electrocution after the first one failed to work properly.
Lynch v. *Donnelly* (1984)	A separation of church and state case in which the Court said that the city of Pawtucket, Rhode Island, could include a nativity scene in its holiday display because the scene formed part of an ensemble with Santa's sleigh and reindeer and a Christmas tree.
Mapp v. *Ohio* (1961)	A rights of the accused/exclusionary rule case in which the Court overturned the conviction of Dollree Mapp for possession of obscene materials because police had found pornographic books in her apartment after searching it without a warrant despite her verbal refusal to let them in.
Marbury v. *Madison* (1803)	The Court ruled for the first time an act of Congress unconstitutional, thereby establishing the principle of judicial review.
McCollum v. *Board of Education* (1948)	A "release time" program case in which the Court would not allow such a program in Champaign, Illinois, because school classrooms were being used for religious purposes.
McCulloch v. *Maryland* (1819)	The Court's ruling upheld the constitutionality of a creation of the Bank of the United States and denied to the states the power to tax it because "the power to tax involves the power to destroy." The ruling clarified the doctrine of implied powers of the national government.
Miller v. *California* (1973)	A freedom of speech/obscenity case in which the Court created a formal list of requirements as a legal test of obscenity. They are that (1) the average person finds that it violates contemporary community standards; (2) the work taken as a whole appeals to prurient interest in sex; (3) the work shows patently offensive sexual conduct; and (4) the work lacks serious redeeming literary, artistic, political, or scientific merit.

***Minersville School District* v. *Gobitis* (1940)**	A free exercise of religion/flag salute case in which the Court held that because the flag was a symbol of national unity, requiring that it be saluted was not an infringement on the free exercise of religion.
***Miranda* v. *Arizona* (1966)**	A rights of the accused/right to remain silent case in which a mentally disturbed suspect, Ernesto Miranda, had been arrested, questioned for two hours, and confessed to the crime of kidnapping and rape. His conviction was reversed by the Court on the basis of the Fifth and Sixth Amendments. Now people are read their rights, including the right to remain silent.
***Mueller* v. *Allen* (1983)**	An excessive entanglement case in which the Court upheld a Minnesota tax law giving parents a state income-tax deduction for the cost of textbooks, transportation for elementary and secondary schoolchildren, and tuition whether the children go to private or public schools.
***Murray* v. *Giarratano* (1989)**	An Eighth Amendment/capital punishment case in which the Court held that indigent death-row inmates have no constitutional right to a lawyer for a second round of state court appeals.
***Myers* v. *United States* (1926)**	The presidential removal power case in which the Court held unconstitutional an 1876 law that required Senate consent before the president could dismiss a postmaster.
***Near* v. *Minnesota* (1931)**	A freedom of press/prior restraint case in which a Minnesota law prohibiting the publication of malicious and scandalous newspapers or magazines was held to be invalid because it constituted unconstitutional prior restraint in violation of the First and Fourteenth Amendments.
***New York Times* v. *United States* (1971)**	A freedom of press/prior restraint case involving the publication of sensitive government documents relating to the government's policy in Vietnam from 1945 to 1967. The U.S. government attempted to suspend the publication of the so-called *Pentagon Papers*, but the Court held that the government could only prosecute after publication, not before.
***In re Oliver* (1948)**	A Sixth Amendment/right to a public trial case in which the Court ruled that not only must a trial be speedy, but it also must be held in public.
***Penry* v. *Lynaugh* (1989)**	An Eighth Amendment/capital punishment case in which the Court held that mentally retarded persons may be executed for murder.
***Plessy* v. *Ferguson* (1896)**	A civil rights case in which the Court ruled that state laws enforcing segregation by race were constitutional when accommodations were equal as well as separate. (Subsequently overturned by *Brown v. Board of Education of Topeka.*)
***Powell* v. *Alabama* (1932)**	A Sixth Amendment right to counsel case in which the Court ruled that the accused has a right to a lawyer in capital punishment cases.

Table of Court Cases—*Continued*

***Powell* v. *McCormack* (1969)**	A congressional qualifications case in which the Court ruled that the House of Representatives could not exclude any elected member who met the Constitution's requirements for citizenship, residence, and age.
***Reed* v. *Reed* (1971)**	A civil rights/gender classification case in which the Court ruled against an Idaho law that gave fathers preferences over mothers in taking care of their children's estates.
***Regents of the University of California* v. *Bakke* (1978)**	A civil rights/reverse discrimination case in which the Court allowed the University of California, Davis Campus, School of Medicine to admit students on the basis of race if the school's aim is to combat the effects of past discriminations. The Court held, nonetheless, that Bakke must be admitted to the medical school because its admissions policy had used race as the *sole* criterion for a limited number of "minority" positions.
***Reno* v. *American Civil Liberties Union* (1997)**	A free speech case in which the Court held that certain provisions in the Communications Decency Act, passed by Congress in 1996 to regulate obscenity on the Internet, were unconstitutional because they restrained too much adult speech.
***Reynolds* v. *Sims* (1964)**	A congressional reapportionment case in which the Court ruled that both chambers of a state legislature must be apportioned with equal populations in each district. This "one-person, one-vote" principle had already been applied to congressional districts in *Wesberry v. Sanders*.
***Reynolds* v. *United States* (1879)**	A free exercise of religion case in which the Court held that Reynolds, a Mormon living in Utah who had been convicted of polygamy, had violated federal law. The Court ruled that polygamy was a crime and therefore could not be excused as religious practice. Hence, people are free to believe and worship as they wish so long as their conduct does not violate laws that protect the safety, health, or morals of the community.
***Richmond* v. *Croson* (1989)**	A civil rights/reverse discrimination case in which the Court ruled that any program that favors blacks over whites has to be judged by the same constitutional test applicable to any law that favors whites over blacks.
***Richmond Newspapers, Inc.* v. *Virginia* (1980)**	A freedom of press/gag order case in which the Court ruled that actual trials must be opened to the public except under unusual circumstances.
***Robinson* v. *California* (1962)**	A Eighth Amendment/no cruel and unusual punishment case in which the Court ruled that the Fourteenth Amendment extends the Eighth Amendment to the states. Here the Court struck down a California law that defines drug addiction as a crime to be punished rather than an illness to be treated.

***Rochin* v. *California* (1952)**	A due process of law/procedural due process case, sometimes referred to as "the stomach pumping case," in which a suspected illegal drug user was taken to a hospital and administered a liquid that forced him to vomit. Morphine capsules thereby recovered were used to convict him of violating the state's narcotics laws. The Court overruled the conviction, holding that it violated the Fourteenth Amendment's guarantee of procedural due process.
***Roe* v. *Wade* (1973)**	A privacy case in which the Court ruled that state antiabortion laws were unconstitutional except when they applied to the last three months of pregnancy.
***Rostker* v. *Goldberg* (1981)**	A civil rights/gender classification case in which the Court upheld the U.S. government selective service law that requires only men to register for the draft.
***Schenck* v. *United States* (1919)**	A free speech case involving the clear and present danger test in which the Court upheld the Espionage Act of 1917, which made it a crime to encourage resistance to the military draft. The Court said that a person who encourages draft resistance during a war is a "clear and present danger."
***Smith* v. *Allwright* (1944)**	A voting rights case in which the Court declared that the white primary was a violation of the Fifteenth Amendment. The Court reasoned that the political party was actually performing a state function in holding a primary election and therefore not acting as a private group.
***South Carolina* v. *Katzenbach* (1966)**	A voting rights case in which the Court held that Congress had acted correctly by passing the Voting Rights Act as a way to implement the Fifteenth Amendment guarantee of the right to vote to every citizen of the United States regardless of race, color, or previous condition of servitude.
***Stone* v. *Graham* (1980)**	A separation of church and state case in which the Court would not allow a Kentucky law that required the Ten Commandments to be posted in all public classrooms.
***Teitel Film Corporation* v. *Cusack* (1968)**	A freedom of press/motion picture case in which the Court held that the government can ban a film if at a judicial hearing it is proven to be obscene.
***Thornhill* v. *Alabama* (1940)**	A freedom of speech/picketing case in which the Court held that picketing was a form of expression protected by the First and Fourteenth Amendments. Nonetheless, picketing may be prevented if it is set in a background of violence, and even peaceful picketing may be controlled if it is being done for an illegal purpose.

Table of Court Cases—*Continued*

***United States* v. *Nixon* (1974)**	A presidential executive privilege case in which the Court ruled that President Nixon had to hand over secret tapes containing his Oval Office conversations while in the White House. The Court ruled that executive privilege could not be used to prevent evidence from being heard in criminal proceedings.
***U.S. Term Limits, Inc.* v. *Thornton* (1995)**	A term limits case in which the Court held that a state does not have the authority to establish term limits for members of the U.S. Congress. Because the U.S. Constitution does not mention such limits, they can be established only by an amendment to the Constitution
***Walz* v. *New York City Tax Commission* (1970)**	A separation of church and state case in which the Court ruled that tax exemptions for churches do not violate the First Amendment, but rather show the state's "benevolent neutrality" toward religion.
***Wesberry* v. *Sanders* (1964)**	A Fourteenth Amendment/congressional districting case in which the Court ruled that the state of Georgia's formation of congressional districts created such huge population differences that they violated the Constitution. This case was the basis of the Court's ruling later requiring one person, one vote.
***West Virginia Board of Education* v. *Barnette* (1943)**	A free exercise of religion/flag salute case in which the Court held that laws requiring a flag salute were an unconstitutional interference with the free exercise of religion.
***Wilkinson* v. *Jones* (1987)**	A freedom of speech and press/cable TV case in which the Court held that state government cannot regulate independent cable programming. The case involved a Utah law prohibiting the cable broadcast of indecent material between 7 A.M. and midnight.
***Yates* v. *United States* (1957)**	A free speech and national security case in which the Court said that merely advocating the overthrow of a government is not illegal, because such speech only addresses people's belief as opposed to causing them to undertake actions against the government.
***Zorach* v. *Clauson* (1952)**	A "release time" case in which the Court upheld a New York City program because that program required religious classes to be held in private places and not on school campuses.

Presidents and Vice Presidents of the United States

GEORGE WASHINGTON

Born: February 22, 1732
Died: December 14, 1799
Dates in office: 1789–1797
Profession before presidency: Planter
Political party: None
State of birth: Virginia

1

George Washington took his oath of office as the first president of the United States on the balcony of Federal Hall on Wall Street in New York City. Understanding the precedent-setting role of his position, Washington acted cautiously as president, working to flesh out the framework of government that was described in the Constitution.

Vice president: John Adams
(see John Adams's listing under Presidents)

JOHN ADAMS

Born: October 30, 1735
Died: July 4, 1826
Dates in office: 1797–801
Profession before presidency: Lawyer
Political party: Federalist
State: Massachusetts

2

On at least two occasions, John Adams went against popular public opinion. As a lawyer, Adams defended the British soldiers who killed three Americans at the Boston Massacre in 1770, feeling a mob mentality was taking over the colony. As president, Adams ignored public sentiment for war with France and instead coaxed France to accept neutrality rights at sea with the United States in exchange for most-favored-nation status.

Vice president: Thomas Jefferson
(see Jefferson's listing under Presidents)

THOMAS JEFFERSON

Born: April 13, 1743
Died: July 4, 1826
Dates in office: 1801–1809
Profession before presidency: Planter
Political party: Democratic-Republican
Home State: Virginia

3

Not known for his eloquence, Thomas Jefferson was the "silent member" of the Continental Congress. He used his writing skills to draft the Declaration of Independence at age 33. During Jefferson's first term as president, he approved the purchase of the vast Louisiana Territory for a paltry $15 million dollars. However, he had originally sent his negotiators to buy only West Florida and New Orleans.

Vice president: Aaron Burr
Home State: New Jersey
Political party: Democratic-Republican
Profession: Lawyer

Vice president: George Clinton
Home State: New York
Political party: Democratic-Republican
Profession: Lawyer

JAMES MADISON

Born: March 16, 1751
Died: June 28, 1836
Dates in office: 1809–1817
Profession before presidency: Lawyer
Political party: Democratic-Republican
Home State: Virginia

4

The shortest and slightest president, James Madison stood about 5 feet 4 inches and weighed just 100 pounds. Madison contributed to the ratification of the Constitution with his co-authored *Federalist* essays. According to Daniel Webster, "Madison had as much to do as any man in framing the Constitution, and as much to do as any man in administering it."

Vice president: George Clinton
Home State: New York
Political party: Democratic-Republican
Profession: Lawyer

Vice president: Elbridge Gerry
Home State: Massachusetts
Political party: Democratic-Republican
Profession: Importer and shipper

JAMES MONROE

Born: April 28, 1758
Died: July 4, 1831
Dates in office: 1817–1825
Profession before presidency: Lawyer
Political party: Democratic-Republican
Home State: Virginia

5

James Monroe faced a nation's fears that Spain might attempt to retake its former colonies in Latin America and that Russia might extend its claims in Alaska to the Oregon Territory. He consequently declared to Congress in 1823 a warning to European nations about intervention in the Western Hemisphere. The message came to bear his name: the Monroe Doctrine.

Vice president: Daniel D. Tompkins
Home State: New York
Political party: Democratic-Republican
Profession: Lawyer

JOHN QUINCY ADAMS

Born: July 11, 1767
Died: February 23, 1848
Dates in office: 1825–1829
Profession before presidency: Lawyer
Political party: Democratic-Republican
Home State: Massachusetts

6

John Quincy Adams was the only president who was the son of a president. Adams ambitiously proposed a strong program sponsored by the federal government to link the sections of

the nation with highways and canals, to create a national university, and to build an astronomical observatory. The programs were largely passed over by Congress, however. Adams obtained only the extension of the Cumberland Road into Ohio and the construction of the Chesapeake and Ohio Canal.

Vice president: John C. Calhoun
Home State: South Carolina
Political party: Democratic-Republican
Profession: Lawyer

ANDREW JACKSON

Born: March 15, 1767
Died: June 8, 1845
Dates in office: 1829–1837
Profession before presidency: Lawyer
Political party: Democratic
Home State: South Carolina

7

As a major general in the War of 1812, Andrew Jackson became a national hero due to his victory over the British at New Orleans. More than any president who came before him, Jackson was elected by the popular vote of common citizens. Later, as president, he recommended eliminating the electoral college.

Vice president: John C. Calhoun
Home State: South Carolina
Political party: Democratic-Republican
Profession: Lawyer

Vice president: Martin Van Buren
(see Van Buren's listing under Presidents)

MARTIN VAN BUREN

Born: December 5, 1782
Died: July 24, 1862
Dates in office: 1837–1841
Profession before presidency: Lawyer
Political party: Democratic
Home State: New York

8

Only about 5 feet 6 inches tall, Martin Van Buren, the "Little Magician," was elected vice president on Andrew Jackson's ticket in 1832. He won the presidency in 1836. A severe economic slump plagued Van Buren's term. Over nine hundred banks closed across the country. Many of Van Buren's deflationary measures contributed to the prolonged depression.

Vice president: Richard M. Johnson
Home State: Kentucky
Political party: Democratic
Profession: Lawyer

WILLIAM H. HARRISON

Born: February 9, 1773
Died: April 4, 1841
Dates in office: 1841
Profession before presidency: Lawyer
Political party: Whig
Home State: Virginia

9

William H. Harrison was the last president born a British subject. His presidency lasted exactly one month. He caught a cold, which turned into pneumonia, while delivering his inaugural address. Shortly before he died, he spoke his last words: "I wish you to understand the true principles of the government. I wish them carried out. I ask nothing more."

Vice president: John Tyler
(see Tyler's listing under Presidents)

JOHN TYLER

Born: March 29, 1790
Died: January 18, 1862
Dates in office: 1841–1845
Profession before presidency: Soldier
Political party: Whig
Home State: Virginia

10

As vice president, John Tyler took the office of president upon the death of William H. Harrison. He became known as "a president without a party" after the Whigs expelled him for failing to go along with them on their plan to establish a national bank. Nevertheless, Tyler was able to enact much positive legislation. For example, his "Log Cabin" Bill allowed settlers to claim and later purchase 160 acres of land before it was put on the public market.

JAMES K. POLK

Born: November 2, 1795
Died: June 15, 1849
Dates in office: 1845–1849
Profession before presidency: Lawyer
Political party: Democratic
Home State: North Carolina

11

James K. Polk was a candidate committed to the nation's "Manifest Destiny," the belief that the United States was divinely destined to rule from sea to sea. He urged reannexation of Texas and reoccupation of Oregon. He also favored acquiring California. These views plunged Polk and the United States into, among other things, the Mexican War. This conflict lasted from 1846 to 1848, when the border between the two countries was fixed at the Rio Grande.

Vice president: George M. Dallas
Home State: Pennsylvania
Political party: Democratic
Profession: Lawyer

ZACHARY TAYLOR

Born: November 24, 1784
Died: July 9, 1850
Dates in office: 1849–1850
Profession before presidency: Soldier
Political party: Whig
Home State: Virginia

12

Zachary Taylor was nicknamed "Old Rough and Ready" from his days as a general in the Mexican War. President Taylor was a former slave owner who told the Southern states that threatened secession that he would personally lead the Union army against them if any of them tried to secede. Taylor's only son, Richard, served in the Civil War as a general in the Confederate army.

Vice president: Millard Fillmore
(see Fillmore's listing under Presidents)

MILLARD FILLMORE

Born: January 7, 1800
Died: March 8, 1874
Dates in office: 1850–1853
Profession before presidency: Lawyer
Political party: Whig
Home State: New York

13

Millard Fillmore embraced the compromise between slave and free states that Zachary Taylor had opposed. Called the Compromise of 1850, it included bills that admitted California as a free state; settled the Texas boundary; granted territorial status to New Mexico; approved the controversial Fugitive Slave Act, which required the federal government to assist in returning escaped slaves to their masters; and abolished slave trade in the District of Columbia.

FRANKLIN PIERCE

Born: November 23, 1804
Died: October 8, 1869
Dates in office: 1853–1857
Profession before presidency: Lawyer
Political party: Democratic
Home State: New Hampshire

14

Franklin Pierce entered the presidency on the heels of tragedy. Just two months before he took office, he and his wife saw their eleven-year-old son killed in a train wreck. Then the tranquility of the years after the Compromise of 1850 ended when Senator Stephen Douglas proposed the Kansas-Nebraska Act, which said in part that the residents of the new territories could decide the slavery question themselves. The result was a rush into Kansas, where southerners and northerners battled in a prelude to the Civil War.

Vice president: William R. King
Home State: North Carolina
Political party: Democratic
Profession: Lawyer

JAMES BUCHANAN

Born: April 23, 1791
Died: June 1, 1868
Dates in office: 1857–1861
Profession before presidency: Lawyer
Political party: Democratic
Home State: Pennsylvania

15

James Buchanan was the only president who never married. He served at a frightful time for the fast-dividing nation. Buchanan misread the political realities of his time. He thought that the problems between North and South could be solved constitutionally through the Supreme Court. In his inaugural address, he said that the Supreme Court was about to settle the situation "speedily and finally."

Vice president: John C. Breckinridge
Home State: Kentucky
Political party: Democratic
Profession: Lawyer

ABRAHAM LINCOLN

Born: February 12, 1809
Died: April 15, 1865
Dates in office: 1861–1865
Profession before presidency: Lawyer
Political party: Republican
Home State: Kentucky

16

Abraham Lincoln constantly reminded the world that the issues of the Civil War involved more than North versus South, slave versus free. At Gettysburg, he proclaimed "that this nation, under God, shall have a new birth of freedom—and that government of the people, by the people, for the people shall not perish from the earth." On January 1, 1863, Lincoln issued the Emancipation Proclamation, which declared slaves free within states controlled by the Confederacy. He was assassinated on Good Friday, April 14, 1865, by John Wilkes Booth at Ford's Theatre in Washington, D.C.

Vice president: Hannibal Hamlin
Home State: Maine
Political party: Republican
Profession: Lawyer

Vice president: Andrew Johnson
(see Andrew Johnson's listing under Presidents)

ANDREW JOHNSON

Born: December 29, 1808
Died: July 31, 1875
Dates in office: 1865–1869
Profession before presidency: Tailor
Political party: National Union
Home State: North Carolina

17

To Andrew Johnson fell the task of reconstructing the nation after the Civil War and Abraham Lincoln's death. Johnson restored legal rights to the Southern states swiftly, since in his view they had never technically left the Union (because the Union was indissoluble). Johnson faced impeachment by the House when he allegedly violated the Tenure of Office Act by wrongly dismissing the secretary of war. He was tried by the Senate and acquitted by one vote.

ULYSSES S. GRANT

Born: April 27, 1822
Died: July 23, 1885
Dates in office: 1869–1877
Profession before presidency: Soldier
Political party: Republican
Home State: Ohio

18

Ulysses S. Grant became commander of all Union armies in March 1864. Robert E. Lee formally surrendered to Grant at Appomattox, Virginia, on April 9, 1865. As president, Grant clashed with speculators, whose attempt to corner the gold market greatly disrupted American business. Grant realized his shortcomings as president. He said, "It was my fortune, or misfortune, to be called to the office of Chief Executive without any previous political training."

Vice president: Schuyler Colfax
Home State: New York
Political party: Republican
Profession: Deputy auditor

Vice president: Henry Wilson
Home State: New Hampshire
Political party: Republican
Profession: Shoe factory owner

RUTHERFORD B. HAYES

Born: October 4, 1822
Died: January 17, 1893
Dates in office: 1877–1881
Profession before presidency: Lawyer
Political party: Republican
Home State: Ohio

19

Rutherford B. Hayes won the most disputed election in American history. Hayes's election depended upon disputed electoral votes in Louisiana, South Carolina, and Florida. He needed every electoral vote from those states to win; a panel established by Congress determined that Hayes did indeed win the election: 185 electoral votes to 184 over Governor Samuel J. Tilden of New York.

Vice president: William A. Wheeler
Home State: New York
Political party: Republican
Profession: Lawyer

JAMES A. GARFIELD

Born: November 19, 1831
Died: September 19, 1881
Dates in office: 1881
Profession before presidency: Lawyer
Political party: Republican
Home State: Ohio

20

On July 2, 1881, James A. Garfield was strolling in a Washington, D.C., railroad station. He was shot in the back by Charles Guiteau, a man who had been rebuffed by the president for an appointment to a diplomatic post following the election. Garfield lay wounded in the White House for weeks. Alexander Graham Bell, the inventor of the telephone, designed an electrical device in an attempt to find the bullet still lodged in the president. On September 6, Garfield, seemingly recuperating, was taken to a New Jersey resort. He died there on September 19.

Vice president: Chester A. Arthur
(See Arthur's listing under Presidents)

CHESTER A. ARTHUR

Born: October 5, 1829
Died: November 18, 1886
Dates in office: 1881–1885
Profession before presidency: Lawyer
Political party: Republican
Home State: Vermont

21

Chester A. Arthur was appointed by President Grant as collector of the port of New York in 1871. He was responsible for collection of about 75 percent of the nation's duties from ships that landed within his jurisdiction. The customhouse was riddled with scandal, including the proven charge that employees were expected to kick back part of their salaries to the Republican Party. As president, Arthur sought to rid himself of machine politics. In 1883, Congress passed the Pendleton Act, which protected employees against removal from their jobs for political reasons.

GROVER CLEVELAND

Born: March 18, 1837
Died: June 24, 1908
Dates in office: 1885–1889; 1893–1897
Profession before presidency: Lawyer
Political party: Democratic
Home State: New Jersey

22

Grover Cleveland was the only president to leave the White House and return for a second term four years later. After his defeat by Benjamin Harrison in 1888, Cleveland returned to his law practice in New York City, seemingly retired from active political life. In his second term, the nation faced a great depression. When railroad workers went on strike in Chicago, Cleveland said, "If it takes the entire army and

navy of the United States to deliver a postcard in Chicago, that card will be delivered."

Vice president: Thomas A. Hendricks
Home State: Ohio
Political party: Democratic
Profession: Lawyer

BENJAMIN HARRISON

Born: August 20, 1833
Died: March 13, 1901
Dates in office: 1889–1893
Profession before presidency: Lawyer
Political party: Republican
Home State: Ohio

23

Benjamin Harrison was the grandson of William H. Harrison, the nation's ninth president. Benjamin Harrison signed the Sherman Anti-Trust Act in 1890, the first of the antitrust laws to curb the abuse of monopolies that conspired to restrict trade. Harrison was defeated for reelection in 1892 by Grover Cleveland, the man he had triumphed over four years earlier.

Vice president: Levi P. Morton
Home State: Vermont
Political party: Republican
Profession: Businessman and banker

(See earlier entry) GROVER CLEVELAND

Vice president: Adlai E. Stevenson
Home State: Kentucky
Political party: Democratic
Profession: Lawyer

WILLIAM MCKINLEY

Born: January 29, 1843
Died: September 14, 1901
Dates in office: 1897–1901
Profession before presidency: Lawyer
Political party: Republican
Home State: Ohio

25

During William McKinley's term, the United States intervened in the Spanish-American War and destroyed the Spanish fleet outside Santiago harbor in Cuba, captured Manila, in the Philippines, and occupied Puerto Rico. McKinley followed public opinion in annexing the acquired territories (except Cuba). McKinley was assassinated in 1901. He was shot while standing in a receiving line at a Pan American Exposition in Buffalo, New York.

Vice president: Garret A. Hobart
Home State: New Jersey
Political party: Republican
Profession: Lawyer

Vice president: Theodore Roosevelt
(see Theodore Roosevelt's listing under Presidents)

William H. Taft was appointed a federal circuit judge at thirty-four years old. He always would prefer law to politics. Nevertheless, he rose politically through presidential appointments and was nominated as Theodore Roosevelt's Republican successor in 1908. Taft was uncomfortable as president. After he was defeated for reelection, he was appointed chief justice of the Supreme Court of the United States by President Warren G. Harding. He considered the appointment his greatest honor. "I don't even remember being President," he said.

Vice president: James S. Sherman
Home State: New York
Political party: Republican
Profession: Lawyer

THEODORE ROOSEVELT

Born: October 27, 1858
Died: January 6, 1919
Dates in office: 1901–1909
Profession before presidency: Author
Political party: Republican
Home State: New York

26

Theodore Roosevelt was not quite forty-three years old when he took over as president for the slain William McKinley. Roosevelt was a charismatic man who led the American people and Congress toward progressive reforms and a strong foreign policy. Roosevelt staunchly defended the right by the United States to use military force, if necessary, to defend the principles of the Monroe Doctrine. His famous words were "Speak softly and carry a big stick; you will go far."

Vice president: Charles W. Fairbanks
Home State: Ohio
Political party: Republican
Profession: Lawyer

WOODROW WILSON

Born: December 29, 1856
Died: February 3, 1924
Dates in office: 1913–1921
Profession before presidency: Educator
Political party: Democratic
Home State: Virginia

28

Woodrow Wilson's campaign slogan for reelection in 1916 was "He kept us out of war." But after his election, Wilson knew that the United States could not remain neutral in the world war. On April 2, 1917, he asked Congress to declare war on Germany. Early the next year, Wilson set forth his famous Fourteen Points, the only basis, he insisted, on which lasting peace could be made. The armistice was signed on November 11, 1918.

Vice president: Thomas R. Marshall
Home State: Indiana
Political party: Democratic
Profession: Lawyer

WILLIAM H. TAFT

Born: September 15, 1857
Died: March 8, 1930
Dates in office: 1909–1913
Profession before presidency: Lawyer
Political party: Republican
Home State: Ohio

27

WARREN G. HARDING

Born: November 2, 1865
Died: August 2, 1923
Dates in office: 1921–1923
Profession before presidency: Editor
Political party: Republican
Home State: Ohio

29

Warren G. Harding was a master of the great phrase, and this, combined with his handsome looks, won him a landslide election in 1920. Harding appeared to be on his way to carrying out his campaign promise of "less government in business and more business in government" when word got to him that some of his friends were using their official positions for their own gain. Harding said, "My friends, they're the ones keeping me walking the floor nights." Harding died in office of a heart attack while in San Francisco in 1923. A historians' poll in 1962 ranked him, along with Ulysses S. Grant, as the worst of the presidents.

Vice president: Calvin Coolidge
(see Coolidge's listing under Presidents)

CALVIN COOLIDGE

Born: July 4, 1872
Died: January 5, 1933
Dates in office: 1923–1929
Profession before presidency: Lawyer
Political party: Republican
Home State: Vermont

30

Calvin Coolidge's father, a notary public, administered his son the oath of office at their family home upon learning of the death of President Warren G. Harding. Coolidge quickly became a popular president, known for his dry wit. Once, a woman sitting next to him at a dinner party confided that she had bet that she could get at least three words from him in conversation. "You lose," he quietly responded.

Vice president: Charles G. Dawes
Home State: Ohio
Political party: Republican
Profession: Lawyer

HERBERT C. HOOVER

Born: August 10, 1874
Died: October 20, 1964
Dates in office: 1929–1933
Profession before presidency: Engineer
Political party: Republican
Home State: Iowa

31

Herbert C. Hoover gained international attention during World War I by leading the distribution of food and supplies to war-torn Europe. He was the secretary of commerce under Presidents Harding and Coolidge before being nominated for president in 1928. Hoover became a scapegoat for the depression that plagued the nation after the stock market crash of 1929. Under the later Truman and Eisenhower administrations, Hoover was appointed to head the commissions that reorganized the executive departments.

Vice president: Charles Curtis
Home State: Kansas
Political party: Republican
Profession: Lawyer

FRANKLIN D. ROOSEVELT

Born: January 30, 1882
Died: April 12, 1945
Dates in office: 1933–1945
Profession before presidency: Lawyer
Political party: Democratic
Home State: New York

32

Franklin D. Roosevelt became president in the midst of the Great Depression. He declared in his inaugural address, "The only thing we have to fear is fear itself." He pledged that his primary task was to put people back to work. By 1935, the nation's economy had recovered somewhat, but Roosevelt's New Deal policies were being criticized increasingly by American businessmen and bankers. Roosevelt was elected to three more terms, the most for any president. After the bombing of Pearl Harbor, Roosevelt directed the United States into World War II.

Vice president: John N. Garner
Home State: Texas
Political party: Democratic
Profession: Lawyer

Vice president: Henry A. Wallace
Home State: Iowa
Political party: Democratic
Profession: Writer and editor

Vice president: Harry S Truman
(see Truman's listing under Presidents)

HARRY S TRUMAN

Born: May 8, 1884
Died: December 26, 1972
Dates in office: 1945–1953
Profession before presidency:
    Businessman
Political party: Democratic
Home State: Missouri

33

Harry S Truman was only vice president for a few weeks when President Franklin D. Roosevelt died on April 12, 1945. As president, Truman made some of the most important decisions in history. He ordered the atomic bomb to be dropped on two cities in Japan at the close of World War II. In June 1945, he witnessed the signing of the Charter of the United Nations. Truman won a close election in 1948 over Republican Thomas Dewey and proudly displayed an early edition of the Chicago Tribune that proclaimed otherwise: "Dewey Defeats Truman."

Vice president: Alben W. Barkley
Home State: Kentucky
Political party: Democratic
Profession: Lawyer

DWIGHT D. EISENHOWER

Born: October 14, 1890
Died: March 28, 1969
Dates in office: 1953–1961
Profession before presidency: Soldier
Political party: Republican
Home State: Texas

34

Dwight D. Eisenhower was the commanding general for the Allied forces in Europe in World War II. As president, he concentrated on maintaining world peace. Eisenhower sent federal troops to Little Rock, Arkansas, to ensure compliance with the federal court order to desegregate the schools. He pointed to peace as his administration's legacy. "The United States never lost a soldier or a foot of ground in my administration. We kept the peace," he said.

Vice president: Richard M. Nixon
(see Nixon's listing under Presidents)

JOHN F. KENNEDY

Born: May 29, 1917
Died: November 22, 1963
Dates in office: 1961–1963
Profession before presidency: Author
Political party: Democratic
Home State: Massachusetts

35

John F. Kennedy was the youngest president to die. He was assassinated in Dallas, Texas, in November 1963. Kennedy won a close election over Richard M. Nixon, due in part to Kennedy's performance in a series of televised debates. He was the first Roman Catholic president. At his inauguration, he declared, "Ask not what your country can do for you—ask what you can do for your country."

Vice president: Lyndon B. Johnson
(see Lyndon B. Johnson's listing under Presidents)

LYNDON B. JOHNSON

Born: August 27, 1908
Died: January 22, 1973
Dates in office: 1963–1969
Profession before presidency: Teacher
Political party: Democratic
Home State: Texas

36

Lyndon B. Johnson's "Great Society" program became the agenda for his administration. Aid to education, attack on disease, Medicare, urban renewal, war on poverty, and the removal of obstacles to the right to vote were many of the recommendations that Johnson sent to Congress. The escalating Vietnam War was Johnson's downfall; controversy over the war fueled protests at home. Johnson declined to seek reelection in 1968.

Vice president: Hubert H. Humphrey
Home State: South Dakota
Political party: Democratic
Profession: Pharmacist, teacher

RICHARD M. NIXON

Born: January 9, 1913
Died: April 22, 1994
Dates in office: 1969–1974
Profession before presidency: Lawyer
Political party: Republican
Home State: California

37

Richard M. Nixon succeeded in bringing an end to the Vietnam War and improving relations with the Soviet Union and China. His election in 1968 was a political comeback. He had been defeated for the presidency in 1960 and for governor of California in 1962. Nixon's presidency ended in the Watergate scandal, in which a break-in of the Democratic headquarters during the 1972 reelection campaign was tied to his administration. Faced with the prospect of impeachment, Nixon resigned on August 9, 1974. He was the only president to resign the office.

Vice president: Spiro T. Agnew
Home State: Maryland
Political party: Republican
Profession: Lawyer

Vice president: Gerald R. Ford
(see Ford's listing under Presidents)

GERALD R. FORD

Born: July 14, 1913
Dates in office: 1974–1977
Profession before presidency: Lawyer
Political party: Republican
Home State: Nebraska

38

In September 1974, Gerald R. Ford granted former president Nixon "a full, free and absolute pardon for all offenses against the United States which he has committed or may have committed or taken part in" during his term in office. Gradually, Ford chose a presidential cabinet of his own. Ford won the Republican nomination for president in 1976 but lost the election to Jimmy Carter. At his inauguration, President Carter began: "For myself and for our nation, I want to thank my predecessor for all he has done to heal our land."

Vice president: Nelson A. Rockefeller
Home State: Maine
Political party: Republican
Profession: Businessman

JAMES E. CARTER, JR.

Born: October 1, 1924
Dates in office: 1977–1981
Profession before presidency:
   Businessman
Political party: Democratic
Home State: Georgia

39

James E. ("Jimmy") Carter, Jr., began campaigning for the presidency in December 1974. His two-year campaign gained momentum, and he was a first-ballot nominee of the Democratic Party. Carter established a national energy program during his administration and sought to improve the environment. His greatest foreign policy accomplishment was the Camp David agreement of 1978 between Egypt and Israel.

Vice president: Walter F. Mondale
Home State: Minnesota
Political party: Democratic
Profession: Lawyer

RONALD W. REAGAN

Born: February 6, 1911
Dates in office: 1981–1989
Profession before presidency: Actor
Political party: Republican
Home State: Illinois

40

As president of the Screen Actors Guild, Ronald W. Reagan became tangled in disputes involving communism. His political views subsequently changed from liberal to conservative. As president, Reagan obtained legislation to stimulate economic growth, curb inflation, increase employment, and strengthen national defense. His "peace through strength" foreign policy is credited as one of the reasons for the collapse of the Communist bloc shortly after his second term.

Vice president: George H. W. Bush
(see Bush's listing under Presidents)

GEORGE H. W. BUSH

41

Born: June 12, 1924
Dates in office: 1989–1993
Profession before presidency:
    Businessman
Political party: Republican
Home State: Massachusetts

George H. W. Bush pledged a return to traditional American values and aimed to make America "a kinder and gentler nation." Bush's handling of the brief Persian Gulf War in 1991 increased his popularity. One of Bush's primary domestic goals was to put an end to "the scourge of drugs" that racked the nation.

Vice president: J. Danforth Quayle
Home State: Indiana
Political party: Republican
Profession: Lawyer

WILLIAM J. B. CLINTON

42

Born: August 19, 1946
Dates in office: 1993—
Profession before presidency: Governor of
    Arkansas
Political Party: Democrat
Home State: Arkansas

Running a campaign that focused on change, William Jefferson Blythe Clinton was swept into the presidency in an election that saw the first upturn in voter turnout since the election of John F. Kennedy. On election night he spoke at a victory rally in Little Rock, Arkansas and said, "My fellow Americans, with high hopes and brave hearts, in massive numbers, the American people have voted to make a new beginning."

Vice president: Albert Gore, Jr.
Home State: Tennessee
Political Party: Democrat
Profession: Journalist

State Statistics

State	Capital	Size (in square miles)	Population	Order Admitted	Date Admitted	Number of Congressional Districts
Alabama	Montgomery	51,705	4,319,154	22	December 14, 1819	7
Alaska	Juneau	591,004	609,311	49	January 3, 1959	1*
Arizona	Phoenix	114,000	4,554,966	48	February 14, 1912	6
Arkansas	Little Rock	53,187	2,522,819	25	June 15, 1836	4
California	Sacramento	158,706	32,268,301	31	September 9, 1850	52
Colorado	Denver	104,091	3,892,644	38	August 1, 1876	6
Connecticut	Hartford	5,018	3,269,858	5	January 9, 1788	6
Delaware	Dover	2,044	731,581	1	December 7, 1787	1*
District of Columbia	Washington	69	528,964	—	June 10, 1800**	1*
Florida	Tallahassee	58,644	14,653,945	27	March 3, 1845	23
Georgia	Atlanta	58,910	7,486,242	4	January 2, 1788	11
Hawaii	Honolulu	6,471	1,186,602	50	August 21 , 1959	2
Idaho	Boise	83,564	1,210,232	43	July 3, 1890	2
Illinois	Springfield	57,871	11,895,849	21	December 3, 1818	20
Indiana	Indianapolis	36,413	5,864,108	19	December 11, 1816	10
Iowa	Des Moines	56,275	2,852,423	29	December 28, 1846	5
Kansas	Topeka	82,277	2,594,840	34	January 29, 1861	4
Kentucky	Frankfort	40,409	3,908,124	15	June 1, 1792	6
Louisiana	Baton Rouge	47,752	4,351,769	18	April 30, 1812	7
Maine	Augusta	33,265	1,242,051	23	March 15, 1820	2
Maryland	Annapolis	10,460	5,094,289	7	April 28, 1788	8
Massachusetts	Boston	8,284	6,117,520	6	February 6, 1788	10
Michigan	Lansing	58,527	9,773,892	26	January 26, 1837	16
Minnesota	Saint Paul	86,614	4,685,549	32	May 11, 1858	8
Mississippi	Jackson	47,689	2,730,501	20	December 10, 1817	5
Missouri	Jefferson City	69,697	5,402,058	24	August 10, 1821	9
Montana	Helena	147,046	878,810	41	November 8, 1889	1
Nebraska	Lincoln	77,355	1,656,870	37	March 1, 1867	3
Nevada	Carson City	110,561	1,676,809	36	October 31, 1864	2
New Hampshire	Concord	9,279	1,172,709	9	June 21, 1788	2
New Jersey	Trenton	7,787	8,052,849	3	December 18, 1787	13
New Mexico	Santa Fe	121,593	1,729,751	47	January 6, 1912	3
New York	Albany	52,735	18,137,226	11	July 26, 1788	31

* Congressional districts at large
** Became seat of the federal government

State	Capital	Size (in square miles)	Population	Order Admitted	Date Admitted	Number of Congressional Districts
North Carolina	Raleigh	52,669	7,425,183	12	November 21, 1789	12
North Dakota	Bismarck	70,702	640,883	39	November 2, 1889	1*
Ohio	Columbus	44,787	11,186,331	17	March 1, 1803	19
Oklahoma	Oklahoma City	69,956	3,317,091	46	November 16, 1907	6
Oregon	Salem	97,073	3,243,487	33	February 14, 1859	5
Pennsylvania	Harrisburg	46,043	12,019,661	2	December 12, 1787	21
Rhode Island	Providence	1,212	987,429	13	May 29, 1790	2
South Carolina	Columbia	31,113	3,760,181	8	May 23, 1788	6
South Dakota	Pierre	77,116	737,973	40	November 2, 1889	1*
Tennessee	Nashville	42,144	5,368,198	16	June 1, 1796	9*
Texas	Austin	266,807	19,439,337	28	December 29, 1845	30
Utah	Salt Lake City	84,899	2,059,148	45	January 4, 1896	3
Vermont	Montpelier	9,614	588,978	14	March 4, 1791	1*
Virginia	Richmond	40,767	6,733,996	10	June 25, 1788	11
Washington	Olympia	68,139	5,610,362	42	November 11, 1889	9
West Virginia	Charleston	24,231	1,815,787	35	June 20, 1863	3
Wisconsin	Madison	56,153	5,169,677	30	May 29, 1848	9
Wyoming	Cheyenne	97,809	479,743	44	July 10, 1890	1*

* Congressional districts at large

Map of the United States

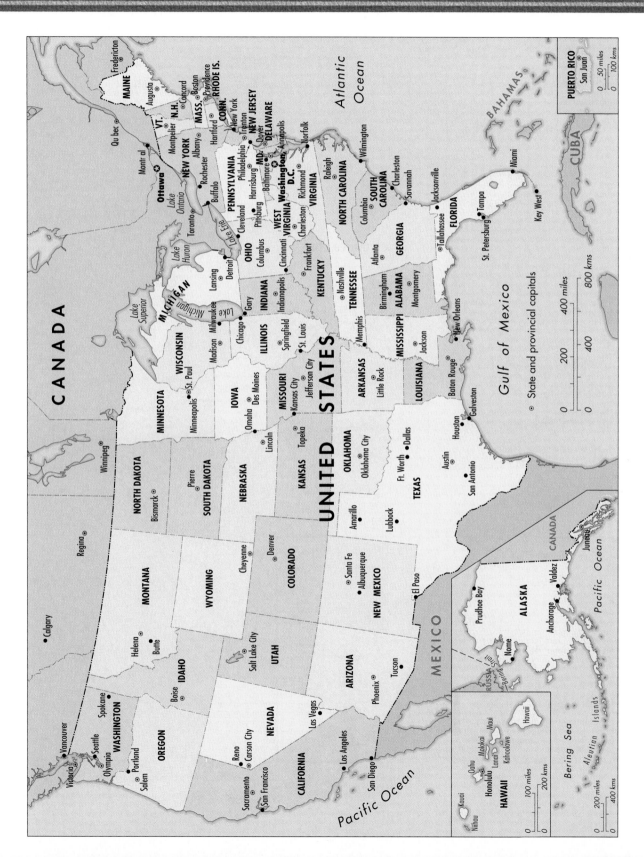

Map of the World

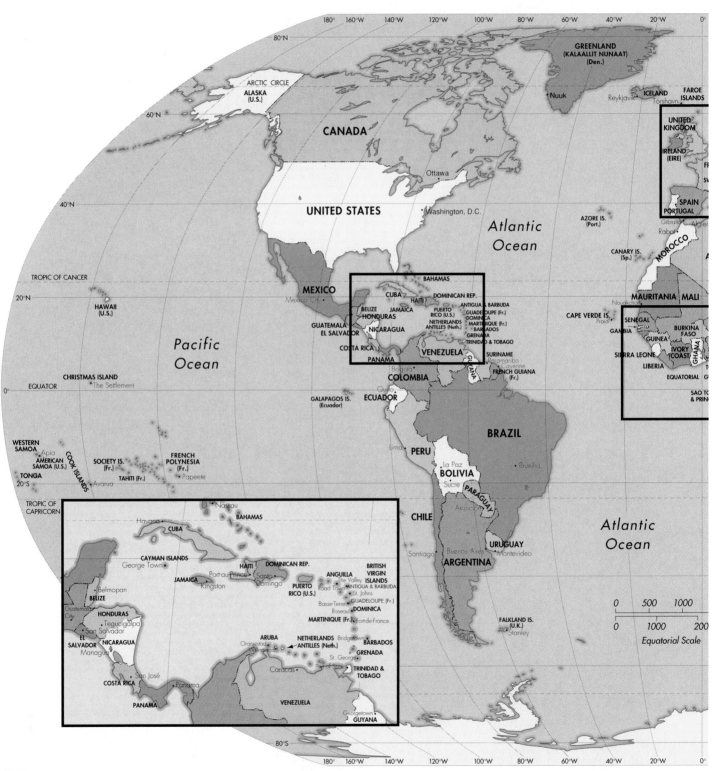

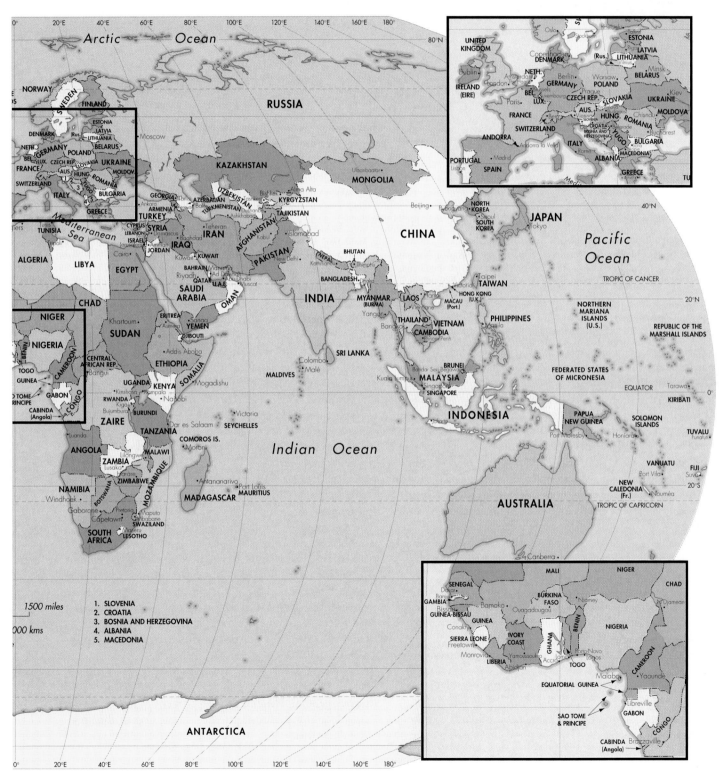

Glossary

A

ability-to-pay principle A taxation principle under which those with higher incomes pay more in taxes than those with lower incomes, regardless of the number of government services they use.

abridge Deprive or diminish.

absentee ballots Votes that are mailed in by the voters, rather than cast at the polls.

absolute monarchs Monarchs who have complete and unlimited power.

absolute monarchy A government in which rulers hold complete and unlimited power. (Compare with *constitutional monarchy.*)

acquittal The pronouncement that a defendant in a criminal case is found not guilty of the charges.

act of admissions A bill passed by Congress that admits a state into the Union.

administrative assistant A person hired to manage a lawmaker's office, supervise his or her schedule, and give advice. (Administrative assistants also work for other types of professionals.)

affirmative action Job hiring policies that allow special considerations for traditionally disadvantaged groups (such as women or racial minorities) in an effort to overcome the present effects of past discrimination.

agenda A list or program of goals to be accomplished. In government, agenda setting usually involves deciding which public policy questions will be debated, considered, or carried out.

Aid to Families with Dependent Children (AFDC) A social program, funded in part by the federal government and administered by the state, that provides financial assistance to impoverished families with children.

alien One who is not a citizen of the state or nation in which she or he lives.

allegiance Loyalty and service to one's country and government.

alliance Association of two or more nations joined together for mutual benefit.

ambassador A diplomat of high rank who represents his or her government to a foreign country.

amendments Written changes or additions to a law or body of laws, such as the United States Constitution.

amnesty A governmental grant of pardon to a large group of individuals.

Anti-Federalists A political group that opposed the adoption of the Constitution because of the document's centralist tendencies and that attacked the framers of the Constitution for failing to include a bill of rights.

appellate court A court that reviews decisions reached by lower (usually trial) courts.

appellate jurisdiction Authority of a court to review decisions reached by lower courts.

apportioned Seats in a legislative body are distributed (apportioned) among electoral districts based on state population.

appropriation The authorization of money for a specific purpose; money approved by the legislature as funding for the activities of another branch of government.

appropriation bills Bills that formally set aside money for a specific purpose.

armistice A temporary agreement between opponents to stop fighting (also called a *cease-fire*).

arraignment A preliminary court proceeding in which the defendant hears the charges and enters his or her plea.

assembly A gathering of people for a common purpose.

assimilation The process in which people are absorbed into the cultural tradition of a different population or group.

at large The election of an official by the voters of an entire governmental unit such as a state or county, rather than by voters of a subdivision of that area.

attaché Member of an embassy staff who serves in a particular capacity.

attack ads A form of negative campaign advertising in which the character of a candidate's opponent is attacked.

attorney general Head of the Department of Justice who is appointed by the president and is a member of the president's cabinet.

Australian ballot A secret ballot that is prepared, distributed, and tabulated by government officials at public expense. The method was introduced to the United States from Australia in 1888 and replaced an open ballot.

authoritarian A concentration of power in a leader who is not constitutionally responsible to the people.

authority The power to influence thought, opinion, and behavior. (Legal authority can be defined as the power to make and enforce laws.)

autocracy A government in which the power and authority are in the hands of a single person.

B

bad-tendency rule The doctrine holding that speech, religious practice, or other First Amendment freedoms may be permissibly curtailed if such expressions might lead to some "evil."

bail Money that a prisoner may be required to deposit with a court to obtain his or her release and to guarantee that he or she will appear in court at a designated time.

balance the ticket A method by which a presidential candidate chooses a vice presidential candidate who possesses complementary characteristics and thus improves the chances of winning an election.

ballot A printed voting form.

bandwagon effect A propaganda technique that attempts to persuade people to support a candidate or issue because large numbers of other people are supposedly doing so.

bankruptcy The state of being legally unable to pay debts.

bench trial A trial before a judge, without a jury.

benefits-received principle A system of taxation in which those who use a particular government service support it with taxes in proportion to the benefits they receive from it.

biased sample A polling sample that does not accurately represent the population.

bicameral legislature A legislature made up of two chambers or parts. The United States has a bicameral legislature, composed of the House of Representatives and the Senate. (Compare with *unicameral legislature*.)

biennially An event that occurs once every two years.

bilateral treaties Treaties between two nations.

bills Proposed laws.

bill of attainder Legislative act that inflicts punishment on particular persons or groups without granting them the right to a trial.

blanket primary A primary in which all candidates' names are printed on the same ballot, regardless of party affiliation. In a blanket primary, voters may choose candidates from more than one party.

block grants A type of funding program in which the federal government gives money to state and local governments to use in broadly defined areas of public policy, such as criminal justice or mental health.

boroughs Administrative subunits of a city. In Alaska, a borough is the equivalent of a county.

boycott An organized refusal by consumers to buy specific goods, usually in protest against certain conditions of production or manufacturing.

budget Spending plan for government submitted by the president to Congress in January of each year.

budget deficit The shortage of funds caused by spending more than is allotted for expenses, or than is collected in revenues.

burden of proof The obligation that rests with the prosecution to prove whether a defendant is guilty of a crime.

bureaucracy A large organization that is structured hierarchically to carry out specific functions.

bureaucrat A person employed by a bureaucracy.

business cycles Cycles of economic activity consisting of recession, recovery, growth, and decline.

busing (for integration) A system of transporting public school students from the neighborhoods where they live to schools in other areas. The aim of busing is to eliminate school segregation based on residential patterns.

C

cabinet An advisory group selected by the president to assist with decision making. A cabinet is traditionally composed of the heads of the executive departments and other officers whom the president may choose to appoint.

calendar A schedule of the order in which bills will be taken up by committee or on the floor.

Calendar of General Orders A schedule that lists bills to be considered by a legislative body, such as the Senate.

campaign manager An individual hired by a candidate to be in charge of the candidate's election campaign.

canvasses Communications undertaken to solicit information or political support. Volunteer citizens often help their political parties by distributing campaign literature door-to-door and asking people to vote for their candidates.

capital Any kind of property (such as machines, buildings, tools, or money) used to produce other goods and services.

capital cases Criminal cases in which the sentence might involve the death penalty.

capitalism An economic system in which the individuals own the factors of production and have the right to use those resources in any way they choose within the limits of the law. (Also called a *market system* or a *free enterprise system*.)

case law A history of cases that, when taken together, form precedents for later judicial decisions.

casework A form of social work in which members of Congress directly involve themselves in the problems and needs of individual citizens.

caseworkers Members of congressional staffs who manage the numerous requests for help from constituents.

categorical grants Federal grants-in-aid to states or local governments for use on very specific programs or projects.

caucus A closed meeting of party leaders to select party candidates or decide on policy.

cease-fire See *armistice*.

censorship The suppression of material (such as books, plays, music, and so on) deemed objectionable on moral, political, or other grounds.

censure An official reprimand of a legislator by his or her peers.

census An official count of the population of a city, state, or nation. A census is performed for the whole United States every ten years.

chancellors Judges in colonial times who resolved judicial disputes on the basis of fairness rather than on specific laws.

chargé d'affaires Member of an embassy who ranks below the ambassador and who may temporarily assume the duties of the ambassador.

charter A document issued by a government that grants rights to a person, group of persons, or a corporation to carry on a certain activity.

checks and balances A major principle of American government in which each of the three branches is given the means to check (to restrain or balance) the actions of the others.

chief administrator plan A plan for county government in which a chief administrative officer shares responsibilities in certain key areas with the county board or with other individuals.

chief diplomat The role of the president in recognizing and interacting with foreign governments.

chief executive Head of the executive branch of government, the president of the United States.

chief of staff The person who directs the president's office in the White House and serves as presidential adviser.

city manager An official appointed by an elected city council to administer city government.

civil disobedience The activity of nonviolent protest used to draw attention to certain laws and issues.

civil law Laws that regulate disputes between private citizens over noncriminal matters, such as contractual agreements, domestic relations, and business practices.

civil liberties Individual rights protected by the Constitution against the powers of the government.

civil rights Constitutionally guaranteed rights and freedoms of Americans.

civil rights movement A political and social movement that began in the 1950s and organized blacks, whites, and people of other races to end the policies of segregation. It sought to establish equal opportunities in the political and economic sectors and to end policies that erected barriers against people because of race.

civil service The term used for the system governing the civilian employees of the government and generally for those who obtained employment through the merit system.

civil service examinations Employment examinations given as part of the civil service system to ensure that government jobs go only to qualified people.

clear and present danger rule The rule or test, first proposed by Justice Oliver Wendell Holmes, which holds that free speech cannot be limited unless it clearly endangers the society the government is designed to protect.

clemency proceedings Proceedings in which a governor may grant a pardon or reprieve for those convicted of a crime.

clerk of the House A non-member staff officer of the House of Representatives.

closed primary The most widely used primary system, in which voters may nominate only candidates from the party with which they are registered.

cloture A limiting of debate by a legislature in order to get an immediate vote on the question being discussed.

cloture rule A Senate rule that imposes a one-hour limit on the amount of time a senator may speak about a bill or issue.

coalitions Alliances of political groups that cooperate to gain a majority vote.

coattail effect The influence a popular or unpopular candidate for top office can have on voter support of other candidates of the same party.

Cold War The ideological, political, and economic impasse that existed between the United States and the Soviet Union after World War II.

collective security The policy of forming international defense alliances to increase the security of each member nation.

colonial empire A group of colonized nations held under the rule of a single imperial power.

command economic system An economic system in which the government controls the factors of production and makes all decisions about their use.

commerce clause The section of the Constitution that grants Congress the power to regulate trade among the states and with foreign countries.

commercial speech Advertising statements that describe

products; have some degree of First Amendment protection.

commission plan A plan for municipal government that consists of a commission of three to nine members who have both legislative and executive powers.

committee of the whole A procedure that the House of Representatives uses to expedite its business by creating itself into one large committee.

common law A body of law that originated in England in which individual judges decided cases in accordance with prevailing customs. As similar decisions were applied to similar cases, a legal standard developed for the nation. Common law forms the basis of the American legal system.

communism Economic and political system based on the theories of Karl Marx. In such a system, the entire economy is based on collective ownership and government control of property and the means of production. Individuals are expected to contribute to the economy according to their ability and are given income according to their needs. Also an economic and political system implemented in countries such as China and, until recently, the Soviet Union, in which the state controls the production and distribution of goods and the government is directed by a single authoritarian leader or party.

Communist bloc A group of countries that fell under Soviet rule after World War II.

commute To reduce a criminal sentence imposed by a court of law.

competition Rivalry among producers or sellers of similar goods to increase sales and profits.

concurrent jurisdiction A sharing of legal authority between federal and state courts.

concurrent majority A principle advanced by John C. Calhoun that states that democratic decisions should be made only with the agreement of all segments of society affected by the decision. Without their agreement, a decision should not be binding on those whose interests it violates.

concurrent powers Powers held by both the federal and state governments in a federal system.

concurrent resolution A congressional measure that deals with matters requiring the action of the House and Senate, but for which a law is not needed. Intended to express an opinion or an official policy, concurrent resolutions must be passed by both chambers of Congress, but do not require the president's signature and do not have the force of law.

concurring opinion A statement written by a justice who agrees (concurs) with the court's decision, but for reasons different from the majority opinion.

confederal government, confederal system A league of independent sovereign states, joined together by a central government that has only limited powers over them.

confederation A league of independent states that are united only for the purpose of achieving common goals.

conferees Members of a conference committee.

conference committee A special joint committee appointed to reconcile differences when a bill passes the two houses of Congress in different forms.

conference report A report submitted by a conference committee after it has drafted a single version of a bill.

congressional district The geographic area within a state that is served by one representative in Congress.

congressional immunity A privilege set out in the Constitution that guarantees freedom of speech to members while they are conducting congressional business. Protects the freedom of legislative debate.

conscription Compulsory enrollment in the armed services.

consensus General agreement among the citizenry on an issue.

consent Permission and agreement of the governed.

consent of the governed The principle that government is based on the will of the people and as such can be abolished by the people.

conservatives Those with a set of political beliefs that include a limited role for government, support for traditional values, and preference for the status quo.

consideration That which each party receives of value when signing a contract.

consolidation The joining of two or more governmental units to form one unit.

constituents The voters in a legislator's home district.

constitutional initiative A process that allows citizens to propose a constitutional amendment through petitions signed by a required number of registered voters.

constitutional monarchy A government in which kings or queens share governmental power with elected lawmakers.

consul A member of the American consulate whose job is to promote American business interests in foreign cities.

consulate Office of the consul.

containment A U.S. diplomatic policy first adopted by the Truman administration to keep communist power contained within its existing boundaries and thus "build situations of strength" around the globe.

contempt Disrespect for or willful disobedience of the rules or orders of a court or legislative body.

contempt of Congress Disrespect for or willful disobedience of Congress.

contempt of court Showing disrespect for the court or disobeying a court order.

contiguous Adjoining.

contract A legal agreement involving an exchange of promises between two people or groups of people.

controller See *comptroller.*

convening The formal opening of each term of Congress. The Twentieth Amendment of the Constitution reset the date at January 3 of each odd-numbered year unless Congress sets another date.

Cooley's rule Derived from an 1871 decision by Michigan Judge Thomas Cooley, who stated that cities should be able "to rule from the home," that is, to govern themselves instead of being governed by the state government.

cooperative federalism The theory that the states and the federal government should cooperate in solving problems.

copyright The exclusive legal right of a person to publish, reproduce, or sell his or her own literary, musical, or artistic creations.

council-manager plan A plan for municipal government in which an elected city council appoints a professional manager who acts as the chief executive.

Council of Economic Advisors A staff agency in the executive office that advises the president on measures to maintain stability in the nation's economy. The council helps the president prepare an annual economic report for Congress and develops economic plans and budget recommendations for maintaining employment, production, and purchasing power.

councils of governments Voluntary political organizations of counties and municipalities concerned with areawide problems, formed to coordinate multiple governmental units.

county A governmental unit set up by the state to administer state law and business at the local level. Counties are drawn up by area, rather than by rural or urban criteria.

county board The governing body of a county, elected by voters to carry out county business.

county borough A local governmental unit in Great Britain.

county-manager plan Plan for county government in which policies are made by an elected body and are carried out by a manager hired by and responsible to that body.

Credentials Committee A committee that convenes at each political party's national convention to inspect the claims of prospective delegates and determine which may participate.

criminal law A body of law that defines crimes and determines punishment for committing them. The government is the prosecutor in criminal cases since crimes are against the public order.

currency power The power granted to Congress by the Constitution to coin money and regulate its value.

cyber strike A strike organized in cyberspace, using the Internet.

D

death taxes Estate and inheritance taxes levied by the state.

debt financing The sale of bonds to finance long-term improvements.

decentralization The shifting of power from the federal government to state and local governments.

de facto **segregation** Racial segregation that occurs not as a result of deliberate intentions but because of previous social and economic conditions and residential patterns.

defense policy Policies that further the defense of the nation, particularly through military preparedness.

de jure **segregation** Racial segregation that occurs because of laws or administrative decisions by public agencies.

delegated, expressed, or enumerated powers Those powers directly granted to the federal government by the Constitution as stated in Article I, Section 8.

delegates People who are authorized to speak, vote, or otherwise act on behalf of others. (Representatives from state political parties to a national party convention serve as *delegates* to that convention.)

deliberative organ A group or organization that deliberates, discusses, and decides important issues.

democracy A system of government in which the people have ultimate political authority. The word is derived from the Greek *demos* (people) and *kratia* (authority).

denaturalization The loss of citizenship through due process of law. Often used for those who used fraud or deception in the naturalization process or for those who are thought to be obstructing the functions of government.

Dennison **rule** An 1861 ruling by the U.S. Supreme Court that upheld the right of the governor of Ohio to refuse an extradition request by the governor of Kentucky for a "free man of color" on charges that he had helped a slave escape to freedom.

deported Forced to leave a country.

depression A major slowdown of economic activity characterized by high unemployment and business downturns and failures.

détente A French word used to refer to the relaxation of tensions between the United States and the Soviet Union under the administration of President Richard Nixon.

deterrence The United States policy adopted after World War II of using the threat of massive retaliation to discourage aggression by its enemies.

devolution The transfer of powers to political subunits.

dictatorship A form of government in which absolute power is exercised by a single person who has usually obtained his or her power by the use of force.

Dillon's rule A principle outlined by John F. Dillon's *Commentaries on the Law of Municipal Corporations* (1911), which states that municipal corporations possess only those powers that the states expressly grant to them.

diplomacy The process by which states establish and maintain political relations with each other through such means as treaties, agreements, and alliances.

diplomat A person who carries out the means of diplomacy on behalf of his or her native country.

direct democracy A system of government in which political decisions are made by the people themselves rather than by elected representatives. This form of government was widely practiced in ancient Greece.

direct primary An election within a party in which the voters select the candidates who will run on the party ticket in the subsequent general election.

direct tax A tax that must be paid by the person on whom it is levied.

disability A physical or mental impairment that "substantially limits" a person's everyday activities.

disenfranchise To deprive voters of the ability to vote.

dissenting opinion A statement written by a justice in which he or she dissents from the conclusion reached by the majority of the court. The justice expounds his or her own views about the case.

district attorney An attorney who initiates and conducts legal action on behalf of the state, especially in criminal proceedings.

diversity of citizenship A legal concept that applies to cases arising between citizens of different states, or between a foreign country and citizens of a state or of different states.

divine right theory A theory that the right to rule by a king or a queen was derived directly from God rather than from the consent of the people.

division of powers A basic principle of federalism provided in the U.S. Constitution, by which powers are divided between units of government (such as the federal and state governments), on a geographic basis.

doctrine A particular position, policy, or principle.

domestic policy Policies that affect a nation's internal affairs.

doubling time The rate at which a population will double, e.g., every five years or every thirty years.

draft Compulsory service in the military.

draft registration The process by which 18-year-old males are required to present themselves as available for the draft should a draft be enacted.

dual citizenship The condition of being a citizen of two sovereign nations or of both a state and a nation.

dual federalism A system of government in which both the federal and state governments maintain diverse but sovereign powers.

due process clause The constitutional guarantees set out in the Fifth and Fourteenth Amendments to the Constitution that government will not illegally or arbitrarily deprive a person of life, liberty, or property. (Also called *due process of law.*)

due process of law (Also called *due process clause.*) The constitutional requirement that the government may not act unfairly or arbitrarily.

E

earned income tax credit (EITC) A program created in 1975 which gives back to low-income workers part or all of their Social Security taxes.

economic sanctions Refusal to trade with a foreign nation as a means of expressing disapproval of that nation's political or economic policies.

economic system The way in which a nation uses its resources to satisfy people's needs and wants.

elastic clause Article I, Section 8 of the Constitution, which gives Congress the power to make all laws "necessary and proper" to carry out its functions.

elected chief executive plan A plan for county government in which the executive officer, such as a mayor, is elected directly by the voters and works with the county board.

electoral college The group of electors who are selected by the voters in each state to officially elect the president and vice president. The number of electors in each state is equal to the number of each state's representatives in both houses of Congress.

electoral college A unique American institution, created by the Constitution, providing for the selection of the president by electors chosen by the state parties, subject to the laws of each state.

electorate All the citizens entitled to vote in a given election.

electors Those individuals chosen early in the presidential election year by state laws and political party apparatus. The electors cast ballots for the president and vice president in order to make the formal selection of president and vice president.

electronic democracy A democracy in which the voting population is able to vote on important policy issues as they arise, via online voting forums.

embassy The official residence and offices of an ambassador.

enabling act A law passed by Congress that allows a territory to draw up a constitution and become eligible for statehood.

enemy aliens Citizens of those nations with which the United States is at war.

enumerated powers See *delegated, expressed, or enumerated powers.*

environmental impact statement A statement mandated by the Environmental Policy Act that must show the costs and benefits of federal actions that could significantly affect the quality of the environment.

equal employment opportunity (EEO) A goal of the 1964 Civil Rights Act to end discrimination based on race, color, religion, sex, or national origin in conditions of employment and to promote employers to foster equal job opportunities.

Equal Employment Opportunity Commission (EEOC) The organization responsible for administering federal laws prohibiting employment discrimination.

equalization A method for adjusting the amount of money that a state must supply to receive federal funds, which takes into account the wealth of the state and its ability to tax its citizens.

equal protection clause Clause in the Fourteenth Amendment that forbids any state to deny to any person within its jurisdiction the equal protection of the laws. This is the major constitutional restraint on the power of governments to discriminate against persons because of race, national origin, or sex.

espionage The practice of spying to obtain information about the plans and activities of a foreign power.

establishment clause A part of the First Amendment that prohibits the establishment of a church officially supported by the federal government. It has been applied to prevent government aid to religious schools, prayer in public schools, and the teaching of religious fundamentalist theories of creation (as opposed to scientific theories of evolution).

evolutionary theory A theory that holds that government evolved over time as families first joined together into clans and then into tribes: Out of the tribes a leader emerged, which eventually gave rise to the gradual establishment of government.

excessive entanglement theory A rule applied by the Supreme Court to maintain the separation of church and state. To be constitutional, government aid to religious school groups must meet three requirements: (1) the purpose must be clearly secular; (2) it must neither advance nor inhibit religion; and (3) it must avoid excessive entanglement of government and religion.

excise taxes A tax levied on certain actions, such as the manufacture or sale of certain commodities such as tobacco or liquor, within a country.

exclusionary rule The rule that any illegally obtained evidence cannot be used at the court trial of the person from whom the evidence was seized. The rule is based upon the Supreme Court interpretation of the Fourth and Fourteenth Amendments.

exclusive jurisdiction A court's authority to hear cases that fall outside the legal scope of other courts.

executive agreements Binding international agreements made between chiefs of state that do not require legislative sanction.

executive authority A person with strong and wide-reaching administrative powers who oversees the executive branch of a system.

Executive Office of the President (EOP) Nine staff agencies that assist the president in carrying out major duties. Established by President Franklin D. Roosevelt by executive order under the Reorganization Act of 1939.

executive order A rule or regulation issued by a chief executive (such as a president or governor) that has the effect of law.

executive privilege The right of the president (or other officials named by the president) to refuse to appear before, or to withhold information from, a legislative committee on the grounds that revealing the information in question may threaten national security.

expatriation The act of voluntarily renouncing (giving up) citizenship in one's nation of origin.

exports Goods that a nation produces and sells to other nations.

ex post facto **law** A criminal law that made certain acts a crime and then punished people for committing the acts before the laws were passed. Ex post facto laws are prohibited by the Constitution.

expressed powers See *delegated, expressed, or enumerated powers*.

expulsion The forced removal of a member of Congress for misconduct.

extradition A process by which fugitive suspected criminals are returned to the jurisdiction of the prosecuting state.

extraordinary majority A majority that is greater than 50 percent plus one. The U.S. Constitution, for example, requires extraordinary majorities of two-thirds of the House and Senate for Congress to propose a Constitutional Amendment.

F

factions Groups or cliques within a larger group.

federal budget The federal government's itemized plan for the expenditure of funds over a certain period of time.

federal government A term that refers to the central or national government, particularly in the United States.

federal question Arises whenever the cause of action of a plaintiff is based at least in part on the United States Constitution, a treaty, or a federal law. Federal questions can be addressed only by the federal judiciary.

Federal Reserve System The central bank of the United

States. "The Fed" was established in 1913 and is led by a board of governors.

federal system A form of government in which a written constitution provides for a separation of powers between a central government and several regional governments. This separation is established by an authority superior to both the central and regional governments, such as a written document. In the United States, the division of powers between the federal government and the fifty states is explained by the Constitution.

federalism A system in which some powers belong to the national, or federal, government while others belong to the states.

Federalists Those who favored a strong central government and the new Constitution.

felony A serious criminal offense punishable by imprisonment. The penalties range from one year in prison to death.

"fighting words" Words that when uttered by a public speaker are so inflammatory they could provoke the average listener to violence.

filibuster Unlimited debate to halt action in the Senate.

First Continental Congress The first gathering of delegates from twelve of the thirteen colonies for the purpose of drafting a federal constitution. The Congress was held in Philadelphia in 1774.

fiscal policy The discretionary adjustments of government expenditures and/or taxes in order to achieve national economic goals, such as high employment and price stability.

fiscal year The twelve-month period that is determined for bookkeeping or accounting purposes. The government's fiscal year runs from October 1 through September 30.

flat tax A single tax rate, with no permitted deductions, used for everyone after a certain amount of initial yearly income has been earned.

food stamps Government-issued coupons that can be used to purchase food.

force theory A theory of the origins of government that holds that when strong persons or groups conquered territories, they forced everyone living in those territories to submit to their will.

foreign policy A nation's political and economic goals with respect to other nations; the techniques and strategies used to achieve those goals.

foreign service The cadre of officials in the State Department who serve in foreign countries.

franchise The legal right to vote. The franchise was extended to African Americans by the Fifteenth Amendment, to women by the Nineteenth Amendment, and to all citizens ages eighteen and over by the Twenty-Sixth Amendment.

franking privilege A privilege that allows members of Congress to send material through the mail by substituting their facsimile signature (frank) for postage.

free exercise clause The provision of the First Amendment that guarantees the free exercise of religion.

fugitive An individual wanted for committing a crime who has fled from prosecution.

full faith and credit clause Article VI, Section I of the Constitution, which requires states to recognize one another's laws and court decisions. It ensures that rights established under deeds, wills, contracts, and other civil documents in one state will be honored by other states.

Fundamental Orders of Connecticut America's first written constitution which called for a representative assembly, made up of elected representatives from each town to serve in that assembly and to make laws. It also called for the popular election of a governor and judges.

fundamental rights Those basic rights necessary for the concept of an ordered liberty such as voting and freedom of religion.

fund-raisers Events paid for by candidates staged in order to raise funds for campaign costs.

G

gag orders Orders issued by judges that restrict publication of news about a trial in progress or a pretrial hearing in order to protect the accused's rights to a fair trial.

gender gap The difference in political opinions between men and women. A term used to describe the difference in the percentages of votes cast for a particular candidate by women and by men. The term was widely used after the 1980 election and brought up again before the 1992 election.

general election Regularly scheduled statewide elections at which voters make the final selection for public office-holders.

generalization An oversimplification that doesn't hold true in every specific case.

general jurisdiction The authority of a court to decide all matters that come before it.

general-law city A city operating under state laws that apply to all local government units of a similar type.

gerrymandering The practice of redrawing legislative district boundary lines to obtain voting advantages for a political party or group.

glittering generalities A propaganda method that uses broad, sweeping statements that sound impressive but have little real meaning.

global warming The gradual increase in average climatic temperatures throughout the world.

government The institutions and processes through which

public policies are made for a society.

government bonds Certificates bought by individuals and companies as a means of loaning money to the government. In exchange for borrowing the money, the government promises to repay buyers the full amount of the loan, plus interest, at a later time.

government corporation An agency of government that is run as a business enterprise. Such an agency is established when the activity is primarily commercial, produces revenue, and requires greater flexibility than permitted in most government agencies.

grand jury A jury, consisting of six to twenty-three persons, that hears criminal charges against individuals and determines whether there is enough evidence to justify holding a trial.

grandfather clause A method used by Southern states to exempt whites from state taxes and literacy laws as a means of denying the franchise to black voters. The clause allowed anyone who could prove that his grandfather had voted before 1867 to vote in current elections.

Great Compromise Roger Sherman's plan to resolve the large-state/small-state controversy during the Constitutional Convention. He proposed a bicameral legislature in which representation in the lower chamber (the House of Representatives) would be based on population, and each state, regardless of size, would have an equal number of representatives in the upper chamber (the Senate).

green vote A vote from those who favor stronger laws to protect and preserve the environment.

greenhouse effect The trapping of heat inside the earth's atmosphere, which is a result of pollution caused largely by the burning of fossil fuels and the emission of carbon dioxide.

grievances Complaints.

H

habeas corpus An order designed to prevent illegal arrests and imprisonments; it demands that a prisoner be brought before the court and that the detaining officer show why the prisoner should not be released.

hereditary peers Members of the British nobility who become so by birth. There are over 700 hereditary peers with titles such as baron, viscount, earl, and duke. These are all members of the House of Lords.

hereditary ruler Someone who rules because he or she is the son or daughter of a previous ruler.

home-rule city A city with a charter that allows local voters to frame, adopt, and amend their own charter.

hopper The box in the House of Representatives, near the clerk's desk, into which new bills are dropped.

horizontal federalism The rules laid out in the Constitution that prevent any one state from setting itself apart from the others by, for example, creating its own foreign policy.

House of Commons The lower and more powerful house of Parliament in Great Britain.

House of Lords The upper chamber of Parliament in Great Britain.

House Rules Committee A permanent committee of the House of Representatives that provides the rules under which bills can be considered, debated, and amended.

human rights Term referring to the rights and privileges of all human beings. These rights are stated in the Declaration of Independence as life, liberty, and the pursuit of happiness. They are guaranteed and protected by the Bill of Rights.

hung jury A jury that cannot agree unanimously on a verdict.

I

ideologues A term applied to individuals whose political opinions are very strong, either at the liberal or conservative extremes.

ideology A set of beliefs about the nature of people and the institutions of government.

illegal aliens Individuals who enter the United States without a legal permit or who enter as tourists and stay longer than their tourist status allows.

image building A process of molding a candidate's image to meet the particular needs of the campaign by using public and private opinion polls and other media-related devices.

immigrants People who move to a new country for the purpose of establishing permanent residency and becoming citizens.

immunity Protection against being brought to trial for certain actions.

impeach To bring a formal charge against a public official for misconduct or wrongdoing in office.

implied powers The powers of the federal government that are implied by the expressed powers in the Constitution, particularly in Article I, Section 8.

impoundment The process by which the president can refuse to spend money that Congress has appropriated for a certain purpose.

incarceration Imprisonment.

income transfer The transfer of income from one group to another, as with the farm program, and the transfer from one generation to another, as occurs in the Social Security program.

incorporation The process of setting up a city through the granting of a charter by the state.

incorporation theory The view that most of the protections of the Bill of Rights are incorporated into the Fourteenth

Amendment's protection against infringement from state governments.

incumbent An official who is presently holding office.

independent executive agency A federal agency with a specific function that reports directly to the president.

independent regulatory agency Responsible for a specific type of public policy. Its function is to create and implement rules that regulate private activity and protect the public interest in a particular sector of the economy.

independents Voters who do not regularly identify themselves with a political party or support candidates of a particular party.

indictment A formal finding by a grand jury that there is sufficient evidence against a particular person to warrant a criminal trial.

indirect democracy See *representative democracy*.

indirect tax A tax levied on an individual or business but passed on to another party for payment.

inflation A general increase in prices.

information A statement issued by a prosecutor that there is enough evidence to bring the accused person to trial, without the use of a grand jury.

information warfare The deliberate impairment of another nation's electronic communications systems—a possible peril of the electronic world.

inherent powers The powers of the federal government which, although not expressly granted by the Constitution, belong to it by virtue of its role as the government of a sovereign state.

initiative A procedure by which voters can propose a change in state and local laws by means of gathering signatures on a petition and submitting it to the legislature for approval.

in-kind subsidy Assistance that is given in forms other than cash, such as food stamps.

institutions Organizations and establishments in a society that are devoted to the promotion of a particular cause. Some of the institutions in our government are the legal system, Congress, and the social welfare system.

intelligence Information gathered about the capabilities and intentions of foreign governments.

interdependence The condition of individuals, organizations, and nations being dependent upon one another.

interest group An organized group of individuals sharing common objectives who actively attempt to influence policy through lobbying, the publication of public opinion polls, and other methods.

interim committees Legislative committees that function between legislative sessions. Such committees study particular issues and report their findings in the next legislative session.

Internet A system connecting more than 150 million computers and eighty thousand networks around the world.

interstate commerce Trade between two or more states.

interstate compact An agreement between two or more states to cooperate on a policy or problem. Minor compacts are made without congressional approval, but any compact that tends to increase the power of the contracting states relative to other states or relative to the federal government generally requires the consent of Congress.

interventionism A political policy of changing or preserving the internal political affairs of foreign nations.

intrastate commerce Trade among different regions in the same state.

iron curtain Described the political boundaries between the democratic countries in Europe and the Soviet-controlled communist countries in Eastern Europe.

iron triangle Term used for a three-way alliance between legislators, bureaucrats, and interest groups to make or preserve policies that benefit their respective individual interests.

isolationism A political policy of noninvolvement in world affairs.

issue ads Political advertisements for ballot initiatives or propositions.

J

joint committees Legislative committees composed of members from both houses of Congress.

joint resolution A legal measure, similar to a bill, passed by Congress and signed by the president which has the force of law.

judicial activism A doctrine that advocates an active role for the Supreme Court in enforcing the Constitution and in using judicial review. An activist court takes a broad view of the Constitution and involves itself in legislative and executive matters.

judicial circuit One of the twelve courts that heard appeals from district courts located within their respective circuits.

judicial implementation The process by which court decisions are translated into policy.

judicial restraint A doctrine that holds that the Supreme Court should rarely use its power of judicial review or otherwise intervene in the political process.

judicial review The power of the courts to determine the constitutionality of the actions of the executive, legislative, and judicial branches of government. First established in *Marbury v. Madison* (1803).

jurisdiction The power of a court to try and decide certain cases.

jury duty The responsibility of all citizens, if called, to serve on a jury for a criminal trial.

jus sanguinis The "law of the blood," as grounds for American citizenship, states that a child born on foreign soil becomes an American citizen at birth if at least one of the parents is a U.S. citizen, and if that citizen has lived in the United States for at least ten years after the age of 14.

jus soli The "law of the soil," as grounds for American citizenship, states that all persons born in the United States are American citizens.

justice court A local court that hears minor civil and criminal cases, performs marriages, and legalizes documents.

justice of the peace A local judicial official who presides over the activities of the justice court.

K

keynote speaker A person of national renown chosen to speak and rouse enthusiasm at a political party's national convention.

kitchen cabinet The name given to a president's unofficial advisors who help him with policy and decisions. The name was coined during Andrew Jackson's presidency.

Kyoto Protocol A 1997 agreement among industrial nations to reduce emissions of greenhouse gases.

L

labor force All individuals over 16 who are working or who are actively looking for a job.

law clerk Recent law school graduates who work for justices by performing much of the research and preliminary drafting necessary for the justices to form an opinion.

legal tender Legitimate currency for trade or purchasing.

legislative assistants Aides to lawmakers who make sure that the lawmakers are well informed about the bills they must deal with.

legislative correspondents Aides to lawmakers who handle their correspondence.

legislative director Aide to a lawmaker who directs and manages the lawmaker's staff.

legislative power The authority to make laws.

legislatures Government bodies primarily responsible for the making of laws.

legitimacy The legal authority of the officials, acts, and institutions of government, conferred by the people on the grounds that the government's actions are an appropriate use of power and that the government is a legally constituted authority.

libel Defamation of character in writing.

liberalism A political ideology whose advocates prefer an active government in dealing with human needs, support individual rights and liberties, and place a priority on social needs over military needs.

liberals Those who hold a set of political beliefs that includes the advocacy of active government intervention to improve the welfare of individuals, support for civil rights, and political change.

lieutenant governor A state official who acts as governor should the governor be absent from the state, become disabled, or die. He or she may act as president of the state senate.

limited government A form of government based on the principle that government should perform only the functions that the people have given it the power to perform.

limited jurisdiction The authority of a court to hear only specific kinds of cases.

line-item veto A power used by an executive branch to veto one or more provisions of a bill while allowing the remainder of the bill to become law.

line organizations Government or corporate groups that provide direct services or products for the public.

literacy tests A voting requirement once used by Southern states that demanded that citizens prove they could read in order to qualify to vote. Primarily used to deny African Americans the right to vote, literacy tests are now outlawed.

lobbying All the efforts by individuals or organizations to affect the passage, defeat, or contents of legislation. The term comes from the lobby of the legislature itself, where petitioners used to corner legislators and speak about their concerns.

lobbyist A person who usually acts as an agent for a group that seeks to bring about the passage or defeat of legislative bills, to influence their content, or to influence administrative actions.

loopholes Legal ways of evading certain legal requirements.

loose constructionists Those who believe that the Constitution should be interpreted loosely and who give broad definitions to the powers of the federal government.

loose monetary policy A policy designed to stimulate the economy by making credit inexpensive and widely available.

M

Madisonian Model The model of government devised by James Madison in which the powers of the government are separated into three branches: executive, legislative, and judicial.

magistrate A local judicial official with limited jurisdiction.

magistrate courts Lower courts in a small town or city.

Magna Carta The great charter that King John of England was forced to sign in 1215 as protection against the absolute powers of the monarchy. It included such fundamental rights as trial by jury and due process of law.

majority floor leader The chief spokesperson of the majority party in the Senate who directs the legislative program and sets the party strategy.

majority leader The leader of the majority party in the House. The majority leader of the House is elected by the caucus of party members to act as spokesperson for the party and to keep the party together.

majority opinion The written statement of the views of the majority of judges in support of a decision made by the court on which they preside.

majority party The party that holds over half the seats in the legislature.

majority rule A political system in which a majority determines the outcome of elections. A simple majority requires 50 percent plus one of the vote, whereas an extraordinary majority requires more than 50 percent plus one of the vote.

malapportionment A condition that results when, based on population and representation, the voting power of citizens in one district becomes more influential than the voting power of citizens in another district.

managed news coverage The skillful manipulation of the media to increase the quantity and quality of news coverage.

mandatory preference poll A type of primary election in which delegates are required to vote for the candidate chosen by the voters at the national convention.

mandatory sentencing A system by which specific crimes carry fixed terms of imprisonment.

marginal tax rate The percentage of additional dollars that must be paid in income taxes. The marginal tax rate is applied to the highest tax bracket only.

market The activity of buying and selling goods and services.

market economic system The opposite of a command economic system; otherwise known as capitalism.

markup session A meeting in which congressional conference committee members decide which changes, if any, should be made on a bill.

Marshall Plan A massive program of economic recovery for the nations of Europe after World War II. Named after former Secretary of State George C. Marshall, Jr., who had that post from 1947 to 1949.

mass media The technical means of communication (especially radio, newspapers, and television) designed to reach, inform, and often influence large numbers of people.

matching funds The funds a state must pay (or "match") when issued many categorical grants. Some programs require states to raise only 10 percent of the funds; others require an even share.

Mayflower Compact A document that stated that laws were to be made for the general good of the people, drawn up by Pilgrim leaders in 1620 on the voyage of the *Mayflower*.

mayor-administrator plan A plan for city government used in large urban areas in which the mayor plays a prominent political role. The mayor appoints a chief administrative officer whose function is to free the mayor from routine administrative tasks.

mayor-council plan A plan for city government in which the mayor is an elected chief executive and the council is the legislative body.

Members of Parliament Normally the elected officials of the House of Commons in Great Britain, but may also include the appointed members of the House of Lords.

merit The standard qualifications and performance criteria used to hire and promote government employees.

merit system The system used to select, promote, and retain government employees based on competitive exams and performance reviews.

minimum wage The minimum hourly wage that workers must be paid as determined by the federal government.

ministers Cabinet members in a parliamentary government.

minor parties Political parties that are less widely supported in a governmental system. In the United States any party other than one of the two major parties (Republican and Democratic) is considered a minor party.

minority floor leader The party officer in the Senate who commands the minority party's policies and directs its legislative program and strategy.

minority leader The leader of the minority party in the House.

minority party The party with fewer members in each house of Congress.

***Miranda* warnings** The guidelines set by the Supreme Court in the case of *Miranda v. Arizona* (1966) establishing the *Miranda* rules, which require that criminal suspects be informed of their rights at the time of arrest.

Missouri Plan A method of selecting judges in which judges are first nominated by a special committee and then appointed by the governor. After serving an initial term, the judicial appointment is either confirmed or rejected at the general election.

mistrial A trial that is canceled because the judge believes it has not been fair in some way.

mixed economy An economic system that contains characteristics of both a command economy and a pure market economy. The mix may vary so that any economic system may lean more toward one pure type than another.

moderates People with political views that are in the middle ground between liberal and conservative.

monarchy A system of government ruled by a hereditary monarch (a king or a queen).

monetary policy Changes in the rate of growth of the money supply and in the availability of credit.

monopoly An industry or company that has total control over the sale of a product or service and does not face competition.

Monroe Doctrine The policy statement included in President Monroe's 1823 annual message to Congress, which set out three principles: (1) European nations should not establish new colonies in the Western Hemisphere; (2) European nations should not intervene in the affairs of independent nations of the Western Hemisphere; and (3) the United States should not interfere in the affairs of European nations.

multilateral treaties Treaties among three or more nations.

multiparty system An electoral system in which three or more political parties compete for public offices.

municipal home rule The power vested in a local unit of government to draft or change its own charter and to manage its own affairs.

municipalities Local units of government that have the authority to govern urban or city areas.

mutual-assured destruction (MAD) A theory that held that as long as the United States and the Soviet Union both had nuclear forces that were large, invulnerable, and somewhat equal, then neither nation would take the chance of waging war with the other.

mutual defense alliance An agreement among allied nations to support one another in case of an attack by enemy forces.

N

name calling A propaganda method that attaches a negative or unpopular label to a person to discredit that person's public image.

nation An area within a particular geographic boundary within which an organized government makes and enforces laws without the approval of a higher authority.

National Assembly The lower house of the French legislature.

national convention The meeting held by each major party every four years to select presidential and vice presidential candidates, to choose a national committee, to write a party platform, and to conduct party business.

national debt The total amount of money the national government owes as a result of borrowing and interest on borrowing. This occurs when the government exceeds its budget and spends more funds than it collects.

National Diet Through its constitution, Japan has a Parliament that is called the National Diet. It consists of two houses—the House of Councilors and the House of Representatives.

national party chairperson Individual who directs the work of the party national committee.

national party committee The political party leaders who direct party business during the time between the national party conventions. The group leads the party's national organization.

national security The nation's protection from unwanted interference, threat, or takeover from other nations. A sense of freedom and independence for the nation.

National Security Council (NSC) A council that advises the president on domestic and foreign matters concerning the safety and defense of the nation. This staff agency of the Executive Office was established by the National Security Act of 1947.

nationalists Individuals who feel strong loyalty and devotion to their nation.

nationality Membership in a particular nation or country.

natural aristocracy Officials whom President Thomas Jefferson placed in the executive bureaucracy.

natural rights Rights that do not come from governments but are inherent within every single man, woman, and child by virtue of the fact that he or she has been born and is a human being.

naturalization The legal process by which an individual born a citizen of one country becomes a citizen of another.

naturalized citizens Citizens from other countries who legally become American citizens. The naturalization process involves meeting certain requirements of residency, literacy, and acceptance of the principles of American government.

Navigation Acts Restrictions placed on colonial activity from 1651 to 1750 by Great Britain, which include the condition that only English ships could be used for trade within the British Empire.

necessary and proper clause Article I, Section 8 of the Constitution, which gives Congress the power to make all laws "necessary and proper" for the federal government to carry out its responsibilities.

negative campaign advertising Advertising in a political campaign aimed at discrediting and damaging the opposing candidate.

neutral competency Federal bureaucrats are expected to exhibit neutral competency, which means that they are supposed to apply their technical skills to their jobs without regard to political issues.

neutrality A position of not being aligned with either side in a dispute or conflict, such as a war.

New Deal A program ushered in by the Roosevelt administration in 1933 designed to help the United States out of the Great Depression. It included many government spending and public assistance programs, in addition to thousands of regulations of economic activity.

New England town A governmental unit in the New England states that combines the roles of city and county governments. "Town" includes a central village and surrounding rural areas, and practices direct democracy.

new federalism A plan to limit the federal government's role in regulating state governments, in order to give the states increased power to decide how they should spend all government revenues.

New Jersey Plan A plan proposed by William Paterson of New Jersey during the Constitutional Convention, which called for equal representation by all states (thereby favoring the smaller states).

no contest A plea in a criminal case in which the defendant neither admits or denies the charges. The principal difference between a plea of guilty and a plea of no contest is that the latter may not be used against the defendant in a civil action.

nominating convention An official meeting of a political party to choose its candidates and select delegates.

nomination A party's naming and endorsing of a particular person as a candidate for public office.

nonpartisan elections Elections held without the participation of political parties to fill certain offices, such as judicial, city, or school board positions.

nonresident aliens Aliens who expect to stay in a foreign country for a short, specified time.

Northwest Ordinance A 1787 congressional act that established a basic pattern for how states should govern new territories north of the Ohio River.

O

obscenity A form of speech that is not protected under the First Amendment. A work that taken as a whole appeals to a prurient interest in sex by depicting sexual conduct as specifically defined by legislation or judicial interpretation in a patently offensive way, and that lacks serious literary, artistic, political, or scientific value.

off-budget items A category outside an official budget.

office-group ballot A ballot on which candidates are listed according to the office for which they are running.

Office of Management and Budget (OMB) Assists the president in preparing the proposed annual budget, which the president must submit to Congress in January of each year.

old-age pensions Retirement plans giving people money after they stop working.

one-party system An electoral system in which only one political party exists, is legal, or has any chance of winning elections.

open primary A direct primary in which voters may cast ballots without having to declare their party orientation.

opinion The statement of a court or judge concerning the decision reached in a case. It expounds the law as applied to the case and details the reasons on which the judgment was based.

opposition The next largest party in a parliamentary government, next to the ruling party. Leaders of the opposition appoint their own potential cabinet members, who "shadow" particular members of the ruling cabinet, and hope to some day replace them.

oral arguments The verbal arguments presented by opposing counsel.

original jurisdiction The legal authority of a court to hear the first presentation of a case.

oversight function The power of Congress to follow up on laws it has passed to ensure that they are being properly enforced and administered.

P

pardon The act of granting a prisoner release from punishment. A pardon can be granted by a president or a governor before or after a criminal conviction.

parishes A term used in Louisiana to describe administrative units of local government.

Parliament The name of the national legislative body in countries governed by a parliamentary system, as in England and France.

parliamentary democracy A form of democracy in which the executive leadership (which usually consists of a prime minister and his or her cabinet) is chosen by and responsible to a democratically elected parliament.

parole The release of a prisoner before the completion of his or her prison sentence.

partisan elections Elections in which candidates running for office are identified by their political parties.

partisan politics Politics in support of a particular party's ideology.

partisan preference The preference of one party over another by voters or legislators.

party identification Linking oneself to a particular party.

party identifiers People who think of themselves as belonging to a particular party but who do not actively participate in party efforts.

party platform The document drawn up by each party at the national convention that outlines the policies and positions of the party. The platform is submitted to the entire convention for approval.

party ticket A list of candidates for various offices that belong to one political party.

party-column ballot A form of ballot used in general elections in which candidates are listed in one column under their respective party names. This ballot emphasizes voting along party lines rather than for particular individuals.

passports Government-issued certificates that identify a person as a citizen of that government's country and authorize the person to travel abroad.

patent A license granted to an inventor that gives exclusive rights to manufacture and sell the invention for a specified period of time.

patronage A system of rewarding party faithfuls and workers with government employment and contracts.

peer group A group of people who share relevant social characteristics such as age and economic status. Peer groups play an important role in shaping individual attitudes and beliefs.

peers Individuals who are one's equals.

petit jury A group of up to twelve persons who hear the facts of a civil or criminal case in a court of law and give a verdict; also called *trial jury*.

petition A request that individuals submit to government officials. The petition may involve government policy or it may be a request to become a citizen.

picketing A form of protest in which workers on strike publicly march in an attempt to raise public awareness of a certain controversy and to persuade consumers not to deal with the employer until the strike is settled.

pigeonhole Filing a bill away or putting it aside for no further action. The term is borrowed from the old-time desks in committee rooms of Congress that had small compartments or "pigeonholes" for filing papers.

plain folks A method of propaganda that attempts to attract people to a political figure by portraying him or her as just an average American.

plaintiff A person who files suit in a court of law.

planks Issues or beliefs that make up a political party's platform.

plea bargaining Agreements between a prosecutor and a defense attorney whereby a defendant pleads guilty to a lesser charge in exchange for a lighter sentence. The prosecutor is willing to plea bargain in order to move the case through an extremely crowded court and to be ensured that the case will result in a guilty plea.

plurality A situation in which a candidate wins an election by receiving more votes than the others but does not necessarily win a majority. Most federal, state, and local laws allow for elections to be won by a plurality vote.

pocket veto A special veto power used by the chief executive after the legislature has adjourned. Bills that are not signed by the chief executive die after a specified period of time and must be reintroduced if Congress wishes to reconsider them.

police power The authority of the states to legislate for the protection of the health, safety, and welfare of the people.

policy voting When people vote for candidates who share their stands on certain key issues.

political action committees Committees that are established by and represent the interests of corporations, labor unions, or special interest groups. PACs raise money and give donations to campaigns on behalf of the groups they represent.

political consultant A professional hired by a political candidate to devise strategy, create campaign themes, and manage the image building of a candidate's political campaign.

political machines Organizations within a political party that control elections by granting favors in exchange for votes or money.

political participation The ways in which individuals can participate in the political process, such as by voting, serving on juries, helping with political campaigns, and running for political office.

political party A group of organized citizens with a broad set of common beliefs who join together to elect candidates to public office and determine public policy.

political patronage A system of appointing people to political positions on the basis of service to the party rather than on any qualifications or merits.

political philosophy A set of notions or ideas about how people should be governed.

political socialization The process by which individuals develop political beliefs and form opinions about political issues. Important forces in this process include the family and the educational system.

politics The authoritative allocation of resources for a society; the process of deciding who gets what, when, and how in a society.

poll tax A special tax that had to be paid before voting. The Twenty-Fourth Amendment outlawed the poll tax in federal elections, and in 1966 the Supreme Court declared it unconstitutional in all elections.

popular vote A vote cast by someone other than an elector; the number of actual votes cast in an election.

pork barrel Appropriations for local projects that improve legislators' popularity in their own districts.

power The possession of control, authority, or influence over others.

power of recognition The power of the executive branch to accept the legal existence of another country's government.

preamble An introductory statement to an official document that usually explains the document's goals and purposes.

precedent A court rule that sets a standard for subsequent legal decisions in similar cases.

precinct The smallest voting district at the local level.

preference poll A type of primary election in which voters may cast separate votes for candidates and for convention delegates.

preferred-position doctrine A Supreme Court test that requires that limitations be applied to the First Amendment only to avoid imminent, serious, and important evils.

preliminary hearing A court hearing at which evidence is submitted and testimony heard to determine whether there is enough reason to continue with court proceedings.

president of the Senate The role given by the Constitution to the vice president of the United States. As presiding officer, he or she may call on members to speak, put questions to a vote, and may cast a vote only in the event of a tie.

president *pro tem* The temporary presiding officer of the Senate in the absence of the vice president.

presidential democracy A democracy in which the people elect both the president and the legislature. (Compare with *parliamentary democracy*.)

presidential succession The legal procedure by which government leaders succeed the presidency should the president die, become disabled, or be removed from office.

press conferences Scheduled interviews with the media.

press secretary A member of the White House staff who holds press conferences for reporters and lets people know what the president thinks about current national and international issues.

pressure groups Private organizations that use persuasion and pressure to see that laws are passed in favor of their interests.

preventive detention Holding accused felons without bail if judges feel that the suspect, if released, will commit another crime.

primary An election held before a general election in which candidates from the same party compete for the party nomination.

prime minister The chief executive in a parliamentary system who is elected by the legislature from among its own members.

principle of federalism A system of government in which the power to govern is shared by a central (or federal) government and state governments, as outlined in a written constitution.

prior restraint The restraining of an action before it has actually occurred. Government censorship of documents or broadcasts before they are published or aired is an example of prior restraint.

private bills A legislative measure that applies only to certain persons or places, rather than to the nation as a whole.

private property Goods owned by individuals or groups rather than by government.

privileges and immunities clause A section of the Constitution that requires states not to discriminate against one another's citizens in such areas as legal protection, access to the courts, freedom to travel, and property rights.

probable cause Sufficient evidence to believe that a crime has been committed. Reasonable grounds for issuing a search warrant against an individual, his or her home, or personal possessions.

probation The suspension of a criminal sentence by a judge on the grounds that the individual maintain good behavior and be supervised by a probation officer for a specified period of time.

procedural due process A provision in the Constitution that states that the law must be carried out in a fair and orderly manner.

profit The amount of money left over after all the expenses of running a business have been paid.

profit incentive The desire to make money that motivates people to produce, buy, and sell goods and services.

progressive taxation A system of taxation in which individuals pay a higher percentage of additional tax dollars as income rises. In this way, the marginal tax rate exceeds the average tax rate.

Prohibition The fourteen-year era (from 1920 to 1933) during which it was illegal in the United States to manufacture, transport, or consume intoxicating beverages. Prohibition began with the Eighteenth Amendment and was repealed by the Twenty-First Amendment.

project grant An assistance grant that state and local agencies can apply for directly, so that funds can be allocated to where they are needed.

propaganda The spreading of ideas, information, or rumor for the purpose of helping or injuring an institution, a cause, or a person.

proportional taxation A system of taxation in which the tax *rate* remains constant regardless of a person's income.

prosecuting attorney The official who represents the government and initiates and carries out legal proceedings.

prototype A model.

public bills A legislative measure that applies to the nation as a whole.

public debt See *national debt*.

public defender The attorney appointed to represent a defendant in a criminal case should the defendant be unable to hire an attorney.

public interest groups Groups that are formed with the broad goal of working for the "public good."

public opinion Opinions and attitudes shared by significant numbers of people on social and political issues.

public opinion poll A random survey to discover popular views on matters of public importance.

public policies Policies that affect the public at large. Public policies are typically carried out by the legislative and executive branches of local, state, and federal government.

pure speech The freely voiced, peaceful expression of thoughts, ideas, or opinions, at home or in public.

Q

quorum The minimum number of legislators who must be present for a legislative body to conduct business.

quotas Rules enforced by the government that state that a certain number of jobs, promotions, or other types of selections must be given to members of certain groups.

R

radical left Persons on the extreme left side of the political spectrum who do not believe in working within the established political processes to achieve their goals and who often want to destroy the established governmental system.

radical right In the political spectrum, those who resist change more strongly than do moderates or conservatives. The radical right includes reactionaries and fascists who are willing to actively fight against social change.

random sample A cross-section of a population that has been polled on a specific issue.

ratify To formally approve or give final consent to a constitution, constitutional amendment, or treaty.

ratings systems Systems by which interest groups evaluate (rate) the performance of legislators based on how the legislators have served the interest groups.

rational-basis test A method used by the Supreme Court to ensure equal legal protection to all individuals. It applies to suspected discrimination situations that affect diverse individuals.

reactionaries People who resist change much more strongly than do either moderates or conservatives. Reactionaries not only do not want society to change, they are willing to actively fight against social change.

realigning election An election in which the electorate turns away from the dominant party and replaces it with a new dominant party.

reapportionment The redrawing of legislative district lines, usually after a census is taken, in accordance with population changes indicated by the census.

recall A procedure that allows voters to dismiss an elected official from a state or local office before the official's term is expired.

recall election An election that gives citizens the power to remove an elected official from office before the end of his or her term.

recesses Periods of time during which a legislative or judicial body is not in session.

recession A period of time in which the rate of economic growth is consistently lower than usual.

record vote (also **roll-call vote**) A method of voting in a legislature in which legislators call out their votes on an issue. A computer records each vote electronically and display boards show how each member has voted.

referendum A form of direct democracy in which legislative or constitutional measures are first decided upon by the legislature and then presented to the voters for approval.

refugees People who must flee from danger in their native countries and find residence outside their homeland.

registration Entering one's name onto a list of eligible voters. Registration requires meeting certain age, residency, and citizenship requirements.

regressive taxation A system of taxation in which individuals pay a lower percentage of tax dollars as income rises. In this way, the marginal tax rate is less than the average tax rate.

released time The time students are given away from regular public school classes to attend religious instruction sessions.

relocation camps Camps established during World War II to house Japanese Americans who were required to dispose of their property, were excluded from "military areas," and subjected to curfews.

repeal To rescind or do away with legislation.

representative assembly A law-making body that is composed of individuals who represent the population.

representative democracy (also **indirect democracy**) A system of democracy in which the people elect representatives who work within government on behalf of the people. (Compare with *direct democracy*.)

representative government A government in which the people, by whatever means, choose a limited number of individuals to determine policy for all citizens.

representatives Officials who are elected to a legislative office for a specific time for the purpose of determining policy for all citizens.

reprieve A postponement of a criminal sentence imposed by a court of law. The president or governor has the power to grant reprieves and usually does so for humanitarian reasons.

reprimand An official reproach used by Congress for a member guilty of misconduct.

republic The name given to a nation in which the supreme power rests in those who are entitled to vote and is exercised by elected representatives who are responsible to voters and who govern according to law. (Compare with *representative democracy*.)

republican form of government A system of government in which the supreme power rests with the voters, who elect representatives to operate the government for them.

reserved powers Powers that are neither granted to the federal government nor expressly forbidden to the states and are therefore retained by the states or by the people.

residency A requirement that a person live within a state for a specified period of time in order to qualify to vote.

resident aliens People who have immigrated to the United States to establish permanent residence.

resulting powers The accumulation of several expressed powers that results in a certain power of the federal government.

revenue bills Bills that involve the raising of money for the government. According to the Constitution, revenue bills must originate in the House of Representatives.

revenue-sharing program A program in which the federal government allocates funds to states and cities with virtually no strings attached. Recipient governments can use the funds in any way they see fit.

reverse discrimination The assertion that affirmative action programs that require preferential treatment or quotas discriminate against those who have no minority status.

review courts See *appellate courts*.

revolution The popular overthrow of an established government or political system and its replacement with a new system of government. Famous revolutions include the American (1775–83), the French (1789–99), Russian [February Revolution (March 17, 1917) and October Revolution (November 7, 1917)], and the Second Russian Revolution, which occurred in August of 1991.

rider An amendment or provision attached to a bill that is not related to the subject of the bill.

roll-call vote See *record vote*.

rule of law A basic principle of government that accompanies constitutional supremacy which states that government shall be carried out according to established law, and that both those who govern and those who are governed will be bound by this law.

run-off election A repeat election between the two front runners in a prior election when no candidate has received a majority of votes. Run-off elections are usually held in places where the law requires a majority vote.

S

sabotage A destructive act intended to hinder a nation's defense efforts.

sacrifice principle A principle of taxation that holds that the sacrifices people make to pay their taxes should be fair.

samples Small numbers of people who represent a cross-section of the total population that has been polled on a specific issue.

sampling error The level of confidence in the findings of a public opinion poll.

search engines Internet Web sites (such as Yahoo, WebCrawler, Excite, and Lycos) which allow the user to search for specific topics on the Internet.

search warrant An order issued and authorized by a judge that gives police the power to search a specific place in connection with a particular crime.

searches and seizures The methods used by law enforcement officials to look for and collect the evidence they need to convict individuals suspected of crimes as referred to in the Fourth Amendment.

secession The act of formally withdrawing from membership in an alliance; the withdrawal of a state from the federal union.

Second Continental Congress The congress of the colonies that met in 1775 to assume the powers of a central government and establish an army.

seditious speech Speech intended to promote resistance to lawful authority and that especially advocates the violent overthrow of a government.

segregation The enforced separation, often by discriminatory means, of racial, ethnic, or other groups from the rest of the population in education, housing, or other areas.

select committees Temporary legislative committees established for a special purpose.

selectmen Individuals chosen by a township to serve on the local board and manage the daily affairs of the town.

self-incrimination Providing damaging information or testimony against oneself in a court of law.

self-nomination Announcing one's own desire to run for public office.

senatorial courtesy An unwritten rule that an executive appointment to a certain state must first be approved by the senators of that state.

seniority An unwritten rule followed in both houses of Congress that specifies that members with longer terms of continuous service will be given preference when committe chairpersons and holders of other significant posts are selected.

seniority rule In Congress, the practice of the majority party caucus choosing the longest-serving member of a particular committee to be a committee chairperson.

sentence The punishment imposed by a court of law on an individual who is found guilty of a crime.

separate-but-equal doctrine A doctrine long held by the Supreme Court, which declared that segregation in schools and public accommodations did not imply the superiority of one race over another. It held that the Equal Protection Clause of the Fourteenth Amendment did not forbid racial segregation as long as the facilities for blacks were equal to those provided for whites. The doctrine was overturned in the *Brown v. Board of Education* decision of 1954.

sessions Regular periods of time during which legislative bodies assemble and conduct business.

shield laws Laws that protect reporters in courts of law against disclosing their sources and revealing other confidential information.

simple resolutions Legislation that deals with matters affecting only one chamber of Congress and is passed by that chamber alone.

single-member district system A method of election in which only one candidate can win election to each office.

single-member districts Electoral districts from which single officeholders are chosen by voters.

slander The public utterance of a statement that holds a person up for contempt, ridicule, or hatred and thus damages the person's reputation.

social conflict Friction between groups within a society. Sometimes social conflict is resolved by violence, other times by the judicial system, and other times by changes in customs and traditions.

social contract theory A theory of society that states that individuals voluntarily agree to create an organized society in order to secure mutual protection and welfare. A theory derived from Hobbes, Locke, and Rousseau.

Social Security A government insurance program of obligatory saving financed from payroll taxes imposed on both employers and employees. Workers pay for the benefits while working and receive the benefits after they retire.

socioeconomic factors Social and economic factors such as age, income, education, and occupation.

soft money Contributions to political parties, instead of to particular candidates.

Solid South A term used to describe the tendency of the southern states to vote Democratic after the Civil War.

solidarity Mutual agreement within a group.

sound bite A several-second comment that captures a thought and has an immediate impact on viewers but that gives little or no relevant information.

sovereignty The supreme and independent authority that a government possesses within its own territory.

speaker The presiding officer in the lower house of a state legislature.

Speaker of the House The presiding officer in the House of Representatives, always a long-time member of the majority party and often the most powerful and influential member of the House.

special election An election held whenever an issue must be decided before the next regular election is held.

special sessions Unscheduled sessions of Congress ordered by the president.

speech plus A verbal expression of opinions, ideas, or beliefs combined with some sort of action such as marching or demonstrating.

split-ticket voting The act of voting for candidates from more than one political party in the same election.

spoils system An arrangement under which the political party that wins an election gives government jobs to its own party members.

sponsors Legislators who draft and propose bills.

Stamp Act An act passed by the British Parliament in 1765 which placed the first direct tax on the colonies. The Stamp Act required the use of tax stamps on all legal documents, newspapers, pamphlets, playing cards, and certain business agreements.

standing committees Permanent committees within the House or Senate that consider bills within a subject area.

standing vote A method of voting in the legislature in which those who favor a measure and those who oppose it are required to stand up to show their vote.

State of the Union Address An annual message from the president to Congress in which a legislative program is proposed. The message is aimed not only at Congress but to the American people and to the world.

status quo The existing state of affairs.

statutory law A law passed by a legislature.

straight-ticket voting The act of voting exclusively for candidates of the same party in an election.

straw poll A survey of opinions taken to estimate the strength of opposing candidates or the popularity of a proposed law.

strict constructionists Those who believe that the Constitution should be interpreted strictly and feel that the federal government should have only those powers specifically named in the Constitution.

strong mayor-council plan A plan for city government in which the mayor is the chief executive and has almost complete control over hiring and firing employees and preparing the budget.

subcommittees Divisions of larger committees that deal with a particular part of the committee's policy area.

subpoena A legal writ that requires a person to give a testimony in court.

substantive due process The Constitutional requirement that the laws used in accusing and convicting persons of crimes must be fair.

suffrage See *franchise*.

suffragists Those who advocated for women's right to vote.

Sugar Act A tax, imposed by the British Parliament in 1764, on all sugar imported into the American colonies.

summit meeting A conference between the heads of two or more nations.

summons A notice that calls on a defendant to appear in court.

super-majority vote Used by the General Assembly of the United Nations. Important questions are decided by a majority vote or by a super-majority vote of two-thirds, depending on the importance of the matter.

superpowers The nations with the greatest economic and military power.

Supplemental Security Income (SSI) A government program that establishes a minimum income for the aged, the blind, and the disabled.

supremacy clause Article VI, Section 2 of the Constitution, which establishes the Constitution and federal laws as superior to all state and local legislation.

suspect classification A test used by the Supreme Court to determine if the classification of individuals based on race, national origin, or sex has in any way denied those individuals equal protection of the law.

symbolic speech The expression of beliefs, opinions, or ideas through forms other than speech or print.

T

talk radio Talk shows broadcast over the radio.

teller vote A method of voting in a legislature in which those who favor a measure and those who oppose it are required to walk down an aisle to show their vote.

Temporary Assistance to Needy Families (TANF) Funds, in the form of grants, turned over to the states by the U.S. government; restrictions include a two-year limit on benefits unless recipient is working, and a five-year maximum for benefits.

tenure The period of time during which a public official holds office.

term See *tenure*.

testimonials A propaganda technique that involves persuading people to support an issue or candidate because well-known individuals, such as a prominent government official or famous entertainers, offer such support.

third parties Political parties other than the two major parties, usually composed of dissatisfied groups that have split from the major parties.

Three-Fifths Compromise A compromise reached during the Constitutional Convention in which it was agreed that three-fifths of all slaves were to be counted both for tax purposes and for representation in the House of Representatives.

tight monetary policy A policy designed to slow the economy by making credit expensive and in short supply.

tolerance A fair and objective attitude toward those whose opinions, race, religion, and nationality differ from one's own.

totalitarian A ruler who rules without the consent of the governed.

town manager system A system adopted by some New England towns in which voters elect selectmen who then appoint professional town managers.

town meeting A traditional form of New England town government at which direct democracy is practiced.

townships Local government units that are subdivisions of counties and have similar governing procedures.

tracking polls Polls that track public opinion of candidates on nearly a daily basis as election day approaches.

trade organizations Organizations that usually support policies that benefit business in general and work toward seeking policy goals that benefit their particular membership.

transfer A propaganda technique that involves associating a candidate with a respected person, group, or symbol.

treason Article III, Section 3 of the Constitution states that treason "shall consist in levying war against (the United States), or in adhering to their enemies, giving them aid and comfort."

treaty A formal agreement between the governments of two or more countries.

trial courts A court of original jurisdiction that hears civil and criminal cases.

trial jury See *petit jury*.

two-party system A political system in which two strong and established parties compete for political offices.

tyranny The arbitrary or unrestrained exercise of power by an oppressive individual or government.

U

unanimous Being of one mind; agreement.

unanimous opinion Agreement by all judges on the same court decision.

unconstitutional Contrary to constitutional provisions and so invalid.

undocumented aliens illegal aliens.

unicameral legislature A legislature with only one legislative body. (Compared with *bicameral legislature*.)

unincorporated areas Areas not located within municipal boundaries.

unitary government, unitary system A centralized governmental system in which local or subdivisional governments exercise only those powers given to them by the central government.

U.S. Treasury Bonds See *government bonds*.

urban areas Highly populated communities.

V

veto A latin word meaning "I forbid"; the refusal by an official, such as the president or governor, to sign a bill into law.

veto power A constitutional power that enables the chief executive (president or governor) to reject legislation and return it to the legislature with reasons for the objection. This prevents or delays the bill from becoming law.

veto session A session in which state legislators can consider bills vetoed by the governor and attempt to override the governor's veto, if enough popular support within the legislature exists.

Virginia Plan A fifteen-resolution plan proposed by Governor Edmund Randolph of Virginia during the Constitutional Convention. It recommended an entirely new national government favoring the larger states; it included a bicameral legislature, a national executive branch, and a national court system.

visa A permit to enter another country, issued from the country one wishes to enter.

voice vote A method of voting in a legislature.

voir dire A French phrase meaning "to speak the truth"; refers to the process by which prospective jurors are examined to ensure their judgments will be impartial.

vote of confidence Support from the parliament for the existing government.

voter turnout The percentage of eligible citizens who actually take part, or "turn out" in the election process.

W

waived Relinquished or given up.

War Powers Act The law passed in 1973 that spells out the conditions under which the president can commit troops to war without congressional approval.

ward A local unit of a party organization.

warrant An order issued by a court authorizing a public official to proceed in a specified manner, such as a search warrant.

weak mayor-council plan Plan for city government in which the mayor is elected as chief executive officer; the council is elected as the legislative body. The mayor has only limited powers and little control over staffing and budgeting, and is often elected for a two-year term.

Western bloc The democratic nations that emerged victorious after World War II, led by the United States.

whips Assistant floor leaders who aid the majority and minority floor leaders.

whistle-blower A government employee who calls public attention to fraud, mismanagement, or waste in his or her own agency or department.

White House Press Corps A group of reporters assigned to cover the presidency full time.

winner-take-all system A system in which the presidential candidate who wins the preference vote in a primary automatically wins the support of all the delegates chosen in the primary.

World Wide Web The leading information retrieval service of the Internet.

writ of *certiorari* A written order issued by a higher court to a lower court to send up the record of a case for review.

writ of *habeas corpus* An order requiring officials to explain to a judge in court why a prisoner is being held; provided for in Article I, Section 9, of the Constitution.

writ of *mandamus* A written order issued by a court commanding an official of the government to perform a specified lawful duty or act.

write-in candidate Someone who will campaign without being listed on the ballot, and will ask voters to write his or her name on the ballot on election day.

Z

zoning The method by which local governments regulate how property may be used.

A

ability-to-pay principle/principio de capacidad de pago Principio impositivo por el cual aquellos con mayores ingresos pagan más impuestos que los de menores ingresos, sin tener en cuenta la cantidad de servicios públicos que utilizan.

abridge/abreviar Reducir o disminuir.

absentee ballot/voto por ausencia Voto enviado por correspondencia en lugar de ser emitido durante el sufragio.

absolute monarchs/monarcas absolutos Monarcas que tienen plenos poderes, sin límites. (Compare con *monarcas constitucionales*).

absolute monarchy/monarquía absoluta Gobierno en el cual los dirigentes tienen un poder completo e ilimitado.

acid rain/lluvia ácida Lluvia que contiene una gran concentración de agentes químicos que forman ácidos, debido, por lo general, a la contaminación industrial del aire, combinada con vapor de agua.

acquittal/absolución Momento en que el acusado de un crímen, es hallado inocente de culpa y cargo.

act of admissions/acta de admisión Decreto pasado por el Congreso, en el que se admite un estado dentro de la Unión.

administrative assistant/asistente administrativo Persona empleada para dirigir la oficina de un legislador, supervisar sus horarios y prestar ayuda. (Los asistentes administrativos también trabajan con otros profesionales).

administrative councils/consejos administrativos Unidades locales de gobierno de Gran Bretaña.

affirmative action/política de afirmación Política de empleos, que da consideración especial a grupos de menores ventajas (como las mujeres o minorías raciales) en un esfuerzo por reducir los efectos presentes, de las discriminaciones del pasado.

agenda/agenda Lista o programa de metas por lograr. En el gobierno, una agenda de deliberaciones indica cuáles cuestiones públicas se van a debatir, considerar o establecer.

agents of political socialization/agentes políticos Grupos de personas que tienen influencia en las opiniones políticas de otros.

Aid to Families with Dependent Children (AFDC)/Ayuda para Familias con Menores Programa social difundido en parte por el gobierno federal y administrado por cada estado, que brinda asistencia financiera a las familias pobres con hijos menores de edad.

alien/extranjero(a) Individuo que no es ciudadano del estado o nación en que reside.

allegiance/obediencia Lealtad y servicio a su país o a su gobierno.

alliance/alianza Asociación de dos o más naciones, para beneficio mutuo.

ambassador/embajador(a) Diplómata de alto rango que representa a su gobierno, en un país extranjero.

amendments/enmiendas Cambios, o agregados por escrito, a una ley o cuerpo de leyes, tales como la Constitución de los Estados Unidos.

American's Creed/Doctrina Americana Principios emanados de la Declaración de Independencia, que incluyen derechos naturales, gobierno limitado, igualdad ante la ley, y gobierno por consentimiento del gobernado.

amnesty/amnistía Concesión de perdón por parte del gobierno, a un grupo grande de individuos.

Anti-Federalists/anti-federalista Grupo político que se oponía a la adopción de la Constitución, debido a las tendencias centralistas del documento y que atacó los que la redactaron, por no haber incluído una declaración de derechos.

appellate court/tribunal de apelaciones Tribunales que revisan las decisiones de los juzgados menores.

appellat jurisdiction/jurisdicción de apelaciones Autoridad del tribunal para revisar las decisiones de los juzgados menores.

apportioned/adjudicados Las bancas del cuerpo legislativo están distribuídas (apportioned) entre los distritos electorales, en base a la cantidad de población del estado. (Ver también *apportionment*).

apportionment/distribución Distribución y asignación de bancas (asientos) del cuerpo legislativo, según los distritos electorales. La asignación basada en la población del estado, es de 435 bancas en la Cámara de Representantes.

appropriation/consignación Autorización de fondos para un propósito específico; dinero aprobado por la legislatura para fomentar actividades de otra rama del gobierno.

appropriation bill/decreto de consignación Decreto que formalmente asigna los fondos para un propósito específico.

armistice/armisticio Acuerdo temporario entre dos adversarios, para detener la lucha (se llama también *alto el fuego*).

arraignment/instrucción de cargos Proceso preliminar del tribunal, en el cual el acusado se entera de los cargos y hace su declaración.

assembly/asamblea Reunión de personas con un fin común.

assimilation/asimilación El estado es absorbido por cierta población o grupo, dentro de una tradición cultural.

at large/elección general Elección de una autoridad mediante el voto de una unidad gubernamental completa, como un estado o un país, en lugar de una subdivisión de una zona.

attaché/agregado Miembro del cuerpo de una embajada, que presta servicios dentro de una rama en particular.

attack ads/campaña de ataque Forma de campaña publicitaria negativa, en la cual la personalidad del candidato es atacada por su opositor.

attorney general/juez supremo Cabeza del Departamento de Justicia, designado por el presidente y que pertenece al gabinete del presidente.

auditor/auditor Persona que examina los registros y cuentas, para verificar su validez.

Australian ballot/sufragio "australiano" Voto secreto preparado, distribuído, y tabulado por las autoridades, como gasto público. Este método fue introducido en los Estados Unidos desde Australia, en 1888, y reemplazó al voto abierto.

authoritarian/autoritario Concentración del poder en un dirigente que no es responsable constitucionalmente ante su pueblo.

authority/autoridad Poder para influenciar el pensamiento, la opinión y el comportamiento. (La autoridad legal se puede definir, como el poder para dictar y ejecutar leyes).

autocracy/autocracia Gobierno en el que el poder y la autoridad, están en manos de una sola persona.

B

bad-tendency rule/regla de mala intención Doctrina que sostiene que la palabra, la práctica religiosa o cualquier otra libertad de la Primer Enmienda, podrían ser restringidas lícitamente, si tal expresión pudiera provocar cierto mal.

bail/fianza Dinero que un acusado debe depositar en los tribunales, para obtener su libertad bajo palabra y para garantizar su presencia en la corte, en el momento determinado.

balance the ticket/equilibrar la fórmula Método por el cual un candidato a presidente elige un candidato a vicepresidente que posea características complementarias y que de esta forma, mejore sus posibilidades de ganar una elección.

ballot/balota Formulario impreso para votar.

bandwagon effect/adhesión a la causa popular Técnica de propaganda que intenta persuadir a la gente para que apoyen a cierto candidato o propuesta, mencionando que grandes números de personas están supuestamente haciendo lo mismo.

bankruptcy/bancarrota Estado en que es legalmente imposible pagar las deudas.

bench trial/tribunal Juicio ante un juez, sin jurado.

benefits-received principle/principio de beneficios recibidos Sistema impositivo por el cual aquellos que utilizan algún servicio público en particular, lo mantienen, pagando impuestos proporcionales al beneficio que reciben.

biased sample/caso tendencioso Elección que no representa con exactitud a la mayoría.

bicameral legislature/legislatura bi-cámara Legislatura compuesta por dos cámaras o partes. Los Estados Unidos tienen una legislatura bi-cámara, compuesta por la Cámara de Representantes y el Senado. (Compare con *unicameral legislatura/legislatura de una cámara*).

biennially/bienal Evento que sucede una vez cada dos años.

bilateral treaties/tratados bilaterales Tratados entre dos naciones.

bill/declaración Propuesta de ley.

bill of attainder/decreto de proscripción Acto legislativo que propone un castigo a cierto individuo o grupo, sin garantizar el derecho a un juicio.

blanket primary/primaria absoluta Primaria en que todos los nombres de los candidatos están impresos en la misma boleta, sin tener en cuenta su afiliación. En una primaria absoluta, los votantes pueden elegir candidatos de más de un partido.

block grants/concesiones en bloque Tipo de programa por el que el gobierno federal entrega dinero a un estado para ser usado en áreas públicas generales, como justicia criminal o salud mental.

boroughs/barrios Sub-unidades administrativas de una ciudad. En Alaska, un barrio es equivalente a un condado.

boycott/boicot Negativa organizada de los consumidores, por la compra de ciertos artículos específicos, por lo general como protesta ante las condiciones de producción o elaboración.

budget/presupuesto Plan de gastos del gobierno, sometido por el presidente ante el Congreso, en enero de cada año.

budget deficit/déficit presupuestario Cuando el gobierno federal gasta más de lo que recibe.

burden of proof/comprobación de evidencia Obligación de la fiscalía de probar que el acusado es culpable de un crímen.

bureaucracy/burocracia Gran organización que está estructurada jerárquicamente, para llevar a cabo funciones específicas.

bureaucrats/burócratas Aquellos empleados por la burocracia.

business cycle/ciclo comercial Ciclo de actividad económica que consiste en recesión, recuperación, crecimiento, y baja.

busing/transporte escolar (para integración) Sistema de transporte público de estudiantes desde los barrios en que viven, a otras áreas. La intención de este busing (transporte) es de eliminar la segregación estudiantil, basada en lugares de residencia.

C

cabinet/gabinete Grupo consejero seleccionado por el presidente, para asistirlo en la toma de decisiones. El gabinete está compuesto tradicionalmente por los directivos de los departamentos ejecutivos y otras autoridades, seleccionados por el presidente .

calendar/calendario Orden en que los decretos serán considerados por la comisión o por la cámara.

Calendar of General Order/Calendario de Ordenes Generales Programa que indica los decretos que serán considerados por un cuerpo legislativo, como puede ser, el Senado.

campaign manager/administrador de la campaña Individuo empleado por el candidato para estar a cargo de la campaña electoral del candidato.

canvasses/corredores Solicitud a domicilio de votos o encuesta de la opinión pública, a lo largo de un área específica.

capital cases/casos capitales Casos criminales en los cuales la sentencia puede ser la pena de muerte.

capitalism/capitalismo Sistema económico en el cual los individuos son poseedores de los bienes de producción y tienen el derecho a usar aquellos recursos de la forma en que quieran, dentro de los límites de la ley (también llamado *sistema de mercado o sistema de libre empresa*).

card stacking/puntos a favor Técnica de propaganda que enfatiza todos los argumentos favorables de un asunto o de un candidato, pero que no señala argumentos negativos.

case law/ley de precedentes Historia de los casos que tomados en conjunto, forman los precedentes, para futuras decisiones judiciales.

casework/estudio de casos Forma de trabajo social por el cual los miembros del Congreso, se dedican personalmente a los problemas y necesidades de cada ciudadano en particular.

caseworkers/estudiosos del caso Miembros del personal del Congreso, que manejan los numerosos pedidos de ayuda de los constituyentes.

categorical grants/concesiones categóricas Fondos de ayuda del gobierno federal hacia los estados o gobiernos locales, para colaborar con programas o proyectos, muy específicos.

caucus/junta electoral Reunión a puertas cerradas de los dirigentes de un partido, para elegir al candidato de un partido o decidir sobre una política especial.

cease-fire/cese el fuego Ver *armistice/armisticio*.

censorship/censura Eliminación del material (como libros, obras de teatro, música, etc.) considerados como inconvenientes para la moral, la política, u otro motivo.

censure/censura Reprimenda oficial a un legislador(a), por parte de sus pares.

census/censo Recuento oficial de la población de una ciudad, estado o nación. En los Estados Unidos se realiza un censo cada diez años.

chancellors/magistrados Jueces en épocas coloniales que resolvían disputas judiciales en base a la equidad, en lugar de aplicar leyes específicas.

chargé díaffairs/encargado de asuntos Miembro de una embajada con rango inferior al embajador, que puede asumir temporariamente los deberes del embajador.

charter/carta Documento publicado por el gobierno que garantiza derechos a una persona, grupo de personas o una corporación, para que lleven a cabo cierta actividad.

checks and balances/control y balance Principio mayor del gobierno americano por el cual cada una de las tres ramas, tiene los medios para controlar (contrarrestar o equiparar) las acciones de las otras.

chief administrator plan/cargo de administrador municipal Sistema de gobierno local, mediante el cual el administrador comparte responsabilidades en ciertas áreas claves, con la junta del condado u otros individuos.

chief diplomat/diplómata mayor Rol del presidente en reconocer y obrar en forma recíproca con los gobiernos extranjeros.

chief executive/director ejecutivo Jefe del cuerpo ejecutivo de gobierno.

chief of staff/jefe del estado mayor Persona que dirige la oficina del presidente en la Casa Blanca y que sirve como el consejero presidencial.

city manager/director municipal Oficial designao por un concejal electo para administrar el gobierno de la ciudad.

civil disobedience/desobediencia civil Acción de una

protesta no-violenta con intenciones de llamar la atención sobre ciertas cuestiones o leyes.

civil law/ley civil Cuerpo de leyes que regula las disputas privadas entre ciudadanos, sobre asuntos no-criminales, tales como contratos, cuestiones domésticas y prácticas comerciales.

civil liberties/libertades civiles Derechos individuales protegidos por la Constitución, contra los poderes del gobierno.

civil rights/derechos civiles Derechos y libertades de los americanos, garantizados constitucionalmente.

civil rights movement/movimiento de derechos civiles Movimiento político y social que comenzó en 1950, y que organizó a los negros y blancos, y gente de otras razas, para terminar con las políticas de segregación. Trató de establecer oportunidades iguales en los sectores políticos y económicos, y de eliminar las políticas que levantaban barreras contra la gente de otra raza.

civil service/administración pública Término que se aplica a los empleados civiles del gobierno y que por lo general, obtienen empleo en base al sistema jerárquico.

Civil Service Commission/Comisión de la Administración Pública Agencia central del personal del gobierno federal.

civil service examination/exámen de la administración pública Exámen de admisión tomado por la administración pública para asegurar que los empleados del gobierno estén bien capacitados.

clear and present danger/riesgo claro y presente Regla propuesta por el Juez Oliver Wendell Holmes, que establece que la libertad de palabra no puede ser limitada a menos que perjudique claramente a la sociedad, a la cual el gobierno debe proteger.

clemency proceedings/procedimientos de clemencia Procedimientos por los cuales un gobernador puede perdonar o suspender la sentencia de alguien acusado de un crimen.

clerk of the House/empleado de la Cámara Personal no-miembro oficial de la Cámara de Representantes.

closed primary/primaria cerrada Sistema más difundido de elección primaria, mediante el cual los votantes pueden solamente elegir candidatos del partido en el cual están registrados.

cloture/clausura Limitación de un debate por parte de la legislatura, con el objeto de votar de inmediato sobre el asunto en cuestión.

cloture rule/regla de clausura Regla del Senado que impone un límite de una hora, al tiempo en que un senador puede hablar sobre una ley o asunto.

coalitions/coaliciones Alianzas de grupos políticos que cooperan para obtener un voto mayoritario.

coattail effect/efecto faldero Influencia que puede tener en una votación a un cargo mayor, un candidato popular o no, por parte de otros candidatos de su mismo partido.

Cold War/Guerra Fría Desaveniencia ideológica, política y económica que existió entre los Estados Unidos y la Unión Soviética, luego de la Segunda Guerra Mundial.

collective security/seguridad colectiva Política de formar alianzas internacionales de defensa, para aumentar la seguridad de cada nación miembro.

colonial empire/imperio colonial Grupo de naciones colonizadas bajo el dominio de un sólo poder imperial.

command economic system/sistema económico comandado Sistema económico mediante el cual el gobierno controla los factores de la producción y toma todas las decisiones sobre su aplicación.

commerce clause/cláusula comercial Sección de la Constitución que garantiza al Congreso el poder de regular el comercio entre los estados y con los países extranjeros.

commercial speech/alocución comercial Oraciones publicitarias que describen ciertos productos; tienen cierto grado de protección bajo la Primer Enmienda.

commission plan/comisión municipal Gobierno municipal que consiste en una comisión de tres a nueve miembros, que tienen ambos poderes: legislativo y ejecutivo.

committee of the whole/comisión de la totalidad Procedimiento que usa la Cámara de Representantes para acelerar su trámite, transformándose en una mayor comisión.

common law/derecho común Cuerpo de leyes originado en Inglaterra, mediante el cual los jueces individuales decidían los casos, de acuerdo con las costumbres en uso. Como se aplicaban decisiones similares en casos similares, se desarrolló un código legal para toda la nación. Este derecho común fue la base del sistema legal americano.

common law marriage/matrimonio consensual Cuando un hmbre y una mujer viven durante cierto tiempo, por ejemplo siete años, contínuamente juntos como marido y mujer, se los considera como dentro de un matrimonio consensual, tratado igual que los otros matrimonios.

communism/comunismo Sistema económico y político basado en las teorías de Karl Marx. En tal sistema, toda la economía está basada en la propiedad colectiva y en el control del gobierno de la propiedad y los medios de producción. Se espera que los individuos contribuyan con la economía de acuerdo con su habilidad, y se les da un ingreso de acuerdo a sus necesidades. También es un sistema político y económico implementado en países como la China y, hasta hace poco, la Unión Soviética, por el cual el estado controla la producción y la distribución de alimentos y el gobierno está dirigido por un único líder o partido autoritario.

Communist bloc/Bloque comunista Grupo de naciones que cayó bajo control soviético, luego de la Segunda Guerra Mundial.

commute/conmutar Reducir una sentencia criminal impuesta por un tribunal.

competition/competencia Rivalidad entre los productores y los vendedores de productos similares, para aumentar las ventas y las ganancias.

comptroller (también controller)/interventor Oficial que controla las cuentas y supervisa los asuntos financieros de una corporación o cuerpo de gobierno.

concurrent jurisdiction/jurisdicción concurrente Compartir la autoridad legal entre los tribunales federales y los de los estados.

concurrent majority/mayoría concurrente Principio emitido por John C. Calhoun, estableciendo que las decisiones democráticas deberían hacerse sólo con el consentimiento de todos los segmentos de la sociedad afectados por tal decisión. Sin este consentimiento, la decisión no puede comprometer aquellos intereses que está violando.

concurrent powers/poderes concurrentes Dentro del sistema federal, poderes a cargo del gobierno federal al igual que de los estados.

concurrent resolution/resolución concurrente Medida del congreso que trata los asuntos que necesitan acción por parte de la Cámara y el Senado, para la cual no se necesita una ley. Intenta expresar una opinión o una política oficial. Las resoluciones concurrentes deben pasar ambas Cámaras del Congreso, pero no requieren la firma del presidente, ni tienen fuerza de ley.

concurring opinion/opiniones coincidentes Declaración escrita de un magistrado indicando está de acuerdo (concuerda) con la decisión de la corte, pero que expresa razones diferentes a la opinión de la mayoría.

confederal system/sistema confederado Liga de estados soberanos independientes, unidos bajo un gobierno central que sólo tiene poderes limitados sobre ellos.

confederation/confederación Liga de estados independientes que están unidos sólo con el propósito de lograr metas comunes.

conferees/deliberante Miembro que participa en una conferencia.

conference committee/comisión de la conferencia Comisión conjunta especial elegida para reconciliar las diferencias cuando un decreto pasa ambas cámaras, bajo diferentes formas.

conference report/informe de la conferencia Informe sometido por la comisión de la conferencia, luego de haber redactado una sola versión del decreto.

congressional district/distrito congresional Area geográfica dentro de un estado que está cubierta por un representante en el Congreso.

congressional immunity/inmunidad congresional Privile-gio establecido en la Constitución, que garantiza la libertad de palabra para los miembros, mientras están ocupados en asuntos del Congreso. Protege la libertad de debate legislativo.

conscription/conscripción Alistado obligatorio en las fuerzas armadas.

consensus/consenso Acuerdo general de la ciudadanía, sobre una cuestión.

consent/consentimiento Permiso o acuerdo de los gobernados.

consent of the governed/consentimiento de los gobernados Principio de que el gobierno está basado en la voluntad del pueblo, y como tal, sólo puede ser abolido por el pueblo.

conservatives/conservadores Aquellos que tienen ideas políticas que incluyen rol limitado del gobierno, apoyo por los valores tradicionales y preferencia por un status quo.

consideration/consideración Aquello que cada parte recibe de valor, cuando firma un contrato.

consolidation/consolidación Unión de dos o más unidades gubernamentales, para formar una sola unidad.

constituents/electores Votantes de un distrito donde reside el legislador.

constitutional initiative/iniciativa constitucional Proceso que permite proponer una enmienda constitucional a través de peticiones firmadas por un número necesario de votantes empadronados.

constitutional monarchy/monarquía constitucional Gobierno en el que los reyes o reinas comparten el poder con legisladores electos.

consul/cónsul Miembro del consulado americano cuya tarea es la promoción de intereses comerciales americanos, en ciudades extranjeras.

consulate/consulado Oficina del cónsul.

containment/contención Política diplomática de EE.UU. adoptada por primera vez por la administración de Truman, para que el poder comunista quedara encerrado dentro de los límites existentes y de ese modo, "crear situaciones de poder" alrededor del mundo.

contempt/rebeldía Falta de respeto, o desobediencia voluntaria de las reglas u órdenes de la corte o cuerpo legislativo.

contempt of Congress/rebeldía ante el Congreso Falta de respeto o desobediencia voluntaria ante el Congreso.

contiguous/contiguo Adjunto.

contract/contrato Convenio legal sobre un intercambio de promesas entre dos personas o grupos de personas.

controller/interventor Ver *Comptroller*.

convening/convocación Apertura formal de cada término del Congreso. La Enmienda Doce de la Constitución dispone el día 3 de enero de cada año impar (nono) para la convocación, salvo que el Congreso disponga otra fecha.

Cooley's rule/regla de Cooley Derivada de una decisión del juez Thomas Cooley, quien en 1871, estableció que las ciudades debían ser "gobernadas desde los hogares," es decir, auto-gobernadas, en lugar de dirigidas por el gobierno del estado.

cooperative federalism/federalismo cooperativista Teoría de que los estados y el gobierno federal deben cooperar entre sí, para resolver los problemas.

copyright/derechos de autor Derecho legal exclusivo de una persona para publicar, reproducir, o vender su obra literaria, musical, o creación artística.

council-manager plan/concejal-director Medida de gobierno municipal por la que un concejal municipal electo designa a un profesional, como director ejecutivo.

Council of Economic Advisors/Consejo Económico Personal de la oficina del director ejecutivo que aconseja al presidente sobre medidas para mantener la estabilidad de la economía nacional. El consejo ayuda al presidente a preparar su informe económico anual al Congreso y desarrolla planes económicos y recomendaciones presupuestarias, para mantener el poder adquisitivo, productivo y laboral.

councils of governments/concejos municipales Organizaciones políticas voluntarias de los condados y municipalidades, que se dedican a problemas locales, formadas para coordinar unidades múltiples de gobierno.

county/condado Unidad gubernamental establecida por el estado, para administrar la ley y los negocios a nivel local. Los condados están designados por área, en lugar de criterio urbano o rural.

county board/junta del condado Cuerpo gobernante del condado, elegido por los votantes para llevar a cabo asuntos locales.

county boroughs/barrios del condado Unidad local de gobierno de Gran Bretaña.

county-manager plan/director del condado Gobierno del condado en que las políticas son establecidas por un cuerpo electo, y se llevan a cabo por un director, empleado por y responsable ante ese cuerpo.

Credentials Committee/comisión de credenciales Comisión convocada en cada convención nacional partidaria, para inspeccionar los reclamos de futuros delegados y determinar quiénes pueden participar.

criminal law/derecho criminal Cuerpo de leyes que define crímenes y determina el castigo por cometerlos. El gobierno es el fiscal en los casos criminales, ya que estos crímenes atentan contra el orden público.

currency power/poder para circular moneda Poder otorgado al Congreso mediante la Constitución, para emitir moneda y regular su valor.

cyberstrike/huelga cibernético Huelga organizada en el espacio cibernético, utilizando el Internet.

D

death taxes/impuestos por fallecimiento Impuestos sobre las propiedades y las herencias, establecidos por el estado.

debt financing/financiación de la deuda Venta de valores para financiar las mejoras a largo plazo.

decentralization/descentralización Translado del poder desde el gobierno federal hacia los estados o gobiernos locales.

de facto* segregation/segregación *de facto Segregación racial que ocurre, no como resultado de intenciones deliberadas, sino por condiciones previas sociales y económicas, o lugares de residencia.

defense policy/política de defensa Protección de la nación mediante la preparación del ejército.

de jure* segregation/segregación *de jure Segregación racial que ocurre debido a leyes o decisiones administrativas, por parte de las agencias públicas.

delegated, expressed, or enumerated powers/poderes delegados, ratificados o enumerados Poderes que son otorgados al gobierno federal directamente por la Constitución, según el Artículo 1, Sección B.

delegates/delegados Personas que están autorizadas para hablar, votar o de algún modo, actuar en nombre de otras. (Los representantes de los partidos políticos de los estados, en la convención nacional, sirven como *delegados* a tal convención).

deliberative organ/órgano deliberante Organo que delibera, discute y decide sobre cuestiones importantes.

democracy/democracia Sistema de gobierno en el cual la gente posee la máxima autoridad política. La palabra deriva del griego *demos* (gente) y *kratia* (autoridad).

denaturalization/desnaturalización Pérdida de la ciudadanía debido a un proceso legal. Se aplica con frecuencia a quienes han causado fraudes durante el proceso de naturalización, o a quienes se estima han obstruído las funciones del gobierno.

Dennison Rule/regla de Dennison Reglamentación de 1861, de la Suprema Corte de EE.UU., que defendió el derecho del gobernador de Ohio, de rechazar el pedido de extradición por parte del gobernador de Kentucky, de un "hombre de color, libre", bajo cargos de haber ayudado a un esclavo, a escapar hacia su libertad.

departments/departamentos Palabra francesa usada para las divisiones geográficas en que se dividen los gobiernos locales.

deportation/deportación Proceso legal por el cual una nación devuelve extranjeros a sus países de origen.

deported/deportado Obligado a abandonar el país.

depression/depresión Caída de la actividad ecoómica, caracterizada por gran tasa de desempleo, bajas y fracasos en los negocios.

détente/cese Palabra francesa usada para el cese de hostilidades entre los Estados Unidos y la Unión Soviética, bajo la administración del presidente Richard Nixon.

deterrence/aterrorizar Política que adoptó Estados Unidos luego de la Segunda Guerra Mundial, amenazando con una venganza masiva, para desanimar la agresión de sus enemigos.

devolution/devolución Transferencia de los poderes a unidades políticas menores.

dictatorship/dictadura Forma de gobierno en que el poder absoluto es ejercido por una sola persona, la que obtuvo su poder por lo general, mediante el uso de la fuerza.

Dillon's rule/regla de Dillon Principio detallado por John F. Dillon en sus Comentarios *sobre la Ley de las Corporaciones Municipales* (1911), que establece que las corporaciones municipales tienen sólo aquellos poderes que el estado expresamente les garantiza.

diplomacy/diplomacia Proceso mediante el cual las naciones establecen y mantienen entre sí, relaciones políticas, a través de tratados, acuerdos y alianzas.

diplomat/diplómata Persona que lleva a cabo tareas de diplomacia, en nombre de su país de origen.

direct democracy/democracia directa Sistema de gobierno en el que las decisiones políticas son tomadas directamente por el pueblo, en lugar de sus representantes electos. Esta forma de gobierno fue ampliamente practicada en la antigua Grecia.

direct primary/primaria directa Elección dentro de un partido, en la que los votantes eligen a los candidatos que estarán en la fórmula del partido de la siguiente elección general.

direct tax/impuesto directo Impuesto que debe ser pagado por la persona en quien está gravado.

disability/incapacidad Impedimento físico o mental que "limita substancialmente" las actividades cotidianas de la persona.

disenfranchise/exención Privar a los votantes de su posibilidad de votar.

dissenting opinion/opinión en disenso Declaración escrita por parte de un juez(a), por la que disiente con las conclusiones a que llegó la mayoría de la corte. El juez expone su punto de vista sobre el caso.

district attorney/fiscal del distrito Abogado que inicia y conduce una acción legal en nombre del estado, especialmente en un proceso criminal.

diversity of citinzenship/diversidad de ciudadanía Concepto legal que se aplica a los casos que surgen entre ciudadanos de distintos estados, o entre extranjeros y ciudadanos de un estado o de diferentes estados.

divine right theory/teoría de derecho divino Teoría que sugiere que el mandato de un rey o de una reina estaba derivado directamente de Dios, en vez del consentimiento del pueblo.

division of powers/división de poderes Principio básico de federalismo que parte de la Constitución de los EE.UU., mediante el cual los poderes están divididos, en base geográfica, entre unidades del gobierno (como gobiernos federal y de los estados).

doctrine/doctrina Posición, política, o principio, particulares.

domestic policy/política doméstica Política que afecta los asuntos internos de la nación.

doubling time/tiempo de duplicación Tasa en que la población se duplica, por ejemplo, cada cinco años, o cada treinta años.

draft/conscripción Servicio militar obligatorio.

draft registration/inscripción para conscripción Proceso por el cual los jóvenes de 18 años deben anotarse como candidatos para la conscripción, en caso de establecerse un servicio militar obligatorio.

dual citizenship/ciudadanía doble Condición de un ciudadano que pertenece a dos naciones soberanas, o a un estado y una nación.

dual federalism/federalismo doble Sistema de gobierno mediante el cual ambos gobiernos el federal y el del estado, mantienen poderes diversos, pero soberanos.

due process clause/cláusula de proceso legal Garantía constitucional establecida en las Enmiendas Quinta y Sexta de la Constitución, por las que el gobierno no puede privar ilegal o arbitrariamente a una persona, de su vida, su libertad o su propiedad. (Llamado también *due process of law/debido proceso legal*).

E

earned income tax credit (EITC)/beneficio sobre impuesto a las ganancias Programa creado en 1975 que devuelve a los trabajadores de bajos ingresos, parte de o el total de los impuestos por jubilación.

economic sanctions/sanciones económicas Resistencia a comerciar con una nación extranjera, como medio para expresar el desacuerdo por su política y sus pautas economicas.

economic system/sistema económico Forma en que una nación emplea sus recursos para satisfacer las necesidades y deseos de su pueblo.

elastic clause/cláusula elástica Artículo 1, Sección 8, de la Constitución, que otorga al Congreso el poder de dictar todas las leyes "necesarias y apropiadas" para cumplir sus funciones.

elected chief executive plan/elección de funcionarios municipales Programa del gobierno de un condado mediante el cual el director en jefe, como puede ser el alcalde, es elegido directamente por los votantes y trabaja con la junta del condado.

electoral college/colegio electoral Grupo de electores seleccionados por los votantes en cada estado, para elegir oficialmente al presidente y al vice-presidente. El número de electores de cada estado, es igual al número de representantes que tiene dicho estado en ambas cámaras del Congreso.

electoral college system/sistema de colegio electoral Institución única americana, creada por la Constitución, que permite la elección del presidente mediante electores elegidos por los partidos de los estados, de acuerdo a las leyes de cada estado.

electorate/electorado Todos los ciudadanos aptos para votar, en una elección dada.

electors/electores Aquellos individuos elegidos al comienzo del año de elecciones presidenciales, según las leyes de los estados y dispositivos de los partidos políticos. Los electores emiten votos para presidente y vice-presidente, con el objeto de hacer una selección formal de presidente y vice presidente.

electronic democracy/democracia electrónica Cantidad de votantes que pueden votar sobre medidas políticas importantes, mediante foros electivos, a través del Internet.

embassy/embajada Residencia oficial y oficinas de un embajador.

enabling act/acta de permiso Ley emitida por el Congreso que permite a un territorio a establecer una constitución y poder optar a transformarse en un estado.

enemy aliens/extranjeros enemigos Ciudadanos de aquellos países que están en guerra con los Estados Unidos.

enumerated powers/poderes ennumerados Ver *delegated, expressed, or enumerated powers.*

environmental impact statement/declaración sobre impacto ecológico Declaración hecha por el Acta sobre Pautas del Medio Ambiente, por la que se deben los perjuicios y beneficios de las acciones del gobierno federal, que podrían afectar significativamente la calidad del medio ambiente.

equal employment opportunity/igualdad de oportunidad de empleo (EEO) Intención del Acta de Derechos Civiles de 1964, de terminar con la discriminación en base a raza, religión, sexo, o nacionalidad, para el empleo y la promoción de empleados, con el fin de fomentar igualdad de oportunidades.

Equal Employment Opportunity Commission (EEOC)/

Comisión de Igualdad de Empleos Organización responsable de administrar las leyes federales que prohíben la discriminación de empleados.

equalization/compensación Método para ajustar la cantidad de dinero que un estado debe suministrar, para recibir fondos federales. Este método toma en cuenta las riquezas del estado y sus recursos impositivos.

equal protection clause/cláusula de igual protección Cláusula de la Enmienda Décimocuarta, que prohibe a un estado, negar a cualquier persona, dentro de su jurisdicción, igual protección ante la ley. Esta es la mayor limitación constitucional de los poderes del gobierno, en contra de discriminar contra las personas en base a su raza, nacionalidad, o sexo.

espionage/espionaje Práctica de espiar para obtener información sobre los planes y actividades de una potencia extranjera.

establishment clause/cláusula de fundación Parte de la Primer Enmienda que prohibe el establecimiento de una iglesia oficial, mantenida por el gobierno federal. Se la aplica para evitar que el gobierno preste ayuda a las escuelas religiosas, fomente la oración en las escuelas públicas, o la enseñanza de fundamentos religiosos sobre la creación (opuestos a las teorías científicas de la evolución).

evolutionary theory/teoría de la evolución Teoría que mantiene que el gobierno evolucionó a lo largo del tiempo, a medida que las familias se unieron en clanes y luego en tribus. De estas tribus surgió un líder que eventualmente dió lugar al establecimiento gradual de un gobierno.

excessive entanglement theory/teoría de implicación excesiva Regla aplicada por la Corte Suprema, para mantener una separación entre la iglesia y el estado. Para ser constitucional, la ayuda del gobierno a los grupos religiosos debe cumplir con tres requerimientos: (1) el motivo debe ser claramente secular; (2) no debe fomentar ni inhibir la religión; y (3) debe evitar la implicación del gobierno con la religión.

excise taxes/impuestos internos Dentro de un país, impuestos cargados sobre ciertas acciones, como la fabricación o venta de ciertos artículos, como ser, tabaco o licor.

exclusionary rule/regla de exclusión Regla que evita que cualquier evidencia obtenida en forma ilegal, pueda ser usada en un juicio contra la persona de quien se ha obtenido tal evidencia. Esta regla está basada en la interpretación de las Enmiendas Cuarta y Décimocuarta, por parte de la Corte Suprema.

exclusive jurisdiction/jurisdicción exclusiva Autoridad de la corte que permite tratar casos que caen fuera del alcance legal de otras cortes.

executive agreements/acuerdos ejecutivos Acuerdos internacionales que no requieren sanción legislativa, establecidos entre dos jefes de estado.

executive authority/director ejecutivo Persona de gran poder administrativo (público) que supervisa la rama ejecutiva de un sistema.

Executive Office of the President (EOP)/Oficina Ejecutiva del Presidente Nueve agentes que asisten al presidente en sus tareas mayores. Fue establecida por el presidente Franklin D. Roosevelt, mediante orden directiva, bajo el Acta de Reorganización de 1939.

executive order/orden ejecutiva Regla o reglamentación emitida por el director en jefe (como el presidente o gobernador), que tiene efecto de ley.

executive privilege/privilegio ejecutivo Derecho del presidente (u otros oficiales nombrados por el presidente) a no presentarse ante una comisión legislativa, o a no revelar ante esa comisión, cierta información, sobre la base de que revelando tal información, se puede atentar contra la seguridad nacional.

expatriation/expatriación Acto de renunciar voluntariamente a la ciudadanía de su país de origen.

exports/exportaciones Artículos que una nación produce y vende a otras naciones.

ex post facto Leyes criminales que señalan ciertos actos como crímenes y luego castigan a las personas por cometerlos, antes de haber pasado las leyes. Las leyes ex post facto están prohibidas por la Constitución.

expressed powers/poderes expresos Ver *delegated, expressed, or enumerated powers.*

expulsion/expulsión Retirar por la fuerza a algún miembro del Congreso, por mala conducta.

extradition/extradición Proceso por el cual los sospechosos fugitivos, son transladados a la jurisdicción donde son procesados.

extraordinary majority/mayoría extraordinaria Mayoría que es superior al 50 por ciento más uno. La Constitución de los EE.UU., por ejemplo, requiere mayorías extraordinarias de los dos tercios de la Cámara y el Senado, para que el Congreso proponga una Enmienda Constitucional.

F

factions/facciones Grupos o camarillas, dentro de un grupo mayor.

federal budget/presupuesto federal Plan del gobierno federal, bien detallado, sobre gastos de los fondos, a lo largo de un cierto período.

federal government/gobierno federal Término que se refiere al gobierno central o nacional, en particular en los Estados Unidos.

federal question/cuestión federal Surge siempre cuando la causa del demandante esté basada, aunque sea en parte, en la Constitución de los Estados Unidos, en algún tratado o ley federales. Las cuestiones federales se pueden tratar sólo por un tribunal federal.

Federal Reserve System/Fondo de Reserva Federal El banco central de los Estados Unidos, el "Fed" se estableció en 1913, y está dirigido por una junta de directores.

federal system/sistema federal Forma de gobierno en la que una constitución escrita establece una separación de los poderes entre el gobierno central y los distintos gobiernos regionales. Esta separación se establece mediante una autoridad superior a ambos gobiernos, como puede ser un documento escrito. En los Estados Unidos, la división de los poderes entre el gobierno federal y los cincuenta estados, está explicada en la Constitución.

federalism/federalismo Sistema por el cual algunos poderes pertenecen al gobierno nacional o federal, mientras que otros pertenecen a los estados.

federalists/federalistas Aquellos que favorecen un fuerte gobierno central y la nueva Constitución.

felony/delito Seria ofensa criminal que es castigada con prisión. Las penalidades van de un año en prisión, hasta la pena de muerte.

fighting words/palabras provocadoras Palabras usadas por un orador público, tan inflamatorias, que pueden provocar cierta violencia en los espectadores.

filibuster/obstruccionista Debate ilimitado para detener la acción en el Senado.

First Continental Congress/Primer Congreso Continental Primera reunión de delegados de doce de las trece colonias, con el propósito de diagramar una constitución federal. El Congreso tuvo lugar en Philadelphia, en 1774.

fiscal policy/política fiscal Ajustes a discreción de los gastos y/o impuestos del gobierno, con el objeto de lograr metas económicas nacionales, como ser, más empleos y estabilidad en los precios.

fiscal year/año fiscal Período de doce meses que está determinado por la contabilidad o motivos contables. El año fiscal del gobierno va desde el 1 de octubre hasta el 30 de septiembre.

flat tax/impuesto fijo Tasa de impuesto único, que no permite deducciones, usada por todos, a partir de un cierto monto inicial de ingresos anuales.

food stamps/boletos de comida Cupones emitidos por el gobierno, que pueden ser usados para comprar alimentos.

force theory/teoría de la fuerza Teoría sobre los orígenes del gobierno, que mantiene que las personas o los grupos más fuertes, conquistaron territorios y forzaron a los demás habitantes de dichos territorios, a someterse a su voluntad.

foreign policy/política exterior Objetivos políticos y económicos de una nación, con respecto a otras naciones.

Técnicas y estrategias usadas para lograr tales objetivos.

foreign service/servicio exterior Cuadro de funcionarios del Departamento de Estado que opera en el exterior.

franchise/privilegio Derecho legal al voto. Este privilegio fue extendido a los afro-americanos mediante la Enmienda Décimoquinta, a las mujeres mediante la Décimonovena y a todos los ciudadanos a partir de los dieciocho años por la Enmienda Veintiseis.

franking privilege/privilegio de franqueo Privilegio que permite a los miembros del Congreso, enviar material por correo, sustituyendo la reproducción de su firma por franqueo (estampilla).

free enterprise system/sistema de libre empresa Ver *capitalism*.

free exercise clause/cláusula de libertad religiosa Provisión de la Primer Enmienda, que garantiza el libre ejercicio de la religión.

fugitive/fugitivo Individuo acusado de un crímen, que se encuentra prófugo de la fiscalía.

full faith and credit clause/cláusula de fe y confianza Artículo VI, Sección 1 de la Constitución, que exige que los estados reconozcan entre sí, las leyes y decisiones de la corte Asegura que los derechos establecidos en títulos, testamentos, contratos, y otros documentos civiles de un estado, sean honrados por los otros estados.

functional consolidations/consolidación operativa Cooperación de dos o más unidades locales de gobierno, para proveer servicios a sus habitantes.

Fundamental Orders of Connecticut/Decreto Fundamental de Connecticut Primera constitución escrita de América, que establecía una asamblea representativa, constituída por representantes electos de cada ciudad, para dictar leyes. También incluía elecciones populares para gobernador y jueces.

fundamental rights/derechos fundamentales Derechos básicos necesarios para cierta libertad, como el voto, o libertad de religión.

fund-raisers/recaudar fondos Eventos pagados por los candidatos, destinados a obtener fondos para los costos de su campaña electoral.

G

gag orders/orden de silencio Ordenes emitidas por los jueces, para restringir la publicación de noticias acerca de un juicio en proceso o una audiencia previa a un juicio, con el objeto de proteger los derechos del acusado, a un juicio justo.

gender gap/separación de sexos Diferencia entre las opiniones políticas de los hombres y las mujeres. Término usado para describir la diferencia entre los porcentajes de votos de mujeres y de hombres, emitidos para un candidato en particular. Este término fue ampliamente usado luego de las elecciones de 1980 y vuelto a traer para las elecciones de 1992.

general election/elecciones generales Elecciones organizadas a lo largo de la nación, mediante las cuales se toma la decisión final sobre quienes ejercerán la autoridad pública.

general jurisdiction/jurisdicción general Autoridad de la corte para decidir todos los asuntos que aparecen ante ella.

generalization/generalización Sobre-simplificación que no siempre es real, en cada caso específico.

general-law city/ciudad de ley general Ciudad que opera bajo las leyes de un estado, las cuales se aplican a todas las unidades locales similares.

gerrymandering/tergiversar Práctica de rediseñar los límites de los distritos legislativos, con el fin de obtener ventajas electorales para un partido o grupo político.

glittering generalities/deslumbrante Método de propaganda que utiliza declaraciones rutilantes, que suenan bien pero que tiene poco significado real.

global warming/calentamiento terrestre Aumento gradual de las temperaturas a través de todo el planeta.

government/gobierno Instituciones y procesos a través de los cuales se emiten las pautas públicas de una sociedad.

government bonds/bonos del gobierno Certificados comprados por individuos y compañías, como medio para prestar dinero al gobierno. A cambio del préstamo de dinero, el gobierno promete devolver en cierto tiempo, la cantidad total más un interés.

government corporation/corporación del gobierno Agencia del gobierno que opera como una empresa mercantil. Se establece tal agencia cuando la actividad es típicamente comercial, cuando produce ganancias y cuando necesita mayor flexibilidad que la permitida a la mayoría de las agencias del gobierno.

grand jury/jurado de acusación Jurado de veintitrés personas, a quienes se informa sobre los cargos contra los individuos y determinan si existe suficiente evidencia, como para iniciar un juicio.

grandfather clause/cláusula del abuelo Método usado por los estados del sur para eximir a los blancos de pagar impuestos y leyes de alfabetización, como medio para negar a los negros el derecho a votar. La cláusula permitía que cualquiera que pudiera probar que su abuelo había votado antes de 1867, podía votar en las corrientes elecciones.

Great Compromise/Gran Compromiso Plan de Roger Sherman para eliminar la controversia entre estado grande y estado pequeño, durante la Convención Constitucional. Propuso una legislatura de dos cámaras, con una cámara baja, de Representantes y una alta, de Senadores.

green vote/voto verde Voto para aquellos que favorecen las leyes que protegen y mantienen el medio ambiente.

greenhouse effect/efecto invernadero Retención del calor dentro de la atmósfera terrestre, como resultado de la contaminación causada por la combustión de motores y la emisión de dióxido de carbono.

grievances/agravios Quejas.

H

habeas corpus Orden designada para evitar arrestos y encarcelamientos. Requiere que el acusado sea presentado ante la corte y que el oficial que lo detuvo, indique por qué no se debe liberar al prisionero.

hereditary peers/herencia nobiliaria Miembros de la nobleza británica, por nacimiento. Existen más de 700 pares, con títulos tales como barón, vizconde, conde y duque. Todos pertenecen a la Casa de los Lores.

hereditary ruler/soberano hereditario Persona que gobierna porque es el hijo(a) de un soberano anterior.

home-rule city/ciudad autónoma Ciudad con una carta constitucional, que permite a los votantes fraguar, adoptar y reformar, su propia carta.

hopper/buzón Caja de madera en la Cámara de Representantes, en donde se depositan las nuevas propuestas de ley.

horizontal federalism/federalismo horizontal Reglas impuestas por la Constitución para evitar que cualquier estado se separe de los otros, por ejemplo, creando su propia política exterior.

House of Commons/Casa de los Comunes Cámara baja y más poderosa del Parlamento británico.

House of Lords/Casa de los Lores Cámara alta del Parlamento británico.

House Rules Committee/comisión de reglas internas Comité permanente de la Cámara de Representantes que edita las reglas bajo las cuales se consideran, debaten y enmiendan los proyectos de ley.

human rights/derechos humanos Término que se refiere a los derechos y privilegios de todos los seres humanos. Estos derechos están indicados en la Declaración de la Independencia; son derechos a la vida, a la libertad y a la búsqueda de la felicidad. Están garantizados y protegidos por la Declaración de Derechos.

hung jury/jurado en desacuerdo Jurado que no puede decidir por unanimidad sobre un veredicto.

hyperpluralism/hiper-pluralismo Forma de pluralismo en que el gobierno está tan descentralizado y la autoridad tan fragmentada, que no puede lograr ningún cometido.

I

ideologues/ideólogo Término aplicado a los individuos cuyas opiniones son muy firmes, ya sea al extremo liberal como al conservador.

ideology/ideología Conjunto de creencias sobre la naturaleza de las personas y las instituciones de gobierno.

illegal aliens/ilegales Individuos que entran en los Estados Unidos sin permiso legal o que entran como turistas y se quedan más de lo que su estado de turista les permite.

image building/mejorar la imagen Proceso de moldear la imagen de un candidato para cubrir las necesidades particulares de la campaña, usando encuestas sobre la opinión pública y privada, y otros mecanismos publicitarios.

immigrants/inmigrantes Gente que se translada a un nuevo país con el propósito de establecer su residencia permanente y ser ciudadano(a).

immunity/inmunidad Protección para evitar ser procesado por ciertas acciones.

impeach/imputar Presentar cargos contra la autoridad pública, por mala conducta o irregularidades durante su oficio.

implied powers/poderes implícitos Poderes del gobierno federal que estan establecidos en los poderes expresados por la Constitución, en particular en el Artículo 1, Sección 8.

impoundment/retención Proceso por el cual el presidente puede resistirse a invertir dinero que el Congreso ha asignado a un cierto próposito.

incarceration/encarcelación Poner en prisión.

income transfer/transferencia de ingresos Transferencia de ingresos de un grupo al otro, como con el programa agrícola, o transferencia de una generación a la otra, como ocurre con el programa de seguro social.

incorporation/asociación Proceso de incorporar una ciudad mediante el otorgamiento de una carta constitucional, por parte del estado.

incorporation theory/teoría de la incorporación Intención de incluir todas los conceptos de protección de la Declaración de Derechos, dentro de la Enmienda Décimocuarta, para que ningún estado infrinja estos derechos.

incumbent/a cargo Funcionario que posee un cargo en el presente.

independent executive agency/agencia ejecutiva independiente Agencia federal con una función específica, que responde directamente al presidente.

independent regulatory agency/agencia regulatoria independiente Agencia que atiende alguna política pública específica. Su función es la de crear e implementar reglas que regulan la actividad privada y protegen el interés público, en algún sector particular de la economía.

independent/independiente Votantes que no se identifican, por lo general, con algún partido político, o que no apoyan a un candidato en especial.

indictment/encausar El jurado de acusación halla evidencias suficientes contra una persona en particular, como para iniciar un proceso criminal.

indirect democracy/democracia indirecta Ver *representative democracy.*

indirect tax/impuesto indirecto Impuesto gravado sobre un individuo o una empresa, pero que es pasado a una tercer parte, para su pago.

inflation/inflación Aumento general de los precios.

information/información Declaración emitida por el fiscal, sobre la existencia de suficiente evidencia para procesar al acusado, sin necesidad de convocar a un jurado de acusación.

information warfare/guerra informativa Posible peligro del mundo electrónico-perjuicio deliberado del sistema electrónico de comunicaciones, de alguna nación.

inherent powers/poderes inherentes Poderes del gobierno federal, los cuales, a pesar de no estar garantizados expresamente por la Constitución, le pertenecen en virtud de su rol como gobierno de una nación soberana.

initiative/iniciativa Procedimiento mediante el cual los votantes pueden proponer cambios en las leyes estatales o municipales, a través de la reunión de firmas sobre una petición, y sometiéndola a la legislatura para su aprobación.

in-kind subsidy/subsidio distinto Asistencia que se da en otra forma que no sea monetaria, tal como cupones de comida.

institutions/instituciones Organizaciones y establecimientos de la sociedad, que están dedicados a la promoción de una causa en particular. Algunas de estas instituciones de nuestro gobierno son el sistema legal, el Congreso y el sistema de bienestar social.

intelligence/inteligencia Información reunida sobre la capacidad e intenciones de los gobiernos extranjeros.

interdependence/interdependencia Condición de los individuos, las organizaciones y las naciones, de depender unos de los otros.

interest group/grupo de interés Grupo organizado de individuos que comparten objetivos comunes, y que tratan activamente de influenciar la política mediante reuniones antecamerales, publicación de encuestas sobre la opinión pública y otros métodos.

interim committees/comisiones interinas Comités legislativos que funcionan entre sesiones legislativas. Dichos comisiones estudian cuestiones en particular e informan sobre sus hallazgos, durante la siguiente sesión legislativa.

Internet/Internet Sistema que conecta más de 150 millones de computadoras y ochenta mil redes de comunicación, a través del mundo.

interstate commerce/comercio interestatal Comercio entre dos o más estados.

interstate compact/convenio interestatal Acuerdo entre dos o más estados, de colaborar por alguna pauta o problema. Los convenios menores se realizan sin aprobación del Congreso, pero los pactos que tienden a aumentar el poder de los estados contractuales, con respecto al de los otros estados, o con respecto al gobierno federal, requieren por lo general, el consentimiento del Congreso.

interventionism/intervencionismo Política de cambiar o conservar los asuntos políticos internos de las naciones extranjeras.

intrastate commerce/comercio intra-estado Comercio entre las distintas regiones de un mismo estado.

iron curtain/cortina de hierro Describe el límite político entre los países democráticos de Europa y los países comunistas controlados por la Unión Soviética, en Europa del Este.

iron triangle/triángulo de hierro Término usado por una alianza tri-partita entre los legisladores, los burócratas y los grupos de interés, para lograr o conservar pautas que benefician sus respectivos intereses individuales.

isolationism/aislacionismo Política de no-intervención en los asuntos internacionales.

J

joint committees/comisiones conjuntas Comités legislativos compuestos por miembros de ambas Cámaras del Congreso.

joint resolution/resolución conjunta Medida legal, similar a un proyecto de ley, pasada por el Congreso y firmada por el presidente, que tiene fuerza de ley.

judicial activism/activismo judicial Doctrina que promueve un rol activo de la Suprema Corte, para hacer cumplir la Constitución y para la crítica judicial. Un tribunal activista tiene una visión amplia de la Constitución y se dedica a cuestiones legislativas y ejecutivas.

judicial circuit/circuito judicial Doce tribunales que conceden apelaciones de los tribunales del distrito ubicados dentro de sus respectivos circuitos.

judicial implementation/implementación judicial Proceso por el cual las decisiones del tribunal se transforman en regla.

judicial review/crítica judicial Poder de los tribunales para determinar la constitucionalidad de los actos de los poderes ejecutivo, legislativo y judicial, del gobierno. Fue establecida en 1803, *Marbury vs. Madison*.

junkets/excursión Viajes que hacen los miembros del Congreso para obtener información sobre una propuesta legislación, como puede ser un nuevo proyecto de ley de comercio.

jurisdiction/jurisdicción Poder de la corte para encausar y decidir ciertos casos.

jury duty/servicio en jurado Responsabilidad de todos los ciudadanos, de servir en un jurado de proceso criminal, al ser convocados.

jus sanguinis La "ley de la sangre," para indicar ciudadanía americana, declara que un niño nacido en suelo extranjero, es ciudadano americano al nacer, si aunque sea uno de sus padres es ciudadano americano, y si tal ciudadano ha vivido en los Estados unidos por lo menos diez años, a partir de los 14.

jus soli La "ley del suelo," para indicar ciudadanía americana, declara que todas las personas nacidas en los Estados Unidos, son ciudadanos americanos.

justice court/tribunal de justicia Tribunal local que presta audiencias en casos menores, civiles y criminales, realiza matrimonios y legaliza documentos.

justice of the peace/juez de paz Magistrado judicial local que preside las actividades del tribunal de justicia.

K

keynote speaker/orador de apertura Persona de renombre nacional elegida para hablar y encender el entusiasmo en una convención nacional de un partido político.

Kitchen Cabinet/Gabinete de Cocina Nombre dado a los consejeros no-oficiales del presidente, que lo ayudan en alguna reglamentación o decisión. El nombre fue forjado durante la presidencia de Andrew Jackson.

L

labor force/fuerza laboral Todos los individuos mayores de 16 años, que trabajan o que están buscando trabajo activamente.

law clerk/actuario Recién graduado en derecho que trabaja para un juez, haciendo investigación y tomando los apuntes necesarios para que el juez se forme una opinión.

law lords/lores Nueve miembros de la Cámara de los Lores, en Gran Bretaña. Son equivalentes a la Corte Suprema Británica.

legal tender/moneda de curso legal Moneda legítima para comerciar y comprar.

legislative assistants/asistentes legislativos Asistentes de los legisladores, a quienes mantienen bien informados sobre los proyectos de ley que deben tratar.

legislative correspondents/corresponsal legislativo Asistentes de los legisladores, que se ocupan de su correspondencia.

legislative director/director legislativo Asistente del legislador, que dirige y supervisa al personal del legislador.

legislative power/poder legislativo Autoridad para dictar leyes.

legislature/legislatura Cuerpo de gobierno responsable principalmente del dictado de las leyes.

legitimacy/legitimidad Autoridad legal de los funcionarios, actos e instituciones del gobierno, conferida por el pueblo sobre la base de que las acciones del gobierno son el apropiado uso del poder y que el gobierno es una autoridad legalmente constituida.

libel/calumnia Difamación por escrito.

liberalism/liberalismo Ideología política que prefiere un gobierno activo para afrontar las necesidades humanas, apoyar los derechos y libertades individuales y dar prioridad a los asuntos sociales antes que a los militares.

liberal/liberales Quienes mantienen un conjunto de creencias políticas que consisten en la intervención activa del gobierno para mejorar el bienestar de los individuos, para apoyar los derechos civiles y para hacer cambios políticos.

lieutenant governor/vice-gobernador Funcionario del estado que puede reemplazar al gobernador en caso de ausencia, incapacidad o muerte. Puede también actuar como el presidente del senado estatal.

life expectancy/promedio de vida Cantidad de años que se espera que viva cierto grupo de gente.

limited government/gobierno limitado Forma de gobierno basada en el principio de que el gobierno debe cumplir solamente las funciones para las cuales el pueblo le ha dado poder.

limited jurisdiction/jurisdicción limitada Autoridad del tribunal, para dar audiencia sólo a casos específicos.

line-item veto/veto excluyente Poder usado para la rama ejecutiva para vetar una o más provisiones de un proyecto de ley, permitiendo que las restantes se constituyan en ley.

line organizations/organizaciones directas Grupos del gobierno o de las corporaciones, que brindan servicios directos o productos para el público.

literacy tests/pruebas de capacidad Requerimiento para votar usado en cierta ocasión en los estados del sur, que exigía a los ciudadanos probar que podían leer, con el fin de calificar para votar. Usadas, en principio, para negar a los afro-americanos el derecho a votar, las pruebas de capacidad han sido ahora eliminadas.

lobbying/camarilla Conjunto de esfuerzos por parte de individuos y organizaciones, para afectar la aprobación, el rechazo o el contenido de una legislación. El término viene de la cámara (lobby) de la misma legislatura, donde los solicitantes acorralaban a los legisladores para hablarles de sus cuestiones.

lobbyist/camarillero Persona que por lo general actúa como agente para un grupo que trata de conseguir la aprobación o el rechazo de algún proyecto de ley, o para influir en su contenido o en la acción del gobierno.

loopholes/escapatorias Modos legales de evadir ciertos requerimientos legales.

loose constructionists/interpretación libre Aquellos que consideran que la Constitución debe ser interpretada más vagamente y que otorgan más definición a los poderes del gobierno federal.

loose monetary policy/pauta monetaria relajada Política diseñada para estimular la economía, reduciendo el costo de los préstamos y facilitando su obtención.

M

Madisonian Model/Modelo de Madison Modelo de gobierno detallado por James Madison, en el que los poderes del gobierno están separados en tres ramas: ejecutiva, legislativa, y judicial.

magistrate/magistrado Autoridad judicial local, con jurisdicción limitada.

magistrate court/tribunal menor Tribunal menor de una pequeña ciudad o pueblo.

Magna Carta/Carta Magna Gran carta que el rey Juan de Inglaterra fue forzado a firmar, en 1215, como protección contra los poderes absolutos de la monarquía. Incluye derechos fundamentales como: juicio por jurado y proceso legal.

majority floor leader/líder de la mayoría (Senado) Jefe del partido mayoritario del Senado, que dirige el programa legislativo y establece las estrategias partidarias.

majority leader/líder mayoritario (Cámara) Líder del partido mayoritario en la Cámara de Representantes. El líder mayoritario es elegido por la junta electoral de los miembros del partido, para que actúe como portavoz del partido y mantenga unido al partido.

majority opinion/opinión mayoritaria Declaración escrita de los puntos de vista de la mayoría de los jueces, a favor de una decisión hecha por el tribunal que presiden.

majority party/partido mayoritario Partido que ocupa la mitad de las bancas de la legislatura.

majority rule/regla de la mayoría Sistema político en el cual la mayoría determina el resultado de las elecciones. Una mayoría simple necesita el 50 porciento más uno de los votos, mientras que una mayoría extraordinaria necesita más del 50 porciento más uno de los votos.

malapportionment/mala distribución Condición que, basada en la población y la representación, resulta en un poder electoral que tiene más influencia que el poder electoral de los ciudadanos de otro distrito.

managed news coverage/cobertura periodística dirigida Hábil manejo de la prensa para aumentar la cantidad y calidad de las noticias periodísticas.

mandatory preference poll/padrón de preferencia fija Tipo de elección primaria en la cual los delegados deben votar por el candidato elegido por los votantes, en la convención nacional.

mandatory sentencing/sentencia fija Sistema por el cual crímenes específicos llevan períodos fijos de encarcelamiento.

marginal tax rate/impuesto marginal Porcentaje adicional de dinero que debe ser pagado como impuesto a los ingresos. El impuesto marginal se aplica solamente a quienes tienen mayores ingresos.

market/mercado Actividad de comprar y vender productos y servicios.

market economic system/sistema de economía de mercado El opuesto al sistema de economía por mandato; conocido de otra forma como capitalismo.

markup session/sesión correctiva Reunión en la que los miembros de la comisión conferencista del congreso, deciden qué cambios, si los hay, se deben hacer a unproyecto de ley.

Marshall Plan/Plan Marshall Programa masivo de recuperación para los países de Europa, después de la Segunda Guerra Mundial. Fue llamado así por el Secretario de Estado, George C. Marshall, Jr., que estuvo en ese cargo entre 1947 y 1949.

mass media/medios masivos Medios técnicos de comunicación (especialmente la radio, los diarios y la televisión) designado para llegar, informar y a menudo, tener influencia sobre un gran número de personas.

matching funds/aparear fondos Fondos que un estado debe pagar (o "aparear") cuando se le otorgan concesiones. Algunos programas requieren que los estados reúnan sólo el 10 porciento de los fondos; otros necesitan compartir un monto todavía mayor.

Mayflower Compact/Acuerdo del Mayflower Documento que establecía que las leyes estaban escritas para el bienestar de la gente. Fue diseñado por líderes de los Pilgrims (peregrinos), en 1620, durante el viaje del *Mayflower*.

mayor-administrator plan/intendente-administrador Gobierno municipal, usado en grandes áreas urbanas, en el que el intendente tiene un rol político prominente. El intendente elige a un funcionario administrativo en jefe, cuya función es liberarlo de ciertas tareas administrativas.

mayor-council plan/intendente-concejal Gobierno municipal en el que el intendente es un magistrado electo y el concejal es el cuerpo legislativo.

Members of Parliament/Miembros del Parlamento Normalmente, son los funcionarios electos de la Cámara de los Comunes en Gran Bretaña, pero también pueden incluir, a ciertos miembros designados de la Cámara de los Lores.

merit/mérito Criterio de calificación y actuación, usado para emplear y promover a empleados del gobierno.

merit system/sistema jerárquico Sistema usado para seleccionar, promover y conservar empleados del gobierno, basado en exámenes competitivos y análisis de actuación.

minimum wage/salario mínimo Salario mínimo por hora que se debe pagar a los trabajadores, según lo determina el gobierno federal.

ministers/ministros Miembros del gabinete en un gobierno parlamentario.

minor party/partido menor Partido político que es menos apoyado en el sistema de gobierno. En los Estados Unidos, cualquier partido que no sea uno de los partidos mayores (republicano o demócrata), es un partido menor.

minority floor leader/líder de la minoría (Senado) En el Senado, funcionario del partido quien conduce la política del partido minoritario y dirige sus estrategias y programa legislativo.

minority leader/líder minoritario (Cámara) Líder del partido minoritario de la Cámara de Representantes.

minority party/partido minoritatio Partido con menos miembros, en cada cámara del Congreso.

Miranda Rules/Reglas de Miranda En 1966 la Suprema Corte dictaminó que un sospechoso debe ser informado sobre sus derechos constitucionales, en el momento de ser arrestado.

Miranda warnings/advertencias de Miranda (*ver también* Miranda *Rules*) Guía impuesta por la Corte Suprema en el caso *Miranda vs. Arizona* (1966) que establece las Reglas de Miranda: requisito de informar al sospechoso sobre sus derechos, al ser arrestado.

Missouri Plan/Plan de Missouri Método de seleccionar jueces, en el que primero son nominados por una comisión especial y luego son designados por el gobernador. Luego de haber prestado servicio durante un término, se confirma o rechaza su designación jurídica, mediante una elección general.

mistrial/juicio nulo Juicio que ha sido anulado porque el juez considera que de algún modo, no ha sido justo.

mixed economy/economía mixta Sistema económico que contiene características de ambas economías:por mandato y de mercado. Esta forma mixta varía de modo que el sistema económico se puede volcar hacia un tipo o el otro.

moderates/moderados Personas con inclinaciones políticas que están en un terreno medio entre liberal y conservador.

monarchy/monarquía Sistema de gobierno dirigido por un monarca hereditario (rey o reina).

monetary policy/política monetaria Cambios en la tasa de crecimiento de los fondos monetarios y en el aumento de los préstamos.

monopoly/monopolio Industria o compañía que tiene control total sobre la venta de un producto o un servicio, sin enfrentarse a la competencia.

Monroe Doctrine/Doctrina Monroe Declaración política del presidente Monroe, en 1823, durante su mensaje anual al Congreso, en el que ratificó tres principios: (1) las naciones europeas no deberían establecer nuevas colonias en el hemisferio occidental; (2) las naciones europeas no deberían intervenir en los asuntos de las naciones independientes del hemisferio occidental; y (3) los Estados Unidos no deberían intervenir en los asuntos de las naciones europeas.

multilateral treaties/tratados multilaterales Tratados entre tres o más naciones.

multiparty system/sistema multipartidario Sistema electoral en el que tres o más partidos políticos, compiten por cargos públicos.

municipal home rule/reglamento municipal propio Poder investido a una unidad local de gobierno para diseñar o cambiar su propia cartera y manejar sus propios asuntos.

municipalities/municipalidades Unidades locales de gobierno que tienen autoridad para gobernar áreas urbanas.

mutual-assured destruction (MAD)/Destrucción mutua Teoría que consideraba que mientras los Estados Unidos y la Unión Soviética tuvieran ambas, fuerzas nucleares poderosas, invulnerables y de algún modo iguales, ninguna nación arriesgaría una guerra contra la otra.

mutual defense alliance/alianza de defensa mutua Acuerdo entre las naciones aliadas para ayudar una a la otra, en caso de ataque por fuerzas enemigas.

N

name calling/apodos Método de propaganda que deja una marca negativa o no-popular a una persona, para desacreditar su imágen pública.

nation/nación Area dentro de una zona geográfica particular, donde un gobierno organizado dicta y ejecuta leyes, sin la aprobación de una autoridad mayor.

National Assembly/Asamblea Nacional Cámara baja en la legislatura francesa.

national convention/convención nacional Asamblea convocada cada cuatro años, por cada partido principal, para elegir a los candidatos para presidente y vice, selecionar la comisión nacional, redactar la plataforma partidaria y conducir asuntos del partido.

national debt/deuda nacional Monto total de fondos que el gobierno nacional debe, como resultado de préstamos e intereses sobre los préstamos. Esto sucede cuando el gobierno se excede de su presupuesto, y gasta más de lo que colecta.

National Diet/Dieta Nacional A través de su constitución, Japón tiene un Parlamento llamado la Dieta Nacional. Consiste en dos cámaras:la Cámara de Concejales y la de Representantes.

national party chairperson/presidente del partido nacional Individuo que dirige el trabajo del comité del partido nacional.

national party committee/comité del partido nacional Líderes de un partido político que dirigen los asuntos del partido durante el período comprendido entre convenciones nacionales. Este grupo dirige la organización nacional del partido.

national security/seguridad nacional Protección de la nación contra interferencias, amenazas e invasiones no deseadas, por parte de otras naciones. Sentido de libertad e independencia para la nación.

National security Council (NSC)/Consejo Nacional de Seguridad Consejo que coopera con el presidente en asuntos, internos y externos, referentes a la seguridad y defensa de la nación. Esta agencia de personal de la Oficina Ejecutiva, fue establecida por el Acta de Seguridad Nacional, de 1947.

nationalists/nacionalistas Individuos que sienten una fuerte lealtad y devoción por su nación.

nationality/nacionalidad Miembro de una nación o país particular.

natural aristocracy/aristocracia natural Autoridades que el presidente Thomas Jefferson colocó en la burocracia ejecutiva.

natural rights/derechos naturales Derechos que no provienen de los gobiernos, sino que son inherentes a cada hombre, mujer o niño, en virtud de haber nacido y pertenecer a la raza humana.

naturalization/naturalización Proceso legal por el cual un individuo nacido ciudadano de un país, se hace ciudadano de otro.

naturalized citizens/ciudadanos naturalizados Ciudadanos de otros países que legalmente se hacen ciudadanos americanos. El proceso de naturalización comprende ciertos requerimientos de residencia, alfabetismo y aceptación de los principios del gobierno americano.

Navigation Acts/Actas de Navegación Restricciones estipuladas por Gran Bretaña a la actividad colonial, entre 1651 y 1750, que establecían que sólo los barcos ingleses podían comerciar dentro del Imperio Británico.

necessary and proper clause/ "necesarias y adecuadas" Artículo 1, Sección 8, de la Constitución, que otorga al Congreso el poder de dictar todas las leyes "necesarias y adecuadas" para que el gobierno federal pueda llevar a cabo sus responsabilidades.

negative campaign advertising/publicidad negativa Publicidad durante una campaña política, con intenciones de descreditar y perjudicar al candidato opositor.

neutral competency/capacidad neutral Se espera que los burócratas federales expresen neutralidad, es decir, que se supone que aplicarán toda su capacidad técnica en su trabajo, sin tener en cuenta sus inclinaciones políticas.

neutrality/neutralidad Posición de no alineación con ninguna de las partes durante una disputa o conflicto, como puede ser la guerra.

New Deal/Nueva Propuesta Programa diagramado por la administración de Roosevelt, en 1933, para ayudar a los Estados Unidos a salir de la Gran Depresión. Incluía muchos programas de gastos y asistencia pública, junto con miles de reglamentos a la actividad económica.

New England town/Pueblos de Nueva Inglaterra Unidad gubernamental en los estados de Nueva Inglaterra, que combina el rol de ciudad y condado. El "Pueblo" (town) comprende una ciudad central rodeada por áreas rurales donde se practica la democracia directa.

new federalism/nuevo federalismo Plan para limitar el rol del gobierno federal en los gobiernos estatales, con el objeto de dar a los estados mayor poder de decisión sobre dónde invertir toda la recaudación del gobierno.

New Jersey Plan/Plan de Nueva Jersey Plan propuesto por William Paterson de Nueva Jersey durante la Convención Constitucional, que establecía la representación equitativa de todos los estados (favoreciendo de este modo a los estados más pequeños).

no contest/sin disputa Alegato en un caso criminal, en el que el acusado, no admite ni niega los cargos. La diferencia principal entre un alegato de culpabilidad y un alegato "sin-disputa," es que este último no se puede usar en contra del acusado en un caso civil.

nominating convention/convención de nombramiento Asamblea oficial de un partido político, para elegir a sus candidatos y seleccionar delegados.

nomination/nominación En un partido, nombramiento y auspicio como candidato para un cargo público, de una persona en particular.

nonpartisan elections/elecciones independientes Elecciones que tienen lugar sin la participación de partidos políticos para ocupar ciertos cargos, como el judicial, municipal o en un consejo escolar.

nonresident aliens/extranjeros no-residentes Extranjeros que esperan quedarse en otro país durante un corto lapso determinado.

Northwest Ordinance Un acta del Congreso de 1787, que establecía un patrón básico de cómo se debían gobernar los nuevos territorios al norte del Río Ohio.

O

obscenity/obscenidad Forma de palabra que no está protegida bajo la Primer Enmienda. Trabajo que, tomado por entero, insta al interés sexual o la lujuria, mostrando una conducta sexual que se define en forma legal o jurídica, como ofensiva y con seria falta de valor literario, artístico, político, o científico.

off-budget items/artículos fuera de presupuesto Categoría fuera del presupuesto oficial.

office-group ballot/voto por cargo Boleta en la que los candidatos están alineados según el cargo por el que se proponen.

Office of Management and Budget (OMB)/Departamento de Administración y Presupuesto Asiste al presidente en la preparación de su propuesta para el presupuesto anual, que el presidente debe someter al Congreso, en enero de cada año.

old-age pensions/jubilación Plan que da dinero a las personas cuando se retiran y dejan de trabajar.

one-party system/systema uni-partidario Sistema electoral en el cual existe, es lícito y tiene posibilidad de ganar, un solo partido político.

open primary/primaria abierta Primaria directa en la que los votantes pueden emitir su voto sin tener que declarar su orientación partidaria.

opinion/opinión Declaración de un tribunal o juez, referente a la decisión a que se llegó en cierto caso. Expone cómo ha sido aplicada la ley en este caso, y detalla las razones en la que se basó el dictámen.

opposition/oposición El segundo mayor partido en un gobierno parlamentario, próximo al partido dirigente. Los líderes de la oposición designan sus propios miembros del gabinete, quienes "ensombrecen" a ciertos miembros del partido gobernante, con la espera de poderlos reemplazar algún día.

oral arguments/argumentos orales Argumentos verbales presentados por el abogado opositor.

original jurisdiction/jurisdicción original Autoridad legal de un tribunal que presta audiencia a la primer presentación de un caso.

oversight function/supervisión Poder del Congreso para controlar las leyes que pasó y asegurarse de que son ejecutadas y administradas con corrección.

P

pardon/perdón Acto de garantizar a un prisionero su liberación del castigo. El perdón puede ser garantizado por parte del presidente o gobernador, antes o después de la convicción criminal.

parishes/"parroquias" Término usado en Louisiana para describir jurisdicciones administrativas municipales.

Parliament/Parlamento Nombre del cuerpo legislativo nacional en los países gobernados por el sistema parlamentario, como ser Inglaterra y Francia.

parliamentary democracy/democracia parlamentaria Forma de democracia en la que el líder ejecutivo (por lo general un primer ministro y su gabinete), son elegidos(as) por, y responsables ante, un parlamento electo democráticamente.

parole/bajo palabra Liberación de un prisionero antes de haber cumplido su sentencia.

partisan elections/elecciones partidarias Elecciones en las que los candidatos a un cargo, están identificados según sus partidos políticos.

partisan politics/política partidaria Política en apoyo de una ideología particular de un partido.

partisan preference/preferencia partidaria Preferencia de un partido sobre otro, por votantes y legisladores.

party identification/identificación partidaria Vínculo de uno, con un partido en particular.

party identifiers/simpatía partidaria Gente que siente que pertenece a cierto partido en particular, sin participar activamente en los esfuerzos partidarios.

party platform/plataforma de un partido Documento diagramado por cada partido en la convención nacional, que detalla la política y posición del partido. La plataforma es sometida a la convención completa, para su aprobación.

party ticket/boleta partidaria Lista de candidatos para varios cargos, quienes pertenecen a un mismo partido político.

party-column ballot/boleta en bloque Forma de boleta usada en elecciones generales, en la que los candidatos están alistados en columnas, bajo el respectivo nombre del partido. Esta boleta propone votar por una alineación partidaria, en lugar de un candidato en particular.

passports/pasaportes Certificados editados por el gobierno que identifican a la persona como un ciudadano del país de ese gobierno, y autorizan a esa persona a viajar al exterior.

patent/patente Licencia garantizada a un inventor, que le da los derechos exclusivos para la fabricación y venta de tal invención, durante un período específico.

patronage/patrocinio Sistema de retribuir a los fieles y los trabajadores del partido, mediante trabajo y contratos con el gobierno.

peer group/grupo de los pares Grupo de gente que comparten las mismas características sociales, como puede ser edad y situación económica. Los grupos de los pares tienen un rol importante en la formación de las actitudes y creencias de los individuos.

peers/pares Individuos que son iguales a uno.

petit jury/jurado "menor" Grupo de hasta doce personas, quienes en un tribunal jurídico, consideran los hechos de un caso civil o criminal, y dan su veredicto; también se los llama *trial jury (jurado procesal)*.

petition/petición Pedido que los individuos someten a las autoridades de gobierno. La petición puede consistir en una pauta de gobierno o una solicitud para ser ciudadano.

picketing/piquetes Forma de protesta por la cual los trabajadores en huelga, marchan públicamente tratando de despertar el conocimiento público sobre cierta controversia y para evitar que los consumidores hagan tratos con el empleador, hasta que culmine la huelga.

pigeonhole/archivo "palomar" Archivar un projecto de ley o ponerlo de lado, sin mayor acción. El término se originó por los antiguos escritorios del Congreso, que tenían pequeños compartimientos o "palomares" donde guardar los papeles.

plain folks/gente común Método de propaganda que intenta atraer a las personas, hacia una figura política, mostrándola como un americano común.

plaintiff/demandante Persona que presenta una demanda en un tribunal jurídico.

planks/principios Cuestiones y convicciones que constituyen la plataforma de un partido político.

plea bargaining/acuerdo de instancia Acuerdos entre el fiscal y el abogado defensor, mediante el cual el acusado se declara culpable de una pena menor, a cambio de una sentencia más leve. El fiscal prefiere llegar a este acuerdo, con el objeto de acelerar el caso, debido a una sobrecarga de los tribunales y para asegurarse de que el caso terminará con una sentencia de culpabilidad.

plurality/mayoría relativa Situación en que un candidato gana una elección por tener más votos, pero no necesariamente por obtener la mayoría. La mayoría de las leyes federales, estatales y municipales permiten que las elecciones sean ganadas por una mayoría relativa de los votos.

pocket veto/veto implícito Tipo de veto especial usado por el presidente, luego de haber levantado las sesiones de la legislatura. Los proyectos de ley que no están firmados por el presidente, mueren luego de un cierto período específico, y deben ser reintroducidos, si el Congreso desea reconsiderarlos.

police power/poder de la policía Autoridad de los estados para legislar la protección de la salud, la seguridad y el bienestar de la gente.

policy voting/voto político Cuando la gente vota por los candidatos que comparten su misma posición, sobre ciertas cuestiones claves.

political action committees/comisiones de acción política Juntas que son establecidas y representan los intereses de corporaciones, sindicatos o grupos de interés especial. Estos comités colectan dinero y hacen donaciones a las campañas electorales, en nombre de los grupos que representan.

political consultant/consultor político Profesional empleado por un candidato político, para delinear estrategias, crear temas de la campaña y dirigir la composición de la imágen de la campaña política.

political machines/maquinarias políticas Organizaciones dentro de un partido político, que controlan las elec-

ciones, garantizando beneficios a cambio de votos o donaciones.

political participation/participación política Forma en que los individuos pueden participar en un proceso político, ya sea votando, participando en un jurado, ayudando en una campaña política o postulándose para un cargo público.

political party/partido político Grupo de ciudadanos organizados, bajo una amplia gama de intereses comunes, que se unen para elegir candidatos a cargos públicos y determinar su política.

political patronage/amparo político Forma de selecionar individuos para puestos políticos, en base a su servicio en el partido, y no a sus méritos o calificaciones.

political philosophy/filosofía política Paquete de nociones o ideas sobre cómo la gente debería ser gobernada.

political socialization/socialización política Proceso por el cual los individuos desarrollan sus simpatías políticas y forman sus opiniones sobre cuestiones políticas. La familia y el sistema educativo, son factores importantes en este proceso.

politics/política Distribución autoritaria de recursos para una sociedad; proceso que decide quién recibe qué, cuándo y cómo, en una sociedad.

poll tax/impuesto al sufragio Impuesto especial que se debe pagar, antes de votar. La Enmienda Vigésimocuarta, canceló el impuesto al sufragio, en las elecciones federales, y en 1966, la Suprema Corte lo declaró inconstitucional, en todas las elecciones.

popular vote/voto popular Voto emitido por alguien que no es un elector; cantidad real de votos emitidos en una elección.

porkbarrel/favoritismos Consignaciones para proyectos locales, con el objeto de aumentar la popularidad de un legislador, en su propio distrito.

power/poder Posición de control, autoridad o influencia, sobre otros.

power of recognition/poder de reconocimiento Poder de la rama ejecutiva para aceptar la existencia legal del gobierno de otro país.

preamble/preámbulo Introducción a un documento oficial que, por lo general, explica los objetivos e intenciones de dicho documento.

precedent/precedente Decisión de la corte que establece una base para las subsiguientes decisiones legales, de casos similares.

precinct/recinto El menor distrito electoral a nivel local.

preference poll/votación preferente Tipo de elección primaria en la que los votantes pueden emitir votos separados para candidatos y para delegados a la convención.

preferred-position doctrine/doctrina de prioridades Teoría de la Corte Suprema que impone limitaciones a la Primer

Enmienda, solamente para evitar perjuicios inminentes, serios y trascendentes.

preliminary hearing/audiencia preliminar Audiencia del tribunal en la que se presentan las evidencias y se conocen los testimonios, para determinar si existe suficiente motivo para continuar con el proceso judicial.

president of the Senate/presidente del Senado Autoridad conferida por la Constitución al vice-presidente de los Estados Unidos. Bajo esta posición, puede llamar a los oradores, poner cuestiones a votación y en caso de empate, puede emitir su voto.

president *pro tempore*/presidente *pro tempore* Autoridad temporaria que preside el Senado en ausencia del vice-presidente.

presidential democracy/democracia presidencial Democracia en la que el pueblo elige tanto al presidente como a los legisladores. (Compare con *parliamentary democracy/democracia parlamentaria*).

presidential succession/sucesión presidencial Proceso legal mediante el cual un líder de gobierno sucede al presidente, en caso de que éste muera, quede incapacitado o sea destituído.

press conferences/conferencias de prensa Entrevistas organizadas con los medios de comunicación.

press secretary/secretario(a) de prensa Miembro de la Casa Blanca que mantiene conferencias de prensa con reporteros y permite al pueblo conocer lo que piensa el presidente, sobre cuestiones comunes, nacionales e internacionales.

pressure groups/grupos de presión Organizaciones primadas que utilizan la persuasión y la presión, para hacer pasar leyes en favor de sus propios intereses.

preventive detention/detención preventiva Encerrar al acusado sin fianza, si el juez sospecha que el detenido puede cometer otro delito, al ser puesto en libertad.

primary/primaria Elección que tiene lugar antes de una elección general, en la que los candidatos de un mismo partido compiten por la nominación de ese partido.

prime minister/primer ministro Jefe en un sistema parlamentario. Es elegido por la legislatura, entre sus propios miembros.

principle of federalism/principio de federalismo Sistema de gobierno en el que el poder del gobierno está compartido entre un gobierno central (o federal) y gobiernos estatales, de acuerdo a lo definido en una constitución escrita.

prior restraint/restricción previa Limitación de una acción antes de que ocurra en la realidad. Un ejemplo de restricción previa es la censura por parte del gobierno, de documentos o de la difusión radial, antes de que sean publicados o emitidos.

private bills/ley privada Medida de la legislatura que sólo se aplica a ciertas personas o lugares, en lugar de a toda la nación.

private property/propiedad privada Bienes que pertenecen a un individuo o a un grupo, en lugar de al gobierno.

privileges and immunities clause/cláusula de privilegios e inmunidades Sección de la Constitución que impide que unos estados discriminen en contra de los ciudadanos de otros, en áreas tales como protección legal, acceso a los tribunales, libertad de traslado, o derechos a la propiedad.

probable cause/causa probable Evidencia suficiente como para considerar que se a cometido un crimen. Motivo razonable para iniciar una investigación de la residencia o posesiones del individuo.

probation/libertad condicional Suspensión por parte del juez, de la sentencia criminal, sobre la base de que el individuo tenga buen comportamiento y sea supervisado por un oficial, durante un período especificado.

procedural due process/proceder en forma lícita Disposición de la Constitución que declara que se debe llevar a cabo la ley en forma justa y de manera ordenada.

processes/procesos Procedimientos.

profit/ganancia Dinero que resulta luego de haber pagado todos los gastos del negocio.

profit incentive/incentivo de ganar Deseo de hacer dinero, que motiva a la gente para producir, comprar y vender productos y servicios.

progressive taxation/impuestos progresivos Sistema impositivo por el cual el individuo paga mayor porcentaje de impuesto adicional, a medida que aumentan sus ingresos. De este modo, esta tasa extraordinaria de impuestos excede a la tasa promedio.

Prohibition/Prohibición Era de catorce años (1920–1933) en los Estados Unidos, durante la cual era ilegal producir, transportar o consumir bebidas alcohólicas. La Prohibición comenzó con la Enmienda Dieciocho y fue derogada por la Enmienda Veintiuno.

project grant/fondo para proyectos Asistencia a la que los estados o los municipios pueden apelar en forma directa, con el fin de aplicar los fondos donde son necesarios.

propaganda/propaganda Diseminación de ideas, información o rumores, con el objeto de colaborar o injuriar a una institución, una causa o una persona.

proportional taxation/impuesto proporcional Sistema impositivo en el cual la tasa permanece constante, a pesar de los ingresos del individuo.

proportionality/proporcionalidad Concepto sobre la "teoría de sólo una guerra," que señala que el bien a que puede llegarse ganando una guerra, no justifica el daño que causa la misma.

prosecuting attorney/fiscal Autoridad representante del

gobierno, que inicia y conduce los procesos legales.

prototype/prototipo Modelo.

psychoactives/psicoactivas (sicoactivas) Término que se aplica a las drogas que afectan la mente: alcohol, nicotina, cafeína, marihuana, opio, y cocaína.

public bills/leyes públicas Medida legal que se aplica a toda la nación en general.

public defender/defensor público Abogado asignado para representar al acusado en un proceso criminal, en caso de que el acusado no pueda contratar a un abogado por sus propios medios.

public interest groups/grupos de interés público Grupos que se forman con el amplio objetivo, de trabajar para el "bienestar público".

public opinion/opinión pública Opiniones y actitudes sobre cuestiones sociales y políticas, compartidas por un número significativo de personas.

public opinion poll/encuesta de opinión pública Reconocimiento al azar para descubrir los puntos de vista populares, sobre asuntos de importancia pública.

public policies/reglas públicas Política que afecta al público en general. Estos planes de acción pública son llevados a cabo por parte de las ramas legislativa y ejecutiva de los gobiernos locales, estatales y federal.

pure speech/puras palabras Expresión libre y pacífica de ideas, pensamientos u opiniones, hecha en el hogar o en público.

Q

quorum/quorum Cantidad mínima de legisladores que deben presentarse en la legislatura, para conducir su tarea.

quota/cupo Regla impuesta por el gobierno, que declara que cierto número de trabajos, promociones u otro tipo de selecciones, deben ser otorgados a miembros de ciertos grupos.

R

radical left/izquierda radical Personas de la extrema izquierda del espectro político, las cuales no están de acuerdo en trabajar dentro de los procesos políticos establecidos para lograr sus objetivos, sino que intentan destruir el sistema de gobierno establecido.

radical right/derecho radical En el espectro político, aquellos que se resisten al cambio con más firmeza que los moderados o conservadores (incluyendo a reaccionarios o fascistas) que desean oponerse activamente a los cambios sociales.

random sample/muestra al azar Sección de la población en donde se ha realizado una encuesta sobre un asunto específico.

ratification/ratificación Aprobación formal o consentimiento final de una constitución, una enmienda consititucional o un tratado.

ratified/ratificado Aprobar formalmente o dar consentimiento definitivo a una constitución, enmienda constitucional, o tratado.

ratings system/sistema de evaluación Sistema por el cual los grupos de interés estudian el desempeño de los legisladores, basados en los servicios de los legisladores a los intereses del grupo.

rational-basis test/prueba racional Método utilizado por la Suprema Corte para asegurar una protección igual para todos los individuos. Se aplica en casos donde se sospecha discriminación de diversos individuos.

reactionaries/reaccionarios Gente que se resiste al cambio, con mayor firmeza que los moderados o los conservadores. Los reaccionarios, no sólo no desean que la sociedad cambie, sino que están dispuestos a luchar activamente contra todo cambio social.

realigning election/elección realineada Elección en la que el electorado se aleja del partido dominante, y se vuelca en otro nuevo partido dominante.

reapportionment/redistribución Por lo general luego de haber realizado un nuevo senso, es la nueva delineación de los distritos legislativos, de acuerdo con los cambios de población indicados en dicho senso.

recall/deponer Procedimiento que permite a los votantes, destituir a un oficial electo a un cargo local o estatal, antes de que haya expirado el término de su mandato.

recall election/elección de destitución Elección que permite a los ciudadanos el poder para destituir de su cargo a un oficial electo, antes de que haya terminado su mandato.

recesses/recesos Períodos de tiempo durante los cuales, los poderes legislativo o judicial, no están en sesión.

recession/recesión Período de tiempo durante el cual la tasa de crecimiento económico, se mantiene por debajo de lo normal, en forma consistente.

record vote (also **roll-call vote/voto registrado** (también **voto cantado**) Método de votar en la legislatura, mediante el cual los legisladores cantan sus votos sobre un asunto. Una computadora registra cada voto en forma electrónica y exhibe el voto de cada miembro.

referendum/referendum Forma de democracia directa en la que las medidas legislativas o constitucionales, se deciden primero en la legislatura y luego son presentadas a los votantes para su aprobación.

refugees/refugiados Personas que huyen del peligro de sus países de origen, y hallan residencia fuera de su patria.

registration/registro Entrar su nombre en la lista de posibles votantes. El registro requiere ciertas condiciones de edad, residencia y ciudadanía.

regressive taxation/impuesto regresivo Sistema impositivo en el cual los individuos pagan menos porcentaje de dinero a medida que aumentan sus ingresos. De este modo, la tasa de impuesto marginal es menor que la tasa del impuesto medio.

released time/momento de relevo Tiempo en que los estudiantes permanecen fuera de las clases escolares, para asistir a sesiones de instrucción religiosa.

relocation camps/campos de reubicación Campos establecidos durante la Segunda Guerra Mundial, para alojar a los americano-japoneses a quienes se despojaba de sus propiedades. También se los apartaba de las "zonas militares" y se los mantenía bajo toque de queda.

repeal/revocar Derogar o abolir una ley.

representative assembly/asamblea representativa Asamblea que dicta leyes y está compuesta por individuos que representan a la población.

representative government/gobierno representativo Gobierno en el cual el pueblo elige, por cualquier medio, un número limitado de individuos para determinar la política a seguir para todos los ciudadanos.

representatives/representantes Magistrados elegidos para un cargo legislativo, durante un período específico de tiempo, con el propósito de determinar la política a seguir para todos los ciudadanos.

reprieve/suspensión Posponer una sentencia criminal impuesta por un tribunal. El presidente o el gobernador tienen el poder de otorgar este tipo de suspensiones, siendo por lo general, de carácter humanitario.

reprimand/reprimenda Reproche oficial usado por el Congreso contra la conducta de uno de sus miembros.

republic/república Nombre dado a una nación en la que el poder supremo pertenece a quienes votan y es ejercido mediante representantes electos, responsables ante los votantes y de gobernar de acuerdo a la ley. (Compare con *representative democracy.*)

republican form of government/forma de gobierno republicana Sistema de gobierno en el que el poder supremo es ejercido por los votantes, quienes eligen representantes para que gobiernen para ellos.

reserved powers/poderes reservados Poderes que ni son garantizados del gobierno federal, ni prohibidos expresamente a los estados, y que por lo tanto, son conservados por los estados o por el pueblo.

residency/residencia Necesidad de vivir en un estado durante un cierto período de tiempo, para poder obtener el derecho a votar.

resident aliens/extranjeros residentes Gente que ha inmigrado a los Estados Unidos, para establecer su residencia permanente.

resulting powers/poderes resultantes Acumulación de distintos poderes que comprende un determinado poder del gobierno federal.

revenue bills/leyes fiscales Leyes que determinan la recolección de fondos para el gobierno. De acuerdo con la Constitución, las leyes fiscales se deben originar en la Cámara de Representantes.

revenue-sharing program/programa de ingresos fiscales libres Programa mediante el cual el gobierno federal asigna fondos a los estados o las ciudades, sin compromiso alguno. Los gobiernos receptores pueden disponer de estos fondos con toda libertad.

reverse discrimination/discriminación inversa Declaración que asegura que los programas de política de afirmación donde se requieren tratamiento preferencial o cupos, discriminan en contra de quienes no son minorías.

review courts/tribunales de revisión Ver *appellate courts.*

revolution/revolución Derrocamiento popular de un gobierno o sistema político establecidos, y su reemplazo por un nuevo sistema de gobierno. Las revoluciones más famosas fueron la Americana (1775–83), la Francesa (1789–99), las Rusas (de Febrero en marzo 17 de 1917 y de Octubre en noviembre 7 de 1917) y la Segunda Rusa (en agosto de 1991).

rider/adición Enmienda o provisión adjuntas a una ley, las cuales no están relacionadas con la ley en sí.

roll-call vote/voto cantado Ver *record vote.*

rule of law/regla de la ley Principio básico de gobierno que acompaña a la supremacía constitucional, que indica que el gobierno debe proceder de acuerdo con la ley, y que ambos, el gobernante y el gobernado, están sujetos a la ley.

run-off election/elección decisiva Nueva elección entre los dos primeros contendientes de una elección previa, cuando ningún candidato ha recibido la mayoría de los votos. Estas elecciones decisivas tienen lugar cuando la ley requiere un voto mayoritario.

S

sabotage/sabotaje Acto destructivo con intenciones de obstruir los esfuerzos defensivos de una nación.

sacrifice principle/principio de sacrificio Principio impositivo que considera que los sacrificios que los individuos hacen para pagar sus impuestos, deben ser justos.

samples/muestras Pequeños números de personas que representan un sector de la población, sujeto a una encuesta específica.

sampling error/márgen de error Nivel de confianza sobre los resultados de una encuesta de opinión pública.

search engines/caminos de búsqueda Sitios dentro de la Red de Internet (como Yahoo, Web Crawler, Excite, y Lycos) que permiten al usuario, hallar temas específicos en el Internet.

search warrant/orden de investigación Orden dictada y autorizada por un juez, para que la policía investigue un lugar determinado, en conección con un crimen en particular.

searches and seizures/búsqueda y captura Métodos utilizados por los oficiales de la ley, para buscar y colectar la evidencia necesaria con el fin de condenar a los sospechosos de crímenes, según se indica en la Enmienda Cuarta.

secession/secesión Acto de retirarse formalmente de una alianza. Separación de la unión federal por parte de un estado.

Second Continental Congress/Segundo Congreso Continental Congreso de las colonias que se convocó en 1775, para asumir los poderes del gobierno central y organizar un ejército.

seditious speech/discurso sedicioso Discurso con intenciones de promover la resistencia en contra de la autoridad lícita y que convoca al derrocamiento violento de un gobierno.

segregation/segregación Separación forzada y en general por medios discriminatorios, del resto de la población, de grupos raciales, étnicos u otros, aplicada a la educación, vivienda u otras áreas.

select committees/juntas selectivas Comisiones legislativas temporarias, establecidas con un fin especial.

selectmen/administradores municipales Individuos elegidos por el municipio para ejercer un cargo en la junta local y dirigir los asuntos diarios de la ciudad.

self-incrimination/incriminación propia Proveer información o testimonio perjuiciosos contra uno mismo, en un tribunal.

self-nomination/auto-nominación Anuncio del deseo de uno para ser electo a un cargo público.

senatorial courtesy/cortesía senatorial Regla implícita de que un funcionario elegido para cierto estado, debe primero ser aprobado por los senadores de dicho estado.

seniority/antigüedad Regla implícita y seguida por ambas Cámaras del Congreso, que especifica que los miembros que han prestado servicios contínuos durante más tiempo, tienen preferencia cuando se seleccionan a los directores de juntas u otros puestos significativos.

seniority rule/antigüedad Regla que se practica en el Congreso, que consiste en convocar al miembro de más antiguo del partido mayoritario, para que presida el comité.

sentence/sentencia Castigo impuesto por la corte, a un individuo que es hallado culpable de un crimen.

separate-but-equal doctrine/doctrina de "separados pero iguales" Doctrina mantenida durante mucho tiempo por la corte Suprema, que declaraba que la segregación de las escuelas y alojamiento públicos, no indicaban una superioridad de una raza sobre otra. Mantenía que la Cláusula de Igual Protección de la Enmienda Décimocuarta, no prohibía la segregación racial, siempre que los servicios fueran los mismos para los negros que para los blancos. Esta doctrina fue derogada mediante la decisión del juicio *Brown vs. Concejo de Educación*, en 1954.

sessions/sesiones Períodos regulares de tiempo durante los cuales se reunen y ejercen sus funciones, los cuerpos legislativos.

shield laws/leyes de amparo Leyes que en los tribunales, protegen a los reporteros sobre la confidencialidad de sus fuentes de información.

simple resolutions/resoluciones únicas Legislación que sólo trata asuntos de una Cámara del Congreso y la cual es pasada por esa Cámara nomás.

single-member district/distrito de un solo miembro Distritos electorales de los que sólo un funcionario es elegido por los votantes.

single-member district system/sistema de un miembro único Método de elección por el cual sólo un candidato puede ganar las elecciones a cada cargo.

slander/calumnia Expresión pública sobre una persona que la ridiculiza, la desprecia o altera, y por lo tanto, perjudica su reputación.

social conflict/conflicto social Fricción entre grupos dentro de una sociedad. A veces los conflictos sociales se resuelven con violencia, y otras, mediante cambios de costumbres y tradiciones.

social contract theory/teoría del contrato social Teoría de la sociedad que sostiene que los individuos voluntariamente aceptan crear una sociedad organizada, con el objeto de asegurar la protección y el bienestar mutuos. Teoría encabezada por Hobbes, Locke, y Rousseau.

Social Security/Seguro Social (Jubilación) Programa de seguro social del gobierno, con ahorro obligatorio financiado por los impuestos sobre salarios que aportan tanto los empleados como los patrones. Los empleados pagan por los beneficios mientras estén trabajando y reciben los beneficios al jubilarse.

socioeconomic factors/factores socioeconómicos Factores sociales y económicos tales como: edad, ingresos, educación, y ocupación.

soft money/gratificación Contribución que se hace a un partido político, en lugar de a un cierto candidato.

Solid South/Sur Unánime Término usado para describir la tendencia de los estados del sur, de votar por los demócratas, después de la Guerra Civil.

solidarity/solidaridad Acuerdo mutuo dentro de un grupo.

sound bite/acotación Comentario de varios segundos que captura un pensamiento o tiene un impacto inmediato en la audiencia, pero que proporciona poca o ninguna información.

sovereignty/soberanía autoridad suprema e independiente que un gobierno tiene, dentro de su propio territorio.

speaker/presidente El que preside la cámara baja de la legislatura de un estado.

Speaker of the House/Presidente de la Cámara El que preside la Cámara de Representantes y miembro durante mucho tiempo del partido mayoritario; a menudo, el miembro de mayor fuerza e influencia de la Cámara.

special election/elección extraordinaria Elección que tiene lugar siempre que se deba decidir sobre un asunto, antes de que ocurra la próxima elección regular.

special sessions/sesiones extraordinarias Sesiones fuera del programa del Congreso, ordenadas por el presidente.

speech plus/arenga Expresión verbal de opiniones, ideas, o conceptos combinados con algún tipo de acción, como marchas o demostraciones.

split-ticket voting/voto dividido Sufragio por candidatos de más de un partido político, en una misma elección.

spoils system/sistema de privilegios Acuerdo bajo el cual el partido político que gana una elección, otorga cargos públicos a los miembros de su propio partido.

sponsor/promotor Legislador que redacta y propone leyes.

Stamp Act/Ley del Timbre Acta pasada por el Parlamento Británico en 1765, que impuso el primer impuesto directo en las colonias. La Ley del Timbre obligaba al uso de sellos en todos los documentos legales, diarios, panfletos, naipes, y ciertos acuerdos comerciales.

standing committee/comisión permanente Junta permanente dentro de la Cámara o el Senado, que considera las leyes dentro de un área dada.

standing vote/voto de pie Método de votación en la legislatura, por el cual aquellos a favor de una medida y los que se oponen, deben ponerse de pie para expresar su voto.

State of the Union Address/Discurso Anual del Presidente Mensaje anual del presidente al Congreso, en el que propone un programa legislativo. El mensaje no sólo está dedicado al Congreso, sino al pueblo americano y al resto del mundo.

status quo/status quo Estado actual de las cuestiones.

statutory law/ley estatutoria Ley pasada por la legislatura.

straight-ticket voting/voto directo Acto de votar exclusivamente por candidatos del mismo partido, en una elección.

straw poll/encuesta no oficial Reconocimiento de opiniones tomadas para estimar la capacidad de los candidatos de la oposición, o la popularidad de una propuesta de ley.

strict constructionists/estructuralistas estrictos Aquellos que consideran que la Constitución debe ser interpretada estrictamente y que sienten que el gobierno federal debería poseer sólo aquellos poderes específicamente indicados en la Constitución.

strong mayor-council plan/concejo municipal fuerte Gobierno municipal en el que el intendente es el director ejecutivo y tiene casi un control total sobre el empleo y despido de personal y la preparación del presupuesto.

subcommittees/subcomisiones Divisiones de mayores comisiones, que tratan una parte específica dentro del área de la comisión.

subpoena/comparendo Documento legal que exige a la persona a dar testimonio en la corte.

substantive due process/proceso legal esencial Requerimiento constitucional de que la ley aplicada para acusar o condenar a alguien de un crimen, debe ser justa.

succession/sucesión Proceso legal por el cual los líderes de gobierno suceden al presidente, en caso de muerte, incapacidad, o destitución.

suffrage/sufragio Ver *franchise*.

suffragists/sufragistas Aquellos que defendían el voto de la mujer.

Sugar Act/Acta del Azúcar Impuesto decretado por el Parlamento Británico en 1764, sobre todas las importaciones de azúcar de las colonias americanas.

summit meeting/reunión cumbre Conferencia entre las cabezas de estado de dos o más naciones.

summons/comparendo Noticia que requiere la presencia de un acusado, en la corte.

super-majority vote/voto de super-mayoría Es usado por la Asamblea General de las Naciones Unidas. Se toman decisiones muy importantes mediante un voto mayoritario o por super-mayoría de los dos-tercios de los votos, según la importancia del tema.

superpowers/superpotencias Naciones con el mayor poder económico y militar.

Supplemental Security Income (SSI)/Ingreso de Seguro Suplementario Programa del gobierno que establece un ingreso mínimo para los ancianos, los ciegos o incapacitados.

supremacy clause/cláusula de supremacía Artículo VI, Sección 2, de la Constitución, que establece que las leyes de la Constitución y las leyes federales, son superiores a las de los estados y municipios.

suspect classification/clasificación del sospechoso Prueba usada por la Corte Suprema para determinar si la clasificación de los individuos basada en raza, origen nacional, o sexo, ha negado de alguna forma al individuo, la misma protección ante la ley.

symbolic speech/discurso simbólico Expresión de sentimientos, opiniones, o ideas, a través de formas que no sean la palabra o la prensa.

T

talk radio/audiciones Programas de comentarios emitidos por la radio.

teller vote/escrutinio Método de votación en la legislatura, mediante el cual aquellos a favor de una medida y los que se oponen, deben caminar por el corredor para emitir su voto.

Temporary Assistance to Needy Families (TANF)/ Asistencia Temporaria a Familias Necesitadas Fondos en forma de concesiones, que el gobierno federal otorga a los estados. Existen restricciones que limitan los beneficios: dos años para individuos que trabajan y cinco años como máximo.

tenure/tenencia Período de tiempo durante el cual un funcionario público mantiene su cargo.

term/término Vea *tenure*.

testimonials/persuasión Propaganda técnica que consiste en persuadir a la gente para que apoye una cuestión o a un candidato, debido a que individuos reconocidos, como el gobernador o artistas famosos, lo apoyan también.

third parties/tercer partido Partidos políticos que no son los dos partidos mayoritarios, los cuales están compuestos, por lo general, por grupos en desacuerdo, que se han desprendido de los otros partidos.

Three-Fifths Compromise/Compromiso de los Tres-Quintos Compromiso arribado durante la Convención Constitucional, mediante el cual los tres quintos de los esclavos eran considerados tanto por motivos impositivos como para obtener representación en la Cámara de Representantes.

tight monetary policy/política monetaria ajustada Política diseñada para detener la economía, haciendo más caros los préstamos y menos accesibles.

tolerance/tolerancia Actitud justa y objetiva con respecto a los demás, en materia de opiniones, raza, religión, y nacionalidad, que son distintas a la de uno.

totalitarian/totalitario Dirigente que gobierna sin el consentimiento de los gobernados.

town manager system/sistema administrativo municipal Sistema adoptado por algunas ciudades de Nueva Inglaterra, en el cual los votantes eligen a los administradores del municipio, quienes a su vez designan a profesionales como dirigentes municipales.

town meeting/junta municipal Forma tradicional en que los municipios de Nueva Inglaterra, practican su democracia directa.

township/municipio Unidades de gobierno local, que son divisiones de los condados y tienen procesos similares de gobierno.

tracking polls/encuestas registradoras Encuestas que registran la opinión pública de los candidatos, en forma casi diaria, a medida que se aproxima la elección.

trade organizations/organizaciones mercantiles Organizaciones que por lo general apoyan las políticas que benefi-cian al comercio en general, y que se dedican a obtener metas que benefician a sus miembros en particular.

transfer/transferencia Propaganda técnica que consiste en asociar al candidato con una persona, un grupo o un símbolo respetables.

treason/traición Artículo III, Sección 3 de la Constitución declara que la traición "deberá consistir en provocar la guerra en contra (de los Estados Unidos) o en adherirse a sus enemigos, brindándoles ayuda y bienestar".

treaty/tratado Acuerdo formal entre los gobiernos de dos o más países.

trial balloon/globo de prueba Práctica de averiguar la reacción de la opinión pública con respecto a una nueva idea, pero sin publicarla oficialmente.

trial courts/tribunal procesal Corte de jurisdicción original que presta audiencia a casos civiles y criminales.

trial jury/jurado procesal Ver *petit jury*.

two-party system/sistema bi-partito Sistema político en el que dos partidos dominantes y ya establecidos, compiten por cargos políticos.

tyranny/tiranía Ejercicio del poder en forma arbitraria y sin restricciones, por parte de un individuo o gobierno opresivos.

U

unanimous/unánime De pensamiento único. Acuerdo.

unanimous opinion/opinión unánime Acuerdo de todos los jueces sobre la misma decisión de la corte.

unconstitutional/inconstitucional Contrario a las disposiciones constitucionales, y por lo tanto, inválido.

undocumented aliens/extranjeros indocumentados Extranjeros ilegales.

unicameral legislature/legislatura de una cámara Legislatura de un solo cuerpo legislativo. (Compare con *bicameral legislature*).

unincorporated areas/áreas no-incorporadas Areas que no están localizadas dentro de los límites municipales.

unitary government/gobierno unitario Sistema de gobierno centralizado, en el que los gobiernos locales y de las subdivisiones ejercitan sólo aquellos poderes, que el gobierno central les otorga.

urban areas/zonas urbanas Comunidades muy pobladas.

U.S. Treasury Bonds/Bonos del Tesoro de EE.UU. Ver *government bonds*.

V

value-added tax/impuesto al valor agregado Impuesto sobre la diferencia entre el costo que involucra la fabricación de un producto y las ganancias recibidas en el momento de su venta.

veto/veto Del latín, palabra que significa "prohibo." Negativa de una autoridad, como el presidente o el gobernador, a firmar un decreto en ley.

veto power/poder de veto Poder constitucional que permite al ejecutivo en jefe (presidente o gobernador) rechazar una legislación y volverla a la legislatura, junto con las razones para su rechazo. Esto evita o atrasa una propuesta para llegar a ser ley.

veto session/sesión de vetos Sesión en la cual los legisladores de los estados pueden considerar los proyectos de ley que han sido vetados por el gobernador, e intentar contrarrestar ese veto, si existe suficiente apoyo popular dentro de la legislatura.

Virginia Plan/Plan de Virginia Plan de quince resoluciones, propuesto por el gobernador de Virginia, Edmund Randolph durante la Convención Constitucional. Proponía un gobierno nacional totalmente nuevo que favorecía a los estados más grandes. Incluía una legislatura de dos cámaras, una rama ejecutiva nacional y un sistema jurídico nacional.

visa/visa Permiso para entrar a otro país, emitido desde el país de orígen.

voice vote/voto oral Método de votar en la legislatura.

voir dire Palabra francesa que significa "decir la verdad." Se refiere al proceso por el cual los posibles jurados son examinados, para asegurar de que sus decisiones sean imparciales.

vote of confidence/voto de confianza Apoyo del gobierno existente, por parte del parlamento.

voter turnout/concurrencia de votantes Porcentaje de ciudadanos que realmente toman parte, o concurren, al sufragio.

W

waive/desistir Abandonar o renunciar a.

War Powers Act/Acta de Declarar Guerra Ley pasada en 1973, que describe las condiciones bajo las cuales el presidente puede enviar tropas a la guerra, sin la aprobación del Congreso.

wards/cuartel Unidad local de una organización partidaria.

warrant/autorización Orden emitida por la corte que autoriza a un funcionario público a proceder de una manera especificada, como puede ser una autorización de investigación.

weak mayor-council plan/organización municipal "débil" Gobierno municipal en el que el intendente es elegido como administrador ejecutivo, y los concejales son elegidos como el cuerpo legislativo. El intendente tiene solamente poderes limitados y poco control sobre el personal y el presupuesto, y es elegido por lo general, por el término de dos años.

Western Bloc/Bloque Occidental Naciones democráticas que emergieron victoriosas luego de la Segunda Guerra Mundial, encabezadas por los Estados Unidos.

whips/diputados Asistentes del Congreso que prestan ayuda a los líderes de la mayoría y minoría.

whistle-blower/"despierta el avispero" Empleado del gobierno que llama la atención pública sobre fraudes, mala administración o derroches en su propia agencia o departamento.

White House Press Corps/Agencia de Prensa de la Casa Blanca Grupo de reporteros asignados exclusivamente a la presidencia.

winner-take-all system/"el ganador se queda con todo" Sistema en el cual el candidato a presidente que obtiene el voto preferencial en las primarias, automáticamente obtiene el apoyo de todos los delegados elegidos en esa primaria.

World Wide Web/Red Mundial Servicio principal del Internet, para obtener información.

writ of *habeas corpus*/decreto de *habeas corpus* Orden que obliga a los oficiales a declarar al juez, los motivos de la detención de un prisionero. Provisión del Artículo 1, Sección 9, de la Constitución.

writ of *mandamus*/regla de *mandamus* Orden escrita emitida por un tribunal exigiendo a un funcionario del gobierno, que realice un acto o deber lícito específico.

writ of *tertiorari*/regla de *tertiorari* Orden escrita emitida por un tribunal superior a un tribunal menor, para obtener los registros de un caso, para estudiarlos.

write-in candidate/candidato incorporado Alguien que se presenta en una campaña sin haber figurado en la boleta, y que solicita a los votantes que anoten su nombre en la lista, el día de las elecciones.

Z

zoning/división zonal Método por el cual los gobiernos municipales regulan el uso de las propiedades.

Index

413, 414, 457, 478, 480, 482, 483, 486, 492, 547, 622, 627, 629, 631, 632, 661

Business cycles, 577

Business interest groups, 248–249

Busing, 177

C

CAB (Civil Aeronautics Board), 512

Cabinet, 461–464; defined, 80, 461; executive departments and, 505–509; foreign policy and, 620, 622; Hispanics in, 180–181; kitchen, 463; members of, 461–463; roles of, 462, 463–464; women in, 191–192

Calder, Ron, 99

Calendar, 434

Camp David, 455

Campaign(s), 297–309; being "turned off" by, 354; changes in, through the years, 308; costs of, 301, 325; defined, 297; ethics and, 303; financing of, 301–309. *See also* Campaign contributions; Campaign-financing rules; Internet and, 331–334; manager of, 298; negative advertising in, 303, 314, 322–323, 324, 354; nomination and. *See* Nomination; organization of, 298–300; political consultants and, 298, 299, 300; political party's role in, 270; strategy of, 300–301; television's role in, 322–325, 327–328

Campaign advertising; evaluation of, 324–325; in Great Britain, 367; issue, 322; negative, 303, 314, 322–323, 324, 354

Campaign contributions; foreign, 305–306, 307; political action committees (PACs) and, 302, 307; tracking, 333

Campaign financing, 301–309. *See also* Campaign-financing rules

Campaign manager, 298

Campaign-financing rules; avoiding, 304–306; case study on, 366–367; enforcement of, problems with, 303–309; Federal Election Campaign Act (FECA) and, 301–303; foreign contributions and, 305–306, 307; loopholes and, 304; in other countries, 307; reform of, 306–309; soft money and, 304–305, 307–308

Campbell, Ben Nighthorse, 387

Canada; acid rain and, 21; American citizens' travel to, 625; NATO and, 630; state and local government spending in, 712; Western bloc and, 615; World War II and, 614

Candidate(s); campaign of. *See* Campaign(s); election and. *See* Election(s); image building and, 298, 358; nomination of. *See* Nomination; petition and, 292; presidential. *See* Presidential election(s); raising money for, 270; selecting, 268; television and, 322–325, 327; write-in, 292

Cannon, Joseph G. ("Uncle Joe"), 388

Canvasses, 269

Capital punishment, 164, 165–166

Career(s); in community service, 221–222; with local governments, 222; with national government, 220, 221, 222–223. *See also* Civil service; in public service, 221–222; with state governments, 222

Caricature, 92

Carpenter, Mrs. Hervert, 347

Carter, Jimmy, 192, 218–219, 276, 277, 278, 323, 358, 361, 450–451, 454, 456, 468, 483, 486, 520, 622, 627

Carter, Rosalynn, 450–451

Cartoons, political, 92–93

Carville, Chester James, Jr., 300

Case law, 535

Casework, 382

Caseworkers, 393

Castro, Fidel, 17

Caucus(es); in Congress, 424; defined, 388; party, 292–293, 295, 296, 388, 424; presidential, 296

Cause and effect, 409

CBO (Congressional Budget Office), 393–394, 404–405, 408

CBS News, 354

CBS News poll, 245

CBS *Saturday Morning,* 329

CCC (Civilian Conservation Corps), 578

CCC (Commodity Credit Corporation), 516

CEA (Council of Economic Advisers), 468, 490, 578

Cease-fire, 484

Censorship, 134–135

Census; defined, 374; first, 12; taking of, 12, 210, 374

Census Bureau, 210, 211, 374, 375

Center for Auto Safety, 252

Center for Defense Information, 621

The Center for Educational Priorities, 326

Center for National Policy, 625

Center for the Study of Responsive Law, 252

Central Intelligence Agency (CIA), 10, 133, 222, 413, 446, 467, 493, 509, 510, 511; creation and function of, 622; Information Warfare Center of, 335

CEQ (Council on Environmental Quality), 469, 599

Certiorari, writ of, 542

CETA (Comprehensive Employment and Training Act), 578

CFCs (chlorofluorocarbons), 22

Chamber of Commerce of the United States, 248

Chargé d' affaires, 625

Charles I (king of England), 32

Charter, 36

Chávez, César, 181

Checks and balances, 68, 69

The Chicago *Tribune,* 558–559

Chief administrator plan, 684

Chief diplomat, 485–487, 489

Chief executive, 452, 482–483, 489, 508–509

Chief legislator, 487–488, 489

Chief of staff, 465

Chief of state, 481–482, 489

Child Watch of North America, 602

Children's Defense Fund, 508

China; American expansionism and, 613; ancient, divine right theory and, 16; immigrants from, 181–182, 209, 213; United Nations and, 633, 634; World War II and, 614; *See also* People's Republic of China

Chinese Americans, 182–183. *See also* Asian American(s)

Chinese Exclusion Act (1882), 181–183, 209, 213

Chlorofluorocarbons (CFCs), 22

Chomsky, Noam, 119

The Christian Science Monitor, 447, 559

Chrysler, 56

Church. *See* Religion

Churchill, Winston, 485, 615

CIA. *See* Central Intelligence Agency

Cisneros, Henry, 180–181

Citizen(s); citizenship and, 204–207. *See also* Citizenship; initiatives and, 651, 652; naturalized, 206, 207; responsibilities of, 218–220, 328; rights of, 216–218

Citizens' Stamp Advisory Committee, 510

Citizenship, 204–221; African Americans and, 99, 204; by birth, 204, 205; diversity of, 539–540; dual, 217; duties of, 8, 123–124; by *jus sanguinis,* 205; by *jus soli,* 205; laws regarding, changes in, through the years, 218; loss of, 207; for Native Americans, 183; Native Americans and, 183, 205, 206; naturalization and, 204, 206–207. *See also* Naturalization

Citizenship Act (1924), 183, 205, 351

Citrus Growers Association, 523

City(ies); city machines, patronage and, 693–695, 697; general-law, 685; home-rule, 685; planning and, 678–681; U.S., with greatest populations, 211; *See also* Local government(s)

City manager, 690

City of Boerne v. Flores, 550

Civil Aeronautics Board (CAB), 512

Civil disobedience, 178–179

Civil law, 536

Civil law system, 535

Civil liberties; civil rights versus, 172; defined, 120; *See also entries beginning with Freedom*

Civil rights; African Americans and, 174–179; Asian Americans and, 181–183; changes in, through the years, 194; civil liberties versus, 172; civil rights movement and, 177–179; defending, 219; defined, 172; equal protection clause and, 172–174, 194, 195; Hispanic Americans and, 180–181; Native Americans and, 183–185; persons with disabilities and, 185–188; women and, 189–192

Civil Rights Act; of 1957, 39, 351, 436; of

and, 660; compensation of, 656; death or removal of, 654; elections and, 653–654, 668; length of service of, 654; militia and, 659; modern, 653–654, 656; National Guard and, 99–100, 102, 176, 485, 659; pardons and, 660; paroles and, 660–661; powers of, 656–661; qualifications of, 653; reprieves and, 660; selection process and, 653–654, 668

GPO (Government Printing Office), 394, 396, 518

Gramm, Phil, 295

Grand jury, 160, 666–667

Grand Old Party (GOP). *See* Republican Party

Grandfather causes, 348

Grant, Ulysses S., 547

Graphs; bar, 214; line, 592

Gray Panthers, 251, 252

Great Britain; American destroyers loaned to, 485; American expansionism and, 613; American Revolution and. *See* Revolutionary War; American settlements of. *See* American colonies; bureaucracy in, 510; campaign-financing laws in, 307; chief of state in, 481, 482; elections in, 309; gun control in, 250; House of Commons of, 373, 389, 437; House of Lords of, 373, 437; NATO and, 630; Parliament of, 20, 33, 72, 373, 482; political advertising in, 367; queen's role in, 481, 482; right to remain silent in, 158; unwritten constitution of, 72; Western bloc and, 615; World War II and, 614; *See also* England; United Kingdom

Great Compromise (Connecticut Compromise), 52, 53, 373

Great Depression, 108, 237, 244, 267, 271, 278, 279, 464, 477–478, 484, 486, 519, 529, 549, 571, 578

Great Society program, 109, 708

Greece; ancient
direct democracy in, 17, 18, 24; divine right theory and, 16; expatriation and, 207;
communist threat and, 615

Green Party (The Greens), 252, 270, 271, 279–280, 281

Green vote, 358

Greenhouse effect, 600

Greenspan, Alan, 577

Gregg v. Georgia, 165

Grenada, American troops sent to, 79

Grievances, 39

Griswold, Roger, 264

Grossman, Joel, 558

The Group (Warren), 43

Grove, Andrew S., 56

GS (general schedule) ratings, 521

GSA (General Services Administration), 509, 511

Guiteau, Charles J., 518–519

Gun control, 250, 259, 260, 550

Gun-Free School Zones Act (1990), 550

H

H & R Block, 581

Habeas corpus, writ of, 120–121, 418

Hagelin, John, 280

Haiti; American occupation of, 613; American troops sent to, 79, 478, 629; refugees from, 208; U.N. peacekeeping mission to, 637

Hallinan, Terrence, 664

Hamilton, Alexander, 49, 50, 54, 55, 57, 82, 209, 264, 407, 452, 461, 483, 548, 549; biography of, 90

Hand, Learned, 123

Harding, Warren G., 328

Harlan, John, 175

Harper, Ernest, 149–150

Harrison, William Henry, 409, 455, 460

Hart, Gary, 329

Hatch, Orrin, 447, 558

Hatch Act (Political Activities Act) (1939), 519–520, 523

"Hate speech," 224

Hay, John, 613

Hayes, Rutherford, 316

Hazelwood School District v. Kuhlmeier, 135, 542–543

Head Start, 108, 109, 571

Henderson v. Mayor of New York, 209

Henry, Patrick, 51, 55

Hershey Foods, 56

Herter, Albert, 62

Hirabayashi v. United States, 182

Hispanic American(s); bilingual education and, 223, 230; English-only laws and, 224, 230–231; ethnic interest groups and, 253; Hispanic Caucus and, 424; political participation and, 6–7, 180–181; population of, 180, 221; poverty and, 592; voting rights and, 350

Hispanic Caucus, 424

The History of the Rise, Progress, and Termination of the American Revolution (Warren), 43

Hitler, Adolf, 17

Hobbes, Thomas, 14, 33–34

Hollerith, Herman, 210

Holmes, Oliver Wendell, 132–133, 134

Homeless, 592, 594

Home-rule city, 685

Hoover, Herbert, 374

Hopper, 432

Hopwood v. State of Texas, 196

Horizontal federalism, 97

Horton, Willie, 323

House Calendar, 434

House of Commons (Great Britain), 373, 389, 437

House of Lords (Great Britain), 373, 437

House of Representatives, U.S. *See* United States House of Representatives

House Rules Committee, 434

Huang, John, 305–306, 366

Human rights, as goal of American foreign policy, 628–629

Humphrey, Hubert, 276

Hung jury, 160, 539, 669

Hungary; Communist bloc and, 615; democracy and, 629

Hunger of Memory (Rodriguez), 231

Hungry people, helping, 100–101

Hurlbut, People v., 685

Hussein, Saddam, 17, 631, 637

I

IBM (International Business Machines), 210

ICC (Interstate Commerce Commission), 511–512

Iceland, NATO and, 630

Ideologues; average American versus, 245–246; defined, 246

Ideology; defined, 280, 459; judicial appointments and, 547–548; political, personal, discovery of, 459; self-interest versus, 246

Illegal aliens, 208, 213, 215

Image building, 298, 358

Immigrant(s); from China, 181–182, 209, 213; from Cuba, 208; defined, 208; from El Salvador, 208; from Germany, 209; from Haiti, 208; from Ireland, 209; nation of, United States as, 209; from Nicaragua, 208; from Poland, 208; refugees as, 208; from Southeast Asia, 208; *See also* Alien(s); Immigration

Immigration; Asian Americans and, 181–182, 183; controversy over, 56, 212–213, 215; non-citizen and, 207–215; policies on, 209–212; Proposition 187 (California) and, 215; quotas and, 182, 209–211; restricting, 209; *See also* Alien(s); Immigrant(s)

Immigration Act; of 1924, 211; of 1990, 212

Immigration and Naturalization Service, 222

Immigration Reform Act (1996), 212, 213, 215

Immigration Reform and Control Act (1986), 213

Immunity; congressional, 383–384; defined, 415; presidential, 495

Impeachment, 410–411, 491, 494, 545, 654

Implied powers, 92–93, 403, 407–409

Impoundment, 408

Imprisonment, alternatives to, 163–164

Inaugural addresses, 528–529

Income level; party affiliation and, 273; public opinion and, 243; voter turnout and, 356; voting behavior and, 361

Income tax; corporate, 565, 704; evolution of,

Justice Department. *See* United States Department of Justice
Justice of the peace (JP), 662–663

K

Katz v. United States, 154
Kelso, Frank, 191
Kemp, Jack, 272
Kennedy, Anthony, 541, 547
Kennedy, John F., 78–79, 82, 100, 102, 218, 272, 278, 315, 324–325, 409, 428, 454, 455, 456, 460, 495
Kerrey, Bob, 465
Key, V. O., 272
Keynote speaker, 296, 297
Khomeini, Ayatollah Ruhollah, 486
King, Martin Luther, Jr., 100, 171, 172, 177, 178, 243, 349, 485; biography of, 179
King, Rodney, 659
"King Caucus," 293
King's court *(curia regis),* 534–535
Kitchen cabinet, 463
KKK (Ku Klux Klan), 140
Know-Nothing Party, 279
Knox, Henry, 461
Koch, Ed, 329
Korea, student achievement in, 694. *See also* South Korea
"Koreagate," 258
Korean War, 78, 406, 478, 615, 627, 636, 638
Korematsu v. United States, 182
Ku Klux Klan (KKK), 140
Kuhlmeier, Cathy, 542–543
Kuwait, Iraq's invasion of, 13, 241, 478, 492, 598, 631, 637, 638. *See also* Persian Gulf War
Kyoto Protocol, 602, 604, 629, 642–643

L

La Marcha, 181
Labor force, 250
Labor interest groups, 249–250, 335–336
Lake, Anthony, 413, 446, 447
Land; control of, 104, 105; federal ownership of, 105
Landon, Alf, 237
Landry, Steve, 653
Laos, American military support to, 486
Larry King Live, 480
LAs (legislative assistants), 392–393
Lasswell, Harold, 6
Law(s); administration of, 658; American, sources of, 534–536; bankruptcy, 405; of the blood *jus sanguinis,* 205; campaign-financing. *See* Campaign-financing rules; case, 535; citizenship, changes in, through the years, 218. *See also* Citizen(s); Citizenship; civil, 536; civil law system and, 535; "code," 535; codified, 535; common, 534–535; constitutional, 535, 648; criminal, 536;

English-only, 225, 230–231; equal protection under, 172–174, 194, 195; *ex post facto,* 121, 419; gun-control, 250, 259, 260; how Congress makes, 422–445. *See also* Legislative process; immigration, changes in, through the years, 218. *See also* Immigrant(s); Immigration; "Jim Crow," 174; obeying, 124; passed, proposed laws versus, 428; proposed, passed laws versus, 428; rule of, 68; shield, 137; of the soil *jus soli,* 205; statutory, 535–536, 648–649; three-strikes-and-you're-out, 590–591; traffic, 569; unconstitutional, 69
Lawsuits, brought by interest groups, 257–258
Lawyer. *See* Attorney(s)
LCs (legislative correspondents), 393
LD (legislative director), 392–393
League of Nations, 414, 485, 614
League of United Latin American Citizens, 253
League of Women Voters of the United States (LWVUS), 249
Lee, Richard Bland, 274
Lee, Richard Henry, 41
Left, radical, 245
Legal Defense and Education Fund, 253
Legislative assistants (LAs), 392–393
Legislative correspondents (LCs), 393
Legislative director (LD), 392–393
Legislative powers, 372, 402–409
Legislative process; calendar and, 434; changes in, through the years, 442; creation of, 422–445; final stages of, 438–442; House action and, 434–435; introducing, 430, 432; presidential action and, 439–442; scheduling, 434; Senate action and, 435–436
Legislative Reorganization Act (1946), 416
Legislators, ratings systems and, 256–257
Legislature(s); bicameral, 51, 373; colonial, 38; courts checked by, 551–552; defined, 38; state, 659–660
Legitimacy, 41
Legitimate power, 10
Lemon v. Kurtzman, 127–128
Lend-Lease Program, 629
L'Enfant, Pierre-Charles, 677, 678
Leon, United States v., 552
Letter; to the editor, 238; requesting information under the Freedom of Information Act, 513
Leviathan (Hobbes), 34
Lewan, Michael, 308
Libel, 135
Liberals, 244, 245
Libertarian Party, 270, 271, 280
Liberties, civil. *See* Civil liberties
Library of Congress, 339, 383, 393, 394, 396
Lightner, Candy, 256
Lightner, Cari, 256
Limbaugh, Rush, 329, 330

Limited government, 32–33, 68
Limited jurisdiction, 662–663
Lincoln, Abraham, 10, 78, 106, 278, 345, 448, 463, 477, 620; biography of, 205
Line graphs, reading of, 593
Line-item veto, 441–442, 488, 660
Line-Item Veto Act (1996), 441
Lippmann, Walter, 417
Lippo Group, 306
Literacy tests, 348
Literary Digest, 237, 238
"Little Rock Nine," 176
Lobbying, 253–255, 258, 259–260
Lobbyist, 254
Local government(s), 674–699; boroughs and, 682; budgets of, 705; businesses operated by, 705–707; changes in, through the years, 691; cities and, 685. *See also* City(ies); constitutional restrictions on, 648; counties and, 682–685; creation and operation of, 681–686, 688–689; federalism and, 95–96; form(s) of, 681–686, 688–689; functions of, 676–681; incorporation and, 685; intergovernmental transfers and, 707–711; jobs with, 222; municipalities and, 685, 689–695, 697; parishes and, 682; party organization and, 284, 285; revenues of; nontax, 705–707; sources of, 703–711; special districts and, 688; taxation by. *See* Local taxation; towns and townships and, 685–686, 688; unincorporated areas and, 688
Local taxation; importance of, 704–705; limitations on, 702–703; types of, 703–705
Locke, Gary, 658
Locke, John, 13–15, 33–34, 41, 452
Long, Huey, 436
Loopholes, 304
Loose constructionists, 407
Loose monetary policy, 575
Lopez, United States v., 550
Los Angeles Times, 719
Lott, Trent, 390, 429
Louis XVI (king of France), 15
Louisiana Purchase Treaty (1803), 206
Louisiana v. Resweber, 164
Lowenstein, Daniel, 719
Luxembourg; NATO and, 630; population of, 12
LWVUS (League of Women Voters of the United States), 249
Lycos, 336
Lyon, Matthew, 264
Lyons, James, 231

M

Macaulay, Lord Thomas Babington, 675
Machine politics, 284
MAD (mutual-assured destruction), 615–616
MADD. *See* Mothers Against Drunk Driving
Madison, James, 5, 14–15, 49, 50, 51, 54, 55,

Association, 73, 190

National Asian Pacific American Legal Consortium, 253

National Association for the Advancement of Colored People (NAACP), 103, 175, 178, 253, 484

National Association of Bilingual Education, 231

National Association of Manufacturers (NAM), 248

National Association of Social Workers, 253

National Audubon Society, 252

National Black Media Coalition, 326

National Capital Planning Commission, 677

National Cattleman's Association, 523

National Center for Atmospheric Research, 601

National committee, 270, 287, 296, 332, 465, 490, 493

National Consumer Coalition (NCC), 251

National convention, 79, 272, 285, 287, 295–297, 329, 330

National Council of Churches, 253

National debt, 404, 579–580, 582

National Economic Council (NEC), 490

National Education Association (NEA), 252; profile of, 249

National Enquirer, 338

National Environmental Policy Act (NEPA) (1969), 599, 600

National Farmers' Union, 250

National government; agencies of, not subject to state taxation, 702; under the Articles of Confederation, 44–49; beginning of, 57; budget and. *See* Federal budget; checks and balances among branches of, 68, 69; chief executive of. *See* President; drug policy and, 110; education standards and, 114–115; European influence and, 32–35; executive branch of. *See* President; federal system of. *See* Federalism; grants from, 709–711; intergovernmental transfers and, 707–711; jobs with, 220, 221, 222–223. *See also* Civil service; land ownership and, 104, 105; legislative branch of. *See* Congress; United States House of Representatives; United States Senate; major principles of, embodied in Constitution, 66–70; obligations of, to states, 99–102; organization of, 504, 505. *See also* Bureaucracy; powers delegated to, 91–93, 95; powers denied to, 93–94, 96; presidential democracy and, 18; public debt of, 579–580, 582; publications of, 45; regulation of interest groups by, 259–260; representative democracy and, 18, 24; revenues of. *See* Tax(es), taxation; spending by, 402, 404, 571–574, 626–627, 630. *See also* Spending; supremacy of, 102–107; true size of, 572–573; *See also* Federalism

National Grange, 250

National Guard, 99–100, 102, 176, 485, 659

National Highway Traffic Safety Administration, 524

National Indian Youth Council (NIYC), 184

National Labor Relations Board (NLRB), 514

National Law Journal, 558

National Milk Producers Association, 523

National Oceanic and Atmospheric Administration, 515

National Organization for Women (NOW); Legal Defense and Education Fund of, 253; *Media Project* of, 326

National origin; discrimination on basis of, 179, 192, 405; jury service and, 158

National Origins Act (1929), 211

National party chairperson, 287

National party committee, 287

National Railway Passenger Corporation (AMTRAK), 516

National Recycling Coalition, 680

National Republican Party, 275, 278

National Rifle Association (NRA), 248, 250, 260, 441

National Science Foundation (NSF), 511

National security; cyberspace and, 81; defined, 612; national government's obligation to provide for, 10, 99

National Security Act (1947), 622, 625

National Security Council (NSC), 460, 467, 622, 626

National Wildlife Federation (NWF), 247, 251–252

National Woman Suffrage Association, 73, 190, 346–347, 348

National Women's Party, 347

Nationalists, 49

Nation-centered federalism, 109

Native Alaskans, voting rights and, 350

Native American(s); citizenship and, 183, 205, 206; early policies toward, 183–184; online interest groups and, 334; past injustices to, compensation for, 185; population of, 209; voting rights and, 172, 350

Native American Languages Act (1990), 185

NativeNet, 334

NATO (North Atlantic Treaty Organization), 89, 486, 630, 631

Natural Law Party, 280

Natural rights, 14, 41

Naturalization; citizenship by, 204, 206–207; congressional powers and, 407; defined, 206; denaturalization and, 207

Naturalized citizens, 206, 207

Nature Conservancy, 252

Navigation Acts (England), 38

NBC, 332

NBC News/*Wall Street Journal* poll, 333

NCC (National Consumer Coalition), 251

NEA. *See* National Education Association

NEC (National Economic Council), 490

Necessary and proper clause, 92, 103, 105, 407

Negative campaign advertising, 303, 314, 322–323, 324, 354

Negotiation, 77

NEPA (National Environmental Policy Act) (1969), 599, 600

The Netherlands; chief of state in, 482; NATO and, 630

Netscape, 331

Neutrality, 614

New Deal, 108, 109, 363, 464, 496, 519

New England town, 685–686

New federalism, 109

New Jersey Plan, 51–52

New York Stock Exchange, 511

New York Times, 135, 284, 305, 327, 338, 433, 550, 590

New York Times poll, 245

New York Times v. United States, 134

New Zealand, Anzus Pact and, 631

News; coverage of, managed, 323; editorials versus stories and, 161; Internet and, 332–333, 338; stories versus editorials and, 161; TV, how to watch, 616–617

Newspaper(s); critical reading of, 161; daily, weekly versus, 339; student, 542–543

Newsweek, 480

Nicaragua; arms for rebels in, 418; refugees from, 208

Nicholas II (tsar of Russia), 16

Nicholson, Jim, 642

Nielsen Media Research, 322

Nineteenth Amendment, 95, 190, 191, 347, 348, 351

Ninth Amendment, 122

Nixon, Richard M., 109, 218, 276, 278, 315, 324–325, 358, 366, 408, 411, 417, 455, 456, 457, 469, 482, 483, 484, 490, 492, 493, 494, 496, 547

Nixon, United States v., 496

NIYC (National Indian Youth Council), 184

NLRB (National Labor Relations Board), 514

No contest plea, 160

Nominating convention, 293, 294, 295–297

Nomination, 292–297; defined, 268, 292; nominating convention and, 293, 294, 295–297; of presidential candidates, 295–297, 312. *See also* Candidate(s); Presidential election(s); self-, 292

Nonpartisan elections, 294–295, 520

Nonresident aliens, 208

Noriega, Manuel, 79

North, Oliver, 418

North American Free Trade Agreement (NAFTA), 485

North Atlantic Treaty Organization (NATO), 89, 486, 630, 631

North Korea, Korean War and, 478, 636, 638

Northwest Ordinance (1787), 45, 183

Norway, 619; chief of state in, 482; NATO and, 630

NOW. *See* National Organization for Women

NRA (National Rifle Association), 248, 250, 260, 441

NRC (Nuclear Regulatory Commission), 514

NSC (National Security Council), 460, 467, 622, 626
NSF (National Science Foundation), 511
Nuclear Regulatory Commission (NRC), 514
NWF (National Wildlife Federation), 247, 251–252

O

OAS (Organization of American States), 630–631
Obscenity, 135
Obstacle Course, 446
Occupation; public opinion and, 243; voting behavior and, 361
Occupational Safety and Health Administration, 524
O'Connor, Sandra Day, 129, 192, 196, 541, 548; biography of, 149
Off-budget items, 582
Office of Administration, 470
Office of Management and Budget (OMB), 463, 466–467, 494, 578
Office of National Drug Control Policy, 470
Office of Personnel Management (OPM), 220, 221, 222–223, 520–521
Office of Policy Development, 467
Office of Science and Technology Policy, 469–470
Office of Special Counsel (OSC), 521
Office of the U.S. Trade Representative, 470
Office of the Vice President, 458–461, 468–469. *See also* Vice President
Office-group (Massachusetts) ballot, 311
Ogden, Aaron, 106
Oklahoma City bombing, 137
Oklahoma Tax Commission v. Chickasaw Nation, 547
Old-age pensions, 281
OMB (Office of Management and Budget), 463, 466–467, 494, 578
Omnibus Crime Control and Safe Streets Act (1968), 154–155
"One person-one vote" rule, 377
One-party system, 267
Open Door Policy, 613
Open primary, 294
Operating budgets, 705
Operation Head Start, 108, 109, 571
Operation PUSH (People United to Save Humanity), 268
Opinion(s); concurring, 544; dissenting, 544; fact versus, 550; majority, 544; private, 236; public. *See* Public opinion; unanimous, 544; United States Supreme Court, 543–544, 545
Opinion leaders, public opinion and, 243
Opinion polls. *See* Public opinion poll(s)
OPM (Office of Personnel Management), 222, 223, 520–521
Oral arguments, 543, 544
Ordinary scrutiny, 173

Oregon v. Smith, 131
Organization chart, reading of, 503
Organization of American States (OAS), 630–631
Organization of Chinese Americans, 253
Original jurisdiction, 538
O'Rourke, P. J., 475
OSC (Office of Special Counsel), 521
Out of Order (Patterson), 323
Oversight function, 416, 417
Ozone layer, depletion of, 21–22

P

PA (prosecuting attorney), 664–665
Pages, congressional, 435
Paine, Thomas, 40, 203, 346
Panama, American troops sent to, 79, 478, 622
Pardon, 483, 660
Parishes, 682
Parks, Rosa, 177
Parliament (Great Britain), 20, 33, 72, 373, 437, 482
Parliamentary democracy, 18, 19, 20
Parochial schools, aid to, 127–128
Parole, 164, 660–661
Partisan politics, 509
Party identification, 357–358
Party identifiers, 271
Party platform, 272
Party ticket, 287; balancing of, 459–460
Party-column ballot, 311
Passports, 625
Pataki, George, 329
Patent, 407
Paterson, William, 51
Patronage, 221, 284, 488, 692–695, 697
Patterson, Thomas, 323
PBS *Newshour,* 231
Peace Corps, 220, 622
Peaceable assembly, 140
Pearl Harbor, 182, 214
Peers, 32
Peña, Federico, 180–181
Pendleton Act (Civil Service Reform Act) (1883), 518–519, 523
Pennsylvania Charter of Privileges, 37–38
Pennsylvania Frame of Government, 37
Pentagon Papers, 134
People; political parties and, 271–272; role of, 123. *See also* Citizenship; *See also* Person(s)
People United to Save Humanity (PUSH), 268
People v. Hurlbut, 685
People's Party, 481
People's Republic of China; American recognition of, 486; ethics and interdependence and, 26; National Day in, 11; one-party system in, 267, 270; population of, 12; program to destroy Tibet's culture and, 11; religious practice in, 126; territory of, 12; *See also* China, ancient

Percentages, figuring and using, 696
Perkins, Frances, 191–192
Perot, H. Ross, 277, 280, 281, 282, 405
Perry, Clifton, 257
Persian Gulf War, 13, 79, 241, 406, 478, 492, 598, 632, 637, 638
Person(s); accused of crime. *See* Crime(s), persons accused of; all equal access for, 186–187; equality of, 20; with disabilities, rights of, 185–189; elderly, interest groups for, 251; homeless, 592, 594; *See also* People
Personal freedoms, 20, 118–145; changes in, through the years, 141; our system of, 120–126 *See also entries beginning with Freedom*
Personal income tax, 565, 703–704
Pesticide Control Act (1972), 601
Petit jury, 669
Petition; to be listed on ballot, 292; defined, 120, 292; freedom of. *See* Freedom of petition; of government, 120
Petition of Rights (England), 32
Philadelphia (Constitutional) Convention, 49–53
Philip Morris, 366
The Philippines; bilateral treaty with United States and, 631; control of, by United States, 613; Western bloc and, 615
Phillips, Howard, 280
Photograph, analysis of, 359
Pigeonhole, 432
Pilgrims, 36, 37, 90
Pinckney, Charles, 346
Planks, 272
Plass, William, 327
Plea(s); arraignment and, 667; bargaining and, 162–163, 670; of no contest, 160
Pledge of Allegiance, 126, 130, 241
Plessy, Homer, 175
Plessy v. Ferguson, 175
"Plum book" (*Policy and Supporting Positions*) (U.S. Government Printing Office), 518
Plunkitt, George Washington, 697
Plurality, 268, 294, 653
Plymouth Company, 37
Pocket veto, 441, 488, 660
Poland; Communist bloc and, 615; democracy and, 616, 629; refugees from, 208
Police power, 648
Police protection, 676, 678
Policy and Supporting Positions ("plum book") (U.S. Government Printing Office), 518
Policy voting, 358, 360
Policymaking; bureaucrats and, 522–525; coordination of, by political parties, 269; federal courts and, 548–554; interest groups and, 253–261; by members of Congress, 385–386
Political action committees (PACs); campaign-finance reform and, 307; contribution limits

Photographer Tom Wachs/Bureau of Engraving and Printing; **508** (left) Corbis-Bettmann; **508** (right) Michael Lewis/Corbis; **510** Digital Stock; **511** Digital Stock; **519** Corbis-Bettmann; **522** ©Robert Rathe/Stock•Boston.

Chapter 20 532-533 Photograph by Franz Jantzen, Collection of the Supreme Court; **534** ©Ellis Herwig/Stock•Boston; **539** ©Dennis MacDonald/PhotoEdit; **541** Photo by Richard Strauss, Smithsonian Institution, Collection of the Supreme Court of the United States; **542** St. Louis Post-Dispatch; **544** ©1993, The Washington Post, Photo by Ray Lustig. Reprinted with permission; **547** (top) Corbis-Bettmann; **547** (bottom) Corbis-Bettmann; **549** Stock Montage, Inc.; **551** Library of Congress/Corbis; **553** AP/Wide World Photos; **554** Collection of the Supreme Court.

Chapter 21 562-563 Jim Sugar Photography/Corbis; **566** Stock Montage, Inc.; **570** James Amos/Corbis; **571** ©James P. Dwyer/Stock•Boston; **572** AP/Wide World Photos; **575** ©Rob Crandall/Stock Boston; **576** Mitchell Jamieson, An Incident in Contemporary American Life, 1941, The U. S. Department of the Interior, Washington, D.C., photographer David Allison; **577** Leif Skoogfors/Corbis; **579** ©Rob Crandall/Stock•Boston; **580** Draper Hill/©1980 The Detroit News.

Chapter 22 586-587 ©95 Jose Fuste Raga/The Stock Market; **589** ©Paul Conklin/PhotoEdit; **590** ©David Woo/Stock•Boston; **592** (top) Joseph Sohm, ChromoSohm Inc./Corbis; **592** (bottom) UPI/Corbis-Bettmann; **596** (top) AP/Wide World Photos; **596** (bottom) ©Jim Borgman/Reprinted with special permission of King Features Syndicate; **597** AP/Wide World Photos; **598** (left) AP/Wide World Photos; **598** (right) Natalie Fobes/Corbis; **599** Chan Lowe, South Florida Sun-Sentinel, ©Tribune Media Services, Inc. All rights reserved. Reprinted with permission. **603** (top) ©Myrleen Ferguson Cate/PhotoEdit; **603** (bottom) Image ©1998 PhotoDisc, Inc.; **605** (top) AP/Wide World Photos; **605** (bottom) Wolfgang Kaehier/Corbis.

Chapter 23 610-611 Digital Stock; **613** Stock Montage, Inc.; **614** Corbis-Bettmann; **615** Boileau/Frankfort State Journal, KY/Rothco;

617 AP/Wide World Photos; **618** AP/Wide World Photos; **620** Reuters/Corbis-Bettmann; **623** Corbis-Bettmann; **624** ©Judy Gelles/Stock•Boston; **625** Wally McNamee/Corbis; **627** Kevin Fleming/©Corbis; **628** ©Diane Lowe Bernbaum/Stock•Boston; **631** Agence France Presse/Corbis-Bettmann; **632** AP/Wide World Photos; **634** Agence France Presse/Corbis-Bettmann; **637** UPI/Corbis-Bettmann; **638** (top) Reuters/Corbis-Bettmann; **638** (bottom) AP/Wide World Photos; **639** Reuters/Corbis-Bettmann.

Chapter 24 646-647 Michigan House of Representatives, photographed by David Trumpie; **649** AP/Wide World Photos; **651** AP/Wide World Photos; **653** AP/Wide World Photos; **654** AP/Wide World Photos; **655** Image ©1998 PhotoDisc, Inc.; **656** AP/Wide World Photos; **658** AP/Wide World Photos; **659** Agence France Presse/Corbis-Bettmann; **661** ©Liederman/Rothco; **662** Culver Pictures Inc.; **663** (top) ©Mark C. Burnett/Stock•Boston; **663** (bottom) Arnie Levin ©1993 from The New Yorker Collection. All rights reserved; **664** AP/Wide World Photos; **666** AP/Wide World Photos; **667** ©A. Ramey/Stock•Boston; **669** AP/Wide World Photos; **670** ©Bob Daemmrich/Stock•Boston.

Chapter 25 674-675 ©Spencer Grant/Stock•Boston; **676** Image ©1998 PhotoDisc, Inc.; **677** Kelly-Mooney Photography/Corbis; **678** Joseph Sohm, ChromoSohm Inc./Corbis; **681** ©Tony Stone Images/Hiroyuki Matsumoto; **683** ©Jeff Greenberg/Photo Researchers; **684** AP/Wide World Photos; **686** (top) ©Dennis Cox; **686** (bottom) Kinora Cliness/Tony Stone Images; **687** ©Gary Wagner/Stock•Boston; **688** Image ©1998 PhotoDisc, Inc.; **691** ©Spencer Grant/Stock•Boston; **692** Mitchell Gerber/©Corbis; **693** AP/Wide World Photos; **695** (top) David H. Wells/Corbis; **695** (bottom) UPI/Corbis-Bettmann.

Chapter 26 700-701 Lowell Georgia/Corbis; **702** AP/Wide World; **704** Karl Hubenthal Cartoon/L.A. Herald-Examiner; **707** AP/Wide World Photos; **708** Digital Stock; **709** ©Greig Cranna/Stock•Boston; **714** ©Bob Daemmrich/Stock•Boston.

The Resource Center 721 Image ©1998 PhotoDisc, Inc.; **771-781** Bureau of Engraving.